POSTCARDS

FROM

AUSTRALIA

Diving the Great Barrier Reef is just one of the many unforgettable experiences awaiting travelers to the land Down Under. © Carl Roessler Photography.

Your gateway to Australia most likely will be Sydney, home of the world-famous Opera House, shown here with its white sails aglow. For details on touring the House and seeing a performance, see chapter 5. © Paul Chesley/Tony Stone Images.

Sydney Harbour buzzes with activity at the start of the annual ferry race. See chapter 4 for details on getting around by ferry and chapter 5 for details on sightseeing cruises. © George Hall/Tony Stone Images.

Sydney's historic Rocks district, with the Harbour Bridge looming in the background. The oldest settlement in Australia is now a lively precinct full of atmospheric pubs, unique boutiques, and top-notch restaurants. See chapters 4 and 5. © Dave Jacobs/Tony Stone Images.

Australia is a study in contrasts, from the sweeping beauty of the Whitsunday Islands, part of the Great Barrier Reef Marine Park; to the lushness of the many rain forest areas; to the almost surreal expanses of the Outback (right). Top photo © Peter Arnold, Inc. Bottom photo © Hans Strand/Tony Stone Images. Photo opposite © David Austen/Tony Stone Images.

You'll have no problem finding a patch of sand all to yourself, like here on Fitzroy Island in Queensland. See chapter 1 for a list of our favorite beaches and chapter 8 for Fitzroy Island.
© Queensland Tourist & Travel Corporation.

Stretching for more than 1,250 miles, the Great Barrier Reef is not just great, it's awesome; see chapter 8. Australia, in fact, has two barrier reefs, the other is off the coast of Western Australia; see chapter 11. © Carl Roessler Photography.

There's no better place than Australia to get face to face with the fishes. For a list of our favorite diving and snorkeling sites, see chapter 1. © Peter Arnold, Inc.

Like a 'roo unexpectedly bounding across the road, the mighty monolith of Ayers Rock (Uluru) seems to pop up out of nowhere from the red desert floor. See chapter 9. © Doug Armand/Tony Stone Images.

The haunting sounds of the didgeridoo capture the spirit of Aboriginal culture. You can learn to play one at the Aboriginal Art and Culture Centre in Alice Springs. See chapter 9. © Paul Souders/Tony Stone Images.

Picturesque today, Port Arthur, on the island-state of Tasmania, was once Australia's most notorious penal colony. You can tour the remains of the church, guard tower, and model prison. See chapter 16. © Greg Probst Photography.

Some dapper chaps confer before the running of "the race that stops the nation," the Melbourne Cup thoroughbred horse race. See chapter 13. © Dave G. Houser Photography.

On the south coast of Victoria winds one of the most scenic drives anywhere, the Great Ocean Road. Along the route you'll pass rain forests, beaches, and dramatic rock formations, such as the stunning Twelve Apostles, shown here. See chapter 14. © Tom Till Photography.

When should I travel to get the best airfare?
Where do I go for answers to my travel questions?
What's the best and easiest way to plan and book my trip?

frommers.travelocity.com

Frommer's, the travel guide leader, has teamed up with **Travelocity.com**, the leader in online travel, to bring you an in-depth, easy-to-use resource designed to help you plan and book your trip online.

At **frommers.travelocity.com**, you'll find free online updates about your destination from the experts at Frommer's plus the outstanding travel planning and purchasing features of Travelocity.com. Travelocity.com provides reservations capabilities for 95 percent of all airline seats sold, more than 47,000 hotels, and over 50 car rental companies. In addition, Travelocity.com offers more than 2,000 exciting vacation and cruise packages. Travelocity.com puts you in complete control of your travel planning with these and other great features:

Expert travel guidance from Frommer's - over 150 writers reporting from around the world!

Best Fare Finder - an interactive calendar tells you when to travel to get the best airfare

Fare Watcher - we'll track airfare changes to your favorite destinations

Dream Maps - a mapping feature that suggests travel opportunities based on your budget

Shop Safe Guarantee - 24 hours a day / 7 days a week live customer service, and more!

Whether traveling on a tight budget, looking for a quick weekend getaway, or planning the trip of a lifetime, Frommer's guides and Travelocity.com will make your travel dreams a reality. You've bought the book, now book the trip!

Other Great Guides for Your Trip:

Frommer's Portable Sydney

Frommer's Australia from $50 a Day

Frommer's New Zealand

Frommer's South Pacific

Here's what the critics say about Frommer's:

"Amazingly easy to use. Very portable, very complete."

—*Booklist*

◆

"The only mainstream guide to list specific prices. The Walter Cronkite of guidebooks—with all that implies."

—*Travel & Leisure*

◆

"Complete, concise, and filled with useful information."

—*New York Daily News*

◆

"Hotel information is close to encyclopedic."

—*Des Moines Sunday Register*

◆

"Detailed, accurate and easy-to-read information for all price ranges."

—*Glamour Magazine*

Australia

2001

by Natalie Kruger & Marc Llewellyn

IDG Books Worldwide, Inc.
An International Data Group Company
Foster City, CA • Chicago, IL • Indianapolis, IN • New York, NY

ABOUT THE AUTHORS

Sydney resident **Marc Llewellyn** (chapters 3, 4, 10, 11, 12, 13, 14, and "Australia in Depth") is one of Australia's premier travel writers and a regular contributor to all of Australia's leading newspaper travel sections and travel magazines. As a member of the Australian Society of Travel Writers, he keeps his suitcase ready packed beneath his bed. He is also the author of *Frommer's Portable Sydney* and co-author of *Frommer's Australia from $50 a Day.*

Natalie Kruger (chapters 2, 5, 6, 7, 8, 9, and the online directory), another Sydneysider, spent 7 years as a public relations consultant for international and Australian airlines, global hotel chains, tourist promotion boards, and tourism industry organizations, until she realized it is more fun to be a travel writer—that way, you get to say what you *really* think. She contributes travel pieces to Australia's top newspapers and magazines, including the prestigious *Weekend Australian,* and is a member of the Australian Society of Travel Writers. She is co-author of *Frommer's Australia from $50 a Day.*

IDG BOOKS WORLDWIDE, INC.

An International Data Group Company
IDG Books Worldwide, Inc.
909 Third Ave.
New York, NY 10022

Find us online at **www.frommers.com**

ISBN 0-7645-6152-9
ISSN 1040-9408

Editor: Lisa Renaud/Dog-Eared Pages
Production Editor: Tammy Ahrens
Design by Michele Laseau
Cartographer: John Decamillis
Photo Editor: Richard Fox
Production by IDG Books Indianapolis Production Department

SPECIAL SALES

For general information on IDG Books Worldwide's books in the U.S., please call our Consumer Customer Service department at 1-800-762-2974. For reseller information, including discounts, bulk sales, customized editions, and premium sales, please call our Reseller Customer Service department at 1-800-434-3422.

Manufactured in the United States of America

5 4 3 2 1

Contents

List of Maps

AN INVITATION TO THE READER

In researching this book, we discovered many wonderful places—hotels, restaurants, shops, and more. We're sure you'll find others. Please tell us about them so that we can share the information with your fellow travelers in upcoming editions. If you were disappointed with a recommendation, we'd love to know that too. Please write to:

Frommer's Australia 2001
IDG Books Worldwide, Inc.
909 Third Ave.
New York, NY 10022

AN ADDITIONAL NOTE

Please be advised that travel information is subject to change at any time—and this is especially true of prices. We therefore suggest that you write or call ahead for confirmation when making your travel plans. The authors, editors, and publisher cannot be held responsible for the experiences of readers while traveling. Your safety is important to us, however, so we encourage you to stay alert and be aware of your surroundings. Keep a close eye on cameras, purses, and wallets—all favorite targets of thieves and pickpockets.

WHAT THE SYMBOLS MEAN

✪ Frommer's Favorites
Our favorite places and experiences—outstanding for quality, value, or both.

The following abbreviations are used for credit cards:

AE	American Express	JCB	Japan Credit Bank
BC	Bankcard	MC	MasterCard
CB	Carte Blanche	V	Visa
DC	Diners Club		

FIND FROMMER'S ONLINE

www.frommers.com offers up-to-the-minute listings on almost 200 cities around the globe—including the latest bargains and candid, personal articles updated daily by Arthur Frommer himself. No other Web site offers such comprehensive and timely coverage of the world of travel.

The Best of Australia

by Natalie Kruger and Marc Llewellyn

Maybe we shouldn't say so, being Aussies ourselves, but Australia has a lot of bests. World bests, that is. It's got some of the best natural scenery, the weirdest wildlife, certainly the most brilliant scuba diving and snorkeling, the best beaches (shut up, California), the oldest rain forest (110 million years and counting), the world's oldest human civilization (some archaeologists say 40,000 years, some say 120,000—who cares? it's old), the best wines (okay, okay, stop browsing the Napa or Bordeaux and come see what we mean), the world's most laid-back people (when they're not from Melbourne and watching Aussie Rules football), the best weather (give or take the odd Wet Season in northern parts), the most innovative east-meets-west-meets-someplace-else cuisine—all bathed in pervasive white sunlight that brings everything up in Technicolor.

"Best" means different things to different people, but scarcely a visitor lands on these shores without having the Great Barrier Reef at the top of their "Best Things to See in Australia" list. So they should, because it really is the Eighth Wonder of the World, a glorious natural masterpiece no one should die without seeing. Also high on most folks' must-see list is Ayers Rock. This monolith must have some kind of magnet inside it designed to attract planeloads of tourists. We're not saying the Rock isn't special, but we think the vast Australian desert all around it is even more so. Sure, come and gawk at the Rock, but spend some time chilling out in the Red Centre wilderness too. The third attraction on most visitors' lists is Sydney, the Emerald City that glitters in the Antipodean sunshine on—here we go with the "bests" again—the best harbor, spanned by the best bridge in the world (shut up, San Francisco).

These "big three" attractions are understandably popular with travelers. What the TV commercials or the travel-agent window displays don't show, however, is how much else there is to see. Like the World Heritage wetlands and Aboriginal rock art of Kakadu National Park, the second Great Barrier Reef on the western coast, and the snowy mountain hiking trails of Tasmania. As planes zoom overhead delivering visitors to the Reef, the Rock, and Sydney, Aussies in charming country towns, on far-flung beaches, on rustic sheep stations, in rainforest villages, and in mountain lodges shake their heads and say sadly, "They don't know what they're missin'." Well, the aim of this chapter is to show you "what you're missin'." All of the country's major attractions are included in our recommendations here, but we've compiled

Australia

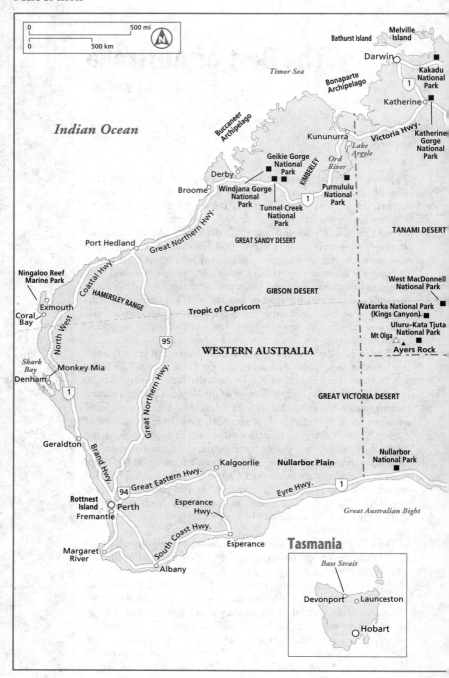

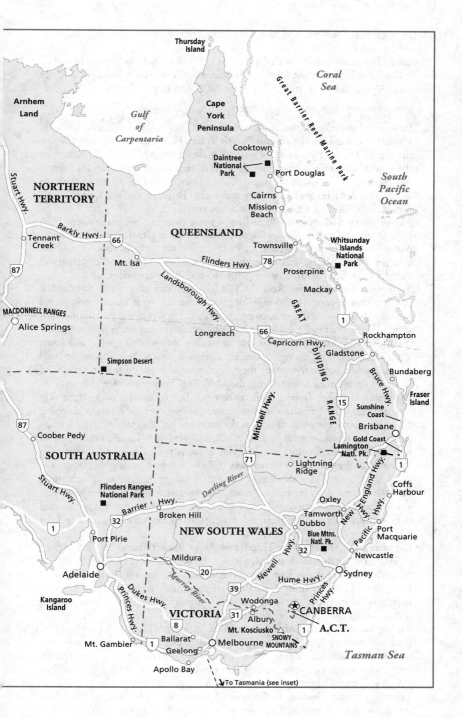

Thursday
Island

Coral
Sea

Arnhem
Land

Gulf
of
Carpentaria

Cape
York
Peninsula

Great Barrier Reef Marine Park

Cooktown
Daintree
National
Park ■   ■ Port Douglas

South
Pacific
Ocean

Stuart Hwy.

NORTHERN
TERRITORY

Barkly Hwy.

66

Tennant
Creek

87

Mt. Isa

QUEENSLAND

Cairns
Mission
Beach

Townsville

Whitsunday
Islands
National
Park ■

Flinders Hwy.   78

Proserpine

Mackay

MACDONNELL RANGES
Alice Springs

Landsborough Hwy.

Longreach   66

Capricorn Hwy.

GREAT

Rockhampton

Gladstone

Bundaberg

Simpson Desert ■

Mitchell Hwy.

DIVIDING

15

Bruce Hwy.

Fraser
Island

87

Coober Pedy

SOUTH AUSTRALIA

71

Lightning
Ridge

RANGE

Sunshine
Coast

Brisbane

Gold Coast
Lamington
Natl. Pk. ■

1

Stuart Hwy.

Flinders Ranges
National Park ■

Hwy.

Barrier Hwy.

Darling River

Oxley

New England Hwy.

Coffs
Harbour

1

32

Broken Hill

NEW SOUTH WALES

Tamworth
Dubbo

Pacific Hwy.

Port
Macquarie

Port Pirie

Blue Mtns.
Natl. Pk. ■

Newcastle

Mildura

Newell Hwy.

32

Adelaide

20

Murray River

Hume Hwy.

Sydney

Kangaroo
Island

Dukes Hwy.

39

Wodonga

Princes Hwy.

CANBERRA

Princes Hwy.

VICTORIA

31

Albury

A.C.T.

8

Mt. Kosciusko 1

Mt. Gambier   1   Ballarat

SNOWY
MOUNTAINS

Geelong

Melbourne

Tasman
Sea

Apollo Bay

↘ To Tasmania (see inset)

3

this list in the belief that you will have a better vacation if you take the road less traveled once or twice.

In the listing below, NSW stands for New South Wales, QLD for Queensland, NT for the Northern Territory, WA for Western Australia, SA for South Australia, VIC for Victoria, TAS for Tasmania, and ACT for the Australian Capital Territory.

1 The Top Travel Experiences

- **Hitting the Rails on the *Indian Pacific* Train:** This 3-day train journey across the Outback regularly—and deservedly—makes it on the "Top Rail Journeys in the World" lists compiled by those glossy travel magazines. It includes the longest straight stretch of track in the world, 478 kilometers (299 miles) across the treeless Nullarbor Plain. Start in Sydney and end in Perth, or vice versa, or just do a section. See "Getting Around Australia," in chapter 2.
- **Experiencing Sydney** (NSW): Sydney is more than just the magnificent Harbour Bridge and Opera House. For one thing, no other city has beaches in abundance like Sydney, and few have such a magnificently scenic harbor. Our advice is to get aboard a ferry, walk from one side of the bridge to the other, and try to spend a week here, because you're going to need it. See chapter 3.
- **Seeing the Great Barrier Reef** (QLD): It's a glorious underwater fairyland, a 2,000-kilometer-long (1,250-mile-long) coral garden with electric colors and bizarre fish life—*and* it comes complete with warm water and year-round sunshine. This is what you came to Australia to see. And what better way to explore it than on a cruise? When you're not snorkeling over stunning coral and clams almost as big as you, diving, calling in at tropical towns, or lazing on deserted island beaches, you're trying out the sun lounges or enjoying the first-rate food aboard your impressive white liner, the **M.V. *Reef Endeavour*.** See chapter 6.
- **Exploring the Wet Tropics Rain Forest** (QLD): Folks who come from skyscraper lands like Manhattan or Los Angeles can't get over the moisture-dripping ferns, the neon-blue butterflies, and the primeval peace of this World Heritage patch of rain forest stretching north, south, and west from Cairns. Hike it, 4WD it, or glide over the treetops in the Skyrail gondola from Cairns. See chapter 6.
- **Bareboat Sailing in the Whitsundays** (QLD): Bareboat means unskippered— that's right, even if you think port is an after-dinner drink, you can charter a yacht, pay for a day's instruction from a skipper, and then take over the helm yourself and explore these 74 island gems. It's easy, really. Anchor in deserted bays, snorkel over dazzling reefs, fish for coral trout from the deck, and feel the wind in your sails. See chapter 6.
- **Exploring the Olgas (Kata Tjuta) and Ayers Rock (Uluru)** (NT): Just why everyone comes thousands of miles to see the big red stone of Ayers Rock is a mystery—that's probably why they come, because the Rock *is* a mystery. Just 50 kilometers (31 miles) from Ayers Rock are the round red heads of the Olgas, a second rock formation more significant to Aborigines and more intriguing to many visitors than Uluru. See chapter 7.
- **Taking an Aboriginal Culture Tour** (Alice Springs, NT): Eating female wasps, contemplating a hill as a giant resting caterpillar, and seeing in the stars the face of your grandmother smiling down at you will give you a new perspective on your own culture. See what we mean on this half-day tour from the Aboriginal Art and Culture Centre in Alice Springs. See chapter 7.
- **Listening to the "Sounds of Silence"** (Ayers Rock, NT): Billed as a "million-star restaurant" because it's outdoors under the Milky Way, this culinary treat is

a fabulous way to soak up the desert. Sip champagne to the twang of a didgeridoo as the sun sets, then settle down to a "bush tucker" feast of emu, kangaroo, and crocodile at white-clothed tables as waiters pour Aussie wines. Some guests even don black tie for the occasion, but wear Reeboks instead of stilettos. Then it's lights out, the music stops, and everyone listens to the eerie sound of silence. See chapter 7.

- **Discovering the Kimberley** (WA): Australia's last frontier, the Kimberley is a romantic cocktail of giant South Sea pearls, red soil, aqua seas, deadly crocodiles, a striking kind of Aboriginal rock art called "Wandjina," and million-acre farms in a never-ending wilderness. Cross it by 4WD on the adventurous Gibb River Road, stay at a cattle station, base yourself on the beach in Broome, or cruise its dramatic island-studded coastline. See chapter 8.
- **Rolling in Wildflowers** (WA): Imagine Texas three times over and covered in wildflowers. That's what the state of Western Australia looks like every spring from August to October when pink, mauve, red, white, yellow, and blue wildflowers bloom their hearts out. Aussies flock to the state big-time for this spectacle, so book ahead. See chapter 9.
- **Drinking in the Barossa Valley** (SA): One of Australia's four largest wine-producing areas, this German-speaking region less than an hour's drive from Adelaide is also the prettiest. Adelaide's restaurants happen to be some of the country's best, too, so test out your wine purchases with the city's terrific food. See chapter 10.
- **Seeing the Sights Along the Great Ocean Road** (VIC): This 106-kilometer (64.5-mile) coastal road carries you past wild and stunning beaches, forests, and dramatic cliff-top scenery—including the Twelve Apostles, 12 pillars of red rock standing in splendid isolation in the foaming Southern Ocean. See chapter 12.
- **Driving Around Tasmania:** The "Apple Isle" is Australia's prettiest state, a picturesque Eden of lavender fields, wineries, snow-topped granite tors, white-water wildernesses, and haunting historic prisons. A bonus is that it's small enough to drive around in a few days. See chapter 14.

2 The Best Outdoor Adventures

- **Horse Trekking in the Snowy Mountains** (NSW): Ride the ranges like the *Man from Snowy River,* staying in bush lodges or camping beneath the stars. See chapter 4.
- **Abseiling in the Blue Mountains** (NSW): Careering backward down a cliff face with the smell of gum trees in your nostrils is not everyone's idea of fun, but you sure know you're alive. Several operators welcome both novices and the more experienced. See chapter 4.
- **Game Fishing off Cairns** (QLD): Battle a black marlin off Cairns and you might snare the world record; that's how big they get down here. Every October, serious anglers worldwide head to Queensland for the Lizard Island Black Marlin Classic at the exclusive Lizard Island Lodge. September to December is the season. See chapter 2 (for the event) or chapter 6 (for the resort).
- **White-Water Rafting on the Tully River** (Mission Beach, QLD): The Grade 3 to 4 rapids of the Tully River swoosh between lush, rain-forested banks. The guides are professional, and the rapids are just hairy enough to be fun. A good choice for first-time rafters. See chapter 6.
- **Four-Wheel-Driving on Fraser Island** (QLD): Burning down 75 Mile Beach in a 4x4 on the biggest sand island in the world is liberating, if not great for the

environment. Paradoxically, the island is an ecologically important zone and popular with nature lovers. Swim its clear blue lakes, hike its eucalypt and rain forests, and fish off the beach. See chapter 6.

- **Canoeing the Top End** (NT): Paddling between the sun-drenched ochre walls of Katherine Gorge really sharpens the senses, especially when a (harmless) freshwater crocodile pops its head up! **Gecko Canoeing** will take you downriver to the rarely explored Flora and Daly River systems to meet Aboriginal communities, shower under waterfalls, hike virgin bushland, and camp in swags on the banks. See chapter 8.
- **Surfing in Margaret River** (WA): A 90-minute surf lesson with four-time Western Australia surf champ Josh Parmateer is a great introduction to the sport—if only to hear Josh's ripper of an Aussie accent! From July to September, Josh shifts his classes to Cable Beach in Broome. See chapters 8 and 9.
- **Sea Kayaking with Sea Lions** (WA): Snorkel with wild sea lions and watch penguins feeding on a sea-kayaking day trip from Perth with **Rivergods.** This Western Australian company also runs multiday sea kayak expeditions past whales, dolphins, and sharks in Shark Bay, and over coral at Ningaloo Reef on the Northwest Cape. See chapter 9. Kayaking is also a great way to explore the Whitsunday Islands, and Dunk Island off Mission Beach in Queensland. See chapter 6.
- **Skiing in the Victorian Alps** (VIC): Skiing in Australia? You bet. When you've had enough of all that coral and sand, you can hit the slopes in Victoria. Where else can you swish down the mountain between gum trees? See chapter 12.

3 The Best Places to View Wildlife

- **Lord Howe Island** (NSW): Taking a swim just offshore as hundreds of enormous fish brush past your face mask as they wait for their daily feed is an amazing experience. The island, a volcanic remnant accessible from Sydney, is home to several species not found anywhere else and is well worth the extra flight to see. See chapter 4.
- **Montague Island** (Narooma, NSW): This little island just offshore from the seaside town of Narooma, on the south coast, is a haven for nesting seabirds, but it's the water around it that's home to the main attractions. Dolphins are common, fairy penguins too, and during the whale-watching season, you're almost sure to spot humpback and southern right whales, some with their calves. See chapter 4.
- **Jervis Bay** (NSW): This is probably the closest place to Sydney where you're certain to see kangaroos in the wild and where you can pet them too. The national park here is also home to hundreds of bird species, including black cockatoos, as well as plenty of possums. See chapter 4.
- **Lone Pine Koala Sanctuary** (Brisbane, QLD): Cuddle a koala (and have your photo taken doing it) at this Brisbane park, the world's first and largest koala sanctuary. Apart from some 130 koalas, lots of other Aussie wildlife—including wombats, Tasmanian devils, 'roos (which you can hand-feed), and colorful parakeets—are on show. See chapter 5.
- **Australian Butterfly Sanctuary** (Kuranda, near Cairns, QLD): Walk through the biggest butterfly "aviary" in Australia and see some of Australia's most gorgeous butterflies, including the electric-blue Ulysses. See many species of butterfly feed, lay eggs, and mate, and inspect caterpillars and pupae. Wearing pink, red, or white encourages the butterflies to land on you. See chapter 6.
- **Wait-a-While Environmental Tours** (QLD): Head into the World Heritage–listed Wet Tropics rain forest behind Cairns or Port Douglas with this

ecotour operator to spotlight big-eyed possums, lizards, pythons, even a platypus, so shy that most Aussies have never seen one in the wild. About once a month, on average, one group will spot the rare and bizarre Lumholtz's tree kangaroo. See chapter 6.

- **Mon Repos Turtle Rookery** (Bundaberg, QLD): Most nights from November to January, giant green, loggerhead, and hawksbill turtles crawl up Mon Repos Beach in Bundaberg to lay their eggs. From late January to March, the babies hatch at night and scamper down to the water. Rangers lead inexpensive tours to watch these magical spectacles. See chapter 6. Heron Island in Queensland (also in chapter 6) and the Northwest Cape in Western Australia (see chapter 9) are two other good turtle-watching sites.

- **Currumbin Wildlife Sanctuary** (The Gold Coast, QLD): Tens of thousands of unbelievably pretty red, blue, green, and yellow rainbow lorikeets have been screeching into this park for generations to be hand-fed by delighted visitors every morning and afternoon. There are 'roos and other Australian animals at the sanctuary, too, but the birds steal the show. See chapter 6.

- **Kakadu National Park** (NT): One-third of Australia's bird species live in Kakadu; so do dingoes, snakes, and lots of dangerous saltwater crocs. A cruise on the Yellow Waters billabong is like cruising through a wetlands theme park. It is at its best later in the Dry Season around September and October, when wildlife converges around the shrinking water. See chapter 8.

- **The Northwest Cape** (WA): For the thrill of a lifetime, go snorkeling with a whale shark. No one knows where they come from, but these mysterious monsters up to 18 meters (60 ft.) long surface in these remote Outback waters every year from March to early June. A mini-industry has sprung up taking snorkelers out to swim alongside the sharks as they feed (on plankton, not snorkelers). See chapter 9.

- **Monkey Mia** (WA): Just about every day, wild bottlenose dolphins come into this remote Outback shore to say hello to visitors. You have to join the queue of tourists and follow the instructions of local rangers, though, because this place gets worldwide publicity and attracts quite a crowd. Even better than the dolphins is a cruise on the *Shotover* catamaran to see some of the area's 10,000 dugongs (manatees), plus turtles, sea snakes, sharks—and more dolphins that come right up to the boat. See chapter 9.

- **Kangaroo Island** (SA): You're sure to see more native animals here—including koalas, wallabies, birds, echidnas, reptiles, seals, and sea lions—than anywhere else in the country, apart from a wildlife park. Another plus: The distances between major points of interest are not great, so you won't spend half the day just getting from place to place. See chapter 10.

4 The Best Places to Experience the Outback

- **Broken Hill** (NSW): There's no better place to experience real Outback life than in Broken Hill. There's the city itself, with its thriving art scene and the Royal Flying Doctor service; a historic ghost town on its outskirts; a national park with Aboriginal wall paintings; an opal mining town nearby; and plenty of kangaroos, emus, and giant wedge-tailed eagles. See chapter 4.

- **Lightning Ridge** (NSW): This opal-mining town is as rough and ready as the stones they pull out of the ground. Meet amazing characters, share in the eccentricity of the place, and visit opal-rush areas with mole-hill scenery made by the old sun-bleached mine tailings. See chapter 4.

- **Uluru–Kata Tjuta National Park** (Ayers Rock, NT): Sure, this magical monolith will enthrall you with its eerie beauty; but the nearby Olgas are more soothing, more interesting, and actually taller than the Rock, so make the time to wander through them too. Hike the Rock's base, burn around it on a Harley-Davidson, saunter up to it on a camel, climb it if you must. Whatever you do, don't go home until you've felt the powerful heartbeat of the desert. See chapter 7.

- **The MacDonnell Ranges** (NT): The Aborigines say these red rocky hills were formed by the Aboriginal caterpillar Dreaming that wriggled from the earth here. To the west of Alice Springs are dramatic gorges, idyllic (and bloody cold) waterholes, and cute wallabies. To the east are Aboriginal rock carvings, and the Ross River Homestead, where you can crack a stockwhip, throw a boomerang, feast on damper and billy tea, and ride a horse in the bush. See chapter 7.

- **Kings Canyon** (NT): Anyone who saw the cult flick *The Adventures of Priscilla, Queen of the Desert* will remember that scene where the transvestites climb a soaring orange cliff and survey the desert floor. That was Kings Canyon, about 320 kilometers (200 miles) from Alice Springs in one direction and Ayers Rock in the other. Trek the dramatic rim or take the easier shady route along the bottom. Don't forget your lipstick, guys. See chapter 7.

- **Finke Gorge National Park** (NT): If you like your wilderness scenic and ancient, come here. Finke Gorge is home to "living fossil" palm trees that survived the ice ages and to what scientists think may be the world's oldest river course. Camp, hike, and just soak up the timeless bush. Visit for a day from Alice Springs or camp out. Access is by four-wheel-drive (4WD) vehicle only. See chapter 7.

- **Elsey Station** (NT): This vast farm got more than its 15 minutes of fame as the setting of the Australian book *We of the Never Never,* an account of isolated Outback life written in 1902 by the station's owner, Mrs. Jeannie Gunn. The title originated in visitors' desire to "never never" leave such remote beauty. Visit for a day and meet the resident Aboriginal kids, or stay longer and canoe the isolated Roper River to Red Lily Lagoon. See chapter 8.

- **The Northwest Cape** (WA): This treeless moonscape of red anthills, spiky spinifex, and blazing heat seems to go on forever, so it's all the more amazing to find a beautiful coral reef on its shore. Drive over the rugged hills in a 4WD, dodging kangaroos along the way; swim with giant manta rays; snorkel right off the beach; scuba dive fabulous coral outcroppings; and laze on blindingly white beaches. This is where the Outback meets the sea. See chapter 9.

- **Coober Pedy** (SA): It may be hot and dusty, but you'll get a true taste of the Outback as you tag along with the local mail carrier as he makes his rounds to the area's remote cattle stations (ranches). It's a 12-hour, 600-kilometer journey along sun-baked dirt roads. See chapter 10.

5 The Best Beaches

- **Palm Beach** (Sydney): At the end of a string of beaches stretching north from Sydney, Palm Beach is long and very white, with some good surfing and a golf course. See chapter 3.

- **Hyams Beach** (Jervis Bay, NSW): This beach in pretty, off-the-beaten-path Jervis Bay is said to be the whitest in the world. You need to wear sunblock if you decide to stroll along it, because the reflection from the sun, even on a cloudy day, can give you a nasty sunburn. The beach also squeaks as you walk. See chapter 4.

- **Four Mile Beach** (Port Douglas, QLD): The sea is turquoise, the sun is warm, the palms sway, and the low-rise hotels starting to line this country beach can't spoil the feeling that it is a million miles from anywhere. But isn't there always a serpent in paradise? The "serpents" in this case are north Queensland's seasonal—and potentially deadly—marine stingers. Come from June to September to avoid them, or confine your swimming to the area in the stinger net the rest of the year. See chapter 6.
- **Mission Beach** (QLD): Azure blue sea, islands dotting the horizon, and lush white sand edged by dense tangled vine forests make this beach a real winner. So does the fact that hardly anyone ever comes here. Cassowaries (giant emu-like birds) hide out in the rain forest, and the tiny town of Mission Beach politely makes itself invisible behind the leaves. Visit from June to September to avoid deadly marine stingers. See chapter 6.
- **Whitehaven Beach** (Whitsunday Island, QLD): It's not a surf beach, but this 6-kilometer (3³/₄-mile) stretch of silica sand on uninhabited Whitsunday Island is pristine, peaceful, and as white as snow. Bring a book, curl up under the rain forest lining its edge, and fantasize that the cruise boat is going to leave without you. See chapter 6.
- **Main Beach** (Sunshine Coast, QLD): The trendy shops of Hastings Street line the white sand and gently rolling surf of this pretty beach. Dust off your designer swimsuit for this one. When you get tired of the scene, you can hike the green walking trails of nearby Noosa National Park. A minute's drive east takes you to another bathing beauty spot, Sunshine Beach. See chapter 6.
- **Surfers Paradise Beach** (Gold Coast, QLD): Actually, all 35 of the beaches on the 30-kilometer (19-mile) Gold Coast strip in south Queensland are worthy of inclusion here. Every one of them has sand so clean it squeaks, great surf, and fresh breezes. Just ignore the tacky high-rises behind you. Surfers will like Kirra and Burleigh Heads. See chapter 6.
- **Cable Beach** (Broome, WA): Is it the South Sea pearls they pull out of the Indian Ocean, the camels loping along the sand, the to-die-for sunsets, the surf, or the red earth meeting the intensely green sea that gives this beach its exotic appeal? Maybe it's the 26 kilometers (16 miles) of glorious white sand. June to September is the only time to swim here, though, when deadly marine stingers are not around. See chapter 8.
- **Cottesloe Beach** (Perth, WA): Perth has 19 great beaches, but this petite crescent is the prettiest. After you've checked out the scene on the sand, join the fashionable set for brunch in the Indiana Tea House, a mock-Edwardian bathhouse fronting the sea. If you're a surfer, head to Scarborough and Trigg. See chapter 9.

6 The Best Diving & Snorkeling Sites

- **Port Douglas** (QLD): Many fabulous dive sites can be found off the shores of Port Douglas, north of Cairns, including Split-Bommie, with its delicate fan corals and schools of colorful fusiliers; Barracuda Pass, with its coral gardens and giant clams; the swim-through coral spires of the Cathedrals; and numerous ribbon reefs. Snorkelers can glide over abundant coral and reef fish life of Agincourt Reef or sail to see great fish life around the Low Isles coral cays just half an hour offshore. See chapter 6.

- **Lizard Island** (QLD): Snorkel over 150-year-old giant clams—as well as lots of gorgeous underwater coral—in the Clam Garden, just off this exclusive resort island northeast of Cairns. Nearby is the famous Cod Hole, where divers can hand-feed a school of giant potato cod. See chapter 6.

- **Green Island** (QLD): This island is made of coral, so you'd expect the snorkeling to be good. Plunge off the beach just about anywhere around the island and marvel at the coral and fish scenes before you. Come over for a day or half day from Cairns or stay at the island's upscale resort. Divers will like it here, too. See chapter 6.

- **Cairns** (QLD): In addition to Green Island (see above), Moore, Norman, Hardy, Saxon, and Arlington reefs and Michaelmas and Upolu cays—all about 90 minutes off Cairns—offer great snorkeling and endless dive sites. Explore on a day trip from Cairns or join a live-aboard adventure. See chapter 6.

- **Coral Sea** (QLD): In this sea east of the Great Barrier Reef off north Queensland, you'll see sharks feeding at Predator's Playground; 1,000-meter (3,280 ft.) drop-offs in the Abyss; large reefs covering hundreds of square miles; and tropical species not found on the Great Barrier Reef. This is not a day-trip destination; numerous dive operators run multiday trips on live-aboard vessels. Visibility is excellent—up to 100 meters (328 ft.). See chapter 6.

- *Yongala* **wreck** (QLD): Sunk by a cyclone in 1911, the 120-meter (394-ft.) SS *Yongala* lies in the Coral Sea off Townsville. Big schools of trevally, kingfish, barracuda, and batfish surround the wreckage; giant Queensland grouper live under the bow, lionfish hide under the stern, turtles graze on the hull, and hard and soft corals make their home on it. It's too far for a day trip; live-aboard trips run from Townsville and Cairns. See chapter 6.

- **Blue Pearl Bay** (QLD): One of the best snorkel spots in the Whitsundays is this patch of reef off Hayman Island. See dazzling coral and colorful fish life, just as good if not better than that on the Outer Great Barrier Reef and a lot closer. Stay at the luxurious Hayman resort or take a sailing day trip from most other island resorts or from the mainland. See chapter 6.

- **The Whitsunday Islands** (QLD): As well as Blue Pearl Bay, these 74 breathtaking islands offer countless dive sites both among the islands themselves and on the Outer Great Barrier Reef 90 minutes away. Bait Reef on the Outer Reef is popular for its cascading drop-offs. Snorkelers can explore not just the outer Reef, but also patch reefs among the islands, and rarely visited fringing reefs around many island shores. See chapter 6.

- **Heron Island** (QLD): If there is a number-one snorkel and dive site in Australia, this is it. If you stayed a week, you couldn't snorkel all the acres of coral stretching from shore. Take your pick each day of 22 dive sites, such as the Coral Cascades, with football trout and anemones; the Blue Pools, favored by octopus, turtles, and sharks; and Heron Bommie, with its rays, eels, and Spanish dancers. Absolute magic. See chapter 6.

- **Lady Elliot Island** (QLD): Gorgeous coral lagoons, perfect for snorkeling, line this tiny coral cay island off the town of Bundaberg. Boats take you farther out to snorkel above manta rays, plate coral, and big fish. Divers can swim through the blow hole, 16 meters (52 ft.) down, and see Gorgonian fans, soft and hard corals, shark, cod, wrasse, barracudas, and loads of reef fish. See chapter 6.

- **Rottnest Island** (WA): Just 19 kilometers (12 miles) off Perth, excellent snorkeling and more than 100 dive sites await you on this former prison island. Wrecks, limestone overhangs, and myriad fish will keep divers entertained. There are no cars, so snorkelers should rent a bike and snorkel gear, buy a map of suggested snorkel trails in 20 pretty bays, and head off to find their own private coral garden. The sunken grotto of Fishhook Bay is great for fish life. See chapter 9.

- **Ningaloo Reef** (WA): A stunningly well-kept secret is how we'd describe Australia's second great barrier reef, stretching some 260 kilometers (163 miles) along the Northwest Cape halfway up Western Australia. Coral starts right on shore, not 90 minutes out to sea as at the Great Barrier Reef. Snorkel or dive with manta rays, and dive to see sharks, angel fish, turtles, eels, grouper, potato cod, and much more. Snorkel with the world's biggest fish, whale sharks up to 18 meters (60 ft.) long, every year from March to early June. See chapter 9.

7 The Best Places to Bushwalk (Hike)

- **Blue Mountains** (NSW): Many bushwalks in the Blue Mountains National Park offer awesome views of valleys, waterfalls, cliffs, and forest. They are all easily reached from Sydney. See chapter 4.
- **Whitsunday Islands** (QLD): Most people think of snorkeling and water sports when they come to these 74 subtropical national-park islands clad in dense rain forest and bush, but every resort island we recommend in chapter 6 has hiking trails. Some are flat; some are hilly. Wallabies and butterflies are common sights en route. South Molle has the best network of trails and 360° island views from its peak. See chapter 6.
- **Lamington National Park** (QLD): Few other national parks in Australia have such a well-marked network of trails as this one, located just 90 minutes from the Gold Coast. In all there are 160 kilometers (100 miles) of tracks. Revel in dense subtropical rain forest, marvel at mossy 2,000-year-old Antarctic beech trees, delight in the prolific wallabies and birds, and soak up the cool mountain air. See chapter 6.
- **Larapinta Trail** (The Red Centre, NT): Soon you will be able to start at Alice Springs and walk this entire 250-kilometer (156-mile) semidesert trail that winds through the stark crimson MacDonnell Ranges. The trail is still under construction, but plenty of day-length and multiday sections are waiting for you now. This one's for the cooler months only. See chapter 7.
- **Kakadu National Park** (NT): Whether you want a pleasant wetlands stroll or a tough overnight hike in virgin bushland, you can find it in this World Heritage–listed park. You'll see red cliffs, cycads, waterfalls, lily-filled lagoons hiding man-eating crocodiles, what looks like Australia's entire bird population, and Aboriginal rock art. See chapter 8.
- **Cape-to-Cape** (WA): Rugged sea cliffs, a china-blue sea, eucalyptus forest, white beaches, and coastal heath are what you will experience hiking between Cape Naturaliste and Cape Leeuwin, in the southwest corner of Western Australia. Walk a short section or tackle the whole 6-day extravaganza. In season, you'll see whales and wildflowers. See chapter 9.
- **Freycinet National Park** (TAS): The trek to Wine Glass Bay passes warty pink granite outcrops, with views over an ocean sliced by a crescent of icy sand. It's prehistorically beautiful. See chapter 14.
- **Cradle Mountain & Lake St. Clair National Park** (TAS): The 80-kilometer (50-mile) Overland Track is the best hike in Australia. The trek, from Lake St. Clair to Cradle Mountain, takes anywhere from 5 to 10 days, depending on your fitness level. Shorter walks, some lasting just half an hour, are also accessible. See chapter 14.

8 The Best Places to Learn About Aboriginal Culture

- **The Umbarra Aboriginal Cultural Centre** (Wallaga Lake, near Narooma, NSW): This center offers boomerang- and spear-throwing instruction, painting with natural ochres, discussions on Aboriginal culture, and guided walking tours of Aboriginal sacred sites. See chapter 4.
- **Tjapukai Aboriginal Cultural Park** (Cairns, QLD): This multimillion-dollar center showcases the history of the local Tjapukai people—their Dreamtime creation history and their often-harrowing experiences since white man arrived—using a film, a superb theatrical work, and a dance performance. Its Aboriginal art and crafts gift shop is one of the country's biggest and best. See chapter 6.
- **Native Guide Safari Tours** (Port Douglas, QLD): Hazel Douglas, an Aborigine who was brought up in the 110-million-year-old Daintree rain forest, takes you on a full-day 4WD rain-forest safari. She shows you how to rustle up a roast dinner using a termites nest, tells you how to know you're in for rain (it's in the way lizards sit on trees), and teaches you how to know when a crocodile is in the water. It's a fabulous insight into the world's oldest culture—one that's almost lost. See chapter 6.
- **Aboriginal Art & Culture Centre** (Alice Springs, NT): You'll get to taste bush food, throw boomerangs and spears, see a dance, and learn about Aboriginal family values in one action-packed half-day tour of this Aborigine-owned center in Alice Springs. Be sure to visit the museum and art gallery, where you can take a 1-hour didgeridoo lesson. See chapter 7.
- **Lilla Aboriginal Tours** (Kings Canyon, NT): Take a short walk with an Aboriginal guide to see sacred paintings in Watarrka National Park. You'll learn the Dreamtime significance of the art, taste bush food, throw a boomerang, and ask questions of your guide about local Aboriginal ways. See chapter 7.
- **Anangu Tours** (Ayers Rock, NT): The Anangu are the owners of Ayers Rock, or Uluru, as it is called in their native tongue. Join them for walks around the Rock as you learn about the poisonous snake men who fought battles here, pick bush food off the trees, throw spears, visit rock paintings, and watch the sun set over the monolith. Their Cultural Centre near the base of the Rock has good displays of cultural and Dreamtime life. See chapter 7.
- **Manyallaluk Tours** (Katherine, NT): This Aboriginal community welcomes visitors to their bush home for the day and teaches them to paint, weave, throw boomerangs, and do other tasks of daily life. A nice, low-key day with opportunities to chat one-on-one with Aboriginal people. See chapter 8.
- **Mangarrayi People** (Katherine, NT): Mike Keighley of **Far Out Adventures** takes tours to beautiful Elsey Station (a ranch) near Katherine, where you visit with the children of the local Mangarrayi people. You'll get to sample bush tucker, learn a little bush medicine, and swim in a vine-clad natural "spa-pool" in the Roper River. See chapter 8.
- **Yamatji Bitja Aboriginal Bush Tours** (Kalgoorlie, WA): Geoffrey Stokes, who was brought up the traditional Aboriginal way in the bush near Kalgoorlie, takes you out tracking emus, foraging for bush food, and even hunting a 'roo for dinner (with a gun, not a boomerang!). Explore the bush, learn about Dreamtime creation myths, and find out what his childhood was like. See chapter 9.
- **Tandanya Aboriginal Cultural Institute** (Adelaide, SA): This is a great place to experience Aboriginal life through Aboriginal eyes. You might catch one of the dance or other performances, although there are plenty of other opportunities to find out more about Aboriginal culture. See chapter 10.

9 The Best of Small-Town Australia

- **Central Tilba** (NSW): Just inland from Narooma on the south coast, this tiny historic hamlet is one of the cutest you'll ever see, complete with its own blacksmiths and leather-work outlets. The ABC cheese factory here offers visitors free tastings, while you can spend hours browsing the antique stalls or simply admiring the period buildings. See chapter 4.

- **Broken Hill** (NSW): Known for its giant silver mines, the quirky town of Broken Hill has more pubs per capita than just about anywhere else. It's also the home of the School of the Air—a "classroom" that transmits its lessons by radio to isolated communities spread over thousands of miles of Outback. Here you'll also find the eccentric Palace Hotel, made famous in the movie *The Adventures of Priscilla, Queen of the Desert,* as well as plenty of colonial mansions and heritage homes. See chapter 4.

- **Port Douglas** (QLD): What happens when trendy Sydneysiders and Melburnites discover a quaint one-street fishing village in tropical north Queensland? Come to Port Douglas and find out. A strip of groovy restaurants and a championship golf course have not diminished "Port's" old-fashioned air. Four Mile Beach is at the end of the street, and boats depart daily for the Great Barrier Reef from the marina. See chapter 6.

- **Mission Beach** (QLD): You'd never know this tidy village, hidden in lush rain forest off the highway, existed if you weren't a well-informed traveler. Aussies know it's here, but few of them bother to patronize its dazzling beach, off-shore islands, and secluded rain-forest trails; so you'll have the place all to yourself. There's great white-water rafting on the nearby Tully River, too. See chapter 6.

- **Broome** (WA): This romantic pearling port on the far-flung Kimberley coast on the Indian Ocean blends Aussie corrugated-iron architecture with red pagoda roofs left by the Chinese pearl divers who settled here. The town combines a sophisticated international ambience with a rough Outback attitude. Play on beautiful Cable Beach (see "The Best Beaches," above) and stay at glamorous Cable Beach Inter-Continental Resort. This is the place to add to your South Sea pearl collection. See chapter 8.

- **Kalgoorlie** (WA): This is it, the real McCoy, the iconic Australian country town. Vibrant Kalgoorlie sits on what used to be the richest square mile of gold-bearing earth ever to see the light of day. It still pumps around 2,000 ounces *a day* out of the ground. Have a beer in one of the gracious 19th-century pubs, peer into the absolutely enormous open-cut gold mine (the world's biggest), and wander the ghost-town streets of its sister town, Coolgardie. See chapter 9.

- **Hahndorf** (SA): A group of Lutheran settlers founded this German-style town, located in the Adelaide Hills just outside the Adelaide, in the 1830s. You'll love the churches, the wool factory and craft shops, and the delicious German food served up in the local cafes, restaurants, and bakeries. See chapter 10.

- **Coober Pedy** (SA): For a fair dinkum (that means "genuine") Outback experience, few places are as weird and wonderful as this opal-mining town in the middle of nowhere. You can visit mines, see wacky museums, and stay in a hotel underground—which is not really that unusual, considering that all the locals live like moles anyway. See chapter 10.

- **Launceston** (TAS): Tasmania's second city is not much larger than your average European or American small town, but it's packed with Victorian and Georgian architecture and plenty of remnants of Australia's convict days. Spend a couple of days here discovering the town and the local scenery, and splurge a little on a stay in a historic hotel. See chapter 14.

10 The Best Museums

- **National Maritime Museum** (Sydney, NSW): The best things about this museum are the ships and submarines often docked in the harbor out front. You can climb aboard and explore what it's like to be a sailor. Inside are some fascinating displays relating to Australia's dependence on the oceans. See chapter 3.
- **Alice Springs Telegraph Station Historical Reserve** (NT): It's not called a museum, but that's what this restored telegraph repeater station out in the picturesque hills by a spring—Alice Springs—really is. From the hot biscuits turned out from the wood-fired oven to the old telegraph equipment tapping away, this 1870s settlement is as real as history can get. See chapter 7.
- **Australian Aviation Heritage Centre** (Darwin, NT): The pride of this hangar is a B-52 bomber on permanent loan from the United States. But there's loads more, and not just heaps of planes, engines, and other aviation paraphernalia—there are detailed stories, jokes, and anecdotes associated with the exhibits. See chapter 8.
- **Warradjan Aboriginal Cultural Centre** (NT): Reader Mari Fagin of Oklahoma City, OK, wrote that this small, stylish museum in Kakadu National Park makes for a "very memorable and moving experience!! This museum is one of the best of its type we've ever seen." Learn about Aboriginal Dreamtime myths and day-to-day life. See chapter 8.
- **Western Australian Maritime Museum** (Perth, WA): Housed in a two-level warehouse in the historic port precinct of Fremantle, Perth, this museum tells tales of the Western Australian coastline since the Dutch first bumped into it and promptly abandoned it as useless in the 1600s. Anyone who ever dreamed of finding a shipwreck laden with pieces of eight will relish the displays of treasure recovered from the deep. See chapter 9.
- **York Motor Museum** (York, WA): This multimillion-dollar collection of veteran, vintage, classic, and racing cars is one of the most wide-ranging in the country. If you're a car buff, don't hang around Perth—get yourself the 99 kilometers (62 miles) to the historic country town of York and make a day of it. See chapter 9.
- **New Norcia Museum and Art Gallery** (New Norcia, WA): The collection of European Renaissance art in this tiny country museum in the Spanish Benedictine monastery town of New Norcia is mind-boggling. The museum also has all kinds of memorabilia from the monks' past—manuscripts, clothing, musical instruments—and gifts from Queen Isabella of Spain. See chapter 9.
- **Migration Museum** (Adelaide, SA): This fascinating museum gives visitors insight into the people who came to Australia, how and where they settled, and how many suffered getting here. Don't expect a lot of musty displays, because this museum is full of hands-on activities. See chapter 10.
- **Australian War Memorial** (Canberra, ACT): Given its name, you might think this museum is a bleak sort of place, but you'd be wrong. The museum gives important insight into the Anzac (Australian and New Zealand Army Corps) spirit, including an evocative exhibit on the tragic battle of Gallipoli. There's also a pretty good art collection. See chapter 13.

11 The Best Luxury Accommodations

- **Ritz-Carlton, Sydney** (☎ **1800/145 004** in Australia, or 02/9252 4600): This grand five-star city hotel combines old-world luxury with a wonderful bar and nice views. I like the top-hatted doorman who valet-parked my rusting 1976 Toyota without a comment. See chapter 3.
- **Park Hyatt Sydney** (☎ **13 12 34** in Australia, or 02/9241 1234): You'll have to book well in advance to snag a room at Sydney's best-positioned property, located at the edge of the city's historic Rocks district. Many rooms have fabulous views across the harbor to the Sydney Opera House. See chapter 3.
- **Lizard Island** (off Cairns, QLD; ☎ **1800/737 678** in Australia, 800/225-9849 in the U.S. and Canada, or 020/7805 3875 in the U.K.): Exclusive Lizard Island has long been popular with Americans for its game fishing, wonderful coral and diving, smart food, and simple upscale lodge accommodations. See chapter 6.
- **Sebel Reef House** (Cairns, QLD; ☎ **1800/079 052** in Australia): Everyone who stays here says the same thing: "It feels like home." Airy rooms look into tropical gardens, waterfalls cascade into the pools, mosquito nets drape over the beds, and you could swear pith-helmeted colonial officers will be back any minute to finish their gin-and-tonics in the clubby Brigadier Bar. Idyllic Palm Cove Beach is just across the road. See chapter 6.
- **Bedarra Island** (off Mission Beach, QLD; ☎ **1800/737 678** in Australia, 800/225-9849 in the U.S. and Canada, or 020/7805 3875 in the U.K.): Presidents and princesses in need of a little time out come to this small rain-forest island ringed by beaches. The timber villas are cozy, and the ultradiscreet staff assures privacy. Best of all, though, is the extravagant 24-hour open bar. See chapter 6.
- **Orpheus Island Resort** (off Townsville or Cairns, QLD; ☎ **1800/077 167** in Australia): Beloved of film stars and others who relish privacy, this resort has simple, attractive rooms; good food; a marvelous sense of seclusion; and a particularly beautiful location in the curve of a palm-lined bay. The only way in is by seaplane. See chapter 6.
- **Hayman** (Whitsunday Islands, QLD; ☎ **1800/075 175** in Australia, or call Leading Hotels of the World at ☎ 800/223-6800 in the U.S. and Canada, 0800/181 123 in the U.K., 1800/409 063 in Ireland, or 0800/44 1016 in New Zealand): Located on Hayman Island in the sybaritic Whitsundays, this is Australia's most glamorous resort. It's got classy rooms, excellent restaurants, staff keen to please, a superb hexagonal swimming pool, and a fleet of gleaming charter boats waiting to spirit you off to the Reef or your own deserted isle. See chapter 6.
- **El Questro Homestead** (The Kimberley, WA; ☎ **08/9169 1777**): Charming country decor spiced up with Indonesian antiques, good cooking, and a dramatic gorge location make this glamorous homestead on a remote million-acre cattle station popular with international jet-setters. Cruise wild gorges, heli-fish for barramundi, and hike to Aboriginal rock art while you're here. See chapter 8.
- **Cable Beach Inter-Continental Resort** (Broome, WA; ☎ **1800/095 508** in Australia, 800/327-0200 in the U.S. and Canada, 020/8847 2277 or 0345/58 1444 outside London in the U.K., 1800/709 300 in Ireland, or 0800/442 215 in New Zealand): Chinatown meets the Outback at this elegant corrugated-iron-and-pagoda-studded resort lying low along glorious Cable Beach in the romantic pearling port of Broome. No international hotel cookie cutter can match the

three to-die-for suites, decorated with superb Asian antiques and paintings by luminaries of the Australian art world. See chapter 8.

- **The Hotel Como** (Melbourne, VIC; ☎ **1800/033 400** in Australia, or 03/9825 2222): Great service, nice rooms, and free plastic ducks make this one of our favorite top-flight Australian hotels. See chapter 11.
- **Hyatt Hotel Canberra** (Canberra, ACT; ☎ **13 12 34** in Australia, 800/ 233-1234 in the U.S. and Canada, or 02/6270 1234): Visiting heads of state and pop stars make this their residence of choice when staying in Canberra. It's only a 2-minute drive from the central shopping district, and a stone's throw from both Lake Burley Griffin and the Parliamentary Triangle. See chapter 13.

12 The Best Moderately Priced Accommodations

- **Explorers Inn Hotel** (☎ **1800/62 3288** in Australia) and **Hotel George Williams** (☎ **1800/064 858** in Australia), both in Brisbane, QLD: These two hotels just around the corner from each other in Brizzie are shining examples of what affordable hotels should be—trendy, clean, and bright with useful facilities like 24-hour front desk, hair dryers, helpful staff, and a pleasant, inexpensive restaurant attached. See chapter 5.
- **The Reef Retreat** (Cairns, QLD; ☎ **07/4059 1744**): It's not often you find so much decorating taste—wooden blinds, teak furniture, and colorful upholstery—at a price you want to pay, but that's what you get at the apartments in trendy Palm Cove, one of Cairns's most desirable beachfront suburbs. There's a swimming pool in the lovely landscaped grounds, but the beach is just a block away. See chapter 6.
- **Archipelago Studio Apartments** (Port Douglas, QLD; ☎ **07/4099 5387**): They may be tiny, but these pretty apartments have a homey atmosphere and are just seconds from spectacular Four Mile Beach. Some units have sea views. The solicitous proprietor is a mine of advice on things to see and do. See chapter 6.
- **South Molle Island** (Whitsunday Islands, QLD; ☎ **1800/075 080** in Australia): At first glance this pretty island resort ain't all that moderately priced, but for an island, it is. Hearty buffet meals, nonmotorized water sports, and other activities are included in the price. See chapter 6.
- **Bahia Beachfront** (the Gold Coast, QLD; ☎ **07/5538 3322**): They're no shakes in the glamour-puss stakes, but these comfortable apartments are big, clean, and airy, and most have great views of the beach right opposite—all for just A$127 (U.S.$82.55) for a double in high season. See chapter 6.
- **Miss Maud Swedish Hotel** (Perth, WA; ☎ **1800/998 022** in Australia): Staying at this slightly musty hotel in the heart of Perth is like staying at grandma's— even if your grandma's house doesn't have Swedish murals on the walls. Friendly staff members who actually look pleased to see you and great food complete the picture. See chapter 9.
- **North Adelaide Heritage Apartments & Cottages** (Adelaide, SA; ☎ **08/8272 1355**): These accommodations actually consist of 18 separate fabulous properties in North Adelaide and Eastwood. The former Friendly Meeting Chaple Hall resembles a small church stocked with Victorian antiques. Another memorable place is the George Lowe Esq. Apartment, done up in the style of a 19th-century gentleman's bachelor pad. See chapter 10.
- **Macquarie Manor** (Hobart, TAS; ☎ **1800/243 044** in Australia, or 03/6224 4999): This lovely place in the heart of Hobart has a variety of heritage rooms with individual appeal. It's just a short walk to the waterfront. See chapter 14.

• **York Mansions** (Launceston, TAS; ☎ **03/6334 2933**): If you feel that where you stay is as important to your visit as what you see, then don't miss out on a night or two here. This National Trust–classified building has five spacious apartments, each with a distinct character. It's like living the high life in the Victorian age. See chapter 14.

13 The Best Alternative Accommodations

• **Underground Motel** (White Cliffs, NSW; ☎ **1800/02 1154** in Australia, or 08/8091 6677): All but two of this motel's rooms are underground in this fascinating opal-mining town. Rooms are reached by a maze of spacious tunnels dug out of the rock. See chapter 4.

• **Daintree Eco Lodge & Spa** (near Port Douglas, QLD; ☎ **1800/808 010** in Australia): These 15 luxury cabins perched high in the tree canopy by a gushing waterfall are Australia's premier rain-forest getaway. Walk the trails, have the tour desk book you on a jungle river cruise, or enjoy an aromatherapy facial in the spa. See chapter 6.

• **Whitsunday Wilderness Lodge** (The Whitsunday Islands, QLD; ☎ **07/3357 3843**): The 10 comfy beachfront cabins are basic, but your vacation at this island eco-retreat will be anything but. Sea kayak, sail, snorkel, hike rain-forest trails, dine with other guests outside under the Milky Way, and maybe even swim with Myrtle, the pet kangaroo. Considering you won't put your hand in your wallet except for wine and maybe a sea-plane trip to the Reef, this is a great value. See chapter 6.

• **Kingfisher Bay Resort & Village** (Fraser Island, QLD; ☎ **1800/072 555** in Australia): If it weren't for the ranger station and natural-history videos in the lobby, the wildlife walks, the guided 4WD safaris, and other eco-activities taking place, you'd hardly know that this hotel is an eco-resort, so comfortable and modern is it. See chapter 6.

• **Binnaburra Mountain Lodge** (☎ **1800/074 260** in Australia) and **O'Reilly's Rainforest Guesthouse** (☎ **1800/688 722** in Australia): both in the Gold Coast Hinterland, QLD: Tucked snugly almost 1,000 meters (3,000 ft.) up on rain-forested ridges, these cozy retreats offer fresh mountain air, daily activities, and instant access to the hiking trails of Lamington National Park. At O'Reilly's you can hand-feed brilliantly colored rain-forest birds every morning. See chapter 6.

• **Emma Gorge Resort** (The Kimberley, WA; ☎ **08/9169 1777**): At this spick-and-span little settlement on the 1-million-acre El Questro cattle station, guests stay in cute safari tents with wooden floors and electric lights, eat at a rustic gourmet restaurant, and join in the many hikes, bird-watching tours, river cruises, and more. A hike up Emma Gorge takes you to an Edenic swimming hole surrounded by red cliffs. See chapter 8.

• **Prairie Hotel** (Flinders Ranges, SA; ☎ **08/8648 4844**): This remarkable tin-roofed, stone-walled Outback pub in the Flinders Ranges has quaint rooms, a great bar out front where you can meet the locals, and some of the best food in Australia. See chapter 10.

• **Cradle Mountain Lodge** (Cradle Mountain, TAS; ☎ **03/6492 1303**): Just minutes from your comfortable cabin are 1,500-year-old trees, moss forests, craggy mountain ridges, limpid pools and lakes, and hordes of scampering marsupials. See chapter 14.

- **Freycinet Lodge** (Freycinet National Park, Coles Bay, TAS; ☎ 03/6257 0101): These eco-friendly bush cabins are right next to one of the nation's best walking tracks. The ocean views from the magnificent restaurant and the surrounding balconies are spectacular. See chapter 14.

14 The Best B&Bs & Guest Houses

- **The Russell** (The Rocks, Sydney; ☎ 02/9241 3543): This B&B, wonderfully positioned in the city's old quarter, is the coziest place to stay in all of Sydney. It's got creaky floorboards, a ramshackle feel, brightly painted corridors, and rooms with immense character. See chapter 3.
- **Echoes Guesthouse** (Katoomba, Blue Mountains, NSW; ☎ 02/4782 1966): Echoes is right on the edge of a dramatic drop into the Jamison Valley. The views from the balconies are breathtaking. See chapter 4.
- **Barrington Guest House** (Barrington Tops National Park, The Hunter, NSW; ☎ 02/4995 3212): Nestled in a valley just outside the Barrington Tops National Park, this charming guest house and luxury cabin property offers magnificent rain-forest walks, plenty of native animals, and excellent activities, such as horseback riding through the bush. See chapter 4.
- **Peppers Anchorage Port Stephens** (Port Stephens, NSW; ☎ 1800/809 142 in Australia, or 02/4984 2555): This low-rise resort is built onto a headland and runs almost directly into the pristine waterways of Port Stephens Bay, just north of Sydney. It's a great place to relax after a day spent watching dolphins and whales swim offshore. See chapter 4.
- **Paddington B&B Waverley** (Brisbane, QLD; ☎ 07/3369 8973): This gorgeous old timber Queenslander house has pretty rooms, and a cool deck within earshot of rainbow lorikeets chirping in the mango trees. The hospitality from your hostess, Annette Henry, makes this a truly lovely place to stay. The cute shops and galleries of fashionable Paddington are right outside your door. See chapter 5.
- **Lilybank Bed & Breakfast** (Cairns, QLD; ☎ 07/4055 1123): This rambling 1890s homestead used to be the Cairns mayor's residence. Today, owners Pat and Mike Woolford welcome guests to its comfy rooms, wide verandas, and blooming gardens. You can also stay in the renovated gardener's cottage. Pat and Mike are loads of fun. See chapter 6.
- **The Rocks** (Townsville, QLD; ☎ 07/4771 5700): Victorian charm has been poured into this old Queenslander with stylish, not frilly, results. Eat off valuable china in the old dining room, bathe in a clawfoot tub in the main bathroom, and meet other guests for sherry on the wide old veranda at dusk. See chapter 6.
- **Marae** (near Port Douglas, QLD; ☎ 07/4098 4900): Lush bushland full of butterflies and birds is the setting for this gorgeous contemporary Queenslander house with hip rooms and an outdoor plunge pool. Host Andy Morris serves a wonderful breakfast, and Cactus, the crazy pet cockatoo, gives you a warm welcome, too. See chapter 6.
- **The Summer House** (Darwin, NT; ☎ 08/8981 9992): Groovy guest rooms with hip furniture, funky bathrooms, louvered windows, and tropical gardens make this small converted apartment block an oasis of cool—in both senses of the word. See chapter 8.
- **Hansons Swan Valley** (near Perth, WA; ☎ 08/9296 3366): Good-bye faded lace, hello art deco—here is a B&B with cutting-edge style for young sophisticates.

Thirty-somethings Jon and Selina Hanson have created a stylish retreat nestled among the Swan Valley vineyards an easy drive from Perth. See chapter 9.

- **Heritage Trail Lodge** (Margaret River, WA; ☎ **08/9757 9595**): How many B&Bs do you know that provide a double Jacuzzi in every room? These salmon-pink cabins abut tall karri forest where parrots flit, streams gush, and peace is attainable. 'Roos hop into the parking lot on occasion, and the fabulous Margaret River wineries surround you. See chapter 9.
- **Hillside Country Retreat** (York, WA; ☎ **08/9641 1065**): Diplomats and assorted VIPs often squeeze in a stay at this charming B&B when they're visiting Perth. Stay in the old-fashioned homestead or the old servants' quarters and marvel at the mounds of historic memorabilia your hosts have amassed. Then explore York's lovely historic streets. See chapter 9.
- **Collingrove Homestead** (Angaston, the Barossa Valley, SA; ☎ **08/8564 2061**): This country house, built in 1856, has a real air of colonial manor farm living, with hallways festooned with hunting trophies, rifles, and oil paintings, and plenty of oak paneling and antiques scattered about. See chapter 10.
- **Robinson's by the Sea** (St. Kilda, Melbourne; ☎ **03/9534 2683**): This 1870s heritage B&B just across the road from St. Kilda beach has a comfortable living room and dining room stocked with antiques and five individually decorated bedrooms. It's a very friendly place and a good value. See chapter 11.

15 The Best Restaurants

- **Mezzaluna** (Sydney, NSW; ☎ **02/9357 1988**): Come here for truly exquisite food, flawless service, and a great view across the city's western skyline. The main dining room opens onto a huge, all-weather terrace kept warm in winter by giant, overhead fan heaters. Don't miss it. See chapter 3.
- **MG Garage** (Sydney, NSW; ☎ **02/9383 9383**): Causing a stir in Sydney with the fashionable crowd, MG Garage is set in a car showroom and serves up great Modern Australian cuisine. See chapter 3.
- **Quay** (Sydney, NSW; ☎ **02/9251 5600**): Sydney's best seafood restaurant offers perhaps the loveliest view in Sydney. Gaze through the large glass windows towards the Opera House, the city skyline, the North Shore suburbs, and the Harbour Bridge. See chapter 3.
- **Sailors Thai** (Sydney, NSW; ☎ **02/9251 2466**): Come here for lunchtime noodles, Thai salads, and won ton soups served on a single stainless-steel table lined with some 40 chairs. Or try inventive Thai cuisine in the à la carte restaurant downstairs. See chapter 3.
- **Salt** (Sydney, NSW; ☎ **02/9332 2566**): You'll need to dress up in your coolest outfit to fit into the scene happening at this modernist restaurant in the Kirketon Hotel in Darlinghurst. Inside it's all sleek and chrome, and the menu is innovative Mod Oz all the way. See chapter 3.
- **Armstrong's** (Brisbane, QLD; ☎ **07/3832 4566**): Innovative Modern Australian cuisine with a French twist is served up at this stylish, intimate venue inside a historic building that used to house medical chambers. Book ahead to secure one of the 40 seats. See chapter 5.
- **Fishlips Bar & Grill** (Cairns, QLD; ☎ **07/4041 1700**): Clever ways with fresh seafood and other Aussie ingredients—such as crocodile—make this cheerful blue beach house on a busy Cairns highway a real winner. This place is the pick of the bunch in Cairns. See chapter 6.

- **Zouí Alto** (Townsville, QLD; ☎ **07/4721 4700**): Townsville is not a place that springs to mind when one is compiling a "Best Restaurants" list, but this rooftop venue fully deserves to be here for faultless Mediterranean fare and fab views of the bay. It's one of the best places to eat on the Queensland coast. See chapter 6.
- **Fraser's** (Perth, WA; ☎ **08/9481 7100**): The city center and Swan River sparkling in the sunshine seem so close that you can almost reach out and touch them from the terrace of this parkland restaurant. Sensationally good Mod Oz food turned out with flare and flavor is what you come here for; seafood is a specialty. Go for a bike ride in Kings Park afterward to work it off. See chapter 9.
- **Newtown House** (Vasse, near Margaret River, WA; ☎ **08/9755 4485**): Chef Stephen Reagan makes intelligent, flavorsome food that beautifully partners with premium Margaret River wines. Stay in his homestead B&B overnight and explore the wineries the next day. See chapter 9.
- **Lamont's** (in the Swan Valley near Perth, WA; ☎ **08/9296 4485**): Hearty, tasty, yet sophisticated fare is what this rustic restaurant in the vineyards is all about. It's worth the 20-minute drive from Perth, but if you can't make the trip, the chef does a mean takeout from her Perth outlet. See chapter 9.
- **Prairie Hotel** (Flinders Ranges, SA; ☎ **08/8648 4844**): Chef Darren ("Bart") Brooks serves up some very high-class cuisine in the middle of nowhere. His "feral" foods, such as kangaroo tail soup and a mixed grill of emu sausages, camel steak, and kangaroo, is remarkable. See chapter 10.
- **Flower Drum** (Melbourne, VIC; ☎ **03/9662 3655**): Praise pours in from all quarters for this upscale eatery serving Cantonese food. The food is exquisite and the service is impeccable. See chapter 11.
- **The Tryst** (Canberra, ACT; ☎ **02/6239 4422**): Canberra has far grander and more expensive restaurants, but this place has found a spot in our hearts for its constantly delicious food. It's also relaxed, feeling almost communal on busy nights. See chapter 13.

Planning Your Trip: 2
The Basics

by Natalie Kruger

This chapter aims to answer all of those practical questions that may pop up as you're planning your trip: how will you get there, how much will it cost, and myriad other pesky details. We've done all the legwork—ferreting out ways to nail down smart deals on airfares, listing package companies, locating outdoor adventure operators, and more—so you won't have to.

1 The Regions in Brief

People who have never visited Australia always wonder why such a huge country has a population of just 18 million people. The truth is, Australia can barely support that many. The vast majority of Australia is harsh **Outback** country, characterized by salt bush plains, arid brown crags, shifting sand deserts, and salt lake country. The soil for the most part is poor in the Outback; it hardly ever rains, and the rivers barely make it to the ocean. Nearly 90% of Australia's population lives in an area that covers only 2.6% of the continent. The only relatively decent rainfall occurs along a thin strip of land around Australia's eastern coastal fringe.

If Australia knows the harsh hand of Mother Nature, though, it also knows her bounty. The Queensland coast is blessed with one of the greatest natural attractions in the world: the Great Barrier Reef. The Reef stretches some 2,000-plus kilometers (1,250 miles) off Gladstone in Queensland to the Gulf of Papua, near New Guinea. It's home to approximately 1,500 kinds of fish and 400 species of corals.

Australia is made up of six states—New South Wales, Queensland, Victoria, South Australia, Western Australia, and Tasmania—and two internal "territories"—the Australian Capital Territory (ACT) and the Northern Territory. The political capital is Canberra, which lies within the boundaries of the ACT.

This book isn't organized strictly along state and territory lines, however. It's organized more in accordance with the way Australians think of the country and the way travelers will experience it. *See the map on pp. 2–3 or the map on the inside cover of this guide to visualize the regions described here.*

NEW SOUTH WALES   Australia's most populated state is also the one most visited by tourists. Principally they come to see **Sydney,** undoubtedly one of the most glamorous cities in the world, with dozens of harbor and ocean beaches scattered within and around the

People are often surprised when they hear that both Melbourne and Brisbane are more than a long day's drive from Sydney, and that it takes the best part of a week to drive from Sydney to Perth. When planning your itinerary, keep in mind that Australia is as big as the whole of western Europe and about the same size as the 48 contiguous U.S. states.

city, and a dramatic mixture of bushland and city development around Harbour itself. Sydney is also a good base for excursions inland, especially to the **Blue Mountains** and the wineries of the **Hunter Valley.**

Farther afield is a string of quaint beachside towns stretching all the way down the southern coast into Victoria. Along the north coast are remnant areas of rain forest, impressive national parks, and a more tropical air, in laid-back hangouts such as Coffs Harbour.

Inland New South Wales is dry and sparsely forested. Its highlights include the area around Broken Hill in the far western part of the state (known for its abundant wildlife and Aboriginal influences), and the Outback opal-mining towns of White Cliffs and Lightning Ridge, which exist in a wacky underground world of their own.

QUEENSLAND   Without a doubt, the biggest draw in Queensland is the **Great Barrier Reef.** Coming to Australia and not visiting the Reef is a bit like going to Paris and skipping the Eiffel Tower. Ogling the tropical fish, weird sea creatures, and endless rainbow-hued corals will be a highlight of your Aussie holiday. The Reef stretches for more than 2,000 kilometers (1,200 miles) right along Queensland's coast, and anywhere from Bundaberg north is a good place to see it. Alluring island resorts are dotted all along the Reef, and while most are expensive, we've found one or two that won't break the bank.

Aside from the Reef, Queensland is also known for its numerous white-sand beaches. The best are on the **Gold Coast** in the state's south, though the **Sunshine Coast** has some lovely ones. **Cairns** and **Port Douglas** in the north have more than their fair share of beaches, too, but unfortunately, deadly box jellyfish call a halt to all ocean swimming from October to May anywhere north of Gladstone. Queensland has yet another aquatic playground—the 74 tropical **Whitsunday Islands.** These mostly uninhabited islands are a paradise for sea kayaking, diving, fishing, hiking through rain forest, and, best of all, sailing.

Away from the coast, the biggest attraction in the state is the lush 110-million-year-old **Daintree Rain Forest,** just north of Port Douglas. The capital, **Brisbane,** has Australia's largest koala sanctuary.

THE RED CENTRE   The eerie silence of **Uluru,** more commonly known as **Ayers Rock,** is what pulls everyone to the sprawling crimson sands of the Red Centre, the heart of the Northern Territory. Most folks discover that they like a nearby giant pebble even more, the towering domes of **Kata Tjuta,** also known as **the Olgas.** A half day's drive from the Rock brings you to **Kings Canyon,** a sheer orange desert gorge popular with hikers. If you visit the Red Centre, try to schedule some time in **Alice Springs.** This laid-back Outback town has the best Aboriginal arts-and-crafts shopping in Australia, some fun Aboriginal tours, a good desert wildlife park, wonderful scenery, hikes through the stark **MacDonnell Ranges,** and even camel rides down a dry riverbed.

Don't make the common mistake of flying into the Rock one day and flying out the next. Give yourself time to soak up the timeless peace of the Aussie desert. One of the best ways to appreciate the Red Centre is on a 3-day 4WD safari, where you camp out under the Southern Cross and cook around a campfire.

THE TOP END   The northwest reaches of Oz, from the dramatic Kimberley in Western Australia to the northern third of the Northern Territory, encompasses what Aussies eloquently dub "the Top End." This is Crocodile Dundee territory, a remote, vast, and hot semidesert region where men are heroes and cows probably outnumber people. Near **Darwin,** the territory's capital, is **Kakadu National Park,** where you can cruise past crocodiles on inland billabongs, bird-watch, and visit ancient Aboriginal rock art sites. Even closer to Darwin is **Litchfield National Park,** where you can take a dip in fern-fringed swimming holes surrounded by majestic red cliffs—stuff straight from Eden. You can cruise the orange walls of **Katherine Gorge,** a few hours south of Darwin, or explore them by canoe. You can even make your own dot painting at an Aboriginal community near **Katherine.**

In the Western Australia section of the Top End, you can visit age-old **Geikie and Windjana gorges,** pearl farms where the world's best South Sea pearls grow, and the charming (in a corrugated-iron sort of way) town of **Broome.** This tract of the country is so underexplored that most Aussies think of it almost as a foreign land. Near Kununurra, on the eastern edge of the Kimberley, is a million-acre **cattle station, El Questro,** where you can camp in comfy safari tents, fish for barramundi, hike through the bush to Aboriginal rock art, and dine every night on terrific modern Oz cuisine. In **Kununurra** you can cruise on the bird-rich and croc-infested Ord River and tour the Argyle Diamond Mine, the world's biggest.

WESTERN AUSTRALIA   One of the least-visited states (largely because distance and high airfares work against it), Western Australia is also the state with the most untamed natural beauty. The seas here teem with whales, and thrill seekers can swim alongside gentle giant whale sharks on the Northwest Cape every fall (Mar to June). Snorkelers gawk at corals and fish on **Rottnest Island,** about 19 kilometers (12 miles) off Perth, and in World Heritage–listed Shark Bay, tourists greet wild dolphins at **Monkey Mia.**

In the southwest "hook" of the continent lies the **Margaret River wine region.** Its wild forests, thundering surf, dramatic cliffs, rich bird life, and wild 'roos make it one of the country's most attractive wine regions. The state's capital, **Perth,** is known for its beaches and its wonderfully restored 19th-century port of Fremantle. One or two hours' drive from the city brings you to some lovely towns, like charming **York,** the state's oldest inland settlement, and the monastery town of **New Norcia.** Inland, the state is mostly wheat fields and desert, but if you have the time and inclination, head west 600 kilometers (375 miles) from Perth to the gold-mining boomtown of **Kalgoorlie.** With its gracious old pubs lining the wide bustling streets, it's just what you think the perfect Aussie country town should be.

SOUTH AUSTRALIA   Stretched out between Western Australia and Victoria is the nation's breadbasket, South Australia. The capital, **Adelaide,** is a stately affair known for its conservatism, parks, and churches. It's a delightful stopover, and it's a base for exploring one of Australia's most illustrious wine regions, the **Barossa Valley.** Big labels like Penfolds, Seppelts, and Wolf Blass are here, but take time to sniff out the many smaller but no less outstanding vineyards. And it's less than an hour from the city!

Bring your binoculars for the giant water-bird sanctuary called the **Coorong,** the south's version of Kakadu. Stay in an underground hotel in the offbeat opal-mining town of **Coober Pedy,** or ride a camel through the craggy, ancient arid lands of the **Flinders Ranges.**

But the greatest of South Australia's attractions (apart from wine, of course!) is **Kangaroo Island,** likely the best place in Australia to see native animals. In a single day—with the right guide—you can spot wallabies, rare birds, sea eagles, echidnas, seals, penguins, and even walk along a beach loaded with sea lions. It's a must-see.

VICTORIA Australia's second-largest city, **Melbourne,** is the capital of Victoria. Melbourne is far more stately than Sydney (more old-world than Californian) and offers an exciting mix of ethnicity and fashion. Areas around Melbourne offer plenty to see and to do, too, including **Phillip Island,** world-famous for its Penguin Parade, where hundreds of tiny penguins dash up the beach to their burrows at dusk; and the historic gold-mining city of **Ballarat.** Victoria is also the site of one of Australia's greatest road trips, the **Great Ocean Road,** which stretches for some 106 kilometers ($64^1/2$ miles) along some of the most scenic coastline you'll ever experience. Then there's the inland, which in Victoria is mostly high country, the stuff of legends, à la *The Man from Snowy River.* The skiing's pretty good around here as well, if you're around in the Down Under winter.

AUSTRALIAN CAPITAL TERRITORY (ACT) Surrounded entirely by New South Wales is the tiny Australian Capital Territory. The ACT is made up of bush land and the nation's capital, **Canberra,** a planned city that's very similar in architectural concept to Washington, D.C. Many outsiders may consider the capital boring, but Canberra can surprise you. It has the country's best museums, so don't automatically exclude it from your itinerary.

TASMANIA Finally, there's the last port before Antarctica: **Hobart,** capital of the island state of Tasmania. Visit the Apple Isle for its beautiful national parks, enormous stretches of wilderness, the world's best trout fishing, and a relaxed pace of life rarely experienced anywhere else. If you're up to it, you could tackle the most well-known hiking trail in Australia, the **Overland Track,** a 85-kilometer (53-mile) route between **Cradle Mountain** and **Lake St. Clair** that passes through highland moors and dense rain forests and traverses several mountains. Another option is a more leisurely visit to **Port Arthur,** Australia's version of Devil's Island, where thousands of convicts brought in to settle the new British colony were imprisoned and died. All of Tasmania is spectacular, but you haven't seen anything until you've experienced **Freycinet National Park,** with its pink granite outcrops set against an emerald-green sea.

2 Visitor Information

The **Australian Tourist Commission (ATC)** is a great source of information if you are connected to the Internet, less so if you are not. Its excellent Web site, **www.australia.com**, has more than 10,000 pages of listings for tour operators, hotels, car-rental companies, specialist travel outfitters, public holidays, maps, distance charts, traveler's firsthand stories, and much more. It provides you with information tailored to travelers from your country of origin, including good-value packages, specials, and deals. By signing up for the free online **Travel Club,** you will be e-mailed news of hot deals, major events, and the like on a regular basis.

The ATC publishes a general **brochure,** a North American version called the *Australian Vacation Planner,* and a version for folks in the United Kingdom,

Europe, and New Zealand called the *Australian Travellers' Guide*. You may find them too general to be of much use. In some countries, the ATC also distributes a brochure on each of the states and the Northern Territory, and logs requests for brochures on a range (very limited so far) of cities or regions, accommodation chains, car and motor-home rental companies, and airlines, which then send their promotional material direct to you. What brochures are available can differ, depending on your country of origin. You can order them online.

The ATC maintains a network of **"Aussie Specialist"** travel agents in several hundred cities across the United States, Canada, the United Kingdom, New Zealand, and several other countries. These agents know better than most how to package an itinerary that's right for you, because they are committed to a continuous training program on the best destinations, hotels, deals, and tours in Oz. Get a referral to the nearest two Aussie Specialists by clicking the "Aussie Specialist" button on the main page on the ATC's Web site; or search the whole list by clicking the "Useful Resources" tab, also on the main page, then the "Contact Us" tab.

If you're online, you can contact the ATC's **Travel Counsellors** for help in piecing together an itinerary, or for answers to any other question about traveling in Australia. They attempt to reply within 48 hours.

No access to the Web? You can contact the **ATC's Aussie Helpline** numbers below to order brochures:

- **United States/Canada:** You can call ☎ **661/775-2000** (a toll call); this is an automated line with recorded information on visas and other aspects of visiting Australia. You can be transferred to an operator who will refer you to your nearest two Aussie Specialists, and log your order for an *Australian Vacation Planner*. Another option is to call ☎ **800/333-4305,** to locate an Aussie Specialist only.
- **United Kingdom:** ☎ **09068/633-235** (charged at 60p/min.).
- **Ireland:** ☎ **01/402-6896.**
- **New Zealand:** ☎ **0800/650 303** (toll-free outside Auckland) or **09/527 1629** (both are called "Aussie Infolines" in New Zealand).

In the United Kingdom and Ireland, the brochure you order will be sent out with a full list of Aussie Specialists in your country. The ATC also has brochure ordering lines in many other countries.

3 Entry Requirements & Customs

ENTRY REQUIREMENTS

Along with a current passport valid for the duration of your stay, the Australian government requires a visa from visitors of every nation (New Zealand citizens are issued a visa on arrival in Australia). This gets up the noses of the United States and other countries who do not make reciprocal demands on Australians, so the Australian government has introduced the **Electronic Travel Authority (ETA)**—an electronic or "paperless" visa that takes the place of a rubber stamp in your passport.

Here's how the ETA works: You give your passport details in person or over the phone to your travel agent or to your airline reservationist when you book your plane ticket. This information will be entered into the airline's reservations system, which is linked to the Australian Department of Immigration and Multicultural Affairs' computer system. Assuming you are not wanted by Interpol, your ETA should be approved in about 6 to 8 seconds while you wait. You can also apply for an ETA at Australian embassies, high commissions, and consulates (see below).

Note the fees below are in Australian dollars; the exact amount charged by the Australian embassy, consulate, or high commission in your country will depend on the foreign currency exchange rate.

Tourists should apply for a **Tourist ETA.** It's free and is valid for as many visits to Australia as you like of up to 3 months each within a 1-year period. Tourists may not work in Australia, so if you are visiting for business, you have two choices: apply for a free **Short Validity Business ETA,** which is valid for a single visit of 3 months within a 1-year period, or pay A$60 (U.S.$39) to apply for a **Long Validity Business ETA,** which entitles you to as many 3-month stays in Australia as you like for the life of your passport.

There are still some situations in which you will need to apply for a visa the old-fashioned way—by taking or mailing your passport, a completed visa application form, and the appropriate payment to your nearest Australian embassy or consulate. This will be the case if your travel agent, airline, or cruise ship (if you plan to arrive in Australia by boat) is not connected to the ETA system. In the United States, Canada, the United Kingdom, Ireland, and many other countries, most agents and airlines are ETA-compatible, but cruise lines are not yet. You will also need to apply for a visa the old-fashioned way if you plan to enter Australia as something other than a tourist or a business traveler—for example, as a full-time, long-term student; a long-term resident; a sportsperson; a performer; or a member of a social group or cultural exchange. If you fall into one of these categories, you will need to apply for a **Temporary Residence visa.** There is a A$60 (U.S.$39) processing fee for non-ETA tourist and business visas for stays of up to 3 months, and A$150 (U.S.$97.50) for business visas for stays between 3 months and 4 years. Non-ETA visa application fees for other kinds of travelers vary, from nil to thousands of dollars. Before shooting off a check, contact the nearest Australian embassy, consulate, or high commission to check what forms of payment they accept.

Apply for non-ETA visas at Australian embassies, consulates, and high commissions. In the **United States,** your state of residence determines where you apply. From California, Arizona, New Mexico, Hawaii, Idaho, Montana, Nevada, New Mexico, Oregon, Utah, and Washington, apply to the Australian Consulate-General, 2049 Century Park E., Level 19, Los Angeles, CA 90067-3238 (☎ 310/229-4800). From anywhere else in the United States, apply to the Australian Embassy, 1601 Massachusetts Ave. NW, Washington, DC 20036-2273 (☎ 202/797-3000). The Australian Embassy Web site is **www.aust.emb.nw.dc.us**. In **Canada,** contact the Australian High Commission, 50 O'Connor St., no. 710, Ottawa, ON K1P 6L2 (☎ 613/783 7665). For business-visa inquiries in the United States and Canada, call ☎ 800/579 7664. In the **United Kingdom,** contact the Australian High Commission, Australia House, The Strand, London WC2B 4LA (☎ 09001/600 333 for 24-hr. recorded information, or 020/7379 4334); or the Australian Consulate, Chatsworth House, Lever Street, Manchester M1 2QL (☎ 0161/228 1344). In **Ireland,** contact the Australian Embassy, Fitzwilton House, Wilton Terrace, Dublin 2, Ireland (☎ 1/676 1517). Travelers from Northern Ireland can lodge their applications in Dublin. The Australian government maintains a Web site tailored for a British audience at **www.australia.org.uk**.

You can obtain an application form for a non-ETA visa via the Internet at the **Australian Department of Immigration and Multicultural Affair**'s Web site (**www.immi.gov.au**). This site also has a good explanation of the ETA system.

Allow at least a month for processing of non-ETA visas.

CUSTOMS & QUARANTINE

WHAT YOU CAN BRING IN   Anyone over 18 can bring into Australia no more than 250 cigarettes or 250 grams of cigars or other tobacco products, 1.125 liters (41 fl. oz.) of alcohol, and "dutiable goods" to the value of A$400 (U.S.$260), or A$200 (U.S.$130) if you are under 18. Broadly speaking, **"dutiable goods"** are luxury items like perfume concentrate, watches, jewelry, furs, plus gifts of any kind. Keep this in mind if you intend to come bearing presents for family and friends in Australia; gifts given to you also count toward the dutiable limit. Your own personal goods that you're taking with you when you leave are usually exempt from duty. Customs officers do not collect duty of less than A$50 (U.S.$32.50) as long as you declared the goods in the first place. If you have something you think may be dutiable but are not sure, contact the nearest Australian embassy or consulate (see above). You can also call the **Australian Customs Service** in Canberra, Australia (☎ **02/6275 6666;** www.customs.gov.au).

Cash in any currency, and other currency instruments such as traveler's checks, under a value of A$10,000 (U.S.$6,500) need not be declared.

Australia is a signatory to the Convention on International Trade in Endangered Species (CITES), which restricts or bans the import of products made from **protected wildlife.** Examples of the numerous restricted items are coral, giant clam, wild cats, monkey, zebra, crocodile or alligator, bear, some types of caviar, American ginseng, and orchid products. You will need an export license from the product's country of origin *and* an import license from Australia to bring restricted items into Australia. Banned items include ivory, tortoise (marine turtle) shell, products from rhinoceros or tiger, and sturgeon caviar. Bear this in mind if you stop in other countries en route to Australia where souvenirs from items such as these may be widely sold. Australian authorities may seize and not return the items to you.

Because Australia is an island, it is free of many agricultural and livestock diseases. To keep it that way, strict quarantine applies to importing plants, animals, and their products, including food. Some items may be held for treatment and returned to you; others may be confiscated; others may be held over for you to take with you when you leave the country. Amnesty trash bins are available before you reach the immigration counters in airport arrivals halls for items such as fruit. Don't be alarmed if, just before landing, the flight attendants spray the aircraft cabin (with products approved by the World Health Organization) to kill potentially disease-bearing insects that entered the plane in a foreign country. For more information on what is and is not allowed entry, contact the nearest Australian embassy or consulate, or contact the **Australian Quarantine and Inspection Service** in Canberra, Australia (☎ **02/6272 3933;** www.aqis.gov.au).

WHAT YOU CAN BRING HOME   Check with your country's Customs or Foreign Affairs department for the latest guidelines—including information on items that are not allowed to be brought into your home country—just before you leave home.

Returning **U.S. citizens** who've been away for 48 hours or more are allowed to bring back, once every 30 days, $400 worth of merchandise duty-free. You'll be charged a flat rate of 10% duty on the next $1,000 worth of purchases. Be sure to have your receipts handy. On gifts, the duty-free limit is $100. You can't bring fresh foodstuffs into the United States; tinned foods, however, are allowed. For more information, contact the **U.S. Customs Service,** 1301 Constitution Ave. (P.O. Box 7407), Washington, DC 20044

(☎ 202/927-6724), and request the free pamphlet *Know Before You Go.* It's also available on the Web at **www.customs.ustreas.gov/travel/travel.htm**.

U.K. citizens should contact HM Customs & Excise Passenger Enquiries (☎ **0181/910-3744**) or visit **www.open.gov.uk**.

For a clear summary of **Canadian** rules, visit the comprehensive Web site of the **Canada Customs and Revenue Agency** at **www.ccra-adrc.gc.ca**.

For New Zealand customs information, contact the **New Zealand Customs Service** at ☎ **09/359-6655,** or go online to **www.customs.govt.nz**.

4 Money

See the "Taxes" section under "Fast Facts: Australia," at the end of this chapter, for details on **Australia's Goods & Services Tax (GST)**.

CASH & CURRENCY

The Australian dollar is divided into 100 cents. Coins come in 5¢, 10¢, 20¢, and 50¢ pieces (all silver in color) and $1 and $2 pieces (gold in color). The 50-cent piece is 12-sided. Prices in Australia often end in a variant of 1¢ and 2¢ (for example, 78¢ or $2.71), a relic from the days before 1-cent and 2-cent pieces were phased out (prices are now rounded up or down to the nearest 5¢). Bank notes come in denominations of $5, $10, $20, $50, and $100.

The Australian Dollar, the U.S. Dollar & the British Pound

For U.S. Readers The rate of exchange used to calculate the dollar values given in this book was U.S.$1 = approximately A$1.54 (or A$1 = U.S.65¢).

For British Readers The rate of exchange used to calculate the pound values in the accompanying table was 1 British pound = A$2.50 (or A$1 = 40p).

Note: International exchange rates can fluctuate markedly. Check the latest rate when you plan your trip. The table below, and all the prices in this book, should be used only as a guide.

A$	U.S.$	U.K.£	A$	U.S.$	U.K.£
0.25	0.16	0.10	30.00	19.50	12.00
0.50	0.33	0.20	35.00	22.75	14.00
1.00	0.65	0.40	40.00	26.00	16.00
2.00	1.30	0.80	45.00	29.25	18.00
3.00	1.95	1.20	50.00	32.50	20.00
4.00	2.60	1.60	55.00	35.75	22.00
5.00	3.25	2.00	60.00	39.00	24.00
6.00	3.90	2.40	65.00	42.25	26.00
7.00	4.55	2.80	70.00	45.50	28.00
8.00	5.20	3.20	75.00	48.75	30.00
9.00	5.85	3.60	80.00	52.00	32.00
10.00	6.50	4.00	85.00	55.25	34.00
15.00	9.75	6.00	90.00	58.50	36.00
20.00	13.00	8.00	95.00	61.75	38.00
25.00	16.25	10.00	100.00	65.00	40.00

ATMS

The fastest, safest, and easiest method of managing money Down Under is to withdraw money directly from your home bank account at an Australian ATM. That way you can get cash when banks and currency exchanges are closed, and your money is safely residing in your bank account back home until you withdraw it. It also means you get the bank exchange rate, not the higher commercial rate charged at currency exchanges. You will be charged a fee for each withdrawal, usually A$4 (U.S.$2.60) or so. (It's your bank back home that's tacking on this charge, not the Aussie bank, so ask your bank what it is.)

All of the biggest banks in Australia—ANZ, Commonwealth, National, and Westpac—are connected to the Cirrus network, which has 465,000 ATMs around the world—and the Plus network, which has 265,000 ATMs worldwide. Both **Cirrus** (☎ 800/424-7787; www.mastercard.com/atm) and **Plus** (☎ 800/843-7587; www.visa.com) networks have automated ATM locators that list the banks in each country that will accept your card. The locators are unwieldy to use, though; instead, ask your bank at home for a directory of international ATM locations where your card is accepted. Most ATMs in Australia accept both four- and six-digit PINs (personal identification numbers), but it's a good idea to request a four-digit PIN from your bank, because these are the most common, not just in Australia but throughout the rest of the world.

Few ATMs have letters on the keypads, so memorize your PIN by number.

In Outback areas, carry cash (several hundred dollars) and a credit card. ATMs are widely available in cities and towns, but they can be conspicuous by their absence in small country towns. Small merchants in remote parts may not cash traveler's checks.

CREDIT CARDS

Visa and MasterCard are universally accepted in Australia, but American Express and Diners Club are considerably less so. Always carry at least a little cash, because many merchants in Australia will not take cards for purchases under A$10 (U.S.$6.50) or so. If your credit card is linked to your bank account, it is good for withdrawing emergency cash from an ATM (just keep in mind that interest starts accruing immediately on credit-card cash advances).

Almost every credit-card company has an emergency toll-free number that you can call if your wallet or purse is stolen. Here are the Australia-wide numbers for the three major cards: **American Express** (☎ 1800/230 100), **MasterCard** (☎ 1800/120 113), and **Visa** (☎ 1800/125 440). Report your stolen wallet to the police, because your credit-card company may require a police report number.

TRAVELER'S CHECKS

Traveler's checks are something of an anachronism from the dark days before ATMs. Major towns and all cities in Australia have 24-hour ATMs, and virtually every establishment, even remote Outback gas stations, accepts credit cards. Traveler's checks are not nearly as widely accepted.

If you do opt to buy traveler's checks, get them in **Australian dollars.** Checks in U.S. dollars are widely accepted at banks, big hotels, currency exchanges, and shops in major tourist regions used to selling to customers from overseas, but chances are shops, restaurants, and any other kind of business will have no idea what the current exchange rate is when you present a U.S. check. Another plus of Australian-dollar checks is that two of the largest

Aussie banks, **ANZ** and **Westpac,** cash them free. It will cost you around A\$5 (U.S.\$3.25) to A\$7 (U.S.\$4.55) to cash checks in foreign currency at an Australian bank.

If you opt to carry traveler's checks, keep a record of their serial numbers, separately from the checks of course. To report lost or stolen **American Express traveler's checks** call ☎ **1800/25 1902** anywhere in Australia.

5 When to Go

When the Northern Hemisphere has winter, Australia, in the Southern Hemisphere, has summer, and vice versa. That means midwinter in Australia is July and August, and the hottest months are November to March. Remember, unlike in the Northern Hemisphere, the farther south you go in Australia, the colder it gets.

HIGH & LOW TRAVEL SEASONS

Airfares to Australia offered by U.S. airlines are lowest from mid-April to late August—that's just the time when it's best to travel in the Red Centre, the Top End, and the Great Barrier Reef!

HIGH SEASON It might surprise you to learn that the peak travel season in the most popular parts of Australia is **winter.** In much of the country—Queensland from around Townsville and northward, all of the Top End and the Red Centre, and most of Western Australia—summer is just too darn hot, too darn humid, too darn wet, or all three. The most pleasant time to travel in these parts is April to September—when daytime temperatures are 19°C to 31°C (66°F to 89°F) and it rarely rains. June, July, and August are the busiest months in these parts; you'll need to book accommodations and tours way in advance then, and you can look forward to paying higher rates then, too.

If I had to pick the one best month to visit Australia, I'd say **September,** when it's warm enough to hit the beach in the southern states on a good day, it's cool enough to tour Ayers Rock, and the humidity and rains have not yet come to Cairns and the Top End. It's also smack bang in the middle of Western Australia's **wildflower season.**

Try to avoid Australia from **Boxing Day (Dec 26) to the end of January,** when Aussies take their summer vacations. Hotel rooms and seats on planes get scarce as hen's teeth, and it's a rare airline or hotel that will discount even one dollar off their full tariffs.

LOW SEASON From **October to March,** intense heat can make touring outdoors all but impossible in the Red Centre, the Top End, and anywhere in Western Australia except Perth and the Southwest. The Top End, the Kimberley, and North Queensland, including Cairns, suffer an intensely hot, humid **Wet Season** from November or December to March or April. In the Top End and Kimberley, this is preceded by an even stickier "build-up" in October and November. Some attractions and tour companies close up shop, floodwaters render others off-limits, and hotels drop their rates.

On the other hand, summer (Dec, Jan, Feb) is a nice time to visit the **southern states**—New South Wales, Victoria, South Australia, Western Australia from Perth on south, and Tasmania. Even in winter, temperatures rarely dip below freezing in these parts, and snow falls only in parts of Tasmania, in the ski-fields of Victoria, and in the Snowy Mountains in southern New South Wales.

Australia's Average Temperatures (°F) and Rainfall

	Jan	Feb	Mar	Apr	May	June	July	Aug	Sept	Oct	Nov	Dec
Alice Springs												
Max	97	95	90	81	73	67	67	73	81	88	93	96
Min	70	69	63	54	46	41	39	43	49	58	64	68
Days of rain	4.8	3.9	8.6	7.8	8	2.6	2.1	2.1	0.6	1.9	3.5	4.4
Cairns												
Max	90	89	87	85	81	79	78	80	83	86	88	90
Min	74	74	73	70	66	64	61	62	64	68	70	73
Days of rain	18.5	18.2	19.7	16.1	11.8	8.2	5.4	5.7	4.9	6.0	10.0	14.7
Darwin												
Max	90	90	91	92	91	88	87	89	91	93	94	92
Min	77	77	77	76	73	69	67	70	74	77	78	78
Days of rain	18	16.9	15.5	11.3	8.0	1.5	1.3	1.5	1.2	5.7	11.4	15.2
Perth												
Max	85	85	81	76	69	64	63	67	70	76	81	73
Min	63	63	61	57	53	50	48	48	50	53	57	61
Days of rain	1.5	1.8	8.3	9.3	12.4	13.8	13.4	12.4	9.0	6.2	2.2	2.0
Sydney												
Max	78	78	76	71	66	61	60	63	67	71	74	77
Min	65	65	63	58	52	48	46	48	51	56	60	63
Days of rain	8.3	9.1	12.3	12.5	12.3	11.0	11.0	8.4	7.9	7.7	7.9	7.2

Source: Australian Tourist Commission Australia Vacation Planner.

HOLIDAYS

In addition to the period from December 26 to the end of January, when Aussies take their summer vacations, the 4 days at **Easter** (from Good Friday through Easter Monday) and all **school holiday periods** are very busy, so book ahead. The school year in Australia is broken into four semesters, with 2-week holidays falling around the last half of April, the last week of June and the first week of July, and the last week of September and the first week of October. Some states break at slightly different dates. There's a 6-week summer/Christmas vacation from mid-December to the end of January.

Almost everything shuts down on **Boxing Day** (Dec 26) and **Good Friday,** and much is closed New Year's Day, Easter Sunday, and Easter Monday. Most things are closed until 1pm, if not all day, on **Anzac Day,** a World War I commemorative day on April 25.

MAJOR NATIONAL HOLIDAYS

New Year's Day	January 1
Australia Day	January 26
Labor Day	First Monday in March (WA)
Eight Hours Day	First Monday in March (TAS)
Labor Day	Second Monday in March (VIC)
Canberra Day	Third Monday in March (ACT)
Good Friday	Varies (Apr 13 in 2001)
Easter Sunday	Varies (Apr 15 in 2001)
Easter Monday	Varies (Apr 16 in 2001)
Anzac Day	April 25
May Day	First Monday in May (NT)
Labour Day	First Monday in May (QLD)

Adelaide Cup	Third Monday in May (SA)
Foundation Day	First Monday in June (WA)
Queen's Birthday	Second Monday in June (except WA)
Royal National Show Day	Second or third Wednesday in August (QLD)
Queen's Birthday	Monday in late September/early October (WA)
Labour Day	First Monday in October (NSW, SA)
Melbourne Cup Day	First Tuesday in November (Melbourne only)
Christmas Day	December 25
Boxing Day	December 26 (usually celebrated on the next Mon if 26th falls on a weekend; if Christmas Day is a Sat and Boxing Day a Sun, then both the following Mon and Tues are holidays)

Australia Calendar of Events

January

✪ **New Year's Eve.** Watching the Sydney Harbour Bridge light up with New Year's Eve fireworks is a treat. The main show is at 9pm, not midnight, so young kids don't miss out. Pack a picnic and snag a Harbour-side spot by 4pm, or even earlier at the best vantage points—Mrs. Macquarie's Chair in the Royal Botanic Gardens and the Sydney Opera House.

• **Sydney Festival.** Highlights of Sydney's summertime visual and performing-arts festival are the free jazz, opera, and classical music concerts held outdoors Saturday nights in the Domain near the Botanic Gardens (take a picnic). Contact booking agent **Ticketek** (☎ 02/9266 4020) or go to www.sydneyfestival.org.au. For 3 weeks in January.

• **Hyundai Hopman Cup,** Perth. Tennis greats from the world's eight top tennis nations are invited to battle it out in a 7-day mixed-doubles competition. Contact the Cup's booking agent, **BOCS Ticketing** (☎ 08/9484 1133), or check www.hopmancup.com.au. Late December or early January.

• **Tamworth Country Music Festival,** Tamworth (459km/287 miles northwest of Sydney), New South Wales. It may look like an Akubra Hat Convention, but this 10-day gathering of rural folk and city folk who would like to be rural folk is Australia's biggest country music festival. The **Tamworth Information Centre** (☎ 02/6755 4300) takes bookings. Second half of January.

• **Australia Day.** Australia's answer to the Fourth of July marks the landing of the First Fleet at Sydney Cove in 1788. Most Aussies celebrate by heading to the nearest beach; in Sydney, there are ferry races and tall ships on the harbor, and fireworks in the evening. January 26.

• **Heineken Classic,** on Perth's outskirts. One of the country's richest golf tournaments with A$1.6 million (U.S.$1,040,000) up for grabs draws top players to the Novotel Vines Resort in the Swan Valley wine region, a 20-minute drive from Perth. Contact the Classic's office (☎ 08/9297 3399; www.heinekenclassic). February 2001; in 2002 the game shifts to Melbourne for 4 years.

March

✪ **Sydney Gay & Lesbian Mardi Gras.** A spectacular street parade of floats, costumes, and dancers, cheered on by several hundred thousand onlookers, followed by a giant gay-only warehouse party. Contact Sydney Gay & Lesbian Mardi Gras (☎ 02/9557 4332; www.mardigras.com.au).

Usually the last Saturday night in February or the first Saturday in March (it'll be Mar 3 in 2001).

✪ **Telstra Adelaide Festival.** This huge event on the international arts scene features enthusiastic performance art, music, dance, and outdoor concerts, as well as a writers week. A summer-party atmosphere takes over Adelaide's city streets every night until late. For tickets and information, contact booking agent **BASS** (☎ **08/8400 2205;** www. adelaidefestival.telstra.com.au). Over 2¹/₂ weeks in March every 2nd year (the next is Mar 1 through 17, 2002).

✪ **Qantas Australian Formula One Grand Prix,** Melbourne. The first Grand Prix of the year on the international FIA Formula One World Championship circuit is battled out on one of its fastest circuits, in Melbourne. Qantas offices worldwide sell tickets. In Australia, call Ticketmaster (☎ **13 1641**); contact Australian Grand Prix Corporation (☎ **03/ 9258 7100**); or order online at www.grandprix.com.au). Four days in the 1st or 2nd week of March.

April

• **Australian Surf Life Saving Championships,** Kurrawa Beach, Gold Coast, Queensland. As many as 6,000 bronzed Aussie and international men and women swim, ski paddle, sprint relay, pilot inflatable rescue boats, perform march-pasts, and resuscitate "drowning" swimmers in front of 10,000 spectators. Contact Surf Life Saving Australia (☎ **02/ 9597 5588;** www.slsa.asn.au). Over 4 days in late March or early April.

June

• **Sydney Film Festival.** World and Australian premieres of leading Aussie and international flicks are shown in the ornate State Theatre and other venues. Contact the Sydney Film Festival (☎ **02/9660 3844;** www. sydfilm-fest.com.au). Over 2 weeks from 1st or 2nd Friday in June.

August

• *Sun-Herald* **City to Surf,** Sydney. Fifty thousand Sydneysiders pound the pavement (or walk, or wheelchair it) in this 14-kilometer (9-mile) "fun run" from the city to Bondi Beach. For an entry form, write to the *Sun-Herald* City to Surf, 201 Sussex St., Sydney, NSW 2000 (☎ **1800/ 55 5514** in Australia, or 02/9282 2833), or enter on the day of the race. Usually the 2nd Sunday in August.

September

• **Floriade,** Canberra. A million tulips, daffodils, hyacinths, and other blooms carpet the banks of Canberra's Lake Burley Griffin in stunning themed flowerbed designs at this spring celebration, which also features performing arts and the like. Contact the Canberra Tourism & Events Corporation (☎ **02/6205 0044;** www.canberratourism.com.au) and see www.floriadeaustralia.com. Over a month from the 2nd or 3rd week of September.

✪ **Henley-on-Todd Regatta,** Alice Springs. Sounds oh-so-sophisticated, doesn't it? It's actually a harum-scarum race down the dry bed of the Todd River in hilarious homemade "boats" made from anything you care to name—an old 4WD chassis, say, or beer cans lashed together. The only rule is has to look vaguely (vaguely) like a boat. Contact the organizers at ☎ **08/8955 1253;** www.henleyontodd.com.au. One Saturday in late September or early October.

• **Honda Indy 300 Carnival,** Surfers Paradise, Queensland. The world's best Indy-car drivers race a street circuit around Surfers Paradise on the glitzy Gold Coast, as part of the international FedEx Championship champ car motor-sport series. Contact **Ticketek** in Brisbane (☎ **13 19 31** in Queensland or 07/3404 6644), or order online at www.indy.com.au. Four days in mid-October.

✪ **Lizard Island Black Marlin Classic,** Lizard Island, Great Barrier Reef, Queensland. Every year 1,000-pounders surface on a line for a few lucky anglers in north Queensland's waters, at this Game Fish Association of Australia event hosted by upscale resort Lizard Island, north of Cairns. Contact the Lizard Island Game Fish Club (☎ 07/5537 4105; e-mail: stevem@ungerboeck.com) to register for the event. Contact Lizard Island (see chapter 6) to book accommodation. A week in October. Book months ahead.

November

- **Melbourne Cup.** If you're not glued to the TV to watch this A$1 million-plus horse race in Melbourne, well, you're probably not an Australian. Women wear hats to the office, files on desks make way for chicken and champagne, and don't even think about flagging a cab at 3:40pm race time. First Tuesday in November.

December

- **Sydney-to-Hobart Yacht Race.** Find a cliff-top spot near the Heads to watch the glorious show of spinnakers as a hundred or so yachts leave Sydney Harbour for this grueling world-class event. Contact Tourism New South Wales (☎ **02/9931 1111;** www.tourism.nsw.gov.au). Starts December 26.

6 The Active Vacation Planner

Australia's generally warm, dry climate and wide-open spaces cry out to even the most dedicated couch potatoes. Most of the operators and outfitters listed below specialize in adventure vacations for small groups. Meals, accommodation, equipment rental, and guides are included in their packages as a rule, though international airfares are usually not. Where you end up spending the night can vary depending on the type of package you select—for example, on a sea-kayaking trip you almost always camp on the beach, on a hiking expedition you may stay at a wilderness lodge, and on a biking trip you often stop over at B&B-style lodgings. If your trip is camping based, you may need to bring your own sleeping bag, or rent one from the adventure operator.

You will find additional information on the outdoor activities discussed below in the relevant regional chapters. Before you hit the outdoors, review the tips on safety later in this section.

SCUBA DIVING

Diving Down Under is one of the best travel experiences in the world. Don't think all of Australia's dive spots are on the Great Barrier Reef, though. Good sites are found all around the coastline. A second barrier reef in **Ningaloo Reef Marine Park** stretches 260 kilometers (163 miles) off the coast of Western Australia (see chapter 9 or check out Exmouth Diving Centre's Web site at www.exmouthdiving.com.au). For a rundown on the country's truly outstanding dive areas, see "The Best Diving & Snorkeling Sites," in chapter 1.

Wherever you find coral in Australia (which is a lot of places), you'll find dive companies offering learn-to-dive courses, day trips, and, in some cases, extended journeys on live-aboard vessels. Most international dive certificates,

August to January is peak visibility time on the Great Barrier Reef, but the marine life will wow you any time of year.

including PADI, NAUI, SSI, and BSAC, are recognized. It's easy to rent gear and wet suits wherever you go, or you can bring your own.

Beginners' courses are known as "open-water certification" and usually require 2 days of theory in a pool at the dive company's premises on land, followed by 2 or 3 days on a live-aboard boat where you make between four and nine dives, including a night dive if you opt for the 5-day course. Open-water certification courses range from an intensive 3 days to a more relaxed 5 days, for which you can expect to pay between A$350 (U.S.$227.50) and A$600 (U.S.$390). Most operators offer courses right up to instructor level. If you're pressed for time, a **PADI Referral course** might suit you. It allows you to do your theory work at home, do a few hours of pool work at a PADI dive center near you in your home country, and then spend just 2 or 3 days in the Australian ocean doing your qualifying dives. Remember to allow time in your itinerary for a medical exam in Australia, and expect the dive instructor to grill you on your theory again before you hit the water.

If you're already a certified diver, remember to bring your "C" card and log book. If you're going to do a dive course, you'll need a medical certificate from an Australian doctor that meets Australian standard AS4005.1, specifically stating that you are fit for scuba diving (an all-purpose physical is not enough). Virtually all dive schools will arrange the medical for you; expect to pay around A$50 (U.S.$32.50) for the consultation. Some courses take as little as 3 days, but 5-day courses are generally regarded as best. Remember, you can fly before you dive, but you must complete your last dive 24 hours before you fly in an aircraft. This catches a lot of people off guard when they are preparing to fly on to their next destination the day after a visit to the Reef. You won't be able to helicopter off the Reef back to the mainland, either. Check to see if your travel insurance covers diving.

If you've never been diving before, you can see what all the fuss is about on an "introductory" dive. Section 1 of chapter 6 contains more information on diving the Great Barrier Reef.

For information on dive regions, operators, and courses, contact the **Australian Tourist Commission** (see "Visitor Information," earlier in this chapter) for diving anywhere in Australia. **Tourism Queensland**'s Web site (www.queensland-holidays.com.au) contains plentiful information on dive operators working the Great Barrier Reef.

If you know exactly where you want to dive, you may obtain an even more detailed list of operators by bypassing the Australian Tourist Commission and contacting the nearest local tourist office for a list of local dive operators. **Dive Queensland** (the Queensland Dive Tourism Association; ☎ **07/4051 1510;** www.great-barrier-reef.net.au) will put you in touch with member dive operators in that state who stick to a code of ethics.

Peter Stone's Dive Australia is a comprehensive 608-page guidebook to more than 2,000 dive sites, plus dive operators, all over Australia. It's published by specialist dive publisher Oceans Enterprises (☎ **03/5182 5108;** www.oceans. com.au). For U.S. readers, the fourth edition (1999) costs A$36 (U.S.$25.20), which includes airmail postage.

BUSHWALKING (HIKING)

With so much unique scenery and so many rare animals and plants to protect, it's not surprising Australia is full of national parks crisscrossed with hiking trails. You're never far from a park with a bushwalk, whether it's an easy stroll to a lookout, or a 963-kilometer (601-mile) odyssey on the Bibbulmun Track in Western Australia.

The best place to get information about bushwalking before you leave home is the **National Parks & Wildlife Service,** or its equivalent in each state, which are listed below. A good Australian bushwalking Web page is at **www. bushwalking.org.au**.

- **NSW National Parks & Wildlife Service** (☎ **02/9585 6333;** www. npws.nsw.gov.au/).
- **Environmental Protection Agency (QLD Parks & Wildlife Service;** ☎ 07/3227 8197; www.env.qld.gov.au).
- **Parks & Wildlife Commission of the Northern Territory** (☎ **08/ 8999 5511;** www.nt.gov.au/paw). The Northern Territory Tourist Commission (see "Exploring the Red Centre," at the beginning of chapter 7) is the official dispenser of information on parks and wildlife matters.
- **Western Australian Department of Conservation and Land Management** (CALM; ☎ **08/9442 0300;** www.calm.wa.gov.au).
- **South Australian Department for Environment and Heritage** (☎ **08/ 8204 1910;** www.denr.sa.gov.au).
- **Parks Victoria** (☎ **03/9816 7066;** www.parks.vic.gov.au).
- **Tasmania Parks and Wildlife Service** (☎ **03/6191 3382;** www.parks. tas.gov.au).

Some parks charge a daily or one-time entry fee; it's usually around A$5 (U.S.$3.25) to A$8 (U.S.$5.20) but is occasionally as much as A$16 or so (U.S.$10.40).

MORE ACTIVE VACATIONS FROM A TO Z

ABSEILING Rappelling is another name for this sport that involves backing down vertical cliff faces on a rope and harness. The ruggedly beautiful **Blue Mountains** near Sydney are Australia's abseiling capital. In the **Margaret River region** in Western Australia, you can do it as mighty breakers crash on the cliffs below. You can even do it in the heart of the city in **Brisbane** on riverside cliffs.

BIKING Australia's flat countryside is ideal for cycling, as Aussies call biking, but consider the heat and the vast distances before trying to cycle from point to point. The rain-forest hills behind **Cairns** hosted the world mountain-biking championships in 1996, and Sydney's **Blue Mountains** have good mountain-biking trails. On **Rottnest Island** off Perth, it's the only mode of transport. All major towns and most resort centers rent regular bikes and mountain bikes.

If you're interested in taking an extended biking trip, get a copy of *Cycling Australia: Bicycle Touring Throughout the Sunny Continent,* by Australian Ian Duckworth (Bicycle Books). This 224-page touring guide outlines eight long trips with maps and detailed route descriptions. Any large bookstore can order it, or it is available for U.S.$14.95 from the **Adventurous Traveler Bookstore** (☎ **800/282-3963** in the U.S. and Canada; www.adventuroustraveler.com), or for £9.95 from the **Quayside Bookshop** in the U.K. (☎ **01626/77-5436;** or order at www.cycling.uk.com).

Remote Outback Cycle Tours (☎ **08/9244 4614;** www.cycletours.com.au) takes novice and expert bike riders, young and old, on extended biking tours through the Red Centre, to Kakadu National Park in the Top End, along the Gibb River Road in the Kimberley, through the vast saltbush plains and into an underground opal mining town in South Australia, or across part of the Nullarbor Plain desert to the Margaret River wine region in southern Western Australia. 4WD vehicles are used some of the time.

BIRD WATCHING Australia's unique position as an island continent ensures it has species you won't see anywhere else. It is probably best known for its many **brilliant parrots,** but you will see species from the wetlands, savannah, mulga scrub, desert, oceans, dense bushland, rain forest, mangroves, rivers, and other habitats. More than half of the country's species have been spotted in the **Daintree Rain Forest** area in north Queensland, and one-third of Australia's species live in wetlands-rich **Kakadu National Park** in the Top End. **The Coorong** in South Australia and **Broome** in the Top End are home to marvelous waterfowl populations.

To get in touch with bird-watching clubs all over Australia, contact **Birds Australia** (☎ **03/9882 2622;** www.birdsaustralia.com.au).

Kirrama Wildlife Tours (☎ **07/4065 5181;** www.gspeak.com.au/kirrama/) operates extended birding expeditions to remote regions in northern Australia. Broome-based ornithologist George Swann of **Kimberley Bird-watching, Wildlife & Natural History Tours** (☎ **08/9192 1246;** e-mail: kimbird@tpg.com.au) tailor-makes birding trips from 3 hours to 21 days throughout the Kimberley.

CANOEING & SEA KAYAKING **Katherine Gorge** in the Northern Territory offers some of the most spectacular flat canoeing in the country. You'll find delightful flat canoeing on the magnificent bird-rich **Ord River** in the Top End, too. Katherine Gorge and the Ord are full of generally harmless freshwater crocodiles, but *never* canoe in saltwater crocodile territory. White-water canoeing can be found in **Barrington Tops National Park** north of Sydney.

Australia's long coastline and rich, warm seas are tailor-made for sea kayaking. Several companies rent kayaks or offer guided expeditions in the **Whitsunday Islands** in north Queensland; to **Dunk Island** off Mission Beach, south of Cairns; and in **Perth, Monkey Mia,** and the **Northwest Cape** in Western Australia.

CAVING Australia doesn't have a lot of caves, but the ones it has are spectacular. The best are the **Jenolan Caves** in the Blue Mountains west of Sydney, a honeycomb of caverns bursting with intricate stalactites and stalagmites; and the 350 limestone caves in the **Margaret River region** in Western Australia. Five are open to the public.

Something Different: Camel Trekking

Camels Down Under? You bet. Australia has one of the world's largest camel populations. Camels were imported to negotiate waterless deserts in the 1900s but were later set free. They are now making a comeback as a popular way to trek the country. Short rambles of an hour or two in **Alice Springs** and at **Ayers Rock** are a novel way to see the Outback. Several companies in **Broome** lead guided rides along Cable Beach. You can also camel trek through **Flinders Ranges National Park** in South Australia.

FISHING   Reef, game, deep sea, beach, estuary, river, and trout fishing—Australia's massive coastline lets you do it all. Drop a line for coral trout on the **Great Barrier Reef;** go for the world record in the Lizard Island Black Marlin Classic near Cairns; hook a fighting "barra" (barramundi) in the **Northern Territory** or the **Kimberley;** or cast for trout in **Tasmania**'s highland lakes.

GOLF   Australians are almost as passionate about golf as they are about football and cricket—after all, before Greg Norman was a Yank, he was an Aussie! **Queensland** has the lion's share of the most stunning resort courses, like the **Sheraton Mirage** in Port Douglas, **Laguna Quays Resort** near the Whitsundays, and the **Hyatt Regency Sanctuary Cove Resort** on the Gold Coast. The **Gold Coast** alone is studded with more than 40 courses. The **Novotel Vines near Perth** is another outstanding resort course. One of the world's best desert courses is at **Alice Springs.** You can play a round of **"bush golf"** in Broken Hill—it's played at night when it's cool with fluorescent golf balls—or hit the links in Lightning Ridge where the "greens" are dusty "browns."

Most courses rent clubs for around A$30 (U.S.$19.50). Greens fees start at around A$20 (U.S.$13) for 18 holes but average A$65 (U.S.$42.25) or more on a championship course.

HORSEBACK RIDING   Horseback-riding operators are everywhere in Australia. A particularly pleasant vacation is a multiday riding and camping trek in the **Snowy Mountains** in New South Wales.

SAILING   The 74 island gems of the **Whitsundays** in Queensland are an out-of-this-world backdrop for sailing. And, no, you don't have to know how to sail—plenty of operators charter "bareboat" yachts (that means unskippered) by the day or the week, even to folks with not a stitch of sailing experience. Perth and Sydney are mad about sailing; head down to the nearest yacht club and see what on-board places are going, especially during summer twilight races. The clubs are often short of sailors and most will welcome out-of-towners.

SURFING   You'll have no trouble finding a good surf beach all along the Australian coast; **Perth** and **Sydney** are blessed with loads of good ones right in the city. Other popular spots include the **Gold Coast** in Queensland, the legendary Southern Ocean swells along **Victoria's southern coast,** and the magnificent sets off **Margaret River** in Western Australia. Just don't take your board much north of the Sunshine Coast in Queensland—the Great Barrier Reef puts a stop to the swell from there all the way to the northern tip of Queensland.

WHITE-WATER RAFTING   The best rapids are the Grade 5 torrents on the **Nymboida** and **Gwydir rivers** behind Coffs Harbour in New South Wales. More Grade 5 rapids await you on the **Johnstone River** in north Queensland, although they must be accessed by helicopter. Loads of tourists who have never held a paddle hurtle down the Grade 3 to 4 **Tully River** near Mission Beach in north Queensland and the gentler Grade 2 to 3 **Barron River** near Cairns. The **Snowy River National Park** in Victoria is another spot popular with rafters. See also "Canoeing & Sea Kayaking," above.

Peregrine Adventures (via Himalayan Travel in the U.S. at ☎ **800/ 225-2380;** 01728/86 2222 in the U.K., or 03/9663 8611; www.peregrine. net.au) runs rafting expeditions in Victoria and on the mighty Franklin River in the wilds of Tasmania. It is represented in Canada by several companies, including WestCan Treks (☎ **800/663-5132** in British Columbia, or 604/734-1066).

MORE OUTFITTERS & ADVENTURE-TRAVEL OPERATORS
AUSTRALIA-BASED OPERATORS
The Adventure Company (☎ 800/388-7333 in the U.S., or 07/4051 4777; www.adventures.com.au) does 1-day and extended trips that incorporate hiking, biking, canoeing, rafting, sea kayaking, scuba diving, and four-wheel-driving in wilderness areas of North Queensland and on the Great Barrier Reef.

MudMaps Australia (☎ 888/MUD-MAPS in the U.S., or 02/6257-4796; www.mudmaps.com) offers 1- to 4-day wilderness tours from Canberra, Sydney, and Melbourne in the Snowy Mountains. The groups are small, your guide is a bushman, the transport is 4WD or minicoach, and you stay at farms and B&B-style accommodation.

Rivergods (☎ 08/9259 0749; www.rivergods.com.au) conducts 1-day and multiday sea kayaking, canoeing, and white-water rafting adventures throughout Western Australia's pristine ocean and rivers, in which whales, sharks, dugongs (manatees), sea snakes, turtles, and dolphins abound. Their "sea kayak with seals" day outing from Perth is popular.

Tasmanian Expeditions (☎ 03/6334 3477; www.tassie.net.au/tas_ex) conducts hiking, cycling, rafting, abseiling, canoeing, and rock-climbing trips throughout Tasmania's national parks and country roads.

U.S.-BASED OPERATORS
The **Great Outdoor Recreation Pages (G.O.R.P.)** site at **www.gorp.com** not only has links to many adventure tour operators to Australia, but also contains articles, sells books and maps, and has links to heaps of sites on Australia with an action slant.

Adventure Express (☎ 800/443-0799 or 415/442-0799; www.adventureexpress.com) sells scuba-diving packages and custom-built itineraries on the Great Barrier Reef. The company claims to meet or beat any competitor's price.

Down Under Answers (☎ 800/788-6685 or 425/895-0895; www.adventour.com) sells diving and sea-kayaking packages in North Queensland, and biking trips in scenic locales throughout the country. A 7-day package combines canoeing, hiking, biking, and snorkeling.

North by Northwest (☎ 949/858-1073; www.north-by-northwest.com) conducts a 10-day bushwalk through the alpine wilds of Tasmania's Cradle Mountain and Lake St. Clair regions.

Outer Edge Expeditions (☎ 800/322-5235 or 517/552 5300; www.outer-edge.com) specializes in ecologically minded camping, diving, hiking, mountain-biking, canoeing, and sea-kayaking packages to such places as the Great Barrier Reef, Ayers Rock, and Kangaroo Island off South Australia.

The World Outside (☎ 800/488-8483 or 303/413-0938; www.theworldoutside.com) runs a 7-day combined hiking, mountain-biking, canoeing, snorkeling, sea-kayaking, and diving packages on the Great Barrier Reef and in the North Queensland rain forest.

TIPS ON HEALTH, SAFETY & OUTDOOR ETIQUETTE DOWN UNDER
Australia has a lot of rough, remote territory typified by incredibly high temperatures, scarce water or none at all, little shade, flash floods, and bushfires. Add to that the deadly snakes and spiders you might meet, and the thought that the nearest gas station, telephone, or person could be hundreds of miles away, and it's a wonder anyone ventures 10 miles from the airport! Extreme

heat and ultraviolet rays can lead to exhaustion, dehydration, sunstroke, and severe sunburn quickly, even if you expend only a small amount of energy.

But follow the tips below and you should make it back home unscathed.

SOME GENERAL RULES OF THUMB

- Don't disturb wildlife, take plant cuttings, or remove rocks, shells, coral, or other pieces of the wilderness. These are offenses in national and marine parks.
- Tell someone where you are going, whether you're taking a 2-hour hike or a 3-week 4WD safari across the country. If you are hiking in a national park, register in the National Parks & Wildlife Service logbook if there is one placed at the start of the walk (don't forget to deregister, or a search party will be out looking for you while you're back at your hotel having dinner). On a longer trip, leave your travel plans with friends, relatives, or the police.
- Carry extra water. It's easy to dehydrate without even knowing it in Australia's extremely hot and arid conditions. Two liters per person per day should be your minimum ration; 1 liter per person per hour is the rule in the Outback and the Top End in summer.
- Don't feed animals, birds, and fish. It makes them unhealthy and causes them to lose their hunting skills.
- Obey fire restrictions. Bushfires are a major threat across Australia. In hot, dry weather, a total fire ban may apply, which means you cannot light a naked flame. Many national parks permit only camp-ovens, not campfires. If you use a campfire, burn only fallen wood, not standing dead trees that could house animals. Extinguish all campfires thoroughly.
- Look at, but don't touch, historic Aboriginal sites such as rock art walls and middens (shell mounds). It can be an offense to disturb them.

BASICS FOR BUSHWALKERS

- Stay on the track. Cutting corners can damage vegetation and cause erosion.
- Whatever you take in, take out. Leave no rubbish, even organic stuff like an apple core (it takes a long time to degrade, it's not the right food for native animals, and it might self-seed and become a pest among native vegetation). For the same reason, don't bury your rubbish.
- Check track conditions and the weather forecast before you go.
- Wear a broad-brimmed hat, sunglasses, sunscreen, sturdy shoes, and a comfortable backpack. Insect repellent should be a key item on your list, because flies can reach plague proportions in dry areas and mosquitoes are common in rain forests.

BEACH SAVVY FOR SWIMMERS & SURFERS

- The signal for "help" in the water is to raise one arm high above your head.
- Never swim alone at beaches not patrolled by lifesavers (lifeguards).
- Always swim between the red and yellow flags denoting a safe swimming zone. Crossed flagpoles or a red flag mean the beach is closed due to extremely dangerous swimming conditions. A yellow flag means conditions are dangerous and swimming is not advised.
- "Rips" are powerful currents that can carry even the strongest swimmer out to sea. If caught in one, don't fatigue yourself struggling. Remain calm, raise one arm high above your head, and wait for help. Try to swim diagonally against the current to shore.
- If you get a cramp, raise one arm and keep the cramped part still.

Aussies love terrorizing wide-eyed visitors with tales of the country's two deadly **spiders,** the funnel web and the redback, but truth is most Australians wouldn't know what a funnel web looked like if it, well, bit them. Spider bites are not all that common. Funnel webs live in holes in the ground (they spin their webs around the entrance to the hole). Redbacks have a habit of resting under toilet seats, in car boots (car trunks), and in dryish areas like garages and garden sheds.

If you go bushwalking, check your whole body carefully. **Ticks** are common, especially in eastern Australia, and can cause severe itching and fever. If you find one attached to you, dab it with methylated spirits or some other noxious chemical. Wait for a while, then pull the tick gently out with tweezers, carefully ensuring you don't leave its head buried inside the wound.

Fish to avoid are stingrays, porcupine fish, stonefish, lion fish, and puffer fish. Never touch an octopus if it has blue rings on it, or a cone shell, and avoid the mainland seas in the northern third of the country in summer, when **marine stingers** (also called box jellyfish) inhabit the coastline. Their sting is very painful and can cause heart failure and death. If you happen to brush past one of these creatures, pour vinegar over the affected site immediately—local councils leave bottles of vinegar on the beach specifically for this purpose. In Sydney, you might come across **"blue bottles."** These long-tentacled blue jellyfish can inflict a generally harmless but painful sting that can last for hours. Sometimes you'll see warning signs on patrolled beaches. The best remedy if you are stung is to apply vinegar or have a very hot shower.

All cuts obtained in the marine environment must be taken seriously, because the high level of bacteria present can quickly cause the cut to become infected. The most common cuts are from **coral.** Contrary to popular belief, coral cannot grow inside your body. However, bacteria can—and very often does—grow inside a cut. The best way to prevent cuts is to wear a wet suit, gloves, and reef shoes. Never, under any circumstances, should you touch a coral head; not only can you get cut, but you can also damage a living organism that took decades to grow. The symptoms of a coral cut can range from a slight scratch to severe welts and blisters. Gently pull the edges of the skin open and remove any embedded coral or grains of sand with tweezers, and scrub the cut well with fresh water. Never use ocean water to clean a cut. If the wound is bleeding, press a clean cloth against it until it stops. If bleeding continues, or the edges of the injury are jagged or gaping, seek medical treatment.

Snakes are common throughout Australia, but you will very rarely see one. The most dangerous land snake is the **taipan,** which hides in the grasslands in northern Australia—one bite contains enough venom to kill up to 200 sheep. If by the remotest chance you are bitten, you must immediately demobilize the limb, wrap that whole section of the limb quite tightly (but not tight enough to restrict the blood flow) with a wide cloth or bandage, and head to the nearest hospital, where antivenin should be available. Keeping calm and moving as little as possible may save your life.

There are two types of **crocodiles** in Australia, the freshwater crocodile, which grows to almost 3 meters (10 ft.), and the dangerous Estuarine (or saltwater) crocodile, which reaches 5 to 7 meters (16 to 23 ft.). Freshwater crocs eat fish and are considered harmless; unfortunately, Estuarine crocs aren't so picky. Estuarine crocs are called "saltwater" crocs but they live mostly in *fresh* water. They are extremely ferocious, move at lightning speed, and are invisible even an inch beneath the water; it is unlikely you would survive an attack.

Never swim in, or stand on the bank of, any river, swamp, or pool in the northern third of Australia, unless you know for certain it's croc free. Don't swim at beaches near estuaries.

7 Health & Insurance

You don't have a lot to worry about healthwise on a trip to Australia. Hygiene standards are high, hospitals are modern, and doctors and dentists are all well educated. Australia's immense distances mean you can sometimes be a long way from a hospital or a doctor, but help is never far away thanks to the **Royal Flying Doctor Service.** No vaccinations are needed to enter the country unless you have been in a yellow-fever danger zone—that is, South America or Africa—in the past 6 days.

WHAT TO DO IF YOU GET SICK AWAY FROM HOME

If you worry about getting sick away from home, you may want to consider medical travel insurance (see the section on travel insurance later in this chapter). In most cases, however, your existing health plan will provide all the coverage you need. Be sure to carry your identification card in your wallet.

If you suffer from a chronic illness, consult your doctor before your departure. For conditions like epilepsy, diabetes, or heart problems, wear a **Medic Alert Identification Tag** (☎ 800/IDALERT; www.medicalert.org), which will immediately alert doctors to your condition and give them access to your records through Medic Alert's 24-hour hotline. Membership is U.S.$35, then U.S.$15 for annual renewal.

Pack prescription medications in your carry-on luggage. Carry written prescriptions in generic, not brand-name, form, and dispense all prescription medications from their original labeled vials. Also bring along copies of your prescriptions in case you lose your pills or run out. Usually a 3-month supply is the maximum quantity of prescription drugs you are permitted to carry in Australia, so if you are carrying large amounts of medication, contact the Australian embassy or consulate in your home country to check that your supply does not exceed the maximum. If you need more medication while you're in Australia, you will need to get an Australian doctor to write the prescription for you.

If you wear contact lenses, pack an extra pair in case you lose one.

If you do get sick, you may want to ask the concierge at your hotel to recommend a local doctor—even his or her own. If you can't find a doctor who can help you right away, try the emergency room at the local hospital. Doctors are listed under "M" for Medical Practitioners in the Australian Yellow Pages.

A Word About Smoking

Smoking in many public areas, such as museums, cinemas, and theaters, is restricted if not banned. Few Oz restaurants totally ban smoking yet; they just have smoking and no-smoking sections. Pubs are a territorial victory for smokers; after a night in one, nonsmokers go home smelling as if they smoked the whole pack (which they probably did, secondhand). Most hotels have smoking and no-smoking rooms. Australian aircraft on all domestic and international routes are completely no-smoking.

WARNING: SUNSHINE MAY BE HAZARDOUS TO YOUR HEALTH

There's a reason Australians have the world's highest death rate from skin cancer—the country's intense sunlight. Limit your exposure to the sun, especially during the first few days of your trip and, thereafter, from 11am to 3pm in summer and 10am to 2pm in winter. Scattered UV rays can bounce off surfaces such city walls, water, and even the ground, and can burn you. Use a broad-spectrum sunscreen with a high protection factor (SPF 30+). Wear a broad-brimmed hat that covers the back of your neck, ears, and face (not a baseball cap), and a long-sleeved shirt to cover your forearms. Kids need more protection than adults do.

Don't even think about coming to Oz without sunglasses, or you'll spend your entire vacation with your eyes shut against Australia's "diamond light" that cuts your eyes like, well, a diamond.

INSURANCE

There are three kinds of travel insurance: trip-cancellation, medical, and lost-luggage coverage. Rule number one: Check your existing policies before you buy any additional coverage.

Trip-cancellation insurance is a good idea if you've paid a large portion of your vacation expenses up front (say, by purchasing a package deal), and it should cost approximately 6% to 8% of the total value of your vacation.

Your existing **health insurance** should cover you if you get sick while on vacation—though if you belong to an HMO, you should check to see whether you are fully covered when away from home. If you need hospital treatment, most health-insurance plans and HMOs will cover out-of-country hospital visits and procedures, at least to some extent. However, most make you pay the bills up front at the time of care, and you'll get a refund after you've returned and filed all the paperwork. Make sure your policy covers medical evacuation by helicopter or Australia's Royal Flying Doctor Service airlift (you might well need this if you become sick or injured in the wilds of the Outback). Your policy should also cover the cost to fly you back home in a stretcher, along with a nurse, should that be necessary. A stretcher takes up three coach-class seats, plus you may need extra seats for a nurse and medical equipment. Medicare only covers U.S. citizens traveling in Mexico and Canada.

Australia has a reciprocal medical-care agreement with Great Britain and New Zealand and a limited agreement with Ireland, under which travelers are covered for most medical expenses for immediately necessary treatment (but not evacuation, ambulances, funerals, dental care, and other expenses) by Australia's national health system. It's still a good idea to buy insurance, though, because Australia's national health-care system typically covers only 85%, sometimes much less, of treatment. Foreign students of any nationality must take out the Australian government's Overseas Student Health Cover as a condition of entry.

Your homeowner's or renter's insurance should cover **lost or stolen luggage.** The airlines are responsible for only a minimal amount if they lose your luggage on an international flight (and for a maximum A$1,600/U.S.$1,040 on domestic flights in Australia), so if you plan to carry anything valuable, keep it in your carry-on bag.

Some credit- and charge-card companies may insure you against travel accidents if you buy plane, train, or bus tickets with their cards, or they may provide collision (but not liability) insurance for car rentals. **American Express** offers its cardholders a free 24-hour **Global Assist** hotline (☎ **800/554-AMEX** in the U.S., or call collect 312/935 3600 from overseas or in Illinois).

If you do require additional insurance, try one of the following companies: **Access America** (☎ 800/284-8300; www.accessamerica.com); **Travel Guard International** (☎ 800/826-1300; www.travel-guard.com); **Columbus Direct** (☎ 020/7375-0011 in London; www.columbusdirect.com), which insures U.K. residents and British passport holders only; and **The Divers Alert Network** (☎ 800/446-2671; www.diversalertnetwork.org), which insures scuba divers and provides a diving medical-emergency hotline.

8 Tips for Travelers with Special Needs

FOR TRAVELERS WITH DISABILITIES Most hotels, major stores, museums, attractions, and public rest rooms have wheelchair access. Many smaller lodges and even B&Bs are starting to cater to guests with disabilities. National parks make an effort to include wheelchair-friendly pathways, too. Taxi companies in bigger cities can usually supply a cab equipped for wheelchairs. TTY facilities are still limited largely to government services, unfortunately.

For information on all kinds of facilities and services in Australia for people with disabilities (not just travel-related organizations), contact **National Information Communication Awareness Network (NICAN),** P.O. Box 407, Curtin, ACT 2605 (☎ **1800/806 769** voice and TTY in Australia, or 02/6285 3713; www.nican.com.au). This free service can put you in touch with accessible accommodations and attractions throughout Australia, as well as with travel agents and tour operators who understand your needs.

A World of Options, a 600-plus page book of resources for travelers with disabilities, costs U.S.$35 (U.S.$30 for members) from **Mobility International USA** (☎ **541/343-1284,** voice and TTY; www.miusa.org). **Twin Peaks Press** (☎ **360/694-2462;** www.home.pacifier.com/~twinpeak) publishes travel-related books for people with disabilities.

FOR GAY & LESBIAN TRAVELERS Sydney is the most gay-friendly city in the world after San Francisco, and across most of Australia, the gay community has a high profile and lots of support services. The annual **Sydney Gay & Lesbian Mardi Gras,** culminating in a huge street parade and gay-only party on the last Saturday in February, is a high point on the city's calendar.

The **International Gay & Lesbian Travel Association** (IGLTA; ☎ **800/448-8550** or 954/776-2626; www.iglta.org) can link you up with gay-friendly hotels, travel agents, and other travel organizations.

One of the biggest travel agencies specializing in gay travel in Australia is **Jornada,** 263 Liverpool St., Darlinghurst, NSW 2010 (☎ **1800/672 120** in Australia, or 02/9360 9611; www.jornada.com.au).

Some services you may find useful are the **Gay & Lesbian Counselling Service of NSW** (☎ **02/9207 2888** for the administration office), which runs a hotline from 4pm to midnight daily (☎ 1800/805 379 in Australia, or 02/9207 2800). The **Albion Street Centre** (☎ 02/9332 1090 for administration, or **1800/451 600** in Australia outside Sydney and 02/9332 4000 in Sydney for the information line) in Sydney is an AIDS clinic and information service.

FOR SENIORS Seniors—often referred to as "pensioners" by Aussies— visiting Australia from other countries don't always qualify for the discounted entry prices to tours, attractions, and events that Australian seniors enjoy, but mostly they do. Always inquire about discounts when booking hotels, airline flights, train or bus tickets, and so on. The best ID to bring is something that shows your date of birth, or something that marks you as an "official" senior, like a membership card from the **American Association of Retired Persons** (AARP; ☎ **800/424-3410** in the U.S.; www.aarp.org). Membership in AARP is open to working or retired people over 50 and costs U.S.$8 a year. AARP has a Purchase Privileges program that entitles members to discounts of 10% to 50% on a wide range of travel operators including airlines, many hotels, cruise lines, rental cars, and more.

Elderhostel (☎ **877/426-8056** toll-free in the U.S. and Canada; www.elderhostel.org) is a nonprofit organization that sells educational package tours, including ones to Australia, for travelers 55 years and over. Recent itineraries in Australia included Great Barrier Reef study cruises, Outback camping trips, bushwalking tours in Tasmania, and visits to Lord Howe Island off the east coast of Australia and Kangaroo Island off the south coast.

FOR FAMILIES Australians travel widely with their own kids, so facilities for families, including family passes to attractions, are common. A great accommodation option for families travelling Down Under are serviced or unserviced apartments. Both are widely available almost everywhere you go in Oz. Not only do they offer a living room, a kitchen, often two bathrooms, and the blissful privacy of a separate bedroom for adults, but they also usually cost considerably less than a hotel room. Just about all hotels in Australia will arrange baby-sitting given a day's notice.

International airlines and domestic airlines within Australia charge 67% of the adult fare for kids under 12. Most charge 10% for infants under 2 not occupying a seat. As a general rule, Australian transport companies, attractions, and tour operators charge around half price or 60% for kids.

Rascals in Paradise (☎ **800/U RASCAL** in the U.S. and Canada; www. rascalsinparadise.com) sells family vacation packages to Australia.

These places have great kids clubs: Mercure Resort Surfers Paradise on the Gold Coast, and Daydream Island Resort and South Molle Island Resort, which are both in the Whitsunday Islands (see chapter 6).

FOR STUDENTS **STA Travel** (☎ **800/781-4040** in the U.S., 020/7361 6144 in the U.K., and 1300/360 960 in Australia; www.statravel.com) and **Council Travel** (☎ **800/2-COUNCIL** in the U.S.; www.counciltravel.com) both specialize in affordable airfares, bus and rail passes, accommodation, insurance, and tours and packages for students and young travelers. Both issue **International Student Identity Cards (ISIC).** This is the most widely recognized proof in Australia that you really are a student. As well as assuring you of discounts on a huge range of travel, tours, and attractions, it comes with a 24-hour emergency help line and a global voice/fax/e-mail messaging system with discounted international telephone calls. Available to any full-time student over 12, in the United States it costs U.S.$20.

Ask STA Travel for a list of its many offices across Australia so you can keep the discounts flowing (and aid lines open) as you travel.

The **Australian Youth Hostels Association** (YHA; ☎ **02/9261 1111;** www.yha.org.au), which is the Australian arm of Hostelling International, has more than 150 hostels in Australia. Rates range from A$10 (U.S.$6.50) to A$24 (U.S.$15.60). You don't have to join the association to stay at its hostels, but members receive discounted rates and myriad other discounts—on car rentals, bus travel, and tours, for example—that can repay the membership fee many times over. It's best to join before you arrive in Australia. In the United States, contact **Hostelling International** (☎ **202/783-6161;** www.hiayh.org). The 12-month membership is free if you are 17 or under, U.S.$25 if you are 18 to 54, and U.S.$15 if you are 55 years or older.

9 Booking a Package or Escorted Tour

It's possible to buy a package tour to Australia that includes airfare and, say, 5 nights in a decent hotel for less than the cost of the airfare alone. Because each element of a package—airfare, hotel, tour, car rental—costs the package company much less than if you had booked the same components yourself, packages are a terrific value and well worth investigating.

There are two kinds of "package tours"—independent and escorted. **Independent packages** usually include some combination of airfare, accommodations, and car rental, with an occasional tour or shopping discount voucher book thrown in. Aside from the cost savings, the main advantage is that you travel on your own pace and according to your own interests—no tour buses and no group sightseeing. Your car and hotel arrangements are already booked, leaving you free to get on with your day instead of fussing about finding a hotel for the night.

Escorted tours have different advantages—you don't have to carry your own luggage, for starters. Nor do you need to constantly plan ahead, and if you have free time, there is someone to advise you on fun things to do and even to make your tour bookings for you. A significant argument for escorted tours is that you usually have a well-informed guide who can offer interesting tidbits about the country as you go along, so you'll probably learn more than you would on your own. You also get to meet and travel with other people, though your time won't be your own to schedule flexibly and a lot of your enjoyment may depend on whether you like your guide and your fellow travelers. Escorted tours tend to be more expensive because you're paying for the guide, but most meals are included.

The airlines themselves are often a good source of package tours. Check newspaper ads, the Internet, or your travel agent. **Austravel** (☎ **800/ 633-3404** in the U.S. and Canada, or 0870/055 0239 in the U.K.; www. austravel.net) and **Inta-Aussie South Pacific** (☎ **800/531-9222** in the U.S.; www.inta-oz.com) are two American companies offering independent packages Down Under.

Escorted tours are available from **Collette Tours** (☎ **800/340-5158** in the U.S., 416/626 1661 in Canada, or 0189/581 2333 in the U.K. through Adventures Unlimited, Inc.; www.collettetours.com) and **Maupintour** (☎ **800/255-4266** in the U.S. and Canada; www.maupintour.com). Collette Tours has an office in Australia. **Connections** (call Adventure Plus ☎ **510/ 654 1879** in the U.S., Goway ☎ **800/387-8850** in Canada, The Imaginative Traveller ☎ 020/8742 8612 in the U.K., or 07/3839 7877 in Australia; www.connections1835.com.au) and **Contiki** (☎ **800/CONTIKI** in the U.S. and Canada, 020/8290 6777 in the U.K., or 02/9511 2200 in Australia; ww.contiki.com) specialize in escorted tours for 18- to 35-year-olds. These trips attract a lot of Australians too, so they are a good way to meet locals. Connections also does a Connections Plus range of active holidays for people of any age.

The following companies offer both independent and escorted tours: **ATS Tours** (☎ **800/423-2880** in the U.S. and Canada; www.atstours.com),

Goway (☎ 800/387-8850 in the U.S. and Canada; www.goway.com), **Qantas Vacations** (☎ 800/348-8139 in the U.S. and 800/268-7525 in Canada; www.qantasvacations.com), **Sunbeam Tours** (☎ 800/955-1818 in the U.S. and Canada; www.sunbeamtours.com), **Swain Australia Tours** (☎ 800/22-SWAIN in the U.S. and Canada; www.swaintours.com), Swain Australia's budget travel division, **Downunder Direct** (☎ 800/642-6224 in the U.S. and Canada; www.downunderdirect.com), and **United Vacations** (☎ 800/917-9246 in the U.S. and Canada; www.unitedvacations.com). Swain Australia is owned and largely staffed by Aussies. Sunbeam Tours, Swain Australia, and Goway have offices in Australia. **ANZA Travel** (☎ 800/269-2166 in the U.S., or 800/667-4329 in Canada; www.anza-travel.com) specializes in special-interest vacations with an active bent, such as golfing, sailing, and fishing.

10 Flying to Australia

There's no doubt about it—Australia is a loooong flight from anywhere except New Zealand. Sydney is a 14-hour nonstop flight from Los Angeles, longer if your flight stops in Honolulu. From the east coast, add $5^1/_2$ hours. If you're coming from the states via Auckland, add transit time in New Zealand plus another 3 hours for the Auckland-Sydney leg. If you are coming from the United Kingdom, brace yourself for a flight of more or less 12 hours from London to Asia; then possibly a long day in transit, because flights to Australia have a nasty habit of arriving in Asia early in the morning and departing around midnight; and finally the 8- to 9-hour flight to Australia.

Sydney, Cairns, Melbourne, Brisbane, Adelaide, Darwin, and Perth are all international gateways, but most airlines fly only into Sydney, and some also fly to Melbourne.

THE MAJOR CARRIERS

Here are toll-free reservations numbers and Web sites for the major international airlines serving Australia. The "13" prefix in Australia means the number is charged at the cost of a local call from anywhere in the country.

MAJOR CARRIERS FLYING FROM NORTH AMERICA
- **Air New Zealand** (☎ 800/262-1234 in the U.S.; in Canada: 800/663-5494 for English, 800/799-5494 for French, or 604/606-0150 in Vancouver; or 13 24 76 in Australia; www.airnz.com)
- **Canada 3000** (☎ 888/CAN3000 in Canada, 416/259-1118 in the U.S., or 1300/55 3301 in Australia; www.canada3000.com)
- **Canadian Airlines** (☎ 800/665-1177 in Canada, 800/363-7530 for French in Canada outside Québec; 800/426-7000 in the U.S. or 1300/655 767 in Australia; www.cdnair.ca)
- **Qantas** (☎ 800/227-4500 in the U.S. and Canada; 13 13 13 in Australia; www.qantas.com)
- **United Airlines** (☎ 800/241 6522 in the U.S. and Canada; 13 17 77 in Australia; www.ual.com)

MAJOR CARRIERS FLYING FROM THE U.K.
- **British Airways** (☎ 0845/773-3377 in the U.K.; 1800/626-747 in Ireland; or 02/8904 8800 in Sydney, 07/3223 3133 in Brisbane, 1300/134 001 in Canberra, 03/9603 1133 in Melbourne, 08/8238 2138 in Adelaide, and 08/9425 7711 in Perth; www.britishairways.com)

- **Cathay Pacific** (☎ **0345/581 581** in the U.K.; 13 17 47 in Australia; www.cathaypacific.com)
- **Malaysia Airlines** (☎ **020/7341 2020** in the U.K.; 1/676-2131 in Ireland; 13 26 27 in Australia; www.malaysiaairlines.com.my)
- **Qantas** (☎ **0345/747-767** in the U.K.; 13 13 13 in Australia; www. qantas.com.au)
- **Singapore Airlines** (☎ **0870/608 8886** in the U.K.; 1/671-0722 in Ireland; 13 10 11 in Australia; www.singaporeair.com)
- **Thai Airways International** (☎ **020/7499 9113** in the U.K.; 1300/ 651 960 in Australia; www.thaiair.com)

FINDING THE BEST AIRFARE

If you're flying from the United States, keep in mind that the airlines' low season is mid-April to the end of August—this is when you'll find the cheapest fares, and this happens to be the best time to travel most parts of Australia. High season is December through February, and shoulder season is September through November, and again from March to mid-April.

Keep an eye out for special deals offered throughout the year. Unexpected lows in airline passenger loads often lead airlines to put cheap offers on the market. The catch is these usually have a short lead time, requiring you to travel in the next 6 weeks or so. Some deals involve taking a circuitous route, via Fiji or Japan, for instance. Canada 3000 has good rates from Vancouver in low season and often has promotional specials.

Austravel (☎ **800/633 3404** in the U.S. and Canada) publishes a quarterly guide to airfares, carriers, stopovers, and flying times to Australia. Some travel agents and wholesalers specializing in cheap fares to Australia include **Austravel** (☎ **800/633-3404** in the U.S. and Canada, or 0870/055 0239 in the United Kingdom; www.austravel.net); **Downunder Direct,** which is a division of Swain Australia (☎ **800/642 6224** in the U.S. and Canada; www.downunderdirect.com); and **Goway** (☎ **800/387-8850** in the U.S. and Canada; www.goway.com).

Consolidators, also known as "bucket shops," are another good source for low fares. Consolidators buy seats in bulk from the airlines and then sell them back to the public at low prices, sometimes even below even the airlines' discounted rates. There's nothing shady about the reliable ones—basically, they're just big travel agents that get discounts for buying in bulk and pass some of the savings on to you. Before you pay, however, ask for a confirmation number from the consolidator and then call the airline itself to confirm your seat. Be prepared to book your ticket with a different consolidator—there are many to choose from—if the airline can't confirm your reservation. Also be aware that consolidator tickets are usually nonrefundable or come with stiff cancellation penalties. Some of the more reliable consolidators include **Cheap Tickets** (☎ **800/377-1000;** www.cheaptickets.com), **Council Travel** (☎ **800/ 226-8624;** www.counciltravel.com), **STA Travel** (☎ **800/781-4040;** www. sta.travel.com), and **1-800-FLY-CHEAP** (www.flycheap.com).

Another good source of good deals are "rebaters" such as **Travel Avenue** (☎ **800/333-3335** in the U.S. or 312/876-6866; www.travelavenue.com), which rebate part of their commissions to you.

You can also search the Internet for cheap fares. *See "Planning Your Trip: An Online Directory," on p. 67, for valuable advice on how to make the Web work for you.*

IN-FLIGHT COMFORT

To relieve the discomfort on this long-distance flight, wear loose clothing and a roomy pair of shoes, because your feet will swell en route. Drink plenty of water and go easy on the alcohol. To while away the hours, consider traveling with an airline that offers in-seat videos. Requesting a bulkhead or exit-door seat will give you more leg room. Some airlines allow you to request seats when you book, but others allocate seats only at check-in—in that case, be early to beat savvy Aussies queuing for the same thing!

Jet lag is a foregone conclusion on such a long trip, so don't plan to climb Ayers Rock the first morning you arrive, or book opera tickets for your first evening. There is no "cure" for jet lag, but you will fight it by getting plenty of sleep on the flight and not overeating. Try to acclimatize yourself to the local time as quickly as possible. Stay up as long as you can the first day, then try to wake up at a normal hour the next morning.

On such a long journey, it makes sense to break the trip with a 1-night stopover if you have time. If you're coming from the United States, this will probably be Honolulu or maybe Fiji; if you're coming from Europe, you have any number of Asian cities—Bangkok, Singapore, Hong Kong—in which to spend a night or two. If you're coming from Europe and you have a long lay-over in Asia, I strongly recommend you book a day room at a hotel with a 6pm checkout. Wandering around a humid, crowded city at 2pm when your body thinks it's 3am is not fun.

11 Getting Around Australia

The one big mistake tourists make Down Under (apart from getting sun-burned) is failing to comprehend the vast distances between the most popular locations. Every Sydney hotelier has a tale to tell about the tourist who comes down to the front desk complaining their room doesn't have a view of Ayers Rock, 2,841 kilometers (1,765 miles) away, or asking what time the afternoon boat to the Great Barrier Reef leaves. Don't try to cram too much in one trip.

While traveling overland may make sense in Europe or North America, fly-ing in Australia is the best way to go. People who go by train, bus, or car are often disappointed at Australia's flat, unchanging vistas of desert, wheat fields, and gum trees—and this dull scenery literally goes on for days. A good com-promise is to take to the air for long trips and save the land travel for short hops of no more than a few hours. Try not to backtrack, because it eats up valuable time and money.

BY PLANE

Australia is a big country with a small population to support its air routes—hence, high airfares. This section contains some tips to help you beat them.

Domestic travel is almost entirely operated by **Qantas** (☎ 800/227-4500 in the U.S. and Canada; 0345/747-767 in the U.K.; 0800/808-767 in New Zealand; 13 13 13 in Australia; www.qantas.com) and **Ansett** (☎ 0800/ 736 409 in New Zealand; 13 13 00 for domestic flights and 13 14 14 for international flights in Australia; www.ansett.com.au). Ansett's overseas repre-sentation is handled by **Air New Zealand** (☎ 888/4-ANSETT in the U.S. or Canada; 020/8741 2299 in the U.K.).

Most of the time Qantas and Ansett airfares on the same route match each other to within a dollar, and both airlines maintain virtually identical stan-dards of in-flight service and safety. Both own or are affiliated with a number of regional airlines covering almost every part of Australia, whose schedules and fares are linked into the parents' reservations systems. Australia's air network is not as well developed as that of North America or Europe, so don't assume there is a direct flight to your chosen destination, or that there is a flight every hour or even every day. *Note:* All flights in Australia are no-smoking.

FARES FOR INTERNATIONAL TRAVELERS   Qantas and Ansett typically offer international travelers a discount of around 30% off the full fares that Australians pay for domestic flights. So if the full fare for Australians is A$1,000, international visitors pay only around A$700—which works out to U.S.$455! Not bad. To qualify for these fares if you find yourself buying a ticket once you arrive in Australia, quote your passport number and international ticket number when making your reservation.

AIR PASSES   If you are planning on whipping around to more than one city, purchasing an Air Pass from either Qantas or Ansett is much cheaper than buying regular fares. *You must buy these passes before you arrive in Australia; residents of Australia and New Zealand cannot purchase them.*

With **Qantas's Boomerang Pass,** for example, you must purchase a minimum of two coupons (and a maximum 10) priced at U.S.$155/Can$230 or U.S.$185/Can$270 per coupon for travel within a zone, or U.S.$195/Can$290 or U.S.$235/Can$345 per coupon for travel between zones. The difference between the higher and lower fares depends on the airline's yield management system, so your coupons may cost the lower or higher amount depending on the day you buy them. Air passes are a great value when you consider that the regular Sydney-Cairns fare is A$599, which works out to U.S.$389.35, compared to the coupon fare of just U.S.$155 or $185!

Coupons are also good for travel to and from New Zealand and to the most popular South Pacific nations. The pass is also good for domestic travel within New Zealand aboard Ansett New Zealand and around the South Pacific with Air Pacific. Zone 1 covers Western Australia; Zone 2 covers the Red Centre and Darwin; Zone 3 covers major towns in South Australia, Tasmania, Victoria, New South Wales, and Queensland; and Zone 4 covers many small towns in the east coast states, including island gateways like Hayman Island, Hamilton Island, Gladstone, and Rockhampton. You must book your first coupon destination before you arrive, but you can book the rest as you go. Another beauty of these fares is that they are refundable and changeable; you will incur a U.S.$45/Can$50 fee to make changes after the coupons have been ticketed. **Ansett's G'Day Pass** is similar, although the pricing and zone structure may differ somewhat. Many small towns, some island resorts, and many airports served by subsidiaries of Qantas and Ansett are not covered by the air passes, but passes will still get you loads of places.

BY TRAIN

The rail network in Australia is mostly good only for long-distance travel between state capitals and the towns in between. Australia's trains are clean, comfortable, and safe, and service standards and facilities are perfectly adequate.

Most long-distance trains have smart sleepers with big windows, electric outlets, wardrobes, hand basins, and fresh sheets and blankets. First-class sleepers have en suite bathrooms, and meals are often included in the fare. Second-class sleepers use shared shower facilities, and meals are not included. Some second-class sleepers are private cabins; on other trains you share with strangers. Single cabins are usually of broom-closet dimensions but surprisingly comfy. The food ranges from okay to pretty darn good. You can smoke in some trains in the club cars, rarely in the dining car or in your sleeper, and on some trains smoking is prohibited altogether.

Important Advice: Australian rail schedules are no match for the snappy frequency of European rail travel—some trains operate only once a week—so check the timetable before you get your other travel arrangements in place. And because Australia doesn't have that many trains, they're often fully booked—so make reservations well in advance whenever you can.

Australia's rail routes are managed either by the private enterprise **Great Southern Railway** (☎ **13 21 47** in Australia or 08/8213 4592; www.gsr. com.au), which runs the *Indian Pacific,* the *Overland* (Melbourne-Adelaide), and the *Ghan* (Sydney-Melbourne-Adelaide-Alice Springs), or by one of the following government bodies: **Queensland Rail** (☎ **13 22 32** in Australia, or 07/3235 1000; www.qr.com.au, or check the unofficial site www.qroti.bit. net.au), which handles rail within that state; **Countrylink** (☎ **13 22 32** in Australia or 02/9379 1298; www.countrylink.nsw.gov.au), which manages travel within New South Wales and to Canberra, Melbourne, and Brisbane; and **Westrail** (☎ **13 10 53** in Western Australia or 1800/099 150 from elsewhere in Australia, or 08/9326 2222; www.westrail.wa.gov.au), which operates trains in Western Australia.

Outside Australia, the umbrella organization **Rail Australia** (www. railaustralia.com.au) handles inquiries and makes reservations for all longdistance trains, with the exception of Westrail services. Call Rail Australia's overseas agents: **ATS Tours** (☎ **800/423-2880**) in the United States, **Goway** (☎ **800/387-8850**) in Canada, **Leisurail** (☎ **0870/750 0222**) in the United Kingdom, and **Tranz Rail** (☎ **03/372 8209**) in New Zealand.

Possibly the most luxurious train in the world, the *Great South Pacific Express* is an ultra-opulent new locomotive with lavish turn-of-the-century decor. It's a joint venture between the Queensland government and Venice Simplon-Orient-Express. It plies the Brisbane-Cairns route weekly, incorporating the scenic rail trip to Kuranda (see chapter 6) and a side trip by seaplane or helicopter to a private pontoon on the Great Barrier Reef. The route extends to or from Sydney around once a month. The scenery is dull, dull, dull; you make this trip for the train itself. Fares range from A$2,830 to $4,690 (U.S.$1,839.50 to $3,048.50) per person, twin-share, for the Brisbane-Cairns leg. Contact **Venice Simplon-Orient Express** (☎ **630/ 954-2945** in the U.S., 020/7805 5100 in the U.K.), **Walshes World in New Zealand** (☎ **09/379 3708**), or **Orient-Express Trains and Cruises** in Australia (☎ **1800/000 395** in Australia or 07/3247 6595). Two Web sites have more information: www.orient-expresstrains.com and www.gspe.com.

The only train linking Sydney, Adelaide, and Perth is the ✪ *Indian Pacific,* which makes a 3-day Outback run. Most folks take it for the experience rather than as a way to get to Perth. The ultraluxurious *Great South Pacific Express* detailed above plies the Sydney-Cairns route. The *Overland* links Adelaide and Melbourne. The *Ghan* traverses a loop in the desert between Sydney, Melbourne, Adelaide, and Alice Springs. Countrylink runs fast *XPTs* (Express Passenger Trains, which despite their name stop at points en route) linking Sydney with Melbourne, Canberra, Brisbane, and the New South Wales town of Dubbo; trains from Sydney to the farming town of Griffith and the Outback town of Broken Hill; and *Xplorer* trains linking Sydney with Canberra and the New South Wales country towns of Tamworth, Armidale, and Moree. In Queensland, the *Queenslander* runs Brisbane-Cairns in all-first-class-sleepers configuration, while the comfortable *Sunlander* does the same route with seats and economy sleepers. The economy-seat–only *Spirit of the Tropics* runs Brisbane-Townsville, and the high-speed *Tilt* train does the Brisbane-Rockhampton route.

Both **Countrylink** and **Queensland Rail** (see above) offer a wide range of **rail packages** that include accommodations and sightseeing throughout New South Wales, as far west as Broken Hill and Lightning Ridge, as far south as Canberra and Melbourne, and throughout Queensland.

RAIL PASSES National and state rail passes are available from **Rail Australia** (see above) at its overseas agents. *National passes must be bought before you arrive and are available only to holders of non-Australian passports.* Unfortunately for parents, only the Queensland's Sunshine Railpass offers a discount for kids, who must be ages 4 to 15 years.

The national **Austrail Pass** is good for economy seats and sleepers on intrastate, interstate, and even suburban city train networks around the country. It comes in 14-, 21-, and 30-day versions and costs between A$660 (U.S.$429) and A$1,035 (U.S.$672.75). You can buy 7-day extensions for A$340 (U.S.$221). An alternative pass, the **Austrail Flexipass,** allows you to travel for any 8, 15, 22, or 29 days, consecutive or not, within a 6-month period. An 8-day Flexipass is A$550 (U.S.$357.50), with the price going up to A$1,440 (U.S.$936) for a 29-day Flexipass. *Note:* You cannot use the 8-day pass on the Adelaide–Perth route or the Sydney–, Melbourne–, or Adelaide–Alice Springs routes.

State passes are available in New South Wales, Victoria, Queensland, and Western Australia, and can be purchased after you arrive in Australia. These individual passes are described in the regional chapters later in this book.

BY BUS

Bus travel in Australia is a big step up from the low-rent affair it can be in the United States. Terminals are centrally located and well lit, the coaches are clean and air-conditioned, you sit in comfy adjustable seats, videos are shown on board, and the drivers are polite and even comment on points of interest along the way sometimes. Some buses even have rest rooms. Unlike Australia's train service, there are few places the extensive bus network won't take you. Buses are totally no-smoking.

Greyhound Pioneer Australia (☎ **13 20 30** in Australia, or 07/3258 1600; www.greyhound.com.au; no relation to Greyhound in the U.S.) and **McCafferty's** (☎ **13 14 99** in Australia, or 07/4690 9888; www.mccaffertys. com.au) are the two big national coach operators. As well as point-to-point services, both coach companies offer a range of tours at popular locations on their networks. McCafferty's has many international agents, including **Inta-Aussie South Pacific** (☎ **310/568-2060**) in the United States, **Goway** (☎ **800/387-8850**) in Canada, and **Bridge the World** (☎ **020/7911 0900**) in the United Kingdom.

BUS PASSES Bus passes are a great value. Day Passes are good for 7, 10, 15, or 21 days of travel (and also 30 days in McCafferty's case), consecutive or not, within a 1- to 2-month period depending on how many days you buy. McCafferty's fares range from A$560 (U.S.$364) for a 7-day pass to A$1,345 (U.S.$874.25) for a 30-day pass. The passes are valid for travel in any direction, and backtracking is allowed. The McCafferty's pass must be bought before you arrive in Australia, while Greyhound Pioneer's passes are available only in Oz.

If you know where you are going and are willing to obey a "no backtracking" rule, a better deal is a **Travel Australia** (McCafferty's) or **Aussie Explorer**

Here are some sample bus fares and travel times, to give you an idea of what you're getting yourself into as you step aboard. McCafferty's and Greyhound's fares are usually almost identical, to within a couple of dollars. All fares and travel times are one-way.

Route	Travel Time	Fare
Broome–Darwin	26$\frac{1}{2}$ hr.	A$234.50 (U.S.$152.40)
Sydney–Brisbane	17 hr.	A$82.50 (U.S.$53.65)
Cairns–Brisbane	28$\frac{1}{2}$ hr.	A$155.10 (U.S.$100.80)

Note: These are the fares you'll pay if you buy your ticket in Australia—fares and passes will be considerably cheaper if you're a student, a senior, a backpacker cardholder, or a YHA/Hostelling International member. Take note, you may have to buy them before you leave home to qualify for discounts.

(Greyhound Pioneer) pass. These passes allow unlimited stops in a generous time frame on a preset one-way route (though you are sometimes permitted to travel the route in either direction). Some routes allow backtracking on specific legs where it's necessary (Darwin to Kakadu National Park, say). You must book the next leg of your trip 24 hours ahead.

As an example, **McCafferty's "Sun and Centre"** pass takes in Ayers Rock, Alice Springs, Kings Canyon, Katherine, Darwin, Kakadu National Park, Mt. Isa, Cairns, and the whole east coast down to Sydney. The pass is valid for 6 months and costs A$725 (U.S.$471.25) for travel only, or A$810 (U.S.$526.50) with some extra tours thrown in at certain popular destinations. McCafferty's does not serve Western Australia, so if you want a pass that covers the whole country, go for Greyhound Pioneer's **All Australian Pass** for A$1,722 (U.S.$1,119.30); it's valid for a year.

Greyhound Pioneer has an **Aussie Kilometre Pass** that allows unlimited stops in any direction within the mileage you buy. Passes are available in increments of 1,000 kilometers (625 miles). Prices range from A$226 (U.S.$146.90) for 2,000 kilometers (1,250 miles)—enough to get you from Cairns to Brisbane—to A$1,617 (U.S.$1,051.05) for a whopping 20,000 kilometers (12,500 miles). McCafferty's has a similar product called an **Australian Roamer Pass,** which is available only to students, holders of selected backpacker cards, and members of YHA/Hostelling International.

BY CAR

Not only are Australia's roads not great, but there are not many of them. The taxes of the population of 18 million people get spread pretty thin when it comes to maintaining roads in a country roughly the size of the continental United States. Most highways are two-lane affairs with the occasional rut and pothole, often no outside line markings, and sometimes no shoulders to speak of.

When you are poring over the map of Australia, remember that what looks like a road may be an unsealed (unpaved) track suitable for 4WD vehicles only. Many roads in the Top End are passable only in the Dry Season (about Apr to Nov). If you plan to do some serious long-distance driving, get a decent road map (see below for sources).

You cannot drive across the middle of the country (except along the north-south Stuart Highway linking Adelaide and Darwin) because most of it is desert. Instead, in most places you must travel around the edge on Highway 1. The map on the inside front cover of this book marks the major highways.

Sample Driving Distances & Times

Here are a few sample road distances between popular points and the minimum time it takes to drive between them.

Route	Distance	Approx. Driving Time
Cairns–Sydney	2,495km (1,559 miles)	29 hr. (allow 4 to 5 days)
Sydney–Melbourne	873km (546 miles)	15 hr. (allow 1 to 2 days)
Sydney–Perth	4,131km (2,581 miles)	51 hr. (allow 6 to 7 days)
Adelaide–Darwin	3,024km (1,890 miles)	31 hr. (allow 4 to 6 days)
Perth–Darwin	4,163km (2,602 miles)	49 hr. (allow 6 to 8 days)

Your current **driver's license** or an **international driver's permit** is fine in every state of Australia. By law you must carry your license with you when driving. The minimum driving age is 16 or 17, depending on which state you visit, but some rental-car companies require you to be 21, or even 26 sometimes, if you want to rent a 4WD vehicle.

CAR RENTALS

Think twice about renting a car in tourist hot spots such as Cairns. In these areas most tour operators pick you up and drop you back at your hotel door, so having a car isn't worth the expense.

The "big four" car-rental companies all have extensive networks across Australia:

- **Avis** (☎ **1800/13 6333** in Australia; 800/230-4898 in the U.S.; 800/272-5871 in Canada; 0870/590 0500 in the U.K.; 21/28 1111 in Ireland; 09/526 2847 in New Zealand; www.avis.com)
- **Budget** (☎ **1300/36 2848** in Australia; 800/527 0700 in the U.S.; 800/268-8900 in Canada; 0645/60 6060 in the U.K.; 09/375 2222 in New Zealand; www.drivebudget.com)
- **Hertz** (☎ **13 30 39** in Australia; 800/654-3001 in the U.S.; 800/263-0600 in English, 800/263-0678 in French in Canada, or 416/620-9620 in Toronto; 0870/844 8844 in the U.K.; 1/676 7476 in Ireland; 0800/654 321 in New Zealand; www.hertz.com)
- **Thrifty** (☎ **1300/367 227** in Australia; 800/THRIFTY in the U.S. and Canada; 0800/96 3163 in the U.K.; 1800/51 5800 in Ireland; 09/309 1111 in New Zealand; www.thrifty.com)

A small sedan good for zipping around a city or touring a wine region will cost around A$70 (U.S.$45.50) a day. A feistier vehicle with enough grunt to get you hundreds of miles from state to state will cost around A$85 (U.S.$52.25) to A$100 (U.S.$65) a day. Rentals of a week or longer usually reduce by A$5 (U.S.$3.25) a day or so.

A regular car will get you to most places in Australia, but because the country has a high number of unsealed roads, it can make sense to rent a **four-wheel-drive (4WD) vehicle.** All of the major car-rental companies rent them. They are more expensive than a regular car at around A$150 (U.S.$97.50) per day, or around A$130 (U.S.$84.50) a day for rentals of a week or longer.

All of the rates quoted here are only a guide. Many smaller local companies, and the big guys too, do competitive specials, especially in tourist areas with distinct off-seasons. Advance purchase rates, usually 7 to 21 days, can offer significant savings.

INSURANCE Insurance for loss of, or damage to, the car, and third-party property insurance are usually included in the rate, but *read the rental agreement* before you set off, because the fine print contains key information the smiling front desk staff never tell you. For example, damage to the car body may be covered, but not damage to the windshield or tires, or damage caused by water.

The deductible, known as "excess" in Australia, on insurance may be as high as A$2,000 (U.S.$1,300) for regular cars and up to $5,500 (U.S.$3,575) on 4WDs and campervans. You can reduce or avoid it by paying a premium of around A$7 to $16 (U.S.$4.55 to $10.40) per day on a car or 4WD, and around A$22 to A$44 (U.S.$14.30 to $28.60) per day on a campervan. The amount of the premium depends on the vehicle type and the extent of reduction you choose. Your rental company may bundle personal accident insurance and baggage insurance into this premium; but your own travel insurance policy may cover these last two items, so check you are not doubling up. And again, check the conditions; some excess reduction payments do not reduce excesses on single-vehicle accidents, for example.

ONE-WAY RENTALS Australia's great distances often make one-way rentals a necessity, for which car-rental companies can charge a hefty penalty amounting to hundreds of dollars. A one-way fee usually applies to campervan renters too—for example, Maui charges a A$165 (U.S.$125.85) fee on most routes, and Britz charges A$200 (U.S.$130).

CAMPERVANS Campervans (as Aussies call motor homes) are popular in Australia. Generally a good deal smaller than the enormous RVs in the United States, they come in two-, three-, four-, or six-berth versions, and they usually have everything you need, such as a minifridge/freezer (icebox in the smaller versions), microwave oven, gas cooker, cooking and cleaning utensils, linen, and touring information including maps and camping ground guides. All have showers and toilets, except for some two-berthers. Four-wheeldrive campers are available, but they are small and usually lack hot water, a toilet, a shower, and air-conditioned sleeping quarters. This last facility is a necessity in most parts of the country from November to March. The minimum allowed driver age is usually 21 years.

Australia's biggest campervan-rental company is **Britz Campervan Rentals and Tours** (☎ **1800/331 454** in Australia, or 03/9417 1888; 805/373-8320 in the U.S.; 08705/143-609 in the U.K.; 0800/83 1900 in New Zealand; 0990/143-609 in the United Kingdom; www.britz.com). Other major national operators include **Maui** (☎ **1800/227 279** in Australia or 02/9556 6100; www.maui-rentals.com) and **Hertz Campervans** (☎ **1800/33 5888** in Australia or Auto-Rent Hertz ☎ 1800/030 500 in Tasmania, or 08/8271 8281; or your nearest Hertz office in your home country; www.hertz.com).

Frustratingly, most local councils take a dim view of you pulling over by the roadside to camp for the night. I think this is absurd in Australia's wide-open spaces. Instead, you will likely have to stay in a campground.

Insurance Alert

Damage to a rental car caused by an animal (hitting a kangaroo, for instance) is not covered by car-rental companies' insurance policies, nor is driving on an unpaved road—and Australia has a lot of those.

A Money-Saving Tip

One nifty way to cut an average of 30% off your car-rental rate is to join the Australian Youth Hostels Association (YHA), the Aussie arm of Hostelling International (see "For Students" under "Tips for Travelers with Special Needs," earlier in chapter). Along with a host of other discounts, membership entitles you discounts from Avis, Budget, and Hertz.

For a two-berth campervan with shower or toilet, Britz's 2000/2001 rates were between A$106 (U.S.$68.90) and A$203 (U.S.$131.95) per day, over a 4- to 20-day rental period. For a four-berth with shower and toilet over the same period, you are looking at between A$150 (U.S.$97.50) and A$265 (U.S.$172.25) per day. Rates vary with the seasons. May and June are the slowest months; December and January are the busiest. It's sometimes possible to get better rates by booking in your home country before departure. Renting for longer than 3 weeks knocks around A$10 (U.S.$6.50) or more off the daily rate. Most companies will demand a minimum 4- or 5-day rental. It's wise to give the company your itinerary before booking, because some routes, such as the ferry across to Tasmania, or in a 4WD campervan's case the Gibb River Road in the Kimberley, may need the company's special permission. Campervan rental companies may not permit you to drive your two-wheel campervan on unsealed roads.

ON THE ROAD IN AUSTRALIA

GAS   The price of petrol (gasoline) will elicit a cry of dismay from Americans and a whoop of delight from Brits. Prices go up and down a lot, but very roughly, you're looking at around A80¢ a liter (or U.S.$1.96 per U.S. gallon) for unleaded petrol in New South Wales, as little as A60¢ a liter (or U.S.$1.47 per U.S. gallon) in Queensland, and A95¢ a liter (or U.S.$2.33 per U.S. gallon), or more, in the Outback. One U.S. gallon equals 3.78 liters. Most rental cars take unleaded gas, and campervans run on diesel, which costs around A70¢ to A$1 a liter (U.S.$1.72 to $2.45 per U.S. gallon), depending on your location. Petrol stations (also called "roadhouses" in rural areas) can be few and far between in the Outback, so fill up at every opportunity.

DRIVING RULES   Australians drive on the left, which means you give way to the right. Left turns on a red light are *not* permitted unless a sign says so.

Roundabouts (traffic circles) are common at intersections; approach these slowly enough to stop if you have to, and give way to all traffic on the roundabout. You are supposed to flash your indicator light as you leave the roundabout (even if you're going straight ahead, as technically that's a left turn), but most Aussies never bother and it's not a rule that's enforced.

The only curly driving rule is Melbourne's requirement that drivers turn *right* from the *left* lane. This allows the city's trams to carry on uninterrupted in the right lane. Pull into the left lane opposite the street you are turning into, and make the turn when the traffic light in the street you are turning into becomes green.

The maximum permitted blood alcohol level when driving is 0.05, which equals approximately two 200 milliliter (6.6 fl. oz.) drinks in the first hour for men, one for women, and one drink per hour for both sexes after that. The police set up random breath-testing units (RBTs) in cunningly disguised and unlikely places all the time, so it is easy to get caught. You will face a court appearance if you do.

The **speed limit** is 60 kilometers per hour (37.5 m.p.h.) in urban areas and 100 kilometers per hour (63 m.p.h.) or 110 kilometers per hour (69 m.p.h.) in most country areas. Speed-limit signs are black numbers circled in red on a white background.

Drivers and passengers, including taxi passengers, must wear a **seatbelt** at all times when the vehicle is moving forward, if a belt is fitted in the car. You can be fined if you don't. Young children are required to sit in the rear seat in a child-safety seat or harness; car-rental companies will rent these to you, but be sure to book them ahead. Tell the taxi company you have a child when you book a cab so that they can send a car with the right restraints.

MAPS   The maps published by the state automobile clubs listed later in "Auto Clubs" will likely be free if you are a member of an affiliated auto club in your home country. However, they mostly dispense road maps with little tourism information, and you will probably have to wait until you arrive Down Under to collect them.

Two of the biggest map publishers in Australia are **HEMA Maps** (☎ **07/3290 0322**; www.hemamaps.com.au) and **Universal Press** (☎ **02/9857 3700**; e-mail: sales@unipress.com.au). Both publish a big range of state and city maps. HEMA has an especially strong list of regional maps ("Gold Coast" and "The Red Centre" are just a few), while Universal produces a complete range of street directories by city, region, or state under the "UBD" and "Gregory's" labels. HEMA produces maps to Kakadu and Lamington National Parks, and a Wine Map of Australia.

Both companies produce a range of national atlases. HEMA's 112-page "Australia Touring Atlas" doubles as a good road atlas, in a ring-bound form or a lighter perfect-bound version. It also publishes a dedicated "Australia Road Atlas" with a 4WD section—good if you plan to go off the trails covered by this guide—and an Australian atlas on CD. I think Universal's best is the 180-page ring-bound "UBD Motoring Atlas of Australia," which helpfully publishes street maps of small regional towns in each state. A new "Gregory's Road Atlas of Australia" will be available from Universal in 2001. I find HEMA's maps easiest to read.

Both HEMA and Universal Press maps are distributed in the United States by **Map Link** (☎ **805/692-6777**; www.maplink.com). HEMA maps are sold by Barnes & Noble and most specialist map stores in the United States and Canada. Universal Press maps are distributed in the United Kingdom by Edward Stanford's (☎ **020/7240-3611**).

In Australia, auto clubs (see below), bigger newsagents, and bookstores are your best source of maps. Petrol stations stock a limited range relating to the route they are on.

ROAD SIGNS   Australians navigate by road name, not road number. The easiest way to get where you're going is to familiarize yourself with the major towns along your route and follow the signs toward them.

AUTO CLUBS   Every state and territory in Australia has its own auto club. Your auto association back home almost certainly has a reciprocal agreement with Australian clubs, possibly entitling you to free maps, accommodation guides, and emergency roadside assistance. Don't forget to bring your membership card.

Even if you're not a member, the clubs are a good source of advice on local traffic regulations, touring advice, road conditions, traveling in remote areas, and any other motoring questions you may have. They sell maps, accommodation guides, and camping guides to nonmembers at reasonable prices. You can drop into numerous regional offices as well as the head office locations listed here. None will mail maps overseas; you'll have to pick those up on arrival.

- **New South Wales & ACT:** National Roads and Motorists' Association (NRMA), 74–76 King St. at George Street, Sydney, NSW 2000 (☎ **13 21 32** in New South Wales, or 02/9848 5201)
- **Victoria:** Royal Automobile Club of Victoria (RACV), 550 Princes Hwy., Noble Park, VIC 3174 (☎ **13 19 55** in Australia, or 03/9790 2211). A more convenient city office is located at 360 Bourke St., Melbourne.
- **Queensland:** Royal Automobile Club of Queensland (RACQ), 300 St. Pauls Terrace, Fortitude Valley, QLD 4006 (☎ **13 19 05** in Australia, or 07/3361 2444). A more convenient city office is in the General Post Office building at 261 Queen St., Brisbane.
- **Western Australia:** Royal Automobile Club of WA (RAC), 228 Adelaide Terrace, Perth, WA 6000 (☎ **08/9421 4444**)
- **South Australia:** Royal Automobile Association of South Australia (RAA), 41 Hindmarsh Sq., Adelaide, SA 5000 (☎ **08/8202 4600**)
- **Northern Territory:** Automobile Association of the Northern Territory (AANT), 79–81 Smith St., Darwin, NT 0800 (☎ **08/8981 3837**)
- **Tasmania:** Royal Automobile Club of Tasmania (RACT), corner of Murray and Patrick streets, Hobart, TAS 7000 (☎ **13 27 22** in Tasmania, or 03/6232 6300)

All these clubs except the AANT can be accessed on the Web at **www. aaa.asn.au**.

Road Conditions & Safety

Long distances, unsealed roads, and wildlife are all potential driving hazards. Here are some of the most common dangers and ways to avoid them:

FATIGUE   Fatigue is a killer on Australia's long roads. Be sure to take a 20-minute break every 2 hours, even if you don't feel tired.

KANGAROOS & OTHER WILDLIFE   It's a sad fact, but Skippy is a road hazard. Avoid driving between dusk and dawn in country areas, because this is when 'roos feed and are most active. If you hit one, always stop and check its pouch for live joeys (baby kangaroos), because females usually have one in the pouch. Wrap the joey tightly in a towel or old sweater, don't feed or over-handle it, and take it to a vet in the nearest town or call one of the following wildlife care groups: **Wildlife Information & Rescue Service** (WIRES) in New South Wales (☎ 1800/641 188 or 02/8977 3333); **Wildlife Care Network** in Victoria (☎ 0500/540 000); **Wildcare** in Queensland (☎ 07/5530 6634); **RSPCA Wildlife** in the ACT (☎ 02/6287 8100); **FAWNA Inc.** in Western Australia (☎ 08/9753 2118); **Wildcare Inc.** in the Northern Territory (☎ 08/8999 5511); the **Kangaroo (& Wildlife) Information & Rescue Service** (KRIS; ☎ 017/869 891 is a mobile telephone) or **Fauna Rescue of S.A.** (☎ **08/8289 2920**) in South Australia; or **Wildcare** in Tasmania (☎ **03/6233 6556**). Most vets will treat native wildlife free of charge.

Some major highways run through unfenced stations (ranches), where sheep and cattle pose a threat. Cattle like to rest on the warm bitumen road at night, so put your lights on high beam to spot them. If an animal does loom up before you, slow down but never swerve or you may roll, and, if you have to, hit it. Tell station owners within 24 hours if you have hit their livestock.

Car-rental companies will not insure for animal damage to the car, which should give you an inkling of how common an occurrence this is.

ROAD TRAINS   Road trains consist of as many as three big truck carriages linked together to make a "train" up to 53.5 meters (175 ft.) long. If you're in front of one, give them plenty of warning when you brake, because they need a lot of distance in which to slow down. Allow over half a mile (at least 1 clear km) before you pass one, but don't expect the driver to make it easy for you— "truckies" are notorious for their lack of concern for motorists.

UNSEALED ROADS   Many of Australia's country roads are unsealed (unpaved). They are usually bone-dry, which makes them a lot more slippery than they look, so travel at a moderate speed on these—35 kilometers per hour (20 m.p.h.) is not too cautious and anything over 60 kilometers per hour is dangerous. Don't over-correct if you veer to one side. Keep well behind any vehicles in front because the dust they throw up can block your vision.

FLOODS   Floods are common in the Top End and north of Cairns from November or December to March or April (the Wet Season). Never cross a flooded road unless you are sure of its depth. Crocodiles may be in the water, so do not wade in to test it! Fast-flowing water is dangerous, even if very shallow. When in doubt, stay where you are and wait for the water to drop, because most flash floods subside in 24 hours. Check the road conditions ahead at least once a day in the Wet Season.

What to Do If Your Vehicle Breaks Down

If you break down or get lost, *never* leave your vehicle. Many a motorist, often an Aussie who should know better, has died wandering off on some crazy quest for help or water, knowing full well that neither is to be found for maybe hundreds of miles. Most people who get lost do so in hot Outback spots; if that happens to you, conserve your body moisture level by doing as little as possible and staying in the shade of your car. Put out distress signals in patterns of three—three yells, three columns of smoke, and so on. The traditional Outback call for help is "coo-*ee*," with the accent on the "ee" and yodeled in a high pitch; it travels a surprisingly long way.

   The state auto clubs listed above provide free **breakdown emergency assistance** to members of many affiliated automobile associations around the world.

Tips for Four-Wheel Drivers

Always keep to the 4WD track and leave gates as you found them. On an extended trip or in very remote areas, be prepared. Carry 5 liters (1.3 gal.) of drinking water per person per day (dehydration occurs fast in the Australian heat); enough food to last 3 or 4 days more than you think you will need; a first-aid kit; spare fuel; a jack and two spare tires; spare fan belts, radiator hoses, and air-conditioner hoses; a tow rope; and a good map that marks all gas stations. In seriously remote areas outside the scope of this book, or if you're planning to travel off-road, carry a high-frequency and CB radio (even

---

Emergency Breakdown Assistance

The emergency breakdown assistance telephone number for every Australian auto club is ☎ **13 11 11** from anywhere in Australia. It is billed as a local call. If you are not a member of an auto club back home that has a reciprocal agreement with the Australian clubs, you'll have to join the Australian club on the spot before they will come tow/repair your car. This costs only around A$60 (U.S.$39), not a big price to pay when you're stranded. In the Outback, the charge may be considerably higher. Most car-rental companies also have emergency assistance numbers.

if you have a cell phone, it may not work in the Outback). Obtain permission from the owners before venturing onto private station (ranch) roads. Advise a friend, your hotel manager, the local tourist bureau, or a police station of your route and your expected time of return or arrival at your destination.

12 Tips on Accommodations

Note: All accommodations listed in this book have private bathrooms unless otherwise noted.

HOTELS It's a rare hotel room that does not have reverse-cycle air-conditioning for heating and cooling, a telephone, a color TV, a clock-radio, a minirefrigerator if not a minibar, an iron and ironing board, and self-serve tea and coffee. Private bathrooms are standard, although they often have only a shower, not a tub. If you are prepared to forego the convenience and pre-dictability of a chain, there are any number of moderately priced, individually run hotels that often offer a little more personal warmth and style than the big guys.

SERVICED APARTMENTS Serviced apartments are the accommodation of choice for many Aussie families and business travelers. Not only do you get a fully furnished apartment with one, two, or three separate bedrooms and a spacious living room, but you also get a kitchen, a laundry, and often two bathrooms. In other words, you get all the facilities of a hotel suite and more, often for less than the cost of a four-star hotel room. The apartment inventory in Australia is enormous and ranges from clean and comfortable to luxurious, and rates vary accordingly. You can find a nice two-bedroom apartment for between A$120 and $220 (U.S.$78 to $143). Most can be rented for just 1 night, but some proprietors will insist on a minimum 3-night stay, or even a week in high season in popular vacation spots.

Medina Serviced Apartments (☎ 1300/300 232 in Australia, or 02/9360 1699; www.medinaapartments.com.au) has a chain of mid-range to upscale properties in Sydney, Melbourne, Brisbane, and Canberra. Australia's biggest apartment chain is the Quest Apartment Accommodation Group (☎ 0800/ 944 400 in New Zealand, 1800/334 033 in Australia, or 03/9347 8622; www.questapartments.com.au). It has mostly upscale properties, in every state and territory except the Northern Territory.

MOTELS & MOTOR INNS Australia's plentiful motels are neat and clean, if often a little dated. You can count on them to provide air-conditioning, a telephone, a color TV, a clock-radio, a minirefrigerator or minibar, and self-serve tea and coffee. Most have only showers, not bathtubs. Some have restaurants attached, and many have swimming pools. Motor inns offer a greater range of facilities and a generally higher standard of rooms than motels. Rates average A$70 to $95 (U.S.$45.50 to $61.75) double.

BED-AND-BREAKFAST INNS B&Bs are cheap and plentiful in Australia. It is easy to find charming rooms for A$80 (U.S.$52) or less for a double, and rarely will you pay more than A$100 (U.S.$65) for a double per night. Bath-room facilities are often shared, although many properties these days have private, if not always en suite, bathrooms.

Travel agents rarely list B&Bs because the establishments are not big enough to pay commission, so they can be hard to find. A great source is *The Australian Bed & Breakfast Book* by J. Thomas (published by Moonshine Press in Australia, by Pelican Press in the U.S.), which lists hundreds of high-quality B&Bs across Australia. In Australia, it's widely available in book-shops and newsagents; you can also order it easily on www.amazon.com or www.bn.com. In the United Kingdom, contact Moonshine Press (☎ 01422/845 085). The entire book is posted on the Web at **www.bnb.co.nz**.

What Next? Productions Pty. Ltd. (☎ **03/9537 0833;** e-mail: jhawley@micronica.com.au) publishes two exquisite color guides titled *Beautiful B&Bs & Small Hotels,* a Tasmania edition featuring 104 properties and a Victoria/South Australia edition featuring 240 properties. The properties listed are more upscale than most, roughly in the A$100 to $200 (U.S.$65 to $130) price range for a double; each book contains six 10% discount vouchers. A guide to New South Wales should be added to the series by the time you read this. The guides sell for A$26.95 (U.S.$17.50) in Australian bookstores.

The Northern Territory Bed & Breakfast Council's Web site provides an **index of Australian B&B directories on the Web:** www.bed-and-breakfast.au.com/dirdir.htm (note: the address reads "au.com," *not* "com.au").

PUBS Aussie pubs are really made for having a few drinks, not spending the night, but many offer rooms upstairs, usually with shared bathroom facilities. Because most pubs are decades old, the rooms may be either cutely old-fashioned or just plain old. Pub accommodations are dying out in the cities but are still common in the country. Australians are rowdy drinkers, so sleep-ing over the front bar can be hellishly noisy; but the pub's saving grace is incredibly low rates. Most charge per person, not per room, and you will rarely pay more than A$50 (U.S.$32.50) per person a night. I have found rooms for as little as A$20 (U.S.$13) a night.

FARMSTAYS The Aussie answer to the dude ranch is a farmstay, where you get involved in farm duties, tour the property, or just relax under a gum tree. Accommodations on farms can be anything from a basic bunkhouse (ask if it's air-conditioned, because most farms are in very hot areas) to rustically luxuri-ous digs that would do Ralph Lauren proud. Do some research on your chosen farm—a lot of activities are seasonal, some farmers will not want you getting involved in dangerous work, not all will offer horse riding, and "farm" can mean different things in different parts of Australia. If you like green fields and

---

Meet the People Down Under

If you want to see an Australian Rules football game in the company of a knowledgeable local in the game's birthplace of Melbourne or swim at Bondi Beach with a Sydneysider, get in touch with **Friends Overseas—Australia,** 68-01 Dartmouth St., Forest Hills, NY 11375 (☎ **718/261 0534;** e-mail: awhyte@mail.idt.net). This meet-the-people program is designed to match visitors to Oz with friendly Aussies of like age and interests, so you can spend time with them, without staying in their homes. Send a stamped, self-addressed envelope to the above address. The membership fee is U.S.$25.

If you want to stay with an Aussie family and really get involved in their life, even sitting at their table, **Homestay Network,** 5 Locksley St., Killara, NSW 2071 (☎ **02/9498 4400;** e-mail: thenetwork@bigpond.com; www.sydney.citysearch.com.au—you will find it under Visiting Sydney, then Where to Stay, then Guesthouses), can place you in one of some 2,000 homes in the greater Sydney area. They can try to match your interests with your host's. Prices vary widely, but expect to pay about A$150 (U.S.$97.50) per double with breakfast.

Planning Basics

black-and-white dairy cows, Victoria is the place for you. If checking fences on a dusty 500,000-acre Outback station (ranch) sounds wildly romantic, not only are you crazy, but you should head to Western Australia or the Northern Territory.

Australian Farm & Country Tourism (☎ 03/9614 0892; www.factv. com) dispenses free brochures, one for each state, that detail the style of accommodation, activities, and rates at a huge range of farmstay properties in Victoria, New South Wales, Queensland, South Australia, and Western Australia. Rates vary widely, but expect to pay about A$85 (U.S.$55.25) for a double without meals.

Fast Facts: Australia

American Express   For all travel-related customer inquiries regarding any American Express service, including reporting a lost card, call ☎ **1800/230 100.** To report lost or stolen traveler's checks there is a separate line (☎ **1800/251 902**).

Business Hours   Banks open Monday to Thursday 9:30am to 4pm, and until 5pm on Friday. General business hours are Monday through Friday 8:30am to 5:30pm. Shopping hours are usually 8:30am to 5pm weekdays and 9am to 4pm or 5pm on Saturday. Many shops close Sundays, although major department stores and shops aimed at tourists, like opal stores, are open 7 days.

Car Rentals   See "Getting Around Australia," earlier in this chapter.

Climate   See "When to Go," earlier in this chapter.

Currency   See "Money," earlier in this chapter.

Customs   See "Entry Requirements & Customs," earlier in this chapter.

Dates   Australians write their dates day, month, year: January 5, 1968, is 05/01/68.

Driving Rules   See "Getting Around Australia," earlier in this chapter.

Drugstores   These are called "chemists" or "pharmacies." Australian pharmacists are permitted to fill only prescriptions written by Australian doctors.

Electricity   The current is 240 volts AC, 50 hertz. Sockets take two or three flat, not rounded, prongs. North Americans and Europeans will need to buy a converter before they leave home (don't wait until you get to Australia, because Australian stores sell only converters for Aussie appliances to fit American and European outlets). Some hotels have 110V outlets for electric shavers or dual voltage, and some will lend converters; but don't count on it. Power does not start automatically when you plug in an appliance; you need to flick the switch located beside the socket to the "on" position.

Embassies/Consulates   Most diplomatic posts are in Canberra: **British High Commission,** Commonwealth Avenue, Canberra, ACT 2600 (☎ 02/6270 6666); **Embassy of Ireland,** 20 Arkana St., Yarralumla, ACT 2600 (☎ 02/6273 3022); **High Commission of Canada,** Commonwealth Avenue, Yarralumla, ACT 2600 (☎ 02/6270 4000); **New Zealand High Commission,** Commonwealth Avenue, Canberra, ACT 2600 (☎ 02/6270 4211); and the **United States Embassy,** 21 Moonah

Place, Yarralumla, ACT 2600 (☎ 02/6214 5600). Embassies or consulates with posts in state capitals are listed in "Fast Facts" in the relevant state chapters.

Emergencies   Dial ☎ **000** anywhere in Australia for police, ambulance, or the fire department. This is a free call from public and private telephones and needs no coins.

Etiquette   Australia's laid-back disposition means it's first names from the start, handshakes all round, and no standing on ceremony, mate. Always return a "shout" (round) at the pub, and don't butt in if there's a queue (line).

Holidays   See "When to Go," earlier in this chapter.

Information   See "Visitor Information," earlier in this chapter.

Liquor Laws   Hours vary from pub to pub, but most are open daily from around 10am to 10pm or midnight. The minimum drinking age is 18. Random breath tests to catch drunk drivers are common, and drunk-driving laws are strictly enforced. Getting caught drunk behind the wheel will mean a court appearance, not just a fine. The maximum permitted blood alcohol level is 0.05. Alcohol is sold only in liquor stores, or "bottle shops" attached to a pub, and rarely in supermarkets.

Mail   A postcard costs A$1 (U.S.65¢) to the United States, Canada, the United Kingdom, or New Zealand.

Maps   See "Getting Around," earlier in this chapter.

Pets   Leave 'em at home. You will be back home planning your next vacation before Fluffy clears quarantine in Oz.

Police   Dial ☎ **000** anywhere in Australia. This is a free call from public and private telephones and requires no coins.

Safety   Violent crime is uncommon. Guns are strictly controlled. Purse snatchers are the same threat in capital cities and tourist areas that they are all over the world.

Taxes   In 2000, Australia introduced a 10% Goods and Services Tax (GST) on most products and services. Your international airline ticket to Australia is not taxed, nor are your domestic airline tickets for travel within Australia *if you bought them outside Australia*. International airline tickets bought in Australia, and domestic legs of that international journey, are not taxed. If you buy more domestic Australian airline tickets once you arrive in Australia, you will pay GST on them.

Through the Tourist Refund Scheme (TRS), Australians and international visitors can claim a refund of the GST (and of a 14.5% wine tax called Wine Equalisation Tax, or WET) paid on a purchase worth more than A$300 (U.S.$195) from a single outlet, within the last 30 days before you leave Australia. More than one item may be included in that A$300. For example, you can claim back the GST you paid on 10 T-shirts each worth A$30, as long as they were bought from a single store. You do this as you leave Australia by presenting your receipt, known in tax office parlance as a "tax invoice," to the Australian Customs Service's TRS booths, located beyond passport control in the international terminal departure areas at most international airports (listed below). If you buy several things on different days from one store, which individually are worth less than A$300 but together add up to A$300 or more, you must ask the store to total all purchases on one tax invoice (or receipt)—now there's a nice piece of bureaucracy to remember Australia by! Carry the items in your carry-on baggage, as you must show them to Customs. You can use the goods before you leave Australia and still claim the refund, but you cannot claim a refund on things you have consumed (film you shoot off in the camera, say, or food). You cannot claim a refund on alcohol other than wine. Allow an extra 15 minutes to stand on line and get your refund.

You can also claim a refund if you leave Australia as a cruise passenger from these ports: Circular Quay or Darling Harbour in Sydney, Cairns, Darwin, or Fremantle (Perth). If your cruise departs from elsewhere in Australia, or if you are flying out from an airport other than Sydney, Melbourne, Brisbane, Adelaide, Cairns, Perth, Darwin or Coolangatta (Gold Coast), telephone the **Australian Customs Service** (☎ **1300/ 363 263**) to see if you can still claim the refund.

Items bought in duty-free stores will not be charged GST. Nor will items you export—such as an Aboriginal painting, say, that you buy in a gallery in Alice Springs and have shipped straight to your home outside Australia.

Basic groceries are not GST taxed, but restaurant meals are.

Other taxes include departure tax of A$30 (U.S.$19.50), which was included in the price of your airline ticket when you bought it; landing and departure taxes at some airports, also included in the price of your ticket; and "reef tax," officially dubbed the Environmental Management Charge, of A$4 (U.S.$2.60) for every person over the age of 4 every time he or she enters the Great Barrier Reef Marine Park (this charge goes toward park upkeep).

Telephone & Fax   To call Australia from North America: Dial the international access code (**011**), then Australia's country code (**61**), then the area code (we've given the area code for every number listed in this book), then the local number. The local area codes found throughout this book all begin with "0"; you drop the "0" if you're calling from outside Australia, but you need to dial it as part of the area code if you're calling from another city or town within Australia. For example, to ring the Sydney Opera House (☎ **02/9250 7111**); from the United States, dial 011-61-2-9250-7111.

To call Australia from the United Kingdom: Dial the international access code (**00**), and then follow the instructions above.

To make an international call from Australia: Dial the international access code (**0011**—note it has two zeros, unlike the international access code from North America), then the country code (1 for the U.S. and Canada, 44 for the U.K., 353 for Ireland, 64 for New Zealand, 27 for South Africa), then the area code, and finally the local number. Dial ☎ 0012 instead of 0011, and the operator will call back within minutes to tell you what your call cost (handy when you are calling from someone's home and you want to reimburse them correctly). To find out the per-minute international call charges to any country, dial ☎ 12552. To find out a country code, call ☎ 1222 or look in the back of the Australian White Pages.

To make an international credit-card or collect call from Australia: Dial one of the following access codes to your country. **United States:** AT&T Direct (☎ 1800/881 011), Sprint (☎ 1800/881 877), MCI

(☎ 1800/881 100), Worldcom (☎ 1800/881 212), or Bell Atlantic (☎ 1800/881 152). **United Kingdom:** BT (☎ 1800/881 440, or 1800/881 441 for automated service only) or Mercury (☎ 1800/881 417). **Ireland:** 1800/881 353. **New Zealand:** ☎ 1800/881 640.

To use a calling card from some pay phones, you will need to deposit A40¢ to put the call through, but this is usually refunded when you hang up.

To make a long-distance call within Australia: Dial the area code, including the initial zero, followed by the number you are calling. Australia's area codes are New South Wales and the A.C.T., 02; Victoria and Tasmania, 03; Queensland, 07; and South Australia, Western Australia, and the Northern Territory, 08. Long-distance calls within Australia on Telstra's network are cheaper before 7am and after 7pm Monday through Friday and anytime on weekends.

Australia's toll-free numbers: Australian phone numbers starting with 1800 are toll-free; numbers starting with 13 or 1300 are charged at the local fee of 25¢ from anywhere in Australia. Numbers beginning with 1900 (or 1901, 1902, and so on) are pay-for-service lines (like 900 numbers in the United States); expect to be charged as much as A$5 (U.S.$3.25) a minute.

Local Calls: Local calls in Australia are untimed and cost a flat A40¢ from a public telephone, or A25¢ from a private phone in a home or office. At the time we wrote this, telephone companies were throwing around the idea of introducing timed local calls.

To avoid juggling for change to use at pay phones, consider buying a **Telstra Smart Phonecard** (which you swipe in the pay phone; not all public telephones take swiped Phonecard or credit cards yet, though) or a **PhoneAway card,** which you use by dialing access codes printed on the card. Both contain a prepaid allotment of call time for local, long-distance, international, and cell-phone calls. PhoneAway cards have a personalized Voicemail voice and fax box. Both cards are widely sold at newsagents, Telstra shops, tourist information booths, and other outlets. PhoneAway cards are also sold at Australia Post offices, Traveland travel agencies, and some duty-free stores.

Mobile Calls: Australia has the world's biggest per-capita uptake of cellular or "mobile" telephones. They are available for daily rental at major airports and in big cities. Before you bring your own cell phone into Australia, check with your telephone provider at home that your device will work on Australia's digital network.

Operator Assistance: To reach the operator for help making a call, dial ☎ **1234.** To make a collect or "reverse charges" call, dial the operator at ☎ **12550.**

To find out a telephone number, call Directory Assistance at ☎ **1223** for numbers within Australia, or ☎ **1225** for overseas numbers.

Time Eastern Standard Time (EST, also written as AEST sometimes) covers Queensland, New South Wales, the Australian Capital Territory, Victoria, and Tasmania. Central Standard Time is used in the Northern Territory and South Australia, and Western Standard Time (WST) is the standard in Western Australia. When it's noon in New South Wales, the A.C.T., Victoria, Queensland, and Tasmania, it's 11:30am in South Australia and the Northern Territory and 10am in Western Australia. All states except Queensland, the Northern Territory, and Western Australia observe daylight saving time from the last Sunday in October (the first Sun in Oct in Tasmania's case) to the last Sunday in March. Not all states switch over to daylight saving on the same day or in the same week.

The east coast of Australia is GMT (Greenwich Mean Time) plus 10 hours. When it is noon on the east coast, it is 2am in London that morning, and 6pm in Los Angeles and 9pm in New York the previous night. These times are based on standard time, so allow for daylight saving in the Australian summer, or in the country you are calling. New Zealand is 2 hours ahead of the east coast of Australia.

Tipping   Waiters get paid decently enough in Australia that you are not expected to supplement their income. It is customary to tip 5% or round up to the nearest A$10 for a substantial meal in a restaurant (but not for a casual sandwich and cup of coffee). Some passengers round up to the nearest dollar in a cab, but it's okay to insist on every last 5-cent piece of change back from the driver. Tipping bellboys and porters is sometimes done, but not really expected. No one tips bar staff, barbers, or hairdressers.

Water   Water is fine to drink everywhere except Port Douglas, where you should stick to the bottled variety. In the Outback, the taps may carry warm brackish water from underground called "bore water" for showers and laundry, while drinking water is collected in rainwater tanks.

Planning Your Trip: An Online Directory

Frommer's Online Directory will help you take better advantage of the travel-planning information available online. Section 1 lists general Internet resources that can make any trip easier, such as sites for obtaining the best possible prices on airline tickets. In section 2 you'll find some top sites specifically for Australia.

This is not a comprehensive list, but a discriminating selection to get you started. Recognition is given to sites based on their content value and ease of use. Inclusion here is not paid for—unlike some Web-site rankings, which are based on payment. Finally, remember that this is a press-time snapshot of leading Web sites; some undoubtedly will have evolved, changed, or moved by the time you read this.

1 The Top Travel-Planning Web Sites

by Lynne Bairstow

Lynne Bairstow is the co-author of *Frommer's Mexico,* and the editorial director of *e-com* magazine.

WHY BOOK ONLINE?

Online agencies have come a long way over the past few years, now providing tips for finding the best fare and giving you suggested dates or times to travel that yield the lowest price if your plans are at all flexible. Other sites even allow you to establish the price you're willing to pay, and they check the airlines' willingness to accept it. However, in some cases, these sites may not always yield the best price. Unlike a travel agent, for example, they may not have access to charter flights offered by wholesalers.

Online booking sites aren't the only places to reserve airline tickets—all major airlines have their own Web sites and often offer incentives (bonus frequent-flyer miles or net-only discounts, for example) when you buy online or buy an e-ticket.

The new trend is toward conglomerated booking sites. By June 2001, a consortium of U.S. and European-based airlines is planning to launch a Web site called **Orbitz.com** that will offer fares lower than those available through travel agents. United, Delta, Northwest, American, and Continental have initiated this effort, based on their success at selling airline seats on their own sites.

Check Out Frommer's Site

We highly recommend **Arthur Frommer's Budget Travel Online** (**www. frommers.com**) as an excellent travel-planning resource. Of course, we're a little biased, but you'll find indispensable travel tips, reviews, monthly vacation giveaways, and online booking. Among the most popular features of this site are the regular "Ask the Expert" bulletin boards, which feature Frommer's authors answering your questions via online postings.

Subscribe to Arthur Frommer's Daily Newsletter (**www.frommers.com/ newsletters**) to receive the latest travel bargains and inside travel secrets in your e-mailbox every day. You'll read daily headlines and articles from the dean of travel himself, highlighting last-minute deals on airfares, accommodations, cruises, and package vacations.

Search our Destinations archive (**www.frommers.com/destinations**) of more than 200 domestic and international destinations for great places to stay and dine, and tips on sightseeing. Once you've researched your trip, the online reservation system (**www.frommers.com/booktravelnow**) takes you to Frommer's favorite sites for booking your vacation at affordable prices.

The best of the travel-planning sites are now highly personalized; they store your seating preferences, meal preferences, tentative itineraries, and credit-card information, allowing you to quickly plan trips or check agendas.

In many cases, booking your trip online can be better than working with a travel agent. It gives you the widest variety of choices, control, and the 24-hour convenience of planning your trip when you choose. All you need is some time—and often a little patience—and you're likely to find that the fun of online travel research will greatly enhance your trip.

WHO SHOULD BOOK ONLINE?

Online booking is best for travelers who want to know as much as possible about their travel options, for those who have flexibility in their travel dates, and for bargain hunters.

One of the biggest successes in online travel for both passengers and airlines is the offer of last-minute specials, including Internet-only fares that must be purchased online. Another advantage is that you can cash in on incentives for booking online, such as rebates or bonus frequent-flyer miles.

Business and other frequent travelers also have found numerous benefits in online booking, because the advances in mobile technology provide them with the ability to check flight status, change plans, or get specific directions from handheld computing devices, mobile phones, and pagers. Some sites will even e-mail or page a passenger if their flight is delayed.

Online booking is increasingly able to accommodate complex itineraries, even for international travel. The pace of evolution on the Net is rapid, so you'll probably find additional features and advancements by the time you visit these sites. The future holds ever-increasing personalization and customization for online travelers.

TRAVEL-PLANNING & -BOOKING SITES

Below are listings for sites for planning and booking travel. The following sites offer domestic and international flight, hotel, and rental-car bookings, plus news, destination information, and deals on cruises and vacation packages. Free (one-time) registration is required for booking.

Travelocity (incorporates Preview Travel). www.travelocity.com; www.previewtravel.com; www.frommers.travelocity.com

Travelocity is Frommer's online travel-planning and booking partner. Travelocity uses the SABRE system to offer reservations and tickets for more than 400 airlines, plus reservations and purchase capabilities for more than 45,000 hotels and 50 car-rental companies. An exclusive feature of the SABRE system is its **Low Fare Search Engine,** which automatically searches for the three lowest-priced itineraries based on a traveler's criteria. Last-minute deals and consolidator fares are included in the search. If you book with Travelocity, you can select specific seats for your flights with online seat maps, and also view diagrams of the most popular commercial aircraft. Its hotel finder provides street-level location maps and photos of selected hotels. With the **Fare Watcher** e-mail feature, you can select up to five routes and receive e-mail notices when the fare changes by $25 or more.

Travelocity's **Destination Guide** includes updated information on some 260 destinations worldwide—supplied by Frommer's.

Note to AOL Users: You can book flights, hotels, rental cars, and cruises on AOL at keyword: Travel. The booking software is provided by Travelocity/ Preview Travel and is similar to the Internet site. Use the AOL "Travelers Advantage" program to earn a 5% rebate on flights, hotel rooms, and car rentals.

Expedia. expedia.com

Expedia is Travelocity's major competitor. It offers several ways of obtaining the best possible fares: **Flight Price Matcher** service allows your preferred airline to match an available fare with a competitor; a comprehensive **Fare Compare** area shows the differences in fare categories and airlines; and **Fare Calendar** helps you plan your trip around the best possible fares. Its main limitation is that like many online databases, Expedia focuses on the major airlines and hotel chains, so don't expect to find too many budget airlines or one-of-a-kind B&Bs here.

TRIP.com. www.trip.com

TRIP.com began as a site geared toward business travelers, but its innovative features and highly personalized approach have broadened its appeal to leisure travelers as well. It is the leading travel site for those using mobile devices to access Internet travel information.

TRIP.com includes a trip-planning function that provides the average and lowest fare for the route requested, in addition to the current available fare. An on-site "newsstand" features breaking news on airfare sales and other travel specials. Among its most popular features are Flight TRACKER and intelliTRIP. **Flight TRACKER** allows users to track any commercial flight en route to its destination anywhere in the U.S., while accessing real-time FAA-based flight monitoring data. **intelliTRIP** is a travel search tool that allows users to identify the best airline, hotel, and rental-car rates in less than 90 seconds.

In addition, the site offers e-mail notification of flight delays, plus city resource guides, currency converters, and a weekly e-mail newsletter of fare updates, travel tips, and traveler forums.

Yahoo Travel. www.travel.yahoo.com

Yahoo is currently the most popular of the Internet information portals, and its travel site is a comprehensive mix of online booking, daily travel news, and destination information. The **Best Fares** area offers what it promises, plus

More people still look online than book online, partly due to fear of putting their credit-card numbers out on the Net. Secure encryption, and increasing experienced buying online, has removed this fear for most travelers. In some cases, however, it's simply easier to buy from a local travel agent who can deliver your tickets to your door (especially if your travel is last-minute or if you have special requests). You can find a flight online and then book it by calling a toll-free number or contacting your travel agent, though this is somewhat less efficient. To be sure you're in secure mode when you book online, look for a little icon of a padlock at the bottom of your Web browser.

provides feedback on refining your search if you have flexibility in travel dates or times. There is also an active section of Message Boards for discussions on travel in general and specific destinations.

LAST-MINUTE DEALS & OTHER ONLINE BARGAINS

There's nothing airlines hate more than flying with lots of empty seats. The Net has enabled airlines to offer last-minute bargains to entice travelers to fill those seats. Most of these are announced on Tuesday or Wednesday and are valid for travel the following weekend, but some can be booked weeks or months in advance. You can sign up for weekly e-mail alerts at the airlines' own sites or check sites that compile lists of these bargains, such as **Smarter Living** or **WebFlyer** (see below). To make it easier, visit a site that will round up all the deals and send them in one convenient weekly e-mail.

Important Note: See section 10, "Flying to Australia," in chapter 2 for the Web addresses of airlines serving Australia. These sites offer schedules and flight booking, and most have pages where you can sign up for e-mail alerts about late-breaking bargains. See also "Booking a Package or Escorted Tour," in chapter 2, for the Web sites of companies that specialize in travel to Australia.

Bid for Travel. www.bidfortravel.com
Bid for Travel is another of the travel auction sites, similar to Priceline (see below), which are growing in popularity. In addition to airfares, Internet users can place a bid for vacation packages and hotels.

Cheap Tickets. www.cheaptickets.com
Cheap Tickets has exclusive deals that aren't available through more mainstream channels. One caveat about the Cheap Tickets site is that it will offer fare quotes for a route, and later show that this fare is not valid for your dates of travel—most other Web sites, such as Expedia, consider your dates of travel before showing what fares are available. Despite its problems, Cheap Tickets can be worth the effort because its fares can be lower than those offered by its competitors.

LastMinuteTravel.com. www.lastminutetravel.com
Suppliers with excess inventory come to this online agency to distribute unsold airline seats, hotel rooms, cruises, and vacation packages. It's got great deals, but an excess of advertisements and slow-loading graphics.

Moment's Notice. www.moments-notice.com
As the name suggests, Moment's Notice specializes in last-minute vacation deals. You can browse free, but if you want to purchase a trip, you have to join Moment's Notice, which costs $25.

Check Your E-mail While You're on the Road

You don't have to be out of touch just because you don't carry a laptop while you travel. Web browser–based free e-mail programs make it much easier to stay in e-touch.

Just open a freemail account at a browser-based provider, such as **MSN Hotmail (hotmail.com)** or **Yahoo! Mail (mail.yahoo.com)**. AOL users should check out **AOL Netmail,** and **USA.NET (www.usa.net)** comes highly recommended for functionality and security. You can find hints, tips, and a mile-long list of freemail providers at www.emailaddresses.com.

Be sure to give your freemail address to the family members, friends, and colleagues with whom you'd like to stay in touch while you're Down Under. All you'll need in order to check your freemail account while you're away from home is a Web connection, easily available at Internet cafes, copy shops, and cash- and credit-card Internet-access machines (often available in hotel lobbies or business centers). After logging on, just point the browser to **www.hotmail.com**, **www.yahoo.com**, or the address of any other service you're using. Enter your user name and password, and you'll have access to your mail, for both receiving and sending messages to friends and family back home, for just a few dollars an hour.

This guide also lists specific locations of cybercafes in Sydney, Melbourne, and a few other destinations. Cybercafes come and go and are becoming more widespread, so you're likely to find them in more and more cities across Australia by the time you travel.

✪ **1travel.com. www.1travel.com**
Here you'll find deals on domestic and international flights and hotels. 1travel. com's **Saving Alert** compiles last-minute air deals so you don't have to scroll through multiple e-mail alerts. And **Farebeater** searches a database that includes published fares, consolidator bargains, and special deals exclusive to 1travel.com. *Note:* The travel agencies listed by 1travel.com have paid for placement.

✪ **Priceline.com. travel.priceline.com**
Priceline lets you "name your price" for domestic and international airline tickets and hotel rooms. You select a route and dates, guarantee with a credit card, and make a bid for what you're willing to pay. If one of the airlines in Priceline's database has a fare lower than your bid, your credit card will automatically be charged for a ticket.

But you can't say when you want to fly—you have to accept any flight leaving between 6am and 10pm on the dates you selected, and you may have to make a stopover. No frequent-flyer miles are awarded, and tickets are non-refundable and can't be exchanged for another flight. So if your plans change, you're out of luck. Priceline can be good for travelers who have to take off on short notice (and who are thus unable to qualify for advance-purchase discounts). But be sure to shop around first, because if you overbid, you'll be required to purchase the ticket—and Priceline will pocket the difference between what it paid for the ticket and what you bid.

Priceline says that over 35% of all reasonable offers for domestic flights are being filled on the first try, with much higher fill rates on popular routes (New York to San Francisco, for example). They define "reasonable" as not more than 30% below the lowest generally available advance-purchase fare for the same route.

Smarter Living. www.smarterliving.com

Best known for its e-mail dispatch of weekend deals on 20 airlines, Smarter Living also keeps you posted about last-minute bargains.

Travelzoo.com. www.travelzoo.com

At this Internet portal, more than 150 travel companies post special deals. It features a Top 20 list of the best deals on the site, selected by its editorial staff each Wednesday night. This list is also available via an e-mailing list, free to those who sign up.

WebFlyer. www.webflyer.com

WebFlyer is a comprehensive online resource for frequent flyers and also has an excellent listing of last-minute air deals. Click on "Deal Watch" for a round-up of weekend deals on flights, hotels, and rental cars from domestic and international suppliers.

2 The Top Web Sites for Australia

by Natalie Kruger

GENERAL SITES FOR AUSTRALIA

See "Getting Around Australia," in chapter 2, for a complete rundown of domestic airlines and rail operators. I've listed each company's Web site there, so you can check out prices and schedules online.

Aussie.com.au. www.aussie.com.au

One of Australia's biggest online business directories, this site links you to a huge range of accommodations, tours, rental-car companies, and other travel-related providers. The search engine is not very discriminating, so it can be hard to sort out the appealing from the irrelevant.

Australian Broadcasting Corporation (ABC). www.abc.net.au

The ABC is Australia's publicly funded radio and television broadcaster. Check the latest news, see what topics are getting Aussies hot under the collar, and buy books, videos, CDs, and merchandise related to many facets of Australian life. The soft-toy dolls spun off from the popular "Bananas in Pajamas" TV show make good gifts for kids.

Australian Bureau of Meteorology. www.bom.gov.au

How cold does it *really* get in Sydney? Find out here, and check forecasts, average temperatures and rainfall, and other climatic considerations for just about any point in Australia that you care to visit.

Australian Embassy, Washington, D.C. www.austemb.org

While not aimed only at holiday-makers, this site posts loads of links to sites on tourism, as well as cultural and educational matters; briefings on the economy, trade, sports, geography, and the Aussie people; events listings; and more. It's written with North Americans in mind.

Australian Tourism Net. www.atn.com.au

It's not comprehensive, but this wide-ranging site connects you to many accommodations, car-rental companies, outdoor adventure operators, and more. It also has a detailed national parks guide.

✪ Australian Tourist Commission. www.australia.com

Australia's official tourism marketing board site has more than 10,000 easy-to-use pages detailing accommodations, tour operators, destinations, travel tips, hot airfare package deals from your country, links to Aussie Specialist travel agents, and much, much more. The "Special Interests" tab is a good place to start.

✪ Dive-Oz. www.diveoz.com

A fabulous resource for anyone diving Down Under. This well-maintained site sports ever-growing directories of dive sites, dive operators, dive boats, wrecks, dive clubs, and dive buddies, as well as a scuba news section, a photographic gallery, discussion forums, and links. There's ample detail in every listing. It covers diving not just on the Great Barrier Reef, but elsewhere in Queensland and all over Australia as well.

✪ Eating and Drinking in Australia. www.miettas.com.au

Mietta O'Donnell ran an acclaimed Melbourne restaurant before turning to publishing *Mietta's Eating and Drinking in Australia 2000* and other dining guides. See extracts from that and her other books here, including thoughtful, unbiased reviews of a couple of hundred of Australia's seriously good restaurants, cafes, and wine bars (organized by price), complete with opening hours, credit cards, and other details. The focus is on editorial, not on advertising.

Lone Pine Koala Sanctuary. www.koala.net

For fact sheets on all kinds of Aussie wildlife from hairy-nosed wombats to whiptail wallabies, check out the site of Australia's first and biggest koala sanctuary, which is in Brisbane. A kids' section has printable koalas to color in, koala face masks to make, and puzzles.

Opals. www.opals.net.au

Opals are at the top of the shopping list for many visitors Down Under. This site has a good description of how the country's national gemstones are formed, the different colors and varieties available, how to care for them, and how to buy a good one.

✪ Orbit Australia. www.pi.se/~orbit/aust.html

Firsthand reports from travelers to Oz make this a great site, especially since many of them take the road less traveled. Written in a quirky voice, the site also has travel tips and plenty of referrals to tour companies, hotels, and the like.

South Sea Pearls. www.paspaleypearls.com

The romantic green seas of Broome in Australia's northwest grow the world's most luscious South Sea pearls. The beautiful site of Australia's premier pearling dynasty, the Paspaleys, has a fascinating explanation of how pearls are farmed, and what marks a good pearl from a bad one.

SYDNEY

✪ CitySearch Sydney. www.sydney.citysearch.com.au

Pick up cool suggestions on sporting activities, restaurants, dance clubs, bars, shops, attractions, concerts, theater, art exhibitions, and festivals, as well as current film listings and lifestyle features on this excellent, densely packed site. Click the "Visiting Sydney" tab for links to an extensive accommodations directory, rental cars, baby-sitters, doctors, churches, shops selling anything from wine to Aussie fashions, and much more.

Sydney Travel Guide. www.travelsydney.com

Written for travelers rather than locals (like CitySearch Sydney above), this site provides a comprehensive rundown of things to see and do, not just in the most popular haunts of Sydney, but in weekender destinations outside the city.

NEW SOUTH WALES

NSW National Parks & Wildlife. www.npws.nsw.gov.au
This official site provides an overview of New South Wales's and the Australian Capital Territory's national parks, though it lacks much useful detail. It lists ranger-station telephone numbers for every park.

Tourism New South Wales. www.tourism.nsw.gov.au
It can be hard to extract the information you want from the site of the state's official tourism marketing board, because the information is mostly search-based, and the content on individual accommodations, tour providers, and event organizers is often sparse, with frustratingly few links. You will get a good overview of the state's regions, though.

QUEENSLAND

Bed & Breakfast and Farmstay Association of Far North Queensland, Inc. www.bnbnq.com.au
Link to the Web sites of B&Bs and farmstays in and around Cairns, Port Douglas and the Daintree rain-forest area, Mission Beach, and Townsville.

Cairns Online. www.cairns.aust.com
A detailed source for travelers containing links to the Web sites of a huge range of fishing charters, cruise boats, yachting trips, wildlife attractions, rain-forest safaris, tour operators, accommodations, and more. It covers not only Cairns but Kuranda, Port Douglas, and the Cape York Peninsula as well.

Environmental Protection Agency. www.env.qld.gov.au
Click the "Search" tab to link to a description of all Queensland's national parks, including major things to see and do in each one, hiking-trail descriptions, campsites and fees, tips on exploring, when to go, visitor facilities, and more.

Queensland Bed & Breakfast Association. www.bnb.au.com
More than 65 properties, some of them lovely old timber Queenslander houses with wide verandas, can be located and booked on this site. Many are in Brisbane and southern Queensland.

Tourism Queensland. www.queensland-holidays.com.au
The state's official tourism marketing board site provides a comprehensive, detailed, and easy-to-use rundown on accommodations, attractions, tour operators, transport providers, and events throughout the state, searchable by city/town, region, type, or special interest. Click the "North American" tab on the home page for details tailored to American travelers.

Tourism Tropical North Queensland. www.tnq.org.au
If you're visiting Cairns, Port Douglas, Mission Beach, or most other parts of north Queensland, north Queensland's official tourism marketing site links you to Web sites of ample Great Barrier Reef cruises, dive operators, 4WD rain-forest safaris, tour providers, accommodations, and more. It has tips on getting around north Queensland, too.

NORTHERN TERRITORY

Northern Territory Bed & Breakfast Council. www.bed-and-breakfast. au.com
Locate and book not only B&Bs but also country homesteads and lodges in and around Alice Springs, Katherine, and Darwin.

Northern Territory Tourist Commission. **www.nttc.com.au**
An excellent site, this is your best source of information on touring the Territory and its national parks, including Uluru–Kata Tjuta National Park (Ayers Rock).

WESTERN AUSTRALIA

Department of Conservation and Land Management (CALM).
www.calm.wa.gov.au
Find out more about all the state's national parks in detail. You can also check out the latest science- and nature-based holidays offered by CALM's excellent "Landscope Expeditions" program.

Western Australia Bed & Breakfast Association. **www.travelaustralia. com.au/wabba**
Find and book B&Bs, farmstays, and other cute places to stay throughout the state from this site.

Western Australian Tourism Commission. **www.westernaustralia.net**
This relatively new site needs more and better content on sights, attractions, and tour operators to flesh out its good bones. Still, the overviews and accommodations listings are helpful now. It has ample photographs and videos.

SOUTH AUSTRALIA

Department for Environment and Heritage. **www.environment.sa.gov.au**
Click the "Parks & Wildlife" tab to link to a brief overview of every one of the state's national parks, including entry fees.

South Australian Tourism Commission. **www.visit-southaustralia.com.au**
The state's official tourism marketing board site lists accommodations, tours, transport, and events using a search engine (search by region and/or for choices tailored to your interests, such as "Kid's Activities"). Loads of tips on traveling the state.

VICTORIA

✪ CitySearch Melbourne. **www.melbourne.citysearch.com.au**
Like CitySearch Sydney (see above), this site is a fabulous resource if you're heading to Melbourne.

Parks Victoria. **www.parkweb.vic.gov.au**
Everything you need to know about every national park in Victoria is here, from things to see and do, to how to get there, to animal and plant notes.

✪ Stepping Out. **www.tracks.vic.gov.au**
A tremendous guide to the state's most picturesque short- and long-distance walking and biking trails. Terrific for bushwalkers. Why don't all states have a site like this?

Tourism Victoria. **www.visitvictoria.com**
Search for accommodations, tour operators, and events on this site, home of the state's official tourism marketing board. It has a brief but helpful Melbourne restaurant guide.

AUSTRALIAN CAPITAL TERRITORY

Canberra Tourism. **www.canberratourism.com.au**
The site of the national capital's tourism promotion board helps you find what you're interested in by category, such as "sport," "wine," or "shopping," as well as listing accommodations, tours, events, and more.

Online Directory

CitySearch Canberra. **www.canberra.citysearch.com.au**
This Canberra version of CitySearch Sydney (see above) is not as full as the Sydney site but is still a great resource.

TASMANIA

Tasmania Parks and Wildlife Service. **www.parks.tas.gov.au**
Explore all of Tasmania's national parks on this site, which lists how to get to each park, entry frees, things to see and do, and much more.

Tourism Tasmania. **www.tourism.tas.gov.au**
As well as detailed listings of accommodations sorted by type and location, Tasmania's official tourism marketing board site helpfully categorizes the state's attractions by nature, culture, history, and food and wine.

Online Directory

Sydney

by Marc Llewellyn

Sunny, sexy, and sophisticated, Sydney is basking in its worldwide reputation as the shining star of the southern hemisphere. Fresh from hosting the 2000 Olympic Games, Sydney is without question one of the most attractive cities on earth. Some people compare it to San Francisco—it certainly has that relaxed California feel—but the gateway to Australia is more than just a clone of an American city.

First off, of course, there's the Sydney Opera House, one of the most recognized buildings in the world. This white-sailed construction, designed by Danish architect Jørn Utzon and caught mid-billow over the waters of Sydney Cove, is the pride of the city, as you might expect. But there's far, far more on offer, not the least of which is that other great Sydney icon, the Sydney Harbour Bridge. You can walk across the pathway beside the trains and traffic and then catch the CityRail train back into town from the other end, while those with a daredevil spirit can venture across catwalks and ladders to the top of the main arch for 360-degree views across the Opera House and the ferries and sailboats below.

Sydney's greatest summer offerings are, of course, the beaches. With more than 20 strung along the city's oceanfront and dozens more dotted around the harbor, you'll be spoiled with choices. The most famous of them all is **Bondi,** a long strip of golden sand legendary for its Speedo-clad lifesavers and surfboard riders. Take time to stroll along the 2-mile coastal path that leads off across the clifftops, via cozy Tamarama beach (dubbed "Glamourama," for its chic sun worshippers), to glorious Bronte Beach, where you can cool down once more in the crashing waves of the Pacific.

Another beach favorite is **Manly,** reached by a 30-minute ferry trip from Circular Quay. Once in Manly, you can pick up some fish-and-chips and head for the main beach, which is flanked by a row of giant Norfolk Island Pines that come alive with the chatter of hundreds of colorful lorikeets at dusk.

The best time to return to the city is in the early evening, when the lights of the skyscrapers around Circular Quay are streaked like rainbows across the inky water of the harbor, and the sails of the Opera House and the iron girders of the Harbour Bridge are lit up. It's a truly magical experience.

If you prefer to keep your feet firmly on the ground, Sydney is a great city for walking. One of the best outings is the 10-kilometer (6.2-mile) hike from Manly to Spit Bridge, which offers extensive harbor views and traverses part of the Sydney Harbour National Park (most visitors to Sydney are surprised by the extent of native vegetation so close to the city's skyscrapers). Another great place to stroll is The Rocks, with its early colonial buildings, the three oldest pubs in Sydney (the sandstone Fortune of War Hotel, the Hero of Waterloo, and the Lord Nelson), and cute boutiques and winding lanes thick with convict and seafaring relics.

History is also enshrined in its many museums and art galleries, while modern Sydney comes alive in the more recent tourist developments around Darling Harbour and the restaurant and entertainment area nearby at Cockle Bay. At Darling Harbour, you'll find the world-class Sydney Aquarium, and lots of restaurants where you can sample Sydney's acclaimed "Modern Australian" cuisine, which combines the freshest of ingredients with Asian spices and Mediterranean flavors.

Sydney is one of the biggest cities in the world (it can take 2 hr. of driving to break free of its outskirts), but fortunately, most sites of interest to visitors are concentrated in a relatively compact area around one of the finest urban harbors in the world. In the pages that follow, I'll show you the very best Sydney has to offer.

1 Orientation

ARRIVING

BY PLANE **Sydney International Airport** is 8 kilometers (about 5 miles) from the city center. The international and domestic terminals are separate but are linked by regular free shuttle buses. In both terminals, you'll find free luggage carts, wheelchairs, a post office (open Mon through Fri from 9am to 5pm), mailboxes, duty-free shops (including one before you go through customs on arrival), restaurants, bars, stores, showers, luggage lockers, and tourist information desks. There are also a State Transit Kiosk selling bus, train, and ferry tickets; a New South Wales Travel Centre desk offering cheap deals on hotels; and a Thomas Cook currency exchange. The airport is completely no-smoking.

Getting into Town from the Airport A new train link from both the international and the domestic airports was opened in mid-2000. Unfortunately, the line uses existing (often very shabby) rolling stock, has no room for luggage, and gets very crowded during rush hours (approximately 7 to 9am and 4 to 6:30pm). If you have lots of luggage and you're traveling into the city at these times, it's probably best to take an airport bus (see below) or a taxi. The train takes 10 minutes to reach Central, and from there you can connect with other CityRail trains. Trains leave every 15 minutes or so and cost $9 (U.S.$5.85) one-way and A$12 (U.S.$7.80) return.

Fast and comfortable green-and-yellow **Airport Express buses** travel between the city center and both the international and the domestic terminals from 5am to 11pm. The number 300 bus runs to and from Circular Quay, The Rocks, Wynyard, and Town Hall every 15 minutes Monday to Friday and approximately every 30 minutes early mornings, nights, weekends, and public holidays. The trip to Circular Quay takes about 45 minutes. Bus 350 runs to and from Kings Cross, Potts Point, and Elizabeth Bay every 20 minutes and takes around 30 minutes to reach Kings Cross. Both buses travel via Central Station (around 20 min. from the International Terminal).

Bus 351 leaves for Coogee, Bronte, and Bondi beaches every 30 minutes. It takes around 55 minutes to reach Bondi Beach from the International Terminal. Bus 352 travels among Central, Chinatown, Darling Harbour, the Star City casino, the Sydney Fish Markets, and Glebe, approximately every 30 minutes. The trip time is about 30 minutes to Darling Harbour and 50 minutes to Glebe.

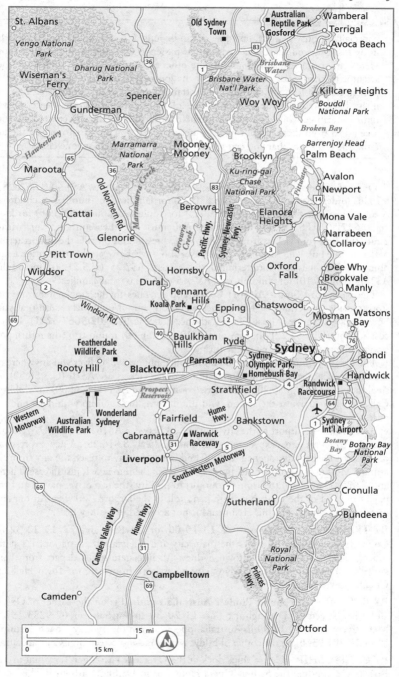

St. Albans

Yengo National
Park

Dharug National
Park

36

Wiseman's
Ferry

Spencer

Gunderman

Hawkesbury

65

36

Maroota

Old Northern Rd.

Marramarra
National
Park

Marramarra Creek

Cattai

Glenorie

Pitt Town

Windsor

2

Windsor Rd.

69

Mooney
Mooney

Berowra

Berowra Creek

Pacific Hwy.

Sydney-Newcastle Hwy.

Hornsby

Dural

Pennant
Hills

Koala Park

Epping

7

40

Baulkham
Hills

Featherdale
Wildlife Park

Rooty Hill

4

Blacktown

Prospect
Reservoir

Parramatta

Western
Motorway

Australian
Wildlife Park

Wonderland
Sydney

7

Fairfield

Hume
Hwy.

Cabramatta

Warwick
Raceway

Liverpool

31

5

Southwestern Motorway

69

Camden Valley Way

Hume Hwy.

31

Camden

Campbelltown

69

Old Sydney
Town

Australian
Reptile Park

Gosford

83

1

Brisbane
Water

Brisbane Water
Nat'l Park

Woy Woy

Broken Bay

Mooney

Brooklyn

Ku-ring-gai
Chase
National Park

83

Elanora
Heights

Wamberal

Terrigal

Avoca Beach

Killcare Heights

Bouddi
National Park

Barrenjoey Head

Palm Beach

Avalon

Newport

14

Mona Vale

Narrabeen

Collaroy

Pittwater

3

Oxford
Falls

Dee Why

Brookvale

14

Manly

1

1

Chatswood

3

2

Mosman

Watsons
Bay

76

Ryde

Sydney
Olympic Park,
Homebush Bay

Sydney

Bondi

4

4

Randwick
Racecourse

Handwick

70

Strathfield

5

64

Bankstown

1

Sydney
Int'l Airport

Botany
Bay

Botany Bay
National
Park

5

7

1

Sutherland

Cronulla

Bundeena

Royal
National
Park

Princes Hwy.

Otford

0   15 mi

0   15 km

N

A Taxi Tip

Especially in busy periods, taxi queues can be long and cab drivers may try to cash in by insisting you share a cab with other passengers waiting in line at the airport. Here's the scam: After dropping off the other passengers, the cab driver will then attempt to charge you the full price of the journey, despite the fact that the other passengers paid for their sections. You certainly won't save any money sharing a cab if this happens, and your journey will be a long one. I find it's often better to wait until you can get your own cab, or catch an airport bus to the city center (and then take a taxi from there to your hotel, if necessary). If you are first in line in the taxi rank, the law states that you can refuse to share the cab with anyone else.

One-way tickets for all buses cost A$7.70 (U.S.$5) for adults, A$4.40 (U.S.$2.85) for kids under 16, and A$16.50 (U.S.$10.75) for families (any number of children). A round-trip ticket costs A$11 (U.S.$7.15) for adults, A$5.50 (U.S.$3.60) for kids, and A$27.50 (U.S.$17.90) for families. You must use the return portion within 2 months. Buy your tickets from the Airport Express booth outside the airport terminal, or on the bus. The Airport Express buses also travel between the international and domestic terminals; an interterminal ticket costs A$2.75 (U.S.$1.80) for adults, A$1.65 (U.S.$1.10) for children, and A$7.15 (U.S.$4.65) for families.

The **Kingsford Smith Airport Coach** also operates to the city center from bus stops outside the terminals. This service will drop you off (and pick you up) at your hotel (pickups require at least 1 hour's advance notice; call ☎ **02/9667 3221**). Tickets cost A$6.50 (U.S. $4.22) one-way and A$10 (U.S.$6.50) round-trip (the return portion can be used at any time in the future).

The **Bondi Jetbus** (☎ **0500/886 008** mobile phone) will deliver you anywhere on the eastern beaches, including Bondi and Bronte. Tickets are A$10 (U.S.$6.50) for single adult, A$8 (U.S.$5.20) each for two or more, and A$4 (U.S.$2.60) for children. Call when you arrive at the airport, and they'll come pick you up within 15 minutes or less.

A **taxi** from the airport to the city center costs between A$16 and $20 (U.S. $10.40 to $13). To Kings Cross expect to pay around A$25 (U.S.$16.25). A new expressway, the Eastern Distributor, opened in 2000 and is a faster way to reach the city from the airport. Most taxis use this route, but it's best to ask them to take it just in case. There's an A$3.30 (U.S.$2.15) toll from the airport to the city (the taxi driver pays it and you pay at the end of the trip), but there is no toll to the airport. *Warning:* An ongoing dispute with Visa means this credit card is not accepted in Sydney taxis.

BY TRAIN Central Station (☎ **13 15 00** for CityRail, and ☎ **13 22 32** for Countrylink interstate trains) is the main city and interstate train station. It's at the top of George Street in downtown Sydney. All interstate trains depart from here, and it's a major CityRail hub. Many city buses leave from here for Town Hall and Circular Quay.

BY BUS The **Greyhound-Pioneer Australia terminal** is on the corner of Oxford and Riley streets in Darlinghurst (☎ **13 20 30** in Australia or 02/9283 5977). **McCafferty's** (☎ **13 14 99** in Australia) operates from the **Sydney Coach Terminal** (☎ **02/9281 9366**) on the corner of Eddy Avenue and Pitt Street, near Central Station.

BY CRUISE SHIP Cruise ships dock at the **Overseas Passenger Terminal** in The Rocks, just opposite the Sydney Opera House, or in Darling Harbour if The Rocks facility is already occupied by another vessel.

BY CAR   Drivers coming into Sydney from the north enter the city on the Pacific Highway; drivers approaching from the south enter the city via the Hume and Princes highways; and those coming from the west enter the city via the Great Western Highway.

VISITOR INFORMATION

The **Sydney Visitor Centre,** 106 George St., The Rocks (☎ **02/9255 1788**), is a good place for maps, brochures, and general tourist information; it also has two floors of excellent displays on The Rocks. The office is open daily from 6am to 6pm. Also in The Rocks is the **National Parks & Wildlife Centre** (☎ **02/9247 8861**), in Cadmans Cottage, 110 George St. If you are in Circular Quay, the **CityRail Host Center** (no phone), opposite No. 5 jetty, has a wide range of brochures and a staff member on hand to help with general inquiries. It's open daily 9am to 5pm.

Elsewhere, the **Sydney Convention and Visitors Bureau** (☎ **02/9235 2424**) operates an information kiosk in Martin Place, near Castlereagh Street, Monday through Friday from 9am to 5pm. The **Manly Visitors Information Centre** (☎ **02/ 9977 1088**), right opposite Manly beach near the Corso, offers general information but specializes in Manly and the northern beaches. If you want to inquire about destinations and holidays within Sydney or the rest of New South Wales, call **Tourism New South Wales**'s helpline at ☎ **13 20 77** in Australia.

Electronic information on cinema, theater, exhibitions, and other events can be accessed through **Talking Guides** (☎ **13 16 20** in Australia). You'll need a code number for each topic, which you can find on page 3 of the A-K section of the Sydney Yellow Pages phone directory. The service costs the same as a local call.

Good **Web sites** include **CitySearch Sydney** (www.sydney.citysearch.com.au), for events, entertainment, dining, and shopping; and **City of Sydney** (www.cityofsydney. nsw.gov.au), the official information site.

CITY LAYOUT

Sydney is one of the largest cities in the world by area, covering more than 1,730 square kilometers (668 square miles) from the sea to the foothills of the Blue Mountains. The jewel in Sydney's crown is its harbor, which empties into the South Pacific Ocean though head lands known simply as North Head and South Head. On the southern side of the harbor are the high rises of the city center; the Sydney Opera House; a string of beaches, including Bondi; and the inner-city suburbs. The Sydney Harbour Bridge and a tunnel connect the city center to the high rises of the North Sydney business district and the affluent northern suburbs and beautiful ocean beaches beyond.

The city's main thoroughfare, **George Street,** runs up from **Circular Quay** (pronounced "key"), past Town Hall and on past Central Station. A whole host of streets bisect the city parallel to George, including Pitt, Elizabeth, and Macquarie streets. **Macquarie Street** runs up from the Sydney Opera House, past the Royal Botanic Gardens, colonial architecture, and Hyde Park. **Martin Place** is a pedestrian thoroughfare that stretches from Macquarie to George streets. It's about half-way between Circular Quay and Town Hall—in the heart of the city center. The easy-to-spot **AMP Centerpoint Tower,** facing onto the pedestrian-only **Pitt Street Mall,** is the main city-center landmark. Next to Circular Quay and across from the Opera House is **The Rocks,** a cluster of small streets that was once city slums but is now a tourist attraction. From Town Hall, roads converge at Kings Cross in one direction and Darling Harbour in the other.

The Neighborhoods in Brief

South of the Harbour

Circular Quay This transport hub for ferries, buses, and CityRail trains is tucked between the Harbour Bridge and the Sydney Opera House. The Quay, as it's known to the locals, is a good spot for a stroll, and its outdoor restaurants and street musicians are very popular. The Rocks, the Royal Botanic Gardens, the Contemporary Art Museum, and the start of the main shopping area (centered on Pitt and George streets) are all just a short walk away. To reach the area via public transportation, take a CityRail train, ferry, or city-bound bus to Circular Quay.

The Rocks This small historic area, just a short stroll west of Circular Quay, is packed with colonial stone buildings, intriguing back streets, boutiques, pubs, tourist stores, and top-notch restaurants and hotels. It's the most exclusive place to stay in the city because of its beauty and its proximity to the Opera House and the harbor. Shops here are geared mostly toward Sydney's yuppies and wealthy Asian tourists—don't expect many bargains. On weekends, a portion of George Street is blocked off for The Rocks Market, with its many street stalls selling touristy souvenirs and crafts. To reach the area via public transportation, take any bus bound for Circular Quay or The Rocks (via George Street) or a CityRail train or ferry to Circular Quay.

Town Hall Right in the heart of the city, this area is home to all the main department stores and to two Sydney landmarks, the Town Hall and the Queen Victoria Building (QVB). In this area are also the AMP Centrepoint Tower and the boutique-style chain stores of Pitt Street Mall. Farther inland along George Street (on the same side of the street as the Town Hall) are major cinema complexes, the entrance to Sydney's Spanish district (around Liverpool Street), and the city's small Chinatown. To reach the area via public transportation, take any bus from Circular Quay via George Street, or take a CityRail train to the Town Hall stop.

Darling Harbour Designed from scratch as a tourist area, Darling Harbour now features Sydney's main convention, exhibition, and entertainment centers; a huge waterfront promenade; the Sydney Aquarium; the giant-screen Panasonic IMAX Theatre; the Sega World theme park; the Australian Maritime Museum; the Powerhouse Museum; a major food court; and plenty of shops. Star City, Sydney's casino and theater complex, opened in Darling Harbour in late 1997. But until Cockle Bay Wharf opened in early 1999 (near the Sydney Aquarium on the city side of Darling Harbour) and brought with it a few good bars and restaurants, few Sydneysiders ever visited the place. To reach the area via public transportation, take a ferry from Circular Quay (wharf 5), the monorail from Town Hall, or the light rail (tram) from Central Station. Or you can simply walk down the side road to the right of the Queen Victoria Building as you are facing it, and across the pedestrian bridge which spans the water.

Central The congested and badly polluted crossroads area around Central Station, the city's main train station, has little to recommend it. The Sydney Central YHA is located here.

Darlinghurst Wedged between grungy Kings Cross and upscale Oxford Street, this extroverted and grimy terraced suburb is home to some of the Sydney's finest cafes, though it's probably wise not to walk around here at night. Take the CityRail train to Kings Cross and head right from the exit.

Kings Cross & the Suburbs Beyond "The Cross," as it's known, is famous as the city's red-light district—though it's also home to some of the city's best-known nightclubs and restaurants. It also houses plenty of backpacker hostels, as well as some

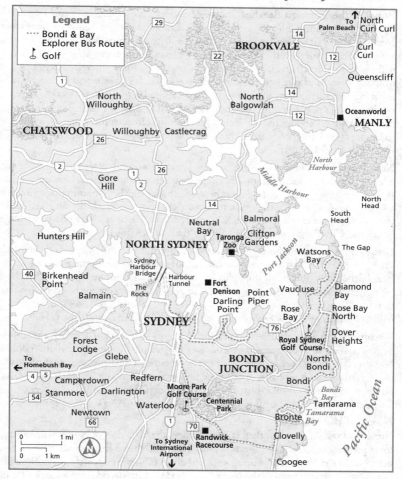

upscale hotels. The main drag, Darlinghurst Road, is quite short, but it's crammed with strip joints, prostitutes, drug addicts, drunks, and down-at-the-heel street kids. Fortunately, there's a heavy police presence. Beyond the strip clubs and glitter, the attractive suburbs of Elizabeth Bay, Double Bay, and Rose Bay hug the waterfront. To reach the area via public transportation, take bus 324, 325, or 327 from Circular Quay; bus 311 from Railway Square, Central Station; or a CityRail train to Kings Cross station.

Paddington/Oxford Street   This inner-city suburb, centered on trendy Oxford Street, is known for its expensive terrace houses, off-the-wall boutiques and bookshops, and popular restaurants, pubs, and nightclubs. It's also the heart of Sydney's very large gay community (the world's largest after San Francisco) and has a liberal scattering of gay bars and dance spots. To reach the area via public transportation, take bus 380 or 382 from Circular Quay (via Elizabeth Street); 378 from Railway Square, Central Station; or 380 and 382 from Bondi Junction.

Bondi & the Southern Beaches   Some of Sydney's most glamorous surf beaches—Bondi, Bronte, and Coogee—can be found basking along the South Pacific Ocean coastline southeast of the city center. Bondi is a disappointment to many tourists who are expecting more than this former working-class suburb has to offer. It does have a wide sweep of beach (which is crowded in summer), some interesting eateries and drinking holes, and plenty of attitude. On weekends, it's a favorite with macho suburbanites, who stand next to their souped-up cars and attempt to look cool. To reach the beaches via public transportation, take bus 380 or 382 to Bondi Beach from Circular Quay or a CityRail train to Bondi Junction to connect with same buses; bus 378 to Bronte from Railway Square, Central Station (via Oxford Street); or bus 373 or 374 to Coogee from Circular Quay.

Newtown   This popular student area is centered around congested King Street, which is lined with many alternative shops, bookstores, and cheap ethnic restaurants. People-watching is an interesting sport here—see how many belly-button rings, violently colored hair-dos, and Celtic arm tattoos you can spot. To reach the area via public transportation, take bus 422, 423, 426, or 428 from Circular Quay (via Castlereagh Street and City Road), or take the CityRail train to Newtown Station.

Glebe   A mecca for young professionals and students, this inner-city suburb is known for its cafes, restaurants, pubs, and shops spread out along the main thoroughfare, Glebe Point Road. All this, plus its location just 15 minutes from the city and 30 minutes from Circular Quay, makes it a good place to stay for budget-conscious travelers. To reach Glebe via public transportation, take bus 431, 433, or 434 from Millers Point, The Rocks (via George St.), or bus 459 from behind Town Hall.

Watsons Bay   Watsons Bay is known for The Gap—a section of dramatic sea cliffs—as well as several good restaurants, such as Doyles on the Beach, and the popular Watsons Bay Hotel beer garden. It's at the northern end of the easternmost peninsula in the harbor and is a terrific spot to spend a sunny afternoon. To reach the area via public transportation, take bus 324 or 325 from Circular Quay, or a ferry from Circular Quay (wharf 2) on Saturdays and Sundays.

North of the Harbour

North Sydney   Just across the Harbour Bridge, the high-rises of North Sydney attest to its prominence as a major business area. That said, there's little on offer for tourists here, except the possibility of being knocked down on some extremely busy thoroughfare. Take a CityRail train to the North Sydney stop. Chatswood (take a CityRail train from Central or Wynyard stations) has some pretty good suburban-type shopping, and Milsons Point, just across the bridge, has a fairly decent pub called the Kirribilli Hotel and a couple of restaurants and cafes worth checking out if you've walked across the Harbour Bridge.

The North Shore   Ferries and buses provide good access to these wealthy neighborhoods across the Harbour Bridge. The gorgeous Balmoral Beach, the Taronga Zoo, and upscale boutiques are the main attractions in Mosman. Take bus 250 from North Sydney to Taronga Zoo, or a ferry from Circular Quay (wharf 2) to Taronga Zoo and a bus from there to Balmoral Beach.

Manly & the Northern Beaches   Half an hour away by ferry, or just 15 minutes by the faster JetCat, Manly is famous for its beautiful ocean beach and scores of cheap restaurants. Farther north are more magnificent beaches popular with surfers. Unfortunately, there is no CityRail train line to the northern beaches. The farthest beach from the city, Palm Beach, has magnificent surf and lagoon beaches, nice walking paths, and a scenic golf course. To reach the area via public transportation, take the ferry or JetCat from Circular Quay (wharves 2 and 3) to Manly. Change at Manly interchange for various buses to the northern beaches, numbers 148 and 154 through 159. You can also take bus L90 from Wynyard Station.

West of the City Center

Balmain   Located west of the city center, a short ferry ride from Circular Quay, Balmain was once Sydney's main ship-building area. In the past few decades the area has become trendy and expensive. The suburb has a village feel about it, and it is filled with restaurants and pubs and hosts a popular Saturday market in the grounds of the local church. Take bus 441, 442, or 432 from Town Hall or George Street, or a ferry from Circular Quay (wharf 5), and then a short bus ride up the hill to the main shopping area.

Homebush Bay   This was the main site of the Sydney 2000 Olympic Games. Here you'll find the Olympic Stadium, the Aquatic Center, and the Homebush Bay Information Center, as well as parklands and a water-bird reserve. To reach the area via public transportation, take a CityRail train from Circular Quay to the new Olympic Park station.

2 Getting Around

BY PUBLIC TRANSPORTATION

State Transit operates the city's buses and the ferry network, CityRail runs the urban and suburban trains, and Sydney Ferries runs the public passenger ferries. Some private bus lines operate buses in the outer suburbs. In addition, a monorail connects the city center to Darling Harbour, and a light rail line (tram) runs between Central Station and Wentworth Park in Pyrmont.

For timetable information on buses, ferries, and trains, call the **Infoline** at ☎ **13 15 00** daily from 6am to 10pm. Pick up a Sydney Transport Map (a guide to train, bus, and ferry services) at any rail, bus, or ferry information office.

MONEY-SAVING TRANSIT PASSES   Several passes are available for visitors who will be using public transportation frequently—all work out to be much cheaper than buying individual tickets. The SydneyPass is a good buy if you plan to do *a lot* of sightseeing, but in my opinion you're better off with the flexibility offered by some of the other passes listed below.

The **SydneyPass** allows 3, 5, or 7 days of unlimited travel on buses and ferries, including the high-speed JetCat to Manly, the Red Sydney Explorer Bus (see below), the Blue Bondi and Bay Explorer Bus, the Airport Express Bus, and all harbor cruises operated by State Transit. A 3-day pass costs A$75 (U.S.$48.75) for adults, A$62 (U.S.$40.30) for children under 16, and A$218 (U.S.$141.70) for families; a 5-day pass is A$98 (U.S.$63.70) for adults, A$84 (U.S.$54.60) for children, and A$280 (U.S.$182) for families; a 7-day pass is A$120 (U.S.$78) for adults, A$100 (U.S.$65) for children, and A$330 (U.S.$214.50) for families. (State Transit defines a "family" as two adults and any number of children from the same family.) Buy the SydneyPass at the airport, Countrylink offices, Public Transport ticket offices, Circular Quay ferry ticket offices, and anywhere else the SydneyPass logo is displayed; proof of overseas residence is required.

A **Weekly Travel Pass** allows unlimited travel on buses, trains, and ferries. There are six different passes (denoted by color) depending on the distance you need to travel. The passes most commonly used by visitors are the **Red Pass** and the **Green Pass.** The Red Pass costs A$28 (U.S.$18.20) and covers all transportation within the city center and the immediate surroundings. This pass will get you aboard inner

Sydney Transportation Systems

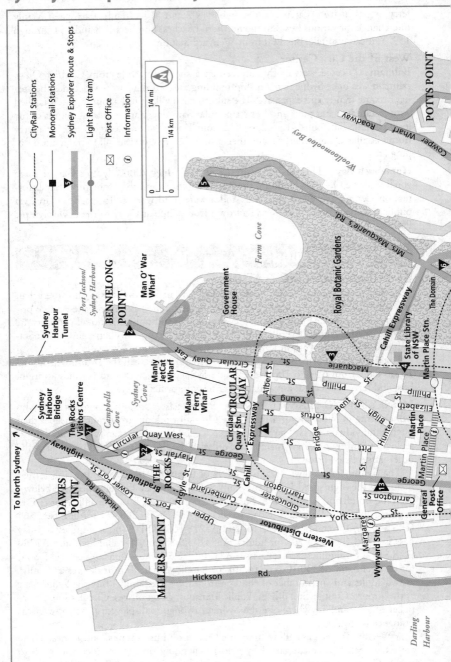

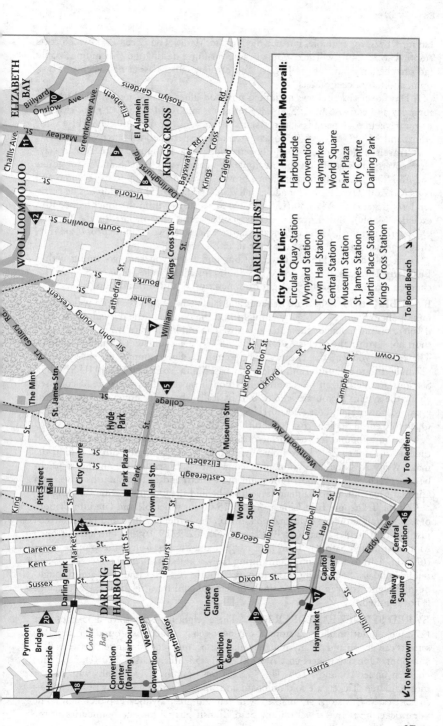

City Circle Line:
Circular Quay Station
Wynyard Station
Town Hall Station
Central Station
Museum Station
St. James Station
Martin Place Station
Kings Cross Station

TNT Harborlink Monorail:
Harbourside
Convention
Haymarket
World Square
Park Plaza
City Centre
Darling Park

ELIZABETH BAY

WOOLLOOMOOLOO

KINGS CROSS

DARLINGHURST

CHINATOWN

DARLING HARBOUR

Cockle Bay

Roslyn Gardens
El Alamein Fountain
Billyard
Onslow Ave.
Challis Ave.
Macleay St.
Greenknowe Ave.
Elizabeth
Darlinghurst Rd.
Bayswater Rd.
Kings Cross Rd.
Craigend St.
Victoria
South Dowling St.
Bourke St.
Cathedral St.
Palmer St.
Sir John Young Crescent
Art Gallery Rd.
The Mint
St. James Stn.
William St.
College St.
Hyde Park
Liverpool St.
Burton St.
Oxford St.
Campbell St.
Crown St.
Wentworth Ave.
Park St.
Elizabeth St.
Castlereagh St.
Pitt Street Mall
City Centre
Park Plaza
Town Hall Stn.
King St.
Market St.
Druitt St.
Bathurst St.
George St.
Goulburn St.
Hay St.
Campbell St.
Dixon St.
Chinese Garden
Exhibition Centre
World Square
Capitol Square
Haymarket
Railway Square
Central Station
Eddy Ave.
Ultimo St.
Harris St.
Western Distributor
Convention Center (Darling Harbour)
Convention
Darling Park
Pyrmont Bridge
Harbourside
Clarence St.
Kent St.
Sussex St.
Kings Cross Stn.
Museum Stn.

To Bondi Beach
To Redfern
To Newtown

87

harbor ferries, for example, but not the ferry to Manly. The Green Pass, which costs A$36 (U.S.$23.40), will take you to more far-flung destinations, including Manly (aboard the ferry but not the JetCat). You can buy either pass at newsagents or bus, train, and ferry ticket outlets.

A **DayRover ticket** allows unlimited travel on buses, ferries, and CityRail services for a day and costs A$22 (U.S.$14.30) for adults and A$11 (U.S.$7.15) for children if you travel in peak periods (journey starts before 9am), or A$17.60 (U.S.$11.45) for adults and A$8.80 (U.S.$5.70) for children outside peak periods (after 9am).

A **Travelten ticket** offers 10 bus or ferry rides for a discounted price. A blue Travelten covers two sections on the bus route and costs A$10.40 (U.S.$6.75) for adults and A$4.80 (U.S.$3.10) for children; a brown Travelten covers up to five sections and costs A$17.60 (U.S.$11.45) for adults and A$8.80 (U.S.$5.75) for children. The Ferryten ferry ticket costs A$23.30 (U.S.$15.15) for 10 trips within the inner harbor (this excludes Manly). Buy Travelten tickets at newsagents, bus depots, or the Circular Quay ferry terminal. These tickets are transferable, so if two or more people are traveling together, you can all use the same ticket.

For a full day's unlimited travel by bus and ferry, you can't go wrong with a **Bus/Ferry Daypass.** It costs A$13 (U.S.$8.45) for adults and A$6.50 (U.S.$4.25) for children 4 to 15, and can be bought from newsagents and at bus depots.

BY PUBLIC BUS   Buses are frequent and fairly reliable. They cover a wide area of metropolitan Sydney—though you might find the system a little difficult to navigate if you're visiting some of the outer suburbs. The minimum fare (which covers most short hops within the city) is A$1.40 (U.S.90¢) for a 4-kilometer (2.5-mile) "section." The farther you go, the cheaper each section is. For example, the 44-kilometer (27-mile) trip to beautiful Palm Beach, way past Manly, costs just A$4.40 (U.S.$2.85). Sections are marked on bus-stand signs (though most Sydneysiders are as confused about the system as you are sure to be). Basically, short city hops, such as Circular Quay to Town Hall, cost A$1.40 (U.S.90¢), and slightly longer ones, say Circular Quay to Central Station, cost A$2.50 (U.S.$1.65).

Most buses bound for the northern suburbs, including night buses to Manly and the bus to Taronga Zoo, leave from Wynyard Park on Carrington Street, behind the main Wynyard CityRail station on George Street. Buses headed to the southern beaches, such as Bondi and Bronte, and the western and eastern suburbs leave from Circular Quay. Buses to Balmain leave from behind the Queen Victoria Building.

Call the **Transport Info Line** at ☎ **13 15 00** for timetable and fare information, or ask the staff at the bus-information kiosk on the corner of Alfred and Loftus streets, just behind Circular Quay CityRail station (☎ **02/9219 1680**). The kiosk is open Monday through Saturday from 8am to 8pm and Sunday from 8am to 6pm. Buses run from 4am to around midnight during the week, less frequently on weekends and public holidays. Some night buses to outer suburbs run after midnight and throughout the night. You can purchase single tickets onboard from the driver; exact change is not required.

BY RED SYDNEY EXPLORER BUS   These bright red buses travel a 35-kilometer (22-mile) circuit, making 22 stops at top sightseeing attractions around the city. Passengers can get on and off anytime they like. Buses run every 20 minutes between 9am and 3pm. One-day tickets cost A$27 (U.S.$17.55) for adults, A$20 (U.S.$13) for children under 16, and A$65 (U.S.$42.25) for a family of two adults with two or more children. Tickets are sold on board and are valid only on the day of purchase—so start early. Bus stops are marked with red-and-green Sydney Explorer signs. The same ticket gives free travel on any State Transit bus within the boundaries of the Explorer circuit until midnight on the day of purchase.

BY BLUE BONDI & BAY EXPLORER BUS   This bus operates on the same prin-ciple as the Red Sydney Explorer Bus but visits Sydney's famous Bondi Beach and the scenic harbor suburbs of Double Bay, Rose Bay, and Watsons Bay. The bus covers a 45-kilometer (28-mile) route and stops at 20 locations, including Circular Quay, the oceanfront suburbs of Bronte and Clovelly, the Royal Randwick Racecourse, and the Sydney Cricket Ground. Buses run every 30 minutes between 9am and 6pm. The one-day fare is A$27 (U.S.$17.55) for adults, A$20 (U.S.$13) for children under 16, and A$72 (U.S.$46.80) for families.

BY FERRY & JETCAT   The best way to get a taste of a city that revolves around its harbor is to jump aboard a ferry. The main ferry terminal is at Circular Quay. Tickets can be bought at machines at each wharf (there are also change machines) or at the main Circular Quay ticket offices just opposite wharf 4. For ferry information call ☎ **13 15 00,** or visit the ferry information office opposite wharf 4. Timetables are available for all routes.

One-way journeys within the inner harbor (virtually everywhere except Manly and Parramatta) cost A$4 (U.S.$2.60) for adults and A$1.80 (U.S.$1.20) for children. The ferry to Manly takes 30 minutes and costs A$5 (U.S.$3.25) for adults and A$2.80 (U.S.$1.85) for children. It leaves from wharf 3. The rapid JetCat service to Manly takes 15 minutes and costs A$6.30 (U.S.$4.10) for adults and children alike. After 7pm, all trips to and from Manly are by JetCat at ferry prices. Ferries run from 6am to midnight.

Sydney Ferries also operates a special **Summer Harbour Beaches service** between Manly, Watsons Bay, and Balmoral on weekends only. This loop service allows you to get on and off when you want and rejoin a later ferry. Tickets, valid for 1 day, cost A$11 (U.S.$7.15) for adults and A$5.50 (U.S.$3.60) for children and include the return fare to Circular Quay. Timetables are available from the ferry information office opposite wharf 4.

BY CITYRAIL   Sydney's publicly owned train system is a cheap and relatively effi-cient way to see the city. The system is limited, though, with many tourist areas—including Manly, Bondi Beach, and Darling Harbour—not connected to the railway network. CityRail trains have a reputation of running late and out of timetable order. All train stations have automatic ticket machines, and most have ticket offices.

The off-peak (after 9am) round-trip fare within the city center is A$2.20 (U.S.$1.45). Before 9am the same journey will cost you A$3.40 (U.S.$2.20). Infor-mation is available from **InfoLine** (☎ **13 15 00**) and at the **CityRail Host Centers** located opposite wharf 4 at Circular Quay (☎ **02/9224 2649**) and at Central Station (☎ **02/9219 1977**); both centers are open daily from 9am to 5pm.

BY HARBOUR EXPRESS   Matilda Cruises (☎ **02/9264 7377**) operates the high-speed **Matilda Rocket** that runs between Darling Harbour and Circular Quay daily from 9:30am to 4:30pm. The Rocket leaves Darling Harbour Aquarium Wharf on the half hour and Circular Quay Commissioner Steps (a small wharf opposite the Museum of Contemporary Art) at a quarter to the hour. The boat stops off at the Opera House and the Harbourside Festival Marketplace at Darling Harbour and includes commentary along the way. You get on and off when you want. The fare is A$19.50 (U.S.$12.70) for adults and A$10 (U.S.$6.50) for children 5 to 12; children under 5 are free; families are $48 (U.S.$31.20). Buy tickets on the boat.

BY METRO MONORAIL   The metro monorail, with its single overhead line, is seen by many as a blight on the city and by others as a futuristic addition. The mono-rail connects the central business district to Darling Harbour. The system operates Monday through Wednesday from 7am to 10pm, Thursday through Saturday from

Sydney Ferries

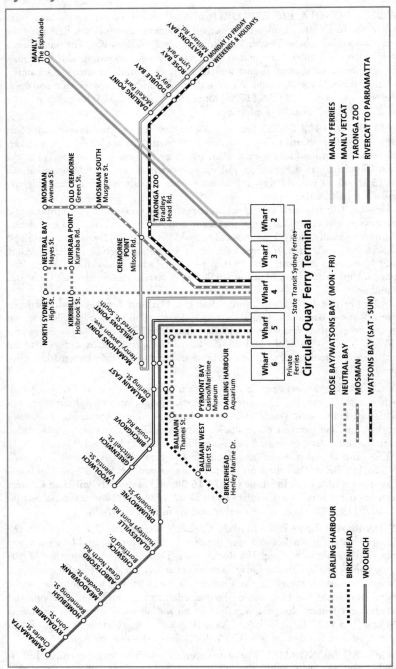

7am to midnight, and Sunday from 8am to 10pm. Tickets are A$3.50 (U.S.$2.30); children under 5 ride free. An all-day monorail pass costs A$7 (U.S.$4.50) for adults and A$20 (U.S.$13) for a family. The trip from the city center to Darling Harbour takes around 12 minutes. Look out for the gray overhead line and the plastic tubelike structures that are the stations. Call **Metro Monorail** at ☎ **02/8584 5288** for more information.

BY METRO LIGHT RAIL   A system of "trams" opened in late 1997 with a route that traverses a 3.6-kilometer (2.2-mile) track between Central Station and Wentworth Park in Pyrmont. It provides good access to Chinatown, Paddy's Markets, Darling Harbour, the Star City casino, and the Sydney Fish Markets. The trams run every 10 minutes. The one-way fare is A$2.20 or $3.30 (U.S.$1.40 or $2.15), depending on distance—check at the station. The round-trip fare is A$3.30 or $4.50 (U.S.$2.15 or $2.90). There are no discounted fares for children. A family day pass costs $A20 (U.S.$13). Call **Metro Light Rail** at ☎ **02/8584 5288** for details.

BY TAXI

Taxis are a relatively economical way to get around Sydney. Several taxi companies service the city center and suburbs. All journeys are metered and cost A$2.50 (U.S.$1.60) before you even go anywhere. It's A$1.27 (U.S.83¢) per kilometer after the initial drop. It's another A$1.10 (U.S.70¢) if you call for a cab. You must also pay extra for waiting time, for luggage weighing over 25 kilograms (55 lb.), if you cross either way on the Harbour Bridge or through the Harbour Tunnel (A$2.20/U.S.$1.40), and if you take the Eastern Distributor from the airport (A$3.30 to U.S.$2.15). An extra 10% will be added to your fare if you pay by credit card (note: Visa cards are not accepted).

Taxis line up at ranks in the city, such as those found opposite Circular Quay and Central Station. They are also frequently found in front hotels. A small yellow light on top of the cab means it's vacant. Cabs can be particularly hard to get on Friday and Saturday nights and between 2 and 3pm everyday, when tired cabbies are changing shift after 12 hours on the road. Tipping is not necessary, but appreciated. Some people prefer to sit up front with the driver, but it's certainly not considered rude if you don't. It is compulsory for all passengers to wear seat belts in Australia. The **Taxi Complaints Hotline** (☎ 1800/648 478 in Australia) deals with problem taxi drivers. Taxis are licensed to carry up to four people.

The main cab companies are **Taxis Combined Services** (☎ **02/9332 8888**); **RSL Taxis** (☎ **02/9581 1111**); **Legion Cabs** (☎ **13 14 51**); and **Premier** (☎ **13 10 17**).

BY WATER TAXI

Harbour Taxis, as they are called, operate 24 hours a day and are a quick and convenient way to get to waterfront restaurants, harbor attractions, and some suburbs. They can also be hired for private cruises of the harbor. A journey from Circular Quay to Watsons Bay, for example, costs about A$55 ($35.75) for two. Extra passengers cost just A$6 (U.S.$3.90); some taxis can hold up to 28 people. An hour's sightseeing excursion around the harbor costs A$181 (U.S. $117.65) for two. The two main operators are **Taxis Afloat** (☎ **02/9955 3222**) and **Water Taxis Combined** (☎ **02/9810 5010**).

BY CAR

Traffic restrictions, parking problems, and congestion can make driving around the city center a frustrating experience, but if you plan to visit some of the outer suburbs or take excursions elsewhere in New South Wales, then renting a car will give you more flexibility. The **NRMA**'s (National Roads and Motorists' Association—the New South Wales auto club) emergency breakdown service can be contacted at ☎ **13 11 11.**

Car-rental agencies in Sydney include **Avis,** 214 William St., Kings Cross (☎ **02/ 9357 2000**); **Budget,** 93 William St., Kings Cross (☎ **13 28 48,** or 02/9339 8888); **Dollar,** Domain Car Park, Sir John Young Car Park (☎ **02/9223 1444**); **Hertz,** corner of William and Riley streets, Kings Cross (☎ **02/9360 6621**); and **Thrifty,** 75 William St., Kings Cross (☎ **02/9380 5399**). Avis, Budget, Hertz, and Thrifty also have desks at the airport. Rates average about A$45 (U.S.$29.25) per day for weekly rentals and around A$80 (U.S.$52) for single-day rentals.

You can rent a campervan from **Campervan Rentals** (☎ **1800/246 869** in Australia or 02/9797 8027; fax 02/9716 5087) or **Britz Campervans,** 182 O'Riordan St., Mascot, NSW 2020 (☎ **1800/331 454** in Australia or 02/9667 0402). Both companies allow you to drop off your van at most state capitals, or in Cairns, though Britz charges an extra A$165 (U.S.$107.25) for the convenience.

Fast Facts: Sydney

American Express   The main AMEX office is at 92 Pitt St., near Martin Place (☎ **02/9239 0666**), open Monday through Friday from 8:30am to 5:30pm and Saturday from 9am to noon. If you've lost your traveler's checks, then you need to head to the head office at 175 Liverpool St. (☎ **02/9271 1111**). It's a locked security building so you'll need to call ahead first.

Baby-sitters   Dial an Angel (☎ **02/9416 7511** or 02/9362 4225) offers a well-regarded baby-sitting service.

Business Hours   General office and banking hours are Monday through Friday from 9am to 5pm. Many banks, especially in the city center, are also open from around 9:30am to 12:30pm on Saturdays. Shopping hours are usually 8:30am to 5:30pm daily (9am to 5pm on Sat), and most stores stay open until 9pm on Thursdays. Most city-center stores are open from around 10am to 4pm on Sundays.

Camera Repair   The **Camera Service Centre,** 1st Floor, 203 Castlereagh St. (☎ **02/9264 7091**), is a tiny place up a flight of stairs not far from the Town Hall CityRail station. It repairs all kinds of cameras on the spot, or within a couple of days if parts are needed.

Currency Exchange   Most major bank branches offer currency-exchange services. Small foreign-currency exchange offices are clustered at the airport and around Circular Quay and Kings Cross. **Thomas Cook** can be found at the airport; at 175 Pitt St. (☎ **02/9231 2877**), open Monday to Friday from 6:45am to 5:15pm and Saturday from 10am to 2pm; in the Kingsgate Shopping Center, Kings Cross (☎ **02/9356 2211**), open Monday to Friday from 9am to 5pm; and on the lower ground floor of the Queen Victoria Building (☎ **02/9264 1133**), open Monday to Saturday from 9am to 6pm (until 9pm Fri), and Sunday from 11am to 5pm.

Dentist   A well-respected dentist office in the city is **City Dental Practice,** Level 2, 229 Macquaire St. (near Martin Place; ☎ **02/9221 3300**). For dental problems after hours, call **Dental Emergency Information** (☎ **02/9369 7050**).

Doctor   The **Park Medical Centre,** Shop 4, 27 Park St. (☎ **02/ 9264 4488**), in the city center near Town Hall, is open Monday through Friday from 8am to

6pm; consultations cost A$40 (U.S.$26) for 15 minutes. (*Note:* If you plan to take a dive course while in Australia, get your medical exam done here. It costs A$70/U.S.$45.50, which is about the cheapest in Australia.) The **Kings Cross Travelers' Clinic,** Suite 1, 13 Springfield Ave., Kings Cross, just off Darlinghurst Road (☎ **1300/369 359** in Australia or 02/9358 3066), is a great place for travel medicines and emergency contraception pills, among other things. Hotel visits in the Kings Cross area cost A$80 (U.S.$52); consultations cost A$40 (U.S.$26). The **Travelers' Medical & Vaccination Centre,** Level 7, 428 George St., in the city center (☎ **02/9221 7133**), stocks and administers all travel-related vaccinations and medications.

Embassies/Consulates   All foreign embassies are based in Canberra. You'll find the following consulates in Sydney: **United Kingdom,** Level 16, Gateway Building, 1 Macquarie Place, Circular Quay (☎ **02/9247 7521**); **New Zealand,** 1 Alfred St., Circular Quay (☎ **02/9247 1344**); **United States,** 19–29 Martin Place (☎ **02/9373 9200**); **Canada,** Level 5, 111 Harrington St., The Rocks (☎ **02/9364 3000**).

Emergencies   Dial ☎ **000** to call police, the fire service, or an ambulance. Call the **Emergency Prescription Service** (☎ **02/9235 0333**) for emergency drug prescriptions, and the NRMA for car breakdowns (☎ **13 11 11**).

Eyeglass Repair   **Perfect Vision,** Shop C22A, in the Centerpoint Tower, 100 Market St. (☎ **02/9221 1010**), is open Monday through Friday from 9am to 6pm (until 9pm Thursday) and Saturday from 9am to 5pm.

Holidays   See "When to Go," in chapter 2. New South Wales also observes Labour Day on the first Monday in October.

Hospitals   Make your way to **Sydney Hospital,** on Macquarie Street, at the top end of Martin Place (☎ **02/9382 7111** for emergencies). **St. Vincents Hospital** is on Victoria and Burton streets in Darlinghurst (near Kings Cross; ☎ **02/9339 1111**).

Hotlines   Contact the **Poisons Information Center** at ☎ **13 11 26;** the **Gay and Lesbian Counseling Line** (4pm to midnight) at ☎ **02/9207 2800;** the **Rape Crisis Center** at ☎ **02/9819 6565;** and the **Crisis Center** at ☎ **02/ 9358 6577.**

Internet Access   **Global Gossip,** at 770 George St., near Central Station (☎ **02/9212 1466**), and 111 Darlinghurst Rd., Kings Cross (☎ **02/9326 9777**), offers Internet, e-mail, and computer access for A$2 (U.S.$1.30) for 10 minutes or A$10 (U.S.$6.50) per hour. It's open daily from 8am to midnight. Elsewhere in the city, the **Surfnet Café** (☎ **02/9976 0808**), next to the public library in Manly, is open Monday through Saturday from 9am to 9pm and Sunday from 9am to 7pm; the **Internet Café,** Level 3, Hotel Sweeney, 236 Clarence St. (☎ **02/9261 5666**), is open Monday through Friday from 10am to 9pm and Saturday from noon to 6pm; and the **Well Connected Café,** 35 Glebe Point Rd., Glebe (☎ **02/9566 2655**), is open Monday through Thursday from 10am to 11pm, Friday and Saturday from 10am to 6pm, and Sunday from noon to 10pm.

Luggage Storage   You can leave your bags at the International Terminal at the airport. A locker here costs A$5 (U.S.$3.25) per day, or you can put them in the storage room for A$7 (U.S.$4.55) per day per piece. The storage room is open from 4:30am to the last flight of the day. Call ☎ **02/9667 9848** for information.

An Important Note on Taxes

Beginning July 1, 2000, Australia adopted a **10% Goods and Services Tax (GST)** on most goods sold in Australia and most services. The GST applies to most travel-related goods and services, including transport, hotels, tours, and restaurants. By law, the tax has to be included in the advertised price of the product, though it doesn't have to be displayed independently of the pretax price. While we've endeavored to include the GST throughout this book, some post-GST prices were not available at the time of writing. Be sure to ask whether it's been included in any prices you're quoted.

Otherwise, leave luggage at the cloakroom at **Central Station,** near the front of the main building off George Street (☎ **02/9219 4395**). Storage at the rail station costs A$4.50 (U.S.$2.90) per article per day. The **Travelers Contact Point,** 7th floor, 428 George St. (above the Dymocks bookstore; ☎ **02/9221 8744**), stores luggage for A$15 (U.S.$9.75) per piece per month.

Newspapers   The *Sydney Morning Herald* is considered one of the world's best newspapers and is available throughout metropolitan Sydney. The equally prestigious *Australian* is available nationwide. The metropolitan *Telegraph Mirror* is a more casual read. The *International Herald Tribune, USA Today,* the *British Guardian Weekly,* and other U.K. newspapers can be found at Circular Quay newspaper stands and most newsagents.

Pharmacies   Most suburbs have pharmacies that are open late. For after-hours referral, contact the **Emergency Prescription Service** (☎ **02/9235 0333**).

Police   In an emergency dial ☎ **000.** Make nonemergency police inquiries through the Sydney Police Centre (☎ **02/9281 0000**).

Rest Rooms   These can be found in the Queen Victoria Building (second floor), most department stores, at Central Station and Circular Quay, near the escalators by the Sydney Aquarium, at Darling Harbour, and in the Harbourside Festival Marketplace in Darling Harbour.

Safety   Sydney is an extremely safe city overall, but as anywhere else, it's good to keep your wits about you and your wallet hidden. If you wear a money belt, keep it underneath your shirt. Be wary in Kings Cross and Redfern at all hours and around the cinema strip on George Street near Town Hall station in the evening—it's a hangout for local gangs. Other places of concern are the back lanes of Darlinghurst and along the Bondi restaurant strip after midnight, when the drunks spill out. Several people have reported thieves operating at the airport on occasions. If traveling by train at night, travel in the carriages next to the guard's van, marked with a blue light on the outside.

Taxis   See "Getting Around," earlier in this chapter.

Telephones   Sydney's public phone boxes take coins (40¢ for local calls), while many also take credit cards and A$10 (U.S.$6.50) phone cards available from newsagents. **Global Gossip,** at 770 George St., near Central Station (☎ **02/ 9212 1466**), and 111 Darlinghurst Rd., Kings Cross (☎ **02/9326 9777**), offers cheap international telephone calls.

To call Australia from the United States, dial the international access code (**011**), then Australia's country code (**61**), then the area code (be sure to drop the first zero of the area code), then the number you want to call. For example, to call the Sydney Opera House (☎ **02/9250 7111**) from the United States, dial **011 61 2 9250 7111.**

To call the United States from Australia, dial the international access code (**0011;** note that it has two zeros, not one like the international access code from the United States), then the country code for the United States (**1**), then the area code and number you want to call.

Travelers Assistance   Travelers Contact Point, at Level 7, 428 George St. (☎ **02/9221 8744**), offers an in-house employment agency for working holidays, an Australia-wide mail forwarding service, Internet access, luggage storage, and short-term mobile phones.

Useful Telephone Numbers   For phone directory/assistance, call ☎ **013** for local numbers, ☎ **0175** for interstate numbers, or ☎ **0103** for international numbers. You can reach the Travelers Aid Society at ☎ **02/9211 2469.** For transit information, call the InfoLine at ☎ **13 15 00** (daily from 6am to 10pm). For the local forecast, call ☎ **1196.**

3 Accommodations

Hotels are generally clustered around the main tourist spots, with the more expensive ones generally occupying the prime positions. Those in The Rocks and around Circular Quay are just a short stroll from the Sydney Opera House, the Harbour Bridge, the Royal Botanic Gardens, the ferry terminals, and the train station, and are close to the main shopping areas.

Hotels around Darling Harbour offer good access to the local facilities, including museums, the Sydney Aquarium, the Star City casino, the IMAX Theatre, and Sega World. Most Darling Harbour hotels are a 10-minute walk, or a short monorail or light rail ride, from Town Hall and the central shopping district in and around the AMP Centerpoint Tower and the Pitt Street Mall.

More hotels are grouped around Kings Cross, Sydney's red-light district. While some of the hotels found here are among the city's best, in this area you'll also find a range of cheaper lodgings, including several backpacker hostels. Kings Cross can be unnerving at any time, but especially so on Friday and Saturday nights, when the area's strip joints and nightclubs are doing their best business. Staying here does have its advantages, though: you get a real inner-city feel and it's close to some excellent restaurants and cafes centered around the Kings Cross/Darlinghurst and Oxford Street areas.

Glebe, with its many ethnic restaurants, is another inner-city suburb popular with tourists. It's well served by local buses, as well as Airport Express Bus route 352.

If you want to stay near the beach, check out the options in Manly and Bondi, though you should consider their distance from the city center and the lack of CityRail trains to these areas. A taxi to Manly from the city will cost around A$33 (U.S.$21.45), and to Bondi around A$22 (U.S.$14.30).

The prices given below for very expensive and expensive hotels are the **"rack rates,"** the official published rates, which almost nobody pays. Always ask about discounts rates, package deals, and any other special offerings when booking a hotel, especially if you are traveling in winter, when hotels are less likely to be full. Ask about weekend discounts, corporate rates, and family plans. **Serviced apartments** are also well worth considering, because you can save a bundle by cooking your own meals; many also have free laundry facilities.

Rooms at all of the following hotels have private bathrooms unless otherwise specified. Almost all hotels offer no-smoking rooms; inquire when you make a reservation

If you turn up in town without a reservation, you should definitely make use of the **New South Wales Travel Centre** desk (☎ 02/9667 6050) on the Arrivals Level of the International Terminal. It represents every Sydney hotel and offers exceptional discounts—up to 50%—on rooms that haven't been filled that day. The desk is open from 6am to the last flight of the day and also offers discounts on tours (to the Blue Mountains, for example), and cheap tickets for flights within Australia.

if it's important to you. Most moderately priced to very expensive rooms will have a hair dryer, tea- and coffee-making facilities, and access to an iron and ironing board. In moderate to expensive hotels, there's an increasing trend to rip off guests with pay-per-view movie channels (around A$14/U.S.$9.10 per movie), rather than to providing full access to a range of free cable TV channels. All hotel prices below include the GST (except, for some reason, the Hotel 59).

NEAR CIRCULAR QUAY
VERY EXPENSIVE

All Seasons Premier Menzies. 14 Carrington St., Sydney, NSW 2000. ☎ **1300/363 600** in Australia, or 02/9299 1000. Fax 02/9290 3819. www.menzies.com.au. E-mail: menziesres@ menzies.com.au. 446 rooms. A/C MINIBAR TV TEL. A$328–$355 (U.S.$213–230.75) double; A$525 (U.S.$341.25) suite. Extra person A$43 (U.S.$28). Children under 12 stay free in parents' room. Ask about special packages. AE, BC, DC, JCB, MC, V. Parking A$24 (U.S.$15.60). CityRail: Wynyard.

The 14-story Menzies was built in 1963 as Sydney's first premier hotel. It's positioned right in the center of town and sports one of the city's few public clocks on top of its impressive facade. Rooms are compact and newly refurbished, decorated with colonial furniture and outfitted with fax machines and all the mod cons (modern conveniences). Deluxe rooms, as you'd expect, are slightly larger and a touch more upscale. Though it took A$14 million (U.S.$9.1 million) to modernize it in 1997, this hotel has retained its grande dame appeal. One room is suitable for travelers with disabilities.

Dining: The Carrington Restaurant serves high-class à la carte meals and fabulous lunch and dinner buffets. A brasserie offers snacks, lunch, and afternoon tea in a very elegant atmosphere.

Amenities: Indoor pool, sauna, spa, massage, gym, concierge, 24-hour room service, free daily newspapers, nightly turndown, shoe shine, laundry, valet, business services, gift shop, newsstand, currency exchange.

○ **Hotel Inter-Continental Sydney.** 117 Macquarie St., Sydney, NSW 2000. ☎ **1800/ 221 828** in Australia (outside New South Wales), or 02/9253 9000. Fax 02/9240 1240. www.sydney.interconti.com. E-mail: sydney@interconti.com. 498 units. A/C MINIBAR TV TEL. A$451–$594 (U.S.$293–386) double; from A$864 (U.S.$561) suite. Extra person A$66 (U.S.$42.90). Children under 15 stay free in parents' room. AE, BC, DC, JCB, MC, V. Parking A$22 (U.S.$14.30). CityRail, bus, or ferry: Circular Quay.

Wonderfully positioned opposite the Royal Botanic Gardens and just a stroll away from many other main attractions, the hotel is situated in the former Treasury building (later the VD clinic), built between 1849 and 1917. All rooms were elegantly refurbished to unite 19th-century classicism with the best of the 20th century. Half of the rooms have a harbor view, and all come complete with everything you'd expect, and some features, like a toaster, that might surprise you. Special rooms for business travelers are slightly larger (and more expensive) and come with dedicated business facilities: modem lines, printer, scanner, and fax machine.

Dining/Diversions: Afternoon tea, lunch, and cocktails are taken in the white marbled Cortile, the building's architectural focal point. The Cortile features live classical music Wednesday to Sunday. One One Seven, the hotel's fine-dining venue, is picking up quite a good reputation. The 30-Something Lounge on the 31st floor has panoramic views over Sydney Harbour and the Royal Botanic Gardens and serves good pizzas and pasta. Sketches Bar and Bistro serves freshly made pasta (see "Dining," below). Café Opera is an informal buffet specializing in sushi and wok-prepared foods.

Amenities: Indoor pool, sauna, spa, gym, power-walking classes, massage therapists, concierge, 24-hour room service, free daily newspapers, nightly turndown, shoe shine, laundry, valet, baby-sitting, business center, secretarial services, hair/beauty salon, gift shop, newsstand, early-arrivals/late-departures lounge, currency exchange.

✪ **Ritz-Carlton Sydney.** 93 Macquarie St., Sydney, NSW 2000. ☎ **1800/145 004** in Australia, or 02/9252 4600. Fax 02/9252 4286. www.ritzcarlton.com.au. E-mail: rdarley@rcdb.zip.com.au. 106 units. A/C MINIBAR TV TEL. A$495 (U.S.$321.75) double, A$525 (U.S.$341.25) deluxe harbor-view double; A$555–$3,000 (U.S.$360.75–$1,950) suite. AE, BC, DC, MC, V. Parking A$25 (U.S.$16.25). CityRail, bus, or ferry: Circular Quay.

Talk about plush! This is Sydney's most deluxe hotel—from the moment the doorman doffs his top hat to you, you enter the world of the aristocracy. The lobby is cozy and elegant, with plenty of antiques scattered around and the slight scent of cigar smoke and aged brandy in the air. It has a prime location, just a short walk from Circular Quay and the Opera House, and just across the road from the Royal Botanic Gardens. Rooms are exceptionally large and luxurious with good-size marble bathrooms. Most rooms have a small balcony. The rooms on the east side of the hotel have the best views across the gardens. Most rooms are accessible to wheelchairs. In 1999, both *Condé Nast Traveler* and *Travel & Leisure* voted this "the best hotel in Australia."

Dining: The Dining Room serves up fine cuisine in a well-heeled atmosphere. The Bar serves a buffet meal at lunchtime and has promotional evenings, such as Oyster night.

Amenities: Indoor pool, sauna, gym, massage, concierge, 24-hour room service, free daily newspapers, nightly turndown, shoe shine, laundry, valet, baby-sitting, business center, secretarial services, hair/beauty salon, gift shop, newsstand, currency exchange.

IN THE ROCKS
VERY EXPENSIVE

✪ **ANA Hotel Sydney.** 176 Cumberland St., The Rocks, Sydney, NSW 2000. ☎ **1800/801 088** in Australia, or 02/9250 6000. Fax 02/9250 6250. www.anahotel.com.au. 563 units. MINIBAR TV TEL. A$429–$456.50 (U.S.$278.85–$296.70) double depending on view; deluxe corner rooms with views A$676.50 (U.S.$439.70); from A$704 (U.S.$457.60) suite. Extra person A$44 (U.S.$28.60). Children stay free in parents' room. Ask about packages. AE, BC, DC, JCB, MC, V. Parking A$19 (U.S.$12.35). CityRail or ferry: Circular Quay.

For a room with a view, you're not going to do better than this ultramodern landmark hotel. All rooms look out either onto Darling Harbour or across the Opera House and Harbour Bridge. Try to book a room on the 20th floor or above, because from here Sydney is laid out at your feet, with the ferries buzzing around below you like wind-up bathtub toys. If you really want to splurge, book a corner room for an extraordinary vista. Rooms are comfortably furnished and decorated to blend with sky, city, and sea. The hotel is popular with tour groups, particularly from Japan.

Dining/Diversions: The Lilyvale restaurant serves delicious Modern Australian dishes, The Rocks Teppanyaki is the hotel's popular Japanese food outlet, and the

Central Sydney Accommodations

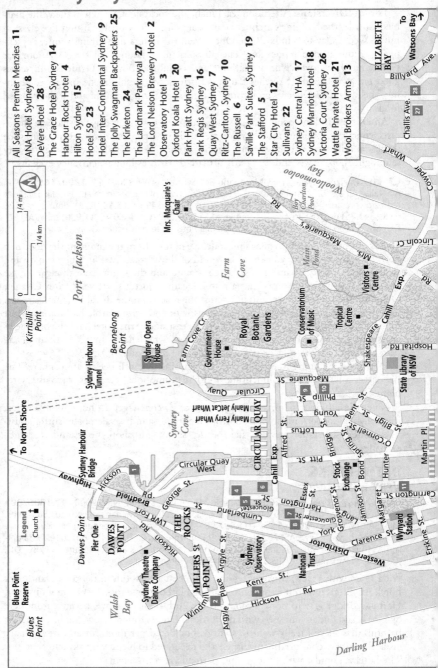

All Seasons Premier Menzies **11**
ANA Hotel Sydney **8**
DeVere Hotel **28**
The Grace Hotel Sydney **14**
Harbour Rocks Hotel **4**
Hilton Sydney **15**
Hotel 59 **23**
Hotel Inter-Continental Sydney **9**
The Jolly Swagman Backpackers **25**
The Kirketon **24**
The Landmark Parkroyal **27**
The Lord Nelson Brewery Hotel **2**
Observatory Hotel **3**
Oxford Koala Hotel **20**
Park Hyatt Sydney **1**
Park Regis Sydney **16**
Quay West Sydney **7**
Ritz-Carlton, Sydney **10**
The Russell **6**
Saville Park Suites, Sydney **19**
The Stafford **5**
Star City Hotel **12**
Sullivans **22**
Sydney Central YHA **17**
Sydney Marriott Hotel **18**
Victoria Court Sydney **26**
Wattle Private Hotel **21**
Wool Brokers Arms **13**

Lobby Lounge serves up cocktails and a view of the landscaped gardens, though it can get noisy when tour groups arrive.

Amenities: Indoor pool, spa and sauna, fitness center, massage, concierge, 24-hour room service, free daily newspapers, nightly turndown, shoe shine, laundry, valet, baby-sitting, business center, meeting facilities, hair/beauty salon, sundry/gift shop, currency exchange, early arrivals/late departures lounge.

☺ Observatory Hotel. 89–113 Kent St., Sydney, NSW 2000. ☎ **1800/806 245** in Australia, or 02/9256 2222. Fax 02/9256 2233. www.observatoryhotel.com.au. 100 units. A/C MINIBAR TV TEL. A$405–$440 (U.S.$263.25–$286) double; from A$500 (U.S.$325) suite. Extra person A$66 (U.S.$42.90) extra. Children under 14 stay free in parents' room. AE, BC, DC, JCB, MC, V. Parking A$25 (U.S.$16.25). Bus: 339, 431, or 433 to Millers Point.

This exclusive hotel, a 10-minute walk uphill from The Rocks and George Street, is a turn-of-the-century beauty competing for top-hotel-in-Sydney honors. Up there with the Ritz-Carlton Sydney (see above) for unadulterated style, it's fitted out with antiques, objets d'art, and the finest carpets, wallpapers, and draperies. It's renowned for its personalized service. Rooms are plush, are quiet, and come with all the modern amenities, including CD players, VCRs, dataports, voice mail, multiple telephones, hair dryers, and in-room movies. The huge bathtub is a great place for a glass of champagne and some take-away sushi. Some rooms have city views while others look out over the harbor. Three rooms are equipped for travelers with disabilities.

Dining/Diversions: The ☺ **Galileo Restaurant** offers very good food in an elegant candlelit atmosphere with silk wallpaper, polished walnut furniture, and original Venetian etchings and Australian Impressionist works of art. The Globe Bar feels like an old-world colonial English club.

Amenities: The chemical-free indoor pool here is one of the best in Sydney (note the fiber-optic lights on the ceiling that depict the Southern Hemisphere constellations). The well-equipped health club (with exercise equipment, sauna, and steam room) offers everything from massage and beauty therapies to a free float in the flotation tank for early arrivals coming in from overseas. Tennis courts, concierge, 24-hour room service, newspaper delivery, nightly turndown, twice-daily maid service, dry cleaning/laundry, business center, free BMW limo service to the central business district on weekdays, conference facilities.

☺ Park Hyatt Sydney. 7 Hickson Rd., The Rocks, Sydney, NSW 2000. ☎ **02/9241 1234.** Fax 02/9256 1555. www.sydney.hyatt.com. 158 units. A/C MINIBAR TV TEL. A$722–$777 (U.S.$469.30–$505) double depending on view; A$886–$996 (U.S.$575.90–$647) executive studio; from A$1,324 (U.S.$860) suite. Extra person A$55 (U.S.$35.75). Children under 18 stay free in parents' room. Ask about lower weekend rates and packages. AE, BC, DC, JCB, MC, V. Parking A$20 (U.S.$13). CityRail, bus, or ferry: Circular Quay.

This artistically curving property on The Rocks foreshore is without a doubt the best-positioned hotel in Sydney. It's literally right on the water, with some rooms having fantastic views directly across the harbor to the Sydney Opera House. Its location and general appeal mean it's usually full and frequently has to turn guests away. The room rates have skyrocketed here in the past year or so; unless you are really looking for a splurge, plenty of places around are far cheaper and offer better value. But that fantastic location still earns this place a star in my opinion.

The building itself is a pleasure to look at, and from a ferry on the harbor it looks like a wonderful addition to the toy-town feel of The Rocks. The marble lobby is elegant, and every possible luxury has been incorporated into the rooms. Room rates here really depend on views; the least expensive units have only glimpses of the harbor. Each of the 33 executive suites has two balconies with a telescope.

Dining/Diversions: Verandah on the Park offers good buffet food either indoors or in a fabulous location on the edge of the harbor. No. 7 at the Park is more formal and has excellent harbor views. The bar has a fireplace and resembles an English club.

Amenities: Outdoor pool, health club, gym, steam room, sauna, spa, massage, concierge, butler, 24-hour room service, nightly turndown, free newspaper, laundry, shoe shine, valet, baby-sitting, business center, lobby shop.

Quay West Sydney. 98 Gloucester St. (corner of Essex St.), The Rocks, Sydney, NSW 2000. ☎ **1800/805 031** in Australia, 0800/444 300 in New Zealand, or 02/9240 6000. Fax 02/9240 6060. www.mirvachotels.com. 132 units. A/C MINIBAR TV TEL. A$374–$473 (U.S.$243–$307) 1-bedroom apt depending on view; A$599.50 (U.S.$389) 2-bedroom apt. Extra person A$30 (U.S.$19.50). Ask about weekend packages and rates for long-term stays. AE, BC, DC, JCB, MC, V. Parking A$16.50 (U.S.$10.70). CityRail, bus, or ferry: Circular Quay or Wynyard.

The very best serviced-apartment complexes, like this one, can even outdo superior five-star hotels. Quay West is a hard-hitting competitor to its rivals in and around The Rocks area—it's got everything they have and more. The lobby is plush and hotel-like. The apartments are very spacious, each with a fully equipped kitchen, a laundry, a CD player, a foldout sofa in the living room as well as a queen-size bed in a separate bedroom, a dining table seating six, and a balcony. Bathrooms are large and feature a separate tub and shower. Some rooms have fantastic views over the Harbour Bridge and the harbor—but you pay through the nose for them (in fact, all the rooms have rocketed in price since a year ago). The 28-story apartment building has a spa, sauna, gym, beautiful indoor Roman-style swimming pool with great views, and the high-quality Carrington Restaurant.

EXPENSIVE

Harbour Rocks Hotel. 34–52 Harrington St., The Rocks, Sydney, NSW 2000. ☎ **1800/251 210** in Australia, or 02/9251 8944. Fax 02/9251 8900. E-mail: harbo@ozemail.com.au. 55 units. MINIBAR TV TEL. A$264–$308 (U.S.$171.60–$200) double. Penthouse suite A$550 (U.S.$357.50). Extra person A$33 (U.S.$21.45). Children under 12 stay free in parents' room. AE, DC, JCB, MC, V. Parking A$18 (U.S.$11.70) across the road. CityRail or ferry: Circular Quay.

This four-story, heritage-listed boutique hotel is right in the heart of the Rocks. Rooms are clean and well appointed with free videos thrown in; but there is no elevator, so guests have to climb the stairs. Rooms vary in size, with some being quite large and others much smaller; bathrooms also vary in size, and none (except the penthouse suite) has a tub. There's one room equipped for travelers with disabilities on the ground floor.

Dining/Diversions: The beautiful Harbor Rocks Café overlooks a leafy balcony, perfect for those sultry summer evenings. Live local jazz bands play in the bar area on Friday nights and Sunday afternoons.

Amenities: Limited room service, laundry service, secretarial services, coin-operated laundry, baby-sitting.

The Stafford. 75 Harrington St., The Rocks, Sydney, NSW 2000. ☎ **02/9251 6711.** Fax 02/9251 3458. www.citysearch.com.au/syd/thestafford. E-mail: staffordsydney@bigpond. com. 61 units. A/C TV TEL. A$231–$270 (U.S. $150–$175.50) studio double; A$275 (U.S. $178.75) 1-bedroom apt; A$308 (U.S. $200) executive 1-bedroom apt; A$292 (U.S.$189.80) terrace house; A$369 (U.S. $239.85) 1-bedroom penthouse. Extra person A$17 (U.S.$11). Children under 12 stay free in parents' room. Ask about lower weekly rates. AE, BC, DC, JCB, MC, V. Parking A$15 (U.S.$9.75). CityRail or ferry: Circular Quay.

Along with Quay West Sydney (see above), the Stafford offers the best positioned serviced apartments in Sydney, right in the heart of The Rocks, very close to the harbor and Circular Quay, and a short stroll from the central business district. The property consists of modern apartments in a six-story building (the best units, for their harbor and Opera House views, are on the top three floors) and seven two-story terrace houses dating from 1870 to 1895. While Stafford isn't as exclusive as Quay West, it's still highly recommended for its location, spacious rooms, and fully equipped kitchen. There are an outdoor pool, a gym, a spa and sauna, and a complimentary self-service laundry.

MODERATE

The Lord Nelson Brewery Hotel. At the corner of Kent and Argyle sts., The Rocks, Sydney, NSW 2000. ☎ **02/9251 4044.** Fax 02/9251 1532. E-mail: lordnelson.com.au. 10 units, 8 with private bathroom. TV TEL. A$160 (U.S.$104) double without bathroom, A$180 (U.S.$117) double with bathroom. Extra person A$15 (U.S. $9.75). Rates include continental breakfast. AE, BC, DC, MC, V. Parking not available. CityRail or ferry: Circular Quay.

Sydney's oldest pub was established in 1841 after serving as a private residence since its construction in 1836. It's an attractive, three-story sandstone building with a busy pub on the ground floor, a good brasserie on the second, and hotel accommodations on the third. The "small" rooms are true to their name, with room for not much more than a bed and a small TV. For an extra A$30 (U.S.$19.50) you get lots more space. From its creaky floorboards and bedroom walls made from convict-hewn sandstone blocks, to the narrow corridors and the wood fire and homemade beer down in the bar, the Lord Nelson positively wallows in colonial atmosphere.

✪ **The Russell.** 143A George St., The Rocks, Sydney, NSW 2000. ☎ **02/9241 3543.** Fax 02/9252 1652. www.therussell.com.au. 29 units, 19 with private bathroom. TV TEL. A$110–$150 (U.S.$71.50–$97.50) double without bathroom; A$180–$229 (U.S.$117–$148.85) double with bathroom; A$230 (U.S.$149.50) suite. Extra person A$15 (U.S.$9.75). Rates include continental breakfast. AE, BC, DC, MC, V. Parking not available. CityRail or ferry: Circular Quay.

This is the coziest place to stay in The Rocks, and perhaps in all of Sydney. It's more than 100 years old, and it shows its age wonderfully in the creak of the floorboards and the ramshackle feel of its brightly painted corridors. Every room is totally different in style, size, and shape; all come with a queen-size bed and half have cable TV (others can have a TV moved in if requested). All rooms have immense character, including a series of rooms added on in 1990 above the Fortune of War Hotel next door. There are no harbor views, but from some rooms you can see the tops of the ferry terminals at Circular Quay. Guests have the use of a comfortable sitting room, a living room scattered with magazines and books, and a rooftop garden. Boulders restaurant serves good food on the ground floor.

NEAR TOWN HALL
VERY EXPENSIVE

The Grace Hotel Sydney. 77 York St., Sydney, NSW 2000. ☎ **1800/682 692** in Australia, or 02/9299 8777. Fax 02/9299 8189. www.gracehotel.com.au. E-mail: sales@gracehotel.com.au. 382 units. A/C MINIBAR TV TEL. A$374–$396 (U.S.$243–$257) double; A$572 (U.S.$371) suite. Extra person A$49.50 (U.S.$32.20). Children under 17 stay free in parents' room. AE, BC, DC, MC, V. Parking A$27.50 (U.S.$17.90). CityRail: Wynyard.

Situated within the historic Grace Building, a replica of the Chicago Tribune Building and one of Australia's finest examples of commercial Gothic architecture, The Grace is one of the city's newest centrally located hotels. The lobby has marble flagstones, stained-glass windows, a lace ironwork balcony, art deco furniture and light fittings, and high ceilings supported by marble columns. Guest rooms vary in size (the more expensive doubles are called "deluxe"; the cheaper ones are "executive"), with either king-size beds or a pair of doubles, and are fronted by almost surreally wide corridors. Each room has three telephones, computer connections, and an in-room safe. Three are suitable for travelers with disabilities.

Dining: The Grace Deli & Cafe on the lobby level serves snacks and beverages in a relaxed, informal atmosphere and is a good place for a gourmet take-away or sidewalk dining. Breakfast, lunch, and à la carte evening meals are served in the second-floor brasserie. There's a good pasta bar located in the Grace Wine Bar on the Mezzanine Level.

Amenities: Heated outdoor swimming pool, sauna, gym, massage, concierge, 24-hour room service, free daily newspaper, nightly turndown on request, shoe shine, laundry, valet, baby-sitting, postal and business services, express checkout, currency exchange.

Hilton Sydney. 259 Pitt St., Sydney, NSW 2000. ☎ **1800/222 255** in Australia, or 02/9266 2000. Fax 02/9265 6065. www.hilton.com. 585 units. A/C MINIBAR TV TEL. A$420–$465 (U.S.$273–$302.25) double; A$550–$1,500 (U.S.$357.50–U.S.$975) suite. Extra person A$45 (U.S.$29.25). Children under 18 stay free in parents' room. AE, BC, DC, JCB, MC, V. Parking $27 (U.S.$17.55). CityRail: Town Hall.

Right in the middle of town and close to all major shops, the Hilton is a 1970s conglomerate with a decidedly ugly facade fronting both Pitt and George streets. The lackluster gold lobby—if you can find it (the main entrance is hidden away in a warren of concrete)—is dimly lit and houses a popular cafe and boutique shops. The rooms were refurbished in 1999 and are the first in Australia to have a fully electronic mini-bar system (aimed at preventing disputes with guests). Many rooms, especially from the 32nd floor up, have panoramic views of the AMP Centrepoint Tower, the Harbour Bridge, and neighboring skyscrapers. The higher priced doubles are "executive" rooms and have access to a meeting room and an evening buffet.

Dining/Diversions: Two of Sydney's best bars are in the Hilton: the stunning Marble Bar, with its extravagant central-European feel, and the popular English-style Henry the Ninth Bar. The hotel has two restaurants.

Amenities: Outdoor pool, sauna, spa, gym, massage, concierge, 24-hour room service, free daily newspaper, nightly turndown, shoe shine, laundry, valet, baby-sitting, business center, tour desk, gift shop, newsstand, currency exchange.

Sydney Marriott Hotel. 36 College St., Sydney, NSW 2010. ☎ **1800/025 419** in Australia, or 02/9361 8400. Fax 02/9361 8599. www.marriott.com. E-mail: sydneymarriott@ mirvachotels.com.au. 241 units. A/C MINIBAR TV TEL. A$396 (U.S.$257.40) "deluxe" double; A$655 (U.S.$425.75) junior suite; A$809 (U.S.$525.85) king suite. Extra person A$25 (U.S.$16.25). Children under 12 stay free in parents' room. Ask about lower weekend rates and discount packages. AE, BC, DC, JCB, MC, V. Free parking. CityRail: Museum.

The Marriott is finely positioned right opposite Hyde Park in the city center. It's a short walk from the major shopping areas around Town Hall, and a hop, skip, and a jump from the beginning of fashionable Oxford Street, with its nightlife and burgeoning

Where to Stay During Gay & Lesbian Mardi Gras

The Saville Park Suites (see below) is a fabulous place from which to watch Sydney's annual Gay and Lesbian Mardi Gras, held every February (the parade is usually on the last Sat in Feb or the first Sat in Mar). Make your plans early, though, because most rooms are booked a year in advance. Four-night Mardi Gras packages range from around A$1,538 to $1,992 (U.S.$999.70 to $1,295). Sullivans hotel (see p. 108) on Oxford Street is also another popular place to stay during Mardi Gras.

restaurant scene. The rooms are typical four-star variety, but they include such extras as plates, cutlery, toasters, and microwaves; one-third of the rooms also have hot plates. The views from the park-facing rooms are fabulous. All rooms have impressive triangular bathtubs. Many Frommer's readers have recommended this property.

Dining/Diversions: Windows on the Park offers à la carte meals with nice views over Hyde Park. The property also features a coffee shop and a cocktail bar.

Amenities: Heated outdoor pool and sundeck with nice views, health club, small gym, steam room, sauna, spa, concierge, arrivals lounge, 24-hour room service.

EXPENSIVE

Saville Park Suites, Sydney. 16–32 Oxford St., Sydney, NSW 2010. ☎ **1800/221 2599** in Australia, or 02/8268 2599. Fax 02/8268 2599. www.savillesuites.com.au. E-mail: sydney@shg.com.au. 135 units. A/C MINIBAR TV TEL. A$230 (U.S.$149.50) 1-bedroom apt; A$255 (U.S.$165.75) 2-bedroom apt. Extra person A$25 (U.S.$16.25). Children under 15 stay free in parents' room. Ask about special rates. AE, BC, DC, JCB, MC, V. Parking A$5 (U.S.$3.25). CityRail: Museum.

Although the serviced apartments here are pleasant and nicely furnished and the complex is very well situated right at the start of Oxford Street and just a short walk across Hyde Park from the Pitt Street Mall shopping area, I feel it's overpriced. You may be able to negotiate a cheaper rate with the management, though; it never hurts to ask. All rooms have a sofa and a couple of armchairs, a separate kitchen, a balcony, and a bathroom with a smallish tub and separate shower. All come with a laundry and an iron and board. You can ask for a microwave. There's a small-but-functional outdoor pool, a sauna, and a spa; guests get free membership at a gym just down the road. Zipp, the fun-looking restaurant, is open for lunch and dinner daily except Monday.

INEXPENSIVE

Park Regis Sydney. 27 Park St. (at Castlereagh St.), Sydney, NSW 2000. ☎ **1800/221 138** in Australia, or 02/9267 6511. Fax 02/9264 2252. www.parkregis.com.au. E-mail: res@parkregissydney.com.au. 120 units. A/C TV TEL. A$165 (U.S.$72.80) double; A$198 (U.S.$128.70) suite. Extra person A$22 (U.S.$14.30). Children under 14 stay free in parents' room. Ask about lower rates available through Aussie auto clubs. AE, BC, DC, JCB, MC, V. Free parking. CityRail: Town Hall. Monorail: Park Plaza.

This hotel occupies the top 15 floors of a 45-story building just 2 blocks from Hyde Park and Town Hall. There's nothing spectacular about the place. The lobby is plain and functional; the rooms are light, modern, and equally practical. The bathrooms have showers but no tubs. Many of the guests are business travelers, which gives the hotel a corporate feel. Nevertheless, it's a relatively good value considering the location. Rooms at the front have views over the city and park. There's a rooftop pool.

☉ Sydney Central YHA. 11 Rawson Place (on the corner of Pitt St., right outside Central Station), Sydney, NSW 2000. ☎ **02/9281 9111.** Fax 02/9281 9199. www.yha.com.au. E-mail: sydcentral@yhansw.org.au. 151 rms or 532 beds (54 twin rms). A$24–$29 (U.S.$15.60–$18.85) dorm bed; A$72 (U.S.$46.80) twin without bathroom, A$80 (U.S.$52) twin with bathroom. Non-YHA members pay A$3 (U.S.$1.95) extra. BC, JCB, MC, V. Parking A$10 (U.S.$6.50). CityRail: Central.

This award-winning youth hostel is one of the biggest and busiest in the world, with a 98% year-round occupancy rate. You'll have to book early to secure a place. Opened in 1987 in a historic nine-story building, it offers far more than standard basic accommodation. In the basement is the Scu Bar, a very popular drinking hole with pool tables and occasional entertainment. There are also a bistro selling cheap meals, a convenience store, two fully equipped kitchens, and an entertainment room with more pool tables and e-mail facilities, TV rooms on every floor, and an audiovisual room showing movies. If you want more, try the heated swimming pool and the sauna! Rooms are clean and basic. The YHA is completely accessible to travelers with disabilities. Check the YHA Web site for other great hostels in Sydney, including the **Glebe Point YHA** in Glebe; the **Sydney Beachhouse YHA,** in the beachside suburb of Collaroy; and **Pittwater YHA,** in Ku-ring-gai National Park (accessible only by boat and a fabulous way to experience the "bush" around Sydney).

AT DARLING HARBOUR
EXPENSIVE

Star City Hotel. 80 Pyrmont St., Pyrmont, Sydney, NSW 2009. ☎ **1800/700 700** in Australia, or 02/9777 9000. Fax 02/9657 8344. www.starcity.com.au. E-mail: reservations@ starcity.com.au. 491 units. A/C MINIBAR TV TEL. A$350–$370 (U.S.$154.70–$163.80) double, depending on view; from A$510 (U.S.$331.50) and way up for apts. Extra person A$40 (U.S.$26). Ask about special packages. AE, BC, DC, JCB, MC, V. Parking A$15 (U.S.$9.75). Ferry: Pyrmont Bay. Monorail: Harbourside. Light rail: Star City. Free shuttle buses run from the central business district.

Opened at the end of 1997, this A$900 million (U.S.$585 million) gambling and entertainment complex includes Sydney's newest five-star hotel. Pay the extra money for a room with truly spectacular views over Darling Harbour. The four split-level Royal Suites are quite spectacular, each with three TVs, a giant spa, a full kitchen, two bathrooms, its own sauna, and the services of the former butler to the governor of Queensland. Standard rooms, on the other hand, are somewhat sterile. Executive suites are very nice though.

Dining/Diversions: The ✪ **Astral** restaurant is the top-flight dining choice here, offering top-rated cuisine and the best service I've come across in Sydney. Other major restaurants are Al Porto, serving Italian, and the Lotus Pond, serving Chinese; there are also a couple of bistro-style places, including the very busy Garden Room, where for $18 (U.S.$11.70) you can eat as much as you want (including prawns, roasts, pizzas, and desserts). The gaming rooms are sectioned into four areas; there are also two theaters, the 2,000-seat Lyric Theatre (the largest in Sydney) and the 900-seat Showroom, which presents Las Vegas–style productions.

Amenities: Heated outdoor pool, sauna, spa, massage, concierge, 24-hour room service, free daily newspaper, nightly turndown, shoe shine, laundry, valet, business center, shopping arcade, newsstand, beauty salon, currency exchange.

INEXPENSIVE

Wool Brokers Arms. 22 Allen St., Pyrmont, NSW 2009. ☎ **02/9552 4773.** Fax 02/9552 4771. E-mail: woolbrokers@ozemail.com.au. 26 units, none with private bathroom. TV. A$79 (U.S.$51) double; A$98(U.S.$63.70) triple; A$120 (U.S.$78) family room for 4. *These discounted prices are for Frommer's readers only.* Rates include continental breakfast. Extra person A$20 (U.S.$13). AE, BC, MC, V. Parking A$9 (U.S.$5.85) nearby. Bus: 501 from central business district or Central Station. Light Rail: Convention Centre.

You'll find this friendly 1886 heritage building on the far side of Darling Harbour, next to the Novotel hotel and hidden behind a monstrous above-ground parking garage. It's set on a noisy road, so unless you're used to traffic, avoid rooms at the front. Rooms are simply furnished with a double bed, a refrigerator, tea-and-coffee-making facilities, and a sink. Room 3 is one of the nicer ones. Family rooms have a king-size bed, a set of bunks, and two singles through an open doorway. There are 19 shared bathrooms, a coin-operated laundry, and a self-service breakfast room. It's a good place for a few nights. Stay anywhere else around here and you'll be forking out at least three times as much.

IN KINGS CROSS & THE SUBURBS BEYOND
VERY EXPENSIVE

The Landmark Parkroyal. 81 Macleay St., Potts Point, NSW 2011. ☎ **02/9368 3000.**
Fax 02/9357 7600. www.sphc.com.au. E-mail: reservations@landmark.parkroyal.com.au.
463 units. A/C MINIBAR TV TEL. A$327–$439 (U.S.$212–$285) double; A$950 (U.S.$617) suite.
Extra bed A$30 (U.S.$19.50). Children under 14 stay free in parents' room. Ask about weekend
and other excellent money-saving packages. AE, BC, DC, JCB, MC, V. Parking A$15 (U.S.$9.75).
CityRail: Kings Cross, then about a 1km (¹/₂-mile) walk. Bus: 311 from Circular Quay.

This top-flight hotel is where airline pilots stay when they're stopping off in Sydney.
Though not slap bang in the city center, it's just a 5-minute walk from Kings Cross station and very close to some of the city's best restaurants. The grand lobby leads to the
restaurant, which serves an interesting buffet. The recently refurbished guest rooms are
good sized and have large windows that open. Some rooms have spectacular views over
the inner harbor, the Heads, and parts of the city; others have good skyline views; while
still others look over the Sydney Opera House and the Harbour Bridge. Bathrooms are
small but come with a tub/shower combination. Guests on the two club floors (the
16th and 17th) receive complimentary breakfast and drinks every evening.

Dining: The hotel's restaurant serves a seafood buffet and Asian gourmet foods.

Amenities: Small outdoor pool, free access to nearby gym, concierge, 24-hour
room service, free daily newspaper, nightly turndown, shoe shine, laundry, valet, baby-
sitting, gift shop, jogging track, courtesy limo.

Ritz-Carlton Double Bay. 33 Cross St., Double Bay, NSW 2028. ☎ **800/241-3333** in the
U.S. and Canada, 0800/443 030 in New Zealand, 0800/234 000 in the U.K, 1300/361 180 in
Australia, or 02/9362 4455. Fax 02/9362 4744. www.ritzcarlton.com. 140 units. A/C MINI-
BAR TV TEL. A$349–$409 (U.S.$226.85–$265.85) double; from A$499 (U.S.$324.35) suite.
A$399–$449 (U.S.$259–$291) Club floor. AE, BC, DC, JCB, MC, V. Parking A$15 (U.S.$9.75).
CityRail: Edgecliff, then about a 1km (¹/₂-mile) walk. Bus: 325 or 324 from Circular Quay.
Ferry: Double Bay.

Madonna, the late Princess Diana, Tom Jones, George Bush, Neil Diamond—they've
all stayed in this five-star darling of the rich and famous, situated about 4 kilometers
(2.5 miles) from the city center in Sydney's poshest harborside suburb. The grand
lobby is decked out in a maritime theme, the corridors are somberly lit, and antiques
and Persian rugs are scattered tastefully here and there. The large guest rooms are done
in Regency style and are almost unnervingly quiet. Everything you would expect at the
best in town is here, from the enormous TV and the fluffy bathrobes down to designer
bathtub salts and a perfect, single rose. Most rooms have balconies with water views.

Dining/Diversions: The Grill serves good continental cuisine in an intimate, elegant environment; the plush Bar is popular for cigars and brandy; and The Lobby
Lounge is wonderfully civilized for breakfast and a favorite lunch and afternoon tea
spot for the local social set.

Amenities: Heated rooftop pool, fitness center, concierge, 24-hour room service,
nightly turndown, twice-daily maid service, valet, baby-sitting, separate kosher kitchen,
business center, meeting facilities, sundry/gift shop, currency exchange.

EXPENSIVE

The Kirketon. 229 Darlinghurst Rd., Darlinghurst. ☎ **02/9332 2011.** Fax 02/9332 2499.
www.kirketon.com.au. E-mail: info@kirketon.com.au. 40 units. A/C MINIBAR TV TEL. A$220
(U.S.$143) junior room, A$275 (U.S.$178.75) premium room, A$365 (U.S.$237.25) execu-
tive room. Rooms only for 1 or 2 people. AE, BC, DC, MC, V. Free parking in garage around
the corner (ask in advance for directions).

If you want to stay somewhere a bit offbeat, and fancy yourself as a hip, fashionable
type, then this boutique hotel in busy Darlinghurst is a fascinating option. Rooms are

lightly stocked with modernist furniture and custom-made fittings, including mirrored headboards on the beds, sleek bathrooms hidden away behind mirrored doors, and interestingly textured bedspreads. There are all the usual conveniences, plus extras like CD players and dataports. All in all, it's quite fun if you like this sleek sort of thing, though personally I found it jarred with my more conventional tastes. Junior rooms are quite compact, some of the premium rooms come with a tub as well as shower, and the quite large executive rooms have VCRs. Some have small balconies, but because they overlook the busy, noisy (especially at night) main road, I wouldn't consider these much of a benefit. The best junior room is number 330, the best premium room is number 340, and the best executive room is number 323.

Dining/Diversions: There are a designer bar and cocktail lounge downstairs, and the hip Salt (see "Dining," later in this chapter) restaurant, which at the time of writing was the flavor of the month.

Amenities: Complimentary access to gym across the road, concierge, room service, nightly turndown, laundry service, postal and business services, baby-sitting, express checkout.

INEXPENSIVE

DeVere Hotel. 44–46 Macleay St., Potts Point, NSW 2011. ☎ **1800/818 790** in Australia, 0800/441 779 in New Zealand, or 02/9358 1211. Fax 02/9358 4685. www.devere.com.au. E-mail: info@devere.com.au. 98 units. A/C TV TEL. A$107.90 (U.S.$70) double; A$140.60 (U.S.$91.40) superior room; A$162.40 (U.S.$105.50) executive room; A$206 (U.S.$133.90) suite. Extra person A$32.70 (U.S.$21.25). Children under 12 stay free in parents' room. AE, BC, DC, MC, V. Parking at nearby Landmark Hotel A$12 (U.S.$7.80) per exit. CityRail: Kings Cross. Bus: 311 from Circular Quay.

The DeVere has been recommended by several readers who commented on the friendly staff and the bargain-basement room prices when booked at the Tourism New South Wales Travel Centre at the Sydney airport. Although the rooms are very modern, they are a little too standard gray corporate for my liking (though the owner says some are now yellow). Superior rooms are a bit larger, and the executive room is larger still and comes with nicer furniture. However, they are certainly a bargain compared to similar, but far more expensive, rooms elsewhere in Sydney. The suites have views of Elizabeth Bay, a spa bath, and a king-size bed rather than a queen. Some suites have a pretty useless kitchenette with no cooking facilities. Some standard rooms have an extra single bed. Breakfast is available from A$8 (U.S.$5.20).

✪ **Hotel 59.** 59 Bayswater Rd., Kings Cross, NSW 2011. ☎ **02/9360 5900.** Fax 02/9360 1828. www.interspace.net.au/inns/hotel59. E-mail: hotel59@enternet.com.au. 8 units. A/C TV TEL. A$115–$135 (U.S.$74.75–$87.75) double. Extra person A$15 (U.S.$9.75), extra children 2–12 A$10 (U.S.$6.50). Rates include cooked breakfast. BC, MC, V. Limited parking A$5 (U.S.$3.25). CityRail: Kings Cross.

This popular and friendly B&B is well worth considering if you want to be near the Kings Cross action, but just far enough away to get a decent night's sleep. Deluxe rooms have either a queen- or king-size bed and a combined shower and tub, while the smaller standard rooms come with a double bed and a shower (no tub). If you bring your kids here—or to any other Kings Cross area hotel—they'll get an eyeful of prostitutes and sex bars on the way to and from the CityRail station. The two large superior rooms come with two single beds and two more that can be locked together to form a king, and a separate living room. One unit has a small kitchen with a microwave and hot plates. All rooms are very clean and comfortable and have private bathrooms. There is also a small guest lounge with a TV. A fully cooked breakfast is served up in the cafe below. A flight of stairs (there's no elevator) might make this a bad choice for travelers with mobility problems.

The Jolly Swagman Backpackers. 27 Orwell St., Kings Cross, NSW 2011. ☎ **1800/805 870** in Australia, or 02/9358 6400. Fax 02/9331 0125. www.jollyswagman.com.au. E-mail: stay@jollyswagman.com.au. 53 units. A$16 (U.S.$10.40) dorm bed; A$22 (U.S.$14.30) per person in double. Ask about 3-day, 5-day, and weekly deals. MC, V. On-street metered parking. CityRail: Kings Cross.

This is one of the best of the backpacker hostels that dot the area between Darling-hurst Road and Victoria Street in Kings Cross. The good thing about this place is that it has two sister properties right near by, so you're almost certain to get a room. The 18 dorm rooms in this property have only two sets of bunk beds in each, which means things don't get too crowded—and couples traveling together will often find they get the room to themselves. There are also plenty of twin and double rooms to go around, as well as two female-only dorms. The atmosphere is young and typical backpacker, with cheap meals (all under A$5/U.S.$3.25) served in the ground-floor cafe. There's a guest kitchen, two TV rooms, a laundry, an ironing room, bag storage, free movies, 24-hour Internet access, and a 24-hour travel agency. Each room is spotless and comes with a security locker.

Victoria Court Sydney. 122 Victoria St., Potts Point, NSW 2011. ☎ **1800/630 505** in Australia, or 02/9357 3200. Fax 02/9357 7606. www.VictoriaCourt.com.au. E-mail: info@ VictoriaCourt.com.au. 22 units. A/C TV TEL. A$99–$115 (U.S.$64.35–$74.75) double, depending on the season; A$165 (U.S.$107.25) deluxe double with sundeck; A$250 (U.S.$162.50) honeymoon suite with balcony. Rates include buffet breakfast. Extra person A$20 (U.S.$13). AE, BC, DC, MC, V. Free parking in secured lot. CityRail: Kings Cross.

This cute little place is made up of two 1881 terrace houses joined together; it's situated near a string of backpacker hostels and popular cafes in a leafy street running parallel to sleazy Darlinghurst Road. The glass-roofed breakfast room on the ground floor is a work of art decked out with hanging ferns, giant bamboo, wrought-iron tables and chairs, and a trickling fountain. Just off this is a peaceful guest lounge stacked with books and newspapers. The very plush rooms come with either king- or queen-size beds but lack a tub in the bathroom. There's a coin-op laundry just down the road.

IN PADDINGTON/OXFORD STREET
MODERATE

Oxford Koala Hotel. Corner of Oxford & Pelican sts., Darlinghurst (P.O. Box 535, Darlinghurst, NSW 2010). ☎ **1800/222 144** in Australia (outside Sydney), or 02/9269 0645. Fax 02/9283 2741. www.oxfordkoala.com.au. 330 units (including 78 apts), some with shower only. A/C TV TEL. A$135–$155 (U.S. $87.75–$100.75) double; A$185–$205 (U.S. $120.25–$133.25) 1-bedroom apt. Extra person A$25 (U.S.$16.25). Children under 12 stay free in parents' room. AE, BC, DC, JCB, MC, V. Parking A$15 (U.S.$9.75) a day. Bus: 380 or any bus traveling via Taylor Square.

This place offers great value. A very popular tourist hotel, it's well located just off trendy Oxford Street, a 5- to 10-minute bus trip from the city center and Circular Quay. There are 13 floors of rooms in this tower block; rooms on the top floor have reasonable views over the city. Superior rooms are very comfortable and more spacious than standard rooms and have better furniture. All come with either shower/tub combinations or just showers. Good-sized apartments come with a full kitchen and are serviced daily. On the premises are a swimming pool, a restaurant, and a cocktail bar.

Sullivans. 21 Oxford St., Paddington, NSW 2021. ☎ **02/9361 0211.** Fax 02/9360 3735. www.sullivans.com.au. E-mail: sydney@sullivans.com.au. 64 units (all with showers only). A/C TV TEL. A$125 (U.S.$81.25) double. AE, BC, DC, MC, V. Limited free parking. Bus: 378, or 380 from Circular Quay.

About half of this boutique hotel's guests come from overseas, mainly from the U.S. and the U.K. There's also a small corporate following. Sullivans is right in the heart of the action in one of Sydney's most popular shopping, entertainment, restaurant, and gay pub and club areas. The hotel is particularly popular with Americans during the Gay and Lesbian Mardi Gras, held over the month of February. Rooms are cozy, with queen-size beds and refrigerators. There are free loaner bicycles, a small swimming pool, and a garden courtyard.

INEXPENSIVE

Wattle Private Hotel. 108 Oxford St. (at corner of Palmer St.), Darlinghurst, NSW 2010. ☎ **02/9332 4118.** Fax 02/9331 2074. E-mail: wattlehotel@yahoo.com.au. 12 units. A/C MINIBAR TV TEL. A$99 (U.S.$64.35) double. Extra person A$11 (U.S.$7.15). Rates include continental breakfast. BC, MC, V. No parking. Bus: Any bus to Taylor Square from Circular Quay.

This attractive Edwardian-style house built between 1900 and 1910 offers homey accommodations in the increasingly fashionable inner-city suburb of Darlinghurst, known for its great cafes, nightlife, and restaurants. Rooms are on four stories, but there's no elevator; so if you don't fancy too many stairs, ask for a room on the lower floor. Rooms are smallish but are opened up by large windows. Twin rooms have a better bathroom, with a tub. The decor is a jumble of Chinese vases, ceiling fans, and contemporary bedspreads. Laundry facilities are on the premises. The owners are very friendly.

IN GLEBE
MODERATE

✪ **Tricketts Luxury Bed & Breakfast.** 270 Glebe Point Rd., Glebe, NSW 2037. ☎ **02/9552 1141.** Fax 02/9692 9462. www.citysearch.com.au/syd/trickettsbandb. 7 units. A$154–A$176 (U.S.$100–$114) double; A$198 (U.S.$128.70) honeymoon suite. Rates include continental breakfast. No credit cards. Free parking. Bus: 431 from George St., or Airport Express bus 352 from airport.

As soon as I walked into this atmospheric old place, I wanted to ditch my modern Sydney apartment and move in. Your first impression as you enter the tessellated tiled corridor of this 1880s Victorian mansion is the amazing jumble of plants and ornaments, the high ceilings, the Oriental rugs, and the leaded windows. Guests play billiards over a decanter of port, or relax among magazines and wicker furniture on the balcony overlooking the fairly busy Glebe Point Road. The bedrooms are quiet and homey (no TVs). My favorites are number 2, with its wooden floorboards and king-size bed, and number 7, with its queen-size bed, extra single bed, and very large bathroom. Rooms all have showers. There's a nice courtyard out the back with a barbecue.

INEXPENSIVE

Alishan International Guest House. 100 Glebe Point Rd., Glebe, NSW 2037. ☎ **02/9566 4048.** Fax 02/9525 4686. 19 units (all with shower only). www.alishan.com.au. E-mail: kevin@alishan.com.au. TV. A$30 (U.S.$19.50) dorm bed; A$100 (U.S.$65) double; A$145 (U.S.$94.25) family room. Extra person A$15 (U.S.$9.75). AE, BC, MC, V. Secured parking available for 6 cars, otherwise free on-street parking. Bus: 431 or 433 from George St., or Airport Express route 352 from airport.

The Alishan is another quiet place with a real Aussie feel. It's at the city end of Glebe Point Road, just 10 minutes by bus from the shops around Town Hall. Standard dorm rooms are spotless, are light and bright, and come with two sets of bunks. Each double has a double bed, a sofa, and an armchair. Grab room 9 if you fancy sleeping on one of two single mattresses on the tatami mat floor, Japanese-style. There are also a BBQ area, a TV room, a laundry, and Internet access.

IN BONDI

Bondi Beach is a good place to stay if you want to be close to the surf and sand, though if you're getting around by public transport, you'll need to catch a bus to Bondi Junction, then a train to the city center (you can stay on the bus all the way, but it takes forever).

EXPENSIVE

Swiss-Grand Hotel. Corner of Campbell Parade and Beach Rd. (P.O. Box 219), Bondi Beach, NSW 2026. ☎ **1800/655 252** in Australia, 800/344-1212 in the U.S., 0800/951 000 in the U.K., 0800/056 666 in New Zealand, or 02/9365 5666. Fax 02/9365 9710. www.swissgrand. com.au. 230 units. A/C TV TEL. A$297 (U.S.$193) double, A$341 (U.S.$221) double with ocean view; suites from A$385 (U.S.$250). Extra person A$44 (U.S.$28.60). AE, BC, DC, MC, V. Free parking. Bus: 380 from Circular Quay.

Situated right on Bondi Beach, overlooking the Pacific, the Swiss-Grand is the best hotel in Bondi. The lobby is grand indeed, with high ceilings and stylish furniture. Rooms are spacious, and all come with a separate tub and shower in a rather luxurious bathroom. All rooms have two TVs; some have spas. All ocean-fronting rooms have balconies. The hotel is very popular with families, tour groups, and honeymooners, who come here for the proximity to the beach, as well as the touch of romance this oceanside lookout offers.

Dining: The Garden Terrace has good views over the beach, and the stylishly elegant Epic Brassiere offers an impressive buffet. The lobby bar is relaxed and has live piano music in the evenings.

Amenities: Rooftop and indoor swimming pools, spa, fitness center.

MODERATE

Ravesi's on Bondi Beach. Corner of Hall St. and Campbell Parade, Bondi Beach, NSW 2026. ☎ **02/9365 4422.** Fax 02/9365 1481. E-mail: Ravesis@wheretostay.com.au. 16 units. A/C TV TEL. A$115.50 (U.S.$75) standard double; A$176–$181.50 (U.S.$114–$118) double with side view; A$209–$236.50 (U.S.$135.85–$153.75) one-bedroom suite. Penthouse $324.50 (U.S.$210). Extra person A$20 (U.S. $13). Two children under 12 stay free in parents' room. AE, BC, DC, MC, V. Parking at the Swiss-Grand Hotel nearby for A$5 (U.S.$3.25) for 24 hr. CityRail: Bondi Junction; then bus 380. Bus: 380 from Circular Quay.

Right on Australia's most famous golden sands, this art deco boutique property offers Mediterranean-influenced rooms with a beachy decor. Standard doubles are spacious but quite basic (they don't have air-conditioning, though you hardly need it with the ocean breeze). The one-bedroom suites are good for families, with two sofa beds in the living room. A split-level one-bedroom suite has a bedroom upstairs and a single sofa bed in the living area. Rooms 5 and 6 and the split-level suite have the best views of the ocean. All rooms have Juliet balconies, and the split-level suite has its own terrace. If you're a light sleeper, request a room on the top floor because the popular Ravesi's Restaurant can cook up quite a bit of noise on busy nights.

IN MANLY

If you decide to stay at my favorite beachside suburb, keep in mind that the ferries from the city stop running at midnight. Taxi fare from the city is around A$35 (U.S.$22.75), or you can catch a night bus from the stand behind Wynyard Station.

If you're looking for a super-cheap place to stay, consider the **Manly Backpackers Beachside,** 28 Ragland St. (☎ **02/9977 3411**), where a double with a bathroom goes for A$55 (U.S.$35.75); or the ✪ **Wharf Backpackers,** 48 E. Esplanade (☎ **02/ 9977 2800**), opposite the ferry terminal, with doubles for A$40 (U.S.$26).

EXPENSIVE

✪ **Manly Pacific Parkroyal.** 55 N. Steyne, Manly, NSW 2095. ☎ **800/835-7742** in the U.S. and Canada, or 02/9977 7666. Fax 02/9977 7822. www.parkroyal.com.au. 169 units. A/C MINIBAR TV TEL. A$283–$327 (U.S.$184–$212) double, depending on view; A$512 (U.S.$332.80) suite. Extra person A$32 (U.S.$20.80). AE, BC, DC, JCB, MC, V. Parking: $10 (U.S.$6.50). Ferry or JetCat: Manly.

If you could bottle the views from this top-class hotel—across the sand and through the Norfolk Island Pines to the Pacific Ocean—you'd make a fortune. Standing on your private balcony in the evening with the sea breeze in your nostrils and the chirping of hundreds of lorikeets is nothing short of heaven. The Manly Pacific is the only hotel of its class in this wonderful beachside suburb. There's nothing claustrophobic here, from the broad expanse of glittering foyer to the wide corridors and spacious rooms. Each standard room is light and modern with two double beds, a balcony, limited cable TV, and all the necessities, from bathrobes to an iron and ironing board. Views over the ocean are really worth the extra money. The hotel is a 10-minute stroll, or a A$4 (U.S.$2.60) taxi ride, from the Manly ferry.

Dining/Diversions: Gilbert's Restaurant has fine dining and views of the Pacific. Nells Brasserie & Cocktail Bar serves a buffet breakfast and dinner daily. The Charlton & Star Bar and Grill has live bands every evening from Wednesday to Sunday and attracts a young crowd.

Amenities: Rooftop spa, pool, gym, sauna, concierge, 24-hour room service, laundry.

MODERATE

Manly Lodge. 22 Victoria Parade, Manly, NSW 2095. ☎ **02/9977 8655.** Fax 02/9976 2090. www.manlylodge.com.au. 24 units. A/C TV. Standard double A$132–A$154 (U.S.$85.80–$100) peak season, A$107.80–$132 (U.S.$69.70–$85.80) off-season; deluxe double A$154–$198 (U.S.$100–$128) peak season, A$132–$154 (U.S.$85.50–$100) off-season; family suite with spa A$264–$330 (U.S.$171.60–$214.50) peak season, A$187–$262 (U.S.$121.55–$170) off-season. Peak season is Christmas, Easter, and school holidays. Rates include continental breakfast. Extra person A$30 (U.S.$19.50); children under 10 A$16.50 (U.S.$10.70) extra. Ask about weekly rates; management will also negotiate off-season prices. AE, BC, MC, V. Free parking. Ferry or JetCat: Manly.

At first sight, this ramshackle building halfway between the main beach and the harbor doesn't look like much—especially the cramped hostel-like foyer bristling with tourist brochures. But don't let that put you off. Some of the rooms here are lovely, and the whole place has a nice atmosphere about it and plenty of character. Double rooms are unexceptional, with a double bed, stone or carpet floors, a TV and VCR, and either a spa or a tub/shower combination. Some of the standard doubles and all of the deluxe doubles have a kitchen. Family rooms have a set of bunk beds and a double in one room, and a shower. Family suites are very classy: each has a small kitchen area, one double and three singles in the bedroom, and two sofa beds in the living area. The lodge also has a communal spa, sauna, gym, laundry, table tennis, and even an Olympic-size trampoline.

Periwinkle–Manly Cove Guesthouse. 18–19 E. Esplanade, Manly, NSW 2095. ☎ **02/9977 4668.** Fax 02/9977 6308. 18 units, 11 with private bathroom. TV. A$126 (U.S.$81.90) double without bathroom; A$165 (U.S.$107.25) double with bathroom; A$148 (U.S.$96.20) triple without bathroom; A$176 (U.S.$114.40) triple with bathroom. Harbor-view units A$11 (U.S.$7.15) extra. Extra person A$33 (U.S.$21.45). Rates include continental breakfast. BC, MC, V. Free parking. Ferry or JetCat: Manly.

Nicely positioned just across the road from one of Manly's two harbor beaches, the Periwinkle is just a short walk from the ferry, the shops along the Corso, and the main ocean beach. Rooms are small and come with a double bed, a small TV, and a refrigerator. Some have a shower and toilet; otherwise, you'll have to make do with one of four shared bathrooms (one has a tub). A full kitchen next to a pleasant-enough communal lounge means you could save money by not eating out. Rooms 5 and 10 are the nicest and have screened balconies overlooking the harbor (but no bathrooms). For atmosphere, I prefer the Manly Lodge (see above). No smoking inside.

INEXPENSIVE

✪ **Manly Paradise Motel and Beach Plaza Apartments.** 54 N. Steyne, Manly, NSW 2095. ☎ **1800/815 789** in Australia, or 02/9977 5799. Fax 02/9977 6848. www. manlyparadise.com.au. E-mail: enquiries@manlyparadise.com.au. 40 units. A/C TV TEL. A$95–$145 (U.S.$61.75–$94.25) double motel unit; A$265 (U.S.$172.25) 2-bedroom apt. Extra person A$20 (U.S.$13). Ask about lower rates for long-term stays. AE, BC, DC, MC, V. Free secured parking. Ferry or JetCat: Manly.

I walked into this place after taking a good look around the modern Manly Waterfront Apartment Hotel next door and immediately felt more at home here. The motel and the apartment complex are separate but share the same reception area. Though there is one motel room that goes for A$90 (U.S.$58.50), it's a bit small for my liking; the rest of the irregularly shaped rooms are big yet cozy and come with a shower (no tub) and a springy double bed. Though there is no restaurant, you can get breakfast in bed. My only concern is that the traffic outside can make it a little noisy during the day (but, hey, you'll probably be on the beach anyway). Some rooms have glimpses of the sea. A swimming pool (with views) on the roof is shared with the apartment complex.

The apartments are magnificent—very roomy, with thick carpets. They're stocked with everything you need, including a private laundry, a full kitchen with dishwasher, and two bathrooms (one with a tub). The sea views from the main front balcony are heart-stopping.

ON THE NORTH SHORE
EXPENSIVE

Duxton Hotel. 88 Alfred St., Milsons Point, NSW 2061. ☎ **02/9955 1111.** Fax 02/9955 3522. www.duxton.com. 165 units. A/C MINIBAR TV TEL. A$291.50 (U.S.$189.50) double; A$374 (U.S.$243) suite. Extra person A$22 (U.S.$14.30). AE, BC, DC, MC, V. Free parking. CityRail: Milsons Point.

One of the newest hotels on the North Shore, the four-star Duxton Hotel is at the far end of the Harbour Bridge, right opposite the Milsons Point CityRail station. Some rooms and all suites have fabulous views of the yachts moored in Lavender Bay and across the water to the Harbour Bridge and the Opera House. Rooms are light and comfortable, with satellite TV and pay-per-view movies. The hotel is especially popular with business travelers.

Dining: The hotel's restaurant has an extensive selection of finely prepared Modern Australian dishes.

Amenities: Small pool and sauna, concierge, 24-hour room service, free daily newspaper, laundry, baby-sitting, business center.

INEXPENSIVE

✪ **Buena Vista Hotel.** 76 Middle Head Rd., Mosman, NSW 2095. ☎ **02/9969 7022.** Fax 02/9968 2879. 14 units, none with private bathroom. TV. A$82.50 (U.S.$53.60) double; A$99 (U.S.$65) family room. Rates double over Christmas and New Year's. Rates include continental breakfast. AE, BC, DC, MC, V. Ferry: Taronga Zoo, then a 5-min. bus ride. Bus: Taronga Zoo from Wynyard Station.

If you want to see how wealthy Sydneysiders live (but without paying high prices), then come and stay in this exclusive suburb just a 10-minute walk from Taronga Zoo.

The rooms above this popular local pub, just down the road from some of Sydney's most exclusive boutiques, are clean and comfortable, and a bargain by Sydney standards. Each comes with a springy queen-size bed or two singles, a small TV, and a sink; a few have balconies. All except room 13 have good city views. The best is room 1, which is larger and brighter than the rest and comes with a large balcony with good views. Family rooms come with a double bed, a foldout sofa bed, and a trundle bed—all in one room. All rooms share nice bathrooms. The fabulous Balmoral Beach is a 10-minute walk away, or just 5 minutes by bus. Ask hotel staff for ferry times and bus/ferry connection details from Taronga Zoo and Mosman wharves. Taxi from city around $22 (U.S.$14.30).

AT THE AIRPORT

The two airport hotels listed below also accommodate guests for short-term stays between flights. Sample costs for the Sheraton are A$60 (U.S.$39) for 2 hours and A$70 (U.S.$45.50) for 4 hours.

EXPENSIVE

Sheraton Sydney Airport Hotel. Corner of O'Riordan and Robey sts. (P.O. Box 353), Mascot, Sydney, NSW 2020. ☎ **1800/073 535** in Australia, 800/325-3535 in the U.S. and Canada, 0800/353 535 in the U.K., 0800/443 535 in New Zealand, or 02/9317 2200. Fax 02/9317 2200. 314 units. A/C MINIBAR TV TEL. A$240–$265 double (U.S.$156–$172.25); from A$390 (U.S.$253.50) and up for suites. Extra person A$25 (U.S.$16.25). Children under 17 stay free in parents' room. Ask about discount packages and weekend rates. AE, BC, DC, JCB, MC, V. A$5 (U.S.$3.25) self-parking fee for up to 10 days.

This is the only five-star airport hotel in Australia. Opened in 1992, it has the largest rooms, each with a king-size bed or two doubles, in-house movies, access to airport information, and good-size bathrooms with tubs. It's just 7 minutes from the airport via a free pickup service. There are also a fine gym and a good outdoor swimming pool.

Dining/Diversions: The two restaurants here serve buffet and à la carte meals. There's also a lounge bar.

Amenities: Pool, spa and sauna, fitness center, massage, concierge, 24-hour room service, laundry, valet, free daily newspapers, nightly turndown, business center, meeting facilities, baby-sitting, currency exchange.

MODERATE

Sydney Airport Parkroyal. Corner of O'Riordan St. and Bourke Rd., Mascot, NSW 2020. ☎ **1800/621 859** in Australia, or 02/9330 0600. Fax 02/9667 4517. www.parkroyal. com.au. E-mail: gm@syd-airport.parkroyal.com.au. 244 units. A/C MINIBAR TV TEL. A$185 (U.S.$120.25) double; A$390 (U.S.$253.50) suite. Extra person A$25 (U.S.$16.25). Children under 15 stay free in parents' room. Ask about special weekend rates and packages. AE, BC, DC, JCB, MC, V. Free parking.

The Parkroyal is a modern hotel with all the facilities you'd expect except a swimming pool. Rooms are of a moderate size, with either a king- or queen-size bed, in-house movies, and facilities to access the airport arrival and departure information. Free shuttle buses take 5 minutes to and from the airport. The Parkroyal's service can be variable, but you'll probably not be here for too long.

Amelia's Brasserie and the Biggles Bar and Cafe both serve up food. There's also a comfortable bar. Other facilities include a fitness center, concierge, 24-hour room service, laundry, free daily newspapers, business and meeting facilities, and currency exchange.

4 Dining

Sydney is a gourmet paradise, with an abundance of fresh seafood, a vast range of vegetables and fruit always in season, prime meats at inexpensive prices, and top-quality chefs making international names for themselves. You'll find that Asian and Mediterranean cooking have had a major influence on Australian cuisine, with spices and herbs finding their way into most dishes. Immigration has brought with it almost every type of cuisine you could imagine, from African to Tibetan, from Russian to Vietnamese, with whole areas of the city dedicated to one type of food, while other areas are a true melting pot of styles.

Sydney is a great place to try "Modern Australian," or "Mod Oz," cuisine, which has been applauded by chefs and food critics around the world as one of the most important food trends going. Modern Australian cuisine emphasizes very fresh ingredients and a creative blend of simple European styles with touches of Asian influence. (Some foodies complain, however, that some restaurants use the label "Modern Australian" as an excuse to serve skimpy portions—like one lamb chop atop a miniscule dollop of mashed potatoes.)

The **Cockle Bay Wharf complex,** on the city side of Darling Harbour, has an array of new and highly recommended restaurants, including **Ampersand** (see below), and the Southern Mediterranean–influenced **Coast** (☎ **02/9267 6700**). Other popular restaurants here include **Chinta Ria, The Temple of Love** (see below); the bustling **Blackbird** (☎ **02/9283 7385**), a cafe with gourmet pizzas; the fiery south Indian **Tandoori Connection** (☎ **02/9283 6707**); and the **Tiara Japanese Brasserie** (☎ **02/9264 5822**).

Sydney's **cheap eats** are congregated in inner-city areas: along King Street in Newtown, Crown Street in Darlinghurst, and Glebe Point Road in Glebe. There are also inexpensive joints scattered among the more upscale restaurants in Kings Cross and along trendy Oxford Street. There are some good food courts around Chinatown, including the **Sussex Street Food Court,** on Sussex Street, which offers Chinese, Malay, Thai, Japanese, and Vietnamese meals for between A$4 and $7 (U.S.$2.60 and $4.55).

I would avoid the takeout booths settled among the ferry wharves at Circular Quay. Recent revelations showed that some of them harbor nasty bugs. **Quay Seafoods,** the fish-and-chip shop opposite the bottle shop is an exception; it serves up some of the best french fries in Sydney.

NEAR CIRCULAR QUAY
VERY EXPENSIVE

Bennelong Restaurant. In the Sydney Opera House, Bennelong Point. ☎ **02/9250 7548** or 02/9250 7578. Reservations recommended. Main courses A$30–$37 (U.S.$19.50–$24). AE, BC, DC, MC, V. Fri noon–2:30pm; Mon–Sat 7–10:30pm. CityRail, bus, or ferry: Circular Quay. MODERN AUSTRALIAN.

If you go to Bondi, you have to swim in the Pacific. Similarly, if you visit the Opera House, you have to eat at the Bennelong—although I do keep hearing rumors about arrogant service. The restaurant is as uniquely designed as the building itself, with tall glass windows furrowing around in an arch and grabbing the harbor and Circular Quay by the throat. Diners munch on main courses like roasted tuna steak and roasted tomato with tomato-and-chili jam, or red emperor (a local fish) with sweet-and-sour eggplant baked in clay. Many patrons would miss the first half of the opera they've paid a fortune to see rather than leave the Bennelong before eating dessert.

What to Know About BYO

Most moderate and inexpensive restaurants in Sydney are BYO, as in "bring your own bottle, though some places may also have extensive wine and beer lists of their own. More and more moderately priced restaurants are introducing "corkage" fees, which mean you pay anywhere from A$1 to $4 (U.S.65¢ to $2.60) per person for the privilege of the waiter opening your bottle of wine. Very expensive restaurants discourage BYO.

✪ **Forty One.** Level 41, Chifley Tower, 2 Chifley Sq. ☎ **02/9221 2500.** Reservations required. Lunch main courses Mon–Fri A$28 (U.S.$18.20). Sun lunch: 3 courses A$85 (U.S.$55.25), 4 courses A$95 (U.S.$61.75), 5 courses A$110 (U.S.$71.50). Mon–Sat dinner: 3 courses A$75 (U.S.$48.75), 4 courses A$85 (U.S.$55.25), 5 courses A$95 (U.S.$61.75). AE, BC, DC, MC, V. Sun–Fri noon–4pm; Mon–Sat 6:30pm–late. CityRail: Wynyard. MODERN AUSTRALIAN.

Powerful people, international celebrities, and average Sydneysiders out for a special celebration all come here to feel exclusive. This restaurant has won some 32 awards from 1994 to 1998 for its cooking, including the Restaurant and Catering Association's 1998 Award for best restaurant in Sydney. The views over the city are terrific, the service is fun, the cutlery is the world's best, and Swiss chef Dietmar Sawyere has given the food a wickedly good Asian slant. In all, it's a very glamorous place to experience the best of Australian cuisine. Try the specialty crown roast wild hare, with braised Belgian endive and chartreuse jus. The seared yellowfin tuna on sesame and miso English spinach is another favorite. If there are 6 to 10 people in your group, rent one of the three special private dining rooms.

EXPENSIVE

Botanic Gardens Restaurant. In the Royal Botanic Gardens. ☎ **02/9241 2419.** Reservations recommended. Main courses A$18–$25 (U.S.$11.70–$16.25). AE, BC, DC, MC, V. Daily noon–2:30pm. Bus or ferry: Circular Quay. MEDITERRANEAN.

You couldn't ask for a better prelude to a meal than strolling through the Royal Botanic Gardens, next to the Sydney Opera House. Enjoying lunch on the wisteria-covered balcony in the middle of Sydney's most beautiful park is a treat every visitor should enjoy. Main courses include the very popular roast loin of lamb with warm salad and couscous. Just reminiscing about the desserts, such as the rhubarb compote with zabaglione and shortbread, makes my mouth water.

Sydney Cove Oyster Bar. No. 1 Eastern Esplanade, Circular Quay East. ☎ **02/9247 2937.** Main courses A$20–$23.50 (U.S.$13–$15.30). 10% surcharge weekends and public holidays. AE, BC, DC, MC, V. Mon–Sat 11am–11pm, Sun 11am–8pm. CityRail, bus, or ferry: Circular Quay. SEAFOOD.

Just before you reach the Sydney Opera House you'll notice a couple of small shedlike buildings with tables and chairs set up to take in the stunning views of the harbor and

A Word About Smoking

Smoking is allowed in the vast majority of Sydney's restaurants, but if you do light up you'll find you won't be the most popular person in the place. Some restaurants have a no-smoking section. Moves to ban smoking in restaurants were underway at press time, so check before you puff.

Central Sydney Dining

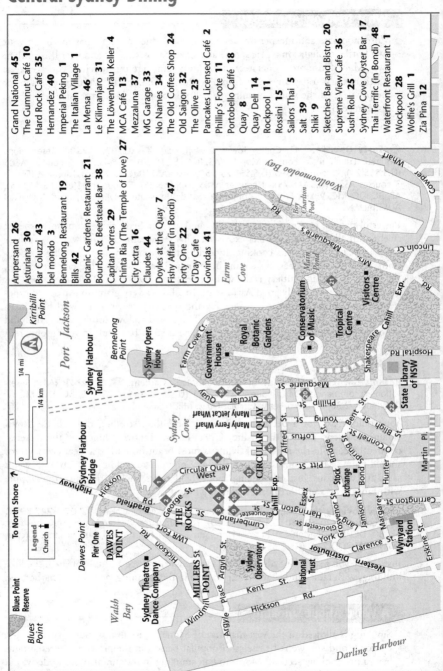

Ampersand **26**
Asturiana **30**
Bar Coluzzi **43**
bel mondo **3**
Bennelong Restaurant **19**
Bills **42**
Botanic Gardens Restaurant **21**
Bourbon & Beefsteak Bar **38**
Capitan Torres **29**
Chinta Ria (The Temple of Love) **27**
City Extra **16**
Claudes **44**
Doyles at the Quay **7**
Fishy Affair (in Bondi) **47**
Forty One **22**
G'Day Cafe **6**
Govindas **41**

Grand National **45**
The Gumnut Café **10**
Hard Rock Cafe **35**
Hernandez **40**
Imperial Peking **1**
The Italian Village **1**
La Mensa **46**
Le Kilimanjaro **31**
The Löwenbräu Keller **4**
MCA Café **13**
Mezzaluna **37**
MG Garage **33**
No Names **34**
The Old Coffee Shop **24**
Old Saigon **32**
The Olive **23**
Pancakes Licensed Café **2**
Phillip's Foote **11**
Portobello Caffé **18**
Quay **8**
Quay Deli **14**
Rockpool **11**
Rossini **15**
Sailors Thai **5**
Salt **39**
Shiki **9**
Sketches Bar and Bistro **20**
Supreme View Cafe **36**
Sushi Roll **25**
Sydney Cove Oyster Bar **17**
Thai Terrific (in Bondi) **48**
Waterfront Restaurant **1**
Wockpool **28**
Wolfie's Grill **1**
Zia Pina **12**

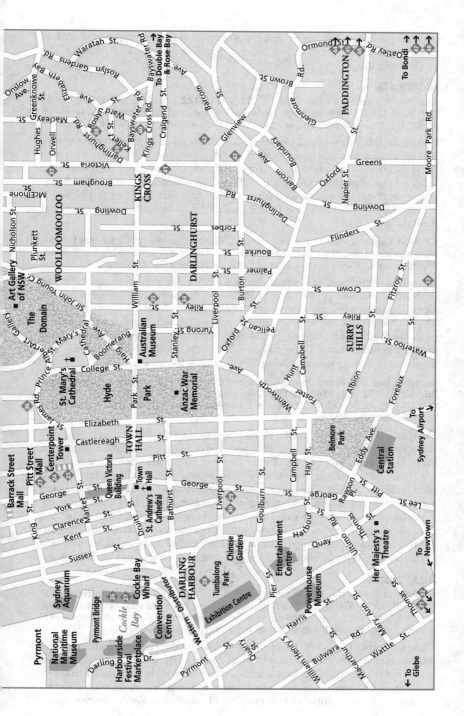

the Harbour Bridge. The first of these is a Sydney institution, serving some of the best oysters in town. Light meals such as Asian-style octopus and seared tuna steak are also on the menu.

MODERATE

City Extra. Shop E4, Circular Quay. ☎ **02/9241 1422.** Main courses A$10.30–$17.65 (U.S.$6.70–$11.50). 10% surcharge midnight–6am, Sun, and public holidays. Daily 24 hr. AE, BC, DC, MC, V. CityRail, bus, or ferry: Circular Quay. ITALIAN/AUSTRALIAN.

Because this place stays open 24 hours, it's convenient if you get the munchies at 3am. It's also conveniently located right next to the Manly ferry terminal. The plastic chairs and tables placed outside make it a pleasant spot to while away an inexpensive meal. A range of pastas are on offer, as well as salads, pies, steaks, ribs, fish, and Asian-influenced dishes. There's also a fat selection of desserts. That said, I agree with several friends of mine who believe the food is much nicer and a better value next door at Rossini (see below).

✪ **MCA Café.** Museum of Contemporary Art, Circular Quay West. ☎ **02/9241 4253.** Main courses A$19–$20 (U.S.$12.30–$13). 10% surcharge weekends and public holidays. AE, BC, DC, MC, V. Daily noon–2:30pm. CityRail, bus, or ferry: Circular Quay. SEAFOOD.

If you find yourself sitting at one of the 16 outside tables here, count yourself as one of the most fortunate people lunching in Sydney. The views over the ferries and the Opera House are wonderful, and you are far enough away from the crowds at Circular Quay to watch the action without feeling a spectacle yourself. Whether you sit outside or in, the food is great. Most of the dishes are seafood, but there are some pasta and meat dishes on the menu. The signature dishes are the trevally with a lemon olive and parsley salad, and the smoked salmon lasagna with eggplant caviar.

Sketches Bar and Bistro. In the Hotel Inter-Continental, 117 Macquarie St. (enter from Bridge St.). ☎ **02/9240 1210.** Reservations recommended. Pasta A$10.90–$17 (U.S.$7–$11). AE, BC, DC, MC, V. Mon–Fri 5:30–9:30pm, Sat 5:30–10:30pm. CityRail, bus, or ferry: Circular Quay. PASTA.

Sketches is a favorite with people on their way to the Opera House and those who really know a bargain when they taste one. Here's how it works: After getting the barman's attention, point to one of three different-sized plates stuck to the bar above your head—the small size is adequate if you're an average eater, the medium plate is good for filling up after a hard day of sightseeing (and no lunch), and I've yet to meet a man who can handle the large serving with its accompanying bread, pine nuts, and parmesan cheese. Then, with ticket in hand, head toward the chefs in white hats and place your order. There are 12 pastas to choose from and several sauces, including carbonara, marinara, pesto, vegetarian, and some unusual ones to dishearten pasta purists, such as south Indian curry. Meals are cooked in front of you while you wait.

INEXPENSIVE

✪ **Freckle Face Café.** 32A Burton St., Kirribilli. ☎ **02/9957 2116.** Main courses A$7 (U.S.$4.55) eat in, A$6.50 (U.S.$4.20) takeout. No credit cards. Mon–Sat 7am–4pm. CityRail or ferry: Milsons Point. Take the left exit from the Milsons Point CityRail station, walk downhill to the traffic lights, cross the road, and it's in the street opposite. CAFE.

There's no better to place to refuel after a walk across the Harbour Bridge than this intimate cafe near the Milsons Point CityRail station on the north side of Sydney Harbour. Freckle Face specializes in sandwiches, bagels, Turkish bread, focaccia, and very good coffee. The smoked salmon, baby spinach, and cream cheese on toasted Turkish bread is one of my favorites, and the biscuits and cakes (especially the flourless orange

You Paid What?

47,000 hotels, 700 airlines, 50 rental car companies. And a few million ways to save money.

Travelocity.com
A Sabre Company

Go Virtually Anywhere.

Will you have enough stories to tell your grandchildren?

Yahoo! Travel

Do You YAHOO!?

and almond cake) are gorgeous. There are good breakfasts here for A$7.50 (U.S.$4.90), including fruit salads, muesli, fruit bread, and egg dishes. Everything is made on the premises. The staff is very friendly, so say hello to Jackie and Victoria—two freckle-faced sisters.

Portobello Caffé. No.1 Eastern Esplanade, Circular Quay East. ☎ **02/9247 8548.** Main courses A$8 (U.S. $5.20). 10% surcharge Sun and public holidays. AE, BC, DC, JCB, MC, V. Minimum credit-card purchase A$30 (U.S.$19.50). Daily 8am–11:50pm. CityRail, bus, or ferry: Circular Quay. PIZZA/SANDWICHES.

Sharing the same address as the Sydney Cove Oyster Bar (and the same priceless views), the Portobello Caffé offers first-class gourmet sandwiches on Italian wood-fired bread, small but delicious gourmet pizzas, breakfast croissants, snacks, cakes, and hot and cold drinks. Walk off with sensational ice cream in a cone for around A$3 (U.S.$1.95).

Quay Deli. E5 Alfred St. (next to the pharmacy under the Circular Quay CityRail station). ☎ **02/9241 3571.** Menu items A$1.80–$5.50 (U.S.$1.20–$3.60). No credit cards. Mon–Fri 5am–6:45pm, Sat 9am–4pm. DELI.

If you're looking for a sandwich or something to take with you on a harbor cruise or on your walk through the Royal Botanic Gardens, you can't go wrong buying it here. Everything is fresh and tasty, and there are all sorts of goodies to choose from, including gourmet sandwiches and simple take-out foods such as olives, Greek dishes, pasta, fruit salads, green salads, homemade rissoles, meat, pies, and the best English-style custard tarts around. The shop also carries a stock of biscuits, tea, coffee, and other supplies. The service is friendly and professional. Plenty of tourists simply buy a couple of fresh bread rolls and a piece of cheese from here, pick up a bottle of wine from the bottle shop just around the corner, and then take off to the Royal Botanical Gardens for a cheerful meal.

✪ **Rossini.** Shop W5, Circular Quay. ☎ **02/9247 8026.** Main courses A$10–$15 (U.S.$6.50–$9.75). No credit cards. Daily 7am–10pm. CityRail, bus, or ferry: Circular Quay. ITALIAN.

This cafeteria-style Italian restaurant opposite ferry wharf 5 at Circular Quay is wonderfully positioned for people-watching. The outside tables are perfect spots for breakfast or a quick bite before a show at the Opera House. Breakfast croissants, Italian donuts, muffins, and gorgeous Danish pastries cost just A$2 (U.S. $1.30), and bacon and eggs just A$8 (U.S. $5.20). Wait to be seated for lunch or dinner, make your choice, pay your money at the counter, take a ticket, and then pick up your food. Meals, including veal parmigiana, cannelloni, ravioli, chicken crepes, and octopus salad, are often huge, and while not the best Italian you'll ever eat, they are tasty enough. Coffee fanatics I know rate the Rossini brew as only average, though.

✪ **Supreme View Café.** Level 14. Law Courts Building, Queens Square, 184 Phillip St. ☎ **02/9230 8224.** Main courses $A8–$13 (U.S.$5.20–$8.45); coffee and cake A$5 (U.S.$3.25). No credit cards. Daily 7am–5pm. CAFE.

This fabulous, largely undiscovered restaurant/cafe offers great-value food and absolutely fantastic views reaching over Hyde Park and even to the harbor. It's very large inside, has panoramic windows, and serves meals from the counter. Breakfasts are hearty and include bacon and eggs, omelets, and cereals. All-day dishes include the likes of sandwiches, Caesar salad, homemade pies, pastas, and lasagna. Even if you're not hungry, it's well worth popping in for a coffee. The cafe is particularly handy if you're staying in the lower Oxford street area.

IN THE ROCKS
VERY EXPENSIVE

bel mondo. 3rd floor in the Argyle Department Store, 18–24 Argyle St., The Rocks. ☎ **02/ 9241 3700**. E-mail: reservations@belmondo.com.au. Reservations recommended well in advance. Main courses A$26.50–$45.50 (U.S.$17.20–$29.60). 10% surcharge Sun and public holidays. AE, BC, DC, MC, V. Mon–Fri 12:30–2:30pm; Mon–Thurs 6:30–10:30pm, Fri–Sat 6:30–11pm, Sun 6:30–10pm. CityRail, bus, or ferry: Circular Quay. NORTHERN ITALIAN.

With its uncomplicated northern Italian cuisine, bel mondo has deservedly positioned itself alongside the very best of Sydney's upscale restaurants. At this family-run affair, chef Stefano Manfredi is helped out in the kitchen by his mum, Franca, a pasta diva in her own right. The restaurant is large and long with high ceilings, and the energetic pace and the banging and clashing coming from the open kitchen give the place a New York feel. Standout appetizers include grilled sea scallops with soft polenta and pesto. Favorite main courses include roast lamb with rosemary and roast potatoes, potato gnocchi with burned butter and parmesan, and barbecued duck with balsamic vinegar. The wine list is very extensive.

bel mondo's **Antibar** is cheaper and more relaxed; it offers a good selection of antipasto and lighter meals (from A$13.50 to $21.50/U.S.$8.80 to $14) and features jazz on Friday evenings from 5:30 to 7:30pm.

✪ **Quay**. On the upper level of the Overseas Passenger Terminal, Circular Quay West, The Rocks. ☎ **02/9251 5600**. Reservations recommended well in advance. Main courses A$40–$50 (U.S.$26–$32.50). A$6 (U.S.$3.90) per person surcharge Sun and public holidays. AE, BC, DC, JCB, MC, V. Mon–Fri noon–3pm; Mon–Sun 6–10pm. CityRail, bus, or ferry: Circular Quay. SEAFOOD.

Without question, Quay is Sydney's best seafood restaurant—and with its enviable location on top of the cruise-ship terminal, it offers perhaps the loveliest view in Sydney, too. In good weather, when the sun sparkles off the water and through the large glass windows, the Opera House, the city skyline, the North Shore suburbs, and the Harbour Bridge all look magnificent. At night, when the lights from the city wash over the harbor and the bridge and the Opera House's sails are all lit up, the view is even better. The signature dishes are the basil-infused tuna, the Kangaroo Island roast chicken with ravioli and truffles (which the *Sydney Morning Herald* named the city's best dish in 1999), and the popular char-grilled beef tenderloin on mashed potatoes. The service is exemplary. Expensive, yet select, this restaurant has tempted all the big-name visitors to Sydney. Believe me, they tell all their friends.

✪ **Rockpool**. 109 George St., The Rocks. ☎ **02/9252 1888**. Reservations required. Main courses A$38 (U.S.$24.70). AE, BC, DC, MC, V. Mon–Sat 6–11pm. CityRail, bus, or ferry: Circular Quay. MODERN AUSTRALIAN.

The Rockpool is an institution in Sydney, known for its inventive food. It's approached by a steep ramp and opens up into two stories of ocean-green carpet, designer chairs, and stainless steel. Along with the bar, the kitchen—with its busy chefs and range of copper pots and pans—is very much at the center of things. Menus change regularly, but you can expect to find anything from a dozen fresh oysters and spanner crab with lemon ravioli, to fish cooked with coconut milk and Indian garam masala and served with snow peas and semolina noodles. On my last visit, the desserts were a letdown after the fabulous main courses.

EXPENSIVE

Doyles at the Quay. Overseas Passenger Terminal, Circular Quay West. ☎ **02/9252 3400**. Main courses A$20–$33 (U.S.$13–$21.45). BC, DC, JCB, MC, V. Daily 11:30am–2:45pm; Mon–Sat 5:30–9:30pm, Sun 5:30–9pm. CityRail, bus, or ferry: Circular Quay. SEAFOOD.

Dining in The Rocks

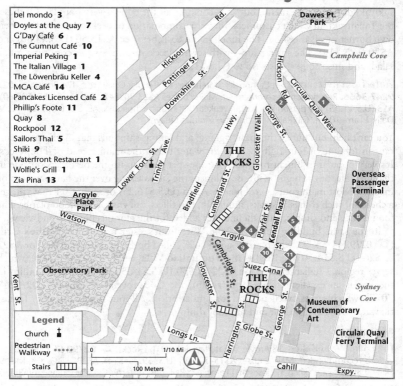

bel mondo **3**
Doyles at the Quay **7**
G'Day Café **6**
The Gumnut Café **10**
Imperial Peking **1**
The Italian Village **1**
The Löwenbräu Keller **4**
MCA Café **14**
Pancakes Licensed Café **2**
Phillip's Foote **11**
Quay **8**
Rockpool **12**
Sailors Thai **5**
Shiki **9**
Waterfront Restaurant **1**
Wolfie's Grill **1**
Zia Pina **13**

Legend

Church ✝
Pedestrian Walkway •••••
Stairs ▭▭▭

0 ——— 1/10 Mi
0 ——— 100 Meters

Just below Quay (see above) is Doyles, a name synonymous with seafood in Sydney. Most customers sit outside to enjoy the fabulous views across the harbor, though a set of thick green railings does somewhat interrupt the view of the Opera House. Businesspeople and tourists come here if they don't want to lay out the cash for Quay, or if they fancy a more relaxed style. The most popular dish here is basically pricey fish-and-chips (choose from ocean trout, garfish, John Dory, swordfish, whiting, and salmon). You can also pick up a dozen oysters for A$20 (U.S.$13) or a lobster for A$65 (U.S.$42.25).

A second Doyles, **Doyles on the Beach** (☎ 02/9337 2007), at Watsons Bay, serves fabulous food. Nearby is a third Doyles, **Doyles Fisherman's Wharf** (☎ 02/9337 1572), located on the ferry wharf; it used to be a take-out joint but now has sit-down service.

Shiki. Clock Tower Square, corner of Argyle and Harrington sts., The Rocks. ☎ **02/9252 2431.** Reservations recommended well in advance. Meals around A$30 (U.S.$19.50) per person. AE, BC, DC, JCB, MC, V. Mon–Fri noon–2:30pm; Mon–Sun 6–10pm. TRADITIONAL JAPANESE.

Shiki is making a name for itself as a top-flight traditional Japanese choice. Though you can eat at Western-style tables, or the sushi bar, there are also five tatami rooms available, where you sit around a raised table on Japanese mats. Either way you can enjoy some good views over The Rocks (it's especially magical at night, when the ferry lights strung across the area's trees are lit up). There is plenty of sushi, sashimi, and sukiyaki dishes on the menu, but "pot-cooking" at the table is very popular. Of these, the Tobanyaki, in which customers simmer a combination of beef and seafood on their own burner, steals the show. The lunch menu costs between A$13.50 (U.S.$8.80) and A$20 (U.S.$13). The sushi plate—with seven pieces of sushi, six pieces of tuna roll, a salad, and miso soup—costs A$20 (U.S.$13).

Waterfront Restaurant. In Campbell's Storehouse, 27 Circular Quay West, The Rocks. ☎ **02/ 9247 3666.** Reservations recommended. Main courses A$23.90–$42.50 (U.S.$15.50–$27.60). A$3 (U.S.$1.95) per person surcharge weekends and public holidays. AE, BC, DC, JCB, MC, V. Daily 11am–10pm. CityRail, bus, or ferry: Circular Quay.

You can't help but notice the mast, rigging, and sailing-ship sails that mark this restaurant in the line of four right next to the water below the main spread of The Rocks. It's very popular at lunchtime, when businesspeople snap up the best seats outside in the sunshine, but at night, with the colors of the city washing over the harbor, it can be magical. Most main courses cost a hefty A$25 (U.S.$16.25) or so, but for that you get a choice of such things as steaks, mud crab, fish fillets, prawns, or a seafood platter. The food is nice and simple, with the markup added for the glorious position and views.

In the same building you'll find the Waterfront's sister restaurants **Wolfie's Grill** (☎ 02/9241 5577), which serves good char-grilled beef and seafood dishes for A$22 to $26 (U.S.$14.30 to $16.90), and **The Italian Village** (☎ 02/9247 6111), which serves regional Italian cuisine for A$22 to $30 (U.S.$14.30 to $19.50). The third in the line is an excellent Chinese restaurant, the ✪ **Imperial Peking** (☎ 02/9247 7073), which serves excellent food for similar prices. All four restaurants offer fantastic water views and indoor and outdoor dining.

MODERATE

The Löwenbräu Keller. 18 Argyle St. (at Playfair St.), The Rocks. ☎ **02/9247 7785.** Reservations recommended. Main courses A$15–$21.50 (U.S. $9.75–$14). AE, BC, DC, JCB, MC, V. Daily 9:30am–2am (kitchen closes at 11pm). CityRail, bus, or ferry: Circular Quay. BAVARIAN.

Renowned for celebrating Oktoberfest every day for the past 20 years, this is a place where Aussies let their hair down. You can come for lunch and munch a club sandwich or focaccia in the glassed-off atrium while watching the daytime action of The Rocks. For a livelier scene, head here on a Friday or Saturday night, when mass beer-sculling (chugging) and yodeling are accompanied by a brass band, and costumed waitresses ferry foaming beer steins about the atmospheric, cellarlike bowels. Hearty southern German and Austrian fare and no fewer than 17 varieties of German beers in bottle or on tap are served. There's a good wine list, and, surprisingly, vegetarians are well catered to.

Pancakes Licensed Café. 10 Hickson Rd. (enter from Hickson Rd. or George St.), The Rocks. ☎ **02/9247 6371.** Reservations not accepted. Main courses A$12.95–$21.95 (U.S.$8.40–$14.30); breakfast (served 24 hr.) A$8.95–$11.95 (U.S.$5.80–$7.80). AE, BC, DC, JCB, MC, V. Daily 24 hr. CityRail, bus, or ferry: Circular Quay. AMERICAN COFFEE-SHOP FARE/PANCAKES.

Buttermilk and chocolate pancakes, and French crepes filled with seafood, chicken and mushrooms, vegetables in a basil-cream sauce, or smoked ham and cheese are the most popular dishes served up in this old warehouse done up in art deco style. The beef ribs, pastas, and pizzas are also good sellers.

Phillip's Foote. 101 George St., The Rocks. ☎ **02/9241 1485.** Main courses A$20 (U.S.$13) weekdays, $21 (U.S.$13.65) weekends. AE, BC, JCB, MC, V. Mon–Sat noon–midnight, Sun noon–10pm. CityRail, bus, or ferry: Circular Quay. BARBECUE.

Venture behind this historic pub and you'll find a popular courtyard strung with tables and benches and large barbecues. Choose your own steak, lemon sole, trout, chicken,

The Sydney Cove, 39 Argyle St., The Rocks (☎ **02/9247 8833**). *We simply have to tell you about this amazing "sleeper" restaurant—the best in town in my opinion . . . The appetizer that I ate for lunch as a main course—the crostini with hommus taziki, olive tapenade, baby kalamata olives, salsa, and caper berries—was the most delicious thing I have ever put in my mouth. I went back 2 days in a row to have this dish, and I would recommend flying [to Sydney] from L.A. just to taste it.*
                                      —Did Carr Reuben, Pacific Palisades, Calif., U.S.

or pork and throw it on the barbie. It's fun, it's filling, and you might even meet some new friends while your meal's sizzling.

✪ **Sailors Thai.** 106 George St., The Rocks. ☎ **02/9251 2466.** Reservations required well in advance in restaurant; not accepted in canteen. Main courses A$14–$34 (U.S. $9.10–$22.10) in restaurant, A$11–$16 (U.S.$7.15–$10.40) in canteen. AE, BC, DC, MC, V. Restaurant Mon–Fri noon–2pm, Mon–Sat 6–10pm; canteen daily noon–8pm. CityRail, bus, or ferry: Circular Quay. THAI.

With a reputation as hot as the chilies in its jungle curry, Sailors Thai canteen attracts lunchtime crowds who come to eat great-tasting noodles and the likes of pork and prawn wonton soup, red curry with lychees, and Thai salads at its single stainless-steel table lined with some 40 chairs. Four other tables overlook the cruise-ship terminal and the quay. Downstairs, the à la carte restaurant serves inventive food that's a far cry from what you'd find at your average Thai restaurant, like sir-fried pineapple curry with chilies and cashew nuts, or a wonderfully glutenous coconut ash pudding, made from the ash of burnt coconuts cooked with licorice root, coconut water, rice flower, and sugar.

INEXPENSIVE

G'Day Café. 83 George St., The Rocks. ☎ **02/9241 3644.** Main courses A$3–$7 (U.S.$1.95–$4.55). AE. Sun–Thurs 5am–midnight, Fri–Sat 5am–3am. CityRail, bus, or ferry: Circular Quay. CAFE.

According to the manager, about half of the tourists who come to Sydney visit this little place in the heart of The Rocks. That's not surprising, considering it offers simple but satisfying food at around half the price you'd expect to pay in such a tourist precinct. The interior is uninspiring, but out back there's a pleasant leafy courtyard. Among the offerings are focaccia sandwiches, hearty soups, salads, burgers, lasagna, chili con carne, and beef curry.

The Gumnut Cafe. 28 Harrington St., The Rocks. ☎ **02/9247 9591.** Main courses A$6.90–$13 (U.S.$4.50–$8.45). AE, BC, DC, MC, V. Daily 8am–5pm. CityRail, bus, or ferry: Circular Quay. MODERN AUSTRALIAN.

A hearty lunch in a courtyard shaded from the sun by giant cream umbrellas—ah, heaven. With a great location in the heart of The Rocks, this restaurant also has an extensive indoor seating area, so it's a perfect place to take a break from all that sightseeing. The breakfast specials (A$8.50/U.S.$5.50) are very popular with guests from surrounding hotels, while at lunchtime it's always bustling with tourists and local office workers. Lunchtime blackboard specials cost A$11 (U.S. $7.15). More regular fare includes the disappointing Ploughman's Lunch (why spoil a traditional English meal of bread, cheese, and pickles by limiting the bread and adding unappealing vegetables and salad?), the better chicken and leek pies, and pasta and noodle dishes. Filling Turkish bread sandwiches cost between A$7.70 and $9 (U.S.$5 and $5.85). The courtyard is heated in winter, making it quite cozy.

Zia Pina. 93 George St., The Rocks. ☎ **02/9247 2255.** Reservations recommended well in advance. Main courses A$7.80–$19 (U.S.$5–$12.35). AE, BC, DC, JCB, MC, V. Daily noon–3pm; Sun–Mon 5–9pm, Tues–Thurs 5–10:30pm, Fri–Sat 5–11:30pm. CityRail, bus, or ferry: Circular Quay. PIZZA/PASTA.

With 10 tables crammed downstairs and another 24 upstairs, there's not much room to breathe in this cramped traditional pizzeria and spaghetti house. But squeeze in between the close-fit bare-brick walls and wallow in the clashes and clangs coming from the hard-working chefs in the kitchen. Pizzas come in two sizes; the larger feeds two people. Servings of delicious gelato go for a cool A$4 (U.S.$2.60).

NEAR TOWN HALL

○ **Capitan Torres**. 73 Liverpool St. (just past the cinema strip on George St., near Town Hall). ☎ **02/9264 5574.** Main courses A$16.50–$19 (U.S.$10.70–$12.35); tapas A$5.50–$9.90 (U.S.$3.60–$6.40). AE, BC, DC, JCB, MC, V. Daily noon–3pm; Mon–Sat 6–11pm, Sun 6–10pm. CityRail: Town Hall. SPANISH.

Sydney's Spanish quarter, based on Liverpool Street (a 10-min. walk from Town Hall station and just past Sydney's main cinema strip), offers some great restaurants, of which Capitan Torres is my favorite. Downstairs is a tapas bar with traditional stools, Spanish serving staff, and lots of authentic dark oak. Upstairs on two floors is a fabulous restaurant with heavy wooden tables and chairs and an atmosphere thick with sangria and regional food. The garlic prawns are incredible, and the whole snapper is a memorable experience.

The tapas are better, though, at **Asturiana** (☎ **02/9264 1010**), another Spanish restaurant a couple of doors down on the same street.

The Olive. Shop 18, Strand Arcade. ☎ **02/9231 2962.** Main courses A$4–$6.30 (U.S.$2.60–$4). Cash only. Mon–Sat 6am–4pm. CityRail, bus, or monorail: Town Hall. ITALIAN/SANDWICHES.

This tiny little sandwich shop in the Strand Arcade, just off the Pitt Street Mall between Town Hall and the AMP Centerpoint Tower, is a tasty lunch option in the city. You can feast on authentic Italian pastas and pizzas, focaccias, and spicy rissoles, or gourmet sandwiches filling enough to last you through a hectic afternoon of sightseeing.

○ **Sushi Roll**. Sydney Central Plaza (downstairs in the food hall next to Grace Brothers department store on Pitt Street Mall). ☎ **02/9233 5561.** Sushi rolls A$1.70 (U.S.$1.10) each. No credit cards. Mon–Wed and Fri–Sat 8am–7pm, Thurs 8am–10pm, Sun 10am–6pm. SUSHI.

The fresh, simple food served up at this bargain-basement take-out booth is certainly a healthy alternative to most fast food. A large range of sushi and nori rolls peek out from behind the counter here, and you can eat at the tables opposite.

AT DARLING HARBOUR & THE COCKLE BAY WHARF
VERY EXPENSIVE

✪ **Ampersand**. Cockle Bay Wharf Complex. ☎ **02/9264 6666.** Reservations required. Main courses A$32–$39.50 (U.S.$20.80–$25.70). AE, BC, DC, MC, V. Mon–Fri noon–3pm, Mon–Sat 6–10:30pm. Monorail or ferry: Darling Harbour. FRENCH.

The upscale Ampersand was an immediate hit following its opening in late 1998. It's the premier restaurant at the new Cockle Bay Wharf development on the city side of Darling Harbour. Its team of world-renowned chefs is led by Sydney icon Tony Bilson. The food can be stunning and reflects Bilson's views on using the finest and freshest ingredients as he tries to emulate the classic French Michelin-starred restaurants. The restaurant itself is light and contemporary and has sparkling views across the harbor. Sample dishes include the roasted venison with beetroot and celeriac puree, and baked fillet of salmon with a scallop crust and basil and spinach tapenade.

Something Fishy

If you like fresh seafood at cheap prices, then saunter down to the **Sydney Fishmarket,** on the corner of Bank Street and Pyrmont Bridge Road, Pyrmont (☎ **02/9660 1611,** or call the Fishline at ☎ 02/9552 2180 for information on special events such as seafood cooking classes). The major fish retailers here sell sashimi at the cheapest prices in Sydney, but if you prefer your seafood cooked, then don't miss out on these two fabulous outlets.

First off there's **Musumeci Seafoods,** found outside the large blue retail arcade. It's little more than a stall with a hot plate, but you won't find baby octopus cooked better in any of Sydney's glitzy restaurants. Seafood combinations are also offered, with a small plate (easily enough for one person) costing just A$5.50 (U.S.$3.60), and a large plate A$11 (U.S.$7.15). Musumeci's is open Friday and Sunday from 7am to 4pm and Saturday from 6am to 4pm.

Also mouthwatering are the stir-fries at nearby **Christies,** a seafood retailer inside the main retail building. Here, you pick your own seafood, such as fresh calamari or mussels, and your own sauce; they throw it straight in a wok and cook it for you on the spot. Stir-fries or great Asian-style seafood noodle dishes cost just A$5.50 (U.S.$3.60). Christies cooks are on the job daily from 7am to 7pm.

To get to the Fishmarket, take the light rail (tram) from Central Station, Chinatown, or Darling Harbour to the Fishmarket stop, or you can walk from Darling Harbour (follow the signs).

✪ **MG Garage.** 490 Crown St., Surry Hills. ☎ **02/9383 9383.** Reservations required. Main courses A$28–$36 (U.S.$18.20–$23.40). AE, BC, DC, MC, V. Mon–Fri noon–2:30pm; Mon–Sat 6:30–10pm. MODERN AUSTRALIAN.

This fine-dining restaurant has caused quite a stir in Sydney, and not just because it's in a car showroom. It's a glamorous, modern eatery with good service and a fashionable crowd. Tables are difficult to get, so you'll need to book at least a week in advance. Among the offerings you might find are the steam fillet of beef with dumplings, and roast pigeon with pine mushrooms.

Wockpool. In the Imax Theatre, Southern Promenade, Darling Harbour. ☎ **02/9211 9888.** Main courses A$28–$35 (U.S.$18.20–$22.75); noodles, laksas, and soups at lunchtime A$12–$14 (U.S.$7.80–$9.10). AE, BC, DC, MC, V. Daily noon–3pm, Sun–Thurs 6–10pm, Fri–Sat 6–11pm. Ferry: Darling Harbour. Monorail: Convention Center. MODERN ASIAN.

With great views of Darling Harbour, this adventuresome child of co-owners Neil Perry and chef Kylie Kwong has taken off big-time. The main dining room is light and spacious with glass walls opening up across the water. The essence up here is Chinese with a twist, and the Sichuan duck and stir-fried spanner-crab omelet are always on the menu. Other dishes to go for are whole steamed snapper with ginger and shallot, rock lobster, and mud crab. The lunchtime noodle bar is always happening, with tourists, locals, and business types crunched up along the bar or around the tables, tucking into light meals such as noodles (of course), laksas, and soups.

MODERATE

✪ **Chinta Ria (The Temple of Love).** Cockle Bay Wharf Complex. ☎ **02/9264 3211.** Main courses A$12–$25 (U.S.$7.80–$16.25). AE, BC, DC, MC, V. Daily noon–2:30pm and 6–11pm. Ferry or monorail: Darling Harbour. MALAYSIAN.

Cockle Bay's star attraction for those who appreciate good food and a fun ambience without paying a fortune, Chinta Ria serves up fairly good "hawker-style" (read: cheap and delicious) Malaysian food. Chinta Ria is on the roof terrace of the three-story Cockle Bay development, in a round building dominated by a giant golden Buddha in the center. While the food is indeed good, the atmosphere is even more memorable. The service is slow, but who cares in such an interesting space, with plenty of nooks and crannies and society folk to look at? There are seats outside (some get the noise of the highway), but the best views unfold inside. The hot-and-sour soup—a broth made with tofu, mushrooms, bamboo shoots, and preserved cabbage—makes an interesting starter, and I recommend the chili prawns and the *Hokkeien Char* (soft-cooked egg noodles with extras) as main dishes.

IN KINGS CROSS/DARLINGHURST
EXPENSIVE

✪ **Mezzaluna**. 123 Victoria St., Potts Point. ☎ **02/9357 1988.** Reservations recommended. Main courses A\$19.50–\$31 (U.S.\$12.70–\$20). A\$3 (U.S. \$2) surcharge Sun. AE, BC, DC, MC, V. Tues–Sun noon–3pm and 6–11pm. Closed public holidays. CityRail: Kings Cross. MODERN ITALIAN.

Exquisite food, flawless service, and an almost unbeatable view across the city's western skyline have all helped Mezzaluna position itself firmly among Sydney's top restaurants. A cozy, candlelit place with plain white walls and polished wooden floorboards, the main dining room opens up onto a huge, all-weather terrace kept warm in winter by giant overhead braziers. The restaurant's owner, well-known Sydney culinary icon Beppi Polesi, provides an exceptional wine list to complement a menu that changes daily. There's always a fabulous risotto on the menu, though, while other delights may include rack of lamb roasted with olives and oregano and served with baked baby eggplant, or grilled fillet of Atlantic salmon on rocket with a borlotti bean puree. Whatever you choose, you can't go wrong. I highly recommend this place; it's where I took my girlfriend for her birthday.

✪ **Salt**. In the Kirketon Hotel, 229 Darlinghurst Rd., Darlinghurst. ☎ **02/9332 2566.** Reservations required. Main courses \$28–\$35 (U.S.\$18.20–\$22.75). AE, BC, DC, MC, V. Open Sun–Fri noon–3pm. Daily 6–11pm. MODERN AUSTRALIAN.

This is the in place for the fashion crowd. You'll need to dress up in your coolest outfit to fit into the scene here. Inside, it's all sleek and chrome, with tables just big enough for two. The food is innovative and cutting-edge and could include anything from quails' eggs encrusted with salt and sugar, to a delicate raw belly of salmon lacquered with shallot and ginger.

MODERATE

The **Hard Rock Cafe** is at 121–129 Crown St. (CityRail: Museum; then walk across Hyde Park, head down the hill past the Australian Museum on William Street, and turn right onto Crown Street. Sydney Explorer Bus: Stop 7.) It's most crowded on Fridays and Saturdays between 7:30 and 10:30pm.

Bourbon & Beefsteak Bar. 24 Darlinghurst Rd., Kings Cross. ☎ **02/9358 1144.** Reservations recommended Fri–Sun. Main courses A\$8.50–\$23.95 (U.S.\$5.50–\$15.60). A\$2 (U.S.\$1.30) surcharge weekends and public holidays. AE, BC, DC, MC, V. Daily 24 hr. (happy hour 4–7pm). CityRail: Kings Cross. INTERNATIONAL.

The Bourbon & Beefsteak has been a popular Kings Cross institution for more than 30 years, and it still attracts everyone from visiting U.S. sailors and tourists to businesspeople and ravers. The fact that it's open 24 hours means many people never seem to leave—occasionally you'll find someone taking a nap in the bathroom. The American-themed restaurant is busy at all hours, churning out steaks, seafood, salads, Tex-Mex, ribs, seafood specials, and pasta. Breakfast is served daily from 6 to 11am.

Every night there's live music in the Piano Bar from 5 to 9pm, followed by a mixture of jazz, Top 40, and rock and roll until 5am. A disco downstairs starts at 11pm every night (finishing at 6am), and a larger one takes off in The Penthouse at the Bourbon bar on Friday and Saturday nights. The music is geared toward the 18-to-25 crowd, both locals and tourists.

INEXPENSIVE

Govindas. 112 Darlinghurst Rd., Darlinghurst. ☎ **02/9380 5155.** Dinner A$13.90 (U.S.$9), including free movie. AE, BC, MC, V. Daily 6–11pm. CityRail: Kings Cross. VEGETARIAN.

When I think of Govindas, I can't help smiling. Perhaps it's because I'm reliving the happy vibe from the Hare Krishna center it's based in, or maybe it's because the food is so cheap! Or maybe it's because they even throw in a decent movie with the meal (the movie theatre is on a different floor). The food is simple vegetarian, served buffet style and eaten in a basic room off black lacquer tables. Typical dishes include pastas and salads, lentil dishes, soups, and casseroles. It's BYO and doctrine-free.

✪ **No Names.** 2 Chapel St. (or 81 Stanley St.), Darlinghurst. ☎ **02/9360 4711.** Main courses A$6–$14 (U.S.$3.90–$9.10). No credit cards. Daily noon–2:30pm and 6–10pm. CityRail: Kings Cross or Town Hall, then a 10-min. walk. ITALIAN.

This fabulous cafeteria-style Italian joint is the place to go in Sydney for a cheap and cheerful meal. Downstairs you can nibble on cakes or drink good coffee, but upstairs you have a choice between spaghetti and several meat or fish dishes. The servings are enormous and often far more than you can eat. You get free bread, and simple salads are cheap. Help yourself to free cordials (concentrated fruit juice, to which you add water).

IN NEWTOWN

The inner-city suburb of Newtown is three stops from Central Station by CityRail train, and 10 minutes by bus from central Sydney. Its main drag, King Street, is clustered with inexpensive restaurants offering food from around the world.

Le Kilimanjaro. 280 King St., Newtown. ☎ **02/9557 4565.** Reservations not accepted. Main courses A$8.50–$9.50 (U.S.$5.50–$6.20). No credit cards. CityRail: Newtown. AFRICAN.

With so many excellent restaurants to choose from in Newtown—they close down or improve quick enough if they're bad—I like Kilimanjaro because it's the most unusual. It's a tiny place, with very limited seating on two floors. Basically, you enter, you choose a dish off the blackboard menu (while standing), and then you are escorted to your seats by one of the waiters. On a recent visit I had couscous, some African bread (similar to an Indian chapatti), and the *Saussou-gor di guan* (tuna in a rich sauce). Another favorite dish is *Yassa* (chicken in a rich African sauce). All meals are served on traditional wooden plates.

✪ **Old Saigon.** 107 King St., Newtown. ☎ **02/9519 5931.** Reservations recommended. Main courses A$10–$40 (U.S.$6.50–$26). AE, BC, DC, MC, V. Wed–Fri noon–3pm; Tues–Sun 6–11pm. BYO only. CityRail: Newtown. VIETNAMESE.

Another Newtown establishment bursting with atmosphere, the Old Saigon was owned until 1998 by a former American Vietnam War correspondent who loved Vietnam so much he ended up living there and marrying a local, before coming to Australia. Just to make sure you know about it, he's put up his own photos on the walls

Jumping Java Joints

Debate rages over which cafe serves the best coffee in Sydney, which has the best atmosphere, and which has the tastiest snacks. The main cafe scenes are centered around Victoria Street in Darlinghurst, Stanley Street in East Sydney, and King Street in Newtown. Other places, like Balmoral Beach on the north shore, Bondi Beach, and Paddington, all have their favored hangouts, too. (Unlike in the U.S., it's very rare to have free refills of coffee in Australian restaurants and cafes.)

Here are some of my favorite java joints: The **Old Coffee Shop,** ground floor of the Strand Arcade (☎ **02/9231 3002**), is Sydney's oldest coffee shop, with an old-world feel and tasty snacks. ✪ **Bills,** 433 Liverpool St., Darlinghurst (☎ **02/9360 9631**), is a bright and airy (and a bit pretentious) hangout serving nouveau cafe–style food. **Hernandez,** 60 Kings Cross Rd., Potts Point (☎ **02/9331 2343**), is a tiny, zany, cluttered cafe serving 20 types of coffee. At **Cafe Niki,** 544 Bourke St., Surry Hills (☎ **02/9319 7517**), you can munch on light Italian meals in the cozy booths. **Bar Coluzzi,** 322 Victoria St., Darling-hurst (☎ **02/9380 5420**), was the first cafe in Sydney to serve real espresso when the rest of the city was still drinking Nescafé. And last but not least, ✪ **Balmoral Boatshed Kiosk,** 2 The Esplanade, Balmoral Beach (☎ **02/9968 4412**), is a beautiful, rustic cafe right on the water that's popular with families on weekend mornings.

and strewn the place with homemade tin helicopters. His Vietnamese brother-in-law has taken over the show, but the food is still glorious; the spicy squid dishes are among my favorites. A popular pastime is grilling your own thin strips of venison, beef, wild boar, kangaroo, or crocodile over a burner at your table, then wrapping the meat up in rice paper with lettuce and mint, then dipping it in a chili sauce. I highly recommend this place for a cheap night out.

IN PADDINGTON/OXFORD STREET

The top end of Oxford Street, which runs from Hyde Park in central Sydney toward Bondi, has a profusion of trendy bars and cafes, with a scattering of cheaper places among the more glamorous ones. In addition to La Mensa, my other favorite places in the area are **Claudes,** 10 Oxford St., Woolhara (☎ **02/9331 2325**), which offers expensive French cuisine in a hushed, intimate atmosphere, and ✪ **Grand National,** 161 Underwood St., Paddington (☎ **02/9363 3096**), which offers fabulous Modern Australian food at moderate prices in elegant surrounds (try the fish pie!). Claudes is open for dinner Tuesday to Saturday, and Grand National is open for dinner daily and lunch Wednesday to Friday and Sunday.

La Mensa. 257 Oxford St., Paddington. ☎ **02/9332 2963.** Reservations recommended. Main courses A\$10.50–\$19.50 (U.S.\$6.90–\$12.70). AE, BC, DC, MC, V. Mon–Thurs 11am–10pm, Fri 11am–11pm, Sat 9am–11pm, Sun 9am–10pm. Bus: Oxford St. ITALIAN/MEDITERRANEAN.

Though I find clean-cut, minimalist interiors like the one here to be increasingly boring, La Mensa has the added zest of a gourmet food and vegetable store tacked on. There's a communal table seating about 20 people, as well as other smaller tables both inside and out. Main courses might include a salad of salmon, asparagus, and poached egg; a pumpkin, pea, and leg ham risotto; grilled swordfish with chickpeas and braised tomatoes; and Tuscan-style baby chicken and potatoes.

AT BONDI BEACH

Fishy Affair. 152–162 Campbell Parade, Bondi Beach. ☎ **02/9300 0494.** Main courses A$14.40–$21 (U.S.$9.40–$13.65) AE, BC, JCB, MC, V. Mon–Sat noon–3pm, Mon–Thurs 6–10pm, Fri–Sat 6–10:30pm, Sun noon–10pm. Bus: Bondi Beach. SEAFOOD.

The Fishy Affair is a standout among the many good restaurants and cafes along the Beach's main drag. Sitting outside watching the beach bums saunter past while tucking into great fish-and-chips is a great way to spend an hour or so. The herb-crusted Atlantic salmon steak and the smoked salmon salad are both truly delicious.

✪ **Thai Terrific.** 147 Curlewis St., Bondi Beach. ☎ **02/9365 7794.** Reservations recommended on Fri–Sat nights. Main courses A$10–$18 (U.S.$6.50–$11.70). Cash only. Daily noon–11pm. Bus: 380 to Bondi Beach. THAI.

Thai Terrific by name, terrific Thai by nature. This truly superb place just around the corner from the Bondi Hotel is run with flair and coolly efficient service. The large back room can be quite noisy, so if you prefer less din with your dinner, sit at one of the small sidewalk tables outside. Servings are enormous: two main courses are easily enough to fill three people. The *tom yum* soups and the prawn or seafood *laksa* noodle soups are the best I've tasted in Australia and are very filling. I also highly recommend the red curries.

Equally nice (and quieter) is the Bangkok-style **Nina's Ploy Thai Restaurant,** 132 Wairoa Ave. (☎ **02/9365 1118**), at the corner of Warners Avenue at the end of the main Campbell Parade strip. Main courses here go for A$9 to $14 (U.S. $5.90 to $9.10); it's cash only. The locals rave about this place.

IN MANLY

Manly is 30 minutes from Circular Quay by ferry, or 15 minutes by JetCat. Take-out shops lining **The Corso,** the pedestrian mall between the ferry terminal and the main Manly Beach, offer everything from Turkish kebabs to Japanese noodles. If you've got a hankering for french fries, don't miss **Manly Ocean Foods,** three shops down from the main beach on The Corso; they serve the best in Sydney. But steer away from the A$6.50 (U.S.$4.30) fish-and-chips (the shark is not the best in my opinion) and spend a couple of dollars extra on barramundi, salmon, perch, or snapper. Another excellent take-out option is **Shakespeares,** at 13 The Corso (☎ **02/9977 5909**), on the left side of The Corso as you walk toward the main beach (1 block up from the ferry terminal). It sells a wide range of fabulous gourmet pies, including several excellent vegetarian options, for around A$4.20 (U.S.$2.80) each.

✪ **Ashiana.** 2 Sydney Rd., Manly. ☎ **02/9977 3466.** Reservations recommended. Main courses A$9.90–$15.90 (U.S.$6.50–$10.40). AE, BC, MC, V. Daily 5:30–11pm. Ferry or JetCat: Manly. INDIAN.

You'll be hard pressed to find a better cheap Indian restaurant in Sydney. Tucked away up a staircase next to the Steyne Hotel (just off The Corso and near the main beach), Ashiana has won a few prizes for its traditional spicy cooking. It's Anglified Indian food (much creamier than you'll find in India); but portions are large and filling, and the service is very friendly. The butter chicken is magnificent, while the *malai kofta* (cheese and potato dumplings in a mild, creamy sauce) is the best this side of Bombay. Beer is the best drink with everything. Work off the heavy load in your stomach with a beachside stroll afterward.

Café Tunis. 30/31 S. Steyne, Manly. ☎ **02/9976 2805.** Main courses (big enough for 2) A$17–$21 (U.S.$11–$13.70). AE, BC, DC, MC, V. Daily 7am–10pm. Ferry or JetCat: Manly. TUNISIAN.

Right on the beach, with fabulous views across the ocean, Café Tunis dishes out huge, value-for-money portions of North African specialties. My favorite starter is the fresh tuna with vegetables and egg deep-fried in pastry. It's big enough for a main dish. Real main courses include couscous royale, with lamb, chicken, and spicy sausage. It's large enough for two. The grilled seafood platter is very popular and is also big enough for you and a friend. Café Tunis is open for breakfast—eggs, especially the egg Benedict, are a specialty—and for lunch, when fish-and-chips is the favorite. You can try the authentic Tunisian desserts at lunch, too.

Green's Eatery. 1–3 Sydney Rd., Manly. ☎ **02/9977 1904.** Menu items A$2–$6.20 (U.S.$1.30–$4). Cash only. Daily 8am–6pm. Ferry or JetCat: Manly. VEGETARIAN.

Of the many choices in Manly, this nice little vegetarian place, just off The Corso on the turnoff just before the Steyne Hotel, does the best lunchtime business. The food is healthy and good quality. The menu includes 11 different vegetarian burgers, vegetable curries and noodle dishes, patties and salads, soups, smoothies, and wraps. They serve some exceptionally nice cakes here, too, which despite being incredibly wholesome are still surprisingly tasty. On a nice day you can sit outside.

IN NORTH SYDNEY

✪ **L'Incontro Italian Restaurant.** 196 Miller St. (at McLaren St.), North Sydney. ☎ **02/9957 2274.** Reservations recommended. Main courses A$19.50–$36.50 (U.S.$12.70–$23.70). AE, BC, DC, MC, V. Mon–Fri noon–3pm; Mon–Sat 6–10pm. CityRail: North Sydney. NORTHERN ITALIAN.

Less than 10 minutes by train from the city center—plus a 5-minute stroll up Miller Street (turn right up the hill as you exit the train station and take the first right)—this little beauty in an easy-to-miss turn-of-the-century house is a good place for moderately priced Italian. Dishes are beautifully prepared and served in this stylish trattoria, which seems as far removed from the modern yuppie bistro as you can get. The food is exquisite. The courtyard, with its vines and ferns, is delightful in summer. Menus change regularly, so pray for the baked rainbow trout cooked with almonds and red wine butter—it's simply the best fish I've ever tasted.

5 Seeing the Sights

The biggest problem with visiting Sydney is fitting in everything you want to do and see. Of course, you won't want to miss the starred attractions like the Opera House and the Harbour Bridge. Everyone seems to be climbing over the arch of the bridge these days on the BridgeClimb Tour, so look up for the tiny dots of people waving to the ferry passengers below.

You should also check out the native Aussie wildlife in the Taronga Zoo and the Sydney Aquarium, stroll around the "tourist" precinct of Darling Harbour, and get a dose of Down Under culture at the Australian Museum. Also try to take time out to visit one of the nearby national parks for a taste of the Australian bush. If it's hot take your "cozzie" and towel to Bondi Beach or Manly.

Whatever you decide to do, you won't have enough time. So don't be surprised if you find yourself planning your next trip before your first visit is even finished.

Suggested Itineraries

If You Have 1 Day   In the morning, make your way down to **Circular Quay** to look around the **Opera House** and admire the **Sydney Harbour Bridge.** Then head over to **The Rocks,** stopping off at The Rocks Visitors Centre to pick up maps and extra information and check out the fascinating exhibits on the top two floors. Have lunch around Circular Quay or The Rocks, or jump on a ferry, to Darling Harbour or Manly perhaps, and eat on board. A walk around The Rocks should be at the top of your agenda for the early afternoon. You can either follow the self-guided walking tour in this chapter, or book ahead for one of The Rocks Walking Tours (see "Harbor Cruises & Other Organized Tours," below). Spend the rest of the afternoon browsing around the stores, or head to **Taronga Zoo** by ferry to get a glimpse of some Australian wildlife. An option for the late afternoon, or dinner, is to take a **harbor cruise.**

If You Have 2 Days   On the 2nd day, head down to Circular Quay again and take the ferry beneath the Harbour Bridge and across to **Darling Harbour.** At Darling Harbour, visit **Sydney Aquarium** for its giant sharks, seals, underwater ocean tunnels, and Barrier Reef displays. Then visit the **National Maritime Museum.** Take the monorail to Town Hall in time for sunset at the top of the **AMP Centrepoint Tower.**

If You Have 3 Days   If the weather's good, head to the beach. Go to either **Bondi Beach,** where you can take the cliff walk to Bronte Beach and back, or take the ferry to **Manly** (see section 2, "Getting Around," earlier in this chapter). If you have time in the afternoon, I highly recommend visiting the **Featherdale Wildlife Park**—it's in the suburbs, but it's really worth the trek. Have dinner at Circular Quay with a view of the harbor and the lights of the Opera House and Harbour Bridge.

If You Have 4 Days or More   On your 4th day, get out of town. Go bushwalking in the **Blue Mountains,** wine tasting in the **Hunter Valley,** or dolphin spotting at **Port Stephens** (see chapter 4 for details on all three).

THE OPERA HOUSE & SYDNEY HARBOUR

Sydney Harbour is the focal point of Sydney and one of the features—along with the beaches and the easy access to surrounding national parks—that make this city so special. It's entered through the Heads, two bush-topped outcroppings (you'll see them if you take a ferry or JetCat to Manly). Beyond them, the harbor laps at some 240 kilometers (149 miles) of shoreline before stretching out into the Parramatta River. Visitors are often awestruck by the harbor's beauty, especially at night, when the sails of the Opera House and the girders of the Harbour Bridge are lit up, and the waters are swirling with the reflection of lights from the abutting high-rises—reds, greens, blues, yellows, and oranges. During the day, it buzzes with ferries pulling in and out of busy Circular Quay, sleek tourist craft, tall ships, giant container vessels making their way to and from the wharves of Darling Harbour, and hundreds of white-sailed yachts. The greenery along the harbor's edges is perhaps a surprising feature, and, all thanks to the Sydney Harbour National Park, a haven for native trees and plants, and a feeding and breeding ground for lorikeets and nectar-eating bird life. In the center of the harbor is a series of islands, the most impressive being the tiny isle supporting Fort Denison, which once housed convicts and acted as part of the city's defense.

The best way to see Sydney Harbour, of course, is from the water. Several companies operate tourist craft for fare-paying customers (see "Harbor Cruises & Other Organized Tours," later in this chapter), but it's easy enough just to hop on a regular

passenger ferry (one-way tickets are just A$3.20/U.S.$2; see "Getting Around," earlier in this chapter). The best ferry excursions are over to the beachside suburb of **Manly** (come back after dusk to see the lights ablaze around The Rocks and Circular Quay); to **Watsons Bay,** where you can have lunch and wander along the cliffs; to **Darling Harbour,** for all the area's entertainment and the fact that you travel right under the Harbour Bridge; and to **Mosman,** just for the ride and to see the grand houses that overlook exclusive harbor inlets.

✪ **Sydney Opera House.** Bennelong Point. ☎ **02/9250 7111** for guided tours and inquiries. Fax 02/9250 7624. www.soh.nsw.gov.au. E-mail: infodesk@soh.nsw.gov.au. For bookings, call ☎ **02/9250 7777;** fax 02/9251 3943; e-mail: bookings@soh.nsw.gov.au. Box office open Mon–Sat 9am–8:30pm, Sun 2 hr. before performance. Tours A$13.50 (U.S.$8.80) adults, A$9.30 (U.S.$6) children (family discounts available); backstage tours A$21.90 (U.S.$14.20). Tours run Mon–Sun 8:30am–5pm, subject to theater availability (tour sizes are limited; be prepared to wait). See information on tours and tickets below. CityRail, bus, or ferry: Circular Quay. Sydney Explorer bus: Stop 2. Parking: Daytime A$6 (U.S.$3.90) per hour; evening A$20 (U.S.$13) flat rate.

Only a handful of buildings around the world are as architecturally and culturally significant as the Sydney Opera House. But the difference between the Opera House and the Taj Mahal, the Eiffel Tower, or the Great Pyramids of Egypt is that this great white-sailed construction caught mid-billow over the waters of Sydney Cove is a working building, not just a monument—it's a full-scale performing-arts complex with five major performance spaces.

The biggest and grandest of the lot is the 2,690-seat **Concert Hall,** which has just about the best acoustics of any man-made building of its type in the world. Come here to experience opera, of course, but also chamber music, symphony, dance, choral performances, and even on occasion rock and roll. The **Opera Theatre** is smaller, seating 1,547, and hosts opera, ballet, and dance. The **Drama Theatre,** seating 544, and the **Playhouse,** seating 398, specialize in plays and smaller-scale performances. In March 1999, a new theater, the Boardwalk, seating 300 for dance and experimental music, opened on the site of the old library.

The history of the building is as intriguing as the design. The New South Wales Government raised the money needed to build it from a public lottery. Danish Architect Jørn Utzon won an international competition to design it. From the start, the project was controversial, with many Sydneysiders believing it was a monstrosity. Following a disagreement, Utzon returned home without ever seeing his finished project, and the interior fell victim to a compromise design, which, among other things, left too little space to perform full-scale operas. And the cost? Initially the project was budgeted at a cool A$7 million (U.S.$5.44 million), but by the time it was finished in 1973, it had cost a staggering A$102 million (U.S.$66.3 million), most raised through even more lotteries. Since then, continual refurbishment and the major task of replacing the asbestos-infected grouting between the hundreds of thousands of white tiles that make up its shell has cost many millions more.

Tours & Tickets: Guided tours of the Opera House last about an hour and are conducted daily from 9am to 4pm, except Good Friday and Christmas. Though guides try to take groups into the main theaters and around the foyers, be aware that tour itineraries can change, because the Opera House is not a museum but a workplace, and there's almost always some performance, practice, or setting up to be done. Reservations are essential. Tours include approximately 200 stairs (tours for people with disabilities can be arranged). Specialized tours, focusing on the building's architectural and engineering configurations, for example, can also be arranged.

The Tourism Services Department at the Sydney Opera House can book combination packages, including dinner and a show; a tour, dinner, and a show; or a champagne interval performance. Prices vary depending on shows and dining venues. Visitors from overseas can buy tickets by credit card and then pick them up at the box office on arrival, or contact a local tour company specializing in Australia. Tickets for performances vary from as little as A$9.50 (U.S.$6.20) for children's shows to A$150 (U.S.$97.50) for good seats at the opera. Plays cost between A$35 and $45 (U.S.$22.70 and $29.25) on average.

Free performances are given outside on the Opera House boardwalks on Sunday afternoons and during festival times. The shows range from musicians and performance artists to school groups.

Sydney Harbour Bridge.

One thing so few tourists do, but which takes only an hour or so, is to walk right across the Harbour Bridge. The bridge, completed in 1932, is 1,150 meters (3,795 ft.) long and spans the 503-meter (1,600-ft.) distance from the south shore to the north. It accommodates pedestrian walkways, two railway lines, and an eight-lane road. The 30-minute stroll across offers some excellent harbor views. From the other side, you can take a CityRail train from Milsons Point train station back to the city (to Wynyard, Town Hall, or Central stations).

As you walk across the bridge, you should stop off at the **Pylon Lookout** (☎ **02/9247 3408**), located at the southeastern pylon. Admission is just A$3 (U.S.$1.95). From the top of this bridge support, you are 89 meters (591 ft.) above the water and get excellent views of Sydney Harbour, the ferry terminals of Circular Quay, and beyond. An interesting museum here charts the building of the bridge. Reach the pylon by walking to the far end of George Street in The Rocks toward the Harbour Bridge. Just past the Mercantile Pub on your left you'll see some stone steps that take you onto Cumberland Street. From there, it's a 2-minute walk to the steps underneath the bridge on your right. Climb four flights of stairs to reach the bridge's Western Footway, then walk along to the first pylon. *Note:* Climbing up inside the pylon involves 200 steps. The Pylon Lookout is open daily from 10am to 5pm (closed Christmas).

A Walk on the Wild Side: Climbing the Harbour Bridge

For years, only bridge painters and maintenance staff had the opportunity to view Sydney from the top of the main Harbour Bridge arch. But since October 1998, Sydneysiders and tourists have been able to experience the spectacular view and the exhilarating achievement of climbing to the top of one of Australia's icons. You'll don specially designed "Bridge Suits" and be harnessed to a static line. You'll also have to take a breath test (for alcohol), and you can't carry anything on the climb, including cameras or video recorders. The experience takes 3 hours all told.

Check in at the **BridgeClimb** base at 5 Cumberland St., The Rocks (☎ **02/9240 1100** or 02/8274 7777; www.bridgeclimb.com). The office is open daily from 8am to 6pm, and climbers leave in small groups every 10 minutes or so. Climbs cost A$117 (U.S.$76) for adults and A$96 (U.S.$62.40) for children ages 12 to 16 on weekdays during the day; A$142 (U.S.$92.30) for adults and $118 (U.S.$76.70) for children for night climbs during the week and weekend day climbs; and A$164 (U.S.$106.60) for adults and $140 (U.S.$91) for children on Saturday and Sunday nights. Children under 12 are not allowed to climb.

Central Sydney Attractions

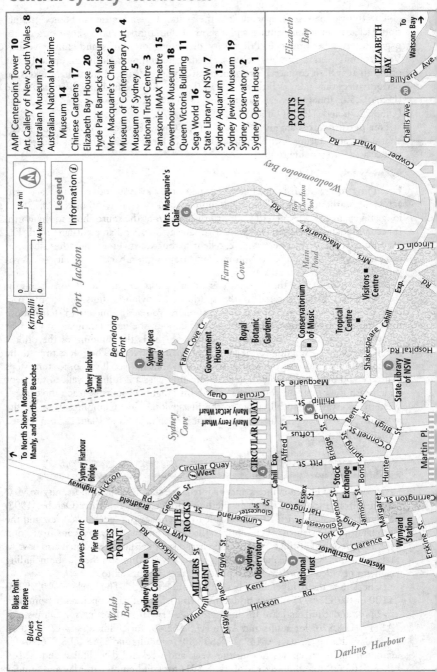

AMP Centerpoint Tower **10**
Art Gallery of New South Wales **8**
Australian Museum **12**
Australian National Maritime
Museum **14**
Chinese Gardens **17**
Elizabeth Bay House **20**
Hyde Park Barracks Museum **9**
Mrs. Macquarie's Chair **6**
Museum of Contemporary Art **4**
Museum of Sydney **5**
National Trust Centre **3**
Panasonic IMAX Theatre **15**
Powerhouse Museum **18**
Queen Victoria Building **11**
Sega World **16**
State Library of NSW **7**
Sydney Aquarium **13**
Sydney Jewish Museum **19**
Sydney Observatory **2**
Sydney Opera House **1**

Legend

Information *i*

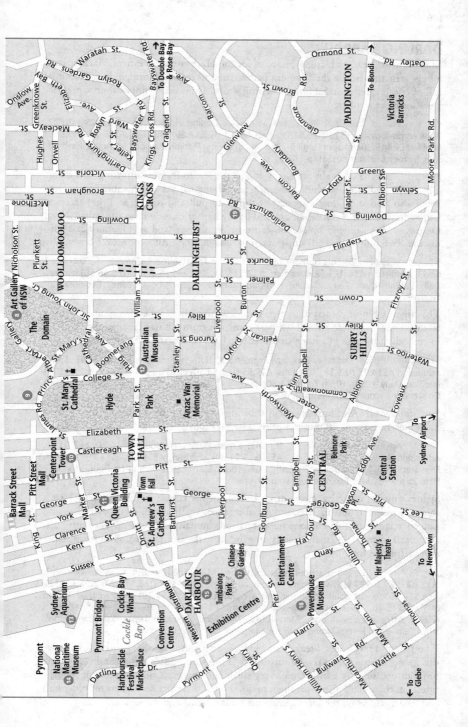

DARLING HARBOUR

Many tourists head to Darling Harbour for the **Harbourside Festival Marketplace,** a huge structure beside the Pyrmont pedestrian and monorail bridge that's crammed full of cheap eateries and a few interesting shops. However, Sydney's tourist precinct has a lot more to offer.

✪ **Australian National Maritime Museum.** Darling Harbour. ☎ **02/9298 3777.** www.anmm.gov.au. A$20 (U.S.$13) adults, A$12 (U.S.$7.80) children, A$50 (U.S.$32.50) families. Daily 9:30am–5pm (until 6:30pm in Jan). Ferry: Darling Harbour. Monorail: Harbourside. Sydney Explorer bus: Stop 18.

Modern Australia owes almost everything to the sea, so it's not surprising that there's a museum dedicated to ships ranging from Aboriginal vessels to submarines. Here you'll also find ships' logs, all sorts of things to pull and tug at, and the Americas Cup–winning boat *Australia II.* Docked in the harbor outside is an Australian Naval Destroyer, *The Vampire,* which you can clamber all over, and an Oberon Class submarine. Two fully rigged tall ships were installed in 1999. Allow at least 2 hours.

Chinese Garden. Darling Harbour (adjacent to the Entertainment Centre). ☎ **02/9281 6863.** Admission A$4 (U.S.$2.60) adults, A$2 (U.S.$1.30) children, A$10 (U.S.$6.50) families. Daily 9:30am–dusk. Ferry: Darling Harbour. Monorail: Convention. Sydney Explorer bus: Stop 19.

The largest Chinese garden of its type outside China offers a pleasant escape from the city concrete. It was designed by expert gardeners from China's Guangdong Province to embody principles of garden design dating back to the 5th century.

Panasonic IMAX Theatre. Southern Promenade, Darling Harbour. ☎ **02/9281 3300**. Admission A$14.95 (U.S.$9.70) adults, A$9.95 (U.S.$6.50) children 3–15, A$35 (U.S.$22.75) families. Daily 10am–10pm (until 11:30pm Fri and Sat). Ferry: Darling Harbour. Monorail: Convention. Sydney Explorer bus: Stop 20.

Four different IMAX films are usually showing on the gigantic eight-story-high screen. Each flick lasts about 50 minutes or so. The 3-D movies cost A$1 (U.S.65¢) extra.

Powerhouse Museum. 500 Harris St., Ultimo (near Darling Harbour). ☎ **02/9217 0111.** Admission A$8 (U.S.$5.20) adults, A$2 (U.S.$1.30) children, A$18 (U.S.$11.70) families. Free admission 1st Sat of every month. Daily 10am–5pm. Ferry: Darling Harbour. Monorail: Harbourside. Sydney Explorer bus: Stop 17.

Sydney's most interactive museum is also one of the largest in the Southern Hemisphere. Inside the post-modern industrial interior you'll find all sorts of displays and gadgets relating to the sciences, transportation, human achievement, decorative art, and social history. The many hands-on exhibits make this fascinating museum especially attractive for kids.

Sega World. Darling Harbour (between the IMAX Theatre and Chinese Gardens). ☎ **02/9273 9273.** www.segaworld.com.au. Admission A$28 (U.S.$18.20) adults, A$22 (U.S.$14.30) for an adult accompanying a child, A$22 (U.S.$14.30) children over 130cm (4'3"), A$15 (U.S.$9.75) children under 130cm (4'3"), and free for children under 90cm (2'11"). Entry includes all rides. Mon–Thurs 11am–8pm, Fri 11am–10pm, Sat 10am–10pm, Sun 10am–8pm. Ferry: Darling Harbour. Monorail: Convention.

If you fancy a few hours' break from the kids, or if you're just a big kid yourself, give this indoor theme park a try. Simulators, 3-D rides, computer games, and the like are fun, but occasionally a little lame. Very small children can't ride a couple of the best rides, but there's still plenty for them to do, though this place seems best for older kids and teenagers. Avoid the huge queues on Friday nights and weekends.

○ **Sydney Aquarium.** Aquarium Pier, Darling Harbour. ☎ **02/9262 2300.** Admission A$18 (U.S.$11.70) adults, A$8 (U.S.$5.20) children, A$41 (U.S.$26.65) families. The Aquarium Link ticket, available from CityRail train stations, combines Aquarium admission with a ferry ride. Daily 9am–10pm. Seal Sanctuary closes at 7pm in summer. CityRail: Town Hall. Ferry: Darling Harbour. Sydney Explorer bus: Stop 20.

This is one of the world's best aquariums and should be near the top of any Sydney itinerary. The main attractions are the underwater walkways through two enormous tanks—one containing an impressive collection of creatures you can find in Sydney Harbour, and the other full of giant rays and Grey Nurse Sharks. Other excellent exhibits include a giant Plexiglas room suspended inside a pool patrolled by rescued seals, and a truly magnificent section on the Great Barrier Reef, where thousands of colorful fish school around coral outcrops. Also on display are a couple of saltwater crocodiles and some tiny fairy penguins. Try to visit during the week when it's less crowded.

OTHER TOP ATTRACTIONS: A SPECTACULAR VIEW, SYDNEY'S CONVICT HISTORY & MORE

AMP Centrepoint Tower. Pitt and Market sts. ☎ **02/9229 7444.** Admission A$10 (U.S.$6.50) adults, A$4.50 (U.S.$2.90) children. Daily 9am–10:30pm. CityRail: St. James or Town Hall. Sydney Explorer bus: Stop 14.

The tallest building in the Southern Hemisphere is hard to miss: it resembles a giant steel pole skewering a golden marshmallow. Standing more than 300 meters (1,860 ft.) tall, it offers stupendous 360-degree views across Sydney and as far as the Blue Mountains. Fortunately, an elevator takes you to the indoor viewing platform. Don't be concerned if you feel the building tremble slightly, especially in a stiff breeze—I'm told it's perfectly natural. Below the tower are three floors of stores and restaurants.

Hyde Park Barracks Museum. Queens Sq., Macquarie St. ☎ **02/9223 8922.** Admission A$6 (U.S.$3.90) adults, A$3 (U.S.$1.95) children, A$15 (U.S.$9.75) families. Daily 9:30am–5pm. CityRail: St. James or Martin Place. Sydney Explorer bus: Stop 4.

These Georgian-style barracks were designed in 1819 by the convict/architect Francis Greenway. They were built by convicts and inhabited by fellow prisoners. These days modern displays here house relics, log books, and other artifacts from the days of early settlement. Don't miss the room full of ships' hammocks in which visitors can lie and listen to fragments of prisoner conversation. The courtyard cafe is excellent.

Museum of Contemporary Art (MCA). 140 George St., Circular Quay West. ☎ **02/ 9252 4033.** www.mca.com.au. Free Admission. Daily 10am–6pm (5pm in winter). CityRail, bus, ferry: Circular Quay. Sydney Explorer bus: Stop 1.

This imposing sandstone museum set back from the water on The Rocks side of Circular Quay offers wacky, entertaining, inspiring, and befuddling displays of what's new (and dated) in modern art. It houses the J. W. Power Collection of more than 4,000 pieces, including works by Andy Warhol, Christo, Marcel Duchamp, and Robert Rauschenberg, as well as temporary exhibits. Guided tours are offered Monday to Saturday at noon and 2pm, and Sunday at 2pm.

○ **Old Sydney Town.** Pacific Hwy., Somersby. ☎ **02/4340 1104.** Admission A$18 (U.S.$11.70) adults, A$10.50 (U.S.$6.80) children. Wed–Sun 10am–4pm; daily during school holidays. Somersby is near the town of Gosford, 84km (52 miles) north of Sydney. To reach Gosford by car, take the Pacific Hwy. and the Sydney-Newcastle Fwy. (F3); the trip takes about an hour. CityRail trains leave from Central Station for Gosford every 30 min. From Gosford, take the bus marked Old Sydney Town (15-min. ride).

You can spend quite a few hours on a nice day wandering around this outdoor theme park bustling with actors dressed up like convicts, sailors, and the like. You'll see plenty

Great Deals on Sightseeing

The **Privileges Card** is a great way to save money if you plan to visit Sydney's biggest attractions. The card costs A$25 (U.S.$16.25), is good for up to a month, and can be used in Sydney, Canberra, and Melbourne. In Sydney, all the major attractions offer some sort of discount if you show a Privileges Card, such as two-for-one admission or reduced-price admission if you're traveling alone. You'll also get discounts on harbor cruises (typically 20%), as well as discounts at certain restaurants (sometimes up to 20% off dinner for four). You can apply for the card over the Internet (www.privilegescard.com) or get one at tourist information centers in Sydney; you'll receive a booklet with details on where you can save. Call Privileges at ☎ **02/6254 1375.** If you book in advance, the company can arrange to have the card sent to your hotel.

Another money-saving option is the **Sydney Bonus Ticket,** which includes admission to the AMP Centrepoint Tower and the Sydney Aquarium, as well as a morning or afternoon harbor cruise with Captain Cook Cruises. You can also use the card to receive discounts while shopping in the AMP Centrepoint Tower shopping complex. The card costs A$39 (U.S.$25.30) for adults and A$29 (U.S.$18.90) for children. You can get the ticket from any of the participating operators or at the desk as you enter Centrepoint from Pitt Street Mall.

If you plan to hit the sights in Darling Harbour, you'll want to know about the **Super Ticket.** It includes a ride on the monorail, entry to both the Sydney Aquarium and the Chinese Gardens, a 2-hour cruise on the Matilda Harbour Express, a meal at the Sydney Aquarium cafe, and discounts on a coach tour of the site of the Sydney Olympic Games at Homebush Bay. The Super Ticket costs A$29.90 (U.S.$19.40) for adults and A$19.90 (U.S.$12.90) for children 3 to 15. It's available at monorail stations, the Sydney Aquarium, and Darling Harbour information booths.

of stores, buildings, and ships from the old days of the colony, and performances are staged all day. It's Australia's version of an American Wild West theme town.

The Sydney International Aquatic and Athletic Centres. Sydney 2000 Olympic Site, Olympic Park, Homebush Bay. ☎ **02/9752 3666.** Tours A$12 (U.S.$7.80) adults, A$8 (U.S.$5.20) children, A$40 (U.S.$26) families. Tours run hourly Mon–Fri 10am–3pm and Sat–Sun noon and 2pm. CityRail: Olympic Park.

This is the best Olympic swimming complex in the world, as well as the athletic center where the Olympic athletes trained. Tours last 90 minutes; otherwise, you can look around yourself for A$2.50 (U.S.$1.60). If you fancy a few laps afterward, be prepared to pay an additional A$5 (U.S.$3.25) for adults and A$4 (U.S.$2.60) for children.

MUSEUMS, GALLERIES, HISTORIC HOUSES & MORE

Art Gallery of New South Wales. Art Gallery Rd., The Domain. ☎ **02/9225 1744.** www.artgallery.nsw.gov.au. Free admission to most galleries. Special exhibitions vary, though expect to pay around A$12 (U.S.$7.80) adults, A$7 (U.S.$4.55) children. Daily 10am–5pm. Tours of general exhibits Tues–Fri 11am, noon, 1pm, and 2pm; Mon 1 and 2pm; call for week-end times. Tours of Aboriginal galleries Tues–Fri 11am, Sat and Sun 1pm. Free Aboriginal performance Tues–Sat noon. CityRail: St. James. Sydney Explorer bus: Stop 6.

The numerous galleries here present some of the best of Australian art and many fine examples by international artists, including good displays of Aboriginal and Asian art.

You enter from The Domain parklands on the third floor of the museum. On the fourth floor you will find an expensive restaurant and a gallery often showing free photography displays. On the second floor is a wonderful cafe overlooking the wharves and warships of Wooloomooloo. Every January and February there's a fabulous display of the best work created by school students throughout the state.

Australian Museum. 6 College St. ☎ **02/9320 6000.** www.austmus.gov.au. Admission A$8 (U.S.$5.20) adults, A$3 (U.S.$1.95) children, A$19 (U.S.$12.35) families. Special exhibits cost extra. Daily 9:30am–5pm. Closed Christmas. CityRail: Museum, St. James, or Town Hall. Sydney Explorer bus: Stop 15.

Though nowhere near as impressive as, say, the Natural History Museum in London or similar museums in Washington or New York, Sydney's premier natural history museum still ranks in the top five of its kind in the world. Displays are presented thematically. The best displays are in the Aboriginal section, with its traditional clothing, weapons, and everyday implements. There are some sorry examples of stuffed Australian wildlife too. Temporary exhibits run from time to time.

Customs House. Alfred St., Circular Quay. ☎ **02/9320 6429.** Free general admission. Admission to Djamu Gallery A$8 (U.S.$5.20) adults, A$2 (U.S.$1.30) children. Daily 9:30am–5pm. CityRail, bus, or ferry: Circular Quay.

This museum, across the large square opposite the Circular Quay CityRail station and the ferry wharves, opened in December 1998. It's worthwhile to take a look inside just for the stunning architecture. Once inside, you'll be hooked on the interesting series of modern art objects displayed on the ground floor, and the traveling exhibits on the third floor. The Djamu Gallery, on the second floor, has four small rooms of Aboriginal and South Pacific items—the overspill from the Australian Museum. Outside in the square is a cafe selling reasonably priced coffee, cakes, sandwiches, and the like.

Elizabeth Bay House. 7 Onslow Ave., Elizabeth Bay. ☎ **02/9356 3022.** Admission A$6 (U.S.$3.90) adults, A$3 (U.S.$1.95) children, A$15 (U.S.$9.75) families. Tues–Sun 10am–4:30pm. Closed Good Friday and Christmas. Bus: 311 from Circular Quay. Sydney Explorer bus: Stop 10.

This magnificent example of colonial architecture was built in 1835 and was described at the time as the "finest house in the colony." Visitors can tour the whole house and get a real feeling of the history of the fledgling settlement. The house is situated on a headland and has some of the best harbor views in Sydney.

Museum of Sydney. 37 Phillip St. ☎ **02/9251 5988.** Admission A$6 (U.S.$3.90) adults, A$3 (U.S.$1.95) children under 15, A$12 (U.S.$7.80) families. Daily 9:30am–5pm. CityRail, bus, or ferry: Circular Quay. Sydney Explorer bus: Stop 3.

You'll need your brain in full working order to make the most of the contents of this three-story post-modern building that encompasses the remnants of Sydney's first Government House. This place is far from being a conventional showcase of history; instead, it's a rather minimalist collection of first-settler and Aboriginal objects and multimedia displays that invite museumgoers to discover Sydney's past for themselves. Some Frommer's readers have criticized the place, saying it's not just minimalist; it's simply unfathomable. By the way, that forest of poles filled with hair, oyster shells, and crab claws in the courtyard adjacent to the industrial-design cafe tables is called *Edge of Trees.* It's a metaphor for the first contact between Aborigines and the British.

St. James Church. Queens Sq., Macquarie St. ☎ **02/9232 3022.** Daily 9am–5pm.

Sydney's oldest surviving colonial church, begun in 1822, was designed by the Government architect Francis Greenway. At one time the church's spire served as a landmark for ships coming up the harbor, but today it looks totally lost amidst the skyscrapers. It's well worth seeking out though, especially for the plaques on the wall, which pay testament to the hard early days of the colony when people were lost at sea, were "speared by blacks," or died while serving the British Empire overseas.

St. Mary's Cathedral. College and Cathedral sts. ☎ **02/9230 1414.** Mon–Tues 6:30am–6:30pm; Sat 8am–7:30pm; Sun 6:30am–7:30pm.

Sydney's most impressive worship place is a giant construction wedged between The Domain and Hyde Park. The original St. Mary's was built in 1821, but the chapel was destroyed by fire. Work on the present cathedral began in 1868 but, due to lack of funds, remained unfinished until work began in 1999 to build the two spires. The stained-glass windows inside are particularly impressive. St. Mary's is Roman Catholic and was built for Sydney's large population of Irish convicts. In perhaps Sydney's worst pre-Olympic planning, the beautiful brown sandstone building was marred by a wide stretch of dark grey paving outside, which has now become a battleground between skateboarders and city-council rangers.

State Library of NSW. Macquarie St. ☎ **02/9273 1414.** Free admission. Mon–Fri 9am–9pm; Sat, Sun, and selected holidays 11am–5pm. Closed New Year's Day, Good Friday, Christmas, and Boxing Day (Dec 26). CityRail: Martin Place. Sydney Explorer bus: Stop 4.

The state's main library is divided into two sections, the Mitchell and Dixon Libraries, located next door to one another. A newer reference-library complex nearby has two floors of reference materials, local newspapers, and microfiche viewers. If you are in this area of town at lunchtime, I highly recommend the library's leafy **Glasshouse Café,** in my opinion one of the best lunch spots in Sydney. The older building contains many older and more valuable books on the ground floor, and it often hosts free art and photography displays in the upstairs galleries. A small library section in the Sydney Town Hall building has international newspapers.

Sydney Jewish Museum. 148 Darlinghurst Rd. (at Burton St.), Darlinghurst. ☎ **02/9360 7999.** Admission A$7 (U.S.$4.55) adults, A$5 children (U.S.$3.25), A$16 (U.S.$10.40) families. Cash only. Mon–Thurs 10am–4pm; Fri 10am–2pm; Sun 11am–5pm. Closed Jewish holidays, Christmas, and Good Friday. CityRail: Kings Cross.

This is considered one of the best Jewish museums in the world. Harrowing exhibits include documents and objects relating to the Holocaust, mixed with soundscapes, audiovisual displays, and interactive media. There are also a museum shop, a resource center, a theater, and a traditional kosher cafe.

Sydney Observatory. Observatory Hill, Watson Rd., Millers Point. ☎ **02/9217 0485.** Admission free in daytime; guided night tours (reservations essential) A$10 (U.S.$6.50) adults, A$5 (U.S.$3.25) children, and A$25 (U.S.$16.25) families. Daily 10am–5pm. CityRail, bus, or ferry: Circular Quay.

The city's only major museum of astronomy offers visitors a chance to see the southern skies through modern and historic telescopes. The best time to visit is during the night on a guided tour, when you can take a close-up look at some of the planets. Night tours are offered at 8:15pm from the end of May to the end of August and at 6:15 and 8:15pm the rest of the year; be sure to double-check the times when you book your tour.

Vaucluse House. Wentworth Rd., Vaucluse. ☎ **02/9337 1957.** Admission A$6 (U.S.$3.90) adults, A$3 (U.S.$1.95) children, A$15 (U.S.$9.75) families. House Tues–Sun 10am–4:30pm. Grounds daily 7am–5pm. Free guided tours. Closed Good Friday and Christmas. Bus: 325 from Circular Quay.

This house overlooking Sydney Harbour includes lavish entertainment rooms and impressive stables and outbuildings. It was built in 1803 and was the home of Charles

Wentworth, the architect of the Australian Constitution. It's set in 27 acres of gardens, bushland, and beach frontage—perfect for picnics.

'ROOS, KOALAS & OTHER AUSSIE WILDLIFE

Australian Reptile Park. Pacific Hwy., Somersby. ☎ **02/4340 1022.** Admission A$11.95 (U.S.$7.75) adults, A$5.95 (U.S.$3.85) children. Daily 9am–5pm. Closed Christmas. Somersby is near the town of Gosford, 84km (52 miles) north of Sydney. To reach Gosford by car, take the Pacific Hwy. and the Sydney-Newcastle Fwy. (F3); the trip takes about an hour. CityRail trains leave from Central Station for Gosford every 30 min. From Gosford, take the bus marked Australian Wildlife Park (10-min. ride).

What started off as a one-man operation supplying deadly snake antivenin in the early 1950s has ended up a nature park teeming with the slippery-looking creatures. But it's not all snakes and lizards here. You'll also find Eric, a 15-foot-long saltwater crocodile; an alligator lagoon with some 50 American alligators; and plenty of somewhat-cuddlier creatures, such as koalas, platypus, wallabies, dingoes, and flying foxes. The park is set in beautiful bushland laced with nature trails.

✪ **Featherdale Wildlife Park.** 217 Kildare Rd., West Pennant Hills. ☎ **02/9622 1644.** Admission A$13 (U.S.$8.45) adults, A$6.50 (U.S.$4.20) children 4–14. Daily 9am–5pm. CityRail: Blacktown station, then take bus 725 to park (ask driver to tell you when to get off). By car: take the M4 motorway to Reservoir Rd., turn off, travel 4km (2^1/$_2$ miles), then turn left at Kildare Rd.

If you visit only one wildlife park in Sydney, make it this one. The selection of native Australian animals is excellent, and, most importantly, the animals are very well cared for. You could easily spend a couple of hours here despite the park's compact size. You'll have the chance to hand-feed plenty of friendly kangaroos and wallabies, and get a photo taken next to a koala (there are many here, both the New South Wales variety and the much larger Victorian type). The park offers twice-daily bus tours, which include hotel pickup and drop-off.

Koala Park. 84 Castle Hill Rd., West Pennant Hills. ☎ **02/9484 3141** or 02/9875 2777. Admission A$10 (U.S.$6.50) adults, A$5 (U.S.$3.25) children. Daily 9am–5pm. Closed Christmas. CityRail: Pennant Hills station via North Strathfield (45 min.), then take bus nos. 651–655 to park.

Unless you want to go all the way to Kangaroo Island in South Australia, it's unlikely you're going to spot as many koalas in the trees as you can find here. In all, there are around 55 koalas roaming within the park's leafy boundaries. Koala cuddling sessions are free, and take place at 10:20am, 11:45am, 2pm, and 3pm daily. There are also wombats, dingoes, kangaroos, wallabies, emus, and native birds here. You can hire a private guide to take you around for A$70 (U.S.$45.50) for a 2-hour session, or hitch onto one of the free "hostess" guides who wander around the park like Pied Pipers.

Oceanworld. West Esplanade, Manly. ☎ **02/9949 2644.** Admission A$14.50 (U.S.$9.40) adults, A$7.50 (U.S.$4.90) children, A$39 (U.S.$25.35) families. Daily 10am–5:30pm. Ferry or JetCat: Manly.

Though not as impressive as the Sydney Aquarium, Oceanworld can be combined with a visit to the wonderful Manly Beach (see below) for a nice day's outing. There's a pretty good display of Barrier Reef fish, a pool of giant saltwater turtles, and yet more giant sharks.

Taronga Zoo. Bradley's Head Rd., Mosman. ☎ **02/9969 2777.** Admission A$16 (U.S.$10.40) adults, A$8.50 (U.S.$5.50) children 4–15, and A$41.50 (U.S.$27) families. Zoopass (includes entry, round-trip ferry from Circular Quay, and Aerial Safari cable-car ride from ferry terminal to upper entrance of zoo) A$21 (U.S.$13.65) adults, A$10.50 (U.S.$6.80) seniors and children. Daily 9am–5pm (Jan 9am–9pm). Ferry: Taronga Zoo. At the Taronga Zoo wharf, a bus to the upper zoo entrance costs A$1.20 (U.S.80¢), or you can take a cable car to the top for A$2.50 (U.S.$1.60). The lower zoo entrance is a 2-min. walk up the hill from the wharf, but it's better on the legs to explore the zoo from the top down.

Taronga has the best view of any zoo in the world. Set on a hill, it looks out over Sydney Harbour, the Opera House, and the Harbour Bridge. The main attractions here are the fabulous chimpanzee exhibit, the gorilla enclosure, and the Nocturnal Houses, where you can see some of Australia's many nighttime marsupials out and about, including the platypus and the cuter-than-cute bilby (the official Australian Easter bunny). There is an interesting reptile display, a couple of rather impressive Komodo dragons, a scattering of indigenous Australian beasties—including a few koalas, echidnas, kangaroos, dingoes, and wombats—and lots more. The kangaroo and wallaby exhibit is very unimaginative; you'd be better off going to Featherdale Wildlife Park (see below) for happier-looking animals. Animals are fed at various times during the day. The zoo can get very crowded on weekends, so I strongly advise visiting during the week or going very early in the morning on weekends. Interestingly, the three sun bears near the lower ferry entrance were rescued by an Australian businessman, John Stephens, from a restaurant in Cambodia, where they were to have their paws cut off one by one and served up as an expensive soup.

HITTING THE BEACH

One of the big bonuses of visiting Sydney in the summer months (Dec, Jan, and Feb) is that you get to experience the beaches in their full glory.

Most major city beaches, such as Manly and Bondi, have lifeguards on patrol, especially during the summer months. They check the water conditions and are on the lookout for "rips"—strong ocean currents that can easily pull a swimmer far out to sea. Safe places to swim are marked by red and yellow flags. You must always swim between these flags, never outside them. If you are using a foam or plastic body board or "boogie board" it's also advisable to use them between the flags. Fiberglass surfboards must generally be used outside the flags. For more tips on safe swimming, see the section "Beach Savvy for Swimmers & Surfers," in chapter 2.

One of the first things visitors wonder when they hit the water in Australia is *Are there sharks?* The answer is yes, but fortunately, they're rarely spotted near shore. In reality, sharks have more reason to be scared of us than we do of them, because most of them end up as the fish portion in your average packet of fish-and-chips (you might see shark fillets sold as "flake"). Though some beaches, such as the small beach next to the Manly ferry wharf in Manly and a section of Balmoral Beach, have permanent shark nets, most rely on portable nets that are moved from beach to beach periodically to prevent territorial sharks from setting up home alongside bathers.

Another common problem off Sydney's beaches are **"blue bottles"**—small blue jellyfish, often called "stingers" in Australia and "Portuguese-Man-o'-Wars" elsewhere. You'll often find these creatures washed up along the beach; they become a nuisance when there's a strong breeze coming off the ocean and they're blown in to shore (watch for warning signs on the shoreline). Blue bottles deliver a hefty punch from their many stinging cells, and you will feel a severe burning sensation almost immediately. Minute individual cells often break off the body of the creature, and they can cause minor itching. Or you might be hit by a whole blue bottle, which will often stick to your skin and wrap its tentacles around you. If you are stung, ask a lifeguard for some vinegar to neutralize any stinging cells that haven't yet sprung into action. Otherwise, a very hot bath or shower can help relieve the pain, which can be very intense and last for up to a day.

SOUTH OF SYDNEY HARBOUR

Sydney's most famous beach is **Bondi.** In many ways, it's like a funky Southern California beach, with plenty of tanned in-line skaters. Though the beach is nice, it's cut off from the cafe and restaurant strip that caters to beachgoers by a big ugly road that pedestrians have to funnel across in order to reach the sand. To reach Bondi Beach, take the CityRail train to Bondi Junction, then transfer to bus 380. You can also catch bus 380 directly from Circular Quay.

If you follow the water along to your right at Bondi, you'll come across a very scenic cliff-top trail that takes you to **Bronte Beach** (a 20-min. walk), via gorgeous little **Tamarama,** a boutique beach known for its dangerous rips. Bronte has better swimming than Bondi. To get to Bronte, catch bus 378 from Circular Quay, or pick up the bus at the Bondi Junction CityRail station.

Clovelly Beach, farther along the coast, is blessed with a large rock pool carved into a rock platform and sheltered from the force of the Tasman Sea. This beach is accessible for visitors in wheelchairs via a series of ramps. To reach Clovelly, take bus 339 from Circular Quay.

The cliff walk from Bondi will eventually bring you to **Coogee,** which has a pleasant strip of sand with a couple of hostels and hotels nearby. To reach Coogee, take bus 373 or 374 from Circular Quay (via Pitt, George, and Castlereagh streets, and Taylor Square on Oxford Street) or bus 314 or 315 from Bondi Junction.

NORTH OF SYDNEY HARBOUR

The best harbor beach can be found at ✪ **Balmoral,** a wealthy North Shore hangout complete with its own little island and some excellent cafes and an upmarket restaurant. The beach itself is split into three separate parts. As you look toward the sea, the middle section is the most popular with sunbathers, while the wide expanse of sand to your left and the sweep of surreally beautiful sand to your right have a mere scattering. Reach Balmoral via a ferry to Taronga Zoo and then a 5-minute ride on a connecting bus from the ferry wharf (or take the special summer ferries, which also stop off at Watsons Bay and Manly).

Farther up on the north shore you'll find ✪ **Manly,** a long curve of golden sand edged with Norfolk Island Pines. (Don't be fooled by the two small beaches on either side of the ferry terminal as some people have been, including Arthur Conan Doyle. The novelist traveled to Manly by ferry and, presuming the small beach near the ferry station was the best the suburb had to offer, did not bother to disembark.) Follow the crowds shuffling through the pedestrianized "Corso" to the main ocean beach. You'll find one of Sydney's nicest walks here too. Looking at the ocean, head right along the beachfront and follow the coastal path to the small and sheltered Shelly Beach, a nice area for snorkeling and swimming (there's also a small food stand here, next to the beachfront restaurant, selling drinks and snacks). Follow the bitumen path up the hill

Grin & Bare It

If getting an all-over tan is your thing, you have a couple of options in Sydney. You can either head to the nudist beach at Lady Jane Bay, which is a short walk from Camp Cove Beach (accessed from Cliff Street in Watsons Bay). Or you can try Cobblers Beach, which is accessed via a short but steep bush track that leads from the far side of the playing-field oval next to the main HMAS Penguin naval base at the end of Bradley's Head Road in Mosman. Be prepared for a largely male scene—as well as the odd boatload of beer-swigging peeping toms.

to the parking lot. Here, a track cuts into the bush and leads toward a fire wall, which marks the entrance to Sydney Harbour National Park. Around here you'll get some spectacular ocean views across to Manly and the northern beaches (the headland farthest in the distance is Palm Beach). The best way to reach Manly is on a ferry or JetCat from Circular Quay.

Farther along the north coast are a string of ocean beaches, including the surf spots of **Curl Curl, Dee Why, Narrabeen, Mona Vale, Newport, Avalon,** and finally ✪ **Palm Beach,** a very long and beautiful strip of sand, cut from the calmer waters of **Pittwater** by sand dunes and a golf course. Here you'll also find the Barrenjoey Lighthouse, which also offers fine views along the coast (see the "Greater Sydney" map, later in this chapter, for a map of this area). Buses 136 and 139 run from Manly to Curl Curl, while bus 190 runs from Wynyard to Newport and then via the other northern beaches as far as Palm Beach.

PARKS & GARDENS
IN SYDNEY

THE ROYAL BOTANIC GARDENS   If you want to see the best of Sydney's green spaces, head for the Royal Botanic Gardens (☎ **02/9231 8111**), next to the Sydney Opera House. The gardens were laid out in 1816 on the site of a farm dedicated to supplying food for the fledgling colony. It's informal in appearance, with a scattering of duck ponds and open spaces, though several areas are dedicated to particular plant species, such as the rose garden, the cacti and succulents display, and the central palm and the rain-forest groves. **Mrs. Macquarie's Chair,** along the coast path, offers superb views of the Opera House and the Harbour Bridge (it's a favorite stop for tour buses). The giant sandstone building dominating the gardens nearest to the Opera House is **Government House,** which was once the official residence of the Governor of New South Wales (he moved out in 1996 in the spirit of republicanism). The pleasant gardens are open to the public daily from 10am to 4pm, and the house is open for inspection Friday to Sunday from 10am to 3pm. Entrance to both is free. If you plan to park around here, note that parking meters cost upwards of A$3 (U.S.$1.95) per hour, and you need A$1 coins.

A popular walk takes you through the Royal Botanic Gardens to the **Art Gallery of New South Wales.** The gardens are open daily from 7am to dusk. Admission is free.

HYDE PARK   In the center of the city is Hyde Park, a favorite with lunching businesspeople. Of note here are the **ANZAC Memorial** to Australian and New Zealand troops killed in the wars, and the **Archibald Fountain,** complete with spitting turtles and sculptures of Diana and Apollo. At night, avenues of trees are lit up with twinkling lights, giving the place a magical appearance.

MORE CITY PARKS   Another Sydney favorite is the giant **Centennial Park** (☎ **02/9339 6699**), usually accessed from the top of Oxford Street. It was opened in 1888 to celebrate the centenary of European settlement, and today it encompasses huge areas of lawn, several lakes, picnic areas with outdoor grills, cycling and running paths, and a cafe. It's open from sunrise to sunset. To get there, take bus 373, 374, 377, 380, 396, or 398 from the city.

A hundred years later, **Bicentennial Park,** at Australia Avenue, in Homebush Bay, came along. Forty percent of the park's total 100 hectares (247 acres) is general parkland reclaimed from a city landfill; the rest is the largest remaining remnant of wetlands on the Parramatta River and is home to many species of both local and migratory wading birds, cormorants, and pelicans. At 1:30pm Monday through Friday, a tractor train takes visitors around the park on a 1- to 1¹/₂-hour guided trip. Tours cost A$8 (U.S.$5.20) for adults and A$7 (U.S.$4.55) for children. Follow park signs to the **visitor information office** (☎ 02/9763 1844), open Monday through Friday from 10am to 4pm, and Saturday and Sunday from 9:30am to 4:30pm. To reach the park, you can either take a CityRail train to Strathfield and then take bus 401 to Homebush Bay (ask the driver when to get off), or take a CityRail train directly to the Homebush CityRail station.

BEYOND SYDNEY

SYDNEY HARBOUR NATIONAL PARK   You don't need to go far to experience Sydney's nearest national park. The Sydney Harbour National Park stretches around parts of the inner harbor and includes several small harbor islands (many first-time visitors are surprised at the amount of bushland still remaining in prime real-estate territory). The best walk through the Sydney Harbour National Park is the **Manly to Spit Bridge Scenic Walkway** (☎ 02/9977 6522). This 10-kilometer (6-mile) track winds its way from Manly (it starts near the Oceanarium), via Dobroyd Head to Spit Bridge (where you can catch a bus back to the city). The walk takes between 3 and 4 hours, and the views across busy Sydney Harbour are fabulous. Maps are available from the **Manly Visitors Information Bureau,** right opposite the main beach (☎ 02/9977 1088).

Other access points to the park include tracks around Taronga Zoo (ask the zoo staff to point you toward the rather-concealed entrances) and above tiny Shelly Beach, opposite the main beach at Manly.

Also part of the national park is the recently restored **Fort Denison,** the easily recognizable fortified outcrop in the middle of the harbor between Circular Quay and Manly. The fort was built during the Crimean War due to fears of a Russian invasion, and later acted as a penal colony. Note: Renovations to Fort Denison started in 2000; the fort is due to reopen for tours in early 2001. Pick up maps of Sydney Harbour National Park at Cadmans Cottage, in The Rocks (☎ 02/9247 8861).

Another great walk in Sydney can be combined with lunch or a drink at Watsons Bay. A 15-minute bush stroll to **South Head** is accessed from the small beach outside the Watsons Bay Hotel. Walk to the end of the beach (to your right as you look at the water), then up the flight of steps and bear left. There are some great views of the harbor from the lighthouse here.

MORE NATIONAL PARKS   Forming a semicircle around the city are Sydney's biggest parks of all. To the west is the **Blue Mountains National Park** (see chapter 4), to the northeast is **Ku-ring-gai Chase National Park,** and to the south is the magnificent **Royal National Park.** All three parks are home to marsupials like echidnas and wallabies, numerous bird and reptile species, and a broad range of native plant life. Walking tracks, whether they stretch for half an hour or a few days, make each park accessible to the visitor.

Ku-ring-gai Chase National Park (☎ 02/9457 9322 or 02/ 9457 9310) is a great place to take a bushwalk through gum trees and rain forest on the lookout for wildflowers, sandstone rock formations, and Aboriginal art. There are plenty of tracks through the park, but one of my favorites is a relatively easy 2.5-kilometer (1.5-mile) tramp to **The Basin** (Track 12). The well-graded dirt path takes you down to a popular estuary with a beach and passes some significant Aboriginal engravings. There are also some wonderful water views over Pittwater from the picnic areas at **West Head.** Pick up a free walking guide at the park entrance, or gather maps and information in Sydney at the National Parks & Wildlife Service's center at **Cadmans Cottage,** 110 George St., The Rocks (☎ 02/9247 8861). The park is open from sunrise to sunset, and admission is A$9 (U.S.$5.85) per car. You can either drive to the park or catch a ferry from Palm Beach to The Basin. Ferries run on the hour (except at 1pm) from 9am to 5pm daily and cost A$3.50 (U.S.$2.30) one-way or A$7 (U.S.$4.55) return; call ☎ **02/9918 2747** for details. Shorelink bus 577 runs from the Turramurra CityRail station to the nearby park entrance every hour on weekdays and every 2 hours on weekends; call ☎ **02/9457 8888** for details. There is no train service to the park. Camping is allowed only at The Basin (☎ **02/9457 9853**) and costs A$10 (U.S.$6.50) for two people booked in advance.

While in the area, you could visit the **Ku-ring-gai Wildflower Garden,** 420 Mona Vale Rd., St Ives (☎ **02/9440 8609**), which is essentially a huge area of natural bush-land and a center for urban bushland education. There are plenty of bushwalking tracks, self-guided walks, and a number of nature-based activities. It's open daily from 8am to 4pm. Admission is A$2.50 (U.S.$1.60) for adults, A$1 (U.S.65¢) for children, and A$6 (U.S.$3.90) for families.

To the south of Sydney is the remarkable **Royal National Park,** Farrell Avenue, Sutherland (☎ **02/9542 0648**). It's the world's oldest national park, having been gazetted as such in 1879 (Yellowstone, in the United States, was established in 1872 but wasn't designated as a national park until 1883). Severe bushfires almost totally destroyed the whole lot in early 1994, but the trees and bush plants have recovered remarkably. There's no visitor center, but you can pick up park information at park entrances, where you'll have to pay a A$9 (U.S.$5.85) per-car entry fee.

There are several ways to access the park, but my favorites are the little-known access points from Bundeena and Otford. To get to Bundeena, take a CityRail train from Central Station to Cronulla. Just below the train station you'll find Cronulla Wharf. From there, hop on the delightful ferry run by **National Park Ferries** (☎ **02/9523 2990**) to Bundeena; ferries run hourly on the half hour (except 12:30pm). After you get off the ferry, the first turn on your left just up the hill will take you to **Bundeena Beach.** It's another 5 kilometers (3 miles) or so to the wonder-fully remote **Little Marley Beach,** via Marley Beach (which has dangerous surf). The ferry returns to Cronulla from Bundeena hourly on the hour (except 1pm). The fare is A$2.40 (U.S.$1.55) each way.

An alternative way to reach the park is to take the train from Central Station to **Otford,** then climb the hill up to the sea cliffs. If you're driving, you might want to follow the scenic cliff-edge road down into Wollongong. The entrance to the national park is a little tricky to find, so you may have to ask directions. A 2-hour walk from the sea cliffs through beautiful and varying bush land and a palm forest will take you to **Burning Palms Beach.** There is no water along the route. The walk back up is steep, so attempt this trek only if you're reasonably fit. Trains to the area are irregular, and the last one departs around 4pm; so give yourself at least 2¹/₂ hours for the return trip to the train station to make sure you don't get stranded. It's possible to walk the 26 kilometers (16 miles) from Otford to Bundeena, or vice versa, in 2 days (take all your food, water, and camping gear).

ESPECIALLY FOR KIDS

There are plenty of places kids can have fun in Sydney, but the recommendations below are particularly suitable for youngsters (all of the places are reviewed in full above).

Taronga Zoo (see p. 141) is an all-time favorite with kids, where the barnyard ani-mals, surprisingly, get as much attention as the koalas. If your kids want hands-on contact with the animals, though, you'd better head to **Featherdale Wildlife Park** (see p. 141), where they can get their photo taken next to a koala, and hand-feed and stroke kangaroos and wallabies.

Sega World (see p. 136) in Darling Harbour will entertain the kids for a few hours, but the trouble is adults can't resist the rides, too. Just as interactive are the exhibits just crying out to be touched and bashed at the **Powerhouse Museum** (see p. 136).

The sharks at **Oceanworld** (see p. 141) in Manly and at the **Sydney Aquarium** (see p. 137) in Darling Harbour are big lures for kids, too, and the thrill of walking through a long Plexiglas tunnel as giant manta rays perch over their heads will lead to more squeals of excitement. Another fascinating outing for both adults and children is to crawl around inside a navy destroyer at the **National Maritime Museum** (see p. 136)—if you're lucky, there may even be a submarine to explore, too.

And, of course, what kid wouldn't enjoy a day at the beach, and Sydney's got plenty to choose from, like **Bondi** or **Manly.**

6 Great City Strolls

Sydney is relatively compact, so it's a wonderful city for exploring on foot. The first walking tour below, through The Rocks, is a "must-do" for any first-time visitor.

Walking Tour 1: On The Rocks

Start: The Rocks Visitor Centre and Exhibition Gallery, 106 George St.
Finish: George Street.
Time: Allow around an hour, longer if you stop to shop.
Best times: Any day, though Saturday brings The Rocks Market and big crowds on George Street.

The Rocks is the site of the oldest settlement in Australia. Initially, convict-built timber houses lined the rocky ridge, which gave the area its name, and dockyard buildings lined the water's edge. In the 1840s a range of more permanent stone buildings was erected, including most of the pubs and shops still standing today. Slums grew up, too, and when the bubonic plague came to Sydney in 1900, the government set about demolishing most of the shanty buildings. Between 1923 and 1932 a large portion of the historic stone cottages in the area were pulled down to make way for construction of the Harbour Bridge. In the 1970s the government decided to pull the lot down and replace it with giant office blocks and a hotel. Local residents stood together, though, and following a 2-year "Green Ban" by the Builders' Labourers Federation, during which they refused to touch any historic building, the government relented.

Start your walk at:

1. **The Sydney Visitor Centre,** 106 George St., The Rocks (☎ **02/9255 1788**), open daily from 9am to 6pm. This excellent visitor center has plenty of information on Sydney, but also a whole range of Australiana books. Upstairs, on two levels, is a fascinating gallery of photographs, explanatory texts, an audio-visual presentation, and objects relating to The Rocks. The building itself is part of the former Sydney Sailors' Home built in the 1860s.

   Outside on George Street, turn left, then turn left again at the first small avenue you come to. Walking down toward the water, you'll see:

2. **Cadmans Cottage,** built in 1816. This small white building was the headquarters of the government body that regulated the colony's waterways. It's named after John Cadman, a pardoned convict who became the government coxswain, and who lived here from 1827 to 1846. Turn toward the water, look to the right, and you'll see a row of historic buildings:

3. **The Sailors' Home,** built in 1864, is the first of them. Sydney was a rough old town in those days, and no sooner had a sailor left his ship with his wages than he was likely to lose them in the brothels, pubs, and opium dens; gamble it away; or be mugged by gangs of "larrikins" who patrolled the back lanes. Concerned local citizens built this home to provide stricken sailors with lodging and food.

4. **The Coroners Court** (1907), next door, used to sit above the now-demolished morgue (or "Dead House," as it was called). Before the Coroners Court was built, bodies would often be dissected for autopsy on the bar of the Observer Tavern across the street, over a few beers. Notice the exposed original foreshore rocks displayed beneath an arch on the wall.

5. **Mariners Church,** built in 1856, is a neoclassical building mostly obscured by later buildings.

6. **Australasian Steam Navigation Company Building,** built in 1884, has a fabulous Flemish clock tower that was once used for spotting incoming ships. Take a look inside the Natural Australian Furniture Shop at the amazing wooden rafters. It was used as a storehouse, but before that the location was occupied by the home of the prominent merchant Robert Campbell.

7. **Campbell's Storehouse** (1838 and 1890) was where Robert Campbell stored his tea, sugar, cloth, and liquor, which he imported from Asia. This wonderful pair of gabled buildings now houses four popular restaurants. From here retrace your steps back to a short flight of stairs that takes you up to Hickson Road. Turn left onto George Street, then cross the road, and turn left onto:

8. **Atherden Street,** the shortest street in Sydney; it was named after a local landowner. Notice the natural rock wall at its end that gave The Rocks its name. Turn left onto Playfair Street. Notice the markings in the rock walls where old slum dwellings used to be affixed. A little way along you'll see some steps. Follow them up to:

9. **Foundation Park,** an interesting artist's impression of what it was like inside the remaining structure of an old house in The Rocks. There wasn't much room, as you'll see. Follow the steps up to your right to Gloucester Walk. Follow this along until you get to Argyle Street. Turn left and walk down the hill, and on the corner of George Street you'll find a nice place to:

☕ **TAKE A BREAK** The historic **Orient Hotel** has dining areas upstairs, or you could just refresh yourself with a glass of local beer from the bar (order a "schooner" if you're really thirsty, or a smaller "midi").

When you're refreshed, head back up Argyle Street, where you'll find a great archway across the road.

10. **The Argyle Cut** was made by chain gangs chipping away at a mass of solid rock in a bid to link The Rocks to Cockle Bay (now Darling Harbour). The project was started in 1843, but 2 years later the use of convict labor for government projects was prohibited in the colony. In 1859 it was finally blasted through with explosives. At the top of the hill to your right is:

11. **Garrison Church,** built in 1839, a wonderful little Anglican church with stained-glass windows. It's engraved at the base with the names of children who died prematurely. In the early years soldiers sat on one side of the church, and free settlers sat on the other. To keep the riffraff out, people had to pay for their pew, which was then name-tagged. Return back along Argyle Street the way you came and turn right onto Harrington Street.

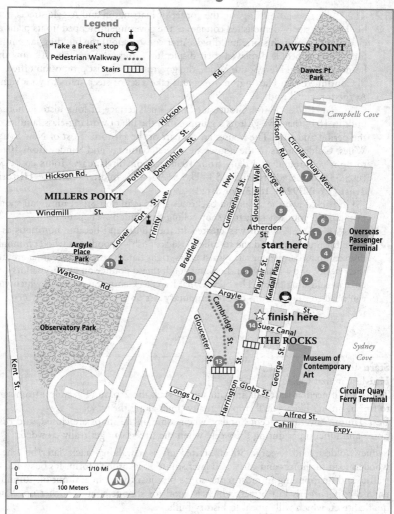

Legend
Church
"Take a Break" stop
Pedestrian Walkway
Stairs

DAWES POINT

Dawes Pt. Park

Campbells Cove

Hickson Rd.

MILLERS POINT

Windmill St.

Hickson Rd.

Hickson St.

Downshire St.

Pottinger

Lower Fort St.

Trinity Ave.

Argyle Place Park

Watson Rd.

Observatory Park

Kent St.

Bradfield Hwy.

Cumberland St.

Gloucester Walk

George St.

Circular Quay West

Atherden St.

start here

7

8

6

1

5

4

3

2

Overseas Passenger Terminal

Playfair St.

Kendall Plaza

9

Argyle St.

10

12

finish here

14 Suez Canal

THE ROCKS

Cambridge St.

Gloucester St.

Harrington St.

Globe St.

George St.

13

Longs Ln.

Museum of Contemporary Art

Sydney Cove

Circular Quay Ferry Terminal

Alfred St.

Cahill Expy.

0   1/10 Mi
0   100 Meters
N

12. The Clocktower Building, on the corner of Harrington and Argyle streets, was built on the site of demolished cottages as the government stepped up its plans to clear the area of its historic buildings. After construction, the building lay empty for 5 years as people displayed their displeasure. Ironically, perhaps, it's now the home of Tourism New South Wales, the government tourist promotion office.

Continue down Harrington Street and take a set of steep stairs to your right. At the top you'll find:

13. Susannah Place, 58–64 Gloucester St., a small terrace of four historic houses built in 1844 that give visitors a glimpse into the life of working-class families of the period and later. The houses are all part of the Historic Trust of New South Wales. Guided tours of the houses are offered Saturday and Sunday from 10am to 5pm year-round and daily from 10am to 5pm in January. Tours cost A$5 (U.S.$3.25) for adults, and A$3 (U.S.$1.95) for children. Call the **Historic Trust** (☎ **02/9241 1893**) for details.

Go back down the stairs and backtrack on Harrington Street until you spot a thin lane to your left next to a shop selling didgeridoos. The lane is:

14. The Suez Canal, which was created in the 1840s and became notorious as a place for prostitutes and the so-called "Rocks Push"—hoodlums who commonly dressed up as dandies in satin waist coats, tight flared pants, a bandanna around their necks, and a jaunty hat. Looking good, they'd pounce on unwary sailors and citizens and mug them. The Suez Canal leads to George Street, from which you can head to the Museum of Contemporary Art or to Circular Quay.

Walking Tour 2: The City Streets

Start: Town Hall.
Finish: Circular Quay.
Time: You'll need at least half an hour just to walk the 2^1/$_2$km (1^1/$_2$ miles) from start to finish, but it's likely you'll stop off many times along the way.
Best Times: Any time except Sunday, when some of the shops are closed, and rush hours and lunchtimes during the week, when the streets can get really crowded.

Sydney's oldest road, George Street, started off as a walking track, later became a wooden road for horses and carts, and later still took its asphalt form. It's busy, full of traffic, and unappealing in most parts, so it's best just to dip in and out of. Running parallel to George is Pitt Street, which is good for shoppers, and, farther up, Macquarie Street, which will appeal to history buffs.

Begin your walk at:

1. Town Hall (1889). Every city has to have a place to roll a red carpet into, and this is Sydney's. This impressive sandstone building is home to the Lord Mayor's council, and it also acts as an exhibition space and a concert hall. Visitors are welcome to have a look around the lower floor. Adjacent to Town Hall is:

2. The Queen Victoria Building (1883), a fabulous piece of architecture with some 200 shops on four levels. It's been described as the best arcade in the world by more than a few high-profile architects. Inside it's all arches, filtered light, Romanesque columns, ornate plasterwork, stained-glass windows, and lace ironwork. It started off life as a produce market but fell into disrepair from the 1930s on, before rising phoenix-like from its mothballs in 1986. If you're around on the hour, look out for the amazing clock that displays English history in pop-up book form.

AT&T Direct® Service

AT&T Access Numbers

Aruba	800-8000	Czech Rep. ▲	00-42-000-101
Australia ●	1-800-551-155	Egypt ●(Cairo)†	510-0200
Austria ●	0800-200-288	France	0-800-99-0011
Bahamas	1-800-872-2881	Germany	0800-2255-288
Barbados +	1-800-872-2881	Greece ●	00-800-1311
Belgium ●	0-800-100-10	Guam	1-800-2255-288
Bermuda +	1-800-872-2881	Hong Kong	800-96-1111
Cayman Isl.+	1-800-872-2881	Hungary	06-800-01111
China, PRC ▲	10811	India ✱,➤	000-117
Costa Rica	0-800-0-114-114	Ireland ✓	1-800-550-000

AT&T Direct® Service

AT&T Access Numbers

Aruba	800-8000	Czech Rep. ▲	00-42-000-101
Australia ●	1-800-551-155	Egypt ●(Cairo)†	510-0200
Austria ●	0800-200-288	France	0-800-99-0011
Bahamas	1-800-872-2881	Germany	0800-2255-288
Barbados +	1-800-872-2881	Greece ●	00-800-1311
Belgium ●	0-800-100-10	Guam	1-800-2255-288
Bermuda +	1-800-872-2881	Hong Kong	800-96-1111
Cayman Isl.+	1-800-872-2881	Hungary	06-800-01111
China, PRC ▲	10811	India ✱,➤	000-117
Costa Rica	0-800-0-114-114	Ireland ✓	1-800-550-000

Israel●	1-800-94-94-949	Philippines●	105-11
Italy●	172-1011	Portugal▲	0800-800-128
Jamaica●	1-800-872-2881	Singapore	800-0111-111
Japan●▲	005-39-111	Spain	900-99-00-11
Malaysia●	1800-80-0011	Switzerland●	0-800-89-0011
Mexico●▽	01-800-288-2872	Thailand《	001-999-111-11
Neth. Ant.●	001-800-872-2881	Turkey●	00-800-12277
Netherlands●	0800-022-9111	U.K.	0800-89-0011
New Zealand●	000-911	U.K.	0800-013-0011
Panama	800-001-0109	Venezuela	800-11-120

FOR EASY CALLING WORLDWIDE

1.Just dial the AT&T Access Number for the country you are calling from. 2.Dial the phone number you're calling. 3.Dial your card number.

For access numbers not listed ask any operator for **AT&T Direct®** Service. In the U.S. call 1-800-331-1140 for a wallet guide listing all worldwide AT&T Access Numbers.

Visit our **Web** site at: www.att.com/traveler
Bold-faced countries permit country-to-country calling outside the U.S.

- ● Public phones may require coin or card deposit to place call.
- + Outside of Cairo, dial "02" first.
- ▲ May not be available from every phone/payphone.
- ♦ Public phones and select hotels.
- ✓ Use U.S. access number in N. Ireland.
- 《 When calling from public phones, use phones marked "Lenso."
- ▽ When calling from public phones, use phones marked "Ladatel."
- ✗ Not available from public phones.
- ▼ Available from phones with international calling capabilities or from most Public Calling Centers.
- ○ From St. Maarten or phones at Bobby's Marina, use 1-800-872-2881.

When placing an international call *from* the U.S., dial 1 800 CALL ATT.

© 1/2000

Israel●	1-800-94-94-949	Philippines●	105-11
Italy●	172-1011	Portugal▲	0800-800-128
Jamaica●	1-800-872-2881	Singapore	800-0111-111
Japan●▲	005-39-111	Spain	900-99-00-11
Malaysia●	1800-80-0011	Switzerland●	0-800-89-0011
Mexico●▽	01-800-288-2872	Thailand《	001-999-111-11
Neth. Ant.●	001-800-872-2881	Turkey●	00-800-12277
Netherlands●	0800-022-9111	U.K.	0800-89-0011
New Zealand●	000-911	U.K.	0800-013-0011
Panama	800-001-0109	Venezuela	800-11-120

FOR EASY CALLING WORLDWIDE

1.Just dial the AT&T Access Number for the country you are calling from. 2.Dial the phone number you're calling. 3.Dial your card number.

For access numbers not listed ask any operator for **AT&T Direct®** Service. In the U.S. call 1-800-331-1140 for a wallet guide listing all worldwide AT&T Access Numbers.

Visit our **Web** site at: www.att.com/traveler
Bold-faced countries permit country-to-country calling outside the U.S.

- ● Public phones may require coin or card deposit to place call.
- + Outside of Cairo, dial "02" first.
- ▲ May not be available from every phone/payphone.
- ♦ Public phones and select hotels.
- ✓ Use U.S. access number in N. Ireland.
- 《 When calling from public phones, use phones marked "Lenso."
- ▽ When calling from public phones, use phones marked "Ladatel."
- ✗ Not available from public phones.
- ▼ Available from phones with international calling capabilities or from most Public Calling Centers.
- ○ From St. Maarten or phones at Bobby's Marina, use 1-800-872-2881.

When placing an international call *from* the U.S., dial 1 800 CALL ATT.

© 1/2000

TIMBUKTU   KALAMAZOO

AT&T Direct® Service

The easy way to call home from anywhere.

Global
connection
with the AT&T
Network | **AT&T**
direct
service

For the easy way to call home, take the attached wallet guide.

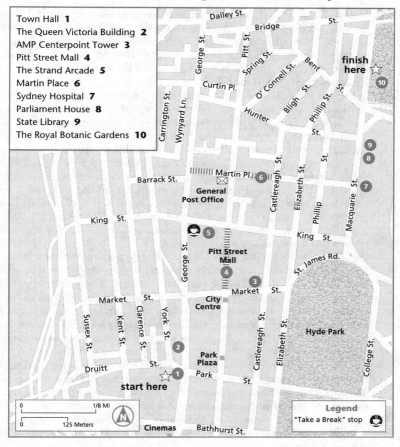

Town Hall **1**
The Queen Victoria Building **2**
AMP Centerpoint Tower **3**
Pitt Street Mall **4**
The Strand Arcade **5**
Martin Place **6**
Sydney Hospital **7**
Parliament House **8**
State Library **9**
The Royal Botanic Gardens **10**

finish here

start here

Legend
"Take a Break" stop

Leaving the building at the far end, cross over the road and walk down Market Street to:

3. **AMP Centrepoint Tower,** which has some good shopping and a cheap food court on its lower levels. Don't miss out on catching an elevator to the top (see "Other Top Attractions," earlier this chapter). Find your way out of the Pitt Street entrance again and you're on:

4. **Pitt Street Mall.** This pedestrian-only shopping street has a couple of excellent record shops and some well-stocked fashion boutiques. At the end of the mall turn left into:

5. **The Strand Arcade (1892).** This Victorian thoroughfare runs between Pitt and George streets on three levels. There are some interesting shops here.

   TAKE A BREAK **The Old Coffee Shop,** on the ground floor of the Strand Arcade, is a terrifically atmospheric place to rest up and get a cup of reasonable coffee. They serve good cakes, too. When you've had your fill, head back out to George Street and continue walking to:

6. **Martin Place.** This closed-off street is a strange-looking, often wind-blown "square," but it's all that the city center has to call a plaza. Lunchtime sees crowds munching on sandwiches as they listen to free performances (beginning at 12:15pm). The sturdy building to your left as you enter Martin Place is the original General Post Office. Continue right up to the end and you'll arrive at Macquarie Street. Across the road is the:

7. **Sydney Hospital.** The original hospital on this site was huge and was known as the "Rum Hospital" following its construction in 1816 (after a design by Government architect Francis Greenway) because its builders were paid in the form of a 3-year monopoly to import rum into the colony. This more modern building was constructed in 1894, and it offered far better conditions than in the old days, when nurses often stole their patient's food and operations were performed on the kitchen table. Notice Il Porcellino, the bronze pig in the front yard; it's a copy of a statue that stands in Florence, Italy. It's supposed to bring good luck if you put a donation in the box and stroke its nose. The south wing of the Rum Hospital became a branch of the Royal Mint following the 1850s gold rushes. Today, it acts as a museum concentrating on Australian currency. There's a restaurant upstairs that is reportedly a good lunch spot.

8. **Parliament House** (☎ **02/9230 2111**) is where the state's politicians argue over how they'll spend the public's money. It was originally a wing of the Rum Hospital, but it was converted to the more sober business of government in 1828. Visitors can pop in and see the action when parliament is sitting. Question time, starting at 2:15pm on Tuesdays, Wednesdays, and Thursdays, is the best time to visit, but you must book in advance. Free guided tours are available on nonsitting days at 10am, 11am, and 2pm. Bookings are essential. Next to Parliament House is:

9. **The State Library,** split into two separate parts. The older sandstone building on the corner of Macquarie and Bent streets holds a wide range of important historical books, while the newer section next door has two levels of reference materials. Continue on Macquarie Street to the entrance just across Bent Street of:

10. **The Royal Botanic Gardens.** At this end of the gardens is the Rose Garden. From here walk downhill to the sea, then follow the sea wall to your left all the way to Circular Quay.

Walking Tour 3: The Bridge, the House & the Gardens

Start: Milsons Point CityRail Train Station.
End: The Art Gallery of New South Wales.
Time: Around 2 hours.
Best times: Anytime but peak traffic hours, when the Harbour Bridge becomes a bit too smoggy.

This walk takes in some of Sydney's major icons, the Harbour Bridge and the Opera House, as well as a wander through the Botanic Gardens to the Art Gallery of New South Wales.

Start your walk at:

1. **Milsons Point CityRail Train Station,** which is just one stop from the Wynyard station across Sydney Harbour. Just around the corner from the train station (literally a 20-sec. walk), you'll find a set of steps that lead to the Harbour Bridge walkway.

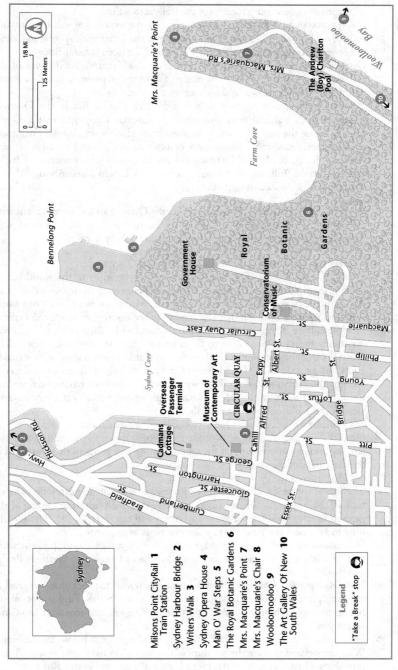

1/8 Mi
125 Meters

Mrs. Macquarie's Rd.

Woolloomooloo Bay

The Andrew (Boy) Charlton Pool

Farm Cove

Bennelong Point

Government House

Royal Botanic Gardens

Conservatorium of Music

Circular Quay East

Macquarie St.

Sydney Cove

Overseas Passenger Terminal

Museum of Contemporary Art

CIRCULAR QUAY

Cadmans Cottage

George St.

Harrington St.

Gloucester St.

Cumberland St.

Bradfield St.

Hickson Rd.

Hwy.

Cahill Expy.

Alfred St.

Albert St.

Phillip St.

Young St.

Loftus St.

Bridge St.

Pitt St.

Essex St.

Sydney

Milsons Point CityRail Train Station **1**
Sydney Harbour Bridge **2**
Writers Walk **3**
Sydney Opera House **4**
Man O' War Steps **5**
The Royal Botanic Gardens **6**
Mrs. Macquarie's Point **7**
Mrs. Macquarie's Chair **8**
Wooloomooloo **9**
The Art Gallery Of New South Wales **10**

Legend
"Take a Break" stop

Surprisingly, few tourists attempt the walk across the:

2. **Sydney Harbour Bridge,** though I guarantee the experience will stay in your memory. The walk takes you from one side to the other with spectacular views in between. You could stop off at the Pilon Lookout (see Harbour Bridge in "The Opera House & Sydney Harbour," earlier in this chapter). At the end of the walkway on the Sydney side of the bridge, follow the steps down into The Rocks and make your way down to the waterfront to the:

3. **Writers Walk,** which starts just past a fig tree planter beside the Overseas Passenger Terminal and carries on through Circular Quay and to the Opera House. Along the way are a series of round brass plaques set into the brick footpath that celebrate the achievements of both Australian and overseas writers. Look out for A. B. "Banjo" Patterson, Henry Lawson, D. H. Lawrence, Charles Darwin, David Williamson, Kenneth Slessor, Jack London, and Aboriginal poet Oodgeroo Noonuccal, among others.

☕ **TAKE A BREAK   Rossini,** in Circular Quay, is an Italian restaurant with chairs out front (see section 4, "Dining," earlier in this chapter). It's a good place for a coffee, an ice cream, or a good-sized lunch if you're hungry.

After you've refueled, continue along Circular Quay to the:

4. **Sydney Opera House.** The best looking modern building in the world has its roots firmly in the colonial past. It stands on Bennelong Point, named after an Aborigine befriended by Governor Macquarie. Macquarie built him a hut where the Opera House now stands to encourage other Aborigines to see the benefits of white culture. Bennelong later died in a quarrel with others of his tribe; he had eventually found it impossible to fit in either white or Aboriginal society. The original name for the point site, though, was Cattle Point, named after six cows and a bull kept there. (The herd escaped and ran off into the forest when the convict guarding them fell asleep. They were found 7 years later, having bred up into quite a herd.) Walk up the Opera House steps, where you can get a very unusual view of the building's two main shells.

Continue on around the Opera House until you reach the:

5. **Man O' War Steps.** This set of stone steps going down to the water acted as a landing and embarkation point for sailors coming and going in their warships in the early days of the colony.

Next proceed to:

6. **The Royal Botanic Gardens,** entered just by the sea wall. You can follow the sea wall all the way around Farm Cove, or alternatively dip into the middle of the gardens to take advantage of the shady groves and rain-forest walks. The gardens used to be where the First Fleet's vegetable plots were planted.

7. **Mrs. Macquarie's Point** is at the far end of the sea wall. Up on top of the small cliff here is one of the best spots to see the Opera House and Harbour Bridge together.

8. **Mrs. Macquarie's Chair** is simply a bench cut out of the rock that was used as a resting place for Governor Macquarie's wife on her walks. Find it just up the hill on the asphalt footpath. Walk up to the parking lots and across the headland, where you'll see:

9. **Wooloomooloo.** The long warehouse-type buildings down below are the Finger Wharves; beyond that are the warships of the Australian navy (and visiting American ships when they're in port). From here, walk up Art Gallery Road to:

10. The Art Gallery of New South Wales. End your trip here with a browse around the galleries. When you've finished, retrace your steps to the far end of the motor bridge, where an entry will take you back into the Botanic Gardens. Alternatively, walk across the parkland opposite the gallery, called The Domain, and you'll end up on Macquarie Street near Martin Place CityRail train station.

7 Harbor Cruises & Other Organized Tours

For details on the Red Sydney Explorer bus, see "Getting Around," earlier in this chapter.

HARBOR CRUISES

The best thing about Sydney is the harbor, so you shouldn't leave without taking a harbor cruise. **Sydney Ferries** (☎ 13 15 00) offers a 1-hour morning harbor cruise with commentary departing Circular Quay, wharf 4, daily at 10 and 11:15am. It costs A$14 (U.S.$9.10) for adults, A$9.50 (U.S.$6.20) for children under 16, and A$37.50 (U.S.$24.40) for families (any number of children under 16). A 2^1/$_2$-hour afternoon cruise explores more of the harbor and leaves from Wharf 4 at 1pm on weekdays and 1:30pm on weekends and public holidays. This tour costs A$21 (U.S.$13.65) for adults, A$12.50 (U.S.$8.10) for children, and A$54.50 (U.S.$35.40) for families. The highly recommended 1^1/$_2$-hour **evening harbor tour,** which takes in the city lights as far east as Double Bay and west to Goat Island, leaves Monday through Saturday at 8pm from Wharf 5. The evening tour costs A$18 (U.S.$11.70) for adults, A$11.50 (U.S.$7.50) for children, and A$47.50 (U.S.$30.90) for families.

If you miss the Mississippi, another option is a trip on a paddle steamer. The *Sydney Showboat* (☎ 02/9552 2722) departs from Campbells Cove in The Rocks. A daily lunch cruise running from 12:30 to 2pm costs A$52 (U.S.$33.80) for adults and A$31 (U.S.$20.15) for children 4 to 12; it includes a good buffet lunch, a jazz band, and commentary. Daily coffee cruises depart at 10:30am, 2:30pm, and 5:15pm, and cost A$19 (U.S.$12.35) for adults and A$11.50 (U.S.$2.50) for children. A daily dinner cruise that runs from 7:30 to 10pm costs A$120 (U.S.$78) for adults and A$72 (U.S.$46.80) for children; a deluxe version of the cruise, including a cabaret, dancers, a magician, singers, a juggler, and a more upscale menu, costs A$163 (U.S.$105.95) for adults and A$98 (U.S.$63.70) for children. A Starlight dinner cruise without entertainment on the same boat costs A$79 (U.S.$51.35) for adults, and A$47.50 (U.S.$30.90) for children. You can buy tickets near the overseas terminal in Circular Quay.

If you're going to splurge on a cruise, though, the best are aboard the fully rigged replica of **Captain Bligh's** *Bounty* (☎ 02/9247 1789). The boat was built for the remake of *Mutiny on the Bounty* (the one with Mel Gibson and Anthony Hopkins). Standard 2-hour lunch cruises run Monday through Friday and cost A$55

Harbor Cruise Tickets & Info

There's one-stop shopping for tickets and information on all harbor cruises at the **Australian Travel Specialists** (☎ 02/9247 5151; www.atstravel.com.au). Find outlets at jetties no. 2 and no. 6 at Circular Quay, at Manly Wharf in Manly, at the Harbourside Festival Marketplace at Darling Harbour, and inside the Oxford Koala Hotel on Oxford Street.

(U.S.$35.75) for adults. Two-and-a-half–hour dinner cruises depart daily in high season (Oct 1 to Apr 30) and Friday and Saturday only from May to Sept, and cost A$85 (U.S.$55.25) for adults. On Saturday and Sunday, a 2¹/₂-hour buffet lunch sail costs A$80 (U.S.$52) for adults, and a 1¹/₂-hour predinner sail costs A$45 (U.S.$29.25) for adults. There's a 40% discount for children under 12 on all cruises.

Alternatively, you can cruise like a millionaire aboard the **M.V. Oceanos** (☎ **02/9555 4599**), a 72-foot luxury motor cruiser. A 3-hour cruise, which leaves Campbells Cove at 12:30pm daily, costs A$69 (U.S.$44.85) per person and includes a quality seafood lunch. Booking a day in advance is essential. **Sail Venture Cruises** (☎ **02/9262 3595**) also has a range of cruises aboard their catamarans.

Captain Cook Cruises. Departing jetty no. 6, Circular Quay. ☎ **02/9206 1111.** www.captcookcrus.com.au.

This major cruise company offers several harbor excursions on its sleek vessels, with commentary along the way.

The Harbour Highlights cruise runs at 9:30am, 11am, 12:45pm, 2:30pm, and 4pm daily and takes in most of the main points of interest in 1¹/₄ hours. Cruises cost A$18 (U.S.$11.70) for adults and A$13 (U.S.$8.45) for children. The 1¹/₂-hour Sundowner cruise takes in the last of the sun's rays starting out at 5pm daily; it costs the same as the Harbour Highlights cruise.

The *Sydney Harbour Explorer* departs at 9:30am, 11:30am, 1:30pm, and 3:30pm and combines visits to five major Sydney attractions with a 2-hour cruise. You can get off where you like and join the boat again later. Tickets cost A$20 (U.S.$13) for adults and A$12 (U.S.$7.80) for children. An Aquarium & Zoo Cruise, costing A$32 (U.S.$20.80) for adults and A$18 (U.S.$11.70) for children, includes the *Sydney Harbour Explorer* cruise and admission to the Sydney Aquarium or Taronga Zoo.

The company also offers a 1¹/₂-hour Luncheon Cruise, which leaves daily at noon. It costs A$47 (U.S.$30.55) for adults and A$35 (U.S.$22.75) for children. A Showtime Dinner Cruise leaves nightly at 7:30pm and includes a cabaret and dinner; it costs A$89 (U.S.$57.85) for adults and A$50 (U.S.$32.50) for children.

Superior meals are served aboard the **John Cadman Cruising Restaurant boat.** A nightly 1¹/₂-hour Sunset Dinner cruise departs at 5:15pm and costs A$65 (U.S.$42.25) for adults and A$30 (U.S.$19.50) for children, which includes a two-course meal and drinks. A second dinner cruise leaves at 7:30pm nightly and takes about 2¹/₂ hours to cruise the harbor, while guests indulge in a fine three-course meal and bop away on the dance floor. Adults cost A$89 (U.S.$57.85); children, A$50 (U.S.$32.50). Reservations are essential.

Matilda Cruises. Departing Aquarium Wharf, Darling Harbour. ☎ **02/9264 7377.** www.matilda.com.au.

The modern Matilda fleet is based at Darling Harbour (but all cruises also pick up a Circular Quay) and offers 1-hour sightseeing tours, morning and afternoon coffee cruises, and daily lunch and dinner cruises. One-hour sightseeing cruises leave Darling Harbour eight times daily beginning at 9:30am (six times daily in winter beginning at 10:30am) and cost A$18 (U.S.$11.70) for adults, A$9 (U.S.$5.85) for children 5 to 12, and A$44 (U.S.$28.60) for a family. Two-hour coffee cruises leave Darling Harbour at 9:30am and 3:05pm and cost A$24 (U.S.$15.60) for adults and A$12 (U.S.$7.80) for children. Two-hour lunch cruises leave at 12:15pm daily and cost A$49.50 (U.S.$32.20) for adults and A$24.50 (U.S.$15.90) for children. Three-hour dinner cruises leave at 7pm and cost A$95 (U.S.$61.75) for adults and A$48 (U.S.$31.20) for children. All boats dock at Circular Quay's Eastern Pontoon (near The Oyster Bar, before you get to the Sydney Opera House), 20 minutes after picking up passengers at Darling Harbour.

WALKING TOURS

The center of Sydney is surprisingly compact, and you'll find you can see a lot in a day on foot. (See the walking tours earlier in this chapter for routes to follow on your own.) If you want to learn even more about Sydney's early history, then consider a guided tour with **The Rocks Walking Tour** (☎ **02/9247 6678**), based at the Shop K4, Kendall Lane (off Argyle Street, The Rocks). Excellent walking tours leave Monday through Friday at 10:30am, 12:30pm, and 2:30pm, and Saturday and Sunday at 11:30am and 2pm (In Jan only 10:30am and 2:30pm). The 1¹/₂-hour tour costs A$13.50 (U.S.$8.80) for adults, A$8.50 (U.S.$5.50) for children 10 to 16, and A$33.50 (U.S.$21.80) for families. Accompanied children under 10 are free.

For other historical walks contact **Sydney Guided Tours** (☎ **02/9660 7157**). The company's owner, Maureen Fry, has been in the business for over 12 years and employs trained guides qualified in specific disciplines, such as history, architecture, and botany. She offers a range of tours including an introductory tour of Sydney, a tour of historic Macquarie Street, and many others. Walking tours cost A$15 (U.S.$9.75) for 2 hours as part of a group (call in advance to find out what's available), or A$150 (U.S.$97.50) for a 2-hour personalized tour (for 1 to 10 people).

A walking tour with a difference is **Unseen Sydney's History, Convicts, and Murder Most Foul** (☎ **02/9555 2700**). The tour is fascinating and fun, with the guide dressed up in old-time gear and theatrical storytellers spinning yarns about Sydney's mysteries and intrigue. The 1¹/₂-hour tour leaves at 6:30pm sharp from Circular Quay Tuesday and Thursday through Saturday. It costs A$18 (U.S.$11.70) for adults and A$14 (U.S.$9.10) for children.

8 Staying Active

BIKING   The best place to cycle in Sydney is in **Centennial Park.** Rent bikes from **Centennial Park Cycles,** 50 Clovelly Rd., Randwick (☎ **02/9398 5027**), which is 200 meters from the Musgrave Avenue entrance. (The park has five main entrances.) Standard bikes cost A$8 (U.S.$5.20) for the first hour, A$12 (U.S.$7.80) for 2 hours, and A$17 (U.S.$11.05) for 3 or 4 hours. Mountain bikes can be hired for the day to take on bush trails elsewhere. They cost A$30 (U.S.$19.50) for 8 hours, or A$40 (U.S.$26) for 24 hours.

Bicycles in The City, 722 George St. (near Central Station; ☎ **02/9280 2229**), rents mountain bikes from A$5 (U.S.$3.25) per hour, or A$25 (U.S.$16.25) per day. You can rent in-line skates here, too, for the same daily rate with all protective gear. (Helmets are compulsory in Australia.)

GOLF   Sydney has more than 90 golf courses and plenty of fine weather. For general information on courses, call the **New South Wales Golf Association** (☎ **02/9264 8433**). The 18-hole championship course at **Moore Park Golf Club,** at Cleveland Street and Anzac Parade, Waterloo (☎ **02/9663 1064**), is the nearest to the city. Visitors are welcome every day except all day Friday and Sunday mornings. Greens fees are A$24 (U.S.$15.60) Monday through Friday, and A$27 (U.S.$17.55) Saturday and Sunday.

One of my favorite courses is **Long Reef Golf Club,** Anzac Avenue, Colloroy (☎ **02/9982 2943**). This northern beaches course is surrounded by the Tasman Sea on three sides and has gorgeous views. Greens fees are A$25 (U.S.$16.25) midweek, and A$35 (U.S.$22.75) on weekends.

IN-LINE SKATING   The best places to go in-line skating are along the beachside promenades at Bondi and Manly beaches and in Centennial Park. **Manly Blades,**

49 North Steyne (☎ **02/9976 3833**), rents skates for A$10 (U.S.$6.50) for the first hour and A$5 (U.S.$3.25) for each subsequent hour, or A$20 (U.S.$13) per day. Lessons are A$20 (U.S.$13), including 1-hour skate hire and a half-hour lesson. **Bondi Boards & Blades,** 148 Curlewis St., Bondi Beach (☎ **02/9365 6555**), offers the same hourly rates, with daily rentals costing A$28 (U.S.$18.20). There's a free lesson at Bondi Boards & Blades every Tuesday afternoon. **Total Skate,** 36 Oxford St., Paddington, near Centennial Park (☎ **02/9380 6356**), also has the same hourly rates, with a whole day costing A$30 (U.S.$19.50). Lessons at 5pm on Sunday are free if you rent skates.

JOGGING   The **Royal Botanic Gardens, Centennial Park,** or any **beach** are the best places to kick-start your body. You can also run across the Harbour Bridge, though you'll have to put up with the car fumes. Another popular spot is along the sea cliffs from Bondi Beach to Bronte Beach.

PARASAILING   If being strapped to a harness and a parachute 100 meters above Sydney Harbour while being towed along by a speed boat is your idea of fun, contact **Sydney Harbour Parasailing and Scenic Tours** (☎ **02/99776781**). A regular flight will see you in the air for 6 to 7 minutes at the end of a 100-meter line. Flights cost A$39 (U.S.$25.35) per adult. For A$49 (U.S.$31.85), you can get 8 to 10 minutes in the air and 150 meters of line on a "super flight." Tandem rides, for children and adults, are also available. The boat departs next to the Manly ferry wharf in Manly.

SCUBA DIVING   Plenty of people learn to dive in Sydney before taking off for the Barrier Reef. Don't expect beautiful coral reefs, though. **Pro Dive,** 27 Alfreda St., Coogee (☎ **02/9665 6333**), offers a 4-day learn-to-dive program costing $345 (U.S.$224.25). A day of diving for registered divers costs A$105 (U.S.$68.25).

SURFING   **Bondi Beach** and **Tamarama** are the best surf beaches on the south side of Sydney Harbour, while **Manly, Narrabeen, Bilgola, Colloroy, Long Reef,** and **Palm** beaches are the most popular on the north side. Most beach suburbs have surf shops where you can rent a board. At Bondi beach, the **Bondi Surf Co.,** 72 Campbell Parade (☎ **02/9365 0870**), rents surfboards for A$30 (U.S.$19.50) for 3 hours or A$40 (U.S.$26) a day. Body boards rent for A$20 (U.S.$13) for 3 hours. In Manly, **Aloha Surf,** 44 Pittwater Rd., Manly (☎ **02/9977 3777**), rents surfboards for A$35 (U.S.$22.75) per day or A$20 (U.S.$13) for half day. Call **Manly Surf School** (☎ **0418 717 313** mobile phone) for information on surf lessons.

SWIMMING   The best place to swim indoors in Sydney is the **Sydney International Aquatic Centre,** at Olympic Park, Homebush Bay (☎ **02/9752 3666**). It's open Monday through Friday from 5am to 9:45pm, and Saturday, Sunday, and public holidays from 7am to 7pm. Entry costs A$4.50 (U.S.$2.90) for adults and A$3.50 (U.S.$2.30) for children.

Another good bet is the **North Sydney Olympic Pool,** Alfred South Street, Milsons Point (☎ **02/9955 2309**). Swimming here costs A$3.20 (U.S.$2.10) for adults and A$1.50 (U.S.$.1) for children. More world records have been broken in this pool than in any other pool in the world. In 1999, the pool went through major renovations.

TENNIS   There are hundreds of places around the city to play one of Australia's most popular sports. A nice spot is the **Miller's Point Tennis Court,** Kent Street, The Rocks (☎ **02/9256 2222**). It's run by the Observatory Hotel and is open daily from 7:30am to 10pm. The court costs A$25 (U.S.$16.25) per hour. The **North Sydney Tennis Centre,** 1A Little Alfred St., North Sydney (☎ **02/9371 9952**), has three courts available daily from 6am to 10pm. They cost A$14 (U.S.$9.10) until 5pm on weekdays and A$18 (U.S.$11.70) at other times.

WINDSURFING   My favorite spot to learn to windsurf or to set out onto the harbor is at **Balmoral Beach,** in Mosman on the North Shore. Rent boards at **Balmoral Windsurfing, Sailing and Kayaking School & Hire,** 3 The Esplanade, Balmoral Beach (☎ **02/9960 5344**). Windsurfers cost A$25 (U.S.$16.25) per hour, and lessons cost A$145 (U.S.$94.25) for 5 hours teaching over a weekend. This place also rents fishing boats.

YACHTING   **Balmoral Boat Shed,** Balmoral Beach (☎ **02/9969 6006**), rents catamarans, 12-foot aluminum runabouts, canoes, and surf skis. The catamarans and runabouts cost A$30 (U.S.$19.50) for the first hour (with an A$80/U.S.$52 deposit); a full day costs A$110 (U.S.$71.50). Other vessels cost A$10 (US.$6.50) per hour with an A$10 (U.S.$6.50) deposit.

Sydney by Sail (☎ **02/9280 1110**, or 0419/367 180 mobile phone) offers daily introductory sailing cruises on the harbor aboard luxurious 34- and 38-foot yachts. A maximum of six people sail aboard each boat, and they leave from the National Maritime Museum at Darling Harbour. Ninety-minute introductory sails cost A$49 (U.S.$31.85) per person with the more popular 3-hour sail costing A$89 (U.S.$57.85). Reservations are essential.

9 Spectator Sports

CRICKET   The **Sydney Cricket Ground,** at the corner of Moore Park and Driver Avenue, is famous for its 1-day and test (multiday) matches, played generally from October to March. Phone the **New South Wales Cricket Association** at ☎ **02/9339 0999** for match details.

FOOTBALL   In this city, "football" means rugby league. If you want to see burly chaps pound into each other (without any protective gear) while chasing an oval ball, then be here between May and September. The biggest venue is the **Sydney Football Stadium,** Moore Park Road, Paddington (☎ **02/9360 6601**). Match information is available at ☎ **1900 963 133.** Buy tickets at **Ticketek** (☎ **02/9266 4800**).

HORSE RACING   The best-known and most central of Sydney's four horse-racing tracks is **Randwick Racecourse,** Alison Street, Randwick (☎ **02/9663 8400**). The biggest race day of the week is Saturday. Entry costs A$8 (U.S.$5.20) per person. Call the **Sydney Turf Club** at ☎ **02/9930 4000** with questions about other Sydney-area tracks.

SURFING CARNIVALS   Every summer these uniquely Australian competitions bring large crowds to Sydney's beaches as surf clubs compete against each other in various water sports. Contact the **Surf Lifesaving Association** (☎ **02/9597 5588** for times and locations.

YACHT RACING   While sailing competitions take place on the harbor most summer weekends, the start of the **Sydney to Hobart Yacht Race** on Boxing Day (Dec 26) is something not to be missed. The race starts from the harbor near the Royal Botanic Gardens. Contact **Tourism New South Wales** (☎ **02/9931 1111**) or **Tourism Tasmania** (☎ **03/6230 8169**) for more information.

10 Shopping

Sydney's shopping is not as good as Melbourne's, but you'll still find plenty of places to flex your credit cards. Most shops of interest to the visitor are located in The Rocks and along George and Pitt streets (including the shops below the AMP Centrepoint Tower and along the Pitt Street Mall). Other shopping precincts worth checking out are Mosman on the North Shore and Double Bay in the eastern suburbs for exclusive boutique shopping, Chatswood for its general shopping centers, the Sydney Fishmarket for the sake of it, and the various weekend markets (listed below).

You won't want to miss the **Queen Victoria Building (QVB),** on the corner of Market and George streets. This Victorian shopping arcade is one of the prettiest in the world and has some 200 boutiques—mostly men's and women's fashion—on four levels. The arcade is open 24 hours, but the shops do business Monday to Saturday from 9am to 6pm (Thurs to 9pm) and Sunday 11am to 5pm.

Several other arcades in the city center also offer good shopping potential, including the **Royal Arcade,** under the Hilton Hotel; the **Imperial Arcade,** near the AMP Centrepoint Tower; **Sydney Central Plaza,** beside the Grace Brothers department store on Pitt Street Mall; and the **Skygarden Arcade,** which runs from Pitt Street Mall to Castlereagh Street. The **Strand Arcade** (running between Pitt Street Mall and George Street) was built in 1892 and is interesting for its architecture and small boutiques, food stores and cafes, and the Downtown Duty Free store on the basement level.

On **Pitt Street Mall** you'll find record shops, including HMV; a branch of The Body Shop; and fashion boutiques such as Just Jeans, Jeans West, Katies, and Esprit.

Regular shopping hours are generally Monday to Friday from 8:30 or 9am to 6pm (Thurs until 9pm), Saturday from 9am to 5 or 5:30pm, and Sunday from 10 or 10:30am to 5pm. Exceptions are noted in the store listings below.

SYDNEY SHOPPING FROM A TO Z
ABORIGINAL ARTIFACTS & CRAFTS

Aboriginal & Tribal Art Centre. 1st floor, 117 George St., The Rocks. ☎ **02/9247 9625.**

This center carries a wide range of desert paintings and bark paintings, mostly of very high quality. Collectibles such as didgeridoos, fabrics, books, and boomerangs are on sale, too. Open daily from 10am to 5pm.

Coo-ee Aboriginal Art Gallery and Shop. 98 Oxford St., Paddington. ☎ **02/9332 1544.**

The proprietors of Coo-ee collect artifacts and fine art from more than 30 Aboriginal communities and dozens of individual artists throughout Australia. The gallery also stocks the largest collection of limited-edition prints in Australia. There are also plenty of hand-painted fabrics, T-shirts, didgeridoos, boomerangs, sculpture, bark paintings, jewelry, music, and books. Don't expect bargain prices, though; you pay for the quality here. Open Monday to Saturday from 10am to 6pm and Sunday from 11am to 5pm.

Didj Beat Didjeridoo's. Shop 2, The Clock Tower Sq., Corner of Argyle and Harrington sts. ☎ **02/9251 4289.**

Here you'll find the best selection of didgeridoos in Sydney. The pieces are authentic and well priced. Open daily from 10am to 6:30pm.

Gavala Aboriginal Art & Cultural Education Centre. Harbourside Festival Marketplace, Darling Harbour. ☎ **02/9212 7232.**

I'd head here first if I were in the market for a decent boomerang or didgeridoo. Gavala is entirely owned and operated by Aborigines, and there are plenty of authentic Aboriginal crafts for sale, including carved emu eggs, grass baskets, cards, and books. A first-rate painted didgeridoo will cost anywhere from A$100 to $450 (U.S.$65 to $292.50). Gavala also sponsors cultural talks, didgeridoo-making lessons, and storytelling sessions. Open daily from 10am to 9pm.

Discount Shopping

If you're looking for bargains, head to Foveraux Street between Elizabeth and Waterloo streets in Surry Hills for factory clearance shops selling end-of-the-run, last season's fashions, and seconds at deep discounts.

If you're really keen on bargain shopping, you might want to consider joining up with **Shopping Spree Tours** (☎ **1800/625 969** in Australia, or 02/9360 6220), which offers tours to factory outlets and warehouses selling everything from clothes to cookware to electrical appliances. Full-day tours cost A$60 (U.S.$39) for adults and A$16.50 (U.S.$10.70) for children 3 to 12 and include pickup at your hotel, visits to 8 to 10 outlets and warehouses, and a two-course lunch at a good restaurant. Tours depart at 8:15am daily except Sunday and public holidays.

Original & Authentic Aboriginal Art. 79 George St., The Rocks. ☎ **02/9251 4222.**

Quality Aboriginal art is on offer here from some of Australia's best-known painters, including Paddy Fordham Wainburranga, whose paintings even hang in the White House in Washington, and Janet Forrester Nangala, whose work has been exhibited in the Australian National Gallery in Canberra. Expect to pay in the range of A$1,000 to $4,000 (U.S.$650 to $2,600) for the larger paintings. There are some nice painted pots here, too, costing from A$30 to $80 (U.S.$19.50 to $52). Open daily from 10am to 6:30pm.

ART PRINTS & ORIGINALS

Done Art and Design. 1 Hickson Rd., The Rocks. ☎ **02/9247 2740.**

The art is by Ken Done, who's well known for having designed his own Australian flag, which he hopes to raise over Australia should it cut ties to Britain and abandon its present banner. The clothing designs—which feature printed sea- and beachscapes, the odd colorful bird, and lots of pastels—are by his wife, Judy. Ken Done's gallery is just off George Street, in the Rocks. Open daily from 10am to 5:30pm.

Ken Duncan Gallery. 73 George St., The Rocks (across from The Rocks Visitor Centre). ☎ **02/9241 3460.** Fax 02/9241 3462.

This photographer-turned-salesman is making a killing from his exquisitely produced large-scale photographs of Australian scenery. Open daily from 9am to 8pm.

BOOKS

You'll find a good selection of specialized books on Sydney and Australia for sale at the **Art Gallery of New South Wales,** the Garden Shop in the **Royal Botanic Gardens,** the **Museum of Sydney,** the **Australian Museum,** and the **State Library of New South Wales.**

Abbey's Bookshop. 131 York St. (behind the Queen Victoria Building). ☎ **02/9264 3111.**

This interesting, centrally located bookshop specializes in literature, history, crime, and mystery, and has a whole floor on language and education.

Angus & Robertson Bookworld. Pitt Street Mall, 168 Pitt St. ☎ **02/9235 1188.**

One of Australia's largest bookshops, with two stories of books—including a good guidebook and Australiana section—and games.

Dymocks. 424–428 George St. (just north of Market St.). ☎ **02/9235 0155.**

The largest of four book department stores in the city, Dymocks has three levels of general books and stationery. There's a reasonable travel section here with plenty of guides. Open Monday to Wednesday and Friday from 9am to 6pm, Thursday from 9am to 9pm, Saturday from 9am to 5pm, and Sunday from 10am to 5pm.

Gleebooks Bookshop. 49 Glebe Point Rd., Glebe. ☎ **02/9660 2333.**

Specializing in art, general literature, psychology, sociology, and women's studies, Gleebooks also has a secondhand store (with a large children's department) down the road at 191 Glebe Point Rd. Open daily 8am to 9pm.

✪ **Goulds Book Arcade.** 32–38 King St., Newtown. ☎ **02/9519 8947.**

Come here to search for unusual dusty volumes. Located about a 10-minute walk from the Newtown CityRail station, the place is bursting at the seams with many thousands of secondhand and new books. You can browse for hours here. Open daily from 8am to midnight.

✪ **Travel Bookshop.** Shop 3, 175 Liverpool St. (across from the southern end of Hyde Park, near the Museum CityRail station). ☎ **02/9261 8200.**

Hundreds of travel guides, maps, Australiana titles, coffee-table books, and travel accessories line the shelves of this excellent bookshop. Open Monday to Friday from 9am to 6pm and Saturday from 10am to 5pm.

CRAFTS

Australian Craftworks. 127 George St., The Rocks. ☎ **02/9247 7156.**

This place showcases some of Australia's best arts and crafts, collected from some 300 Australian artists from around the country. It's all displayed in a former police station built in 1882, a time of economic depression when mob riots and clashes with police were common in this area. The cells and administration areas are today used as gallery spaces. Open daily from 8:30am to 7pm.

✪ **The puppet shop at the rocks.** 77 George St., The Rocks. ☎ **02/9247 9137.**

I can't believe I kept walking past the sign outside this place for so many years without looking in. Deep down in the bowels of a historic building, I eventually came across several cramped rooms absolutely packed with puppets, costing from a couple of dollars to a couple of hundred. The owners make their own puppets— mostly Australian in style (emus, koalas, and that sort of thing)—as well as import things from all over the world. Wooden toys abound, too. It's the best shop in Sydney! Open daily from 10am to 5:30pm.

Telopea Gallery. Shop 2 in the Metcalfe Arcade, 80–84 George St., The Rocks. ☎ **02/9241 1673.**

This shop is run by the New South Wales Society of Arts and Crafts, which exhibits works made by its members, all of whom are New South Wales residents. There are some wonderful glass, textile, ceramic, jewelry, fine-metal, and wood-turned items for sale. Open daily from 9:30am to 5:30pm.

DEPARTMENT STORES

David Jones (☎ **02/9266 5544**) is the city's largest department store, selling everything from fashion to designer furniture. You'll find the women's section on the corner of Elizabeth and Market streets, and the men's section on the corner of Castlereigh and Market streets.

Grace Brothers (☎ **02/9238 9111**) is similar to David Jones, but the building is newer and flashier. It's located on the corner of George and Market streets. Both stores are open Monday to Wednesday and Friday to Saturday from 9am to 6pm, Thursday from 9am to 9pm, and Sunday from 11am to 5pm.

DUTY-FREE SHOPS

Sydney has several duty-free shops selling goods at a discount. To take advantage of the bargains, you need a passport and a flight ticket, and you must export what you buy. The duty-free shop with the best buys is **Downtown Duty Free,** which has two city outlets, one on the basement level of the Strand Arcade, off Pitt Street Mall (☎ **02/9233 3166**) and one at 105 Pitt St. (☎ **02/9221 4444**). Five more stores are found at Sydney International Airport and are open from the first to the last flight of the day.

FASHION

The best places to shop for fashion are the Queen Victoria Building and the Sydney Central Plaza (on the ground floor of the mall next to the Grace Brothers department store on Pitt Street Mall). Otherwise, the major department stores and Pitt Street Mall outlets will keep you up-to-date.

Australian Outback Clothing

R.M. Williams. 389 George St. (between Town Hall and Central CityRail stations). ☎ **02/ 9262 2228.**

Moleskin trousers may not be the height of fashion at the moment, but you never know. R.M. Williams boots are famous for being both tough and fashionable. You'll find Akubra hats, Driza-bone coats, and kangaroo-skin belts here, too.

Thomas Cook Boot & Clothing Company. 790 George St., Haymarket. ☎ **02/9212 6616.** www.thomascookclothing.com.au.

Located on George Street between Town Hall and central CityRail stations, this place specializes in Australian boots, Driza-bone coats, and Akubra hats. There's another shop at 129 Pitt St., near Martin Place (☎ **02/9232 3334**).

Unisex Fashions

Country Road. 142–146 Pitt St. ☎ **02/9394 1818.** www.countryroad.com.au.

This chain store has outlets all across Australia as well as in the United States. The clothes, for both men and women, are good quality but tend to be quite expensive. You'll find other branches in the Queen Victoria Building and the Skygarden Arcade, and in Bondi Junction, Darling Harbour, Double Bay, Mosman, and Chatswood.

Mostrada. Store 15G, Sydney Central Plaza, 450 George St. ☎ **02/9221 0133.**

If you're looking for good-quality leather items at very reasonable prices, then this is your place. Leather jackets for men and women go for between A$199 (U.S.$129.35) and A$899 (U.S.$584.35), with an average price of around A$400 (U.S.$260). There are also bags, belts, and other leather accessories on offer.

Men's Fashion

Esprit Mens. Shop 10G, Sydney Central Plaza, 450 George St. ☎ **02/9233 7349.**

Not so cheap, but certainly colorful, clothes come out of this designer store where bold hues and fruity patterns are the in thing. Quality designer shirts cost around A$60 (U.S.$39).

Gowings. 45 Market St. ☎ **02/9264 6321.**

Probably the best all-round men's clothing store in Sydney, Gowings sells quality clothing on two levels, with more formal attire sold in the basement. Upstairs, things go weird, with an eclectic mix of gardening equipment, gourmet camping gear, odds and ends for the extrovert, a good range of Australian bush hats, and R.M. Williams boots (well-priced at around A$200/U.S.$130 a pair). There's a similar store at 319 George St. (☎ **02/9262 1281**), near Wynyard CityRail station.

Outdoor Heritage. Shop 13G, Sydney Central Plaza, 450 George St. ☎ **02/9235 1560.**

Quality clothing with a yachting influence is what you'll find at this good-looking store specializing in casual, colorful gear.

Women's Fashion

In addition to the places listed below, head to Oxford Street (particularly Paddington), for more avant-garde designers.

Carla Zampatti. 143 Elizabeth St. ☎ **02/9264 3257.**

One of more than 30 Carla Zampatti stores around Australia offering stylish fashions at hard-to-swallow prices. Open Monday to Saturday from 10am to 5pm.

Dorian Scott. 105 George St., The Rocks. ☎ **02/9221 8145.**

Probably the best place to go for hand-knit sweaters—called "jumpers" in Australia—Dorian Scott has a wide range of colorful garments from more than 200 leading Australian designers. While some items go for A$80 (U.S.$52), others will set you back hundreds. You'll also find clothing accessories for men, women, and children in this two-story emporium, including Hot Tuna surfware and Thomas Cook adventure clothing. Open Monday to Saturday from 9:30am to 7pm and Sunday from 10am to 6pm. There are also two Dorian Scott stores at Sydney International Airport (☎ **02/9667 3255**) and another at the Inter-Continental Hotel at 117 Macquarie St. (☎ **02/9247 1818**).

FOOD

The goodies you'll find in the downstairs food section of the **David Jones** department store on Castlereigh Street (the men's section) will be enough to tempt anyone off their diet. It sells the best of local and imported products to the rich and famous.

Coles. Wynyard Station, Castlereagh St., Wynyard (directly opposite the Menzies Hotel and the public bus stands). ☎ **02/9299 4769.**

One of the few supermarkets in the city center, this place is a good bet if you want to cater for yourself or are after ready-made food (including tasty sandwiches) and cheap soft drinks. Open daily 6am to midnight.

Darrell Lea Chocolates. At the corner of King and George sts. ☎ **02/9232 2899.**

This is the oldest location of Australia's most famous chocolate shop. Pick up some wonderful handmade chocolates, as well as other unusual candies, including the best licorice this side of the Kasbah.

Sydney Fishmarket. At the corner of Bank St. and Pyrmont Bridge Rd., Pyrmont. ☎ **02/9660 1611.**

Finding out about what people eat can be a good introduction to a new country, and, in my opinion, nowhere is this more fascinating than a visit to the local fish market. Here you'll find seven major fish retailers selling everything from shark to Balmain bugs (a kind of squat crayfish), with hundreds of species in between. Watch out for the local pelicans being fed the fishy leftovers. There are also a Doyles restaurant and a sushi bar, a couple of cheap seafood eateries, a fruit market, and a good deli. The retail sections are open daily from 7am to 4pm. Get here by Light Rail (get off at the Fishmarket stop), or walk from Darling Harbour. Parking is A$2 (U.S.$1.30) for the first 3 hours.

GIFTS & SOUVENIRS

The shops at **Taronga Zoo,** the **Oceanarium** in Manly, the **Sydney Aquarium,** and the **Australian Museum** are all good sources for gifts and souvenirs. There are many shops around **The Rocks** worth browsing, too.

⭐ **Australian Geographic.** Harbourside Festival Marketplace, Darling Harbour. ☎ **02/ 9212 6539.** AMP Centrepoint Tower, Pitt St. ☎ **02/9231 5055.**

A spin-off from the Australian version of *National Geographic* magazine, this store sells good-quality crafts and Australiana. On offer are camping gadgets, telescopes and binoculars, garden utensils, scientific oddities, books and calendars, videos, music, toys, and lots more.

National Trust Gift and Bookshop. Observatory Hill, The Rocks. ☎ **02/9258 0154.**

You can pick up some nice souvenirs, including books, Australiana crafts, and indigenous foodstuffs, here. An art gallery on the premises presents changing exhibits of paintings and sculpture by Australians. There's also a cafe. Closed Monday.

⭐ **The Wilderness Society Shop.** AMP Centrepoint Tower, Castlereagh St. ☎ **02/9233 4674.**

Australiana is crawling out of the woodwork at this cute little craft emporium dedicated to spending all its profits on saving the few remaining untouched forests and wilderness areas of Australia. You'll find some quality craft items, cute children's clothes, books, cards, and knickknacks.

MARKETS

Balmain Market. On the grounds of St. Andrew's Church, Darling St., Balmain. ☎ **02/ 9555 1791.**

Active from 8:30am to 4pm every Saturday, this popular market has some 140 vendors selling crafts, jewelry, and knickknacks. Take the ferry to Balmain (Darling Street); the market is a 10-minute walk up Darling Street.

Paddington Bazaar. On the grounds of St. John's Church on Oxford St., on the corner of Newcome St. (just follow the crowds). ☎ **02/9331 2646.**

At this Saturday-only market you'll find everything from essential oils and designer clothes to New Age jewelry and Mexican hammocks. Expect things to be busy from 10am to 4pm. Take bus 380 or 389 from Circular Quay.

Paddy's Markets. At the corner of Thomas and Hay sts., in Haymarket, near Chinatown. ☎ **1300/361 589** in Australia, or 02/9325 6924.

A Sydney institution, Paddy's Markets has hundreds of stalls selling everything from cheap clothes and plants to chickens. It's open Friday to Sunday from 9am to 4:30pm. Above Paddy's Markets is **Market City** (☎ **02/9212 1388**), which has three floors of fashion stalls, food courts, and specialty shops. Of particular interest is the largest Asian-European supermarket in Australia, on level 1, and the **Kam Fook yum cha** Chinese restaurant on level 3, also the largest in Australia.

The Rocks Market. On George St., The Rocks. ☎ **02/9255 1717.**

Held every Saturday and Sunday, this very touristy market has more than 100 vendors selling everything from crafts to housewares, posters, jewelry, and curios. The main street is closed to traffic from 10am to 4pm to make it easier to stroll around.

MUSIC

Birdland. 3 Barrack St. ☎ **02/9299 8527.** www.birdland.com.au.

This is the best store in Sydney for jazz and blues, and it stocks a sizable collection of rare items. The staff is very knowledgeable.

HMV Music Stores. Pitt Street Mall. ☎ **02/9221 2311.**

This is one of the best music stores in Sydney. The jazz section is impressive. CDs in Australia are not cheap, with most new releases costing around A$30 to $35 (U.S.$19.50 to $22.75).

Red Eye Records. Tank Stream Arcade (downstairs), at the corner of King and Pitt sts. (near Town Hall). ☎ **02/9233 8177** (new recordings), or 02/9233 8125 (secondhand CDs). www.redeye.com.au.

These two shops, tucked away downstairs in a small arcade not far from Pitt Street Mall and the Strand Arcade, are directly across from one another. The larger store sells a wide range of modern CDs, but the smaller store sells a great collection of quality secondhand and end-of-the-line CDs for around A$20 (U.S.$13) each.

Sounds Australian. In the Argyle Stores department store, The Rocks. ☎ **02/9247 7290.** Fax 02/9241 2873.

Anything you've ever heard that sounds Australian you can find here. From rock and pop to didgeridoo and country, it's all here. Fortunately, if you haven't a clue what's good and what's bad, you can spend some time listening before you buy. The management is extremely knowledgeable.

OPALS

ANA House Sydney. 37 Pitt St. ☎ **02/9251 2833.**

When you're buying good opals, it's always a good idea to bargain, and this is one of the best places to do it in the city. The shop sells some good stones, as well as all the usual touristy trinkets. There's a special VIP viewing room off to the side of the main sales floor if you're interested in buying real quality. Upstairs is a decent souvenir shop.

Australian Opal Cutters. Suite 10, Level 4, National Building, 250 Pitt St. ☎ **02/9261 2442.** www.opal.citysearch.com.au

Learn more about opals before you buy at this shop. The staff here will give you lessons about opals to help you compare pieces.

WINE

Australian Wine Centre. 1 Alfred St., Shop 3 in Goldfields House, Circular Quay. ☎ **02/9247 2755.** www.wine.ptylimited.com.

This is one of the best places in the country to pick up Australian wines by the bottle or the case. The shop stocks a wide range of wines from all over Australia, including bottles from small boutique wineries you're unlikely to find anywhere else. Individual tastings are possible at any time, though there are formal tastings every Thursday and Friday from 4 to 6pm. Wine is exported all over the world from here, so if you want to send home a crate of your favorite, you can be assured it will arrive. The center owns the wine bar and bistro next door, which is open Monday to Saturday from 6am until late. You can drink here without dining.

11 Sydney After Dark

Australians are party animals when they're in the mood, and whether it's a few beers around the barbie with friends or an all-night rage at a trendy dance club, they're always on the lookout for the next event. You'll find that alcohol plays a big part in the Aussie culture. The best way to find out what's on is to get hold of the "Metro" section of the Friday *Sydney Morning Herald* or the "Seven Days" pullout from the Thursday *Daily Telegraph*.

THE PERFORMING ARTS

If you have an opportunity to see a performance in the ✪ **Sydney Opera House,** jump at it. The "House" is actually not that impressive inside, but the walk back after the show toward the ferry terminals at Circular Quay, with the Sydney Harbour Bridge lit up to your right and the crowd all around you debating the best part of this play or who dropped a beat in that performance—well, it's like hearing Gershwin while on the streets of New York. You'll want the moment to stay with you forever. For more on Sydney's most famous performing-arts venue, see the beginning of this chapter.

Sydney is also blessed with plenty of theaters, many more than I have space for here. Check the *Sydney Morning Herald,* especially the Friday edition, for information on what's currently in production.

Australian Ballet. Level 15, 115 Pitt St. ☎ **02/9223 9522.** www.austballet.telstra.com.au.

Based in Melbourne, the Australian Ballet tours the country with its performances. The Sydney season, at the Opera House, is from mid-March until the end of April. A second Sydney season runs from November to December.

Australian Chamber Orchestra. Opera Quays, 2 E. Circular Quay. ☎ **02/9357 4111;** box office ☎ **02/8274 3888.** www.aco.com.au.

Based in Sydney, this well-known company performs at various venues around the city, from nightclubs to specialized music venues, including the Concert Hall in the Sydney Opera House.

Belvoir Street Theatre. 25 Belvoir St., Surry Hills. ☎ **02/9699 3444.** Tickets around A$34 (U.S.$22.10).

The hallowed boards of the Belvoir are home to Company B, which pumps out powerful local and international plays upstairs in a wonderfully moody main theater, formerly part of a tomato-sauce factory. Downstairs, a smaller venue generally shows more experimental productions, such as Aboriginal performances and dance.

Capital Theatre. 13–17 Campbell St., Haymarket (near Town Hall). ☎ **02/9320 5000.** Ticket prices vary.

Sydney's grandest theater plays host to major international and local productions like, gag, Australian singing superstar Kylie Minogue. It's also been the Sydney home of musicals such as *Miss Saigon* and *My Fair Lady.*

Her Majesty's Theatre. 107 Quay St., Haymarket (near Central Station). ☎ **02/9212 3411.** Ticket prices average A$55–$75 (U.S.$35.75–$48.75).

A quarter of a century old, this large theater is still trawling in the big musicals. Huge productions that have run here include *Evita* and *Phantom of the Opera.*

Opera Australia. 480 Elizabeth St., Surry Hills. ☎ **02/9699 1099;** bookings ☎ **02/9319 1088.** www.opera-australia.org.au.

Opera Australia performs at the Sydney Opera House's Opera Theatre. The opera season runs January to March and June to November.

Money-Saving Tip

A good way to save money on entertainment in Sydney is through a visit to the **Half-Tix** office at 201 Sussex St. (four streets behind the Queen Victoria Building; ☎ **02/9286 3310;** www.halftix.com.au). Here you can buy discount tickets to shows, theatre, some live music events, museum exhibitions, and bus tours. It's open 9am to 5pm Monday to Friday, and 10am to 3pm on Saturday.

Sydney Symphony Orchestra. Level 5, 52 William St., East Sydney. ☎ **02/9334 4644;** box office ☎ **02/9334 4600.** www.symphony.org.au.

Sydney's finest symphony orchestra is conducted by the renowned Edo de Waart. It performs throughout the year in the Opera House's Concert Hall. The main symphony season runs from March to November, and there's a summer season in February.

Wharf Theatre. Pier 4, Hickson Rd., The Rocks. ☎ **02/9250 1777.** www.sydneytheatre. com.au. Ticket prices vary.

This wonderful theater is situated on a refurbished wharf on the edge of Sydney Harbour, just beyond the Harbour Bridge. The long walk from the entrance of the pier to the theater along old creaky wooden floorboards builds up excitement for the show. The Sydney Theatre Company is based here, a group well worth seeing, whatever production is running. Dinner before the show at the Wharf's restaurant offers special views of the harbor.

THE CLUB & MUSIC SCENE
LIVE MUSIC

✪ **The Basement.** 29 Reiby Place, Circular Quay. ☎ **02/9251 2797.** www.basement.com.au. Cover A$9–$10 (U.S.$5.85–$6.50) for local acts, A$20–$25 (U.S.$13–$16.25) for international performers.

Australia's hottest jazz club also manages to squeeze in plenty of blues, folk, and funk. Acts appear every night; pick up a schedule at the door. A Blue Note Bar specializing in jazz opened in July 1998.

The Bridge Hotel & Brasserie. 135 Victoria St., Rozelle. ☎ **02/9810 1260.** Cover A$5–$25 (U.S.$3.25–$16.25).

Come on a Sunday afternoon and you're assured of getting the blues. Friday and Saturday nights offer blues, rock, or house music depending on the whim of the management. The three-level beer garden out the back is nice on a sunny day.

The Harbourside Brasserie. Pier One, Hickson Rd., Walsh Bay (behind The Rocks). ☎ **02/ 9252 3000.** www.ozemail.com.au/~harbrass. Cover A$8–$20 (U.S.$5.20–$13) depending on performer.

Eat to the beat of soul and rhythm and blues at this not-bad eatery. Comedy nights attract big acts. Drinks are expensive.

Metro. 624 George St. ☎ **02/9264 2666.** Cover varies.

A medium-size rock venue with space for 1,000, the Metro is the best place in Sydney to see local and international acts. Tickets sell out quickly.

Soup Plus. 383 George St. (near the Queen Victoria Building). ☎ **02/9299 7728.** Cover A$5 (U.S.$3.25) Mon–Thurs; A$25 (U.S.$16.25) Fri and Sat, including 2-course meal and show.

On my last visit to this cavernous jazz bar, it seemed such a pity that the cover charge forced me to eat the bistro-style food, which really was poor. However, some mellow blues cheered me up in the end.

DANCE CLUBS

Blackmarket. 111–113 Regent St., Chippendale, at the corner of Meagher St. (5-min. walk from Central Station). ☎ **02/9698 8863.** Cover A$15 (U.S.$9.75).

This wacky place is known for its Friday-night Hellfire Club (from 11pm to 4am), where Sydneysiders of all persuasions hang out to watch jelly wrestling and live sadomasochism shows. It's all in (relatively) good taste, though, with nothing too brutal, and it attracts a fun-loving crowd from students to office workers (about 50/50 male and female). Some people make the effort to dress up. There's some good music on offer, too, in the dark and moody interior. Ravers continue on, or drop in after working the night shift, at the Day Club, offering dance music from 4am to 2pm on Saturday (you can stay on free after the Hellfire Club) and 4am to 6pm on Sunday.

Bourbon & Beefsteak Bar. 24 Darlinghurst Rd., Kings Cross. ☎ **02/9358 1144.** Cover A$7.50 (U.S.$4.90) Fri–Sat.

Right in the middle of Sydney's red-light district, this 24-hour restaurant and night spot freaks out to dance music downstairs nightly from 11pm to 5am. It's popular with both young backpackers and the 25-to-35 crowd.

Byblos. 169 Oxford St., Darlinghurst. ☎ **02/9331 7729.** Cover A$15–$20 (U.S.$9.75–$13).

"Upmarket nightclubbing for the likes of models and beautiful people from the [affluent] north shore of Sydney," is how the manager described this place to me. The interior is pseudo-Roman with lots of pillars. The club offers hard-core club/dance music. Dress code is fashionable, with a shirt collar required for men and no sneakers.

Cauldron. 207 Darlinghurst Rd., Darlinghurst. ☎ **02/9331 1523.** Cover A$10 (U.S.$6.50).

This intimate and trend-setting nightclub is firmly established as part of "the scene." Tuesday night offers retro music, on Wednesday and Saturday it's house, and on Thursday and Friday it's funk/R&B. A stylish dress code applies.

Mister Goodbar. 11a Oxford St., Paddington. ☎ **02/9360 6759.** Cover A$15–$20 (U.S.$9.75–$13) Fri–Sat.

A young, trendy, local crowd inhabits Mister Goodbar's two good-size dance floors, which offer reggae on one floor and hip-hop on the other on Wednesdays, and disco and funk other days.

Riche Nightclub. In the Sydney Hilton, 259 Pitt St. ☎ **02/9266 2000.** Cover A$12 (U.S.$7.80) Fri and Sun, A$15 (U.S.$9.75) Sat.

This hot spot for dancing is popular with the local over-25 club set, as well as with hotel guests wanting to shake their booties to typical "dance" music.

GAY & LESBIAN CLUBS

With Sydney having the largest gay community outside San Francisco, it's no wonder there's such a happening scene here. The center of it all is **Oxford Street,** though **Newtown** has established itself as a major gay hangout, too. For information on news

---

It's a Festival!

The annual **Sydney Festival** kicks off just after New Year's and continues until the last week of the month, with recitals, plays, films, and performances held at venues throughout the city, including Town Hall, the Royal Botanic Gardens, the Sydney Opera House, and Darling Harbour. Some of the events are free. "Jazz in The Domain" and "Symphony in The Domain" are two free outdoor performances held in the Royal Botanic Gardens outside the Art Gallery of New South Wales; each event (which generally takes place on the 3rd and 4th weekend in Jan) attracts tens of thousands of Sydneysiders. For more information on the Sydney Festival, contact **Festival Ticketec** (☎ 02/9266 4111). You can also buy tickets and find out about performances on the Web at **www.sydneyfestival.org.au.**

and events concerning gays and lesbians, pick up a copy of the *Sydney Star Observer,* available at art-house cinemas and many cafes and stores around Oxford Street.

✪ **Albury Hotel.** 2–6 Oxford St. (near Barcom Ave.). ☎ **02/9361 6555.** No cover.

An institution, the Albury is a grande dame offering drag shows nightly in the public bar, and knockout Bloody Marys in the cocktail lounge.

✪ **Imperial Hotel.** 35–37 Erskineville Rd., Erskineville (near Union St.). ☎ **02/9519 9899.** No cover.

A couple of minutes' walk from King Street in Newtown, the Imperial is a no-attitude gay venue with a pool and cocktail bar out front and a raging cabaret venue out back. Sydney's best full-production drag shows happen late on Thursday, Friday, and Saturday nights, with dancing in between.

Midnight Shift. 85 Oxford St. (near crown St.). ☎ **02/9360 4319.** Cover A$5 (U.S.$3.25) Sat.

The beat here is sleazy, groovy, and dance party. A favorite with the denim-and-leather set, and the odd drag queen, this place gets more energetic as night becomes day. This is the original gay hangout on the Oxford Street strip.

Newtown Hotel. 174 King St., Newtown. ☎ **02/9557 1329.** No cover.

The octagonal bar here is the center of a casual drinking and cruising scene. The place kicks up its heels during late-night drag shows and powerfully camp discos.

77 Night Club. 77 William St., East Sydney. ☎ **02/9361 4981.** Cover A$8–$10 (U.S.$5.20–$6.50).

This basement venue, beneath a tower block and prestige car salesroom, is an odd one out location-wise, but its moody interior is a hot spot for alternative, dance, progressive house, and jungle music.

Taxi Club. 40 Flinders St., Darlinghurst (near Taylor Sq., Oxford St.). ☎ **02/9331 4256.** Cover A$10 (U.S.$6.50) Fri–Sat.

"Tacky Club," as it's affectionately known, is good for commercial dance music and midweek cabaret shows. It's open 24 hours.

THE BAR SCENE

Most of Australia's drinking holes are known as "hotels," after the tradition of providing room and board alongside a good drink in the old days. Occasionally you might hear them referred to as pubs. You tend to find the term "bar" used in upscale hotels and trendy establishments.

Bondi Hotel. 178 Campbell Parade, Bondi Beach. ☎ **02/9130 3271.** No Cover.

This huge, whitewashed conglomerate across the road from Bondi Beach offers pool upstairs, a casual beer garden outside, and a resident DJ Thursday to Sunday from 8pm to 4am. There's also a free nightclub on Friday nights. Watch yourself; too much drink and sun turns some people nasty here.

The Friend in Hand. 58 Cowper St., Glebe. ☎ **02/9660 2326.**

In the same location as the fantastically cheap Caesar's No Names spaghetti house, The Friend in Hand offers cheap drinks, poetry readings on Tuesday evenings from 8:30pm, a trivia night on Thursday evenings from 8:30pm, and the distinctly unusual Crab Racing Party every Wednesday from around 8pm. Crab fanciers buy a crustacean for A$3 (U.S.$1.95), give it a name, and send it off to do battle in a race against around 30 others. Victorious crustaceans win prizes for their owners.

Cocktails with a View

There's nothing better than a fabulous view rising above the lip of a full cocktail glass. One of the best places in town to drink in the view with your libations is **Horizon,** the cocktail bar at the very top of the multistory ANA Hotel in The Rocks (☎ **02/9250 6000**). The views of The Rocks, Circular Quay, and out across Sydney Harbour are spectacular. It's open from noon to 1am daily, except on Sunday, when it closes at midnight. Go at night for the city lights.

Another good option is a cocktail (or champagne) in the **Bennelong Bar** in the Sydney Opera House (☎ **02/9250 7548**). Sit next to the window and you'll be treated to a very special view of the Opera House sails and the boats coming into Circular Quay, and the best view of the Harbour Bridge in the city. Cocktails here average a steep A$11 (U.S.$7.15). It's open from Monday to Saturday from 5:30 to 11:30pm and Saturday for lunch.

For more dramatic 360-degree sky-high views, head to **The Summit Skylounge,** Level 47, Australia Square, 265 George St. (☎ **02/9247 9777**). It's open daily from 6pm to around midnight, and cocktails cost A$12.50 (U.S.$8.15). The place slowly revolves to take in the view, which can be a bit off-putting. Don't expect plush surrounds or particularly good service here, either.

The International, 14th floor, Victoria Street, Kings Cross (☎ **02/9360 9080**), offers a buzzing art deco cocktail lounge with lots of wood paneling, dim lighting, and leather booths. Cocktails cost A$12 (U.S.$7.80). It's open daily from 5:30 to 11:30pm.

Henry the Ninth Bar. In the Sydney Hilton, 259 Pitt St. ☎ **02/9266 2000.**

This mock-Tudor drinking hole gets very busy on Friday and Saturday nights. They serve up some good ales in an oaky atmosphere. An Irish band whips up the patrons on Thursday and Friday nights; a cover band does the same on Wednesday and Saturday nights. A good-value happy hour brings beer prices tumbling Monday to Thursday from 5:30 to 7:30pm, Friday from 5:30 to 8:30pm, and Saturday from 8 to 10pm.

Hero of Waterloo Hotel. 81 Lower Fort St., The Rocks. ☎ **02/9252 4553.**

This 1845 landmark was allegedly the stalking ground of press gangs, who'd whack unsuspecting landlubbers on the head, push them down a trapdoor out the back, and cart them out to sea. Today, this strangely shaped drinking hole is popular with the locals, and it hosts old-time jazz bands (the musicians are often in their 70s and 80s) on Saturday and Sunday afternoons from 1:30 to 6:30pm, and Irish and cover bands Friday to Sunday evenings from 8:30pm.

Jacksons on George. 178 George St., The Rocks. ☎ **02/9247 2727.** Cover A$10 (U.S.$6.50) for nightclub Fri–Sat after 10pm.

A popular drinking spot, this place has four floors of drinking, eating, dancing, and pool playing, and it is a popular haunt with tourists and after-work office staff. Pool is expensive here at A$3 (U.S.$1.95) a game (you'll need to ask the rules, because Australians have their own), and drinks have a nasty habit of going up in price without warning as the evening wears on. The nightclub plays commercial dance, and there's a smart/casual dress code. Happy hour is Monday to Friday from 5 to 7pm, when drinks cost about one-third less than normal.

✪ **Lord Dudley Hotel.** 236 Jersey Rd., Woollahra. ☎ **02/9327 5399.**

The best way to get to this great English-style pub is via the Edgecliff CityRail station (between Kings Cross and Bondi Junction). From there, it's a 5-minute walk up the hill outside the station and then take a right onto Jersey Road. The Lord Dudley has the best atmosphere of just about any drinking hole in Sydney, with log fires in winter, couches to relax in, three bars, and a restaurant.

✪ **Lord Nelson Hotel.** At Kent and Argyle sts., The Rocks. ☎ **02/9251 4044.**

Another Sydney landmark, the Lord Nelson rivals the Hero of Waterloo for the title of "Sydney's oldest pub." A drink here is a must for any visitor. The drinks are sold English style, in pints and half-pints, and the landlord even makes his own prize-winning beers. Of these beers, Three Sheets is the most popular, but if you can handle falling over on your way home, you might want to try a drop of Quail (a pale beer), Victory (based on an English bitter), and a dark beer called Admiral. You can get some good pub grub here, too. Upstairs there's a more formal brasserie.

✪ **Marble Bar.** In the Sydney Hilton, 259 Pitt St. ☎ **02/9266 2000.**

Once part of a hotel demolished in the 1970s, the Marble Bar is unique in that it's the only grand cafe-style watering hole in Australia. With oil paintings, marble columns, and brass everywhere, it's the very picture of 15th-century Italian Renaissance architecture. It's a tourist attraction in itself. Live music, generally jazz or soul, is played here Tuesday through Saturday beginning at 8:30pm. Dress smart on Friday and Saturday evenings. Drinks are normally very expensive, but the happy hour (daily from 7 to 9pm) cuts prices down to what you'd pay during normal drinking hours elsewhere.

The Mercantile. 25 George St., The Rocks. ☎ **02/9247 3570.**

Sydney's original Irish bar is scruffy and loud when the Irish music's playing in the evening. It's an essential stop on any self-respecting pub crawl in The Rocks. The Guinness is some of the best in Sydney. Irish bands kick off every night at around 8am.

✪ **Watsons Bay Hotel.** 1 Military Rd., Watsons Bay. ☎ **02/9337 4299.**

If it's a sunny afternoon, don't waste it; get over to Watsons Bay for the best food you'll find in the sun anywhere. The beer garden serves very good seafood and BBQ meat dishes, while you sip your wine or beer overlooking the harbor. Nearby are the fabulous Doyles Wharf Restaurant and Doyles at the Beach take-away.

MOVIES

The best movie theater in town is the ✪ **Hayden Orpheum Picture Palace,** 380 Military Rd., Cremorne (☎ **02/9908 4344**). This six-screen art deco gem is an experience in itself, especially on Saturday and Sunday evenings when a Wurlitzer pops up from the center of the Cinema 2 stage, and a musician in a tux gives a stirring rendition of times gone by. Eat "Jaffas," round candy-coated chocolates, if you want to fit in. Tickets are A$11.50 (U.S.$7.50) adults, A$7.50 (U.S.$4.90) children; Tuesday A$7.50 (U.S.$4.90) adults, A$4.50 (U.S.$2.90) children.

THE CASINO

Star City. 80 Pyrmont St., Pyrmont (adjacent to Darling Harbour). ☎ **02/9777 9000.** No cover. Open 24 hr. Ferry: Pyrmont (Darling Harbour). Monorail: Casino.

This huge entertainment complex has 15 main bars, 12 restaurants, two theaters—the Showroom, which presents Las Vegas–style revues, and the Lyric, Sydney's largest theater—and a huge complex of retail shops. All the usual gambling tables are here, in four main gambling areas. In all, there are 2,500 slot machines to gobble your change.

New South Wales

by Marc Llewellyn

Mountains, forests, beaches, Outback, rivers, country, and Sydney: these are the seven wonders of New South Wales. With so much to see in such a big state, you're not going to see all the major attractions in one hit, so as with any trip to Australia, you must prioritize.

If you have just a few days to spare, you should certainly head out to the Blue Mountains, part of the Great Dividing Range that separates the lush eastern coastal strip from the more arid interior. Although they are really hills rather than mountains, they are nevertheless spectacular, with tall eucalyptus trees, deep river valleys, waterfalls, and craggy cliffs. Another option is to spend a day in the vineyards of the lower Hunter (also known as the Hunter Valley). If you have a few more days, I recommend heading to Barrington Tops National Park, north of the Hunter, for a dose of rain forest and native animals, or down to the pristine beaches of Jervis Bay on the south coast for gorgeous scenery and some great bushwalks.

For longer trips, you have three main touring options. You can head north toward the Queensland border on the 964-kilometer (600-mile) route to Brisbane. On the way you'll pass pretty seaside towns, deserted beaches, and tropical hinterland. Another option is to travel along the south coast 1,032 kilometers (640 miles) to Melbourne. Along the way are some of the country's most spectacular beaches, quaint hamlets, some good opportunities to spot dolphins and whales, and extensive national parks.

If you want to experience another side of Australia—the Outback—then you need to head west across the Blue Mountains. You are sure to see plenty of kangaroos, emus, reptiles, and giant wedge-tailed eagles. The main Outback destinations in New South Wales are the extraordinary opal mining town of Lightning Ridge, where you can meet some of the most eccentric *fair-dinkum* (that means "authentic" or "genuine") Aussies you'll come across anywhere, and the city of Broken Hill.

EXPLORING THE STATE

VISITOR INFORMATION The **Sydney Visitors Centre,** 106 George St., The Rocks (☎ **13 20 77** in Australia; www.tourism.nsw.gov.au), will give you general information on what to do and accommodations throughout the state. Otherwise, **Tourism New South Wales** (☎ **02/9931 1111**) will direct you to the regional tourist office in the town or area you are interested in.

New South Wales

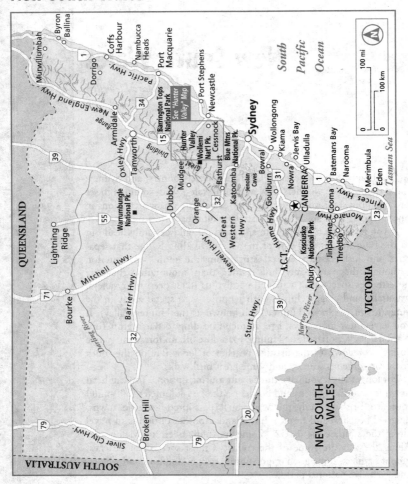

GETTING AROUND **By Car** From Sydney, the **Pacific Highway** heads along the north coast into Queensland, and the **Princes Highway** hugs the south coast and runs into Victoria. The **Sydney–Newcastle Freeway** connects Sydney with its industrial neighbor and the vineyards of the Hunter. The **Great Western Highway** and the **M4 Motorway** head west to the Blue Mountains, while the **M5 Motorway** and the **Hume Highway** are the quickest (and least interesting) ways to get to Melbourne.

The state's automobile association, the **National Roads and Motorists' Association (NRMA),** 151 Clarence St., Sydney (☎ **13 11 22** in Australia; www.aaa.asn.au), offers free maps and touring guides to members of overseas motoring associations, including the AAA in the United States, the CAA in Canada, the AA and RAC in the United Kingdom, and the NZAA in New Zealand.

By Train **Countrylink** (☎ **13 22 32** in Australia) trains travel to most places of interest in the state and as far south as Melbourne in Victoria and across the border into southern Queensland. Countrylink also has a range of rail holidays and has teamed up with **Ansett** (☎ **13 13 00** in Australia) and its affiliates to offer cheap one-way plane tickets, so you can combine the rail experience with the convenience of getting either to or from your destination by air. Countrylink also has special rates for car hire through Thrifty.

In 1999, one of the great trains of the world, *The Ghan,* began operating from Sydney to Alice Springs. It's an expensive 2-day, 2-night trip, and reviews are mixed. First-class sleepers cost A$1,095 (U.S.$711.75) for adults and A$734 (U.S.$477) for children. Otherwise, it's A$750 (U.S.$487.50) for adults and A$502 (U.S.$326.30) for children in an economy sleeper, and A$372 (U.S.$241.80) for adults and A$186 (U.S.$120.90) for children in an economy seat. Call **Great Southern Railways** (☎ **08/8213 4530**) for more information and bookings, or check out the timetables and fares at www.gsr.com.au/fares.htm.

By Plane   Ansett (☎ **13 13 00** in Australia), **Qantas** (☎ **13 13 13** in Australia), **Hazelton Airlines** (☎ **13 17 13** in Australia), and **Eastern Australia Airlines** (book through Qantas) fly to most major cities and towns within the state. See "Getting Around Australia," in chapter 2, for details on air passes.

1 The Blue Mountains

The ✪ **Blue Mountains** are where Sydneysiders go to escape the humidity and crowds of the city and suburbs. But in the fledgling days of the colony, the mountains posed one of the most difficult barriers to early exploration of the interior. In 1813, three explorers—Gregory Blaxland, William Charles Wentworth, and William Lawson—managed to conquer the sheer cliffs, valleys, and dense forest, and cross the mountains (which are hardly mountains at all, but rather a series of hills covered in bush and ancient fern trees) to the plains beyond. There they found land urgently needed for grazing and farming. The Great Western Highway and Bells Line of Road are the access roads through the region today—winding and steep in places, they are surrounded by Blue Mountains and Wollemi national parks.

The area is known for its spectacular scenery, particularly the cliff-top views into the valleys of gum trees and across to craggy outcrops that tower up from the valley floor. It's colder up here than down on the plains, and the clouds can sweep in and fill the canyons with mist in minutes, while waterfalls cascade down sheer drops, spraying the dripping fern trees that cling to the gullies.

The Blue Mountains, which derive their name from the ever-present blue haze (caused by light striking the droplets of eucalyptus oil that evaporate from the leaves of the dense surrounding forest), are also one of Australia's best-known adventure playgrounds. Rock climbing, caving, abseiling, bushwalking, mountain biking, horseback riding, and canoeing are all practiced here throughout the year.

BLUE MOUNTAIN ESSENTIALS

VISITOR INFORMATION   You can book accommodations or pick up maps, walking guides, and other information at **Blue Mountains Tourism,** with locations at Echo Point Road, Katoomba, NSW 2780 (☎ **1300/653 408** in Australia or 02/4739 6266), and on the Great Western Highway at Glenbrook, a small settlement 61 kilometers (42 miles) from Sydney (same telephone number). The Katoomba information center is an attraction in itself, with giant glass windows overlooking a gum forest and cockatoos and colorful lorikeets feeding on seed dispensers. Be sure to pick up a copy of the *Blue Mountains Pocket Guide,* a free guide to dining, accommodations, bushwalking, and entertainment in the area. Both offices are open from 9am to 5pm daily (the office at Glenbrook closes at 4:30pm on Sat and Sun).

Travel Tips

Try to visit the Blue Mountains on weekdays, when most Sydneysiders are at work and prices are much lower. Note, too, that the colder winter months (June, July, and Aug) are actually the busiest time in the Blue Mountains. This period is known as Yuletide—the locals' version of the Christmas period, when most places offer traditional Christmas dinners and roaring log fires.

The **National Park Shop,** Heritage Centre, at the end of Govetts Leap Road, Blackheath (☎ 02/4787 8877; www.npws.nsw.gov.au), is run by the National Parks and Wildlife Service and offers detailed information about the Blue Mountains National Park. The staff can also arrange personalized guided tours of the mountains. The shop is open daily from 9am to 4:30pm (closed Christmas).

GUIDED TOURS FROM SYDNEY   Many private bus operators offer day trips from Sydney. Shop around; some offer a guided coach tour where you just stretch your legs occasionally, while others let you get the cobwebs out of your lungs with a couple of longish bushwalks. One highly recommended operator is **Oz Trek Adventure Tours,** P.O. Box 319, Potts Point, NSW 2011 (☎ **02/9360 3444;** www.oztrek. com.au; e-mail: info@oztrek.com.au). Their trips include a tour of the Olympic site, a visit to Glenbrook National Park (where you'll see kangaroos and wallabies in the wild), tours of all the major Blue Mountain sites, and a 1¹/₂-hour bushwalk. It costs just A$49 (U.S.$31.85) for adults (prices vary for children depending on age).

Wonderbus (☎ **02/9555 9800;** e-mail: info@wonderbus.com.au; www.wonderbus. com.au) tours are good fun for all ages and include most of the major sites and a short bushwalk. Day tours leave Sydney at approximately 7:30am from The Rocks and 8:15am from Central Station (Bay 15 on Pitt Street) and return after 7pm and cost A$70 (U.S.$45.50) for adults and A$55 (U.S.$35.75) for children. Wonderbus also sells overnight packages, with accommodation in the YHA hostel in Katoomba, or, for a higher price, with an upgrade to your own room at the pleasant Clarendon Guest House.

Cox's River Escapes, P.O. Box 81, Leura, NSW 2780 (☎ **02/4784 1621,** or mobile 0407 400 121), offers highly recommended tours for those wanting to get off the beaten track. Half-day trips with morning or afternoon tea cost A$110 (U.S.$71.50); full-day trips with morning tea, lunch, and afternoon refreshments and entry into Jenolan Caves cost A$220 (U.S.$143).

AAT Kings, Shop 1, corner of Alfred Street and ferry wharf no. 1, Circular Quay (☎ **02/9518 6095;** www.aatking.com.au), operates three typical big bus tours of the mountains, taking in all the usual sights, with a couple of short walks included. One tour includes a visit to Jenolan Caves. Tours range in cost from A$78 to A$110 (U.S.$50.70 to $71.50) for adults, and A$39 to A$48 (U.S.$25.35 to $31.20) for children. Another large operator, **Australian Pacific Tours** (☎ **1300 655 965**), offers a similar trip with a visit to the Australian Wildlife Park and a quick visit to the Sydney Olympic site at Homebush Bay. This tour costs A$94 (U.S.$61.10) for adults and A$47 (U.S.$30.55) for children.

BUSHWALKING & OTHER ACTIVE PURSUITS

Whereas almost every other activity costs money, ✪ **bushwalking (hiking)** is the exception to the rule that nothing in life is free. There are some 50 walking trails in the Blue Mountains, ranging from routes you can cover in 15 minutes to the 3-day **Six Foot Track** that starts just outside Katoomba and finishes at Jenolan Caves. If

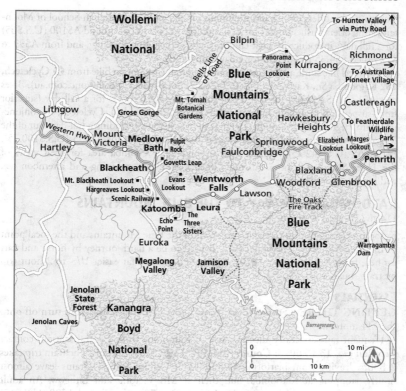

you're planning to do some bushwalking, I highly recommend picking up a copy of *Sydney and Beyond—Eighty-Six Walks in NSW,* by Andrew Mevissen (Macstyle Publishing). It features eight walks in the Blue Mountains, from easy 1-hour treks to 6-hour tramps. Buy it at bookshops and tourist information centers. Before setting off on any bushwalk by yourself, always tell someone where you're going—plenty of people get lost every year. For other outdoor safety advice, see "Tips on Health, Safety & Outdoor Etiquette Down Under," in section 6 of chapter 2.

✪ **Great Australian Walks,** 81 Elliot St., Balmain, NSW 2041 (☎ **1300 360 499** in Australia or 02/9555 7580; www.walkaustralia.com), is a superb operator offering walks in the Blue Mountains. I had great fun on their 3-day Six Foot Track Walk from Katoomba to Jenolan Caves. Though not a wilderness trek, it goes through nice pockets of rain forest and open gum forests and traverses pretty farming country.

One of the best adventure operators in the area is **High 'n' Wild,** 3/5 Katoomba St., Katoomba, NSW 2780 (☎ **02/4782 6224;** e-mail: info@high-n-wild.com.au; www.high-n-wild.com.au), offering abseiling (aka rappelling), rock climbing, and, for those who like things a bit tamer, river floats on inflatable air beds.

Other excellent adventure operators are **The Blue Mountains Adventure Company,** P.O. Box 242, Katoomba, NSW 2780 (☎ **02/4782 1271;** e-mail: bmac@bmac. com.au), located in Katoomba at 84a Bathurst Rd. (above The Summit Gear Shop); and the **Australian School of Mountaineering,** 166b Katoomba St., Katoomba, NSW 2780 (☎ **02/4782 2014;** e-mail: asm@pnc.com.au). Both operators can organize rock climbing, abseiling, and canyoning expeditions, while the Blue Mountains Adventure

Company also offers caving and mountain biking, and the Australian School of Mountaineering offers bushcraft and survival training. Expect to pay around A$100 (U.S.$65) for a full day's introductory rock-climbing course including abseiling, and from A$99 to $125 (U.S.$64.35 to $81.25) for a day's canyoning.

If you feel like some adventure on your own, rent a mountain bike from ✪ **Cycletech,** 182 Katoomba St., Katoomba (☎ **02/4782 2800;** e-mail: cycltech@pnc.com.au). Bikes cost A$17 (U.S.$11.05) for half a day and A$25 (U.S.$16.25) for a full day (superior front-suspension mountain bikes cost A$45/U.S.$29.25 a day). Cycletech, in conjunction with High-n-Wild, also offers a range of bicycle tours including a full-day tour of the Megalong Valley area and another around Blackheath, both for A$155 (U.S.$100.75). For A$65 (U.S.$42.25) you can cycle around the Katoomba area for great views of the Three Sisters and more. All tours include bike hire, morning and afternoon tea, and lunch.

KATOOMBA: GATEWAY TO THE BLUE MOUNTAINS
114km (71 miles) W of Sydney

Katoomba (pop. 11,200) is the largest town in the Blue Mountains and the focal point of the Blue Mountains National Park. It used to be a hard journey by horse and cart up here from Sydney in the 1870s, but these days it's a far easier 1¹/₂- to 2-hour trip by train, bus, or car.

ESSENTIALS
GETTING THERE   From Sydney, travel along Parramatta Road and turn off onto the M4 motorway.

Frequent rail services connect Sydney to Katoomba from Central Station; contact **CityRail** (☎ **13 15 00**) or **Countrylink** (☎ **13 22 32**) for details. The train trip takes 2 hours, leaving from platforms 12 and 13 of Central Station. Trains leave almost hourly, stopping at Katoomba, and then at Mt. Victoria and Lithgow. An adult day-return round-trip ticket costs A$11.80 (U.S.$7.70) off-peak and A$20 (U.S.$13) during commuter hours. A child's day-return round-trip ticket costs A$3 (U.S.$1.95).

GETTING AROUND   If you take the train to Katoomba from Sydney, walk up the stairs from the station onto Katoomba Street; at the top of the street you'll see the Savoy, a former theater but now a restaurant. Coaches operated by **Mountain Link** (☎ **1800/801 577** in Australia, or 02/4782 3333) meet most trains from Sydney outside this theater or opposite at the Carrington Hotel (check the signs for your particular destination) and take passengers to the main Blue Mountains attractions, including Echo Point, the Three Sisters, the Skyway, Leura Village, the Gordon Falls, and Blackheath, as well as other drop-off points for good views. Single-ride tickets to one destination cost between A$1.80 and $3.60 (U.S.$1.20 and $2.35) depending on the distance.

The **Blue Mountains Bus Company** (☎ **02/4782 4213**) also runs buses through Katoomba, Leura, Wentworth Falls, and as far as Woodford every hour. Buses leave from either the Carrington Hotel or the Savoy. Fares are similar to Mountain Link's.

You can also connect with the **Blue Mountains Explorer Bus.** This red double-decker bus leaves from outside Katoomba train station every half hour from 9:30am. It stops at 27 major attractions and various resorts, craft galleries, and tearooms. You can get on and off as often as you want. Tickets cost A$20 (U.S.$13) for adults, A$10 (U.S.$6.50) for children, and A$50 (U.S.$32.50) for families. Weekdays you can take a 3-hour **Blue Mountains Highlights Tour,** which costs A$37.50 (U.S.$24.40) for

High on the Hog

A thrilling way to see the Blue Mountains is on the back of a chauffeur-driven Harley-Davidson. **Blue Thunder Bike Tours** (☎ **02/4571 1154**) leave from Manly Wharf in Sydney (but they'll pick you up anywhere in the city). Rides cost A$80 (U.S.$52) for the first hour, A$130 (U.S.$84.50) for 2 hours, A$255 (U.S.$165.75) for half a day, and A$360 (U.S.$234) for a full day with lunch. The same company runs Hot Heritage Tours, operating out of the Blue Mountains (pickup anywhere in the Mountains), for the same prices.

adults, A$18.75 (U.S.$12.20) for children, and A$88 (U.S.$57.20) for families; tours leave Katoomba train station Monday through Friday at 10:30am, 11:30am, and 2pm. For details contact **Fantastic Aussie Tours** (☎ **1300/300 915** in Australia, or 02/4782 1866; e-mail: info@fantastic-aussie-tours.com.au).

Combined rail/bus tours from Sydney can be purchased at any **CityRail** (☎ **13 15 00** in Australia) station.

EXPLORING THE AREA

The most visited and photographed attraction in the Blue Mountains is the unusual rock formation known as the **Three Sisters.** The best place to view these astonishing-looking pinnacles is from **Echo Point Road,** right opposite the Blue Mountains Tourism office. Other good lookouts include Evans Lookout, Govetts Leap, and Hargreaves Lookout, all at Blackheath (see below).

One thing you have to do in the Blue Mountains is take a ride on the **Scenic Railway,** the world's steepest. It consists of a carriage on rails that is lowered 415 meters (1,360 ft.) down into the Jamison Valley at a maximum incline of 52 degrees. Originally it was used to transport coal and shale in the 1880s from the mines below. The trip takes only a few minutes there and back; at the bottom there are some excellent walks through forests of ancient tree ferns. Another popular attraction is the **Skyway,** a cable car that travels 300 meters (990 ft.) above the Jamison Valley. The trip takes 6 minutes round-trip. The Scenic Railway and the Skyway (☎ **02/4782 2699**) each cost A$7 (U.S.$4.55) round-trip for adults and A$3 (U.S.$1.95) for children, and operate from 9am to 5pm daily (last trip at 4:50pm). They leave from the ticket office at 1 Violet St., Katoomba (follow the signs).

Canyons, waterfalls, underground rivers—the Blue Mountains has them all, and before you experience them in person you can catch them on the (giant) silver screen in *The Edge* at the **MAXVISION Cinema,** 225–237 Great Western Hwy., Katoomba (☎ **02/4782 8900;** boxoffice@edgecinemas.com.au). The special effects and extra-large screen (18 × 24m, or 59 × 79 ft.) make you feel like you're part of the action. The 38-minute film is shown at 10am, 11:40am, 12:30pm, 1:20pm, 2:50pm, and 5:15pm. Tickets are A$13.50 (U.S.$8.80) for adults, A$9 (U.S.$5.85) for children, and A$42 (U.S.$27.30) for families. Another movie (titles vary) is shown between screenings of *The Edge*. The cinema is a 5- to 10-minute walk from the train station. The cinema is open daily from 9am to 9:30pm, with recent-release movies shown on part of the giant screen in the evenings. There are a restaurant and a snack bar on the premises.

ACCOMMODATIONS

There are plenty of places to stay throughout the Blue Mountains, including historic guest houses, B&Bs, resorts, motels, and homestays.

Very Expensive

✪ **Echoes Guesthouse.** 3 Lilianfels Ave., Katoomba, NSW 2780. ☎ **02/4782 1966.** Fax 02/4782 3707. www.ozemail.com.au/echoes. E-mail: echoes@ozemail.com.au. 13 units. MINIBAR TV TEL. Weekend $710 (U.S.$461.50) double for 2 nights, including 1 dinner and 2 breakfasts; midweek A$285 (U.S.$185.25) double with breakfast. AE, BC, DC, MC, V. Free parking.

Despite being less expensive than Lilianfels (see below) across the road, Echoes has by far the superior views. It's right on the edge of the dramatic drop into the Jamison Valley, and most guests can sit on their balconies and simply take in the fantastic scenery. Rooms are smaller than at Lilianfels, and quite simply furnished. All have under-floor heating, and two corner rooms have Jacuzzis. Upstairs is a large deck offering more legendary views, plus a lounge with an open fire, a restaurant serving French cuisine, and a bar—all with large windows. The property also has a sauna.

Lilianfels Blue Mountains. Lilianfels Ave., Katoomba, NSW 2780. ☎ **1800/ 024 452** in Australia, or 02/4780 1200. Fax 02/4780 1300. E-mail: reservations@lilianfels.com.au. www.slh.com. 85 units, 1 cottage. A/C MINIBAR TV TEL. A$315–$380 (U.S.$204.75–$247) double; A$430–$585 (U.S.$279.50–$380.25) suite; A$950 (U.S.$617.50) cottage. Extra person A$50 (U.S.$32.50). Ask about off-season packages. AE, BC, DC, MC, V. Free parking.

Set just over a road from Echo Point, this Victorian country-house hotel—a member of the Small Luxury Hotels of the World—has some impressive views. Remarkably, it has also managed to combine the facilities of a top-class resort and the coziness of a guest house. Rooms are very spacious and furnished with antiques. Most come with king-size beds and both a tub and a shower. Those with views are more expensive. The living areas are just as grand, with roaring log fires and more antiques. The lounge, which overlooks the Jamison Valley, is the property's best feature. On the grounds is a freestanding 1889 cottage. Meant for two, it has a sitting room, a bedroom with a four-poster bed, a spa, an intimate fireplace, and its own private gardens. Lilianfels also has a billiards room, a library and reading room, a tennis court, and a French bowls lawn.

Dining/Diversions: Darley's Restaurant is set in historic surrounds and offers very good meals. Lilian's is more casual but equally good, while the Lobby Lounge is perfect for light meals and teas.

Amenities: Heated indoor pool; health club with flotation tank, herbal bath, gym, sauna, and Jacuzzis; room service; dry cleaning/laundry; nightly turndown; secretarial services; massage therapist and beautician; mountain bikes.

Expensive

Avonleigh Guest House. 174 Lurline St., Katoomba, NSW 2780. ☎ **02/4782 1534.** Fax 02/4782 5688. 12 units (some with shower only). Weekend A$125–$160 (U.S.$81.25–$104) per person double, including breakfast and dinner; midweek A$65 (U.S.$42.25) per person double, including breakfast, A$105 (U.S.$68.25) per person double, including breakfast and dinner. AE, BC, DC, MC, V.

This three-star 1902 property is a cozy mountain hangout with a Victorian feel. The rooms are comfortable and varied, each with antique furniture, a queen or double bed, and a nice-sized bathroom with a shower and a tub, or just a shower. The living room has high ceilings, velvet chairs, double cameo couches, and sprays of dried flowers. There's free tea and coffee in the lounge all day, and in cooler months there are open fires as well as central heating. Plenty of American and German guests stay here. Children are not encouraged, and the stairs could make it difficult for travelers with disabilities.

Moderate

The Cecil. 108 Katoomba St., Katoomba, NSW 2780. ☎ **02/4782 1411.** Fax 02/4782 5364. 23 units, 4 with private bathroom. Weekend A$110 (U.S.$71.50) double; midweek A$90 (U.S.$58.50) double. Rates include substantial breakfast. Children under 15 half price. Ask about multinight midweek discounts and tour packages. AE, BC, DC, MC, V.

Right in the center of town, this lovely old property has comfortable rooms. Rooms above the second floor (numbers 30 to 35) on the east side have great views, with room 33 offering the very best—a breathtaking vista across the mountains. Five rooms renovated in 1988 have small attached bathrooms with showers. There are a cozy lounge area with a TV, a game room with a pool table and Ping-Pong table, a good library, and a small terraced garden out the back. Three-course dinners cost A$25 (U.S.$16.25). The breakfasts are huge enough to sustain you for a whole day's walking.

Echo Point Holiday Villas. 36 Echo Point Rd., Katoomba, NSW 2780. ☎ **02/4782 3275.** Fax 02/4782 7030. 5 villas, 2 cottages (all with shower only). TV. Fri–Sat and public holidays A$132 (U.S.$85.80) villa; Sun–Thurs A$105 (U.S.$68.25) villa. Weekend A$220 (U.S.$143) cottage; midweek A$180 (U.S.$117) cottage. Linen A$6 (U.S.$3.90) extra per person in villas. Minimum 2-night stay required. Extra person A$10 (U.S.$6.50). AE, BC, DC, MC, V.

These are the closest self-contained accommodations to the Three Sisters Lookout. The two front-facing villas are the best because of their beautiful mountain views. Some villas have one double and two single beds, plus a foldout double bed in the lounge room. Bathrooms contain a shower, a washing machine and dryer, and a hair dryer. The villas also come with modern, fully equipped kitchens, and there are barbecue facilities in the backyard. The cottage is also fully self-contained and has a bathroom, central heating, and access to nice gardens.

Three Explorers Motel. 197 Lurline St., Katoomba, NSW 2780. ☎ **02/4782 1733.** Fax 02/4782 1146. 14 units. TV. Fri–Sat A$109 (U.S.$70.85) double; A$182 to A$211 (U.S.$118.30–$137) spa suite. Sun–Thurs A$94 (U.S.$61) double; A$164 (U.S.$106.60) spa suite. Public holidays A$132 (U.S.$85.80) double. Ask about packages and discounts for Aussie auto club members. Extra adult A$16 (U.S.$10.40) in double, A$22 (U.S.$14.30) in spa suite. Extra child under 13 A$13 (U.S.$8.45). AE, BC, DC, MC, V.

Staying in a motel isn't the ideal Blue Mountains experience, but it does offer some advantages. The main selling point of this motel is that it's just a 5-minute walk from Echo Point; it's also very quiet. Rooms here vary in size, from those just large enough to fit one queen-size bed to large family units with six beds. Standard rooms are comfy and come with an attached bathroom with shower. The spa suites have a queen-size bed in the main living area, a separate bedroom with a second queen-size bed, and a large bathroom. Breakfast can be served in your room, and each night there is a choice of four main courses costing around A$14 (U.S.$9.10). There are also a laundry and video rental.

Inexpensive

Katoomba Mountain Lodge. 31 Lurline St., Katoomba, NSW 2780. ☎ and fax **02/4782 3933.** 23 units, none with private bathroom. Sun and Mon–Thurs A$42–$52 (U.S.$27.30–$33.80) double; Fri–Sat (2-night package) A$132 (U.S.$85.80) double. A$10–$15 (U.S.$6.50–$19.75) dorm bed. AE, BC, DC, MC, V.

This 2¹/₂-star property is quite cozy, with rooms looking out across the mountains. Dorm rooms are clean and come with three to six beds. Doubles are basic and lack a TV, but are certainly adequate for a couple of nights. All share bathrooms. On the premises you'll find a TV lounge with a log fire, a BYO dining room, a laundry,

A Shopping Stop

If you're into hats, then you shouldn't miss **The Hattery,** 171 Lurline St., Katoomba (☎ **02/4782 5003**), which stocks more than 25 styles, from famous Akubra bush hats to women's hats, English Tweeds, and Panama Straws. The shop is open daily from 9am to 5pm.

and a game room. The staff can arrange tour packages. Breakfast costs an additional A$9 (U.S.$5.85) per person, and dinner and breakfast costs an extra A$20 (U.S.$13) per person.

DINING

Katoomba Street has many ethnic dining choices, whether you're hungry for Greek, Chinese, or Thai. Restaurants in the Blue Mountains are generally more expensive than equivalent places in Sydney.

Lindsay's. 122 Katoomba St., Katoomba. ☎ **02/4782 2753.** Reservations recommended. Main courses A$14–$23.50 (U.S.$9.10–$15.30). AE, BC, JCB, MC, V. Sat–Sun noon–3pm; daily 6pm–midnight. INTERNATIONAL.

Swiss chef Beat Ettlin has been making waves in Katoomba ever since he left some of the best European restaurants behind to try his hand at dishes such as panfried crocodile nibbles on pumpkin scones with a ginger dipping sauce. The food in this upscale, New York–style speakeasy is as glorious as its decor—Tiffany lamps, sketches by Australian artist Norman Lindsay, and booths lining the walls. The three-level restaurant is warmed by a cozy fire surrounded by an antique lounge stage and resounds every night with piano, classical music, or a jazz band. The menu changes every few weeks, but a recent popular dish was grilled veal medallions topped with Balmain bugs (small saltwater crayfish) with potato and béarnaise sauce.

Paragon Café. 65 Katoomba St., Katoomba. ☎ **02/4782 2928.** Menu items vary in price. AE, MC, V. Tues–Fri 10am–3:30pm, Sat–Sun 10am–4pm. CAFE.

The Paragon has been a Blue Mountains institution since it opened for business in 1916. Inside, it's decked out with dark wood paneling, bas-relief figures guarding the booths, and chandeliers. The homemade soups are delicious. The cafe also serves pies, pastas, grills, seafood, waffles, cakes, and a Devonshire tea of scones and cream.

The Pavilion at Echo Point. 35 Echo Point Rd., Katoomba. ☎ **02/4782 7055.** Main courses A$11–$19 (U.S.$7.15–$12.35). AE, BC, DC, MC, V. Mon–Fri 8:30am to 5pm, Sat–Sun 8am to 6pm (will also be opening evenings from June). MODERN AUSTRALIAN/SNACKS.

This miniature version of Sydney's Queen Victoria Building is so close to Echo Point that it looks like a shove will send it tumbling over the edge. Light fills the three-story building through a rooftop glass atrium and huge windows on the top two floors. On the ground level are a few stores; on the middle level is a food court with a burger/pie outlet, a bakery, and an ice-cream counter; and on the top level is a cafe serving dishes such as baked camembert in puff pastry, battered fillets of trout on a vegetable fritter, and oven-baked baby barramundi with lemon and parsley butter. The food is good for the price, but the views from the terrace and balcony are even better.

TrisElies. 287 Bathurst Rd., Katoomba. ☎ **02/4782 4026.** Reservations recommended. Main courses A$12–$25 (U.S.$7.80–$16.25). AE, MC, JCB, V. Fri–Sun noon–midnight; Mon–Thurs 5pm–midnight. TRADITIONAL GREEK.

Perhaps it's the belly dancers and the plate smashing, or the smell of moussaka, but as soon as you walk through the door of this lively eatery, you feel like you've been transported to an authentic Athenian taverna. The restaurant folds out onto three tiers of tables, all with a good view of the stage where every night Greek or international performances take place. The food is solid Greek fare—souvlaki, traditional dips, fried haloumi cheese, Greek salads, casseroles like mother could have made, whitebait, and sausages in red wine—with a few Italian and Spanish extras. If it's winter, come in to warm up beside one of two log fires.

LEURA

107km (66 miles) W of Sydney, 3km (2 miles) W of Katoomba

The fashionable capital of the Blue Mountains, Leura is known for its gardens, its pretty old buildings (many of them holiday homes for Sydneysiders), and its cafes and restaurants. The National Trust has classified Leura's main street as an urban conservation area. Just outside Leura is the **Sublime Point Lookout,** which has spectacular and unusual views of the Three Sisters formation in Katoomba. From the southern end of **Leura Mall,** a cliff drive takes you all the way back to Echo Point in Katoomba; along the way you'll get some spectacular views across the Jamison Valley.

ACCOMMODATIONS

Fairmont Resort. 1 Sublime Point Rd., Leura, NSW 2780. ☎ **1800/786 640** in Australia, or 02/4782 5222. Fax 02/4784 1685. www.fairmont.com.au. E-mail: reservations@fairmont. com.au. 230 units. A/C MINIBAR TV TEL. Weekend A$174–$246 (U.S.$113–$159.90) double, A$302–$530 (U.S.$196.30–$344.50) suite. Midweek A$136–$210 (U.S.$88.40–$136.50) double; A$258–$472 (U.S.$167.70–$306.80) suite. Extra person A$35 (U.S.$22.75). Children under 16 stay free in parents' room. Ask about cheaper rates through Aussie auto clubs. 2-night minimum stay on weekends. AE, BC, DC, JCB, MC, V.

If you don't like B&Bs or guest houses, opt for this award-winning resort. It opened in 1988 as the Blue Mountains' only deluxe hotel-style accommodation. Rooms are rather luxurious; the valley-view rooms on the upper floors have the best outlooks and cost the most. The resort is popular with Sydneysiders, who come up to enjoy the recreational facilities and the Blue Mountains' best golf course, which is just across the road.

Dining: Both Jamison's and The Terrace offer exquisite dining with excellent service. There are also a bistro and a buffet.

Amenities: Indoor and outdoor swimming pools, health club, gym, spa, sauna, four floodlit tennis courts, two squash courts, adjacent Leura Golf Course, children's center and supervised activity program, concierge, 24-hour room service, laundry, valet, nightly turndown, massage, baby-sitting, business center, gift shop.

A TEAROOM

Bygone Beautys Tea Room. 20–22 Grose St., Leura. ☎ **02/4784 3117.** Devonshire tea A$6.50 (U.S.$4.20); light meals around A$8 (U.S.$5.20), afternoon tea A$12.50 (U.S.$8.10) per person or A$22 (U.S.$14.30) for 2 people. BC, MC, V. Daily 10am–5pm. Closed Christmas and New Year's. LIGHT MEALS/DEVONSHIRE TEA.

Everyone has to try a Devonshire tea in the Blue Mountains. It's just part of the experience. This is one of the more unusual places to partake. It's set amid the largest private antiques emporium in the Blue Mountains, yet it's still cozy in an Edwardian kind of way. As well as your scones and cream, you can treat yourself to a light lunch—such as soup, chicken casserole, a beef curry with rice—or a traditional afternoon tea, with sandwiches, scones, homemade biscuits and cakes, all served on fine china and silver. You can browse the antiques when you finish dining.

WENTWORTH FALLS

103km (62 miles) from Sydney, 7km (4 miles) from Katoomba

This pretty little town has numerous craft and antique shops, but the area is principally known for its magnificent 935-foot-high waterfall, situated in **Falls Reserve.** On the far side of the falls is the **National Pass Walk**—one of the best in the Blue Mountains. It's cut into a cliff face with overhanging rock faces on one side and sheer drops on the other. The views over the Jamison Valley are spectacular. The track takes you down to the base of the falls to the **Valley of the Waters.** Climbing up out of the valley is quite a bit more difficult, but just as rewarding.

ACCOMMODATIONS

If you want to stay in a historic cottage, then consider **Bygone Beautys Cottages,** 20–22 Grose St., Leura, NSW 2780 (☎ **02/4784 3117;** e-mail: info@bygonebeauty. com.au). Nine of the 17 self-contained cottages the group owns are in Wentworth Falls; the others are in Leura and Bullaburra. Prices range from A$62 to $100 (U.S.$40.30 to $65) per person midweek, and A$77.50 to $130 (U.S.$50.40 to $84.50) per person on weekends (with a minimum 2-night stay).

✪ **Whispering Pines, The Sandpatch, and Woodlands.** 178–186 Falls Rd., Wentworth Falls, NSW 2782. ☎ **02/4757 1449.** Fax. 02/4757 1219. 4 units in main building, 1 4-bedroom cottage at Sandpatch, 1 3-bedroom cottage at Woodlands. TV TEL. Whispering Pines: weekend A$160–$220 (U.S.$104–$143); midweek A$100–$150 (U.S.$65–$97.50). Sandpatch: A$180 (U.S.$117) per couple per night plus A$25 (U.S.$16.25) per extra person (4 people minimum). Woodlands: weekend A$200–$220 (U.S.$130–$143) per couple plus A$25 (U.S.$16.25) per extra person (4 people minimum on weekends); midweek A$120 (U.S.$78) per couple and A$25 (U.S.$16.25) per extra person. All properties require a minimum 2-night stay on weekends. AE, BC, DC, MC, V.

Whispering Pines is a grand heritage guest house set in 4 acres of rambling woodland gardens right at the head of Wentworth Falls. Built in 1898, it continues to foster a kind of Victorian luxury. Rooms are cozy and filled with period antiques. If you really want to get away from it all, then the Sandpatch property just down the road is for you. It has two large bedrooms and guest living rooms with Persian rugs, polished floorboards, and all the antiques and added modern luxuries you could ask for. Two people can rent the cottage, but they must pay the four-person rate (it sleeps eight). There are a full kitchen, a CD player, and a VCR. Woodlands is a wood cottage tucked away in the bush, with three bedrooms, a lounge room with fire, a spa bath, a laundry room, and a full kitchen. The property was undergoing renovation as of this writing, so prices here may change.

A NICE SPOT FOR LUNCH

Conservation Hut Café. At the end of Fletcher St., Wentworth Falls. ☎ **02/4757 3827.** Menu items A$6–$14 (U.S.$3.90–$9.10). BC, MC, V. Daily 9am–5pm. CAFE.

This pleasant cafe is in the national park itself on top of a cliff overlooking the Jamison Valley. It's a good place for lunch on the balcony if you're famished after the Valley of the Waters walk, which leaves from just outside. It serves all the usual cafe fare: burgers, salads, sandwiches, and pastas. There are plenty of vegetarian options too. There's a nice log fire inside in winter.

MEDLOW BATH

150km (90 miles) W of Sydney, 6km (3$^1/_2$ miles) E of Katoomba

A cozy place, with its own railway station, a secondhand bookstore, and a few properties hidden between the trees, Medlow Bath has one claim to fame: the **Hydro Majestic Hotel** (☎ **02/4788 1002**), a must-do stop for any visitor to the Blue Mountains. The historic Hydro Majestic has fabulous views over the Megalong Valley; the best time to appreciate the views is at sunset with a drink on the terrace. (You can't stay over as of this writing, but there are plans afoot to turn this place back into a proper hotel with overnight accommodations.) Also drop into Medlow Bath's **Old Post Office,** now a musty secondhand bookshop and antiques store.

ACCOMMODATIONS

The Chalet. 46–50 Portland Rd., Medlow Bath, NSW 2780. ☎ **02/4788 1122.** Fax 02/4788 1064. 8 units, 4 with private bathroom. TV TEL. Weekend $A250–$290 (U.S.$162.50–$188.50) per person for 2-night stay in double, including dinner and breakfast. Midweek A$60–$70 (U.S.$39–$45.50) per person with breakfast. Restaurant open Wed–Sat. AE, BC, DC, MC, V.

When you stay at this recently renovated guest house, originally built in 1892, you are buying a bit of a bygone era. The heritage-listed cottage is set away from the main road in 3 acres of gardens and lawns. Inside, it is bisected by a long checkerboard-tiled hall-way. On one side is a lounge, with a fireplace, flowery sofas, lace curtains, doilies, and arrangements of plastic flowers. Next door is an impressive wood-paneled dining room, with a beamed ceiling and crisp table linens, another blazing fireplace, and jazz on Saturday evenings. Guests may also use the clay tennis court outside. Four of the eight rooms are suitable for families, and four have private bathrooms. All are comfortable and homey. The Chalet prides itself on its contemporary food, and although the menu is limited and lacks a vegetarian option, it's excellent. The Chalet is strictly BYO (bring your own) when it comes to alcohol.

BLACKHEATH

114km (71 miles) W of Sydney, 14km (9 miles) W of Katoomba

Blackheath is the highest town in the Blue Mountains at 3,495 feet. The **Three Brothers** at Blackheath are not as big or as famous as the Three Sisters in Katoomba, but you can climb two of them for fabulous views. Or you could try the **Cliff Walk** from **Evans Lookout** to **Govetts Leap** (named after a surveyor who mapped the region in the 1830s), where there are magnificent views over the **Grose Valley** and **Bridal Veil Falls.** The 1^1/$_2$-hour tramp passes through banksia, gum, and wattle forest, with spectacular views of peaks and valleys. The town itself has some interesting tearooms and antiques shops.

One of the nicest ways to get around is on horseback. **Werriberri Trail Rides** (☎ **02/4787 9171**), found at the base of the Blue Mountains, 10 kilometers (6 miles) from Blackheath on Megalong Road in the Megalong Valley, offers guided half-hour to 3-hour rides through the Megalong Valley. Suitable for beginners to advanced riders. Half-hour rides cost A$17 (U.S.$11).

ESSENTIALS

GETTING THERE   The Great Western Highway takes motorists west from Katoomba to Blackheath. CityRail trains also stop at Blackheath.

VISITOR INFORMATION   **The Heritage Centre** (☎ **02/4787 8877;** www. npws.nsw.gov.au; e-mail: bluemountainsgeneral@npws.nsw.gov.au), operated by the National Parks and Wildlife Service, is close to Govetts Leap Lookout on Govetts Leap Road. It has information on guided walks, camping, and hiking, as well as information on local European and Aboriginal historic sites. It's open daily from 9am to 4:30pm.

ACCOMMODATIONS

✪ **Jemby-Rinjah Lodge.** 336 Evans Lookout Rd., Blackheath, NSW 2785. ☎ **02/4787 7622.** Fax 02/4787 6230. E-mail: jembyrin@pnc.com.au. 10 cabins, 3 lodges. Cabins (occupied by up to 2 adults and 2 children): Fri–Sun and public holidays A$160–$225 (U.S.$104–$146.25); Mon–Thurs A$115–$167 (U.S.$74.75–$108.55). Extra adult A$22 (U.S.$14.30), extra child A$14 (U.S.$9.10). Linen Hire A$13.50 (U.S.$8.80) per bed. Larger lodges available for groups of 8 with dinner B&B packages priced at A$98.50 (U.S.$65) per night. AE, BC, JCB, MC, V.

The Blue Mountains National Park is just a short walk away from this interesting alternative option. There are nine standard cabins (seven two-bedroom cabins and two one-bedroom loft cabins), one deluxe cabin called Treetops Retreat, and three pole-frame lodges. The cabins are right in the bush, can sleep up to six people, and are well spaced. Each has a slow combustion heater, carpets, a bathroom, a fully equipped kitchen, and a lounge and dining area. There are also automatic laundry and barbecue areas nearby. The lodges each have five bedrooms, two bathrooms, and a common lounge area with a circular fireplace. Composting toilets, walkways, and solar heating help protect the environment. You can rent linens, but bring your own food. Free pickup can be arranged from Blackheath train station. Treetops Retreat has a Japanese hot tub, TV and VCR, stereo, and three private balconies with bush views. It sleeps two, making it a perfect romantic getaway.

The nearby walking trails take you to the spectacular Grand Canyon; the Grose Valley Blue Gum forests; and Walls Cave, a resting place for local Aborigines 10,000 years ago.

DINING

⊙ **Cleopatra.** 118 Cleopatra St., Blackheath, NSW 2785. ☎ **02/4787 8456.** Fax 02/4787 6238. 3-course meal A$75 (U.S.$48.75). AE, BC, DC, MC, V. Mon–Sat 7:30–11pm; Sun 1–3:30pm. FRENCH.

The *Sydney Morning Herald*'s "Good Food Guide" consistently rates this restaurant as the best outside Sydney. It's also won the American Express restaurant award for the best restaurant in western New South Wales for 6 years. The dining room, in a hidden treasure of a National Trust house, is comfortable and warm and furnished with tasteful antiques. On the menu you could find appetizers such as duck-neck sausage of duck and pork, flavored with truffle juice and cognac; or a salad of mussels, baby squid, and prawns with fresh borlotti beans. A standout among the main courses is the Tasmanian salmon covered with a purée of black olives, with spring onions, olive oil, and lemon juice. A classic dessert is the hot chocolate pudding with a liquid chocolate center served with fresh mint sauce. Lunch in summer is served in the garden.

If you anticipate being too full to move after dinner, you can stay in one of the house's five cozy **rooms and apartments.** Midweek, they rent for A$180 to $230 (U.S.$117 to $149.50) per person including dinner and breakfast, and on weekends from A$385 to $495 (U.S.$250.25 to $321.75) per person including 2 nights' accommodation, two dinners, and one lunch.

JENOLAN CAVES

182km (113 miles) W of Sydney, 70km (42 miles) SW of Katoomba

The winding road from Katoomba eventually takes you to a spur of the Great Dividing Range and a series of underground limestone caves considered to be some of the world's best. They were known to the local Aborigines as "Binoomea," meaning "dark place." Millions of people have come to see the amazing stalactites, stalagmites, and underground rivers and pools since the caves were opened up to the public in 1866.

GETTING THERE

It's a 1½-hour drive from Katoomba to the caves. CityRail trains run to Katoomba and link up with daily Jenolan Caves excursions run by **Fantastic Aussie Tours** (☎ **02/4782 1866**). The CityRail Link Ticket, which is a combination train ticket/bus tour, costs A$60 (U.S.$39) for adults and A$30 (U.S.$19.50) for children. The tour alone from Katoomba costs A$64 (U.S.$41.60) for adults and A$32

(U.S.$20.80) for children, so the Link Ticket is well worthwhile to buy. These prices include cave entry. You can purchase Link Tickets at any rail station.

Day trips from Sydney are operated by **AAT King's** (☎ **02/9252 2788**) and **Australian Pacific Tours** (☎ **02/9252 2988**). Coach tours depart from the coach terminal at Circular Quay. Since a day trip involves spending 6 hours on a bus, I recommend staying overnight, either in Jenolan Village or somewhere else in the Blue Mountains.

EXPLORING THE CAVES

There are nine caves open to the public, with guided tours conducted at the **Jenolan Caves Reserves Trust** (☎ 02/6359 3311; www.jenolancaves.org.au). The first cave tour starts at 10am weekdays and 9:30am weekends and holidays. The final tour departs at 4:30pm (5pm in warmer months). Tours last 1 to 2 hours, and each costs A$12 to $50 (U.S.$7.80 to $32.50) for adults, and A$8 to $10 (U.S.$5.20 to $6.50) for children under 15. Family concessions and multiple cave packages are available. The best all-round cave is **Lucas Cave; Imperial Cave** is best for seniors. **Adventure Cave Tours,** which include canyoning, last from 3 hours to all day and cost from A$40 to $100 (U.S.$26 to $65) per person.

ACCOMMODATIONS

The Gatehouse Jenolan. Jenolan Caves Village, NSW 2790. ☎ **02/6359 3322.** Fax 02/6359 3227. 13 units. Weekend rates: 4-person dorm room A$90 (U.S.$58.50), 6-person dorm room A$110 (U.S.$71.50). Weekday rates: 4-person dorm room A$65 (U.S.$42.25), 6-person dorm room A$80 (U.S.$52). Linen rental A$3 (U.S.$1.95) per person. AE, BC, MC, V.

The Gatehouse is a clean and cozy budget-style lodge, with a separate cottage nearby. It's located opposite the caves. The Gatehouse sleeps 66 people in all, in seven six-bed rooms and six four-bed rooms in the main building. The cottage can accommodate up to four couples. There are also two common rooms, lockers, washing machines and dryers, basic kitchen facilities, and a barbecue area. There are outdoor barbecues on the premises, and apparently at least one ghost.

Jenolan Caves House. Jenolan Caves Village, NSW 2790. ☎ **02/6359 3322.** Fax 02/6359 3227. www.jenolancaves.com.au. E-mail: bookings@jenolancaves.com. 101 units, some with bathroom. TV TEL. Weekend rates: Grand Classic A$310 (U.S.$201.50), Classic A$240 (U.S.$156), Traditional A$150 (U.S.$97.50), Mountain Lodge A$205 (U.S.$133.25). Weekday rates: Grand Classic A$220 (U.S.$143), Classic A$170 (U.S.$110.50), Traditional A$100 (U.S.$65), Mountain Lodge A$140 (U.S.$91). Family rooms also available. AE, BC, DC, MC, V.

This heritage-listed hotel was built between 1888 and 1906 and is one of the most outstanding structures in New South Wales. The main part of the enormous three-story building is constructed of sandstone and fashioned in Tudor-style black and white. Around it are several scattered cottages and former servants' quarters. Rooms vary within the main house from simple budget bunk rooms to "traditional" rooms with shared bathrooms and "classic" rooms with private bathrooms. The traditional and classic rooms are both old-world and cozy, with heavy furniture and views over red-tile rooftops or steep vegetated slopes. Mountain Lodge rooms are found in a separate building behind the main house and are more motel-like.

The lodge's bar fills up inside and out on summer weekends; Trails Bistro sells snacks (bring your own if you're a vegetarian, though). Chisolms at Jenolan is a fine-dining restaurant serving very good Modern Australian cuisine.

2 The Hunter Valley: Wine Tasting & More

Cessnock: 190km (114 miles) N of Sydney

The Hunter Valley (or simply "the Hunter") is the oldest commercial wine-producing area in Australia, as well as being a major site for coal mining. Internationally acclaimed wines have been pouring out of here since the early 1800s. Though the region falls behind the major wine-producing areas of Victoria in terms of volume, it has the advantage, from the traveler's point of view, of being just 2 hours from Sydney.

People come here to visit the vineyards' "cellar doors" for free wine tasting, to enjoy the rural scenery, to sample the area's highly regarded cuisine, or to escape from the city for a romantic weekend. The whole area is dedicated to the grape and the plate, and you'll find many superb restaurants hidden away between the vineyards and farmland.

In the **Lower Hunter,** centered on the towns of Cessnock and Pokolbin, you'll find more than 50 wineries, including well-known producers such as Tyrell, Roth-bury, Lindemans, Draytons, McGuigans, and McWilliams. Many varieties of wine are produced here, including semillon, shiraz, chardonnay, cabernet sauvignon, and pinot noir.

Farther north, the **Upper Hunter** offers the very essence of Australian rural life, with its sheep and cattle farms, historic homesteads, more wineries, and rugged bush-land. The vineyards here tend to be larger than those in the south, and produce more aromatic varieties, such as traminers and Rieslings. This being the southern hemi-sphere, the harvest months are February to March.

The Upper Hunter eventually gives way to the forested heights of the World Heritage–listed site nearest to Sydney, Barrington Tops National Park. The park is ruggedly beautiful and is home to some of the highest Antarctic beech trees in the country. It also abounds with animals, including several marsupial species, and an abundance of bird life.

HUNTER VALLEY ESSENTIALS

GETTING THERE   To get to the wine-producing regions of the Hunter, leave Syd-ney via the Harbour Bridge or Harbour Tunnel and follow the signs for Newcastle. Just before Hornsby, turn off the highway and follow the signs for Cessnock. The trip will take about 2¹/₂ hours. Barrington Tops National Park is reached via the Upper Hunter town of Dungog.

A rental car should cost you from A$45 (U.S.$29.25) a day from Sydney, and you might put in around A$40 (U.S.$26) worth of petrol or so for a couple of days of touring. In the Hunter, contact **Hertz,** 1A Aberdare Rd., Cessnock (☎ **13 30 39** in Australia, or 02/4991 2500).

Keynes Buses (☎ **1800/043 339** in Australia, or 02/6543 1322) runs coaches to Scone in the Hunter Valley from Sydney's Central Station. Buses depart Monday to

Wine-Tasting Tips

The best year ever for red wines in this part of Australia was 1988, when a long, hot summer produced fewer but more intensely flavored grapes. Stock up on anything you can find from this vintage. At the other end of the scale, 1997 was a very bad year in the Hunter.

Some wineries routinely offer some of their inferior wines for tastings. I've made a habit of specifically asking for a list of their premium wines available for tasting. Most wineries usually have a bottle or two of their better wines uncorked for those with a serious interest.

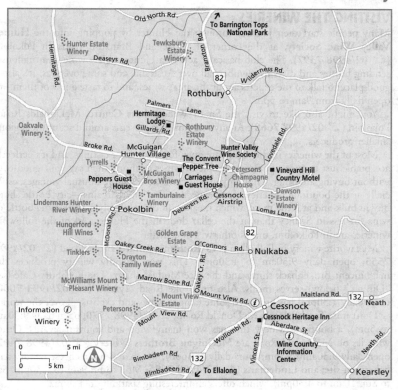

Saturday at 3pm and arrive in Scone at 6:50pm; there's a second service on Fridays leaving at 6pm, and on Sunday the bus leaves at 6:40pm. Round-trip tickets are A$74 (U.S.$48.10) for adults and A$38 (U.S.$24.70) for children.

ORGANIZED TRIPS FROM SYDNEY   Several companies offer day trips to the Hunter Valley from Sydney. **Wonderbus Tours** (☎ **02/9555 9800;** www.wonderbus. com.au; e-mail: info@wonderbus.com au) operates a fun trip that combines wine tasting in the Hunter Valley, a visit to Oakdale Farm (a native animal reserve) near Port Stephens, and dolphin spotting at Port Stephens. The trip costs A$180 (U.S.$117) for adults and A$135 (U.S.$87.75) for children 5 to 12, including lunch and wine. An optional extra is a 30-minute ride on a high-speed boat called the *Foxy* in Port Stephens; it's A$65 (U.S.$42.25) adults, A$35 (U.S.$22.75) for children.

Wonderbus also offers a tour visiting five vineyards (instead of the three in the above trip) with lunch, costing $140 (U.S.$91). Another option is a tour including a morning horse ride, lunch, and afternoon wine tour by horse and carriage costing $240 (U.S.$156).

VISITOR INFORMATION   **Wine Country Visitors Information Centre,** Turner Park, Aberdare Road, Cessnock, NSW 2325 (☎ **02/4990 4477;** www.winecountry. com.au; e-mail: info@winecountry.com.au), is open Monday to Friday from 9am to 5pm, Saturday from 9:30am to 5pm, and Sunday from 9:30am to 3:30pm. The staff can make accommodation bookings and answer any questions. The **Dungog Visitors Information Centre,** on Dowling Street, Dungog (☎ **02/4992 2212**), has plenty of information on the Barrington Tops area.

VISITING THE WINERIES

Many people start their journey through the Hunter by popping into the **Hunter Valley Wine Society,** at the corner of Broke and Branxton roads in Pokolbin (☎ **02/4998 7397**). The club basically acts as a Hunter Valley wine clearinghouse, sending bottles and cases to members all over Australia, and some overseas. It's also a good place to talk to the experts about the area's wines, and to taste a few of them. It's open daily from 9am to 5pm.

You might also like to visit the **Small Winemakers Centre,** McDonalds Road, Pokolbin (☎ **02/4998 7668**). At any one time it represents around six of the region's smaller producers.

Most of the wineries in the region are open for cellar-door tastings, and it's perfectly acceptable just to turn up, taste a couple of wines or more, then say your good-byes without buying anything. Though you will come across some unusual vintages, especially at the boutique wineries, don't expect to find any bargains—city bottle shops buy in bulk and at trade price, which means you can probably get the same bottle of wine for less in Sydney than at the cellar door in the Hunter. All of the following wineries are in Polkolbin, unless otherwise specified.

My favorite winery in Polkolbin is ✪ **Rothbury Estate,** Broke Road (☎ **02/4998 7555;** open daily 9:30am to 4:30pm). This very friendly winery produces the magnificent Brokenback shiraz and the nice Mudgee shiraz. The Rothbury Café (see "Dining," below) serves meals. Also on Broke Road, **Tyrell's** (☎ **02/4993 7000;** tours daily 1:30pm) has produced some famous wines and exports all over the world.

Don't miss **Tamburlaine,** McDonald Road (☎ **02/4998 7570;** open daily 9:30am to 5pm), a boutique winery that has won many wine and tourism awards. Other wineries on McDonald Road are **McGuigan Brothers Winery** (☎ **02/4998 7402;** open daily 9:30am to 5pm; tours daily at noon), which also has a cheese factory and bakery on-site; and **Lindemans** (☎ **02/4998 7684;** Mon to Fri 9am to 4:30pm, Sat to Sun 10am to 4:30pm), which offers an interesting sparkling red shiraz.

Peterson's Champagne House, at the corner of Broke and Branxton roads (☎ **02/ 4998 7881;** daily 9am to 5pm), is the only specialist champagne winery in the Hunter. **McWilliams Mount Pleasant,** Marrowbone Road (☎ **02/4998 7505;** daily 10am to 4:30pm; tours daily at 11am), is famed for both its Elizabeth Semillon, which has won 15 trophies and 134 gold medals over 12 years, and its Lovedale Semillon, which has won 24 trophies and 38 gold medals.

Drayton Family Wines, Oakey Creek Road (☎ **02/4998 7513;** Mon to Fri 9am to 5pm, Sat to Sun 10am to 5pm), produces some spectacular shiraz. The Hunter's largest winery, **Hunter Estate Winery,** Hermitage Road (☎ **02/4998 7777;** daily 10am to 5pm), crushes some 6,500 tons of grapes a year. Come here for excellent semillon and shiraz; there are tours daily 11am and 2pm.

If you want to taste the grapes in season, head to **Tinklers,** Pokolbin Mountains Road (☎ **02/4998 7435;** daily 10am to 4pm). It sells some 30 varieties of eating grapes between December and March, and nectarines, plums, peaches, and vegetables

---

Don't Drink & Drive

Australia's drunk-driving laws are strict and rigidly enforced. If you're interested in tasting some grapes in the Hunter Valley, choose a designated driver or take a guided tour (see above). Both easily identifiable and unmarked police cars regularly patrol the vineyard regions.

at other times of the year. It also offers wine tasting and free vineyard walks at 11am on Saturday and Sunday.

Mount View Estate, Mount View Road in Mount View (☎ **02/4990 3307;** daily 10am to 5pm), is the Australian pioneer of Verdelho wines, made from a grape attributed to Portugal but also grown in small quantities in Italy and France. It's a very crisp and dry white wine, which I like with seafood. On the same road is **Peterson's Vineyard** (☎ **02/4990 1704;** Mon to Sat 9am to 5pm, Sun 10am to 5pm), which produces fine chardonnay, semillon, and shiraz.

DAY TOURS, HOT-AIR BALLOON RIDES & OTHER FUN STUFF

If you don't have a car, you'll have to get around as part of a tour, as there is no public transportation between the wineries.

Hunter Valley Day Tours, P.O. Box 59, Paterson 2421 (☎ **02/4938 5031;** www.huntertourism.com/daytours; e-mail: daytours@hunterlink.net.au), offers a wine and cheese tour with pickup from your Hunter accommodation. The tour runs from 10:15am to 3:45pm and goes to as many wineries as they can fit in. Tours costs A$80 (U.S.$52) for adults, A$30 (U.S.$19.50) for children, including lunch. A longer rain-forest and winery tour includes a walk and lunch in the Watagan Mountains, followed by an afternoon of wine tasting. The tour costs A$110 (U.S.$71.50) for adults, A$30 (U.S.$19.50) for children, including morning tea and lunch.

If you're a die-hard romantic, consider touring the wineries by horse and carriage. **Somerset Carriages** (☎ **02/4998 7591**) offers all-day excursions in either a two-person Victoria carriage or a six-person Landau carriage. Included on the trip are visits to four wineries and a gourmet picnic lunch with wine. Excursions cost A$130 (U.S.$84.50) per person for one to three people, and A$105 (U.S.$68.25) per person for four to six people.

Another tranquil way to see the wineries is from above. **Balloon Aloft,** in Cessnock (☎ **1800/028 568** in Australia, or 02/4938 1955), offers year-round dawn balloon flights that include a post-flight champagne and optional breakfast costing A$15 (U.S.$9.75). Flights last about an hour and cost A$205 (U.S.$133.25) for adults on weekdays and A$230 (U.S.$149.50) on weekends. Children ages 7 to 12 fly for A$130 (U.S.$84.50) daily.

If you like adventure, try **Grapemobile Bicycle and Walking Tours** (☎ **0500/804 039** in Australia, or 02/4991 2339). This company supplies you with a mountain bike, helmet, guide, and support bus, and takes you on a peaceful meander through the wineries. Tours cost A$98 (U.S.$63.70), including a restaurant lunch. The company also runs a walking tour for A$89 (U.S.$57.85), including wine tasting and lunch.

ACCOMMODATIONS

The Hunter Valley is far more expensive on weekends and during public holidays, when room prices jump significantly and some properties insist on a 2-night stay. It's worthwhile checking out the information board located inside the Wine Country Visitors Information Centre (see "Visitor Information," above) for special deals, but most of the rooms on offer tend to be in nondescript motels.

IN CESSNOCK

Staying in Cessnock is a good idea if you don't have a car and are relying on local tour companies to pick you up and show you around the area.

Cessnock Heritage Inn. Vincent St. (P.O. Box 714), Cessnock, NSW 2325. ☎ **02/4991 2744.** Fax 02/4991 2720. www.hunterweb.com.au/heritageinn.html. E-mail: heritageinn@ hunterweb.com.au. 13 units. TV TEL. Weekend A$50 (U.S.$32.50) per person with breakfast. Midweek A$55 (U.S.$35.75) double without breakfast; A$75 (U.S.$48.75) double with full breakfast. AE, BC, MC, V.

This 1920s building, built as a pub, is right in the center of Cessnock, so there's easy access to all the local pubs and restaurants. All the rooms are done in country style, with dried grasses, floral drapes, and the like. All are quite large with high ceilings but differ greatly. All have ceiling fans and free video movies.

In Ellalong

Ellalong Hotel. 80 Helena St., Ellalong, NSW 2325. ☎ and fax **02/4998 1217.** 10 units, none with private bathroom. Sat A$75 (U.S.$48.75); Fri A$65 (U.S.$42.45); Sun–Thurs A$55 (U.S.$35.75) per double. Rates include country breakfast. No credit cards. Inquire about dinner packages.

This 1924 pub, located only 11 kilometers (7 miles) from Cessnock, has a good Aussie country atmosphere. All rooms have a real out-in-the-country style with solid wood dressers and bouquets of dried flowers. Some have just a double bed, while others squeeze in an extra single. Rooms 1 and 2 are the best, as they have fantastic views across to the Brokenback Ranges from their verandas. Lunch and dinner are served in the restaurant, and counter meals are served up in the bistro.

In Pokolbin

✪ **Carriages Guest House.** Halls Rd., Pokolbin, NSW 2321. ☎ **02/4998 7591.** Fax 02/4998 7839. 10 units. A/C TV TEL. A$150 (U.S.$97.50) double, A$195–$210 (U.S.$126.75–$236.50) suite; A$245 (U.S.$159.25) spa suite. Rates include breakfast. Minimum 2-night stay on weekends. Ask about 10%–20% discounts midweek. AE, BC, MC, V.

Tucked away on 36 acres, a kilometer off the main road, Carriages is a secluded retreat in the heart of Pokolbin. The main house is a two-story double-gabled building. A new two-suite cottage called the Gatehouse is on a separate part of the grounds. In the main house, downstairs rooms open up onto a veranda and are furnished with antique country pine. Upstairs, the two lofty gable suites center on huge fireplaces. The Gatehouse suites offer five-star luxury; although they're new, the stained-glass windows and rescued timber give them a rustic feel. Breakfast is served in your room, and Robert's restaurant is just next door. The friendly owner, Ben Dawson, enthuses about how he'll take Frommer's readers up to the top of a nearby hill where they can see plenty of wild kangaroos.

✪ **The Convent Pepper Tree.** In the Pepper Tree Complex, Halls Rd., Pokolbin, NSW 2320. ☎ **02/4998 7764.** Fax 02/4998 7323. www.peppers.com.au. 17 units. A/C MINIBAR TV TEL. Weekends A$658–$732 (U.S.$427.70–$475.80) double for 2 nights. Midweek A$296–$327 (U.S.$192.40–$212.55) double. Rates include breakfast and predinner wine and canapés. Children under 5 stay free in parents' room; children 5–15 A$20 (U.S.$13) extra. AE, BC, DC, MC, V.

This remarkable place started out in life in 1909, when it was ordained as a convent for the Brigidine nuns. In 1990, the structure was dismantled and ferried some 600 kilometers (372 miles) from Coonamble in central New South Wales to its present position. A year later, it opened as a hotel. Rooms are elegant and spacious, with French baroque–inspired decor, including cherub prints and figurines, plaster frieze ceilings, and yards of drapery. French doors open onto private verandas overlooking patches of bushland. King rooms are larger and have wicker lounge areas. There are an elegant sitting area where drinks are served, and a light and airy breakfast room serving the best breakfasts in the Hunter. Also on the premises are a pool, spa, and tennis court. Free bikes are also available. The Pepper Tree Complex includes Pepper Tree Wines and the excellent Robert's Restaurant (see "Dining," below).

Hermitage Lodge. At Gillards and McDonalds Rd., Pokolbin, NSW 2320. ☎ **02/4998 7639.** Fax 02/4998 7818. www.ozemail.com.au/~hlodge/. E-mail: hlodge@ozemail.com.au. 10 units. A/C TV TEL. Weekend A$155 (U.S.$100.75) standard double; A$200–$230 (U.S.$130–$149.50) spa suites. Midweek A$95 (U.S.$61.75) standard double, A$130–$140 (U.S.$84.50–$91) spa suites. Rates include continental breakfast. Extra person A$10 (U.S.$6.50). Minimum 2-night stay on weekends. Ask about discounts for midweek multinight stays. AE, BC, MC, V.

If you want to be right in the heart of vineyard country, stay here. The property is surrounded by vineyards. Standard rooms are large and sunny and nicely decorated with queen-size beds and a double sofa bed, an iron and ironing board, a hair dryer, a fridge, and tea- and coffee-making facilities. The spa suites are larger with queen-size beds and double sofas, cathedral ceilings, spa baths, and separate showers. The more expensive suites have a separate bedroom, bathrobes, and daily newspaper. Breakfast is served in all rooms. Frommer's readers can rent bicycles free. An outdoor swimming pool was put in early in 1999, and there are free laundry facilities. There's a great Italian restaurant, called Il Cacciatore, on the premises, too.

✪ **Peppers Guest House.** Ekerts Rd., Pokolbin, NSW 2321. ☎ **02/4998 7596.** Fax 02/4998 7739. www.peppers.com.au. 47 units, 1 cottage. MINIBAR TV TEL. A$289 (U.S.$187.85) "classic" double; A$300 (U.S.$195) "vintage" double; A$347 (U.S.$225.55) heritage suite. Ask about midweek packages. AE, BC, DC, MC, V.

This tranquil escape is set in beautiful bush gardens. So peaceful is it that kangaroos hop up to the veranda in the evenings looking for treats. The "classic" rooms downstairs have French doors that you can fling open with abandon, while upstairs rooms express just a tad more old-fashioned charm and come with air-conditioning. All rooms have king-size beds (and hair dryers) and are furnished with colonial antiques. Guests don't come here for action; they come to relax. The Pampering Place offers massages, facials, and a gentle 30-minute trail that winds through the bush. Tennis courts, an indoor swimming pool, and bicycles and boules are also on offer. There's a pleasant guest lounge with an open fireplace and a bar. The inn's restaurant, **Chez Pok,** is an upscale establishment with mismatched china and a reputation for good country food.

Vineyard Hill Country Motel. Lovedale Rd., Pokolbin, NSW 2321. ☎ **02/4990 4166.** Fax 02/4991 4431. 8 units. A/C MINIBAR TV TEL. Weekend A$128 (U.S.$83.20) 1-bedroom unit; A$198 (U.S.$128.70) 2-bedroom unit. Midweek A$88 (U.S.$57.20) 1-bedroom unit, A$150 (U.S.$97.50) 2-bedroom unit. Extra person A$15 (U.S.$9.75). Ask about midweek and long weekend packages. AE, BC, MC, V.

"Motel" is a bit of a misnomer for this place; it's more aptly described as a "fully self-contained chalet." Units are modern, each with a separate bedroom, a lounge and dining area, a full kitchen, and a balcony with views across a valley of vineyards to the Brokenback Ranges in the distance. It's all terrifically rural, with cows wandering about and kangaroos and possums creeping around at dusk. There's no restaurant, but there is a gourmet deli on the premises. In the garden are a large swimming pool and a spa.

IN THE UPPER HUNTER

✪ **Barrington Guest House.** Salisbury (via Dungog), NSW 2420. ☎ **02/4995 3212.** Fax 02/4995 3248. 20 rain-forest cottages, 21 guest-house units (13 with private bathroom). A$149 (U.S.$96.85) per person in cottage; A$215 (U.S.$139.75) self-catering cottage (minimum 2-night stay; 2nd night A$193 (U.S.$125.45). A$76 (U.S.$49.40) per adult in a guesthouse room without bathroom, A$116 (U.S.$75.40) with bathroom. All rates include

Something Special: A Cattle Station in the Upper Hunter

Located just off the Golden Highway, 1 hour north of Mudgee, 2½ hours west of Cessnock, and 4 hours northwest of Sydney, **Runnymeade,** Highway 84, Runnymeade, Cassilis, NSW 2329 (☎ **02/6376 1183;** fax 02/6376 1187), a 2,000-acre sheep-and-cattle station, is a perfect place to experience Australia's agricultural life. The ranch offers farm-style lodgings in a 1930s California-style bungalow. Two rooms have their own showers, while the third shares the hosts' bathroom down the hall. The homestead offers an open fire in the living room (and a rarely used TV). There are plenty of native birds in the gardens, and kangaroos are common. May is the best time to see sheepshearing, and August is the best time to witness lambing and calving. The hosts, Libby and David Morrow, are very good company, and guests rave about them. David offers 1-hour tours of the property for around A$30 (U.S.$19.50) per "Toyota-load," and other tours throughout the district.

Doubles go for A$80 to $90 (U.S.$52 to $58.50). Rates include breakfast, but dinner is A$20 (U.S.$13) per person extra (BYO wine or beer). No credit cards.

activities; all rates except self-catering cottages include meals. Ask about packages. AE, BC, MC, V. The property is about 3½ hours from Sydney and 1½ hours from the main Hunter wine region. Free pickup from Dunoog railway station.

Barrington Guest House is nestled in a valley just outside Barrington Tops National Park—the closest World Heritage site to Sydney. It retains an old-world charm and serves bacon and eggs for breakfast, scones and cream, and vegetables boiled soft enough for your dentures. The place has lace tablecloths in the dining room, a log fire beneath a higgledy-piggledy brick chimney, dark mahogany walls, high ceilings, and personalized service—despite the communal mealtimes and the lack of a menu. Rooms range from the original guest-house chambers adjoining the dining room, to new and almost luxurious two-story self-contained cottages (sleeping up to five) that cling to a hillside.

This place is very popular with older travelers during the week but attracts a range of ages on the weekends. The grounds attract plenty of animals from the surrounding national park and act as a wildlife reserve for several rescued kangaroos. Activities include horseback riding, guided walks through the magnificent rain forest, "billy tea" tours, and night spotting for quolls (native cats) and possums, not to mention bush dancing, tennis, film evenings, and skeet shooting.

DINING
IN CESSNOCK

Amicos. 138 Wollombi Rd., Cessnock. ☎ **02/4991 1995.** Reservations recommended. Main courses A$8.90–$15.90 (U.S.$5.80–$10.40); pizzas A$12.50–$16.50 (U.S.$8.20–$10.70). 10% discount for take-out orders. BC, MC, V. MEXICAN/ITALIAN PIZZERIA.

You can't mistake the Mexican influence in the decor, with bunches of chili peppers, cow skulls, ponchos, masks, and frescoes, but the Mediterranean/Italian connection is more evident in the menu. Mexican dishes include the usual nachos, enchiladas, burritos, barbecued chicken, and the like, while there are a few pastas and Mediterranean dishes, such as crumbed lamb brains, too. The pizzas are pretty good; one could just about serve four people.

IN POKOLBIN

In addition to the restaurants below, Chez Pok, in Peppers Guest House (see "Accommodations," above), has a reputation as one of the better places in the area.

Blaxland's Restaurant. Broke Rd., Pokolbin. ☎ **02/4998 7550.** Reservations recommended. Main courses A$26.40–$27.80 (U.S.$17–$18). A$2 (U.S.$1.30) per person surcharge weekends and public holidays. AE, BC, DC, MC, V. Daily noon–3pm and 7–10pm. MODERN INTERNATIONAL.

This very atmospheric restaurant revolves around a winery theme, with pictures of vineyards on the walls, one of the most comprehensive Hunter wine lists in the area, and even the owner's homemade vintages on the menu. The building itself has been recycled from the ruins of an 1829 colonial mansion, with wooden trusses holding up the ceiling and exposed sandstone block walls. The signature dishes are the salmon and sea perch tempura appetizers, and the roast duck with fresh steamed vegetables main course. Hugely popular, too, are the three medallions of beef, veal, and lobster served with three sauces. A large open fire brings a glow to the white tablecloths in winter.

Café Enzo. At the corner of Broke and Ekerts Rd. (adjacent to Peppers Creek Antiques, near Peppers Guest House), Pokolbin. ☎ **02/4998 7233.** Main courses A$10–$18 (U.S.$6.50–$11.70). Devonshire tea A$7.50 (U.S.$4.90). AE, BC, DC, MC, V. Wed–Sun 10am–5pm (until 10pm Sat nights). MODERN AUSTRALIAN.

This charming little cafe offers a nice ambience and good cuisine. Pastas, pizzettas, antipasti, and steaks dominate the menu. The pizzetta with char-grilled baby octopus, squid, and king prawns, Kalamata olives, fresh chili and onion, and freshly shaved parmigiano is particularly nice. Cakes and cheese plates are a specialty.

Casuarina Restaurant. Hermitage Rd., Pokolbin. ☎ **02/4998 7888.** Reservations recommended. Main courses A$27–$34 (U.S.$17.55–$22.10). $3 (U.S.$1.95) per person surcharge weekends and public holidays. AE, BC, DC, MC, V. Open daily 7–11pm. MODERN AUSTRALIAN.

This superb restaurant has taken a slew of awards for its cooking in recent years. The surroundings are elegant, with lots of antiques below the very high wooden ceilings. The restaurant specializes in flambés, with its signature dish being the flambé of chili lobster and prawn (for two people). Other meals to write home about are the Thai-style chicken curry and the Caesar salad.

✪ **Robert's Restaurant.** In the Pepper Tree complex, Halls Rd., Pokolbin. ☎ **02/4998 7330.** Main courses A$29–$31 (U.S.$18.85–$20). A$3 (U.S.$1.95) per person surcharge weekends and public holidays. AE, BC, DC, JCB, MC, V. Daily noon–5pm and 7–11pm. MODERN AUSTRALIAN.

Chef and owner Robert Molines has become a legend in Hunter Valley gourmet circles for consistently coming up with great dishes that perfectly complement the region's wines. His restaurant is known for its eclectic mix of antiques and his country-style dishes, such as rabbit with olives and vegetables, rack of lamb from the wood-fired oven, and twice-roasted duckling. The meat-free specialty is the wild mushroom risotto.

The Rothbury Café. Upstairs at the Rothbury Estate, Broke Rd., Pokolbin. ☎ **02/4998 7363.** Main courses A$16–$18 (U.S.$10.40–$11.70). AE, BC, DC, MC, V. Daily noon–3pm. MODERN AUSTRALIAN.

This second-floor cafe has some of the best views across the valley; occasionally you can even spot kangaroos grazing in the farmers' fields across the way. The cafe has a Mediterranean feel about it, with timber tables loaded with bread and olives. Signature dishes are the chickpea-battered squid with yogurt and eggplant relish for a first course, and the venison and beetroot pie or the braised oxtail with orange, walnuts, olives, and polenta for main courses. Desserts include the fabulously rich chocolate-chestnut torte with berries.

3 Port Stephens: Dolphin- & Whale Watching

209km (130 miles) N of Sydney

Port Stephens Bay, just 2^1/$_2$ hours north of Sydney, should be at the top of any New South Wales itinerary. It's a perfect add-on to a trip to the Hunter Valley (see above). Though you can come up from Sydney for the day, I highly recommend staying in the general area for at least 1 night.

The sheltered Port Stephens Bay itself is more than twice the size of Sydney Harbour and is as clean as a newly poured bath. The sea literally jumps with fish, and the creamy islands and surrounding Tomaree National Park boast more species of birds than even Kakadu National Park in the Northern Territory. Two pods of bottle-nosed dolphins, around 70 individuals in all, call the bay home, and you're almost certain to see some on a dolphin-watching cruise. Port Stephens is also a fabulous place to watch whales during their migration to the breeding grounds farther north (roughly from June to mid-Nov, though less frequently in Aug). There is also a large breeding colony of koalas in Lemon Tree Passage on the south side of the Tomaree Peninsula, which makes up the southern shoreline of the bay.

The main town, **Nelson Bay** (pop. 7,000), is on the northern side of the peninsula. The township of Shoal Bay, farther along, has a nice beach edged with wildflowers. Another small resort town, **Anna Bay,** is the largest development on the southern side of the peninsula and has good surf beaches nearby. The Stockton Bight stretches some 35 kilometers (22 miles) from Anna Bay south to the large industrial town of Newcastle. The beach here is popular with ocean fishermen, who have the awful habit of driving their 4WDs along it. The Stockton Sand Dunes, which run behind the beach, are the longest in the Southern Hemisphere.

Opposite the Tomaree Peninsula, across the bay, are the small tourist townships of Tea Gardens and Hawks Nest, both at the mouth of the Myall River. See the Wonderbus tour of The Hunter (above) for details on a tour to Port Stephens.

ESSENTIALS

GETTING THERE   Take the Sydney–Newcastle Freeway (F3) to its end, then follow the Pacific Highway signs to Hexham and Port Stephens. **Port Stephens Coaches** (☎ **1800/045 949** in Sydney, or 02/4982 2940) travel between Port Stephens and Newcastle, and to Nelson Bay from Sydney daily at 2pm. **Buses** from Sydney leave from Eddy Avenue, near Central Station; the journey takes 3^1/$_2$ hours. A one-way ticket costs A$26 (U.S.$16.90) for adults and A$18 (U.S.$11.70) for children.

VISITOR INFORMATION   The **Port Stephens Visitor Information Centre,** Victoria Parade, Nelson Bay (☎ **1800/808 900** in Australia, or 02/4981 1579; www.portstephens.org.au; e-mail: tops@hunterlink.net.au), is open Monday to Friday from 9am to 5pm and Saturday and Sunday from 9am to 4pm.

A Horse Ride Through the Dunes

You can ride a horse through the dunes with **Sahara Horse Trails** (☎ **02/4981 9077**). A 2-hour trip costs A$40 (U.S.$26), and a half-day excursion is A$60 (U.S.$39). Bookings are required 1 day in advance.

SEEING THE AREA

Several operators have vessels offering **dolphin- and whale-watching cruises.** Some of the best are aboard *Imagine* (☎ **02/4984 9000;** www.imagineportstephens. hunterlink.au), a 50-foot catamaran operated by Frank Future and Yves Papin, two real characters. They offer a daily "Island Discovery" trip that includes dolphin watching and a trip around the offshore islands. The 4-hour cruise departs from **D'Albora Marina** in Nelson Bay daily at 11am and costs $39 (U.S.$25.35) for adults, and A$19 (U.S.$12.35) for children 4 to 14, including lunch.

Four-hour whale-watching tours cost the same and leave at 11am from June 1 to November 15. You're most likely to spot humpback whales, but there's also a chance to see Minke and southern right whales.

A morning dolphin-watching cruise runs from 9am to 10:30am daily during summer and costs A$15 (U.S.$9.75) for adults, A$7 (A$4.55) for children, and A$38 (U.S.$24.70) for families. If you happen to be around on the weekend nearest a full moon, ask about the company's overnight **"Full Moon Tours."**

Another operator, *Advance II* (☎ **02/4981 0399**), offers 2-hour dolphin cruises for A$18 (U.S.$11.70) and a 3-hour whale-watch cruise for A$43 (U.S.$27.95). The **Port Stephens Ferry Service** (☎ **02/4981 3798** or 0419/417 689 mobile phone) operates a 2¹/₂-hour "Early Bird Dolphin Watch" daily at 8:30am with a stop-off at Tea Gardens. A similar 3¹/₂ cruise departs at noon (you can eat lunch at Tea Gardens), and a 2-hour dolphin-watching cruise departs at 3:30pm. All cruises cost A$15 (U.S.$9.75) for adults, A$8 (U.S.$5.20) for children, and A$35 (U.S.$22.75) for families.

ACCOMMODATIONS

Port Stephens is very popular with Sydneysiders, especially during the Christmas holidays, the month of January, and Easter, so you'll need to book well in advance at those times.

✪ **Peppers Anchorage Port Stephens.** Corlette Point Rd., Corlette, NSW 2315. ☎ **1800/ 809 142** in Australia, or 02/4984 2555. Fax 02/4984 0300. 80 units. Weekend A$280 (U.S.$182) double; A$380 (U.S.$247) suite. Midweek A$225 (U.S.$146.25) double; A$319 (U.S.$207.35) suite. Ask about midweek packages. AE, BC, DC, MC, V.

This low-rise resort, split into a main guest house and four separate lodges, is built onto a headland and runs almost directly into the bay—it's stopped from sliding in only by a boardwalk and a picturesque marina. Rooms are light and luxurious; the suites each have a good-size whirlpool, perfect for two. Rooms on the top floor have a large balcony, from which you have uninterrupted views across the bay and the islands; those below have their own private verandas. Two rooms are designed for wheelchairs. A nearby beach is the perfect spot for a sunset stroll. There are a gym, communal spa, and swimming pool; childcare facilities; and a kids club on public holidays. Merrettes Restaurant offers exceptional local seafood and has a superb vegetarian menu.

Port Stephens Motor Lodge. 44 Mangus St., Nelson Bay, NSW 2315. ☎ **02/4981 3366.** Fax 02/4984 1655. A/C TV TEL. 17 units. A$60–$110 (U.S.$39–$71.50) standard double (depending on season); A$100 (U.S.$65) family unit on weekdays and A$120 (U.S.$78) on weekends. Extra person A$10 (U.S.$6.50), extra person under 15 A$5 (U.S.$3.25). AE, BC, DC, MC, V.

Surrounded by tall trees and gardens, this motor lodge is a peaceful place to stay and a short stroll from the main township. The standard rooms are quite plain, with raw-brick walls, comfy double beds (and an extra single bed in most rooms), private balconies, and attached showers with hip-tubs (small tubs you can sit in beneath the shower). Adjacent to the lodge is a self-contained family unit with two bedrooms, a laundry, and water views. There are a swimming pool and a barbecue area and a coin-op laundry on the grounds.

Salamanda Shores. 147 Soldiers Point Rd., Soldiers Point, NSW 2317. ☎ **1800/655 029** in Australia, or 02/4982 7210. Fax 02/4982 7890. E-mail: salamanda@fastlink.com.au. 90 units. A/C TV TEL. A$108.90 (U.S.$70.80) standard double; A$160.60 (U.S.$104.40) sea-view room with spa; $229 (U.S.$148.90) family suite; $264 (U.S.$171.60) penthouse. Ask about packages. AE, BC, DC, MC, V.

Salamander Shores looks like a beached, ramshackle paddle steamer. It's all white-painted bricks and rails and stairs, fixed to the bay by a jetty. Set in a well-tended, sloping garden, this five-story hotel retains a certain 1960s charm, despite under-going selective modernization. Many of the renovated rooms have spas and large balconies with extensive views of the bay. When the sun rises over the water and the garden is full of lorikeets and corellas, it couldn't be more picture-perfect.

The hotel has three bars and two restaurants, one serving simple, well-priced seafood and the other with a piano player and candles for those more intimate moments with your credit card. There are also an outdoor pool, a sauna, and a bottle shop and pub. My only complaint is that it seems a little understaffed for such a large place.

DINING

Most people head down to Nelson Bay for their meals because of the great views across the bay. You'll also find a host of cheap take-out joints here.

The Pure Pizza Cafe. D'Albora Marina. ☎ **02/4984 2800.** Main courses A$9–$16.50 (U.S.$5.90–$10.70). Daily 11am–11pm. AE, BC, DC, MC, V.

Perfect for takeout, this pizza and pasta place offers regular-size pizzas suitable for two for A$10 to A$12 (U.S.$6.50 to $7.80), and a lunchtime pizza for one for just A$6 (U.S.$3.90). Family-size pizzas cost A$20 (U.S.$13) on average. Also on offer are filling pastas, as well as ribs and chicken wings.

Rob's on the Boardwalk. D'Albora Marina. ☎ **02/4984 4444.** Main courses A$9.50–$22.50 (U.S.$6.20–$14.60). Daily 8am until the last customer leaves. AE, BC, DC, MC, V. CAFE.

You can pick up a hearty American breakfast at this busy cafe overlooking the bay, or a snack throughout the day. The Caesar salad is popular, as are the half-dozen oysters for A$12.50 (U.S.$8.20). One of the best mains is the mixed seafood bouil-labaisse, while the prime scotch fillet with sautéed forest mushrooms, Jerusalem artichokes, gratin potatoes, and a red wine sauce would temp the most red-blooded carnivore.

Rock Lobster. D'Albora Marina. ☎ **02/4981 1813.** Main courses A$15–$29 (U.S.$9.75–$18.85). Seafood platter for 2 A$95 (U.S.$61.75). Daily 11:30am–2:30pm and 5:30–9pm. AE, BC, DC, MC, V. SEAFOOD.

Eat inside or out at this peaceful yet stylish restaurant. The plump Port Stephens oysters should be enough to tempt you to start, while main courses such as smoked salmon in layers of wonton pastry with salad and wasabi sauce, or calamari flavored with chili and coriander in bread crumbs with spicy passion-fruit dip should fill you up. There are usually a couple of meat dishes and a vegetarian option on the menu, too.

4 North of Sydney Along the Pacific Highway: Australia's Holiday Coast

The Pacific Highway leads over the Sydney Harbour Bridge and merges into the Sydney-Newcastle Freeway. It travels on into Newcastle, an industrial seaside town, and skirts the recreational areas of Tuggerah Lake and Lake Macquarie (neither of great interest compared to what's beyond). From here on, the Pacific Highway stays close to the coast until it reaches Brisbane, some 1,000 kilometers (620 miles) from Sydney.

Though the road is gradually being upgraded, the conditions vary, and the distances are long. Travelers should be aware that the route is renowned for its accidents. Though you could make it to Brisbane in a couple of days, you could also easily spend more than a week stopping off at the attractions along the way. The farther north you travel the more obviously tropical the landscape gets. By the time visitors reach the coastal resort town of Coffs Harbour, temperatures have noticeably increased and banana palms and sugar-cane plantations start to appear.

Along the coast, you'll find excellent fishing and some superb beaches, most of them virtually deserted. Inland, the Great Dividing Range, which separates the wetter eastern plains from the dry interior, throws up rain forests, extinct volcanoes, and hobby farms growing tropical fruit as you head even farther north toward the Queensland border. Along the way, too, is a series of national parks, most of them requiring detours of several kilometers. Those you shouldn't miss out on include the Dorrigo and Mount Warning national parks, both of which offer some of the country's best and most accessible rain forests.

PORT MACQUARIE
423km (262 miles) N of Sydney

Port Macquarie (pop. 28,000) is roughly halfway between Sydney and the Queensland border. The main attractions here are some spectacular beaches, including Flynn's, which can offer exceptional surfing. Boating and fishing are other popular pastimes.

ESSENTIALS
GETTING THERE   From Sydney, motorists follow the Pacific Highway and then the Sydney-Newcastle freeway (F3). **Eastern Australia Airways** (☎ **02/9691 2333**) flies between Sydney and Port Macquarie. The coach trip from Sydney takes about 7 hours.

VISITOR INFORMATION   The **Port Macquarie Visitor Information Centre,** at the corner of Clarence and Hay streets, under the Civic Centre (☎ **1800/025 935** in Australia, or 02/6581 8000; www.portmacquarieinfo.com.au; e-mail: vicpm@ midcoast.com.au), is open Monday to Friday from 8:30am to 5pm and Saturday and Sunday from 9am to 4pm.

EXPLORING THE AREA
The Billabong Koala and Wildlife Park, 61 Billabong Dr., Port Macquarie (☎ **02/6585 1060**), is a family-owned nature park where you can get up close to hand-raised koalas, kangaroos, emus, wombats, many types of birds, and fish. You can pet the koalas at 10:30am, 1:30pm, and 3:30pm. There are also barbecue facilities, picnic grounds, and a restaurant. Allow 2 hours to fully experience this recommended wildlife park. It's open daily from 9am to 5pm; admission is A$8 (U.S.$5.20) for adults and A$5 (U.S.$3.25) for children.

The 257-passenger vessel *Port Venture* (☎ **02/6583 3058**) leaves from the wharf at the end of Clarence Street Tuesday, Thursday, Friday, Saturday, and Sunday at 10am and 2pm for a 2-hour scenic cruise on the Hastings River. Cruises cost A$17 (U.S.$11) for adults, A$7 (U.S.$4.55) for children 6 to 14, and A$42 (U.S.$27.30) for families. Reservations are essential. The boat also travels up the river on a 5-hour Barbecue Cruise every Wednesday morning leaving at 10am. It docks at a private bush park along the way, and passengers can tuck into a traditional Aussie barbecue of steaks, fish, and salad. You can then fish, take a bushwalk, go swimming, or take a 20-minute 4WD trip. The cruise costs A$32 (U.S.$20.80) for adults, A$15 (U.S.$9.75) for children, and A$80 (U.S.$52) for families. A 4-hour barbecue cruise also leaves on Monday at 10am. It costs A$30 (U.S.$19.50) for adults, A$13 (U.S.$8.45) for children, and A$75 (U.S.$48.75) for families.

ACCOMMODATIONS

El Paso Motor Inn. 29 Clarence St., Port Macquarie, NSW 2444. ☎ **1800/027 965** in Australia, or 02/6583 1944. Fax 02/6584 1021. 55 units. A/C MINIBAR TV TEL. A$87 (U.S.$56.55) standard double; A$97 (U.S.$63) deluxe double; A$130 (U.S.$84.50) spa rooms; A$150 (U.S.$97.50) suite. Extra person A$10 (U.S.$6.50). A$30 (U.S.$19.50) per room surcharge Easter, Christmas, and some long weekends. BC, DC, MC, V.

Located right on the waterfront, this place offers standard motel-type rooms; the more expensive deluxe doubles are a little larger and have newer furniture and a fresher coat of paint. Two rooms have whirlpools. Some, including the third-floor three-room suite (which has great ocean views) have kitchenettes. The motel also has a heated pool, a sauna, a hot tub, a recreation room, a licensed restaurant overlooking the sea, and a cocktail bar.

COFFS HARBOUR: BANANA CAPITAL OF OZ

150km (93 miles) N of Port Macquarie, 572km (355 miles) N of Sydney, 427km (265 miles) S of Brisbane

The relaxed capital of Australia's Holiday Coast is bounded by rain forests, beaches, and sand. The state's "banana republic" headquarters (the area produces more bananas than anywhere else in Australia) is bordered by hillsides furrowed with neat rows of banana palms. Farther inland, the rolling hills plateau into the mystical Dorrigo National Park, one of the best examples of accessible rain forests anywhere in the world. Also inland is the Nymboida River, known for its excellent white-water rafting.

Coffs Harbour itself is a rather disjointed place, with an old town center retail area; the Jetty Strip (with restaurants and fishing boats) near the best swimming spot, Park Beach; and a new retail area called The Plaza. Wide sweeps of suburbia separate these three areas, making it a difficult town to negotiate if you don't have a car.

ESSENTIALS

GETTING THERE It takes around 7 hours to drive from Sydney to Coffs Harbour without stops; from Brisbane it takes around 5 hours. The Pacific Highway in this region is notoriously dangerous; there have been many serious accidents in recent years involving drivers enduring long hours behind the wheel. Ongoing road-widening projects are supposed to improve things.

Ansett (☎ **13 13 00** in Australia), **Qantas** (☎ **13 13 13** in Australia), and **Eastern Australian Airlines** fly nonstop to Coffs Harbour from Sydney. Several coach companies, including **Greyhound-Pioneer** (☎ **13 20 30** in Australia) and **McCafferty's** (☎ **13 14 99** in Australia), make the trip from Sydney in about 9 hours. A **Countrylink** (☎ **13 22 32** in Australia) train from Sydney costs A$75 (U.S.$48.75).

VISITOR INFORMATION   The **Coffs Harbour Visitors Information Centre** (☎ **1800/025 650** in Australia or 02/6652 1522) is just off the Pacific Highway, at the corner of Rose Avenue and Marcia Street, 2 blocks north of the city center. It's open daily from 9am to 5pm.

GETTING AROUND   If you don't have a car, you can get around with **Coffs Harbour Coaches** (☎ **02/6652 2877**), which runs day trips around the local area on weekdays (including a town tour on Mon, and a trip to the magnificent Dorrigo National Park on Wed). ✪ **Blue Tongue Transport** (☎ **02/6651 8566**, or 1800 258 386 in Australia) offers smaller group tours of Dorrigo National Park daily costing A$50 (U.S.$32.50) for adults and A$40 (U.S.$26) for children; a morning city tour for A$11 (U.S.$7.15); and an upmarket afternoon champagne tour of town for A$22 (U.S.$14.30).

CHECKING OUT THE BIG BANANA & OTHER THINGS TO DO

You can't miss the 10-meter (33-ft.) reinforced concrete banana alongside the highway at the **Big Banana Theme Park** (☎ **02/6652 4355**), 3 kilometers (2 miles) north of town. The park includes an air-conditioned, diesel-powered train that takes visitors on a 1-hour tour of the 45-acre banana plantation that contains some 18,000 banana trees. Along the route it passes various off-the-wall exhibits relating to farming, Aborigines, and local history. It stops at the property's hydroponic glasshouses and at a viewing platform and cafeteria, which serves up banana cake, banana bread, banana splits, banana shakes, and so on. The park is open daily from 9am to 4:30pm (3pm in winter). Admission is free, but the train tour costs A$10 (U.S.$6.50) for adults, A$6 (U.S.$3.90) for children, and A$25 (U.S.$16.25) for families. I had my doubts about this place before I visited, but I must admit I ended up enthusing about it—even if it was just about the wackiness.

The **Coffs Harbour Zoo** (☎ **02/6656 1330**), 10 minutes north of town on the Pacific Highway, has plenty of breeding koalas (you can pet them), as well as wombats, kangaroos, dingoes, Tasmanian Devils (don't pet them!), water birds, and aviaries. The award-winning native gardens are full of wild birds expecting a feed. The zoo is open daily from 8:30am to 4pm. Admission is A$12 (U.S.$7.80) for adults, A$6 (U.S.$3.90) for children, and A$30 (U.S.$19.50) for families.

A free natural attraction is **Mutton Bird Island,** which you can get to via the Coffs Harbour jetty. A steep path leads up the side of the island, but the views from the top are worth it. Between September and April the island is home to thousands of shearwaters (or mutton birds), which make their nests in burrows in the ground.

If you prefer fish, try diving with gray nurse sharks, manta rays, and moray eels with **Island Snorkel and Dive** (☎ **02/6654 2860**) or **Dive Quest** (☎ **02/6654 1930**). The *Pamela Star* (☎ **02/6658 4379**) offers good-value deep-sea fishing trips including all tackle and bait, and lunch, for A$60 (U.S.$39). The boat leaves Coffs Harbour jetty at 7:30am and returns at 1:30pm daily.

For a taste of gold-rush fever, head to **George's Gold Mine,** 40 kilometers (25 miles) west of Coffs Harbour on Bushman's Range Road (☎ **02/6654 5355** or 02/6654 5273). You get to go into a typical old-timer gold mine, see the "stamper battery" crushing the ore, and pan for gold yourself. The mine is open Wednesday through Sunday (daily during school and public holidays) from 10:30am to 4pm. Admission is A$9 (U.S.$5.85) for adults, A$4.50 (U.S.$2.90) for children, and A$26 (U.S.$16.90) for families.

You might also like to visit **Kiwi Down Under Farm** (☎ **02/6653 4449**), a fascinating organic farm growing kiwi fruit and macadamia nuts, among other things. No nasty sprays are used here. Free 30- to 45-minute guided tours of the property leave at 2, 3, and 4pm on weekends and school holidays. The tea shop on the premises serves amazing scones and jam for A$4.50 (U.S.$2.90) and excellent vegetarian lunches for A$8.50 (U.S.$5.50). The farm is 14 kilometers south of Coffs Harbour; turn off at Gleniffer Road, just south of Bonville, and follow the signs for 4 kilometers (2.5 miles).

SHOPPING FOR ARTS & CRAFTS

There are several recognized "craft drives" in the area, where tourists can go in search of quality souvenirs. Pick up a free copy of *Discover the Coffs Harbour Region* from the tourist information center for more details on the dozens of craft shops in the area. One of the best is the **Australian Wild Flower Gallery** (☎ 02/6651 5763), just off West High Street and Bennetts Road. Wolfgang Shultze carves intricate designs out of pewter, silver, and gold to make detailed animal- and plant-inspired jewelry, charms, and spoons. Pieces cost between A$5 (U.S.$3.25) and A$36 (U.S.$23.40). The gallery is open daily from 9am to 5pm.

On the way to or from the Dorrigo rain forest, stop off at the township of **Bellingen,** 20 minutes south of Coffs Harbour on Waterfall Way. It's a pleasant place with several interesting craft shops. Among the best are **The Old Church** (☎ 02/6655 0438), 8 Church St. (just off the main road), crammed full of wooden craft items, cards, furniture, wacky mobiles, incense, hats, and knickknacks, and surrounded by gardens and fruit trees. It's open daily from 8:30am to 5:30pm.

EXPLORING THE RAIN FORESTS & OTHER OUTDOOR ADVENTURES

Coffs Harbour's main tourist attraction is its position as a good base for exploring the surrounding countryside. You must see the World Heritage–listed ✪ **Dorrigo National Park,** 68 kilometers (42 miles) west of Coffs Harbour, via Bellingen. Perched on the Great Dividing Range that separates the lush eastern seaboard from the arid interior, the rain forest here is the best I've seen in Australia (it's a desperate pity that so much of it fell to the axes of early settlers). Entry to the rain forest is free.

The **Dorrigo Rainforest Centre** (☎ 02/6657 2309) is the gateway to the park and has extensive information on the local rain forest. Just outside is the 21-meter (69-ft.) high **Skywalk,** which offers a bird's-eye view of the forest canopy. There are several rain-forest walks leaving the Rainforest Centre, the Glade Picnic Area (about 1km away), and the Never-Never Picnic Area (a 10km drive along Dome Road). Most tracks are suitable for wheelchairs. Bring a raincoat or an umbrella; it's not called a rain forest for nothing. The **Dorrigo Tourist Information** office (☎ 02/6657 2486) is in the center of Dorrigo township.

One of the best tour operators in the area is the award-winning **Mountain Trails 4WD Tours** (☎ 02/6658 3333). Full-day tours that include visits to two rain-forest areas and a good lunch cost A$80 (U.S.$52) for adults and A$60 (U.S.$39) for children under 16. Half-day tours of one rain forest cost A$56 (U.S.$36.40) for adults and A$40 (U.S.$26) for children.

For less-motorized action, try horseback riding through the rain forest with **Valery Trails,** 23 kilometers (14 miles) southwest of Coffs Harbour (☎ 02/6653 4301). Two-hour rides leave at 10am and 2pm daily and cost A$35 (U.S.$22.75) per person; advance booking is essential.

More exciting still are ✪ **white-water rafting** trips on the furious Nymboida River with ✪ **Wow Rafting,** 1448 Coramba Rd., Coramba via Coffs Harbour, NSW 2450 (☎ 1800/640 330 in Australia, or 02/6654 4066). Full-day trips, including morning tea, high-energy snack, and a barbecue meal, cost A$153 (U.S.$99.45). These adventurous trips operate year-around, depending on water levels. A 2-day trip costs A$325 (U.S.$211.25), including all meals and overnight camping. If the water level in the Nymboida is low, you raft on the Goolang Creek, which offers a shorter run but is still thrilling. Most of the rapids are grade 3; some of them can be pretty hairy. The rafting guides are real characters; although they're safety conscious, you're sure to be dunked a few times.

Rapid Rafting 2,000 (☎ **1800 629 797** in Australia, or 02 6652 1741) also runs rafting trips on the Goolang River, costing A$77 (U.S.$50) for a half-day trip, and A$120 (U.S.$78) for a full day.

Looking for yet another adrenaline rush? Then head to the **Raleigh International Raceway** (☎ **02/6655 4017**), where you can zip around the track behind the wheel of your very own . . . Go-Kart. It's located 23 kilometers (14 miles) south of Coffs Harbour and 3 kilometers (2 miles) along Valery Road off the Pacific Highway north of Nambucca Heads. Six high-speed laps cost A$16 (U.S.$10.40), 11 cost A$23 (U.S.$14.95), and 16 cost A$32 (U.S.$20.80). It's open daily from 9am to 5pm (6pm in summer).

The *Pacific Explorer* catamaran (☎ **0418/663 815** mobile phone, or 02/6652 7225 after working hours) operates **whale-watching trips** between June and October; the 2¹/₂ cruises cost A$44 (U.S.$28.60). Between November and May, they run half-day dolphin-watching cruises for the same price.

ACCOMMODATIONS

Coffs Harbour is a popular beachside holiday spot with plenty of motels along the Pacific Highway offering standard roadside rooms from between A$35 (U.S.$22.75) and A$49 (U.S.$31.85) per night. Vacancy signs are common except during Australian school holiday periods and the Christmas and Easter periods (when Coffs really fills up). A few to try are the **Caribbean Motel,** 353 High St. (☎ **02/6652 1500**), with doubles ranging from A$55 to A$120 (U.S.$35.75 to $78), depending on the season and the view; and the **Coffs Harbour Motor Inn,** 22 Elizabeth St. (☎ **02/6652 6388**), with doubles ranging from A$72 to $108 (U.S.$46.80 to $70.20).

✪ **Pelican Beach Centre Resort.** Pacific Hwy., Coffs Harbour, NSW 2450. ☎ **1800/02 8882** in Australia, 800/835-7742 in the U.S. and Canada, or 02/6653 7000. Fax 02/6653 7066. 112 units. A/C MINIBAR TV TEL. A$98–$170 (U.S.$63.70–$110.50) standard room for 1 or 2; A$205–$265 (U.S.$133.25–$172.25) family room for up to 4; A$265–$420 (U.S.$172.25–$273) suite. Extra person A$25 (U.S.$16.25). Ask about packages and discounts. The higher rates apply Dec 26–Jan 18. AE, BC, DC, MC, V.

This Bali-style resort complex is situated 7 kilometers (4.2 miles) north of Coffs Harbour beside a long stretch of creamy sand (the beach is dangerous for swimming, though). Terraced over six levels, the resort's rooms all have balconies and many have ocean views. Standard rooms are light and modern, with either twin or queen beds. Family rooms have a kitchenette and dining area and one queen and two single beds divided by a half wall. Suites have a separate bedroom, kitchenette, lounge area, and spa bath. Two rooms are equipped for travelers with disabilities.

Outside in the landscaped gardens are three tennis courts, a mini golf course, a volleyball court, and a lagoonlike heated pool. There are also indoor and outdoor spas, a sauna, a gym, and a barbecue area. A game room and a kids club that operates on weekends and school holidays keep the kiddies out of your hair. Award-winning Shores Restaurant offers indoor and terrace dining. Taxis operate from the resort to the town center for A$3 (U.S.$1.95) each way.

Sanctuary Resort. Pacific Hwy., Coffs Harbour, NSW 2450. ☎ **02/6652 2111.** Fax 02/6652 4725. 37 units. A/C TV TEL. A$88 (U.S.$57.20) standard double; A$93.50 (U.S.$60.80) superior double; A$150 (U.S.$97.50) executive double. Extra person A$13.50 (U.S.$8.80). Holiday surcharges. Ask about Aussie auto-club discounts. AE, BC, DC, MC, V.

If you like animals, you'll love this animal sanctuary/guest-house complex 2 kilometers (1¼ miles) south of town. Wandering around the grounds are wallabies, kangaroos, peacocks, and several species of native birds. The rooms are comfortable, with the more expensive rooms being larger and more recently renovated. The executive room comes with a spa.

In Nearby Nambucca Heads

If you're really looking to get away from it all, consider staying in the small town of Nambucca (pronounced "nam-*buck*-a") Heads, 44 kilometers (27 miles) south of Coffs Harbour. They practically roll up the streets after 6pm here. The **Nambucca Valley Visitor Information Centre** (☎ **02/6568 6954;** e-mail: nambuct@midcoast. com.au), on the Pacific Highway on the southern entrance to town, is open daily from 9am to 5pm.

Beilby's Beach House. 1 Ocean St., Nambucca Heads, NSW 2448. ☎ **02/6568 6466.** Fax 02/6568 5822. E-mail: beilbys@midcoast.com.au. 5 units, 3 with private bathroom. TV. A$40–$50 (U.S.$26–$32.50) double without bathroom; A$60–$75 (U.S.$39–$48.75) double with bathroom; A$80–$100 (U.S.$52–$65) family room. Rates include breakfast. BC, MC, V.

If you're looking for a peaceful place to stay, then come to Beilby's (named after the beach here). The standard rooms are basic but comfortable enough and have either a queen or a double bed. Three come with attached showers. The family room is basically two small rooms with an adjoining door. All rooms have verandas overlooking a bush garden. There are polished floorboards throughout, a large swimming pool in the garden, a guest kitchen, a large covered barbecue area, a guest laundry, Internet facilities, and computer games for the kids. It's a short walk through the bird-filled bush to the beach. While a few backpackers stay here, the guests range from young couples to families and senior citizens.

Scotts Guesthouse. 4 Wellington Dr., Nambucca Heads, NSW 2448. ☎ **02/6568 6386.** Fax 02/6569 4169. E-mail: 8 units. TV. A$70–$110 (U.S.$45.50–$71.50) double (depending on season). Extra person A$20 (U.S.$13). A$15 (U.S.$9.75) extra child. Rates include breakfast. AE, BC, DC, MC, V.

Scotts, a friendly B&B run by an Irish couple, offers good motel-style rooms in a modernized 1887 house not far from the beach. All rooms are spacious and very modern, and have good-sized balconies with nice views. Each comes with a queen-size bed, a shower, and a fridge. Family rooms have an extra double sofa bed and a single. Try to get room number 1 for the best views.

Dining

Seafood Mama's. Pacific Hwy. ☎ **02/6653 6733.** Reservations recommended. Main courses A$12.50–$25 (U.S.$8.10–$16.25). AE, BC, DC, MC, V. Tues–Sat 6–10pm. ITALIAN/SEAFOOD.

Seafood Mama's is right on the ocean, near the Pelican Beach and the older Nautilus resorts, 7 kilometers (4.2 miles) north of Coffs Harbour. This award-winning Italian restaurant offers a mean barbecue seafood dish of octopus, prawns, fish, calamari, and mussels. Also on the menu in this rustic, bottles-hanging-from-the-ceiling Italian joint are some well-regarded veal and steak dishes, and plenty of pastas. It's cheerful, friendly, and informal, and it does takeout and hotel deliveries.

BYRON BAY: A BEACH BOHEMIA
78km (48 miles) SE of Murwillumbah

The sun's rays hit Byron, the most easterly point on the Australian mainland, before anywhere else. This geographical position is good for two things: you can spot whales close to shore as they migrate north in June and July, and it's holistically attractive to the town's "alternative" community. Painters, craftspeople, glassblowers, and poets are so plentiful they almost fall from the macadamia nut trees. The place is loaded with float tanks, "pure body products," beauty therapists, and massage centers. Though Byron Bay attracts squadrons of roving backpackers each summer to its party scene and discos, many of the locals simply stay at home, sipping their herbal tea and preparing for the healing light of the coming dawn. Families love Byron Bay for the beautiful beaches, and surfers flock here for some of the best surfing in the world.

ESSENTIALS

GETTING THERE   If you're driving up the north coast, leave the Pacific Highway at Ballina and take the scenic coast road via Lennox Head. It's around 10 hours by car from Sydney, and 2 hours (200km, 124 miles) south of Brisbane. **Ansett** flies from Sydney to Ballina, 20 kilometers (12.4 miles) south of Byron Bay. The **Coolangatta airport** is just north of the Queensland border, 112 kilometers (69.5 miles) away. **Countrylink** (☎ **13 22 32** in Australia) runs daily trains from Sydney to Byron Bay; the one-way fare is A$92 (U.S.$59.80) one-way for adults and A$46 (U.S.$29.90) for children. **Greyhound Pioneer** (☎ **13 20 30** in Australia) buses from Sydney take around 13¹/₂ hours; the one-way coach fare is A$69 (U.S.$44.85).

ORGANIZED TOURS FROM SYDNEY   An unusual way to get to Byron is on a 5-day surf safari from Sydney with **Aussie Surf Adventures,** P.O. Box 614, Toukley, NSW 2263 (☎ **1800/113 044** in Australia or 0414/863 787 mobile). The trips leave 8:30am every Monday (between Sept and May) from Sydney's Circular Quay, stopping off for surfing, body boarding, fishing, and nature walks along the way. Beginners to experienced surfers are welcomed. Included are all meals, surfing lessons, surfing equipment, accommodation, and return bus to Sydney. Trips cost A$380 (U.S.$247).

A highly recommended 3-day tour is with the very likable Ivan from the **Pioneering Spirit** (☎ **1800/672 422** in Australia or 0412/048 333 mobile phone; www.users. omcs.com.au/pioneering). Suitable for adventurous travelers, the trip by minibus leaves Sydney every Friday and stops off along the way for swimming, native animal spotting, a tour of the Hunter Valley and Dorrigo National Park, and bushwalking. Accommodations are in basic but interesting buildings. The trip costs A$235 (U.S.$152.75) and includes transport and all meals (except lunch), accommodations, and entry fees.

VISITOR INFORMATION   The **Byron Visitors Centre**, 80 Jonson St., Byron Bay, NSW 2481 (☎ **02/6685 8050**), is open daily from 9am to 5pm. A half hour farther south is the **Ballina Tourist Information Centre,** on the corner of Las Balsas Plaza and River Street, Ballina (☎ **02/6686 3484**), open daily from 9am to 5pm. Two good Web sites on the area are **www.byronbay.net.au** and **www.byrontobush.com.au**.

SPECIAL EVENTS   Byron really goes to town during its Easter weekend **Blues Festival,** and on the first Sunday of every month when the extraordinary local **craft market** brings hippies and funky performers out from the hinterland.

HITTING THE SURF & SAND
Many accommodations in Byron Bay offer free surfboards for guests. If yours doesn't, head to the **Byron Bay Surf Shop,** on Lawson Street near Fletcher Street

(☎ **02/6685 7536**), which rents boards for A$12 (U.S.$7.80) for 4 hours and A$20 (U.S.$13) for 24 hours. The shop can also arrange surf lessons for around A$25 (U.S.$16.25) per hour.

Wategos Beach and an area off the tip of Cape Byron called **"The Pass"** are two particularly good surf spots, though since each of Byron's major beaches faces a different direction, you are bound to find the surf is up on at least one. **Main Beach,** which stretches along the front of the town (it's actually some 50km, 31 miles, long), is good for swimming. West of Main Beach is **Belongil Beach,** which acts as an unofficial nudist beach when the authorities aren't cracking down on covering up. **Clarke's Beach** curves away to the east of Main Beach toward Cape Byron.

The **Cape Byron Lighthouse** on Cape Byron is one of Australia's most powerful. It's eerie to come up here at night to watch the stars and see the light reach some 40 kilometers (25 miles) out to sea. A nice walk just south of town goes through the rain forest of the **Broken Heads Nature Reserve.**

The best place to dive around Byron Bay is at **Julian Rocks,** about 3 kilometers (2 miles) offshore. Cold currents from the south meet warmer ones from the north here, which makes it a good spot to find a large variety of marine sea life. **Byron Bay Dive Centre,** 111 Jonson St. (☎ **02/6685 7149**) charges A$70 (U.S.$45.50) for the first dive and A$35 (U.S.$22.75) for each subsequent dive. **Sundive,** in the Byron Hostel complex on Middleton Street (☎ **02/6685 7755**), has cheaper initial dives at A$60 (U.S.$39) each.

EXPLORING THE HILLS & RAIN FORESTS

Behind Byron you'll find hills that could make the Irish weep, as well as rain forests, waterfalls, and small holdings burgeoning with tropical fruits. A good operator taking trips inland is **Forgotten Country Ecotours** (☎ **02/6687 7843**). **Byron Bay to Bush Tours** (☎ **02/6685 6889,** or 0418/662 684 mobile; e-mail: bush@mullum. com.au) operates day trips to the hippie hangout of Nimbin and up into the rain forest, visiting a macadamia nut farm on the way and having a barbecue on their own organic farm. The trip leaves at 11am Monday to Saturday and costs A$30 (U.S.$19.50). This company also operates trips to the Sunday market at Channon on the second Sunday of each month and the one at Bangalow on the fourth Sunday. These trips cost A$15 (U.S.$9.75).

ACCOMMODATIONS

Real-estate agents **Elders R Gordon & Sons** (☎ **02/6685 6222;** e-mail: eldersbb@ omcs.com.au) can book rooms and cottages in Byron Bay and in the hinterland.

The Byron Bay Waves Motel (The Waves). Corner of Lawson and Middleton Sts. (P.O. Box 647), Byron Bay, NSW 2481. ☎ **02/6685 5966.** Fax 02/6685 5977. www.byronwaves.com. E-mail: info@byronwaves.com. A/C TV TEL. 19 units. A$125–$235 (U.S.$81.25–$152.75) double depending on season; A$225–$375 (U.S.$146.25–$243.75) suite; A$300–$490 (U.S.$195–$318.50) penthouse. Extra person A$20 (U.S.$13), extra child under 16 A$20 (U.S.$13). AE, BC, DC, MC, V.

This exceptional motel is just 60 meters (195 ft.) from Main Beach and just around the corner from the town center. The rooms are very nice; each comes with a queen-size bed, a marble bathroom with shower and a king-size tub, a safe, a refrigerator, an iron, a hair dryer, and tea- and coffee-making facilities. Four rooms on the ground floor have a courtyard, and one room is suitable for travelers with disabilities. Toasters, in-house massage, and beauty treatments are also available. The suites have a king-size bed and a large balcony. The penthouse is a very plush, fully self-contained one-bedroom apartment. There are six family rooms; each sleeps three adults, or two adults and two children.

Byron Central Apartments. Byron St., Byron Bay, NSW 2481. ☎ **02/6685 8800.** Fax 02/6685 8802. E-mail: byroncentral@one.net.au. 26 units. TV TEL. A$90–$180 (U.S.$58.50–$117) standard apt. (depending on season). Higher rates apply Christmas/New Year period; low season is Apr–Sept. Ask about discounts for multiple-night stays. AE, BC, DC, MC, V.

The apartments here have ceiling fans, full kitchens, queen-size beds and sofa beds, and free in-house movies. Those on the first floor come with balconies. There are also a few loft-style apartments with separate dining, lounge, and sleeping areas. Units for people with disabilities are available. The landscaped, mostly concrete surrounds house a saltwater pool and a barbecue. There's also a laundry. The apartments are a 2-minute walk from the main beach and town.

✪ **Holiday Village Backpackers.** 116 Jonson St., Byron Bay, NSW 2481. ☎ **02/6685 8888.** Fax 02/6685 8777. 42 units, 13 with bathroom. A$50–$55 (U.S.$32.50–$35.75) double in hostel; A$55 (U.S.$35.75) self-contained double. A$19–$21 (U.S.$12.35–$13.65) dorm bed. BC, DC, MC, V.

Byron Bay's original hostel is still one of the best. It's located in the center of town next door to Woolworth's supermarket and only a few minutes' walk from the bus and train stops, the main beach, and the town center. It's classified as a five-star backpackers, which is as good as it gets. Dorm rooms are clean, and doubles in the hostel are above average and come with a double bed, a fan, and a wardrobe. For a couple of dollars more, you can stay in a fully self-contained unit with a separate bedroom, lounge, and kitchen area. On the premises are a volleyball court, a pool and hot tub, a TV and video lounge (there's a video library), barbecues, a basketball hoop, Internet and e-mail access, and free surfboards, body boards, and bicycles.

✪ **Taylor's Guest House.** 160 McGettigan's Lane, Ewingsdale, Byron Bay, NSW 2481. ☎ **02/6684 7436.** Fax 02/6684 7526. 5 units, 1 cottage. TV. A$200 (U.S.$130) double; A$330 (U.S.$214.50) cottage. Rates include breakfast, cakes and biscuits, and predinner champagne cocktails. Surcharge of 20% (50% for the cottage) at Christmas and Easter. AE, BC, DC, MC, V. Not suitable for children.

This truly beautiful guest house is set in five secluded acres of gardens and rain forest. Rooms here vary in price depending on whether you stay for 1 night or more. The guest rooms are lavishly decorated in a country style and come with either queen- or king-size bed. The cottage is huge, has wraparound verandas and long French windows and is done up in bright Santa Fe–style colors. The cottage also comes with a laundry and has the largest bed in Australia—an 8-foot by 7-foot antique English "Emperor" bed. Outside in the garden is a very large swimming pool. A three-course dinner here costs A$50 (U.S.$32.50).

DINING

Beach Hotel Barbecue. In the Beach Hotel, at Bay and Johnson Sts. ☎ **02/6685 6402.** Main courses A$3.90–$13.50 (U.S.$2.50–$8.80). No credit cards. Daily noon–3pm. PUB/BARBECUE.

The outdoor meals served at this pub near the beach make it very popular with visitors and locals alike. About the cheapest thing on the menu is the burger; the most expensive, a steak. The Beach Hotel Bistro here is open from 10am to 9pm daily and serves coffee, cakes, and snacks throughout the day; a full lunch menu is served from noon to 3pm and dinner from 6 to 9pm.

Earth 'n' Sea. 11 Lawson St. ☎ **02/6685 6029.** Reservations recommended. Main courses A$11–$21 (U.S.$7.15–$13.65). AE, BC, MC, V. Daily 5:30–11pm. PIZZA/PASTA.

This popular spot has been around for years and offers a fairly extensive menu of pastas and pizzas, including some unusual combinations such as prawns, banana, and pineapple. Pizzas come in three sizes; the small is just enough to satisfy the average appetite.

The Pass Café. At the end of Brooke Dr., on Cape Byron Walking Track, Palm Valley. ☎ **02/6685 6074.** Main courses A$7–$12 (U.S.$4.55–$7.80). BC, MC, V. Daily 8–11:30am and noon–3pm. MEDITERRANEAN.

Though not as well located, the Pass Café rivals Rae's Restaurant and Bar (see below) for breakfasts and lunches. If you happen to be heading to or from the local rain forest on the Cape Byron Walking Track, you'll find this a great place to stop off. Breakfast items range from simple fresh fruit and muffins to gourmet chicken sausages. Lunch specials include Cajun chicken, octopus, and calamari salad, as well as fresh fish, meat dishes, and plenty of good vegetarian options.

Rae's Restaurant and Bar. Watago's Beach, Byron Bay. ☎ **02/6685 5366.** Reservations recommended. Dinner main courses A$18–$28 (U.S.$11.70–$18.20); lunch A$14–$26 (U.S.$9.10–$16.90). AE, BC, DC, MC, V. Daily 7–10pm; Sat–Sun noon–3pm. MODERN AUSTRALIAN/SEAFOOD.

You can't beat Rae's for location or food. It's right on the beach, about a 2-minute drive from the town center, and has a secluded, privileged air about it in the nicest of ways. Inside it's all Mediterranean blue and white, which perfectly complements the incoming rollers hitting the sand. The menu changes daily, but you may find the likes of grilled Atlantic salmon, red curry of roast beef fillet, braised lamb shanks, and yellow fin tuna. If you have any special dietary requirements, tell the chef, and he'll go out of his way to please you.

Next door to the restaurant and part of the same establishment is **Rae's on Watago's,** an exclusive guest house offering luxury accommodations.

✪ **Raving Prawn.** Feros Arcade (between Jonson and Lawson sts.). ☎ **02/6685 6737.** Reservations recommended. Main courses A$15–$24 (U.S.$9.75–$15.60). AE, BC, DC, MC, V. Tues–Sat 6–10pm (until around 9pm in winter). Open daily during school holidays. SEAFOOD.

Fish cover the walls at this excellent place, but there's more than that on the menu. You can tuck into veal, chicken, or vegetarian dishes if you want to, but I wouldn't miss out on the fabulous signature dish, the jewfish (a kind of grouper) with an herb-mustard crust. The forest-berry tart is the best dessert on the menu.

MURWILLUMBAH

321km (200 miles) N of Coffs Harbour, 893km (554 miles) N of Sydney, 30km (19 miles) S of Queensland border

The main town of the Tweed Valley, Murwillumbah is a good base for touring the surrounding area, which includes **Mount Warning,** picturesque country towns, and countryside dominated by sugarcane and banana.

ESSENTIALS

GETTING THERE Murwillumbah is inland from the Pacific Highway. The nearest airport is at **Coolangatta,** 34 kilometers (21 miles) away just over the Queensland border. **Countrylink** trains (☎ **13 22 42** in Australia) link Murwillumbah with Sydney, taking 12 hours and 40 minutes. **Greyhound Pioneer** (☎ **13 20 30** in Australia) buses run from Sydney to Murwillumbah; the trip takes 14¹/₂ hours.

VISITOR INFORMATION The **Murwillumbah Visitors Centre,** at the corner of the Pacific Highway and Alma Street, Murwillumbah, NSW 2484 (☎ **02/6672 1340**), is worth visiting before heading out to see more of the Tweed Valley or the beaches to the east. Another option is the **Tweed Heads Visitors Centre,** at the corner of Bay and Wharf streets, Tweed Heads, NSW 2485 (☎ **07/5536 4244**). Both are open Monday to Friday from 9am to 5pm, and Saturday from 9am to 1pm.

SEEING THE AREA

If you're looking for a Big Avocado to go with your Coffs Harbour Big Banana, then head for **Tropical Fruit World,** on the Pacific Highway (☎ **02/6677 7222**), 15 kilometers (9 miles) north of Murwillumbah and 15 kilometers south of Coolangatta. The Tweed Valley's top attraction grows some 400 varieties of tropical fruit, which can be discovered on an interesting 1¹/₂-hour tractor-train tour of the 200-acre tropical fruit plantation, as well as on 4WD rain-forest drives and riverboat rides. It's open daily 10am to 5pm. Also on the property are a kiosk, fruit market, and gift shop. Admission to food and shopping areas is free. Guided tours cost A$22 (U.S.$14.50) for adults, A$12 (U.S.$7.80) for children 4 to 12.

The 1,154-meter (3,815-ft.) **Mount Warning** is part of the rim of an extinct volcano that formed from volcanic action some 20 to 23 million years ago. You can hike around the mountain and to the top of it on trails in the Mount Warning World Heritage Park.

ACCOMMODATIONS & DINING

✪ **Crystal Creek Rainforest Retreat.** Brookers Rd., Upper Crystal Creek, Murwillumbah, NSW 2484. ☎ **02/6679 1591.** Fax 02/6679 1596. 7 cabins. TV. A$210–$225 (U.S.$136.50–$146.25). Ask about lower midweek rates and weekly specials. BC, MC, V. Not suitable for children. Pickup service from the airport and bus and train stations is available.

Crystal Creek is tucked away in a little valley of grazing cows just 25 minutes by car from the Pacific Highway. Self-contained cabins nestle on the edge of a rain forest bordering the Border Ranges National Park, a World Heritage Site. There are plenty of native birds, possums, echidnas, wallabies, and bandicoots around and about. Though the water is always cold, guests can swim in the natural pools and laze around on hammocks strung up in the bush. Cabins have two comfortable rooms, a balcony, a kitchen, a barbecue, and plenty of privacy. Appropriately for an eco-lodge, everything inside is green, even the sheets. Two new glass-terrace cabins overlook the rain forest and mountain and have a king-size bed and a double spa.

Several tours are offered, including 4WD rain-forest tours and visits to local country markets and arts-and-crafts galleries. Bird watching and canoeing are popular on the nearby lake. Guests cook their own food or eat at the casual restaurant. Crystal Creek won a 1998 NSW Tourism Award for Excellence, in the category of Unique Attraction. No smoking.

THE TWEED VALLEY AFTER DARK

The clubs up here on the border of Queensland are huge. They tend to offer cheap bistro meals, plus pricier ones in the more upscale restaurants, inexpensive drinks at the bar, entertainment, and hundreds of poker machines. The biggest in New South Wales is the **Twin Towns Services Club,** Wharf Street, Tweed Heads (☎ **07/5536 2277**). Another worth checking out is **Seagulls Rugby League Club,** Gollan Drive, Tweed Heads (☎ **07/5536 3433**). Major entertainers such as Tom Jones and Joe Cocker have played here over the past few years. It's open 24 hours.

To gain admittance to these "private" clubs, you must sign the registration book just inside the door.

✪ LORD HOWE ISLAND: AN IDEAL GETAWAY

702km (435 miles) NE of Sydney; due E of Port Macquarie

Why fly another 2 hours when the last thing you probably want to do after the long journey here is see another plane? Well, paradise is worth the effort. Australia's best known World Heritage–listed island is a tiny, extremely panoramic, palm-treed

Something Special

For a remarkable experience on Lord Howe Island, visit Ned's Beach at around 5pm every afternoon to see the locals feed schools of giant fish, including kingfish well over 2 meters (6 ft.) long. Snorkeling as the fish thrash around gulping down bread and restaurant scraps is truly memorable.

volcanic remnant just 11 kilometers (less than 7 miles) long and no more than 2 kilometers (about 1.5 miles) wide. Animals and plants have had the past 7 million years, with no bridge to the mainland, to evolve into unique life forms such as the indigenous flightless Woodhen. Lord Howe is also home to large colonies of seabirds, as well as the most southern coral reef in the world. Few cars, incredible fishing, fabulous walks, and nice beaches also help make this place a delightful, and relatively undiscovered, getaway.

ESSENTIALS

GETTING THERE **Eastern Australia Airlines** (☎ **02/9691 2333**) flies to Lord Howe from Sydney most days. The trip takes 2 hours. **Sunstate Airlines** (book through Qantas ☎ **13 13 13** in Australia) flies from Brisbane. For good-value package deals, contact the **Pacific & International Travel Company (PITC),** 91 York St., Sydney, NSW 2000 (☎ **13 27 47** in Australia, or 02/9244 1811).

VISITOR INFORMATION **Tourism New South Wales** (☎ **02/9931 1111**) can direct you toward relevant information about Lord Howe, or you can look up the island on the Internet (www.lordhowe.com.au).

ENJOYING THE ISLAND

Popular activities are swimming, surfing, snorkeling, scuba diving, tennis, golf, fishing, hiking, and bird watching. The most common form of transport on the island is bicycle.

The daylong hike through the palm forests to the top of the mist-shrouded **Mount Gower** is considered one of Australia's toughest and best; a guide is essential. **Ron's Ramble** (book the day before at Thompson's Store on Ned's Beach Road) is much easier and offers a fascinating insight into the island's history, geology, plants, and animals. A 3-hour ramble costs A$15 (U.S.$9.75).

Daylong **boat cruises,** including snorkeling on the reef and visiting seabird colonies, cost A$20 (U.S.$13). **Scuba diving** on the reef with **Pro Dive** costs from A$60 (U.S.$39). Fishing gear and glass-bottomed boat tours can also be arranged through Thompson's Store.

ACCOMMODATIONS & DINING

Beachcomber Lodge. Lord Howe Island, NSW 2898. ☎ **13 27 47** (for Pacific & International Travel Company, which handles reservations to island). 8 units. TV TEL. From A$77 (U.S.$50) per person with full breakfast. 50% discount for children up to 12; children under 3 free. AE, BC, DC, MC, V.

Cheaper than Pinetrees and right near Ned's Beach and the roosting colonies of mutton birds, this property has reasonable rooms, each with fridge, bathroom, fan, and tea/coffeemaker. Superior rooms are well appointed with separate living rooms and large bathrooms. Meals are hearty and traditional, but served only on Saturday, Sunday, and Wednesday.

✪ **Pinetrees Lodge.** Lagoon Rd., Lord Howe, NSW 2898. ☎ **02/6563 2177.** Fax 02/6563 2156. www.pinetrees.com.au. E-mail: info@pinetrees.com.au. Sydney booking office:

72 Erskine St. (☎ **02/9262 6585**). 27 units, 7 cottages. From A$195 (U.S.$126.75) per person double; from A$395 (U.S.$256.75) per person garden cottage. Higher rates in summer (Dec–Jan). 4-night packages available. Children under 10 half price. Rates include all meals. AE, MC, V (for bookings in Sydney office only).

Pinetrees is an upscale old-fashioned guest house opened in 1900. The beautifully renovated accommodations consist of motel-style units and cottages—all set in stunning gardens opposite the lagoon. There are also a tennis court, a small library, and a pool table. Evening meals are among the best on the island.

Somerset Holiday Accommodation. Neds Beach Rd., Lord Howe Island, NSW 2898. ☎ **02/6563 2061.** Fax 02/6563 2110. 25 units. TV TEL. From A$150 (U.S.$97.50) double. AE.

The centrally located Somerset is surrounded by nice gardens and has clean and simple two-room apartments with solar-heated shower, microwave, and fridge. Outdoor barbecues are available on which to cook your catch, but there is no restaurant.

5 South of Sydney Along the Princes Highway

There are two main roads leading south out of Sydney: the Hume Highway and the Princes Highway. Both routes connect Sydney to Melbourne, but the Hume Highway is quicker. That means that trucks and anyone in a hurry won't be on the scenic, coastal Princes Highway. It takes almost twice as long to get to Melbourne via this road, but you take it for the many attractions along the route, not for speed.

KIAMA

119km (74 miles) S of Sydney

Kiama (pop. 10,300) is famous throughout the nation for its **blowhole.** In fact, there are two, a large one and a smaller one, but both spurt sea water several meters into the air. The larger one can jet water up to 60 meters (195 ft.), but you need a large swell and strong southeasterly winds to force the sea through the rock fissure with enough force to achieve that height. The smaller of the two is more consistent but fares better with a good northeasterly wind.

Pick up a map from the Kiama Visitors Centre (see below) to guide you around a Heritage Walk, which takes in the historic precinct of this pretty harborside village, including a row of National Trust workers cottages built in 1896, open from 10am to 5pm daily.

ESSENTIALS

GETTING THERE   From Sydney, travel south on the Princes Highway via the steel-works city of Wollongong. There's also a regular **train** service from Sydney and Greyhound-Pioneer (☎ **13 20 30** in Australia) **coach** service. The trip takes about 2 hours.

VISITOR INFORMATION   The **Kiama Visitors Centre** at Blowhole Point, Kiama (☎ **02/4232 3322;** www.kiama.net/tourism.htm; e-mail: kiamatourism@ozemail.com.au), is open daily from 9am to 5pm.

ACCOMMODATIONS & DINING

Kiama Terrace Motor Lodge. 45–51 Collins St., Kiama, NSW 2533. ☎ **02/4233 1100.** Fax 02/4233 1235. 50 units (3 with shower only). A/C TV TEL. A$95–$135 (U.S.$61.75–$87.75) double. Extra person A$10 (U.S.$6.50). Reservations can be made through Best Western (☎ 800/780-7234 in the U.S. and Canada, 0800/39 3130 in the U.K., 0800/237 893 in New Zealand, or 13 17 79 in Australia). Ask about weekend packages and lower rates through Aussie auto clubs. AE, BC, DC, MC, V.

Kiama's only four-star motel has pleasant rooms; 22 of the more expensive ones have a whirlpool bath. Two rooms offer facilities for travelers with disabilities. Meals can be brought to your room or eaten in a roadside restaurant serving up good seafood. Facilities include a self-service laundry, a barbecue, and a saltwater pool.

✪ JERVIS BAY: AN OFF-THE-BEATEN-TRACK GEM
182km (113 miles) S of Sydney

Booderee National Park at Jervis Bay is nothing short of spectacular. You should make a trip here even if it means cutting time out of your Sydney itinerary. How does this grab you: miles of deserted beaches, the whitest sand in the world, kangaroos you can pet, lorikeets who mob you for food during the daytime and possums who do the same at night, pods of dolphins, some great walks through gorgeous bushland, and a real Aboriginal spirituality-of-place? I could go on, but it's best you see it for yourself.

ESSENTIALS
GETTING THERE   It's best to reach Jervis Bay via Huskisson, 24 kilometers (15 miles) southeast of Nowra on the Princes Highway. Approximately 16 kilometers (10 miles) south of Nowra, turn left onto the Jervis Bay Road to Huskisson. The entrance to Booderee National Park is just after Huskisson. It's about a 3-hour drive from Sydney.

   Australian Pacific Tours (☎ 02/9247 7222; www.aptours.com.au) runs a dolphin-watching cruise to Jervis Bay from Sydney every day between early October and mid-April, and Monday and Thursday in winter. The 12-hour trip—7 hours of which are on the bus—includes a visit to the Kiama blowhole, a 3-hour luncheon cruise looking for bottlenose dolphins, and a stop off on the way back at Fitzroy Falls in the Southern Highlands. The trip costs A$116.50 (U.S.$75.70) for adults and A$108.50 (U.S.$70.50) for children.

VISITOR INFORMATION   For information on the area, contact the **Shoalhaven Visitors Centre,** corner of Princes Highway and Pleasant Way, Nowra (☎ **1800/024 261** in Australia, or 02/4421 0778; www.shoalhaven.nsw.gov.au). Pick up maps and book camping sites at the **Booderee National Park** office (☎ **02/4443 0977**), located just beyond Huskisson; it's open daily from 9am to 4pm. **Hyams Beach Store** (☎ **02/4443 0242**) has an accommodation guide listing 34 rental properties from A$100 (U.S.$65) a weekend.

SEEING THE AREA
If you want to see the best spots, you'll need to pay the park entrance fee of A$7.50 (U.S.$4.90). The entrance sticker lasts 7 days. Some of the places you could visit include ✪ **Hyams Beach,** reputed to have the whitest sand in the world. Notice how it squeaks when you walk on it. Wear sunscreen! The reflection off the beach can burn your skin in minutes on a sunny day. **Hole in the Wall Beach** has interesting rock formations and a lingering smell of natural sulfur. **Summer Cloud Bay** is secluded and offers excellent fishing.

   Dolphin Watch Cruises, 74 Owen St., Huskisson (☎ **1800/246 010** in Australia, or 02/4441 6311), runs a hardy vessel out of Huskisson on the lookout for the resident pod of bottlenose dolphins—the company claims you have "more than a 95% chance of seeing them." Lunch cruises run daily at 1pm, and a coffee cruise runs at 10am on Saturdays, Sundays, and holidays. The 2^1/$_2$-hour lunch cruise costs A$35 (U.S.$22.75) for adults and A$19.50 (U.S.$12.70) for children. The 2-hour coffee cruise costs A$20 (U.S.$13) for adults and A$10 (U.S.$6.50) for children. It's possible to see humpback and southern right whales in June, July, September, and October.

ACCOMMODATIONS & DINING

If you have a tent and camping gear, all the better. **Caves Beach** is a quiet spot (except when the birds chorus at dawn) located just a stroll away from a good beach; it's home to resident Eastern Grey kangaroos. A campsite here costs A$8 (U.S.$5.20) per tent in winter and A$10 (U.S.$6.50) in summer and on public holidays. It's about a 250-meter (¼-mile) walk from the car park to the campground. **Greenpatch** is more brown than green, but you get your own area and it's suitable for campervans. It's infested with over-friendly possums around dusk. A campsite here costs A$13 (U.S.$8.45) in winter and A$16 (U.S.$10.40) in summer.

For supplies, head to the area's main towns, **Huskisson** (pop. 930) and **Vincentia** (pop. 2,350). The **Huskisson RSL Club,** overlooking the wharf area on Owen Street (☎ **02/4441 5282**), has a good cheap bistro and a bar. You'll have to sign in just inside the main entrance door.

Huskisson Beach Tourist Resort. Beach St., Huskisson, Jervis Bay, NSW 2540. ☎ and fax **02/4441 5142.** 38 units. TV. Fri–Sat A$65–$80 (U.S.$42.25–$52) cabin; Sun–Thurs A$50–$75 (U.S.$32.50–$48.75) cabin. BC, DC, MC, V.

This resort is the very pinnacle of cabin accommodation on this part of the east coast. Cabins vary in price depending on size, but even the smallest has room enough for a double bed, triple bunks, and a small kitchen with microwave. Larger cabins have two separate bedrooms. There are a swimming pool, a game room, a full-size tennis court, and barbecue facilities on the grounds.

✪ **Jervis Bay Guest House.** 1 Beach St., Huskisson, NSW 2540. ☎ **02/4441 7658.** Fax 02/4441 7659. www.oztourism.com.au/~gdaymate/jervis. 4 units. A$140–$220 (U.S.$91–$143) double depending on season. Rates include breakfast. BC, DC, MC, V. After the Jervis Bay Hotel, take the 2nd road to the left and follow it to the end. Children under 16 not allowed.

This new guest house has four distinctly different rooms, all with private bathroom. One room has a Jacuzzi and two rooms face the water. All rooms have plush robes and hair dryers. Breakfast is a hearty affair and could include emu sausages or thick slabs of bacon, followed by a tropical fruit platter.

Jervis Bay Hotel. Owen St., Huskisson, NSW 2540. ☎ **02/4441 5001.** 7 units, none with private bathroom. A$55 (U.S.$35.75) double, A$80 to A$100 (U.S.$52–$65) family room. AE, BC, DC, MC, V.

Rooms at the "Huskie Pub," as it's known, are clean and simple, with not much more than a double bed and coffee- and tea-making facilities. One family room has two small rooms, with a double in one and a set of bunks in the other. Shared bathrooms are down the hall. There are also a little common room and ironing facilities. The pub below is popular with locals and the odd tourist who comes to eat pretty reasonable bistro food, play pool, and listen to bands on the weekends. The bar closes around 10pm during the week and no later than 11:45pm on Friday and Saturday nights. The Thai restaurant across the road is pretty good.

A Safety Warning

Jervis Bay is notorious for its car break-ins, a situation that the local police force has been unable to bring under control. If you park your car anywhere in the national park, remove all valuable items, including things in the trunk.

BATEMANS BAY

275km (171 miles) S of Sydney

This laid-back holiday town offers good surfing beaches, arts-and-crafts galleries, boat trips up the Clyde River, good game fishing, and bushwalks in Morton and Deua national parks.

ESSENTIALS

GETTING THERE   Batemans Bay is about a 5¹/₂- to 6-hour drive from Sydney. **Premier Motor Service** (☎ **1300/368 100** in Australia, or 02/4423 5233) runs coaches to Batemans Bay from Sydney's Central Station.

VISITOR INFORMATION   Batemans Bay Visitor Information Centre, at the corner of Princes Highway and Beach Road (☎ **1800/802 528** in Australia, or 02/4472 6800), is open daily from 9am to 5pm.

GAME FISHING & A RIVER CRUISE

If you fancy some serious fishing, contact **OB1 Charters,** Marina, Beach Road, Batemans Bay (☎ **1800/641 065** in Australia, or ☎/fax 02/4472 3944). The company runs full-day game fishing trips and morning snapper fishing trips (afternoon snapper trips in summer, too). Expect to encounter black marlin, blue marlin, giant king fish, mako sharks, albacore tuna, yellow-fin tuna, and blue tuna in winter. The trip includes all tackle and bait, and afternoon and morning teas, but you must provide your own lunch. It costs A$150 (U.S.$97.50) per person. Snapper trips include all gear and bait, and morning or afternoon tea for A$75 (U.S.$48.75).

A river cruise on the **MV Merinda,** Innes Boatshed, Orient Street, Batemans Bay (☎ **02/4472 4052**), is a pleasant experience. The 3-hour cruise leaves at 11:30am daily and travels inland past townships, forests, and farmland. It costs A$20 (U.S.$13) for adults, A$10 (U.S.$6.50) for children, and A$50 (U.S.$32.50) for families; a fish-and-chips lunch is A$6 (U.S.$3.90) extra, and a seafood basket for two is A$12 (U.S.$7.80).

A NICE PLACE TO STAY

The Esplanade. 23 Beach Rd. (P.O. Box 202), Batemans Bay, NSW 2536. ☎ **1800/659 884** in Australia, or 02/4472 0200. Fax 02/4472 0277. 23 units. A/C TV TEL. A$95 (U.S.$61.75) double; A$140–$300 (U.S.$91–$195) suite. Extra person A$15 (U.S.$9.75). Children under 18 stay free in parents' room. AE, BC, DC, MC, V.

This four-star hotel is right on the Batemans Bay river estuary and close to the town center. Rooms are light and well furnished, and all have kitchenettes and balconies (some with good water views). Some doubles and suites have whirlpools; they cost the same as non-spa rooms, so specify if you want one when booking. Eat at the hotel's à la carte restaurant or at the Batemans Bay Soldiers' Club just opposite, which has a restaurant, a bistro, cheap drinks, and a free evening kids club.

NAROOMA

345km (214 miles) from Sydney

Narooma is a pleasant seaside town with beautiful deserted beaches, an interesting golf course right on a headland, a natural rock formation in the shape of Australia (popular with camera-wielding tourists), and excellent fishing. However, its major attraction is ✪ **Montague Island,** the breeding colony for thousands of shearwaters (or mutton birds, as they're also called) and a hangout for juvenile seals.

Just 18 kilometers (11 miles) farther south is ✪ **Central Tilba,** one of the prettiest towns in Australia and the headquarters of the boutique **ABC Cheese Factory.** You'll kick yourself if you miss this charming historical township (pop. 35, but attracting 1 million visitors annually).

ESSENTIALS

GETTING THERE   Narooma is a 7-hour drive from Sydney down the Princes Highway. **Premier Motor Service** (☎ **1300/368 100** in Australia, or 02/4423 5233) runs coaches to Narooma from Sydney's Central Station.

VISITOR INFORMATION   The **Narooma Visitors Centre,** Princes Highway, Narooma (☎ **02/4476 2881;** www.naturecoast-tourism.com.au), is open daily from 9am to 5pm.

WHAT TO SEE & DO: WHALES, GOLF & MORE

A must if you're visiting the area is a boat tour with ❂ **Narooma Charters** (☎ 02/ 4476 2240). It offers spectacular tours of the coast on the lookout for dolphins, seal colonies, and little penguins, and also includes a tour of Montague Island. Morning and afternoon tours take 3¹/₂ hours and cost A$66 (U.S.$42.90) for adults, A$49.50 (U.S.$32.20) for children and A$198 (U.S.$128.70) for families. A 4¹/₂-hour tour includes some of the world's best whale watching (between mid-Sept and early Dec) and costs A$88 (U.S.$57.20) for adults, A$71.50 (U.S.$46.50) for children, and A$297 (U.S.$193) for a family of four. The last time I went on this trip, we saw no fewer than eight humpback whales, some of them mothers with calves. The company also offers game fishing from February to the end of June and scuba diving in the seal colonies from August to the end of December. Dives cost A$66 (U.S.$42.90) for a double dive, plus approximately A$33 (U.S.$21.45) for gear rental.

   The Narooma Golf Club, Narooma (☎ **02/4476 2522**), has one of the most interesting and challenging coastal courses in Australia. A round of golf will cost you A$25 (U.S.$16.25).

   While you're in the area, I recommend stopping off at the ❂ **Umbarra Aboriginal Cultural Centre,** Wallaga Lake, just off the Princes Highway on Bermagui Road (☎ **02/4473 7232;** ubbarra@acr.net.au). The center offers activities such as boomerang and spear throwing, and painting with natural ochres for A$6.25 (U.S.$4) per person or A$20 (U.S.$13) for a family. There are also discussions, Aboriginal archival displays, and a retail store. It's open Monday to Friday from 9am to 5pm and Saturday and Sunday from 9am to 4pm (closed Sun in winter). The center's guides also offer 2- to 4-hour 4WD/walking trips of nearby **Mount Dromedary** and **Mumbulla Mountain,** taking in sacred sites. The tours cost A$45 (U.S.$29.25) per person. Reservations are essential.

   If you want to attempt Mt. Dromedary without a guide, ask for directions in Narooma. The hike to the top takes about 3 hours.

ACCOMMODATIONS

Whale Motor Inn. Princes Hwy., Narooma, NSW 2546. ☎ **02/4476 2411.** Fax 02/4476 1995. 17 units. A/C TV TEL. A$70–$125 (U.S.$45.50–$81.25) double; A$80–$125 (U.S.$52–$81.25) suite. Extra person A$10 (U.S.$6.50). AE, BC, DC, MC, V.

This nice and quiet motor inn has the best panoramic ocean views on the south coast and the largest rooms in town. Standard rooms have a queen-size and a single-person sofa bed. The standard suites have a separate bedroom, two additional sofa beds, and a kitchenette. Executive and spa suites are very spacious, are better furnished, and have a kitchenette and a large balcony or patio. The restaurant, Harpoons, specializes in local seafood. There's also a swimming pool.

MERIMBULA

480km (385 miles) S of Sydney, 580km (464 miles) NE of Melbourne

This seaside resort (pop. approx. 7,000) is the last place of interest before the Princes Highway crosses the border into Victoria. Merimbula is a good center from which to discover the surrounding **Ben Boyd National Park** and **Mimosa Rocks National Park,** both of which offer bushwalking. Another park, **Bournda National Park,** is situated around a lake and encompasses good walking trails and a surf beach.

Golf is the game of choice in Merimbula itself, and the area's most popular course is the **Pambula-Merimbula Golf Club** (☎ 02/6495 6154), where you can spot kangaroos grazing on the 27 fairways. It costs A$14 (U.S.$9.10) for nine holes, or A$25 (U.S.$16.25) for the day. Another favorite is **Tura Beach Country Club** (☎ 02/6495 9002), known for its excellent coastal views. A round of 18 holes costs A$20 (U.S.$13).

Eden, 20 kilometers (12.4 miles) south of Merimbula, was once a major whaling port. The rather gruesome **Eden Killer Whale Museum,** on Imlay Street in Eden (☎ 02/6496 2094), is the only reason to stop off here. It has a dubious array of relics, including boats, axes, and remnants of the last of the area's killer whales, called Old Tom. The museum is open Monday to Saturday from 9:15am to 3:45pm, Sunday from 11:15am to 3:45pm. In January it's open daily from 9:15am to 4:45pm daily. Admission is A$5 (U.S.$3.25) for adults and A$1.50 (U.S.$1) for children. Thankfully you can still see a scattering of whales off the coast in October and November.

ESSENTIALS

GETTING THERE　The drive from either Sydney or Melbourne takes about 7 hours. Both **Kendell Airlines** (☎ 1800/338 8894 in Australia) and **Hazelton Airlines** (☎ 13 17 13 in Australia) operate flights to Merimbula. The **Greyhound-Pioneer** (☎ 13 20 30 in Australia) bus trip from Sydney takes more than 8 hours.

VISITOR INFORMATION　The **Merimbula Tourist Information Centre,** at Beach Street, Merimbula (☎ 1800/150 457 in Australia, or 02/6495 1129), is open daily from 9am to 5pm (10am to 4pm in winter).

SPECIAL EVENTS　Jazz fans should head for the **Merimbula Jazz Festival** held over the long Queens Birthday weekend, the second weekend in June. A country-music festival takes place the last weekend in October.

ACCOMMODATIONS

Ocean View Motor Inn. Merimbula Dr. and View St., Merimbula, NSW 2548. ☎ **02/6495 2300.** Fax 02/6495 3443. E-mail: oceanview@acr.net.au. 20 units. A/C TV TEL. A$60–$110 (U.S.$39–$71.50) double (depending on season). Extra person A$10 (U.S.$6.50). BC, MC, V.

This pleasant motel has good water views from 12 of its rooms (the best are numbers 9, 10, and 11). The rooms are spacious and modern, with plain brick walls, patterned carpets, and one long balcony serving the top six rooms. Fourteen rooms have kitchenettes. All have showers. It's a friendly place, with a medium-size outdoor saltwater pool and a Laundromat on the premises. Breakfast is served to your room for A$7 (U.S.$4.55) extra.

6 The Snowy Mountains: Australia's Ski Country

Thredbo: 519km (322 miles) SW of Sydney, 208km (129 miles) SW of Canberra, 543km (331 miles) NE of Melbourne

Made famous by Banjo Patterson's 1890 poem, the "Man from Snowy River," the Snowy Mountains are most commonly used for what you'd least expect in Australia:

skiing. It starts to snow around June and carries on until September. During this time hundreds of thousands of people from all over the country flock here to ski at the major ski resorts: Thredbo and Perisher Blue, and to a lesser extent Charlotte Pass and Mount Selwyn. It's certainly different skiing here, with ghostly white gums as the obstacles instead of pine trees.

The whole region is part of the **Kosciuszko** (pronounced ko-zi-*os*-co) **National Park,** the largest alpine area in Australia. During the summer months, the park is a beautiful place for walking, and in spring, the profusion of wildflowers is exquisite. A series of lakes in the area, including the one in the resort town of Jindabyne, are favorites with trout fishermen.

Visitors stay at either **Jindabyne,** 62 kilometers (39 miles) south of Cooma, or **Thredbo Village,** 36 kilometers (20 miles) southwest of Jindabyne. Jindabyne is a pretty bleak-looking resort town on the banks of the man-made Lake Jindabyne, which came into existence when the Snowy River was dammed to provide hydro-electric power.

Thredbo Village is set in a valley of Mt. Crackenback and resembles a European-style resort. From here, the **Crackenback Chairlift** provides easy access to the top of Mt. Kosciuszko, which at 2,228 meters (7,352 ft.) is Australia's highest peak. The mountain has stunning views of the alpine region and some good walks.

Thredbo was the scene of a 1997 disaster that gripped the nation. At 11:40pm on a dark wintry night of July 30, a freak landslide tumbled down the hillside from the Alpine Way and smashed into two ski lodges. Twenty people were buried under the wreckage, and for days rescuers tried to shore up the hill and slowly pick through the rubble, all the while aware it could all shift again at any moment and bury them too. Ultimately there was only one survivor, a ski instructor who had managed to make it through freezing conditions for more than 36 hours.

SNOWY MOUNTAIN ESSENTIALS

GETTING THERE   From Sydney, the Parramatta Road runs into the Hume Highway in the suburb of Ashfield. Follow the Hume Highway south to Goulburn, where you turn onto the Federal Highway toward Canberra. From there take the Monaro Highway to Cooma, then follow the Alpine Way through Jindabyne and on to Thredbo. In winter, you may need chains for the snowy roads; you can rent them from local service stations. The trip takes around 7 hours from Sydney with short breaks.

Impulse Airways, a subsidiary of Ansett (☎ **13 13 00** in Australia), has daily flights from Sydney to Cooma. A connecting bus to the ski fields takes about 1 hour and is available from June to October. It's run by **Snowy Mountain Hire Cars** (☎ **02/6456 2957**) and costs A$48 (U.S.$31.20) one-way.

In winter only (from around June 19 to Oct 5), **Greyhound Pioneer** (☎ **13 20 30** in Australia) operates daily **buses** between Sydney and Cooma, via Canberra. The journey takes around 7 hours from Sydney and 3 from Canberra. A one-way ticket costs A$50 (U.S.$32.50).

VISITOR INFORMATION   Pick up information about the slopes and accommo-dation options either at the **Cooma Visitors Centre,** 119 Sharp St., Cooma, NSW 2630 (☎ **02/6450 1740**), or at the **Snowy Region Visitor Centre,** Kosciuszko Road, Jindabyne, NSW 2627 (☎ **02/6450 5600**).

HITTING THE SLOPES & OTHER ADVENTURES

Obviously, skiing is the most popular activity around here. More than 50 ski lifts serve the combined fields of Perisher Valley, Mt. Blue Cow, Smiggins Holes, and Guthega. Perisher Valley offers the best overall ski slopes; Mt. Blue Cow is generally very crowded; Smiggins Holes offers good beginner runs; and Guthega has nice light, powdery snow and less-crowded conditions. Thredbo has some very challenging runs and the longest downhill runs. A day's ski pass costs around A$62 (U.S.$40.30) for adults and A$36 (U.S.$23.40) for children.

For up-to-date ski information call **Perisher Blue** at ☎ **02/6459 4485; Thredbo** at ☎ **02/6459 4100; Charlotte Pass** at ☎ **02/6457 5247;** or **Mt. Selwyn** at ☎ **02/ 6454 9488.**

A ski-tube train midway between Jindabyne and Thredbo on the Alpine Way travels through the mountains to Perisher Valley and then to Blue Cow. It costs A$10 (U.S.$6.50) a day for adult skiers and A$6 (U.S.$3.90) for child skiers; A$22 (U.S.$14.30) for nonskiing adults and A$11 (U.S.$7.15) for nonskiing children. Prices are cheaper in summer. You can rent ski gear at numerous places in Jindabyne and Thredbo.

In summer, the region is popular for hiking, canoeing, fishing, and golf. Thredbo Village has tennis courts, a 9-hole golf course, and mountain-bike trails.

ACCOMMODATIONS

You'll have to book months ahead to find a place to stay during the ski season (especially on weekends). And, don't expect to find a lot of bargains. The **Kosciuszko Accommodation Centre,** Nuggets Crossing, Jindabyne, NSW 2627 (☎ **1800/026 354** in Australia, or 02/6456 2022), can help find and book accommodations in the area. Other private agents who can help find you a spot for the night include **The Snowy Mountains Reservation Centre** (☎ **02/6456 2633**) and the **Thredbo Resort Centre** (☎ **1800/020 622** in Australia).

IN THREDBO

Riverside Cabins. Thredbo, NSW 2625. ☎ **1800/026 333** in Australia, or 02/6459 4299. Fax 02/6459 4195. 36 units. TV TEL. Winter A$145–$350 (U.S.$94.25–$227.50) double. Summer A$110–$150 (U.S.$71.50–$97.50) double. Ask about weekly rates. AE, BC, DC, MC, V.

These studio and one-bedroom cabins are above the Thredbo River and overlook the Crackenback Range. They're also a short walk from the Thredbo Alpine Hotel and local shops. Most rooms have balconies.

Thredbo Alpine Apartments. Thredbo, NSW 2628. ☎ **1800/026 333** in Australia, or 02/6459 4299. Fax 02/6459 4195. 35 units. TV TEL. Winter weekends (July 30–Sept 2) A$204–$429 (U.S.$132.60–$278.85) 1-bedroom apt.; A$281–$610 (U.S.$182.65–$396.50) 2-bedroom apt.; A$383–$748 (U.S.$248.95–$486.20) 3-bedroom apt.; midweek rates approximately 20% cheaper. Summer A$120 (U.S.$78) 1-bedroom apt.; A$150 (U.S.$97.50) 2-bedroom apt.; A$170 (U.S.$110.50) 3-bedroom apt. Ask about weekly rates. AE, BC, DC, MC, V. Underground parking.

These apartments are very similar to the Riverside Cabins (see above) and are managed by the same people. All have balconies with mountain views. Some have queen-size beds. There are limited daily maid service and in-house movies.

Thredbo Alpine Hotel. P.O. Box 80, Thredbo NSW 2625. ☎ **02/6459 4200.** Fax 02/6459 4201. 65 units. MINIBAR TV TEL. Winter A$220–$478 (U.S.$143–$310.70) double. Summer A$147–$180 (U.S.$95.55–$117) double. Ask about weekly rates and packages. Rates include breakfast. AE, BC, DC, MC, V.

The center of activity in Thredbo after the skiing is finished for the day is this large resort-style lodge. Rooms vary; those on the top floor of the three-story hotel were refurbished in 1998 and have a king-size bed instead of a standard queen. The rooms are all wood paneled. Thredbo's only nightclub is here. There are also a swimming pool, a sauna, and a hot tub.

Following in the Footsteps of the Man from Snowy River

☉ **Horseback riding** is a popular activity for all those wanting to ride like the "Man from Snowy River." **Reynella Kosciusko Rides,** located in Adamanaby, 44 kilometers (27 miles) northwest of Cooma (☎ **02/6454 2386**), offers multinight tours through the Kosciusko National Park from October to the end of April. The trips are all-inclusive and include camping and homestead accommodations. Shorter rides are offered by **Jindabyne Trail Rides** (☎ **02/6456 2421**). Gentle 1¹/₂-hour rides on the slopes above Jindabyne cost about A$20 (U.S.$13) per person.

IN JINDABYNE

Station Resort. Dalgety Rd., Jindabyne, NSW 2627. ☎ **02/6456 2895.** Fax 02/6456 2544. 250 units (all with shower only). A$199–A$409 (U.S.$129.35–$265.85) per person 2-night weekend package, A$339–A$769 (U.S.$220.35–$499.85) 5-night midweek package. AE, BC, DC, MC, V.

The largest resort in the Snowy Mountains accommodates 1,400 guests and is situated on 50 rural acres. It's open only during the ski season, roughly mid-June to mid-October and offers only weekend or midweek packages. Rooms are spacious and comfortable, sleeping four to seven people. Book well in advance. There are three restaurants, two bars, and a nightclub on the property. Rates include ski-lift tickets for Perisher Blue ski resort. The property is 6 kilometers (4 miles) from Jindabyne.

7 Outback New South Wales

The Outback is a powerful Australian image. Though it's hot and dusty, and prone to flies, it can also be a romantic place, where wedge-tailed eagles float in the shimmering heat and where you can spin around in a circle and follow the unbroken horizon. If you drive out here, you have to be constantly on the lookout for emus, large flightless birds that dart across roads open-beaked and wide-eyed. When you turn off the car engine, it's so quiet you can hear the scales of a sleepy lizard, as long as your forearm, scraping the rumpled track as it turns to taste the air with its long, blue tongue.

The scenery out here is like a huge canvas with a restricted palette of paint: blood red for the dirt, straw yellow for the blotches of Mitchell grass, a searing blue for the surreally large sky. There is room to be yourself in the Outback, and you'll soon find out that personalities can easily roam toward the eccentric side. It's a hard-working place, too, where miners, sheep and cattle farmers, and assorted other types try to eke out a living in Australia's hard center.

✪ LIGHTNING RIDGE: OPALS GALORE

765km (474 miles) NW of Sydney, 572km (355 miles) SW of Brisbane

Lightning Ridge, or "The Ridge" as the locals call it, is perhaps the most fascinating place to visit in all of New South Wales. Essentially, it's a hard-working opal-mining town stuck out in the arid far northern reaches of New South Wales—where summer temperatures regularly hover around the 45°C (113°F) mark. Lightning Ridge thrives off the largest deposit of black opal in the world. Good quality opals from here can fetch a miner around A$8,000 (U.S.$5,200) per carat, and stones worth upwards of A$500,000 (U.S.$325,000) each are not unheard of. Tourists come here to get a taste of life in Australia's "Wild West." A popular tourist activity in the opal fields is to pick over the old white heaps of mine tailings. Stories (perhaps tall tales) abound of tourists finding overlooked opals worth thousands of dollars.

Outback Driving Tips

Most of the places covered below are accessible by 2WD cars, though you should never attempt to travel on dirt tracks after a rain. Always make sure you have plenty of water and fuel, and never wander off the main tracks unless you have a detailed local map of the area and have told someone when to expect to hear from you.

I strongly recommend you visit the **Grawin** and **Glengarry opal fields,** each about an hour or so from Lightning Ridge on a dirt track barely suitable for 2WD cars (check with locals before you go). These full-on frontier townships are bristling with drills and hoists pulling out bucket loads of dirt and buzzing with news of the latest opal rush.

ESSENTIALS

GETTING THERE   From Sydney, it takes about 9 hours to drive to Lightning Ridge, via Bathurst, Dubbo, and the fascinating town of Walgett. **Countrylink Holidays** (☎ **13 28 29** in Australia) offer a 3-night/4-day Lightning Ridge tour from Sydney for A$373 (U.S.$242.45) for adults and A$187 (U.S.$121.55) for children, including accommodation, some meals, and entrance fees; train fare is additional, so ask about specials. **Hazelton Airlines** (☎ **13 17 13** in Australia) also flies to Lightning Ridge.

VISITOR INFORMATION   The **Lightning Ridge Tourist Information Centre** on Morilla Street (☎ **02/6829 0565**) is open Monday to Friday from 8:30am to 4pm.

SPECIAL EVENTS   If you're in Australia around Easter, make sure you come to Lightning Ridge for the **Great Goat Race** and the rodeo.

SEEING THE TOWN

Any visit to Lightning Ridge should start with an orientation trip with **Black Opal Tours** (☎ **02/6829 0368**). The company offers a 5-hour tour of the opal fields for A$60 (U.S.$39) per person. Also ask about their shorter tours as well as their 2- and 3-day tours of the area.

Among the many points of interest is the 15-meter-tall (50-ft.) homemade **Amigo's Castle,** which dominates the worked-out opal fields immediately surrounding the modern township of Lightning Ridge. Complete with turrets, battlements, dungeons, and a wishing well, the castle has been rising out of these arid lands for the past 17 years, with every rock scavenged from the surrounding area and lugged in a wheelbarrow or in a rucksack on Amigo's back. Amigo (a local gent known by this nickname) hasn't taken out insurance on the property, so there are no official tours, though if he feels like a bit of company he'll show you around.

The ✪ **Artesian Bore Baths,** 2 kilometers (1 mile) from the post office on Pandora Street, are free of charge, open 24 hours a day, and said to have therapeutic value. The water temperature hovers between 40°C and 50°C (104°F to 122°F). It's an amazing place to visit at night with the stars out above.

The **Bevan's Black Opal & Cactus Nursery** (☎ **02/6829 0429**) contains more than 2,000 species of cactus and succulent plants, including many rare specimens. Betty Bevan cuts her own opals, many of which are on display. Admission is A$4 (U.S.$2.60).

There are plenty of opal shops, galleries, walk-in opal mines, and other distinctly unique things to see in Lightning Ridge. You might want to take a look at **Gemopal**

Pottery (☎ **02/6829 0375**), on the road to the Bore Baths. The resident potter makes some nice pots out of clay mine tailings and lives in one of his five old Sydney railway carriages.

ACCOMMODATIONS & DINING

The Wallangulla Motel. Morilla St. (at Agate St.), Lightning Ridge, NSW 2834. ☎ **02/6829 0542.** Fax 02/6829 0070. 43 units. A/C TV TEL. A$55–$83 (U.S.$35.75–$53.95) double; A$77–A$94 (U.S.$50–$61) triple; A$108–A$121 (U.S.$70.20–$78.65) family room with spa. AE, BC, DC, MC, V.

The best motel in town offers two standards of rooms, the cheaper rooms being in an older section of the property. Newer rooms are better furnished and generally nicer; they're worth the extra money. Two large family rooms each have two bedrooms and a living room; one has a whirlpool. Guests can use the barbecue facilities, and there is a special arrangement with the Bowling Club over the road for meals there to be charged back to your room. The Bowling Club has a restaurant with pretty good food and a very cheap bistro.

❂ BROKEN HILL

1,157km (717 miles) W of Sydney, 508km (315 miles) NE of Adelaide

At heart, Broken Hill—or "Silver City" as it's been nicknamed—is still very much a hard-working, hard-drinking mining town. Its beginnings can be traced back to 1883 when the trained eye of a boundary rider named Charles Rasp noticed something odd about the craggy rock outcrops at a place called the Broken Hill. Today, the city's main drag, Argent Street, bristles with finely crafted colonial mansions, heritage homes, hotels, and public buildings. Look deeper and you see the town's quirkiness. Around one corner you'll find the radio station built to resemble a giant wireless set with round knobs for windows, and around another the headquarters of the Housewives Association, which ruled the town with an iron apron for generations. Then there's the Palace Hotel—made famous in the movie *The Adventures of Priscilla, Queen of the Desert*—with its high painted walls and a mural of Botticelli's *Birth of Venus* on the ceiling two flights up. There are 23 pubs for the town's 24,500 inhabitants (down from 73 at the turn of the century), but also plenty of houses of worship.

ESSENTIALS

GETTING THERE   By car, take the Great Western Highway from Sydney to Dubbo, then the Mitchell Highway to the Barrier Highway, which will take you to Broken Hill.

There are regular **flights** on **Kendell Airlines** (☎ **1800/338 8894** in Australia) from Adelaide, and **Hazelton Airlines** (☎ **13 17 13** in Australia) from Sydney. **Southern Australian Airlines** (book through Qantas, ☎ **13 13 13** in Australia) also connects Broken Hill to Adelaide, Melbourne, and Mildura.

The *Indian Pacific* **train** stops here on its way to Perth. It departs Sydney at 2:55pm on Monday and Thursday and arrives at Broken Hill at 9am the next morning. The fare is A$395 (U.S.$256.75) for adults and A$265 (U.S.$172.25) for children in a first-class sleeper, A$276 (U.S.$179.40) for adults and A$182 (U.S.$118.30) for children in an economy sleeper, and A$117 (U.S.$76) for adults and A$59 (U.S.$38.35) for children in an economy seat. The train also runs between Sydney and Adelaide via Broken Hill. Call **Great Southern Railways** (☎ **08/8213 4530**) for more information and bookings, or check out the timetables and fares on their Web site (www.gsr.com.au/fares.htm).

Greyhound-Pioneer (☎ **13 20 30** in Australia) runs buses from Adelaide for A$69.30 (U.S.$45); the trip takes 7 hours. The 16-hour trip from Sydney costs A$111.10 (U.S.$71.50).

VISITOR INFORMATION   The **Broken Hill Tourist and Travelers Centre,** at Blende and Bromide streets, Broken Hill, NSW 2880 (☎ **08/8087 6077;** www.murrayoutback.org.au), is open daily from 8:30am to 5pm. The **National Parks & Wildlife Service** (NPWS) office is at 183 Argent St. (☎ **08/8088 5933**), and the **Royal Automobile Association of South Australia,** which offers reciprocal services to other national and international auto-club members, is at 261 Argent St. (☎ **08/8088 4999**).

Note: The area code in Broken Hill is **08,** the same as the South Australia code, not 02, the New South Wales code.

GETTING AROUND   Silver City Tours, 380 Argent St. (☎ **08/8087 3144**), conducts tours of the city and surrounding Outback. City tours take around 4 hours and cost A$32 (U.S.$20.80) for adults and A$10 (U.S.$6.50) for children. They also offer a range of other tours of the area. **Broken Hill Outback Tours,** 160–170 Crystal St. (P. O. Box 199), Broken Hill, NSW 2880 (☎ **1800/670 120** in Australia, or 08/8087 7800), conducts 3- to 6-day tours of the area.

Hertz (☎ **08/8087 2719**) rents 4WD vehicles suitable for exploring the area.

EXPLORING THE TOWN

With the largest regional public gallery in New South Wales and 27 private galleries, Broken Hill has more places per capita to see art than anywhere else in Australia. The **Broken Hill City Art Gallery,** Chloride Street, between Blende and Beryl streets (☎ **08/8088 5491**) houses an extensive collection of Australian colonial and impressionist works. Of particular interest is the *Silver Tree,* a sculpture wrought from pure silver mined from beneath Broken Hill and dedicated to the discoverer of the first mineral deposits, Charles Rasp. This is also a good place to see works by the "Brushmen of the Bush," a well-known group of artists, including Pro Hart, Jack Absalom, Eric Minchin, and Hugh Schultz, who spend many days sitting around campfires in the bush trying to capture its essence in paint. The gallery is open Monday to Friday from 10am to 5pm, and Saturday and Sunday from 1 to 5pm. Admission is A$3 (U.S.$1.95) for adults, A$2 (U.S.$1.30) for children, and A$6 (U.S.$3.90) for families.

Other galleries worth visiting around town include **Absalom's Gallery,** 638 Chapple St. (☎ **08/8087 5881**), and the **Pro Hart Gallery,** 108 Wyman St. (☎ **08/8087 2441**). All are open daily. Pro Hart's gallery is really worth a look. Apart from his own works—including works based on incidents and scenes relating to Broken Hill—his gallery is crammed with everything from a bas-relief of Salvador Dalí to a landscape by Claude Monet.

To get a real taste of mining in Broken Hill, take an underground tour at **Delprat's Mine** (☎ **08/8088 1604**). Visitors go 120 meters (396 ft.) below the surface. Children under 6 are not allowed. Tours run Monday to Friday at 10:30am and Saturday at 2pm. The 2-hour tour costs A$23 (U.S.$14.95) for adults and A$18 (U.S.$11.70) for children.

What Time Is It, Anyway?

Broken Hill runs its clocks to Central Standard Time, to correspond with South Australia. The surrounding country, however, runs half an hour faster at Eastern Standard Time.

Be sure not to miss the School of the Air and the Royal Flying Doctor Service base, both of which help show the enormity of the Australian interior. The **School of the Air**—the largest schoolroom in the world, with students scattered over 800,000 square kilometers (312,000 square miles)—conducts lessons via two-way radios. Visitors can listen in on part of the day's first teaching session Monday through Friday at 8:30am (except public holidays). Bookings are essential and must be made through the **Broken Hill Tourist and Travelers Centre** (see "Visitor Information" above). Tours costs A$2 (U.S.$1.30) per person. The **Royal Flying Doctor Service base** is at the Broken Hill Airport (☎ **08/8080 1777**). The service maintains communication with more than 400 outback stations, ready to fly at once in case of an emergency. The base at Broken Hill covers 25% of New South Wales, as well as parts of Queensland and South Australia. Continuous explanatory lessons are held at the base Monday to Friday from 9am to noon and 1 to 5pm, Saturday and Sunday from 10am to 4pm. Admission is A$3 (U.S.$1.95) for adults, free for children.

WHAT TO SEE & DO NEARBY

VISITING A GHOST TOWN   At least 44 movies have been filmed in the Wild West town of **Silverton** (pop. 50), 23 kilometers (14 miles) northwest of Broken Hill. It's the Wild West Australian-style, though with camels instead of horses sometimes placed in front of the **Silverton Pub,** which is well worth a visit for its kitschy Australian appeal. Silverton once had a population of 3,000 following the discovery of—guess what?—silver in 1882. But within 7 years almost everyone had left. There are some good art galleries here, as well as a restored jail and hotel.

DISCOVERING ABORIGINAL HANDPRINTS   Mootwingee National Park, 130 kilometers (80 miles) northeast of Broken Hill, was one of the most important spiritual meeting places for Aborigines on the continent. Groups came from all over the country to peck out abstract engravings on the rocks with sharpened quartz tools and to sign their handprints to show they belonged to the place. The ancient, weathered fireplaces are still here, laid out like a giant map to show where each visiting group came from. Hundreds of ochre outlines of hands and animal paws, some up to 30,000 years old, are stenciled on rock overhangs. The fabulous 2-hour Outback trip from Broken Hill to Mootwingee is along red-dirt tracks not really suitable for two-wheel-drives and should not be attempted after a heavy rain.

It's best to tour Mootwingee National Park with a guide, rather than on your own. Call the park at ☎ **08/8088 5933,** or book direct through **Mootwingee Heritage Tours** (☎ **08/8088 7000**), which organizes inspections of the historical sites every Wednesday and Saturday morning at 10:30am Broken Hill time (11am Mootwingee, or Eastern Standard, Time). The tours may be canceled in very hot weather. The **NPWS office** in Broken Hill (☎ **08/8088 5933**) also has details. You can camp at the **Homestead Creek** campground for A$11 (U.S.$7.15) a night. It has its own water supply.

EXPLORING WHITE CLIFFS   White Cliffs, 290 kilometers (180 miles) east of Broken Hill, is an opal-mining town bigger than it looks. To escape the summer heat, most houses are built underground in mine shafts, where the temperature is a constant 23°C (73°F). Prospecting started here in 1889, when kangaroo shooters found the colorful stones scattered on the ground. A year later the rush was on, and by the turn of the century about 4,000 people were digging and sifting in a lawless, waterless hell of a place.

Today, the country looks like an inverted moonscape, pimpled with bone-white heaps of gritty clay dug from the 50,000 mine shafts that surround the town. These days, White Cliffs is more renowned for its eccentricity. Take **Jock's Place,** for

---

A Fabulous Place to Enjoy the Sunset

Just outside Broken Hill, in the **Living Desert Nature Park,** is the best collection of sculptures this side of Stonehenge. Twelve sandstone obelisks, up to 3 meters (10 ft.) high and carved totemlike by artists from as far away as Georgia, Syria, Mexico, and the Tiwi Islands, make up the Sculpture Symposium. Surrounding them on all sides is brooding mulga scrub. It's fantastic at sunset.

---

instance, an old underground museum full to the beams with junk pulled from old mine shafts.

Then there's a house made of beer flagons and a nine-hole ✪ **dirt golf course** where the locals play at night with fluorescent green golf balls. If you fancy an after-hours round of golf in the dirt (and who doesn't?), contact the secretary of the **White Cliffs Golf Club,** John Painter (☎ 08/8091 6715 after hours). He'll be happy to supply you with a golf club or two and a couple of balls for A$2 (U.S.$1.30). Otherwise, put A$2 (U.S.$1.30) in the black box at the first tee if you have your own clubs—but be warned, bush playing can damage your clubs, and crows often make off with the balls. Visitors can play daily day or night, but if you want some company, turn up on Sunday, when club members shoot it out.

ACCOMMODATIONS: ABOVE GROUND & BELOW

One option is to rent a local cottage from **Broken Hill Historic Cottages** (☎ 08/8087 9966) for A$80 (U.S.$52) a night, or **Sue Spicer's Holiday Cottages** (☎ 08/8087 8488), which rents fully equipped cottages for A$65 (U.S.$42.25) per night and up.

Broken Hill Overlander Motor Inn. 142 Iodide St., Broken Hill, NSW 2880. ☎ **08/8088 2566.** Fax 08/8088 4377. Reservations can be made through Best Western (☎ 800/780-7234 in the U.S. and Canada, 0800/39 3130 in the U.K., 0800/237 893 in New Zealand, or 13 17 79 in Australia). 15 units. A/C TV TEL. A$80–$102 (U.S.$52–$66.30) double, A$130 (U.S.$84.50) 2-bed unit. Extra person A$10 (U.S.$6.50). AE, BC, DC, JCB, MC, V.

This is my favorite place to stay in Broken Hill, although admittedly that's not really saying much in this Outback town. It's set way back from the road, has nice green areas with a pool and barbecue facilities, and is very quiet. There are also a whirlpool and sauna on the premises. The more expensive four-star rooms are much nicer than the cheaper variants, and considerably larger. Two family rooms sleep up to six in a combination of single and queen-size beds.

Mario the Palace Hotel. 227 Argent St., Broken Hill, NSW 2880. ☎ **08/8088 1699.** Fax 08/8087 6240. 51 units, 10 with private bathroom. A/C TV TEL. A$40 (U.S.$26) double without bathroom; A$50–$60 (U.S.$32.50–$39) double with bathroom. AE, BC, DC, MC, V.

With its high painted walls, a mural of Botticelli's *Birth of Venus* on the ceiling two flights up, and an office crammed with stuffed animal heads and crabs, the Palace Hotel is an intriguing sanctuary for the night. The owners have put a lot of work into restoring the place. The more expensive doubles are larger and come with a small lounge area, but all are comfortable and cool. Ten double rooms come with an attached shower. Mario has owned the place for "donkey's years" as he says, but he has plans to sell it.

✪ **Underground Motel.** Smiths Hill (P.O. Box 427), White Cliffs, NSW 2836. ☎ **1800/02 1154** in Australia, or 08/8091 6677. Fax 08/8091 6654. 30 units, none with private bathroom. A$79 (U.S.$51.35) double. Extra person A$24 (U.S.$15.60). BC, MC, V.

I love this place; it's worth making the scenic trip out to White Cliffs just to stay here for the night. All but two of the rooms are underground; they're reached by a maze of spacious tunnels dug out of the rock and sealed with epoxy-resin to keep out the damp and the dust. The temperature below ground is a constant 22°C (71°F), which is decidedly cooler than a summer day outside. Rooms are comfortable though fairly basic, and toilets and showers are shared. Turn the light off and it's as dark as a cave. Upstairs are a bar and a dining room, where every night guests sit around large round tables and dig into the roast of the day (vegetarians are catered to, also). There's also a pool on the premises.

DINING

The best place for a meal Aussie-style is at one of the local clubs. You'll find one of the best bistros at the **Barrier Social & Democratic Club,** at 218 Argent St. (☎ **08/ 8088 4477**). It serves breakfast, lunch, and dinner. There's also a whole host of Chinese restaurants around town, including the **Oceania Chinese Restaurant** on Argent Street (☎ **08/8087 3695**), which has a A$7 (U.S.$4.55) lunch special. You can get a late-night snack at the **International Deli** (☎ **08/8087 3427**), on Oxide Street (near Beryl Street); it's open until midnight.

5 Brisbane

by Natalie Kruger

Queensland's capital, Brisbane, is just what a subtropical capital should be. Cradled within a curve of the stately Brisbane River, its palm tree–lined streets shade gracious sandstone and limestone colonial civic buildings, its gardens swell with mango and banana trees, and the weather forecast always seems to be "fine." (Brisbane is rarely cold enough for an overcoat in winter, though summer can be unpleasantly hot and sticky.)

Is there much to see? Well, not if you're into touristy stuff. The major visitor attraction is the country's largest koala sanctuary, where you can cuddle one of these cutie-pies free. Instead, you'll come here for a pleasant outdoorsy city, packed with welcoming parks, a healthy performing-arts scene, and alfresco dining.

Brisbane (pronounce it "*Briz*-bun" if you want to fit in) is renowned for its charming timber cottages and houses, which are set atop stilts to catch the breeze and underneath provide dark, cool relief from the worst of the midday sun. It's an architectural style dubbed "Queenslander." Many houses have been converted into delightful B&Bs or rainbow-colored cafes and shops selling antiques, fashion, and desirable housewares.

The best way to enjoy Brisbane is to stroll the city streets and admire the architecture, drop into the excellent Queensland Art Gallery, in-line skate or bike along the river, have a beer in the courtyard of a pub, or wend your way downriver on the CityCat ferries. If it's a weekend, browse one of the colorful handcrafts markets. There's even a man-made beach in the city center. Folks here are very laidback (smart shorts and deck shoes will get you into most places).

Australia's third-biggest city (pop. 1.3 million), Brisbane is located on the southern coast of the state. Because it's less than a 2-hour drive south from the Sunshine Coast and 80 minutes north of the Gold Coast, it's the perfect springboard for a day trip to either spot.

1 Orientation

ARRIVING

BY PLANE Twenty-three airlines fly into Brisbane. International flights come from Europe, Asia, New Guinea, the South Pacific, and New Zealand, though flights from North America arrive via Sydney. **Ansett** (☎ 13 13 00 in Australia) and **Qantas** (☎ 13 13 13 in Australia) have plentiful daily flights from most Australian state capital

Greater Brisbane

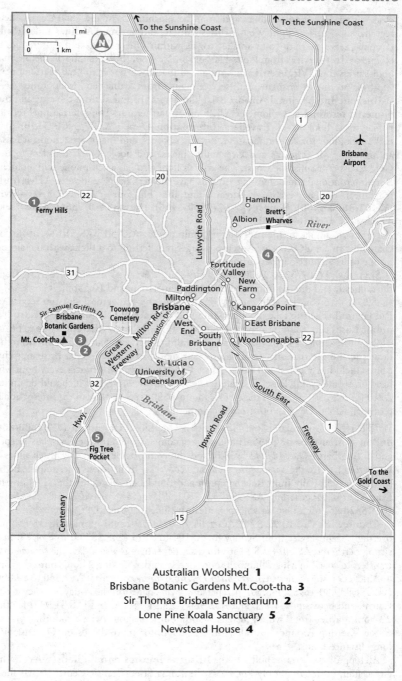

Australian Woolshed **1**
Brisbane Botanic Gardens Mt.Coot-tha **3**
Sir Thomas Brisbane Planetarium **2**
Lone Pine Koala Sanctuary **5**
Newstead House **4**

cities, either direct or via Sydney, and from the Sunshine Coast and Gold Coast. Their regional subsidiaries **Flight West Airlines** (Ansett) and **Sunstate Airlines** and **Airlink** (Qantas) serve the city from smaller towns within Queensland, and Ansett flies a couple of daily services from Coffs Harbour in New South Wales. Shortly before this book's press time, **Virgin Atlantic** announced that it was about to headquarter a new "no-frills" airline in Brisbane, with service mainly from Sydney and Melbourne.

Brisbane International Airport is 16 kilometers (10 miles) from the city, and the **domestic terminal** is 2 kilometers (1.25 miles) farther out. The international terminal's arrivals floor has a **Travellers' Information Desk** (☎ 07/3406 3190) that makes bookings for accommodation, car rental, tours, and major attractions; it's also an agent for McCafferty's and Greyhound buses, and books coach transfers to the Gold Coast and Sunshine Coast. The arrivals floor also has a cell-phone rental outlet. Both international and domestic terminals have showers, baggage lockers, ATMs (cash machines), currency-exchange bureaus, and the "big four" car-rental desks—**Avis** (☎ 07/3860 4200), **Budget** (☎ 07/3860 4466), **Hertz** (☎ 07/3860 4522), and **Thrifty** (☎ 07/3860 4588).

An interterminal shuttle runs every 15 minutes for A$2.50 (U.S.$1.65), or free of charge if you are a Qantas or Ansett passenger transferring to a flight with the airline or one of its alliance partner airlines.

Skytrans (☎ 07/3236 1000) runs a city shuttle every 45 minutes departing from the domestic and international terminals between 5:15am and 10:55pm. It costs A$11 (U.S.$7.15) to your hotel in the city, Spring Hill, and Kangaroo Point (no service to Paddington). The trip takes about 30 minutes. Advance bookings are not needed. No **public buses** run from the airport. From May 1, 2001, a new **Airtrain** is due to begin a 22-minute service approximately every 15 minutes between 5am and 11pm from the domestic and international terminals to four suburban rail stations in Brisbane's city center, including Central and Roma Street Transit Centre. Two services every hour will head on to the Gold Coast. The fare was not set as we wrote, but it should be under A$10 (U.S.$6.50). A taxi to the city is around A$20 (U.S.$13) from the international terminal, A$24 (U.S.$15.60) from the domestic.

BY TRAIN   Queensland Rail's long-distance division, **Traveltrain** (☎ 1800/806 468 in Australia, or 07/3235 1000; www.qr.com.au) operates the first-class sleeper and sitting berth *Queenslander* weekly and the comfortable *Sunlander* three times a week from Cairns, the *Spirit of the Tropics* twice weekly from Townsville, and the high-speed *Tilt* train daily from Rockhampton and Bundaberg. Fares for the 31-hour trip from Cairns range from A$156 (U.S.$101.40) for a *Sunlander* seat to A$505 (U.S.$328.25) for a first-class sleeper, meals included, aboard the *Queenslander.*

Countrylink (☎ 13 22 32 in Australia, or 02/9379 1298) runs a daily 13¹/₂-hour overnight train service from Sydney for A$104 to $145 (U.S.$67.60 to $94.25) in a sitting berth and A$240 (U.S.$156) for a sleeper. There is also a daytime service that transfers to coach in Murwillumbah south of the border, tacking 2 hours onto the trip.

A ticket on the opulent ***Great South Pacific Express*** costs from A$2,830 to $4,690 (U.S.$1,839.50 to $3,048.50) per person, twin-share for the 4-day journey from Cairns, and between A$1,770 and A$2,980 (U.S.$1,150.50 and U.S.$1,937) for the 22-hour journey from Sydney. It makes both journeys about twice a month.

See "Getting Around Australia," in chapter 2, for more details on Queensland's long-distance trains.

All long-distance trains pull into the **Brisbane Transit Centre** at Roma Street in the city center, more commonly known as the Roma Street Transit Centre. It has food outlets, showers, a tour desk, and lockers. Most city and Spring Hill hotels are a few blocks' walk or a quick cab ride away.

Queensland Rail CityTrain (☎ **07/3235 5555,** or call **Transinfo** at ☎ **13 12 30** in Queensland) provides roughly two trains every hour from the Sunshine Coast. The train departs from Nambour; Sunshine Coast bus company **Sunbus** (☎ **07/5492 8700**) runs a linking bus (route X12) to Nambour station from Noosa Heads five times a day. The bus trip takes 45 minutes and costs A$6.70 (U.S.$4.35); the train trip takes a further 2 hours and costs A$9.70 (U.S.$6.30). CityTrain provides a half-hourly service daily from Robina station on the Gold Coast. The fare for the 1 hour, 20 minute trip is A$8.30 (U.S.$5.40).

BY BUS   McCafferty's (☎ **13 14 99** in Australia) and **Greyhound Pioneer** (☎ **13 20 30** in Australia) each have between three and five daily services from Cairns and four or five a day from Sydney, stopping at most towns en route. A one-way Cairns–Brisbane ticket costs around A$156 (U.S.$100.40), and the trip takes around 28¹/₂ hours. The Sydney-Brisbane trip takes about 17¹/₂ hours (via the coastal Pacific Highway or the inland New England Highway) and costs A$77 (U.S.$50.05) one-way.

Coachtrans (☎ **07/5588 8777** for administration, or call Transinfo for route and timetable information) provides 12 daily public bus services from the Gold Coast to six stops in downtown Brisbane, terminating at the Roma Street Transit Centre. The trip can take up to 2¹/₂ hours; opt for one of the five express services to keep traveling time to around 2 hours or less. The single adult fare is A$13 (U.S.$8.45). There is no need to book; simply hail the bus en route.

Bus company **Suncoast Pacific** (☎ **07/5443 1011** Sunshine Coast or **07/3236 1901** Brisbane) runs one or two daily services from Hervey Bay, and nine daily services from Noosa Heads, to Brisbane for A$22 (U.S.$14.30); trip time: about 3 hours.

All long-distance coaches pull into the Brisbane Transit Centre (see "By Train," above).

BY CAR   The **Bruce Highway** from Cairns enters the city from the north, and the **Pacific Highway** enters from Sydney in the south. There is no highway east from Alice Springs or Ayers Rock to Brisbane.

VISITOR INFORMATION

Brisbane Tourism, P.O. Box 12260, Elizabeth St., Brisbane, QLD 4002 (☎ **07/3221 8411;** e-mail: enquiries@visitbrisbane.com.au; www.brisbanetourism.com.au), has an information center in the Queen Street Mall near Albert Street (☎ **07/3229 5918**). It's open 9am to 5pm Monday through Thursday, to 7pm on Friday, and to 4pm on Saturday; Sunday it's open 10am to 4pm. There is a smaller outlet in City Hall at King George Square between Adelaide and Ann streets at Albert Street.

A good source of information on dining, performing arts, galleries, shopping, and other facets of Brisbane's laid-back lifestyle is the color weekly *Brisbane News,* free from newsstands, cafes, hotel lobbies, and the like.

CITY LAYOUT

The city center sits on the north-bank "tip" of an almost 180° curve of the Brisbane River. At the very tip are the **City Botanic Gardens.** The 30-meter (98-ft.) sandstone cliffs of **Kangaroo Point** rise on the eastern side of the south bank; on the west side of the south bank are the South Bank Parklands and Queensland Cultural Centre, known collectively as **South Bank.** Five kilometers (3 miles) to the west, **Mt. Coot-tha** (pronounced "*Kew*-tha") looms up modestly, providing a vantage point for gazing over the city.

MAIN ARTERIES & STREETS   All city center **east-west streets** are named after female British monarchs and princesses, and all **north-south streets** after their male counterparts. The "female" streets start with Ann in the northwest followed by Adelaide, Queen, Elizabeth, Charlotte, Mary, Margaret, and Alice. From northeast to southwest, the "male" streets run Edward, Albert, George, and William. William becomes North Quay, flanking the river's northeast bank. **Brunswick Street** is the main thoroughfare running through Fortitude Valley and New Farm.

Queen Street is the city's main thoroughfare; it is a pedestrian mall between Edward and George streets. **Roma Street** exits the city diagonally to the northwest, leading you to Milton and Rosalie (via Milton Road) and Paddington (via Petrie Terrace).

STREET MAPS   *The Brisbane Map*, free from Brisbane Tourism (see "Visitor Information," above) or your concierge, is a great detailed lightweight color map that shows the river and outlying suburbs as well as the city. It also shows parking lots and one-way traffic directions.

The Neighborhoods in Brief

City Center   Queen Street Mall, right in the heart of town, is popular with shopaholics and cinemagoers, especially on Friday nights, when stores stay open until 9pm. The **Eagle Street** financial/legal precinct boasts some great riverside restaurants. Much of Brisbane's gorgeous colonial architecture is in the city center, too.

The city center is the most convenient place to stay, but because **Spring Hill** is just a few blocks (uphill) from the city center, it almost counts as downtown.

Kangaroo Point   This area is a short drive (less than 2km/1^1/$_4$ miles) over the Story Bridge from the city center. It can also be reached via one of the cross-river ferries (trip time: 3 min.) that depart every 10 or 15 minutes from 5:30am until midnight. Kangaroo Point has a few good hotel choices, but other than that, it's not really an area of tourist interest.

South Bank   A 7-minute walk across Victoria Bridge, at the western end of Queen Street, takes you to South Bank, a kind of peaceful public playground composed of the Queensland Cultural Centre and the parks, rain-forest walks, artificial beach, and restaurants of South Bank Parklands. Come here to see a play, meet for dinner, shop in weekend markets, or just chill out on the riverbank.

Fortitude Valley   Ten years ago, this suburb of derelict warehouses just east of the city center was a no-go zone. Today, it's a stomping-ground for street-smart young folk who meet in restored pubs and eat in cool cafes. Chinatown is here, too. Take Turbot Street, then Wickham Street, to "the Valley's" main drag, Brunswick Street. Many buses depart from City Hall for the Valley; or take the train to "Fortitude Valley" station.

New Farm   This posh residential suburb is fast becoming the city's hip destination for cafe-hopping, shopping, and cinema-going. Merthyr Street is where most of the action is, especially on Friday and Saturday nights. It's embryonic, but getting bigger all the time. From the intersection of Wickham and Brunswick streets, follow Brunswick southeast for 13 blocks to Merthyr; or take bus 190 or 191.

Paddington   If you think this hilltop suburb a couple of miles west of the city is the prettiest in Brisbane, you are in good company. Quaint, brightly painted Queenslander cottages line the main street, Given Terrace, which becomes Latrobe Terrace as it winds west along a ridge top. Many of the houses have been turned into inviting shops and cafes, and the street is never empty of people browsing for antiques, lapping up coffee and cake, or just strolling the streets to admire the architecture. Take bus 374 or 375.

Park Road   A street rather than a neighborhood, this commercial-district avenue in Milton, a few miles west of town, is the city's unofficial Italian quarter. It buzzes with white-collar office workers who quaff alfresco cappuccinos, scout interior-design stores, and stock up on European designer rags. Take the train to Milton station, or it's an easy 30-minute riverside walk along North Quay and Coronation Drive.

West End   This small inner-city enclave, located the next suburb southwest from South Bank, is alive with ethnic restaurants, alternative cafes, and quirky houseware and fashion stores. Most action is at the intersection of Vulture and Boundary streets. Take bus 190 or 191.

2 Getting Around

BY PUBLIC TRANSPORTATION

For questions about bus, train, and ferry timetables and routes as far afield as the Sunshine and Gold Coasts, call **Transinfo** (☎ **13 12 30** in Queensland). Bus and ferry timetables, route maps, single tickets, and passes are available at **Brisbane Transport** outlets (most convenient are the **Brisbane Administration Centre,** downstairs at 69 Ann St., and on Level A in the **Myer Centre,** 91 Queen Street Mall). Train timetables are available at the station.

A single sector or zone on the bus or ferry costs A$1.40 (U.S.90¢), and A$1.50 (U.S.$1) on the train. You may transfer from one bus or ferry route to another, or from bus to ferry and vice versa, within the same zone, within a 2-hour period, without having to buy another ticket. Children under 5 travel free on trains, buses, and ferries, while 5- to 15-year-olds pay half fare. Seniors and students not resident in Australia pay full fare.

MONEY-SAVING PASSES   Day Rover passes cost A$7 (U.S.$4.55) for 1 day's unlimited travel on both buses and ferries, or $8.50 (U.S.$5.55) for 1 day's unlimited travel on the suburban train network. Apart from the Australian Woolshed, most attractions are not on the train lines. On weekends and public holidays, it's cheaper to buy an **Off-Peak Saver pass,** which lets you travel on buses and ferries all day for A$4 (U.S.$2.60). Weekly passes and Ten Trip Saver tickets are also available.

On **weekends and public holidays,** round-trip CityTrain suburban train fares drop to the price of a single ticket.

You can buy all tickets and passes at Brisbane Transport outlets listed above; you can buy single tickets, Day Rover passes, and Off-Peak Saver passes on the bus; on the ferry you can buy only single ferry tickets; and you can buy single train tickets and Day Rover train passes at the train station. Any of 300 news agencies displaying a yellow-and-white BUS & FERRY TICKETS SOLD HERE banner sells bus/ferry passes. Check out the excellent ✪ **City Sights bus tour,** described under "Bus Tours" in the "Exploring Brisbane" section, later in this chapter; it entitles you to unlimited travel on buses and ferries for the day.

BY BUS   Most buses depart from City Hall at King George Square at Adelaide Street. Many are wheelchair accessible. They operate from around 5am or 6am to 11pm weekdays, sometimes with fewer services on weekends, especially on Sunday, when many routes stop around 5pm. Look for the blue-and-white stops. A ticket costs A70¢ (U.S.50¢).

From Monday to Friday (excepting public holidays) from 7am to 5:40pm, the smart way to get around the city center is aboard the **City Circle bus 333,** which does a loop every 5, 10, or 20 minutes around Roma Street, Wickham Terrace, Wharf Street, up Ann Street, along North Quay, down Adelaide Street, along Eagle Street, and then Mary and Albert streets.

Brisbane

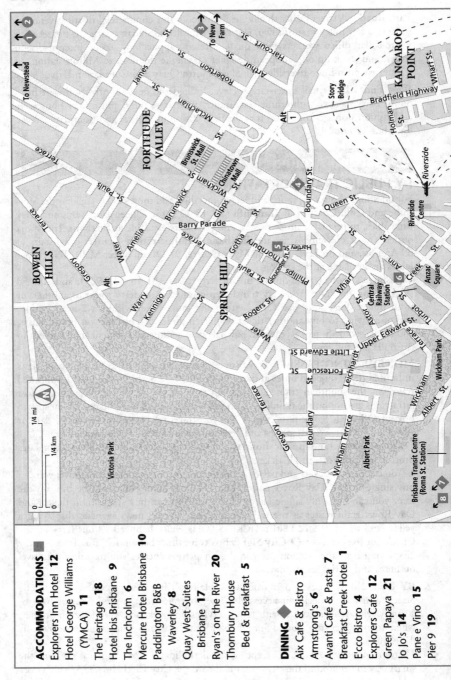

ACCOMMODATIONS
Explorers Inn Hotel **12**
Hotel George Williams
(YMCA) **11**
The Heritage **18**
Hotel Ibis Brisbane **9**
The Inchcolm **6**
Mercure Hotel Brisbane **10**
Paddington B&B
Waverley **8**
Quay West Suites
Brisbane **17**
Ryan's on the River **20**
Thornbury House
Bed & Breakfast **5**

DINING
Aix Cafe & Bistro **3**
Armstrong's **6**
Avanti Cafe & Pasta **7**
Breakfast Creek Hotel **1**
E'cco Bistro **4**
Explorers Cafe **12**
Green Papaya **21**
Jo Jo's **14**
Pane e Vino **15**
Pier 9 **19**

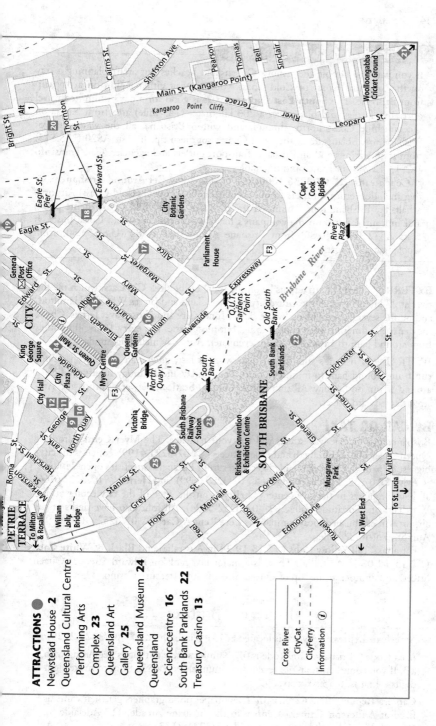

ATTRACTIONS ●

Newstead House **2**
Queensland Cultural Centre
    Performing Arts
    Complex **23**
    Queensland Art
    Gallery **25**
    Queensland Museum **24**
    Queensland
    Sciencecentre **16**
South Bank Parklands **22**
Treasury Casino **13**

Cross River ——
CityCat - - - -
CityFerry - - - -
Information ⓘ

233

Hitting Brisbane and the Beaches

If you want to sample the famous Queensland beaches but aren't planning a stay on the Sunshine Coast or Gold Coast, you can visit either region on a day trip from Brisbane. The **South East Explorer pass** is good for a day's unlimited travel on trains, ferries, and buses over a 206-kilometer (129-mile) area from Noosa on the Sunshine Coast north, through and within Brisbane, all the way south of Brisbane to Coolangatta at the Gold Coast's southern tip. It costs A\$20 (U.S.\$13) from train stations and all Brisbane Transport outlets and agencies. Call **Transinfo** (☎ **13 12 30**) for routes and timetables.

Coachtrans (☎ **07/3236 1000**) sells a 3- to 4-day **Get Around Brisbane** pass that includes return transfers from Brisbane or Coolangatta (Gold Coast) Airports, a half-day Brisbane tour, unlimited travel to five major Gold Coast theme parks, and unlimited travel on the company's many daily Brisbane–Gold Coast buses. It costs A\$72 (U.S.\$46.80) from Brisbane Airport and A\$82 (U.S.\$53.30) from Coolangatta Airport.

BY FERRY   Plenty of attractions lie on the route of the sleek **CityCats,** which ply the river at 27 knots between the University of Queensland and Brett's Wharf at Hamilton, and on the several routes made by the slower Inner City and Cross River ferries. Check the departure times for your chosen route, but most ferries run every 10 to 30 minutes from around 6am to around 11pm, or even later, every day including Sunday.

BY TRAIN   Brisbane's suburban rail network is fast, quiet, safe, and clean. Trains run from around 5am to midnight, until 1am Friday and Saturday nights, and until around 11pm on Sunday. All trains leave **Central Station,** between Turbot and Ann streets at Edward Street.

BY CAR OR TAXI

Brisbane's grid of one-way streets will test your patience. The **Myer Centre,** fronting Queen Street Mall at Elizabeth and Albert streets (☎ **07/3221 4199**), contains the city's biggest carpark and has reasonable rates; enter from Elizabeth Street. It's open 24 hours.

Avis (☎ 07/3221 2900), **Budget** (☎ 07/3220 0699), and **Hertz** (☎ 07/3221 6166) all have branches in the city center. **Thrifty** is on the edge of the city center at 325 Wickham St., Fortitude Valley (☎ 07/3252 5994). All four also have desks at the airport. An established local company is **Letz Rent A Car** (☎ 07/3252 4811) at 925 Ann St., Fortitude Valley.

For a taxi, call **Yellow Cabs** (☎ **13 19 24** in Australia) and **Black & White Cabs** (☎ **13 10 08** in Australia). There is a major taxi rank on Edward Street at Queen Street, and another at the top of Queen Street by the Treasury Casino.

Fast Facts: Brisbane

American Express   AMEX is located at 131 Elizabeth St. (☎ **07/3229 2729**).

Area Code   Brisbane's area code is 07. Numbers are eight digits beginning with a 3. If you come across an old seven-digit number, pop a 3 in front to make eight digits—that is, 07/3xxx xxxx.

Camera Repair   The *Courier-Mail* newspaper photographers get their cameras fixed at **Anderson Camera Centre,** in the Brisbane Arcade, 117 Adelaide St. between Edward and Albert streets (☎ **07/3221 3133**).

Consulates   The United States, Canada, Ireland, and New Zealand have no representation in Brisbane. The **British Consul General** is at Level 26, Waterfront Place, 1 Eagle St. (☎ **07/3223 3200**).

Currency Exchange   Travelex, Lennons Plaza, Queen Street Mall between Albert and George streets (☎ **07/3229 8610**), is open Monday to Friday from 9am to 6pm, Saturday from 9:30am to 5pm, and Sunday from 10:30am to 4pm.

Dentist   The Adelaide and Albert Street Dental Centre (☎ **07/3229 4121**), located at Travellers Medical Service (see "Doctor," below), is open Monday to Friday 8am to 6pm and is on call 24 hours.

Doctor   Travellers Medical Service is located on the second floor, 245 Albert St. at Adelaide Street diagonally opposite City Hall (☎ **07/3211 3611**). It's open Monday to Friday 7:30am to 7pm, Saturday 9am to 5pm, and Sunday 10am to 4pm; doctors are on call for home visits 24 hours.

Emergencies   Dial ☎ **000** for fire, ambulance, or police help in an emergency. This is a free call from a private or public telephone and needs no coins.

Eyeglass Repair   OPSM in the Myer Centre, 91 Queen Street Mall (☎ **07/ 3229 2913**), and also in the Wintergarden complex, is a reputable chain retailer and repairer of eyeglasses.

Hospitals   Royal Brisbane Hospital, about a 15-minute drive from the city center at Herston Road, Herston (☎ **07/3636 8111**), has an emergency room.

Internet Access   Internet cafe **Café Escape** (☎ **07/3210 6671**) is on the second floor at 43 Queen Street Mall.

Luggage Storage/Lockers   Lockers cost A$2 (U.S.$1.30) on Level A in the **Myer Centre,** 91 Queen Street Mall (☎ **07/3221 4199**). The **Brisbane Transit Centre** on Roma Street also has suitcase-sized lockers for $5 per 24 hours.

Newspapers/Magazines   *The Courier-Mail* (Mon through Sat) and the *Sunday-Mail* are Brisbane's daily newspapers.

Pharmacies   The **T&G Day & Night Pharmacy,** Queen Street Mall near Albert Street (☎ **07/3221 4585**), is open Monday through Friday 7:30am to 9pm, Saturday 8am to 9pm, and Sunday 9:30am to 5:30pm.

Police   Dial ☎ **000** in an emergency, or police headquarters (☎ **07/3364 6464**); this is a free call from all private and public telephones. Police are stationed beside the Brisbane Tourism information booth on Queen Street Mall at Albert Street 24 hours (☎ **07/3220 0752**).

Safety   Brisbane is relatively crime free, but groups of kids have been known to attempt muggings in lonely areas late at night. Stick to well-lit streets and busy precincts.

Tax   A nationwide goods and services tax (GST) of 10% applies to most items, including restaurant meals, tours, and accommodation. Brisbane has no separate hotel tax.

Time Zone   Brisbane is GMT plus 10 hours. It does not observe daylight savings time, which means it's on the same time as Sydney and Melbourne in winter, and 1 hour behind those cities from October to March, when they go to daylight savings. For the exact local time, call ☎ **1194.**

3 Accommodations

Brisbane has not only some lovely one-of-a-kind five-star hotels and serviced apartments, but also charming B&Bs in gracious Queenslander houses, holiday apartments near the city, and some smart little midtown hotels at the low-priced end of the scale. The city center is the most convenient place to stay; but because Spring Hill is just a few blocks (uphill) from the city center, it almost counts as downtown, and Paddington is a short bus or cab ride away. To stay at Kangaroo Point, drive or bus less than 2 kilometers (1¼ miles) over the Story Bridge, or take one of the cross-river ferries (trip time: 3 min.) that depart every 10 or 15 minutes from 5:30am until midnight.

Don't forget to ask about packages at city hotels, especially on weekends, when the business travelers have all gone home. Such deals often offer a remarkable value.

IN THE CITY CENTER
VERY EXPENSIVE

The Heritage. Edward St. (between Margaret and Alice sts.), Brisbane, QLD 4000. ☎ **1800/773 700** in Australia, or 07/3221 1999. Fax 07/3221 6895. www.beaufort-hotels. com/brisbane. E-mail: reservations@theheritage.com.au. 252 units. A/C MINIBAR TV TEL. A$418 (U.S.$271.70) double, A$638–$3,080 (U.S.$414.70–$2,002) suite. Extra person A$39 (U.S.$25.35). Children under 13 stay free with existing bedding. Ask about packages. AE, BC, DC, JCB, MC, V. Free valet parking. Airport shuttle. Train: Central, then taxi or walk 6 blocks. Bus: City Circle 333. Ferry: Edward St.

The historic Heritage is one of Brisbane's most beautiful hotels; its marble lobby is dotted with brocade loungers, enormous still-life oils, gilt mirrors, and palms. It's also one of the few city hotels to have river views from every room—especially stunning at night from the southern rooms when the Story Bridge lights up. The plush rooms are not enormous, but all fit a king-size bed (or twins), have modem and fax lines, and offer free and pay-per-view movies. What must be the biggest bathrooms in Brisbane sport small TVs to watch from the tub. A riverside boardwalk leads from the hotel to the Eagle Street Pier restaurants on one side, and the Botanic Gardens abut the hotel on the other. Queen Street Mall is an easy 6-block walk.

Dining/Diversions: Siggi's, in a historic sandstone building, is one of Brisbane's grandest fine-dining restaurants; Kabuki serves teppanyaki; and the alfresco Brasserie does all-day dining riverside. You can order cigars with your cognac in Siggi's Wine Bar; a pianist plays nightly in the lobby lounge, and the courtyard Pavilion Bar is a hit with the Friday after-work crowd.

Amenities: Smallish outdoor heated lap pool and sundeck, Jacuzzi, sauna, gym, jogging track in adjacent Botanic Gardens, 24-hour butler service on every floor, concierge, nightly turndown, 24-hour room service, complimentary newspaper, babysitting, beauty salon/hairdresser, boutiques and convenience store, tour and car-rental desk, currency exchange, business center, conference facilities.

✪ **Quay West Suites Brisbane.** 132 Alice St. (between Albert and George sts.), Brisbane, QLD 4000. ☎ **1800/672 726** or 07/3853 6000. Fax 07/3853 6060. www.mirvachotels. com.au. E-mail: reservationqwb@mirvachotels.com.au. 96 units. A/C MINIBAR TV TEL. A$317–$338 (U.S.$206.05–$219.70) 1-bedroom apt; A$370–A$490 (U.S.$240.50–$318.50) 2-bedroom apt. Extra person A$30 (U.S.$19.50). Ask about weekend and other packages. AE, BC, DC, JCB, MC, V. Valet A$8 (U.S.$5.20); no self-parking. Airport shuttle. Bus: City Circle 333. Ferry: Edward St. (CityFerry and Cross River Ferry); or Riverside (CityCat), then a 10-minute walk.

My husband stays at these stylish serviced apartments whenever he visits Brisbane, not because they have all the amenities of a five-star hotel, but for the staff's down-to-earth friendliness. Their Queensland-meets-Mediterranean elegance is to die for. Each has a laundry, a dining area, one or two separate bedrooms, a granite-top kitchen, bathrooms with Siena marble countertops, two TVs, a stereo, pay-per-view movies, bathrobes, a hair dryer, and a big terra-cotta balcony overlooking the City Botanic Gardens across the road. Style devotees with a sense of vamp will like the plunge-pool flanked by stone rams, and the sandstone pavilion over the Jacuzzi. You're 4 blocks from Queen Street Mall and close to the river.

Dining/Diversions: McMahon's restaurant does casually sophisticated fare inside or in the leafy Italian-style terrace; Fraser's is the small lobby bar.

Amenities: 24-hour room service, concierge, gym overlooking the heated outdoor plunge pool, sundeck, sauna, jogging tracks in the Botanic Gardens, dry cleaning/laundry, shoeshine, complimentary newspaper, secretarial services, babysitting, tour and car-rental desk, small conference rooms, business center, safes.

EXPENSIVE

Mercure Hotel Brisbane. 85–87 North Quay (between Ann and Turbot sts.), Brisbane, QLD 4000. ☎ **1300/65 6565** in Australia, 800/221-4542 in the U.S. and Canada, 020/8283 4500 in the U.K., 0800/44 4422 in New Zealand, or 07/3236 3300. Fax 07/3236 1035. www.hotelweb.fr. E-mail: res@mercurehotelbrisbane.com.au. 194 units. A/C MINIBAR TV TEL. A$185–$196 (U.S.$120.25–$127.40) double, A$201 (U.S.$130.65) studio suite, A$229 (U.S.$148.85) executive suite. Extra person A$22 (U.S.$14.30). Children under 16 stay free in parents' room with existing bedding. Ask about packages. AE, BC, DC, JCB, MC, V. Discounted parking approx. A$8.50 (U.S.$5.55) per day midweek, A$5 (U.S.$3.25) weekends for limited number of cars in Kings carpark adjacent to hotel. Airport shuttle. Train: Roma St. Bus: City Circle 333. Ferry: North Quay (CityCat and CityFerry).

Sweeping views of the Brisbane River come with many of the rooms at this bright little 14-story hotel across the water from South Bank. Renovated in 1998, the compact rooms are not grand, but they get down to business with comfortable, unassuming furniture and new bathrooms with hair dryers and plenty of counter space. Rooms without water views have nice city outlooks. Roma St. Transit Centre, Queen Street Mall, South Bank Parklands, and Queensland Cultural Centre are a walk away.

Dining/Diversions: Quays is a sunny, contemporary restaurant serving breakfast, lunch, and dinner. The large, slightly shabby bar is awaiting a refurb but has great freeway/river views.

Amenities: Small outdoor pool and sundeck, sauna, Jacuzzi, 24-hour room service, complimentary newspapers, tour desk, conference facilities. The YMCA gym is just behind the hotel.

MODERATE

Hotel Ibis Brisbane. 27–35 Turbot St. (between North Quay and George St.), Brisbane, QLD 4000. ☎ **1300/65 6565** in Australia, 800/221-4542 in the U.S. and Canada, 020/8283 4500 in the U.K., 0800/44 4422 in New Zealand, or 07/3237 2333. Fax 07/3237 2444. www.hotelweb.fr. E-mail: res@ibisbrisbane.com.au. 218 units. A/C TV TEL. A$174 (U.S.$113.10) double. Extra person A$22 (U.S.$14.30). Children under 16 stay free in parents' room with existing bedding. Ask about packages. AE, BC, DC, JCB, MC, V. Parking A$5–A$12 (U.S.$3.25–$7.80) in Queensland Place open-air public carpark 1 block away (enter off Roma St.) or use Mercure Hotel Brisbane's parking arrangements (see above). Airport shuttle. Train: Roma St. Bus: City Circle 333. Ferry: North Quay (CityCat and CityFerry).

Rooms at this sister property to the Mercure just around the corner (see above) are bigger than the Mercure's, so they're a good value if you don't mind doing without a few of its slightly ritzier sibling's amenities—no river vistas, no porters, no minibar, no pool. Rebuilt inside a gutted building in 1998, the rooms are almost new, furnished in a contemporary decor, with irons, sizable work desks, and small but smart bathrooms that have hair dryers. Maintenance standards could be better (my room had marks on the wall and carpet lifting at the edge), but the fittings are a decent quality. Among the amenities are limited room service, laundry/dry cleaning, currency exchange, and fax/photocopy services.

✪ **The Inchcolm.** 73 Wickham Terrace (next to the Novotel), Brisbane, QLD 4000. ☎ **13 2400** in Australia, 1877/444 3524 in the U.S. and Canada, 0800/892 407 in the U.K., 1800/554 952 in Ireland, 0800/803 524 in New Zealand, or 07/3226 8888. Fax 07/ 3226 8899. www.inchcolmhotel.com.au. Email: info@inchcolmhotel.com.au. 35 units (some with shower only, some with Jacuzzis). A/C MINIBAR TV TEL. A$110–$143 (U.S.$71.50–$92.95) double, A$130–$173 (U.S.$84.50–$112.45) 1- and 2-bedroom apt. Extra person A$10 (U.S.$6.50). AE, BC, DC, MC, V. Free valet parking for 14 cars. Airport shuttle. Train: Central. Bus: City Circle 333.

Housed in a one-time doctors' chambers in Brisbane's "medico row," this heritage-listed Flag hotel is one of the best values in Brisbane. It was renovated in 1999, fitted out with modern extras like French fabrics, original artworks, firm beds, new bathrooms, kitchenettes, desks, laptop outlets, iron and boards, hair dryers, and free in-room movies. It still retains many of its gracious old features, like rare silky oak paneling, big picture windows, and a caged elevator. It pulls guests from five-star hotels nearby who like the boutique ambience and the personal service from the friendly managers, Dave and Carol Barry. Each accommodation has an individual configuration—some are one big room, others have separate bedrooms. There are secretarial and dry-cleaning/laundry services weekdays, and the magnificent Armstrong's (see "Dining," below) does room service. There are no porters.

Up on the third floor is a cute bonsai version of a pool too small to do anything but dip in, but the little sundeck is a great perch from which to admire the leafy city views. Queen Street Mall is a 5-minute downhill walk.

The Sebel of Brisbane. Albert St. at Charlotte St., Brisbane, QLD 4000. ☎ **1800/888 298** in Australia, or 07/3224 3500. Fax 07/3211 0277. www.mirvachotels.com.au. E-mail: ressob@ mirvachotels.com.au. 190 units. A/C MINIBAR TV TEL. A$110–$125 (U.S.$71.50–$81.25) studio; A$145–$160 (U.S.$94.25–$104) 1-bedroom suite; A$200–$230 (U.S.$130–$149.50) 2-bedroom suite. Extra person A$25 (U.S.$16.25). Children under 14 stay free in parents' room with existing bedding. Ask about packages. AE, BC, DC, JCB, MC, V. Valet parking A$8 (U.S.$5.20); no self-parking. Airport shuttle. Train: Central. Bus: City Circle 333.

A studio at this 30-story "suite hotel" is just as big as a standard hotel room (the one-bedroom suites are even bigger), *and* you get extras like a kitchenette or full kitchen with dishwasher and microwave (and a washer/dryer in suites), bathrobes, Nintendo, instant Internet connections, voice mail, and a modish decor with loads of light. The Sebel was built in May 1999, just a block from Queen Street Mall. Rooms begin at the sixth floor, so all offer some kind of view from the furnished balcony, whether of the city, the Botanic Gardens, and/or the river and its prettily illuminated sandstone cliffs. All have windows that open, irons, pay-per-view movies, and hair dryers; bedroom suites have a second TV in the bedroom and a CD player.

Palette's is a casually minimalist restaurant/bar on-site; it offers quick modern cuisine and cafe fare, open all day. The intersection outside buzzes with more smart, inexpensive cafes of the same ilk. There's a small heated lap pool with a petite sundeck overlooking the city, plus a small children's pool, a sauna, a small gym (with a personal fitness trainer by arrangement), 24-hour room service, dry cleaning/laundry, conference facilities, and currency exchange.

INEXPENSIVE

✪ **Explorers Inn Hotel.** 63 Turbot St. (near George St.), Brisbane, QLD 4000. ☎ **1800/ 62 3288** in Australia, or 07/3211 3488. Fax 07/3211 3499. www.powerup.com.au/~explorer.

E-mail: explorer@powerup.com.au. 58 units (all with shower only). A/C TV TEL. A$75.90–$97.90 (U.S.$49.35–$63.65) double, A$97.90 (U.S.$63.65) family. AE, BC, DC, MC, V. Parking A$5–A$12 (U.S.$3.25–$7.80) per day in Queensland Place open-air public carpark across the road (enter off Roma St.). Airport shuttle. Train: Roma St. Bus: City Circle 333. Ferry: North Quay (CityCat and CityFerry).

You'll be floored when you see such spruce decor and terrific value in one place— and in the heart of town, too! Each tiny but shipshape room at this former YWCA was designed by its architect owners to contain a narrow slip of desk, a minifridge, individually controlled air-conditioning, and a bathroom not much bigger than the shower cubicle it holds. The front desk lends hair dryers. South Bank, the casino, the Roma Street Transit Centre, and Queen Street Mall are all close by, and the friendly staff is on hand 24 hours to help with booking tours and sending e-mails.

○ **Hotel George Williams (YMCA).** 317–325 George St. (between Turbot and Ann sts.), Brisbane, QLD 4000. ☎ **1800/064 858** or 07/3308 0700. Fax 07/3308 0733. 42 units (some with shower only). www.ymca.org.au. E-mail: hgw@ymca.org.au. A/C TV TEL. A$99 (U.S.$64.35) double. Extra person A$17 (U.S.$11.05). Children under 4 stay free in parents' room. Free crib. Ask about packages. AE, BC, DC, MC, V. Limited free parking; adjacent open-air parking approx. $6 per day. Airport shuttle. Train: Roma St. Bus: City Circle 333. Ferry: North Quay (CityCat and CityFerry).

It's hard to believe this groovy joint is a YMCA. Your room looks like it belongs in an interior-design magazine, with vivid bedcovers, chrome chairs, and artsy bedside lamps on chrome stands, and the place has an air of refined privacy. Units are small, but each has a minuscule bathroom, a wardrobe, a minifridge, a hair dryer, and self-serve tea and coffee. Among the amenities are a 24-hour front desk, safe-deposit boxes, free use of the YMCA gym downstairs, and a hip cafe serving cheap nosh. You're around the corner from the Explorers Inn Hotel, above.

○ **Thornbury House Bed & Breakfast.** 1 Thornbury St., Spring Hill, Brisbane, QLD 4000. ☎ **07/3832 5985.** Fax 07/3832 7255. www.babs.com.au/thornbury.htm. E-mail: thornburyhouse@primus.com.au. 6 units (all with bathroom, 5 with shower only). TV. A$99 (U.S.$64.35) double. A$420 (U.S.$273) apt weekly. Rates include full breakfast. AE, BC, MC, V. Free parking in vacant lot across street; metered on-street parking. Airport shuttle. Train: Central.

A 15-minute walk to nearby Spring Hill from the city center brings you to this charming 1886 Queenslander cottage on a quiet street in this semi-commercial area. Hostess Michelle Bugler has decked out every room individually with Oriental rugs, comfortable beds, bathrobes, hair dryers, and lovely old furniture and knickknacks. One has a tub and is air-conditioned. Those without en suite bathrooms have their own pretty, impeccably clean private bathrooms down the hall. Downstairs is a self-contained apartment with contemporary decor. Michelle serves a scrumptious breakfast in the ferny courtyard, a cool and restful place to be on a humid Brisbane day, where you can help yourself to tea, coffee, cookies, and the newspaper all day long. Guests may use Michelle's microwave and laundry, and there's a pay phone in the hall. No smoking indoors.

IN KANGAROO POINT

Ryan's on the River. 269 Main St. (at Scott St.), Kangaroo Point, Brisbane, QLD 4169. ☎ **07/3391 1011.** Fax 07/3391 1824. www.ryans.com.au. E-mail: reservations@ryans.com.au. 24 units (all with shower only). A/C TV TEL. A$99–$149 (U.S.$64.35–$96.85) double. Rates include continental breakfast. Extra person A$10 (U.S.$6.50). AE, BC, DC, MC, V. Free parking. Airport shuttle. Ferry: Thornton St. from Edward St. or Eagle Street Pier (Cross River Ferry); the ferry makes the 3-min. crossing to the city every 10–15 min. 5:30am–midnight.

Its small-scale ambience and river/city views from every room make this hotel a great value. Rooms on the south have partial city and water views, those on the north are quieter and have great views of the city and Story Bridge (which lights up beautifully at night), while those on the west get the Full Monty, a superb river and city vista that must be the envy of every five-star hotel in Brisbane. Renovated in 1998, the rooms are big, light, and comfortable, with modern bathrooms, hair dryers, and balconies. The ferry stop is right outside, and a riverside pedestrian/bike path traces the opposite bank from the city all the way to South Bank Parklands. Breakfast is served up with those wonderful city views out by the small saltwater pool.

IN PADDINGTON

✪ **Paddington B&B Waverley.** 5 Latrobe Terrace at Cochrane St., Paddington, Brisbane, QLD 4064. ☎ **07/3369 8973** or 0419/74 1282 mobile. Fax 07/3876 6655. www.babs. com.au/paddington. 4 units (all with shower only; tub available in the additional shared bathroom). TV. A$99 (U.S.$64.35) double. A$418 apt (U.S.$271.70) weekly. Extra person A$20 (U.S.$13). Rates for regular rooms (not apts) include full breakfast. AE, BC, DC, MC, V. Free parking. Bus: 374, 375.

Right on the lively shopping strip in trendy Paddington, this three-story 1888 Queenslander house was beautifully renovated in 1995 as a B&B. It retains most of its original features: tongue-in-groove walls, high ceilings, and polished timber floors. Your delightfully friendly hostess, Annette Henry, has decorated the big air-conditioned rooms in great style, with chiropractic mattresses, pretty prints and quilts, and attractive modern bathrooms with hair dryers. You can also stay in two self-contained apartments downstairs. She cooks a hearty breakfast (ask for her bacon and corn muffins) and encourages guests to use her cozy lounge and fireplace, and the lofty rear deck where rainbow lorikeets can be heard frolicking in the mango trees. Facilities include a laundry and a pay phone. No smoking indoors.

4 Dining

Visitors—even Sydneysiders and Melbournites—are surprised to find Brisbane has a sophisticated dining scene. Stylish bistros and cafes are beginning to line Merthyr Street in New Farm; cute cafes are plentiful in Paddington; Asian eateries are a good budget choice around the intersection of Vulture Street and Boundary Street in West End; and in Fortitude Valley ("the Valley" for short), you'll find Chinatown. There's a streetful of upscale but laid-back restaurants on Park Road in Milton, many with a Mediterranean flavor, and in town you can find slick riverfront restaurants at Eagle Street Pier and Riverside. The intersection of Albert and Charlotte streets buzzes with inexpensive, good-quality cafes.

IN THE CITY CENTER
EXPENSIVE

✪ **Armstrong's.** In the Inchcolm Hotel, 73 Wickham Terrace (next to the Novotel). ☎ **07/3832 4566.** Reservations recommended. Main courses A$19.50–$28 (U.S.$12.70– $18.20); midsize meals A$15–$19.50 (U.S.$9.75–$12.70). AE, BC, DC, MC, V. Mon–Fri 7–9:30am and noon–2:30pm; Sat–Sun 7:30–10am; Mon–Sat 6pm–late. MODERN AUSTRALIAN.

From this chic spot in a National Trust–classified hotel, chef Russell Armstrong serves exquisite fare—try his ballantine of Barossa chicken and sand crab on green and blond asparagus with champagne broth, or a barbecued fillet of reef fish and Japanese eel on warm rice wakami salad with lime wasabi mayonnaise. And save room for dessert. Other chefs say Russell is the best chef in Brisbane, and the local food critics seem to agree. The restaurant seats just 40, so it's very intimate and quite formal. Smoking in the bar only.

✪ **e'cco bistro.** 100 Boundary St. (at Adelaide St.). ☎ **07/3831 8344.** Reservations required. Main courses A$23.50–$24.50 (U.S.$15.30–$15.95). AE, BC, DC, MC, V. Tues–Fri noon–2:30pm; Tues–Sat 6–10:30pm. Also open Mon Nov–Christmas. Closed Christmas until 2nd week of Jan. MODERN AUSTRALIAN.

A former winner of Australia's top restaurant award (the Remy Martin Cognac/Gourmet Traveller Restaurant of the Year), this buzzing bistro is famous for simple food done well. That may be a warm salad of prawn, fennel, grain mustard, chili, and lime oil for starters, followed by lamb cutlets with black olive and herb mash, English spinach, and balsamic roasted red onion. The restaurant is housed in a 76-year-old tea warehouse on the city fringe, renovated with bold colors, clean-lined timber seats, and lots of light. It sells wine, but you can BYO wine for a corkage fee of $4 per bottle.

Pier Nine. Eagle Street Pier, 1 Eagle St. ☎ **07/3229 2194.** Reservations recommended. Main courses A$20–$40 (U.S.$13–$26). AE, BC, DC, JCB, MC, V. Daily 11:30am–10pm; supper daily 10–11pm. Bus: City Circle 333. Ferry: Riverside (CityCat); Edward St. or Riverside (CityFerry); Eagle Street Pier (Cross River Ferry). MODERN AUSTRALIAN SEAFOOD.

Ask a Brisbanite for the best seafood restaurant in town, and this light-filled contemporary restaurant overlooking the river and Story Bridge is where they'll send you. Fresh local Moreton Bay bugs (a kind of crustacean) and oysters shucked to order and done any of five ways (say, with a green mango, cucumber, and tomato salad plus gin and lime dressing) are specialties; so is Atlantic salmon (from Tasmania), which might be done with caramelized asparagus and artichoke hearts and raspberry balsamic glaze. It's always busy, so prepare to cool your heels at the oyster bar if you turn up without a reservation.

MODERATE

Jo Jo's. On the 2nd floor, Queen Street Mall at Albert St. ☎ **07/3221 2113.** Reservations not needed. Main courses A$7–$19 (U.S.$4.55–$12.35). AE, BC, DC, MC, V. Daily 9:30am–late. Happy Hour daily 4:30–6pm. INTERNATIONAL/CAFE FARE.

Three different menus—char-grill, Thai, and Mediterranean—are on offer at this unpretentious spot overlooking the mall. Locals have been dropping in here for years to take a shopping pit stop, or to eat after the cinema, because the food is well-priced and good. Char-grilled grain-fed rib fillet, Thai prawns with chili and basil, fettuccine with spinach, pine nuts and chicken, and gourmet sandwiches are some of your options. The wine list is only so-so, but prices are reasonable.

Pane e Vino. Albert St. at Charlotte St. ☎ **07/3220 0044.** Reservations recommended at lunch. Main courses A$11.90–$19.90 (U.S.$7.75–$12.95); foccacias and panini A$7–$8.50 (U.S.$4.55–$5.55); breakfast A$1.50–$8.90 (U.S.$1–$5.80). AE, BC, DC, MC, V. Sun–Thurs 7:30am–10pm, Fri–Sat 7:30am–11:30pm. Bus: City Circle 333. MODERN ITALIAN/CAFE FARE.

A laid-back attitude attracts cool java drinkers and a higher-powered corporate lunch set to this contemporary open-sided cafe on a busy street corner. Sit inside in the modish decor of polished concrete floors and sleek timber, or choose a sidewalk table. The simple but sophisticated all-day menu boasts things like grilled King schnapper on creamed zucchini with tomato, olive, and basil butter sauce. There's also a wide variety of lighter risottos and pastas, huge focaccias and tasty panini (say, prosciutto, mushroom, onion, and provolone). Fry-ups, omelets, and "door stops" are served at breakfast.

INEXPENSIVE

Explorers Café. 63 Turbot St. (near the corner of George St.). ☎ **07/3211 3488.** Reservations recommended at lunch. Main courses A$9.90–$16.90 (U.S.$6.45–$11) dinner, A$5.50–$13.90 (U.S.$3.60–$9) lunch, A$1–$9.90 (U.S.65¢–$6.45) breakfast. AE, BC, DC, MC, V. Daily 7–9:30am and 6–8pm; Mon–Fri noon–2pm; open for coffee all day. Happy Hour Mon–Fri 5–6pm. Train: Roma St. Bus: City Circle 333. INTERNATIONAL.

What a find! you'll think as you stumble upon this basement restaurant under the Explorers Inn Hotel. Breakfasts like cereal and juice can be had for a couple of dollars, and decent lunches like a seafood basket with fries and salad cost A$9.90 (U.S.$6.45). City office workers think the place is a find, too, so book in the morning to get ahead of them for lunch. At night the meals get a bit beefier—chicken satay, rib fillet, and the like. The ambience is warm and dignified for such a low-cost joint, with exposed brick walls, potted palms, trendy sisal matting, and a cool corrugated iron bar. Note the kitchen closes early at night.

IN EAST BRISBANE

✪ **Green Papaya.** 898 Stanley St. (at Potts St.), East Brisbane. ☎ **07/3217 3599.** Reservations recommended. Main courses A$10–$25 (U.S.$6.50–$16.25); average A$16 (U.S.$10.40). Set 4-course menus A$28–$33 (U.S.$18.20–$21.45). AE, BC, DC, MC, V. Tues–Sun 6–10pm. Closed Christmas–early Jan. Located on the river's south bank, one suburb southeast of Kangaroo Point, a 10-min. drive from town and 1 block from the Wolloongabba Cricket Ground. NORTH VIETNAMESE.

A large and loyal horde of followers descends upon the two bright yellow-and-blue rooms here for simple, exquisitely delicate dishes made of ultrafresh ingredients assembled by chef/proprietress Lien Yeomans. If you don't know your Bo Cay Ngot (spicy beef) from your Nom Du Du (green papaya salad), the staff willingly deciphers the menu. They do takeout also. Licensed and BYO bottled wine only (no beer or spirits).

IN NEW FARM

Aix Café + Bistro. 83 Merthyr Rd. ☎ **07/3358 6444.** Reservations recommended on weekends. Main courses A$9.50–$16.50 (U.S.$6.20–$10.75); sandwiches and light meals from A$4.90 (U.S.$3.20). AE, BC, DC, MC, V (min. charge A$20 (U.S.$13). Daily 7am–midnight. Bus: 190. MODERN AUSTRALIAN CAFE/BISTRO.

Chic decor, affordable dishes, and a "drop in anytime" atmosphere attract a wide range of locals to this open-fronted eatery and bar on New Farm's hip strip. Chef Michel Thompson turns out dishes with flair and fresh ingredients, whether it's an herb-coated loin of lamb with Italian roast vegetable salad, mint pesto, and red wine jus, or

A Pub with Grub

There's no better place to meet the locals than at the **Breakfast Creek Hotel,** 2 Kingsford Smith Dr. (at Breakfast Creek Road), in Albion (☎ 07/3262 5988), an ornate gabled National Trust–listed pub overlooking the river. Order a XXXX ("Fourex") beer pulled "off the wood" (from the keg); take a seat in the beer garden on plastic seats under umbrellas; and choose from affordable steaks, chicken, and fish off the blackboard menu, all uniformly served with mushroom or chili sauce, an Idaho potato with bacon sauce, and coleslaw. Be prepared for big crowds on footy nights. There's a band on Sunday afternoons. (*Tip:* Wear thongs—what Aussies call flip-flops—and you'll blend in seamlessly.) Lunch and dinner are served daily; the bars are open until 10 or 11pm. (Train: Albion. Bus: 300 or 322. Wickham Street becomes Breakfast Creek Road; the hotel is just off the route to the airport.)

his signature char-grilled salmon with salade niçoise. Loads of inexpensive and stylish pastas, pizzas, and sandwiches on Turkish flat bread, panini, and bruschetta are an alternative to a main course. Many high-class Aussie wines are sold by the glass. Take note, Yanks—the breakfast menu includes pancakes with bacon and maple syrup!

IN MT. COOT-THA

The Summit. At the Mt. Coot-tha Lookout, Sir Samuel Griffith Dr., Mt. Coot-tha. ☎ **07/ 3369 9922.** Reservations recommended Fri and Sat nights. Main courses A$16.90–$26.90 (U.S.$11–$17.50). Prix-fixe 3-course menu A$38.50 (U.S.$25). Sun brunch A$11.90 (U.S.$7.75) adults, A$6.90 (U.S.$4.50) child under 12. 3-course early-bird menu A$19.90 (U.S.$12.95) available from 3pm if you finish by 7pm. AE, BC, DC, JCB, MC, V. Daily 11:30am–midnight; Sun brunch from 8am. Bus: 471. From Roma Street Transit Centre, take Upper Roma St. and Milton Rd. 3.5km (2 miles) west to the Western Freeway roundabout at Toowong Cemetery, veer slightly right into Sir Samuel Griffith Dr., and go approx. 3km (2 miles). MODERN AUSTRALIAN.

You'd be hard-put to find a nicer setting than this mountain-top Queenslander house. Part 19th century, part sympathetic new extension, the restaurant is wrapped by covered decks with a super city view. Try panfried Moreton Bay prawns on preserved lemon risotto, or maybe roast kangaroo loin with a peppered cherry muffin, a wild mushroom ragout, and sautéed beans. There are also pastas and cuts off the grill. Come at night to catch the city lights.

IN BARDON

Avanti Cafe & Pasta. 57 MacGregor Terrace, Bardon. ☎ **07/3369 4375.** Main courses A$9.50–$16.95 (U.S.$6.20–$11). AE, BC, DC, MC, V. Daily 10am–10pm. Bus: 375. Take Roma St. out of the city, veer right into Petrie Terrace, almost immediately left into Caxton St., which becomes Given Terrace and then Latrobe Terrace. Follow Latrobe to the end and turn right into MacGregor. ITALIAN.

Brisbanites love this classic Italian joint so much they named it runner-up in the recent *Courier-Mail* newspaper's People's Choice city restaurant awards. It serves all your Italian faves in a casual indoor setting—octopus salad, chicken breast stuffed with camembert, sun-dried tomatoes and fresh spinach in pesto sauce, and a long litany of pastas, many of which make the most of Brisbane's fresh local seafood. BYO.

5 Exploring Brisbane

THE TOP ATTRACTIONS: TALK TO THE ANIMALS

✪ **Australian Woolshed.** 148 Samford Rd., Ferny Hills. ☎ **07/3872 1100.** Admission to ram show, sheep shearing, dog show, and animal farm A$15 (U.S.$9.75) adults, A$11 (U.S.$7.15) seniors and students, A$10 (U.S.$6.50) children 3–14, A$42.50 (U.S.$27.65) families. Admission to billy tea and damper A$6 (U.S.$3.90) adults, A$4 (U.S.$2.60) children 3–14. Waterslide A$5.50 (U.S.$3.60) for 1 hr., A$7.50 (U.S.$4.90) for 4 hr., or A$9.50 (U.S.$6.20) all day; open 9:30am–5pm weekends, and public and school holidays. Minigolf A$5.50 (U.S.$3.60) 9 holes. Daily 7am–5pm (Ram Show 8am, 9:30am, 11am, 1pm, and 2:30pm). Closed Christmas and until 1pm Anzac Day. Train: Ferny Grove station, then a 1km (just over 1/2 mile) paved level walk. Take Kelvin Grove Rd. from the city; it becomes Enoggera Rd., which becomes Samford Rd.; the trip is 14km (9 miles).

Remember in the movie *Babe* how that piglet got supposedly dumb sheep to make some smart moves in the show arena? That's just what happens in the Woolshed's Ram Show—eight well-behaved rams from the major Australian breeds walk calmly through the audience when their name is called and take their place on a dais with their name on it. Amazing! Set in eucalypt parkland, this sheep-farm theme park is the next-best thing to visiting a fair dinkum Aussie sheep station. The ram parade is followed by a display of sheep shearing and an entertaining sheepdog demonstration, and a visit to the animal farm where kids (and you) can milk a cow, bottle-feed baby farm animals, hand-feed kangaroos and emus, and see wombats. At 9am, 10:30am, and 12:30pm, a stockman prepares *billy tea* (basically, tea brewed up in a metal pot with a gum leaf thrown in) and *damper* (Australian-style campfire bread), accompanied by an Australian stockwhip-cracking display and a recital of bush poetry. A highlight is the chance to have your photo taken cuddling a koala for A$12.50 (U.S.$8.15) for a 5 × 7-inch or A$16.50 (U.S.$ 10.75) for an 8 × 10-inch print. The digital photo can be transferred to stickers, a T-shirt (A$30/U.S.$19.50), or even a floppy disk to use as computer wallpaper in just a few minutes; I can vouch for the quality. A barn-style restaurant serves breakfasts and lunches by the country plateful (open 7am to 2pm). The gift shop has won awards for the quality of its merchandise. The sheepskin and woolen products are particularly good.

About once a month on a Friday or Saturday night, the Woolshed hosts a traditional bush dance featuring spoon-playing, sing-alongs, a live bush band, and a barbecue dinner. Tickets cost A$38.50 (U.S.$25) per person at the door, A$33.50 (U.S.$21.80) if you pay a week in advance (you'll need to reserve in advance anyway). Minimum entry age is 18.

Allow at least 90 minutes to 2 hours to enjoy everything, plus traveling time.

✪ **Lone Pine Koala Sanctuary.** Jesmond Rd., Fig Tree Pocket (11km/7 miles from city center). ☎ **07/3378 1366.** Admission A$13 (U.S.$8.45) adults, A$8–$10.50 (U.S.$5.20–$6.85) seniors, A$10.50 (U.S.$6.85) students, A$8.50 (U.S.$5.55) children 3–13, A$31.90 (U.S.$20.75) family pass for 2 adults and 3 children. Daily 7:30am–5pm; 1:30–5pm on Anzac Day (Apr 25); 7:30am–4pm Christmas.

Lone Pine was Australia's first koala sanctuary, and with 130 of these adorable "bears" that are not really bears, it's still the biggest. Koala cuddling is outlawed in New South Wales and Victoria, because it is thought to stress the animals, but the ones working the photo rounds here seem well cared for and relaxed. You can cuddle them any time of the day free and get a digital photo taken holding one for A$11.80 (U.S.$7.70), plus around 10% for GST tax. For an extra charge you can have the photo transferred to a sheet of 16 stickers, to an A3 calendar, or to a disk as a still shot (good for posting on your personal Web site) and in 5-second movie format. Once you have purchased one photograph, your companions can take unlimited shots of you with their own camera. Lone Pine sounds touristy, but it really isn't. There's no razzle-dazzle, and the focus is very much on conservation education in a low-key, natural setting.

Lone Pine is not just about koalas. Within its 20-hectare (49-acre) bushland grounds you can hand-feed free-roaming kangaroos and emus (in a large natural pen), and see wombats, Tasmanian devils, bats, and other Aussie wildlife. Animal talks take place throughout the day. There are a gift shop, an e-mail terminal, a restaurant, and a cafe, and you are free to bring a picnic to eat overlooking the river.

Getting There: The **M.V. *Miramar*** (☎ **07/3221 0300**) cruises to Lone Pine up the Brisbane River, departing North Quay next to Victoria Bridge (beside the casino) at 10am. The 19-kilometer (12-mile) trip passes Queenslander homes, a bat colony,

Chow Time!

A good time to visit Lone Pine is 2 to 2:30pm daily, when the koalas are given fresh eucalyptus leaves. The normally lethargic critters are more active around mealtime.

Strollin', Strollin' . . .

Strolling is one of the nicest things to do in this warm, leafy city full of colonial-era architecture. Arm yourself with the excellent free ✪ *Heritage Trail Maps* from the Brisbane Tourism information booths. There are separate Heritage Trail Maps for the city center, the riverfront, the cute Queenslander cottages and shops of Paddington (my favorite), Fortitude Valley, peaceful Toowong Cemetery a 10-minute drive from the city, and the early seaside suburb of Sandgate. Driving trails exist for the posh residential suburbs of New Farm, nearby, and Hamilton, a 10-minute drive toward the airport.

Ambling among the Moreton Bay strangler figs, rain forest, duck ponds, palm groves, and flower beds of the **City Botanic Gardens** makes a blissfully cool reprieve on a summer's day. The rotunda near the Alice Street entrance has free maps to walk trails. Free guided walks leave the rotunda at 11am and 1pm Monday through Saturday. The Gardens are free and open 24 hours.

---

and native bush, all with commentary from the captain. You have 2 hours to explore Lone Pine; the boat gets back in the city at 2:50pm. The fare is A$16 (U.S.$10.40) for adults and A$9 (U.S.$5.85) for children 3 to 13, including transfers from city hotels (these are not always available on weekends), and discounted adult entry to Lone Pine of ($10.50 (U.S.$6.30). Cruises depart every day except Christmas and Anzac Day.

If you want to **drive,** take Milton Road to the roundabout at Toowong Cemetery, then the Great Western Freeway toward Ipswich. Take the Fig Tree Pocket exit, turn right onto Fig Tree Pocket Road, and go through one roundabout to Gunnin Street and Lone Pine. It is about 20 minutes from the city center by car. A taxi is about A$18 (U.S.$11.70). Bus 430 goes direct to the Sanctuary daily every hour from Koala Platform "N" in the Myer Centre on Queen Street Mall (enter off Albert Street). The fare is A$2.80 (U.S.$1.90).

MORE ATTRACTIONS

Brisbane Botanic Gardens Mt. Coot-tha. Mt. Coot-tha Rd., Toowong, 8km (5 miles) from the city. ☎ **07/3403 2535** Visitor Centre. Admission free. Daily 8am–5pm (5:30pm in summer). Bus: 471 stops in gardens. See "Bus Tours" at the end of this section for details on Brisbane Transport's daily bus tour.

A 10-minute drive from the city brings you to these 52-hectare (128-acre) gardens at the base of Mt. Coot-tha. They feature diverse Aussie natives and exotics, an arid zone, a giant glass dome housing rain forest, a cactus house, fragrant plants, a Japanese garden, a bonsai house, a bamboo grove, and an Aboriginal plant trail. There are lakes, picnic areas and walking trails, usually a horticultural show or arts-and-crafts display on weekends, and a cafe. Free 1-hour guided tours leave the Visitor Centre at 11am and 1pm Monday through Saturday (except public holidays).

Mt. Coot-tha Lookout. Sir Samuel Griffith Dr., Mt. Coot-tha. Free admission. Daily 24 hr. Bus: 471.

It may be more of a hill than a mountain, but sweeping views nonetheless await you from the city's best viewpoint. Look out over the city right out to Moreton Bay, then opt for something yummy from The Summit restaurant (see "Dining," earlier in this chapter) or the inexpensive **Kuta Café** (☎ **07/3369 9922**) right next door. It's open daily from 7am to 11pm, to midnight Friday and Saturday.

Newstead House. Newstead Park, Breakfast Creek Rd. at Newstead Ave., Newstead. ☎ **07/ 3216 1846.** Admission A$4.40 (U.S.$2.90) adults, A$3.30 (U.S.$2.20) seniors, A$2.20 (U.S.$1.45) children 6–17, and $11 (U.S.$7.15) family. Mon–Fri 10am–4pm; Sun and most public holidays 2–5pm. Closed Christmas, Boxing Day (Dec 26), Good Friday, and Anzac Day (Apr 25). Bus: 300, 306, 322.

Brisbane's oldest surviving home has been restored to late Victorian splendor in a peaceful park overlooking the Brisbane River, a 5-minute drive from the city. Wander the rooms, admire the exterior dating from 1846, and, on Sundays between March and November from 2 to 4:30pm, take Devonshire tea. The U.S. Army occupied the house in World War II, and the first American war memorial built in Australia is on the grounds.

Queensland Cultural Centre. At South Bank across Victoria Bridge at the western end of Queen St. Train: South Brisbane. Ferry: South Bank (CityCat) and Old South Bank (CityFerry). Bus: Many buses that depart Adelaide St. near Albert St. cross the Victoria Bridge and stop outside. Plentiful underground parking. The Centre is a 7-min. walk from town.

Adjacent to South Bank Parklands (see above), this modernistic low-rise complex stretching along the riverbank houses many of the city's performing-arts venues as well as the state art gallery and museum in a series of interlinked buildings. Indoor/ outdoor spaces filled with Brisbane's wonderful light make the **Queensland Art Gallery** in Melbourne Street (☎ **07/3840 7350**) a particularly uplifting space in which to appreciate works by diverse Australian painters, sculptors, and other artists, many of them modern pieces. This is one of the better galleries in Australia. Admission is free; a charge may apply to special exhibitions. Free guided tours of the collections run daily at 11am, and at 1pm Monday through Friday and on Sunday, and 2pm on Saturday. The gallery opens daily from 10am to 5pm; closed Good Friday, Christmas, and until noon on Anzac Day (Apr 25).

The **Queensland Museum,** on the corner of Grey and Melbourne streets (☎ **07/ 3840 7555**), displays an eclectic assortment ranging from natural-history specimens and fossils to a World War I German tank. Admission is free, except to special exhibitions, and it is open daily from 9:30am to 5pm; closed Christmas and Good Friday.

The **Queensland Performing Arts Complex,** on the corner of Grey and Melbourne streets (☎ **07/3840 7100** administration, 07/3840 7482 to book tours of the venues, or 13 62 46 box office), houses the 2,000-seat **Lyric Theatre** for musicals, ballet, and opera; the 1,800-seat **Concert Hall** for orchestral performances; the 850-seat **Optus Playhouse** for plays; and the 315-seat **Cremorne Theatre** for theater-in-the-round, cabaret, and experimental works.

✪ **Queensland Sciencentre.** 110 George St. between Mary and Charlotte sts. ☎ **07/ 3220 0166.** Admission A$8 (U.S.$5.20) adults; A$6 (U.S.$3.90) seniors, students, and children 5–15; A$2.50 (U.S.$1.65) children 3–4; and A$28 (U.S.$18.20) family pass. Tickets allow unlimited multiple reentry throughout the day. Daily 10am–5pm. Closed Good Friday and Christmas, and until 1pm Anzac Day (Apr 25). Bus: City Circle 333. Ferry: QUT Gardens Point (CityCat and CityFerry).

Adults love this hands-on science museum as much as the kids 12 and under for which it was designed. Become part of a battery, see walls expand before your eyes, create your own tornado, carry a briefcase with a mind of its own—these and other amazing feats demonstrating the principles of science cover three fascinating floors. Interactive shows run throughout the day.

Sir Thomas Brisbane Planetarium. In the Brisbane Botanic Gardens at Mt. Coot-tha (see above). ☎ **07/3403 2578.** Wed–Sun noon–7pm for bookings, or 07/3403 2535 Gardens information center for inquiries. Reservations are not necessary but advisable. Admission A$10

(U.S.$6.50) adults, A$8.50 (U.S.$5.55) seniors and students, A$6 (U.S.$3.90) children under 15 (not recommended for children under 6), A$28 (U.S.$18.20) family. Wed–Fri 3:30 and 7:30pm; Sat 1:30, 3:30, and 7:30pm; Sun 1:30 and 3:30pm. Bus: 471.

If you haven't spied the Southern Cross yet, you will during this fascinating astronomical show that re-creates the Brisbane night sky on the domed ceiling of a theaterette. The show explores some exciting "big" questions, like "Is there life on Mars?" Kids will like this place.

South Bank Parklands. At South Bank across the Victoria Bridge at the western end of Queen St. ☎ **07/3867 2051** for the Visitor Information Centre, 07/3867 2020 for recorded entertainment information line. Free admission. Park daily 24 hr. Visitor Information Centre (located in Stanley Street Plaza) daily 9am–6pm (until 10pm Fri). Train: South Brisbane or Vulture St. Ferry: South Bank (CityCat) and Old South Bank (CityFerry). Bus: Countless bus routes depart Adelaide St. near Albert St., cross the Victoria Bridge, and stop at the Queensland Cultural Centre; walk through the Centre to South Bank Parklands. Plentiful underground parking; access off Grey St. The Parklands are a 7-min. walk from town.

This delightful 16-hectare (40-acre) complex of parks, restaurants, playgrounds, street theater, cinemas, weekend markets, and even an artificial palm-lined lagoon with real sand is the city's breathing space, stretching for 1 kilometer (over half a mile) along the Brisbane River opposite downtown. Folks stroll the meandering pathways, swim, read the paper over a latte, meet friends for dinner or a barbecue, picnic on the banks, or take in a 3-D movie at the **IMAX cinema** (☎ **07/3844 4222**).

RIVER CRUISES

Guided cruises along the Brisbane River aboard the *Club Crocodile River Queen* **paddle wheelers** (☎ **07/3221 1300**) are a good way to take in the city's charming timber Queenslander homes on stilts, and its subtropical foliage—especially lovely in October/November when jacaranda trees burst into mauve flower all over town. The boats depart the Eagle Street Pier, 1 Eagle St., at 12:15 and 7:30pm. A variety of cruise options and prices is offered. Cheapest are the 90-minute lunchtime "Coffee, Tea & Cookies" cruises at A$19 (U.S.$12.35); most expensive is the seafood buffet dinner cruise at A$55 (U.S.$ 35.75). Expect to pay about A$4 (U.S.$2.60) more on public holidays.

BUS TOURS

Brisbane's public transport provider, **Brisbane Transport** (☎ **13 12 30** in Australia), runs two bus tours. They're a good value because they offer unlimited access to buses, ferries, and CityCats for the day. Tickets for either tour cost A$15 (U.S.$9.75) for adults, A$10 (U.S.$6.50) for children 5 to 15, and A$30 (U.S.$19.50) for a family. The ✪ **City Sights** tour takes you in an old-fashioned tram-style bus to 19 major points of interest in a running loop around the city center, South Bank, Fortitude Valley, and West End. Hop, on and off and repeat the trip as often as you like. The

---

River Cruises on the Cheap

One of the cheapest "tours" in town is a ride on the fast ✪ **CityCat ferries.** Head downstream under the Story Bridge past Newstead House to a budding "restaurant row" at Brett's Wharf; or glide upriver past the city and South Bank to the University of Queensland's lovely campus (take a peek at its Great Court while you're there). A ticket one way in either direction will set you back a whopping A$3.20 (U.S.$2.10).

route takes 80 minutes without stopping. The tour departs daily every 40 minutes from 9am to 12:20pm and 1:40 to 4:20pm. Buy tickets on board or at any Brisbane Transport newsagency or outlet. They entitle you to discounted admission to some attractions en route. You can join the route anywhere, but the most central stop is Stop 2 at City Hall in Adelaide Street at Albert Street.

6 Enjoying the Great Outdoors

Outdoor Pursuits (☎ 07/3397 7779) is an adventure/training company in its own right and is also a booking agent for many outdoor activities in and around Brisbane—white-water rafting, sea kayaking (as far away as Fraser Island), parachuting, waterskiing, horse riding, ballooning, 4WD tours, and many more.

ABSEILING & ROCK CLIMBING   Right in the heart of the city, the even face of the Kangaroo Point cliffs just south of the Story Bridge are a breeze for first-time abseilers to scale. Outdoor Pursuits (see above) stages $3^1/_2$-hour rock-climbing sessions up the cliffs every second Sunday from 8:30am for A\$33 (U.S.\$21.45) per person. At 1pm you can abseil back during a 4-hour session for A\$38.50 (U.S.\$25) per person, in which you fit at least four or five descents. A package combining both experiences is A\$60.50 (U.S.\$39.35).

BIKING   Bike tracks stretch for 400 kilometers (219 miles) in Brisbane. A great scenic route sweeps from just west of the Story Bridge, through the City Botanic Gardens, and out to the University of Queensland's campus, mostly along the river; it's about 9 kilometers ($5^1/_2$ miles), all up. **Brisbane Bicycle Sales and Hire,** 87 Albert St. (☎ 07/3229 2433), rents bikes from A\$9 (U.S.\$5.85) an hour up to A\$20 (U.S.\$13) for the day including helmets, which must be worn by law in Oz. They also supply Brisbane City Council's free bike maps, or pick one up at Brisbane Tourism booths (see "Visitor Information," above) or the Brisbane Administration Centre at 69 Ann St.

IN-LINE SKATING   In-line skaters can use Brisbane's excellent network of bike/pedestrian paths. See "Biking," above, for where to find a map, or just head down to the City Botanic Gardens at Alice Street and find your own way out along the river. **SkateBiz,** 101 Albert St. (☎ 07/3220 0157), rents blades and protective gear for A\$10/U.S.\$6.50 (the price goes up to A\$12/U.S.\$7.80 on Sun) for 2 hours. All-day rental is A\$25 (U.S.\$16.25). Bring a photo ID. The store is open daily.

7 Shopping

Brisbane's best shopping is centered on **Queen Street Mall.** Fronting the mall at 171–209 Queen St. under the Hilton is the three-level **Wintergarden** shopping complex (☎ 07/3229 9755), housing mostly upscale jewelers and Aussie fashion designers. Farther up the mall at 91 Queen St. at Albert Street is the **Myer Centre** (☎ 07/3221 4199), which has Brisbane's biggest department store and some 200 moderately priced stores, mostly fashion, over five levels. Its top floor has a mini-roller coaster and other fun stuff for kids. The historic **Brisbane Arcade,** 160 Queen Street Mall, boasts the boutiques of Queensland's best designers such as the **Keri Craig Emporium** downstairs (☎ 07/3229 4255) for feminine but practical clothes, and **Tim Lindgren** (☎ 07/3220 0116) for sexy suits and evening gowns. Just down the mall, you'll find the **Broadway on the Mall** arcade (☎ 07/3229 5233), stocking affordable fashion, gifts, and accessories on two levels. The city's most upscale department store is **David Jones,** 194 Queen Street Mall (☎ 07/3243 9000).

Opals are your best jewelry bet in Queensland. Present your passport and airline ticket to claim a tax-free discount. **Quilpie Opals,** in Lennons Plaza, 68 Queen Street Mall (☎ **07/3221 7369**), is a respected store selling black, boulder, and white gems unmounted or set as jewelry.

For genuine boomerangs and didgeridoos, paintings on bark, canvas, and paper, and many other crafts made by Aborigines from all areas of Queensland, shop at **Queensland Aboriginal Creations,** 199 Elizabeth St. (☎ **07/3224 5730**). It's opposite the Hilton.

The trendy suburb of ✪ **Paddington,** just a couple of miles from the city by cab, or take bus 374 or 375, is the place to go for antiques, books, art, handcrafts, one-of-a-kind clothing designs, and unusual gifts. The shops—cute, colorfully painted Queenslander cottages—line the main street, Given Terrace, which becomes Latrobe Terrace. Don't miss the second wave of shops around the bend from the first lot.

Authentic retro 1950s and 1960s fashion, old LPs (vinyl lives!), secondhand crafts, and all kinds of junk and treasure are up for sale at the **Brunswick Street Markets,** Brunswick Street Mall in Fortitude Valley. Hang around in one of the nearby cafes and listen to live folk bands. It's held Saturday 7am to 4pm.

Friday night is a fun time to visit the **South Bank Craft Village Markets,** Stanley Street Plaza, South Bank Parklands (☎ **07/3870 2807**), when this buzzing outdoor handcrafts market, with stalls housed in colorful tents, is lit by lanterns. All goods for sale on Friday and Sunday are Australian made. The market is held Friday 5 to 10pm, Saturday 11am to 5pm, and Sunday 9am to 5pm.

Brisbane's glamour set likes trawling the riverfront **Eagle Street Pier Craft Market** (☎ **0414/888 041**), dubbed the Riverside Markets by locals, at the Eagle Street Pier, 1 Eagle St., for attractive housewares, colorful pottery, handmade toys, painted flower-pots, and other stylish wares. It's held Sunday 8am to 4pm.

8 Brisbane After Dark

Ticketek (☎ **13 19 31** in Queensland, 07/3404 6644 outside Queensland, 1900/93 9277 for a recorded events information service) is a major booking agent for festivals, rock concerts, performing-arts events, and sports. There is an A$2.20 (U.S. $1.45) fee per ticket.

The *Brisbane News* (see "Visitor Information," earlier in this chapter) lists performing arts, jazz and classical music performances, art exhibitions, rock concerts, and public events. The free weekly street mag *Time Off,* found in bars and cafes, carries a complete guide to live music gigs.

THE PERFORMING ARTS

Most of Brisbane's performing arts are staged at the Queensland Performing Arts Complex (PAC) within the Queensland Cultural Centre at South Bank (see "Exploring Brisbane," above). **QTIX** (☎ **13 62 46** in Australia) is the booking agent for all events here. You can avoid the A$6 (U.S.$3.90) service charge by buying tickets in person at the QTIX box office at the PAC between 9am and 9pm Monday through Saturday, at the South Bank Parklands Visitor Information Centre, or at Rocking Horse Records, 101 Adelaide St. Among the highlights here are the **Queensland Theatre Company** (☎ **07/3840 7000** administration, 13 6246 box office), one of Australia's best, performing mostly at the Performing Arts Complex. The **La Boite Theatre** performs fresh, fringy all-Australian plays, usually in a tiny theater-in-the-round on the city center's edge at 57 Hale St., Petrie Terrace (☎ **07/3369 1622** box office and administration). **Opera Queensland** (☎ **07/3875 3030** administration,

13 62 46 box office) is a smallish but creditable company staging three traditional works a year, usually at the Performing Arts Complex. The **Queensland Symphony Orchestra** (☎ **07/3377 5000** for administration, 13 62 46 for box office) plays several series of classical and contemporary music at the Performing Arts Complex and occasionally at other more intimate venues such as City Hall.

THE CLUB & MUSIC SCENE

The ground floor of the busy Centra Brisbane hotel, next to the Roma Street Transit Centre, is the unlikely setting for the **Centra Brisbane Jazz & Blues Bar,** on Roma Street (☎ **07/3238 2222**), one of Brisbane's best live jazz venues. No cover Wednesday through Thursday, A$5 (U.S.$3.25) after 8:30pm Friday through Saturday; cover varies for major visiting acts. A mixed crowd in their 20s to 40s listens to a lucky dip of jazz, blues, and soul.

    Friday's, upstairs in the Riverside Centre, 123 Eagle St. (☎ **07/3832 2122**), a riverfront bar/restaurant/nightclub complex, is a haunt for young professionals and university students drawn by unbeatable drinks deals. The dance action starts around 11pm. Every second Wednesday from 6pm the Wine Club treats over-30s to all the drinks, food, and live bands they can handle for A$25 (U.S.$16.25). Live music plays on the terrace Sunday afternoons. Friday is the big night. Cover is usually A$5 to $7 (U.S.$3.25 to $4.55).

    A smart mid-30s to mid-40s crowd gathers at sophisticated **Margaux's,** on the fifth floor of the Brisbane Hilton, 190 Elizabeth St. (enter from Queen Street Mall; ☎ **07/3234 2000**), to dance and chat over cocktails and supper. There's a cover charge of A$5 (U.S.$3.25) on Saturdays.

    Super-cool young groovers dance to an all-night beat at Wonder Bar nightclub, upstairs in the historic **Empire Hotel,** 339 Brunswick St. at Ann Street, Fortitude Valley (☎ **07/3852 1216**), where the cover is A$6 (U.S.$3.90) on weekend nights. Boppers of all ages hit the popular Empire Bar downstairs, which doubles as a friendly pub by day.

PUBS & BARS

Downstairs at the **City Rowers Tavern,** Eagle Street Pier, 1 Eagle St. (☎ **07/3221 2888**), you'll find a modern tavern with great river views, the riverfront Fish Café, an affordable grill restaurant, a DJ Monday to Saturday, and a live band Sunday afternoons. Upstairs is a disco opening Wednesday to Saturday. Every night sees some kind of drinks special, and in the disco there is sometimes karaoke, and even male strippers. Neighborhood office workers drink up big at the 5 to 8pm Happy Hour Monday to Saturday. Cover in the nightclub is A$7 (U.S.$4.55), or free before 9pm on Saturdays.

    The city's premier mixed girl/guy gay venue, the **Hotel Wickham,** 308 Wickham St., Fortitude Valley (☎ **07/3852 1301**), is a pub by day, a club with DJs by night. Tuesday is boys' night, Wednesday is karaoke, and Thursday is a drag show.

    Jameson's Restaurant & Bar, 475 Adelaide St. (☎ **07/3831 7633**), has a funky and convivial downstairs bar that might have anything from house music and "rare groove" funk to 1970s and 1980s dance tunes or a jazz duo. Literary nights, fun debates, comedy cabarets, and other entertainment take center stage here sometimes. The cutting-edge Oz cuisine restaurant upstairs has great views of the illuminated Story Bridge.

    Kick back on the wide wooden veranda, lounge in the beer garden, or order a steak at the **Plough Inn,** South Bank Parklands (☎ **07/3844 7777**), a re-created traditional Aussie country pub. Live bands play Friday and Saturday nights and Sunday afternoon, and karaoke is a regular fixture.

The young style set sip cocktails to laid-back jazz, funk, and groove music at the **Press Club,** within the Empire Hotel complex, 339 Brunswick St. at Ann Street, Fortitude Valley (☎ **07/3852 1216**), a serenely elegant lounge bar and restaurant housed in a former newspaper printery.

ROLLING THE DICE

Treasury Casino. On Queen St. between George and William sts. ☎ **1800/506 888** in Australia, or 07/3306 8888. Must be 18 years old to enter; neat casual attire required (no beachwear, but jeans, shorts, and deck shoes are okay; jeans are not permitted in Club Conrad on 3rd floor, where bets are a minimum A$25 (U.S.$16.25). Open 24 hr. Closed 3am–midnight Christmas and Good Friday, and 3am–1pm Anzac Day (Apr 25).

A casino is housed in this sandstone Edwardian Baroque building that was built in 1886 as, ironically enough, the state Treasury offices. Three levels of 104 gaming tables offer roulette, blackjack, baccarat and minibaccarat, big six, craps, sic-bo, Keno and sports betting, 1,200 slot machines, and a VIP gaming room.

6 Queensland & the Great Barrier Reef

by Natalie Kruger

Queensland is where Aussies go for their holidays. "Beautiful one day, perfect the next" is the state tourism authority's marketing slogan, and that's not a bad way to sum up the state's embarrassment of riches—great beaches, great weather (except for the summer Wet Season in the north), and, of course, the Great Barrier Reef. A necklace of white sandy beaches graces most of the coastline, and off that dangles a string of the world's most beautiful islands and coral atolls. In the southern end of the state, just above the border with New South Wales, the beaches and theme parks of the Gold Coast attract tourists by the bucket-load. In the state's northern reaches, from Townsville on up, is another drawing card: a tangly 110-million-year-old rain forest that is home to rare primitive plants and animals.

Queensland is a big producer of bananas and pineapples, and one of the world's biggest sugar producers. Most of this stuff is grown on the warm, wet coastline, and that's where you'll spend most of your time too. Much of the inland is vast, dry grassland of little interest unless you're a beef farmer or a mining conglomerate.

Brisbane (covered separately in chapter 5) is the state's relaxed capital. It has a pleasant tropical feel, but consider basing yourself on the Gold Coast or the Sunshine Coast for the beaches and taking side trips to Brisbane.

North of Brisbane, the world's largest sand island, ✪ **Fraser Island,** attracts hard-drinkin' four-wheel-drivin' fishermen and ecotourists. Beyond that lies a tiny, little-visited coral cay, ✪ **Lady Elliot Island.** The gateway to the island, **Bundaberg,** is home to a wonderful marine turtle rookery on the beach from November to March. Keep going north and you reach **Gladstone,** the gateway to the Great Barrier Reef's most spectacular island, coral-wreathed **Heron Island.** As you proceed up the coast, you begin to pass one tropical island after another, until you hit 74 of them in the beautiful Whitsunday area. The **Whitsundays** are a sailor's dream, and hugely popular for their island resorts, water sports, and Great Barrier Reef day trips.

North of the Whitsundays is **Townsville,** an unprepossessing place that is the gateway to two island resorts. One, **Magnetic Island,** is cheerfully down-market, pretty, and affordable; the other, **Orpheus Island,** is pristine, beautiful, and pricey. Heading north from Townsville is popular **Dunk Island,** ultraprivate **Bedarra Island,** and the lovely rain-forest settlement of **Mission Beach** hidden in the jungle. White-water rafting is a big thing to do in the rain-forested hills around here.

Next you come to **Cairns,** with rain-forest hills and villages to explore, posh island resorts, and a harbor full of cruise and dive boats waiting to take you to the Reef. Cairns is a fine base, but savvy folks these days head an hour north to the trendy village of **Port Douglas,** where country sugar farmers rub shoulders with city golfers in the main street. Port Douglas is next door to **Daintree National Park.** Beyond that, the countryside gets wild and remote. Few people have penetrated **Cape York Peninsula,** the forested, roadless northern tip of Australia that juts up toward New Guinea.

EXPLORING THE QUEENSLAND COAST

VISITOR INFORMATION   Tourism Queensland operates a Web site at **www. queensland-holidays.com.au** (click the "North American Site" tab on the Web site home page for advice tailored to American travelers) that's a great resource for information on traveling the state.

Whether or not you're on the Web, contact the local tourism bureau of the area of the state you want to visit. Their contact details appear under "Visitor Information" in each section of this chapter.

You'll also find excellent information via the **Great Barrier Reef Visitors Bureau,** a private company offering itinerary planning and booking services for a wide range of accommodations and tours throughout north Queensland. Contact them at ☎ **07/ 3876 4644** or online at www.great-barrier-reef.com.

WHEN TO GO   Australia's winter (June to Aug) is high season in Queensland; the water can be a touch chilly but is still swimmable. Water temperature rarely drops below 22°C (72°F). August through January is peak visibility time for divers. Summer is hot and sticky across the entire state. North Queensland (Mission Beach, Cairns, and Port Douglas) gets a monsoonal **Wet Season** from November or December to March or April, which brings heavy rains, high temperatures, extreme humidity, and cyclones. It's no problem to visit then, but if the Wet turns you off, consider the beautiful Whitsundays. These are generally beyond the reach of the rains and the worst of the humidity (although not beyond the reach of cyclones).

GETTING AROUND   The **Bruce Highway** connects Brisbane and Cairns. It's mostly a narrow two-lane highway, not in super condition, bordered by dreary eucalyptus scenery most of the way.

The **Royal Automobile Club of Queensland (RACQ),** 300 St. Pauls Terrace, Fortitude Valley, QLD 4006 (☎ **13 19 05** in Australia, or 07/3361 2444), dispenses maps

Life's a Beach

Which Queensland beach is right for you? If it's surf you're after, head to the Gold Coast or the Sunshine Coast near Brisbane, as the Great Barrier Reef puts a stop to the swell north of Hervey Bay or thereabouts. North of Gladstone, deadly box jellyfish known as "stingers" are a real wet blanket, putting a stop to all swimming on the mainland (but not the islands; these critters hug the shore) in summer from October to May. Never swim in unprotected seas at that time. Most popular beaches have net enclosures for safe swimming. If you love swimming, you don't want to swim in nets, and you're visiting in stinger season, head to an island (or choose a hotel with a good pool)!

Choose a cay (such as Michaelmas Cay, Upolu Cay or Green Island off Cairns, the Low Isles off Port Douglas, Beaver Cay off Mission Beach, or Heron Island off Gladstone) if you can't swim well. That way you can wade in to the coral off a shallow sandy shore.

and driving advice. A more convenient city office is in the General Post Office building at 261 Queen St., Brisbane. For road-condition reports, call ☎ **07/3219 0900.**

1 Exploring the Great Barrier Reef

It's the only living structure on Earth visible from the moon; at 348,700 square kilometers (238,899 square miles), it's bigger than the United Kingdom. It stretches for over 2,000 kilometers (1,250 miles) from Lady Elliot Island off Bundaberg to just south of Papua New Guinea. It's home to 1,500 kinds of fish, 400 species of corals, 4,000 kinds of clams and snails, and who knows how many sponges, worms, starfish, and sea urchins. In short, the ✪ **Great Barrier Reef** is the Eighth Wonder of the World.

The Reef is not a plant but one big conglomeration of tiny animals called coral polyps. Coral polyps coat themselves in limestone, and as they die, their bodies cement into reef, onto which more living coral grows.

You will see three kinds of reef on the Great Barrier Reef—fringe, ribbon, and platform. **Fringe reef** grows along the mainland and island shores. **Ribbon reefs** are long, thin "streamers," found only north of Cairns. **Platform reefs,** or patch reefs, are splotches of coral emerging up off the continental shelf all along the Queensland coast; they are the most common kind. Islands in the Great Barrier Reef Marine Park are either "continental," meaning they are part of the Australian landmass, or "cays," which are piles of crushed dead coral and sand amassed over time by water action. Cays are surrounded by sensational coral and fish life, while coral around continental islands ranges from terrific to nonexistent.

To see the Reef, you can snorkel it, fish it (recreational fishing is permitted in most zones), fly over it, and dive it. Most of the Reef lies an average of 65 kilometers (41 miles) off the coast, though isolated patch reefs and island fringing reefs lie closer to the mainland.

A good overview is provided by ✪ **Reef Teach** (☎ 07/4031 7794), which is a slide-show presentation by Paddy Colwell, an enthusiastic marine biologist and scuba diver. He tells you everything you need to know, from how coral has sex, to what dangerous critters to avoid, to how to take successful underwater photos. Presentations take place Monday to Saturday, at 6:15pm at 14 Spence St. (at Abbott Street), Cairns. The cost is A$13 (U.S.$8.45).

Townsville is the headquarters of the **Great Barrier Reef Marine Park Authority** (☎ 07/4750 0700; www.gbrmpa.gov.au or www.reefHQ.org.au), and a visit to its showcase, ✪ **Reef HQ** (see section 4, "The North Coast: Mission Beach, Townsville & the Islands," later in this chapter) is a superb introduction to this underwater fairyland.

CHOOSING A GATEWAY TO THE REEF

Lots of overseas travelers believe that Cairns is the best place from which to access the Reef. Not so. Cairns is a fine place from which to see it; but the quality of the coral is just as good off any town down the Queensland coast, so don't worry too much about which part of the Reef is "best." The outer Reef is pretty much equidistant from any point along the coast—about 90 minutes by high-speed catamaran. It is closest at Mission Beach (an hour away) and farthest away at Townsville (where it's about 2½ hr. away).

The main gateways, taken north to south, are **Port Douglas, Cairns, Mission Beach, Townsville,** the **Whitsunday Islands,** and **Bundaberg. Heron Island** off Gladstone is actually on the Reef itself. For my money, the Whitsundays area is pick

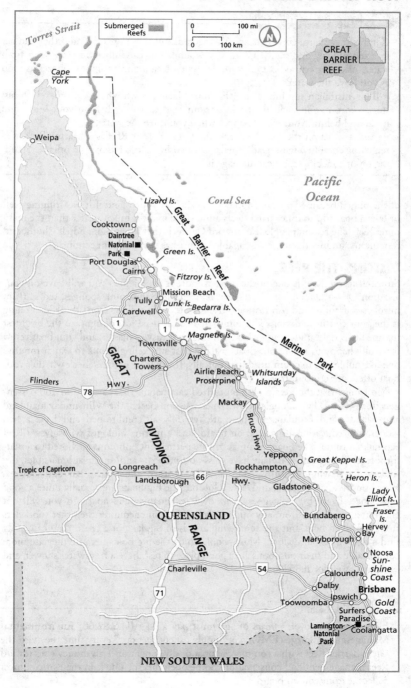

The Great Barrier Reef

Submerged Reefs

0   100 mi
0   100 km

GREAT
BARRIER
REEF

Torres Strait

Cape York

Weipa

Pacific Ocean

Lizard Is.   *Coral Sea*

Cooktown
Daintree
Nationial ■
Park ■
Port Douglas
Cairns

Green Is.

Fitzroy Is.

Mission Beach
Tully   Dunk Is.
Cardwell   *Bedarra Is.*

Orpheus Is.

Magnetic Is.

Townsville
Charters
Towers   Ayr
Airlie Beach
Proserpine   *Whitsunday Islands*

GREAT   Flinders   Hwy.   78

Mackay

Bruce Hwy.

DIVIDING

Yeppoon
Tropic of Capricorn   Longreach   Rockhampton   *Great Keppel Is.*
Landsborough   66   Hwy.   Gladstone   *Heron Is.*

Lady Elliot Is.

QUEENSLAND

RANGE   Bundaberg
Maryborough   Hervey Bay

Fraser Is.

Noosa
Sun-shine Coast
Charleville   54   Caloundra
Dalby   **Brisbane**
71   Toowoomba   Ipswich   *Gold Coast*
Surfers Paradise
Lamington-Nationial Park   Coolangatta

NEW SOUTH WALES

Reef Safety Warnings

Coral is very sharp; coral cuts aren't dangerous but they're painful, and they can get infected quickly and badly. Clean any wounds out carefully, and rinse with fresh water. Ask your cruise-boat crew for antiseptic cream and apply it to grazes as soon as you leave the water.

The Australian sun burns you *fast*. You're facing down when you snorkel, so put sunscreen on your back, the backs of your legs, especially behind your knees and neck, and behind your ears. Reapply when you leave the water.

And a word on the Reef's safety—the Great Barrier Reef is a Marine Park, and removing coral (living or dead), shells, or any other natural item is an offense. Standing on or touching coral can damage it.

of the bunch because you can snorkel every day off your island if it has fringing reef, or take a boat trip to inner patch reefs among the islands, much nearer than the main outer reef. The reason people lean toward Cairns is that it has more hotels, shops, and restaurants, and its Boeing 747–capable airport has the best connections.

VISITING THE REEF

Snorkeling the Reef is one of the most wondrous experiences you will have on your vacation Down Under. You'll see green and purple clams, pink sponges, red starfish, purple sea urchins, and fish from electric blue to neon yellow. Don't think snorkeling is the poor cousin to diving. The coral's rich colors need lots of light, so the brightest marine life is right under the surface. Snorkeling is easy to master, and your boat's crew is usually happy to tutor you. Boats usually post snorkeling scouts to watch for anyone in trouble and to count heads periodically. If you wear glasses, check whether your boat offers prescription masks.

Most folks visit the Reef on big motorized catamarans that carry up to 400 passengers from Cairns, Port Douglas, Townsville, Mission Beach, the Whitsunday mainland and islands, and Bundaberg. These are typically air-conditioned and have a bar, videos, and educational material on board, and a marine biologist who gives a Reef eco-talk en route. The boats tie up at private permanent pontoons anchored to a platform reef. The pontoons usually have glass-bottom boats and/or semisubmersibles, dry underwater viewing platforms, sundecks, shaded seats, sometimes a bar, and showers. Four hundred passengers sounds like a lot, but the big boats are actually quite a good experience. Every big boat goes to its own reef many miles apart, so you will not encounter passengers from any other vessel. Sure, you encounter the other snorkelers from your own boat, but the snorkeling area is so big it's not a crush. You can easily find a place to explore alone. Most people enjoy the big boats because they are more comfortable and their pontoons are a good place to rest, have a freshwater shower, and eat lunch at tables and chairs.

The Reef Tax

Every passenger over 4 years of age must pay a A$4 (U.S.$2.60) **Environmental Management Charge (EMC),** commonly called "reef tax," every time they visit the Great Barrier Reef with a commercial boat or dive operator. This money goes toward Reef management and conservation. Some operators include it in their prices; most collect it from you on board.

An alternative to the "big" boats is the multitude of smaller boats, which take no more than 30 or so passengers. The advantages? They typically visit two or three Reef sites rather than just one; the crew gives you personal attention; and you have the coral pretty much to yourself. The drawbacks? You have only the cramped deck to sit on when you get out of the water; and your traveling time to the Reef may be half an hour or so longer. If you're a nervous snorkeler, you may feel safer on a big boat where you are surrounded by 300 other folks in the water. Small boats operate from Port Douglas, Cairns, and the Whitsundays. Big boats operate from all those places, and Mission Beach and Bundaberg also. You can travel as a snorkel-only passenger on most dive boats too, but be warned that what constitutes a brilliant dive site does not necessarily make for a good snorkel site.

Most day-trip fares include your snorkel gear—fins, mask, and snorkel—a plentiful buffet lunch, morning and afternoon refreshments, and, on the big boats that have pontoons, free use of the underwater viewing chambers and glass-bottomed boat rides. Some boats may charge A$5 (U.S.$3.25) or so extra for a wet suit, which you will probably want only in midwinter.

If your cruise offers a **"snorkel safari,"** take it! These small-group expeditions led by a marine biologist show you stuff you would never find on our own, such as a clownfish family, an eel, or a coral that oozes its own sunscreen. They are worth the extra cost of A$25 (U.S.$16.25) or so.

A day trip to the Reef also offers you a great opportunity to go ✪ **diving**—even if you've never dived before. Most snorkel and dive boats offer "introductory" dives for around A$55 to $85 (U.S.$35.75 to $55.25). These allow anyone to dive to a depth of 6 meters (20 ft.) in the company of an instructor. You will complete a medical questionnaire on board; then, after a 30-minute briefing session on the boat and a practical lesson in shallow water, you make a foray of 20 to 40 minutes into a magical underwater world. Introductory dives are also called "resort" dives, because many resorts offer a similar thing, giving you a couple of hours' instruction in the resort pool before taking you to a nearby reef to dive.

MULTIDAY CRUISES ALONG THE REEF

I highly recommend a cruise aboard the 168-passenger ✪ **M.V. *Reef Endeavour,*** which makes 3- and 4-night forays from Cairns along the Great Barrier Reef, calling at islands, coral cays, and outer reefs. The crew is fun, the food is excellent, and the itinerary is perfectly paced. My husband and I loved every minute of our 4-day northbound itinerary, as we toured tropical Cooktown, hiked and snorkeled from a deserted white beach on Lizard Island, climbed Cook's Look on Lizard Island at dawn with the entire ship's complement, snorkeled at Two Isles coral cays, and snorkeled Ribbon Reef No. 5 on the outer reef. I would venture to say that this itinerary is more interesting than the 3-day southbound one. Ask about the annual golf cruise. The ship has a marine naturalist on board, glass-bottom and dive boats, an ample sundeck, a pool, two Jacuzzis, a sauna, a cocktail lounge, and live nightly entertainment. All 75 large comfortable cabins—with air-conditioning, telephones, and bathrooms—are on the outside, with sea views. Fares for the 4-night trip range from A$1,399 to $1,904 (U.S.$909.35 to $1,237.60) per person, twin-share. The cruise departs weekly. Book through **Captain Cook Cruises** (☎ **800/6754-8888** in the U.S. and Canada; 020/8748 9167 in the U.K.; 0800/44 6389 in New Zealand, or 1800/221 080 in Australia, or 02/9206 1100 [Sydney sales office]; www.captaincook.com.au).

Which Great Barrier Reef Resort Is Right for You?

Island	Access	Coral Rating	Beaches	Accommodations & Dining
FAR NORTH				
Lizard	Cairns	3	sand	Lodge-style luxury rooms & villas; fine dining with sea views
Green	Cairns	3	coral sand	Stylish rooms; fine dining
Fitzroy	Cairns	2*	coral sand	Simple cabins; also bunkhouses
NORTH				
Orpheus	Townsville & Cairns	2	sand	Attractive rooms; good seaside dining
Magnetic	Townsville	1	sand	Big range of motels, hotels, apartments, and camping
Hayman	Hamilton Island & Airlie Beach	2*	coral sand	Five-star luxury rooms; range of excellent dining options
Hamilton	Hamilton Island Airport & Airlie Beach	1	sand	Hotels and apartments (some high-rise), plus Polynesian bures; good dining venues
Long	Hamilton Island (by helicopter only)	1	sand	Whitsunday Wilderness Lodge: simple but comfortable cabins; hearty camp-oven meals served communally under the stars
South Molle	Hamilton Island & Airlie Beach	1*	sand	Slightly old but renovated rooms; average to good buffet dining (rates include meals)
Hook	Airlie Beach	2	sand	Very basic cabins & dorm beds; basic cafe & bar
Dunk	Mission Beach & Cairns	1*	sand	Decent mid-range rooms; several dining choices
Bedarra	Mission Beach & Cairns	1	sand	Relaxed but luxurious ; lodge-style rooms; fine dining in romantic setting; 24-hour open bar

Coral Rating: 1 is limited, 2 is good, 3 is excellent, 3+ (Heron Island only) is out of this world!

*accessible by boat only

Sports/Activities	Day Trips to Outer Reef	Comments
Game fishing, diving, water sports (mostly nonmotorized), tennis, hiking, many beaches	yes	Private & exclusive
Snorkeling, diving, water sports (mostly nonmotorized), parasailing, rain-forest trails, lovely beach	yes	Exquisite, very small resort; superb snorkeling; busy in daytime with day-trippers
Snorkeling, diving, water sports (nonmotorized), rain-forest hiking	yes	Affordable resort aimed at 18–35s
Snorkeling, diving, game fishing, water sports (nonmotorized)	yes (charter only)	Secluded; blissfully peaceful; pretty beach; beautiful location
Huge range of watersports, snorkeling, diving, horseback riding, extensive hiking	yes	Suburb of Townsville; not glamorous but affordable; national park island; wild koalas to see; many deserted beaches
Large range of water sports & activities, snorkeling, diving, sailing cruises, kids' club, yachts and luxury boats for charter, tennis, squash, extensive fitness center, hiking, game-fishing trips, rocky tidal beach		Australia's best luxury resort
Biggest range of watersports & land-based activities, snorkeling, diving, tennis, game fishing, hiking, kids' club, marina	yes	Upscale resort with widest array of activities; beach of thin sand/rock; busy, "man-made" atmosphere
Snorkeling, diving, hiking, sailing, sea kayaking; all-inclusive rates include daily excursions	yes (by seaplane only)	Eco-retreat in idyllic location; small sand/rock beach; max. 20 guests
Wide array of water sports, snorkeling, cruises, diving, extensive hiking, tennis, kids' club	yes	Pleasant mid-range resort in pretty location; pretty beach
Snorkeling, diving, very limited watersports (nonmotorized), hiking	yes	Cheap, low-key resort aimed at student crowd
Large range of water sports, diving, cruises, horseback riding, kids'club, tennis, extensive hiking, game fishing, beaches	yes	Pleasant resort for all ages
Limited nonmotorized water sports (more activities nearby at Dunk Island), snorkeling, game fishing, tennis, limited hiking, beaches	yes	Utter privacy; max. 30 guests

(continues)

Which Great Barrier Reef Resort Is Right for You? (*cont.*)

Island	Access	Coral Rating	Beaches	Accommodations & Dining
MID-NORTH				
Great Keppel	Rockhampton	2*	sand	Comfortable rooms; big range of dining venues
SOUTH				
Heron	Gladstone	3+	coral	Comfortable rooms, good dining
Lady Elliot	Bundaberg	3	coral	Basic lodge-style rooms and permanent tents; basic food

Coral Rating: 1 is limited, 2 is good, 3 is excellent, 3+ (Heron Island only) is out of this world!

*accessible by boat only

DIVING THE REEF

An almost endless choice of small day-trip dive boats and large live-aboard vessels ply the Reef. Many are based in Cairns or Port Douglas because the greatest number of dive sites are there, but you can also dive the Reef from Mission Beach, Townsville, the Whitsundays, and Bundaberg.

A typical day trip will include two dives. You can expect to save about $20 on quoted prices if you have your own gear. Rates will be higher in diving's high season from June to December. Some companies offer videos (for around A$60/U.S.$39) of your dive, guided dives for about A$15 (U.S.$9.75) extra, and underwater camera hire for about A$50 (U.S.$32.50). Most dive boats welcome beginners who want to take a first-time dive in the company of an instructor. A tip for live-aboard passengers: Make sure your boat has hot, not cold, showers!

Don't forget to bring your "C" certification card. It's also a good idea to bring along your dive log. Remember not to fly for at least 12 hours after diving, preferably 24.

"The Active Vacation Planner," in chapter 2, has more pointers on diving in Australia.

Virtually every Great Barrier Reef dive operator offers dive courses. Most island resorts offer them, too. You will find dive schools in Cairns, Port Douglas, Mission Beach, Townsville, and the Whitsunday Islands. Several dive companies do courses in Woongarra Marine Park abutting the mainland at Bundaberg; strictly speaking, the Park is not part of the Great Barrier Reef Marine Park, but it is close to Great Barrier Reef sites like Lady Musgrave Island and Lady Elliot Island and has some of the best shore diving in Australia.

Feeling Green?

If you are inclined to be seasick, come prepared with medication or your own acupressure wristbands. Some boats sell a ginger-based natural antiseasickness pill, but it doesn't always work! Take your medication *before* you set sail; once you're underway, it's generally too late.

Sports/Activities	Day Trips to Outer Reef	Comments
Huge range of water sports & activities (many free), skydiving, diving, tennis, hiking, kids' club, beaches	no	Mid-range resort for 18- to 35-year-old action fiends
Snorkeling, reef walking, diving, cruises, bird watching, diving, beach, limited watersports	yes—the island is *on* the Reef	Superb snorkeling; sea turtles nest on beach
Snorkeling, diving, reef-walking, bird watching	yes—the island is *on* the Reef	Excellent snorkeling; sea turtles nest on beach; small & very limited beaches; old facilities; sparse vegetation

Most dive companies teach from beginner level ("open-water certification") through to Advanced, Rescue, Dive Master, and Dive Instructor level. Courses usually commence every day or every week. Prices vary quite a bit, but a rough guide is around A$550 (U.S.$357.50) for a 5-day open-water certification course, or A$440 (U.S.$286) for the same course over 4 nights.

Companies offering dive courses appear under the relevant regional sections throughout this chapter.

2 Cairns

346km (216 miles) N of Townsville; 1,807km (1,129 miles) N of Brisbane

When international tourism to the Great Barrier Reef boomed a decade or two ago, Cairns (pronounced "cans") boomed with it. This sugar-farming town on the north Queensland coast now has a collection of five-star hotels in its tiny center, deluxe island resorts bobbing offshore, big cats in the harbor waiting to whisk snorkelers to the Reef, and souvenir shops springing up where the corner store used to be.

Cairns is not just close to one natural wonder; it's close to two. Sure, the Great Barrier Reef is nearby, but a couple of hours north lies a precious 110-million-year-old rain forest, the Daintree, where plants that are fossils elsewhere in the world exist in living color. The Daintree is part of the Wet Tropics, a World Heritage–listed area that stretches from north of Townsville to beyond Cairns, and it houses one-half of Australia's animal and plant species. From Cairns, you can glide over the rain-forest canopy in a gondola to the mountain village of Kuranda, where the only things that interrupt the green are hiking trails, gorges, and towering waterfalls.

Downtown Cairns has little to recommend it. Although the city is edged by lovely green mountains, there are no beaches right in town, the shopping is lackluster, and good restaurants are scant. If you plan to spend more than a day or two in the area, consider basing yourself at one of the pretty beach suburbs north of the city, in Kuranda, or in Port Douglas (see "Port Douglas, Daintree & the Cape Tribulation Area" section, later in this chapter), an hour's drive north.

ESSENTIALS

GETTING THERE   By Plane   Qantas (☎ **13 13 13** in Australia) and **Ansett** (☎ **13 13 00** in Australia) have many direct flights daily from Sydney and Brisbane. Qantas flies direct from Darwin once a day. Flights with both airlines from Melbourne are direct only on weekends. At press time, neither had flights from the Whitsunday Islands. Ansett and Qantas affiliate **Airlink** (book through Qantas) flies daily from Alice Springs, and daily or every 2nd day from Ayers Rock. **Flightwest Airlines** (book through Ansett) and **Sunstate Airlines** (book through Qantas) fly many times a day from Townsville. International flights land in Cairns from several Asian cities, Papua New Guinea, and New Zealand.

Cairns Airport is 8 kilometers (5 miles) north of downtown. A 5-minute under-cover walk or an A$2 (U.S.$1.30) shuttle ride connects the international and domestic terminals. Kids 12 and under ride free. Both the domestic terminal and the inter-national terminal's arrivals hall have showers, baby change rooms, ATMs, currency exchange, accommodation boards with free booking telephones, booking counters for Australia Coach and Coral Coaches (see below), and taxi and limousine ranks. Both terminals have lockers big enough for a suitcase for between A$4 and $8 (U.S.$2.60 and $5.20) per day. Baggage trolleys are free for arriving international passengers, and A$2 (U.S.$1.30) for everyone else. Avis, Budget, Hertz, and Thrifty (see "Getting Around," below) have desks at both terminals.

Airport shuttle **Australia Coach** (☎ **07/4031 3555**) picks up right outside the arrivals halls at both terminals and transfers you to city hotels (but not northern beaches accommodations) for A$7 (U.S.$4.55), or A$3 (U.S.$1.95) for kids ages 2 to 12. It runs approximately half-hourly and meets major domestic flights. Reservations for the airport-city run are rarely needed. **Coral Coaches** (☎ **07/4031 7577**) meets most flights between 6am and 8:15pm for door-to-door transfers to all city, northern beaches, and Port Douglas accommodations. Five trips a day require reservations; the rest are on a first-come, first-served basis (I would still book ahead). The fare is A$7.40 (U.S.$4.80) to the city, A$11.40 (U.S.$7.40) to Trinity Beach, and A$14.80 (U.S.$9.60) to Palm Cove. Children 4 to 14 pay half price; seniors get a 40% discount.

A **taxi** from the airport costs around A$10.50 (U.S.$6.85) to the city, A$26 (U.S.$16.90) to Trinity Beach, and A$34 (U.S.$22.10) to Palm Cove. The flagfall on weekdays from 6am to 8pm, and from 6am to 1pm Saturdays, is A$1.90 (U.S.$1.25); outside those times, at night and on public holidays it is A$3 (U.S.$1.95). A 60¢ (U.S.40¢) booking fee applies if you book the cab instead of hailing it. Call **Black & White Taxis** (☎ **13 10 08** in Cairns, or 07/4051 5333).

By Train   The first-class sleeper and sitting berth *Queenslander* (weekly) and the comfortable seat and sleeper *Sunlander* (three times a week) make the 31-hour trip from Brisbane, calling at most towns and cities en route. Both are operated by Queensland Rail's long-distance division, **Traveltrain** (☎ **1800/806 468** in Australia, or 07/3235 1000; www.qr.com.au). They pull into the **Cairns Central terminal** on McLeod Street at Shields Street in the center of town. There is no train from Port

---

Staying Connected

You can surf the Web and check your e-mail at **Travellers' Contact Point,** in the offices of The Adventure Company, 2nd floor, 13 Shields St. (☎ **07/4041 4677**), for A$1 (U.S.65¢) per hour. You can also send and receive faxes, and have snail-mail sent here. It's open daily from 8am to 8pm.

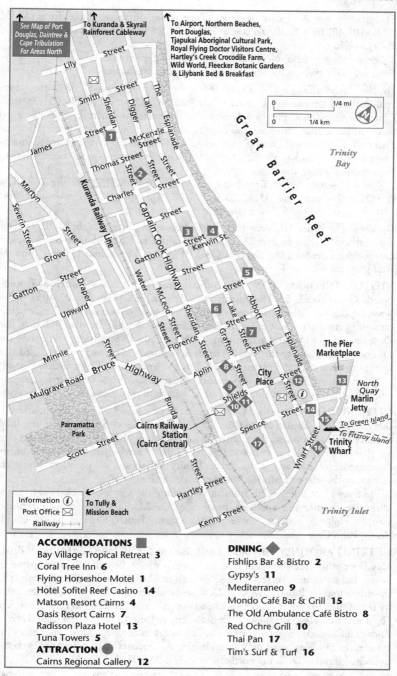

Cairns

See Map of Port Douglas, Daintree & Cape Tribulation For Areas North

To Kuranda & Skyrail Rainforest Cableway

To Airport, Northern Beaches, Port Douglas, Tjapukai Aboriginal Cultural Park, Royal Flying Doctor Visitors Centre, Hartley's Creek Crocodile Farm, Wild World, Fleecker Botanic Gardens & Lilybank Bed & Breakfast

Great Barrier Reef

Trinity Bay

0   1/4 mi
0   1/4 km

Lily Street

Smith Street

Sheridan Street

Digger Street

Lake Street

The Esplanade

McKenzie Street

James Street

Thomas Street

Charles Street

Captain Cook Highway

Gatton Street

Street

Kerwin St.

Street

Street

Street

Street

Abbott Street

Lake Street

Grafton Street

The Esplanade

Martyn Street

Severin Street

Grove Street

Draper Street

Upward Street

Kuranda Railway Line

Water Street

McLeod Street

Sheridan Street

Florence Street

Gatton Street

Minnie Street

Bruce Highway

Mulgrave Road

Aplin Street

Shields Street

City Place

The Pier Marketplace

North Quay Marlin Jetty

To Green Island

To Fitzroy Island

Bunda Street

Parramatta Park

Cairns Railway Station (Cairn Central)

Spence Street

Wharf Street

Trinity Wharf

Scott Street

Hartley Street

Kenny Street

Trinity Inlet

Information (i)
Post Office ⊠
Railway

To Tully & Mission Beach

ACCOMMODATIONS ■
Bay Village Tropical Retreat **3**
Coral Tree Inn **6**
Flying Horseshoe Motel **1**
Hotel Sofitel Reef Casino **14**
Matson Resort Cairns **4**
Oasis Resort Cairns **7**
Radisson Plaza Hotel **13**
Tuna Towers **5**
ATTRACTION ●
Cairns Regional Gallery **12**

DINING ◆
Fishlips Bar & Bistro **2**
Gypsy's **11**
Mediterraneo **9**
Mondo Café Bar & Grill **15**
The Old Ambulance Café Bistro **8**
Red Ochre Grill **10**
Thai Pan **17**
Tim's Surf & Turf **16**

Douglas or the Northern Territory. Fares from Brisbane range from A$156 (U.S.$101.40) for a *Sunlander* seat to A$505 (U.S.$328.25), meals included, aboard the *Queenslander*.

For details on the opulent *Great South Pacific Express* that runs from Sydney or Brisbane to Cairns, see "Getting Around Australia," in chapter 2.

By Bus McCafferty's (☎ 13 14 99 in Australia or 07/4051 5899 for Cairns terminal) and **Greyhound Pioneer** (☎ 13 20 30 in Australia or 07/4051 3388 for Cairns terminal) buses pull into **Trinity Wharf Centre** on Wharf Street in the center of town. Buses from Brisbane stop at most towns and cities on the Bruce Highway. From Alice Springs and Darwin, buses travel via Tennant Creek, the Outback mining town of Mt. Isa, and Townsville. McCafferty's has five services a day from Brisbane; Greyhound Pioneer, three.

The 46-hour Sydney–Cairns trip costs A$249.70 (U.S.$162.30), the 28¹/₂ hour trip from Brisbane costs A$167.20 (U.S.$108.70), and the 41-hour journey from Darwin costs A$335.50 (U.S.$218.10).

By Car The **Bruce Highway** from Brisbane enters Cairns from the south. To reach the northern beaches or Port Douglas from Cairns, take **Sheridan Street** in the city center, which becomes the **Captain Cook Highway.** The nearest highway from the west joins the coast in Townsville.

VISITOR INFORMATION The official tourism bureau is **Tourism Tropical North Queensland,** 51 The Esplanade, Cairns, QLD 4870 (☎ 07/4051 3588; www.tnq.org.au). Its information center is a particularly good source of information on tour operators, not just in Cairns and its environs, but also in Mission Beach, Port Douglas and the Daintree rain forest, Cooktown and Cape York to the north, and Outback Queensland to the west. It's open daily from 8:30am to 5:30pm (closed after 1pm public holidays, and closed all day Christmas and Boxing Day, which is Dec 26).

Another useful Web site is **www.cairns.aust.com**. Oodles of free tourist guides are available at the airport, in your hotel lobby, and from tour desks.

CITY LAYOUT Downtown Cairns is laid out on a grid 5 blocks deep, bounded in the east by **The Esplanade** and in the west by **McLeod Street,** where the long-distance train station and the Cairns Central shopping mall are located. In between are shops, offices, and restaurants. Cruises to the Great Barrier Reef leave from the eastern edge of this area, from either **Trinity Wharf** on Wharf Street beside the Hilton, or the adjacent **Marlin Marina** beside the Pier mall.

Heading 15 minutes north from the city along the Captain Cook Highway, you start to encounter the **northern beaches** of the Marlin Coast (really suburbs of Cairns): Holloway's Beach, Yorkey's Knob, Trinity Beach, Kewarra Beach, Clifton Beach, Palm Cove, and Ellis Beach.

GETTING AROUND **By Bus** Local **Sunbus** (☎ 07/4057 7411) buses depart City Place at the intersection of Lake and Shields streets. Buy all tickets and passes on board, and try to have correct change. You can hail buses anywhere it's convenient for the driver to stop. Buses 1, 1A, and 2X (a seasonal June-to-Nov express service) travel to Trinity Beach; and 1, 1B, 1X (weekend express), and 2X travel to Palm Cove. The "N" route runs along the highway from the city to Palm Cove all night until dawn on Friday and Saturday nights, stopping at all beaches in between. Most other buses run from early morning until almost midnight. A "Beaches" pass allowing 24 hours' unlimited travel as far as the northern beaches is A$8.95 (U.S.$5.80).

By Car Avis (☎ 07/4051 5911), **Budget** (☎ 07/4051 9222), **Hertz** (☎ 07/4051 6399), and **Thrifty** (☎ 07/4051 8099) all have offices in Cairns city and airport.

Croc Alert!

Crocodiles inhabit Cairns waterways, even in the 'burbs! Do not swim in, or even stand on the bank of, any river, stream, estuary, or mangrove.

One of the biggest local outfits, **Sugarland Car Rentals** (☎ 07/4052 1300; www. sugarland.com.au) has reasonable rates, 18 vehicle types including 4WDs, and offices in Cairns, Palm Cove, and Mission Beach. Most major campervan companies have offices in Cairns (see "Getting Around Australia," in chapter 2, for their contact details).

By Taxi & Limo   Call **Black & White Taxis** at ☎ 13 10 08. For a transfer or guided tour by town car or stretch limo, try **Black & White Limousines** (☎ 13 19 08 in Cairns, or 07/4051 5074). Cairns has several limousine operators.

WHAT TO SEE & DO IN & AROUND CAIRNS

If you're staying in Cairns, also check out what there is to see and do in and around Port Douglas (see section 3 of this chapter) and Mission Beach (see section 4 of this chapter). Many tour operators in Port Douglas, and a few in Mission Beach, offer free or affordable transfers from Cairns.

LEARNING ABOUT ABORIGINAL CULTURE

✪ **Tjapukai Aboriginal Cultural Park.** Off the Captain Cook Hwy. (beside the Skyrail terminal), Smithfield. ☎ **07/4042 9900.** Admission A$27 (U.S.$17.55) adults, A$13.50 (U.S.$8.80) children 4–14. Ask about packages that include lunch, a guided Magic Space tour, and optional transfers. Daily 9am–5pm. Closed Christmas and New Year's Day. Bus: 1C, 1E, 1G, 1H. Book shuttle transfers from Cairns and northern beaches hotels (A$14/U.S.$9.10 adults and A$7/U.S.$4.55 children) through the park. The park is approx. 15 min. north of Cairns and 15 min. south of Palm Cove along the Captain Cook Hwy.

Nowhere else in Australia are you likely to learn so much about Aboriginal culture in one place. The Tjapukai (or Djabugay) are the Aboriginal tribe indigenous to Cairns; their name means "people of the rain forest." This center was founded in 1987 by Don Freeman, a former Broadway director and accountant, and by Judy Freeman, a French-Canadian show dancer. Although Don and Judy are still heavily involved, the park is 51% owned by the Aboriginal people who work in it.

Housed in striking premises incorporating Aboriginal themes and colors, the park is based around three performances: First, there's a stirring film on how the white man's arrival in Cairns 120 years ago affected the Tjapukai. Next you move to the Creation Theatre for a really impressive high-tech reenactment of the Dreamtime creation. The third performance is an energetic dance by Aboriginal men, performed in the open-sided Dance Theatre. Each show takes 20 to 25 minutes and is designed to flow into the next one. It's good to do them in the order listed here, although you can wander through at your own pace in any way you like. The shows mostly commence hourly or every 2 hours, so there is always something on or about to start; only the dance troupe breaks for lunch.

Throughout the day there are ongoing didgeridoo demonstrations, spear- and boomerang-throwing lessons, and short talks on "bush tucker" (native foods). The gallery and gift shop is the best place in town to buy authentic Aboriginal art, didgeridoos, boomerangs, and quality gifts and souvenirs. And a tip for your tummy: The buffet lunch is excellent. Allow at least $2^1/_2$ hours to see the lot.

MORE ATTRACTIONS

In Cairns

Cairns Regional Gallery. Shields St. at Abbott St. ☎ **07/4031 6865.** Admission A$6 (U.S.$3.90) adults; A$3 (U.S.$1.95) seniors, students, and children; free admission Fri. Daily 10am–6pm. Closed Good Friday and Christmas.

Paintings, sculpture, and other works by a changing array of Australian and international artists, much of it with a modern skew, make this one of Australia's best nonmetropolitan galleries. It devotes plenty of space to Aboriginal and Torres Strait Islander artists.

Flecker Botanic Gardens. Collins Ave. (3km northwest of the city), Edge Hill. ☎ **07/4044 3398.** Admission free; guided walks A$4.50 (U.S.$2.95) adults, children under 13 free. Mon–Fri 7:30am–5:30pm, Sat–Sun and public holidays 8:30am–5:30pm. Bus: 7. Take Sheridan St. out of the city and turn left into Collins Ave.

These city-owned gardens are a 38-hectare (93-acre) Shangri-La of wetlands, orchids, lakes, palms, fruit trees, and walking trails. Guided walks take place at 1pm Monday to Friday. It has a cafe and bookshop.

Royal Flying Doctor Visitors Centre. 1 Junction St., Edge Hill (10-min. drive from the city). ☎ **07/4053 5687.** Admission A$5 (U.S.$3.25) adults, A$2.50 (U.S.$1.65) children, A$15 (U.S.$9.75) family pass for 2 adults and unlimited kids. Mon–Sat 9am–5pm. Closed all public holidays. Bus: 6, 6A.

Many folks are fascinated by the Royal Flying Doctor Service, the free aero-medical service that provides a "mantle of safety" for all Outback Australians. Here at the Cairns base, you can watch a film, chat with the guides about how the service began, browse through memorabilia, and board a former RFDS plane. Allow 45 minutes.

Two Wildlife Parks

Hartley's Creek Crocodile Farm. Captain Cook Hwy. (40km/25 miles north of Cairns, 25km/16 miles south of Port Douglas). ☎ **07/4055 3576.** Admission (including GST): A$16 (U.S.$10.40) adults, A$14.50 (U.S.$9.45) students, A$8 (U.S.$5.20) children 4–15, A$40 (U.S.$26) family pass for 2 adults and unlimited kids. Entry tickets are valid for unlimited repeat visits over 3 days. Daily 8:30am–5pm. Closed Christmas. Transfers available through Coral Coaches (☎ 07/4031 7577).

This working crocodile farm tucked away in the rain forest may be small, but it has loads of gigantic crocs on display. At 9:15am you can see them get fed. At 10am, the Aussie Icon Show presents famous Aussie critters like wallabies, followed by a farm tour at 11am. Kids can pet koalas at the mammal talk at 1pm, and a snake in the 2pm snake show; at 3:45pm you can have your photo taken holding a live croc; at 4pm it's koala feeding time; and at 4:15pm the cassowaries eat. The highlight is the 45-minute "croc attack" show at 3pm. This place is a good stop en route to Port Douglas. Crocs never move much except to eat, so turn up at feeding or show time to see them in action (the same advice applies to visiting Wild World, below).

Wild World: The Tropical Zoo. Captain Cook Hwy. (22km/14 miles north of Cairns), Palm Cove. ☎ **07/4055 3669.** Admission A$20 (U.S.$13) adults, A$10 (U.S.$6.50) children 4–15; Cairns Night Zoo experience A$69 (U.S.$44.85) adults, A$34.50 (U.S.$22.45) children 4–15. Kangaroo feed A$1 (U.S.65¢) per bag. Daily 8:30am–5pm; Cairns Night Zoo Mon–Thurs and Sat 7–10pm. Closed Christmas. Bus: 1B. Transfers available through Coral Coaches (☎ 07/4031 7577).

Most of the popular Aussie animals are on show here. You'll see kangaroos, emus, and rainbow lorikeets (all of which you can hand-feed), cassowaries, dingoes, wombats (which you can pet at 2:30pm), snakes, lizards, and birds in a walk-through aviary. A photo of you cuddling a koala is an extra A$11.50/U.S.$7.50; photos are taken at 11:15am and 2:30pm. Some kind of talk or show takes place every 15 to 30 minutes or so throughout the day, such as koala talks and crocodile feeding.

Many Aussie critters are nocturnal, so they can be more interesting to see at night than by day. If you would like to take the park's **Cairns Night Zoo tour,** book by 4pm that day, earlier if you want hotel transfers. This evening includes a wildlife spotlighting walk on which you can pat a koala and a possum and feed 'roos, a BBQ dinner with beer and wine, billy tea and damper, supper, and dancing to a live Aussie bush ballad or two.

DIVING & SNORKELING THE GREAT BARRIER REEF

Several large catamarans, a few sailing vessels, and many small dive boats make day trips to the Great Barrier Reef from Cairns. The two biggest are run by Great Adventures and Sunlover Cruises. Daily cruises with **Great Adventures** (☎ 07/4044 9944) take about 90 minutes in air-conditioned 300-passenger catamarans to a three-level pontoon on Norman or Moore reefs, with an underwater observatory and a kids' pool. You get at least 3 hours on the Reef. Free semisubmersible rides, a marine biology talk, snorkel gear, and lunch is included in the cost of A$139 (U.S.$90.35) adults, A$69.50 (U.S.$45.20) children ages 4 to 14, and A$347.50 (U.S.$225.90) for a family of four. Hotel transfers are available from Cairns, the northern beaches, and Port Douglas for an extra charge. Guided snorkel tours are A$15 (U.S.$9.75) extra, introductory dives are A$88 (U.S.$57.20) extra, and certified dives cost A$60 (U.S.$39) for one dive, A$88 (U.S.$57.20) for two, or A$175 (U.S.$113.75) for the whole day—cruise, lunch, snorkeling, and two dives.

You can depart Cairns earlier with Great Adventures and spend around 2 hours on Green Island en route (see below). This cruise costs A$155 (U.S.$100.75) adults, A$85.50 (U.S.$55.60) kids, or A$387.50 (U.S.$251.90) families. Guests at Green Island Resort can join the cruise for A$110 (U.S.$71.50).

Sunlover Cruises (☎ 1800/810 512 in Australia, or 07/4050 1333) includes free snorkel safaris and hotel pickups from Cairns and the northern beaches in its two outer Reef trips aboard 320-passenger air-conditioned catamarans. The first stops at Fitzroy Island for a rain-forest walk and a snorkel lesson, then heads to Moore Reef. You spend about an hour on Fitzroy Island and about 3 hours on the Reef. The journey takes 55 minutes to Fitzroy, and a further 45 minutes to the Reef. The trip costs A$142 (U.S.$92.30) adults, A$71 (U.S.$46.15) kids 4 to 14, and A$335 (U.S.$217.75) for a family of four. Sunlover's second trip also picks up passengers at Palm Cove (a 50-min. journey) before heading to Arlington Reef (a further 75 min.). You spend almost 4 hours on the Reef. This trip costs A$126 (U.S.$81.90) adults, A$63 (U.S.$40.95) kids, and A$315 (U.S.$204.75) families. Introductory dives on either trip cost A$93 (U.S.$60.45). Certified dives cost A$83 (U.S.$53.95) for one dive; there is not always time for a second one. Pontoons at both reefs have underwater observatories, semisub coral viewing boats, and a marine-life touch tank, and both trips include a marine biology presentation.

Both companies offer scenic **helicopter** flights over the Reef from their pontoons. The Reef is spectacular from the air. Ask about fly/cruise and fly/fly day trips.

You can board the Port Douglas–based **Quicksilver Wavepiercers** in Cairns or Palm Cove. The fare for the whole day from Cairns or Palm Cove is A$160 (U.S.$104) adults, A$82.50 (U.S.$53.65) kids 4 to 14. The second child travels free in a family package. Ask about fly/cruise packages incorporating a helicopter flight to the Reef one-way and the Quicksilver boat the other. Passengers can also transfer by coach to join Port Douglas–based 30-passenger snorkeling specialist **Wavelength.** Both boats are described in section 3, later in this chapter.

Ocean Spirit Cruises (☎ 1800/644 227 in Australia, or 07/4031 2920) operates two sailing cats taking 150 or 100 passengers to Michaelmas Cay or Upolu Cay, two sandy islands surrounded by reefs. Michaelmas is home to 27,000 sea birds; you may spot dugongs (manatee) off Upolu. The trip includes a 2-hour sail to either cay, a snorkel safari, guided beach walks, a marine biology presentation, semisubmersible rides, lunch, and a free glass of bubbly and live music on the way home. You get about 4 hours on the Reef. The trip to Michaelmas is A$150 (U.S.$97.50) adults, and A$415 (U.S.$269.75) for a family of four. The trip to Upolu costs A$122 (U.S.$79.30) adults, and A$330 (U.S.$214.50) for families. Children 4 to 14 pay half price. Hotel transfers from Cairns and the northern beaches are free; transfers from Port Douglas are available at extra cost. Introductory dives cost A$85 (U.S.$55.25), and certified dives cost A$53 (U.S.$34.45) for one or A$85 (U.S.$55.25) for two. A package to Upolu containing an introductory dive costs A$180 (U.S.$117) per person. Both boats depart daily.

As a cheaper alternative to these "big guys" above, Pat and Mike Woolford of Lilybank Bed & Breakfast recommend **Seahorse** (☎ 07/4041 1919). This 20-passenger 15.2-meter (50-ft) sailing schooner visits Upolu Cay daily for just A$60 (U.S.$39) per adult and A$35 (U.S.$22.75) kids 3 to 13. Like the big guys, it has an onboard marine naturalist; unlike many big guys, it does a free snorkel safari. Introductory dives are a very cheap A$45 (U.S.$29.25); a certified dive is a terrifically low A$25 (U.S.$16.25). This isn't a flashy boat, but happy Lilybank guests told me they had a decent lunch, sailed back with a wine/cheese/fruit platter, and liked the personal attention from the crew.

Divers have countless dive sites to choose from within a 2-hour boat ride from shore. There are more sites farther afield, too, like the famous ✪ **Cod Hole off Lizard Island,** where you can hand-feed giant potato cod. It is accessible on a day trip from exclusive Lizard Island (see "Accommodations," below); otherwise, it is usually accessed on a 4-day live-aboard trip from Cairns offered by a number of dive operators. One hundred to 200 kilometers offshore, beyond the Great Barrier Reef, the ✪ **Coral Sea** boasts huge cliffs, 30-meter (100-ft.) visibility, and big fish like whaler sharks, hammerheads, and barracuda.

You can dive with the boats mentioned above, but divers will likely get more out of a trip with a dedicated dive boat. Among the established dive operators offering day trips, live-aboard expeditions, and learn-to-dive courses are **Down Under Dive** (☎ 1800/079 099 in Australia, or 07/4031 1288; www.downunderdive.com.au), **Tusa Dive** (☎ 07/4031 1248; www.tusadive.com), and **Deep Sea Divers Den** (☎ 07/4031 2223; www.divers-den.com). Large Townsville dive operator **Mike Ball Dive Expeditions** (☎ 07/4031 5484; www.mikeball.com) also runs live-aboard trips from Cairns. This is not an exhaustive list of Cairns' many dive operators. You can find many more through **Dive Queensland** (☎ 07/4051 1510; www.great-barrier-reef. net.au), an association of dive operators whose members stick to a code of ethics. Remember, island resorts offer diving, too.

EXPLORING THE ISLANDS

You don't have to go all the way to the outer Reef to see coral. Less than an hour from the city wharf, Green Island has snorkeling equal to that on the Great Barrier Reef. Fitzroy Island has rain-forest walks, coral accessible by dive and snorkel boat trips from the island, and water sports. See "Accommodations," later in this section, for details of the resorts on both islands.

✪ **GREEN ISLAND** Twenty-seven kilometers (17 miles) east of Cairns is Green Island, a 15-hectare (37-acre) Great Barrier Reef coral cay surrounded by dazzling coral and marine life. Here you can rent snorkel gear, windsurfers, and paddle-skis;

A Travel Tip

Unless you know what tours you want to take, it often pays to wait until you get to Cairns to book them. Local travel agents, your hotel or B&B host, and other travelers are all good sources of advice. Cairns has some 600 tour operators, so even in peak season, it's rare for a tour to be booked up more than 24 hours in advance.

take glass-bottom boat trips; go parasailing; take an introductory or certified dive; walk vine-forest trails; or laze on the beach. The beach is coral sand, so it's a little rough underfoot. Day visitors can use one of Green Island Resort's pools, its main bar, its casual or upscale restaurants, and its lockers and showers; they can buy basics, ice cream, and beachwear. If you don't snorkel, it's worth the meager admission charge to see the magical display of clown fish, potato cod, and anemones at the little underwater observatory, despite its cloudy old viewing windows. The island has a small attraction called **Marineland Melanesia,** where you can see old nautical artifacts, primitive art, a turtle and reef aquarium, and live crocodiles, including Cassius, said to be the biggest saltwater croc in captivity. Admission is A$8.50 (U.S.$5.55) adults, A$4 (U.S.$2.60) kids; croc shows are at 10:30am and 1:45pm.

Great Adventures (☎ 07/4044 9944) and **Big Cat Green Island Reef Cruises** (☎ 07/4051 0444) both make half- and full-day trips to Green Island from Cairns. Expect to pay around A$50 (U.S.$32.50) for a half-day trip with snorkel gear or a glass-bottom boat cruise. A full-day trip can be as much as A$90 (U.S.$58.50), but Big Cat makes a day trip for as little as A$49 (U.S.$31.85). Big Cat's boat is slower, but you still get 5¹/₂ hours on the island. Both companies pick up from hotels in Cairns, the northern beaches, and Port Douglas for a little extra; Big Cat runs to the island direct from Palm Cove also. Boat transfers alone with the island's ferry operator, Great Adventures, are A$44 (U.S.$28.60) adults, A$22 (U.S.$14.30) kids 4 to 14, round-trip.

You can stay for dinner at Green Island Resort's pretty restaurant, Emerald's, and return on Great Adventures' 10:30pm staff run; it's an appealing alternative to Cairn's lackluster dining scene. Bookings are essential; the 10:30pm boat runs only Tuesday, Wednesday, Friday, and Sunday.

FITZROY ISLAND   It may not have the off-the-beach coral and wide beaches of Green Island, but equally scenic Fitzroy Island is a hilly rain-forested national park 45 minutes offshore that offers good diving. Here you can rent windsurfers, catamarans, and canoes; hike to the mountain-top lighthouse; view coral from a glass-bottom boat or take a short boat trip from the island to snorkel it; take a beginners' or certified dive; and swim in the modest pool. A day trip is simply the price of the ferry fare at A$36 (U.S.$23.40) round-trip, or A$18 (U.S.$11.70) for kids 4 to 14. Book through **Raging Thunder Adventures** (☎ 07/4030 7990). Raging Thunder also runs guided **sea-kayak expeditions** around Fitzroy Island. The trips include transfers from your Cairns hotel and a boat transfer to the island, 3 hours of kayaking, snorkeling gear, lunch on a deserted beach, and a rain-forest walk to the lighthouse. The full-day trip costs A$110 (U.S.$71.50).

EXPLORING THE WET TROPICS RAIN FOREST

The dense rain forest that blankets the hills behind Cairns is part of the ✪ **Wet Tropics of Queensland World Heritage Area** that stretches from Cooktown to Townsville. Unchanged by ice ages and other blips on the geological timeline, its animals and plants retain primitive characteristics from the days when Australia belonged

---

A Wildlife-Viewing Tip

If you want to spot rain-forest wildlife, join a specialist tour. To avoid contact with humans on the coast, rain-forest animals are increasingly retreating to higher altitudes; however, most tour operators in Daintree National Park stick to the lowlands. Rain-forest animals are shy, camouflaged, nocturnal, or all three, so evening spotlighting trips offer the most wildlife-viewing bang for your buck.

---

to Gondwana, the supercontinent it occupied with Africa, India, South America, and Antarctica. It shelters 65% of Australia's bird species, 60% of its butterfly species, and many of its frogs, reptiles, bats, marsupials, and orchids.

I saw seven possum species here, including the cute black-and-white Herbert River variety, gliders, musky-rat kangaroos, eastern water dragons and Boyd's forest dragons (lizards), a sawshell turtle, flying foxes, glowworms, neon-blue Ulysses butterflies, and (a rare sight even for an Aussie) two platypuses in the wild on a wildlife-spotting trip with ✪ **Wait-A-While Environmental Tours** (☎ **07/4033 1153**). Using low-wattage bulbs and binoculars, a knowledgeable naturalist guide led our group of eight (that's the maximum) into restricted parts of the forest. Tours depart Cairns daily at 2pm, return around midnight or 1am, and include dinner at a country restaurant and a fun candle-lit supper in the forest. The cost is A$132 (U.S.$85.80) for adults and A$99 (U.S.$64.35) for children under 15. Of the two itineraries, the Atherton Tableland one is best for spotting wildlife. Highly recommended.

I have yet to try it, but **Uncle Brian's Fun, Falls & Forest** (☎ **07/4050 0615**) got rave reviews from American travelers I spoke to. This rain-forest adventure packs gentle hiking, singing under waterfalls, natural water-sliding, platypus-spotting, forest picnics, and the odd giggle-making surprise into a day trip. It departs Cairns Monday, Wednesday, Friday, and Saturday, and costs A$60 (U.S.$39) per person.

A WET TROPICS VILLAGE: A SIDE TRIP TO KURANDA

Few travelers visit Cairns without making a day trip to the pretty mountain village of Kuranda, 34 kilometers (21 miles) west of the city within the Wet Tropics. Although it's undeniably touristy, the cool mountain air and mist-wrapped, jungly scenery cannot be spoiled, no matter how many visitors clutter the streets. The town is easily negotiated on foot, so pick up a visitors' guide and map at the Skyrail station or train station when you arrive.

GETTING THERE

Getting to Kuranda is part of the fun. Some people drive up on the winding 25-kilometer (16-mile) road, but the most popular routes are to chuff up the mountain-side in a scenic train, or to glide silently over the rain-forest canopy in the world's longest cable-car route, the Skyrail Rainforest Cableway. Most folk combine the two; they take Skyrail on the way up to Kuranda (mornings are best for camera hounds) and the train back down to Cairns in the afternoon. Both routes traverse the 2,820-hectare (6,965-acre) Barron Gorge National Park.

BY SKYRAIL The ✪ **Skyrail Rainforest Cableway** (☎ **07/4038 1555**) is a magnificent feat of engineering and one of Australia's best attractions. One of 114 six-person gondolas leaves every few seconds from the Skyrail terminal in Cairns for the 7.5-kilometer (4¹/₂-mile) journey over lush virgin rain forest. The view of the coast as you ascend is wonderful, and once you're over the range, nothing but green spreads to the horizon. En route, you can choose to make two stops. At **Red Peak station,** explore the dripping palm fronds on a signposted raised boardwalk (hang around for the free guided walks that run every 20 min.). At the second stop, you can get out and view **Barron Falls,** magnificent after heavy rain, and visit a **Rainforest Interpretative Center.** The one-way trip takes about 40 minutes, or about 90 minutes if you make the two stops.

A ticket is A$30 (U.S.$19.50) one-way, A$45 (U.S.$29.25) round-trip for adults; A$15 (U.S.$9.75) one-way, A$22.50 (U.S.$14.65) round-trip for children 4 to 14; and A$75 (U.S.$48.75) one-way, A$112.50 (U.S.$73.15) round-trip for families. With transfers from your Cairns or northern beaches hotel, round-trip tickets are A$59 (U.S.$38.35) adults, A$29.50 (U.S.$19.20) children, and A$147.50 (U.S.$95.90) families; or A$73 (U.S.$47.45) adults, A$36.50 (U.S.$23.75) kids, and A$182.50 (U.S.$118.65) families from Port Douglas. You must book a seat on a gondola, specifying a 15-minute segment in which you will travel. The cable way operates daily from 8am to 5pm (closed Christmas and New Year's Day), with last boarding at the Cairns end at 3:45pm sharp. The Skyrail terminal is on the Captain Cook Highway at Kamerunga Road, Caravonica Lakes, 15 kilometers (9 miles) north of downtown. The signposted turnoff is to your left at a major roundabout. Buses 1C, 1E, 1G, and 1H stop there.

BY SCENIC RAILWAY   The 34-kilometer (21-mile) **Kuranda Scenic Railway** (☎ **1800/620 324** in Australia, or 07/4031 3636) hugs a fern-covered mountainside, traverses gorges, makes a photo stop at Barron Falls, rises 328 meters (1,076 ft.), and goes through 15 tunnels before emerging at the pretty fern-smothered Kuranda station. The trip to or from Cairns takes 90 minutes. The train, a historic locomotive, departs Cairns Central at 8:30 and 9:30am every day except Christmas (no 9:30am train on Sat) and leaves Kuranda at 2 and 3:30pm (no 2pm trip on Sat). Fares are A$29.60 (U.S.$19.25) adults, A$19.80 (U.S.$12.90) Australian seniors and students (no discounts for international visitors), and A$15 (U.S.$9.75) kids 4 to 15. A pass for a family of four is A$74.80 (U.S.$48.65).

SKYRAIL/TRAIN COMBINATION TICKETS   Many travelers opt for a package of Skyrail travel in one direction and the Kuranda Scenic Railway trip in the other. Three-way packages are also available that combine Skyrail and Kuranda Scenic Railway with entry to Tjapukai Aboriginal Cultural Park, or to Rainforestation Nature Park. The packages offer convenience rather than savings. All are available with optional transfers from Cairns, northern beaches and Port Douglas accommodations, and transfers between Skyrail and the nearest Kuranda Scenic Railway train station at Freshwater, 7 kilometers (4 miles) away. Adult prices without hotel transfers, but including the Skyrail-Freshwater transfer, are A$64.60 (U.S.$42) for a Skyrail/Scenic Railway duo, A$91.60 (U.S.$59.55) for the Skyrail/Scenic Railway/Tjapukai trio, and A$102.60 (U.S.$66.70) for the Skyrail/Scenic Railway/Rainforestation option. Kids 4 to 14 pay about half price; a second child in a family of four travels free. Skyrail, Kuranda Scenic Railway, and the Tjapukai park sell packages.

OTHER WAYS TO GET THERE   White Car Coaches (☎ **07/4091 1855**) operates several daily bus services to Kuranda departing from 48 Spence St., Cairns. The fare is A$7 (U.S.$4.55) adults and A$3.50 (U.S.$2.30) kids 4 to 12.

EXPLORING KURANDA

Kuranda is known for two markets that sell locally made arts and crafts, fresh produce, boomerangs, toys, T-shirts, and jewelry. The small "original" markets, behind the Kuranda Market Arcade, open Wednesday through Friday and Sunday, mainly sell cheap imports these days. The 90-stall **Heritage markets** (☎ **07/4093 8060**), open daily from 9am to 3pm, offer better quality and a wider variety.

You may find higher quality again at the **Kuranda Arts Co-operative,** 20 Coondoo St. (☎ 07/4093 9026), where some 50 local artisans sell furniture, paintings, and other works. It is open from 10am to 4pm daily. Kuranda also has stores selling opals, Australian-made handicrafts, crocodile and kangaroo leather goods, paintings and prints, stationery, Aboriginal art and artifacts, Akubra hats, books, and all manner of other stuff, most of it with some kind of Australiana motif.

An array of short, easy **walking trails** wind from Kuranda through the rain forest and along the Barron River. Brian Clarke of ✪ **Kuranda Rainforest Tours** (☎ 07/4093 7476) runs informative 45-minute river cruises departing regularly from 10:15am to 2:30pm from the riverside landing across the footbridge near the train station. He also runs a daily 1-hour 400-meter nature walk through the forest leaving at 11:45am. Brian is a former professional crocodile hunter and has lived in the rain forest for over 30 years. The cruise or the walk costs A$12.50 (U.S.$7) for adults, A$6 (U.S.$3.50) for kids 5 to 15, and A$30 (U.S.$8.15) for families. Combined cruise/walk tickets are cheaper. Buy tickets on board.

KURANDA'S NATURE PARKS

Kuranda has several small wildlife attractions, including two small but lovely walk-through aviaries. **Birdworld** (☎ 07/4093 9188), located behind the Heritage Markets off Rob Veivers Drive, has more eye-catching species, showing rain-forest birds from around the world, including macaws. It's open daily from 9am to 4pm; admission is A$10 (U.S.$6.50) for adults, A$9 (U.S.$5.85) for seniors, and A$3 (U.S.$1.95) for school-age children. ✪ **The Aviary,** 8 Thongon St. (☎ 07/4093 7411), is good for seeing a wider range of Australian species, especially colorful parrots. It's open from 10am to 4pm; admission is A$10 (U.S.$6.50) for adults, A$9 (U.S.$5.85) for seniors and students, A$4.50 (U.S.$2.95) for kids 4 to 16, and A$25 (U.S.$16.25) for a family of four. Both aviaries are closed Christmas.

✪ **Australian Butterfly Sanctuary.** 8 Rob Veivers Dr. ☎ **07/4093 7575.** Admission A$11.50 (U.S.$7.50) adults, A$10.50 (U.S.$6.85) seniors, A$5 (U.S.$3.25) students and children 5–16, family pass A$28 (U.S.$18.20) for 2 adults and 2 children; extra children A$4 (U.S.$2.60). Daily 9:45am–4pm. Free guided tours depart from 10am approx. every 15 min.; last tour departs 3:15pm. Closed Christmas.

A lovely array of more than 1,500 tropical butterflies—including the electrifyingly beautiful "Ulysses blue" and the Cairns birdwing, Australia's largest species—is housed in a lush walk-through enclosure here. Definitely take the free tour for a neat insight into the butterfly's life cycle. *A tip:* Wear pink, red, or other bright colors and the creatures will likely land on you.

Rainforestation Nature Park. On the Kennedy Hwy., a 5-min. drive from the center of Kuranda. ☎ **07/4093 9033.** See prices below. Daily 9am–4pm. Closed Christmas. A shuttle costing A$6 (U.S.$3.90) adults, A$3 (U.S.$1.95) children, and $13.75 (U.S.$8.95) family round-trip departs 1/2-hourly from Skyrail and train terminals 10:15–11:15am and Australian Butterfly Sanctuary 10:45am–2:45pm.

At this 40-hectare (99-acre) complex, you can plunge into a lake in a World War II amphibious Army Duck on a tour of the rain-forest ecosystem. You can also see a performance by Aboriginal dancers, learn about Aboriginal legends, throw a boomerang

---

A Travel Tip

Bring some warm clothing to Kuranda in winter (June to Aug). It never gets to freezing, but it does get nippy up in the mountains.

and play a didgeridoo, and see artifacts and Aboriginal dwellings on the Dreamtime Walk. In the wildlife park, you can have your photo taken cuddling a koala and hand-feed 'roos. You can pay to do any of these activities separately, or do all of them (except cuddle a koala) in a package that costs A$32.50 (U.S.$21.15) for adults, A$16.25 (U.S.$10.50) for kids 4 to 14, or A$81.25 (U.S.$52.80) for a family of five. Koala photos are A$11.50 (U.S.$7.50). The 45-minute Army Duck runs on the hour from 10am; the dancers perform at 11:30am and 2pm; and the Dreamtime Walk, which takes about 30 minutes, leaves at 11am, noon, 1:30pm, and 2:30pm.

WHITE-WATER RAFTING & OTHER OUTDOOR ACTIVITIES

The **Adventure Company** (☎ 800/388-7333 in the U.S., or 07/4051 4777), **RnR Rafting** (☎ 07/4051 7777) and **Raging Thunder Adventures** (☎ 07/4030 7990) serve as one-stop booking shops for a panoply of action pursuits in and around Cairns, like hot-air ballooning, skydiving, jet-boating, horse riding, ATV (all-terrain vehicle) safaris, parasailing, and rafting. Ask them about multipursuit packages.

For details on diving and snorkeling the Great Barrier Reef, see "Exploring the Great Barrier Reef," earlier in this chapter.

BIKING   The 1996 World Mountain Bike Championships were held in the wild rain-forest hills behind the city. **Dan's Mountain Biking** (☎ 07/4033 0128) runs a range of tours, priced from A$65 (U.S.$42.25) for a half day to A$125 (U.S.$81.25) for a day.

BUNGEE JUMPING   A. J. Hackett Bungy (☎ 07/4057 7188) launches thrill seekers from a platform in the rain forest, 20 minutes north of town on McGregor Road. A jump costs A$99 (U.S.$64.35), with free transport from Cairns and northern beaches hotels.

FISHING   Cairns is the giant black-marlin capital of the world. Catches weighing in at more than 1,000 pounds hardly raise an eyebrow in this neck of the woods. The ✪ **game fishing season** is September to December; October/November is peak. Book early then, because boats are reserved months ahead. **Destination Cairns Marketing,** Shop 5 in the Hilton hotel complex, Wharf Street (☎ 1800/807 730 in Australia or 07/4051 4107), can book you a charter. You will pay around A$400 (U.S.$260) per person per day for heavy-tackle game fishing, A$190 to $250 (U.S.$123.50 to $162.50) for light tackle stuff, A$100 to $145 (U.S.$65 to $94.25) for reef fishing, and A$120 (U.S.$78) for a day or A$60 (U.S.$39) for a half day in the Cairns Inlet estuary.

GOLF   Cairns's best course, the championship **Paradise Palms Golf Course** at Clifton Beach (☎ 07/4059 1166), abuts the ranges in the northern suburbs. Nine holes are A$60 (U.S.$39), 18 holes are A$100 (U.S.$65), cart included. Greens fees entitle you to a free hour on the tennis court and use of the swimming pool and sauna. No public transport operates there. **Koala Golf** (☎ 07/4032 2718) runs day trips to Paradise Palms and four other courses, including the plush fairways at the Sheraton Mirage Port Douglas.

SKYDIVING   Great views of the rain-forest and sea will greet you as you plummet to earth in tandem with an instructor with one of Cairns's several skydiving companies. At **Paul's Parachuting** (☎ 07/4051 8855), prices range from A$228 to $348 (U.S.$148.20 to $226.20); the higher the jump, the higher the price. Pickups from hotels as far away as Port Douglas are included.

WATER SPORTS   Cairns Parasail & Watersport Adventures (☎ 07/4031 7888), on the ground floor of the Pier Marketplace by the Esplanade, offers parasailing, jet-ski rental, and "chariot" rides (an inflatable two-seat contraption pulled by a speed-boat) in Trinity Harbour. Each activity costs A$65 (U.S.$42.25), or A$25 (U.S.$16.25) for the chariot ride; that includes free pickup from city hotels.

○ **WHITE-WATER RAFTING** Several companies offer white-water rafting trips from Cairns on the Grade 3 to 4 Tully River, 90 minutes south near Mission Beach; white-water rafting on the Grade 3 Barron River in the hills behind the city; and heli-rafting adventures on the Grade 4 to 5 rapids of the inland Johnstone River. One of the best outfitters is ○ **RnR Rafting** (☎ **07/4051 7777**).

One-day trips on the **Tully River** are suitable for all ages and abilities and are the most popular. You can do this if you're staying in Cairns or Port Douglas. For details, see "The North Coast: Mission Beach, Townsville & the Islands," later in this chapter.

The gentler **Barron River** is a good choice for the timid. Half-day trips with RnR Rafting featuring 2 hours' rafting depart twice a day and cost A$79 (U.S.$51.35) from Cairns or A$90 (U.S.$58.50) from Port Douglas.

ACCOMMODATIONS

High season in Cairns includes 2 weeks at Easter, the period from early July to early October, and the Christmas holiday through January. Book ahead in those periods. During the **low season,** from November to June, always ask about discounted rates, because many hotels will be willing to negotiate.

The major drawback of staying in Cairns city? There's no beach, just unswimmable mudflats. To reach the sand, head 20 to 30 minutes north of downtown to the northern beaches.

Don't think you have to stay in Cairns city if you don't have a car. Most tour and cruise operators will pick you up and drop you off in Cairns, on the northern beaches, or even in Port Douglas (see section 3, later in this chapter).

IN CAIRNS

Unless noted otherwise, all accommodations below are within walking distance of shops, restaurants, cinemas, the casino, the tourist office, bus terminals, the train station, and the departure terminals for Great Barrier Reef cruises.

Very Expensive

○ **Hotel Sofitel Reef Casino.** 35–41 Wharf St., Cairns, QLD 4870. ☎ **1800/808 883** in Australia, 800/221 4542 in the U.S. and Canada, 020/8283 4500 in the U.K., 0800/44 4422 in New Zealand, or 07/4030 8888. Fax 07/4030 8777. www.hotelweb.fr. E-mail: res@ reefcasino.com.au. 128 units. A/C MINIBAR TV TEL. A$380–$600 (U.S.$247–$390) double; A$710–$2,190 (U.S.$461.50–$1,423.50) suite. Extra person A$33 (U.S.$21.45) extra. Children under 15 stay free in parents' room using existing bedding. AE, BC, DC, JCB, MC, V. Free valet and self-parking. Airport shuttle.

Arguably the most stylish five-star property in Cairns, this six-story hotel is 1 block from the water, with partial water views from some rooms, and nice city/hinterland outlooks from others. All the rooms, which have lots of light and higher-quality fittings than the average five-star digs, come with Jacuzzis, VCRs, pay-per-view movies, modem jacks, safes, bathrobes, hair dryers, and small balconies with smart timber furniture. The town casino is attached to the hotel.

Dining/Diversions: In addition to dinner shows in the Conservatory (see "Cairns After Dark," below), Anthia's offers fine dining, Pacific Flavors Brasserie does a good-value "Hot Wok" Asian buffet, and the heritage-listed Customs House coffee shop serves light meals. There is a lobby bar.

Amenities: Smallish rooftop pool with a nice large sundeck, Jacuzzi, gym, sauna, massage, concierge, 24-hour room service, twice-daily maid service, baby-sitting, dry cleaning/laundry, business center, secretarial services, express checkout, currency exchange, tour desk, lobby shop.

Radisson Plaza Hotel. Pierpoint Rd., Cairns, QLD 4870. ☎ **1800/333 333** in Australia and New Zealand, 800/333-3333 in the U.S. and Canada, 0800/37 4411 in the U.K., 1800/55 7474 in Ireland, or 07/4031 1411. Fax 07/4031 3226. www.radissoncairns.com.au. E-mail: reservations@radissoncairns.com.au. 219 units. A/C MINIBAR TV TEL. A$347–$517 (U.S.$225.55–$336.05) double, A$693 (U.S.$450.45) suite. Extra person A$33 (U.S.$21.45). Children under 17 stay free in parents' room using existing bedding. AE, BC, DC, JCB, MC, V. Free outdoor self-parking; undercover and valet parking A$5 (U.S.$3.25). Airport shuttle.

Everyone goes "wow!" when they enter the rain-forest lobby of this low-rise hotel on Trinity Bay. Tall trees (real ones) and cockatoos (papier-mâché) give the place a great atmosphere. Sporting the best views of any city-center hotel, the rooms were renovated in 1999 with smart maple entryways and a gold and navy decor. Each has a VCR, pay-per-view movies, a balcony, and a view of the harbor, the city, tropical gardens, or the big free-form pool. The bathrooms all have marble and maple fittings, big corner tubs, and hair dryers. The hotel is connected to The Pier shopping mall and is next to the Great Barrier Reef cruise terminals.

Dining/Diversions: The formal Sirocco restaurant has stunning harbor views in the day. There are also a casual restaurant and a poolside cafe/bar. The Trinity Blue cocktail bar is a nice relaxing spot overlooking the water.

Amenities: Large swimming pool and sundeck, Jacuzzi, children's pool, game room, poolside Ping-Pong and snooker, gym, sauna, in-room massage, concierge, tour desk, 24-hour room service, dry-cleaning/laundry service, baby-sitting, secretarial services, business center, conference facilities, express checkout.

Expensive

Matson Resort Cairns. The Esplanade (at Kerwin St.), Cairns, QLD 4870. ☎ **1800/079 105** in Australia, or 07/4031 2211. Fax 07/4031 2704. www.matsonresort.com.au. E-mail: res@matsonresort.com.au. 342 units. A/C MINIBAR TV TEL. A$220–$260 (U.S.$143–$169) double; A$150 (U.S.$97.50) studio; A$165–$310 (U.S.$107.25–$201.50) apt. (to sleep 2–5). Extra person A$25 (U.S.$16.25). Ask about Reef and golf packages. AE, BC, DC, JCB, MC, V. Free parking for 177 cars. Courtesy transfers to and from airport.

Not glitzy but well-run, the 14-story Matson is a 20-minute waterfront walk from downtown. All the accommodations have been refurbished over the past 3 years. The one- and two-bedroom apartments look out to the sea; hotel rooms have sea or mountain views. The rooms are spacious, but the bathrooms are not, perhaps reflecting the hotel's Japanese market. All units have hair dryers and pay-per-view movies; some have dataports. Out back are cheaper studios and apartments, a tad worn, but a good value. Out front is a pretty free-form pool and sundeck.

Dining: The Crystal Twig restaurant and bar offer fine dining 5 nights a week, but you may prefer the fun concoct-it-yourself wok-fries, pasta lunches, and Sunday barbecues in the Coral Hedge restaurant off the lobby.

Amenities: Three swimming pools, extensive gym with aerobics and karate classes, massage, two day/night tennis courts, sauna, Jacuzzi, 7-11 store, pantry-stocking service in apartments, 24-hour room service, Sony PlayStations for rent, safes for rent, secretarial services, tour desk, currency exchange, salon, conference facilities.

Oasis Resort Cairns. 122 Lake St., Cairns, QLD 4870. ☎ **1300/65 6565** in Australia, 800/221-4542 in the U.S. and Canada, 020/8283 4500 in the U.K., 0800/44 4422 in New Zealand, or 07/4080 1888. Fax 07/4080 1889. www.oasis-cairns.com.au. E-mail: info@oasis-cairns.com.au. 314 units. A/C MINIBAR TV TEL. A$197–$219 (U.S.$128.05–$142.35) double; A$328 (U.S.$213.20) suite. Extra person A$32.50 (U.S.$21.15). Children under 17 stay free in parents' room using existing bedding. Free crib. Ask about packages. AE, BC, DC, JCB, MC, V. Free valet and self-parking. Airport shuttle.

So what if downtown Cairns doesn't have a beach? You've got a neat little sandy one right here—and a swim-up bar to boot—at the large free-form swimming pool at this attractive six-story resort built in 1997. All the colorful, contemporary rooms have views over the tropical gardens, mountains, or the pool; smart bathrooms with hair dryers; safes; and pay-per-view movies. The suites, with a TV in the bedroom and a large Jacuzzi bathtub, could well be the best-value suites in town.

Dining/Diversions: The attractive Springs buffet restaurant overlooks the pool, and the swim-up bar does light meals. Live music plays some nights in the lobby bar.

Amenities: Concierge, room service, complimentary newspaper delivery on request, dry cleaning/laundry, baby-sitting, children's pool, gym, tour desk, small conference facilities, express checkout, currency exchange, lobby shop.

Moderate

✪ **Bay Village Tropical Retreat.** Corner of Lake and Gatton sts., Cairns, QLD 4870. ☎ **07/4051 4622.** Fax 07/4051 4057. www.bayvillage.com.au. E-mail: reservations@bayvillage. com.au. 63 units (most with shower only). A/C TV TEL. A$123.30 (U.S.$80.15) double, A$137.50 (U.S.$89.40) studio, A$192.50 (U.S.$125.15) 2-bedroom apt. Extra person A$22 (U.S.$14.30). Children under 15 stay free in parents' room using existing bedding. Crib A$5.50 (U.S.$3.60). AE, BC, DC, MC, V. Free parking (for limited number of cars); ample on-street parking. Free airport shuttle.

An inviting swimming pool and sundeck tucked in a lush garden courtyard, plus a fashionable decor, make this two-story hotel a half mile from downtown a charming choice for its price range. All rooms are a decent size, but the studios are especially roomy. Parents will like the separate bedroom in the family rooms. The bathrooms are compact but smartly done, with hair dryers. Among the facilities are a pleasant restaurant and 24-hour bar, a free barbecue, room service, and a friendly staff who run the tour desk.

Tuna Towers. 145 The Esplanade (at Minnie St.), Cairns, QLD 4870. ☎ **07/4051 4688.** Fax 07/4051 8129. www.ozemail.com.au/~tunatowr. E-mail: tunatowers@bigpond.com. 60 units. A/C MINIBAR TV TEL. A$124 (U.S.$80.60) double, A$140 (U.S.$91) studio apt. double; A$167 (U.S.$108.55) suite. Extra person A$10 (U.S.$6.50). AE, BC, DC, JCB, MC, V. Limited free parking; some on-street parking. Airport shuttle.

The harbor views at this multistory motel and apartment complex are better than those at most of the five-star hotels in Cairns. Two blocks from town, the accommodations are a good size, with fresh, appealing furnishings, and modern bathrooms with hair dryers. Studios and suites have kitchenettes. If your balcony does not have a water vista, it has a nice aspect of the city or mountains instead. There are a small, not very private pool and Jacuzzi in front, and a pleasant restaurant and cocktail bar. The front desk exchanges currency and runs a tour desk.

Inexpensive

Coral Tree Inn. 166–172 Grafton St., Cairns, QLD 4870. ☎ **07/4031 3744.** Fax 07/4031 3064. www.coraltreeinn.com.au. E-mail: reservations@coraltreeinn.com.au. 58 units (some with shower only). A/C TV TEL. A$106 (U.S.$68.90) double, $136 (U.S.$88.40) suite. Extra person $10 (U.S.$6.50). Children 12 and under stay free in parents' room using existing bedding. Ask about packages. AE, BC, DC, MC, V. Free parking (for limited number of cars); ample on-street parking. Airport shuttle.

This cheery little resort-style motel a 5-minute walk from town is a good value. Its focal point is a sunny communal kitchen and barbecue that overlooks the small but pretty palm-lined pool and sundeck, where you can join fellow guests over free coffee.

The smallish motel rooms are basic but were pleasantly spruced up in 1998 with white paint, terra-cotta tile or freshly carpeted floors, and new bathrooms (reception has hair dryers). Front desk books tours and exchanges foreign currency. Breakfast of fruit, yogurt, toast, cereal, juice, and coffee is A$8 (U.S.$5.20).

Flying Horseshoe Motel. 281–289 Sheridan St., Cairns, QLD 4870. ☎ **1800/814 171** in Australia, or 07/4051 3022. Fax 07/4031 2761. www.flyinghorseshoe.com.au. E-mail: flying-horseshoe@bestwestern.com.au. 50 units (all with shower only). A/C MINIBAR TV TEL. A$95–$105 (U.S.$61.75–$68.25) double, A$115–$125 (U.S.$74.75–$81.25) studio apt. Extra adult A$10 (U.S.$6.50); extra child under 15 A$5 (U.S.$3.25). AE, BC, DC, JCB, MC, V. Free parking. Bus: all "1" series, 7, N. Call the motel for a free pickup at the airport, train station, or bus terminal.

Well-maintained rooms await you at this Best Western about 10 blocks from the city center. The managers encourage guests to mingle by staging a nightly hearty buffet around the small pool, and the tropical gardens run to a Jacuzzi. All rooms have hair dryers. The studio apartments are by the highway, so expect some traffic noise. The staff book tours and rental cars, and can arrange dry cleaning, baby-sitting, room service at breakfast and dinner, and secretarial services. The bus to the city stops just across the road.

✪ **Lilybank Bed & Breakfast.** 75 Kamerunga Rd., Stratford, Cairns, QLD 4870. ☎ **07/4055 1123.** Fax 07/4058 1990. www.lilybank.com.au. E-mail: hosts@lilybank.com.au. 5 units (3 with shower only). A/C. A$77–$99 (U.S.$50.05–$64.35) double. Extra person A$27.50 (U.S.$17.90). Rates include full breakfast. AE, BC, MC, V. Free parking. Bus: 1E, 1F, 1G. A taxi is approx. A$14 (U.S.$9.10) from the airport or A$15.50 (U.S.$10.10) from the city. Children not permitted.

This big 1890s Queenslander homestead, originally the mayor's residence, is in a leafy suburb a 10-minute drive from the city. Your hosts, Mike and Pat Woolford, are wonderfully engaging and know all there is to know about touring Cairns. All the homey rooms are individually decorated with nice touches such as patchwork quilts, and pleasant bathrooms with hair dryers. Breakfast is a grand affair of tropical fruits, Pat's home-baked croissants, and great hot dishes (try the banana pancakes). A rock-lined saltwater pool beckons in the lovely gardens, guests have their own TV lounge and kitchen/dining room, and there is phone, fax, and e-mail access. Many tours pick up at the door, and restaurants and a nice pub are a stroll away. No smoking indoors.

ON THE NORTHERN BEACHES

Cairns has a string of white sandy beaches starting 15 minutes north of the city center. Most have just two or three restaurants and a handful of shops, and usually a tour desk and a rental-car outlet. **Trinity Beach,** 15 minutes from the airport, is secluded, elegant, and scenic. The most upscale is **Palm Cove,** 20 minutes from the airport. Here cute, rainbow-hued shops and tasteful apartment blocks nestle among giant paperbarks and palms fronting a postcard-perfect beach. It has several advantages over other beach suburbs: A 9-hole resort golf course and a gym are within walking distance, the Quicksilver Wavepiercer Great Barrier Reef cruise boat picks up passengers here daily, and it has the greatest choice of places to eat. Add 5 to 10 minutes to the traveling times above to reach the city.

Very Expensive
✪ **Sebel Reef House.** 99 Williams Esplanade, Palm Cove, Cairns, QLD 4879. ☎ **1800/079 052** in Australia, or 07/4055 3633. Fax 07/4055 3305. www.reefhouse.com.au. E-mail: info@reefhouse.com.au. 69 units (some with shower only). A/C MINIBAR TV TEL. A$270–$435 (U.S.$175.50–$282.75) double, A$435–$556 (U.S.$282.75–$361.40) suite. Extra person

A$30 (U.S.$19.50). Children under 14 stay free in parents' room using existing bedding. AE, BC, DC, MC, V. Free parking (for limited number of cars); ample on-street parking. Courtesy airport shuttle. Bus: 1, 1B, 1X, 2X, N.

I could happily spend my life between the bougainvillea-clad white walls of this gorgeous boutique hotel. Martha Stewart herself would approve of the airy terra-cotta or white-tiled interiors with rustic handmade artifacts, white wicker furniture, and mosquito nets draped over the beds. My favorite are the Verandah rooms that look onto the pool, waterfalls, and lush gardens; they have small kitchenettes (and in some cases Jacuzzis) *outside* on a generous terrace. Every room has a VCR and CD player, bathrobe, portable telephone, toaster, hair dryer, and coffee plunger.

Dining/Diversions: Lovely Coral's Restaurant is open to the breeze and in earshot of the waves. It serves casually elegant meals. The Poolside Cafe serves lunch until late in the day. In the Brigadier Bar, it's easy to fancy you're Somerset Maugham penning the next big novel as you down another Singapore Sling.

Amenities: Two small but attractive swimming pools, two Jacuzzis, massage, room service (limited hours), nightly turndown, tour desk, dry cleaning/laundry, guest laundry, baby-sitting, safes (at a fee), meeting room.

Expensive

Courtyard by Marriott Great Barrier Reef Resort. Williams Esplanade (at Veivers Rd.), Palm Cove, Cairns, QLD 4879. ☎ **800/321-2211** in the U.S. and Canada, 0800/221 222 in the U.K. or 171/591 1500 in London, 0800/441 035 in New Zealand, 1800/251 259 in Australia or 02/9251 5522 in Sydney, or 07/4055 3999 for the resort. Fax 07/4055 3902. www.courtyard.com. Email: res@courtyard.com. 189 units. A/C MINIBAR TV TEL. A$237–$296.50 (U.S.$154.05–$192.75) double; A$312–$388 (U.S.$202.80–$252.20) suite. Extra person A$32.50 (U.S.$21.15). Children under 17 stay free in parents' room using existing bedding. Ask about packages. AE, BC, DC, JCB, MC, V. Bus: 1, 1B, 1X, 2X, N. Courtesy resort shuttle to and from airport, city wharf, and train station.

A sprawling free-form pool and sundeck winding beneath a miniforest of palms is the focal point of this comfortable four-story resort right opposite the beach. All the same reasonable size, the rooms were renovated in 1999. All have hair dryers and pay-per-view movies. Pool-view rooms have the most restful vistas; the "ocean view" is largely obscured by trees, and some "garden views" really just look onto the street.

Dining/Diversions: The Garden Terrace opens onto the pool and serves à la carte menus and themed buffets. The Golden Cane Bar and Sunken Plaza, a poolside sunken lounge bedecked with greenery, is a nice cocktail spot. A coffee shop sells sweet treats.

Amenities: Small gym, day/night tennis court, bicycle rental, Jacuzzi, Ping-Pong, billiards table, kids' pool and playground equipment, room service, safes (at a fee), baby-sitting, laundry, tour desk, gift shop, currency exchange, conference facilities.

Moderate

✪ The Reef Retreat. 10–14 Harpa St., Palm Cove, Cairns, QLD 4879. ☎ **07/4059 1744.** Fax 07/4059 1745. www.reefretreat.com.au. E-mail: sales@reefretreat.com.au. 36 units (17 with shower only, 13 with Jacuzzi also). A/C TV TEL. A$130 (U.S.$84.50) studio; A$140–$160 (U.S.$91–$104) suite; A$250 (U.S.$162.50) 2-bedroom apt. (to sleep 4). Extra person A$22 (U.S.$14.30) adult. Children under 3 free in parents' room using existing bedding. Crib A$22 (U.S.$14.30). Twice-weekly servicing; 1 free servicing for stays of 5 days or longer (extra servicing A$16/U.S.$10.40 per clean). AE, BC, DC, MC, V. Free parking. Bus: 1, 1B, 1X, 2X, N. Airport shuttle.

Tucked back one row of buildings from the beach is this gem—a three-story collection of roomy, contemporary studios and suites built around a swimming pool and Jacuzzi in an almost mystically peaceful grove of palms and silver paperbarks. Either

Safe Swimming

All of the northern beaches have small, netted enclosures for safe swimming from October to May, when deadly box jellyfish (stingers) render all mainland beaches in north Queensland off-limits.

built or renovated 4 to 6 years ago, all units have fresh white interiors, cool tile floors, cedar blinds, smart teak and cane furniture, hair dryers, a living area, a kitchenette, a coffee plunger, a balcony or patio (a kitchenette *on* the balcony in the case of the Spa suites), and views over the pool, garden, or sea through the trees. The studios are a terrific value, much larger than the average hotel room. Management stages a fun guest barbecue every Thursday. *Note:* There's no elevator.

Inexpensive

✪ **Absolute Beachfront Bed & Breakfast.**6–10 Peacock St., Trinity Beach, Cairns, QLD 4879. ☎ **07/4055 6664.** Fax 07/4055 6179. www.absolutebeach.com.au. E-mail: kay@absolutebeach.com.au. 3 units (all with shower only, 1 also with Jacuzzi). A/C TV. A$95–$130 (U.S.$61.75–$84.50) double. Extra person A$20 (U.S.$13) extra. Rates include full breakfast. BC, MC, V. Free parking. Bus: 1, 1A, 3X, N. Airport shuttle. Free airport transfers for guests staying 3 or more nights. Children not permitted.

"Absolute Luxury" is just as good a moniker for this architecturally stunning timber house, which won the "Queensland Design Home of the Year" award in 1999. From the gorgeous open-fronted living room, the only obstacle between you and the sand is the pool set in palm-studded lawns. The contemporary rooms, each a little different, have such features as Balinese four-poster beds, polished limestone or timber floors, Oriental rugs, VCRs, and hip bathrooms (check out the one with sea views from the Jacuzzi!). A rain-forest headland walk is a stroll in one direction, Trinity Beach's one or two restaurants the other. Owners Kay and John Lane leave you to your own devices, so this is a good retreat for those who like privacy. No smoking indoors.

Palm Cove Saray'i.95–97 Williams Esplanade, Palm Cove, QLD 4879. ☎**1800/805 708** or 07/4055 3734. Fax 07/4059 1022. www.sarayi.com.au. E-mail: info@sarayi.com.au. 24 units (some with shower only, 7 with Jacuzzis). A/C TV TEL. High season (mid-June to Nov) A$89–$122 (U.S.$57.85–$79.30) double, A$160–$215 (U.S.$104–$139.75) suite. Low season A$79–$110 (U.S.$51.35–$71.50) double, A$150–$195 (U.S.$97.50–$126.75) suite. Extra person $17.50 (U.S.$11.40). Children under 4 stay free in parents' room with existing bedding. 6% discount for early direct bookings. Weekly rates available. AE, BC, DC, MC. V. Free parking for limited number of cars; ample on-street parking. Bus: 1, 1B, 1X, 2X, N. Airport shuttle.

Built in 1998, this hotel opposite the beach resembles a white-columned, turreted Turkish palace. The large rooms don't match the opulent exterior, but they are a good value, with tile floors, fresh white and blue decor, kitchenettes, clean bathrooms, and hair dryers. Some of the suites have ocean views and Jacuzzis. Out back a handful of old rooms remain, with severely dated furniture and scant natural light—pay the extra few dollars for a new room. Up on the roof are a pool and sundeck, sauna, and Jacuzzi. There are also a seafood restaurant, a bar, and a tour and car-rental desk.

ON AN ISLAND

Several island resorts are located off Cairns. They afford you safe swimming year-round, because the October-to-May infestations of deadly marine stingers don't make it to the islands.

Very Expensive

⊙ **Green Island Resort.** 27km/17 miles east of Cairns. P.O. Box 898, Cairns, QLD 4870. ☎ **1800/67 3366** in Australia, or 07/4031 3300. Fax 07/4052 1511. www. greenislandresort.com.au. E-mail: res@greenislandresort.com.au. 46 units. A/C MINIBAR TV TEL. A$440 (U.S.$286) double; A$550 (U.S.$357.50) suite. Extra person A$66 (U.S.$42.90). Ask about packages. AE, BC, DC, JCB, MC, V. Great Adventures (☎ 07/4044 9944) runs transfers (50 min.) from Cairns 3 times a day for A$44 (U.S.$28.60) adults, A$22 (U.S.$14.30) children 4–14, A$110 (U.S.$71.50) family, round-trip. Helicopter and seaplane transfers are available through resort.

Step off the beach at this Great Barrier Reef national-park island, and you are surrounded by acres of coral. That's because Green is a coral cay, not a continental island like most others off Cairns. The resort itself is little more than a high-class cluster of rooms tucked away in a dense vine forest. Each room is private, roomy, and very elegantly outfitted with polished wooden floors. All have a balcony looking into the forest, hair dryers, and safes. Windsurfing, paddle-skiing, canoeing, diving and snorkeling (both on the island and on day trips to the outer Reef), learn-to-dive courses, glass-bottom boat trips, walking rain-forest trails, parasailing, and beach volleyball are the activities available, or you can simply laze on the abundant beach of coarse white coral sand. Helicopter and seaplane flights and cruises are available to the Outer Reef. Many activities and equipment are free for guests, such as nonmotorized sports, snorkel gear, and glass-bottom boat trips, while there's a charge for scuba diving and other activities using fuel. Both the island and the resort are small, so you can feel a bit cramped when the day-trippers from Cairns descend; but after most of them leave at 4:30pm, the place is blissfully peaceful.

Dining/Diversions: Beautiful indoor/outdoor Emerald's restaurant overlooks the pool and serves stylish à la carte meals. Burgers and the like are sold during the day from the casual Grill, and there are a cocktail bar, a pool bar, and an ice-cream store.

Amenities: A wide array of water sports and other activities (see above), two freshwater swimming pools (one guests-only), small lounge with complimentary tea and coffee, 24-hour room service, free movies, concierge, laundry/dry cleaning, guest laundry, secretarial services, Internet access, meeting room, currency exchange, resort store, boutique.

⊙ **Lizard Island.** 240km/149 miles N of Cairns; 27km offshore. P&O Australian Resorts, GPO Box 478, Sydney, NSW 2001. ☎ **1800/737 678** in Australia, 800/225-9849 in the U.S. and Canada, 020/7805 3875 in the U.K., 02/9277 5050 (Sydney reservations office) or 07/4060 3999 (the island). Fax 02/9299 2477 (Sydney reservations office) or 07/4060 3991 (the island). www.poresorts.com.au. E-mail: resorts_reservations@poaustralia.com.au. 40 units (all with shower only). A/C MINIBAR TEL. A$1,260–$1,600 (U.S.$819–$1,040) double. Extra person A$340 (U.S.$221). Rates include all meals and many activities. Ask about packages; some combine stays at Silky Oaks Lodge (Port Douglas), Sebel Reef House (Cairns), and Bedarra Island (off Mission Beach). AE, BC, DC, JCB, MC, V. Transfers are by twice-daily 1-hour flight from Cairns on Transtate Airlines (book through Qantas or Ansett); round-trip advance purchase fare is A$380 (U.S.$247) per person. Aircraft luggage limit 15kg (33 lb.) per person. Air-charter transfers also available. No children under 10.

Black marlin, huge potato cod so tame divers can pet them, snorkeling right off the beach, and isolation—that's what lures well-heeled Americans, Europeans, and Aussies to this exclusive resort. Lizard is a rugged 1,000-hectare (2,470-acre) national-park island on the Great Barrier Reef, grassy and sparse but beautiful, ringed by 24 white sandy beaches, with stunning fringing reefs and giant clams. No day-trippers bother you. Many activities are free: snorkeling and glass-bottom boat trips, windsurfing, sailing catamarans, glass-bottom paddle-skis, dinghies, fishing tackle, tennis, and hiking trails, such as the muscle-straining 545-meter ($^1/_3$-mile) climb to Cook's Look, where

Captain Cook spied his way out of the treacherous reefs in 1770. You pay for fishing trips, and diving trips to various nearby Reef sites, including Cod Hole. The dive shop conducts introductory dives, night dives, and 5-day learn-to-dive courses. Lizard's waters are home to world-record black marlin, and half- and full-day game fishing trips are available.

The resort underwent a renovation in July 2000. Accommodations, which are free-standing lodges tucked under palms along the beach or up the cliff, are of elegant timber and stone construction, in a casual tropical style, with earth-toned finishes, a CD player, modem outlets, bathrobes, a hair dryer, and a balcony facing the sea. The larger open-plan villas and one-bedroom suites, some of them split-level, have big decks and the best views.

Dining/Diversions: Tables edge a wide curving veranda overlooking the sea at Osprey's restaurant, where chef Genevieve Copland turns out terrific à la carte fare with French and Asian influences. Her menu changes daily. Romantic dinners at candle-lit tables on the beach can be requested. Picnic hampers are free. A comfy lounge bar serves cocktails.

Amenities: Wide array of sports and activities (see above); swimming pool; "pampering center" for facials, massages, and the like; day/night tennis court; small gym; nightly turndown; laundry; currency and traveler's checks exchange (limited); safe-deposit boxes; guest fax; boutique.

Moderate/Inexpensive

Fitzroy Island. 35km/22 miles SE of Cairns. P.O. Box 1109, Cairns, QLD 4870. ☎ **07/ 4051 9588.** Fax 07/4052 1335. www.fitzroyislandresort.com.au. E-mail: sales@ragingthunder. com.au. 8 cabins (all with shower only); 32 bunkhouses, none with private bathroom. Cabins A\$220 (U.S.\$143) double. Extra person A\$35 (U.S.\$22.75). Bunkhouses A\$31 (U.S.\$20.15) per person per bed (sharing with up to 3 other people); A\$116 (U.S.\$75.40) double (sole use); A\$150 (U.S.\$97.50) family bunkhouse. AE, BC, DC, JCB, MC, V. Round-trip transfers 3–4 times daily from Cairns (approx. 45 min.) cost A\$36 (U.S.\$23.40) adults, A\$18 (U.S.\$11.70) children 4–14.

This low-key, friendly rain-forest island is one of the few affordable island resorts on the Great Barrier Reef. It's targeted at a younger crowd looking for action and eco-fun in a pristine, beautiful location. It's no glamour-puss palace, but the place was revamped in 2000 to sport a new Hard Rock Cafe–style restaurant, spruced-up linens and upholstery, and a makeover around the small pool area. Fitzroy is a continental island offering little in the way of fringing coral and only a few narrow strips of coral sand. What it does have are catamarans, outrigger canoes, and surf skis; glass-bottom boat rides; and hiking trails through dense national-park forest to a lighthouse. Divers can make drift dives over the reefs dotted around the island to see manta rays, reef sharks, turtles, and plenty of coral. There is good snorkeling at two points around the island that you can reach twice a day on the dive boat, at an extra fee. You can also catch the Sunlover Cruises day trip to the outer Great Barrier Reef.

Each of the modestly comfortable beach cabins has a queen-size bed in front and two bunks in the back, fans, a TV, a minifridge, an iron, and a hair dryer, and a large balcony with views through the trees to the sea. Forty-four new cabins are on the drawing board for 2001. The bunkhouse accommodations are basic fan-cooled carpeted rooms with bunks and/or beds. Bunkhouse guests can use the communal kitchen if they BYO supplies from the mainland.

Dining/Diversions: The restaurant is moderately priced, a kiosk sells cheap take-out food, and the poolside grill and bar does casual meals. The Raging Thunder Beach Bar, billed as "the only nightclub on the Reef," really gets going Friday and Saturday nights.

Amenities: Dive shop conducting introductory and certified dives and certification courses, other water sports (see above), small swimming pool, volleyball, tour desk, boutique.

DINING

IN CAIRNS

Expensive

✪ **Fishlips Bar & Grill.** 228 Sheridan St. (between Charles St. and McKenzie St.). ☎ **07/ 4041 1700.** Reservations recommended. Main courses A$17.50–$31 (U.S.$11.40–$20.15); most dishes under A$22 (U.S.$14.30). AE, BC, DC, JCB, MC, V. Fri noon–2:30pm; daily 6pm–late. Bus: All "1" series, 7. MOD OZ/SEAFOOD.

Ask locals where they go for seafood themselves, and they'll direct you to this cute bluebird-blue beach shack about 2 kilometers (1¼ miles) from town on a nondescript section of Sheridan Street. Chef Ian Candy is famous not just for seafood but also for his wok-tossed crocodile on sweet-potato mash in a herb tuille with pumpkin-seed salsa. Barramundi usually shows up in two incarnations—perhaps beer-battered with rough-cut chips (fries) and fresh tartar sauce, or dressed up in red-pepper pesto butter on spring olive potato mash. Plenty of nonseafood options and a vegetarian choice appear on every menu. Dine in the Mediterranean-chic interior complete with portholes, or on the small front deck. Licensed, and from Sunday to Thursday BYO also (wine only; no BYO beer or spirits).

Red Ochre Grill. 43 Shields St. (at Sheridan St.). ☎ **07/4051 0100.** Reservations recommended. Main courses A$8.50–$18 (U.S.$5.55–$11.70) at lunch, A$18–$25 (U.S.$11.70–$16.25) at dinner. Australian game platter A$32 (U.S.$20.80) per person, seafood platter A$42 (U.S.$27.30) per person. AE, BC, DC, JCB, MC, V. Mon–Sat noon–3pm; daily 6pm–late. GOURMET BUSH TUCKER.

If you accuse this restaurant of using weird and wonderful Aussie ingredients as a gimmick to pull in crowds, you will eat those words when you taste the possum wontons, eucalyptus-smoked salmon, or kangaroo sirloin with wild mushroom risotto and Australian pepperleaf mustard sauce. The food is too good to be a trick! With its terracotta floors, groovy indoor and sidewalk seating, and Aboriginal art for sale on the wall, the place is slick enough for a night out but informal enough for a casual meal. Check out the rundown of bush tucker ingredients on the menu—that way you will know when you're chewing on a fat, slimy witchetty grub. Just kidding.

Moderate

Gypsy's Restaurant. 41A Shields St. ☎ **07/4051 5530.** Reservations recommended. Main courses A$16–$22 (U.S.$10.40–$14.30); A$12 (U.S.$7.80) pasta specials. Daily 11am–midnight (bar open until 2am). AE, BC, DC, MC, V. MODERN AUSTRALIAN.

Part restaurant, part cocktail bar, part dance club—no one seems to know just what Gypsy's is, but locals love it. Sit outside or in the cavernous interior, which will sport a trendy new decor, a dance floor, and disco lights by the time you get here. The menu has ample choices like char-grilled Scotch fillet with roast zucchini, fried kumara sherds, and a garlic shallot cabernet jus; dakka-crusted lamb fillet with a warm vegetable salad, eggfruit and chili relish on a beetroot, and orange jus; pastas; and vegetarian/vegan options. After 10pm from Wednesday to Saturday, a live band strikes up anything from soft melodies to Top 40, and everyone hits the dance floor. Licensed and BYO wine only (no BYO beer or spirits).

✪ **Mediterraneo.** 74 Shields St. ☎ **07/4051 4335.** Reservations recommended on weekends. Main courses A$17.50–$21.80 (U.S.$11.40–$14.20); pasta A$12.50–$15.50 (U.S.$8.15–$10.10). BC, MC, V. Tues–Sun 6pm–late. ITALIAN.

If I lived in Cairns, I'd eat at this Italian joint every night. The food is cooked with flair and flavor, and the service is friendly. Choices include loads of pastas such as fettuccine with bugs (a kind of cray), prawns, scallops, garlic, herbs, and white-wine and tomato sauce, and updated classics such as chicken panfried in rosemary with a pesto and tomato sauce. The decor is trendy but not showy, just a polished concrete floor, framed sketches on the wall, and timber tables. There's also a courtyard out the back. BYO.

Mondo Café Bar & Grill. In the Hilton Cairns, Wharf St. ☎ **07/4050 2000.** Reservations not accepted. Main courses A$8.75–$21 (U.S.$5.70–$13.65). AE, BC, DC, JCB, MC, V. Daily 11am–11pm for snacks and drinks; lunch Mon–Sat noon–2:30pm, Sun noon–6pm; dinner Sun–Thurs 6–10pm, Fri–Sat 6:30–10:30pm. EAST-MEETS-WEST CAFÉ FARE.

Set near the water with outdoor seating and inlet views, this sleek cafe and cocktail bar is frequented by hip locals, corporate types, and "southerners" from Sydney and Melbourne. Drop by for a coffee, order a bar snack like "Shanghainese" chicken ribs, or stay for bigger meals like "barra-ratat," which is barramundi on Asian ratatouille with soy/ginger cream. There's a wide range of wines, spirits, and liqueurs, plus live music some nights.

Thai Pan. 43–45 Grafton St. ☎ **07/4052 1708.** Reservations recommended. Main courses A$15.70–$19.50 (U.S.$10.20–$12.70). AE, BC, DC, MC, V. Daily 5:30–10:30pm. LAO/THAI.

Delicately fragrant curries and carefully prepared stir-fries and soups are served up in this humble brick restaurant. Try the *pad gratium* (tender beef fried in a complex garlic sauce with crisp vegetables); one of the many seafood dishes, such as the mixed seafood cooked in basil and a hint of chili; or one of the plentiful vegetarian choices. As with many Asian restaurants, the wine list is unremarkable, so bring your own. Licensed and BYO.

Inexpensive

In addition to checking out the places below, head to **The Esplanade** along the seafront; it's lined with cheap cafes, pizzerias, fish-and-chips places, food courts, and ice-cream parlors.

The Old Ambulance Café Bistro. 135 Grafton St. (at Aplin St.). ☎ **07/4051 0511.** Main courses A$9.80–$14.50 (U.S.$6.40–$9.45). AE, BC, DC, MC, V. Mon 7am–6pm, Tues–Thurs 7am–10:30pm, Fri–Sat 7am–11:30pm. LIGHT FARE.

This trendy little terra-cotta–tiled place used to be an ambulance station, but the wailing sirens have been replaced by young city workers and moms with strollers. Drop in by day for a coffee, a toasted focaccia sandwich, or a baked potato with ham and mushroom topping. Dinner is heartier but still light: risotto, a steak sandwich, or maybe smoked pork-loin cutlets with mustard sauce, salad, and potato.

✪ **Tim's Surf 'n' Turf.** Upstairs at Trinity Wharf, 28–34 Wharf St. (at the end of Abbott St.). ☎ **07/4031 6866.** Reservations accepted only for groups of 8 more. Main courses A$7.15–$20.90 (U.S.$4.65–$13.60); many dishes under A$13 (U.S.$8.45). Kids' menu A$3.50–$4.50 (U.S.$2.30–$2.95). No credit cards. Daily noon–2:30pm and 5:30–9:30pm. STEAK/SEAFOOD.

For huge meals at unbeatable prices, you can't go wrong at this cheerful chain outlet overlooking Trinity Inlet. Most restaurateurs would charge outrageous prices given a prime waterfront location like this, but not Tim, bless 'im! The seafood platters, oysters, pastas, roasts, quiche, and a long list of other simple dishes are all fresh and cooked with skill. The highlight is the mighty grain-fed steaks.

ON THE NORTHERN BEACHES

Colonies. Upstairs in the Paradise Village shopping center, Williams Esplanade, Palm Cove. ☎ **07/4055 3058.** Reservations recommended at dinner. Main courses A$18.50–$23.90 (U.S.$12–$15.55). Daily 7:30am–10:30pm. Closed part of Feb and/or Mar. AE, BC, DC, MC, V. Bus: 1, 1B, 1X, 2X, N. MODERN AUSTRALIAN/CAFÉ FARE.

It may not have ocean frontage, but you are still within earshot of the waves from the veranda of this cheery little aerie tucked behind a seafront building. The atmosphere is simple enough for a morning coffee, and special enough at night for a full-fledged banquet, such as barbecued barramundi, oysters, mussels, salmon, and prawns, or New York steak. The long menu includes loads of inexpensive choices at both lunch and dinner, such as pastas, Thai green chicken curry, and chicken breast on olive panini. Licensed and BYO.

Far Horizons. At the Angsana Resort and Spa, 1 Veivers Rd. (at the southern end of Williams Esplanade), Palm Cove. ☎ **07/4055 3000.** Reservations recommended. Main courses A$20.50–$28.50 (U.S.$13.35–$18.50). AE, BC, DC, JCB, MC, V. Daily 6:30am–midnight (last orders 9:45pm). Bus: 1, 1B, 1X, 2X, N. MODERN AUSTRALIAN.

You can't quite twiddle your toes in the sand, but you are just yards from the beach at this open-fronted restaurant that should be sporting a smart new decor by the time you arrive. The menu is best described as "laid-back fine dining," which could be tasty King Island beef, or bugtails (a kind of lobster) panfried with steamed bok choy and sweet soya beurre blanc. In nice weather, the staff sometimes sets up dining on the lawn under the palm trees between the restaurant and the beach. On Friday and Saturday nights, a guitar player strums in the cocktail bar.

CAIRNS AFTER DARK

Cairns is not big on after-hours action. The **Hotel Sofitel Reef Casino,** 35–41 Wharf St. (☎ **07/4030 8888**), has two levels of blackjack, baccarat, reef routine, roulette, sic-bo, money wheel, Keno, and slot machines. It's open 10am to 4am Monday through Thursday, and 24 hours from 10am Friday until 4am Monday (and closed Good Friday, Anzac Day, and Christmas). The hotel also puts on a dinner show, where you sit among rain-forest plants in a giant glass-domed **Conservatory.** Last time I went the food was good, and the show was a rather average illusion performance. It takes place every night except Sunday and costs A$80 (U.S.$52) per person. The hotel also has Cairns's hottest nightclub, **Nightclub 1936,** located underground. It's open Friday and Saturday from 9:30pm to 3am; cover is A$5 (U.S.$3.25).

    Gypsy's (see "Dining," above) is another popular night spot; you don't have to eat there to dance there, and it charges no cover. If you're under 35 or so and it's Friday or Saturday night, you may want to take the 6:30pm boat to the DJs or live bands at the **Raging Thunder Beach Bar** on Fitzroy Island (see "Accommodations," above). The boat costs A$12 (U.S.$7.80) round-trip and departs for Cairns at midnight. Book through **Raging Thunder Adventures** (☎ **07/4030 7990**).

3 Port Douglas, Daintree & the Cape Tribulation Area

Port Douglas: 67km (42 miles) N of Cairns; Mossman: 19km (12 miles) N of Port Douglas; Daintree: 49km (31 miles) N of Port Douglas; Cape Tribulation: 34km (21 miles) N of Daintree

The quaint fishing and sugar farming village of ✪ **Port Douglas** (pop. approximately 3,000) has the distinction of being the only place in the world where two World Heritage areas—the Daintree rain forest and the Great Barrier Reef—lay side by side. Just over an hour's drive north from Cairns, Port Douglas may be a one-horse town, but

Port Douglas, Daintree & Cape Tribulation

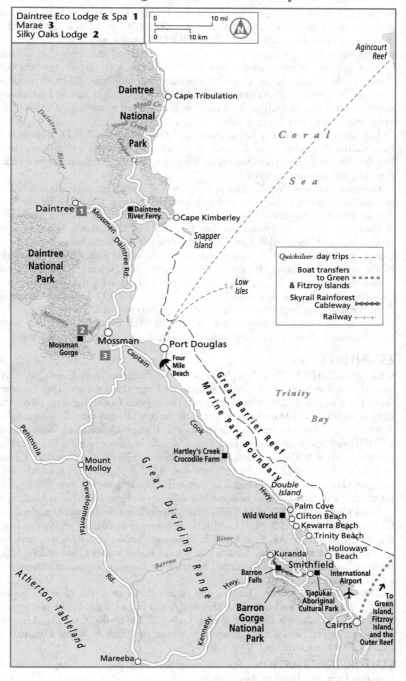

Daintree Eco Lodge & Spa **1**
Marae **3**
Silky Oaks Lodge **2**

0   10 mi
0   10 km

Agincourt
Reef

Daintree

Cape Tribulation

National

Myall Cr.

Noah Creek

Park

Daintree River

C o r a l

S e a

Daintree **1**

Daintree
River Ferry

Cape Kimberley

*Snapper
Island*

Mossman Daintree Rd.

**Daintree
National
Park**

Mossman River

*Low
Isles*

Quicksilver day trips —————
Boat transfers
to Green
& Fitzroy Islands ●●●●●
Skyrail Rainforest
Cableway ━━━━━
Railway +++++

2

Mossman
Gorge **3**

Mossman

Captain

Port Douglas

Four
Mile
Beach

Great Barrier Reef

Marine Park Boundary

Trinity

Bay

Peninsula

Cook

Mount
Molloy

Hartley's Creek
Crocodile Farm

*Double
Island*

Developmental

Hwy.

Palm Cove
Wild World   Clifton Beach
Kewarra Beach
Trinity Beach

G r e a t   D i v i d i n g   R a n g e

River

Barron

Kuranda

Holloways
Beach

Barron
Falls

Smithfield

International
Airport

A t h e r t o n   T a b l e l a n d

Rd.

Kennedy

Hwy.

**Barron
Gorge
National
Park**

Tjapukai
Aboriginal
Cultural Park

Cairns

To
Green
Island,
Fitzroy
Island,
and the
Outer Reef

Mareeba

it's got a cute main street with a handful of stylish shops, some trendy restaurants that attract trendy Sydneysiders and Melburnites, a clutch of five-star resorts and deluxe eco-retreats, and a beautiful 4-mile beach called ✪ **Four Mile Beach.**

Folks often base themselves in "Port," as the locals call it, rather than Cairns, because they like the rural surroundings, the peaceful beach, the proximity to the rain forest, the slow pace, and the charming absence of tall buildings and tacky development (so far, anyway). Don't think you'll be isolated here; many reef and rain-forest tours originate in Port Douglas, and many tours discussed in the Cairns section earlier in this chapter pick up from here.

The Great Barrier Reef is just as pretty and accessible from Port Douglas as it is from Cairns. The town is the departure point for several snorkel and dive vessels to the Reef, including the large Quicksilver Wavepiercers and several smaller boats that cater to small intimate groups.

Daintree National Park lies a short drive north of town. This wild tract of rain forest, mountain rivers, mangroves, and hilly coastal headlands is part of the vast Wet Tropics World Heritage Area that stretches from Cooktown in the north to Townsville in the south. It is a true treasure, both ecologically and aesthetically. While ice ages rose and fell and Noah bobbed about on the briny, the rain forest hereabouts did not change much in the last 110 million years. It's home to rare plants that are key links in the story of evolution. In the 76,000-hectare (187,720-acre) park, you'll find cycads, dinosaur trees, fan palms, giant strangler figs, basket ferns, staghorns, and elkhorns. Exploring the park is easy on one of the many 4WD day safaris operating from Port Douglas. Nighttime crocodile-spotting tours on the Daintree River vie for popularity with early-morning cruises to see the incredibly rich bird life, while pythons, lizards, frogs, and electric blue Ulysses butterflies attract photographers.

ESSENTIALS

GETTING THERE   Port Douglas is a 65-minute drive from Cairns, in parts through rain forest and on a narrow winding road that skirts the sea. Take Sheridan Street north out of the city when it becomes the Captain Cook Highway; follow the signs to Mossman and Mareeba until you reach the Port Douglas turnoff on your right.

Another pleasant transport mode is aboard a giant **Quicksilver Wavepiercer** (☎ **07/4099 5500**) catamaran. One departs Cairns at 8am and Palm Cove jetty at 8:30am to arrive at Marina Mirage in Port Douglas at 9:30am. Transfers from Cairns or Palm Cove are A$22 (U.S.$14.30) one-way, A$32 (U.S.$20.80) round-trip, half price for kids 4 to 14. Stay on board in Port and go straight to the Great Barrier Reef for the day, and it costs less. A courtesy bus collects you from your Cairns hotel.

Coral Coaches (☎ **07/4031 7577**) makes eight daily runs to Port Douglas from Cairns city hotels for A$20.50 (U.S.$13.35) one-way, and makes 17 trips a day from the Cairns airport for A$25 (U.S.$16.25) one-way. Seniors pay 40% less; fares for children 4 to 14 are half price. Coaches meet most flights between 6am and 8:15pm. Booking is a must on five of the airport runs; it's not necessary on the other trips, but a good idea anyway.

There is no train to Port Douglas, and no scheduled air service. A small airport handles light aircraft and helicopter charters. A taxi from Cairns would run around A$94 (U.S.$61.10); call **Black & White Taxis** (☎ **13 10 08** in Cairns). Limo or town-car transfers from Cairns are another option; try **Black & White Limousines** (☎ **13 19 08** in Cairns, or 07/4051 5074).

VISITOR INFORMATION   For information before you go, contact the **Port Douglas Daintree Tourism Association,** P. O. Box 511, Port Douglas, QLD 4871

☎ **07/4099 4588;** www.pddt.com.au). It has no visitor information office in Port Douglas itself. Instead, drop by the several private tour booking centers in town. One of the biggest and most centrally located is the **Port Douglas Tourist Information Centre,** 23 Macrossan St. (☎ **07/4099 5599**), open daily from 7:30am to 6pm.

GETTING AROUND   Budget (☎ **07/4099 4690**) and **Avis** (☎ **07/4099 4331**) have offices in Port Douglas; Hertz and Thrifty do not. Several local companies rent cars and 4WDs; **Crocodile Car Rentals** (☎ **07/4099 5555**) has a good range. It insists you rent a 4WD for use beyond the Daintree River. Avis and Budget will permit a conventional 2WD across the river until the paved road switches to dirt road 2.5 kilometers (1½ miles) short of Cape Tribulation; beyond that, you will need to rent a 4WD. There are a couple of taxi and limo outfits in town (try **Nautilus Chauffeured Limousines** at ☎ **07/4099 5565**), and a bike rental store.

Coral Coaches (☎ **07/4099 5351**) makes a local circuit, stopping at popular places like Rainforest Habitat, Four Mile Beach, and Marina Mirage. Fares range from A$1.30 to $3.20 (U.S.85¢ to $2.10). The bus runs hourly from 7:30 until 9am, then half-hourly until midnight. You can catch it outside Salsa Bar in Macrossan Street.

Cruise and fishing boats depart Marina Mirage, an upscale retail/marina complex on Dickson Inlet in Wharf Street, a 10-minute walk from the main street, Macrossan Street.

EXPLORING THE REEF & THE RAIN FOREST

SNORKELING & DIVING THE GREAT BARRIER REEF   The waters off ✪ **Port Douglas** boast just as many wonderful reefs as Cairns, as close, if not closer, to shore. The closest site, the ✪ **Low Isles,** lies only 15 kilometers (9 miles) northeast. These two tiny coral cays are covered in lush vegetation and surrounded by fine coral sand and 55 acres of coral. The coral is not quite as good as the outer Reef's, but the fish life is rich and the proximity makes for a more relaxing day.

Several boats operate day trips to dive and snorkel the outer Reef. Most popular are the air-conditioned ✪ **Quicksilver Wavepiercer** (☎ **07/4099 5500**) catamarans which carry 300 or 400 passengers every day to Agincourt Reef, a ribbon reef 39 nautical miles (72km/45 miles) offshore. After the 90-minute trip and a talk from a marine biologist, you tie up at a two-story pontoon, where you spend 3½ hours on the Reef. Snorkel gear, semisubmersible coral viewing rides, and the pontoon's dry underwater viewing chamber are free. The days costs A$150 (U.S.$97.50) for adults, half price for kids 4 to 14, and A$362.50 (U.S.$235.65) for a family, plus an extra A$5 (U.S.$3.25) for transfers from your hotel. Snorkel safaris led by a marine biologist cost A$31 (U.S.$20.15), and introductory dives cost A$107 (U.S.$69.55). Qualified divers can make one dive for A$67 (U.S.$43.55) or two for A$104 (U.S.$67.60), all gear included, at a possible 20 sites on Agincourt Reef. It's a good idea to book snorkel safaris and dives in advance. Helicopter flights over the Reef from the pontoon are A$98 (U.S.$63.70) per person. You can even fly by helicopter one-way to the pontoon, and cruise the other way with Quicksilver, for a total of A$325 (U.S.$211.25) per person.

Safety Tips

The **tap water** is not safe for drinking in Port Douglas. Most hotels provide free bottled water. Deadly **marine stingers** (box jellyfish) infest the waters offshore from October to May; swim only in the stinger nets on Four Mile Beach during those months. **Crocodiles** inhabit this region, so never swim in, or stand on the bank of, any stream, river, or estuary.

Quicksilver operates the smaller 24-meter, 80-passenger **Quicksmart,** which moors at two sites at Agincourt Reef away from the crowds, not at the pontoon. A day trip is A$110 (U.S.$71.50) adults, A$85 (U.S.$55.25) kids 4 to 14. Quicksmart caters to first-time and certified divers, but serious divers may be better to travel with Quicksilver's 21-passenger dive boat, **Silverblue** (☎ **07/4099 4544**). It visits 3 of a possible 40 sites over nine reefs daily. A day trip with two dives costs A$185 (U.S.$120.25) plus A$15 (U.S.$9.75) for a third dive, all gear included. Introductory divers pay A$185 (U.S.$120.25) for a single dive, plus A$40 (U.S.$26) if they want a second dive. Hotel pickups aboard Quicksmart and Silverblue are free from Port Douglas, A$10 (U.S.$6.50) from Cairns and the northern beaches.

An emphasis on conservation and education is key aboard snorkeling specialist **Wavelength** (☎ **07/4099 5031**), whose 15-meter (50-ft.) boats carry a maximum 30 passengers. The boats visit three Reef sites daily, compared to most operators' one site. The 90-minute trip gives you about 5 hours on the coral. The cost, including lunch, reef education talks, and a snorkel safari, is A$123 (U.S.$79.95) adults, A$83 (U.S.$53.95) kids 2 to 12, and A$394 (U.S.$256.10) for a family of four. Round-trip transfers from Cairns hotels are A$25 (U.S.$16.25), or A$20 (U.S.$13) from the northern beaches. The company also does a morning trip on Wednesdays and Saturdays to the Low Isles, 30 minutes away, for A$83 (U.S.$53.95) adults, A$60 (U.S.$39) kids, and A$223 (U.S.$144.95) for a family.

Several sailing boats make full-day trips to the Low Isles, including the large 30-meter (98-ft.) sailing catamaran *Wavedancer* (☎ **07/4099 5500**), operated by Quicksilver. After the 1-hour sail to the isles, it moors at a pontoon where you snorkel or take a glass-bottom boat ride, walk along the beach with a marine biologist, take a snorkel safari, or laze under thatched umbrellas on the sand. The trip costs A$100 (U.S.$65) per person, with lunch. Children 4 to 14 pay half price, and families pay A$250 (U.S.$162.50). For no extra cost, you can connect by Quicksilver Wavepiercer (see "Getting There," earlier in this chapter) or coach from the northern beaches or Cairns. Introductory scuba dives cost an extra A$87 (U.S.$56.55) per person.

Quicksilver Dive (☎ **07/4099 5050;** www.quicksilverdive.com.au), operated by the company that runs the Quicksilver Wavepiercers to the Reef, does 4-day learn-to-dive courses and 2-day referral courses, and will tailor "exclusive" courses for individuals, couples, friends, or colleagues who don't want to go with a larger group.

EXPLORING DAINTREE NATIONAL PARK Just about everyone who comes to Port Douglas takes a guided 4WD day trip into the beautiful Daintree National Park. The park is in several patches. You will want to visit the southern inland section containing Mossman Gorge, and the rugged northern Cape Tribulation section, which sweeps down to sandy beaches and fringing coral reefs.

You can rent a 4WD and explore on your own, but you may not see much except palm fronds and ferns without a guide to interpret it all. Most companies cover pretty much the same territory and sights, including a 1-hour Daintree River cruise to spot crocs, a visit to the short but interesting Marrdja Botanical Walk in the mangroves, an isolated beach stroll, lunch at a pretty spot somewhere in the forest, and a visit to Mossman Gorge. Some also go to the Bloomfield Falls deeper north in Cape Tribulation National Park. Expect to pay about A$110 (U.S.$71.50) for an adult and about A$75 (U.S.$48.75) for a child. Trips that include Bloomfield Falls are about A$30 (U.S.$19.50) more. You may not see much wildlife on these trips, because rain-forest animals are shy, camouflaged, nocturnal, or all three! Keep your eyes peeled for a cassowary, though, large flightless black birds with a red-and-blue neck and a bony crown on their heads. Floods and swollen creeks can quash your trip in the Wet Season, especially January through April, so keep your plans flexible then. Among the best

Drat Those Aussie Mozzies!

Mozzies, as Aussies call mosquitoes, love the rain forest as much as people do, so throw some insect repellent in your day pack when touring the Daintree and Cape Tribulation. Aerogard and RID are two effective brands.

established operators are **Trek North Safaris** (☎ 07/4051 4328), **BTS Tours** (☎ 07/4099 5665), and **De Luxe Safaris** (☎ 07/4098 2097).

If your chosen safari does not visit **Mossman Gorge,** 19 kilometers (12 miles) northwest of Port Douglas near the sugar town of Mossman, try to get there on your own. The silvery river gushing over big boulders (the eggs of the Rainbow Serpent to Aboriginal people) and the network of short forest walks are magical. Bring your swimmers, but don't climb on the rocks or enter the river except at designated swimming spots, because strong currents claimed the life of at least one tourist recently. **Coral Coaches** (☎ 07/4099 5351) makes 10 daily runs to the gorge from its Grant Street depot in Port Douglas, or from your hotel. Book a seat. The round-trip fare is A$22 (U.S.$14.30). Maybe pack a picnic, or have afternoon tea or lunch at Silky Oaks Lodge (see the box "Dining in the Rain Forest," below).

A 1-hour croc-spotting cruise on the Daintree River is high on the list of most visitors. You are not guaranteed to see crocodiles, but chances are you will. To see the Daintree's bird life, take an early-morning cruise when birds are active. To see the most wildlife, ironically, you are best to go at night. Most Daintree rain-forest day tours include a river cruise, but if yours does not, a variety of boats from open-sided "river trains" to small fishing boats run short cruises. Most leave from the Daintree River ferry crossing. Take the Captain Cook Highway from Port Douglas 19 kilometers north to Mossman, where it becomes the Mossman-Daintree Road, and follow it for 24 kilometers (15 miles) to the signposted ferry turnoff on your right. The ferry is 5 kilometers (3 miles) from the turnoff. One of the best operators catering to wildlife enthusiasts is Dan Irby's **Mangrove Adventures** (☎ 07/4090 7017), whose small, open boats can get up side creeks the bigger boats can't. Dan is a wildlife artist and photographer; he takes no more than 10 people at a time on 2-, 3-, and 4-hour cruises. He also does a night cruise. A 2-hour trip costs A$38.50 (U.S.$25).

More than half of Australia's bird species have been recorded within a 200-kilometer (125-mile) radius of these parts. **Fine Feather Tours** (☎ 07/4094 1199) leads full-day bird-watching safaris through the Wet Tropics and to dryer inland grasslands (that's the start of the Outback) for A$145 (U.S.$94.25), and a morning cruise on the bird-rich Daintree River for A$90 (U.S.$58.50).

It's not in the rain forest, but the **Rainforest Habitat wildlife sanctuary** (☎ 07/4099 3235) is not just as good as the real thing—it's better. That's because more than 200 Wet Tropics species that you normally wouldn't spot in the wild are gathered here for you to see up close. The highlight is the walk-through aviary, but you can also see crocodiles, hand-feed kangaroos, and have your photo taken with (but not holding) a koala (photos from 10 to 11am and 3 to 4pm). A donation is requested for photos. I recommend the free guided tours that leave on the hour from 9am until the last one at 3pm. Rainforest Habitat is on Port Douglas Road at the turnoff from the Captain Cook Highway. It's open daily from 8am to 5:30pm (last entry 4:30pm); admission is A$18 (U.S.$11.70) adults, A$16.20 (U.S.$10.55) seniors and students, A$9 (U.S.$5.85) kids 4 to 14, and a second child free with a family. From 8 to 11am, it serves a great champagne buffet breakfast for A$34 (U.S.$22.10) adults and A$17 (U.S.$11.05) kids, including admission. Allow 90 minutes here.

To see rain-forest critters in the wild, join a wildlife-spotting walk with **Wait-A-While Environmental Tours** (☎ 07/4033 1153). These are described in "Exploring the Wet Tropics Rain Forest," in the "Cairns" section, earlier in this chapter. Port Douglas visitors can join the Daintree tour that departs at 3pm Monday, Wednesday, and Thursday and gets back around midnight or 1am; it costs A$121 (U.S.$78.65) for adults, A$88 (U.S.$57.20) for kids under 15.

DISCOVERING ABORIGINAL CULTURE A full-day Daintree rain-forest tour with a full-blood Aboriginal woman, Hazel Douglas of ✪ **Native Guide Safari Tours** (☎ 07/4098 2206; www.internetnorth.com.au/native), is a terrific alternative to the mainstream safari operators. A vivacious member of the local Gugu (or Kuku) tribe, Hazel grew up the traditional Aboriginal way right here in this forest. Her stories are spellbinding, whether it's how a birdcall warns that you're about to step on a death adder, or how a leaf can stun fish for dinner if you screw it up and throw it into the river. Her driver, Thomas, tells the area's history from a European perspective. Never mind that Hazel's vehicle is a little old and not air-conditioned; I can't recommend her tour highly enough. Passengers from Cairns or the northern beaches transfer up from their hotels on the Quicksilver Wavepiercer catamaran, and return by coach or catamaran. The trip costs A$120 (U.S.$78) for adults and A$80 (U.S.$52) for children 3 to 14, plus A$10 (U.S.$6.50) extra from Cairns and the beaches.

On a 1-hour guided walk through the rain forest with ✪ **KuKu-Yalanji Dreamtime Tours** (☎ 07/4098 1305), you will learn about bush medicines and foods, see paint get made, hear "Dreamtime" (Aboriginal creation story) legends, and see sacred sites and cave paintings. (The KuKu-Yalanji are this region's native tribe.) Then you sit down to billy tea and damper in a bark "warun." Tours depart Monday to Friday at 10am, 11:30am, 1pm, and 2:30pm from the KuKu-Yalanji community on the road to Mossman Gorge (1km/half a mile before the Gorge parking lot) and cost A$15 (U.S.$9.75) adults, A$12 (U.S.$7.80) seniors, and A$7.50 (U.S.$4.90) children. Transfers from Port Douglas or Silky Oaks Lodge are available.

MORE TO SEE & DO

Remember that in addition to the companies below, some outdoor-activity companies in Cairns provide inexpensive or free pickups from Port Douglas hotels. See "White-Water Rafting & Other Outdoor Activities," in the "Cairns" section, earlier in this chapter.

A key "activity" in Port Douglas is simply lazing in the gentle surf of ✪ **Four Mile Beach,** a 5-minute walk from the main street. From October to May, swim only in the stinger safety net.

Visitor greens fees on the championship **Sheraton Mirage golf course** (see "Accommodations," below) are A$135 (U.S.$87.75) for 18 holes, plus A$35 (U.S.$22.75) for clubs and A$10 (U.S.$6.50) for shoes, or you can wear regular sports shoes. Contact the **Pro Shop** (☎ 07/4099 5537).

A couple of companies provide rain-forest horseback riding. **Wonga Beach Equestrian Centre** (☎ 07/4098 7583) does 2¹/₂-hour rides through the forest, along Wonga Beach (with time for a swim), through sugar-cane fields, and into orchards to taste tropical fruits like rambutans and mangoes. The ride costs A$65 (U.S.$42.45), including 35-minute transfers from Port Douglas.

Bike 'n' Hike (☎ 07/4099 4650 for the booking agent) takes you biking, hiking, swimming under waterfalls in the rain forest, or descending the tough 14-kilometer (9-mile) Bump Track. Half-day trips cost A$60 (U.S.$39) and full-day trips cost

A$82 (U.S.$53.30). Pickups from your Port Douglas hotel are free; transfers from Cairns and Palm Cove are available at a fee.

Every Sunday, a colorful handicrafts and fresh food **market** sets up on the lawns under the mango trees beside Dickson Inlet at the end of Macrossan Street. Stalls sell everything from foot massages to fresh coconut milk. It runs from 7:30am to 1pm. While you're here, take a peek, or attend a nondenominational service, inside the pretty timber St. Mary's By The Sea church.

ACCOMMODATIONS

Port Douglas Accommodation Holiday Rentals (☎ **1800/645 566** in Australia, or 07/4099 4488; www.portdouglasaccom.com.au) has a wide range of apartments and homes for rent.

High season in Port Douglas is generally from June 1 through October 31.

VERY EXPENSIVE

Sheraton Mirage Port Douglas. Davidson St. (off Port Douglas Rd.), Port Douglas, QLD 4871. ☎ **1800/07 3535** in Australia; 800/325-3535 in the U.S. and Canada; 00800/325 353535 in the U.K., Ireland, and New Zealand; or 07/4099 5888. Fax 07/4099 4424. www.sheraton-mirage.com.au. E-mail: info@sheraton-mirage.com.au. 394 units. A/C MINI-BAR TV TEL. A$557–$743 (U.S.$362.05–$483.95) double; A$879–$1,099 (U.S.$571.35–$714.35) 2-, 3-, or 4-bedroom villa. Extra person A$66 (U.S.$42.90). Children under 17 stay free in parents' room using existing bedding. Rates include full breakfast. Discounted rates for 14-day and 30-day advance bookings. AE, BC, DC, JCB, MC, V. Free valet and self-parking. Helicopter transfers available.

One of Australia's most luxurious properties, this low-rise Sheraton has 5 acres of swimmable saltwater pools, and a championship Peter Thomson–designed 18-hole golf course. It helps to have a car to stay here: it is a tad too far from Port's main street to hoof it, and though it's on the beach, the stinger nets and lifeguards are really too far up the sand to walk. If you're going to pay these rates, upgrade to an extra-large Mirage room with a corner Jacuzzi and king beds. They're better value than the unexciting standard rooms. One hundred privately owned two-, three-, and four-bedroom luxury villas with golf course, garden, or sea views are rented out by Sheraton; the decor varies, but all have a Jacuzzi and two bathrooms and TVs. A free shuttle runs from 9am to 6pm to the golf course's country club/health center, to Marina Mirage shopping center, and into town.

Dining/Diversions: Both Macrossan's, serving formal modern Australian fare, and the Japanese Zai offer dinner. Lagoon's is an all-day buffet and à la carte venue with some seating by the pool. The Plantation Bar has a sports screen, a jukebox, a pizza menu, and live bands some nights. There's a swim-up pool bar, and live piano plays in the Daintree Lounge lobby bar nightly.

Amenities: 18-hole championship golf course, country club and pro shop, aquatic driving range (with targets in a lake), putting green, group and private golf clinics, gym, two saunas, 25-meter lap pool, nine day/night tennis courts and lessons, massage, float tanks, Jacuzzi, bike rentals, game room, children's pool, baby-sitting, daily day care for kids under 5, kids' club for children ages 5 to 15 during school vacations (for a fee), tour desk, 24-hour room service, dry cleaning/laundry, turndown, complimentary newspaper, secretarial services, currency exchange, salon, business center, conference facilities, express checkout, gift shop.

EXPENSIVE

✪ **The Peninsula Boutique Hotel.** 9–13 The Esplanade, Port Douglas, QLD 4871. ☎ **1800/676 674** in Australia, or 07/4099 9100. Fax 07/4099 5440. www.peninsulahotel. com.au. E-mail:peninsulahotel.com.au. 34 units. A/C TV TEL. A$280–$320 (U.S.$182–$208) double. Rates include continental breakfast. Ask about packages. AE, BC, DC, MC, V. Complimentary round-trip transfers from your Cairns hotel, Cairns airport, wharf, or train terminal.

Built in 1999 over three levels, this intimate studio apartment hotel fronting Four Mile Beach is one of the nicest places to stay in town. Every one features an open-plan living room/bedroom, a contemporary kitchenette, and a groovy bathroom boasting a giant double tub (or Jacuzzi, in some units). Two people fit perfectly; corner apartments are a little bigger. The decor is a stylish melange of terra-cotta, mosaic tiles, granite, and wicker, with classy extra touches like a CD player, VCR, boxed Twining's teas, and plunger coffee. All have hair dryers and in-room safes. Most have great beach views from the roomy balcony or patio, while a few look onto the hip green and mauve complex of petite art deco-ish pools, waterfalls, hot and cold Jacuzzis, and sundeck rising and falling on several levels. A 2-minute walk brings you to the main street.

Dining/Diversions: The beachfront Sands Café/Bar is lovely (see "Dining"). Inside is a sleek, diminutive cocktail bar.

Amenities: Swimming pool and Jacuzzi (note: no kids under 15 without an adult in either), bicycle rental, book exchange, tour desk, currency exchange, laundry/dry cleaning, picnic hamper service, modem line.

MODERATE

✪ **Archipelago Studio Apartments.** 72 Macrossan St., Port Douglas, QLD 4871. ☎ **07/ 4099 5387.** Fax 07/4099 4847. www.archipelago.com.au. E-mail: archipelago@portdouglas. tnq.com.au. 21 units (all with shower only). A/C TV TEL. High season A$109–$164 (U.S.$70.85–$101.60) double; low season A$87–$135 (U.S.$56.55–$87.75) double. Extra person A$15 (U.S.$9.75). BC, MC, V. Free parking. Children under 3 not permitted.

They may not be the newest or biggest digs in town, but I like these sweet, homey apartments, 10 seconds from the beach and a 2-minute walk from town, for their location, and the cheery hospitality of proprietor Wolfgang Klein. Most suit only three people max, but all are freshened up annually and boast neat cane furniture, bright bedcovers, little kitchenettes, and compact, newly tiled bathrooms with hair dryers. You can opt for a tiny and rather dark Garden unit with a patio; or upgrade to a lighter, larger Balcony unit. The most expensive ones are actually quite roomy and have side-on views of Four Mile Beach from the balcony. Housekeeping services will cost you A$20 (U.S.$13) extra. There are a small pool and sundeck, a Jacuzzi, a BBQ, and a laundry. Wolfgang advises on tours and books them for you.

Port Douglas Retreat. 31–33 Mowbray St. (at Mudlo St.), Port Douglas, QLD 4871. ☎ **07/4099 5053.** Fax 07/4099 5033. www.portdouglasretreat.com.au. E-mail: info@ portdouglasretreat.com.au. 36 units (all with shower only). A/C TV TEL. High season A$141 (U.S.$91.65) double; low season A$101 (U.S.$65.65) double. Crib A$5 (U.S.$3.25) per night. AE, BC, MC, V.

This well-kept two-story studio apartment complex on a quiet street, featuring the white-battened balconies of the Queenslander architectural style, is a good value, because even some of the ritzier accommodation houses in town can't boast its lagoon-like pool hedged in by dense jungle, wrapped by an ample shady sundeck that cries out to be lounged on with a good book and a cool drink. The apartments are not enormous, but are fashionably furnished with terra-cotta tile floors, wrought-iron beds, cane seating, colorful bedcovers, kitchenettes, and free in-house movies. Borrow a hair dryer from the front desk. All have large furnished balconies or patios looking into tropical gardens (some on the ground floor open onto the common-area boardwalk, so maybe ask for a first-floor unit). The managers run a tour desk. Town and the beach are a 5-minute walk away. No smoking indoors.

INEXPENSIVE

Port O'Call Lodge. Port St. (at Craven Close), Port Douglas, QLD 4871. ☎ **1800/892 800** in Australia, or 07/4099 5422. Fax 07/4099 5495. www.portocall.com.au. E-mail: info@portocall.com.au. 28 units (all with shower only). High season (June–Sept.) A$85–$95 (U.S.$55.25–$61.75) double; shoulder season (May and Oct) A$75–$85 (U.S.$48.75–$55.25) double; low season (Nov–Apr) A$65–$75 (U.S.$42.25–$48.75) double. A$21 (U.S.$13.65) dorm bed (A$19.50/U.S.$12.70 for YHA/Hostelling International members). Extra person A$11 (U.S.$7.15). Children under 3 free. BC, MC, V. Free parking. The hotel operates a free door-to-door minibus to and from Cairns Mon, Wed, and Sat.

Backpackers, families, and anyone on a budget seem to treat this modest motel like a second home, swapping travel stories as they cook up a meal in the communal kitchen. Located on a suburban street a 10-minute walk from town, the rooms are spacious, light, and fresh with tiled floors, plenty of baggage space, air-conditioning, and compact bathrooms with old but neat fixtures (BYO hair dryer). Only the Deluxe rooms have TVs, clock radios, tea and coffee, and minifridges. At night the bistro around the nice free-form pool is the place to be (see "Dining," below). The front desk runs a tour desk and rents bikes; Quicksilver does free introductory dives in the pool; and there are a kiosk, Internet access, pay phones, a guest safe, and a laundry.

A LUXURY B&B IN THE COUNTRY

○ **Marae.** Lot 1, Ponzo Rd., Shannonvale (P.O. Box 133, Port Douglas, QLD 4871). ☎ **07/ 4098 4900.** Fax 07/4098 4099. www.marae.com.au. E-mail: marae@internetnorth.com.au. 3 units (2 with shower only). A/C TV. A$100 (U.S.$65) double. Rates include full breakfast. Minimum 2-night stay required. BC, MC, V. From Port Douglas take the Captain Cook Hwy. toward Mossman for 10km (6 miles), turn left onto the Mt. Molloy turnoff and follow for 1km (just over ¹/₂ mile), then turn right onto Ponzo Rd. for 2km (1¹/₄ miles); Marae's driveway is on your left. You will need a car because tour operators and bus services do not call (or take taxis). No children under 13.

Andy Morris has turned this architecturally stunning timber home into a haven of glamour in the countryside. Set on a hillside 15 kilometers (9 miles) north of Port Douglas, the house's rustic-meets-sleek contemporary bedrooms have white mosquito nets and smart linens on timber beds, and elegant bathrooms with hair dryers. One bathroom is private, but not en suite. You will love chilling out in the gorgeous big living room, whose walls open outward on poles, Dutch hopper-style, to let in the breeze; to one side is a gourmet kitchen. Andy serves a breakfast of pancakes, croissants, tropical fruit, and anything you like. Wallabies and bandicoots (a small marsupial) feed in the garden, kingfishers and honey eaters use the plunge pool overlooking the valley, and butterflies are everywhere. You can laze on two decks, or wander the rain-forest trails of Mossman Gorge a few miles away, but most guests end up playing with the Jack Russell terriers and Cactus, the irrepressible pet cockatoo.

TWO HIDEAWAYS IN THE RAIN FOREST

○ **Daintree Eco Lodge & Spa.** 20 Daintree Rd., Daintree, QLD 4873 (4km/2¹/₂ miles south of Daintree village). ☎ **1800/808 010** in Australia, or 07/4098 6100. Fax 07/4098 6200. www.daintree-ecolodge.com.au. E-mail: info@daintree-ecolodge.com.au. 15 units (10 with shower only). A/C MINIBAR TV TEL. A$434.50–$489.50 (U.S.$282.45–$318.20) double. Extra person A$66 (U.S.$42.90). Children under 4 stay free in parents' room using existing bedding. Rates include full breakfast. Ask about 3-night packages. AE, BC, DC, MC, V. Scheduled minibus picks up and drops off once a day at Port Douglas hotels, Cairns hotels, and Cairns airport for A$49.50/U.S.$32.20 (Port Douglas) or A$55/U.S.$35.75 (Cairns) per person, one-way. Transfers at any time are available at higher cost. Private car transfers A$143 (U.S.$92.95) from Port Douglas or A$165 (U.S.$107.25) from Cairns, per car, one-way. Limousine and helicopter transfers can be arranged. The lodge is 98km (61 miles) north of Cairns and 40km (25 miles) north of Port Douglas. Take the Captain Cook Hwy. north to Mossman, where it becomes the Mossman-Daintree road; follow this all the way to the lodge.

Acclaimed nature documentary maker David Attenborough described a stay at this luxury eco-resort as "one of the most magical experiences of my life." Who wouldn't think so, after waking up suspended over a burbling creek in a swish villa in the rainforest canopy? Forever winning awards for its "green tourism" ethos, this place hosts only a small number of guests and has a position right in the primeval forest (rather than on the forest's edge like Silky Oaks Lodge, below) that gives it a special sense of peace. Don't think "eco" means sacrificing creature comforts: the big rooms were refurbished in 2000 and boast marble floors, exotic timber and bamboo furniture, coffee plungers, and smartly tiled bathrooms with robes and hair dryers. Five have Jacuzzis on the balcony. You may be disappointed to encounter the fine insect screens around your quarters, even the balcony, but they are essential for blocking mosquitoes. All drinking and shower water is pure rainwater from the waterfall.

A new health spa dishes out all kinds of treatments, from the Jalaynba Rain Treatment (in which six shower heads pummel you as you recline on a timber "wet bed") to the Secret Sacred Treatment (a women-only "pilgrimage" to the lodge's waterfall for a body treatment involving natural ochres found at its base). You can join a yoga or Ki (based on Japanese Aikido) session, laze by the petite solar-heated pool and sundeck, walk rain-forest trails leading from the lodge, join members of the local Aboriginal Kuku tribe on a bush tucker and native medicine stroll, or take a 4WD day trip to modern-day Aboriginal communities. The tour desk books 4WD jungle safaris, Daintree river wildlife-spotting cruises, horseback riding, and snorkeling, diving, and fishing trips to the Great Barrier Reef. The Baaru House Restaurant and Bar, built over a lily-filled pond, serves gourmet bush tucker in what I call a "deluxe tree-house" atmosphere. Amenities include laundry service and a gift shop.

Silky Oaks Lodge. 7km (4 miles) west of Mossman; 27km (17 miles) from Port Douglas. c/o P&O Australian Resorts, GPO Box 478, Sydney, NSW 2001. ☎ **1800/737 678** in Australia, 800/225-9849 in the U.S. and Canada, 020/7805 3875 in the U.K., 02/9277 5050 (Sydney reservations office) or 07/4098 1666 (lodge). Fax 02/9299 2477 (Sydney reservations office) or 07/4098 1983 (lodge). www.poresorts.com.au. E-mail: resorts_reservations@ poaustralia.com.au. 60 chalets. A/C MINIBAR TEL. A$426 (U.S.$276.90) double. Extra person A$65 (U.S.$42.25). Rates include continental breakfast. Ask about packages; some combine stays at Dunk, Bedarra, and Lizard islands and Sebel Reef House (all described in this chapter). AE, BC, DC, JCB, MC, V. Free morning and afternoon shuttle from Port Douglas. Coral Coaches makes morning and afternoon transfers from Port Douglas for A$14.80 (U.S.$9.65) one-way, A$29.60 (U.S.$19.25) round-trip. Town-car transfers A$125 (U.S.$81.25) per car one-way from Cairns city or airport; stretch limousine transfers available. Take the Captain Cook Hwy. to Mossman, where it becomes the Mossman-Daintree Rd.; follow this approx. 3.5km (2 miles) past Mossman and turn left onto Finlayvale Rd. at the small white-on-blue SILKY OAKS sign. No children under 6.

From the main complex of this upscale lodge at Mossman Gorge, you look straight down onto the picturesque Mossman River, where you can swim (croc-free!). Despite its peaceful setting, the place has a rather bustling air because of the high number of guests, plus visitors to the restaurant. Accommodations are in petite chalets scattered through a mixture of rain forest and man-made gardens; a few have river frontage and some have Jacuzzis. Each has elegant timber floors, attractive furnishings, bathrobes, a hair dryer, a CD player, and a double hammock to string up on your veranda. You can have a massage on your balcony, too.

Guided nature walks, mountain bikes, and evening nature slide shows are free, and there are a daily activities program, a day/night tennis court, a lovely free-form swimming pool and sun lounges, and a wallaby sanctuary where you can feed the animals. A beautiful open-sided restaurant serves elegant meals, and there's a cocktail lounge. Among the amenities are turndown, currency exchange, a boutique, laundry service, a laundry, and meeting rooms. Plans were underway for a health/beauty spa as I wrote. The tour desk books Great Barrier Reef cruises, rain-forest 4WD safaris, and other activities throughout the Cairns region. A car is necessary to access Mossman Gorge's lovely walking trails across the river.

WHERE TO DINE IN PORT DOUGLAS

✪ **Nautilus.** 17 Murphy St. (entry also from Macrossan St.), Port Douglas. ☎ **07/4099 5330.** Reservations required. Main courses A$25.90–$36 (U.S.$16.85–$23.40). AE, BC, DC, JCB, MC, V. Daily 6:30pm–late. TROPICAL/SEAFOOD.

If it's good enough for Bill and Hillary, it might be good enough for you. President Clinton and the First Lady dined here in November 1996 during a visit Down Under and by all accounts loved it. The restaurant is extremely popular for its magical outdoor setting under palm trees and stars, and for its cleverly cooked seafood. A typical dish is grilled yellowfin tuna on a salad of roasted peppers, pink papaw, and avocado with black sesame dressing. There are plenty of nonseafood choices too. If you want a meal fit for a president, order what he ordered—a fresh seafood tapas plate, followed by deep-fried coral trout with sweet chili sauce and Asian spices, rounded off with a hot mango soufflé.

On the Inlet. 3 Inlet St. ☎ **07/4099 5255.** Reservations recommended. Main courses A$16–$25 (U.S.$10.40–$16.25); seafood platter for 2 A$95 (U.S.$61.75). AE, BC, DC, JCB, MC, V. Daily noon–3:30pm; 5:30pm–late. Happy Hour with snacks 4–6pm. SEAFOOD.

No-nonsense seafood and a no-fuss atmosphere make this waterside venue popular with the locals. It's nothing flashy—just white plastic chairs on a shady deck with nice views. Kick back over a long lunch, which might include fried calamari with tartar sauce to start, followed by a stack of chilled Moreton Bay bugs. Or you could try the sizzling garlic prawns for an appetizer and a seafood plate of fried fish, calamari, prawns, scallops, and fries for a main course. From the Sunset Bar, you can watch sting rays and grouper feed in the depths below. A take-out section up front serves calamari, prawns, or fish-and-chips. The restaurant doubles as a seafood wholesaler, so you know the fish is fresh.

Port O' Call Bistro & Bar. At the Port O' Call Lodge, Port St. at Craven Close. ☎ **07/4099 5422.** Main courses A$8.50–$11.50 (U.S.$5.55–$7.50). BC, MC, V. Daily 6–9pm; Happy Hour 5–7pm (bar opens 4pm).

Locals patronize this casual open-sided bistro and bar at the Port O' Call Lodge (see "Accommodations," above) almost as often as guests do, because it serves tasty food in hearty portions at painless prices. The atmosphere is fun and friendly, with tiki torches set around the pool. You have plenty of choices, such as char-grilled steak or reef fish, vegetarian lasagna, chicken schnitzel, or a homemade steak pie. Most meals come with a baked potato and salad. Tuesday night is the popular (U.S.$5.60) curry night with little over A$10 (U.S.$6.50), and Sunday is roast night.

✪ **Salsa Bar & Grill.** 38 Macrossan St. ☎ **07/4099 4922.** Reservations recommended, especially at dinner. Main courses A$19–$22.50 (U.S.$12.35–$14.65). AE, BC, DC, JCB, MC, V. Mon–Sat noon–late, Sun 7:30am–late. MODERN AUSTRALIAN/CALIFORNIAN.

Groovy decor, affordable prices (especially at lunch), and first-rate food add up to constantly buzzing crowds at this smart alfresco joint. My vegetable and goat-cheese

Dining in the Rain Forest

At **Baaru House** restaurant at Daintree Eco Lodge & Spa (see "Accommodations," above), you dine in an airy insect-screened timber pole house, surrounded by the noises of crickets, frogs, birds, and rushing water. The signature dish on the "gourmet bush tucker" menu is wild baby barramundi wrapped in native ginger leaves (grown in the resort's rain forest) and melaleuca bark. Main courses range from A$21.50 to $29.50 (U.S.$14 to $19.20). It's open daily from 7 to 10am, noon to 2pm, and 6 to 9pm.

At the **Tree House Restaurant** at Silky Oaks Lodge (see "Accommodations," above), the menu is upscale Modern Australian fare, and you dine at polished timber tables on a large veranda above the Mossman River. It's open all day, serving meals from 7 to 10am (until 11am for à la carte), noon to 2:30pm, and 6 to 9pm. Main courses are A$16.50 to $19.50 (U.S.$10.75 to $12.70) at lunch, A$19.50 to $25 (U.S.$12.70 to $16.25) at dinner. Breakfast is A$15 (U.S.$9.75) continental, or an extra A$10 (U.S.$6.50) for hot fare. Afternoon tea is served from 2:30 to 5pm. There is also a three-course à la carte lunch package featuring round-trip transfers from Port Douglas at 11:30am (back at 3pm) for A$49 (U.S.$31.85) per person. Bring your swimsuit and take a dip in the picturesque river beforehand. Kids under 6 not permitted.

Treetops restaurant at the Radisson Treetops Resort, Port Douglas Road (☎ **07/4030 4333**), cooks sophisticated à la carte dishes over an open flame in five open-sided "tree houses" set high in the rain-forest canopy overlooking the lagoon. Each tree house has several tables. The three-course prix-fixe menu, with choices for each course, is A$57 (U.S.$37.05). Open for dinner only.

burrito with black bean–corn salsa was out of this world. You could chow down on the calamari stack with smoked tomato salsa for lunch, or the crispy skinned chicken and smoked salmon with wild lime beurre blanc for dinner. Whatever you choose, save room for dessert. Try the ultracontemporary bar next door for a pre- or post-dinner cocktail.

✪ **Sands Café/Bar.** At the Peninsula Boutique Hotel, 9–13 The Esplanade. ☎ **07/4099 9100.** Reservations recommended. Main courses A$17.50–$24.50 (U.S.$11.40–$15.95). AE, BC, DC, MC, V. Daily 7:30am–2:30pm, Fri–Sun 7:30am–late (may open for dinner nightly in high season). MODERN AUSTRALIAN.

Port's only beachfront dining venue is this simple, stylish, alfresco cafe/restaurant across the road from the waves. It serves adventurous breakfasts like polenta and pecan flapjack; satisfying lunches like smoked chicken, spinach, and parmesan risotto (highly recommended); and modish dinners like Moroccan lamb cutlets on chick pea salsa and sweet potato mash (recommended too). A very smart wine list completes the picture. Watch for the monthly Full Moon dinners, when the moon rises over the sea through the palms.

4 The North Coast: Mission Beach, Townsville & the Islands

For years the lovely town of ✪ **Mission Beach** was something of a well-kept secret. Farmers retired here; then those who liked to drop out and chill out discovered it. Today, it's a petite, prosperous, and stunningly pretty rain-forest town tucked in dense, dense jungle. Even now you'll encounter few crowds, so clever has Mission Beach been at staying out of sight, out of mind, and off the tourist trail. The beach here is one of the most gorgeous in Australia, a long white strip fringed with tangled vine forests. A scattering of idyllic islands can be seen decorating the seascape just offshore.

The nearby **Tully River** is the white-water rafting capital of Australia (although the folks on the Nymboida and Gwydir rivers in New South Wales might argue about that).

From Mission Beach, it's a short ferry ride to **Dunk Island,** a large rain-forested resort island that welcomes day-trippers. You can even ✪ **sea kayak** there from the mainland. Mission Beach is closer to the Great Barrier Reef than any other point along the coast—just an hour away—and cruise boats depart to the Reef daily from the jetty, stopping en route at Dunk Island.

Just south of Dunk Island is one of Australia's most exclusive island resorts, **Bedarra Island,** which hosts just 30 lucky guests at a time, who get to soak up its glorious rain forest, unspoiled beaches, and 24-hour open bar.

A few hours' drive south brings you to the city of **Townsville,** also a gateway to the Great Barrier Reef, but more important to visitors as a gateway to **Magnetic Island,** a picturesque, laid-back haven for water-sports enthusiasts and hikers.

The drive from Cairns to Townsville through sugarcane fields, cloud-topped hills, and lush bushland is a pretty one—one of the most picturesque stretches in Queensland.

MISSION BEACH: THE CASSOWARY COAST
140km (88 miles) S of Cairns; 240km (150 miles) N of Townsville

Tucked off the Bruce Highway, the exquisitely pretty township of Mission Beach has managed to duck the tourist hordes. It's actually a string of four beachfront towns: South Mission Beach, Wongaling Beach, Mission Beach proper, and Bingil Bay. Dense jungle hides the towns from view until you come around the corner and discover tidy villages full of small-scale hotels, neat shops, and a handful of smart little restaurants. Most commercial activity is centered around the small nucleus of shops and businesses in Mission Beach proper.

The jungle around the town is cassowary country. **Cassowaries,** an endangered species, are flightless birds about the size of an emu; they have black plumage, red and blue necks, and bony cones on their heads that give them a rather dashing *Jurassic Park* look. Signs on the road from the highway warn you to slow down and watch out for them crossing the road.

ESSENTIALS
GETTING THERE   From Cairns, take the Bruce Highway south to the turnoff at tiny El Arish. From the turnoff, it's 25 kilometers (16 miles) to Mission Beach. It's a 90-minute trip. From Townsville, there's a turnoff just north of Tully that leads 18 kilometers (11 miles) to Mission Beach.

> **Safety Tips**
>
> **Crocodiles** inhabit the waterways around Mission Beach. Do not swim in, or stand on the bank of, any river, stream, or estuary.
>
> It's frustrating, but the area's 14 kilometers (9 miles) of beaches are all but off-limits in the deadly **marine stinger** season from October through April or May. Swim only in the stinger nets at Mission Beach and South Mission Beach then.
>
> **Cassowaries** can kill with their powerful claws. If you confront one, back slowly away and hide behind a tree.

Mission Beach Bus & Coach (☎ **07/4068 7400**) operates four door-to-door shuttles a day from Cairns for A$28 (U.S.$18.20) per person, and from the Cairns airport for A$33 (U.S.$21.45) per person. One service a day runs from the northern beaches at A$38 (U.S.$24.70) per person. **McCafferty's** (☎ **13 14 99** in Australia) and **Greyhound Pioneer** (☎ **13 20 30** in Australia) coaches both stop in Mission Beach proper (not South Mission Beach) several times daily on their Cairns–Brisbane–Cairns runs. Trip time from Brisbane is over 26 hours.

Four trains a week on the Cairns–Brisbane–Cairns route call at the nearest train station, Tully, about 20 kilometers (13 miles) away. The fare is A$24.20 (U.S.$15.75) from Cairns for the 3¼-hour trip; from Brisbane fares range from A$173 (U.S.$112.45) for a seat to A$449 (U.S.$291.85) for a first-class sleeper. Call Queensland Rail's long-distance division, **Traveltrain** (☎ **1800/806 468** in Australia, or 07/3235 1122). A taxi from Tully to Mission Beach with **Tully Taxis & Buses** (☎ **07/4068 3937**) is about A$40 (U.S.$26).

VISITOR INFORMATION The **Mission Beach Visitor Centre,** Porters Promenade, Mission Beach, QLD 4852 (☎ **07/4068 7099;** www.missionbch.com), is at the northern end of Mission Beach proper. It's open Monday to Saturday from 9am to 5pm, until 4pm Sundays.

GETTING AROUND The local bus (☎ **07/4068 7400,** or call the driver's cell phone at 0419/745 875) travels day and night between all the beach communities, stopping at all the accommodations listed below, Clump Point Jetty, and Wongaling Beach near the Dunk Island water taxi. The only car-rental company in town is **Sugarland Car Rentals** (☎ **07/4068 8272**). The taxi company is **Mission Beach Taxi Service** (☎ **07/4068 8155**).

WHAT TO SEE & DO

SNORKELING & DIVING THE GREAT BARRIER REEF Mission Beach is the closest point on the mainland to the Reef, 1 hour by the air-conditioned **Quick Cat** catamaran (☎ **1800/654 242** in Australia, or 07/4068 7289). The trip includes a 45-minute stop at Dunk Island, then 3 hours on sandy Beaver Cay on the Outer Reef. On Sunday, "Adventurers and Backpackers Day," the boat bypasses Dunk and goes straight to the Reef, giving you 4 hours on the coral. The boat departs Clump Point Jetty every day except Tuesday. On Sunday, the trip is a great-value A$68 (U.S.$44.20); other days it costs A$134 (U.S.$87.10) for adults, A$67 (U.S.$43.55) for children 4 to 14, and A$335 (U.S.$217.75) for a family of four, including a free pickup from your hotel. An introductory dive costs A$77 (U.S.$50.05) for the first and A$33 (U.S.$21.45) for the second. Prebook these to ensure a place. Certified dives cost A$55 (U.S.$35.75) for the first, A$33 (U.S.$21.45) for the second. You can connect to this trip by coach from your Cairns or northern beaches hotel for an extra charge.

Mission Beach Dive Charters (☎ **07/4068 7277**) operates dive day trips and open-water certification courses.

WHITE-WATER RAFTING ON THE TULLY A day spent rafting through the jungle on the Grade 3 to 4 Tully River involves hair-raising but manageable rapids punctuated by calm stretches. You don't need experience, just agility and enthusiasm. I highly recommend ✪ **RnR Rafting** (☎ **07/4051 7777**), whose trip includes 5 hours on the river with fun expert guides, a riverside BBQ lunch, and a video screening of your antics afterward. Trips run daily and cost A$128 (U.S.$83.20) from Mission Beach, A$138 (U.S.$89.70) from Cairns and northern beaches, and A$149 (U.S.$96.85) from Port Douglas. Minimum age is 13.

A Travel Tip

There is no bank in Mission Beach, and only one ATM, located within Mission Beach Resort at Wongaling Beach. That's a drive from Mission Beach proper or South Mission Beach.

EXPLORING THE RAIN FOREST & COAST   Several companies offer sea kayaking along the unspoiled island-dotted shoreline and guided nature walks in the rain forest. Ingrid Marker of **Sunbird Adventures** (☎ 07/4068 8229; www.sunbird. com.au) does half-day sea-kayaking expeditions for A$48 (U.S.$31.20), and nighttime nature walks for A$25 (U.S.$16.25). Ingrid knows heaps about Aboriginal tracking, foods, and medicines.

Ask the Mission Beach Visitor Centre for their free maps marking the town's **seaside and jungle walking trails.**

A DAY TRIP TO DUNK ISLAND   Day-trippers can pop over to Dunk Island to swim, snorkel (the coral isn't great; the best spot is off Muggy Muggy Beach and Naturist Beach), hike, and pay to use the water-sports equipment. A A$25 (U.S.$16.25) day pass entitles you to use one of the pools and includes a A$15 (U.S.$9.75) lunch credit. **Dunk Island Ferry & Cruises** (☎ 07/4068 7211) gets you there for A$26 (U.S.$16.90) for adults and A$11 (U.S.$7.15) for kids 10 to 14 (free for younger kids), round-trip. Free snorkeling gear is included with a A$20 (U.S.$13) refundable deposit. The boat departs daily from Clump Point Jetty, a quick drive or a 40-minute walk from Mission Beach proper.

The **Dunk Island Express water taxi** (☎ 07/4068 8310) runs six times a day from Wongaling Beach. Be ready to get your feet wet when you land. The round-trip fare is A$26.40 (U.S.$17.15) adults, half price for kids 4 to 14.

A novel way to explore the island is by sea kayak with Ingrid Marker of **Sunbird Adventures** (see above). Ingrid says if you can pedal a bike for an hour, you can sea kayak for the hour it takes to get to the island. You glide over reefs looking for sea turtles; picnic on oysters, mussels, and other fresh produce (all organic) in Hidden Palm Valley; and then hike the rain forest to look for Aboriginal bush tucker. Bring snorkel gear if you like. The full day trip costs A$80 (U.S.$52).

ACCOMMODATIONS IN MISSION BEACH

✪ **The Horizon.** Explorer Dr., South Mission Beach, QLD 4852. ☎ **1800/079 090** in Australia, or 07/4068 8154. Fax 07/4068 8596. www.thehorizon.com.au. E-mail: info@ thehorizon.com.au. 55 units. A/C MINIBAR TV TEL. A$195–$230 (U.S.$126.75–$149.50) double. Extra person A$30 (U.S.$19.50). Rates may be higher Christmas–early Jan. AE, BC, DC, MC, V.

Beguiling views across the pool to Dunk Island make this hillside resort a truly lovely hideaway. Boardwalks lead through dense rain forest to the smart contemporary rooms, even the least expensive of which are spacious and have luxurious bathrooms fitted with hair dryers. All but a handful have some kind of sea view. A half-dozen retain the older-style bathrooms from a previous resort development, but the views from these are the best. There are a poolside restaurant and cocktail bar, and tennis courts. A short, steep path down the hill leads to the beach.

Mackays. 7 Porters Promenade, Mission Beach, QLD 4852. ☎ **07/4068 7212.** Fax 07/ 4068 7095. 22 units (some with shower only). TV TEL. A$77–$99 (U.S.$50.05–$64.35) double, A$99 (U.S.$64.35) 1- and 2-bedroom apt. Higher rates at Easter. Extra adult A$16.50

(U.S.$10.75); extra child under 14 A$6.60 (U.S.$4.30). Ask about packages that include white-water rafting, Reef trips, Dunk Island cruises, and more. BC, MC, V.

This white-lattice motel 80 meters (260 ft.) from the beach is delightful. The friendly Mackay family repaints the rooms annually, adorns every stair with hibiscus flowers, and provides a tour desk. Each spacious room has white-tiled floors, cane sofas, colorful bedcovers, and very clean bathrooms (hair dryers are at the front desk). Rooms in the newer section are air-conditioned, and some have views of the lovely granite-lined pool and gardens. Those in the older wing have garden views from a communal patio and no air-conditioning. The packages are a terrific value.

ACCOMMODATIONS ON DUNK ISLAND

Dunk Island. Off Mission Beach. c/o P&O Australian Resorts, GPO Box 478, Sydney, NSW 2001. ☎ **1800/737 678** in Australia, 800/225-9849 in the U.S. and Canada, 020/7805 3875 in the U.K., 02/9277 5050 (Sydney sales and reservations office) or 07/4068 8199 (the island). Fax 02/9299 2477 (Sydney sales and reservations office) or 07/4068 8528 (the island). www.poresorts.com.au. E-mail: resorts_reservations@poaustralia.com.au. 147 units (73 with shower only). A/C MINIBAR TV TEL. A$380–$590 (U.S.$247–$383.50) double. Rates include full breakfast. Extra adult A$90 (U.S.$58.50), extra child 3–14 A$45 (U.S.$29.25). Ask about packages; some combine stays at Bedarra Island and Silky Oaks Lodge (both described elsewhere in this chapter). AE, BC, DC, JCB, MC, V. Transtate Airlines makes 3 daily 45-min. flights from Cairns (book through the resort); advance-purchase fare A$200 (U.S.$130) adults, A$136.72 (U.S.$88.90) child 3–14, round-trip. Aircraft luggage limit 16kg (35 lb.) per person. Dunk Island Ferry & Cruises (☎ 07/4068 7211) makes 1 or 2 daily round-trip ferry transfers from Mission Beach for A$26 (U.S.$16.90) adults. *Including* the ferry fare, the company does daily door-to-door coach connections from Port Douglas for A$108 (U.S.$70.20), Cairns city and airport for A$75 (U.S.$48.75), and Cairns northern beaches (A$85/U.S.$55.25) adult. Fares for children 4–14 are half price. Note: Ferry occasionally lands on beach, meaning wet feet. Airport pickups must be booked. Transfers also available by air charter and "Quick Cat" Great Barrier Reef cruise boat (see earlier in this chapter).

Just 5 kilometers (3 miles) offshore from Mission Beach, Dunk is a thickly rainforested 12-square-kilometer (7½-square-mile) island that attracts everyone from honeymooners to families to retired couples. The island is renowned for bird life and neon-blue Ulysses butterflies, which you spy on the 13 kilometers (8 miles) of walking trails. Coral reefs just offshore are not extensive, though you will find some coral at Muggy Muggy and Naturist beaches. Divers join the Quick Cat (described earlier in this chapter) or dive with mainland-based operators.

Among the free activities are snorkel gear and lessons, windsurfing, catamaran sailing, paddle-skiing, fishing tackle, a 6-hole golf course (pay for balls and tees), day/ night tennis courts, squash and racquetball courts, fitness classes and aqua-aerobics, beach and pool volleyball, badminton, croquet, bocce, archery, and a basketball hoop. You pay for guided jet-ski tours, "Discover Scuba" sessions in the pool, parasailing, waterskiing, tube rides, tandem skydiving, sport-fishing trips, dinghies, sunset champagne sails, horse riding, and mountain bikes. A yacht calls to make trips around nearby islands, and a game fishing boat collects here regularly.

All four kinds of low-rise accommodations are comfortable rather than glamorous, with tile floors, nice cane furniture, hair dryers, and colorful furnishings. Not all have sea views; those that do are the most recently renovated (in 1999).

Dining/Diversions: In 2000, A$2 million (U.S.$1.3 million) was spent to spruce up the restaurants and central complex. You have a sidewalk cafe, an à la carte seafood dinner restaurant (both have sea views), a beach hut cafe, a pool bar for light lunches, and a pleasant cocktail bar. Beach barbecues are held from time to time.

Amenities: A "Spa of Peace and Plenty" was added in 2000, offering trendy health treatments. Daily activities program (see above), three-tiered swimming pool and sundeck, daily kids' club for kids 3 to 14 (at a fee), baby-sitting, playground, private artists' colony in the rain forest selling works Monday and Thursday (10am to 1pm), boutique, laundry, currency exchange, safe-deposit boxes, conference facilities.

BEDARRA ISLAND: THE ULTIMATE LUXURY GETAWAY

Only a mile long, Bedarra is home to an exclusive 15-room resort favored by the rich, the famous, and anyone who treasures privacy. The Duchess of York has stayed here, and so has Princess Caroline of Monaco. The staff is discreet, and day-trippers are banned. Rain forested and fringed by beaches, Bedarra is a few miles south of Dunk Island, above.

✪ **Bedarra Island.** Off Mission Beach. c/o P&O Australian Resorts, GPO Box 478, Sydney, NSW 2001. ☎ **1800/737 678** in Australia, 800/225-9849 in the U.S. and Canada, 020/7805 3875 in the U.K., 02/9277 5050 (Sydney sales and reservations office) or 07/4068 8233 (the island). Fax 02/9299 2477 (Sydney sales and reservations office) or 07/4068 8215 (the island). www.poresorts.com.au. E-mail: resorts_reservations@poaustralia.com.au. 15 villas. A/C MINIBAR TV TEL. A$1,600–$1,730 (U.S.$1,040–$1,124.50) double. Rates include all meals and 24-hr. open bar. Ask about packages; some combine stays at Dunk Island (see above), Silky Oaks Lodge, and Lizard Island (both described in this chapter). AE, BC, DC, MC, V. Air or coach/ferry transfer to Dunk Island from Cairns (see above), then free 15-min. boat transfer. Water transfers can be arranged from Mission Beach. No children under 16.

Bedarra is one of those rare and fabulous places that throws not just meals but vintage French champagnes, fine cognacs and wines, and other potable treats into the price, shocking though that price may be. If you feel like Louis Roederer Champagne at 3am, help yourself. Refurbished in 1999, both the restaurant/cocktail bar and the villas have an appealing "rustic elegant" tropical look, with timber walls and polished wood floors, pitched ceilings with exposed beams, and quality wicker furniture. Each villa is tucked into the rain forest with a balcony and sea views. All come with generous living areas, king beds, VCR and CD players, bathrobes, hair dryers, and the important things in life, like double hammocks on the veranda and big double bathtubs.

The emphasis here is on relaxation. Walk along rain-forest trails, fish off the beach, snorkel, or take a catamaran, paddle-ski, or windsurfer out on the water. These activities are free; chartering a yacht or game fishing boat costs extra. To visit the Great Barrier Reef, you will need to transfer to Dunk Island to join the Quick Cat catamaran (see earlier in this chapter). Many guests do nothing more strenuous than have the chef pack a gourmet picnic with a bottle of bubbly and set off in a dinghy in search of a deserted beach. Dress at night is smart casual.

Dining/Diversions: The timbered restaurant has an attractive open veranda overlooking the sea and a menu that changes daily. The emphasis is on fresh seafood and tropical fruits. The Bedarra Bar is open 24 hours.

Amenities: Secluded swimming pool and sundeck, Jacuzzi, day/night tennis court, massage (in your room or on the beach), water sports (see above), library, boutique, currency exchange (limited), laundry service, nightly turndown.

DINING IN MISSION BEACH

Friends. Porters Promenade (opposite Campbell St.), Mission Beach. ☎ **07/4068 7107,** or 07/4068 7440 (9am–5pm). Reservations recommended. Main courses A$12.50–$22 (U.S.$8.15–$14.30). AE, BC, MC, V. Mon–Sat 6:30pm–late. Open Sun on long weekends. Closed for 1 month during Feb–Mar. HOME COOKING.

The cozy interior and a hearty menu favoring local seafood make this place a long-standing favorite with locals. Appetizers include mussels Normandy, oysters done three ways, and garlic prawns; main courses feature lamb shanks; eye fillet steak with

Dianne, mushroom, or green peppercorn sauce; and chicken hotpot. Settle in with a homemade dessert and liqueur coffee after dinner. Licensed and BYO.

TOWNSVILLE & MAGNETIC ISLAND
346km (216 miles) S of Cairns; 1,371km (857 miles) N of Brisbane

Townsville is a bit like Cairns without the crowds, the palms, or the touristy ambience. Unglamorous but friendly, this industrial and army-base town nestles on the Coral Sea below the pink face of Castle Rock, which juts 300 meters (about 1,000 ft.) straight up above town. Townsville's low-key charms may not put it at the top of your list, but you could easily spend a pleasant couple of days here if you're driving down the coast from Cairns. Divers come to visit the SS *Yongala* wreck and a couple of other remote Coral Sea reefs that are less crowded than the Great Barrier Reef sites farther north. The headquarters of the Great Barrier Reef Marine Park Authority is here, where you can visit a marvelous man-made living reef in a giant tank at **Reef HQ.** Cruises depart to the real thing most days from the harbor, although at $2^{1}/_{2}$ hours away, the Reef is farther from shore here than anywhere else along the coast.

Just 5 miles offshore is "Maggie," or **Magnetic Island,** a popular playground for all kinds of water sports, diving, snorkeling, national-park hiking, and spotting koalas in the wild. This unpretentious but pretty island is just a half-day drive from Cairns plus a short ferry ride, so it makes a nice side trip. Although far enough north to be hot and sticky in summer, Townsville comes under a rain shadow, saving it from the worst of the summertime Wet Season rains.

ESSENTIALS
GETTING THERE   Townsville is on the Bruce Highway, a 3-hour drive north of Airlie Beach and $4^{1}/_{2}$ hours south of Cairns. The Bruce Highway breaks temporarily in the city. From the south, take Bruce Highway Alt. 1 route into the city. From the north, the highway leads into the city as Ingham Road.

Ansett (☎ 13 13 00 in Australia), **Qantas** (☎ 13 13 13 in Australia), and their respective subsidiaries **Flight West Airlines** and **Sunstate Airlines** (book through the parent airlines) have many flights a day from Cairns, and several from Brisbane. Sunstate flies from Proserpine and Hamilton Island airports in the Whitsundays.

Airport Transfers & Tours (☎ 07/4775 5544) runs a door-to-door airport shuttle. It meets only flights from Brisbane, not from Cairns or elsewhere. A trip into town is A$6 (U.S.$3.90) one-way or A$10 (U.S.$6.50) return, less if there are two of you. Reservations are not needed.

The *Queenslander* (weekly) and the *Sunlander* (three times a week) stop at Townsville on their Brisbane–Cairns–Brisbane routes. The twice-weekly *Spirit of the Tropics* from Brisbane terminates in Townsville. The trip from Cairns takes about 7 hours and costs A$47.30 (U.S.$30.75). Fares for the 23- or 24-hour journey from Brisbane range from A$124 (U.S.$80.60) for a sitting berth to A$455 (U.S.$295.75) for a first-class sleeper. Call Queensland Rail's long-distance division, **Traveltrain** (☎ 1800/806 468 in Australia, or 07/3235 1122).

Greyhound Pioneer (☎ 13 20 30 in Australia) and **McCafferty's** (☎ 13 14 99 in Australia) coaches stop at Townsville many times a day on their Cairns–Brisbane–Cairns routes. The fare from Cairns is around A$44 (U.S.$28.60); trip time is 6 hours. The fare from Brisbane is around A$130 (U.S.$84.50); trip time is $22^{1}/_{2}$ hours.

VISITOR INFORMATION   For an information packet, contact **Townsville Enterprise Limited,** P.O. Box 1043, Townsville, QLD 4810 (☎ 07/4726 2728; www.tel.com.au). It has two **Information Centres.** One is in the heart of town on

Flinders Mall (☎ **1800/801 902** in Australia, or 07/4721 3660); it's open Monday through Friday from 9am to 5pm, and weekends from 9am to 1pm. The other is on the Bruce Highway 10 kilometers (6 miles) south of the city (☎ **07/4778 3555**); it is open daily from 9am to 5pm. Townsville Enterprise supplies information on **Magnetic Island,** but also check the island's Web site at www.magnetic-island.com.au.

GETTING AROUND   Local **Sunbus** (☎ **07/4725 8482**) buses depart Flinders Street Mall. Car-rental chains include **Avis** (☎ **07/4721 2688**), **Budget** (☎ **07/4725 2344**), **Hertz** (☎ **07/4775 5950**), and **Thrifty** (☎ **07/4725 4600**).

Detours Coaches (☎ **07/4721 5977**) runs tours to most attractions in and around Townsville.

THE TOP ATTRACTIONS IN TOWN

Museum of Tropical Queensland. 78–102 Flinders St. E. ☎ **07/4726 0600.** Admission A$9 (U.S.$5.85) adults; A$6.50 (U.S.$4.25) seniors and students; A$5 (U.S.$3.25) children 4–16; A$24 (U.S.$15.60) families of 5. Daily 9am–5pm. Closed Christmas and Good Friday, and until 1pm Anzac Day (Apr 25).

This attraction should be reopened when you arrive, in new A$20 million (U.S.$13 million) premises. The pride of the place will be relics from *The Pandora*, a 24-gun frigate that was carrying 14 recaptured mutineers from the infamous *Bounty* when it struck the reef off Townsville in 1791 and went down with 31 crew and four prisoners. The museum will also have dinosaur fossils; a giant re-creation of a coral polyp; Aboriginal artifacts; a hands-on science center for kids; and displays of Australia's wildlife. Allow 2 hours.

✪ **Reef HQ.** 2–68 Flinders St. ☎ **07/4750 0800.** Admission A$16 (U.S.$10.40) adults, A$13.80 (U.S.$9) seniors and students, A$7 (U.S.$4.55) children 4–14, A$38 (U.S.$24.70) family pass. Daily 9am–5pm. Closed Christmas.

This is the Great Barrier Reef Marine Park Authority's headquarters. The highlight is a 2.5-million-liter (650,000-gallon) aquarium that houses a complete living reef ecosystem, brimming with colorful fish, anemones, starfish, corals, and sea cucumbers. There are also a vast range of smaller live tanks, excellent educational displays, and a touch pool. On the daily program may be shark feeding, baby turtle talks for kids, guided tours, films, and the chance to ask questions of divers in the aquarium as you sit in the theaterette and watch them. Even if you visit this wonderful attraction after you visit the Reef, it's still good. Allow at least 90 minutes.

EXPLORING THE GREAT BARRIER REEF FROM TOWNSVILLE

The Great Barrier Reef is 2¹/₂ hours by boat from Townsville, about an hour longer than it takes to reach from elsewhere in Queensland. The only Reef operator to offer fishing, **Pure Pleasure Cruises** (☎ **1800/079 797** or 07/4721 3555) operates a 186-passenger air-conditioned catamaran to a pontoon on Kelso Reef. The cruise costs A$125 (U.S.$81.25) for adults, A$114 (U.S.$74.10) for seniors and students, A$64.50 (U.S.$41.95) for children 5 to 15, and A$314.50 (U.S.$204.45) for a family of two adults and up to three children. Optional snorkeling tours are A$15 (U.S.$9.75) extra, and glass-bottom boat rides over the coral are free. A new pontoon, due to be in place by the time you read this, will have an underwater observatory. Introductory dives cost A$66 (U.S.$42.90) for the first and A$33 (U.S.$21.45) for the second, while certified divers can make one dive for a very reasonable A$33 (U.S.$21.45) and two dives for just A$55 (U.S.$42.90); all gear is included. Fishing for sweetlip, coral trout, and other reef beauties is free. In high season, cruises depart Tuesday, Wednesday, and Friday through Sunday; in low season (Oct through Mar), Wednesday, Friday, Saturday, and Sunday. The boat picks up at Magnetic Island en route, and hotel pickups are free. You get about 4 hours on the Reef.

The sunken remains of the ✪ **SS *Yongala*** lie off the coast in 30 meters (98 ft.) with good visibility. A cyclone sent the boat and 49 passengers and 72 crew to the bottom of the sea in 1911. Today it's surrounded by a mass of coral and rich marine life, including barracuda, grouper, rays, and turtles. Townsville-based **Mike Ball Dive Expeditions** (☎ **07/4772 3022;** 800/952-4319 in the U.S.; www.mikeball.com) runs a variety of 2- to 13-day trips to the wreck on a fleet of live-aboard dive boats. Some combine Great Barrier reefs and remoter Coral Sea reefs, and visits to Cod Hole north of Cairns. The company also does learn-to-dive courses.

ACCOMMODATIONS

Centra Townsville. 334 Flinders Mall, Townsville, QLD 4810. ☎ **1800/079 903** in Australia, 800/835-7742 in the U.S. and Canada, 0345/581 666 in the U.K. or 020/8335 1304 in London, 0800/801 111 in New Zealand, or 07/4772 2477. Fax 07/4721 1263. www. centra.com.au. E-mail: reservations@townsville.centra.com.au. 198 units. A/C MINIBAR TV TEL. A$198 (U.S.$128.70) double, A$198–$330 (U.S.$128.70–$214.50) suite. Extra person A$30 (U.S.$19.50). Children under 18 stay free in parents' room using extra bedding. Free crib. Ask about weekend rates, advance-purchase rates, and packages. AE, BC, DC, JCB, MC, V. Free valet parking.

The "Sugar Shaker" (you'll know why when you see it) has been Townsville's favorite hotel for years, especially with the corporate set. Right on Flinders Mall, it's a stroll from Reef HQ, Museum of Tropical Queensland, and Magnetic Island ferries. The rooms are fitted out in sleek blonde-wood decor, and because the 20-story building is circular, every one faces the city, the bay, or Castle Hill. All have hair dryers. The place is well-run, with lots of extras like free tea and coffee in the lobby, women's and men's gyms, free newspaper on request, and 24-hour room service. The star attraction, though, is the rooftop pool and sundeck.

✪ **The Rocks.** 20 Cleveland Terrace, Townsville, QLD 4810. ☎ **07/4771 5700,** or 0416/044 409 mobile telephone. Fax 07/4771 5711. www.therocksguesthouse.com. E-mail: therocks@ultra.net.au. 8 units, 1 with bathroom (shower only). A$97–$107 (U.S.$63.05–$69.55) double. Rates include continental breakfast. AE, BC, DC, MC, V. Airport shuttle.

If you have a weakness for colonial Victoriana, you will sigh with delight when you enter this exquisite old Queenslander home. Joe Sproats and Jenny Ginger have furnished it with 19th-century antiques; even your meals are served on collectible dinnerware. Every room is individually decorated. My favorite is the lavender pitch-ceilinged one that served as an operating theater when U.S. forces occupied the house in World War II. Five are air-conditioned, and there are hair dryers and laundry facil-ities. One of the two shared bathrooms has a cast-iron clawfoot tub. Complimentary sherry is served at 6pm on the veranda overlooking Cleveland Bay, and Jenny cooks up Sri Lankan dinners on request (at extra cost). Guests have the run of the house, including the fax, a portable telephone, and Internet access; an outdoor Jacuzzi; and a billiards table (antique, of course). The Strand is a minute's stroll away, and town and the Magnetic Island ferries are 10 minutes on foot.

Seagulls Resort. 74 The Esplanade (enter off Primrose St.), Belgian Gardens, Townsville, QLD 4810. ☎ **1800/079 929** in Australia, or 07/4721 3111. Fax 07/4721 3133. www.seagulls. com.au. E-mail: resort@seagulls.com.au. 70 units (all with shower only). A/C TV TEL. A$99–$110 (U.S.$64.35–$71.50) double; A$139 (U.S.$90.35) 2-bedroom apt. Extra adult A$15 (U.S.$9.75), extra child under 14 A$9 (U.S.$5.85). AE, BC, DC, MC, V. Airport shuttle. Bus: 4, 5, 5A, 7.

This popular low-key hotel 2.5 kilometers (1½ miles) from town is built around an inviting free-form pool in 1.2 hectares (3 acres) of tropical gardens. The rooms don't have water views, but they are a good size, refurbished in 1997 with modest decor. The pleasant poolside restaurant and bar attracts locals, and there are a tour desk, room service at dinner, a small tennis court, a BBQ, a kids' wading pool, and a playground. A free shuttle runs to town and the Magnetic Island ferries several times a day, and most tour companies pick up at the door.

DINING

You'll find more restaurants and cafes on **Palmer Street,** an easy stroll across the river from Flinders Mall. Try the pleasant courtyard restaurant out back of the beautifully restored **Australian Hotel,** 11 Palmer St. (☎ **07/4771 4339**). Errol Flynn is said to have stayed here.

Michel's Cafe and Bar. 7 Palmer St. ☎ **07/4724 1460.** Reservations recommended. Main courses A$10.90–$23 (U.S.$7.10–$14.95). AE, BC, DC, MC, V. Tues–Fri 11:30am–2pm; Tues–Sun 5:30–10pm. MODERN AUSTRALIAN.

This big contemporary space is packed with Townsville's hip crowd every time I visit. Owner/chef Michel Flores works in the open kitchen, where he can keep an eye on the excellent service. The big menu covers everything from light stylish pizzas and warm salads to hefty mains like Louisiana blackened rib fillet and kangaroo.

✪ **Zouí Alto.** On the 14th floor at Aquarius on the Beach, 75 The Strand. ☎ **07/4721 4700.** Reservations recommended. Main courses A$17.50–$22 (U.S.$11.40–$14.30). AE, BC, MC, V. Fri 12:30–3pm; Mon–Sat 6:30–9:30pm. Bus: 7. MODERN AUSTRALIAN.

Not only is this one of the best restaurants in Townsville, but it's one of the best in the country. Chef Mark Edwards, who's cooked for the King of Norway, turns out terrific food, while his effusive wife, Eleni, runs the front of the house, which is decked out in splashes of Mediterranean color and Greek urns. Main courses include ravioli with clever fillings—like pumpkin and blue vein cheese, sweet potato and ginger, or sun-dried tomato and goat's cheese—and blue-eye cod in chili and tomato jam on a mound of champ with coriander and peanut pesto. Go before sunset for the great views of Castle Hill on one side and the bay on the other.

A SIDE TRIP TO MAGNETIC ISLAND
8km (5 miles) E of Townsville

More a suburb than a side trip, "Maggie" is a delightful 51-square-kilometer (20-square-mile) island, 20 minutes from Townsville by ferry. It has a population of just 2,500, but it gets busy with Aussie tourists from the mainland who zip about in mini-mokes (mini cars; see below) to the small settlements dotted around the island. Still, the peace-seeker will find plenty of unspoiled nature, especially because over half of the island is national park. Maggie is off the international tourist trail and it's definitely a flip-flops kind of place, so leave your Prada stilettos in your suitcase.

GETTING THERE & GETTING AROUND   **Sunferries** (☎ **07/4771 3855**) runs up to 14 services a day from the 168–192 Flinders St. East terminal near Reef HQ or the Breakwater terminal on Sir Leslie Thiess Drive. A courtesy coach brings you from your hotel for the 10:30am ferry, and it collects three times a day from the Transit Centre where long-distance coaches pull in. Round-trip tickets are A$14 (U.S.$9.10) for adults, A$12 (U.S.$7.80) for students, A$7 (U.S.$4.55) for seniors and children 5 to 15, and A$29 (U.S.$18.85) for a family of five. Tickets combining the ferry with a Magnetic Island bus pass or mini-moke rental can save you a couple of dollars.

A vehicular ferry takes cars to the island, but most people rent a mini-moke (mini cars that don't go much faster than the island's 60kmph [37.5 m.p.h.] speed limit). **Holiday Moke Hire** (☎ **07/4778 5703**), near the jetty on the island, rents them for

A$35 (U.S.$22.75) a day, plus A30¢ (U.S.20¢) per kilometer. An all-day pass on the frequent **island bus service** costs A$11 (U.S.$7.15) for adults, A$5.50 (U.S.$3.60) seniors and kids up to 15, and A$27.50 (U.S.$17.90) families.

Out & About on the Island

There is no end to the things you can do on Maggie: snorkeling, swimming in one of a dozen or more bays, waterskiing, parasailing, horseback riding, biking, tennis, golf, scuba diving, sea kayaking, sailing or cruising around the island, fishing, and more. There is a catch, though: deadly **marine stingers** (box jellyfish) inhabit Maggie's waters from October to May (in summer)! Outside the safe swimming enclosure at Picnic Bay, you can enter the water only with a full-length Lycra stinger-suit that most water-sports companies provide.

Most activities are spread out around the island's four settlements: **Picnic Bay** (where the ferry pulls in), **Nelly Bay, Arcadia,** and **Horseshoe Bay.** One very popular activity is a jet-ski tour circumnavigating the island conducted by **Adrenalin Jet Ski Tours & Hire** (☎ 07/4778 5533). The 3-hour tour on tandem jet skis costs A$99 (U.S.$64.35), which includes a wet suit, goggles, gloves, life jackets, and, in season, stinger suits. Tours depart every morning and afternoon from Horseshoe Bay. Keep your eyes peeled for dolphins, dugongs (manatees), and sea turtles.

Maggie lies within the Great Barrier Reef Marine Park. Outside stinger season, good reef snorkeling is to be had at Florence Bay, Arthur Bay, and Geoffrey Bay, where you can reef-walk at low tide (wear sturdy shoes). There is good swimming at 20 or so pristine (and amazingly deserted) secluded bays. **Alma Bay** is reef free and has shady lawns and a playground. **Pleasure Divers** (☎ 07/4778 5788; e-mail: pleasure.divers@ ultra.net.au) conducts learn-to-dive courses and day trips to dive sites around the island.

Hikers and bird-watchers like exploring Maggie's eucalyptus woods, patches of gully rain forest, and high granite outcroppings. One of the best of the 24 kilometers (13 miles) of **hiking trails** is the first 45 minutes of the 5-kilometer (3-mile) Nelly Bay to Arcadia trail. Another good one is the 2-kilometer (1¼-mile) trail from the Radical Bay turnoff to the Forts, remnants of World War II defenses, which have great sea views. The best place to spot the island's wild **koalas** is on the Forts trail off Horseshoe Bay Road. Carry water, because many trails are nowhere near shops.

Accommodations & Dining

To book a room at one of Magnetic Island's oodles of accommodations, contact **Magnetic Island Holidays** (☎ 07/4778 5155; e-mail: magneticislandholidays@ ultra.net.au). In peak season (June to Sept), some apartments rent by the week only.

The island has a good supply of reasonably priced restaurants, cafes, and take-out joints.

Magnetic Island International Hotel. Mandalay Ave., Nelly Bay, Magnetic Island, QLD 4819. ☎ **1800/079 902** in Australia, or 07/4778 5200. Fax 07/4778 5806. www. magnetichotel.com.au. E-mail: magnetichotel@hotkey.net.au. 96 units (all with shower only). A/C MINIBAR TV TEL. A$154 (U.S.$100.10) double; A$220 (U.S.$143) suite. Extra person A$25 (U.S.$16.25). Children under 14 stay free in parents' room with existing bedding. AE, BC, DC, MC, V. Round-trip coach-ferry-coach transfers from Townsville Airport to island to hotel are A$25 (U.S.$16.25) adults, A$18 (U.S.$11.70) children under 14. Round-trip transfers on ferry only are A$15.60 (U.S.$10.15) adults and A$7.80 (U.S.$5.10) children.

This is the island's premier place to stay. It's located a short drive or bus ride from the ferry, and a long but level walk of about half a dozen blocks from the beach. The rooms, set in motel-style blocks among the gardens and around the pool, are on the small side but nicely decorated in summery colors. All have kitchenettes and hair dryers. In the 4 hectares (10 acres) of tropical gardens, where guests hand-feed wild

Magnetic Island Travel Tips

There is an ATM but no bank on the island. If you do not have a Cirrus- or Plus-connected ATM card, bring cash and a credit card (not every business may cash traveler's checks).

kookaburras every evening, you'll find a swimming pool, a playground, day/night tennis courts, a gym, a tour desk, and a pleasant indoor/outdoor restaurant and bar.

ORPHEUS ISLAND
80km (50 miles) N of Townsville; 190km (119 miles) S of Cairns

In the 1930s, actress Vivien Leigh and novelist Zane Grey were among the stars who sought seclusion at this beautiful island. More recently, rock star Elton John vacationed here. One of the Great Barrier Reef's most exclusive retreats, Orpheus Island Resort is a popular getaway for executives, politicians, and any savvy traveler eager for peace and beauty. Although it takes 74 guests, guest numbers usually sit at around 40 or so. The surrounding waters are home to 340 of the 350 or so coral species found on the Great Barrier Reef, 1,100 species of fish, green and loggerhead turtles, dolphins, manta rays, and, from June to September, humpback whales. The only other people you will see are resort staff, a handful of guests, and the occasional scientist from the James Cook University marine research station in the next bay. Day-trippers are not allowed.

Transfers are by eight-seater Cessna seaplane. There are two flights a day from Townsville and one from Cairns. Fares are A$565 (U.S.$367.25) per person, round-trip, from Cairns (trip time: 1 hr.), and A$350 (U.S.$227.50) per person, round-trip, from Townsville (trip time: 30 min.). Book through the resort. Luggage limit is 25kg (55 lb.) per person.

✪ **Orpheus Island Resort.** Orpheus Island, Great Barrier Reef via Townsville (PMB 15, Townsville Mail Centre, QLD 4810). ☎ **1800/077 167** in Australia, or 07/4777 7377. Fax 07/4777 7533. www.orpheus.com.au. E-mail: orpheus@t140.aone.net.au. 31 units (8 with shower only). MINIBAR. A$1,020–$1,430 (U.S.$663–$929.50) double. Extra person A$255–$360 (U.S.$165.75–$234). Rates include all meals and snacks; drinks cost extra. Ask about packages. AE, BC, DC, MC, V. No children under 15.

The resort is little more than a cluster of rooms lining one of the prettiest turquoise bays you'll find anywhere. Most guests simply snorkel over coral reefs, chill with a magazine in the Polynesian-style Quiet Lounge, or swing in a hammock. Free activities include waterskiing (and lessons), snorkeling, catamaran sailing, canoeing, windsurfing, paddle-skiing, glass-bottom boat rides, fishing, a "Discover Scuba" lesson, and taking a dinghy around the shore to explore some of the island's 1,300 national-park hectares (3,211 acres). You can pay to go game fishing, charter a boat or seaplane to the outer Reef, dive, or do a dive course.

Rooms do not contain TV or telephones, but a TV is hidden away in the gym. The smallest units are the beachfront Terraces; I think they are also the prettiest, with mosquito netting over the beds, tiled floors, and timber shutters. Beachfront Studio rooms are larger and smarter looking, with black-and-white tiled bathrooms with Jacuzzis, and walnut veneer fittings. Larger still are Beachfront Bungalows, more like traditional hotel rooms with Jacuzzis facing a little garden courtyard. All beachfront units are air-conditioned. Up on a hill are palatial two-bedroom villas (not air-conditioned), renovated in 1999. All rooms have hair dryers. Don't expect marbled splendor on Orpheus; the rooms and facilities are attractive and comfortable rather than luxurious—although the complimentary champagne, fruit and chocolates, and fresh flowers in your room when you arrive are extravagant touches. What you are paying for are seclusion and tranquillity. A good many guests are regulars.

Dining/Diversions: The attractive open-sided restaurant and cocktail bar by the sea serves snacks and elegant à la carte meals that make good use of seafood and fresh tropical fruit. Picnic hampers are free.

Amenities: Many water sports (see above), small free-form swimming pool with swim-up bar and sundeck, Jacuzzi, combined gym/billiard room, day/night tennis court, twice-daily maid service, secretarial services, laundry service, boutique.

5 The Whitsunday Coast & Islands

A day's drive or an hour's flight south of Cairns brings you to the dazzling 74 ✪ **Whitsunday islands,** one of the most unsung parts of Australia. No more than 3 nautical miles separates most of them, and together they include countless bays, beaches, coral reefs, and sailing and fishing spots that compose one fabulous Great Barrier Reef Marine Park playground, all sharing the same latitude as Río de Janeiro and Hawaii. The water is at least 22°C (72°F) year-round and the sun shines most of the year.

This is Australia's premier sailing territory. Whether you take a day trip aboard one of the many yachts based on the mainland, book one of the popular 3-day/2-night sailing jaunts, or charter your very own sailboat—known as "bareboat" (unskippered) charter—from the region's plethora of charter outfits, sailing is easy in these calm blue waters. And it's not all that expensive.

Most of the islands are national park, and only a handful are inhabited. Don't expect palm trees and coconuts—these islands are covered with dry-looking pine, eucalyptus, and rain forest full of dense undergrowth, and rocky coral covers far outnumber the few sandy beaches. More than half a dozen islands have resorts offering just about any activity you care to name—snorkeling, scuba diving, sailing, reef fishing, waterskiing, jet skiing, parasailing, sea kayaking, hiking, tennis, squash, and more. Accommodations range from low-key wilderness retreats, to mid-range family havens, to Australia's most luxurious resort, Hayman. The unpretentious village of Airlie Beach is the center of the action on the mainland.

The Whitsundays are just as good a stepping stone to the outer Great Barrier Reef as Cairns. In fact, I think they're better. The outer Reef is about the same distance from the mainland here as it is at Cairns, but most of the islands have some additional fringing reef around their shores, and there are good reefs between the islands you can visit by boat trips.

April to October is the best time to visit. November ain't bad; but December to March is uncomfortably hot and humid, and that's when most rain falls.

WHITSUNDAY ESSENTIALS

GETTING THERE **By Car** The Bruce Highway leads south from Cairns or north from Brisbane to Proserpine, 26 kilometers (16 miles) inland from Airlie Beach. Take the "Whitsunday" turnoff to reach Airlie Beach and Shute Harbour. Allow a good 8 hours to drive from Cairns. There are several car-storage facilities at Shute Harbour. Sandra and Roger Boynton of **Whitsunday Car Security** (☎ **07/4946 9955** or 0419/729 605) collect your car anywhere in the Whitsunday area and store it in locked undercover parking for A$13.50 (U.S.$8.80) per 24 hours.

By Plane There are two air routes into the Whitsundays: Hamilton Island airport, and Proserpine airport on the mainland. **Ansett** (☎ **13 13 00** in Australia) and

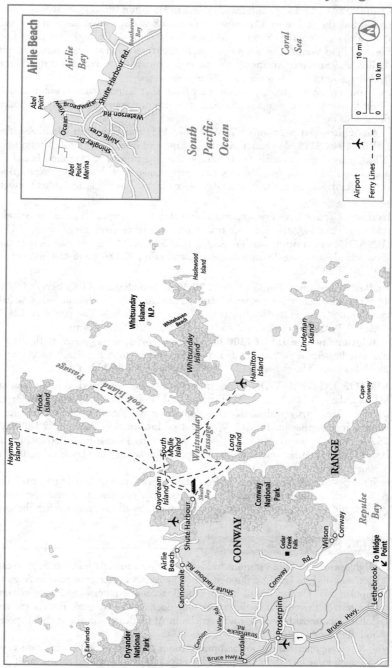

Airlie Beach

Airlie Bay

Abel Point

Ocean View Dr.

Broadwater

Shute Harbour Rd.

Southaven Bay

Waterson Rd.

Airlie Cres.

Shingley Dr.

Abel Point Marina

Coral Sea

10 mi

10 km

Airport

Ferry Lines

South Pacific Ocean

Haslewood Island

Whitsunday Islands N.P.

Whitehaven Beach

Whitsunday Island

Hamilton Island

Lindeman Island

Hook Island

Passage

Hayman Island

South Molle Island

Whitsunday Passage

Long Island

Cape Conway

RANGE

Daydream Island

Shute Bay

Conway National Park

Repulse Bay

Shute Harbour

CONWAY

Conway

Wilson

Airlie Beach

Cedar Creek Falls

Rd.

Cannonvale

Shute Harbour Rd.

Conway

Letherbrook

To Midge Point

Earlando

Dryander National Park

Valley Rd.

Canyon

Foxdale

Strathdickie Rd.

Proserpine

Bruce Hwy.

Bruce Hwy.

1

Qantas (☎ **13 13 13** in Australia) fly direct to Hamilton Island from Sydney. Ansett and Airlink (book through Qantas) fly daily from Brisbane. Ansett has a direct weekly flight from Melbourne. Sunstate Airlines (book through Qantas) flies daily from Cairns. **Flight West Airlines** (book through Ansett) serves Proserpine from Brisbane; **Airlink** and **Sunstate Airlines** (book through Qantas) fly to Proserpine direct from Brisbane, and from Cairns via Townsville.

If you stay on an island, the resort may book your launch transfers automatically. These may appear on your airline ticket, in which case your luggage will be checked through to the island.

Air Whitsunday Seaplanes (☎ **07/4946 9111**) and **Hamilton Island Aviation** (☎ **07/4946 8249**) do charter mainland-island and interisland transfers from small Whitsunday airport near Shute Harbour, Proserpine airport, or Hamilton Island airport. Hamilton Island Aviation uses helicopter, seaplane, or fixed-wing aircraft. Both companies fly charter to the Whitsundays from Cairns, Townsville, and other northern Queensland cities.

By Train Trains from Brisbane and Cairns stop at Proserpine. The one-way fare is A$73.70 (U.S.$47.90) from Cairns. From Brisbane, fares range from A$110 (U.S.$71.50) for a sitting berth to A$376 (U.S.$244.40) for a first-class sleeper. Call Queensland Rail's long-distance division, **Traveltrain** (☎ **1800/806 468** in Australia, or 07/3235 1122).

By Bus **Greyhound Pioneer** (☎ **13 20 30** in Australia) and **McCafferty's** (☎ **13 14 99** in Australia) operate plentiful daily services to Airlie Beach from Brisbane (trip time: around 18 hr.) and Cairns (trip time: 9 to 10^1/₂ hr.). The fare is A$124.30 (U.S.$80.80) from Brisbane and A$71.50 (U.S.$46.50) from Cairns.

Whitsunday Transit (☎ **1300/65 5449** or 07/4945 4011) meets all flights and trains at Proserpine to provide door-to-door transfers to Airlie Beach hotels, or to Shute Harbour. The fare is A$12 (U.S.$7.80), half price for kids 4 to 14.

VISITOR INFORMATION For information before you travel, contact **Tourism Whitsundays,** P.O. Box 83, Whitsunday, QLD 4802 (☎ **07/4946 6673;** fax 07/4946 7387; www.whitsundayinformation.com.au). Another useful Web site is www.whitsunday.net.au. Tourism Whitsundays' **information center** (☎ **1800/801 252** in Australia, or 07/4945 3711) is inconveniently located in Proserpine, on the Bruce Highway in the town's south. It's open Monday to Saturday from 8:30am to 5:30pm and Sunday from 10am to 5pm.

It's easier to pick up information from the countless private booking agents lining Airlie Beach's main street, which all stock a vast range of cruise, tour, and hotel information, and which make bookings free of charge. They all have pretty much the same

---

The Secret of the Seasons

High season is school vacations (mid-Apr, late June to early July, late Sept to early Oct, and mid- to late Dec through Jan). The Aussie winter from June to August is popular, too. During school holidays, book accommodations months in advance. The rest of the year, though, expect tour operators to compete fiercely for your dollars; blackboards outside tour agencies in Airlie Beach will shout about specials and discounted deals.

If you are prepared to book accommodations with just 24 or 48 hours' notice, you can snare some incredibly cheap standby rates at hotels and island resorts in off-peak season, even the swanky ones like Hayman.

stuff; but because some manifest certain boats exclusively, and prices can vary a little from one to the next, shop around. One place that gave me good unbiased advice was **Where? What? & How?,** Shop 1, 283 Shute Harbour Rd. (☎ **07/4946 5255;** icentre@whitsunday.net.au).

GETTING AROUND   Island ferries and Great Barrier Reef cruises leave from **Shute Harbour,** a 10-minute drive south of Airlie Beach on Shute Harbour Road. Most other tour-boat operators and bareboat charters anchor at **Abel Point Marina,** a 15-minute walk west from Airlie Beach.

Avis (☎ **07/4946 6318**), Hertz (☎ **07/4946 4687**), and Thrifty (☎ **07/4946 7727**) have outlets in Airlie Beach and Proserpine Airport (telephone numbers serve both locations). Budget has no Whitsundays office.

Local bus company **Whitsunday Transit** (☎ **1300/65 5449** or 07/4945 4011) runs a half-hourly service between Airlie Beach and Shute Harbour to meet all ferries. The fare is A$3.60 (U.S.$2.35).

Most tour-boat operators pick up guests free from Airlie Beach hotels and call at some or all island resorts.

Whitsunday All Over (☎ **1300/366 494** in Australia, or 07/4946 9499), **Whitsunday Island Adventure Cruises** (☎ **07/4946 5255** for the booking agent), and **FantaSea Cruises** (☎ **1800/650 851** in Australia, or 07/4946 5111) make ferry transfers from Shute Harbour to the islands and between the islands. One-way transfers cost from A$8 (U.S.$5.20) for the short hop from Daydream Island to South Molle Island, to A$24 (U.S.$15.60) from Hamilton Island to the mainland. Children 4 to 14 pay around half price. It is not necessary to book, but do book your arrival and departure ferry so that you don't miss your connections. Don't assume there is a boat leaving every 10 minutes; most islands receive a boat only every 2 to 4 hours, some only once or twice a day.

THE REEF TAX   Don't forget to add a A$4 (U.S.$2.60) per person **Environmental Management Charge** ("reef tax") to the price of all cruises in and around the Great Barrier Reef. This tax goes toward Reef upkeep.

CHOOSING A WHITSUNDAY BASE

The advantages of staying on the mainland? Cheaper accommodations, for a start! Also, the mainland has a choice of restaurants. What it does not have is great swimming, snorkeling, or extensive water sports (although that may change when a new saltwater lagoon is built in the bay at Airlie Beach, planned for completion in 2001).

The advantages of an island? A vast range of water sports, swimming, snorkeling, bushwalking, and the like, many of which are free, is right outside your door. Unlike Airlie Beach, the islands are free of deadly marine stingers. You won't be isolated, because a huge range of Great Barrier Reef cruise boats, "sail and snorkel" yacht excursions, Whitehaven Beach cruises, dive boats, fishing vessels, helicopter flights, day trips to golf resorts, and so on are available from the islands daily or several times a week. Once you're "captive" on an island, however, you may be socked with high food and drink prices. While nonmotorized water sports, such as windsurfers and catamarans, are free of charge on most islands, you pay for activities that use fuel.

Everywhere in the Whitsundays, extreme low tides reveal rocky mudflats, so expect some unsightliness then. Water sports can be limited at low tide.

EXPLORING THE ISLANDS

SNORKELING & DIVING THE GREAT BARRIER REEF   Visitors to the Whitsundays get to have their cake and eat it too; they can visit the outer Reef, as well

Gorgeous Spots Not to Miss

The 6-kilometer (3³/₄-mile) stretch of white silica sand on ✪ **Whitehaven Beach** on uninhabited Whitsunday Island will leave you in raptures. It doesn't have coral; but the swimming is good, and the forested shore is beautiful for strolling. Take a book and chill out. Some sailboats visit it on a day trip, as do several motorized vessels, including the *Lindeman Pacific* (☎ 07/4946 6922) and **FantaSea Cruises** (☎ 1800/650 851 in Australia, or 07/4946 5111).

If you take a sailing and snorkeling trip, try to include ✪ **Blue Pearl Bay** on the itinerary. It is renowned for spectacular coral and fish life.

---

as enjoying some good dive and snorkel sites in and around the islands. Many islands have rarely-visited fringing reefs, which you can explore in a rented dinghy or fishing boat.

FantaSea Cruises (☎ 1800/650 851 in Australia, or 07/4946 5111) makes a daily trip of approximately 2 hours to Hardy Reef from Shute Harbour in a 350-passenger air-conditioned catamaran. En route you can hear a Reef talk by a marine biologist. You anchor at the pontoon, which has an underwater observatory, a semisubmersible for coral viewing, and kids' swimming pools, and spend about 3¹/₂ hours on the Reef. The trip costs A$135 (U.S.$87.75) for adults, A$120 (U.S.$78) for seniors and students, A$68 (U.S.$44.20) for kids 4 to 14, and A$316 (U.S.$205.40) for a family of four. Guided snorkel safaris cost A$22 (U.S.$14.30) extra. The day with an introductory or certified dive is A$190 (U.S.$123.50). Scenic helicopter flights to FantaSea's pontoon, and fly/cruise and fly/fly packages to it are available through **Hamilton Island Aviation** (☎ 07/4946 8249).

FantaSea offers a 2-day, 1-night ReefSleep experience overnighting on the pontoon. Snorkeling at night is a different experience, because the coral is luminescent, and nocturnal fish come out to play. The trip includes a slide presentation from a marine biologist, two scuba dives, night snorkeling, glass-bottom boat trips, two buffet lunches, dinner under the stars with wine, breakfast, and more snorkeling on the second day. You sleep in the quad-share bunkhouse for A$298 (U.S.$193.70) per person, or in a suite with a king-size bed and French champagne for A$350 (U.S.$227.50).

For the day trip (above) and the ReefSleep experience, FantaSea Cruises picks up passengers free at South Molle and Hamilton island resorts. Free coach transfers run from Airlie Beach hotels to the wharf.

One of the best dive day trips within the islands, as opposed to the outer Reef, is **Black Reef** (commonly called Bali Hai Island) offered by **Whitsunday All Over** (☎ 1300/366 494 in Australia, or 07/4946 6900). You'll see marvelous soft shelf and wall coral, tame Maori wrasse, and lots of fish. A dive/cruise package is A$118 (U.S.$76.70) if you prebook.

Whitsunday Dive Charters (☎ 07/4946 5366; www.reefjet.com.au) does a daily two-dive day trip to the 800-hectare (1,976-acre) **Bait Reef** on the outer Reef, a renowned site, for A$165 (U.S.$107.25), or A$170 (U.S.$110.50) with a single introductory dive. Their 68-passenger boat gets you there in a lightning-fast 70 minutes.

Kelly Dive & Sail (☎ 1800/063 454 in Australia, or 07/4946 6122; www.kellydive.com.au) combines Hook Island bushwalking and a stop at gorgeous Whitehaven Beach with diving the islands and outer Reef in 3-day/3-night trips aboard a 101-foot yacht or a 65-foot sailing cat. The trip costs A$450 (U.S.$292.50) or A$495 (U.S.$321.75) in an air-conditioned en suite double cabin, depending on the boat. That includes six dives, or two introductory dives for uncertified divers. Each trip departs twice weekly.

As well as 1-day and live-aboard dive trips, **Reef Dive Whitsunday** (☎ 07/ 4946 6508; www.reefdive.com.au) does dive courses from beginner to instructor level. There are other dive operators in the area; you can also dive on FantaSea Cruises' day trip to the outer Reef (above) and off many sailing boats (below).

Most dive operators depart Airlie Beach; some pick up at the islands.

SAILING, SNORKELING & SEA KAYAKING   A simpler alternative to skippering your own yacht (see "Come Sail with Me," below) is to jump aboard the many yachts offering 3-day island sailing adventures. Take a hand in sailing if you want, snorkel over reefs, call into secluded bays, swim, sunbathe, hike, and generally have a laid-back good time. A few boats offer introductory and qualified scuba diving at extra cost. Most carry a maximum 12 passengers, although some take 20 or more. You typically sleep in comfortable but small berths off the galley, less commonly in petite twin or double cabins. The food is generally good and the showers are hot.

For a 3-day/2-night trip, expect to pay A$300 to $360 (U.S.$195 to $234) per person on a regular yacht and up to A$530 (U.S.$344.50) on a luxury vessel; in off-season you may pay as little as A$250 (U.S.$162.50). **ProSail** (☎ 07/4946 5433; www.prosail.com.au) has a fleet of 10 yachts running 3-day/2-night sails. Tourism Whitsundays can supply you with brochures on other charters.

Myriad yachts will pick you up from Airlie Beach or the islands to take you out just for the day to snorkel over reefs, swim, sail, and dive, and feast on a buffet lunch on a beach or on the boat. Among the best known is *Maxi Ragamuffin* (☎ 07/ 4946 7777), whose day trips cost A$78 (U.S.$50.70) for adults, A$69 (U.S.$44.85) for seniors and students, A$39 (U.S.$25.35) for kids 4 to 14, or A$195 (U.S.$126.75) for a family of four. The day costs A$116 (U.S.$75.40) with a prebooked first-time or regular scuba dive.

✪ **Sea kayaking** is a great way to soak up the islands' natural beauty and maybe spot dolphins and turtles along the way. Daydream Island and North, Mid, and South Molle islands are all within paddling distance of the mainland. **Salty Dog Sea Kayaking** (☎ 07/4946 1388 or 0419/54 4841 mobile phone) rents single kayaks (a tandem one is A$70/U.S.$45.50 per day) and camping gear, and it does guided 1- or 2-day adventures.

ISLAND HOPPING   Day-trippers to Hamilton, Daydream, South Molle, Club Crocodile Long Island, and Hook Island resorts can rent the hotels' water-sports equipment, laze by the beaches and pools, scuba dive, join the resorts' activities programs, hike their trails, and eat at some or all of their restaurants. See "The Whitsunday Island Resorts," later in this chapter, for details on Hamilton, South Molle, and Hook islands. Club Crocodile Long Island is a rather noisy, unpretentious resort that nonetheless has plentiful water sports, picturesque hiking trails, wild wallabies, and a large beach-cum-tidal flat where you can laze on sun lounges. Daydream Island is a mid-range resort, claustrophobically small, but with ample water sports, snorkeling off a small coral beach, a nice free-form pool, and a short hilly rain-forest trail.

You can get to the islands on your own by ferry (see "Getting Around," above), or take an organized day trip that visits one, two, or even three islands in a day. **FantaSea Cruises** (☎ 1800/650 851 in Australia, or 07/4946 5111), **Whitsunday All Over** (☎ 1300/366 494 in Australia, or 07/4946 6900), and **Whitsunday Island Adventure Cruises** (☎ 07/4946 5255 for the booking agent) all offer them, as do several yachts. Whitsunday All Over also does a day trip to ✪ **Bali Hai,** an uninhabited isle where you can snorkel, dive, view the coral from a large submersible, or laze on the sand. Rates for day trips range from A$36.50 to $75 (U.S.$23.75 to $48.75). Whitsunday All Over's "Action Pack" trips are a good value.

Come Sail with Me

What? Me sail my own yacht? Yes, you! One of the absolute delights of a Whitsundays vacation is sailing yourself around the islands on a ✪ **"bareboat,"** or self-skippered, chartered yacht—even if you don't know one end of a boat from another. Sailing is easy in these glorious blue waters where the channels are deep and hazard-free, the seas are protected from big swells by the Great Barrier Reef farther out to sea, and the 74 islands are so close that one is always in sight.

If you have no boating experience, the company may require you to take a skipper along for the first day at a typical extra cost of A$140 (U.S.$91) a day. Even if you think you know what you're doing, you can choose to have a skipper accompany you for an extra fee for the first couple of hours, or overnight, or longer, to help you get the hang of things. In any case, most companies mail you a preparation kit before you leave home, you receive a thorough 2- to 3-hour briefing before departure, and you get easy-to-read maps marking channels, anchorage points, and the few dangerous reefs. Your charter company will radio in twice a day, and you can contact them any time for advice.

Most yachts are fitted for two to eight passengers. Get a boat with two berths more than you need if your budget will bear it, because space is always tight. The boats usually have a galley kitchen, a barbecue mounted on the stern, hot showers and toilet, linen, a radio and/or stereo, a motorized dinghy, and snorkeling equipment. Sleeping quarters are usually not all that luxurious and include a mix of single galley berths, double berths, and perhaps one or two very compact private cabins. You can purchase your own provisions or have the charter company stock the boat for you at an extra cost of about A$30 (U.S.$19.50) per person per day. Some operators will load a windsurfer, fishing tackle, and scuba-diving equipment for an extra fee.

SCENIC FLIGHTS   Expect to pay around A$180 (U.S.$117) for a 1-hour flight over the outer Reef (a spectacular sight from the air), about A$250 (U.S.$162.50) for a seaplane flight to a private Reef pontoon to snorkel for a couple of hours, way up to A$375 (U.S.$243.75), even more, for a helicopter to drop you on a deserted coral-edged island with a champagne seafood picnic and snorkel gear. **Hamilton Island Aviation** (☎ **07/4946 8249**) and **Air Whitsunday Seaplanes** (☎ **07/4946 9111**) both do a big range of such tours. Air Whitsunday also does day trips to posh Hayman (see "The Whitsunday Island Resorts," below), the only operator to do so.

FISHING   Red emperor, coral trout, sweetlip, and schnapper are common catches off the reefs throughout the islands. One of the most popular fishing-tour boats is the 54-foot timber cruiser *Moruya* (☎ **07/4946 6665**), which departs Shute Harbour daily. Boat owners rent dinghies and half-cabin cruisers, with bait and tackle, at Abel Point Marina.

GOLF   Serious golfers should not miss a round on arguably Australia's best resort course, the championship ✪ **Turtle Point** golf course at Laguna Quays Resort, Kunapipi Springs Road, Midge Point (☎ **1800/812 626** in Australia, or 07/4947 7777), a 45-minute drive south of Airlie Beach. An 18-hole round dodging wallabies, goannas, and kookaburras on these difficult fairways will set you back A$55 (U.S.$35.75) midweek, A$66 (U.S.$42.90) weekends, plus A$30 (U.S.$19.50) for

In peak season, you will have to charter the boat for 5 nights. At other times, most companies stipulate a minimum of 5 nights but may rent for 3 nights if you ask. Peak-season dates vary considerably from one company to the next, so shop around.

For a 5-night rental in peak season, expect to pay around A$350 to $600 (U.S.$286.65 to $390) for a four- to six-berth yacht, per boat, per night, although prices can go up to A$1,000 or more (U.S.$650) for a luxury vessel. Rates in the off-season will be around A$30 (U.S.$19.50) less, sometimes much less for luxury vessels. Fuel is included. Your only other expenses should be food, a bond of around A$750 (U.S.$487.50), and mooring fees of between around A$20 and $65 (U.S.$13 to $42.25) per boat per night, should you want to call into one of the island resorts. Some bareboat charter companies sell "sail 'n' stay" packages combining a few days of sailing with a stint at an island resort.

Most charters operate out of either Airlie Beach or Hamilton Island. Some of the better-known ones include **Australian Bareboat Charters** (☎ 1800/ 075 000 in Australia or 07/4946 9381; www.ozemail.com.au/~bareboat), **Queensland Yacht Charters** (☎ 1800/075 013 in Australia, or 07/4946 7400; www.yachtcharters.com.au), **Sail Whitsunday** (☎ 1800/075 045 in Australia, or 07/4946 7070; www.whitsunday.net.au/bareboat/sailwhit.htm), **The Moorings** (☎ 888/952 8420 in the U.S.; www.moorings.com; in Australia, contact the company's broker, Club Seafarer, at ☎ 1300/656 484 or 02/9389 5856; www. seafarer.com.au), and **Whitsunday Rent A Yacht** (☎ 1800/075 111 in Australia, or 07/4946 9232; www.rentayacht.com.au). **Tourism Whitsundays** (see "Visitor Information," above) can furnish you with a complete list of operators.

And you know what? If sailing yourself is looking too much like hard work, most charters will supply a skipper for around A$150 (U.S.$97.50) per day.

clubs, A$10 (U.S.$6.50) for shoes, and A$25 (U.S.$16.25) for a round-trip shuttle transfer.

HIKING & 4WD SAFARIS   Hiking trails from 1 kilometer (just over half a mile) to 5.4 kilometers (3¹/₂ miles) lead through eucalypt and rain forest and down to the beach in **Conway National Park,** which spans Shute Harbour Road between Airlie Beach and Shute Harbour. The trails depart from one of three parking lots along Shute Harbour Road. The **Queensland Parks & Wildlife Service's Whitsunday Information Centre** (☎ 07/4946 7022) on Shute Harbour Road at Mandalay Road, 2.5 kilometers (1¹/₂ miles) northeast of Airlie Beach, has maps.

AIRLIE BEACH
640km (400 miles) S of Cairns; 1,146km (716 miles) N of Brisbane

The little town of Airlie Beach is the focal point of activity on the Whitsunday mainland. The town is only a few blocks long, but you will find an adequate choice of moderately priced accommodations, a small selection of restaurants and bars, a boutique or two, and facilities such as banks and a small supermarket. Despite its name, Airlie Beach has no real beach, just a narrow strip of sand around a curving bay that becomes a rocky mudflat at low tide. The city fathers are planning to build a large seawater lagoon in the bay for tide-free, stinger-free swimming, which may or may not be in place by the time you arrive.

Safety Tips

Deadly **marine stingers** (box jellyfish) may inhabit the Airlie Beach shoreline from October to April. These mangrove creatures hug the mainland, so swimming in the islands is safe year-round.

Never swim in, or stand on the bank of, mainland rivers and estuaries in the Whitsundays, because they are home to **crocodiles**.

ACCOMMODATIONS

Boathaven Lodge. 440 Shute Harbour Rd., Airlie Beach, QLD 4802. ☎ **07/4946 6421.** Fax 07/4946 4808. www.whitsunday.net.au/boathaven. E-mail: boathavn@whitsunday. net.au. 12 units (all with shower only). A/C TV. A$95 (U.S.$61.75) double, studio; A$120 (U.S.$78) 1-bedroom apt.; A$145 (U.S.$94.25) 2-bedroom apt. Extra adult A$20 (U.S.$13); extra child under 15 A$10 (U.S.$6.50). New (2001) studios, apts, and penthouses A$120–$250 (U.S.$78–$162.50). AE, BC, DC, MC, V.

Friendly Jan and Peter Cox run these well-maintained studio and one- and two-bedroom apartments, 400 meters (¹/₄ mile) from town among lovely gardens. All have views over Boathaven Bay, as does the petite pool and Jacuzzi. The simple but attractive one-bedroom apartments are quite new and airy, with big living areas, kitchenettes, modern bathrooms (borrow a hair dryer at reception), indoor palms, and large timber decks. Jan and Peter also advise on tours and make your bookings. By the time you arrive, a second pool and waterfall may have replaced the smaller, older studios near the road, and by mid-2001, 20 more apartments should be gracing the hill behind.

Whitsunday Terraces Resort. Golden Orchid Dr. (off Shute Harbour Rd.), Airlie Beach, QLD 4802. ☎ **1800/075 062** in Australia, or 07/4946 6788. Fax 07/4946 7128. www. whitsunday.net.au/terraces.htm. E-mail: terraces@whitsunday.net.au. 65 units. A/C TV TEL. A$138 (U.S.$89.70) studio, A$149 (U.S.$96.85) 1-bedroom apartment. Extra person A$15 (U.S.$9.75). Rates lower for stays of 3 nights or more. AE, BC, DC, MC, V.

These studio and one-bedroom apartments on a hillside a steep 2-minute walk above Airlie Beach are my pick for the "value with a view" prize. The one-bedroom apartments have especially roomy, light-filled living rooms, and every apartment has a big balcony. All are furnished differently, but to a high standard, and serviced daily. The front desk lends hair dryers. Guests gather around the swimming pool/sundeck/restaurant/cocktail bar, which, like the rooms, has sweeping views over the town to the bay and Twin Cone Island. The friendly managers run a tour desk.

DINING

Mangrove Jack's. In the Airlie Beach Hotel, 16 The Esplanade (enter via Shute Harbour Rd.). ☎ **07/4946 6233.** Reservations recommended. Main courses A$7.90–$19.90 (U.S.$5.15–$12.95); average A$14 (U.S.$9.10). AE, BC, DC, MC, V. Daily 10am–midnight. WOOD-FIRED PIZZA/CAFE FARE.

Sailors, local sugar farmers, Sydney yuppies, and European backpackers all flock to this big open-fronted sports bar/restaurant/cafe. Wood-fired pizza with trendy toppings is the specialty. Our chicken burger came on a gigantic focaccia bun in a field of fries, though I could have done with more pesto on our tasty lamb stack with roasted eggplant, provolone cheese, and baked peanut rosemary pesto. More than 50 wines come by the (big) glass.

THE WHITSUNDAY ISLAND RESORTS
VERY EXPENSIVE

✪ **Hayman.** Hayman Island, Whitsunday Islands, QLD 4801. ☎ **1800/075 175** in Australia, or call Leading Hotels of the World (☎ 800/223-6800 in the U.S. and Canada, 0800/181 123 in the U.K., 1800/409 063 in Ireland, 0800/44 1016 in New Zealand), 03/9866 8085 (Melbourne sales office), or 07/4940 1234 (the island). Fax 03/9866 8665 (Melbourne sales office) or 07/4940 1567 (the island). www.hayman.com.au. E-mail: reserve@hayman.com.au. 214 units (32 with shower only). A/C MINIBAR TV TEL. A$537.08–$840.88 (U.S.$349.10–$546.60) double, A$1,410.50–$1,627.50 (U.S.$916.85–$1,057.90) suite, A$1,844.50–$3,580.50 (U.S.$1,198.95–$2,327.35) penthouse. Children under 15 stay free in parents' room. Children under 15 charged 50% for all dining costs. Ask about packages. AE, BC, DC, JCB, MC, V. Resort launch meets all flights at Hamilton Island Airport for the 55-min. transfer. Launch transfer A$352 (U.S.$228.80) per person round-trip (usually included on your airline ticket and in your airfare). Helicopter and seaplane transfers available. Hayman Island is 33km (21 miles) from Shute Harbour.

This is the most luxurious resort in Australia, more glitzy and glamorous than the low-key atmosphere at pricey Bedarra. Check-in is done over a free glass of bubbly on board the resort's sleek launch that meets you at Hamilton Island airport. Upon reaching the resort, most guests don't take long to find their way through the open-air sandstone lanais, cascading ponds, and tropical foliage to the fabulous hexagonal complex of swimming pools by the sea. Despite the luxurious ambience, Hayman is not at all starchy. Dress code is beachwear by day, smart casual at night (though you could pack something swish for dinner at La Fontaine restaurant).

While Hayman is renowned for the antiques, original landscapes, and fine *objets* gracing its public areas, the four-story accommodations are suitably grand, but relaxing. Every room or suite has a balcony or terrace, bathrobes, hair dryers, free and pay-per-view movies, and valet service (and butler service in the penthouses). My favorites are the West Wing rooms, which were renovated in 2000 with marble floors and bathrooms and tropically elegant furnishings; they have views over the pool, and also to the sea from the third and fourth floors. East Wing rooms are not quite as fashionable, but some guests prefer them because they are larger and more private; they overlook a lagoon and have sea views from the third floor. The least expensive (and smallest) accommodations are Palm Garden rooms, but these are nice, too, with smart Mediterranean-style decor; they overlook gardens. Beachfront rooms are compact but have a Jacuzzi, and open directly onto the coral sand beach. The 11 penthouses each have a different themed decor, such as South Seas, Moroccan, or French Provincial.

An impressive lineup of activities includes snorkeling trips to Blue Pearl Bay (one of the Whitsundays' best snorkeling spots, just off the island), sunset sails, organized hikes through eucalypt and pine forest, dive and snorkel trips to nearby reefs and the outer Reef, and, in season, whale-watching trips. Have the kitchen pack you a picnic, and the staff will spirit you off to a deserted beach or nearby islet for snorkeling. An unexpected hit with many guests is the behind-the-scenes kitchen tour. Few day-trippers are allowed and few tour boats call. Instead, the island has its own fleet of

---

Whale Watching in the Whitsundays

Humpback whales migrate to the Whitsundays every July to September to give birth to their calves. **FantaSea Cruises** (☎ **1800/650 851** in Australia, or 07/4946 5111) runs whale-watching cruises in season; it's not uncommon for whales to come right up to the boat.

launches, cruisers, purpose-built game fishing and dive boats, yachts (with skipper and cook if you like), speedboats, and dinghies, which you can charter or join on excursions just for Hayman guests. The only drawbacks to Hayman are ones it shares with most other Whitsunday resorts: The beach is coarse coral sand, and at low tide the water recedes over rocky mudflats for hundreds of yards, limiting water sports to a 4¹/₂-hour block every 12 hours. Nonmotorized water sports are free.

Dining/Diversions: The food is excellent. Up to four venues open different nights of the week: a formal French restaurant (jacket required, tie optional), a fun Italian trattoria, a pondside Asian restaurant, and Planters restaurant for Mod Oz cuisine. Two casual beachside spots serve breakfast, light meals, and cocktails. Room service delivers picnics anywhere on the grounds and can do candlelit dinner on your balcony. The sophisticated Club Lounge does pre- or after-dinner cocktails; Hernando's casual nightclub has dancing some nights; and the West Wing pool bar does light meals. Live music plays in various restaurants nightly.

Amenities: Three swimming pools (one saltwater and two heated freshwater); many water sports including parasailing, waterskiing, windsurfing, and catamarans; dive center offering dive day trips, courses, and gear rental; extensive fitness center with massage, sauna, float tanks, and personalized fitness programs; five day/night tennis courts with ball machine and coaching; two squash courts; golf target range and putting green; beach volleyball; badminton; hiking trails; weekly movies in the 300-seat entertainment center; billiards; game room; Ping-Pong; library; free daily kids' club for children ages 5 to 14; day care for younger kids; baby-sitting; playground; concierge; tour desk; 24-hour room service; dry cleaning/laundry; twice-daily maid service; nightly turndown; safes; medical center; secretarial services; conference center; express checkout; currency exchange; upscale shopping arcade; florist; salon.

EXPENSIVE

Hamilton Island. Hamilton Island (16km/10 miles SE of Shute Harbour), Whitsunday Islands, QLD 4803. ☎ **1800/075 110** in Australia, or 02/8353 8444 (reservations office in Sydney), or 07/4946 9999 (the island). Fax 02/8353 8499 (reservations office in Sydney) or 07/4946 8888 (the island). www.hamilton.com.au. E-mail: vacation@hamiltonisland.com.au. 750 units (some with shower only). A/C MINIBAR TV TEL. A$269 (U.S.$174.85) bungalow; A$315–$506 (U.S.$204.75–$328.90) apt. (to sleep 5 or 6); hotel A$337–$404 (U.S.$219.05–$262.20) double, A$652–$1,124 (U.S.$423.80–$730.60) suite; Beach Club A$472 (U.S.$306.80) double. Extra person A$27 (U.S.$17.55). Children under 15 stay free in parents' room using existing bedding and eat free from kids' menu at 5 restaurants. No children in Beach Club rooms. Ask about packages. AE, BC, DC, JCB, MC, V. Airlines fly into Hamilton Island Airport. Free airport-resort transfers for all guests. FantaSea Cruises (☎ 1800/650 851 in Australia, or 07/4946 5111) provides by far the cheapest launch transfers from the mainland (Shute Harbour) and most other islands.

More a vacation village than a single resort, Hamilton has the widest range of activities, accommodation styles, and restaurants of any Great Barrier Reef island resort. Thanks to a A$40 million (U.S.$26 million) refurbishment over the past 3 years, the place is looking fresh. Your accommodation choices are extra-large rooms and suites in the high-rise hotel, high-rise one- and two-bedroom apartments, Polynesian-style bungalows in tropical gardens (but too close to the road for real privacy), and hip new (Nov 1999) rooms in the two-story, adults-only Beach Club, which sports glamorously minimalist decor, and a personal "host" to cater to every whim. The best sea views come from the second-floor Beach Club rooms, from floors 5 to 18 of the hotel, and from most apartments. All units have hair dryers. Guests in the hotel section enjoy 16-hour room service, pay-per-view movies, safes, concierge, laundry service and a Laundromat, currency exchange, and express checkout. The apartments, each with two TVs and a VCR, are serviced every 3rd day; guests in this section enjoy a private swimming pool. Jacuzzi Beach Club rooms have VCR, CD player, coffee plunger, bathrobes, Internet access, safes, and complimentary newspapers; guests here enjoy 18-hour room service, laundry service, private swimming pool and bar, and free non-motorized water sports and tennis.

On one side of the island is a marina village with cafes, restaurants, shops, and a yacht club. On the other side is the main complex with accommodations, a large and inviting free-form pool and swim-up bar surrounded by sun lounges with cocktail service, more shops and restaurants, and the wide curve (and rather thin sand) of Cat's Eye Beach. As well as an enormous range of water sports, fishing trips, and cruises, Hamilton offers speedboat rides, Go-Karts, a "wire flyer" flying-fox hang glider, a pistol/clay target/rifle range, minigolf, an aquatic driving range, beach BBQ safaris in an army truck, hiking trails, an Aussie fauna park where you can cuddle a koala, and an extensive daily activities program.

The drawbacks? Because the resort is split by a steep hill, you need to get around by shuttle (which runs half-hourly or hourly between 10am and 8pm at A$5.50/U.S.$3.60 a day), by golf buggy (A$15/U.S.$9.75 per hour or A$55/U.S.$35.75 for 24 hr.), by inexpensive taxi, or on foot. Despite the price, everyone seems to go for the buggies, so the place can feel like rush hour. To get away, hit the beach or the hiking trails, because most of the 750-hectare (1,853-acre) island is virgin bushland. The biggest caveat is that just about every activity—*including* nonmotorized watercraft—costs big-time, whether it's A$25 (U.S.$16.25) an hour for a catamaran, A$40 (U.S.$26) for 50 pistol shots, or a frightening A$250 (U.S.$162.50) for a scuba-diving trip.

Dining/Diversions: As well as 10 restaurants and cafes, you have a bakery, deli, and butcher; an ice-creamery; a (high-priced!) minisupermarket; and two takeouts. Restaurant decor and food are generally a cut above what you'll find at most other Queensland islands. Live entertainment plays nightly, some restaurants have bars attached, and there is a liquor store.

Amenities: A huge range of water sports and activities (see above), dive shop (dive courses, day trips for certified and first-time divers, snorkel safaris, gear rental), game and reef fishing, dinghy rental, gym and aerobics, massage, float tank, day/night tennis courts, squash courts, beach volleyball, mountain bikes. Other amenities include airport, 135-berth marina, tour desk, post office, bank, medical center, pharmacy, hair/beauty salon, video store, Laundromat, shopping arcade, baby-sitting, all-faiths church, secretarial services, business center, large convention center. The Clownfish Club is an accredited child-care center that provides free daily child care for kids in three age groups, from 6 weeks to 14 years.

MODERATE

✪ **South Molle Island.** South Molle Island (7km/4 miles E of Shute Harbour), Whitsunday Islands. (Postal address: P.M.B. 21, Mackay, QLD 4741). ☎ **1800/075 080** in Australia, or 07/4946 9433. Fax 07/4946 9580. www.southmolleisland.com.au. E-mail: info@ southmolleisland.com.au. 200 units (some with shower only, some also with Jacuzzi). AC TV TEL. A$342–$474 (U.S.$222.30–$308.10) double. Extra adult A$171–$237 (U.S.$111.15–$154.05); extra child 3–14 A$55 (U.S.$35.75). Family rates available in some rooms. Rates include all meals. Ask about packages. AE, BC, DC, MC, V. FantaSea Cruises (☎ 1800/ 650 851 in Australia, or 07/4946 5111) and Whitsunday All Over (☎ 1300/366 494 in Australia, or 07/4946 9499) provides launch transfers from the mainland (Shute Harbour) and most other islands.

South Molle is a good-value island choice. It's not glamorous but it's pretty, with many free activities, and all meals included in the rates. The complex, built around a curving white-sand bay, is getting on in years, so expect a nicely maintained but modest collection of accommodations nestled in tropical gardens or along a hillside. Each unit has sea, garden, or golf-course views. Following a 1998–1999 refurbishing, some beachfront units, especially those with Jacuzzis, are looking positively trendy. The front desk lends hair dryers, and there is a Laundromat.

The 405-hectare (1,000-acre) island is a hilly National Park of grasslands, rain forest, and eucalypts with 16 kilometers (10 miles) of walking trails, including a steep climb to Mt. Jeffreys for fabulous 360° views. As well as a basic but pretty 9-hole golf course (small charge for balls), there are catamarans, windsurfers, and paddle-skis (all free), jet skis, water skis, donut rides, a gym, a Jacuzzi and sauna, archery, Ping-Pong, a toddler's pool, a volleyball net, two day/night tennis courts, and fishing tackle and snorkel gear to rent, plus a beauty salon and boutique. The swimming pool is a big, rather-cheerless rectangle, but it is lined with welcoming lounge chairs under palms, as is the beach. A packed daily activities program offers everything from parasailing to coconut-throwing competitions. The dive shop makes dive and snorkel day trips, takes first-timers diving in the bay, and runs courses. The island is rimmed with inlets accessible by hiking or rented dinghy. Snorkeling is not the best, though you will find some pockets of coral; snorkeling safaris to better reefs run some days. Rainbow lorikeets are everywhere, even on your shoulder stealing food at fish feeding time. A free kids' club for tykes 5 and under operates every day, and during Aussie school vacations a free club runs for 6- to 12-year-olds.

Although the dining room lacks sea views, the buffet food is fine; good meals are available at extra cost in Coral's restaurant some nights, and a cafe sells light meals. Some kind of live entertainment plays every night in the large bar, from a staff song-and-dance show to cane toad racing to the Friday-night "Flames of Polynesia" dinner show.

✪ **Whitsunday Wilderness Lodge.** Long Island (16km/10 miles SE of Shute Harbour), Whitsunday Islands. (Postal address: c/o 30 Swan Terrace, Windsor, Brisbane, QLD 4030.) ☎ and fax **07/3357 3843** (Brisbane reservations office) or 07/4946 9787 (the island; all bookings and enquiries to Brisbane office). www.southlongisland.com. E-mail: info@ecoventure. com.au. 10 units (all with shower only). A$1,782 (U.S.$1,158.30) double *for 3 nights*. Rates include all meals, helicopter transfers from Hamilton Island Airport, daily excursions, and equipment. 3-night minimum stay required. Rates decrease with longer stays. 1 night free with 4-night stay over Beachcomber Day (first Tues of every month). BC, MC, V. No children under 15.

If Hayman (see above) is the most luxurious man-made resort in the Whitsundays, then this place best shows off the region's "au natural" luxury. Tucked in a cove under towering hoop pines and palms, this environmentally sensitive lodge on a national-park island is for people who want to explore the wilderness in basic comfort, but without the crowds, noisy water sports, or artificial atmosphere of a resort. It's also a great place to meet other travelers. A maximum 20 guests stay in simple but smart new (1999) cabins facing the sea, each with a double and single bed, modern bathrooms, and a private deck facing the sea. The lodge is solar powered, so electricity-sucking devices like hair dryers and irons are a no-no. There is no TV or radio, there's only one public phone, and breezes replace air-conditioning. Social life centers on an open-sided gazebo by the beach, equipped with a natural-history library and CDs, where everyone dines together at slab tables under the Milky Way on fabulous buffet-style campfire meals. Access is only by a short but stunning helicopter flight from Hamilton Island.

Every morning (except Sun), the resort managers decide what the day's excursion will be, usually aboard the lodge's gleaming 34-foot catamaran. It could be sailing to tidal flats to look for red and purple rhinoceros starfish, sea kayaking the mangroves to spot giant green sea turtles (which are common around the lodge), sailing to South Molle Island to hike, snorkeling the fringing reef on uninhabited islands, or bush-walking to a magical milkwood grove no one else knows about. You don't have to join in; laze in the hammocks, or head off with a free sea kayak and snorkel gear. The beach is more tidal flat than sand, but clean and firm enough to sunbathe on. Wildlife abounds, including Myrtle, the lodge's pet human (actually, she's a kangaroo, but don't tell her). Folks who stay here consider it a plus that no ferries or cruise boats call and that the lodge is inaccessible to day-trippers or hikers from other resorts on this 1,215-hectare (3,001-acre) island. The only available commercial tour (at a fee) is a seaplane flight to snorkel the outer Great Barrier Reef. On Beachcomber Days, guests are asked to help clear debris from the islands' shores in the course of the day's fun. It's easy, and actually fun in itself.

INEXPENSIVE

Hook Island Wilderness Resort. Hook Island (40km/25 miles NE of Shute Harbour), Whitsunday Islands. (Postal address: P.M.B. 23, Mackay, QLD 4741.) ☎ **07/4946 9380.** Fax 07/4946 9470. www.hookis.com. E-mail: enquiries@hookis.com. 20 tent sites; 2 10-bed dormitories; 10 cabins, 4 with bathroom (shower only). A/C. A$66 (U.S.$42.90) cabin with-out bathroom double; extra adult A$22 (U.S.$14.30); extra child 4–14 A$16.50 (U.S.$10.75). A$104.50 (U.S.$67.95) cabin with bathroom double; extra adult A$27.50 (U.S.$17.90), extra child A$22 (U.S.$14.30). Tent site A$14.30 (U.S.$9.30) adult, A$7.70 (U.S.$5) child 4–14. Dorm bed A$22 (U.S.$14.30) adult, A$16.50 (U.S.$10.75) child (linen supplied). Ask about packages. BC, MC, V. Whitsunday Island Adventure Cruises (☎ 07/4946 5255 for the book-ing agent) provides transfers from the mainland (Shute Harbour) at A$35 (U.S.$22.75) per person, round-trip (trip time: 1–1¹/₂ hr.).

This humble collection of cabins and campsites on a white sandy beach is one of the few really affordable island resorts on the Great Barrier Reef. That makes it popular with backpackers and anybody who just wants to dive, rent canoes, play beach volley-ball, visit the underwater observatory, hike, fish in the four-person flat-bottom boat, laze in the pool and Jacuzzi, and chill out. Good snorkeling is footsteps from shore, and the resort's dive center conducts first-time and regular dives off the beach. Hook is a national park and the second-largest Whitsunday island.

You need to be able to get along without room service, in-room telephones, and smart accommodations, because the cabins are just basic huts with beds or bunks sleeping six or eight. All come with fresh bed linen (BYO bath towels), tea- and coffee-making facilities, and a minifridge. BYO hair dryer. There is a casual cafe and bar. A store sells essentials, but try to come with everything you need. Snorkel gear costs A$10 (U.S.$6.50) for the duration of your stay. The staff will drop you off at a deserted beach for A$10 (U.S.$6.50) per person or take you to coral gardens for A$20 (U.S.$13) per person. Apart from Whitsunday Island Adventure Cruises' once-daily launch, and daily day trips to Whitehaven Beach and the outer Reef, almost no sail-boats, fishing boats, or other tours call here.

6 The Central Queensland Coast, the Southern Reef Islands & Fraser Island

Once you get south of the Whitsundays, it's a long drive through uninspiring rural scenery until you hit the beaches of the Sunshine Coast just north of Brisbane. The lackluster rural towns and dearth of resorts in this region suggest there is nothing to see or do, but that's not entirely so.

For a start, the most spectacular Great Barrier Reef island of them all, ✪ **Heron Island,** is in this region, off the coast from Gladstone. Heron's shallow reefs are a nonstop source of enchantment for snorkelers, and its waters boast fabulous dive sites. In summer giant turtles nest on its beaches, and in winter humpback whales are a common sight.

North of Gladstone is Rockhampton, a town you'll most likely use as a stepping stone to **Great Keppel Island,** a friendly resort island popular with 18- to 35-year-old Aussies. To the south off the small town of Bundaberg lies another coral cay, **Lady Elliot Island.** There is nothing tropical or pretty about the island—it's mostly treeless, windswept, and used as a nesting site by tens of thousands of seabirds—but the fringing reef is first-rate. Two little-known attractions in Bundaberg are its good shore scuba diving and an awe-inspiring loggerhead turtle rookery that operates on the beach from November to March. Farther south lies **Fraser Island,** the world's largest sand island, a playground for 4WD fans and nature lovers.

ROCKHAMPTON: GATEWAY TO GREAT KEPPEL ISLAND
1,055km (659 miles) S of Cairns; 638km (399 miles) N of Brisbane

"Rocky" is the unofficial capital of the Queensland's sprawling beef-cattle country, and the gateway to Great Keppel Island, which boasts a sporty resort.

The town has plenty of motels that provide a decent bed for the night. The **Club Crocodile Motor Inn,** Alma Street at Albert Street, Rockhampton, QLD 4700 (☎ **1800/816 441** in Australia, or 07/4927 7433; www.clubcroc.com.au; or book through Flag Choice worldwide), has doubles for A$98 to $109 (U.S.$63.70 to $70.85).

ESSENTIALS
GETTING THERE   Rockhampton is on the Bruce Highway, a 3¹/₂-hour drive south of Mackay, and almost 2 hours north of Gladstone.

Sunstate Airlines and **Airlink** (book through Qantas at ☎ **13 13 13** in Australia) and **Ansett** (☎ **13 13 00** in Australia) have flights from Brisbane, and from Cairns via Townsville and Mackay. Sunstate flies from Bundaberg, and Flight West Airlines (book through Ansett) and Sunstate both fly from Gladstone.

Queensland Rail's long-distance division, **Traveltrain** (☎ **1800/806 468** in Australia, or 07/3235 1122) operates trains to Rockhampton from Brisbane and Cairns. The fare from Brisbane (trip time: 7 to 9¹/₂ hr., depending on the train) is A$70 (U.S.$45.50); fares from Cairns (trip time: 19¹/₂ hr.) range from A$110 (U.S.$71.50) for a sitting berth to A$367 (U.S.$238.55) for a first-class sleeper.

McCafferty's (☎ **13 14 99** in Australia) and **Greyhound Pioneer** (☎ **13 20 30** in Australia) call at Rockhampton on their many daily coach services between Brisbane and Cairns. The fare is A$66 (U.S.$42.90) from Brisbane (trip time: just over 11 hr.) and A$103 (U.S.$66.95) from Cairns (trip time: about 16¹/₂ hr.).

VISITOR INFORMATION   Drop by the **Capricorn Tourism bureau,** whose information center is at the city's southern entrance on Gladstone Road (at the Capricorn Spire; ☎ 07/4927 2055). It's open daily 9am to 5pm.

GETTING AROUND   **Avis** (☎ 07/4927 3344), **Budget** (☎ 07/4926 4888), **Hertz** (☎ 07/4922 2721), and **Thrifty** (☎ 07/4927 8755) have offices in Rockhampton.

GREAT KEPPEL ISLAND
15km (9 miles) E of Rockhampton

Great Keppel Island's resort offers a huge range of water sports and activities, a happening nightlife, and an emphasis on action-oriented youthful fun. That's not to say less active folk won't enjoy the place's surprisingly quiet surroundings while all the 18-to-35s are out playing. More grass and bushland than palmy paradise, the island's 1,454 hectares (3,635 acres) are crisscrossed with walking trails and rimmed with 17 sandy beaches. It has only modest to good coral, and the best snorkeling is a boat trip away.

Day-trippers can pay to do many of the resort's water sports, swim free in one of its pools, eat at the cafe or moderately priced grill, and drink at the Wreck Bar. Stop by the information center near the Wreck Bar to book activities and pick up a walking-trail map.

GETTING THERE   **Keppel Tourist Services** (☎ **1800/77 4488** in Australia, or 07/4933 6744) makes the 35-minute ferry crossing from Rosslyn Bay Harbour, about 55 kilometers (34 miles) east of Rockhampton, four or five times daily. The return fare is A$30 (U.S.$19.50) adults, A$15 (U.S.$9.75) children 5 to 14, and A$75 (U.S.$48.75) for families of four. From Rockhampton, take the Capricorn Coast scenic route no. 10 to Emu Park and follow the signs to Rosslyn Bay Harbour. Approaching Rockhampton from the north, the scenic drive no. 10 turnoff is just north of the city, and from there it's 46 kilometers (29 miles) to the harbor. **Great Keppel Island Security Car Park** (☎ **07/4933 6670**) on the Scenic Highway at Kempsey Avenue provides undercover car storage for A$7 (U.S.$4.55) per day. The car park's free shuttle takes you the 1 kilometer (just over half a mile) to Rosslyn Bay Harbour.

Rothery's Coaches (☎ **07/4922 4320**) runs three daily services from Rockhampton to Rosslyn Bay Harbour for A$14 (U.S.$9.10) adults, A$10.50 (U.S.$6.85) seniors and students, and A$7 (U.S.$4.55) children 4 to 14, round-trip. Ask about a free pickup from the train station or your Rockhampton hotel. The company's airport–Rosslyn Bay Harbour transfer is $24 round-trip.

Guests at Great! Keppel Island Resort can fly from Rockhampton on up to four daily 20-minute services with **Air Whitaker.** The round-trip fare is A$106 (U.S.$68.90) for adults and A$53 (U.S.$34.45) for children 3 to 14. Book through the resort (see below). Air Whitaker also flies from Gladstone.

ACCOMMODATIONS & DINING

Great! Keppel Island Resort. P.O. Box 206, Torquay, QLD 4655. ☎ **1800/245 658** in Australia or 07/4125 6966 (reservations office), or 07/4939 5044 (island). Fax 07/4125 3363 (reservations office) or 07/4439 1775 (island). www.gkeppel.com.au. E-mail: reservations@ keppel.com.au. 192 units (some with shower only). MINIBAR TV TEL. A$330–$470 (U.S.$214.50–$305.50) double. A$135–$175 (U.S.$87.75–$113.75) *per person* triple/ quad-share. Extra child 3–14 A$39 (U.S.$25.35). Rates include full breakfast and many sports. 2- and 3-meal packages per day A$40–$63 (U.S.$26–$40.95) adult, A$23–$35 (U.S.$14.95–$22.75) child. Ask about packages. AE, BC, DC, MC, V.

Just about every water- and land-based sport you can name is in the offing at this friendly resort, from Frisbee golf to champagne tennis, camel rides on the beach to cricket matches. Many pursuits, including catamarans, paddle-skis, and windsurfers, are free. Activities that cost extra include scuba diving, tandem skydiving, parasailing, guided snorkeling safaris, jet skiing, sunset champagne sails, and reef fishing trips, to name only a few. When the sun goes down the fun goes on every night with live bands, karaoke, discos, games nights, or other entertainment in two venues. The credo is "enthusiasm" rather than "chic"; the buildings are decent, but not spanking new or glamorous.

The white-tiled Hillside Villas with sea or tree views are for folks who like smart interiors and air-conditioning. The Beachfront and Garden units were renovated in 2000 and are perfectly comfortable, although not air-conditioned.

Dining/Diversions: As well as the unpretentious Admiral Keppel restaurant, plenty of cheap options are open to you: the poolside lunch menu, the outdoor Anchorage Char Grill, a cafe, and an ice-creamery. Neptunes and the Wreck Bar have nightly entertainment, bands, and discos. The Sunset Lounge does cocktails, and there are a poolside bar and a swim-up bar.

Amenities: Extensive activities (see above), five outdoor swimming pools, two Jacuzzis, three day/night tennis courts, two squash courts, massage, free kids' club for children 3 to 12, hairdresser, boutique, conference facilities, currency exchange, Laundromat.

GLADSTONE: GATEWAY TO HERON ISLAND
550km (344 miles) N of Brisbane; 1,162 (813 miles) S of Cairns

The industrial port town of Gladstone is the departure point for beautiful Heron Island.

ESSENTIALS
GETTING THERE & GETTING AROUND   Gladstone is on the coast 21 kilometers (13 miles) off the Bruce Highway. **Sunstate Airlines** (book through Qantas at ☎ **13 13 13** in Australia) and **Flight West Airlines** (book through Ansett at ☎ **13 13 00** in Australia) both fly from Brisbane (trip time: about 75 min.), and Sunstate operates a "milk run" via Townsville, Mackay, and Rockhampton. Sunstate flies weekly from Bundaberg; Flight West flies weekly from Rockhampton.

Queensland Rail's long-distance division, **Traveltrain** (☎ **1800/806 468** in Australia, or 07/3235 1122) operates trains from Brisbane and Cairns. The fare from Brisbane (trip time: 6 to 8 hr., depending on the train) is A$63 (U.S.$40.95); fares from Cairns (trip time: just under 22 hr.) range from A$114 (U.S.$74.10) for a sitting berth to A$404 (U.S.$262.60) for a first-class sleeper.

McCafferty's (☎ **13 14 99** in Australia) and **Greyhound Pioneer** (☎ **13 20 30** in Australia) operate many daily coach services to Gladstone on their Brisbane–Cairns–Brisbane runs. The fare is A$62 (U.S.$40.30) from Brisbane (trip time: 10¹/₂ hr.) and A$114 (U.S.$74.10) from Cairns (trip time: 19¹/₂ hr.).

Avis (☎ **07/4978 2633**), **Budget** (☎ **07/4972 8488**), **Hertz** (☎ **07/4978 6899**), and **Thrifty** (☎ **07/4972 5999**) all have Gladstone offices.

VISITOR INFORMATION   Gladstone Area Promotion & Development Ltd's **Visitor Information Centre,** in the ferry terminal at Gladstone Marina, Bryan Jordan Drive, Gladstone, QLD 4680 (☎ **07/4972 9922;** www.gladstoneregion.org.au), is open Monday to Friday from 8:30am to 5pm, and Saturday and Sunday from 9am to 5pm.

ACCOMMODATIONS
Country Plaza International. 100 Goondoon St., Gladstone, QLD 4680. ☎ **1800/ 244 904** in Australia, or 07/4972 4499. Fax 07/4972 4921. E-mail: counglad@ fc-hotels.com.au. 80 units. A/C MINIBAR TV TEL. A$120 (U.S.$78) double. Extra adult A$10 (U.S.$6.50); extra child under 13 A$7 (U.S.$4.55). A Heron Island stopover package including full breakfast and transfers to Gladstone Marina costs A$130 (U.S.$84.50) double. AE, BC, DC, MC, V. Free parking for limited number of cars. Free shuttle to and from airport, coach terminal, marina, and train station.

This four-level hotel in the center of town runs a free shuttle to the wharf for guests bound for Heron Island. It also happens to be Gladstone's best hotel. It caters mostly to business travelers, so it has spacious rooms (and two- and three-bedroom apartments), modern bathrooms with hair dryers, a nice restaurant, 24-hour room service, and an outdoor swimming pool and sundeck.

✪ HERON ISLAND: CORAL, MORE CORAL, TURTLES & WHALES
72km (45 miles) NE of Gladstone

When I asked a travel writer friend of mine, who's been to many enviable spots world-wide, to name her favorite place, she replied, "Heron Island." When you see Heron, it's not hard to understand her answer. Step off the beach from this coral cay speck, a national park in its own right smack bang on the Great Barrier Reef, and you enter fields of coral that stretch for miles. The island is home to 22 fabulous dive sites.

Heron is a major rookery for seabirds and giant green and loggerhead turtles. Guests gather on the beach from late November to February to watch the turtles lay eggs, and from February to mid-April to see the hatched babies scuttle down to the water. Humpback whales pass through from June to September.

Heron lacks the myriad of waters ports, rain-forest trails, and off-island tours offered by most other Great Barrier Reef island resorts, so consider another island if you're not an avid snorkeler.

GETTING THERE A courtesy coach transfers air passengers at Gladstone Airport at 10:30am to Gladstone Marina for the 2-hour launch trip to the island. Launches depart at 11am daily (except Christmas); the round-trip fare is A$168 (U.S.$109.20) adults, half price for kids 3 to 14. Helicopter transfers are A$427 (U.S.$277.55) for adults and A$213 (U.S.$138.45) for children 3 to 14, round-trip. A 15-kilogram luggage limit applies on the helicopter (one soft suitcase per person only). Excess bags are stored free at Gladstone Airport.

ACCOMMODATIONS & DINING

✪ **Heron Island.** Via Gladstone, QLD 4680 (P&O Australian Resorts, GPO Box 478, Sydney, NSW 2001). ☎ **1800/737 678** in Australia, 800/225-9849 in the U.S. and Canada, 020/7805 3875 in the U.K., 02/9277 5050 (Sydney reservations office), or 07/4972 9055 (the island). Fax 02/9299 2477 (Sydney reservations office). www.poresorts.com.au. E-mail: resorts_reservations@poaustralia.com. 117 units, 87 with bathroom (86 with shower only). Turtle Cabins A$180 (U.S.$117) per person; A$360 (U.S.$234) double. A$520–$600 (U.S.$338–$390) double; A$800 (U.S.$520) double, Beach House or Point Suite. Extra adult 50% of room rate; extra child 3–14 25% of room rate when sharing with 2 adults. No children in Point Suites or Beach House. Free crib. Rates include 3 meals a day. Ask about accommodation or dive packages. AE, BC, DC, JCB, MC, V.

I bet every guest arriving at Heron dumps his or her suitcase on the bed and heads straight for the coral. Snorkeling lessons are free, and snorkel gear costs A$12 (U.S.$7.80) per day; snorkel boat trips to the reef's edge cost more. If snorkeling isn't your cup of tea, you can still see the coral from a semisubmersible boat, at a fee. The staff runs free guided reef walks, island ecology walks, turtle walks in nesting season, star-gazing nights, and bird-watching walks (speaking of birds, seabirds abound, so pack a big, cheap straw hat for protection from their calling cards). For an extra charge, you can join BBQ fishing and snorkeling cruises to nearby Wilson Island, whale-watching cruises (in season), fishing trips, glass-bottom paddle-ski tours, sunset wine-and-cheese cruises, two daily dive trips, night dives, or a shallow introductory dive (for A$140/U.S.$91). The dive shop runs weekly 6-day open-water dive certification courses.

The resort itself is pleasantly comfortable rather than glamorous. All the nicely furnished rooms come with hair dryers, ceiling fans, bathrobes, and iron, but no telephones or TV. Only the more expensive ones have sea views. Cheaper lodgings are found in the 30 clean quad-share Turtle Cabin bunkrooms (you can request a double bed), which have shared bathroom facilities. To travelers who are not a couple, Turtle Cabins are sold on a "share with stranger" basis. None of the accommodations is air-conditioned; all have fans. The doors have no locks, though safety boxes are available.

Dining/Diversions: The maître d' allocates your table on the first night. Breakfast and lunch are fabulous buffets, and dinner is usually an excellent four-course menu. Coffee and snacks are sold at the cocktail bar/cafe overlooking the reef. Some kind of entertainment plays nightly, be it dancing, movies, or a wildlife slide show. Packed hampers are free.

Amenities: Many water sports and excursions (see above), swimming pool, beach, free day/night tennis court, Junior Ranger program for kids 7 to 12 in Aussie school vacations for a one-off fee of A$50 (U.S.$32.50), baby-sitting (prebook it), national-parks interpretive center, game room, boutique/shop, conference facilities, currency exchange, safe-deposit boxes, Laundromat, pay telephones, one guest TV.

BUNDABERG: GATEWAY TO LADY ELLIOT ISLAND

384km (241 miles) N of Brisbane; 1,439km (900 miles) S of Cairns

The sugar town of Bundaberg is the last point south (or the first point north) from which you can explore the Great Barrier Reef. Divers can also experience some of Australia's best shore diving off Bundaberg's beaches. If you visit the area between November and March, plan an evening at the wonderful ✪ **Mon Repos Turtle Rookery.**

GETTING THERE & GETTING AROUND   Bundaberg is on the Isis Highway, 50 kilometers (31 miles) off the Bruce Highway from Gin Gin in the north and 53 kilometers (33 miles) off the Bruce Highway from just north of Childers in the south.

Flight West Airlines (book through Ansett at ☎ **13 13 00** in Australia) and **Sunstate Airlines** (book through Qantas at ☎ **13 13 13** in Australia) fly from Brisbane. Sunstate also flies from Cairns via Townsville, Mackay, and Rockhampton, and direct from Gladstone.

All trains stop in Bundaberg en route between Brisbane and Cairns. The fare is A$45 (U.S.$29.25) from Brisbane (trip time: 4¹/₂ to 5¹/₂ hr., depending on the train); fares range from A$124 (U.S.$80.60) for a sitting berth to A$414 (U.S.$269.10) for a first-class sleeper from Cairns (trip time: around 24 hr.). Contact Queensland Rail's long-distance division, **Traveltrain** (☎ **1800/806 468** in Australia, or 07/3235 1122).

McCafferty's (☎ **13 14 99** in Australia) and **Greyhound Pioneer** (☎ **13 20 30** in Australia) call here many times a day on their coach runs between Brisbane and Cairns. The 7-hour trip from Brisbane costs around A$46 (U.S.$29.90). From Cairns it is a 22-hour trip, for which the fare is A$125 (U.S.$81.25).

Avis (☎ **07/4152 1877**), **Budget** (☎ **07/4153 1600**), **Hertz** (☎ **07/4155 2403**), and **Thrifty** (☎ **07/4151 6222**) all have offices.

VISITOR INFORMATION   The **Bundaberg District Tourism and Development Board Information Center** is at 271 Bourbong St. at Mulgrave Street, Bundaberg, QLD 4670 (☎ **1800/060 499** in Australia, or 07/4152 2333; www.tourgroups. net). It's open daily from 9am to 5pm.

SNORKELING & DIVING THE GREAT BARRIER REEF

Bundaberg is the departure point for **Lady Musgrave Island,** a 14-hectare (35-acre) national-park coral cay, 52 nautical miles off the coast on the Great Barrier Reef. It is surrounded by a lagoon 8 kilometers (5 miles) in circumference, filled with hundreds of coral and fish species. The air-conditioned 150-passenger *Lady Musgrave* (☎ **1800/072 110** in Australia, or 07/4159 4519; wwww.ozreef.net) makes a

Up Close & Personal with a Turtle

Just after 7pm, we got the call. "We've got hatchers; repeat, hatchers!" came the crackly message over the radio, and 2 minutes later, I was stumbling along the beach in the dark with 69 other excited people.

Our mission? To stare awestruck as baby turtles emerged from their sandy nest on the beach at the ✪ **Mon Repos Conservation Park** at Bundaberg. Every night from mid-November to early February, Aussies and international visitors flock to this isolated shore to see giant female loggerheads inch their way up past the high-tide mark, laboriously dig a hole in the sand, and lay their eggs. Then every evening from January to mid-March, you get to watch the youngsters hatch.

By the time we reached the hole in the sand dug by a ranger to aid the hatchlings, turtles tiny enough to fit in a matchbox were streaming out, little flippers waving. They moved fast because even under cover of night, seabirds, crabs, and dingoes can pounce before they reach the water. Out of 1,000 babies, only 1 survives.

The rangers got us to form two lines down the beach like a guard of honor, and the turtles scampered down between us to the water. Within 15 minutes, all 100 or so were safely in the waves.

Mon Repos Conservation Park is one of the two largest loggerhead turtle rookeries in the South Pacific. The visitor center by the beach has a great educational display on the turtle life cycle and shows films at approximately 7:30pm each night in summer. Visitors can turn up anytime from 7pm; the laying and hatching action goes on through the night, sometimes as late as 7am. Be prepared to wait around; very occasionally, no turtles show. Nesting happens around high tide; hatching usually occurs between 8pm and midnight. Try to get there early to join the first group of 70 people, the maximum allowed at one laying or hatching. Crowds can be 500 strong from mid-December through January. Bring a flashlight if you have one.

The **Mon Repos Conservation Park** (☎ **07/4159 1652** for the visitor center) is 14 kilometers (9 miles) east of town. Follow Bourbong Street toward Burnett Heads as it becomes Bundaberg–Bargara Road. Take the Port Road to the left and look for the Mon Repos signs to the right. Admission is A$4 (U.S.$2.60) for adults, A$2 (U.S.$1.30) for seniors and children 5 to 15, and A$10 (U.S.$6.50) for families.

2¹/₂-hour journey to a pontoon from which you can snorkel the lagoon, take semi-submersible and glass-bottom boat rides over coral, and walk the beach, for A$127 (U.S.$82.55) adults, A$114 (U.S.$74.10) seniors and students, and A$64 (U.S.$41.60) for children 4 to 14. You get around 4 hours on the coral. Introductory dives in the lagoon cost A$66 (U.S.$42.90) extra; certified dives outside it cost A$55 (U.S.$35.75) for one dive, or A$77 (U.S.$50.05) for two. Book dives ahead. The boat departs Monday to Thursday and Saturday, more often in school vacations, from Port Bundaberg, 20 minutes from the city. Transfers to the jetty are available. The boat also does humpback **whale-watch** cruises from mid-August to mid-October.

The best shore diving in Queensland is in Bundaberg's **Woongarra Marine Park.** It has loads of soft and hard corals and nudibranchs, wobbegongs and epaulette sharks, sea snakes, some 60 fish species, and frequent sightings of green and loggerhead turtles. **Salty's Dive Centre** (☎ **07/4151 6422;** www.saltys.net) rents dive gear for A$44 (U.S.$28.60) per day, and will give you a lift down to the beach for A$8 (U.S.$5.20) and point out two good sites. They also conduct boat trips to offshore reefs and aircraft and boat wrecks, 3-night live-aboards around the southern Great Barrier Reef, and 4-day shore-based learn-to-dive courses at a very affordable A$163.90 (U.S.$106.55).

ACCOMMODATIONS

Acacia Motor Inn. 248 Bourbong St., Bundaberg, QLD 4670. ☎ **1800/35 1375** in Australia, or 07/4152 3411. Fax 07/4152 2387. E-mail: acacbund@fc-hotels.com.au. 26 units (all with shower only). A/C MINIBAR TV TEL. A$79.20 (U.S.$51.50) double. Extra adult A$11 (U.S.$7.15), extra child under 12 A$6 (U.S.$3.90). A$5 (U.S.$3.25) crib. AE, BC, DC, MC, V.

This tidy motel a short stroll from the town center offers slightly dated but clean, well-kept rooms at a decent price. All units have hair dryers. Local restaurants do room service, and many are within walking distance. There's a small pool, and the very helpful managers run a tour desk.

LADY ELLIOT ISLAND

80km (50 miles) NE of Bundaberg

The southernmost Great Barrier Reef island, Lady Elliot is a 42-hectare (105-acre) coral cay edged by a wide, shallow lagoon filled with coral.

Reef walking, snorkeling, diving, bird watching, and relaxing are reasons people come to this islet, which is so small you can walk around it in 55 minutes. Green and loggerhead turtles nest on the beach from November to March, and humpback whales pass by from June to September.

Lady Elliot is a sparse, grassy island rookery with narrow coarse-sand beaches, not a lush tropical paradise, so don't come expecting ukuleles and palm trees. Some folks will find it too spartan; others will relish chilling out in a peaceful, unspoiled location with abundant marine life and gorgeous reef all around. Just be prepared for the musty smell and constant noise of those birds, especially in the October-to-February nesting season.

GETTING THERE   Access is by daily 25-minute flight from Bundaberg, or a 40-minute flight from Hervey Bay (flights generally travel via Bundaberg). Book air travel through the resort. Round-trip airfares from Bundaberg or Hervey Bay are A$159 (U.S.$103.35) for adults and A$80 (U.S.$52) for children 3 to 14.

Day trips from Bundaberg or Hervey Bay cost A$199 (U.S.$129.35) for adults and A$99 (U.S.$64.35) for children; these include flights, snorkel gear, a guided snorkel safari, a boat snorkel trip, or a glass-bottom boat ride, a reef walk, an island tour, fish feeding, and lunch. Snorkeling on Lady Elliot can be done only in the 2 or 3 hours either side of high tide; reef walking works only at low tide.

ACCOMMODATIONS

Lady Elliot Island Resort. P.O. Box 5206, Torquay, QLD 4655. ☎ **1800/072 200** in Australia, or 07/4125 5344. Fax 07/4125 5778. www.ladyelliot.com.au. E-mail: reservations@ladyelliot. com.au. 49 units, 29 with bathroom (shower only). A$274–$396 (U.S.$178.10–$257.40) double. Extra person A$137–$198 (U.S.$89.05–$128.70) adult, A$66–$99 (U.S.$43.55–$64.35) child 3–14. Rates include breakfast and dinner. Ask about dive and other packages. AE, BC, DC, MC, V.

You could say Lady Elliot is the least glamorous of all the Great Barrier Reef islands. One of the oldest of Queensland's island resorts, it does not compare with the flashier big-scale complexes farther north, but its lack of pretensions has a charm all its own. If the wildlife reminds you of *The Birds*, the accommodations—which resemble army huts—may make you think you're on the set of *M*A*S*H*. Inside, the rooms are basic. Reef units have a double bed (some have two bunks also), a chair or two, a bathroom, tea and coffee, and a deck with views through the trees to the sea. Island suites are

When you land on the grass airstrip at Lady Elliot Island during nesting season, you'll think you're on the set of Hitchcock's *The Birds*. The air is thick with tens of thousands of swirling noddy terns and bridal terns that nest in every available branch and leave their mark on every available surface, including you (so bring a big cheap straw hat for protection).

more luxurious, with simple but pleasant furnishings including a diminutive living area, one or two separate bedrooms, smart modern bathrooms, a fridge, tea and coffee, and great sea views from the deck. The 14 permanent tents have beds or bunks, electric lighting, a wooden floor, and shared bathroom facilities. All accommodations have fans.

The few resort facilities include a small pool, a gift shop, a dining room, a poolside snack bar, a casual bar with sea views from the deck, and a dive center. There is also a humble reef education center with aquariums, a library, and educational videos. There is no air-conditioning, no keys (secure storage is at the front desk), no TVs or radio, no hair dryers, and only one public telephone. The food is basic. The low-key activities program includes things like guided wildlife and island history walks to the lighthouse, fish feeding, reef fishing, volleyball, and movie screenings. A Reef Ranger program runs for kids in school vacations. Dives cost A$63 (U.S.$40.95) for certified divers and A$121 (U.S.$78.65) for first-timers. The dive shop runs learn-to-dive courses. The island holds a maximum of 140 guests, so you get the reef pretty much to yourself.

FRASER ISLAND: ECO-ADVENTURES & 4WD FUN

1,547km (967 miles) S of Cairns; 303km (189 miles) N of Brisbane; 15km (9 miles) E of Hervey Bay

Situated just off the central Queensland coast, this 165,280-hectare (405,000-acre) World Heritage–listed island—the biggest sand island in the world—attracts a curious but happy mix of ecotourists and Aussie blokes who like fishing. Almost all of Fraser is part of the **Great Sandy National Park.** The island is a pristine vista of eucalyptus woodlands, soaring dunes, fast-flowing gin-clear creeks, ancient rain forest, postcard-blue lakes, ochre-colored sand cliffs, and a stunning 75-mile-long beach. Dingoes, often too shy to show themselves elsewhere in Australia, stroll around in full view here. Bushwalkers delight in the forests, bird-watchers can chase some 240 species, and dugong, dolphins, and humpback whales (from July or Aug through Oct) are common sights.

For ✪ **4WD** fans, though, Fraser's true beauty lies in its complete absence of paved roads. On weekends when the fish are running, it's nothing to see a hundred or so 4WDs lining 75 Mile Beach as their owners cast a line. The heady mix of a big catch, too much beer, and a powerful 4WD leads to so much wild driving up and down the beach that the police do random blood-alcohol breath tests on the sand on Friday and Saturday nights.

Fraser is not a well-known hitching post on the international tourist trail. Some folks find its low-key beauty boring, but if you like your nature natural, it might be your kind of place. You won't be able to see everything in a day—those sandy 4WD trails make for slow going—so allow a couple of days if you want to catch most of the highlights.

ESSENTIALS

GETTING THERE Hervey (pronounced "Harvey") Bay is the main gateway to the island. Take the Bruce Highway to Maryborough, then the 34-kilometer (21-mile) road to Hervey Bay. If approaching from the north, turn off the highway at Torbanlea, north of Maryborough, and cut across to Hervey Bay. Allow 3 hours from the Sunshine Coast, a good 5 from Brisbane.

Guests at Kingfisher Bay Resort (see below) can get to the resort aboard the **Kingfisher Bay Fastcat,** which departs Urangan Boat Harbour at Hervey Bay six times a day. The last trip is at 10:30pm. Round-trip fare for the 40-minute crossing is A$33 (U.S.$21.45) adults and A$16.50 (U.S.$10.75) kids 4 to 14. The resort runs a courtesy shuttle from Hervey Bay's airport and coach terminal to the harbor. You can park free in the open at the Fastcat terminal; **Fraser Coast Secure Vehicle Storage,** at 629 The Esplanade (☎ **07/4125 2783**), a 5-minute walk from the terminal, gives covered parking for A$7.70 to $9.90 (U.S.$5 to $6.45) per 24 hours.

Both **Greyhound Pioneer** and **McCafferty's** coaches stop several times a day in Hervey Bay on their Brisbane–Cairns–Brisbane routes. The 6-hour trip from Brisbane costs around A$37.40 (U.S.$24.30). From Cairns, the fare is A$152.90 (U.S.$99.40) for a 23-hour trip.

The nearest train station is Maryborough West, 34 kilometers (21 miles) from Hervey Bay. Passengers can book a connecting bus service to Hervey Bay via Queensland Rail's long-distance division, **Traveltrain** (☎ **1800/806 468** in Australia, or 07/3235 1122) for A$4.30 (U.S.$2.80). The fare from Brisbane (trip time: $3^1/_2$ or $4^1/_2$ hr., depending on the train) is A$39 (U.S.$25.35). Fares for the $25^1/_2$-hour trip from Cairns range from A$132 (U.S.$85.80) in a sitting berth to A$426 (U.S.$276.90) in a first-class sleeper.

Flight West Airlines (book through Ansett) and **Sunstate Airlines** (book through Qantas) both have 1 or 2 direct daily flights from Brisbane to Hervey Bay.

GETTING THERE & AROUND BY 4WD Four-wheel drive is the only permissible mode of transport on the island. Many 4WD rental outfits are based in Hervey Bay. You'll pay between about A$100 (U.S.$65) and A$160 (U.S.$104) a day, plus around A$20 (U.S.$13) to A$35 (U.S.$22.75) per day to reduce the deductible, which is usually A$4,000 (U.S.$2,600), plus a bond (typically A$500/U.S.$325). You must also buy a **Vehicle Access Permit,** which costs A$30 (U.S.$19.50) from your rental-car company or Urangan Boat Harbour or the Mary River Heads boat ramp, or A$40 (U.S.$26) from a Queensland Parks and Wildlife Service office on the island. Both **Bay 4WD Centre** (☎ **07/4128 2981**; www.bay4wd.com.au) and **Ausbay 4WD Rentals** (☎ **1800/679 479** in Australia, or 07/4124 6177; www.ausbay4wd. com.au) rent 4WDs; offer camping and accommodated 4WD packages; rent camping gear; organize Vehicle Access Permits, barge bookings, camping permits, and secure storage for your own car; and pick you up free from the airport, coach terminal, or your hotel. Ausbay 4WD Rentals allows 1-day rental (at a slightly higher price); Bay 4WD Centre demands a minimum 2.

Four-wheel drives transfer by **Fraser Venture barge** (☎ **07/4125 4444**), which runs at least three times a day from Mary River Heads, 17 kilometers (11 miles) south of Urangan Boat Harbour. The round-trip fare for vehicle and driver is A$77 (U.S.$50.05), plus A$5.50 (U.S.$3.60) per extra passenger. It is a good idea to book a place for the 10-minute crossing.

Kingfisher Bay 4WD Hire (☎ **07/4120 3366**) within Kingfisher Bay Resort (see below) rents 4WDs for A$195 (U.S.$126.75) a day, plus an A$500 (U.S.$325) bond and an A$2,000 (U.S.$1,300) deductible. They allow 1-day rentals. Book well in advance.

Fraser Island Taxi Service (☎ 07/4127 9188) will take you anywhere on the island—in a 4WD, of course. It's based at Eurong on the island's eastern side. A typical fare, from Kingfisher Bay Resort across the island to go fishing on 75 Mile Beach, say, is A$50 (U.S.$32.50). The taxi seats five.

VISITOR INFORMATION   Contact the **Hervey Bay Tourism & Development Bureau,** 10 Bideford St., Hervey Bay, QLD 4655 (☎ **1800/811 728** in Australia, or 07/4124 9609; www.herveybaytourism.com.au). A better source for Web-connected travelers is **www.hervey.com.au**. The **Marina Kiosk** (☎ 07/4128 9800) at Urangan Boat Harbour is a one-stop booking and information agency for all Fraser-related travel. Several Queensland Parks and Wildlife Service information offices are on the island.

ORGANIZED TOURS & PACKAGE DEALS   **Kingfisher Bay Resort** (see below) offers day trips, overnight, and multiday packages from Hervey Bay, as do several tour companies. One of the most established is **Fraser Island Top Tours** (☎ **1800/063 933** in Australia, or 07/4125 3933; www.fraserislandtours.com.au). **Air Fraser Island** (see above) does fly-4WD-fly day trips for A$200 (U.S.$130) double, and overnight fly-4WD-camp-fly trips for A$340 (U.S.$221) double—a good value when you consider the cost of 4WD rental alone. **Fraser Island V.I.P. Tours** (☎ 07/3273 6688; www.fraservip.com.au) does 2-day tours to Kingfisher Bay Resort from the Gold Coast, Brisbane, and Sunshine Coast. **Fraser Island Adventure Tours** (☎ 07/5444 6957) does a good day trip from the Sunshine Coast.

ECO-EXPLORING THE ISLAND

Among Fraser's main attractions are its 40 or so turquoise lakes and tea-colored lakes "perched" in the dunes. A swim off the white, sandy shore of blue ✪ **Lake McKenzie** could be the highlight of your visit. **Lake Birrabeen** is another popular swimming spot. A giant sand dune is gradually engulfing peaceful **Lake Wabby**—that's bad for the lake but good for your photo album. **Basin Lake** shelters many freshwater turtles and birds. The trick to a refreshing swim in the clear shallows of ✪ **Eli Creek** is to wade upstream for a mile or two and let the current carry you back down.

Hiking trails crisscross the island; most take between 1 and 4 hours. One of the nicest is the boardwalk along **Wanggoolba Creek.** It departs from Central Station.

Unfortunately, you shouldn't swim at ✪ **75 Mile Beach,** which sprawls forever along the island's eastern coast, because of strong currents and a healthy shark population. Instead, swim in freshwater lakes and creeks, and in the beach's ✪ **Champagne Pools** (also called the Aquarium); these pockets of soft sand are turned into minispas by bubbling seawater, protected from the worst of the waves by rocks.

When I was a kid, it was a big thing to bring home a bottle full of Fraser's red, ochre, gold, and black sand. These days, people prefer to view the island's famous colored sand in its natural setting—best seen at the 70-meter (230-ft.) **Cathedrals** cliffs, which stretch north of Happy Valley on the island's eastern side.

4WD Fundamentals on Fraser

Getting bogged in Fraser's loose sand tracks is common, and the beach can be dangerous—travel too high, you get trapped in soft sand; travel too low, and a surprise wave can swamp your vehicle. Walk in to test the current before fording Fraser's fast-flowing creeks. Stick to firm tracks, and know the tides so you don't get cut off. Remember, your pace will be much slower on a 4WD trail than on a conventional road. And look out for planes landing on the beach!

Fraser is fishermen's heaven and one of the best **saltwater fly-fishing** spots in the country. Wade in the shallows for golden trevally and bone fish, and cast off the beach for bream, whiting, flathead, and swallowtail. Freshwater fishing is not allowed. Fishing tour boats run from Hervey Bay.

From July/August through October, tour boats from Hervey Bay crowd the straits to see **humpback whales** returning to Antarctica with calves in tow. **Mimi Macpherson** (☎ 07/4124 7247), sister of supermodel Elle, runs a cruise from Urangan Boat Harbour.

A Special Eco-Resort

✪ **Kingfisher Bay Resort & Village.** Fraser Island (PMB 1, Urangan, QLD 4655). ☎ **1800/ 072 555** in Australia, or 07/4120 3333. Fax 07/4120 3326. www.kingfisherbay.com. E-mail: reservations@kingfisherbay.com. 279 units, 247 with bathroom. Hotel A$249 (U.S.$161.85) double or triple (or 2 adult/2 children); extra child A$30 (U.S.$19.50). Villa A$275 (U.S.$178.75) 2-bedroom villa (sleeps 4 or 5), A$352 (U.S.$228.80) 3-bedroom villa (sleeps 6). Minimum 3-night stay in villas. Free crib. Ask about package deals. AE, BC, DC, JCB, MC, V.

Blending into the eucalyptus along Fraser's west coast, this sleek two-story eco-resort mixes a high level of comfort and award-winning architecture with a concern for the island's fragile ecosystem. Everything from the building materials to the waste-disposal system is natural, recycled, or treated. The hotel rooms have contemporary furnishings and balconies, mostly with views into the bush. The attractive two- and three-bedroom villas have spacious living and dining areas, kitchens, and decks. Both rooms and villas have telephones, TVs, and hair dryers, but only the hotel rooms are serviced and air-conditioned (a must from Nov through Mar). Travelers on the resort's Wilderness Adventure package stay in the nicely rustic Wilderness Lodge, sharing bathrooms and living quarters.

An impressive lineup of eco-educational activities includes daily guided 4WD tours and nature walks, canoe trips, fishing, whale-watch cruises in season, and more. A Junior Eco-Ranger program is free for 4- to 15-year-olds on weekends and school vacations. Most tours cost extra.

Dining/Diversions: Elegant Seabelle serves native Australian cuisine; the poolside Maheno is open for breakfast, lunch, and buffet dinner; the pool bar does snacks; and the lively Sandbar serves great pizzas and cheap bar meals. It has discos and entertainment at night. The small on-site village has a bakery and cafe. The kitchen will pack you a picnic hamper if you ask.

Amenities: On-site ranger office; large free-form heated pool and second smaller pool; extensive sundeck; Jacuzzi; hiking trails; water-sports equipment for rent; free daily fishing clinics; guided game-, fly-, and sport-fishing trips; bait for sale; fishing tackle and dinghies for rent; two day/night tennis courts; beach volleyball; game room; tour desk; baby-sitting; kids' club for children under 5 (at a fee); salon; massage; dry cleaning/laundry; currency exchange; general store; fuel; conference facilities.

7 The Sunshine Coast

If not many international visitors make it to the Sunshine Coast, that's probably because they can't elbow their way in past all the upper-crust Sydneysiders and Melburnites filling the hotel rooms and hogging the (very good) restaurant tables. The warm sunshine and miles of pleasant beaches on this stretch of coastline, an easy 2-hour drive north of Brisbane, attract Aussie southerners like flies to a honey pot. If the Gold Coast (see section 9, later in this chapter) is a mini-Florida, all built up and tacky, then the Sunshine Coast is Hawaii, all pineapple plantations and sugarcane.

The Sunshine Coast commences at Caloundra, 83 kilometers (52 miles) north of Brisbane, and runs all the way to Rainbow Beach, 40 kilometers (25 miles) north of Noosa Heads. **Noosa Heads** is where the fashionable action is. Most of the Sunshine Coast's sunbathing, dining, shopping, and socializing takes place on trendy Hastings Street, Noosa's main strip, and on adjacent Main Beach.

In the immediate hinterland lies one of Australia's prettiest scenic routes, the **Blackall Range Tourist Drive,** a winding mountaintop ribbon of craft villages, lush national parks, and terrific coastal views. The Sunshine Coast is home to a neat wildlife park managed by popular television personality **"Crocodile Hunter"** Steve Irwin and his wife, Terri.

SUNSHINE COAST ESSENTIALS

GETTING THERE From Brisbane, take the Bruce Highway 84 kilometers (53 miles) north to the Sunshine Motorway exit, then the motorway 54 kilometers (34 miles) to Noosa Heads. Exits off the motorway to Coolum are signposted. Allow 2 hours.

Flights land at **Sunshine Coast Airport** in Maroochydore, 42 kilometers (26 miles) south of Noosa Heads. **Qantas** (☎ **13 13 13** in Australia) and **Ansett** (☎ **13 13 00** in Australia) fly direct from Sydney, and on Saturday and Sunday from Melbourne. **Sunstate Airlines** (book through Qantas) and Ansett have many daily flights from Brisbane. **Henry's Airport Bus Service** (☎ **07/5474 0199**) meets all flights; door-to-door transfers to Noosa Heads are A$14 (U.S.$9.10) adults and A$7 (U.S.$4.55) kids 5 to 14, one-way. Bookings are not necessary.

Suburban trains make the 2-hour trip from Brisbane every 2 to 4 hours or so (less often on weekends) to Nambour, 41 kilometers (26 miles) southwest of Noosa Heads, from where a connecting Sunbus bus covers the remaining 45-minute (bus route 12x) or 1-hour (route 12) journey to Noosa Heads; call **CityTrain** (☎ **13 12 30** in Queensland, or 07/3235 5555). The train fare is A$9.70 (U.S.$6.30), and the bus fare A$6.70 (U.S.$4.35). Traveltrain's *Queenslander* and *Sunlander* (from Cairns) and *Spirit of the Tropics* (from Townsville) stop at Nambour. Fares for the 30-hour trip from Cairns range from A$138 (U.S.$89.70) for a seat to A$449 (U.S.$291.85) for a first-class sleeper.

Sun-Air (☎ **1800/804 340** in Australia, or 07/5478 2811) makes up to 10 daily door-to-door transfers from Gold Coast and Brisbane hotels, and also from Brisbane Airport. The one-way fare to a Noosa Heads hotel is A$43 (U.S.$27.95) from Brisbane Airport, A$55 (U.S.$35.75) from Brisbane, and A$79 (U.S.$51.35) from the Gold Coast. **McCafferty's** (☎ **13 14 99** in Australia) and **Greyhound Pioneer** (☎ **13 20 30** in Australia) each stop at Noosa Heads once or twice a day en route from Cairns and Brisbane. The fare is around A$16 (U.S.$10.40) from Brisbane, and A$152 (U.S.$98.80) from Cairns (trip time from Cairns: about 27 hr.).

VISITOR INFORMATION Contact **Tourism Sunshine Coast Ltd.,** P.O. Box 246, Mooloolaba, QLD 4557 (☎ **07/5477 7311;** www.sunshinecoast.org). Two other useful Web sites are **www.tourismnoosa.com.au** and **www.sunzine.net/ suncoast/welcome.html**. In Noosa, drop into the **Tourism Noosa Information Centre** (☎ **1800/44 8833** in Australia, or 07/5447 4988) on the roundabout on Hastings Street at Noosa Drive. It's open daily from 9am to 5pm.

GETTING AROUND Major car-rental companies in Noosa Heads are **Avis** (☎ **07/ 5447 4933**), **Budget** (☎ **07/5447 4588**), **Hertz** (☎ **07/5447 2253**), and **Thrifty** (☎ **07/5447 2299**). All have outlets at the airport. The local bus company is **Sunbus** (☎ **13 12 30** in Queensland, or 07/5492 8700).

The Sunshine Coast

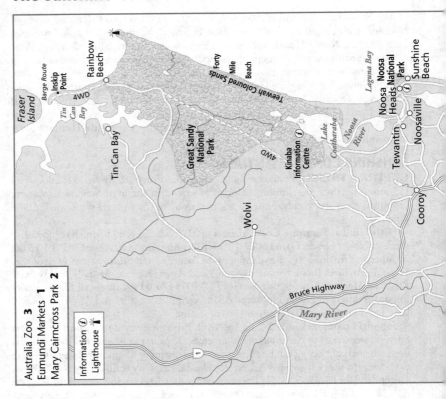

Australia Zoo **3**
Eumundi Markets **1**
Mary Cairncross Park **2**

Information (i)
Lighthouse *

EXPLORING THE AREA

HITTING THE BEACH & OTHER OUTDOOR FUN   Most folks spend their day swimming and surfing on pretty ✪ **Main Beach** in Noosa Heads. If the bikini-clad supermodel look-alikes pose too much of a scene for your taste, hop in a cab or take bus 10 to **Sunshine Beach,** behind Noosa Junction off the David Low Way, about 2 kilometers (1¼ miles) from Noosa Heads. It's less fussy and just as beautiful.

To rent a windsurfer, canoe, kayak, surf ski, catamaran, jet ski, or canopied fishing boat on Noosa River, check out the dozens of rental outfits along **Gympie Terrace** between James Street and Robert Street in Noosaville.

EXPLORING NOOSA NATIONAL PARK   A 10-minute stroll northeast from Hastings Street brings you to the delightful beaches and forests of the 2,280-hectare (5,632-acre) Noosa National Park. Proving that nature and humankind can live in harmony, a koala colony has set up house in the parking lot (or more likely, the parking lot set up house around them). Most scenic in the network of signposted **walking trails** is the 2.7-kilometer (1½-mile) one-way coastal track; keep an eye out for dolphins and whales. The shortest trail is the 1-kilometer (just over half a mile) Palm Grove rain-forest circuit.

"CROCODILE HUNTER'S" THEME PARK   A dozen or more small-scale theme parks thrive on the Sunshine Coast, many based around local produce like ginger or pineapples. Most are crass, commercial, tame, or all three, but one that might spark your interest is Steve and Terri Irwin's ✪ **Australia Zoo** (☎ **07/5494 1134**). You

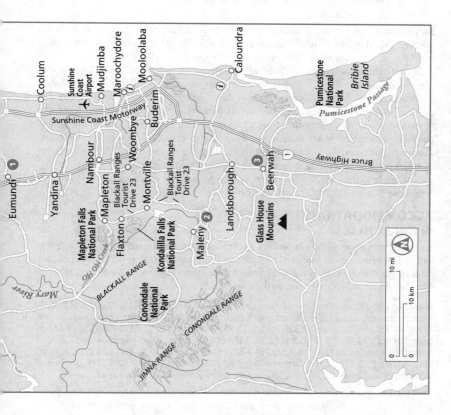

may have seen this fearless couple manhandling crocodiles on their U.S. television show, Animal Planet's *Crocodile Hunter*. Their zoo has crocodiles and other Aussie wildlife like koalas, pythons, and 'roos you can hand-feed, plus non-native ring-ins like camels and Galapagos tortoises. The croc show is the highlight of an ongoing program of talks, photo opportunities, and feeding sessions throughout the day. The zoo is on Glass House Mountains Tourist Drive, Beerwah. Admission is A$15.50 (U.S.$10.10) adults, A$13.50 (U.S.$8.80) seniors and students, A$8 (U.S.$5.20) kids 3 to 14, and A$39.90 (U.S.$25.95) families. It is open daily 8:30am to 4pm; closed Christmas.

A MOUNTAINTOP DRIVE IN THE RAIN FOREST A leisurely half- or full-day drive along the lush rain-forested ridge of the **Blackall Ranges** in the Sunshine Coast hinterland is one of Australia's prettiest days out. Cute villages, crafts shops, cafes, woodland walking trails, homegrown macadamia nuts and avocados for roadside sale, and terrific views of the coast are the main attractions.

If it's Saturday, start at the outdoor ✪ **Eumundi Market** (☎ **07/5442 8581**) in cute Eumundi village, 13 kilometers (8 miles) west of Noosa along the Eumundi Road. Some 300 stalls offer everything from locally grown produce to antique linen to live emu chicks (who knows why!); Brazilian bands, bush poets, or didgeridoo players liven the air. It runs from 6:30am to 2pm.

From Eumundi, take the Bruce Highway to Nambour and turn right onto the Nambour–Mapleton Road just before Nambour. (If you find yourself in town, you've gone too far.) A winding 12-kilometer (7-mile) climb brings you to the village of

Mapleton. It's worth the 4-kilometer detour (2¹/₂ miles) to the 120-meter (400-ft.) waterfalls in **Mapleton Falls National Park.** A 1.3-kilometer (³/₄-mile) circuit departs from the picnic grounds to great views over the Obi Obi Valley.

Back on the main road, travel south 10 kilometers (6 miles) to **Montville,** a cutesy-pie mock-English village that has lost whatever authenticity it had before tourists swamped it. Still, its tree-lined streets, gift shops, galleries, and cafes are pleasant.

Next stop, 13 kilometers (8 miles) on, is **Maleny,** a more modern but less tacky version of Montville, where antiques and handcrafts are the things to look for. Follow the signs around to **Mary Cairncross Park** for spectacular views of the ✪ **Glass House Mountains,** 11 volcanic plugs protruding out of the plains. A 1.7-kilometer (1-mile) rain-forest walking loop takes you past giant strangler figs.

You can backtrack to Noosa the way you came, or drive down to Landsborough to rejoin the Bruce Highway and return northward.

ACCOMMODATIONS
IN NOOSA HEADS

It's low season most of the year on the Sunshine Coast. Most hotels stipulate high season as December 26 to mid- or late-January, the 4-day Easter break, and, depending on how good a year it is, the 2-week school holidays in June to July and September to October. Book well ahead then, and on weekends just to be safe.

Noosa Crest. 2 Noosa Dr., Noosa Heads, QLD 4567. ☎ **07/5447 2412.** Fax 07/5447 2679. www.noosacrest.com.au. E-mail: reception@noosacrest.com.au. 36 units (some with shower only). TV TEL. High season A$329 (U.S.$213.85) 2-bedroom apt.; A$351 (U.S.$228.15) 3-bedroom apt.; A$439–$472 (U.S.$285.35–$306.80) penthouse. No 1-bedroom apts. in high season. Low season A$186 (U.S.$120.90) 1-bedroom apt.; A$219 (U.S.$142.35) 2-bedroom apt.; A$241 (U.S.$156.65) 3-bedroom apt.; A$230–$340 (U.S.$149.50–$221) penthouse. Weekly rates available. AE, BC, DC, MC, V. Free parking. Bus: 1, 10, 10B, 11, 12X.

Distant but great views of Laguna Bay from the rooftop—where there are also a pool, Jacuzzi, and barbecue—make these hillside apartments a great value, especially in low season. Generous in size, all were renovated in late 1998 with smart contemporary decors. Each has a big balcony or patio overlooking gardens; a kitchen; a dining room; a VCR; a stereo; and one or two bathrooms with hair dryer. Only some are air-conditioned. Penthouse guests get private rooftop Jacuzzis, even rooftop pools in some cases. Amenities include a sauna, a tennis court, a tour desk, voicemail, and a security intercom. Housekeeping is weekly. The same hill that delivers the views demands a steep 7-minute walk up from the beach and Hastings Street.

Noosa Village Motel. 10 Hastings St., Noosa Heads, QLD 4567. ☎ **07/5447 5800.** Fax 07/5474 9282. E-mail: noosavillage@bigpond.com.au. 11 units (9 with shower only). TV. High season (Dec 24–Jan 14) A$155 (U.S.$100.75) double; A$190 (U.S.$123.50) family room. Low season A$95 (U.S.$61.75) double; A$135 (U.S.$87.75) family room. Extra person A$11–$15 (U.S.$7.15–$9.75). Discounts for longer stays. Ask about May/June specials. BC, MC, V. Free parking.

All of the nice letters from satisfied guests pinned up on the wall here convinced me that this clean, brightly painted little motel in the heart of Hastings Street was worth recommending—and that was before I saw the pleasant rooms. Each one is freshly painted with a toaster and crockery, a refrigerator, a small but spotless shower, a hair dryer, and a ceiling fan. Rainbow lorikeets play in the palms opposite the balcony. Cheerful proprietors John and Mary Skelton, who are forever sprucing up the place, make tour bookings.

IN THE HINTERLAND

Avocado Grove Bed & Breakfast. 10 Carramar Court, Flaxton, QLD 4560. ☎ and fax **07/5445 7585.** www.babs.com.au/avocado. E-mail: avocadogrove@ozemail.com.au. 4 units, 3 with bathroom (shower only), 1 with private adjacent bathroom. A$105 (U.S.$68.25) double; A$120 (U.S.$78) suite. Weekend rates A$5 (U.S.$3.25) higher; rates are lower for multinight stays. Rates include full breakfast. BC, MC, V. Turn off the Mapleton–Maleny Rd. onto Ensbey Rd.; Carramar Court is the first left.

Noela and Ray Troyahn's Queenslander home lacks sea views, but that doesn't matter when you're ensconced in their cozy rooms, all with country-style furniture, private verandas, fans, and oil heaters. Their house is set on a rural 1 1/2 hectares (3 1/2 acres), where you can picnic on the lawns with lovely views west to Obi Obi Gorge. Noela serves a wonderful breakfast in a hexagonal pagoda as lorikeets play on the bird feeder. Expect an escort to the door by the pug-faced Persian, Apache. Hair dryers are supplied. No smoking indoors.

A LUXURY SPA/GOLF RESORT NEAR NOOSA

One of Australia's best spa resorts is in the small seaside town of Coolum, 19 kilometers (12 miles) south of Noosa Heads, and 7 kilometers (4 1/2 miles) north of the Sunshine Coast Airport. Some tours pick up at the door.

Hyatt Regency Coolum. Warran Rd., off David Low Way (approx. 2km/1 1/4 miles south of town), Coolum Beach, QLD 4573. ☎ **13 12 34** in Australia, 800/633-7313 in the U.S. and Canada, 0845/758 1666 in the U.K. or 020/8335 1220 in London, 0800/44 1234 in New Zealand, or 07/5446 1234. Fax 07/5446 2957. www.coolum.hyatt.com. E-mail: coolum@hyatt.com.au. 324 units (some with Jacuzzis). A/C MINIBAR TV TEL. A$253–$357.50 (U.S.$164.45–$232.75) double, A$325–$869 (U.S.$211.25–$564.85) villa, A$990–$1,540 (U.S.$643.50–$1,001) residence. Rates include continental breakfast. Extra person A$45 (U.S.$29.25). Children under 13 stay free in parents' room using existing bedding. Ask about golf, spa, and other packages. AE, BC, DC, JCB, MC, V. Free valet parking. Resort shuttle meets all flights at Sunshine Coast Airport for A$15 (U.S.$9.75) per person, one-way. Town car transfers from Brisbane Airport A$65 (U.S.$42.25) per person one-way (shared service with other guests); limousine transfers available.

Well-heeled Sydneyites and Melburnites flock to this sprawling bushland resort for two things: its spa and its 18-hole Robert Trent Jones, Jr.–designed course. The spa does everything from aromatherapy baths to triglyceride checks (130 treatments in all) and has massage rooms, aqua-aerobics, yoga, and much more. The golf course was rated in Australia's top five resort courses by *Australian Golf Digest* in 2000. Golf widows and widowers can play tennis; do decoupage in the Creative Arts Center; take the twice-daily free shuttle into Noosa to shop; and surf at the resort's private patrolled beach. A nightly shuttle runs to Noosa Heads restaurants for A$15 (U.S.$9.75) per person, round-trip.

So spread out are the low-rise accommodations that guests rent a bike to get around, or wait 15 minutes for the two free resort shuttles (frustrating sometimes!). Accommodations all sport contemporary, if uninspiring, decor and come as "suites" (a single room divided into living and sleeping quarters); two-bedroom President's Villas with a kitchenette; villas within the Ambassador Club, which has its own concierge, pool, tennis court, and lounge; and two-story, three-bedroom Ambassador Club residences boasting rooftop terraces with a Jacuzzi. All units have hair dryers.

Dining/Diversions: The stylish Fish Tales does modern seafood. The McKenzie Grill overlooks the golf course. An Italian joint, a pizzeria, a take-out deli, a wine cellar, a Thai noodle house, and a bar are all located in the Village Square. Fraser's is a nightly disco. Spike's Bar is next to the pro shop.

Amenities: Health/beauty spa with hairdresser; championship golf course with driving range, putting and chipping greens, and golf lessons; nine swimming pools including 25-meter (82-ft.) heated lap pool; gym; seven day/night tennis courts; two squash courts; golf and tennis pro shop; rental of body boards, canoes, and fishing tackle; nature trail; daily clubs for kids 6 weeks to 12 years old (for a fee); concierge; room service; safes; turndown on request; dry cleaning/laundry; baby-sitting; tour/car rental desk and travel agency; extensive conference facilities; business center; currency exchange.

DINING IN NOOSA HEADS

✪ **Artis.** 8 Noosa Dr. ☎ **07/5447 2300.** Reservations recommended. Main courses A$18.50–$24.50 (U.S.$12–$15.95). AE, BC, DC, MC, V. Daily 6pm–late; may close Sun in winter. Bus: 1, 10, 10B, 11, 12X. MODERN AUSTRALIAN.

Only uninformed tourists turn up at this elegant A-frame restaurant without a reservation. Everyone else knows to book in advance. The food—such as basil- and lime-cured salmon; or a prawn, chicken, and coconut salad with chili, mint, kaffir lime, and coriander—is elaborately presented and darn good. The sleek modern interior manages to be warm and intimate, but on a warm night ask to sit outside on the terrace under the stars and just ignore the noisy traffic. Live jazz plays Wednesday and Friday.

✪ **Season.** 30 Hastings St. ☎ **07/5447 3747.** Reservations not accepted. Light meals and main courses A$10–$22 (U.S.$6.50–$14.30). AE, BC, DC, MC, V. Daily 5:30–10pm. MODERN AUSTRALIAN.

Ever since chef Gary Skelton opened this casual place, it has been full of vacationing Sydneysiders who used to patronize his groovy Sydney pizza joint. The food is unfailingly good. There's a tiny indoor eating room, but most folks line up (sometimes for an hour or more) for a seat at the terrazzo tables on the sliver of a veranda. Choose from a sliding scale of dish sizes, ranging from the roast vegetable salad with baby spinach and feta, up to the char-grilled veal with roast rosemary potatoes and truffle oil. BYO; no smoking.

✪ **Soleil.** Upstairs on Duke St. at Bryan St., Sunshine Beach. ☎ **07/5474 5533.** Reservations essential on weekends. Light meals and main courses A$12.50–$21.50 (U.S.$8.15–$14); fresh fish market price. AE, BC, DC, MC, V. Mon–Sat 6–10pm. Bus: 10. MODERN AUSTRALIAN.

Locals love this award-winning beach shack and bar overlooking Sunshine Beach, with its rough concrete floors, polished decking, and partly outdoor seating. Owner/chef Patrick Landelle trained in France and now creates dishes like quail marinated in Moroccan spice, char-grilled and served on barbecued eggplant. His "Flavours of Japan" sushi and sashimi plate is a favorite. Mondays a cheaper menu partners the speak-easy air and live music in the Luna Lounge bar, and Fridays a DJ plays Motown and bossa sounds. A log fire keeps the place cozy in winter. Licensed and BYO (wine only; no BYO beer or spirits).

8 The Gold Coast

You'll either love the Gold Coast or hate it. Its fans praise its miles of squeaky-clean beaches, its glitzy shops, its summer sunshine, and its pulsing energy. Its detractors—and there are plenty—lament its endless strips of neon-lit motels, cheap souvenir shops, soulless apartment towers, and overexposed sunburned flesh in bikinis and stilettos. In an unabashed development boom that's been going on since the 1950s, so many apartment towers shot up that skyscrapers now cast a spoilsport shadow on beaches in Surfers Paradise in the afternoon.

The Gold Coast

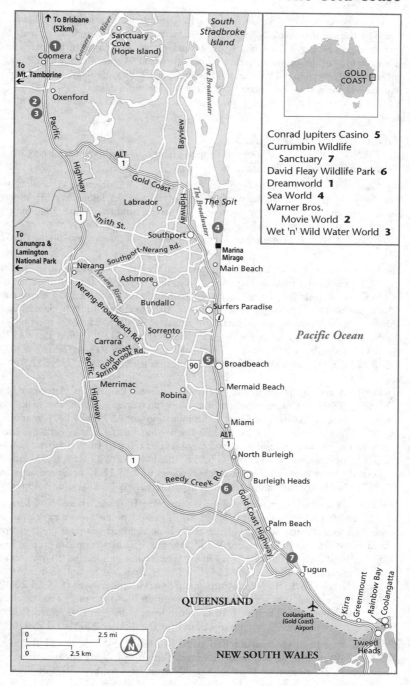

To Brisbane (52km)

Coomera **1**

To Mt. Tamborine

Oxenford

2
3

Pacific

Sanctuary Cove (Hope Island)

South Stradbroke Island

The Broadwater

Bayview

ALT **1**

Gold Coast

Labrador

Highway

The Spit

The Broadwater

Southport

Marina Mirage

Main Beach

Highway

Smith St.

1

To Canungra & Lamington National Park

Nerang

Southport-Nerang Rd.

Nerang River

Ashmore

Bundall

Surfers Paradise *i*

Nerang-Broadbeach Rd.

Sorrento

Pacific Ocean

Carrara

Gold Coast Springbrook Rd.

90 **5** Broadbeach

Merrimac

Pacific

Robina

Mermaid Beach

Highway

Miami

ALT **1**

1

North Burleigh

Reedy Creek Rd.

6 Burleigh Heads

Gold Coast Highway

Palm Beach

7 Tugun

QUEENSLAND

Coolangatta (Gold Coast) Airport

Kirra
Greenmount
Rainbow Bay
Coolangatta

Tweed Heads

NEW SOUTH WALES

Conrad Jupiters Casino **5**
Currumbin Wildlife Sanctuary **7**
David Fleay Wildlife Park **6**
Dreamworld **1**
Sea World **4**
Warner Bros. Movie World **2**
Wet 'n' Wild Water World **3**

GOLD COAST

0 ——— 2.5 mi
0 ——— 2.5 km

N

Theme parks draw big crowds to the Gold Coast. None is as large or as sophisticated as the equivalent parks in the United States, but they're exciting enough to get Aussies hopping on a Gold Coast–bound plane. The three major parks are Dreamworld, a kind of mini-Disneyland of Australiana; Warner Bros. Movie World, a Down Under version of Universal Studios; and Sea World. Golfers will love the Gold Coast's 40-plus golf courses, many of them championship quality.

It's a little too nippy to swim in winter. The best time to visit is between September and April.

GOLD COAST ESSENTIALS

GETTING THERE　　See "Getting Around" for passes that include transfers from Gold Coast or Brisbane airports.

By Car　　From Brisbane, take the South East Freeway 18 kilometers (11¹/₄ miles) to the Pacific Highway at Springwood, take the highway 53 kilometers (33 miles) to Nerang, and then follow the signs to Southport, a commercial hub 3 kilometers (2 miles) north of Surfers Paradise. The trip takes 80 minutes. From Sydney, it's a 928-kilometer (580-mile), 11-hour trip along the crowded and run-down two-lane Pacific Highway.

By Plane　　Ansett (☎ 13 13 00 in Australia) and **Qantas** (☎ 13 13 13 in Australia) fly many times a day from Sydney, and at least once each a day from Melbourne, to **Gold Coast Airport** (known as Coolangatta Airport), at Coolangatta, 25 kilometers (16 miles) south of Surfers Paradise. **Sunstate Airlines** (book through Qantas) and Ansett fly from Brisbane daily. **Coachtrans** shuttles (☎ 07/5588 8747) meet major flights and transfer you to your Surfers Paradise hotel for A$11 (U.S.$7.15), or A$20 (U.S.$13) to Sanctuary Cove. A taxi from the airport with **Regent Taxis** (☎ 07/5588 1234) is around A$30 (U.S.$19.50) to Surfers Paradise, A$50 (U.S.$32.50) to Sanctuary Cove.

The nearest major international gateway is Brisbane. Coachtrans' **Airporter** bus (☎ 07/5588 8777) meets most domestic and international flights and makes as many as 20 trips a day to Gold Coast accommodations for A$35 (U.S.$22.75) adults, A$18 (U.S.$11.70) kids 4 to 14. Book a seat if your flight lands in Brisbane after 7:30pm. The trip takes 90 minutes. Coachtrans makes transfers **from Brisbane hotels to Gold Coast hotels** for A$27.50 (U.S.$17.90) adults, A$13.75 (U.S.$8.95) kids.

Route 1A with local company **Surfside Buslines** (☎ 13 12 30 in Queensland, or 07/5571 6555) runs half-hourly from the airport to Surfers Paradise until 6:45pm.

By Bus　　As well as its airport-to-door service from Brisbane, above, **Coachtrans** (☎ 13 12 30 in Queensland, or 07/5588 8777) runs 11 public buses a day from the Brisbane Transit Centre at Roma Street. Stops include all major theme parks except David Fleay Wildlife Park, and Sea World (*but* the 8:30am service *does* stop at Sea World). About every second service is express, which takes an hour and 20 minutes to Surfers Paradise. The adult fare is A$13 (U.S.$8.45). Bookings are not needed.

McCafferty's (☎ 13 14 99 in Australia) and **Greyhound Pioneer** (☎ 13 20 30 in Australia) each pull into Surfers Paradise between three and five times a day on their Sydney–Brisbane route. The 15- to 16-hour trip from Sydney costs around A$82.50 (U.S.$53.65), while the 90-trip from Brisbane is about A$15.40 (U.S.$10).

By Train　　Suburban **Queensland Rail** trains (☎ 07/3235 5555, or call Transinfo ☎ 13 12 30 in Queensland) depart Brisbane Central and Roma Street stations, on average every 30 minutes or hour, for the 90-minute trip to the suburb of Robina, approximately 10 kilometers (6¹/₄ miles) southwest of Surfers Paradise. The fare is A$8.30 (U.S.$5.40). Numerous Surfers Paradise–bound buses run from Robina station.

From May 1, 2001, a new **Airtrain** is due to begin a 72-minute service every 30 minutes between 5am and 11pm from the domestic and international terminals of Brisbane Airport to Robina station. The fare was not set at press time.

By train from Sydney or other southern cities, you will transfer to a coach in Casino (an overnight trip) or Murwillumbah (a daytime journey), 181 kilometers (113 miles) and 58 kilometers (36 miles) respectively south of Surfers Paradise. The whole trip from Sydney is 14 to 15 hours. The train-coach fare ranges from A$98 (U.S.$63.70) for a seat to A$227 (U.S.$147.55) for a sleeper. Services run daily. Call **Countrylink** at ☎ **13 22 32** in Australia, or 02/9379 1298).

VISITOR INFORMATION   The **Gold Coast Tourism Bureau** has an information kiosk on Cavill Avenue in Surfers Paradise (☎ 07/5538 4419). It's open Monday to Friday from 8:30am to 5:30pm, Saturday from 9am to 5:30pm, and Sunday from 9am to 3:30pm. For material in advance, contact the bureau at P.O. Box 7091, Gold Coast Mail Centre, QLD 9726 (☎ **07/5592 2699;** www.goldcoasttourism.com.au).

ORIENTATION   The heart of the Gold Coast is **Surfers Paradise**—"Surfers" to the locals, pronounced more like "surface"—a forest of high-rise apartment towers, shops, dirt-cheap eateries, bars, and amusement parlors. Its center is the pedestrians-only **Cavill Mall.** Twenty-five minutes north of Surfers is **Hope Island,** a wetlands isle effectively part of the mainland, home to the plush **Sanctuary Cove** golf, resort, shopping, and marina complex.

The **Gold Coast Highway** is the main north–south artery connecting a string of beachside suburbs. North of Surfers is **Main Beach,** home to the Gold Coast's first up-and-coming pocket of cool on the Tedder Avenue cafe strip. Heading south of Surfers, the biggest suburbs are the retail and restaurant precinct of Broadbeach; family-oriented Burleigh Heads; and the sleepy "twin towns" of Coolangatta in Queensland and Tweed Heads just over the state border, popular with young families. West of Surfers lie affluent suburbs, many on a network of canals.

GETTING AROUND   Avis (☎ 07/5539 9388), **Budget** (☎ 07/5538 1344), **Hertz** (☎ 07/5538 5366), and **Thrifty** (☎ 07/5538 6511) have outlets in Surfers Paradise and at Gold Coast Airport.

Coachtrans (☎ **07/5588 8777**) has a 3- to 4-day "Get Around" pass entitling you to unlimited coach pickups from your hotel to major shopping centers, the casino, all restaurants between Main Beach and Broadbeach, and most theme parks, plus unlimited travel on the company's many daily bus services to and from Brisbane. A shopping tour and a trip to Sanctuary Cove are included, as are transfers from and to Gold Coast or Brisbane airports. You book the coach when you want it. The pass is A$45 adults (U.S.$29.25), A$23 (U.S.$14.95) kids 4 to 14 from Gold Coast Airport, or A$77 (U.S.$50.05) adults, A$42 (U.S.$27.30) kids from Brisbane Airport. Families get discounts.

A Gold Pass for a day's unlimited travel with **Surfside Buslines** (☎ **13 12 30** in Queensland, or 07/5571 6555) also entitles you to travel the **Gold Coast Tourist Shuttle,** which makes door-to-door transfers from Coolangatta Airport and to the theme parks. A 1-day pass costs A$12 (U.S.$7.80) adults, A$6 (U.S.$3.90) kids 4 to 14, and A$30 (U.S.$19.50) for a family.

WHAT TO SEE & DO

No fewer than 35 wide, white ✪ **beaches,** with sand so clean it squeaks, stretch for some 30 kilometers (19 miles) along the Gold Coast. The "beaches" are in fact one fabulous long beach interrupted by a few headlands. Step onto it at any point and you will easily spot the nearest red and yellow flags that signal safe swimming. Popular beaches like **Main Beach, Surfers Paradise, Mermaid Beach, Burleigh Heads, Coolangatta, Greenmount,** and others are patrolled by volunteer lifeguards ("life-savers") 365 days a year.

Surfers will find the best breaks at Burleigh Heads and Kirra. **Surfers Beach Club** (☎ 07/5526 7077), on The Esplanade in front of the Paradise Centre at Cavill Mall, rents **surfboards, body boards, bicycles,** and **in-line skates** for A$20 (U.S.$13) per 24 hours (or A$25/U.S.$16.25 for a long surfboard). They give 2-hour surfing lessons for A$50 (U.S.$32.50), board included.

Shangri-La Cruises (☎ 07/5557 8888) and **Island Queen Showboat Cruises** (☎ 07/5557 8800) offer a similar array of sightseeing, shopping, lunch, and dinner cruises on the city's posh canal estates.

Fishing charter boats are mostly based at Marina Mirage on Sea World Drive, oppo-site the Sheraton. **Paul Burt's Reel Action Fishing Charters** (☎ 07/5596 5546 or 014/46 1188) will take you out reef, game, or calm-water fishing for a half or whole day. Prices range from A$30 (U.S.$19.50) per person for a twilight session to A$190 (U.S.$123.50) per person for a day's game fishing.

Grandest of the Gold Coast's 40-plus **golf** courses is the Scottish links–style Thomson-Wolveridge ✪ **Hope Island Golf Club,** at Hope Island Resort on Oxenford-Southport Road, 30 minutes north of Surfers Paradise (☎ 07/5530 9000). A 9-hole round is A$50 (U.S.$32.50), but few resist the whole 18 for A$95 (U.S.$61.75). Other championship fairways include **The Palms** at the Hyatt Regency Sanctuary Cove (see "Accommodations," below); **Lakelands,** Gooding Drive, Merrimac (☎ 07/5579 9000), designed by Jack Nicklaus; and **Royal Pines Resort,** Ross Street, Ashmore (☎ 07/5592 9173). **Koala Golf** (☎ 07/5591 6181) runs day trips to local courses.

Shopping is a big pastime on the Gold Coast. Try the 270 boutiques and depart-ment stores at **Pacific Fair,** next to Conrad Jupiters Casino on the Gold Coast High-way at Hooker Boulevard, Broadbeach (☎ 07/5539 8766), or cruise two levels of upper-crust fashion labels at **Marina Mirage** (☎ 07/5577 0088) on Sea World Drive, Main Beach (across from the Sheraton). The **Marine Village** (☎ 07/5530 8400) next to the Hyatt Regency Sanctuary Cove has 85 upscale gift shops, galleries, boutiques, and restaurants in a marina atmosphere.

Conrad Jupiters Casino, Gold Coast Highway, Broadbeach (☎ 07/5592 1133), is open 24 hours (closed Christmas Day and Good Friday from 3am, and from 3am to 1pm Anzac Day on Apr 25). You must be 18. Don't wear singlets, flip-flops, or beachwear.

THE THEME PARKS

Theme parks thrive among the Gold Coast's holiday crowds, who have money to spend and nothing to do once they've overdosed on sunbathing. The "big three" are **Dreamworld, Sea World,** and **Warner Bros. Movie World.**

Indy Fever!

Traffic comes to a stop—literally—for 4 days every mid-October when V8 Super-cars, Formula Fords, Porsches, and other contestants in the **Honda Indy 300** roar around a 4.5 kilometer (3-mile) circuit on Surfers Paradise streets at up to 300 kilometers per hour (187$^{1}/_{2}$ m.p.h). The Indy is part of the international FedEx Championship champ car motorsport series. For tickets, contact **Ticketek** in Brisbane (☎ 13 19 31 in Queensland, or 07/3404 6644; or order online at www.indy.com.au).

Money-Saving Tip

Sea World, Warner Bros. Movie World, and Wet 'n' Wild Water World sell a **3-Park Super Pass** that gets you a full day's entry to each park, plus a free return visit to the one you like best. It costs A$127 (U.S.$83.10) for adults, and A$82.30 (U.S.$53.50) for seniors and kids ages 4 to 13. You can't buy it at the theme parks; it's sold by any travel agent, Australia Post office, auto-club offices, Ansett or Qantas shopfronts, and some hotel tour desks.

Only Sea World is handily located in the center of town. The other parks are on the Pacific Highway, a 20-minute drive north of Surfers Paradise. You can ride free to and from the "big three," plus Wet 'n' Wild Water World and Currumbin Wildlife Sanctuary, *and* get a free Gold Pass for unlimited bus travel for 24 hours, if you buy your park admission aboard a **Surfside Buslines** (☎ **13 12 30** in Queensland) bus. Park tickets cost the same on the bus as they do at the gates—and you avoid queuing. Take bus 1A to Movie World, Wet 'n' Wild Water World, and Dreamworld; and bus 2, 2A, or 9 to Sea World.

Coachtrans does daily transfers **from Gold Coast hotels** to the "big three" parks plus Wet 'n' Wild Water World and Currumbin Wildlife Sanctuary. Round-trip fares to any one park except Sea World are A$13 (U.S.$8.45) adults, A$8 (U.S.$5.20) kids 4 to 14, or A$36 (U.S.$23.40) for families of four. Round-trip transfers to Sea World are A$7 (U.S.$4.55) adults, A$4 (U.S.$2.60) kids, and A$18 (U.S.$11.70) families. Coachtrans's round-trip transfers **from Brisbane hotels** are A$25 (U.S.$16.25) adults, A$15 (U.S.$9.75) kids, and A$60 (U.S.$39) families. The company also offers airport transfer packages from Coolangatta Airport and Brisbane Airport to the "big three" parks plus Wet 'n' Wild Water World. Book transfers a day ahead if you can, especially in peak season. Call Coachtrans (☎ **1800/426 224** in Australia or 07/5592 3488 for transfers from the Gold Coast, or ☎ **07/3236 1000** for transfers from Brisbane). You can also hail Coachtrans's 11 daily public buses that run between the Gold Coast and Brisbane (see "Getting There," above); a convenient stop to join them in Surfers is the Transit Centre in Beach Road.

Island Queen Showboat Cruises and **Shangri-La Cruises** (see above) incorporate theme-park transfers into some cruises.

Dreamworld. Pacific Hwy. (25km/16 miles north of Surfers Paradise), Coomera. ☎ **1800/ 073 300** in Australia, 07/5588 1111, or 07/5588 1122 (24-hr. info line). Admission (all inclusive except skill games, souvenir photos, and helicopter rides) A$49.80 (U.S.$32.40) adults, A$30.80 (U.S.$20) children 6–13 and seniors. Daily 10am–5pm; Anzac Day (Apr 25) 1:30–6:30pm. Main Street, Plaza Restaurant, and Koala Country open at 9am. Extended hours may operate in school vacations. Closed Christmas.

High-octane rides here, such as the 39-story "Giant Drop" (the world's tallest free-fall ride), "Thunderbolt" (Australia's fastest double-loop roller coaster), and a dozen or so other rides of varying degrees of terror, make the rest of this family-oriented park look tame. Laid out Disney-style—except that Kenny Koala roams the streets instead of Mickey Mouse—its attractions include an Imax theater, an Aussie wildlife park, performing koala cabarets, a river cruise and bushranger show, skills games, a waterslide park, and rides for little kids. A highlight is watching trainers swim and wrestle with five gold and white Bengal tigers. You can be photographed patting a tiger for A$295 (U.S.$191.75)—yes, you read that right—with up to four people in the shot (you must be at least 10 years old), or cuddling a koala for A$12.95 (U.S.$8.40). Book tiger photos. Allow the best part of a day here.

Sea World. Sea World Dr. (3km/2 miles north of Surfers Paradise), The Spit, Main Beach. ☎ **07/5588 2222,** or 07/5588 2205 for recorded show times. Admission (all inclusive except interactive animal experiences, helicopter rides, and powered water sports) A$49.80 (U.S.$32.40) adults, A$31.40 (U.S.$20.40) seniors and children 4–13. Daily 10am–5pm; Anzac Day (Apr 25) 1:30–6:30pm. Closed Christmas.

Although this Sea World isn't as sophisticated as similar parks in the United States, folks flock here to see performing dolphins and sea lions, water-ski shows, aquariums, shark feeding, a 3D pirate movie, a handful of rides including a triple-loop roller coaster, and a playground for little ones featuring such cartoon characters as the Powerpuff Girls. There are also a free waterslide playground and other water sports. A variety of programs (at an extra fee) let you dive with sharks, kiss seals, snorkel with dolphins (A$95/U.S.$61.75; you must be 14 or older), and swim with seals (A$70/U.S.$45.50). Kids can attend a dolphin talk, pat one in shallow water, and have their photo taken with it for A$35 (U.S.$22.75). A long half day oughta do it here.

Warner Bros. Movie World. Pacific Hwy. (21km/13 miles north of Surfers Paradise), Oxenford. ☎ **07/5573 3999,** or 07/5573 8485 for recorded information. Admission (all inclusive) A$49.80 (U.S.$32.35) adults, A$31.40 (U.S.$20.40) seniors and children 4–13. Daily 9:30am–5:30pm; Anzac Day (Apr 25) 1:30–6:30pm. Rides and attractions operate 10am–5pm. Extended hours operate during Christmas–New Year period. Closed Christmas.

Australia's answer to Universal Studios just about matches its U.S. counterpart for thrills and spills. Laid out like a Wild West village, it is based around working film studios where movies such as *The Phantom,* starring Billy Zane, were filmed. Don't miss the hilarious *Police Academy* Stunt Show; the other highlight is the tummy-turning "Lethal Weapon" suspended roller coaster. The park also offers "Batman Adventure—The Ride," an illusion show, a bloopers cinema, a Wild West flume ride, a neat cinema tricks studio tour, and, for young kids, rides and stage shows themed around Looney Tunes characters. Every day sees a Grand Parade starring Warner Bros. Cartoon characters at 11:30am, and "Breakfast with the Stars" and "Lunch with the Legends" song-and-dance shows. Most action happens from 11am to 4pm.

Wet 'n' Wild Water World. Pacific Hwy. (next to Warner Bros. Movie World), Oxenford. ☎ **07/5573 6233,** or 07/5573 2255 for recorded information. Admission A$28.20 (U.S.$18.35) adults, A$19.50 (U.S.$12.70) seniors and children 4–13. Daily Nov–Dec and Feb 10am–5pm, Jan 10am–9pm, Mar–Apr 10am–4:30pm, May–Aug 10am–4pm, Sept–Oct 10am–4:30pm. Open until approx. 9pm on Dive-In Movie nights. Closed Christmas and until 1:30pm Anzac Day (Apr 25).

Hurtling down a seven-story waterslide at 70 kilometers per hour (44 m.p.h.), corkscrewing seven times inside the "Twister" slide, doing the Mammoth Plunge slide in a tube with six mates, and racing head-first down an eight-lane speedslide are some of the thrills at this aquatic fun park. Calm-water fans can float past palmy "islands" in the gentle Calypso Beach current, or splash about in the Wave Pool. Young kids have their own water playground. Every night in January and Saturday nights from September to April is **Dive-In Movie night,** when fans recline on rented rubber tubes in the pool to watch recent-release flicks. The water is heated to 26°C (79°F) year-round.

THE WILDLIFE PARKS

✪ **Currumbin Wildlife Sanctuary.** 28 Tomewin St., off the Gold Coast Hwy. (18km/11 miles south of Surfers Paradise), Currumbin. ☎ **07/5534 1266,** or 07/5598 1645 for the activities program. Admission A$18.50 (U.S.$12) adults, A$10.50 (U.S.$6.85) seniors and children 4–15, A$46.50 (U.S.$30.25) family pass. Daily 8am–5pm. Closed Christmas and until 1pm Anzac Day (Apr 25). Bus: 1A, or Coachtrans (see "Getting There" under "Theme Parks," above).

There's hardly a Queenslander alive who can't show you childhood snapshots of him- or herself draped in the beautiful rainbow lorikeets at this 27-hectare (67-acre) park. The birds flock here in the thousands every day to be hand-fed pans of bread and honey by hundreds of delighted visitors, from 8 to 9:30am and 4 to 5:30pm. While you're here, have your photo taken cuddling a koala (for A$10.95/U.S.$7.10; call for photo session times), hand-feed kangaroos, take a free miniature train ride through wetlands to see a range of Aussie wildlife, see orphaned joeys, walk through an aviary, catch animal talks, and see a daily Aboriginal dance show. Allow 3 hours to see everything.

✪ **David Fleay Wildlife Park.** West Burleigh Rd. (17km/11 miles south of Surfers Paradise), West Burleigh. ☎ **07/5576 2411.** Admission A$13.20 (U.S.$8.60) adults, A$8.80 (U.S.$5.70) seniors and students, A$6.60 (U.S.$4.30) children 4–17, or A$33 (U.S.$21.45) families. Free reentry if rained out. Daily 9am–5pm (nocturnal creatures on show from 11am). Closed Christmas Day and until 1pm Anzac Day. Bus: 4. Take the Gold Coast Hwy. south to Burleigh Heads, veer right onto West Burleigh Rd., and follow it for 1km (just over $1/2$ mile); the park is on the left.

Meander through picturesque mangrove, rain-forest, and eucalyptus habitats, on raised boardwalks, to see a small but intriguing range of Aussie wildlife: koalas (touch but don't hold), a platypus, crocodiles, kangaroos, snakes, dingoes, the rare Lumholtz's tree kangaroo, and lots of Australian birds in the walk-through aviary. A local Aboriginal gives cultural talks. Call for the daily program of talks, free guided tours, and summer-time croc-feeding demonstrations. You might bring a picnic, because the grounds are lovely.

ACCOMMODATIONS

The late fashion designer Gianni Versace designed the 205 hotel rooms and 72 two- and three-bedroom condos at the opulent **Palazzo Versace,** Sea World Drive, The Spit, Main Beach (☎ **07/5509 8000** for the pre-opening office; www. palazzoversace.com.au), which should be open by the time you read this. Rates go from A$660 (U.S.$429) double way up to A$3,960 (U.S.$2,574).

Your best motel choice is the big clean rooms at the **Pink Poodle,** 2903 Gold Coast Hwy. (at Fern St.), Surfers Paradise, QLD 4217 (☎ **13 17 79** in Australia, or 07/5539 9211; www.bestwestern.com.au). This Best Western property is a minute's hop to the beach and a 1.2-kilometer ($3/4$-mile) walk to downtown Surfers. Rates are A$77 to $99 (U.S.$50.05 to $64.35) double, plus an A$30 (U.S.$19.50) surcharge from mid-December to mid-January.

IN SANCTUARY COVE

Hyatt Regency Sanctuary Cove. Casey Rd., Hope Island 20km (12$1/2$ miles) north of Surfers Paradise (P.O. Box 200, Sanctuary Cove, QLD 4212). ☎ **13 12 34** in Australia, 800/633-7313 in the U.S. and Canada, 0845/758 1666 in the U.K., 0800/44 1234 in New Zealand, or 07/5530 1234. Fax 07/5577 6161. www.sanctuarycove.com and www. hyatt.com. E-mail: sanctuary@hyatt.com.au. 247 units. A/C MINIBAR TV TEL. A$207–$338 (U.S.$134.55–$219.70) double; A$202.80–$1,300 (U.S.$131.80–$845) suite. Extra person A$38 (U.S.$24.70). Children under 13 stay free in parents' room. Ask about golf, tennis, massage, theme-park, and other packages. AE, BC, DC, JCB, MC, V. Free valet and self-parking. Bus: 10 (to adjacent Marine Village). Coachtrans shuttle from Brisbane or Gold Coast airports. Helicopter transfers available from both airports. Take the Pacific Hwy. north, exit left on the Oxenford-Mt. Tamborine turnoff, and follow the signs to Sanctuary Cove.

When Queensland real-estate developer Mike Gore announced plans to build a 1,000-plus–acre resort, complete with four man-made harbors, on the marshy backwater of Hope Island on the northern outskirts of the Gold Coast, locals snorted with derision. But when this vision of loveliness arose from the swamp, they dropped the insults, reached for their golf clubs, and checked in. The resort is nowhere near the beach, so guests swim in a Shangri-La of pools dressed with urns and fountains and a 1-acre saltwater pool with a sand "beach." The resort has two championship golf courses: The Palms (open to the public) and the Arnold Palmer–designed The Pines (resort guests only), rated as one of the country's toughest.

One of the five low-rise accommodation wings is the Regency Club, whose guests receive complimentary continental breakfast and evening drinks. All of the spacious rooms have an elegant Queenslander decor, with parquet floors, timber sleigh beds, walk-in wardrobes, and plantation shutters, as well as Internet via the TV, modem outlets, hair dryers, and irons. Adjacent is the upscale Marine Village with 85 shops and restaurants and a cinema.

Dining/Diversions: Wood-fired cuisine is served in The Fireplace nightly, the Cove Cafe is open all day, the pool bar serves snacks, and there is a cocktail bar.

Amenities: Two 18-hole championship golf courses, floodlit driving range, golf swing analysis studio, golf coaching, pro shop; extensive fitness center with nine day/night tennis courts, 25-meter (82-ft.) lap pool with time clock, personal trainers, gym, aerobics and yoga classes, solarium, sauna, Jacuzzi, and a range of massage, health, and beauty practitioners; 330 marina berths; sailing and fishing-boat charter; kids' club for 4- to 12-year-olds (for a fee, usually only on weekends and school vacations); baby-sitting; tour/car-rental desk and travel agency; currency exchange; hairdresser; shops; drugstore; complimentary newspaper; 24-hour room service; laundry/dry-cleaning; express checkout; business and conference center.

IN & NEAR SURFERS PARADISE

Courtyard Surfers Paradise Resort. Gold Coast Hwy. at Hanlan St., Surfers Paradise (P.O. Box 1342, Surfers Paradise, QLD 4217). ☎ **1800/25 1259** in Australia or 02/9251 5522 in Sydney, 800/321-2211 in the U.S. and Canada, 0800/22 1222 in the U.K., 0800/44 1035 in New Zealand, or 07/5579 3499. Fax 07/5592 0026. E-mail via the Web site only. www.courtyard.com. 405 units. A/C MINIBAR TV TEL. A$240–$260 (U.S.$156–$169) double; A$275–$310 (U.S.$178.75–$201.50) suite; A$2,200 (U.S.$1,430) penthouse. Extra person A$35 (U.S.$22.75). Children under 17 stay free in parents' room using existing bedding. Free crib. AE, BC, DC, JCB, MC, V. Free parking. Bus: 1, 1A.

Just a block from the beach, this 36-story Marriott has ocean, city, or green hinterland views from every room. The rooms were renovated in 1999 to be simple but smart; all have balconies and hair dryers. Spa suites have Jacuzzis, and the three-story penthouse has a Jacuzzi outside on the terrace. Shops, restaurants, and the tourism bureau's information outlet are just around the corner on Cavill Mall.

Dining/Diversions: Rez 252 serves modern cuisine all day and night, and the Verandah Bar serves cocktails. There's also a bar by the pool in summer.

Amenities: Swimming pool and sundeck, Jacuzzi, sauna, gym, tennis court, game room, pay-per-view movies, room service, complimentary newspapers in lobby, concierge, tour/car-rental desk, safes, currency exchange, laundry and dry-cleaning service, Laundromat, babysitting, secretarial services, express checkout, conference facilities.

Mercure Resort Surfers Paradise. 122 Ferny Ave., Surfers Paradise, QLD 4217. ☎ **1800/ 07 4111** in Australia, 800/221-4542 in the U.S. and Canada, 0181/283 4500 in the U.K., 0800/44 4422 in New Zealand, or 07/5579 4444. Fax 07/5579 4492. www. mercuresurfers.com.au. Email: mrsp@ozemail.com.au. 405 units. A/C MINIBAR TV TEL. A$191 (U.S.$124.15) double; A$230 (U.S.$149.50) family room. Extra person A$22 (U.S.$14.30). Children under 16 stay free in parents' room using existing bedding. Free crib. Meal pass A$20 (U.S.$13) for 3 daily meals for children under 16. Ask about packages. AE, BC, DC, JCB, MC, V. Free parking. Bus: 1A. Twice-daily shuttle to beach and shopping center A$7 (U.S.$4.55) per family, round-trip.

The Secret of the Seasons

High season on the Gold Coast is Aussie school vacations—from December 26 to mid- or late January, and for 2-week blocks around Easter, late June to mid-July, and late September to early October. Accommodations are booked months in advance, and apartments will be rented only by the week. Most places demand a 4-day minimum stay at Easter and during the Honda Indy 300 motorsport carnival in mid-October.

Outside school holidays, rates can plummet, so ask about discounts and packages then.

If your idea of a holiday is lazing around a leafy complex of heated pools while someone else minds your kids, this place is for you. Child-care professionals look after toddlers aged 6 weeks to 4 years, 365 days a year, for A$20 (U.S.$13) per 4-hour session, while kids 5 to 12 hit the minicars, underwater playground, and other themed areas in the free, supervised Gecko Fun Club. The low-rise rooms are not grand but are comfortable, with pool or garden views, in-room movies, and hair dryers. Some have kitchenettes. Features like a daily activity program (one for kids, one for you), two restaurants and a bar, room service, a gym, a sauna, Jacuzzis, tennis courts, bikes for rent, a basketball court, a playground, a tour/car-rental desk, and A$12 (U.S.$7.80) round-trip transfers to the theme parks make this hotel a good value. A patrolled beach is a few blocks across the highway (which some rooms are close to, incidentally, so ask for a quiet room). Strollers, bottle sterilizers, Sony PlayStations, and even baby monitors you can listen to by the pool can be rented, and the store sells diapers and baby food at supermarket prices.

Good-Value Vacation Apartments

Apartment developers snagged the best beachfront spots when the Gold Coast boomed in the 1970s, so apartment blocks, not hotels, have the best ocean views. As a rule, only the priciest apartments are air-conditioned or have housekeeping service. Most demand a 1-week minimum stay in high season. The two complexes below are particularly good values.

✪ **Bahia Beachfront.** 154 The Esplanade, Surfers Paradise, QLD 4217. ☎ **07/5538 3322.** Fax 07/5592 0318. www.bahia.com.au. E-mail: info@bahia.com.au. 39 units. TV TEL. High season A$127 (U.S.$82.55) 1-bedroom apt., A$172 (U.S.$111.80) 2-bedroom apt for 4 people, A$245 (U.S.$159.25) 3-bedroom apt for 6 people. Low season A$98 (U.S.$63.70) 1-bedroom apt., A$135 (U.S.$87.75) 2-bedroom apt. for 4 people, A$245 (U.S.$159.25) 3-bedroom apt to sleep 6 people. Extra person A$15 (U.S.$9.75). Weekly rates available. AE, BC, DC, JCB, MC, V. Free parking. Bus: 1, 1A.

You get champagne ocean views at a six-pack price at this 13-story complex 800 meters (¹/₂ mile) north of town. Every unit is simply but neatly furnished with a large living room, a modern kitchen, a compact bathroom/laundry, ceiling fans, and a balcony. Many at the front have a mirrored rear wall to reflect the ocean. Only those in the southwest corner or on the first two floors miss out on sea views. All are serviced daily; the front desk has hair dryers. The complex has a tour/car-rental desk, bikes for rent, a kids' pool, a sauna, a Jacuzzi, two tennis courts, a game room, and a barbecue. There's a heated pool, but you will likely make a beeline for the patrolled beach across the road.

Trickett Gardens Holiday Inn. 24–30 Trickett St., Surfers Paradise, QLD 4217. ☎ **1800/ 074 290** in Australia, or 07/5539 0988. Fax 07/5592 0791. www.about-australia.com/ trickett. E-mail: bobmille@fan.net.au. 33 units (all with shower only). A/C TV TEL. High season (Dec 26–mid-Jan) A$132 (U.S.$85.80) 1-bedroom apt., A$160 (U.S.$104) 2-bedroom apt.

Low season A$100 (U.S.$65) 1-bedroom apt., A$108 (U.S.$70.20) 2-bedroom apt. Extra person A$20 (U.S.$13). A$6 (U.S.$3.90) for children under 3 with extra bedding. AE, BC, DC, JCB, MC, V. Free parking. Bus: 1, 1A.

This well-maintained three-story block (not a member of the Holiday Inn chain) 100 meters (a few hundred feet) from the beach and 2 blocks from Cavill Mall is hard to beat for location, price, and comfort. The painted-brick units have modest but neat furnishings, balconies, spacious light living areas, safes, and hair dryers, and are serviced daily. The kitchens and small combined bathrooms/laundries were refurbished in 1999. Out front are a heated pool, Jacuzzi and barbecue. Proprietors Bob and Hilary Miller greet you with a swag of tour brochures, carry your bags, and deliver a daily newspaper. No smoking inside.

DINING

Locals like the trendy restaurant strips in Broadbeach (head to the corner of Surf Parade and Victoria Avenue) and Main Beach (head to Tedder Avenue). Marina Mirage on Sea World Drive at Main Beach has a few upscale eating places with Broadwater views.

Billy T. Bones on the Beachfront Café Bar Grill. Under the Iluka Beach Resort Hotel, The Esplanade at Hanlan St., Surfers Paradise. ☎ **07/5526 7913.** Main courses A$6.90–$17.95 (U.S.$4.50–$11.65); breakfast A$2.50–$9.95 (U.S.$1.65–$6.45). AE, BC, DC, JCB, MC, V. Mon–Fri 11am–10pm, Sat–Sun 6:30am–10pm. Bus: 1, 1A. STEAK/PASTA/SEAFOOD.

For a good meal at bearable prices and a view of the sea, this casual, open-sided spot fits the bill. The long list of lunch and dinner options includes pastas, stir-fry noodles, seafood platters, and big steaks served with an Idaho potato, sour cream, bacon, coleslaw, and mushroom, pepper, or chili sauce. On weekends, look for pancakes and maple syrup with eggs and lean bacon—the last item is hard to find in Australia, my English husband tells me.

Eazy Peazy Thai & Japanezy. Tedder Ave. at Peak Ave., Main Beach. ☎ **07/5591 9000.** Reservations recommended Fri–Sat dinner. Main courses A$9.90–$19.90 (U.S.$6.45–$12.95). AE, BC, DC, MC, V. Tues–Sun noon–3pm; daily 6–10pm. Bus: 2, 9. THAI/JAPANESE.

Have a quick feed at the noodle bar or make a relaxed night of it at this alfresco joint on the corner of happening Tedder Avenue. Everything on the lengthy menu is freshly prepared, from the sushi to the Thai chili beef salad to the marinated fried chicken on light Japanese veggies. Licensed and BYO.

The proprietors also operate an Indian restaurant, **Get It India,** at 14–16 Tedder Ave. (☎ **07/5527 0027**), open daily 10:30am to 10:30pm and offering affordable dishes.

La Porchetta. In the Mark Centre, 3 Orchid Ave. (just off Cavill Mall), Surfers Paradise. ☎ **07/5527 5273.** Reservations recommended. Main courses A$4.40–$13.50 (U.S.$2.85–$8.75). AE, BC, DC, MC, V. Daily 10am–midnight. Bus: 1, 1A. PIZZA/ITALIAN.

Pizza for A$4.40 (U.S.$2.85)? That must be for a slice, we thought. But nope, around six bucks at this bustling alfresco joint buys you the whole shebang, a "small" pizza—about 25 centimeters (10 in.) across—with olives, anchovies, tomato, cheese, and oregano. Two of us pigged out on a medium, easily big enough for three, which had a tasty, crispy crust topped with good-quality Italian sausage and basil. Traditional pastas, steaks, chicken, and seafood dishes all come with salad or vegetables and fries. Be prepared to wait for a table. They do takeout too.

RPR's. On the 21st floor, Royal Pines Resort, Ross St., Ashmore. ☎ **07/5597 1111.** Reservations recommended. No shorts after 6pm. All main courses A$29.50 (U.S.$19.20); Sunset Dining special A$45 (U.S.$29.25) per person for 2 courses and glass of champagne if you are seated by 5:30pm and leave before 7pm. AE, BC, DC, JCB, MC, V. Mon–Sat 5:30–9:30pm. MODERN AUSTRALIAN.

Some of the slickest dishes on the Gold Coast get turned out in this aerie with views of the distant city skyline from every table. Meat dishes such as sage roast chicken breast with truffle mash sit alongside a wide range of fish dishes, including panfried schnapper on sweet-potato gratin with a preserved lemon aioli and sorrel beurre blanc. The quiet cocktail bar has restful hinterland views.

9 The Gold Coast Hinterland: Back to Nature

What a difference half an hour behind the wheel makes! Thirty minutes ago, you were sweating on the beach, but up here in the mountain ranges just inland of the Gold Coast, at an altitude of 500 to 1,000 meters (approximately 1,500 to 3,500 ft.), tree-ferns drip moisture, the air is cool, and the architecture is all cottage charm, not skyscraper brash. Welcome to the rain-forest hills of the Gold Coast hinterland—the "green behind the gold," as the region's tourism spin doctors like to put it.

Two main spots attract the bulk of visitors: Mt. Tamborine and Lamington National Park. **Mt. Tamborine** is all about little conglomerations of oh-so-cute craft shops, tea houses, and lofty mountain roads and hiking trails twisting among ferns and farmland. The mountain views are lovely.

Even more impressive is the 20,500-hectare (50,635-acre) World Heritage–listed ✪ **Lamington National Park,** farther away than Mt. Tamborine, about 90 minutes from the Gold Coast and $2^{1}/_{2}$ hours from Brisbane. Australia's largest reach of subtropical rain forest, mossy 2,000-year-old Antarctic beech trees, giant strangler figs, and misty mountain air characterize Lamington's high narrow ridges and plunging valleys. The winding mountain drives to either of the park's two rather-special ridge-top retreats are so lovely that they're an attraction in themselves. It's possible to visit Lamington as a day trip from either the Gold Coast or Brisbane. However, once you're ensconced up in the forest, you will wish you'd stayed longer, so consider a stay of at least a couple of nights.

MT. TAMBORINE
43km (27 miles) NW of Surfers Paradise; 59km (37 miles) S of Brisbane

More a plateau than a peak, Mt. Tamborine shelters a string of villages just a mile or two apart—**Eagle Heights, North Tamborine,** and **Mt. Tamborine**—which together are what folks usually mean when they say they're off to Mt. Tamborine for the day. Note: Many shops and cafes are open only Thursday, Friday, and weekends.

ESSENTIALS

GETTING THERE   From the Gold Coast, take the Pacific Highway north to the Mt. Tamborine turnoff at Oxenford; it's the first exit after Warner Bros. Movie World. Eagle Heights is the first village you come to, 21 kilometers (13 miles) from the turnoff. From Brisbane, take the Pacific Highway south 36 kilometers (23 miles) to the Mt. Tamborine exit at Beenleigh, then follow the road 23 kilometers (14 miles) to the first village, Tamborine. A number of tour operators run minibus and 4WD day trips from the Gold Coast and Brisbane.

VISITOR INFORMATION   Head to the **Gold Coast Tourism Bureau** kiosk, on Cavill Avenue in Surfers Paradise (☎ **07/5538 4419**), to stock up on information and maps before you head out. Brisbane Tourism outlets (see "Visitor Information," in chapter 5) also have a little information. The **Tamborine Mountain Information Centre** (☎ **07/5545 3200**) is in Dougherty Park, where Geissmann Drive becomes Main Western Road, in North Tamborine; it's open daily from 10:30am to 3:30pm.

EXPLORING THE MOUNTAIN

New Age candles, homemade soaps, maple pecan fudge, framed tropical watercolors, and German cuckoo clocks are some of the stuff you can buy up here. The best place to shop is the strip of galleries, cafes, and shops known as **Gallery Walk** on Long Road, between North Tamborine and Eagle Heights. Eagle Heights has few shops but great coastal views. North Tamborine is mainly a commercial center. Mt. Tamborine itself is mainly residential.

Queensland is not exactly the wine capital of the universe, but up here in the cool air, the state's biggest winery, the boutique **Mount Tamborine Winery,** 32 Hartley Rd. (☎ **07/5545 3981**), northwest of North Tamborine off the Main Western Road, turns out an agreeable drop. The cellar door is open for free tastings from 10am to 4pm daily.

No fewer than nine small national parks dot the mountain. The Mt. Tamborine Information Centre can give you a map marking the parks' walking trails that wind from the streets through palm groves, rain forest, and eucalyptus woodland. Most are reasonably short.

A RAIN-FOREST B&B

✪ **Tamborine Mountain Bed & Breakfast.** 19–23 Witherby Crescent, Eagle Heights, QLD 4721. ☎ **07/5545 3595.** Fax 07/5545 3322. www.babs.com.au/qld/tamborine.htm. E-mail: elfin@onthenet.com.au. 4 units (all with shower only). A/C TV. Sun–Fri A$115 (U.S.$74.75) double, Sat A$135 (U.S.$87.75) double. Rates decrease with longer stay. Weekend package Sat–Sun A$235 (U.S.$152.75) double *for 2 nights.* Extra person A$30–$40 (U.S.$18.75–$26). Rates include full breakfast. BC, MC, V. Children and teenagers not permitted.

Proprietor Elizabeth Finnemore's restful timber home, huddled in rain forest, boasts stunning views to the Gold Coast skyline from the breakfast balcony. It's a delight to laze on the lovely veranda, where rainbow lorikeets, kookaburras, and crimson rosellas demand to be hand-fed. The day I visited, a 6-foot goanna had been sunning itself out there all morning. In winter, you can warm up by the fire in the timber-lined living room. Each of the four purpose-built rooms in the ferny gardens features rustic cypress logs on the outside, and charming Edwardian cottage-style interiors, with individual touches like a four-poster bed or mosquito nets. Appealing heritage tiles and dressers furnish the lovely bathrooms, which sport rainwater showers. Your hosts lend hair dryers. Gallery Walk shopping is a stroll away. No smoking indoors.

LAMINGTON NATIONAL PARK

45–78km (28–49 miles) W of Gold Coast; 77–104km (48–65 miles) S of Brisbane

Lamington is one of the best national parks in Australia for ✪ **hiking.** Blanketing the Macpherson Ranges, the park is crisscrossed with 160 kilometers (100 miles) of well-marked, mostly gentle trails through eucalypt forest and tangled rain forest, past waterfalls, over ferny mountain streams, and along ridges with soaring views across green valleys. They vary in difficulty and length, from 1-kilometer (half-mile) strolls to the 21-kilometer (13-mile) Border Trail that follows the New South Wales–Queensland border for much of the way (fit folks can do it in a day).

One of the park's most magnificent features is **Antarctic beech trees.** Straight from central casting for a medieval fairy-tale movie, these mossy monarchs stand 20 meters (66 ft.) tall and up to 8 meters (26 ft.) around the base. The species is a survivor of a time 55 million years ago, when Australia and Antarctica belonged to the rain-forested supercontinent Gondwana. The trees you see here are about 2,000 years old, suckering off root systems about 8,000 years old. The most picturesque stand is a gnarled old group among lichen-covered granite boulders on the 5-kilometer (3-mile) round-trip Tullawallal walk from Binnaburra Mountain Lodge (see below). The nearest from O'Reilly's Rainforest Guesthouse (see below) are about 45 minutes along the Elabana Falls trail, but they're not as magical a sight.

You should easily spot rosellas of red and blue, stunning black-and-gold Regent bowerbirds, whipbirds (you won't see 'em but their whipcrack call is instantly recognizable), and maybe even a rare lyrebird. That's not the only wildlife you will see. Small wallabies, called pademelons, might graze outside your room. In summer you may spot a giant carpet python curled up in a tree, or goannas. Near streams you may get bailed up by a hissing Lamington spiny crayfish, an aggressive little monster 6 inches long, patterned royal blue and white like a Wedgwood plate. At night, the park comes alive with owls, possums, sugar-gliders, and howling dingoes.

The way to explore is to base yourself at O'Reilly's Rainforest Guesthouse, or at Binnaburra Mountain Lodge (see below). Most of the trails lead from one or the other of these resorts. Guided walks and activities at either resort are for houseguests only; however, both properties welcome day visitors who just want to walk the trails free. Which one you visit is up to you: the drive to Binnaburra is shorter and less treacherously winding, it has prettier views, and the best Antarctic beeches are accessed from it. O'Reilly's has a treetop rope-bridge walk, and bird feeding (sometimes early in the morning; call to check the day's times). Both have cafes, basic picnic supplies, and takeout, and Binnaburra opens its cliffside restaurant to day-trippers (book a table ahead).

It is often 4°C to 5°C (7.2°F to 9°F) cooler here than down on the coast, so bring a sweater, even in summer. In winter, nights get close to freezing.

ESSENTIALS

GETTING THERE   By Car   Roads to both retreats are paved all the way. **O'Reilly's** is 78 kilometers (49 miles) southwest of Surfers Paradise. From Southport just north of Surfers Paradise, head to Nerang on the Nerang–Southport Road for 10 kilometers (6 miles), then head 31 kilometers (19 miles) inland to Canungra. From Canungra, the 37-kilometer (23-mile) road to O'Reilly's climbs steeply and makes a lot of hairpin bends, so take extreme care. Allow an hour for the drive from Canungra, and plan to arrive before dark. From Brisbane, take the Pacific Highway south 36 kilometers (23 miles) to Beenleigh, then the Mt. Tamborine exit for 23 kilometers (14 miles) to Tamborine, then head south 18 kilometers (11 miles) to Canungra.

Binnaburra is 45 kilometers (28 miles) southwest of Surfers Paradise. Head inland to Nerang (see above for directions); the lodge is a further 35 kilometers (22 miles) via the tiny town of Beechmont. The last 10 kilometers (6 miles) are on a winding mountain road. From Brisbane, take the Pacific Highway south for 69 kilometers (43 miles) to Nerang, then follow the directions above.

Allow up to 2¹/₂ hours to reach either resort from Brisbane. From the Gold Coast allow a good 1¹/₂ hours to reach O'Reilly's and an hour to reach Binnaburra. Binnaburra sells unleaded fuel; O'Reilly's has emergency supplies only.

By Coach   Several coach and 4WD tour companies run day trips from the Gold Coast and Brisbane, but I don't recommend these tours—you spend too much time traveling, and not enough time hiking and enjoying the park before you turn around and head back to your hotel.

Binnaburra Mountain Lodge runs a daily shuttle that departs the Surfers Paradise Transit Centre on Beach Road at 1:15pm, Nerang train station on the Brisbane line at 1:30pm, or Coolangatta Airport at 2pm. The fare is A$22 (U.S.$14.30) adults, half price for kids 5 to 16. Book 24 hours ahead.

VISITOR INFORMATION　There is a national-park information office at both **O'Reilly's Rainforest Guesthouse** and **Binnaburra Mountain Lodge** (see below). The **ranger at Lamington National Park,** Green Mountains section (which is at O'Reilly's), Private Mail Bag 4, via Canungra, QLD 4220 (☎ **07/5544 0634**), can send you a visitor information sheet, an application form for bush camping, and a hiking trail map. A good Web site is **www.lamington.nrsm.uq.edu.au**; the park's official site is accessed via **www.env.qld.gov.au**.

ACCOMMODATIONS & DINING

The rates at these two mountaintop retreats include all meals and activities. O'Reilly's also has rates without meals, but you end up paying the same with the meal plan, and even more if you buy all three meals separately at the restaurant. Both places are old and have developed in a higgledy-piggledy fashion over the years, so don't expect whizbang facilities. There is little to choose between them. Binnaburra's lounge and dining room are more atmospheric; the family-owned O'Reilly's is a little homier and more personal, and it has a lovely bar, a rope-bridge treetops walk, 4WD trips, and bird-feeding sessions. Both have ample walking trails of a similar type and distance, daily guided bushwalks, and good food. Their kitchens pack picnic backpacks for all-day hikers. Look into the program of special-interest workshops both properties run throughout the year, focusing on anything from frog watching to gourmet cooking.

✪ **Binnaburra Mountain Lodge.** Beechmont, Lamington National Park, QLD 4211. ☎ **1800/074 260** in Australia, or 07/5533 3622. Fax 07/5533 3658. www.binnaburralodge. com.au. E-mail: info@binnaburralodge.com.au. 40 cabins, 25 with private bathroom (shower only). A$297–$363 (U.S.$193.05–$235.95) double. Extra adult A$135–$165 (U.S.$87.75–$107.25); extra child 5–16 A$49.50 (U.S.$32.20). *Rates include all meals and activities.* Rates decrease with every night you stay. Minimum 2-night stay on weekends, 3-night stay on public holidays, 4-night stay at Easter. AE, BC, DC, JCB, MC, V.

Perched on a hillside with lofty valley views, some of Binnaburra's slab timber cabins built in 1935 are still in use today. They are outfitted with modern comforts, but not 20th-century "inconveniences" such as telephones, radios, or clocks. Guided half- or full-day walks run daily, and abseiling for beginners and advanced folk takes place at least twice a week. Of the 21 trails leading from the lodge, 9 are less than 6 kilometers (3³/₄ miles). Once a week, the resort buses hikers to O'Reilly's so they can spend the day walking back to Binnaburra. Nightly fun might consist of an occasional bush dance or campfire dinner, or more often a wildlife-spotlighting walk or natural-history slide show. There is a nature activities program for kids during school holidays and a neat environmental playground.

While none of the accommodations is grand or large, all are nice enough, with timber walls, neat bedcovers, and heaters and electric blankets. The mud-brick and weatherboard Acacia cabins have the most charm and space and the best valley views. They have private bathrooms. The small Casuarina cabins share clean communal bathrooms, which even include a Jacuzzi. Good for families are the bunkrooms that sleep up to six. The front desk will loan hair dryers. Meals are served at communal tables in the lovely stone-and-timber dining room, which has breathtaking valley views. There are a welcoming lounge with a fire, a bar and observation deck, a craft shop, a natural-history library, a Ping-Pong table, small conference rooms, and a public telephone. Baby-sitting can be arranged.

✪ **O'Reilly's Rainforest Guesthouse.** Via Canungra, Lamington National Park Rd., Lamington National Park, QLD 4275. ☎ **1800/688 722** in Australia, or 07/5544 0644. Fax 07/5544 0638. www.oreillys.com.au. E-mail: reservations@oreillys.com.au. 72 units, 66 with private bathroom (most with shower only). A$304.55–A$401.75 (U.S.$198–$261.15) double, A$509.76 (U.S.$331.35) suite. Extra person A$21.60 (U.S.$14.05). Children under 18 stay free in parents' room using existing bedding; child meal plan A$32.40 (U.S.$21.10) children 10–17, A$16.20 (U.S.$10.55) children 4–9 (or available on a per-meal basis). Free crib. *Rates above include all meals and activities.* Ask about rates without meals (separate meals and meal plans available). Rates decrease with every night you stay. Minimum 2-night stay on most weekends, 3-night stay on long weekends, 4-night stay Easter and Christmas. AE, BC, DC, MC, V.

Snuggled high on a ridge, closed in on three sides by rain forest with views to mountains to the west, this cozy retreat began life in 1926 as the O'Reilly family's dairy farm. It's still run by the family today. A highlight of your stay may be hand-feeding brilliantly colored rain-forest birds each day. Another lovely feature is the rope-suspension walk through the forest canopy, 30 meters (about 100 ft.) aboveground at its highest point. Every day the staff runs guided half- and full-day walks and half-day 4WD bus trips. Every night there is a slideshow, a nature-spotlighting walk, or sometimes a dance or campfire. Of the 19 trails that fan out from the parking lot, one of the nicest is the 7.6-kilometer (5-mile) round-trip walk to Elabana Falls, which takes half a day. On weekends and school holidays a free "Scrub Club" runs for kids over 5.

The resort complex is inviting rather than grand. Most of the rooms are of modestly furnished concrete-block construction, not all that atmospheric but pleasant enough. Each has a small fridge (except for the Tooloona rooms), a heater, and electric blankets. The front desk lends hair dryers. The Tooloona rooms date from the 1930s and are just a small room with a bed and not much else. They share bathrooms. The Elabana rooms, refurbished in 1998 and 1999, are a homey motel-style room. The Bithongabel rooms deliver the most space and atmosphere (the double ones, that is; those for solo travelers are very narrow) and have balconies with lovely sunset views. Some were new-built in 2000 in a stylish enviro-chic style, and eight are air-conditioned. The best digs in Lamington are the three new suites added in 2000, sporting a King-size four-poster and fireplace in the separate bedroom, range views from the Jacuzzi, and balconies looking into the rain forest and ranges. The maître d' assigns you to a communal table in the dining room, where you meet other guests over remarkably good food. The convivial timber bar perched high in a hexagonal aerie is really atmospheric. Among the services and facilities are a cafe and gift shop, a game room, a natural-history library, a public telephone, and baby-sitting.

7

The Red Centre

by Natalie Kruger

The Red Centre is the landscape many of us conjure up when we think of the Outback—vast horizons, fiery red sand as far as the eye can see, mysterious monoliths, cloudless blue sky, harsh sunlight, and the rhythmic twang of the didgeridoo. It's home to sprawling cattle ranches; ancient low mountain ranges; "living fossil" palm trees that survived the Ice Age; cockatoos and kangaroos; red gorges; the Finke River, thought to be the world's first watercourse; pretty water holes; and, of course, Ayers Rock, which the Aborigines call Uluru. Aboriginal people have lived here for tens of thousands of years, long before the Pyramids were a twinkle in a Pharaoh's eye, but the Centre is still largely unexplored by non-Aboriginal Australians. A single highway cuts through it from Adelaide in the south to Darwin in the north, and a few paved roads and 4WD tracks make a lonely spider web across it; but there are many, many areas where non-Aborigines have never set foot.

Alice Springs is the only big town in Central Australia. Let's get one thing straight—Alice Springs and Uluru are not side by side. Never a day goes by when a tourist does not wander into the Alice Springs visitor center after lunch, and says he or she wants to "go see the Rock this afternoon." The Rock is 462 kilometers (289 miles) away. You can see it in a day from Alice, but it takes a big effort.

The Red Centre is more than just a Rock, though. Give yourself a few days to experience all there is to see and do out here—such as visiting the impressive Olgas near Ayers Rock, walking the rim of Kings Canyon, riding a camel down a dry riverbed, poking around Aboriginal rock carvings, swimming in gorge water holes, or staying at an Outback homestead where you can ride horses or learn to throw a boomerang. Many friends and colleagues share my opinion that a stay in Alice Springs gives you an even better flavor for the Outback than Ayers Rock. Go to Ayers Rock, but also allow time for Alice. It can be hard to shed the tourist hordes at Ayers Rock, but if you base yourself in Alice, it's easy to radiate out to less populated but still beautiful attractions like Palm Valley, Ormiston Gorge, and Trephina Gorge Nature Park, each easily handled on a day trip. Too many international visitors (and Australians too) fly in, snap a photo of the Rock, and head home, only to miss the real essence of the desert.

EXPLORING THE RED CENTRE
VISITOR INFORMATION The **Central Australian Tourism Industry Association** (see "Visitor Information" under "Alice

The Red Centre

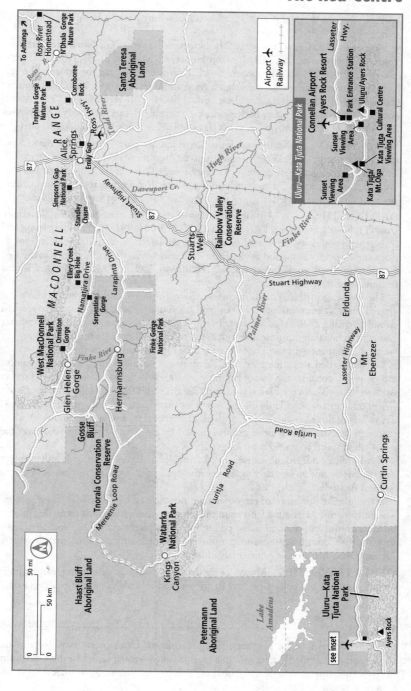

Airport ✈
Railway +–+–+

To Arltunga ↗
Ross River Homestead
N'Dhala Gorge Nature Park
Ross R.
Trephina Gorge Nature Park
Corroboree Rock
Santa Teresa Aboriginal Land
RANGE
Todd River
Ross Hwy.
Alice Springs
Emily Gap
87
Simpson's Gap National Park
Standley Chasm
MACDONNELL
Ellery Creek Big Hole
Namatjira Drive
Serpentine Gorge
Stuart Highway
Davenport Cr.
Hugh River
West MacDonnell National Park
Ormiston Gorge
Finke River
Glen Helen Gorge
Finke Gorge National Park
Larapinta Drive
Hermannsburg
Rainbow Valley Conservation Reserve
Stuarts Well
Finke River
Palmer River
Stuart Highway
Erldunda
87
Gosse Bluff
Tnorala Conservation Reserve
Mereenie Loop Road
Lasseter Highway
Mt. Ebenezer
Luritja Road
Haast Bluff Aboriginal Land
Watarrka National Park
Luritja Road
Curtin Springs
Kings Canyon
50 mi
50 km
0
0
Petermann Aboriginal Land
Lake Amadeus
Uluru–Kata Tjuta National Park
see inset ✈
Ayers Rock

Inset:
Uluru–Kata Tjuta National Park
Lasseter Hwy.
Ayers Rock Resort
Park Entrance Station
Uluru/Ayers Rock
Connellan Airport ✈
Sunset Viewing Area
Kata Tjuta Cultural Centre
Kata Tjuta Viewing Area
Sunset Viewing Area
Kata Tjuta/Mt. Olga

Springs," later in this chapter) can send you a brochure pack. It is your best one-stop source of information.

Most of the Red Centre lies within the Northern Territory. The **Northern Territory Tourist Commission (NTTC),** Tourism House, 43 Mitchell St., Darwin, NT 0800 (☎ **08/8999 3900;** www.nttc.com.au—click on the "U.S." tab for information tailored to American travelers), publishes a good annual guide to Central Australia that details hotels, tour operators, rental-car companies, and attractions. The Commission operates a division that offers package deals on complete trips: **Territory Discoveries** (☎ **1800/621 336** in Australia, or ☎/fax 08/8981 4300; www.ntholidays.com).

WHEN TO GO April/May and September/October have warm sunny days (coolish in May, hot in Oct). Winter (that's June to Aug) means cold days, a sharp wind, and nights as cold as freezing point. Summer (Nov to Mar) is ferociously hot and best avoided. Limit exertions to early morning and late afternoon in summer, and choose air-conditioned accommodations. Rain is rare but can come at any time of year.

DRIVING TIPS The **Automobile Association of the Northern Territory (AANT),** 79–81 Smith St., Darwin, NT 0800 (☎ **08/8981 3837**), offers reciprocal emergency breakdown service to members of affiliated overseas automobile associations and dispenses maps and advice from its Darwin office. It has no office in the Red Centre. For **road conditions,** call ☎ **1800/246 199** in Australia for a 24-hour recorded report.

The few sealed (paved) roads in the Northern Territory are the highways and a few arterial roads. A conventional 2WD car will get you to 95% of all you want to see, but consider renting a 4WD for complete freedom. All the big car-rental chains rent them. Some attractions are on unsealed (unpaved) roads good enough for a 2WD car, but your car-rental company will not insure a 2WD for driving on them.

Outside settled areas, the Northern Territory has no speed limit, but *before* you hit the gas pedal, consider the risk of hitting wild camels, kangaroos, and protected native wildlife. This risk is very high. Locals stick to a comfortable 120 kilometers-per-hour (75 m.p.h.) or less. Cattle lie on the warm bitumen at night, and 'roos feed at dusk, dawn, and night; so avoid driving at night, early morning, and late afternoon. A white road sign bearing a black circle outline crossed by a diagonal black line indicates the point when speed restrictions no longer apply.

Road trains and fatigue caused by driving long distances are two other major threats. For details on safe driving, review the tips in the "By Car" section of "Getting Around Australia," in chapter 2.

If you plan to "go bush" in remote regions not covered by this guide, you may need a permit to cross Aboriginal land from the relevant Aboriginal lands council. This can be a drawn-out bureaucratic affair taking weeks, so plan ahead. The Northern Territory Tourist Commission (above) can put you in touch with the appropriate council. All good road maps mark Aboriginal lands clearly.

OTHER TRAVEL TIPS **Always carry drinking water.** When hiking, carry 4 liters (about a gallon) per person per day in winter, and a liter (¼ gallon) per person *per*

Buzz Off!

Uluru is notorious for plagues of flies in summer. Don't be embarrassed to cover your head with the fly-nets sold in souvenir stores—you'll look like the Dreamtime Beekeeper from Outer Space, but there will be "no flies on you, mate," an Aussie way of saying you are doing the right thing.

hour in summer. Wear a broad-brimmed hat, high-factor sunscreen lotion, and insect repellent.

Bring warm clothing for chilly evenings in winter.

TOUR OPERATORS   No end of coach, minicoach, and 4WD tour operators offer itineraries taking in some or all the highlights of the region. They depart either Alice Springs or Ayers Rock, offering accommodations ranging from spiffy resorts, comfortable motels, and basic cabins to shared bunkhouses, tents, or swags (sleeping bags) under the stars. Most pack a lot into a 2- or 3-day trip, though you can find more leisurely trips that run 6 days or more. A one-way itinerary between Alice and the Rock (often via Kings Canyon), or vice versa, allows you to avoid backtracking.

Contact **AAT Kings** (☎ **03/9274 7422** is the Melbourne central reservations office; www.aatkings.com.au), which specializes in mainstream coach tours but also has 4WD camping itineraries; **Alice Springs Holidays** (☎ **08/8953 1411;** www. alicespringsholidays.com.au), which does upscale soft-adventure tours for a maximum 15 passengers; or **Sahara Outback Tours** (☎ **08/8953 0881;** www.saharatours. com.au), which conducts affordable camping safaris in small groups for all ages. **Austour** (☎ **03/9770 2145;** www.austourtravel.com) does 1- to 2-day tours using a coach, minicoach, or 12-seater 4WD equipped with lounge, videos, and information tapes, staying in tent, lodge, or resort accommodations. Austour also runs 4WD tag-alongs, partly led by an Aboriginal guide, into the Simpson Desert, where you follow the leader driving your own rented 4WD vehicle. Coach operators **Greyhound Pioneer** (☎ **13 20 30** in Australia) and **McCafferty's** (☎ **13 14 99** in Australia) provide inexpensive tours.

Tailormade Tours (☎ **08/8952 1731;** www.ozemail.com.au/~tmade/) and **VIP Travel Australia** (☎ **1800/806 412** in Australia, or 08/8956 2388; www.vipaustralia. com.au) customize luxury tours utilizing stretch limos, minicoaches, and 4WDs.

You can book Sahara Outback Tours, Austour, and Tailormade Tours via **Alice Springs Tour Professionals** (☎ **08/8953 0666;** www.alicetourprofessionals. com.au), a one-stop shop that represents a number of Alice Springs–based coach and 4WD tour specialists. Their tours range from moderately priced to deluxe, for groups big or small, on set or personalized itineraries, in accommodations from five-star resorts to campgrounds.

1 Alice Springs

462km (289 miles) NE of Ayers Rock; 1,491km (932 miles) S of Darwin; 1,544km (965 miles) N of Adelaide; 2,954km (1,846 miles) NW of Sydney

"The Alice," as Australians fondly dub it, is the unofficial capital of Outback Australia. In the early 1870s, a handful of telegraph-station workers struggled nearly 1,000 miles north from Adelaide through uncompromising desert to settle by a small spring in what must have truly seemed like the end of the earth. Alice Springs, as the little place was called, was nothing but a few huts built around a repeater station on the ambitious telegraph line that was to link Adelaide with Darwin and the rest of the world.

Today Alice is a city of 27,000 people, with supermarkets, banks, and nightclubs. It's a friendly, rambling, unsophisticated kind of place. No matter what direction you come from, you will soar for hours over a vast, flat, unchanging landscape to get here. That's why folks are so surprised when they reach Alice Springs and see low but dramatic mountain ranges, rippling red in the sunshine. Many people excitedly mistake them for Ayers Rock, but that baby is almost 300 miles down the road. These hills, jutting their craggy faces up against the streets, are the ✪ **MacDonnell Ranges.**

Many tourists visit Alice only to get to Ayers Rock, but Alice has plenty of charms all its own. The red folds of the MacDonnell Ranges hide striking gorges with shady picnic grounds. A planned 250-kilometer (156-mile) hiking trail is partly ready for your boots now. There are old gold-rush towns to poke around in, quirky museums, wildlife parks, a couple of cattle stations (ranches) that welcome visitors, and one of the world's top-10 desert golf courses. You could easily fill 2 or 3 days in the area.

This is the heart of the Aboriginal Arrernte people's country, and Alice is a rich source of tours, shops, and galleries for anyone with an interest in Aboriginal culture, art, or simple souvenirs. There is a sad side to the town's Aboriginal riches. Not every Aboriginal succeeds in splicing his or her ancient civilization with the 21st century, and the result is dislocated communities living in the riverbed with only alcohol for company.

ESSENTIALS

GETTING THERE By Plane Ansett (☎ **13 13 00** in Australia) makes one direct flight a day from Sydney, Adelaide, Ayers Rock, and Darwin; one or two daily from Cairns; and one a week from Melbourne. **Qantas** (☎ **13 13 13** in Australia) flies direct once a day from Sydney, Adelaide, and Darwin; and its subsidiary **Airlink** (book through Qantas) flies direct from Perth, from Darwin, between 2 and 5 times a day from Ayers Rock, and once or twice a day from Cairns. Ansett and Airlink each operate two weekly services from Broome. Ansett and Qantas flights from most other cities connect via Sydney or Adelaide. **Airnorth** (☎ **1800/627 474** in Australia, 08/8945 2866, or book through Ansett) does a "Centre Run" from Darwin via Katherine and Tennant Creek every day except Sunday.

The **Alice Springs Airport Shuttle** (☎ **1800/621 188** in the Northern Territory, or 08/8953 0310) meets all major flights (but not always those from small towns like Tennant Creek) and transfers you to your Alice hotel door for A$9.90 (U.S.$6.45) one-way or A$16.50 (U.S.$10.75) round-trip, per person. A taxi from the airport to town, a distance of 15 kilometers (9 miles), is about A$21.50 (U.S.$14).

By Train The *Ghan* **train,** named after Afghani camel-train drivers who carried supplies in the Red Centre in the 1800s, makes the 45-hour trip from Sydney via Broken Hill and Adelaide to Alice every week. It also does a weekly 36-hour trip from Melbourne via Adelaide. The twice-weekly 19-hour Adelaide–Alice stretch is treeless and empty, if fascinatingly so, so don't be concerned you'll miss it by overnighting on the train. For fares and schedules, call **Great Southern Railway** (☎ **13 21 47** within Australia, or 08/8213 4592; www.gsr.com.au) or see chapter 2 for its booking agencies abroad.

By Bus Greyhound Pioneer (☎ **13 20 30** in Australia) runs once daily from Adelaide and Darwin. **McCafferty's** (☎ **13 14 99** in Australia) operates four times a week from Adelaide, daily from Darwin. It's about a 19-hour trip from Adelaide, and the fare is around A$148 (U.S.$96.20). The trip is around 21 hours from Darwin and costs about A$157 (U.S.$102.05). Greyhound does a daily run from Ayers Rock; McCafferty's plies this route Sunday, Tuesday, Thursday, and Friday. The trip takes 5³/₄ hours with Greyhound, 7 with McCafferty's. The fare is around A$62 (U.S.$40.30).

By Car Alice Springs is on the Stuart Highway linking Adelaide and Darwin. Allow a very long 2 or a more comfortable 3 days to drive from Adelaide; the same goes from Darwin. From Sydney, connect to the Stuart Highway via Broken Hill and Port Augusta north of Adelaide; from Cairns head south to Townsville, then west via the mining town of Mt. Isa to join the Stuart Highway at Tennant Creek. Both routes are

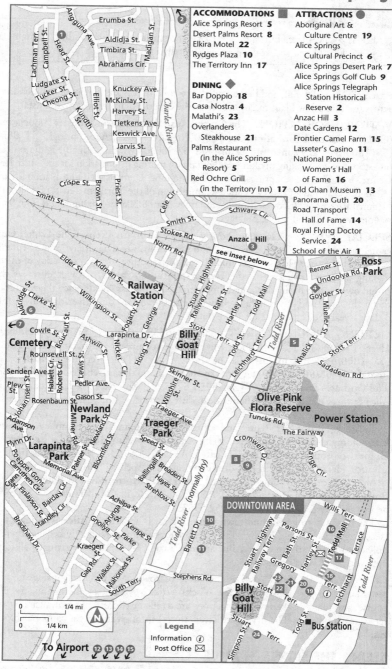

Alice Springs

ACCOMMODATIONS
Alice Springs Resort **5**
Desert Palms Resort **8**
Elkira Motel **22**
Rydges Plaza **10**
The Territory Inn **17**

DINING
Bar Doppio **18**
Casa Nostra **4**
Malathi's **23**
Overlanders
  Steakhouse **21**
Palms Restaurant
  (in the Alice Springs
  Resort) **5**
Red Ochre Grill
  (in the Territory Inn) **17**

ATTRACTIONS
Aboriginal Art &
  Culture Centre **19**
Alice Springs
  Cultural Precinct **6**
Alice Springs Desert Park **7**
Alice Springs Golf Club **9**
Alice Springs Telegraph
  Station Historical
  Reserve **2**
Anzac Hill **3**
Date Gardens **12**
Frontier Camel Farm **15**
Lasseter's Casino **11**
National Pioneer
  Women's Hall
  of Fame **16**
Old Ghan Museum **13**
Panorama Guth **20**
Road Transport
  Hall of Fame **14**
Royal Flying Doctor
  Service **24**
School of the Air **1**

Ross Park

Railway Station

Billy Goat Hill

Anzac Hill
see inset below

Cemetery

Newland Park

Larapinta Park

Traeger Park

Olive Pink Flora Reserve

Power Station

The Fairway

DOWNTOWN AREA

Billy Goat Hill

Bus Station

0   1/4 mi
0   1/4 km

N

To Airport

Legend
Information (i)
Post Office ✉

Safety Tip

Alice is a safe place, but steer clear of dark streets and the riverbed at night, as teenage kids like to accost people and generally cause trouble.

---

extremely long and dull, and best avoided. From Perth it is an even longer, duller drive across the Nullarbor Plain to connect with the Stuart Highway at Port Augusta.

VISITOR INFORMATION The **Central Australian Tourism Industry Association (CATIA) Visitor Information Centre,** 60 Gregory Terrace, Alice Springs, NT 0870 (☎ **1800/645 1299** in Australia, or 08/8952 5800; www.catia.asn.au), is the official one-stop shop for making bookings and obtaining touring information for the entire Red Centre, including Alice Springs, Kings Canyon, and Uluru-Kata Tjuta National Park (Ayers Rock). It has a Parks & Wildlife Commission of the Northern Territory desk with National Park notes. It's open Monday to Friday from 8:30am to 5:30pm and from 9am to 4pm weekends and public holidays.

SPECIAL EVENTS The town hosts a couple of bizarre events. The **Camel Cup** camel race takes place on the second Saturday in July. On a Saturday in late September or early October, folks from hundreds of miles around turn out for a day of mirth making and beer drinking at the **Henley-on-Todd Regatta.** Crowds cheer as the proud owners of gaudily decorated, homemade bottomless "boats" race them on foot down the dry Todd River bed. Well, what else do you do on a river that flows only 3 days a year? See chapter 2 for more details.

GETTING AROUND **Avis** (☎ 08/8953 5533), **Budget** (☎ 08/8952 8899), **Hertz** (☎ 08/8952 2644), local Alice Springs company **Outback Auto Rentals** (☎ **1800/652 133** in Australia, or 08/8953 5333), and **Territory Thrifty Car Rental** (☎ **08/8952 9999**) all rent conventional and 4WD vehicles. Booking agent **The Outback Travel Shop** (☎ **08/8955 5288;** www.outbacktravelshop.com.au) in Alice Springs can give you a better deal with Territory Thrifty than you can get by going direct.

Territory Thrifty Car Rental and Outback Auto Rentals rent complete **camping kits** holding everything you need, including a tent, sleeping bags, and a gas stove. A kit for two people from Territory Thrifty is A$25 (U.S.$16.25) per day. Book them in advance. Hertz is ceasing to rent camping gear after April 1, 2001.

Among Alice's many campervan rental outfits are **Britz Australia** (☎ 08/8952 8814), **Budget Campervan Rentals** (☎ 08/8952 8049), **Hertz Campervans** (☎ 08/8953 5333), and **Maui Rentals** (☎ 08/8952 5353).

The best way to get around town without a car is aboard the **Alice Wanderer bus** (see "Organized Tours," below). Taxi fares are exorbitant, presumably because there is only one prime outfit in town, **Alice Springs Taxis** (☎ **13 10 08**). Virtually all tours pick you up at your hotel.

CITY LAYOUT **Todd Mall** is the heart of town. Most shops, businesses, and restaurants are here or within a few blocks' walk. Most hotels, the casino, the golf course, and many of the town's attractions are a mile or two out of town, just a bit too far to reach on foot. The dry Todd River "flows" through the city a couple of blocks east of Todd Mall.

SEEING THE SIGHTS IN ALICE

✪ **Aboriginal Art & Culture Centre.** 86 Todd St. ☎ **08/8952 3408.** Admission A$2 (U.S.$1.30). Daily 8am–6pm. Closed Christmas and Good Friday.

Set up by the local Southern Arrernte Aboriginal people, this center houses a small but intriguing museum with exhibits on Aboriginal foods, music, and a timeline of Aboriginal history since "contact," as the arrival of Europeans is called. A limited range of artifacts is for sale downstairs, and a huge art gallery of works is for sale upstairs. Allow anywhere from 15 minutes to 2 hours.

Alice Springs Cultural Precinct. Larapinta Dr. at Memorial Ave., 2km (1¼ miles) south of town. ☎ **08/8951 1120.** Incorporating the Museum of Central Australia, Araluen Centre of Arts & Entertainment (☎ 08/8951 1122 box office), Central Australian Aviation Museum, Territory Craft, and the Memorial Cemetery. Admission A$7 (U.S.$4.55) adults; A$4 (U.S.$2.60) children 5–16, seniors, and students; A$18 (U.S.$11.70) family. Daily 10am–5pm. Closed Christmas, New Year's Day, and Good Friday. Take a cab or the Alice Wanderer bus (see "Organized Tours," below).

Several attractions cluster within walking distance of one another here. Along with fossils, natural history displays, and meteorites, the **Museum of Central Australia** houses the **Strehlow Exhibition,** an absorbing display of research into local Aboriginal language and customs. The Araluen Centre of Arts & Entertainment has three art galleries of Aboriginal and contemporary Aussie artists; check out the "Honey Ant Dreaming" stained-glass window in its foyer. The small but interesting **Aviation Museum** preserves the Territory's aerial history with old radios, engines, several aircraft, and wreckage. You can buy craft works, and maybe catch the artists at work, in the **Territory Craft** gallery. The **cemetery** contains graves of key local figures, including "Afghani" (Pakistani) camel herders buried facing Mecca.

✪ **Alice Springs Desert Park.** Larapinta Dr., 6km (3¾ miles) north of town. ☎ **08/8951 8788.** Admission A$18 (U.S.$11.70) adults; A$9 (U.S.$5.85) students and children 5–16, A$40 (U.S.$26) family of 6. Daily 7:30am–6pm (last entry 5pm). Closed Christmas.

By means of a 1.6-kilometer (1-mile) trail through three reconstructed Central Australian habitats, this wildlife and flora park shows you 120 or so of the animal species that live in the desert around Alice, but that you won't spot too easily in the wild, like the big-eared bilby (a marsupial), snakes, and cute thorny devils (lizards). Don't miss the excellent Birds of Prey show at 10am and 3:30pm. A short film, shown hourly, on Australia's 4,500-million-year geological past has a surprise shot at the end—see for yourself! Guides do free talks throughout the day. Allow 3 hours.

Desert Park Transfers (☎ 08/8952 4667) gets you to and from the park from your hotel for A$25 (U.S.$16.25) for adults, and A$16 (U.S.$10.40) students, seniors, and kids 5 to 16. That includes park admission.

✪ **Alice Springs Telegraph Station Historical Reserve.** On the Stuart Hwy. 4km (2½ miles) north of town (beyond the School of the Air turnoff). ☎ **08/8952 3993.** Admission free to picnic grounds and trails; station A$6 (U.S.$3.90) adults, A$4.50 (U.S.$2.95) seniors and students, A$3 (U.S.$1.95) children 5–15. Daily 8am–5pm (picnic grounds and trails open until 9pm). Station closed Christmas; picnic grounds open 365 days a year. Take a cab or the Alice Wanderer bus (see "Organized Tours," below) or the 4km (2½-mile) riverside pedestrian/bike track that starts near the corner of Wills Terrace and Undoolya Rd.

Alice Springs began life as this charming telegraph repeater station in 1871, set by a pretty water hole amid red bouldery hills, sprawling gums full of parrots, and mercifully green lawns. Aided by a printed guide the staff hands out, you wander around the old station master's residence; the telegraph office, with its Morse code machine tap-tapping away; the shoeing yard packed with blacksmith's equipment; and the stables, housing vintage buggies and saddlery. From May to October, "kitchen maids" in period dress serve scones (biscuits) and damper straight from the original wood-fired ovens. The park runs a care program for orphaned kangaroo joeys, so you may see

Earning a Degree from Didgeridoo University

Fancy yourself as a Ray Charles of the desert? Then there's only one place for you to hone your talents—Didgeridoo University, at the Aboriginal Art & Culture Centre (see above).

Paul Ah Chee-Ngala set up his "campus" to satisfy an ever-growing demand from world travelers to master the didgeridoo's evocative rhythms. In truth, the university is an alcove in the culture center, and the degree takes just 1 hour. Classes begin everyday at 1pm and cost A$11.50 (U.S.$7.50) adults, A$5.50 (U.S.$3.60) kids (or are free as part of the Centre's half-day tour described in "Organized Tours," below). Paul guarantees you will be able to make kangaroo hopping sounds on the darn thing by the end of the hour—unless you are the 1 in 30 people who cannot blow through their lips! The trick to didgeridoo playing is to breathe in and out at the same time, a technique known as "circular breathing."

When buying a didgeridoo, keep in mind there is no such thing as a "good" or a "bad" one. Look for one that is resonant and that you like the sound of. The diameter, the wood used, and the unique surface of the wood inside the instrument are what makes each one unique. Didgeridoos were never traditionally painted, so don't worry about selecting an "authentic" design on yours. The pitch of the instrument can vary from a high wail on G to a deep and somber A that was mostly used only by Aboriginal men in important ceremonies. The shorter the didgeridoo, the higher the pitch.

If you can't take a "degree" at the Aboriginal Art and Culture Centre, learn to play the thing in your own living room via an audio lesson on the center's Web site, www.aboriginalart.com.au. The site sells didgeridoos, too.

those hopping around the gift shop. Allow a good hour to see everything, more to walk one of the several hiking trails leading from the grounds. This is a lovely picnic spot.

Frontier Camel Farm. On the Ross Hwy. (4km/2.5 miles from town). ☎ **1800/806 499** in Australia, or 08/8953 0444. Free admission to shop. Admission to display room A$6 (U.S.$3.90) adults, A$3 (U.S.$1.95) children 5–12, A$12 (U.S.$7.80) family. Admission to display room and short camel ride A$10 (U.S.$6.50) adults, A$9 (U.S.$5.85) seniors and students, A$6 (U.S.$3.90) children, A$25 (U.S.$16.25) family. Daily 9am–5pm; camel rides 10:30am–noon daily, also 1–2:30pm Apr–Oct. Closed Christmas, New Year's Day, and Camel Cup Day. Take a cab or the Alice Wanderer bus (see "Organized Tours," below).

You might not associate camels with Australia, but camels' ability to get by without water was key to opening up the arid inland parts of the country to European settlement in the 1800s. With the advent of cars, they were released into the wilds, and today there are more than 200,000 of them roaming central Australia's deserts. Australia even exports them to the Middle East! Here you can take a short camel ride and browse a display of black-and-white photos, videos, and camel memorabilia. A shop sells camel leather, camel wool, camel cosmetics—even camel poo, though who knows why! See "Organized Tours" and the "Dinner in the Desert" boxed story, both below, for details of camel rides down the Todd River.

National Pioneer Women's Hall of Fame. The Old Courthouse, 27 Hartley St. ☎ 08/8952 9006. Admission A$2 (U.S.$1.30). Daily 10am–5pm. Closed mid-Dec to early Feb.

With a collection of photographs, domestic artifacts, and other memorabilia, this engrossing museum tells the stories of more than 100 Aussie women who were pioneers in their fields, be they Olympic gold medalists, priests, or pilots.

Royal Flying Doctor Service (RFDS). 8–10 Stuart Terrace (at the end of Hartley St.). ☎ **08/8952 1129.** Admission A$5.25 (U.S.$3.45) adults, A$2.10 (U.S.$1.40) children 6–15. Mon–Sat 9am–4pm (last tour departs 4pm), Sun and public holidays 1–4pm. Closed Christmas and New Year's Day.

Alice is a major base for this airborne medical service that treats people living and traveling in the Outback. You can see the radio in action handling the odd emergency and, more commonly, routine clinic and diagnosis calls. Half-hour tours of the base and museum begin every 30 minutes and include an interesting short video. It also has a garden cafe and gift shop.

School of the Air. 80 Head St. (2½km/1½ miles from town). ☎ **08/8951 6834.** Admission A$3.50 (U.S.$2.30) adults, A$2.50 (U.S.$1.65) seniors and children 5–16, A$12 (U.S.$7.80) family. Mon–Sat and public holidays 8:30am–4:30pm, Sun 1:30–4:30pm. Closed Christmas, Boxing Day (Dec 26), and New Year's Day; sometimes also closed Good Friday. Bus: 3.

Sitting in on school lessons may not be your idea of a vacation, but this school is different—it broadcasts by radio to a 1,300,000-square-kilometer (501,800-square-mile) "schoolroom" of children on Outback stations. That's a classroom as big as Germany, Great Britain, Ireland, New Zealand, and Japan combined—or twice the size of Texas. You can listen in when classes are in session on weekdays, and any time you may hear taped classes, watch a video, and browse kids' artwork, old radios, and photos.

ORGANIZED TOURS

AROUND TOWN & OUT IN THE DESERT The ○ **Alice Wanderer bus** (☎ **1800/66 9111** in Australia, or 08/8952 2111) does a running loop of town attractions every 70 minutes from 9am, with the last departure at 4pm. Hop on and off as you please, and enjoy the commentary from the driver. It departs daily from the southern end of Todd Mall. Tickets are sold on board and cost A$22 (U.S.$14.30) for adults, A$20 (U.S.$13) for seniors, and A$13 (U.S.$8.45) for students and kids 4 to 14. Call for a free pickup from your hotel.

The bus calls at most of the attractions listed above, plus **Anzac Hill,** for a 2-minute photo stop; the **Road Transport Hall of Fame;** the **Old Ghan Museum,** housing the original *Ghan* train that plied the Adelaide–Alice Springs line from 1929 to 1980; the **Date Gardens;** and **Panorama Guth,** an art gallery housing a 360° painting by artist Henk Guth of central Australian landscapes.

Many Alice-based companies do guided day trips and extended tours not only of Alice, but also of the East and West Macs, Hermannsburg, the Mereenie Loop Road, and Finke Gorge National Park. Not all of the companies listed here go to all those places. Among the reputable companies are **Alice Wanderer Centre Sightseeing Tours** (which also runs the Wanderer service, above; www.ozemail.com.au/~alicwand), doing half- to 3-day tours by minicoach or 4WD; and **Central Oz 4WD Tours** ☎ **1800/240 230** in Australia, or 08/8953 4755; www.highonthehog.com.au), which does only personalized 4WD tours for a maximum four adults and the odd kid. **Alice Springs Tour Professionals** (☎ **1800/673 391** in Australia, or 08/8953 0666; www.alicetourprofessionals.com.au) is one-stop shopping for several reliable tour operators and adventure outfitters. See also "Exploring the Red Centre," at the beginning of this chapter.

High on the Hog (☎ **1800/240 230** in Australia, or 08/8953 4755; the same company as Central Oz 4WD Tours, above) shows you the sights from a Harley-Davidson. Costs range from A$45 (U.S.$29.25) for a 20-minute "Town Blast" to A$460 (U.S.$299) for a daylong burn into the East or West MacDonnell Ranges. Tours are cheaper for advance bookings. Some rides combine bushwalks.

ABORIGINAL TOURS The excellent ✪ **Half-Day Aboriginal Tour** offered by the Aboriginal Art & Culture Centre (see "Seeing the Sights in Alice," above) features an explanation of the Dreamtime creation era; a gentle bush tucker walk; and a chance to throw a boomerang and spear, learn about tools and weapons, hear about Aboriginal culture, beliefs, and family relationships over billy tea and damper, and see a dance performance. The experience wraps up with a 1-hour didgeridoo lesson at 1pm. The tour departs daily at 8am and costs A$82.50 (U.S.$53.60) adults and A$44 (U.S.$28.60) children under 12 (including hotel pickup).

The Aboriginal Art & Culture Centre also stages nightly Aboriginal dinner-show performances at **Red Centre Resort** (book via resort ☎ **08/8952 8955**). They cost A$79 (U.S.$51.35) adults, A$45 (U.S.$29.25) children ages 5 to 14.

At the Walpiri community on an ✪ **Aboriginal Dreamtime & Bushtucker Tour** with Rod Steinert Tours (☎ **08/8558 8377;** www.rstours.com.au), you meet Aboriginal elders who still live a partly Aboriginal lifestyle. These guys are the last of their line at the start of the 21st century. Chat to them about their religious beliefs, hunting skills, and daily life, try throwing a boomerang or spear, watch a male Aboriginal dance (a "corroboree"), sample fat white witchetty grubs (not as bad as they sound!), and, if you wish, buy crafts and artwork painted in front of you. The trip departs daily at 8:30am and returns at 11:30am. The price, which includes hotel pickup, is A$79 (U.S.$51.35) for adults, half-price for kids 3 to 14; or A$59 (U.S.$38.35) adults if you drive yourself to the community 15 kilometers (9 miles) south of Alice.

CAMEL SAFARIS Riding a camel down the dry Todd River is a great way to soak up the landscape. **Frontier Camel Tours** (☎ **1800/806 499** in Australia, or 08/8953 0444) runs a 1-hour ✪ **Camel Ramble** down the riverbed that finishes with a browse through the Frontier Camel Farm's camel display. With transfers from your hotel it costs A$49 (U.S.$31.85) for adults and A$27 (U.S.$17.55) for kids 6 to 12, and it departs daily at 8:30am and 1:30pm April through October, and 8:30am and 3pm November through March. Kids under 6 can join the ride if the cameleer on duty agrees.

HOT-AIR BALLOON FLIGHTS Floating above the desert at dawn as kangaroos bound away beneath is a popular experience in Central Australia. There is a price to pay, though—you have to get up 90 minutes before dawn. Expect to pay upward of A$210 (U.S.$136.50), around 30% less for kids, for a 1-hour flight followed by champagne breakfast in the bush. Kids under 6 are discouraged, because they cannot see over the basket. Contact **Spinifex Ballooning** (☎ **1800/677 893** in Australia, or 08/8953 4800) and **Outback Ballooning** (☎ **1800/809 790** in Australia, or 08/8952 8723). Both do half-hour flights also. Allow all morning, by the time you get back to your hotel.

ACTIVE PURSUITS
BUSHWALKING The 250-kilometer (156-mile) ✪ **Larapinta Trail** winds west from Alice through the sparse red ranges, striking gorges, picturesque semidesert scenery, and rich bird life of the West MacDonnell National Park (see "Road Trips

from Alice Springs," later in this chapter). It is still under construction, but sections 1 to 3 and 8 to 12 of its 13 sections are ready for your boots now. Sections range from easy to hard, and from 8 kilometers (5 miles) to several 23- to 29-kilometer (14- to 18-mile) stretches. Trail maps and information are dispensed by the **Parks & Wildlife Commission of the Northern Territory** office in Alice Springs (☎ 08/8951 8211). Camp facilities are simple at best on popular routes, nonexistent on less traveled sections. Always carry drinking water. The trail may close in extremely hot summer periods.

Alice Wanderer Centre Sightseeing Tours (☎ 1800/66 9111 in Australia, or 08/ 8952 2111) runs transfers to road access points along the trail, where you can mostly pick up a choice of 1-, 2-, or 3-day hikes. **Trek Larapinta** (☎ 08/8953 2933; www.treklarapinta.com.au) leads guided hikes of 1 or more days between April and October.

BIKING A gently undulating 17-kilometer (11-mile) bike trail weaves from **John Flynn's Grave** on Larapinta Drive, 7 kilometers (4 miles) west of town, through the bushland and desert foothills of the MacDonnell Ranges to Simpson's Gap (see "West MacDonnell National Park" below). **Centre Cycles** (☎ 08/8953 2966) on Lindsay Avenue at Undoolya Road rents bikes for A$15 (U.S.$9.75) per day (and a A$50/U.S.$32.50 refundable deposit). *Note:* Carry water, because the two taps en route are a long way apart. Bike in cooler months only.

GOLF The ✪ **Alice Springs Golf Club,** 1 kilometer (half a mile) from town on Cromwell Drive (☎ 08/8952 5440), boasts a Thomson-Wolveridge course rated among the world's top desert courses by touring pros. The course opens from sunup to sundown, about 7am to 6pm in winter, 6am to 6:30pm in summer. For nine holes you will pay A$17.50 (U.S.$11.40), plus A$10 (U.S.$6.50) for clubs, and A$15 (U.S.$9.75) for a cart, which many locals don't bother with. It's best to book a tee time.

SHOPPING AT THE SOURCE FOR ABORIGINAL ART

Top of the shopping list for most travelers to Alice is Aboriginal arts and crafts. You will find no shortage of stuff to buy: linen and canvas paintings, didgeridoos, spears, clapping sticks, coolamons (a dish used by women to carry anything from water to babies), animal carvings, baskets, and bead jewelry, as well as books and CDs. Prices can soar into the thousands of dollars for large canvases by world-renowned painters, but you will find plenty of small works for under A$200 (U.S.$130). Major artworks sell unmounted for ease of shipment, which most galleries arrange on your behalf.

Store hours can vary with the seasons and the crowds, so it pays to check ahead.

A good place to start is the biggest gallery in town, upstairs at the **Aboriginal Art & Culture Centre** (see "Seeing the Sights in Alice," above). You can also order its art, didgeridoos, artifacts, and books over the Internet at **www.aboriginalart.com.au**.

See artists at work when you drop by **Jukurrpa Artists,** on Stott Terrace between Gap Road and Leichhardt Terrace (☎ 08/8953 1052; www.ozemail.com.au/~jukurrpa). This Aboriginal women's cooperative studio/gallery sells the "pattern and dot" paintings of the Western Desert style, plus carvings, craft items, weapons, tools, and seed jewelry.

You can make your own didgeridoo in half a day at **Dust Storm Didgeridoos,** 45 Gap Rd. (☎ 08/8952 2739). Here you can also buy custom-designed and off-the-shelf didges, and boomerangs and other artifacts. This is a private home, so call first.

Aboriginal-owned **Warumpi Arts,** 105 Gregory Terrace (☎ 08/8952 9066), sells wooden artifacts, seed necklaces, and canvas and board paintings in the dramatic, earth-hued designs of the Papunya people, who live 250 kilometers (156 miles) west of Alice. Another Aboriginal-owned gallery, **Papunya Tula Artists,** 78 Todd St. (☎ **08/ 8952 4731**), sells paintings on canvas and linen from Papunya and other artists living in the desert as far as 700 kilometers (438 miles) west of Alice Springs.

Several stores on Todd Mall sell affordable Aboriginal art and souvenirs. The oldest and biggest, the **Original Dreamtime Gallery,** 63 Todd Mall (☎ **08/8952 8861**), stocks a huge selection, and packs, mails, and insures your purchases free of charge anywhere in the world. It also shows visiting exhibitions of Aboriginal art.

Arunta Art Gallery & Bookshop, 72 Todd St. (☎ **08/8952 1544**), stocks some Aboriginal and European artworks, Aboriginal artifacts, and a range of books on Aboriginal art, language, and archaeology, as well as Australian history, geology, wildlife, and biographies.

If you're interested in investing in serious artwork, speak to Roslyn Premont, proprietor of **Gallery Gondwana,** 43 Todd Mall (☎ **08/8953 1577**). She has written a book on desert art, and her gallery sells only top-notch works. Her second gallery, **Gondwana II,** 11 Todd Mall (☎ **08/8953 5511**), stocks elegant crafts and design pieces by Australian artists.

Today's Aboriginal bands mix ancient and hip new rhythms to create some wonderful sounds. For the country's biggest range of indigenous music, head to the **CAAMA** (Central Australian Aboriginal Media Association) store at 101 Todd St. (☎ **08/8952 9207**), inside the association's studios. It also stocks books on Aboriginal art and issues, children's books with Aboriginal story lines, a line of Aboriginal fabrics and cushions, and cute Yamba the Honey Ant dolls, modeled after a kids' character on the local Aboriginal television station, Imparja.

ACCOMMODATIONS

You may pay lower rates than those listed below in the summer off-season from December to March, and sometimes even as late as June. Peak season typically runs from July to October or November.

EXPENSIVE

Alice Springs Resort. 34 Stott Terrace, Alice Springs, NT 0870. ☎ **1800/805 055** in Australia, or 08/8951 4545. Fax 08/8953 0995. www.ayersrock.aust.com. E-mail: reservations@ aliceresort.mtx.net.au. 144 units (108 shower only). A/C MINIBAR TV TEL. A$192–$225 (U.S.$124.80–$146.25) double. Extra person A$20 (U.S.$13). Children under 13 stay free in parents' room with existing bedding. Ask about packages with Ayers Rock Resort and/or Kings Canyon Resort. AE, BC, DC, JCB, MC, V. Free parking. Airport shuttle.

This friendly, well-run low-rise property is a 3-minute walk from town over the Todd River. By mid-2001, the decorators should have done something about that bright green carpet and those peach floral curtains in the 98 rooms not yet renovated, but even if they haven't, you'll likely spend most of your time around the free-form pool under a couple of palms. All the rooms are clean and comfortable, and deluxe rooms are really huge. Thirty-six airy new deluxe rooms built in 1999 sport smart desert-toned decor, balconies, bathtubs as well as showers, bathrobes, and dataports. All units have pay-per-view movies and hair dryers.

Dining/Diversions: The Palms Restaurant serves excellent Mod Oz fare inside in winter and around the pool in summer (see "Dining," below). Happy Hour starts at 5:30pm every night at the pool bar and in the Gumtree Lounge bar, where a fire roars on nippy winter evenings.

Amenities: Solar-heated swimming pool and sundeck, bikes for rent, room service, dry-cleaning and laundry service, tour/car-rental desk, lobby shop, secretarial services, conference facilities, currency exchange, baby-sitting.

Rydges Plaza Alice Springs. Barrett Dr. (1½km/1 mile from town center), Alice Springs, NT 0870. ☎ **1800/675 212** in Australia, 0800/446 187 in New Zealand, or 08/8950 8000. Fax 08/8953 0475. www.rydges.com.au. E-mail: reservations_alice@rydges.com. 235 units. A/C MINIBAR TV TEL. A$207 (U.S.$134.55) double, A$392–$501 (U.S.$254.80–$325.65) suite. Extra person A$25 (U.S.$16.25). Children under 12 free in parents' room with existing bedding. Ask about packages. Free crib. AE, BC, DC, MC, V. Free parking. Airport shuttle.

Located next to the golf club and a walk from Lasseter's Casino, the Rydges is Alice's fanciest resort. A gleaming lobby leads onto the pool and ample sundeck. Three stories of rooms wrap around the pool, all spacious with nice if rather dated fittings. Martha Stewart would freak out if she saw the fluffy pink or blue carpet, but that is due to be replaced by early 2001. Every room has a balcony, some looking onto the pool, some back toward town, others over the red ranges. All have free in-room movies, voice mail, modem lines, hair dryers, and irons.

Dining/Diversions: Nightly barbecues take place outdoors (Sept to Mar), and the informal Balloons does all-day meals and Sunday brunch. There are a quiet lobby bar, a pool bar, and the lively nightclub and cocktail bar, Simpson's Gap Bar, which is a hit with locals.

Amenities: Heated swimming pool, 24-hour room service, dry-cleaning and laundry service, Jacuzzi, sauna, gym, two day/night tennis courts, bike rental, babysitting, tour desk, shops, conference facilities.

MODERATE

The Territory Inn. Leichhardt Terrace (backing on to Todd Mall), Alice Springs, NT 0870. ☎ **1800/089 644** in Australia, or 08/8950 6666. Fax 08/8952 7829. www.aurora-resorts. com.au. E-mail: tti@aurora-resorts.com.au. 108 units (all with shower only, 1 suite with Jacuzzi). A/C MINIBAR TV TEL. A$140–$150 (U.S.$91–$97.50) double, A$210 (U.S.$136.50) suite. Extra person A$15 (U.S.$9.75). Children under 14 stay free in parents' room using existing bedding. AE, BC, DC, JCB, MC, V. Free parking.

This pleasant hotel is smack bang in the center of town. Rooms in the newer wing are your standard modern variety, all clean, large, and decorated nicely enough. Those in the original wing are small and a little dark, but have a pretty heritage theme with floral bedcovers and lace curtains. All have irons and free movies. The courtyard has a barbecue and covered dining area, and there are a tour desk, hair dryers for loan, and a post-checkout shower room. The tiny heated pool and Jacuzzi tucked away are in a utilitarian corner, so this is not the place for chilling out poolside; stay here primarily to be within walking distance of shops and restaurants. Room service is from the marvelous Red Ochre Grill (see "Dining," below).

INEXPENSIVE

✪ **Desert Palms Resort.** 74 Barrett Dr. (1km/½ mile from town), Alice Springs, NT 0870. ☎ **1800/678 037** in Australia, or 08/8952 5977. Fax 08/8953 4176. www.saharatours. com.au/despalms.htm. E-mail: despalms@saharatours.com.au. 80 units (all with shower only). A/C TV TEL. A$92 (U.S.$59.80) double. Extra person A$10 (U.S.$6.50). AE, BC, DC, MC, V. Free coach station/train station/airport shuttle twice daily; free resort-to-town shuttle 4 times daily.

Right next to Lasseter's Casino and the Alice Springs Golf Club (to which guests enjoy honorary social membership), these cabins set behind manicured palms and pink bougainvillea are one of the cheeriest places to stay in Alice. Don't be deterred by their poky prefab appearance; inside they are surprisingly large, well-kept, and inviting, with a pine-pitched ceiling, a minikitchen, a sliver of bathroom sporting new white tiles and fittings, and a pert little furnished front deck. A pretty sundeck and pool with its own little island is out front; there's also a tennis court. The pleasant staff at the front desk loans hair dryers, processes your film, does laundry service, sells basic grocery and liquor supplies, and books your tours.

Bond Springs Outback Retreat, Alice Springs (☎ **08/8952 9888;** www.alice. aust.com/~bondhmst). *Mrs. Janice Heaslip owns and operates the B&B at this huge cattle station north of Alice Springs. It reminded me of the type of Outback station depicted in The Thornbirds, complete with a 'movie-star handsome' tour guide (Mrs. Heaslip's 30-year-old son Ben), who takes guests out in a 4x4 for very informative tours (at an extra charge). It's a lovely home, and Mrs. Heaslip serves marvelous country breakfasts (complete with homemade bread and jams) in her beautiful country kitchen. Guests can also arrange to have dinner with Mrs. Heaslip and station hands. The evening we were there dinner was served under the stars on a long table. . . . All accommodations are clean, tastefully decorated, comfortable, and modern.*
—Mari Fagin, Ph.D., Oklahoma City, Okla., U.S.

Author's Note: The station is 25 kilometers (16 miles) north of town. One homestead room and two self-contained cottages have bathrooms. Two other homestead rooms share a bathroom. All have air-conditioning and heating. The Heaslips run a good range of day trips, overnight bush camps, and tours throughout the Red Centre of up to 3 days. Rates are A$220 to $264 (U.S.$143 to $171.60) double, including breakfast. Ask about 5-day packages combining tours and accommodations at Bond Springs, Kings Canyon Resort, and Ayers Rock Resort. Dinner is A$50 (U.S.$32.50) per person (wines extra). Transfers cost A$35 (U.S.$22.75) from town, or A$65 (U.S.$42.25) from the airport, one-way, per vehicle.

Elkira Motel. 65 Bath St., Alice Springs, NT 0870. ☎ **1800/809 252** in Australia, or 08/ 8952 1222. Fax 08/8953 1370. www.bestwestern.com.au/elkira. E-mail: elkira@bestwestern. com.au. 56 units (some with shower only). A/C TV TEL. A$75–$105 (U.S.$87.65–$68.25) double. Extra person A$10 (U.S.$6.50); extra child under 3 A$5 (U.S.$3.25). AE, BC, DC, MC, V. Free parking. Airport shuttle.

The cheapest rooms we can recommend in the heart of town are at this unpretentious but clean Best Western motel. All were renovated in 1998 with new carpets, floor tiles, wall paneling, and hair dryers. Deluxe rooms have a little more space than the standard rooms, and some have microwaves. Ask for a room away from the road, because the traffic is noisy during the day. Unless money's really tight, the budget rooms are too dated and tiny to consider. There is a modest pool with a barbecue area under lovely big trees, a tour desk, and a reasonably priced restaurant.

DINING
EXPENSIVE

A 1-hour sunset saunter on camelback down the dry Todd River is part of the ✪ **Take a Camel out to Dinner** nights offered by **Frontier Camel Tours** (☎ **1800/806 499** in Australia, or 08/8953 0444) in Alice Springs. Setting off from the Mecca Date Gardens, it's a pretty journey past river red gums while black cockatoos whirl overhead. At the **Frontier Camel Farm** (see "Seeing the Sights in Alice"), you dine on a tasty three-course meal of kangaroo sausages, barramundi, or steak, with wattleseed bread, wine, and beer. The meal is served inside, not out in the sand. The cost of A$95 (U.S.$61.75) for adults and A$70 (U.S.$45.50) for children 6 to 12 includes pickup from your hotel. The rides run nightly year-round, departing at 4pm April through October, and at 5pm November through March.

At **Camp Oven Kitchen's** nightly bush dinners, you sit down at white-clothed, lamplit slab tables in a fire-lit clearing to soup and damper, kangaroo kebabs, roast beef and vegetables, golden syrup dumplings with ice cream, and billy tea. The evening features a night sky talk and bush ballads. The meal, including transfers from your hotel but not including drinks, costs A$76 (U.S.$49.40) for adults and A$61 (U.S.$39.65) for kids under 12. It departs 5:30pm May to September, 6pm October to April. Call **Alice Springs Holidays** (☎ **08/8953 1411;** www.alicespringsholidays.com.au).

Overlanders Steakhouse. 72 Hartley St. ☎ **08/8952 2159.** Reservations required in peak season. Main courses A$17.50–$25 (U.S.$11.40–$16.25); Drover's Blowout A$41.25 (U.S.$26.80). Ask about meal packages with drinks and transfers. AE, BC, DC, JCB, MC, V. Daily 6pm–late. STEAK/AUSSIE TUCKER.

This landmark on the Alice dining scene is famous for its "Drover's Blowout" menu, which assaults the megahungry with soup and damper, then a platter of crocodile vol-au-vents, camel and kangaroo fillet, and emu medallions—these are just the appetizers—followed by Scotch fillet steak in red wine and mushroom sauce, or barramundi, with potatoes and vegetables, followed by dessert. There's a regular menu with a 700-gram (1-lb., 10-oz.) grain-fed steak, plus lots of lighter fare. The barnlike interior is Outback all through, from the rustic bar to the saddlebags hanging from the roof beams. An "Overlanders' Table" seats solo diners together.

✪ **Palms Restaurant.** At the Alice Springs Resort, 34 Stott Terrace. ☎ **08/8951 4545.** Reservations recommended at dinner. Main courses A$21.90–$30.25 (U.S.$14.25–$19.60). AE, BC, DC, JCB, MC, V. Daily 6:30am–10pm. MODERN AUSTRALIAN.

Ask the locals for the best chow in town and this is where they'll send you. It's sophisticated modern food with an east-meets-west twist, such as baby barramundi steamed with lemongrass and ginger on baby bok choy and a kaffir lime beurre blanc. Bush tucker creeps onto the menu, too, in dishes like the crispy chili crocodile cake appetizer on crunchy Asian greens with coriander aioli and red bell-pepper oil. Live piano music plays nightly. No smoking inside until 9pm.

MODERATE

Malathi's Restaurant & Sean's Irish Bar. 51 Bath St. (opposite K-Mart). ☎ **08/8952 1858.** Reservations recommended. Main courses A$13.20–$26 (U.S.$8.60–$16.90); many dishes under A$20 (U.S.$13). AE, BC, DC, MC, V. Restaurant Mon–Sat 5:30pm–late. Bar daily 3:30pm–late. ASIAN/WESTERN.

Located in an unprepossessing building a couple of blocks from Todd Mall, Malathi's serves up an eclectic assortment of Asian dishes plus a few true-blue Aussie choices, such as flavorful King Island steak. Don't be put off by the fusty pink walls, old carpet, and Asian print tablecloths, because the food is outstanding. I can recommend the lamb korma (a kind of mild curry). You might want to try the Lakshmi King prawns cooked in Indian flavors or the Thai coconut curry. They do takeout too. Buy wine at the restaurant or bring your own (but don't BYO beer or spirits). The Irish bar serves cheap stews, live bands (sometimes), and Guinness (always!).

Red Ochre Grill. Todd Mall. ☎ **08/8952 9614.** Reservations recommended at dinner. Main courses A$7.50–$21.50 (U.S.$490–$14) lunch; A$15–$22.50 (U.S.$9.75–$14.65) dinner; buffet breakfast A$10.50–$15 (U.S.$6.85–$9.75). AE, BC, DC, MC, V. Daily 6:30am–10pm. GOURMET BUSH TUCKER.

If you've never tried wallaby mignons on a bed of native pasta and polenta cake with a native berry and red wine cream sauce, or barramundi baked in paperbark with wild lime and coriander butter, here's your chance. The chef at this upscale chain fuses Aussie bush ingredients with dishes from around the world; although the results might sound strange, they're mouthwatering. Opt for the contemporary interior fronting Todd Mall, or dine outside in the attractive courtyard.

INEXPENSIVE

✪ **Bar Doppio.** 2 & 3 Fan Arcade (off the southern end of Todd Mall). ☎ **08/8952 6525.** Reservations not accepted. Main courses A$7–$16 (U.S.$4.55–$10.40); sandwiches average A$6 (U.S.$3.90). No credit cards. Mon–Sat 7:30am–9pm, Sun 10am–4pm. Closed public holidays; may close Christmas–New Year. EAST-MEETS-WEST CAFE FARE.

If you're in need of a dose of cool—style, that is, as well as air-conditioning—this laid-back arcade cafe is the place to chill over good coffee and feast on cheap, wholesome food. Sacks of coffee beans are stacked all over, gypsy music plays, no tables and chairs match, there are world magazines to read, and the staff doesn't care if you sit here all day. It's largely vegetarian, but fish and meat figure on the blackboard menu. Try lamb chermoula cutlets on Gabriella potatoes with rocket, red onion and tomato salad, chicken laksa, Turkish bread sandwiches, or spuds with hot toppings. Hot and cold breakfast choices stay on the menu until 11am. They do takeout. BYO.

✪ **Casa Nostra.** Corner of Undoolya Rd. and Sturt Terrace. ☎ **08/8952 6749.** Reservations strongly recommended. Main courses A$10–$19 (U.S.$6.50–$12.35); most are A$13 (U.S.$8.45). BC, MC, V. Mon–Sat 5pm–late. Closed Christmas–end of Jan. ITALIAN.

The only difference between this cheery homespun Italian family eatery and every other Italian restaurant in the world is that this one has autographed photos of Tom Selleck pinned to the wall. Judging by his scrawled praise, Tom loved eating here (when on location in Alice filming *Quigley Down Under*) as much as the locals do. You've seen the red-checked tablecloths and the basket-clad Chianti bottles before, but the food is surprisingly good. A long list of pastas (like the masterful carbonara), traditional pizzas, and chicken and veal dishes are the main offerings. BYO.

2 Road Trips from Alice Springs

See "Organized Tours," earlier in the "Alice Springs" section, for companies that run coach or 4WD tours of a half day, a full day, or longer to the West and East Macs. Expect to pay about A$100 (U.S.$65) for a full-day trip.

THE WEST MACDONNELL RANGES

WEST MACDONNELL NATIONAL PARK   The approximately 300-kilometer (188-mile) round-trip drive west from Alice Springs into West MacDonnell National Park is a stark but picturesque trip to a series of red gorges, semidesert country, and peaceful swimming holes. You may not stop at every gorge en route; most folks call at two or three and enjoy a picnic lunch at one.

From Alice, take Larapinta Drive west for 18 kilometers (11 miles) to the 8-kilometer (5-mile) turnoff to **Simpson's Gap,** a shady water hole between steep ridges lined with ghost gums. Black-footed rock wallabies hop out on the cliffs in the late afternoon (so you may want to time a visit here on your way back to Alice). There are a couple of short trails, including a 500-meter (1/3-mile) Ghost Gum circuit, and a 17-kilometer (11-mile) round-trip trail to **Bond Gap.** Swimming is not permitted. The place has an information center/ranger station and free barbecues.

Twenty-three kilometers (14 miles) down Larapinta Road and 9 kilometers (5 1/2 miles) down a turnoff is **Standley Chasm** (☎ **08/8956 7440**). This towering cleft in the rock is only a few meters wide but 80 meters (262 ft.) high, reached by a pretty 10-minute creekside trail. Aim to be here at midday, when the walls glow orange in the overhead sun. You may escape the crowds if you walk through the chasm to the upper ramparts. A kiosk sells snacks and drinks. Admission is A$5.50 (U.S.$3.60) for adults and A$4 (U.S.$2.60) seniors and children 5 to 14. The Chasm is open 8am to 6pm daily, with last entry at 5pm (closed Christmas).

Road-Trip Tips for the East & West Macs

Come prepared with food (a picnic perhaps, or meat to barbecue), drinking water, and a full gas tank, because facilities are scarce. Bring your own food if camping. Leaded, unleaded, and diesel fuel sold at Glen Helen Lodge, Hermannsburg, and Ross River Homestead. Wear walking shoes.

Because the water holes in the East and West Macs are mostly spring fed, the water can be intensely cold. Take only short dips to avoid cramp and hypothermia, don't swim alone, and be careful of underwater snags. Some holes dry up with no rain. Don't wear sunscreen because it pollutes a precious source of drinking water for native animals.

Two-wheel-drive rental cars will not be insured on unsealed (unpaved) roads—that means the last few miles into Trephina Gorge Nature Park, the 11-kilometer (7 miles) road into N'Dhala Gorge Nature Park, and the 36-kilometer (22½-mile) road to Arltunga Historical Reserve, all in the East Macs. Some unsealed access roads can be impassable after heavy rain. The West MacDonnell road is sealed to Glen Helen Gorge; a few points of interest may require driving for short lengths on unpaved road. Before setting off, drop into the **Parks and Wildlife Commission of the Northern Territory** desk at the CATIA Visitor Information Centre (see "Visitor Information," above). It can fill you in on road conditions and on the free ranger talks, walks, and slide shows taking place at some points of interest in the West and East Macs from April to October. Entry to all parks and reserves, except for Standley Chasm, is free.

Six kilometers (3¾ miles) past Standley Chasm, you can branch right onto Namatjira Drive and head 42 kilometers (26 miles) to picturesque **Ellery Creek Big Hole.** The water is so nippy that the tourism authority warns swimmers to take a flotation device as a defense against cramping. A 3-kilometer (2-mile) walking trail explains the area's geological history.

Eleven kilometers (7 miles) farther along Namatjira Drive is **Serpentine Gorge,** where a trail leads up to a lookout for a lovely view of the ranges through the gorge walls. Another 12 kilometers (7.5 miles) on are **ochre pits,** which Aboriginal people quarried for body paint and for decorating objects used in ceremonial performances. A 3-hour bushwalk on the Larapinta Trail leads from here to Inarlanga Pass in the Heavitree ranges. Twenty-six kilometers (16 miles) farther west, 8 kilometers (5 miles) from the main road, is **Ormiston Gorge and Pound** (☎ **08/8956 7799** for the ranger station/visitor center). This is a good spot to picnic, swim in the wide deep pool below red cliffs, and walk a choice of trails, such as the 30-minute Ghost Gum Lookout trail or the easy and picturesque 7-kilometer (4-mile) loop through the pound (allow 3 to 4 hours). Because the water hole is wide, the water is good swimming temperature in summer. You can camp here for A$5 (U.S.$3.25) per adult, and A$2 (U.S.$1.30) per kid 5 to 15. The campground has hot showers and free gas barbecues.

A couple of miles on is **Glen Helen Gorge,** where the mighty Finke River cuts through the ranges, with more scenic gorge swimming and helicopter flights. Modest **Glen Helen Resort** (☎ **1800/896 110** in Australia, or 08/8956 7489; www.melanka.com.au) has 25 motel rooms, quad-share bunkhouses, and campgrounds; a restaurant serving three meals a day; a bar; and barbecues for which they sell meat packs. Motel rooms are A$116 (U.S.$75.450) double, bunkhouses are A$64 (U.S.$41.60) per room, a tent site is A$8 (U.S.$5.20) per person, and a powered campsite is A$20 (U.S.$13) double.

TRAVELING THE MEREENIE LOOP ROAD   If you have a 4WD, you can carry on 17 kilometers (11 miles) west past Glen Helen Gorge, link back south and east 99 kilometers (62 miles) to **Hermannsburg** (described below), and then go on 267 kilometers (167 miles) to **Kings Canyon** (see below). This route follows a rough, unsealed road generally referred to as the Mereenie Loop Road, although technically the Mereenie Loop begins at Katapata Pass, some 70 kilometers (44 miles) west of Hermannsburg. There's not much to see, but the desert, low mountain scenery, and wide-open spaces really tell you you're in the Outback, mate! (You can shave off 44 kilometers [28 miles] by not going all the way into Hermannsburg from Glen Helen Gorge, because you have to double back 22 kilometers [14 miles] to rejoin the Loop.) About 55 kilometers (34 miles) from either Glen Helen or Hermannsburg, you can visit **Tnorala (Gosse Bluff) Conservation Reserve,** a spectacular 5-kilometer (3-mile) crater left by a meteorite that smashed to earth 142 million years ago. A 4WD track leads to picnic areas inside the crater.

Allow a long half day to drive from Alice to Kings Canyon via the Mereenie Loop, plus sightseeing time.

Despite what some maps and guides will tell you, the Mereenie Loop Road is really too rough for a conventional 2WD car, and, anyhow, rental companies will not rent you a 2WD car for this trip. Drive your 4WD at a sensible pace to avoid rolling it. The road crosses Aboriginal land, for which you will need a A$2 (U.S.$1.30) per vehicle permit from the **CATIA Visitor Information Centre** in Alice Springs, the gas station in Hermannsburg, or **Kings Canyon Resort.** It comes with a color guide and mud-map, and grants you entry to the Tnorala crater.

Camping and turning off are not permitted anywhere along the road. Take food and plenty of water, and keep the gas tank full.

HERMANNSBURG HISTORICAL PRECINCT   An alternative to visiting the West Mac gorges is to take Larapinta Drive 128 kilometers (80 miles) from Alice Springs to the old **Lutheran Mission** at the **Hermannsburg Historical Precinct** (☎ **08/8956 7402**). Some maps will show this route as an unsealed road, but it is now sealed. Settled by German missionaries in the 1870s, the town has pretty farmhouse-style mission buildings that have been restored. There are a museum, a gallery housing works by famous Aussie artist Albert Namatjira, and tearooms serving a fabulous apple strudel from an old German recipe. The Mission is open daily 9am to 4pm March through November, and daily 10am to 4pm December through February. Admission to the precinct with tea or coffee is A$4.50 (U.S.$2.95) for adults, A$3 (U.S.$1.95) for school-age kids, or A$12 (U.S.$7.80) for a family, plus A$3.50 (U.S.$2.30) per person or A$12 (U.S.$7.80) per family for a guided gallery tour, which departs every hour. The precinct is closed from December 24 to January 2 or 3, and on Good Friday.

From Hermannsburg, you can join up with the Mereenie Loop Road (see above) to Kings Canyon.

✪ FINKE GORGE NATIONAL PARK   Just west of Hermannsburg is the turnoff to the 46,000-hectare (113,620-acre) Finke Gorge National Park, 16 kilometers (10 miles) to the south on an unpaved road. The park is most famous for **Palm Valley,** where groves of rare *Livistona mariae* cabbage palms have survived since central Australia was a jungle millions of years ago. You will need a 4WD to explore this park. Four walking trails between 1.5 kilometers (1 mile) and 5 kilometers (3 miles) take you among the palms or up to a lookout over cliffs; one is a signposted trail exploring Aboriginal culture. There is a campsite about 4 kilometers (2¹/₂ miles) from the palms; it has showers, toilets, and free barbecues. Collect your firewood outside the park. Camping is

A\$5 (U.S.\$3.25) for adults, A\$2 (U.S.\$1.30) for kids 5 to 15. For information, call into the **CATIA Visitor Information Centre in Alice Springs** before you leave, because there is no visitor center in the park. The ranger station (☎ **08/8956 7401**) is for emergencies only.

THE EAST MACDONNELL RANGES

Not as many tourists tread the path on the Ross Highway into the East Macs, but if you do, you'll be rewarded with lush walking trails, fewer crowds, and traces of Aboriginal history. I even spotted wild camels on my visit. At the end of the drive, 86 kilometers (54 miles) from Alice, is the dinky-di (that's Australian for "authentic"— as is "fair dinkum") **Ross River Homestead** (see "Accommodations," below). Day-trippers are welcome. The homestead stages a whip-cracking and billy-tea experience from 10am to noon daily, so consider heading there first, then dropping in on the attractions below as you return.

The first points of interest are **Emily Gap,** 10 kilometers (6 miles) from Alice, and **Jessie Gap,** 7 kilometers (4 miles) on. Jessie is the prettiest picnic spot. You can cool off in the Emily Gap swimming hole if there is any water. Don't miss the "Caterpillar Dreaming" Aboriginal art on the wall, on your right as you walk through. Because the painting is archaeologically important, and this is an Aboriginal sacred site, visitors are asked not to touch it.

At **Corroboree Rock,** 37 kilometers (23 miles) on, you can make a short climb up this rocky outcrop that was important to local Aborigines. The highly polished rock "seat" at the hole high up in it means Aboriginal people must have used this rock for eons.

Twenty-two kilometers (13³/₄ miles) on is the turnoff to **Trephina Gorge Nature Park,** an 18-square-kilometer (7-square-mile) beauty spot with peaceful walking trails ranging from 45 minutes to 4¹/₂ hours. An easy amble between the brick-red walls of the gorge to a water hole takes only a few minutes. The last 5 kilometers (3 miles) of the 9-kilometer (5.5-mile) access road into the park are unsealed, but you can make it in a conventional car.

Not far past the Trephina Gorge Nature Park exit is the turnoff to the gold-rush ghost town of **Arltunga Historical Reserve** (☎ **08/8956 9770** for the visitor center and ranger station), 36 kilometers (23 miles) off the highway on the unsealed Arltunga Road. Gold was found here in 1887 and mined until 1913. You can wander through the romantically ruined stone miners' houses with a self-guiding brochure, explore the underground mines (take a flashlight), visit the restored police station and jail, and fossick (rummage) for riches. A month's fossicking permit for a family is A\$5 (U.S.\$3.25) from the Arltunga Bush Hotel (below). The visitor center is open daily from 8am to 5pm and has a slide show on the difficulties early settlers faced in the early days. These were not inconsiderable. The nearest town was Oodnadatta, 600 kilometers (375 miles) away; it was no thriving metropolis then (or now), and many new settlers walked from there! Close by the Reserve is the **Arltunga Bush Hotel** (☎ **08/8956 9797**), a pub with cold beer, hot meals all day, basic rooms without private bathrooms for A\$38.50 (U.S.\$25) double, and campsites with hot showers for A\$5.50 (U.S.\$3.60) per person. Hotel guests share the campground bathrooms. Bring cash because the hotel lacks a credit-card line connecting it to banks.

N'Dhala Gorge Nature Park, 10 kilometers (6 miles) past Trephina Gorge Nature Park, just before you reach Ross River Homestead, houses an "open-air art gallery" of rock carvings, or petroglyphs, left by the Eastern Arrernte Aboriginal people. There are thought to be some 6,000 rock carvings, hundreds or thousands of years old, in this eerily quiet gorge, along with rock paintings. A 1.5-kilometer (1-mile) signposted trail leads you past some carvings and explains their Dreamtime meanings. A 4WD vehicle is a must to traverse the 11-kilometer (7-mile) access road.

The Ross Highway is sealed all the way to Ross River Homestead. Basic **camping** facilities with pit toilets and barbecues, but no showers, or even drinking water in N'Dhala's case, are available at Trephina and N'Dhala. The camping fee is A$2.50 (U.S.$1.65) for adults and A$1 (U.S.65¢) for kids.

ACCOMMODATIONS

Ross River Homestead. Ross Hwy., 86km (54 miles) east of Alice Springs (P.O. Box 3271), Alice Springs, NT 0871. ☎ **1800/241 711** in Australia, or 08/8956 9711. Fax 08/8956 9823. www.ozemail.com.au/~rrhca. E-mail: rrhca@ozemail.com.au. 48 units, 30 with bathroom (shower only). A/C. Cabin A$79 (U.S.$51.35) double. Extra person A$17 (U.S.$11.05). Bunkhouse quad-share A$20 (U.S.$13) per person with linen. Unpowered campsite A$6 (U.S.$3.90) per adult; powered campsite A$9 (U.S.$5.85) per adult. Lower rates for kids in bunkhouses and campgrounds. AE, BC, DC, MC, V. Coach transfers from Alice Springs A$25 (U.S.$16.25) per person, round-trip.

This fair dinkum 100-year-old station offers both day visitors and overnight guests a condensed taste of Outback life. Overnight accommodations are rustic, roomy log cabins; there are also basic quad-share bunkhouses, with shared bathrooms, and shady campgrounds with a general store.

The whitewashed original homestead has been converted to an atmospheric restaurant with Edwardian furniture, open for breakfast, lunch, and dinner at moderate prices. If enough folks are interested, the homestead does wagon rides to camp-oven cookouts under the stars, sometimes combined with overnight horse and camel camping safaris. Call to check if any are scheduled.

Entry to the homestead, its rustic restaurant and bar, the barbecue, four scenic bushwalking trails, and kangaroo enclosure is free (get feed for them from the stables); so are the pool and Jacuzzi if you patronize the bar or restaurant. A 1-hour horse or camel ride is A$33 (U.S.$21.45); half- and full-day rides are also available. A 30-minute wagon ride is A$8 (U.S.$5.20), and whip-cracking and boomerang-throwing lessons over billy tea and damper, offered from 10am to noon, cost A$5.50 (U.S.$3.60). A 4WD half-day safari at A$55 (U.S.$35.75) should be on offer this year. All activity prices are lower for kids under 12. It's best to book activities ahead.

3 Kings Canyon

Anyone who saw the Australian movie *The Adventures of Priscilla, Queen of the Desert* will remember the stony plateau the transvestites climb to gaze over the majestic plain below. You can stand on that very same spot (wearing sequined underpants is optional) at ✪ **Kings Canyon** in **Watarrka National Park** (☎ **08/8956 7460** for park headquarters), 320 kilometers (200 miles) southwest of Alice Springs as the crow flies. The red sandstone walls of the canyon drop 100 meters (about 330 ft.) to crystal-clear rock pools and centuries-old gum trees.

GETTING THERE

BY PLANE   No regular flights operate, but **Rockayer** (☎ **08/8955 5200** Alice Springs central reservations office, or 08/8956 2345 if you are in Ayers Rock; www.dove.mtx.net.au/~rockayer) does an aerial day trip from Ayers Rock Resort that incorporates the canyon walk at A$410 (U.S.$266.50) per adult, A$380 (U.S.$247) per child 4 to 14.

Rockayer and **Murray Cosson's Australian Outback Flights** (☎ and fax **08/8952 4625;** www.australianoutbackflights.com.au) both offer aerial day trips on a charter basis from Alice Springs. An 8-hour day with Murray Cosson including a flight over the West MacDonnell Ranges and Gosse Bluff meteorite crater, the rim walk, and lunch is around A$410 (U.S.$266.50) per person (based on a minimum two passengers).

BY CAR With a 4WD, you can get to Kings Canyon from Alice Springs on the unpaved Mereenie Loop Road (see "Road Trips from Alice Springs," above).

The regular route is the 480-kilometer (300-mile) trip from Alice Springs south via the Stuart Highway, then west onto the Lasseter Highway, then north and west on the Luritja Road. All three roads are sealed. Uluru (Ayers Rock) is 306 kilometers (191 miles) to the south on a sealed road; from Yulara, take the Lasseter Highway east for 125 kilometers (78 miles), then turn left onto Luritja Road for 168 kilometers (118 miles) to Kings Canyon Resort.

Kings Canyon Resort sells leaded and unleaded petrol and diesel.

BY ORGANIZED TOUR Numerous coach and 4WD tour outfits call at Kings Canyon, with time allowed for the rim walk. See "Exploring the Red Centre," at the beginning of this chapter, for recommended companies.

Uluru Motorcycle Tours (☎ **08/8956 2019;** www.yulara.topend.com.au/ ~harleys) takes you on a 1-day tour by Harley Davidson from Ayers Rock Resort for A$550 (U.S.$357.50) per person (as a passenger) or A$580 (U.S.$377) per person (with you in the driver's seat). Time is allowed to walk the rim.

EXPLORING THE PARK

The way to explore is on the 6-kilometer (3³/₄-mile) walk up the side (short but steep!) and around the rim. Even if you're in good shape, it's a strenuous 3- to 4-hour hike, but well worth the effort. It leads through a maze of rounded sandstone formations called the **Lost City,** across a bridge to the Garden of Eden, a fern-fringed pocket of water holes about half way along, and then back along the other side of the canyon through more sandstone rocks to the starting point. There are lookout points en route. If you visit after the odd occasion when rain falls, the canyon walls will teem with waterfalls. In winter, don't set off too early, because sunlight doesn't light up the canyon walls to good effect until midmorning.

If you're not up to making the rim walk, you can still hike along the shady 2.6-kilometer (0.8-mile) round-trip trail along the mostly dry **Kings Creek bed** on the canyon floor. The trail wanders up to a lookout point and comes back the same way; it takes an hour. Wear sturdy boots, because the ground can be very rocky. This walk is good for very young kids and travelers in wheelchairs for the first 700 meters (half a mile).

Both walks are well signposted. Avoid the rim walk in the middle of the day between September and May; it's too hot.

Apart from campgrounds, the only place to stay in Watarrka National Park is at **Kings Canyon Resort. AAT Kings** provides a coach to and from the resort to the start of the walks for A$38 (U.S.$24.70) per adult, A$19 (U.S.$12.35) kids under 15, round-trip. It departs daily at 6am in summer, 7am in winter (rim walk) and 7am in summer, 8am in winter (creek-bed walk). It's best to book a seat; do this through Kings Canyon Resort.

You can also explore the park from an Aboriginal viewpoint with ✪ **Lilla Aboriginal Tours** (book through Kings Canyon Resort). Aboriginal guides take you on an easy 1-kilometer (0.6-mile) walk to sacred caves and rock-painting sites. You learn about the artworks, hear the Dreamtime events that created the land around you, discover plant medicines and food, and have a go at throwing a spear and a boomerang. The tour lasts

1¹/₂ to 2 hours and departs at 9am, 11am, and 4pm daily (closed mid-Dec to mid-Jan) from the Lilla community, 14 kilometers (9 miles) from Kings Canyon Resort. The resort does transfers for A$20 (U.S.$13) per person, round-trip, or A$30 (U.S.$19.50) for two of you. The tour costs A$29.70 (U.S.$19.30) for adults, A$24.20 (U.S.$15.75) for seniors and students, and is free for kids under 15.

Professional Helicopter Services (☎ **08/8956 7873;** www.phs.com.au) makes 12- to 15-minute scenic flights over the canyon for A$90 (U.S.$58.50) per adult and usually half-price for kids under 13 (depending on their weight, not their age).

ACCOMMODATIONS & DINING

Kings Canyon Resort. Luritja Rd., Watarrka National Park, NT 0872. ☎ **1800/817 622** in Australia, or 08/8956 7442. Fax 08/8956 7410. www.ayersrockresort.com.au. 164 units (128 with bathroom, of which 32 have Jacuzzis); 66 powered campsites and tent sites. A/C TV. High season (July–Nov) A$305–$370 (U.S.$198.25–$240.50) hotel room double; low season (Dec–June) A$256–$321 (U.S.$166.40–$208.65) hotel room double. Extra adult A$22 (U.S.$14.30). Children under 16 stay free in parents' room with existing bedding. A$90–92 (U.S.$58.50–$59.80) double lodge room, A$165–$171 (U.S.$107.25–$111.15) family lodge room (sleeps 5), A$150–$155 (U.S.$107.25–$100.75) quad-share lodge room, or A$40 (U.S.$26) per bed in quad-share lodge room (sharing with strangers). No children in lodge rooms unless you book entire room. Tent sites A$11 (U.S.$7.15) per person; powered sites A$26 (U.S.$16.90) double. Extra person A$10 (U.S.$6.50) adults, A$5 (U.S.$3.25) children 6–15 in powered campsite. Children under 16 dine free at breakfast and dinner buffets at Carmichael's. Ask about packages in conjunction with Ayers Rock Resort and Alice Springs Resort. AE, BC, DC, JCB, MC, V.

This attractive, low-slung complex 7 kilometers (4 miles) from Kings Canyon blends into its surroundings. The nicely decorated hotel rooms have telephones, hair dryers, free movies, and restful range views from the balcony. All but four of the larger deluxe rooms are new (1999) and have desert views from glass-enclosed Jacuzzis. The double, twin, quad, and family lodge rooms are a good low-budget choice, with neatly painted concrete brick walls, tiled floors, heating and air-conditioning, a TV, a minifridge, a dining setting for four, and a communal kitchen and bathroom facilities. The quad-share kind have lockers (should you opt to share with a stranger). Dine in the inexpensive cafe or in **Carmichael's** restaurant, or cook up a steak at the free barbecue area. There are a well-stocked minimart, two bars, two swimming pools, a tour desk, a tennis court, a gift shop, room service, baby-sitting, secretarial services, and a sunset-viewing platform.

4 Uluru-Kata Tjuta National Park (Ayers Rock/The Olgas)

462km (289 miles) SW of Alice Springs; 1,934km (1,202 miles) S of Darwin; 1,571km (976 miles) N of Adelaide; 2,841km (1,765 miles) NW of Sydney

Ayers Rock is the Australia tourism industry's pinup icon, a glamorous red stone that has probably been splashed on more posters than Cindy Crawford has been on magazine covers. Just why people trek from all over the world to gawk at it is a bit of a mystery. For its size? Hardly, for nearby Mt. Conner is three times as big. For its shape? Probably not, when most folks agree the neighboring Olgas are prettier. You can put its popularity down only to the faint shiver up the spine and the indescribable sense of place it evokes in anyone who looks at it. Even taciturn Aussie bushmen reckon it's "got somethin' spiritual about it."

Ayers Rock is commonly known by its Aboriginal name, Uluru. In 1985 the ✪ **Uluru-Kata Tjuta National Park** was returned to its Aboriginal owners, the

Pitjantjatjara and Yankunytjatjara people, together known as the Anangu, who continue to manage the property jointly with the Australian government. People used to speculate that the Rock was a meteorite, but we now know it was formed by conglomerate sediments laid down 600 to 700 million years ago in an ancient inland sea and thrust up above ground 348 meters (1,141 ft.) by geological forces. With a circumference of 9.4 kilometers (6 miles), the Rock is no pebble, especially because two-thirds of it is thought to be underground. On photos it looks like a big smooth blob. In the flesh, it's more interesting—it is dappled with holes and overhangs, and its sides are draped with curtains of stone, creating little coves hiding water holes and Aboriginal rock art.

Don't think a visit to Uluru is just about snapping a few photos and going home. You can walk around the Rock, climb it (although the owners prefer you don't), fly over it, ride a camel to it, motorcycle around it on a Harley-Davidson, trek through the Olgas, eat in an outdoor restaurant, tour the night sky, and join Aboriginal people on some rather special walks. Give yourself at least a couple of days in this area.

Isolation (and a lack of competition?) makes most things expensive at Ayers Rock, whether it be accommodations or meals or transfers. An organized coach tour or 4WD camping safari is often the cheapest way to see the place. The "Exploring the Red Centre" section, at the beginning of this chapter, lists some recommended tour companies.

ESSENTIALS

GETTING THERE   By Plane   Ansett (☎ **13 13 00** in Australia) flies to Ayers Rock (Connellan) Airport direct from Sydney once a day, from Alice Springs once or twice a day, and from Perth four times a week. **Qantas** (☎ **13 13 13** in Australia) flies direct from Sydney daily, and **Airlink** (book through Qantas) flies from Alice Springs two or three times a day, daily from Perth, and twice daily from Cairns. All airlines' flights from most other ports around Australia go via Alice Springs. The airport is 6 kilometers (3³/₄ miles) from Ayers Rock Resort. A free shuttle ferries all resort guests, including campers, to their door.

Murray Cosson's Australian Outback Flights (☎ **08/8952 4625;** www. australianoutbackflights.com.au) does an aerial day trip from Alice Springs that includes scenic flights over the West MacDonnell Ranges, Kings Canyon, Gosse Bluff meteorite crater, and Lake Amadeus; a rental car at Ayers Rock; National Park entry fee; and lunch. Expect to pay around A$520 (U.S.$338) per person (based on a minimum two passengers).

By Bus   Greyhound Pioneer (☎ **13 20 30** in Australia) makes a daily trip from Alice Springs. **McCafferty's** (☎ **13 14 99** in Australia) serves the Rock from Alice on Sunday, Tuesday, Thursday, and Friday. The trip takes about 5¹/₂ hours, and the one-way fare is around A$62 (U.S.$40.30). Both companies drop you to your hotel door at Ayers Rock Resort.

Greyhound Pioneer also does a 2-day tour of Ayers Rock from Alice Springs, looping back to Alice via Kings Canyon on an optional 3rd day.

By Car   Take the Stuart Highway south from Alice Springs for 199 kilometers (124 miles), and turn right onto the Lasseter Highway for 244 kilometers (153 miles) to Ayers Rock Resort. The Rock itself is 18 kilometers (11 miles) farther on. (Everyone mistakes the flat-topped mesa they first see along the way for Ayers Rock; it's Mt. Conner).

If you want to rent a car in Alice Springs and drop it at Ayers Rock, brace yourself for a one-way penalty. Territory Thrifty Car Rental charges a one-way fee of A$80 (U.S.$52) for bookings under 3 days; Hertz charges A$125 (U.S.$81.25) for bookings under 7 days; and Avis charges A$125 (U.S.$81.20) for bookings of 2 days or less.

The Rock in a Day?

You *can* visit Ayers Rock in a day from Alice, but it's a *loooong* day. Most organized coach tours pack a Rock base walk or climb, a visit to the Olgas, a visit to the Uluru-Kata Tjuta Cultural Centre, and a champagne sunset at the Rock into a busy day trip that leaves Alice around 5:30am in winter or 6am in summer and does not get you back until late at night.

Consider a day trip only in the cooler months between May and September. In summer, it's too hot to do much at the Rock between early morning and late afternoon.

As we wrote, Budget did not allow one-way Alice–Ayers Rock rentals. See "Getting Around," in the "Alice Springs" section, for car-rental companies.

VISITOR INFORMATION   For information before you leave home, contact the Central Australian Tourism Industry Association (CATIA), 60 Gregory Terrace, Alice Springs (☎ **1800/645 1299** in Australia, or 08/8952 5800; www.catia.asn.au). By the time you read this, Uluru-Kata Tjuta National Park should have an official Web site at **www.environment.gov.au**. Also try Ayers Rock Resort's site (**www.ayersrockresort.com.au**; click on "Activities" for things to see and do).

The **Ayers Rock Resort Visitor Centre**, next to the Desert Gardens Hotel (☎ **08/8957 7377**), has displays on the area's geology, wildlife, and Aboriginal heritage, plus a souvenir store selling books and videos. It's open daily from 8:30am to 7:30pm. You can book tours at the tour desk in every hotel at Ayers Rock Resort, or visit the **Ayers Rock Resort Tour & Information Centre** (☎ **08/8956 2240**) at the shopping center in the resort complex. It dispenses information on tours as far afield as Kings Canyon and Alice Springs. It's open daily from 8:30am to 8:30pm. Ayers Rock Resort stages a nightly **slide show** as an introduction to the Red Centre's wildlife, geology, and Aboriginal culture.

One kilometer (half a mile) from the base of the Rock is the ✪ **Cultural Centre** (☎ **08/8956 3138**), owned and run by the Anangu, the Aboriginal owners of Uluru. It uses eye-catching wall displays, frescoes, interactive recordings, and videos to tell about Aboriginal Dreamtime myths and laws. It's worth spending some time here to understand a little about Aboriginal culture. A National Park desk here has information on ranger-guided activities; park notes; animal, plant, and bird-watching checklists; a cafe; the Maruku Arts and Crafts gallery selling Aboriginal wares; and a European-style crafts gallery. Open daily from 7am to 5:30pm.

PARK ENTRANCE FEES   Entry to the Uluru-Kata Tjuta National Park is A$16.25(U.S.$10.60) per adult, free for children under 16. At press time, this pass was valid for 5 days; it may be valid for only 3 by the time you arrive. The cost of the pass is included in many organized tours.

ETIQUETTE   You wouldn't like folks photographing your face, church, or backyard without permission, and for the same reason the Anangu ask you not to photograph sacred sites or Aboriginal people without permission. They ask that you approach sacred sites quietly and respectfully.

GETTING AROUND

Every time you want to get from point A to point B at Ayers Rock, it costs. **Ayers Rock Resort** runs a free shuttle every 15 minutes or so around the resort complex between 10:30am and 6pm and 6:30pm and 12:30am (that is, after midnight), but to get to the Rock itself or to the Olgas, you will need to take transfers, join a tour, or have your own wheels.

BY SHUTTLE   The easiest and cheapest way to get around is with **Uluru Express** (☎ **08/8956 2152**). This company provides minibus transport from Ayers Rock Resort to and from the Rock every 45 minutes, and four times a day to the Olgas. Cheapest of all Sunworth's services is a lap of Uluru and a sunset viewing for A$25 (U.S.$16.25); most expensive is a 4-hour trip to the Olgas to walk the Valley of the Winds, followed by sunset back at the Rock, for A$50 (U.S.$32.50). All fares are round-trip.

BY CAR   If there are two of you, it might be cheaper to rent a car than pay for transfers. All roads in the area are sealed, so a 4WD is unnecessary. Expect to pay around A$75 to A$90 (U.S.$48.75 to $58.50) per day for a medium-sized car. Rates drop somewhat in low season. Most car-rental companies will give you the first 100 kilometers (63 miles) free, then charge A25¢ (U.S.16¢) per kilometer after that, or A28¢ (U.S.18¢) per kilometer in a 4WD. Take this into account, because the round-trip from the resort to the Olgas is more than 100 kilometers (63 miles), and that's without driving to the Rock. Only **Avis** (☎ **08/8956 2266**), **Hertz** (☎ **08/ 8956 2244**), and **Territory Thrifty Car Rental** (☎ **08/8956 2030**; book 4WDs through its Darwin office at 08/8924 0000) have outlets at Ayers Rock. All rent regular cars and 4WDs. Booking agent **The Outback Travel Shop** (☎ **08/8955 5288;** www.outbacktravelshop.com.au) in Alice Springs can get you a better deal with Territory Thrifty than you'll get by booking direct.

BY ORGANIZED TOUR   Several tour companies run daily sunrise and sunset viewings, circumnavigations of the Rock by coach or on foot, guided walks at the Rock or the Olgas, camel rides, observatory evenings, visits to the Uluru-Kata Tjuta Cultural Centre, and innumerable permutations and combinations of all these. Some do "passes" containing the most popular activities. Virtually every company picks you up at your hotel. Among the companies are **Uluru Experience** (☎ **1800/803 174** in Australia, or 08/8956 2563; www.ecotours.com.au), which specializes in ecotours for small groups; and large coach operator **AAT Kings** (☎ **08/8956 2171** is the Ayers Rock office; www.aatkings.com.au). **Tailormade Tours** (**08/8952 1731;** www. ozemail.com.au/~tmade/) and **VIP Travel Australia** (☎ **1800/806 412** in Australia, or 08/8956 2388; www.vipaustralia.com.au) do personalized tours and upscale treats like private desert barbecues and champagne tailgate dinners overlooking the Rock or the Olgas.

ABORIGINAL TOURS   Because ✪ **Anangu Tours** (☎ **08/8956 2123**) is owned and run by the Rock's Aboriginal owners, its tours give you firsthand insight into Aboriginal culture. Tours are in the Anangu language, translated to English by an interpreter. On the 2-hour, 2-kilometer (1¼-mile) Liru Walk tour leading from the Cultural Centre to the Rock, you hear Dreamtime stories, discover bush tucker, have a go at throwing a spear, and the like. The walk departs daily at 8:30am April to September, 8am in March and October, and 7:30am November to February, and it costs A$47 (U.S.$30.55) for adults, A$24 (U.S.$15.60) for kids 5 to 15. This doesn't include hotel pickup; if you want that, you will have to join the **Aboriginal Uluru Tour,** which includes sunrise at the Rock and continental breakfast at the Cultural Centre cafe overlooking Uluru, as well as the Liru Walk, for a rather hefty A$98

Water, Water . . .

Fresh water tanks are scarce and kiosks nonexistent in Uluru-Kata Tjuta National Park, so always carry your own drinking water when sightseeing or hiking.

Dinner in the Desert

Ayers Rock Resort's ✪ **Sounds of Silence** dinner is a must. In an outdoor clearing, you'll sip champagne and nibble canapés as the sun sets over the Rock to the strains of a lone didgeridoo, then sit at white-clothed, candlelit tables to a gourmet barbecue of kangaroo, barramundi, and emu, and Aussie wines. After dinner, the lanterns fade, the didgeridoo falls silent, and you are left with stillness. It is the first time some big-city folk have ever heard silence. Next, an astronomer points out the constellations of the Southern Hemisphere's Milky Way. Sounds of Silence is held nightly, weather permitting, and costs A$105 (U.S.$68.25) for adults and A$53 (U.S.$34.45) for children 5 to 16, including transfers from Ayers Rock Resort. It's mighty popular, so book 3 months ahead in peak season. Book through Ayers Rock Resort (see "Accommodations & Dining," under "Uluru-Kata Tjuta National Park (Ayers Rock/The Olgas)," earlier in this chapter).

Couples can dine *a deux* in the desert with Ayers Rock Resort's **"Desert Dinner for a Duo"** experience. This means Australian *méthode champenoise* (sparkling wine) at sunset, a four-course meal over a candlelit table under the stars, and a waiter and chef just for the two of you—at a cool A$250 (U.S.$162.50) per person.

(U.S.$63.70) for adults (or A$79/U.S.$51.35 without breakfast) and A$69 (U.S.$44.85) for kids (or A$54/U.S.$35.10 without breakfast). It departs an hour before sunrise and takes $4^1/_2$ to $5^1/_2$ hours.

The company also does a **Kuniya walk,** where you visit the Kata Tjuta Cultural Centre and the Mutitjulu water hole at the base of the Rock, learn about bush foods, and see rock paintings, before watching the sun set over Uluru. It departs at 2:30pm April through September, 3:30pm October through March, and it costs A$79 (U.S.$51.35) for adults and A$54 (U.S.$35.10) for children with transfers, or A$47 (U.S.$30.55) for adults and A$24 (U.S.$15.60) for kids without.

Ask about family discounts, and slightly cheaper rates for doing more than one tour.

DISCOVERING AYERS ROCK

AT SUNRISE & SUNSET   Sunset is the peak time to catch the Rock's beauty, when fiery oranges, peaches, pinks, reds, and then indigo and deep violet creep across its face as if it were a giant opal. The sunset-viewing car parks are free (as long as you have bought your National Park entry pass). Several companies offer sunset tours from the resort; a coach tour with **AAT Kings** (☎ **08/8956 2171**) departs 90 minutes before sunset, includes a free glass of wine with which to watch the "show," and returns 20 minutes after sundown; the cost is A$28 (U.S.$18.20) for adults, A$25 (U.S.$16.25) seniors and students, and half-price for children 4 to 14.

At sunrise the colors are less dramatic, but the spectacle of the Rock being unveiled by the dawn to birdsong is quite moving. You'll need an early start—most tours leave about 75 minutes before the sun comes up.

CLIMBING IT   Aborigines refer to tourists as "minga"—little ants—because that's what we look like as we crawl up Uluru. Climbing this thing is no picnic—there's sometimes a ferociously strong wind that can blow you right off, the walls are almost vertical in places so you have to hold onto a chain, and it can be freezing cold or insanely hot.

Quite a few people have died climbing the rock from heart attacks, heat stress, exposure, or simply falling off, so if you're not in good shape, have breathing difficulties, heart trouble, or high or low blood pressure, or are just plain scared of heights, don't do it. The Rock is closed to climbers during bad weather; when temperatures exceed 36°C (97°F), which they often do between November and March; and when wind speed exceeds 25 knots, so plan the climb for the stillness of early morning. Wherever you go at Uluru and the Olgas, *bring lots drinking water with you from the resort.*

If all that does not put you off, you will be rewarded with 360° views of the plain far below, the Olgas, and Mt. Conner. The surface is rutted with ravines about 2.5 meters (8 ft.) deep, so be prepared for some scrambling. The climb takes at least 1 hour up for the fit, and 1 hour down. Less sure-footed mountaineers should allow 3 to 4 hours all told.

The Anangu do not like people climbing Uluru, because the climb follows the trail their ancestral Dreamtime Mala men took when they first came to Uluru. They allow people to climb but prefer that they don't.

WALKING, DRIVING, OR BUSING AROUND IT   The easy 9.4-kilometer (6-mile) **Base Walk** circumnavigating Uluru takes about 2 hours, but allow time to linger around the water holes, caves, folds, and overhangs that make up its walls. A shorter walk is the easy 1-kilometer (0.6-mile) round-trip trail from the Mutitjulu parking lot to the pretty water hole near the Rock's base, where there is some rock art. The **Liru Track** is another easy trail; it runs 2 kilometers (1¼ miles) from the Cultural Centre to Uluru, where it links with the Base Walk.

Make time for the free daily 2-kilometer (1¼-mile) ✪ **Mala Walk,** where the ranger, who is often an Aborigine, explains the Dreamtime myths behind Uluru, talks about Aboriginal lifestyles and hunting techniques in days gone by, and explains the significance of the rock art and other sites you see along the way. It leaves the Mala Walk sign at the base of the Uluru climb at 10am May through September, and at a cooler 8am October through April. Allow 1 or 2 hours.

Before setting off, it's a good idea to arm yourself with the self-guided walking notes available for A$1 (U.S.65¢) from the Cultural Centre (see "Visitor Information," above).

A sealed road runs around the Rock.

Uluru Experience (see "Getting Around," above) conducts two guided base tours that give you an insight into natural history, rock art, and Dreamtime beliefs. Both arrive in time for sunrise: one is a 5-hour walk, the other is a 4-hour tour in a vehicle that incorporates short walks to the Rock base and a stop at the Uluru-Kata Tjuta Cultural Centre. Both include breakfast and cost A$98 (U.S.$63.70) for adults and A$65 (U.S.$42.25) for children 6 to 15. Kids under 6 are free but their meals are not included. The 5-hour walk is not suited to kids under 10.

FLYING OVER IT   Several companies do scenic flights by light aircraft or helicopter over Uluru and/or the Olgas, nearby Mt. Conner, the vast white salt pan of Lake Amadeus, and as far as Kings Canyon. As a guide to prices, **Professional Helicopter Services** (☎ **08/8956 2003**) does a 12- to 15-minute flight over Uluru for A$75 (U.S.$48.75) per adult. Kids under 13 usually pay half-price (that depends more on their weight than their age). **Rockayer** (☎ **08/8956 2345**) does a 110-minute Uluru/Olgas/Lake Amadeus/Kings Canyon "joyflight" for A$250 (U.S.$162.50) adults, A$220 (U.S.$143) kids under 15.

MOTORCYCLING AROUND IT   A blast out to the Rock at sunset with **Uluru Motorcycle Tours** (☎ **08/8956 2019;** www.yulara.topend.com.au/~harleys) will set you back A$120 (U.S.$78), or A$180 (U.S.$117) to the Olgas. They drive the bike, you sit behind, hang on, and make like Dennis Hopper in *Easy Rider.* They do

Most tourists do Uluru in the mornings and the Olgas in the afternoon. Beat the crowds by reversing the order: Do the Valley of the Winds walk in the morning and visit Uluru in the afternoon. That way you'll find both places a little more silent and spiritual.

sunrise rides, laps of the Rock, and Rock and/or Olgas tours with walks, also. Self-ride tours are available, at a hefty price.

VIEWING IT ON CAMELBACK   Frontier Camel Tours (☎ **1800/806 499** in Australia, or 08/8956 2444) makes daily forays aboard "ships of the desert" to view Uluru at sunrise and sunset. Amble through red sand dunes with great views of the Rock, dismount to watch the sun rise or sink over it, and ride back to the depot for billy tea and yummy beer bread in the morning, or champagne in the evening. They say a soul travels at the same pace as a camel; it's certainly a peaceful way to see the Rock. The 2-hour rides depart Ayers Rock Resort 1 hour before sunrise, or $1^1/_2$ hours before sunset, and cost A$76 (U.S.$49.40) per person, including transfers from your hotel. Some connect to coach Base Tours of the Rock. Each day between 10:30am and midday you can visit the depot's camels and display free of charge and take a short camel ride for A$10 (U.S.$6.50) for adults, or A$6 (U.S.$3.90) for kids 5 to 12.

EXPLORING THE OLGAS

Although not everyone has heard of massive ✪ **Mt. Olga** (or "the Olgas"), a sister monolith 50 kilometers (31 miles) west of Uluru, many folks who have say she's prettier and more mysterious. Known to the Aborigines as Kata Tjuta or "many heads," the Olgas' 36 momentous red domes bulge out of the earth like turned clay on a potter's wheel. The tallest dome is actually 200 meters (656 ft.) higher than Ayers Rock. The Olgas are more important in Aboriginal Dreamtime legend than Uluru.

Two walking trails take you in among the domes: the 7.4-kilometer ($4^1/_2$-mile) Valley of the Winds walk, which is fairly challenging and takes 3 to 5 hours, and the 2.6-kilometer ($1^1/_2$-mile) Gorge walk, which is easy and takes about an hour. The Valley of the Winds trail is the more rewarding in terms of scenery. Both have lookout points and shady stretches. The Valley of the Winds trail is closed when temperatures rise above 36°C (97°F).

ACCOMMODATIONS & DINING

Ayers Rock Resort not only is in the township of Yulara—it *is* the township. This is the only place to stay at or near Uluru. It is about 16 kilometers (10 miles) from the Rock, outside the national park boundary. Because everyone either is a tourist or lives and works here, the resort has a village atmosphere—with a supermarket; a bank; a post office; child-minding services; a medical center; a hair and beauty salon; several gift, clothing, and souvenir shops; a cinema (both indoor and outdoor); and conference facilities.

You have a choice of six self-contained places to stay, from hotel rooms and apartment buildings to bunkhouses and campsites. All guests may use all the pools, restaurants, and other facilities of every hostelry, except the Sails in the Desert pool, which is reserved for Sails guests. You can book accommodations through the resort's central reservations office in Sydney (☎ **1300/139 889** in Australia, or 02/9339 1040; www.ayersrockresort. com.au; e-mail: reservations@ayersrockresort.com.au). You can also book Kings Canyon Resort and Alice Springs Resort accommodations through this office.

High season is July 1 to November 30. Book well ahead in this period.

Ayers Rock Resort, Alice Springs Resort, and Kings Canyon Resort are operated by the same company, and packages for stays at one, two, or all three resorts are sometimes available. Some include airfares from Australian state capitals, tours, and 4WD safaris. Ask when making your reservation.

As well as the dining options within the hotels below, the resort shopping center has **Gecko's Café,** which offers wood-fired pizzas and Mediterranean cuisine; a bakery; an ice-creamery; and a take-out joint. Kids under 16 dine free at any of the hotels' buffets in the company of an adult.

A tour desk, dry-cleaning and laundry service, and baby-sitting are available at every hostelry and campground. Every single kind of accommodation is air-conditioned.

VERY EXPENSIVE

Sails in the Desert. Yulara Dr., Yulara, NT 0872. ☎ **08/8957 7888.** Fax 08/8957 7475. 232 units (6 with Jacuzzis). A/C MINIBAR TV TEL. High season A$438–$512 (U.S.$282.75–$332.80) double, A$773 (U.S.$502.45) suite. Low season A$403–$470 (U.S.$261.95–$305.50) double, A$717 (U.S.$466.05) suite. Extra person A$22 (U.S.$14.30). AE, BC, DC, JCB, MC, V. Free airport shuttle.

This is the top-of-the-range choice, with elegant, contemporary rooms that were renovated in 1999 in the rich timber-and-stone tones of the desert and Aboriginal art. You do not see the Rock from your room, but most guests are too busy sipping cocktails by the big free-form pool to care. The pool area is shaded by eye-catching white "sails" and surrounded by sun lounges on inviting green lawns. The lobby art gallery regularly has artists-in-residence, both Western and Aboriginal.

Dining/Diversions: The beautiful **Kuniya** serves elegant à la carte European classics with novel bush tucker ingredients; **Winkuku** is a smart buffet venue; and in summer, **Rockpool** serves alfresco Thai fare poolside. The indoor/poolside **Tali Bar** has live piano music nightly.

Amenities: Large heated swimming pool, room service, two day/night tennis courts, putting green, pay-per-view movies, gift shop, secretarial service.

EXPENSIVE

Desert Gardens Hotel. Yulara Drive, Yulara, NT 0872. ☎ **08/8957 7888.** Fax 08/8957 7716. 160 units (100 with shower only). A/C MINIBAR TV TEL. High season A$365–$428 (U.S.$237.25–$278.20) double. Low season A$338–$398 (U.S.$219.70–$258.70) double. Extra person A$22 (U.S.$14.30). AE, BC, DC, JCB, MC, V. Free airport shuttle.

This is the only hotel with views of the Rock (rather distant ones), from some of the 60 deluxe rooms. The accommodations are not as lavish as those at Sails in the Desert, but they're just as comfortable, and smartly done up with creamy walls, botanical prints, and elegant furnishings. All have pay-per-view movies, and bathrooms with hair

---

When You See the Southern Cross for the First Time . . .

There's so little light out in these parts that the night sky in the Red Centre is a dazzler. At the **Ayers Rock Observatory,** you can check out your zodiac constellation and take a 1-hour tour of the Southern Hemisphere heavens (they're different from the Northern Hemisphere stars).

To visit the observatory, you must join a tour with **Uluru Experience** (☎ **1800/ 803 174** in Australia, or 08/8956 2563), which provides hotel pickup and a tour. Tours depart twice a night; times vary. It costs A$30 (U.S.$19.50) for adults, A$22 (U.S.$14.30) for children 6 to 15, and A$63 (U.S.$40.95) for a family.

dryers. You get your own swimming pool and sundeck, the **White Gums** à la carte and buffet restaurant, a poolside bar, a small lobby bar, a gift shop, and room service.

Emu Walk Apartments. Yulara Dr., Yulara, NT 0872. ☎ **08/8957 7888.** Fax 08/8957 7742. 59 apts (all with shower only). A/C MINIBAR TV TEL. High season A$342 (U.S.$222.30) 1-bedroom apt, A$424 (U.S.$275.60) 2-bedroom apt for 4. Low season A$314 (U.S.$204.10) 1-bedroom apt, A$390 (U.S.$253.50) 2-bedroom apt. Extra person A$22 (U.S.$14.30). AE, BC, DC, JCB, MC, V. Free airport shuttle.

These bright, contemporary apartments have full kitchens, laundry areas, and living areas, and are serviced daily. They have room service, pay-per-view movies, and hair dryers. There's no restaurant or pool; but Gecko's Café and the supermarket are close, and you can cool off in the Desert Gardens Hotel pool next door.

Outback Pioneer Hotel and Lodge. Yulara Dr., Yulara, NT 0872. ☎ **08/8957 7888.** Fax 08/8957 7615. 125 units, all with private bathroom; 12 cabins, none with private bathroom; 36 quad-share bunkrooms and 4 20-bed single-sex dorms, none with private bathroom. A/C. High season A$331 (U.S.$215.15) double, $147 (U.S.$95.55) cabin. Low season A$303 (U.S.$196.95) double, A$138 (U.S.$89.70) cabin. Extra person A$22 (U.S.$14.30). Bunkroom bed A$38 (U.S.$24.70), dorm bed A$30 (U.S.$19.50), year-round. No children under 16 in bunkhouses unless you book entire room. AE, BC, DC, JCB, MC, V. Free airport shuttle.

A happy, all-ages crowd congregates at this mid-range collection of hotel rooms, cabins, bunkrooms, and dorms. The decent-sized hotel rooms got a smart refurbishing in 1999; each has an adequately sized bathroom, a minibar, a TV, pay-per-view movies, a telephone, and a hair dryer. Some also have sinks and microwaves. The cabins have double beds and bunks, shared bathroom facilities, and a shared kitchen, but they are still comfortably decked out with self-serve tea and coffee and minirefrigerators. Out by the nice pool, there are plenty of sundeck lounges.

The **Bough House Restaurant and Bar** does à la carte lunch and buffet dinners, and there is a dirt-cheap kiosk; but just about the entire resort gathers nightly at the ✪ **Pioneer Barbeque and Bar.** This rustic barn with big tables, lots of beer, and live music is the place to join the throngs throwing a steak on the communal cook-it-yourself barbie.

INEXPENSIVE

Ayers Rock Campground. Yulara Dr., Yulara, NT 0872. ☎ **08/8956 2055.** Fax 08/8956 2260. 220 tent sites, 198 powered sites, 14 cabins (none with bathroom). A$132 (U.S.$85.80) cabin for up to 6 people. A$13 (U.S.$8.45) per person tent site; A$29 (U.S.$18.85) double powered site. Additional person A$11 (U.S.$7.15) adults, A$5 (U.S.$3.25) children 6–15 in powered site. AE, BC, DC, JCB, MC, V. Free airport shuttle.

Instead of red dust you get blissfully green lawns at this campground, which has its own pool, barbecues, clean communal bathrooms, telephones, Laundromat, and even its own tour desk. If you don't want to camp but you want to travel cheap, consider the cabins. They're clean, modern, and a great value; each has a kitchenette, petite dining furniture, a double bed, and four bunks. They share bathroom facilities. Territory Thrifty Car Rental (☎ **08/8956 2030**) rents camping gear to its customers for A$25 (U.S.$16.25) per day; you must book it ahead. Hertz will cease renting camping gear to customers after April 1, 2001.

Spinifex Lodge. Yulara Dr., Yulara, NT 0872. ☎ **08/8957 7888.** Fax 08/8957 7755. 34 units and 34 quad-share bunkhouses, none with private bathroom. A/C TV TEL. A$135–$145 (U.S.$87.75–$94.25) double or bunkhouse. Extra person A$22 (U.S.$14.30). AE, BC, DC, JCB, MC, V. Free airport shuttle.

If you can handle shared bathrooms, your best budget-wise bet outside camping are these clean, cool, smartly furnished rooms. Both the twin/double rooms and the bunkrooms have kitchenettes, TVs, telephones, and pay-per-view movies. There's no pool, but you can walk a few hundred meters and use the one at Desert Gardens. There's no restaurant either, but a few eateries and the supermarket are next door.

The Top End   8

by Natalie Kruger

The "Top End" is the term Aussies use to refer to the vast sweep of barely inhabited country from Broome on the west coast of Western Australia to Arnhemland in the Northern Territory and eastern Queensland. It is the place Mick "Croc" Dundee called home, a genuine last frontier, a place of wild beauty and, sometimes, hardship.

The rugged northwest portion of Western Australia is known as the Kimberley, where beef cattle farming, pearl farming, and tourism thrive in a rocky moonscape of red cliffs, waterfalls, mighty rivers, sparse gums, and wetland lagoons. Here you can visit a million-acre cattle station rich in ancient Aboriginal rock art sites, tour the world's largest diamond mine, cruise the lush Ord River to see hundreds of native birds, ride a camel on the beach, hike ancient red gorges, visit a working pearl farm, and shop for the world's biggest and best South Sea pearls.

The northern reaches of the Northern Territory are slightly more populated than the Kimberley, but only just. Darwin, the capital, is a smallish city, rich, modern, and tropical. Katherine, to its south, is a small farming town famous for a beautiful river gorge. Here you can drop by on an Aboriginal community, explore vast cattle stations, canoe jungly rivers, and soak in natural thermal pools. To the east of Darwin and Katherine is Kakadu National Park, home to wetlands, crocodiles, and millions of birds—one-third of the country's bird species, in fact. Farther east still is Arnhemland, an endless stretch of rocky ridges and flooding rivers owned by Aboriginal people. Few white folks ever penetrate here.

Life is a bit different in the Top End than elsewhere in Australia, especially in the Northern Territory. It has a slightly lawless image, which I suspect Territorians enjoy cultivating among tenderfoot Aussies from the south. The isolation, the intense humidity in the summer Wet Season, monsoonal floods, human-eating crocodiles, and other dangers breed a tough kind of guy and girl. Mick "Crocodile" Dundee may only be a movie character, but the scriptwriters didn't exaggerate entirely when they invented him.

EXPLORING THE TOP END

Read "Exploring the Red Centre," at the start of chapter 7; it contains information on traveling the entire Northern Territory.

VISITOR INFORMATION   The **Northern Territory Tourist commission** (NTTC), Tourism House, 43 Mitchell St., Darwin, NT 0800

(☎ **08/8999 3900;** www.nttc.com.au—click on the "U.S." tab for information tailored to American travelers), can supply you with information on Darwin, Litchfield National Park, Kakadu National Park, Katherine, and any other destinations in the Territory. The Darwin Region Tourism Association and the Katherine Region Tourist Association (listed in the "Darwin" and "Katherine" sections of this chapter) can also supply useful information about the entire Top End and the Kimberley, not just their respective local regions.

Your best source of information on the Kimberley region is the Broome Tourist Bureau or the Kununurra Tourist Bureau (both listed in section 4 of this chapter). You can also contact the **Western Australian Tourism Commission** (WATC), 16 St. Georges Terrace, Perth, WA 6000 (☎ **08/9220 1700;** www.westernaustralia.net).

WHEN TO GO   The sanest time to visit the Top End is in the winter **Dry Season** ("the Dry"). Not a cloud will grace the sky, and temperatures will be comfortable, even hot in the middle of the day. The Dry runs roughly from **late April to the end of October.** It is high season, so book every tour, hotel, or campsite in advance.

The **Wet Season** ("the Wet") runs **from November** (sometimes as early as Oct) **to March or April,** sometimes a few weeks longer in the Kimberley. While it does not rain 24 hours a day during the Wet, it comes down in buckets when it does, usually for an hour or two each day, mainly in the late afternoon or overnight. The land floods as far as the eye can see, the humidity is murderous, and the temperatures hit nearly 40°C (104°F). The floods cut off many attractions, sometimes suddenly, and some tour companies shut up shop for the season. Cyclones may hit the coast during the Wet, roughly with the same savagery and frequency as hurricanes hit Florida. Many people find the "build-up" to the Wet in October and November, when clouds gather but do not break, the toughest time to be in the Top End.

Having said all that, the Wet is a wonderful time to travel. Waterfalls become massive torrents, fork lightning storms crackle across the afternoon sky, the land turns green, cloud cover keeps the worst of the sun off you, and crowds vanish. Keep your plans flexible to account for floods, take it slow in the heat, and carry loads of drinking water, and you should be okay. Even if you normally camp, sleep in air-conditioned accommodations now. Book tours ahead, because most will operate on a reduced schedule.

GETTING AROUND   The **Automobile Association of the Northern Territory** (AANT), 79–81 Smith St., Darwin, NT 0800 (☎ **08/8981 3837**), and the **Royal Automobile Club of Western Australia** (RACWA), 228 Adelaide Terrace, Perth, WA 6000 (☎ **08/9421 4444**), are both good sources of maps and road advice.

Go-it-alone travelers will like the **Blue Banana** (☎ **08/8945 6800;** www.octa4.net.au/banana), a minibus that does a running loop between Darwin, Kakadu National Park, Katherine, and Litchfield National Park. Jump on and off whenever you like at the 26 stops, pick up the bus on its next trip through (it runs 4 days a week), and get treated to a guided commentary and photo stops en route. The only real rule is that you must book your next leg 24 hours in advance. The whole loop is A$170 (U.S.$110.50), or you can buy a single leg. You're responsible for your own meals, accommodations, and activities. The company rents camping gear.

TRAVELING IN THE WET   Some roads will be underwater throughout the Wet, while others can flood unexpectedly, leaving you cut off for hours, days, or even months. Flash floods pose dangers to unwary motorists. Don't cross a flooded road

The Northern Territory

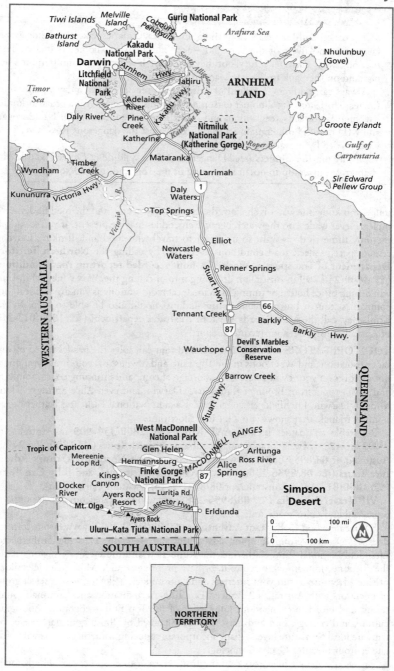

Tiwi Islands
Melville Island
Bathurst Island
Cobourg Peninsula
Gurig National Park
Arafura Sea

Kakadu National Park
Arnhem Hwy.
Darwin
Litchfield National Park
Adelaide River
Daly R.
Daly River
Pine Creek
Katherine
Jabiru
Kakadu Hwy.
Katherine R.
South Alligator R.

ARNHEM LAND

Nhulunbuy (Gove)

Timor Sea

Nitmiluk National Park (Katherine Gorge)
Roper R.

Groote Eylandt

Gulf of Carpentaria

Mataranka

Wyndham
Timber Creek
Kununurra
Victoria Hwy.
Victoria R.

Larrimah

Sir Edward Pellew Group

Daly Waters
Top Springs

Newcastle Waters
Elliot

Renner Springs
Stuart Hwy.

WESTERN AUSTRALIA

Tennant Creek
66
Barkly
Barkly Hwy.
87

Devil's Marbles Conservation Reserve
Wauchope

Barrow Creek
Stuart Hwy.

QUEENSLAND

West MacDonnell National Park
MACDONNELL RANGES
Glen Helen
Mereenie Loop Rd.
Hermannsburg
Finke Gorge National Park
Arltunga
Ross River
Alice Springs
87

Kings Canyon
Docker River
Ayers Rock Resort
Luritja Rd.
Lasseter Hwy.
Mt. Olga
Ayers Rock
Uluru–Kata Tjuta National Park
Erldunda

Tropic of Capricorn

Simpson Desert

0   100 mi
0   100 km

SOUTH AUSTRALIA

NORTHERN TERRITORY

Croc Alert! (& Other Safety Tips)

Saltwater crocodiles are a serious threat in the sea, estuaries, lakes, wetlands, waterfall pools, and rivers of the Top End—even hundreds of kilometers inland. They may be called "saltwater" crocs, but they live in fresh water. Never jump in the water or stand on the bank unless you want to be lunch.

Always carry 4 liters (a gallon) of **drinking water** per person a day when walking (increase to 1 liter/¹/₄ gallon per person *per hour* in summer). Wear a broad-brimmed hat, high-factor sunscreen lotion, and insect repellent containing DEET (Aerogard and RID brands both contain it) to protect against the dangerous Ross River Fever virus carried by mosquitoes.

Deadly **marine stingers** (see "Dangerous Aussie Wildlife & Other Hazards," in chapter 2) put a stop to ocean swimming in the Top End from October to April.

unless you know the water is shallow, the current very gentle, and the road underneath intact. Never wade into the water, because crocodiles may be present. If you're cut off, the only thing to do is wait, so it's smart to travel with food and drinking water in remote parts. Check road conditions every day by calling the **Northern Territory Department of Transport & Works' 24-hour recorded report on road conditions** (☎ 1800/246 199 in Australia); dropping into or calling the AANT (above) in Darwin during office hours; or tuning in to the local radio stations as you drive. Local tour companies, tourist bureaus, and police stations should also be able to help. In the Kimberley, call the **Main Roads Western Australia** department (☎ 1800/013 314 in Australia) for a 24-hour recorded report.

TOUR OPERATORS   Taking an organized tour can solve the hassles posed by distance, isolation, and Wet floods in the Top End, and it will show you things you might not discover on your own. There is no shortage of companies running coach, minibus, and 4WD tours from Broome, Kununurra, Darwin, and even Alice Springs. A loop through Darwin, Litchfield National Park, Kakadu National Park, and Katherine is a popular triangle that shows you a lot in a short time.

Reputable companies include **AAT Kings** (☎ 1800/334 009 in Australia, or 03/9274 7422; www.aatkings.com.au); **Sahara Outback Tours** (☎ 1800/806 240 in Australia, or 08/8953 0881; www.saharatours.com.au); **Northern Territory Adventure Tours** (☎ 08/8936 1300; www.adventuretours.com.au); and **Billy Can Tours** (☎ 1800/813 484 in Australia, or 08/8981 9813; www.billycan.com.au).

VIP Travel Australia (☎ 08/8956 2388; www.vipaustralia.com.au) does luxury organized and tailor-made tours.

Katherine-based ✪ **Far Out Adventures** (☎ 08/8972 2552; www.farout.com.au) does 4WD small-group camping adventures into Kakadu, Darwin, Arnhemland, Litchfield National Park, Katherine, the Kimberley, and more remote regions across the Top End. Join an organized tour, or have proprietor/guide Mike Keighley tailor a private adventure to suit your interests and your budget. Mike is one of a select group of operators with Australia's Advanced Eco Tour Accreditation and Savannah Guide status, and he has a tremendous knowledge of the Top End's geography, Aboriginal culture, and ecology. Fun and personal, accompanied by "bush gourmet" meals, his trips are ideal for nature lovers; many incorporate canoeing wilderness rivers with affiliate ecotour operator Gecko Canoeing.

For details of tour operators running from Darwin to Broome, see "The Kimberley" section, later in this chapter.

1 Darwin

1,489km (923 miles) N of Alice Springs

Named after the founder of evolution himself, Australia's northernmost capital (pop. 97,750), full of proud white civic buildings adorned with pink bougainvillea, has a touch of Asian exoticism about it. It's a modern tropical capital—extremely modern, actually, because most of it was rebuilt after Cyclone Tracy wiped out the city on Christmas Eve 1974. Don't bother bringing along a jacket and tie here. Shorts and sandals will get you most places—even the swankiest official state invitations stipulate dress as "Territory Rig," meaning long pants and a short-sleeved open-necked shirt for men.

The city is most commonly used as a gateway to Kakadu National Park, Katherine Gorge, and the Kimberley. Australians look at you askance when you say you're visiting this place ("What the heck are you going to do in Darwin?"), but I really like its mix of frontier rawness, scenic beauty, and surprisingly sophisticated food. Give yourself at least a day to wander the pleasant streets and parklands, visit the wildlife attractions, and maybe explore the city's World War II history. The wetlands fishing is excellent, as is the shopping for Aboriginal art and the Top End's illustrious South Sea pearls. An easy day trip away is Litchfield National Park, one of the Territory's best-kept secrets.

ESSENTIALS

GETTING THERE   **Qantas** (☎ **13 13 13** in Australia) and **Ansett** (☎ **13 13 00** in Australia) serve Darwin daily from most state capitals; flights either are direct or connect in Alice Springs. Qantas flies direct from Cairns daily, as does Ansett twice a week. Ansett flies daily from Broome, either direct or via Kununurra, and Airlink (book through Qantas) makes a direct Broome–Darwin flight twice a week. **Airnorth** (☎ **1800/627 474** in Australia, or 08/8945 2866, or book through Ansett) flies to Darwin every day except Saturday from Alice Springs via Tennant Creek and Katherine. It also operates an extra service most days from Katherine. There are also direct international flights to Darwin from Asia.

Darwin Airport Shuttle Services (☎ **1800/358 945** in the Northern Territory, or 08/8981 5066) meets every flight and delivers to city hotels (including the MGM Grand) for A$7 (U.S.$4.55) one-way or A$12 (U.S.$7.80) round-trip. Children under 10 travel free. You don't need to book a seat. A cab to the city is around A$15 (U.S.$9.75), or A$17 (U.S.$11.05) at night, on Sundays, and on public holidays.

Greyhound Pioneer (☎ **13 20 30** in Australia) and **McCafferty's** (☎ **13 14 99** in Australia) make a daily coach run to Darwin from Alice Springs. The trip takes around 18¹/₂ hours, and the fare is A$157 (U.S.$102.05). Greyhound also has daily service from Broome via Kununurra and Katherine; this trip takes around 26¹/₂ hours and costs A$234.40 (U.S.$152.40). Both companies run from Cairns via Townsville and Tennant Creek.

Darwin is at the end of the Stuart Highway. Allow at least 2 very long days, 3 to be comfortable, to drive from Alice. The nearest road route from the east is the Barkly Highway, which connects with the Stuart Highway at Tennant Creek, 922 kilometers (572 miles) south. The nearest road from the west is the Victoria Highway, which joins the Stuart Highway at Katherine, 314 kilometers (195 miles) to the south.

There is no train service to Darwin.

VISITOR INFORMATION   The **Darwin Region Tourism Association,** Beagle House, Knuckey Street at Mitchell Street, Darwin, NT 0800 (☎ **08/8981 4300;**

e-mail: drtainfo@ozemail.com.au), is the place to go for maps, bookings, and information. It's open Monday through Friday 8:30am to 5:45pm, Saturday 9am to 2:45pm, and Sunday and public holidays 10am to 1:45pm. It stocks official guides to all the Top End's national parks, too.

CITY LAYOUT   The heart of the city is the **Smith Street pedestrian mall.** One street over is the lively **Mitchell Street Tourist Precinct,** full of backpacker lodges, cheap eateries, and souvenir stores. Two streets past that is the harborfront **Esplanade.** In the **Old Wharf precinct,** near town, are a couple of tourist attractions, a jetty popular with local fishermen, and a working dock. **Cullen Bay Marina** is a "millionaire's row" of restaurants, cafes, and expensive boats; it's about a 25-minute walk northwest of town. A couple of miles northwest of the town center is **Fannie Bay,** where you'll find the Botanic Gardens, sailing club, golf course, museum and art gallery, and casino.

GETTING AROUND   For car and 4WD rentals, call **Avis** (☎ 08/8981 9922), **Budget** (☎ 08/8981 9800), **Hertz** (☎ 08/8941 0944), or **Territory Thrifty Car Rental** (☎ 08/8924 0000).

Darwinbus (☎ **08/8924 7666**) is the local bus company. The city terminus is on Harry Chan Avenue (behind the Commonwealth Bank and Qantas buildings). Get timetables there, or from the Darwin Region Tourism Association.

The **Tour Tub bus** (☎ **1800/63 2225** in Australia, or 08/8981 5233) does a loop of most city attractions and major hotels between 9am and 4pm daily. Hop on and off as often as you like all day for A$22 (U.S.$14.30) for adults, A$13.20 (U.S.$8.60) for children ages 4 to 12. It departs the Knuckey Street end of Smith Street Mall. **Darwin Day Tours** (☎ **08/8981 8696**) has a range of sightseeing tours.

Call **Darwin Radio Taxis** (☎ **131 008**) for a cab. The taxi stand is at the Knuckey Street end of Smith Street Mall.

EXPLORING DARWIN

Darwin's parks, stunning harbor, and tropical clime make it a lovely city for strolling during the Dry. The tourist office has free maps of a Historical Stroll that takes you to 17 points of interest around town. The Esplanade makes a pleasantly short and shady saunter; and the **Darwin Botanic Gardens** (☎ **08/8981 1958**), on Gardens Road 1.5 kilometers (a mile) from town, has paths through palms, orchids, and lawns, plus an Aboriginal plant-use trail. Entry is free daily. Take bus 4 or 6.

The pleasant 5-kilometer (3-mile) trail along **Fannie Bay** from the MGM Grand to the East Point Military Museum is also worth doing. Keep a lookout for the some 2,000 wild wallabies that live on the east side of Alec Fong Lim Drive near the museum.

Darwin has two wildlife parks worth visiting. At the **Territory Wildlife Park** (☎ **08/8988 7200**), 61 kilometers (38 miles) south of Darwin, you can take a free shuttle or walk 6 kilometers (3³/₄ miles) of bush trails to see native Northern Territory wildlife in 12 natural habitats. Bats, bilbies, and birds live in a walk-through aviary; sawfish and stingrays are the residents in a walk-through aquarium; and spiders, crocs, and kangaroos also make their home here (but not koalas, because they don't live in the Territory). Go first thing to see the animals at their liveliest. Take the Stuart Highway for 50 kilometers (31 miles) and turn right onto the Cox Peninsula Road for another 11 kilometers (7 miles). Allow 4 hours to see everything, plus traveling time. Open daily 8:30am to 6pm (last entry at 4pm), and closed Christmas. Admission is A$18 (U.S.$11.70) for adults, A$9 (U.S.$5.85) for seniors and students and children 5 to 16, and A$40 (U.S.$26) for a family of six.

Darwin

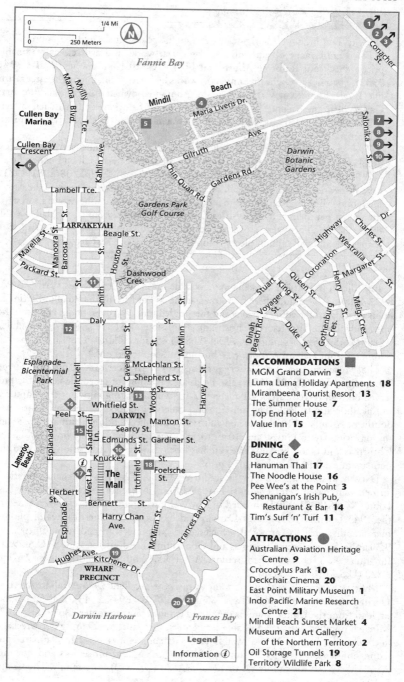

ACCOMMODATIONS ■
MGM Grand Darwin **5**
Luma Luma Holiday Apartments **18**
Mirambeena Tourist Resort **13**
The Summer House **7**
Top End Hotel **12**
Value Inn **15**

DINING ◆
Buzz Café **6**
Hanuman Thai **17**
The Noodle House **16**
Pee Wee's at the Point **3**
Shenanigan's Irish Pub,
  Restaurant & Bar **14**
Tim's Surf 'n' Turf **11**

ATTRACTIONS ●
Australian Avaiation Heritage
  Centre **9**
Crocodylus Park **10**
Deckchair Cinema **20**
East Point Military Museum **1**
Indo Pacific Marine Research
  Centre **21**
Mindil Beach Sunset Market **4**
Museum and Art Gallery
  of the Northern Territory **2**
Oil Storage Tunnels **19**
Territory Wildlife Park **8**

Legend
Information ⓘ

The Darwin Shopping Scene

Darwin's best buys are Aboriginal art and crafts, pearls, opals, and diamonds.

For a great range of authentic Aboriginal artworks and artifacts at reasonable prices, check out **Raintree Aboriginal Fine Arts,** 20 Knuckey St. (☎ **08/8941 9933**). For a heavyweight investment in works by internationally sought-after artists like Emily Kame Kngwarreye, visit the Aboriginal-owned **Aboriginal Fine Arts Gallery,** on the second floor on the corner of Knuckey and Mitchell Streets (☎ **08/8981 1315**). Its Web site at **www.aaia.com.au** is a useful guide to art and artists.

The world's best South Sea pearls are farmed in the Top End seas. Buy, or just drool in the window, at **Paspaley Pearls,** just off Smith Street Mall on Bennett Street (☎ **08/8981 9332**). The **World of Opal,** 44 Smith St. Mall (☎ **08/8981 8981**), has a re-creation of an opal mine in their showroom. If you can't make it to the Argyle Diamond Mine in Kununurra to buy your pink diamond (the world's rarest) at the source, get them at **S. & J. Miles Creative Jewellers,** 27 Smith St. Mall (☎ **08/ 8941 1233**). They also stock the champagne diamonds for which Argyle is renowned, and will fashion pieces within 24 hours for overseas visitors.

In addition to housing a fascinating crocodile museum, **Crocodylus Park** (☎ **08/ 8922 4500**), a 15-minute drive from town at the end of McMillan's Road in Berrimah, holds exciting croc-feeding sessions and free guided tours at 10am, noon, and 2pm. It's open daily 9am to 5pm (closed Christmas). Admission is A$18 (U.S.$11.70) for adults, A$15 (U.S.$9.75) for seniors, and A$9 (U.S.$5.85) for children 5 to 15. The park is 5 minutes from Darwin Airport; take bus no. 5 (Mon to Fri only).

The **Museum and Art Gallery of the Northern Territory,** Conacher Street, Fannie Bay (☎ **08/8999 8201**), also holds an attraction for crocodile fans—the preserved body of Sweetheart, a 5.1-meter (17-ft.) woman-eating saltwater croc captured in Kakadu National Park. The museum and gallery have good sections on Aboriginal, Southeast Asian, and Pacific art and culture. Both gallery and museum are open 9am to 5pm Monday to Friday, and 10am to 5pm weekends and public holidays (closed Christmas and Good Friday). The cafe has lovely bay views. Admission is free to the permanent exhibits. Take bus no. 4 or 6.

Darwin was an Allied supply base during World War II, when many American airmen were based here. The **East Point Military Museum,** East Point Road, East Point (☎ **08/8981 9702**), housed in a WWII gun command post, plays a video of the 1943 Japanese bombing of Darwin and has small but fine displays of photos, memorabilia, artillery, armored vehicles, and weaponry old and new. Open daily 9:30am to 5pm (closed Christmas and Good Friday). Admission is A$8 (U.S.$5.20) for adults, A$6 (U.S.$3.90) for seniors, A$4 (U.S.$2.60) for children under 15, and A$20 (U.S.$13) for a family.

Military or aircraft buffs won't want to miss the excellent ✪ **Australian Aviation Heritage Centre,** 557 Stuart Hwy., Winnellie (☎ **08/8947 2145**). A B-52 bomber on loan from the United States is the prized exhibit, but the center also boasts a B-25 Mitchell bomber, Mirage and Sabre jet fighters, rare Japanese Zero fighter wreckage, and good displays on World War II and Vietnam. Hours are daily 9am to 5pm. Admission is A$8 (U.S.$5.20) for adults, A$5 (U.S.$3.25) for seniors and students, A$4 (U.S.$2.60) for children 6 to 12, and A$20 (U.S.$13) for a family. The Centre is 10 minutes from town; take the no. 5 or 8 bus.

On Kitchener Drive in the Old Wharf precinct, you can walk through the **World War II oil storage tunnels** (☎ **1800/63 2225** in Australia, or 08/8981 5233), which contain a substantial collection of black-and-white photographs of the war in Darwin, each one hauntingly lit up in the dark. Admission is $4. The tunnels are usually closed December 10 to 27, and all of February, and their hours are restricted during the Wet.

On the Esplanade stands a monument to the destroyer U.S.S. *Robert E. Peary*, which went down in Darwin Harbour, with a loss of 88 lives.

At the **Indo Pacific Marine Research Centre** at Stokes Hill Wharf (☎ **08/8981 1294**), you watch a brief film before taking a guided tour of living coral reefs in tanks. The 3¹/₂-hour night show at 7pm (Wed, Fri, and Sun only) is especially good, because coral is luminous in the dark; it's combined with seafood dinner for A$65.45 (U.S.$42.55) adults, A$32.45 (U.S.$21.10) kids under 14. The 1-hour day tour alone is A$15.50 (U.S.$10.10), and A$5.50 (U.S.$3.60) for kids. The Centre opens daily from 9am to 5pm, only to 1pm in the Wet. Between May and October the Centre does 6-hour guided eco-explorations of the city's mangroves and rock pools for A$82.50 (U.S.$53.65) or A$64.90 (U.S.$42.20) for kids.

The Top End's vast wetlands and warm oceans are **fishing** heaven. The big prey is barramundi, but the many other catches include tarpon, salmon, and marlin. Loads of charter boats conduct jaunts from a mere morning to up to 10 days in the river and wetland systems around Darwin, Kakadu National Park, and remote Arnhemland. If you just want to cast a line in Darwin Harbour, **Tour Tub Fishing Charters** (☎ **1800/63 2225** in Australia, or 08/8981 5233) will take you out for A$71.50 (U.S.$46.50) for a half day, or A$132 (U.S.$85.80) for a full day. On the inland wetlands, one of the most experienced operators is **Land-A-Barra Tours** (☎ **08/ 8932 2543**), which takes a maximum three anglers on day trips for A$264 (U.S.$171.60) per person, or extended fishing safaris with meals and basic accommodation for A$407 (U.S.$264.55) per person per day. Prices are cheaper for three people, pricier for a single traveler.

ACCOMMODATIONS

April to October is the peak travel Dry Season; from November to March, the Wet Season, hotels usually drop their rates.

EXPENSIVE

MGM Grand Darwin. Gilruth Ave., The Gardens, Darwin, NT 0800. ☎ **1800/89 1118** in Australia, or 08/8943 8888. Fax 08/8943 8999. E-mail: res@mgmgrand.com.au. 96 units. A/C MINIBAR TV TEL. A$159.50–$198 (U.S.$103.70–$128.70) double; A$236.50–$302.50 (U.S.$153.75–$196.65) suite. Extra person A$44 (U.S.$28.60). Children under 13 stay free in parents' room with existing bedding. AE, BC, DC, JCB, MC, V. Free valet and self-parking. Bus: 4, 6.

Attached to Darwin's casino on Fannie Bay, this rather grand hotel is well priced for such an upscale place. The whole complex resembles a tropical palace with its white blocky architecture and 18 acres of gardens on Mindil Beach. It's worth paying the A$27.50 (U.S.$17.90) extra to guarantee an ocean-facing room so you can watch Darwin's great sunsets. The rooms are a cocktail of European-style/contemporary Spanish furniture, recessed ceilings with ornate friezes, and the tropical elegance of timber louvers and potted palms. All units have pay-per-view movies, hair dryers, iron and boards, and bathrobes; the suites come with Jacuzzis. The Botanic Gardens are nearby, as is a 9-hole public golf course across the road (free for suite guests). A beachside stroll brings you to the Museum and Art Gallery. A free shuttle runs a couple of times a day to the city, which is an A$6 (U.S.$3.90) cab ride away.

Dining/Diversions: E'Voo in the Boardroom offers fine dining overlooking the ocean; the Dragon Court Chinese restaurant is popular with locals; and the Sunset Café serves all-day meals and snacks. The pool bar opens in the Dry. The Cariba Lounge in the casino has live entertainment. Sweetheart's nightclub is located under the hotel.

Amenities: Swimming pool, children's pool, Jacuzzi, sauna, massage, gym, jogging track, day/night tennis court, 24-hour concierge, 24-hour room service, dry-cleaning service, baby-sitting, conference facilities, business center, gift shop, tour desk.

MODERATE

Luma Luma Holiday Apartments. Knuckey St. at Woods St., Darwin, NT 0800. ☎ **1800/ 656 988** in Australia, or 08/8981 1899. Fax 08/8981 1882. 64 units (all with shower only). A/C TV TEL. Dry Season A$134.20 (U.S.$87.25) studio, A$160.60 (U.S.$104.40) 1-bedroom apt (sleeps 4), A$242 (U.S.$157.30) 2-bedroom apt (sleeps 6). Wet Season A$119.90 (U.S.$77.95) studio, A$149.60 (U.S.$97.24) 1-bedroom apt, A$225.50 (U.S.$146.60) 2-bedroom apt. Extra bed A$15 (U.S.$9.75). Free crib. AE, BC, DC, JCB, MC, V. Free parking.

Built in 1997, these nicely decorated, good-size serviced apartments in the city center are perfect for families. Even the one-bedroom apartments sleep four comfortably, but families can take a two-bedroom apartment and the kids get their own bathroom and their own TV in the bedroom. The studios have kitchenettes, while apartments come with full kitchens. Bathrooms are big enough for everyone to spread out all their gear; the front desk lends hair dryers. The complex has a nice big swimming pool, an important consideration in Darwin's heat. Smith Street Mall is just 2 blocks away. No smoking.

Mirambeena Tourist Resort. 64 Cavenagh St., Darwin, NT 0800. ☎ **1800/891 100** in Australia, or 08/8946 0111. Fax 08/8981 5116. www.mirambeena.com.au. E-mail: Info@mirambeena.com.au. 225 units (all with shower only). A/C TV TEL. A$143–179.30 (U.S.$92.95–$116.55) double, A$218.90 (U.S.$142.30) town house (sleeps 4). Extra person A$24.40 (U.S.$15.90). Children under 3 stay free. Ask about lower rates Oct–Apr. AE, BC, DC, MC, V. Free parking for limited cars, plus on-street parking. Bus: 4, 5, 6, 8, 10.

You're just a stone's throw from the city center at this modern hotel complex, where the tempting saltwater swimming pools, the Jacuzzis, and the treetop restaurant, all shaded by the leaves of a sprawling strangler fig, have a castaway island feel. All rooms were refurbished in 1998 to a high standard; each is a decent size and has a hair dryer, an iron and board, free in-room movies, and some kind of garden or pool view, plus minibars on request. Town houses with kitchenettes are good for families, if you can handle sharing the compact bathroom with your kids. The place also has a pool bar and cafe, dry-cleaning service, room service, a gym, a game room, minigolf, bike rental, a children's pool, baby-sitting, a tour desk, conference facilities, secretarial service, and a lobby shop.

Top End Hotel. Mitchell St. at Daly St., Darwin, NT 0801. ☎ **1800/626 151** in Australia, or 08/8981 6511. Fax 08/8941 1253. www.bestwestern.com. E-mail: topendhotelaccommodation@ tmgroup.com.au. 40 units (all with shower only). A/C TV TEL. Dry Season A$152 (U.S.$98.80) double, A$163 (U.S.$105.95) triple. Wet Season A$126 (U.S.$81.90) double, A$138 (U.S.$89.70) triple. Extra person A$20 (U.S.$13) adult, A$16 (U.S.$10.40) child under 12. AE, BC, DC, JCB, MC, V. Free parking. Bus: 4, 5, 6, 8, 10.

Where Can I Swim?

It makes you sigh, especially on Darwin's lovely hot days, but crocodiles render Darwin's lovely turquoise seas a no-swim zone year-round. Locals sunbathe on Casuarina Beach, and swim within view of the sea in Lake Alexander on Alec Fong Lim Drive in East Point Reserve. It's that or hit the hotel pool!

This two-story Best Western hotel has a quiet ambience, despite the trendy complex of bars, restaurants, sports betting outlets, slot machines, and a liquor store on one side. Most of the rooms face a saltwater swimming pool surrounded by a lawn, sun lounges, tall palms, and BBQs rather than the bar complex. The front desk sells meat packs for you to cook up on the barbie. Rooms were renovated at the end of 1998, and each is a good size, with quality fittings, free in-room movies, and a furnished patio or balcony. You're just across the road from fish feeding and the Esplanade, close to restaurants, and a 1-kilometer (half-mile) stroll from Smith Street Mall.

INEXPENSIVE

✪ **The Summer House.** 3 Quarry Crescent, Stuart Park (P.O. Box 104, Parap, NT 0820). ☎ **08/8981 9992.** Fax 08/8981 0009. www.bed-and-breakfast.au.com/ntfsums.htm (note: *not* "com.au"). E-mail: shbb@octa4.net.au. 3 units (all with shower only). A/C TV. A$120 (U.S.$78) double, A$200 (U.S.$130) 2-bedroom apt (sleeps 4). Rates include continental breakfast. Rates A$10 (U.S.$6.50) lower without breakfast. AE, BC, MC, V. Free parking. Bus: 5, 6, 8, 10 only. From the airport, take the Stuart Highway 5km (3 miles) to Stuart Park; turn left onto Woolner Rd., immediately right onto Iliffe St., right onto Armidale St., and immediately left onto Quarry Crescent.

Jill Farrand has created a groovy tropical hideaway in her converted apartment block. Two rooms sport cool white walls, trendy polished concrete floors, and wrought-iron furniture (one has giant Balinese bamboo armchairs and 10-foot-high exotic flower arrangements), while a third has a retro look. All have louvered windows to encourage a breeze, hip mosaic bathrooms (with hair dryers), and one or two bedrooms, a living area, and a kitchenette. Jill delivers a nice continental breakfast in the morning. The place is in a leafy suburb 3 kilometers (2 miles) from town and 5 kilometers (3 miles) from the airport, on the local bus route. A Jacuzzi in the jungly garden is great for cooling off on hot nights. No smoking indoors.

Value Inn. 50 Mitchell St., Darwin, NT 0800. ☎ **08/8981 4733.** Fax 08/8981 4730. www.valueinn.com.au. E-mail: valueinn@valueinn.com.au. 93 units (all with shower only). A/C TV. Dry Season A$73.70 (U.S.$47.95) double. Wet Season A$60.50 (U.S.$39.35) double. Shoulder season (Sept–Nov) A$64.90–$70.40 (U.S.$42.20–$45.80) double. No charge for extra person. AE, BC, MC, V. Free parking for approx. 40 cars.

The cheerful rooms at this neat little hotel in the Mitchell Street Tourist Precinct are extremely compact but tidy, and have colorful modern fittings. Each room is just big enough to hold both a queen-size and a single bed, a minirefrigerator, and a small writing table. The views aren't much, but you'll probably spend your time in the cafes along the street anyhow. Smith Street Mall and the Esplanade walking path are 2 blocks away. There are a public pay phone and a coffee vending machine on each floor, and a teensy garden swimming pool off the car park.

DINING

Cullen Bay Marina, a 25-minute walk from town or a short cab ride, is packed with cool restaurants and cafes. If it's Thursday, don't even think about eating anywhere other than the **Mindil Beach Sunset Market** (see below). The cool crowd hangs at **Roma Bar,** 30 Cavenagh St. (☎ **08/8981 6729**), for good coffee and cheap nosh; it's open 7am to 5pm Monday to Friday, 8am to 2pm weekends.

EXPENSIVE

✪ **Buzz Café.** At the Cullen Bay Marina. ☎ **08/8941 1141.** Reservations recommended in the Dry. Main courses A$14–$25 (U.S.$9.10–$16.25). AE, BC, DC, MC, V. Mon–Fri noon–2am, Sat–Sun 10:30am–2am (including brunch). MODERN AUSTRALIAN.

Local movers and shakers come to this busy outdoor venue to move, shake, and enjoy the terrific views over the marina from the deck. There are some more terrific views from inside the men's bathroom (no, I don't mean views of the guys—girls, get a male to take you in there and show you what I mean!). The food is fresh, flavorsome East-meets-West fare like jungle curry of chicken with snake beans and green pepper-corns, or panfried barramundi on potato mash in a lemon butter sauce. Lots of folks wash the meal down with a cocktail from the bar (try the mango daiquiris).

Pee Wee's at the Point. Alec Fong Lim Dr., East Point Reserve (4km/2¹/₂ miles from town). ☎ **08/8981 6868.** Reservations recommended. Main courses A$21–$24.50 (U.S.$13.65–$15.95). AE, BC, DC, MC, V. Daily 6pm–late; call for opening hours for lunch (Dry Season only). MODERN AUSTRALIAN CREOLE.

Surrounded on three sides by jungly forest, this modern steel-and-glass venue affords views of the turquoise Fannie Bay from every table, inside, out on the deck, or down on the lawn. Some of the dishes don't have much to do with Creole cuisine—would Creoles eat Moreton Bay bug tails (a scrumptious crustacean), panfried and served on risotto with a hint of chili and Grand Marnier butter sauce, and finished with deep-fried rocket leaves?—but the Hot Flushes, whole chilis stuffed with cheese sauce, definitely do. Book ahead because locals like this place.

MODERATE

Hanuman Thai. 28 Mitchell St. ☎ **08/8941 3500.** Reservations recommended. Main courses A$8.50–$20.50 (U.S.$5.55–$13.35). AE, BC, DC, JCB, MC, V. Mon–Fri noon–2:30pm, daily 6:30pm–late. CONTEMPORARY THAI/NONYA/TANDOORI.

This elegant city restaurant works hard as a business lunch venue by day and as a pop-ular rendezvous for couples, families, and more business folk by night. It serves up sophisticated dishes cooked with skill, such as marinated chicken wrapped in pandan leaves with a mild chili and malt sugar sauce, and grilled local Gulf prawns with a sauce of crushed coriander and coconut milk sprinkled with kaffir lime leaf julienne. Desserts are a Thai take on French classics, such as black rice brûlée.

Shenannigan's Irish Pub, Restaurant & Bar. 69 Mitchell St. at Peel St. ☎ **08/8981 2100.** Reservations recommended. Daily specials approx. A$9.50–$14 (U.S.$6.20–$9.10). Main courses A$9–$18. (U.S.$5.85–$11.70). AE, BC, DC, MC, V. Meals daily noon–2:30pm, 6–9pm (snack menu 3–5:30pm); bar open daily 10am–2am. IRISH PUB FARE.

Hearty Irish stews and braised beef and Guinness pies (plus the odd pint of Guinness itself) gets everyone in the mood for eating, talking, and dancing at this convivial bar/restaurant. A friendly mix of solo travelers, families, seniors, and backpackers eat and drink in atmospheric wooden booths, standing up at bar tables, or by the fire. As well as hearty meat dishes, there is a snack menu with lighter stuff like toasted sandwiches, and good-value nightly specials, such as chicken and chili pasta or poached barramundi in white wine sauce with fries and salad.

Cheap Eats & More!

If it's Thursday, join the entire city (well, 8,000 locals, anyhow) at the ✪ **Mindil Beach Sunset Market** to feast at the 60 terrific (and cheap!) Asian food stalls, listen to live bands, wander among 200 arts-and-crafts stalls, and mix and mingle with the masseurs, tarot-card readers, bands, and street performers. The action runs from 5 to 10pm in the Dry (May to Oct). A smaller market of about 40 stalls runs Sun-day between June and September from 4 to 9pm. The beach is a A$6 (U.S.$3.90) cab ride from town, and the Tour Tub does A$4 (U.S.$2.60) transfers between 5 and 9:30pm Thursday from major city hotels and the Knuckey Street end of Smith Street Mall. Or take bus 4.

INEXPENSIVE

The Noodle House. 33 Knuckey St. ☎ **08/8941 1742.** Main courses A$6–$22 (U.S.$3.90–$14.30). AE, BC, MC, V. Mon–Fri 11am–2pm, daily 6–10pm. CHINESE.

Twenty bucks will buy you a huge feed at this unpretentious eatery just around the corner from Smith Street Mall. Tummy-fillers like pineapple-and-chicken fried rice or shredded-beef fried rice are especially cheap. The long menu lists many meat dishes, such as Szechuan beef or chicken and roast duck, and there are the usual Chinese soup suspects. The decor isn't exactly the stuff of romance, but the place has a friendly atmosphere. BYO.

○ **Tim's Surf 'n' Turf.** In the Asti Motel, Smith St. at Packard Place ☎ **08/8981 9979.** Main courses A$6.50–$19 (U.S.$4.30–$12.35) (many dishes around A$10/U.S.$6.50); seafood platter for 2 A$26 (U.S.$16.90). BC, MC, V. Mon–Fri noon–2pm; daily 5:30–9:30pm. STEAK/SEAFOOD.

Locals fairly bash down the door to get into this unpretentious restaurant housed under a cheap motel on the city fringe. The modest surroundings are not the attraction, so what is? Hearty, no-nonsense food cooked well, and served in portions big enough to feed an army. No namby-pamby steaks here—Tim's steaks are monsters up to 800 grams (25¹/₂ oz.), over an inch thick, and grain-fed (a boon in Australia, where the beef is mostly grass-fed and hence a little chewy). Garlic prawns, crocodile schnitzel, lasagna, oysters, quiche, and roast of the day are typical menu items. There are meals for kids too.

DARWIN AFTER DARK

If it's Thursday, you are mad to be anywhere except the Mindil Beach Markets (described earlier). Ditto if it's Sunday evening and you're not at the free ○ **Sunset Jazz,** held once a month from May to October on the lawns at the MGM Grand Casino, Gilruth Avenue, The Gardens, on Mindil Beach.

A good spot to catch Darwin's Technicolor sunsets any night of the week is the super-casual **Darwin Sailing Club,** Atkins Drive on Fannie Bay (☎ **08/8981 1700**). Ask the manager to sign you in. A bistro serves affordable meals, and the bar is open from 10am until midnight, and until 2am Friday and Saturday. The cafes and restaurants of **Cullen Bay Marina** are a good place to be, day or night, but especially for Dry Season sunsets.

Lie back in a deckchair at the **Deckchair Cinema** (☎ **08/8981 0700**) to watch Aussie hits, foreign films, and cult classics under the stars. Movies are screened Wednesday through Sunday in the Dry (Apr or May to Oct or Nov) with late sessions Friday and Saturday nights. As we wrote this, the cinema was looking for a new location; at press time, it was located off Mavie Street behind Old Stokes Hill Power Station near the Wharf (a 20-min. walk from the center of town). Tickets are A$10 (U.S.$6.50).

Darwin Entertainment Centre, 93 Mitchell St. (☎ **08/8981 9022** administration, 08/8981 1222 box office) is the city's main performing-arts venue.

The gaming tables at the **MGM Grand Casino,** Gilruth Avenue, Mindil Beach (☎ **08/8943 8888**), are in play from noon until 4am, and until 6am Saturday and Sunday. Slot machines are in play 24 hours. The dress regulation is neat but casual. **Sweetheart's,** also in the MGM Grand, is a popular nightclub attracting ages 18 to 45.

On most nights, **Shenannigan's Irish Pub,** 69 Mitchell St. at Peel Street (☎ **08/ 8981 2100**), has that wonderful mix of live Irish music, dancing, blarney, and laughter called "craik," oiled by ample Guinness. When the U.S. Marines are in town, they head to **Rorke's Drift,** 46 Mitchell St. (☎ **08/8941 7171**), an English-style pub and cafe. Live jazz, blues, and classic rock and soul play nightly at **Nirvana Restaurant,** 130 Smith St. (☎ **08/8981 2025**), a 1970s relic renowned for good Indian, Malay, and Thai food.

Tracy's Bar, in the Central Darwin Hotel, 122 The Esplanade (☎ **08/8981 5388**), is a pleasant after-work watering hole. The stylish complex of pool bar, DJ, beer garden, grill, sports bar, and upscale restaurant that is the **Top End Hotel,** Mitchell Street at Daly Street (☎ **08/8981 6511**), has something to suit just about everyone.

A SIDE TRIP TO LITCHFIELD NATIONAL PARK
120km (74 miles) S of Darwin

An easy 90-minute drive south of Darwin is a miniature Garden of Eden full of forests, waterfalls, rocky sandstone escarpments, glorious natural swimming holes, and prehistoric cycads that look like they walked off the set of Jurassic Park. ✪ **Litchfield National Park** is much smaller (a mere 146,000 hectares/360,620 acres) and much less famous than its big sister, Kakadu, yet most folks would say it is prettier.

The park's main attractions are the spring-fed swimming holes, like the magical plunge pool at **Florence Falls,** 27 kilometers (17 miles) from the eastern park entrance, surrounded by high sandstone cliffs and monsoon rain forest. It's quite a hike down to the water, so the easily accessible pool at **Wangi Falls,** 49 kilometers (30 miles) from the eastern entrance, actually gets more crowds (it's another beautiful spot, surrounded by cliffs and forests and boasting a pretty viewpoint from the top). More idyllic swimming grottos are to be had a couple of miles away at **Buley Rockhole,** a series of cute birdbathlike rock holes and waterfalls.

There are a number of manageably short walking trails through the park, too, and by the time you arrive, a 70-kilometer (43-mile) hiking circuit around the top of the Tabletop Range may be in place. It will link many waterfalls not currently seen by visitors.

If you have a 4WD vehicle, you can swim at **Sandy Creek Falls,** just under 50 kilometers (31 miles) from the eastern entrance, or visit the **"Lost City,"** a group of sandstone rock formations.

All these swimming holes are regarded as crocodile-free; the same is *not* true of the Finniss and Reynolds rivers in the park, so no leaping into those! Parts of the park are also home to thousands of termite mounds up to 2 meters (6.5 ft.) high.

To get there from Darwin, head south for just over 86 kilometers (53 miles) on the Stuart Highway and follow the park turnoff on the right through the town of Batchelor for 34 kilometers (21 miles). **Northern Territory Adventure Tours** (☎ **1300/654 604** in Australia, or 08/8936 1300) makes day trips from Darwin.

The **Parks & Wildlife Commission** district office in Batchelor, on the corner of Nurdina Street and Pinaroo Crescent (☎ **08/8976 0282**), has maps and information; most locations of interest in the park have signboards. Entry to the park is free.

Roads to most swimming holes in the park are paved, although a few areas are accessible only by 4WD. In the Wet Season (approximately Nov to Apr), some roads in the park may be closed, usually the 4WD ones, and the Wangi water hole may be off-limits due to turbulence and strong currents. Check with the Parks & Wildlife Commission office before you leave Darwin during this time.

There are basic campsites with toilets, showers, and wood-fired barbecues at Florence Falls and Wangi Falls, plus several other sites with fewer facilities throughout the park. You may collect firewood in the park, but not around the campgrounds. The camping fee is A$5 (U.S.$3.25) for adults, A$2 (U.S.$1.30) for kids under 16. A kiosk at Wangi Falls sells basic supplies, but stock up on fuel and alcohol in Batchelor.

2 Kakadu National Park

257km (159 miles) E of Darwin

✪ **Kakadu National Park,** a World Heritage area, is Australia's largest national park at whopping 1,755,200 hectares (4,335,344 acres).

Cruising the lily-clad wetlands to spot fearsome crocodiles, plunging into exquisite natural swimming holes, hiking through spear grass and cycads, fishing for prized barramundi, soaring in a light aircraft over torrential waterfalls during the Wet, photographing the millions of birds flying over the eerie red sandstone escarpment that juts 200 meters (650 ft.) above the floodplain, and admiring superb Aboriginal rock art sites—these are the activities that draw people to Kakadu. Some 275 species of birds and 75 species of reptiles inhabit the park, making it one of the richest wildlife habitats in the country.

The name "Kakadu" comes from "Gagudju," the group of languages spoken in the northern part of the park. No one knows for sure, but it is thought that Aboriginal people have lived in this part of the world for 50,000 years. Today, Aborigines manage the park as its owners, in conjunction with the Australian government. This is one of the few places in Australia where some Aborigines stick to a fairly traditional lifestyle of hunting and living off the land. You won't see them, because they keep away from prying eyes, but their culture is on display at a cultural center and at rock art sites. Kakadu and the vast wilds of Arnhemland to the east are the birthplace of the "x-ray" style of art for which Aboriginal artists are famous.

To nature-loving Aussies, Kakadu is a true ecological jewel. They're right, but be aware that the hefty distances between points of interest in the park, and that sameness that infects so much Australian landscape, can detract from Kakadu's appeal for some folks.

Moves are under way to class the park as "threatened" under World Heritage listing, partly due to uranium mining operations within its boundaries. The mine won't impact your experience of the place, though; it's a mere pinprick on the Kakadu's landscape of 1.7 million-plus hectares.

JUST THE FACTS

VISITOR INFORMATION   Both of the park entrances—the northern station on the Arnhem Highway used by visitors from Darwin and the southern station on the Kakadu Highway for visitors from Katherine—hand out free visitor guides with maps, and in the Dry they issue a timetable of free guided ranger walks, talks, and slide shows taking place that week.

Park headquarters is at the **Bowali Visitor Centre** (☎ **08/8938 1120**) on the Kakadu Highway, 5 kilometers (3 miles) from Jabiru, 100 kilometers (62 miles) from the northern entry station, and 131 kilometers (81 miles) from the southern entry station. This architecturally attractive, environmentally friendly Outback-style center shows good videos every 30 or 60 minutes on the park's natural history and Aboriginal culture, stocks maps and free park notes, has a library and displays, has information officers on hand to help you plan your visit, and has a gift shop and a cafe. It is open daily from 8am to 5pm.

You can also book tours and get information at the **Jabiru Travel Centre,** Shop 6, Tasman Plaza, Jabiru, NT 0886 (☎ **08/8979 2548;** e-mail: wendymchugh@ bigpond.com.au).

Before you arrive, you can find information on Kakadu, and book tours to it, at Darwin's tourist office. You can also contact the rangers at Kakadu National Park (☎ **08/8938 1120;** e-mail: KakaduNationalPark@ea.gov.au). The best Web site on Kakadu is the Northern Territory Tourist Commission's site at **www.nttc.com.au.**

WHEN TO GO   Kakadu has two distinct seasons: Wet and Dry. The Dry Season from May to October is overwhelmingly the best time to go, thanks to temperatures around 30°C (86°F) and sunny days. Many tours, park hotels, and even campsites are booked out a year in advance at this time, so don't travel without reservations.

In the Wet Season, from November through April, floodwaters cover much of the park, some attractions are cut off all season or unexpectedly for days, and the heat and humidity are extreme. Some tour companies do not run during the Wet, and ranger talks, walks, and slide shows are not offered. The upside of visiting during the Wet is that the crowds vanish, the normally brownish vegetation bursts into green, waterfalls swell from a trickle to a roar, and lightning storms are spectacular, especially in the very hot "build-up" to the season in October and November. The landscape can change dramatically from one day to the next as floodwaters rise and fall, so be prepared for surprises, both nice ones (like giant flocks of geese that are here today, gone tomorrow) and unwelcome ones (like blocked roads). Although it can pour down all day, it's more common for the rain to fall in late-afternoon storms and at night. Take it easy in the humidity and don't even think about camping in this heat—stay in air-conditioned accommodations.

GETTING THERE   Follow the Stuart Highway 34 kilometers (21 miles) south of Darwin, and turn left onto the Arnhem Highway all the way to the park's northern entrance station. The trip takes 2¹/₂ to 3 hours. If you're coming from the south, turn off the Stuart Highway at Pine Creek onto the Kakadu Highway, and follow the Kakadu Highway for 79 kilometers (49 miles) to the park's southern entrance station. **Greyhound Pioneer** (☎ **13 2030** in Australia) makes a daily run from Darwin for A$40.70 (U.S.$26.45). The **Blue Banana** bus (see "Exploring the Top End," at the beginning of this chapter) visits the park from Darwin.

FEES & REGULATIONS   The park entry fee of A$16.30 (U.S.$10.60) per adult is valid for 14 days. Children 15 and under enter free.

LOGISTICAL TIPS   Kakadu is a big place—about 200 kilometers (124 miles) long by 100 kilometers (62 miles) wide—so plan to spend a couple of nights here. It's really too far and too big to see much in a day trip from Darwin.

Most major attractions are accessible in a conventional vehicle on sealed (paved) roads, but a 4WD vehicle allows you to get to more falls, water holes, and campsites. **Territory Thrifty** (☎ **08/8979 2552**) rents cars at the **Gagudju Crocodile Hotel;** otherwise, rent a car in Darwin. If you 4WD it, always check the road conditions at the **Bowali Visitor Centre** (☎ **08/8938 1120**). In the Wet Season (late Nov through Apr), call daily to check floodwater levels on all roads, paved and unpaved. The Bowali Visitor Centre, main attractions such as Nourlangie and Yellow Water Billabong, and the towns of Jabiru and Cooinda stay above the floodwaters year-round.

Facilities are limited in Kakadu. The only town of any size is **Jabiru** (pop. 1,455), a mining community where you can find a bank. The only other real settlements are accommodation houses.

A big range of coach, minibus, and 4WD tours and camping safaris taking an average of 1 to 3 days depart from Darwin every day. These are a good idea, because many of Kakadu's geological, ecological, and Aboriginal attractions come to life only with a guide, and the best water holes, lookouts, and wildlife-viewing spots change dramatically from month to month, or even from day to day.

SEEING THE HIGHLIGHTS
EN ROUTE TO KAKADU

En route to the park, stop in at the **Fogg Dam Conservation Reserve** (☎ **08/8988 8009** is the ranger), 25 kilometers (15¹/₂ miles) down the Arnhem Highway plus

Never Smile at a You-Know-What

The Aboriginal Gagudju people of the Top End have long worshipped a giant crocodile called Ginga, but the way white Australians go on about these reptilian relics of a primeval age, you'd think they worshipped 'em, too. There is scarcely a soul in the Northern Territory who will not earbash you with his or her own particular croc story, and each one you hear will be weirder and taller than the last. Aussies may be good at pulling your leg with tall tales, but when they warn you not to swim in crocodile country, they're not kidding. After all, crocodiles are good at pulling your leg too—literally. To be sure you don't end up as lunch, here are some tips:

1. There are two kinds of crocs in Australia, the highly dangerous and enormously powerful saltwater or "estuarine" kind, and the "harmless" freshwater kind, which will attack only if threatened or accidentally stood on. Saltwater crocs can and do swim in the ocean, but they *live* in fresh water.

2. Don't swim in any waterway, swimming hole, or waterfall unless you have been specifically told that it is safe. Take advice only from someone authoritative like a recognized tour operator or a park ranger. You can never be sure where these critters lurk from year to year, because every Wet Season crocs head upriver to breed and spread out over a wide flooded area. As the floodwaters subside in the Dry, they are trapped in whatever waterway they happen to be in at the time—so what was a safe swimming hole last Dry Season might not be so croc-free this year.

3. Never stand on or walk along a riverbank, and stand well back when fishing. A 20-foot croc can be 1 inch beneath the surface of that muddy water yet remain utterly invisible. They move fast, so you won't see him until you're in his jaws.

4. Plant your campsite and clean fish at least 25 meters (82 ft.) back from the bank.

And if you come face to face with a crocodile? Everyone has different advice, but it all boils down to two things: Make your peace with God, or run!

10 kilometers (6 miles) off the highway. Here you'll get a close-up look at geese, egrets, ibis, brolgas, and other wetland birds from boardwalks leading through monsoon forests to raised lookouts. Entry is free every day of the year.

Four kilometers (2¹/₂ miles) down the Arnhem Highway at Beatrice Hill, you may want to stop at the **Window on the Wetlands Visitor Centre** (☎ **08/8988 8188**), a hilltop center with sweeping views across the Adelaide River floodplain and touch-screen information on the wetlands' ecology. It's free and open daily from 7:30am to 7:30pm.

Just past Beatrice Hill on the highway at the Adelaide River (you can't miss the statue of a grinning croc), you can join the **Original Jumping Crocodiles cruise** (☎ **08/8988 8144**) aboard the *Adelaide River Queen* to watch wild crocodiles leap out of the water for hunks of meat dangled over the edge by the boat crew. Reader Mari Fagin of Oklahoma City, OK, says this was one of the highlights of her Australian vacation. "After seeing little crocodile 'action' on our Yellow Waters Cruise, it was awesome and a bit sobering to see the speed and agility of these monsters in pursuit of food," she writes. The 90-minute cruise departs 9am, 11am, 1pm, and 3pm from May to August, and 9am, 11am, and 2:30pm September to April (closed Dec 24 and 25). It costs A$31 (U.S.$20.15) for adults, A$27 (U.S.$17.55) for seniors, and A$18 (U.S.$11.70) for children 5 to 15.

Farther down the track at Annaburroo, stop for a drink at the **Bark Hut Inn** on your left (☎ **08/8978 8988**). Well, pretend you want a drink—you're actually here for an eyeful of the colorfully tough Territory truckies and station hands who often prop up the bar, looking like extras from *Crocodile Dundee*.

TOP PARK ATTRACTIONS

WETLANDS CRUISES   One of the biggest attractions in the park is **Yellow Water Billabong,** a lush lake 50 kilometers (31 miles) south of the Bowali Visitor Centre at **Cooinda** (pop. 20). It's rich with freshwater mangroves, paperbarks, pandanus palms, water lilies, and marvelous swathes of thousands of birds gathering here to drink—sea eagles, honking magpie geese, kites, china blue kingfishers, and jacanas, called "Jesus birds" because they seem to walk on water as they step nimbly across the lily pads. This is also one of the best places in the park to spot saltwater crocs. Cruises in canopied boats with a running commentary depart near Gagudju Lodge Cooinda six times a day from 6:45am in the Dry (May to Nov) and 7am in the Wet (Dec to Apr). A 90-minute cruise costs A$29.70 (U.S.$19.30) for adults and A$14.30 (U.S.$9.30) for children 2 to 14. A 2-hour cruise (available in the Dry only) costs A$34 (U.S.$22.10) for adults and A$15.40 (U.S.$10) for children. Book through Gagudju Lodge Cooinda (see "Accommodations & Dining," below).

Even though it means spending the night in the park and getting up before dawn, the sunrise cruise is especially good, when the dawn silence gets broken by an overture that builds to a full-blown orchestral performance, all courtesy of the birds. In the Wet, when the billabong floods to join up with Jim Jim Creek and the South Alligator River, the bird life spreads far and wide over the park and the crocs head upriver to breed, so don't expect wildlife viewing to be all that spectacular.

Another excellent cruise is the **Guluyambi Aboriginal Culture Tour** (☎ **1800/ 089 113** in Australia, or 08/8979 2411 for booking agent—Kakadu Tours) on the East Alligator River, which forms the border between Kakadu and isolated Arnhemland. Unlike the Yellow Water journey, which focuses on crocs, birds, and plants, this cruise tells you about Aboriginal myths, bush tucker, and hunting techniques. The cruise, limited to 25 passengers, lasts 1 hour and 45 minutes and leaves at 9am, 11am, 1pm, and 3pm daily from May to October. The schedule shifts to a half-day cruise on the Magela Creek system in the Wet, with a climb of Ubirr Rock thrown in. Transportation to the boat in the Dry Season is not included, so you will need to get yourself to the departure point; in the Wet, the trip picks up from the Gagudju Crocodile Hotel at 10am. The cruise costs A$29 (U.S.$18.85) for adults and A$14 (U.S.$9.10) for children 4 to 14.

ABORIGINAL ART & CULTURE   There are as many as 5,000 art sites throughout the park, though the Aboriginal owners make only a few accessible to visitors. The two best are **Nourlangie Rock** and **Ubirr Rock.** Nourlangie, 31 kilometers (19 miles) southeast of the Bowali Visitor Centre, features "x-ray" style paintings of animals and a vivid striped Dreamtime figure of Namarrgon, the "Lightning Man," alongside

---

A Bird-Watching Tip

Early morning and late afternoon are the best times for bird watching, when the birds flock to water holes to drink.

modern depictions of a white man in cowboy boots, a rifle, and a sailing ship. Rangers have told me that Nourlangie is a "tourist" art site and that there is "much better" stuff hidden elsewhere in the park, but this one is pretty impressive! You'll also find rock paintings at **Nanguluwur,** near Nourlangie, and at Ubirr Rock, which is worth the 250 meter steep climb for the great views of the floodplain at sunset. Access to Ubirr can be limited in the Wet, but the views of afternoon lightning storms up here at that time are breathtaking. Unlike most sites in Kakadu, Ubirr is not open 24 hours—it opens at 8:30am from May to November and at 2pm from December to April, and closes every day at sunset. There is a 1.5-kilometer (1-mile) signposted trail around Nourlangie's paintings, a 3.4-kilometer (2-mile) trail at Nanguluwur, and a 1-kilometer (0.6-mile) track at Ubirr. Access to all of these sites is free.

Displays and videos of the bush tucker, Dreamtime creation myths, and lifestyles of the local Bininj Aboriginal people are on show at the ✪ **Warradjan Aboriginal Cultural Centre** (☎ **08/8979 0051**) at Cooinda. This circular building was built in the shape of a pig-nose turtle at the direction of the Aboriginal owners. There are also a quality gift shop selling didgeridoos, bark paintings by local Aboriginal artists, and baskets woven from pandanus fronds. The center is open from 9am to 5pm daily, and admission is free. It is connected to Gagudju Lodge Cooinda and the Yellow Water Billabong by a 1-kilometer (half-mile) trail.

SCENIC FLIGHTS Scenic flights over the floodplains and the surprising palm-filled ravines of the escarpment are well worth doing. In the Wet, make sure your flight includes Jim Jim Falls and Twin Falls, which swell from their Dry Season trickle to a full roaring flood. From the air is also the best way to appreciate the clever crocodile shape of the Gagudju Crocodile Hotel. **North Australian Helicopters** (☎ **08/8972 1666**) does flights from Jabiru lasting from 30 minutes to 1¾ hours for between A$120 (U.S.$78) and A$390 (U.S.$253.50) per person. **Kakadu Air** (☎ **1800/089 113** in Australia, or 08/8979 2411) does 30-minute fixed-wing flights from Jabiru and Cooinda for A$70 (U.S.$45.50) per person and 1-hour flights from Cooinda for A$120 (U.S.$78) per person.

SWIMMING, FISHING & BUSHWALKING IN THE PARK

In the eastern section of the park rises a massive red sandstone escarpment that sets the stage for two magnificent waterfalls, ✪ **Jim Jim Falls** and ✪ **Twin Falls.** In the Dry, the volume of water flowing in them may not be all that impressive, but their settings are magical. Both are accessible by 4WD only, and neither is open in the Wet.

Though folk do swim at Jim Jim, Twin Falls, and other water holes, such as Gubara, Maguk, and Koolpin Gorge, you do so at your own risk. Saltwater crocodiles have been known to slip through the traps rangers set for them alongside popular swimming holes. *Never* swim without checking with a ranger that the water hole is croc-free; if you are unsure, the only place rangers recommend you swim is your hotel pool. A 1-kilometer (half-mile) walk over rocks and through rain forest leads to a deep green plunge pool at Jim Jim Falls, 103 kilometers (64 miles) from the Bowali Visitor Centre. The water is wrapped by an almost perfectly circular 150-meter (490-ft.) cliff. The road may be upgraded by the time you read this, but if not, allow 2 hours to drive the final 60 unpaved kilometers (37 miles) off the highway. Due to floodwaters, Jim Jim Falls may not open until as late as June.

Paddling past the odd "harmless" freshwater crocodile at nearby Twin Falls is great, too. The falls descend into a natural pool edged by a sandy beach and surrounded by bush and high cliffs.

John and Bronwen Malligan of ✪ **Kakadu Gorge and Waterfall Tours** (☎ **08/8979 0111,** or 08/8979 2025 after hours) run an excellent small-group day trip to the falls for active people. You bushwalk into Jim Jim Falls for morning tea, 4WD through the bush, and then paddle in a tandem canoe to Twin Falls for lunch. Tours depart daily from Jabiru and Cooinda from May to November and cost A$130 (U.S.$84.50) for adults, A$110 (U.S.$71.50) for kids 4 to 14 (no kids under 4 allowed). Book in advance for July, the busiest month.

Remember the idyllic pool that Paul Hogan and Linda Koslowski plunged into in *Crocodile Dundee*? That was **Gunlom Falls,** about 170 kilometers (105 miles) south of the Bowali Visitor Centre. A climb to the top of the falls rewards you with great views of southern Kakadu. Access is by 4WD and can be cut off in the Wet.

Kakadu's wetlands are brimful of barramundi, and there is nothing Territorians like more than to hop in a tin dinghy barely big enough to resist a croc attack and go looking for them. John and Bronwen Malligan, mentioned above, also run **Kakadu Fishing Tours** (☎ **08/8979 0111,** or 08/8979 2025 after hours) in a 4.75-meter sportfishing boat. Tours depart from Jabiru, 5 kilometers (3 miles) east of the Bowali Visitor Centre, and cost A$120 (U.S.$78) per person for a half day (A$190 /U.S.$123.50 if there is only one of you) and A$230 (U.S.$149.50) per person for a full day. They also do fly-fishing.

A wide-ranging collection of ✪ **bush and wetlands trails** lead throughout the park, including many short strolls and six half- to full-day treks. Typical trails include a 600-meter (less than ¹/₂-mile) amble through the **Manngarre Monsoon Forest** near Ubirr Rock, an easy 3.8-kilometer (2.4-mile) circular walk at the **Iligadjar Wetlands** near the Bowali Visitor Centre, or a tough 12-kilometer (7.4-mile) trek through rugged sandstone country at Nourlangie Rock.

One of the best wetlands walks is at **Mamukala wetlands,** 29 kilometers (18 miles) from Jabiru. Countless thousands of magpie geese feed here, especially in the late Dry Season around October. An observation platform gives you a good view of them, and a sign explains the dramatic seasonal changes the wetlands undergo. Choose from a 1-kilometer (0.6-mile) or 3-kilometer (1.8-mile) meander. The Bowali Visitor Centre sells hiking trail maps. There are also some challenging unmarked trails along creeks and gorges, for which you will need good navigational skills.

CAMPING IN THE PARK

There are more than 20 campsites, many of them with few facilities, all mostly near popular billabongs and wetlands.

The best-equipped sites are at **Gagudju Lodge Cooinda** (see below). Campers are free to use all of the facilities here, although in extremely busy times the pool may be available only to bungalow guests.

Tent site–only campgrounds with hot showers and toilets are found at **Gunlom, Mardugal Billabong, Muirella Park** near Nourlangie Rock, and **Merl** in the northeast. A ranger visits campgrounds daily to collect a nightly fee of A$5 (U.S.$3.25) per person.

Fewer crowds, no camping fees, and the peace of the bush are the payoffs for going without showers and having only basic toilets, or none, at the free "bush camps"

Bushwalking Tips

Try to plan your walk in the early morning or late afternoon, especially in the Wet, because the heat can dehydrate you quickly. If you want to camp at an undesignated campsite on an overnight walk, you will need a camping permit from the rangers at the Bowali Visitor Centre, which can take a week to arrange.

located throughout the park. Inquire at the park entry stations or at the **Bowali Visitor Centre** for a map marking them.

Some campsites need a 4WD to reach them, and most are closed in the Wet. Gagudju Lodge Cooinda is open year-round.

If you want to camp in the wild rather than at a designated campground, you will need a permit from the **Bowali Visitor Centre.** These can take a week to process, so plan ahead. Bring a mosquito net, because mosquitoes here carry the potentially dangerous Ross River virus. RID and Aerogard are two brands that help protect against it.

ACCOMMODATIONS & DINING

High season is usually April 1 to November 30.

Gagudju Crocodile Hotel. Flinders St. (5km/1¼ miles by road east of Bowali Visitor Centre), Jabiru, NT 0886. ☎ **1800/808 123** in Australia, 800/835 7742 in the U.S. and Canada, 020/8335 1304 or 0345/58 1666 in the U.K., 0800/801 111 in New Zealand, or 08/8979 2800. Fax 08/8979 2707. www.sphc.com.au. E-mail: executivesec@crocodile.sphc.com.au. 110 units. A/C MINIBAR TV TEL. A$275 (U.S.$178.75) double. Expect to pay lower rates in the Wet. Extra adult A$27.50 (U.S.$17.90). Children under 16 free in parents' room. AE, BC, DC, JCB, MC, V.

Some people think this hotel is gross kitsch; others declare it an architectural masterpiece. It was built to the specifications of its owners, the Gagudju Aboriginal people, in the form of their spirit ancestor, a giant crocodile called "Ginga." The building's entrance is the "jaws," the two floors of rooms are in the "belly," and the circular car park clusters are "eggs." Love it or hate it, it is the most luxurious place to stay in Kakadu. Once you're inside, it's a normal hotel with smallish but comfortable modern rooms (though I think the hair dryers could have been crocodile-shaped, too, don't you?). All have irons and boards, and hair dryers. Guests can access the 9-hole golf course, tennis courts, and Olympic-size swimming pool a few blocks away in Jabiru. The lobby doubles as an art gallery selling the works of local Aborigines. You are central to many Park attractions from here. A short bush-walking trail leads to the Bowali Visitor Centre.

Dining/Diversions: The joke is that you get to *have* dinner inside a crocodile instead of *being* dinner inside a crocodile. The Escarpment restaurant uses bush tucker in some of its à la carte and buffet meals and has nightly live entertainment March through December. The small windowless tavern has a pool table, does gourmet pizzas, and stages a disco on Friday nights. There is also poolside service.

Amenities: Room service (Dry Season only), small swimming pool and sundeck, free in-house movies, in-room massage (Dry Season), tour desk and car-rental desk, gift shop, baby-sitting, secretarial services, conference facilities, currency exchange.

Gagudju Lodge Cooinda. Kakadu Hwy. (50km/31 miles south of Bowali Visitor Centre), Jim Jim, NT 0886. ☎ **1800/500 401** in Australia, 800/835-7742 in the U.S. and Canada, 0345/58 1666 in the U.K. or 020/8335 1304 in London, 0800/801 111 in New Zealand, or 08/8979 0145. Fax 08/8979 0148. www.sphc.com.au. Email: COOINDA1@bigpond.com. A/C. 48 bungalows (all with shower only), 84 budget rms (none with bathroom), 57 powered and 310 unpowered campsites. Bungalow A$198 (U.S.$128.70) double. Extra person A$27.50 (U.S.$17.90); children under 13 free. Budget room A$30.80 (U.S.$20) per bed, or $25.30 (U.S.$16.45) per bed for YHA/Hostelling International members. A$12.65 (U.S.$8.25) per adult, powered campsite; A$9.90 (U.S.$6.45) per adult, unpowered campsite. Children 2–12 free in campsite. Expect to pay lower rates in bungalows and budget rooms in the Wet Season. AE, BC, DC, JCB, MC, V.

This pleasantly modest lodge is situated at the departure point for Yellow Water Billabong cruises. The bungalows are simply furnished but big and comfortable; they come with telephones (hair dryers and baby-sitters available on request). The budget rooms are just bunk beds (four have double beds) in a corrugated iron demountable (portable cabin) with shared bathrooms. They rent on a per-bed basis, so you may find yourself sharing with a stranger. Tropical gardens keep the place feeling cool, and there is a small shady pool.

The lodge is something of a town center, so there are a general store, a gift shop, a tour desk, currency exchange, a post office, fuel, and other useful facilities. Cook up a 'roo steak in the nightly do-it-yourself barbecue in the satisfyingly rustic and ultra-casual **Barra Bar & Bistro,** or go for the excellent bush tucker à la carte meals at lunch or dinner in **Mimi's,** which has a really nice "bush sophisticated" ambience. The Barra Bistro does full buffet breakfast and an all-day snack menu, and has live entertainment in the Dry Season most nights. Scenic flights take off from the lodge's airstrip, and the Warradjan Aboriginal Cultural Centre is a 15-minute walk.

3 Katherine

314km (196 miles) S of Darwin; 512km (320 miles) E of Kununurra; 1,177 (736 miles) N of Alice Springs

The local townsfolk in Katherine (pop. 9,450) are understandably proud that more people cruise Katherine Gorge every year than visit Ayers Rock. Dramatic sheer orange walls dropping to a tranquil blue-green river make the gorge a powerful drawing card, all the more so because it's an unexpected delight in the middle of the dry Arnhemland plateau that stretches to the horizon.

The gorge and its surrounding river ecosystem are located in the 292,008-hectare (721,269-acre) **Nitmiluk National Park.** In the Dry, the gorge is a haven not just for cruisers but also for canoeists, who must dodge the odd freshwater crocodile (the "friendly" kind) as they paddle up between its walls. In the Wet, the gorge can become a foaming torrent at times, and jet-boating is sometimes the only way to tackle it. Hikers will find nice trails any time of year throughout the park. Farther afield from Katherine are hot springs to soak in, natural water holes to swim in, uncrowded rivers to canoe, caves to explore, and Aboriginal communities where visitors can learn how to make dot paintings and find bush tucker.

ESSENTIALS

GETTING THERE   Airnorth (☎ **1800/627 474** in Australia, or 08/8945 2866, or book through Ansett) flies once or twice a day from Darwin, and every day except Saturday from Alice Springs via Tennant Creek. It's a 50-minute trip from Darwin and a 3-hour flight from Alice.

McCafferty's (☎ **13 14 99** in Australia) and **Greyhound Pioneer** (☎ **13 20 30** in Australia) stop in Katherine on their Darwin–Alice Springs and Alice Springs–Darwin routes, which both companies run daily. Greyhound also calls daily from Broome via Kununurra. It's a 4-hour trip from Darwin, costing A$45.10 (U.S.$29.30); from Alice it's a 14-hour journey for which the fare is A$154 (U.S.$100.10); and the 22-hour trip from Broome costs A$207.90 (U.S.$135.15).

Katherine is on the Stuart Highway, which links Darwin and Alice Springs. From Alice Springs, allow a good 2 days to make the drive. The Victoria Highway begins in Katherine and heads west to Kununurra. There is no direct route from the east.

VISITOR INFORMATION   The Katherine Region Tourist Association, Stuart Highway at Lindsay Street, Katherine, NT 0850 (☎ **08/8972 2650;** e-mail: krta@ nt-tech.com.au), has information on things to see—not only all around Katherine, but as far afield as Kakadu National Park and the Kimberley. It's open Monday through Friday 9am to 5pm and, in the Dry Season only, weekends 10am to 3pm.

The **Nitmiluk Visitor Centre** (☎ **08/8972 1886**) on the Gorge Road, 32 kilometers (20 miles) from town, dispenses information on the Nitmiluk National Park and sells tickets for gorge cruises, which depart right outside. The ranger station is here also. The Centre has maps; displays on the park's plant life, birds, geology, and Aboriginal history; a gift shop; and a cafe. It's open daily 7am to 7pm, sometimes closing a little earlier in the Wet. Entry to the park is free.

GETTING AROUND   Avis (☎ 08/8971 0520), **Budget** (☎ 08/8971 1333), **Hertz** (☎ 08/8971 1111), and **Territory Thrifty Car Rental** (☎ 08/8972 3183) have outlets in Katherine.

Travel North (☎ **1800/089 103** in Australia, or 08/8972 1044) makes transfers from Katherine hotels to the cruise, canoe, and helicopter departure points at the Nitmiluk Visitor Centre. Round-trip fares are A$17.50 (U.S.$11.40) for adults and A$8.50 (U.S.$5.55) for kids 5 to 15. The company also runs many local tours and activities such as horse-riding dinners on cattle stations, visits to an old homestead, and transfers to as far away as Mataranka Thermal Pools (see below). For personalized tours both off the beaten path and around town, contact **Far Out Adventures** (☎ **08/8972 2552**).

EXPLORING KATHERINE GORGE (NITMILUK NATIONAL PARK)

Cruising the gorge in an **open-sided boat** is the most popular way to appreciate its beauty. Katherine Gorge is actually a series of 13 gorges, but most cruises ply only the first two, because the second gorge is the most photogenic.

All cruises are operated by **Travel North** (☎ **1800/089 103** in Australia, or 08/8972 1044). Most folks take the 2-hour cruise, which departs four times a day and costs A$33 (U.S.$21.45) for adults and A$13 (U.S.$8.45) for children 5 to 15. There is also a daily 4-hour cruise for A$47 (U.S.$30.55) for adults and A$21 (U.S.$13.65) for kids, although you will probably be satisfied with 2 hours. If you want to spend the whole day outdoors, take the 8-hour safari to the fifth gorge (available Apr to Oct only). In addition to cruising, you get to swim, hike for 5 kilometers (3 miles) over sometimes-rough terrain, and have a barbecue lunch. All-day trips cost A$82 (U.S.$53.30) per person, adult or child. Because each gorge is cut off from the next by rapids, all the cruises involve some walking along the bank to transfer to a boat in the next gorge, so wear sturdy shoes.

In the Wet Season, the cruises may not operate on days when the floodwaters really start to swirl. Instead, Travel North runs a **jet boat** those days as far as the third gorge. This 45-minute adventure costs A$38 (U.S.$24.70) for adults and A$28 (U.S.$18.20) for kids 5 to 15. Departure times vary from day to day.

Cruising is nice, but in a ✪ **canoe** you can discover sandy banks and waterfalls, and get up close to the gorge walls, the birds, and those crocs (don't worry, they're the freshwater kind). The gorges are separated by rocks, so be prepared to carry your canoe quite often. A half-day canoe rental from **Travel North** is A$27 (U.S.$17.55) for a single canoe and A$41 (U.S.$26.65) for a double, and full-day rental is A$38 (U.S.$24.70) for a single canoe and A$56 (U.S.$36.40) for a double. There's an A$20 (U.S.$13) refundable deposit, or $60 if you want to camp out on the riverbank overnight.

Once the river gets too high for go-it-alone canoeing during the Wet, Travel North runs guided canoeing adventures instead. These last 5¹/₂ hours and cost $41 per person. In fact, guided paddles are a good idea any time of year as you will learn and see more.

The most knowledgeable such company is ✪ **Gecko Canoeing** (☎ **1800/ 634 319** in Australia, or 08/8972 2224), whose tours are accredited for their ecotourism content. Gecko's owner/guide, Martin Wohling, has attained Australia's elite "Savannah Guide" ecotour guide status. They will pick you up from your accommodation for an all-day escorted canoe safari at a cost of A$93.50 (U.S.$60.80) per person. In the Dry, the company also runs canoeing and camping safaris (with any other activities you like thrown in such as mountain biking, rock climbing, wildlife photography, hiking or fishing) of up to 12 days in little-explored wildernesses nearby, such as the Flora and Daly River systems.

Some 100 kilometers (63 miles) of hiking trails crisscross **Nitmiluk National Park,** ranging in duration from 1 hour to the lookout to 5 days to Edith Falls (see below). Trails—through rocky sandstone-conglomerate terrain and forests, past water holes and along the gorge—depart the Nitmiluk National Park ranger station, located in the Nitmiluk Visitor Centre, where you can pick up trail maps. Overnight walks require a deposit of between A$20 (U.S.$13) and A$50 (U.S.$32.50) per person, payable at the Nitmiluk Visitor Centre.

One of the nicest spots in the Park is actually 42 kilometers (26 miles) north of Katherine, 20 kilometers (12¹/₂ miles) off the Stuart Highway. ✪ **Edith Falls** is a real Eden of natural (croc-free) swimming holes bordered by red cliffs, monsoonal forest, and pandanus trees. A 2.6-kilometer (1¹/₂-mile) round-trip bushwalk from the Falls, which takes about 2 hours, incorporates a dip at the upper pool en route.

More than the gorge itself, the aerial views of the ravine-ridden **Arnhem Plateau,** which stretches uninhabited to the horizon, are arresting. **North Australian Helicopters** (☎ **08/8972 1666**) does 12- and 24-minute flights over the gorge for A$75 (U.S.$48.75) and A$125 (U.S.$81.25). It also does longer flights on to Kakadu National Park.

ABORIGINAL CULTURE TOURS, HOT SPRINGS & MORE

On a 1-day visit to the ✪ **Manyallaluk** Aboriginal community, a 90-minute drive southeast from Katherine, you chat with Aboriginal people about how they balance traditional ways with modern living; take a guided bushwalk to look for native medicines and bush tucker like green ants (they're refreshing!); try lighting a fire with two sticks, weaving baskets, throwing spears, painting on bark, and playing a didgeridoo; take a dip in a natural water hole; and buy locally made Aboriginal art and artifacts at better prices than you may find elsewhere. Lunch is a terrific barbecue featuring stuff like high-grade kangaroo fillet, kangaroo tail, Scotch fillet steak, or barramundi cooked in paperbark on hot coals. Some visitors rush into these tours and expect the community to be a kind of Aboriginal Disney World theme park with a new attraction every 10 minutes, but that's not how it is. It's an unstructured experience (this is the community's home), so it's up to you to take part. A 1-day tour from Katherine costs A$132 (U.S.$85.80) for adults and A$71.50 (U.S.$46.50) for children 6 to 15, or A$99 (U.S.$64.35) adults and A$60.50 (U.S.$39.35) for kids if you drive yourself. The last 35 kilometers (22 miles) of road is unsealed (unpaved), for which rental cars will be insured only if they are 4WD. The tour runs Monday to Friday from April to September; check to see what is happening in the Wet. You can camp overnight for A$5 (U.S.$3.25) adults, A$3 (U.S.$1.95) kids, or A$15 (U.S.$9.75) double for a powered site. Call **Manyallaluk: The Dreaming Place** (☎ **08/8975 4727**).

The Manyallaluk community also does a 2-day experience on request, for very small groups, subject to limited availability. Spend the first day doing the activities above, camp out overnight, and spend the next day exploring areas by 4WD rarely seen by white folks, visiting superb ancient rock art sites and swimming at a remote waterfall. The price is negotiable, but expect it to start at A$400 (U.S.$260) per person. Book ahead.

In the 500-million-year-old **Cutta Cutta Caves** (☎ **08/8972 1940**), 29 kilometers (18 miles) south of Katherine off the Stuart Highway, you will see limestone stalagmites and stalactites and maybe catch a glimpse of the rare resident Orange Horseshoe and Ghost bats. You must take a 1-hour tour to see the caves; these depart six times a day from 9am and cost A$9.50 (U.S.$6.20) adults, A$4.50 (U.S.$2.95) kids 5 to 15.

One hundred and ten kilometers (69 miles) south of Katherine on the Stuart Highway is the town of Mataranka (pop. 665), where you can soak at the ✪ **Mataranka Thermal Pools.** These man-made pools are fed by 34°C (93°F) spring water, which bubbles up from the earth at a rate of 16,495 liters (4,123³/₄ gallons) per minute! It's a real little paradise, surrounded by palms, pandanus, and a colony of flying foxes. The pools are open 24 hours every day, and admission is free. They are 7 kilometers (4 miles) along Homestead Road, which is off the highway 1¹/₂ kilometers (1 mile) south of Mataranka township. The pools are within the grounds of **Mataranka Homestead Tourist Resort** (☎ **08/8975 4544**), less a resort than a low-key collection of motel rooms, cabins, campgrounds, a restaurant or two, and a *très* casual bar. While you're here, inspect some re-created Aboriginal "gunyahs," or bark shelters, and a replica of the slab-hut Elsey Station homestead (see below). From May to September a free homestead tour operates daily at 11am. The homestead and pools lie within the 13,840-hectare (34,185-acre) **Elsey National Park.** A sealed road winds from the homestead along the banks of the Roper River, where there are swimming holes and a couple of walking trails, including a shaded 4-kilometer (2¹/₂-mile) trail into Mataranka Falls. *Note:* Ask the homestead to direct you to croc-free swimming areas. Don't just dive in! The homestead sells handlines to fish for barramundi and rents canoes to take on the river.

Back in town, you can soak your cares away at the pleasantly warm **Katherine Hot Springs,** under shady trees 3 kilometers (2 miles) from town on Riverbank Drive. Entry is free. At the **School of the Air,** Giles Street (☎ **08/8972 1833**), you can sit in on an 800,000-square-kilometer (262,400-square-mile) "classroom" as children from the Outback do their lessons by radio. Forty-five–minute tours begin on the hour from 9am to 2pm (there's no tour at noon). Tours also run during school holidays and public holidays minus the on-air classes. The school is open Monday through Friday 9am to 3pm from mid-March until mid-December. Admission is A$5 (U.S.$3.25) for adults and A$2 (U.S.$1.30) for school-age kids.

Mike Keighley of ✪ **Far Out Adventures** (☎ **08/8972 2552**) runs numerous eco- and cultural-tours around Katherine. One of his best is his "Never Never" tour, an all-day chill-out on a beautiful patch of the 5,000-square-kilometer (1,930-square-mile) ✪ **Elsey Station,** 140 kilometers (88 miles) southeast of Katherine, made famous as the setting of the Aussie book and film *We of the Never Never.* Meet children of the Mangarrayi Aboriginal people, sample bush tucker, learn a little bush medicine, and swim in a vine-clad natural "spa-pool" in the Roper River. The day costs A$200 (U.S.$130) adults, A$150 (U.S.$97.50) kids 5 to 15. Mike has been accepted as an honorary family member of the Mangarrayi people and is a mine of information about Aboriginal culture and the bush. He can extend this trip into an overnight camp/canoe safari to Elsey Falls and the water lilies on **Red Lily Lagoon.**

Mike also runs croc-spotting campfire cruises on the Katherine River Monday, Wednesday, and Friday through Sunday nights from April to October. They cost A$45 (U.S.$29.25) per adult and A$20 (U.S.$13) for kids, departing at 6pm from your hotel.

ACCOMMODATIONS & DINING

The Nitmiluk National Park ranger station in the Nitmiluk Visitor Centre has maps of available "bush campsites" throughout the park. These are very basic sites—no showers, no soaps or shampoos allowed because they pollute the river system, and simple pit toilets or none at all. Most are beside natural swimming holes. You must stop for a camping permit from the ranger station beforehand; the camping fee is A$3 (U.S.$1.95) per person per night.

Travel North (see above) runs the **Gorge Caravan Park** next to the Nitmiluk Visitor Centre. Wallabies sometimes hop into the shady grounds here. Fees are A$7 (U.S.$4.55) per adult, A$4.50 (U.S.$2.95) per child for a tent site, and A$19 (U.S.$12.35) double for a powered site.

Knotts Crossing Resort. Corner Giles and Cameron sts., Katherine, NT 0850. ☎ **08/ 8972 2511.** Fax 08/8972 2628. www.knottscrossing.com.au. E-mail: reservations@knottscrossing. com.au. 123 units (some with shower only; cabins have adjacent private bathroom), 41 powered and unpowered campsites. A/C TV. A$71 (U.S.$46.15) double cabin; A$82 (U.S.$53.30) double "village" room; A$116–$138 (U.S.$75.40–$89.70) double motel room. Extra person A$10 (U.S.$6.50) adult and A$5 (U.S.$3.25) child under 16, cabin or village room; A$11–$16.50 (U.S.$7.15–$10.75) per person extra, motel room. AE, BC, DC, MC, V.

At this low-key resort, you have a choice of huge, well-furnished motel rooms, some with kitchenettes, minibars, and in-room fax machines; cabins with their own private bathrooms just outside the door; or campgrounds, all located among the tropical landscaping. You can also opt for "village" rooms, built in 1998 and smartly furnished with a double bed and bunks, bathroom, kitchenette, TV, telephone, and joint verandah facing a small private garden pool with a barbecue. The cabins have no telephone but offer a little more privacy, each with a kitchenette and TV. Locals meet at the casual bar beside the large pool and Jacuzzi, and Katie's Bistro is one of the smartest places to eat in town. A small sundries store doubles as a tour and car-rental desk.

4 The Kimberley: A Far-Flung Wilderness

Most Aussies would be hard put to name a single settlement, river, or mountain within ◐ **the Kimberley,** so rarely visited and sparsely inhabited is this vast wilderness. This is an old, old land of red rocky plateaus stretching for thousands of square miles, jungly ravines, endless bush, crocodile-infested wetlands, spooky-looking boab trees with trunks shaped like bottles, lily-filled rock pools, lonely island-strewn coastline, droughts in winter, and massive floods in summer. The dry, spreading scenery reminds me a little of Africa or India. In the Dry, the area's biggest river, the Fitzroy, is bone dry, but in the Wet, its swollen banks are second only to the Amazon in the volume of water that surges to the sea. Aqua and scarlet are two colors that will hit you in the eye in the Kimberley—a luminous aqua for the sea, and the fiery scarlet of the fine soil hereabouts called "pindan." The area is famous for Wandjina-style Aboriginal rock art depicting people with circular hair-dos that look more than a little like beings from outer space. It is also known for another kind of rock art known as "Bradshaw figures," sticklike representations of human forms, which may be the oldest art on earth. A mere 25,000 people live in the Kimberley's 420,000 square kilometers. That's three times the size of England.

The unofficial capital of the East Kimberley is **Kununurra.** It's a small agricultural town that serves as the gateway to wildlife river cruises; the Bungle Bungles, a massive labyrinth of beehive-shaped rock formations; and a million-acre cattle station where you can hike, fish, and cruise palm-filled gorges by day and sleep in comfy permanent safari tents or glamorous homestead rooms by night. The main town in the West

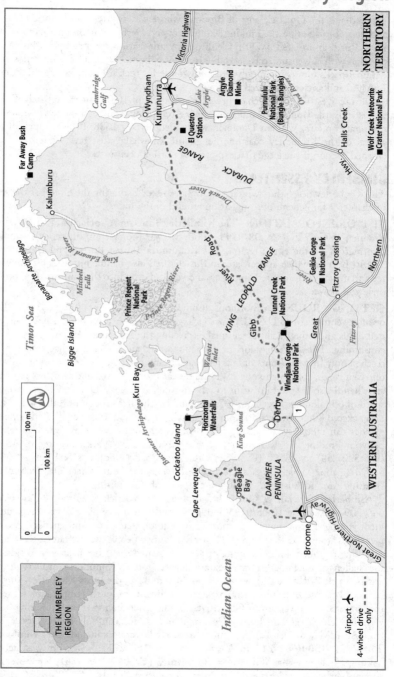

NORTHERN TERRITORY

Victoria Highway

Cambridge Gulf

○ Wyndham

Kununurra ✈

■ Argyle Diamond Mine

Lake Argyle

Purnululu National Park (Bungle Bungles)

Ord River

■ Halls Creek

Hwy

■ Wolf Creek Meteorite Crater National Park

El Questro Station ■

DURACK RANGE

Far Away Bush Camp ■

Durack River

Kalumburu ○

Bonaparte Archipelago

King Edward River

Mitchell Falls

Prince Regent National Park

Prince Regent River

Road

River

KING LEOPOLD RANGE

Geikie Gorge National Park ■

Fitzroy Crossing ○

River

Northern

Bigge Island

Timor Sea

Gibb

Tunnel Creek National Park ■

Great

Fitzroy

Walcott Inlet

Windjana Gorge National Park ■

Brecknock Archipelago Kuri Bay ○

Horizontal Waterfalls ■

Cockatoo Island

King Sound

Derby ○

100 mi

100 km

Cape Leveque

○ Beagle Bay

DAMPIER PENINSULA

WESTERN AUSTRALIA

Great Northern Highway

Broome ○ ✈

Indian Ocean

THE KIMBERLEY REGION

Airport ✈

4-wheel drive only ▬ ▬ ▬ ▬

Kimberley is the Outback port of Broome, whose waters give up the world's biggest and best South Sea pearls. Linking Kununurra and Derby, near Broome, is the Gibb River Road, an isolated 4WD track through cattle-station country that is becoming popular with adventure travelers. The region is home to some of Australia's best national parks too, containing weird and wonderful rock formations like the Bungle Bungles, and ancient fossilized coral reefs.

Off the West Kimberley coast lies a jigsaw puzzle of 10,000 or more barely inhabited islands, the **Bonaparte** and **Buccaneer Archipelagos,** the last named in honor of the pirate's pirate, William Dampier, who sailed here in 1688. In fact, much of the appeal of the Kimberley coastline lies in the knowledge that few Westerners have clapped eyes on it since the first explorers of the 17th century.

KIMBERLEY ESSENTIALS

The Kimberley lies within Western Australia, so see "Exploring the State," at the start of chapter 9 for general tips on getting around in the state.

VISITOR INFORMATION The **Kimberley Tourism Association,** P.O. Box 554, Broome, WA 6725 (☎ **08/9193 6660;** www.ebroome.com/kimberley), supplies information on the entire region. The Kununurra Tourist Bureau and the Broome Tourist Bureau (which appear later in this chapter) also handle inquiries on things to see and do across the entire Kimberley, and you can drop into their information offices once you arrive.

GETTING AROUND Enormous distances, high petrol costs (often A$1 per liter or more, equivalent to U.S.$2.45 per U.S. gallon), Wet Season floods, and very limited roads and other facilities can make traveling the Kimberley expensive and time-consuming. The place has lots of attractions that are so remote that they can be reached only by aerial tours or charter boats. Many more sights are accessible only on unpaved roads, for which your 2WD rental car is not insured and which it probably can't handle, so if you don't want to rely on tours, rent a 4WD. Allow for an average speed of 60 kilometers per hour (37.5 m.p.h.) on the area's rough unsealed roads, and never exceed 80 kilometers per hour (50 m.p.h.), because unexpected dips and smooth patches can take drivers by surprise. Most rental outfits will allow one-way rentals between Broome and Kununurra, or vice versa, at a ball-park surcharge of A$350 (U.S.$227.50) to A$500 (U.S.$325). Review "Road Conditions & Safety," "What to Do If Your Vehicle Breaks Down," and "Tips for Four-Wheel Drivers," in the "Getting Around Australia" section of chapter 2, before setting off.

Kimberley Caravan & Outback Supplies, 65 Frederick St., Broome (☎ **1800/ 645 909** in Australia, or 08/9193 5909) sells and rents every piece of camping equipment you need, from tents and "mozzie" (mosquito) nets to cooking utensils. A complete set is around A$48 (U.S.$31.20) per day for two people; weekly rates are available.

Taking a guided 4WD camping or accommodated safari is a neat way to sidestep the challenges of Kimberley travel. Safaris depart Broome, Kununurra, or Darwin, and last between 2 days and 2 weeks. A popular route is the cross-Kimberley journey between Broome and Kununurra, or vice versa. If you opt for this route, look for tours that traverse the adventurous Gibb River Road, rather than the less interesting highway via Halls Creek and Fitzroy Crossing. Most safaris run only in the Dry Season from April/May to October/November. Respected operators include **East Kimberley Tours** (☎ **1800/682 213** in Australia, or 08/9168 2213; www.comswest.net.au/ ~ektoursb); **Kimberley Wilderness Adventures** (☎ **08/9192 5741;** www.ozemail. com.au/~kwaaust); **Northern Territory Adventure Tours** (☎ **08/8936 1300;** www.adventuretours.com.au); and **Safari Treks** (☎ **08/9271 1271;** www.safaritreks. com.au).

Bird Watching & Bushwalking with Camels

More than one-third of Australia's bird species live in the Kimberley. The blue, green, yellow, and violet Gouldian finch, Nankeen night heron, tawny frogmouth, and hundreds more species get "twitchers," as locals affectionately dub bird-watchers, excited. The **Broome Bird Observatory** research station (☎ 08/ 9193 5600), 25 kilometers (16 miles) out of town on Roebuck Bay, monitors the thousands of migratory wetlands birds that gather here from Siberia. It offers 2-hour tours from Broome of shorebird, mangrove, and bush species, and has basic accommodations and camping facilities for real enthusiasts.

In the cooler Dry Season, bushwalking in this unspoiled environment is delightful. **Kimberley Bushwalks** (☎ 08/9192 7077; www.bushwalks.com) has hit on the neat idea of using pack camels to carry your gear (or you can ride them). It visits places inaccessible by car or boat from Broome, such as forested parts of the Fitzroy River, into the Great Sandy Desert sandhills, through ancient springs and billabongs, and to the Ngyginah Aboriginal people in the purple Mt. Anderson ranges. Some walks have themes like learning to make didgeridoos, stargazing, or meditation and yoga. Prices start at A$120 (U.S.$78) per person for 1-day walks; treks go up to 10 days or more.

Broome Aviation (☎ 08/9192 1369; www.broomeaviation.com) and **King Leopold Air** (☎ 1800/637 155 in Australia, or 08/9193 7155; www.kingleopoldair. com.au), both based in Broome, and **Alligator Airways** (☎ 08/9168 1333; www.hobbit.com.au/~alligator) and **Slingair Heliwork** (☎ 1800/095 500 in Australia, or 08/9169 1300; www.slingair.com.au), both based in Kununurra, run a range of flight-seeing tours all over the Kimberley, lasting from a couple of hours to several days. Some flights incorporate sightseeing on the ground, hiking in national parks, 4WD trips, overnights at fishing camps, or calls into vast cattle stations. Slingair offers a Kimberley Airpass.

KUNUNURRA

827km (517 miles) SW of Darwin; 1,032km (645 miles) E of Broome

Given the arid conditions in the Kimberley, it's quite a surprise to swoop over a field of sugar cane as you come in to land at Kununurra. This little town (pop. 5,000) is a booming agricultural center created by the damming of the mighty Ord River to form **Lake Argyle.**

Kununurra itself (the name is Aboriginal for "Meeting of Big Waters") has little to spark your interest, but it is the gateway to several outstanding attractions. A cruise down the **Ord River** to see wild birds, dramatic cliffs, and crocs is a must. So is a flight over or a hike into the Bungle Bungles (Purnululu National Park), monumental orange domes of rock that look like giant beehives. The world's biggest diamond mine is not in South Africa but out in the rugged Kimberley wilds near Kununurra, and it can be visited by air every day. The town is also a gateway to **El Questro,** a million-acre cattle station where you can hike magnificent gorges, fish, cruise rivers, ride horses, and see some of Australia's most breathtaking Aboriginal art.

ESSENTIALS

GETTING THERE   Ansett (☎ 13 13 00 in Australia) flies from Darwin once or twice a day, and Ansett and its affiliate Airnorth (book through Ansett) fly from Broome most days. Ansett also does direct service from Perth three times a week.

There is no train to Kununurra. **Greyhound Pioneer** (☎ **13 20 30** in Australia) serves the town daily from Broome and daily from Darwin via Katherine. From Broome the trip takes about 13¹/₂ hours, and the one-way fare is A$158.40 (U.S.$103); from Darwin, the trip time is around 9 hours, and the fare is A$118.80 (U.S.$77.25).

Kununurra is 512 kilometers (320 miles) west of Katherine on the Victoria Highway. The Great Northern Highway from Broome connects with the Victoria Highway 45 kilometers (28 miles) west of Kununurra. The Gibb River Road is an alternative 4WD scenic route from Derby near Broome (see later in this chapter); it connects with the Great Northern Highway 53 kilometers (33 miles) west of town.

VISITOR INFORMATION The **Kununurra Tourist Bureau** is at Coolibah Drive, Kununurra, WA 6743 (☎ **08/9168 1177**). Its hours change with the crowds and the season, but it usually opens from 8am to 5pm daily in the Dry. In the Wet it may operate reduced hours weekdays and may even close weekends.

GETTING AROUND **Avis** (☎ 08/9169 1258), **Budget** (☎ 08/9168 2033), **Hertz** (☎ 08/9169 1424), and **Territory Thrifty** (☎ 08/9169 1911) all rent 4WD vehicles, as does local company **Handy Rentals** (☎ **08/9169 1188**). At press time, no company in Kununurra rented camping gear or campervans.

WHAT TO SEE & DO

ON THE ORD RIVER Cruise outfits will offer you the option of cruising the Ord River or Lake Argyle, a massive man-made blue inland sea ringed by stony red cliffs and bigger than 19 Sydney Harbours, but go for the Ord. The Ord River is one of the most picturesque waterways in Australia, lined by bulbous red cliffs in parts, and teeming with all kinds of wetland birds and freshwater crocodiles. Jeff Haley of ✪ **Triple J. Tours** (☎ **1800/242 682** in Australia, or 08/9168 2682) runs excellent cruises along it. There are several itineraries, but the most popular starts with a 70-kilometer (44-mile) coach ride and commentary to Lake Argyle, a wander through a historic homestead, then the 55-kilometer (34-mile) cruise back to Kununurra. The boat travels fast and is a bit noisy, but Jeff pulls in at numerous tranquil spots and does a great picnic lunch on the bank. This costs A$92 (U.S.$59.80) for adults and A$50 (U.S.$32.50) for children 4 to 15, including pickup from your hotel.

Big Waters Kimberley Canoe Safaris (☎ **1800/641 998** in Australia, or 08/9169 1998; www.adventure.kimberley.net.au) offers a 3-day self-guided canoeing/camping safari down the Grade 1 (that means "gentle") Ord River. The company provides transfers from Kununurra to the river, two-person Canadian canoes, camping and cooking gear, watertight barrels, and Styrofoam coolers; you provide the food and the sense of adventure. It costs A$132 (U.S.$85.80) per person. The company also runs an afternoon guided canoe trip for A$44 (U.S.$28.60) per person.

A day on the river to fish for barramundi with **Greg Harman's Ultimate Adventures** (☎ **08/9168 2310**) costs A$190 (U.S.$123.50) per person, if there are two of you. Greg also does trips of up to 10 days to remote fishing camps.

DIAMONDS IN THE ROUGH Turning out an impressive 34 million carats a year—that's about 8 tons of pure diamond, or one-third of total world output—the **Argyle Diamond Mine** is the only mine in the world to produce the rare pink diamond in commercial quantities, as well as champagne, cognac, yellow, green, and white rocks. During a 3¹/₂- to 4-hour visit to the mine, you will see rough and polished gems in the viewing room, see gems get extracted from the huge open-cut mine as long as safety conditions permit that day, and, if you like, buy some. For security reasons, you must join an organized aerial tour with either **Belray Diamond Tours** and its affiliate, **Alligator Airways** (☎ **1800/632 533** in Australia, or 08/9168 1014), or **Slingair Heliwork** (☎ **1800/095 500** in Australia, or 08/9169 1300). I'd recommend you opt for a flight that covers the nearby Purnululu National Park (Bungle Bungles) and Lake Argyle as well, an option both companies offer for around A$325 (U.S.$211.25). Belray Diamond Tours does a coach trip Thursdays only from June to September, but it's a 2½-hour drive each way. The company also does a 3-day aerial/4WD trip incorporating the mine tour and camping and hiking in Purnululu National Park. Kids under 12 are not permitted on mine tours. A couple of jewelry stores in Kununurra sell Argyle diamonds.

SPENDING THE DAY AT EL QUESTRO STATION   You do not have to stay at ✪ **El Questro** (see "Accommodations") to enjoy the wonderful facilities. When aristocratic Englishman Will Burrell bought this million-acre cattle station in 1991, he turned it into a kind of Outback holiday camp where anyone from the members of the international jet set to humble 4WD enthusiasts could revel in its rugged beauty. Although it's a working cattle station, guests don't really get involved in the cow side of things. Instead, they go barramundi fishing and heli-fishing in wetlands and rivers, soak under palm trees in the thermal waters of **Zebedee Springs,** hike the rainforest of **Pentecost Gorge,** take half-day 4WD fishing safaris, cruise tranquil **Chamberlain Gorge,** ride horses across stony plains, photograph towering red rocky ranges, join rangers on bird-watching tours, or explore a rich lode of Aboriginal rock paintings. It's an unspoiled, primeval place.

Day trippers are welcome for a fee of A$10 (U.S.$6.50) or A$5 (U.S.$3.25) if you go only as far as Emma Gorge, plus the regular fees charged for all activities. Children 3 to 12 are half price. The staff at El Questro's office in Kununurra, on Banksia Street, will give you a map and point out all there is to see and do, and you will find the rangers friendly and knowledgeable. Pay there or at the station store near the campground, where you can buy basic supplies and fuel and rent 4WDs and camping gear. Most activities depart here. The station does organized day trips from Kununurra for A$135 (U.S.$87.75) per person. Ask staff to identify which swimming spots are croc-free, and don't swim anywhere else!

You pay for most activities—between A$5 (U.S.$3.25) to walk Emma Gorge and A$360 (U.S.$234) for a half day's heli-fishing. A typical price is A$37 (U.S.$24.05) for a gorge cruise. Guests at Emma Gorge will usually pay A$12 (U.S.$7.80) round-trip to transfer to join tours and activities departing the station store. The tour desk also arranges such off-station activities as day trips on the Ord River, trips to the Argyle diamond mine and the Bungle Bungles, and extended tours throughout the Kimberley as far afield as Broome.

ACCOMMODATIONS

At El Questro

✪ **El Questro Station,** Gibb River Road, 100 kilometers (63 miles) southwest of Kununurra (P.O. Box 909, Kununurra, WA 6743; ☎ **08/9169 1777;** www.elquestro. com.au; e-mail: sales@elquestro.com.au), consists of the three separate facilities described below. Four-wheel–drive transfers from Kununurra cost A$90–$100 (U.S.$58.50–$65) per adult round-trip; children ages 3 to 12 are charged half price. To get there, take the Great Northern Highway 58 kilometers (36 miles) toward Wyndham, then the (unsealed) Gibb River Road 26 kilometers (16 miles) to Emma Gorge Resort, or a further 23 kilometers (14 miles) to the station store. All of the accommodations accept AE, BC, DC, MC, and V.

In addition to the options listed below, there's **Black Cockatoo Riverside Camping.** Forty-five riverside camp locations near the station store are available for a nightly charge of A$16.50 (U.S.$10.75) per adult (less in the Wet Season), and free for children under 12. Campers share shower facilities and use the bungalows' restaurant. Extra, more secluded riverside campsites are a 10-minute drive.

✪ **El Questro Homestead.** See contact details above. 6 units (all with shower only). A/C. A$742.50–$852.50 (U.S.$482.65–$554.15) *per person* per night (including 4WD transfers from Kununurra, meals, open bar, laundry service, and all activities except helicopter flights). Minimum 2-night stay. The homestead is 1 hr., 45 min. by road from Kununurra. Air transfers from Darwin, Kununurra, Broome, Alice Springs, and Ayers Rock available on request. Children under 16 not permitted.

Perched over the Chamberlain River on the edge of a gorge, this homestead is one of the world's most luxurious yet simple getaways. Visitors (make that *wealthy* visitors—no one else could afford those astronomical rates!) come for the sense of seclusion and the wilderness experience. You stay in airy rooms furnished in a blend of Aussie country style and Indonesian antiques, with a view of the gardens and the river from your veranda. Your room has a hair dryer. There's no menu; instead, everyone dines on the same home-cooked gourmet meal at the one big communal table. There are an inviting TV lounge, a tennis court, a Jacuzzi, and a pool with a sundeck.

✪ **Emma Gorge Resort.** See contact details above. 35 tent cabins (17 with bathroom). A$113.30–$154.50 (U.S.$73.65–$100.45) double, A$30 (U.S.$19.50) children 3–12, A$192.50 (U.S.$125.15) family tent with 1 double and 2 single beds. Emma Gorge is 1 hr. by road from Kununurra.

This neatly kept oasis of permanent tents mounted on lush lawns under pandanus palms at the foot of the soaring red Cockburn Range is a great way to "camp" in the wilderness without sacrificing comfort. Although they are "only" tents, the accommodations are very comfortable, for they have wooden floors, electric lights, standing fans, insect screens, nice firm beds, bedside tables, and torches (flashlights) for getting around at night. Those without bathrooms share clean and modern facilities. Reception stocks sundries and souvenirs and lends hair dryers. The bush veranda restaurant and bar serves up gourmet bush tucker meals that would put many big-city restaurants to shame. There's a man-made swimming pool, but most folks walk the 1.6-kilometer (1-mile) trail along lush Emma Gorge to the natural swimming hole and trickling waterfall enclosed by 46-meter (150-ft.) cliffs. This walk is free to guests.

El Questro Bungalows. See contact details above. 12 bungalows (all with shower only). A/C. A$162 (U.S.$105.30) double. Extra person A$32–$33 (U.S.$20.80–$21.45). The Bungalows are 90 min. by road from Kununurra.

These basic but comfortable rooms located by the store at the heart of the station operations are good for families, or anyone without their own transport. Some have single beds and bunks, while eight new ones are quite spiffy, with stylish queen beds and balconies overlooking the Pentecost River. The Steakhouse restaurant and bar serves three meals a day, such as "barra burgers." A swimming hole is nearby.

In Kununurra

Country Club Hotel. 47 Coolibah Dr., Kununurra, WA 6743. ☎ **08/9168 1024.** Fax 08/9168 1189. www.countryclubhotel.com.au. E-mail: cchotel@bigpond.com. 88 units (all with bathroom, 8 with tub). A/C TV TEL. Dry Season A$154 (U.S.$100.10) double, A$203.50 (U.S.$132.30) apt. Wet Season A$132 (U.S.$85.80) double, A$170.50 (U.S.$110.85) apt. Extra person A$22 (U.S.$14.30). Children under 17 stay free in parents' room. AE, BC, DC, MC, V.

Located just down the road from the tourist bureau, this low-rise member of the Flag motel chain is your best bet among Kununurra's modest choice of accommodations. Nestled among tropical gardens, it has a large, lovely shaded pool with sun lounges and poolside dining, a Chinese restaurant, an all-day grill restaurant, and a couple of bars. The rooms are nothing flashy, but they're neat, clean, and modern, with plenty of space. The front desk acts as a tour desk and loans hair dryers.

PURNULULU (BUNGLE BUNGLES) NATIONAL PARK

Rising out of the landscape 250 kilometers (156 miles) south of Kununurra are thousands of enormous sandstone domes 200 to 300 meters (656 to 984 ft.) high called the Bungle Bungles. Thought to be named after either "bundle bundle" grass or the bungle beetle, the Bungle Bungles get their distinctive orange-and-gray stripes from algae found in the permeable layers and mineral graining in nonpermeable layers. The formations are 360 million years old.

The domes look spectacular from the air—and that's the only way to see them in the Wet, because the park is closed to ground traffic from January 1 to March 31. As the waters subside (sometimes not until early June, and they may swell again in late Oct), the soaring gorges and forested creeks at the base of the Bungle Bungles are accessible on foot. Highlights are the beehive-shaped walls of **Cathedral Gorge,** the natural rock pool at **Frog Hole Gorge,** and palm-filled **Echidna Chasm.** Keep an eye peeled for rainbow bee-eaters, flocks of budgerigars, rare nailtail wallabies, and euros, a kind of kangaroo.

There are several basic campgrounds with pit toilets, wood barbecues, and water (boil before drinking) but no showers and no telephones. The camping fee is A$7 (U.S.$4.55) for adults, A$1 (U.S.65¢) for kids under 16. Bring food and fuel with you. For information call the state **Department of Conservation and Land Management,** or CALM (☎ **08/9168 0200**) in Kununurra; there is a ranger station in the park during the season.

GETTING THERE & GETTING AROUND   Most folks take a scenic flight over the park in a light aircraft or helicopter from Kununurra for about A$200 (U.S.$130). The flight takes about 2 hours. Contact **Slingair Heliwork** (☎ **1800/095 500** in Australia, or 08/9169 1300) or **Alligator Airways** (☎ **1800/632 533** in Australia, or 08/9168 1333). Both companies also do a combined air/hiking day trip. Alligator Airways does a 3-day aerial/hiking/camping trip incorporating the Argyle diamond mine tour.

Road access is 4WD only. To explore by car, you will need at least 1 overnight to explore Purnululu's 3,000 square kilometers (1,158 square miles); entry is A$8 (U.S.$5.20) per vehicle. Take the Victoria Highway 45 kilometers (28 miles) west of Kununurra, turn left onto the Great Northern Highway for 201 kilometers (126 miles) to the park turnoff, and allow 2 hours to cover the final tough 53 kilometers (33 miles) from the highway to the park entrance. Turkey Creek, 53 kilometers (33 miles) north of the turnoff, is the nearest place for supplies.

Several companies offer 4WD hiking/camping safaris from Kununurra lasting 2 to 4 days.

TUNNEL CREEK & WINDJANA GORGE NATIONAL PARKS

Windjana Gorge National Park is 240 kilometers (150 miles) east of Broome, 21 kilometers (13 miles) off the Gibb River Road. The massive 350-million-year-old walls of the gorge, which shoot straight up as high as 100 meters (328 ft.) above the sandy desert floor, are actually an old limestone barrier reef. A picturesque 7-kilometer (4-mile)

Driving the Gibb River Road

If you really want to discover the Outback, mate, the Gibb River Road is for you. Traversing this sandy, rocky, unpaved 660-kilometer (413-mile) 4WD track that links the east and west Kimberley is fast becoming a "must do" for seasoned adventure travelers. Populated only by stark red ranges, rivers that flood to the horizon in the Wet and vanish to dustbowls in the Dry, fern-fringed swimming holes and waterfalls, and huge cattle stations, it is a road for self-reliant folk who seek wilderness and know how to change a tire.

Homesteads along the way offer activities such as barramundi fishing in lily-clad water holes, hikes through gorges, and even aerial tours to remote Prince Regent Nature Reserve, **King's Cascade,** Mitchell Falls, the Horizontal Waterfalls, and other spots on the north Kimberley Coast. Some serve meals and have basic accommodations, ranging from campsites with hot showers to rooms at the homestead. They ain't the lap of luxury, but neither is the road.

Expect ribbed "corrugation" on the gravel, soft patches, and bumpy rocks that will limit your speed to 60 kilometers per hour (37.5 m.p.h.) or slower for much of the way. It's possible to drive the road in 2 days (or even 1), but give yourself 3 to 5 days to do some sightseeing. You can count on the road being passable only from May to October; much of it is under water in the Wet.

The road starts on the Great Northern Highway, 53 kilometers (33 miles) west of Kununurra. **El Questro Station** (see "Accommodations" in the "Kununurra" section, above) is the first stop, 33 kilometers (21 miles) along. It finishes in **Derby,** a small coastal town 221 kilometers (138 miles) northeast of Broome. The Great Northern Highway connects Derby with Broome. Windjana Gorge and Tunnel Creek national parks (described in this chapter) are accessed off the road.

To drive the road in a rented 4WD, you will need written permission from your rental-car company. Carry cash (you can forget about ATMs out here, and traveler's checks are not always accepted), spare fuel, enough drinking water and food to last 3 or 4 days longer than you think you'll need, a tool kit, a tire puncture repair kit and a high lift jack, a spare tire, radiator hoses, a spare fan belt, and a first-aid kit. Your rental-car company should provide all of this, except your supplies. If you want to stay in rooms rather than in the campground, book ahead. Even so, carry camping gear in case tire punctures, swollen creeks, or some other circumstance holds you up between homesteads. Some homesteads are private farms not open to the public, and their owners take a dim view of poorly prepared tourists begging them for water, fuel, or food. Swim only where the locals tell you, on account of crocodiles.

Before setting off, obtain a copy of the A$2 (U.S.$1.30) Gibb River Road guide that lists accommodations, the very few fuel stops, and other facilities along the way. It is available from the tourist bureaus in Kununurra and Broome.

Plenty of 4WD safari tours operate on the road between Broome and Kununurra, and even from Darwin, taking between 5 and 10 days. See "Kimberley Essentials" at the beginning of this section for companies to contact.

round-trip trail winds through the gorge, revealing fossilized marine creatures laid down in the Devonian period. This reef is actually part of a much larger barrier reef—comprising hundreds of coral patches, some a couple of miles across, other hundreds of miles wide—created when this part of Australia was an ocean floor. As the ocean floor subsided, those little coral-building creatures kept on building their reefs higher and higher. When the ocean floor pushed up above sea level, the reefs were left high and dry and became the **Napier Ranges.** The **Lennard River,** which carved Windjana Gorge, flows only in the Wet, but freshwater crocodiles, fruit bats, and birds are common year-round in and around the residual pools.

Thirty kilometers (19 miles) southeast of Windjana Gorge is **Tunnel Creek National Park,** where you can explore a cave tunneled by the river through the same ancient limestone reef system. To reach it, you wade through the creek for 750 meters (about half a mile) in the dark. Before you leave Broome, ask your hotel to lend you a torch (flashlight) to reveal the tunnel's stalactites, fish, five bat species including rare ghost bats, and even odd freshwater croc (the "friendly" sort). Wear shoes you can get wet, and expect the water to be cold!

You can include Windjana and Tunnel Creek on a Gibb River Road safari, or visit from Broome (where operators offer coach and 4WD tours). Take the Great Northern Highway east for 187 kilometers (117 miles), take a left onto the Derby Highway for 43 kilometers (27 miles) to Derby, and then head east along the Gibb River Road. *Note:* The last 70 kilometers (44 miles) to Windjana, and from there to Tunnel Creek, are unpaved, so you will need a 4WD. Both parks are usually closed in the Wet from November or December to mid-April.

Camping at Windjana Gorge costs A$7 (U.S.$4.55) for adults, A$1 (U.S.65¢) for kids under 16. The campground has cold showers, toilets, barbecues and wood, and a public telephone, but no food or fuel. There is no camping, food, water, or ranger station in Tunnel Creek National Park.

Neither park has an entry fee.

For park information, and to check accessibility and road conditions outside June to September, call the state **Department of Conservation and Land Management (CALM)** in Broome (☎ **08/9192 1036**).

GEIKIE GORGE NATIONAL PARK

Freshwater versions of saltwater beasties such as sharks, sawfish, and stingrays lurk in the Fitzroy River, which flows through **Geikie Gorge** (pronounced "*Geek*-ee"). Although strictly speaking, the gorge is part of an ancient Devonian reef, like Windjana Gorge and Tunnel Creek, its gold-and-gray 30-meter (98-ft.) walls were built not by coral but by algae. Like Windjana Gorge, its walls show primitive life forms that inhabited a time before reptiles and mammals were around. Today, pandanus palms, wild passion fruit, mangroves, and river gums line the banks, and freshwater crocodiles and all kinds of birds can be seen, especially in the Dry. If you spot a stream of water arching out of the river, that's an archer fish targeting an insect by spitting at it.

There are moves afoot to dam the mighty Fitzroy, which makes sense to some farmers but will wreak havoc on the ecology of fishes and rare birds and flood Aboriginal cultural sites.

The most popular way to experience the park is on a wildlife and geology cruise with the park rangers. They conduct four 1-hour cruises each day in the dry season, fewer in the seasonal cusp around April/May and September/October. Cruises cost A$17.50 (U.S.$11.40) for adults, and just A$2 (U.S.$1.30) for school-age kids. Bookings are not needed. There are also two walking trails to explore, a 1-hour round-trip "reef" trail along the base of the gorge wall, and a 20-minute walk along the riverbank to a fishing and swimming hole.

Cruises run April to November; the gorge is open but may be cut off by floodwaters December to March. There are picnic facilities (buy food in Fitzroy Crossing) but there's no camping.

For inquiries on the cruise schedule and any other matters, call the **Department of Conservation and Land Management (CALM)** in Fitzroy Crossing (☎ 08/9191 5121), or in the Dry Season at the gorge (☎ 08/9191 5112).

Entry to the park is free. The gorge is 418 kilometers (261 miles) east of Broome, so be prepared for a long day. The road is paved all the way. Take care with the water level on the several concrete fords. The nearest town is **Fitzroy Crossing,** 18 kilometers (11 miles) before the entrance (☎ 08/9191 5355 is the Fitzroy Crossing Tourist Bureau). No rangers are based in the park during the Wet. Coach and 4WD day tours are available from Broome.

BROOME

2,250km (1,406 miles) N of Perth; 1,859km (1,161 miles) SW of Darwin

Part rough Outback town, part glam seaside resort, the pearling port of ✪ **Broome** (pop. 11,000) is a fascinating mixture of Australia and Asia you won't see anywhere else. Chinese and Japanese pearl divers used to work the pearling luggers in this isolated little town in the old days, and as the Chinese settled here, they affixed their distinctive architecture to typical Australian buildings. The result is a main street so cute it could be a movie set, with neat rows of Australian corrugated iron stores wrapped by verandas and trimmed with Chinese peaked roofs.

The people are a unique mixture, too, because Anglo-Saxon/Irish Aussies and Chinese, Filipino, and Malayan pearl workers often married Aboriginal women. The Japanese tended to return home rather than settle here, but not all of them made it. Cyclones, the "bends," sharks, and crocodiles all took their toll. The Japanese legacy in the town is a rather eerie divers' cemetery with Asian inscriptions on 900 rough-hewn headstones, incongruously surrounded by the Aussie bush.

For such a small and remote place, Broome is surprisingly sophisticated. Walk the streets of Chinatown and you'll rub shoulders with Aussie tourists, itinerant workers, Asian food-store proprietors, tough-as-nails cattle hands, and well-heeled visitors from Europe and America downing good coffee at a couple of trendy cafes. Broome's South Sea pearls are still its bread and butter, but the old-timber pearling luggers have been replaced with gleaming high-tech vessels equipped with helipads and stainless-steel security doors.

To be honest, it's kinda hard to explain Broome's appeal. There is not all that much to do here really, but it's somehow just a nice place to be. You can shop for pearls, of course, and it's a good base for exploring the wider Kimberley; but most people come to laze by the jade-green Indian Ocean on Cable Beach, ride camels along the sand as the sun plops into the sea, fish the unplundered seas, and soak up the gorgeous reds, blues, and greens of the Kimberley coast.

ESSENTIALS

GETTING THERE   Ansett (☎ 13 13 00 in Australia) has the best service to Broome, with several daily direct flights from Perth and from Darwin (some go via Kununurra), and once a week from Alice Springs. Airlink (book through Qantas) flies from Perth six times a week and has a couple of flights a week from both Alice Springs and Darwin. The trip to Broome from Sydney and other state capitals is a lengthy affair via Perth, or via Alice Springs and Darwin.

Greyhound Pioneer (☎ 13 20 30 in Australia) has a daily service from Perth that takes around 32 hours and extra express services some days that take around 27 hours. The fare is A$271.70 (U.S.$176.60). Greyhound's daily service from Darwin via Katherine and Kununurra takes around 24 hours; the one-way fare is A$234.30 (U.S.$152.30).

There is no train service to Broome.

Broome is 34 kilometers (21 miles) off the Great Northern Highway, which leads from Perth in the south, Kununurra to the east. The Gibb River Road is an alternative 4WD scenic route from Kununurra (see "Driving the Gibb River Road," above).

VISITOR INFORMATION   The **Broome Tourist Bureau** is on the Great Northern Highway (locals call it the Broome Highway) at Bagot Street, Broome, WA 6725 (☎ **08/9192 2222;** www.ebroome.com/tourism). In the Dry, it's open Monday through Friday 8am to 5pm, and Saturday and Sunday 9am to 4pm; in the Wet, it's open Monday to Friday 9am to 5pm, Saturday, Sunday, and public holidays 9am to 1pm.

Book accommodations and tours well ahead in the peak June-to-August season.

GETTING AROUND   ATC Rent A Car (☎ 08/9193 7788), **Avis** (☎ 08/ 9193 5980), **Broome Broome Car Rentals** (☎ 1800/676 725 in Australia, or 08/9192 2210), **Budget** (☎ 08/9193 5355), **Hertz** (☎ 08/9192 1428), and **Thrifty** (☎ 08/9193 6787) all rent conventional cars and 4WDs. For campervans or 4WD campers, contact **ATC Rent A Car** (see above) or **THL Rentals** (☎ 08/9192 2647), who are agents for Britz, Koala, and Maui campervans.

The **Town Bus** (☎ **08/9193 6000**) does an hourly loop of most attractions from 7:20am to 6:15pm daily, more often in the middle of the day in the Dry. A single fare is A$2.50 (U.S.$1.65), and a day pass is A$8 (U.S.$5.20).

Broome Taxis (☎ **08/9192 1133**) operates the airport shuttle to your hotel door. For a cab call Roebuck Taxis (☎ 1800/880 330).

Broome Day Tours (☎ **1800/801 068** in Australia, or 08/9192 1068) runs tours of the town and farther afield to gorges and other natural attractions. **Over the Top Adventure Tours** (☎ **08/9192 3977**) runs 1- and 2-day 4WD tours to hard-to-get-to wilderness spots like the Dampier Peninsula.

WHAT TO SEE & DO

Head to **Chinatown,** in the town center on Carnarvon Street and Dampier Terrace, when you arrive to get a feel for the town. It's not all that Chinese anymore, but most shops, cafes, and galleries are here. The Broome Tourist Bureau gives out maps to a 2-kilometer (1¼-mile) trail taking in the town's historic buildings. When he's not away on tour, Aboriginal actor Stephen "Baamba" Albert presents the seamier side of Broome's history on fun walking tours of Chinatown. A 90-minute morning tour costs A$25 (U.S.$16.25). The tours meet outside Sun Pictures at 8am in the Wet, 9am in the Dry. He also does 2-hour evening tours for A$30 (U.S.$19.50) departing at 4:30pm. Call ✪ **Baamba** (☎ **0417/988 328**).

Probably the most popular Dry Season pastime is lazing on the 22 glorious white sandy kilometers (14 miles) of ✪ **Cable Beach.** The beach is 6 kilometers (3¾ miles) out of town; the town bus runs there regularly. A beach hut near Cable Beach Inter-Continental Resort (see "Accommodations & Dining," below) rents beach and water-sports equipment in the Dry. From November to April the water is off-limits due to deadly marine stingers. Crocodiles, on the other hand, do not like surf, so you should be safe swimming here. Make a point of being at the beach for at least one of the magnificently rosy sunsets in the Dry.

A novel way to experience the beach is on camelback. Several outfits operate. A 1-hour ride with **Red Sun Camel Safaris** (☎ **08/9193 7423** or 0419/954 996) costs A$33 (U.S.$21.45) adults, A$22 (U.S.$14.30) kids 11 to 15, and A$11 (U.S.$7.15) for kids 5 to 10.

Reigning four-time state surf champ ✪ **Josh Parmateer** (☎ **0418/958 264**) gives 2-hour surf lessons on the beach from July to September for A$80 (U.S.$31.85) per

Stairway to the Moon

You've heard of a stairway to heaven? Well, Broome has a stairway to the moon. On the happy coincidence of a full moon and a low 10-meter tide (which happens about 3 consecutive nights a month from Mar to Oct), nature treats the town to a special show as the light of the rising moon falls on the rippled sand and mudflats in Roebuck Bay, looking for all the world like a "staircase to the moon." The best place to see it is from the cliff-top restaurant at the Mangrove Hotel (see "Accommodations & Dining"), or from the food and craft markets held at Town Beach most staircase nights.

person, or A$30 (U.S.$19.50) per person if there are two of you. He supplies the boards, the wet suits, and a guarantee you'll be standing by the end of the lesson!

Definitely drop by the **Pearl Luggers,** 44 Dampier Terrace (☎ **08/9192 2059**). A 75-minute session here includes a look over two restored Broome pearling luggers, a browse through a small well-equipped pearling museum, and an absolutely riveting and hilarious talk about pearl diving as it used to be by former divers Richard "Salty" Baillieu or Steve "Zimmo" Zimmerle. Don't miss it. Admission is A$15 (U.S.$9.75) adults, A$13.50 (U.S.$8.80) seniors and students, A$9 (U.S.$5.85) for kids 8 to 17. The attraction opens 9am to 5pm May to October, 10am to about 2:30pm November to April; tours run 9:30am, 11am, 1pm, and 3pm in the Dry, and 11am and 1pm in the Wet. Closed Christmas.

A dinosaur footprint 120 million years old is on show at very low tide on the cliff at **Gantheaume Point,** 6 kilometers (3³/₄ miles) from town. The town authorities have set a plaster cast of it higher up on the rocks, so you can see it anytime. Bring your camera to snap the point's breathtaking palette of glowing red cliffs, white beach, and turquoise water.

You should also take a peek at the haunting **Japanese pearl divers' cemetery** on Port Drive. Entry is free.

During a tour of the **Willie Creek Pearl Farm** (☎ **08/9193 6000**), 38 kilometers (24 miles) north of town, you will see the delicate process of an oyster getting "seeded" with a nucleus to form a pearl, and learn about pearl farming firsthand from the managers. The tour costs A$17.50 (U.S.$11.40) adults, A$9 (U.S.$5.85) children 5 to 15. Book first. The road to the farm is 4WD-only and tides can cut it off; coach tours operate.

The daily croc-feeding session is the best time to visit the **Malcolm Douglas Broome Crocodile Park,** next to Cable Beach Inter-Continental Resort, Cable Beach Road (☎ **08/9192 1489**).

Several art galleries sell vivid oil and watercolor Kimberley landscapes and a small range of Aboriginal art. A historic pearling master's house, **Matso's,** 60 Hamersley St. (☎ **08/9193 5811**), stocks the biggest range of European and Aboriginal paintings, sculpture, pottery, carvings, and books. It has a lovely veranda cafe and boutique brewery turning out unusual recipes like chili beer. It's open daily from 10am to 5pm; meals are from 8am.

On Saturday from 8am to 1pm, browse the **markets** in the gardens of the colonial **Courthouse** at the corner of Frederick and Hamersley streets. It used to be the official station for the cable from Broome to Java. Don't bet the ranch on this tale being gospel, but locals like to tell you that when the British authorities packed up the building materials for the courthouse in Britain and addressed it to "The Kimberley," they meant them to end up in the Kimberley, South Africa. Instead, the stuff arrived in the

Kimberley, Australia. The town kept the building and so can proudly lay claim to having Australia's only Zulu-proof courthouse.

A number of boats run sunset cruises on Roebuck Bay or off Cable Beach. Fishing for trevally, Spanish mackerel, barracuda, barramundi, queenfish, tuna, shark, sailfish, marlin, salmon (in the May to Aug run), and reef fish is excellent around Broome; fly- and sportfishing are also worth a try. Rent tackle and try your luck from the deep-water jetty near Town Beach 2 kilometers (1¼ miles) south of town, or join one of several charter boats running day trips. **FAD Game Fishing Charters** (☎ **08/9192 3998**) and **Lucky Strike Charters** (☎ **08/9193 7375**) are two of the respected ones. **Pearl Sea Coastal Cruises** (see "Boating the Kimberley Coast," later in this chapter) runs extended live-aboard fishing trips up the coast. Cyclones, rain, high winds, and strong tides can restrict fishing from December to March.

Australia's first family of pearling, the Paspaleys, sell their wonderfully elegant jewelry at ✪ **Paspaley Pearls,** Carnarvon Street at Short Street (☎ **08/9192 2203**). Linney's and Broome Pearls are two other reputable jewelers nearby.

Don't leave without taking in a recent-release movie at the adorable **Sun Pictures** outdoor cinema, Carnarvon Street near Short Street (☎ **08/9192 1077**). Built in 1916, these are the oldest "picture gardens" in the world, where the audience sits in (saggy) canvas deck chairs. Films are even screened through the rain in the Wet. Tickets are A$11 (U.S.$7.15). Open nightly except Christmas.

ACCOMMODATIONS & DINING

✪ **Cable Beach Inter-Continental Resort.** Cable Beach Rd., Broome, WA 6725. ☎ **1800/095 508** in Australia, 800/327-0200 in the U.S. and Canada, 020/8847 2277 or 0345/58 1444 outside London in the U.K., 1800/709 300 in Ireland, 0800/442 215 in New Zealand, or 08/9192 0400. Fax 08/9192 2249. www.interconti.com. E-mail: reserve@broome.wt.com.au. 263 units (some with shower only). A/C TV TEL. High season (July–Sept) A$286–$371 (U.S.$185.90–$241.15) double, A$369–$447 (U.S.$239.85–$290.55) bungalow. Slight discounts in Apr–June; significantly lower rates Oct–Mar. Lower rates for a 3-night stay. Ask about packages. Extra person A$38 (U.S.$24.70). Children under 18 stay free in parents' room. AE, BC, DC, MC, V. Airport shuttle A$6 (U.S.$3.90) per person return. Town bus.

For some Aussies, a visit to Broome is just an excuse to stay at this chic Chinatown-meets-Outback resort, which blends Australian frontier architecture and decor—corrugated iron walls inside as well as out, verandas, Aboriginal art—with Chinese elements like red and green latticework, pagoda roofs, silky red bathrobes, and Asian cotton bedcovers. The huge standard rooms are gorgeous and have a decent-sized living area and balcony. Bungalows (which sleep four to six) have central bedrooms surrounded on three sides by a veranda; 18 new ones will be fitted with kitchens by the time you arrive. All units have pay-per-view movies, hair dryers, and irons and boards. It's tough to match the I'm-a-colonial-pearling-master suites, lavishly decked out with eye-popping antique Asiatica and valuable Australian art. These are truly to die for, so ask about suite packages, which offer remarkably good value. A dune blocks true sea views, because the authorities won't allow buildings visible from the sand. It is a 5-minute drive or a 6-kilometer (3¾ miles) bus ride into town.

Dining/Diversions: Unlike many resorts I can name, this one offers food worth eating. There are Pandanus for elegant dinners in a pondside setting; Sketches pasta bar; all-day dining inside or on the terrace at the casual colonial-style Lord Mac's; and a cafe. The open-sided Kimberley Grill does steaks, and the Walking Wok offers Mongolian stir-fries; both close in the Wet. Two pool bars serve snacks. The popular Sunset Bar has live entertainment on Sundays and a free live sunset every night of the week (in the Dry!). My only gripe? The room-service menu is limited to snacks, and then only at dinner.

Amenities: Guest activities program; family swimming pool and an adults-only chilled pool; Jacuzzi; guests-only section on the beach with free umbrellas and chairs; water-sports equipment for rent in the Dry Season; kids' club for kids 3 to 12 (at a fee); baby-sitting; eight day/night tennis courts and tennis instruction; extremely well-equipped gym offering a variety of massages, yoga, float tank, personal trainers (even cardio-boxing!); concierge; tour desk; art gallery; pearl boutique; resort store; dry cleaning/laundry; conference facilities; business center and secretarial services.

Mangrove Hotel. 120 Carnarvon St., Broome, WA 6725. ☎ **1800/094 818** in Australia, or 08/9192 1303. Fax 08/9193 5169. www.mangrovehotel.com.au. E-mail: mangrovehotel@ bigpond.com. 67 units, all with bathroom (2 with Jacuzzi, 1 with tub). A/C TV TEL. High season (Apr–Oct) A$143–$165 (U.S.$92.95–$107.25) double, A$220 (U.S.$143) suite, A$264 (U.S.$171.60) 2-bedroom apt. Low season (Nov–Mar) A$121–$143 (U.S.$78.65–$92.95) double, A$198 (U.S.$128.70) suite, A$242 (U.S.$157.30) 2-bedroom apt. Extra person A$33 (U.S.$21.45). Children under 3 stay free. Ask about packages in the Wet Season. AE, BC, DC, MC, V. Free airport shuttle.

The best views in Broome are across Roebuck Bay from this cliff-top hotel 5 minutes' walk from town. It's worth hightailing it back from sightseeing just to watch dusk fall over the bay from the lovely Tides Garden outdoor restaurant, where tables and chairs are set out on the lawns under the palms and along the cliff edge. Tides Garden is popular with locals for good, affordable food, and Charter's restaurant inside is one of Broome's best. There's no faulting the clean, well-kept standard rooms; the ultraroomy deluxe rooms with sea views (a good value); the two suites that have Jacuzzis; and the two-bedroom apartment. All have hair dryers and irons and boards. Two swimming pools and two Jacuzzis set in the lawns overlooking the bay, room service, and a tour desk are among the amenities. The town bus stops across the road.

BEYOND BROOME

North of Broome, the Kimberley gets really wild.

Stretching 220 kilometers (138 miles) north of Broome, the **Dampier Peninsula** is home to several Aboriginal communities that sell artworks, and a wonderful pearl-shell church built by missionaries.

The 10,000 or more islands of the **Buccaneer** and **Bonaparte Archipelagos** are mostly uninhabited except for **Cockatoo Island Resort,** P.O. Box 444, Darwin, NT 0801 (☎ **08/8946 4455;** e-mail: cockatooisland@bigpond.com.au), several hundred kilometers north of Broome, a glamorously simple hideaway that puts guests in salmon-pink former miners' huts perched high on a rock wall over the sea. Fishing, taking nature walks, and lazing by the stunning cliff-top pool are the main activities.

Near Derby are the 2-meter-high **Horizontal Waterfalls** at Talbot Bay, created by tides. Much farther north are the tidal whirlpools, gorges, and rain-forested waterfalls of **Walcott Inlet;** the utter isolation of the gorges, rock plateaus, and river of the 600,000-hectare (1,482,000-acre) **Prince Regent Nature Reserve;** and the four tiers of the picturesque **Mitchell Falls.**

There are no roads to most of these places (except for 4WD tracks to the Dampier Peninsula and Mitchell Falls), so you need to explore by plane or by boat. From July to September or later, plane and boat passengers often spot humpback whales along this coast.

BOATING THE KIMBERLEY COAST

Boating this vast and unspoiled coastline is a true adventure. Here you can go fishing in rivers no one has even named yet, hike through spectacular gorges, laze on isolated beaches, see Aboriginal rock art, eat oysters fresh off the rocks, spot giant marine turtles, shower under waterfalls, swim in the odd croc-free rain-forest pool, and generally feel the wilderness is yours for a while. But extremely strong tidal currents of up to 11 meters, high cliffs, sharks, and saltwater crocodiles all pose dangers, so you should be reasonably fit and independent to travel by boat. This is a big region, so you will need to take an extended charter trip lasting anywhere around 5 to 14 days.

Half a dozen or so boat operators run fishing and adventure trips from Broome or Derby 221 kilometers (138 miles) north, or even from Wyndham 105 kilometers (65 miles) northwest of Kununurra, or from Darwin. Some incorporate short inland expeditions on foot, or by light aircraft or 4WD. North Star Charters, below, even travels with its own helicopter for flight-seeing. Some boats take scuba divers to Rowley Shoals, a marvelous outcrop of coral reef and giant clams 260 kilometers (163 miles) west off Broome. Find a vessel that suits you—some offer comfortable private cabins, while others are basic but fun camp-on-the-beach jobs. **North Star Charters** (☎ **08/9192 1829;** www.NorthStarCharters.com.au) and **Pearl Sea Coastal Cruises** (☎ **08/9192 3829;** www.users.bigpond.com/pearlsea) are the first kind; **Buccaneer Sea Safaris** (☎ **08/9191 1991;** e-mail via the Derby Tourist Bureau at derbytb@comswest.net.au) is the second. Contact the Broome Tourist Bureau for an up-to-date list of the boats plying the coast, because some boats come and go from year to year.

The *Coral Princess* makes 10-day Broome–Darwin or reverse voyages from April through October. It's a 35-meter (115-ft.) motorized catamaran carrying no more than 50 passengers in comfortable standard and deluxe staterooms or in budget cabins (all with bathrooms en suite). Facilities include a Jacuzzi, sundeck, cocktail bar, and dining room. The voyages depart about nine times a year and give you the opportunity to go ashore twice daily to swim (in croc-free pools only), fish, hike in spectacular scenery, croc-spot on river cruises, have a BBQ on an island beach, take optional scenic helicopter flights over the Mitchell Falls, and see Aboriginal art. Fares in 2000 ranged from A$4,675 (U.S.$3,038.75) to A$5,495 (U.S.$3,571.75) per person in a double cabin. Contact **Coral Princess Cruises,** Breakwater Terminal, Sir Leslie Thiess Drive, Townsville, QLD 4810 (☎ **1800/079 545** in Australia, or 07/4721 1673; www.coralprincess.com.au); in the United States and Canada, contact **S.H. Enterprises,** PMB #B, Mt. Hermon Road, Scotts Valley, CA 95066 (☎ **800/441 6880** or 831/335 4954; e-mail: Coralpss@aol.com).

9

Perth & Western Australia

by Natalie Kruger

Many international visitors—heck, many east coast Australians!—never make the trek to Western Australia. It's too far away, too expensive to fly to, too big when you get there, they say. That's all true, especially the bit about it being big (it's 2.5 million square kilometers, or 965,000 square miles), but don't dismiss a trip here out of hand. Flights need not be expensive (not if you're an international traveler flying on air-pass coupons—see chapter 2), and some of Australia's best snorkeling and diving, cutest historic towns, most splendid natural scenery, and most fantastic wine regions are here. Every spring (that's Sept to Nov Down Under), most of the state is carpeted in masses of wildflowers. The capital, Perth, has great food, a fabulous outdoor life of biking and beaches, plenty of smallish museums that are well worth a look, and a beautiful historic port called Fremantle.

The Southwest "hook" of the state, below Perth, is far and away the prettiest part of Western Australia to visit, and also the easiest region to visit outside of Perth. Massive stands of karri and jarrah trees stretch to the sky, the surf is world-class, and the coastline is wave smashed and rugged. The Southwest's Margaret River region is responsible for turning out some of Australia's most acclaimed wines.

Head east 400 miles inland from Perth and you strike what, in the 1890s, was the richest square mile of gold-bearing earth ever found in the world. Here the mining town of Kalgoorlie, still Australia's biggest gold producer, fuses ornate 19th-century architecture with a zeal for pumping out nearly 2,000 ounces of gold a day at the dawning of the 21st century. If Australia has an iconic country town, an answer to the Wild West, then Kalgoorlie is it.

Once you drive north of Perth past Geraldton on the Midwest coast, you know you're in the Outback. Orange sand, scrubby trees, and spiky grass called spinifex are all you see for hundreds of miles. About 850 kilometers (531 miles) north of Perth is a special phenomenon: daily visits by wild dolphins to the shores of Monkey Mia. Another 872 kilometers (545 miles) on is one of Australia's best-kept secrets, a 260-kilometer (163-mile) coral reef called Ningaloo, stretching along the isolated Outback shore. It's a second Great Barrier Reef, barely discovered by world travelers or even Aussies themselves. The reef is making a name for itself as a whale-shark habitat, where you can swim with these mysterious 12-meter (40-ft.) fish-monsters every Aussie fall.

Western Australia

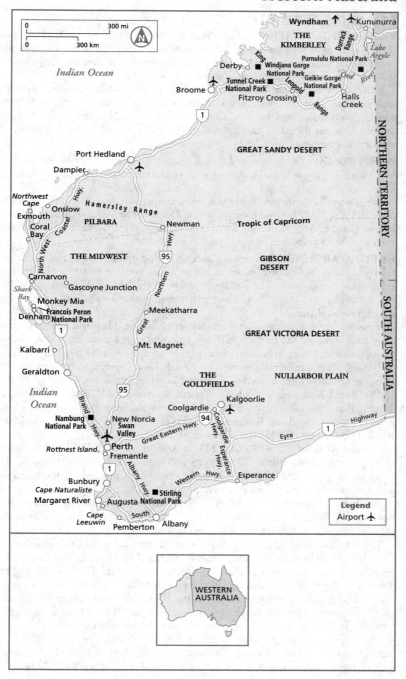

EXPLORING THE STATE

VISITOR INFORMATION   The **Western Australian Tourism Commission (WATC)** is the official source of information on touring the state. Its Web site (**www.westernaustralia.net**) provides a good overview, but it does not yet provide a thorough rundown on what to see and do.

It may be better to contact the WATC's office in Perth, which can send you maps and brochures, dispense advice, and make bookings. See section 1 of this chapter for contact information, and for details on the Perth "W.A. Naturally" office, a good source of tips on the state's national and marine parks (check out their Web site at **www.calm.wa.gov.au**).

WHEN TO GO   Perth is blessed with long, dry summers and mild wet winters. You'll want warm gear in the Southwest winters, but temperatures rarely hit the freezing point.

Much north of Perth, summer is hell, when temperatures soar well into the 40s°C (over 104°F to 120°F). Avoid these parts from December to March; February is worst. Winter (June to Aug) in the mid-, northern, and inland reaches of the state is pleasantly cool, sometimes even hot.

GETTING AROUND   Before you plan a whirlwind driving tour of this state, consider the distances (it's three times as big as Texas) and the mostly arid, flat, and monotonous countryside. The Southwest makes pretty driving; elsewhere, fly, unless you want to count sheep in all those vast brown paddocks you will be whizzing through if you drive.

If you do hit the road, remember that Western Australia is largely devoid of people, gas stations (so keep the gas tank full), and emergency help. Road trains and wildlife pose a road threat more so here than in any other state, so avoid driving at night, dusk, and dawn—all prime animal feeding times. Read "Road Conditions & Safety," in the "Getting Around Australia" section in chapter 2, before setting off.

The Royal Automobile Club of Western Australia (RACWA), 228 Adelaide Terrace, Perth, WA 6000 (☎ **08/9421 4444;** www.aaa.asn.au), is a good source of maps and motoring advice. For a recorded road-condition report, call the state **Main Roads Department** (☎ **1800/013 314** in Australia).

Skywest Airlines (☎ **1800/642 225** in Australia, or 08/9478 9999; or book through Ansett) and **Airlink** (☎ **08/9225 8383;** or book through Qantas) are the state's major regional airlines. Skywest has a range of airfare- and accommodation-inclusive vacation packages departing Perth.

Greyhound Pioneer (☎ **13 20 30** in Australia) is the only interstate coach company serving Western Australia. It travels the highway from Adelaide over to Perth, then up the coast to Broome and across to Darwin.

The only train to Western Australia from outside the state is the ✪ *Indian Pacific* from Adelaide to Perth (see "Getting Around Australia," in chapter 2). Inside the state, long-distance trains run only in the southern third of the state. They are operated by **Westrail** (☎ **13 10 53** in Western Australia, or 08/9326 2222) from Perth to Bunbury south of Perth, Northam eastward in the Avon Valley, and Kalgoorlie. Westrail also runs connecting coach services to the Southwest and the southern coast, and as far north as Kalbarri (but not Monkey Mia) on the Midwest coast.

Motor homes are not necessary because motels are plentiful, but they make good sense if you plan a long-distance state tour. Australia's biggest motor-home outfit, **Britz Campervan Rentals & Tours,** has an office in Perth (☎ **08/9478 3488**).

TOUR OPERATORS   **Australian Pinnacle Tours** (☎ **1800/999 304** in Australia, or 08/9221 5411; www.pinnacletours.com.au) specializes in coach tours around Perth

Tiptoeing Through the Wildflowers

Every year from August to mid-November, Mother Nature blesses just about the entire state of Western Australia with a carpet of 12,000 species of white, yellow, mauve, pink, red, and blue ✪ **wildflowers.**

This annual burgeoning is accompanied by wildflower shows and festivals in country towns throughout the state, and coach and rail tour companies go into overdrive ferrying petal enthusiasts from all around Australia and the globe on wildflower tours. Conveniently, the blossoms cluster in the cooler southern half of the state, where you can easily explore them on day trips from Perth, or on longer jaunts of up to 5 days or so. September and October are usually the best months.

The most popular route is what the tourism authority calls the **Everlasting Trail,** running through sparsely populated farming country north of Perth. It follows the Great Northern Highway to Wubin, 272 kilometers (170 miles) north of Perth, and on to the small country town of Mullewa, another 222 kilometers (139 miles) north, which puts on one of the state's best wildflower shows for a week every late August. From here, head west 98 kilometers (61 miles) to Geraldton and 424 kilometers (265 miles) back to Perth down the Brand Highway for more floral sensations. However, this route has little of interest *except* flowers; instead, I would combine my wildflower watching with wine tasting on a jaunt to the much prettier, less isolated Southwest (see section 3 of this chapter).

If time is short, don't despair. You can see ample blossoms right in **Perth** at the Kings Park & Botanic Garden, which proudly conducts free guided walks through its 200 species during its 10-day Wildflower Festival every September or October.

Because Australian flora is adapted to desert conditions, it tends to sprout on dry, sunny days following a rain shower. For this reason, the Western Australia Tourist Centre (see "Visitor Information," in "Exploring the State," above) runs a **Wildflower Desk** during the season to keep you up to speed on whatever hot spot is blooming brightest that week, and they can book you on one of the many coach, rail, or 4WD wildflower tours.

Interstate buses and trains and regional hotels fill up fast in wildflower season, so book ahead.

and throughout the state. **Overland 4WD Safaris** (☎ 08/9524 7122; www.overland.com.au) runs 4WD safaris from Perth with an off-the-beaten-track bent.

Aerial tours make sense in W.A. Contact **Complete Aviation Services** (☎ 1800/632 221 in Australia, or 08/9478 2749; www.casair.com.au) or **Kookaburra Air** (☎ 08/9354 1158; www.kookaburra.iinet.net.au). Both do tours departing Perth throughout Western Australia, including the Kimberley (see chapter 9) and the Red Centre (see chapter 7). Both offer custom-tailored itineraries as well as preset tours.

✪ **Landscope Expeditions** is an excellent nature lovers' tour program run by the state **Conservation and Land Management Department,** or CALM (☎ 08/9380 2433 is the University of Western Australia, which handles bookings; fax 08/9380 1066 for a free schedule; or check it out at www.calm.wa.gov.au). It has you assisting CALM scientists on research projects, such as reintroducing endangered native species to the Shark Bay World Heritage region, observing solar eclipses from a boat in the remote Houtman Abrolhos Islands, or learning about 17th-century Dutch shipwrecks on the treacherous Zuytdorp Cliffs.

1 Perth

4,405km (2,753 miles) W of Sydney; 2,557km (1,598 miles) S of Broome

If you like Sydney, you'll probably like Perth. It has the same silver skyscrapers glinting in the sun, a remarkably blue sky, the same energetic outdoorsy vibrancy, and, like Sydney, the sparkling Indian Ocean and glorious white beaches just a bus ride from downtown. It likes to boast it gets more sunshine than any other city in Australia, some 300 days a year.

Far from being one of those drab, anonymous capitals that exists only to serve the state's economy, Perth has lots of fun stuff to do. Wander through the impressively restored historic warehouses, museums, and working docks of bustling Fremantle; stock up at the plentiful Aboriginal art and souvenir stores; eat at some of the country's best restaurants (no, they're not all in Sydney and Melbourne); go snorkeling and sea kayaking with wild sea lions; bushwalk through a 1,000-acre park in the middle of the city; and pedal your bike to a great snorkeling spot on ✪ **Rottnest Island,** a miniature reef resort 19 kilometers (12 miles) off-shore.

Perhaps more than other Aussie capitals, Perth gives you several good choices of side trips too: Wander the pretty streets of historic York, drop in on the Benedictine monks in the Spanish Renaissance town of New Norcia, nip out to the Swan Valley vineyards 20 minutes from town, or spend a few days in Margaret River country, one of Australia's most revered wine regions.

ORIENTATION

ARRIVING   By Plane   Ansett (☎ 13 13 00 in Australia) and **Qantas** (☎ 13 13 13 in Australia) fly at least once a day, if not more often, from all mainland state capitals, either direct or with mostly only one stop. **Airlink** (☎ 08/9225 8383, or book through Qantas) flies direct from Alice Springs daily, and once a day from Cairns via Ayers Rock. Airlink and **Skywest Airlines** (☎ 1800/642 225 in Australia, 08/9478 9999, or book through Ansett) operate flights from many small towns within Western Australia. Between them, Ansett and Airlink provide three of four direct services a day from Broome.

Perth International Airport is 20 kilometers (12.5 miles) northeast of the city, and the domestic terminal is 8 kilometers (5 miles) closer. Both have currency exchange bureaus, ATMs, showers, baby change rooms, lockers, internet access stations, direct-dial accommodation boards, post boxes (the news agencies inside sells stamps), and a limited range of tourist information. Mobile (cell) telephones can be rented at the international terminal.

Avis (☎ 08/9277 1177 domestic terminal, 08/9477 1302 international terminal), **Budget** (☎ 08/9277 9277), **Hertz** (☎ 08/9479 4788), and **Thrifty** (☎ 08/9464 7333) all have desks at both terminals.

Feature Tours runs the **airport-city shuttle** (☎ 08/9479 4131), which meets all international and interstate flights. It does not specifically meet intrastate flights. There is no need to book ahead. Transfers to the city from the international terminal cost A$10 (U.S.$6.50) for adults, A$8 (U.S.$5.20) children 2 to 15. Domestic terminal-city transfers are A$8 (U.S.$5.20) for adults and A$6 (U.S.$3.90) for kids. Transfers between the domestic and international terminals are A$8 (U.S.$5.20) for adults, and A$6 (U.S.$3.90) for kids. Qantas runs a free bus between terminals for its passengers. The private **Fremantle Airport Shuttle** (☎ 08/9383 4115) operates eight services a day between the airport and Fremantle hotels on demand, so you must

Perth

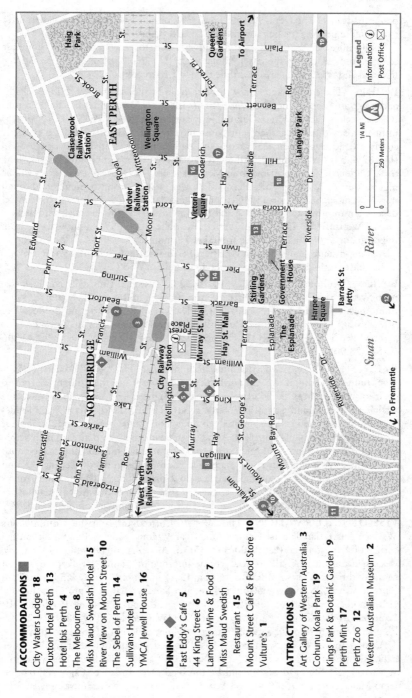

ACCOMMODATIONS
City Waters Lodge **18**
Duxton Hotel Perth **13**
Hotel Ibis Perth **4**
The Melbourne **8**
Miss Maud Swedish Hotel **15**
River View on Mount Street **10**
The Sebel of Perth **14**
Sullivans Hotel **11**
YMCA Jewell House **16**

DINING
Fast Eddy's Café **5**
44 King Street **6**
Lamont's Wine & Food **7**
Miss Maud Swedish
  Restaurant **15**
Mount Street Café & Food Store **10**
Vulture's **1**

ATTRACTIONS
Art Gallery of Western Australia **3**
Cohunu Koala Park **19**
Kings Park & Botanic Garden **9**
Perth Mint **17**
Perth Zoo **12**
Western Australian Museum **2**

Legend
ⓘ Information
☒ Post Office

book in advance. The fare is A$15 (U.S.$9.75), or A$12 (U.S.$7.80) per person for two or more people traveling together, and A$28 (U.S.$18.20) for a family.

Public buses 200, 201, 202, 208, and 209 run to the city from the domestic terminal only. A taxi to the city is about A$25 (U.S.$16.25) from the international terminal and A$20 (U.S.$13) from the domestic terminal.

By Train   The epic 3-day journey to Perth from Sydney via Broken Hill, Adelaide, and Kalgoorlie aboard the ✪ *Indian Pacific* is an experience in itself. The train runs twice a week in each direction. The one-way fare ranges from A$1,431 (U.S.$930.15) in first class with meals and en suite bathroom, to A$974 (U.S.$633.10) in perfectly comfy second class (meals cost extra, and bathrooms are shared), down to A$459 (U.S.$298.35) for the sit-up-all-the-way coach class (not a good idea on this long trip). Connections are available from Melbourne on *The Overland* train. Fares will be higher during Western Australia's wildflower season from September through mid-November. See section 11, "Getting Around Australia," in chapter 2, for contact details. For information, schedules, and reservations on the *Prospector* from Kalgoorlie, call **Westrail** (☎ **13 10 53** in Western Australia, 1800/099 150 in Australia from interstate, or 08/9326 2222). The trip takes 7¾ hours.

All long-distance trains pull into the **East Perth Terminal,** Summers Street off Lord Street, East Perth. A taxi to the city center costs about A$8 (U.S.$5.20).

By Bus   Greyhound Pioneer (☎ **13 20 30** in Australia) runs daily coach service from Sydney, via Canberra and Adelaide (trip time: 54 hr. from Sydney, almost 35 hr. from Adelaide). It also has service daily from Darwin via Kununurra and Broome (trip time: 56 hr.). Travelling from Alice Springs requires a connection in Adelaide. The Sydney–Perth fare is A$341 (U.S.$221.65) and Darwin–Perth is A$506 (U.S.$328.90).

By Car   There are only two road routes from interstate. The 2,423-kilometer (1,514-mile) route from Broome in the north follows the Great Northern Highway (not so great for road quality), the North West Coastal Highway (a decent enough two-lane affair), and the Brand Highway (pretty good). The 2,708-kilometer (1,693-mile) route from Adelaide includes hundreds of miles along some of the world's straightest road on the treeless Nullarbor Plain. Arm yourself with an up-to-date road map before setting off on this route, and carry spare gas. It's not a bad idea to contact the South Australian or Western Australian state auto clubs (listed under "Getting Around Australia," in chapter 2) for more advice on crossing the Nullarbor. Both routes cross mostly featureless and lonely semidesert, sheep ranches or wheat fields most of the way, with very few towns en route. For that reason, I don't recommend either!

VISITOR INFORMATION   The Western Australian Tourism Commission's **Western Australian Tourist Centre,** Albert Facey House, 469 Wellington St. on the corner of Forrest Place (☎ **1300/361 351** in Australia, or 08/9483 1111; www.westernaustralia.net), is the official visitor information source for Perth. It's open Monday through Thursday 8:30am to 6pm (5pm in winter), Friday 8:30am to 7pm (6pm in winter), Saturday 8:30am to 5pm, and Sunday 10am to 5pm (3pm in winter). Another good source of free information and booking is the **Perth Tourist Lounge,** Level 2, Carillon City Arcade off 680 Hay Street Mall (☎ **08/9229 2238**). It's open Monday through Saturday 9am to 5:30pm and Sunday noon to 4pm.

A good source of ideas on nature-based activities and attractions in the state's national and marine parks is the **"W.A. Naturally"** center, 47 Henry St., Fremantle, WA 6160 (☎ **08/9430 8600**), run by the state Department of Conservation and Land Management (CALM)—check out their Web site at **www.calm.wa.gov.au**. The center is open every day except Tuesday from 10am to 5:30pm.

For an untouristy lowdown on the city's restaurants, cultural life, shops, bars, festivals, concerts, and the like, buy the local glossy quarterly magazine *Scoop* (A\$7.95/U.S.\$5.20; www.scoop.com.au) or pick up the free color newspaper, *Perth Weekly.* Both are readily available around town in newsagents, cafes, tour desks, and such places.

CITY LAYOUT   The city center is 19 kilometers (12 miles) upriver from the Indian Ocean, on the north bank of a broad reach of the Swan River. **Hay Street** and **Murray Street** are the two major thoroughfares, 1 block apart; both are bisected by pedestrian malls between William and Barrack streets. It helps to know that Adelaide Terrace and St. Georges Terrace are one and the same street. The name change occurs at Victoria Avenue.

MAPS   Of the many free pocket guides to Perth available at tour desks and in hotel lobbies, *Your Guide to Perth & Fremantle* has the **best street map,** because it shows one-way streets, public toilets and telephones, taxi stands, post offices, police stations, and street numbers, as well as most attractions and hotels. The Royal Automobile Club of Western Australia (see "Exploring the State," at the start of this chapter) is a good source of maps to the entire state.

The Neighborhoods in Brief

City Center   The central business district (called the CBD in Australia) is home to shops and department stores connected by a honeycomb of shopping arcades. A good introduction to Perth's charms is to take in the views from the pedestrian/bike path that skirts the river along Riverside Drive. Within walking distance on the western edge of town is Kings Park & Botanic Garden.

Northbridge   Just about all of Perth's nightclubs, and a good many of its cool restaurants, bars, and cafes, are in this 5-block precinct just north of the railway line, within easy walking distance of the city center. It's roughly bounded by James, Beaufort, Aberdeen, and Lake streets. What locals call the Cultural Centre—an umbrella term that means the Western Australian Museum, the Art Gallery of Western Australia, the State Library, and the Perth Institute of Contemporary Arts—is here too. The free Blue CAT buses deliver you right into the heart of this buzzing precinct.

Subiaco   This well-heeled suburb is on the other side of Kings Park from the city. Saturday morning just wouldn't be Saturday morning for Perth's see-and-be-seen crowd without a stroll through "Subi's" villagelike concoction of cafes, markets, upscale boutiques, antique shops, and art galleries. Intersecting Hay Street and Rokeby (pronounced "Rockerby") Road are the main promenades. Take the train to Subiaco station.

Fremantle   Not only is "Freo" Perth's working port, but it's also Perth's second city heart, and locals' favorite weekend spot to relax, eat, shop, and sail. A careful 1980s restoration of its long-neglected Victorian warehouses saw it emerge as a marvelous living example of a 19th-century seaport—kind of like Fisherman's Wharf in San Francisco without the stale commercial taint. Fremantle is 19 kilometers (12 miles) downriver on the mouth of the Swan.

Scarborough Beach   This is one of Perth's prize beaches, 12 kilometers (7^1/$_2$ miles) north of the city center. The district is a little tatty with that oversupply of cheap take-out food outlets that seem to plague Aussie beaches, but if you like sun, sand, and surf, this is the place to be. You will find supermarkets, bars, restaurants, shops, and surf-gear rental stores here. Allow 15 to 20 minutes to get there by car, 35 minutes on the bus.

A Free Ride

A welcome freebie in Perth is the **Free Transit Zone (FTZ).** You can travel free on trains and buses within this zone at any hour, day or night. It is bounded by Kings Park Road, Fraser Avenue, Thomas Street, and Loftus Street in the west; Newcastle Street in the north; and the river in the south and east. Basically, this means you can travel to Kings Park, Northbridge, east to major sporting grounds, and anywhere in the city center free. Signs mark the FTZ boundaries; just ask the driver if you're unsure.

GETTING AROUND

BY PUBLIC TRANSPORTATION **Transperth** runs Perth's buses, trains, and ferries. For route and timetable information, call ☎ **13 62 13** in Western Australia, or drop into the Transperth InfoCentres at the Plaza Arcade off Hay Street Mall, the Perth Railway Station, the Wellington Street bus station, or the City Bus Port on Mounts Bay Road. You can transfer from bus to ferry to train on one ticket within its expiry time. Travel costs A$1.70 (U.S.$1.10) in one zone (to Subiaco, for instance), and A$2.50 (U.S.$1.65) in two, which gets you most places, including Fremantle. Non-Australian seniors and students don't qualify for discounted fares; kids ages 5 to 14 do.

MultiRider passes give you 10 trips at a savings of 15%; they come in a range of prices good for various numbers of zones. A **DayRider** pass allows 1 day's unlimited travel after 9am on weekdays and all day on weekends and public holidays, and costs A$6.50 (U.S.$4.25). If you're a family, it may be worth getting a MaxiRider, valid for 1 day's unlimited travel for a group of seven people with a maximum of two adults. MaxiRiders are aimed at Perth families and so are valid only weekends, public holidays, after 9am during Western Australian school holidays, after 6pm year-round Monday to Thursday, and after 3pm Friday. They cost A$6.50 (U.S.$4.25). Passes, collectively known as FastCards, are sold at Newspower newsagents and at Transperth InfoCentres. To use the passes, validate them in the machines located on board in the case of buses, and on the platform or wharf in the case of trains and ferries.

Buses and trains run from about 5:30am until about 11:30pm.

By Bus The Wellington Street Bus Station, centrally located next to Perth Railway Station at Forrest Place, and the City Bus Port on the western edge of the city on Mounts Bay Road, are the two main depots. The vast majority of buses travel along St. Georges Terrace. Drivers do not always stop unless you hail. Buy tickets from the driver.

By far the best way to get around town is on the silver, free **CAT (Central Area Transit)** buses that run a continual loop of the city and Northbridge. The Red CAT runs east–west every 5 minutes, Monday through Friday 6:50am to 6:20pm, and once every hour from 10am to 6pm weekends. The Blue CAT runs north–south as far north as Northbridge and south to Barrack Street Jetty every 8 minutes from 6:50am. The last Blue Cat service is at 6:20pm Monday through Thursday, and on Friday it continues every 15 minutes from 6:20pm until 1:05am Saturday morning. It also runs Saturdays from 8:30am to 1am (Sun morning) every 12 minutes, and Sundays every 15 minutes from 10am to 5pm. Look for the silver CAT bus stops. Transperth Info-Centres (see above) dispense free route maps.

The **Perth Tram Co.** tours (see "Whale-Watching Cruises, Tram Trips & Other Tours," later in this chapter) are a good way to get around, too.

By Train   Trains in Perth are fast, clean, and safe. They start from about 5:30am and run every 15 minutes or even more often during the day, and every half hour at night until midnight. NightRider trains depart Perth at midnight, 1am, and 2am Friday and Saturday night, and 3am from December to March, stopping at all stations on all lines. All trains leave from Perth Railway Station opposite Forrest Place on Wellington Street. Buy your ticket before you board, at the vending machines on the platform.

By Ferry   You will probably use ferries only to visit Perth Zoo. They run every half hour or so, more often in peak hour, every day from 6:50am weekdays and 7:50am weekends, until 7:15pm (or until 9:15pm on Fri and Sat nights in summer between Sept and Apr) from the Barrack Street Jetty to Mends Street in South Perth. Buy tickets before you board from the vending machine on the wharf. The trip takes 7 minutes.

BY TAXI   Perth's two taxi companies are **Swan Taxis** (☎ **13 1330**) and **Black & White Taxis** (☎ **08/9333 3333**). Ranks are located at Perth Railway Station, and at both ends of Hay Street Mall.

BY CAR   Perth's signposting is notorious for telling you where you have been, not where you are going—for example, some interstate highways are announced with insignificant signs more suited to a side street.

CarePark, 152–158 St. Georges Terrace between William Street and King Street (☎ **08/9321 0667**) charges A$2.20 (U.S.$1.45) per hour and is open Monday to Friday 6:30am to 8pm (until midnight Fri), Saturday from 8am to 6:30pm, and Sunday from 8:30am to 6:30pm. The charge is a flat A$3 (U.S.$1.95) between 5pm and midnight Friday, and all day Saturday or Sunday. There is no charge for leaving your car in overnight.

The major car-rental companies are **Avis** (☎ **08/9325 7677**), **Budget** (☎ **08/9322 1100**), **Hertz** (☎ **08/9321 7777**), and **Thrifty** (☎ **08/9464 7444**). All have both city and Fremantle outlets. **ATC Rent-A-Car** (☎ **1800/999 888** in Australia but outside Western Australia, or 08/9325 1833) is a locally owned outfit with offices in Monkey Mia and Broome; it also rents camping kits. **Hawk Rent-A-Car** (☎ **08/9221 9688**) is another local operator worth a try.

Fast Facts: Perth

American Express   The bureau, located at 645 Hay Street Mall (☎ **08/9261 2711**), is open Monday through Friday 9am to 5pm and Saturday 9am to noon.

Business Hours   Banks are open Monday through Thursday 9:30am to 4pm and until 5pm Friday. Shopping hours are usually 9am to 5:30pm Monday through Friday (until 9pm on Thurs in the suburbs and Fremantle, and until 9pm Fri in the city), and 9am to 5pm on Saturday. On Sunday most major stores (but not all) open noon to 4pm or later in the city, and from 10am to 6pm in Fremantle.

Currency Exchange   Go to the American Express office (see above) or **Interforex,** Shop 24, London Court off Hay Street Mall (☎ **08/9325 7418**), open daily 9am to 5:30pm, and until 9pm Friday. Interforex has a Fremantle bureau at the corner of William Street and Adelaide Street (☎ **08/9431 7022**) open daily from 8am to 8pm.

Dentist   **Forrest Chase Dental Centre** (☎ **08/9221 4749**) is on the Upper Walkway Level, Forrest Chase shopping complex, 425 Wellington St. opposite

Perth Railway Station. Open daily 8am to 8pm, it can be reached after hours at ☎ **08/9383 1620.**

Doctor   Central City Medical Centre is on the Perth Railway Station concourse, 420 Wellington St. (☎ **08/9221 4747;** this number diverts to an on-call doctor after hours). It is open daily from 7am to 7pm.

Embassies/Consulates   The **United States Consulate-General** is at 16 St. Georges Terrace (☎ **08/9231 9400**). The **Canadian Consulate** is at 267 St. Georges Terrace (☎ **08/9322 7930**). The **British Consulate-General** is at 77 St. Georges Terrace (☎ **08/9221 5400**). The **Irish Consulate** is at 10 Lilika Rd., City Beach (☎ **08/9385 8247**).

Emergencies   Dial ☎ **000** for fire, ambulance, or police in an emergency. This is a free call, and no coins are needed from a public phone.

Hospitals   Royal Perth Hospital in the city center has a public casualty ward (☎ **08/9224 2244**). Enter from Victoria Square, which is accessed from Murray Street.

Luggage Storage/Lockers   The Perth Tourist Lounge, Level 2, Carillon City Arcade, 680 Hay Street Mall (☎ **08/9229 2238**), rents lockers and stores baggage for A$1 (U.S.65¢) for small bags, A$3 (U.S.$1.95) for large ones, during its hours: Monday through Saturday from 9am to 5:30pm, and Sunday noon to 4pm. There are baggage lockers at the international and domestic terminals at the airport.

Pharmacies   Forrest Chase Pharmacy (☎ **08/9221 1691**), on the upper level of the Forrest Chase shopping center on Wellington Street (near the dentist's office listed in "Dentist," above) is open Monday to Saturday 8:30am to 7pm (and until 9pm Fri), and Sunday 10am to 6pm. **Shenton Pharmacy,** 214 Nicholson Rd., Subiaco (☎ **08/9381 1358** business and after hours), will deliver across Perth.

Police   Dial ☎ **000** in an emergency. City Police Station, 1 Hay St., East Perth (☎ **08/9222 1048**), the City Watch police bureau at Perth Railway Station, and Fremantle Police Station, 45 Henderson St. (☎ **08/9430 5244**), are open 24 hours. For general police inquiries call ☎ **13 14 44.**

Safety   Perth is safe, but steer clear of the back streets of Northbridge at night, even if you are not alone, because groups of teenage boys have been known to pick fights.

Time Zone   Western Australian time (WST) is GMT plus 8 hours and has no daylight saving. This means it is normally 2 hours behind Sydney and Melbourne, 3 from October to March when New South Wales and Victoria go to daylight saving. Call ☎ **1194** for the exact local time.

Weather   Call ☎ **1196** for a recorded local weather forecast.

ACCOMMODATIONS

Perth has a surfeit of upscale hotels in the city center, so competition can be high, especially from Friday to Sunday when the staple clientele of business travelers dries up. Ask about lower rates on weekends. If you're not afraid to negotiate, you can strike a good deal on weeknights too, if business is slow across town.

IN THE CITY CENTER
Very Expensive
Duxton Hotel Perth. 1 St. Georges Terrace (at Victoria Ave. next to Perth Concert Hall), Perth, WA 6000. ☎ **1800/681 118** in Australia, or 08/9261 8000. Fax 08/9261 8020.

www.duxton.com.au. E-mail: duxton@global.net.au. 306 units (several with shower only). A/C MINIBAR TV TEL. A$325–$395 (U.S.$211.25–$256.75) double; A$420(U.S.$273) suite. Extra person A$27 (U.S.$17.55). Children under 16 stay free in parents' room with existing bedding. Ask about packages and special upgrade rates. AE, BC, DC, MC, V. Valet parking A$10 (U.S.$6.50); no self-parking. Bus: Red CAT Stop 11 "Victoria Avenue." Airport shuttle.

From the moment you pull up under the sandstone portico and step into the bronze-paneled lobby with its Siena marble floor, you'll be swooning over the Duxton's drop-dead 21st century–meets–art deco glamour. Only a few years old as a hotel, the place was created out of old state tax office chambers. The rooms sport blond Tasmanian oak room furniture with 1930s curves, elegant marquetry patterning, ample bathrooms, pay-per-view movies, and hair dryers. Superior rooms on the corners have extra-large bathrooms; some have Jacuzzis. Ask for the south side if you want uninterrupted views of the river a block away; north-side rooms have city views. Suite and Club Room guests get a light complimentary breakfast and evening drinks in the Club Lounge.

Dining/Diversions: The modern Australian cuisine in the casual streetfront Brasserie is a cut above most hotel fare. The plush lobby bar resembling a formal salon of times gone by opens onto a patio on St. Georges Terrace.

Amenities: Make time to see and be seen lazing around that petite swimming pool colonnaded like a Roman bath. Jacuzzi, health club, sauna, 24-hour room service, free newspaper, in-room massage, baby-sitting, business center, conference rooms, secretarial services, currency exchange, car-rental/tour desk, concierge, laundry/dry-cleaning service, express checkout.

Expensive

✪ The Sebel of Perth. 37 Pier St., Perth, WA 6000. ☎ **1800/999 004** in Australia, or 08/9325 7655. Fax 08/9325 7383. www.mirvachotels.com.au (tip: hit "Perth" tab, then click on the map to access hotel information). E-mail: reservationsebelperth@mirvachotels.com.au. 119 units. A/C MINIBAR TV TEL. A$240–$260 double (U.S.$156–$169), A$302 (U.S.$196.30) suite. Extra person A$25 (U.S.$16.25). Children under 12 stay free in parents' room. Ask about weekend, overnight, honeymoon, and suite packages. AE, BC, DC, JCB, MC, V. Free valet and self-parking. Bus: Red CAT Stop 12 "Town Hall East"; Blue CAT Stop 4 "Town Hall" or 5 "Murray St. Mall East."

Come for the biggest standard hotel rooms in Perth; stay for the atmosphere. This upscale establishment has a friendly ambience that's a welcome contrast to the frosty hauteur of many five-star properties. Nice touches are everywhere—like a free gift with every stay (I received two trendy bottles of aromatherapy oils), free tea and coffee in the lobby every morning, and a weekly General Manager's cocktail party. By the time you get here, the rather-tired rooms should be refurbished in opulent navy and gold. All of them have big desks, acres of benchtop space, walk-in closets, bathrobes, armchairs or sofas, windows that open for fresh air, toasters for do-it-yourself breakfasts, hair dryers, irons and boards, and pay-per-view movies. Every Monday to Friday at 6:15am, you, three other guests, and a senior member of management jump into the hotel's "Cottesloe Express" Rolls Royce and motor in style to fabulous Cottesloe Beach 20 minutes away for a swim, a walk, or a jog. They get you back to the hotel by 7:40am or so. Overnight packages are often less than half the "rack" rates we quote above.

Dining/Diversions: The formal Pyrenees restaurant serves modern Mediterranean cuisine. The poolside Office Bar & Café attracts the local corporate crowd with cheap tasty lunches, and serves coffee and cocktails all day.

Amenities: Heated outdoor swimming pool and small sundeck, discount access to a nearby health club, free bike rental, concierge, 24-hour room service, twice-daily maid service, nightly turndown, laundry/dry-cleaning service, free daily newspaper, business center, conference rooms, secretarial services, baby-sitting, currency exchange, tour and car-rental desk, express checkout.

Moderate

Hotel Ibis Perth. 334 Murray St. (between William and King sts.), Perth, WA 6000. ☎ **1300/65 6565** in Australia, 1800/221-4542 in the U.S. and Canada, 020/8283 4500 in the U.K., 0800/44 4422 in New Zealand, or 08/9322 2844. Fax 08/9321 6314. www. hotelweb.fr. E-mail: gmibisper@bigpond.com. 174 units (all with shower only). A/C MINIBAR TV TEL. A$140.80 (U.S.$91.50) double, A$206.80 (U.S.$134.40) suite. Extra person A$30 (U.S.$19.50). Children 12 and under stay free in parents' room with existing bedding. Ask about weekend packages. AE, BC, DC, JCB, MC, V. Discounted self-parking A$8 (U.S.$5.20) at the nearby Queen Street Carpark. Bus: Red CAT Stop 15 "Murray St. Mall West"; Blue CAT Stop 17 "Hay Street Mall West." Airport shuttle.

Ibis is one of those reputable chain brands of the "four-star facilities at a three-star price" variety. The modern, neat, and comfortable rooms are a bit small, but families will like the separate bedroom for Mum and Dad, and business travelers will like the express checkout and business center. Rooms have pay-per-view movies, hair dryers, and irons and boards. You get plenty for the price, including a free drink on arrival, room service, dry-cleaning service, a car-rental and tour desk, and discounted rates at a nearby gym. Downstairs is a convivial street-front bistro and bar popular with locals. Shops, cinemas, and malls are just a block or two away.

The Melbourne. Corner of Hay and Milligan sts., Perth, WA 6000. ☎ **1800/68 5671** in Australia, or 08/9320 3333. Fax 08/9320 3344. www.melbournehotel.com.au. E-mail: bookings@melbournehotel.com.au. 36 units (all with shower only). A/C MINIBAR TV TEL. A$165 (U.S.$107.25) double; A$190 (U.S.$123.50) suite. Extra person A$25 (U.S.$16.25). Children under 6 stay free in parents' room. AE, BC, DC, MC, V. Valet parking A$10 (U.S.$6.50); no self-parking. Bus: Red CAT Stop 18 "QVI." Airport shuttle.

This long-derelict 1897 hotel in Perth's posh West End, thoroughly restored to its ornate gold-rush–era originality in 1997, is a great value, because its facilities and rooms match most five-star hotels. The public areas have a New Orleans theme, aided by original trappings like pressed metal ceilings, floral carpets, and a polished timber staircase. Rooms drop the Southern splendor in favor of convenience for business travelers (like separate in-room laptop and fax points) but nod to Tara with wooden blinds, summery wall friezes, and brass-trimmed fans. First-floor outside rooms open onto the big veranda; second-floor rooms don't, but have higher ceilings; and inside rooms lack views. The minibars have the kind of stuff you really need—film, vitamin B supplements that fight hangovers, and pantyhose in wearable colors—and rooms also have hair dryers and irons and boards. Additional hotel amenities include 24-hour concierge, limited room service, free daily newspaper, secretarial services, dry-cleaning/laundry service, car-rental desk, babysitting, currency exchange, and conference facilities.

The Orleans Café serves light fare all day, while the exquisitely decorated Louisiana's Restaurant serves Mod Oz fare with a Cajun twist. The atmospheric street-front Mississippi's Bar, resplendent in paneled walls, etched-glass windows, and black-and-white photos of paddle steamers, is a happening place to be on Friday nights.

✪ Miss Maud Swedish Hotel. 97 Murray St. (at Pier St.), Perth, WA 6000. ☎ **1800/998 022** in Australia, or 08/9325 3900. Fax 08/9221 3225. www.missmaud.com.au. E-mail: missmaud@missmaud.com.au. 51 units (41 with shower only). A/C MINIBAR TV TEL. A$112.87–$150.50 (U.S.$73.40–$97.80) double. Extra person A$10.75 (U.S.$7). Rates include full smorgasbord breakfast. AE, BC, DC, JCB, MC, V. Discounted parking A$7.50 (U.S.$4.90) at the Kings Hotel carpark 1 block away on Hay St. between Pier and Irwin sts. Bus: Red CAT Stop 1 "Pier St."; Blue and Weekend CAT Stop 5 "Murray St. Mall East." Airport shuttle.

Staying at this adorable hotel in the heart of town is like staying at Grandma's. Never mind that the bedspread clashes with the carpet, and the paint's peeling off the door (the rooms are gradually getting refurbished, anyhow). You're here for the homey ambience, the cozy rooms sporting wall-sized murals of Scandinavian pine forests, and a staff that's more polite and on the ball than those in most five-star hotels. You also get limited room service, a 24-hour front desk, hair dryers, laundry/dry-cleaning service, a private sundeck tucked away as a little surprise up among the rooftops, and a tour desk. The real Miss Maud, Maud Edmiston, wants guests to feel they are in a European family hotel like in her Swedish homeland, and she succeeds. A fabulous full buffet breakfast is included at Miss Maud Swedish Restaurant downstairs (see "Dining," below).

Sullivans Hotel. 166 Mounts Bay Rd., Perth, WA 6000. ☎ **1800/99 9294** in Australia, or 08/9321 8022. Fax 08/9481 6762. www.sullivans.com.au. E-mail: Perth@sullivans.com.au. 68 units (66 with shower only). A/C TV TEL. A$110–$130 (U.S.$71.50–$84.50) up to 4 people in room, A$150–$175 (U.S.$97.50–$113.75) 1-bedroom apt; A$200 (U.S.$130) 2-bedroom apt. Ask about packages. Weekly rates available. AE, BC, DC, MC, V. Free parking. Bus: 72, 201 (the hotel is within the Free Transit Zone). Airport shuttle.

This family-owned hotel about 1.5 kilometers (1 mile) from town is popular with Europeans for its small-scale ambience. Despite being on the main road into the city, none of the rooms seems to be noisy. They're simply furnished with laminate fittings, not glamorous but clean and large, with hair dryers. Larger deluxe rooms come with desks, safes, and balconies with views over parkland and freeway to the river. There are also two apartments with kitchenettes. Out back is a really pleasant and private swimming pool with a sundeck and BBQ. Bikes are free for guests, and there are a tour/car-rental desk, free movies, room service (no delivery charge), a 24-hour front desk, and an affordable restaurant. The Swan River is a stroll away, and Kings Park is a short, steep walk up the hill.

Inexpensive

City Waters Lodge. 118 Terrace Rd. (between Victoria Ave. and Hill St.), Perth, WA 6000. ☎ **1800/999 030** in Australia, or 08/9325 1566. Fax 08/9221 2794. www.citywaters. com.au. E-mail: perth@citywaters.com.au. 72 units. A/C TV TEL. A$78 (U.S.$50.70) double, A$83 (U.S.$53.95) triple or family apt. to sleep 4, A$118 (U.S.$76.70) 2-bedroom apt. to sleep 5. Weekly rates available. BC, MC, V. Free parking. Bus: Blue CAT Stop 19 "Barrack Square." Airport shuttle.

Try to get one of the apartments on the end of this old but neatly maintained three-story block down by the river, because they have lovely parkland views. The fixtures in these one- and two-bedroom apartments are aging, especially in the kitchen and bathroom, but you get plenty of space, daily servicing, and good-quality mattresses. Two-bedroom units have two TVs and two phones. All rooms received new beds, paint, and carpets in 1999, and by the time you get here, the kitchens and bathrooms will be retiled. The helpful proprietors carry your luggage up the stairs, order in continental breakfast from a nearby deli, and run a tour/car-rental desk. City buses run along St. Georges Terrace a block away, and you're a 5-block walk from Hay Street Mall.

River View on Mount Street. 42 Mount St., Perth, WA 6000. ☎ **08/9321 8963.** Fax 08/9322 5956. www.riverview.au.com (not "riverview.com.au."). E-mail: manager@ riverview.au.com. 50 units (all with shower only). A/C TV TEL. A$75–$85 (U.S.$48.75–$55.25) apt. (sleeps 3). AE, BC, DC, MC, V. Free parking for limited number of cars. Bus: Red CAT Stop 18 "QVI" (located over the freeway footbridge accessed from the corner of St. Georges Terrace and Milligan St.). Airport shuttle.

Situated on a quiet leafy street a short walk from the center of town and Kings Park, these roomy studio apartments in an older-style 1960s block were all totally refurbished in 1999 with trendy new kitchens, smart bathrooms, and fresh carpets, curtains, and fittings. The result is great style at a great price. Some have views of the river a few blocks away, and all have a data jack for laptops. Maid service is weekly. The helpful on-site managers run a tour/car-rental desk, loan hair dryers, and get your dry cleaning done. You will probably breakfast at the excellent Mount Street Café and Food Store downstairs (see " Dining," below), which also sells prepared curries and deli items. Be prepared to hike three stories, because there is no elevator. No smoking.

YMCA Jewell House. 180 Goderich St., Perth, WA 6000. ☎ **1800/998 212** in Australia, or 08/9325 8488. Fax 08/9221 4694. E-mail: jewellhouse@bigpond.com. 250 units, none with private bathroom. A$44–$48.40 (U.S.$28.60–$31.45) double, A$71.80 (U.S.$46.70) family room to sleep 5. AE, BC, DC, JCB, MC, V. Free off-street parking for 16 cars. Bus: Red CAT Stop 4 "Bennett Street." Airport shuttle.

You may not like the dingy carpets and well-used furniture in this 11-story one-time nurses' quarters, but you will love the prices and the river panorama from the south rooms. Bathrooms are communal but clean and should be refurbished by the time you get here. Rooms simply contain beds, a fan, self-serve tea and coffee, and linen and towels, but heck, splash out the extra $4.80 on "deluxe" quarters with a TV and minifridge. BYO hair dryer. Housemaid service is daily. There are 24-hour reception, currency exchange, TV lounges, a wonderfully affordable dining room, and a helpful staff. The Perth Mint is a block away, and Hay Street Mall is a 5-block stroll.

On the Beach

Hotel Rendezvous Observation City Perth. The Esplanade, Scarborough Beach, WA 6019. ☎ **1800/067 680** in Australia, or 08/9245 1000. Fax 08/9245 1345. www. rendezvous.com.au. E-mail: reservations@rendezvous.com.au. 334 units. A/C MINIBAR TV TEL. A$225–$314 (U.S.$146.25–$204.10) double; A$550–$1,320 (U.S.$357.50–$858) suite. Extra person A$33 (U.S.$21.45). Children under 18 free with existing bedding. Ask about overnight packages. AE, BC, DC, JCB, MC, V. Valet parking A$16.50 (U.S.$10.75); self-parking A$6.60 (U.S.$4.30). A courtesy shuttle operates between the hotel, Perth city, Burswood Casino, Fremantle, and a local shopping mall. Bus: 400.

One of the few beachside places to stay in Perth is this 17-story complex right on the never-ending sands of Scarborough Beach. Despite its colossal size, it has a no-fuss ambience that makes it popular with vacationing Aussies. All the rooms, which were renovated in 1998, have balconies with ocean views, and even some standard rooms have Jacuzzis. They all have hair dryers, toasters, irons and boards, bathrobes on request, pay-per-view movies, and modem jacks. The top three floors are given over to the Plaza Club, which does free continental breakfast and drinks at sunset on its lounge balcony.

Dining/Diversions: Savannah's is the east-meets-west "fine-dining" choice, The Pines Grand Buffet and Carvery does just what it says, the Dragon Palace is Chinese, and there are pizzas and tapas from the colorful wood-fired oven in the center of Café Estrada. Several entertainment venues include the Stamford Arms, a traditional British pub popular with locals; the lobby lounge; the pool bar; the Lookout live music lounge; and the Club A nightclub.

Amenities: Large heated free-form swimming pool and sundeck, children's pool, health club, Jacuzzi, sauna, two day/night tennis courts, in-house masseur, beauty salon, childcare center (at a fee), baby-sitting, concierge, 24-hour room service, laundry/dry-cleaning, business center, secretarial services, free newspaper on request, express checkout, conference facilities, currency exchange, car-rental/tour desk, bike rental, small shopping arcade.

IN FREMANTLE

There's a perpetual holiday atmosphere in this picturesque port city. Although you're 19 kilometers (12 miles) from Perth's city center, public transport connections are good, so you could happily explore all of Perth from here—and most of top attractions are in Freo anyhow. There are good restaurants and a happening nightlife too.

✪ **Danum House.** 6 Fothergill St. (at Bellevue Terrace), Fremantle, WA 6160. ☎ **08/9336 3735.** Fax 08/9335 3414. www.staywa.net.au/ads/danum. E-mail: Danum@nettrek.com.au. 2 units (both with shower only). TV. A$90–$110 (U.S.$58.50–$71.50) double. Minimum 2-night stay. Rates include full breakfast. BC, MC, V. Ample on-street parking. Train: Fremantle. Fremantle airport shuttle. Children not permitted.

Cheerful hostess Christine Sherwin has created a warmly welcoming haven in her beautiful Federation (ca. 1909) home within walking distance of town. One room, daringly decked out in bold reds and greens, opens onto a cottage garden. The other very large room has an ornate mantle, floral wallpaper, long drapes, and that most colonial of furnishings, a daybed, as well as a real bed for sleeping. Both sport antiques, ornate ceiling roses and cornices, fireplaces, very high ceilings, and fans, and have a private entrance to the house. Even the bathrooms (one en suite, one with private access) share the colonial decor. Christine serves a hearty cooked breakfast, and you can relax in the comfy lounge over books, CDs, free tea and coffee, and complimentary port and chocolates. Hair dryers and irons are available. No smoking.

Esplanade Hotel Fremantle. Marine Terrace at Essex St., Fremantle, WA 6160. ☎ **1800/ 998 201** in Australia, or 08/9432 4000. Fax 08/9430 4539. www.esplanadehotelfremantle. com.au. E-mail: reservations@esplanadehotelfremantle.com.au. 259 units (some with shower only). A/C MINIBAR TV TEL. A$237–$325 (U.S.$154.05–$211.25) double; A$451 (U.S.$293.15) suite. Extra person A$33 (U.S.$21.45). Children under 12 stay free in parents' room with existing bedding; cribs free. Ask about packages. AE, BC, DC, MC, V. Valet parking A$12 (U.S.$7.80). Train: Fremantle. Fremantle Airport Shuttle (see "Arriving: By Plane," above).

Freo's best hotel is this low-rise 1897 colonial establishment wrapped by two verandas, centered around a buzzing four-story atrium lobby. A new 1996 wing blends in seamlessly. Renovated only a few years ago, the rooms sport all the accoutrements you would expect in a four-and-a-half–star hotel, including balconies, except for those on the inside of the old wing. The views are of the street, the pool, or the distant harbor across a park. Some rooms have Jacuzzis, inside or on the balcony; all have pay-per-view movies, hair dryers, irons and boards, and voice mail. The attractive courtyard pool is a great place to chill out without getting buffeted by the pesky wind known as the "Fremantle Doctor." It's a minute's walk to Freo's cafes, shops, and attractions.

Dining/Diversions: The Atrium Garden Restaurant does a mean buffet breakfast among its three meals a day. Trendier Café Panache does nightly à la carte dinner. Live entertainment plays weekends in the lounge bar, and there's a pool bar.

Amenities: Two heated outdoor swimming pools and sundeck, small health club, three Jacuzzis, sauna, in-room massage, 24-hour concierge, 24-hour room service, laundry/dry cleaning, free daily newspaper, baby-sitting, business center, secretarial services, extensive conference facilities, express checkout, currency exchange, car-rental and tour desk, bike rental, gift shop.

DINING

Perth's restaurant scene is as sophisticated as Sydney's and Melbourne's, with an array of upscale choices, plus terrific, cheap ethnic places (many of which are in "restaurant city," Northbridge).

Don't forget that going BYO (Bring Your Own wine or beer) makes sense to your wallet. Some restaurants charge "corkage" fees on BYO wine, usually A$1 or A$2 per person, but sometimes as much as A$4 (U.S.$2.80) per person.

For an inexpensive pasta, a Turkish bread sandwich, or excellent coffee and cake, you can't beat Perth's homegrown ✪ **DOME** chain of cafes. You will spot their dark green logo at Trinity Arcade between Hay Street Mall and St. Georges Terrace (☎ **08/9226 0210**); 149 James St., Northbridge (☎ **08/9328 8094**); 13 S. Terrace, Fremantle (☎ **08/9336 3040**); 19 Napoleon St., Cottesloe (☎ **08/9383 1071**); 26 Rokeby Rd., Subiaco (☎ **08/9381 5664**); and on Rottnest Island (☎ **08/ 9292 5026**).

Western Australian law bans smoking in enclosed public spaces, including restaurants.

IN THE CITY CENTER
Expensive
✪ **Fraser's.** Fraser Ave. (next to the Visitor Information Centre), Kings Park. ☎ **08/9481 7100.** Reservations required. Main courses A$22–$45 (U.S.$14.30–$29.25); average A$26 (U.S.$16.90). AE, BC, DC, MC, V. Mon–Fri 7–10:30am and noon–3pm, Sat–Sun 7:30–11am and 12:30–3:30pm; daily 6–10:30pm; light meals daily 10pm–late. Closed Good Friday. Bus: 33 stops outside the Visitor Centre; 103, 104, 200, 202, 208, and 209 stop outside the park gates. Red CAT Stop 25 "Havelock Street" is 1 block to the north of the gates. MODERN AUSTRALIAN/SEAFOOD.

What a sensational view from this hilltop restaurant! The city skyscrapers and Swan River look so close you could almost reach out and touch them—and even better, the victuals match the vista. Executive chef Chris Taylor's sure hand with seafood, which composes about 70 percent of the menu, has made the place a finalist in national "restaurant of the year" awards more than once. Seared Atlantic salmon with oyster mushrooms and bok choy is typical, and so is wok-fried baby octopus with chili jam and bean sprouts. The duck is also legendary. The spiced beef chunks with eggplant pahie (curry) and lentil dahl accompanied by chutney and yogurt salsa was possibly the best meal I've ever had. To maximize the view, ask for a seat on the terrace.

Moderate
✪ **44 King Street.** 44 King St. ☎ **08/9321 4476.** Reservations not accepted. Grazing menu A$3.20–$11.50 (U.S.$2.10–$7.50) breakfast, A$9.50–$24 (U.S.$6.20–$15.60) lunch and dinner. AE, BC, DC, MC, V. Daily 7am–late. Bus: Red CAT Stop 28 "King Street"; Blue CAT Stop 1 "Cloisters." MODERN AUSTRALIAN.

Socialites and hip corporate types adorn this sophisticated hangout, whose interior is a mix of industrial design and European cafe with dark timber tables, exposed air ducts, and windows onto the street. Thai spiced roast blue eye trevally with green papaya salad and crispy squid is a typical lunch or dinner choice; lemon curd crepe stack with berry compote is on the breakfast menu. Not only does the menu helpfully list two wine suggestions for each dish, but it also does taster-size glasses from around A$3 (U.S.$1.95) to A$7.50 (U.S.$4.90) from a long wine list, even of top-notch wines like an A$85 (U.S.$55.25) Mountadam merlot. Lots of folks drop in just for coffee, roasted on-site, and the famous cakes. All meals are available as takeout.

Miss Maud Swedish Restaurant. 97 Murray St. at Pier St. (below Miss Maud Swedish Hotel). ☎ **08/9325 3900.** Reservations recommended. Smorgasbord breakfast A$14.50 (U.S.$9.45) Mon–Fri, A$15.50 (U.S.$10.10) Sat–Sun and public holidays; lunch A$21.95 (U.S.$14.25) Mon–Fri, A$23.95 (U.S.$15.60) Sat–Sun and public holidays; dinner A$26.95 (U.S.$17.55) Sun–Thurs, A$29.95 (U.S.$19.50) Fri–Sat. Cheaper smorgasbord prices for children 4–13. À la carte main courses, sandwiches, and light meals A$3.95–$19.50

(U.S.$2.60–$12.70). Dine and leave by 7:15pm Mon–Sat for a A$5 (U.S.$3.25) discount. AE, BC, DC, JCB, MC, V. Open all day for coffee and cake. Meals daily 6:45–10am, noon–3pm, and 5:30–11pm. Bus: Red CAT Stop 1 "Pier St."; Blue CAT Stop 5 "Murray St. Mall East." INTERNATIONAL.

"Good food and plenty of it" is the motto at Miss Maud (Edmiston's) homey establishment, and the crowds packing the place prove it works. Most diners skip the long à la carte menu and go straight for the smorgasbord. At breakfast, that means 50 dishes including pancakes cooked before your eyes. At lunch and dinner you can tuck into soup, 10 salads, a big range of seafood (including oysters at dinner), cold meats, roasts, hot vegetables, pasta, cheeses, European-style breads, half a dozen tortes, fruit, and ice cream—65 dishes in all. Service is fast and polite.

❍ **Mount Street Café and Food Store.** Under the "River View on Mount Street" apartments, 42 Mount St. ☎ **08/9485 1411.** Reservations recommended Thurs–Sun. Main courses A$5.50–$24.50 (U.S.$3.60–$15.95); many meals under A$10 (U.S.$6.50) at breakfast and lunch. BC, MC, V. Summer Sun–Mon 7:30am–4pm, Tues 7:30am–6pm, Wed–Sat 7:30am–10:30pm. Winter Sun–Mon 7:30am–4pm, Tues–Thurs 7:30am–6pm, Fri–Sat 7:30am–10:30pm. Bus: Red CAT Stop 18 "QVI" (located over the freeway footbridge accessed from corner of St. Georges Terrace and Milligan St.). MODERN AUSTRALIAN.

Chef Toby Uhlrich runs the kitchen of this charming alfresco cafe on the edge of the central business district. Come for dinners like milk-fed veal with black-currant glaze on spinach fettuccine; lunches like lemon pepper chicken breast with bacon, salad, and mayo on dark rye with julienne vegetables; and good-value breakfasts like eggs Benedict in huge portions, beautifully presented on dark rye with the freshest asparagus you've ever had. Dine inside at a few tables, or out on the shaded stone terrace. Drop by anytime for cakes and good coffee, but be prepared to fight the regulars for a table. BYO.

Inexpensive

Fast Eddy's Café. 454 Murray St. (at Milligan St.). ☎ **08/9321 2552.** Main courses A$5–$15 (U.S.$3.25–$9.75); average A$10 (U.S.$6.50). BC, MC, V. Daily 24 hr. Red CAT Stop 27 "Milligan St." FAST FOOD.

A hefty menu of steaks, burgers, sandwiches, soups, pancakes, sundaes, milk shakes, and full fry-up brekkies are served all hours at this popular local chain. The fun interior is decked out with 1930s soap powder posters and Coca-Cola advertisements. One side is table service; the same food will cost you about a third of the already-low prices, at the Victorian-era–meets–1950s diner on the other side.

| Great Takeout |

It's a take-out joint, not a restaurant, but some of the tastiest dishes in Perth are at ❂ **Lamont's Wine & Food,** 125 St. Georges Terrace (☎ **08/9321 9907**). Grab some veal ravioli with goat's cheese, roast capsicum, and eggplant; or chicken with chermoula, couscous, pumpkin, and parsley and find a shady tree to eat under. Main courses cost A$7 to $13 (U.S.$4.55 to $8.45), while sandwiches cost between A$5 and A$6.50 (U.S.$3.25 to $4.25). Desserts, such as macadamia tarts and blueberry trifle, are all under A$6 (U.S.$3.90). They also sell their own label of wine. You can eat more of chef Kate Lamont's scrumptious food at her eponymous restaurants at 11 Brown Street, East Perth (☎ **08/9202 1566**), and in the Swan Valley (see "Side Trips from Perth," later in this chapter).

IN NORTHBRIDGE

Vultures. Francis St. at William St., Northbridge. ☎ **08/9227 9087.** Reservations recommended for dinner Fri–Sat. Main courses A$12.50–$22.50 (U.S.$8.15–$14.65); dine-in or take-out sandwiches at lunch Mon–Fri A$6–$9 (U.S.$3.90–$5.85). AE, BC, DC, MC, V. Sun–Thurs noon–1am; Fri–Sat noon–3am. Bus: Blue CAT Stop 9 "TAFE." MODERN AUSTRALIAN.

This large, relaxed, and groovy "coffee lounge cum restaurant" suits all occasions and all types of people, from couples having a romantic dinner in the streetside courtyard to teenage nightclubbers hanging out after a big night. You can even lie down in Balinese four-poster wedding beds instead of sitting at tables, with cushions to sit on and a low coffee table inside. The food is surprisingly good, from light fare—gourmet sandwiches (Mon to Fri), roast chicken nachos, curry laksa—to stylish main courses like veal ribs on parsnip and potato mash with snow peas and a Dijon cream jus. Rainbow-colored cocktails are a specialty.

ON THE BEACH

The Blue Duck. 151 Marine Parade, North Cottesloe. ☎ **08/9385 2499.** Reservations recommended, especially on weekends. Main courses A$2.90–$13.50 (U.S.$1.90–$8.80) breakfast, A$10.50–$25.50 (U.S.$6.85–$16.60) all day menu (many meals under A$20/U.S.$13). Buffet breakfast Sat–Sun and public holidays A$12–$17.50 (U.S.$7.80–$11.40). Kids' menu A$6.50–$8.50 (U.S.$4.25–$5.55). AE, BC, DC, MC, V. Daily 6am–late (from 6:30am in winter). Bus: 71, 72, 73. MODERN AUSTRALIAN.

For ocean views, it's hard to beat this casual restaurant perched right over the sand. Although the interior lacks the balcony's panoramic position, it has an upbeat seaside ambience and is just as packed as the porch. The long all-day menu has lots of light choices like chicken Caesar salad, as well as steaks, grilled fish, gourmet burgers, and wood-fired pizzas with creative toppings. Many dishes have an Asian twist, like the spicy green Thai curry with tiger prawns and reef fish. Licensed and BYO (bottled wine only—no BYO beer or spirits).

✪ **Indiana Tea House.** 99 Marine Parade (on Cottesloe Beach opposite Forrest St.), Cottesloe. ☎ **08/9385 5005.** Reservations recommended. Grazing menu A$10.50–$35 (U.S.$6.85–$22.75); most meals under A$30 (U.S.$19.50). AE, BC, DC, MC, V. Daily 7–10:15am, noon–3pm, 6–9:30pm; open all day for coffee. Bus: 71, 72, 73. MODERN AUSTRALIAN.

The colonial Asian trappings at this delightful turn-of-the-century bathhouse-turned-restaurant on Cottesloe Beach (bamboo birdcages, plaster lions, and palms) make me want to head straight for the tropical timber bar and order a Singapore Sling. Actually, the tasteful stucco building with bay windows and wooden floors is new—it just looks old. The Spice Islands–meets–Down Under food is up-to-date, though. It's a grazing menu of light to full-on dishes, such as Goan spiced mussels with cucumber, chili and mint raita, and garlic naan bread; or char-grilled yellowfin tuna on sesame-crushed potatoes with mango salsa. Seafood is a big item. The place is just as popular with business folk cutting deals as it is with arty types browsing the papers over their caffe latte. Go in the daytime to make the most of those ocean views, or at sunset.

North Cott Café. 149 Marine Parade, North Cottesloe. ☎ **08/9385 0338.** Main courses A$3–$12 (U.S.$1.95–$7.80). No credit cards. Mon–Fri 6:30am–4pm, Sat–Sun 6:30am–5pm. Bus: 71, 72, 73. CAFE FARE.

It's just a humble beach shack with plastic furniture, but this laid-back cafe next to the trendier Blue Duck has the same sea views (from the front three tables, anyhow; try to snare one) and the same breezy ambience. It also has terrific toasted flatbreads with fillings like tandoori chicken, roasted pumpkin, cucumber, and chutney, as well as muffins, juices, sandwiches, topped bruschetta, and salmon salad. Grab a newspaper from the stand and enjoy a lazy brekkie. BYO.

Java Joints

Don't leave Freo without a "short black" (that's an espresso) or a "flat white" (coffee with milk) at the port's "cappuccino strip" on South Terrace. On weekends this street bursts at the seams with locals flocking to alfresco Italian-style cafes serving good java and excellent foccacia, pasta, and pizza. **DOME, Old Papa's,** and **Gino's Trattoria & Cafe** are three to look for.

IN FREMANTLE

There's a Fremantle branch of **Fast Eddy's** (see above) at 13 Essex St. (☎ **08/9336 1671**) and another **Miss Maud Swedish Restaurant** (see above) at 33 S. Terrace (☎ **08/9336 1599**), though this branch serves only the breakfast buffet on weekends.

Gino's Pizzeria. 95 Market St. (behind Gino's Trattoria & Café on South Terrace). ☎ **08/ 9430 6126.** Reservations recommended on weekends; some tables always kept unreserved. Pizzas A$7–$14. (U.S.$4.55–$9.10); main courses A$9.50–$16.90 (U.S.$6.20–$11). AE, BC, DC, JCB, MC, V. Mon–Thurs 6pm–late, Fri–Sun noon–late. Train: Fremantle. WOOD-FIRED PIZZA/ITALIAN.

All the traditional favorites get served up alongside the tastiest wood-fired pizzas in Perth at this lively Italian joint. Servings are huge—one pizza is easily enough for two. The pizza base is high, airy, and crispy, and the toppings are innovative, like blue castello cheese, leek and parsley, or roast lamb with pesto salsa and pine nuts. Traditional main courses such as pasta and veal parmigiana share the menu with trendier offerings such as char-grilled swordfish in a balsamic vinaigrette. The decor is upbeat with terrazzo tables, a groovy concrete and timber floor, and a stainless-steel bar. Licensed and BYO (BYO spirits not permitted).

WHAT TO SEE & DO IN PERTH

Art Gallery of Western Australia. 47 James St. (enter near the walkway opposite Perth Railway Station), Northbridge. ☎ **08/9492 6600** administration, 08/9492 6622 recorded information line. Free admission. Entry fee may apply to special exhibitions. Daily 10am–5pm; from 1pm Anzac Day. Closed Christmas, New Year's, entire month of February, and Good Friday. Train: Perth. Bus: Blue CAT Stop 7 "Culture Centre."

Most outstanding among this state gallery's international and Australian paintings, prints, sculpture, craft, and drawings is the Aboriginal art collection, regarded as the finest in Australia. A free guided tour of a particular collection runs once a day, most days; call for times.

Cohunu Koala Park. Off Mills Rd. E., Gosnells (or located in the suburb of Martin on some maps). ☎ **08/9390 6090.** Admission A$16.50 (U.S.$10.75) adults, A$7.70 (U.S.$5) children 3–13. Animal feed A40¢ (U.S.26¢). Daily 10am–5pm; koala photo sessions 10am–4pm. Closed Christmas. Train: Gosnells on Armadale line plus A$13 (U.S.$8.45) cab. By car: Take Riverside Dr. across Swan River onto Albany Hwy., follow for approx. 25km (16 miles) to Gosnells, turn left onto Tonkin Hwy. and right 1/2 mile later onto Mills Rd. E. (approx. 35-min. drive from city). A cab from the city is approx. A$30 (U.S.$19.50).

This wildlife park is your big chance to have your photo taken cuddling a koala (for A$20/U.S.$13, or A$10 if you take it yourself). You can also feed 100 kangaroos, wallabies, and emus wandering in natural enclosures; see wombats, dingoes, and llamas; and walk through an aviary housing Aussie native birds. Wild water birds collect on the ponds in the park's 18 hectares (45 acres). A small train will ferry you around part of the grounds for an extra A$2 (U.S.$1.30).

Kings Park & Botanic Garden. Fraser Ave. off Kings Park Rd. ☎ **08/9480 3600.** Free admission. Daily 24 hr. The Visitor Information Centre on Fraser Ave. inside the park is open daily 9:30am–4pm (closed Christmas and Good Friday). Bus: 33 stops outside the Visitor Centre and extends into the park on Sat afternoon, and much of the day Sun and public holidays; 103, 104, 200, 202, 208, and 209 stop outside the gates. Red CAT Stop 25 "Havelock Street" is 1 block north of the gates.

On the edge of the city center is Perth's pride and joy, a 400-hectare (988-acre) hilltop park of botanic gardens and uncultivated remnant bushland. Here you can inspect weird and wonderful Western Australian flora, get to know the solitude of the Australian bush, and bike, hike, or drive an extensive network of roads and trails. Visiting the wildflower displays from August to October is a highlight on many Perth residents' calendars. Aboriginal art is on display in the gallery under the city lookout on Fraser Avenue. There are BBQ and picnic facilities, several extensive playgrounds, bikes for rent (behind the Visitor Information Centre), tearooms, and the incomparable Fraser's (see "Dining," above).

Pick up self-guiding maps from the Visitor Information Centre, or join one of the daily free guided walks departing from the giant Karri Log outside it. Walks usually depart 10am and 2pm (but check before you show up) and take 1¹/₂ hours, or up to 3 hours on bushwalks. **The Perth Tram Co.** (☎ **08/9322 2006**) runs 1-hour tours of the park and neighboring University of Western Australia in replica 1899 wooden trams. Tours depart daily from outside the Visitor Information Centre on Fraser Avenue at 11am, 12:15pm, 1:15pm, and 2:15pm (and occasionally at 3:15pm on Sun subject to demand; check with the driver). Tickets cost A$10 (U.S.$6.50) for adults, A$8 (U.S.$5.20) for seniors, A$5 (U.S.$3.25) for children 4 to 14, and A$25 (U.S.$16.25) families. Buy tickets on board.

Perth Mint. 310 Hay St. at Hill St., East Perth. ☎ **08/9421 7425.** Admission A$6.60 (U.S.$4.30) adults, A$5.50 (U.S.$3.60) seniors and students, A$3.30 (U.S.$2.15) school-age children, A$16.50 (U.S.$10.75) families; free admission to the shop. Mon–Fri 9am–4pm, Sat–Sun 9am–1pm. Closed Christmas, New Year's Day, ANZAC Day (Apr 25), and Good Friday.

During the 1890s gold rush, a monthly escort brought gold to this infant mint from Kalgoorlie to be made into coins for Great Britain, Australia, and other countries. Bullion is still traded in this lovely late-Victorian building today, so if you stumble across a gold nugget on your travels through Western Australia, you know where to bring it! You can mint your own medallion for an extra A$15 (U.S.$9.75), handle a A$200,000 (U.S.$130,000) 400-ounce gold bar, see coins being minted, ogle a sizable collection of nuggets, and watch a gold pour on the hour from 10am weekdays, and from 10am to noon inclusive on weekends. A 30-minute free guided tour departs half an hour before every pour. The shop sells gold coins and nugget jewelry.

Perth Zoo. 20 Labouchere Rd., South Perth. ☎ **08/9474 3551** for recorded information, 08/9367 7988 administration. Admission A$11 (U.S.$7.15) adults, A$5.50 (U.S.$3.60) children 4–15, A$30 (U.S.$19.50) family of 4. Daily 9am–5pm. Ferry: Barrack St. Jetty to Mends St. Jetty, South Perth. Bus: 108 or 110 from stand 42, St. Georges Terrace at William St.

This is a good place to see numbats, wombats, Tasmanian devils, echidnas (the Aussie answer to the porcupine), dingoes, kangaroos, koalas, crocodiles, black swans, and just about every other kind of Aussie wildlife in natural habitats. Notable exotic animals

Picture Perfect

For the only photo of Perth you'll need, snap the view over the city and river from the **War Memorial** in Kings Park—it's superb day or night.

include orangutans, Rothschild's giraffes, Asian elephants, and Sumatran tigers. Feeding demonstrations and talks run throughout the day. There are picnic facilities.

Underwater World. Sorrento Quay at Hillarys Boat Harbour, 91 Southside Dr., Hillarys. ☎ **08/9477 7500.** Admission A$17.50 (U.S.$11.40) adults, A$9 (U.S.$5.85) children ages 3–14; A$13.50 (U.S.$8.80) seniors and students, A$44 (U.S.$28.60) family of 4 plus A$5 (U.S.$3.25) per extra child. Daily 9am–5pm. Closed Christmas. Train and bus: Take Joondalup train line (also called the Currambine line) to Warwick, transfer to bus 423 (note: only 3 bus services run Sun). By car, take Mitchell Hwy. 23km (14 miles) north, turn left into Hepburn Ave., and follow signs to the "Oceanarium."

You won't catch performing dolphins a la Sea World, but there's plenty for kids to see here, including a moving walkway through an underwater tunnel of sharks, rays, and turtles; a touch pool that even has a (small!) shark; and lots of aquariums that showcase the marine life of the Western Australian coast, including leafy sea dragons, coral reefs, jellyfish, crocodiles, and dangerous sea critters. Keepers feed the sharks and the touch pool creatures daily. For A$75 (U.S.$48.75), qualified divers can dive with sharks, and for the same fee, anyone over 12 years of age can swim with fur seals on weekends, Wednesdays, and Fridays. Book both experiences well in advance.

Western Australian Museum. Francis St. at Beaufort St. (or enter off James Street Mall), Northbridge. ☎ **08/9427 2700.** Free admission (donation requested). Admission fee may apply to special exhibitions. Daily 9:30am–5pm; ANZAC Day (Apr 25) and Boxing Day (Dec 26) 1–5pm. Closed Christmas and Good Friday. Train: Perth. Bus: Blue CAT Stop 8 "Museum."

Kids will like the dinosaur gallery, the drawers full of insects in the lobby, the mammal and blue-whale skeletons on the well-stocked aquatic zoology floor, the butterfly gallery, and the bizarre "megamouth" shark preserved in a tank set in the ground in the courtyard. The main attraction for grown-ups is one of the best collections of Aboriginal artifacts and rare photographs in the country.

HITTING THE BEACHES

Perth shares Sydney's good luck in having beaches in the metropolitan area—19 of them, in fact, laid end to end along the 35-kilometer (22-mile) Sunset Coast from Cottesloe in the south to Quinns Rocks in the north. Mornings are best, because a strong afternoon wind, known as the "Fremantle Doctor," can be unpleasant, especially in summer. Always swim between the red and yellow flags, which denote a "safe swimming" zone.

A **walk/cycle path** runs alongside 15 beaches from Sorrento Beach in the north all the way down to Port Beach on Fremantle's outskirts in the south. It veers inland for a few miles at Swanbourne, where it also cuts out for a few blocks; you should easily pick it up again.

On weekends and public holidays from the last Saturday in September to the last Sunday in April, the **Sunset Coaster** bus 928 stops hourly during the day at most beaches on its way from Fremantle to Hillarys and beyond. It also operates in the reverse direction. You can take a surfboard under 2 meters on the 928.

All beaches have ample parking. These are the three most popular:

✪ **COTTESLOE** This pretty crescent, graced by the delightful Edwardian-style Indiana Tea House restaurant (see "Dining," above), is Perth's most fashionable beach. It has good, safe swimming, a small surf break, and a kiosk. A couple of good cafes are nearby. Train: Cottesloe, then a walk of several hundred meters. Bus direct to the beach: 71, 72, or 73.

SCARBOROUGH Biggest of them all, Scarborough's white sands stretch for miles from the base of the Hotel Rendezvous Observation City Perth. Swimming is generally safe, and surfers are always guaranteed a wave, although inexperienced swimmers should take a rain check when the surf is rough. The busy shopping precinct across the road means there's always somewhere to buy lunch and drinks. Bus: 400.

TRIGG   Surfers like Trigg best for its consistent swells. It has a kiosk. Bus: 400 to Scarborough, then a 10-minute walk north.

A DAY OUT IN FREMANTLE

The heritage port precinct of ✪ **Fremantle,** 19 kilometers (12 miles) from downtown Perth on the mouth of the Swan River, is probably best known outside Australia as the site of the 1987 America's Cup challenge. Just before that event, the city embarked on a major restoration of its gracious but run-down warehouses and derelict Victorian buildings. The Cup may be gone, but today "Freo" is a bustling district of 150 National Trust buildings, alfresco cafes, museums, galleries, pubs, markets, and shops in a masterfully preserved historical atmosphere. It's still a working port so you will see fishing boats unloading and yachts gliding in and out of the harbor. The ambience is so authentic that locals make a beeline for the place every weekend, resulting in a wonderful hubbub of buzzing shoppers, market stall holders, java drinkers, yachties, tourists, and fishermen. Allow a full day to take in even half the sights—and don't forget to knock back an ale or two on the verandas of one of the gorgeous old pubs.

ESSENTIALS

GETTING THERE   Parking is plentiful, but driving is frustrating in the maze of one-way traffic. Most attractions are within walking distance, so take the train to Fremantle station and explore on foot.

A nice way to get to the port and see Perth's river suburbs at the same time is on the cruises run by several companies once or twice a day from Barrack Street Jetty. See "Whale-Watching Cruises, Tram Trips & Other Tours," later in this chapter, for cruise operators.

GETTING AROUND   The easiest way to explore is on foot. Elaine Berry, of the Western Australian Maritime Museum (see below), leads a 90-minute walking tour for A$10 (U.S.$6.50) for adults, A$7.50 (U.S.$4.90) for seniors, and A$3 (U.S.$1.95) for school-age kids; you must book by calling the museum ☎ **08/9431 8455,** or Elaine at home (☎ 08/9336 1906) on weekends. She schedules the tours for a day and time to suit you.

Check with the Fremantle Tourist Bureau whether the free **Clipper** bus makes a running loop of local attractions; at press time this service had ceased but plans were underway to revive it. **Fremantle Trams** (☎ **08/9339 8719**)—an old tram carriage now on wheels, not tram tracks—conducts various tour routes of 45 or 90 minutes, departing eight times a day from Fremantle Town Hall from 10am, with the last tour at 4pm. Tickets cost A$8 to $10 (U.S.$5.20 to $6.50) for adults, A$6 to $8 (U.S.$3.90 to $5.20) for seniors, A$3 to $5 (U.S.$1.95 to $3.25) for children 15 and under, and A$15 to $20 (U.S.$9.75 to $13) for families. Buy tickets on board.

Fremantle Ghost Walks (☎ **08/9484 1133** is the booking agent, BOCS; 08/9336 1916 for inquiries) leads 1-hour spook saunters Monday (of the Fremantle Arts Centre) and Wednesday (of 10 haunted buildings) at 8pm; tickets are A$12 (U.S.$7.80) adults, A$10 (U.S.$6.50) seniors and students, and A$8 (U.S.$5.20) kids ages 6 to 15, plus a BOCS telephone booking fee of A$6 (U.S.$3.90) per booking.

VISITOR INFORMATION   The **Fremantle Tourist Bureau** is located in Town Hall, Kings Square at High Street, Fremantle, WA 6160 (☎ **08/9431 7878;** www. fremantle.wa.gov.au). It's open Monday through Saturday 9am to 5pm and Sunday 12:30 to 4:30pm.

SEEING THE SIGHTS IN FREMANTLE

You'll want to explore some of Freo's excellent museums and other attractions below, but take time to stroll the streets and admire the 19th-century offices and warehouses, many now painted in rich, historically accurate colors. As soon as you arrive, wander down to the docks—either Victoria Quay, where sailing craft come and go, or Fishing Boat Harbour off Mews Road, where the boats bring in their catches—to get a breath of salt air.

Freo's best **shopping** is arts and crafts, from handblown glass to Aboriginal art to alpaca wool clothing. Worth a look are the assorted art, craft, and souvenir stores on **High Street** west of the mall; the **E Shed markets** on Victoria Quay (open Fri to Sun only, from 9am to 6pm); and **Bannister Street CraftWorks,** an arts cooperative where you often spy the artists at work (open from 11am to 5:30pm; closed Mon). The **Fremantle Markets,** 74 S. Terrace at Henderson Street (☎ **08/9335 2515**), mostly sell cheap imported handicrafts, jewelry, homewares, and clothing, as well as inexpensive food. They're open Friday 9am to 9pm, Saturday 9am to 5pm, and Sunday and any public holidays that fall on a Monday 10am to 5pm.

The most popular watering holes are the **Sail & Anchor,** 64 S. Terrace (☎ **08/9335 8433**), which brews its own Brass Monkey Stout; the **Norfolk,** 47 S. Terrace at Norfolk Street (☎ **08/9335 5405**); and the beautifully restored front bar and garden courtyard at **Phillimore's Café & Bar** at His Majesty's Hotel, on Phillimore Street at Mouat Street (☎ **08/9335 9596**). The happening "cappuccino strip" on South Terrace is good for people-watching.

Fremantle Arts Centre. 1 Finnerty St. ☎ **08/9432 9555.** Free admission. Daily 10am–5pm. Closed Christmas and Good Friday, Boxing Day (Dec 26), and New Year's Day.

Housed in a striking neo-Gothic 1860s building built by convicts, this center contains one of Western Australia's best contemporary arts-and-crafts galleries with a constantly changing array of works. There are a shop selling high-quality Western Australian crafts, a bookshop stocking Australian literature and art books, and a leafy courtyard cafe. Free musical concerts play on the lawn every Sunday between September and April or May from 2 to 4pm.

Fremantle History Museum. 1 Finnerty St. at Ord St. (part of the Fremantle Arts Centre, see above). ☎ **08/9430 7966.** Free admission. Sun–Fri 10:30am–4:30pm, Sat and public holidays 1–5pm. Closed Christmas, Boxing Day (Dec 26), and Good Friday.

Housed in a convict-built former lunatic asylum next to the Fremantle Arts Centre, this small but densely packed museum uses lots of old photographs and personal possessions to paint a realistic picture of what life was like for Fremantle's first settlers, the Aboriginal people they displaced, and later generations up to the present day.

Fremantle Prison. 1 The Terrace. ☎ **08/9430 7177.** Free admission to courtyard. Tours A$10 (U.S.$6.50) adults, A$4 (U.S.$2.60) children 6–15; candlelight tours Wed and Fri. A$12 (U.S.$7.80) adults, A$6 (U.S.$3.90) children. A$2 (U.S.$1.30) discount on admission to Fremantle Trams passengers (see "Getting Around," earlier in the chapter). Daily 10am–5pm (5pm tour excludes women's prison tour), Wed and Fri evening tours from 7pm. Closed Christmas and Good Friday.

Even jails sported attractive architecture back in the 1850s. This picturesque limestone jail, built by convicts who no doubt ended up inside it, was a maximum-security prison until 1991. You can enter the courtyard free of charge, but to see bushranger (highwayman) Joe Moondyne's cell, the gallows, and cell walls featuring some wonderful artwork by the former inmates, you need to take the 75-minute tour which runs every half hour throughout the day. It is followed by a 45-minute tour of the women's cells. You must book for the Wednesday- and Friday-night candlelight tours, which take 90 minutes.

The Roundhouse. 10 Arthur Head (entry over the railway line from High St.). Admission A$2 (U.S.$1.30) donation. Daily 9am–5pm May–Oct., 9am–6pm Nov–April. Closed Good Friday and Christmas.

A peep at this 12-sided jail, the state's oldest public building (built around 1830) will only take a minute. There are no displays or memorabilia, but it's worth a look for history's sake, and for the sea views on the other side. Whaling took place from the beach below the jail in the 19th century, and the time cannon just to its west, a replica of a gun salvaged from an 1878 wreck, is fired daily and a time ball dropped at 1pm, just as it was in the 1800s.

✪ Western Australian Maritime Museum. Cliff St. ☎ **08/9431 8444.** Free admission (donation requested). Daily 9:30am–5pm. Anzac Day and Boxing Day (Dec 26) 1–5pm. Free guided 30-min. tours daily 11am and 2pm. Closed Christmas and Good Friday.

Fascinating archaeological displays of shipwrecks and treasure recovered off the treacherous Western Australian coast are well worth a visit here. Two floors in a historic stone warehouse house displays dating from the 1600s, when Dutch explorers became the first Europeans to encounter Australia, and promptly abandoned its harsh shores as being useless.

WHALE-WATCHING CRUISES, TRAM TRIPS & OTHER TOURS

Boat Torque (☎ **1300/368 686** in Australia, or 08/9221 5844), **Golden Sun** (☎ **08/9325 1616**), and **Oceanic Cruises** (☎ **08/9325 1191**) run an assortment of morning, afternoon, sunset, luncheon, dinner, half-, and full-day cruises on the Swan River, some as far as Fremantle, and to historic homes and vineyards in the Swan Valley. **Captain Cook Cruises** (☎ **08/9325 3341**) cruises on the Perth–Fremantle route only.

From September through November, Perth's waters are alive with **southern right whales** and **humpback whales** returning from the north with their calves. To join a 2- or 3-hour jaunt to watch them, contact Boat Torque, Oceanic Cruises, or the **Rottnest Express** ferry (☎ **08/9335 6406**), which does whale-watch trips between ferry runs. Departure days and times vary from year to year with every cruise operator, so check ahead. The average price is around A$25 (U.S.$16.25), about half price for kids. Most depart Fremantle; Boat Torque also does them from Hillarys Boat Harbour (near Underwater World; see "What to See & Do in Perth," above). The company provides coach connections to Hillarys from Perth.

The Perth Tram Co. (☎ **08/9367 9404**) makes a daily guided running loop of city attractions, the casino, and Kings Park in replica 1899 wooden trams; hop on and off as often as you wish. Tickets, which you buy on board, cost A$12 (U.S.$7.80) for adults, A$10 (U.S.$6.50) for seniors, A$6 (U.S.$3.90) for children 4 to 14, and A$30 (U.S.$19.50) families. City-casino, city–Kings Park and casino–Kings Park single legs are also available. Join anywhere; the tram starts at 565 Hay Street at 9:40am and makes six 90-minute loops a day.

Feature Tours (☎ **1800/999 819** in Australia, or 08/9479 4131; www.ft.com.au) runs half-day and full-day coach tours to many attractions in and around Perth.

ACTIVE PURSUITS

BIKING Bike tracks stretch for miles along the Swan River, through Kings Park, around Fremantle, and all the way down the beaches. There is a great 9.5-kilometer (6-mile) track around Perth Water, the broad expanse of river in front of the central business district, that starts at the Swan River on Riverside Drive in the city and goes over the Causeway bridge, back along the other bank and over the bridge at the

Narrows back to the city. The state Department of Transport's cycling division, Bikewest, publishes bike-route maps to the city. They are available in bike shops, and by the time you read this, they should also be widely available in newsagents.

An hour's rental with **Koala Bike Hire,** located in the carpark behind Fraser's restaurant in Kings Park (☎ **08/9321 3061**), is A$4 (U.S.$2.60), or A$15 (U.S.$9.75) for the day, which includes a helmet (required by law in W.A.), lock, and maps of Kings Park.

CANOEING, KAYAKING & WHITE-WATER RAFTING ✪ **Rivergods** (☎ **08/9259 0749**) runs canoeing, sea kayaking, and white-water rafting adventures on the Swan and other rivers near Perth. The company's 1-day ✪ **sea kayak trip** to **snorkel with wild sea lions** in the Shoalwater Islands Marine Park, just south of Perth, gets rave reviews. You also paddle into limestone caves, and see penguins being fed on Penguin Island. On the return journey you tie your kayaks together, raise a kite, and kayak-sail home! The cost for the day is A$104.50 (U.S.$67.95). Pickup from your hotel is an extra A$10 (U.S.$6.50). This trip runs daily from September or October to June.

FISHING Dhufish, pink snapper, cod, marlin, shark, tuna, and mahimahi run in the ocean off Perth. **Mill's Charters** at Hillarys Boat Harbour, approximately 25 kilometers (15½ miles) north of the city center (☎ **08/9246 5334,** or 08/9401 0833 after hours) runs full-day deep-sea trips aboard 60-foot and 70-foot cruisers for A$75 (U.S.$48.75) weekdays and A$85 (U.S.$55.25) on weekends and public holidays. That includes tackle and bait; BYO lunch and drinks. The company also runs game-fishing day trips, for which you're looking at A$250 (U.S.$162.50) per person. Another great fishing spot is Rottnest Island (see "Side Trips From Perth," below). **Rottnest Malibu Diving** (☎ **08/9292 5111**) rents tackle for beach and jetty fishing, and does fishing tours to the pick of the island's bays in winter months.

GOLF Most convenient to the city is **Burswood Park Golf Course,** part of the Burswood International Resort Casino complex, across the Swan River from town on the Great Eastern Highway, Burswood (☎ **08/9362 7576** for the pro shop). Great city views, and wild black swans and pelicans on the water, make this a pretty course. A 9-hole round is just A$12 (U.S.$7.80) weekdays and A$15 (U.S.$9.75) weekends. A cart for 9 holes is A$20 (U.S.$13), and club rental is A$15 (U.S.$9.75).

Even more scenic are the 27 championship fairways designed by Robert Trent Jones, Jr., at **Joondalup Resort,** Country Club Boulevard, Connolly, a 25-kilometer (15½-mile) drive north of Perth (☎ **08/9400 8811** is the pro shop); and **The Vines Resort** in the Swan Valley (☎ **08/9297 3000** for the resort, or 08/9297 0222 for the pro shop), which has two 18-hole bushland courses. It was ranked No. 1 Golf Resort in Australia by *Golf Australia* magazine in 2000. Kangaroos often come onto the course at Joondalup and The Vines. Expect to pay around A$60 (U.S.$39) to A$80 (U.S.$52) for 9 holes at either resort. **Koala Golf** (☎ **08/9221 2688**) runs day trips to various Perth courses.

SAILING The tallest Tall Ship in Australia, the lovely three-masted barquentine STS *Leeuwin II* (☎ **08/9430 4105**), sails from B Shed at Victoria Quay, Fremantle, when it is not out on charter. Leisurely day trips from 10am to 3pm are A$90 (U.S.$58.50) for adults and A$50 (U.S.$32.50) for children under 13. The ship sometimes does 3-hour sails at breakfast or twilight.

Experienced sailors can sail on Wednesday and Saturday afternoons in summer with members of the **Royal Perth Yacht Club,** Australia II Drive, Crawley (☎ **08/9389 1555;** ask for the sailing administrator), if there is a place free aboard. All-white dress standards apply.

SCUBA DIVING & SNORKELING   Rottnest Island's corals, reef fish, and lime-stone caverns, in 18- to 35-meter (59- to 128-ft.) visibility, are a gift from heaven to Perth divers and snorkelers. Contact **Rottnest Malibu Diving** (☎ **08/9292 5111**) on Rottnest Island (see "Side Trips From Perth," below) to rent gear or join a dive trip. **Diving Ventures,** at 37 Barrack St. in Perth (☎ **08/9421 1052**), conducts dive day trips from Perth to Rottnest Island, and also to the wreck of the HMAS *Swan* off Dunsborough in the state's Southwest, a 250-foot-long destroyer which was scuttled for divers' pleasure a couple of years ago. A day trip to either spot costs A$135 (U.S.$87.75) with two dives, including lunch and all gear. The company also rents scuba gear. It has an outlet at 384 S. Terrace, Fremantle, too.

SURFING   You will find good surfing at many city beaches, Scarborough and Trigg in particular. See the "Hitting the Beaches" section, earlier in this chapter. Rottnest Island (see "Side Trips from Perth," below) also has good breaks. **Murray Smith Surf Centre,** Shop 14, Luna Maxi Mart, Scarborough (☎ **08/9245 2988**), rents long boards for A$20 (U.S.$13) for half a day or A$30 (U.S.$19.50) for the day, plus a A$100 (U.S.$65) refundable deposit. They also rent body boards. **Surfing WA** (☎ **08/9448 0004**) runs hour-long surfing classes for A$40 (U.S.$26) per person, or A$35 (U.S.$22.75) per person for two people. Boards, wet suits, and sunscreen are provided. Lessons run daily at any beach where there are waves. That usually turns out to be Trigg or Scarborough.

THE SHOPPING SCENE

Perth's city center is a major retail precinct. Most shops are located on the parallel **Hay Street** and **Murray Street malls,** located 1 block apart, and in the network of arcades running off them such as the Plaza, City, and Carillon City arcades. **London Court** off Hay Street Mall is a re-created Tudor street lined with one-off fashion, gift, and jewelry shops. Off Murray Street Mall on Forrest Place is the **Forrest Chase shopping center,** housing the Myer department store and boutiques on two gallery levels. Add to your collection of international designer brands on posh **King Street.**

If you want to avoid the chains, skip the city center and spend half a day in fashion-able **Subiaco** or "Subi," where Hay Street and Rokeby Road are lined with smart boutiques, home accessories shops, art galleries, cafes, antique shops, and markets. The Colonnade shopping center at 388 Hay St. showcases groovy young Aussie fashion designers in its Studio 388 section.

Fremantle's shopping is mostly limited to a good selection of crafts, markets, and Aboriginal souvenirs.

Shops are open until 9pm on Friday in the city, and until 9pm on Thursday in Subiaco and Fremantle.

ABORIGINAL ARTS & CRAFTS   **Creative Native,** 32 King St. (☎ **08/9322 3398**), stocks Perth's widest range of Aboriginal arts and crafts, including carvings, boomerangs, bowls, carved emu eggs, a huge range of didgeridoos, and Aboriginal-print merchandise from men's ties to pot holders. Upstairs is a gallery selling original works by some renowned Aboriginal artists. There's another branch at 65 High St., Fremantle (☎ **08/9335 6995**).

Indigenart, The Mossenson Gallery, 115 Hay St., Subiaco (☎ **08/9388 2899**), and 82 High St., Fremantle (☎ **08/9335 2911**), stocks works on canvas, paper, and bark, as well as artifacts, textiles, pottery, didgeridoos, boomerangs, and sculpture, by world-famous and lesser-known Aboriginal artists from all over Australia. Serious collectors should find something they like here.

Desert Designs

Aboriginal artist **Jimmy Pike** grew up in Western Australia's Sandy Desert and began transferring his Dreamtime art and designs to fabrics in 1981. Today his highly successful range of merchandise includes clothing. The children's gear is especially cute. The **Japingka Gallery,** 47 High St., Fremantle (☎ 08/9335 8265), stocks original paintings and limited-edition prints by Jimmy, his artistic partner, Doris Gingingara, and many other Aboriginal artists. It also stocks authentic didgeridoos, artifacts, and stunning high-quality hand-tufted woolen floor rugs in Aboriginal designs. For clothing and accessories featuring designs by Jimmy, Doris, and other leading Aboriginal artists, visit the **Desert Designs** boutique at 114 High Street Mall, Fremantle (☎ **08/9430 4101**).

JEWELRY   Western Australia is renowned for farming the world's best **South Sea pearls** off Broome, for Argyle **diamonds** mined in the Kimberley, and for being one of the world's biggest **gold** producers. Most shops give tax-free prices to international travelers who present their airline ticket and passport; how much that tax amounts to was not clear when we went to print, due to a reshuffling of Australia's tax rates.

   Artisans of the Sea, corner of Marine Terrace and Collie Street, Fremantle (☎ 08/ 9336 3633), is owned by the Kailis family, which runs one of the world's biggest pearling operations in Broome. This store sells elegant South Sea pearl strands and gold jewelry.

   Family-owned sister stores, **Costello's,** Shop 5–6, London Court (☎ 08/9325 8588), and **Swan Diamonds,** Shop 4, London Court (☎ 08/9325 8166), have tasteful, understated jewelry. The designers at **Linneys Jewellers,** 37 Rokeby Rd., Subiaco (☎ 08/9382 4077), turn out sleekly artistic one-of-a-kind pieces. Costello's, Swan Diamonds, and Linneys all use opals, Argyle diamonds, and Broome pearls.

   For opals to suit all budgets, head to **Quilpie Opals,** Shop 6, Piccadilly Arcade off Hay Street Mall (☎ 08/9321 8687).

PERTH AFTER DARK

Scoop and the *Perth Weekly* (see "Visitor Information," earlier in this chapter) are good sources of information on public festivals and concerts, performing arts, classical music, at exhibitions, and the like. Your best guide to hip dance clubs, concerts, gig listings, art-house cinemas, and art galleries is the *X-press newspaper,* free every Thursday at more than 500 pubs, cafes, and live-music venues across town. The *West Australian* and *Sunday Times* newspapers publish a limited amount of entertainment information, including cinema guides.

   Two major booking agents handle bookings to most of the city's major performing arts, entertainment, and sporting events: **BOCS** (☎ 08/9484 1133 for bookings; Yellow Pages Talking Guide 13 16 20 in Perth for recorded event listings) and **Ticketmaster 7** (☎ **13 61 22** for sporting events or 13 61 00 for all other events, or 1902/ 29 1502, a pay-by-the-minute line for recorded events information).

THE PERFORMING ARTS   The West Australian Opera Company and West Australian Ballet usually perform at **His Majesty's Theatre,** 825 Hay St., a restored "grande dame" venue from the early 1900s. Perth's leading theatrical company, the Black Swan Theatre Company, mostly plays at the **Subiaco Theatre Centre,** 180 Hamersley Rd., Subiaco. The **West Australian Symphony Orchestra** (☎ 08/9326 0000 for bookings, or call BOCS) usually performs at the **Perth Concert Hall,**

5 St. Georges Terrace next to the Duxton Hotel. Blessed with the best acoustics of any such venue in Australia, it has housed performances by the London Philharmonic, comedian Billy Connolly, and blues icon B B King. Book opera, ballet, and the Black Swan Theatre Company through BOCS.

The monthlong **Perth International Arts Festival** (books through BOCS) showcases contemporary performing and visual arts every January, February, or March, many events taking place outdoors. In summer, look for outdoor concerts at **Perth Zoo** (☎ **08/9474 3551** for recorded information, 08/9367 7988 administration) and outdoor concerts, plays, and movies in **Kings Park** (☎ **08/9480 3600**).

PUBS & DANCE CLUBS　　Northbridge houses most of city's lively pubs and dance clubs. Don't forget Freo has good pubs, too (we recommend three in "A Day Out in Fremantle," earlier in this chapter).

For a trendy take on the traditional corner pub, head to **The Brass Monkey,** 209 William St. at James Street, Northbridge (☎ **08/9227 9596**). Downstairs are several bars and a beer garden; upstairs is the Monkey Bar cocktail bar (open Fri and Sat nights only, when a DJ plays) and a nice veranda brasserie. Stand-up comedy plays Wednesday night in the Monkey Bar for an A$8 (U.S.$5.20) cover.

In Subiaco, suits flock to the "Subi," also known as the **Subiaco Hotel,** 465 Hay St. at Rokeby Road, Subiaco (☎ **08/9381 1028**), a popular historic pub with a stylish cafe. It's big on Friday night.

Metropolis, 146 Roe St., Northbridge (☎ **08/9228 0500**), is a huge complex of dance floors and bars over several levels, where live Aussie and touring bands play. If your "dancing 'til 6am" days are over but you still know how to hit the dance floor, hit it at **Margeaux's,** a nightclub popular with 30-, 40- and 50-somethings, located in the Perth Parmelia Hilton, 14 Mill St. (☎ **08/9215 2000**). It opens Wednesday, Friday, and Saturday nights.

THE CASINO　　A 2,000-seat showroom that hosts the likes of Gene Pitney and opera singer Andrea Bocelli is located in the **Burswood International Resort Casino,** on the Great Eastern Highway just over the river from the city (☎ **08/9362 7646** for guest information; for show bookings call 08/9484 7000 for the box office or call BOCS—see above). Live bands, disco, or karaoke play nightly in the Cabaret Lounge free, and there are nine restaurants and five bars within the resort/casino complex. On the gaming floor are 126 tables, 1,160 video gaming machines, a VIP players' room, and a Keno Lounge. Except for Christmas Day, Good Friday, and Anzac Day, the casino is open 24 hours. Dress standards are smart casual—no jeans or T-shirts at night, for example. It's about an A$10 (U.S.$6.50) cab ride from the city, or take a train to Burswood station.

2 Side Trips from Perth

ROTTNEST ISLAND: GETTING FACE-TO-FACE WITH THE FISHES
19km (12 miles) W of Perth

The delightful wildlife reserve of ✪ **Rottnest Island** just off the Perth coast is like the city's own Great Barrier Reef in miniature. Its jewel-bright turquoise waters, warm currents, rocky coves, and many sheltered beaches harbor **coral reefs** and 360 kinds of fish that make for fabulous snorkeling. You may spot humpback whales from September to December, and dolphins surfing the waves anytime. The island is also home to 10,000 **quokkas,** cute otterlike marsupials that reach up to your knees. A wonderful thing about Rottnest is that there are no cars. Everyone gets around by bike (or bus, if you tire of pedaling). The island is 11 kilometers (7 miles) long and 4.5 kilometers (3 miles) across at its widest point.

ESSENTIALS

GETTING THERE   **Boat Torque** (☎ 1800/368 686 or 08/9221 5844) and **Oceanic Cruises** (☎ 08/9325 1191) each operate services at least three times a day from Perth (trip time: about 1 hr., 45 min.), and as many as six times a day from Fremantle (trip time: about 25 min.). The **Rottnest Express** ferry (☎ 08/9335 6406) runs four or five times a day from Fremantle only. Typical round-trip fares from Perth are A$50 (U.S.$32.50), or it's A$34 (U.S.$22.10) round-trip from Fremantle. This includes a free coach pickup from your Perth hotel for Perth departures. You pay about A$5 (U.S.$3.25) more if you return on a later day. Most boat operators offer day-trip and accommodation packages.

   Kookaburra Air (☎ 08/9354 1158) does half-day, full-day, and 2-day trips, on either a fly/fly or a fly/cruise basis, departing Jandakot Airport, a 20-minute drive from downtown Perth. Return pickups from your hotel are included, but tours are not; you spend your time on the island however you wish. A full-day fly/fly trip costs $150 (U.S.$97.50) per adult, and A$75 (U.S.$48.75) per child ages 3 to 12.

VISITOR INFORMATION   For information before you arrive, write to the **Rottnest Island Authority,** E Shed, Victoria Quay, Fremantle, WA 6160 (☎ 08/9432 9300; www.rottnest.wa.gov.au). The **Rottnest Island Visitor Centre** (☎ 08/9372 9752) is right at the end of the jetty.

GETTING AROUND   Ferries pull into the jetty in the main town, called "Settlement" at Thomson Bay. **Bell-A-Bike Rottnest** (☎ 08/9292 5105), next to the Rottnest Hotel near the jetty, rents 2,300 bikes in every size, speed, and type imaginable, as well as holders for everything from surfboards to babies. An 18-speed bike is A$18 (U.S.$11.70) for a 9-hour day (plus an A$25 (U.S.$16.25) refundable deposit), including a helmet (compulsory in Oz) and lock. There is no need to book a bike.

   The yellow **Bayseeker** bus does regular circumnavigations calling at all the best bays. An all-day ticket costs A$5 (U.S.$3.25) for adults, A$3 (U.S.$1.95) for seniors and students, A$2 (U.S.$1.30) children 4 to 12, and A$12 (U.S.$7.80) for families of four. Buy tickets on board.

   A free bus runs regularly between the airport and the five small communities around the island.

SNORKELING, DIVING, SURFING & FISHING

Most people come to Rottnest to snorkel, swim, surf, dive, or fish. As soon as you arrive, rent a bike and your preferred aquatic gear, and pedal around the coast until you come to a beach that suits you. (Don't forget to carry drinking water and food, because the only shops are at Settlement.) The Basin, Little Parakeet Bay, and Little

Island Orientation Tours

Many first-time visitors take the 2-hour **Island Bus Tour** because it is a good introduction to the bays and the island's cultural and natural history—and because it includes a stop to pet the quokkas. It costs A$12 (U.S.$7.80) for adults, A$9 (U.S.$5.85) for seniors and students, A$6 (U.S.$3.90) for kids 4 to 12, and A$32 (U.S.$20.80) families of four. Departure times vary, but you can expect them to run twice a day, usually around 10:30am and 1:30pm. Buy tickets from the Visitor Centre.

Salmon Bay are good snorkel spots. The Visitor Centre sells A$5 (U.S.$3.25) maps to suggested snorkel trails in 20 bays. Surfers should try Cathedral Rocks or Strickland Bay. Fishermen will catch squid, salmon, and tailor, as well as all kinds of reef fish. **Rottnest Malibu Diving** (☎ 08/9292 5111), near the jetty, rents snorkel gear, dive gear, wet suits, surfboards, body boards, aqua-bikes, and fishing tackle. The company conducts trips to some of the 100-plus dive sites around Rottnest. Some feature lime-stone caverns and some of the island's 14 shipwrecks. A shore or boat dive with all gear included is A$60.50 (U.S.$39.30). If you have never dived before but want to try, a 1- to 2-hour theory lesson followed by a boat dive is A$121 (U.S.$78.65).

FOR HISTORY BUFFS

Rottnest has quite a bit to offer history buffs, who may want to walk (45-min. trip), cycle, or take the train to the Oliver Hill 1930s gun emplacements, which has intact 9.2-inch guns and battery tunnels housing an engine room, a plotting room, and observation posts. You can explore the 1.5-kilometer (1-mile) heritage trail on your own (buy a map from the Visitor Centre for a dollar or so), or take a guided 1-hour tour on the hour between 11am and 2pm inclusive. The train fare, which includes the tour except for the last trip of the day, costs A$9 (U.S.$5.85) for adults, A$6 (U.S.$3.90) for seniors and students, A$4.50 (U.S.$2.95) for children 4 to 12, and A$24 (U.S.$15.60) for families of four. It departs from the station near the Visitor Centre hourly from 10:30am to 2:30pm inclusive.

Volunteer guides run free 1-hour historical walking tours of architectural points of interest around Thomson Bay, many of them built in the 19th century, like the Gov-ernor's residence, the chapel, the octagonal prison, the small museum (open daily from 11am to 4pm), and the former Boys' Reformatory. They depart from the Environment Office at 11:30am and 2:30pm daily. Another 1-hour heritage trail takes you to the memorial marking de Vlamingh, the Dutch explorer who named the island Rott Enest (Rat Nest) in 1696 when he mistook quokkas for varmints. Self-guiding maps to both these trails are sold at the Visitor Centre for a dollar or two.

ACCOMMODATIONS & DINING

Call the **Rottnest Island Authority's accommodation booking service** (☎ 08/ 9432 9111) to book one of the island's 250-plus holiday homes, apartments, cabins, historic cottages, or the campground. Don't expect anything too new or upscale. Water and electricity restrictions mean no accommodation is air-conditioned. Book well in advance all through summer and during Western Australian school vacations.

Apart from the good restaurants at the hotels listed below and a couple of lackluster take-out joints, your only other dining option is the excellent DOME cafe at the jetty.

Shoulder season is usually April to May, and again from September to November or December. Winter is June to August.

Rottnest Hotel. Rottnest Island, WA 6161. ☎ **08/9292 5011.** Fax 08/9292 5188. 18 units (all with shower only). TV. Summer A$165–$185 (U.S.$107.25–$120.25) double; shoulder A$120–$140 (U.S.$78–$91) double; winter A$100–$120 (U.S.$65–$78) double. Rates include continental breakfast. Extra person A$40 (U.S.$26). AE, BC, DC, MC, V.

This appealing 1864 building near the jetty, once the state governor's summer resi-dence, is now the local pub where day-trippers gather in the sports bar, the upscale restaurant, or the large open-air beer garden to admire the ocean views over an ale or two. The building contains pleasant, modern, motel-style rooms renovated 4 years ago, some with a small patio and sea views. The rooms here, or the Lakeside units at Rottnest Lodge, below, are the pick of the places to stay on the island.

Rottnest Lodge Resort. Rottnest Island, WA 6161. ☎ **08/9292 5161.** Fax 08/9292 5158. www.rottnestlodge.com.au. E-mail: lodge@rottnestlodge.com.au. 80 units (all with shower only). TV TEL. High season (approx. Dec 20–Jan 30) rate on application; expect to pay more than A$200 (U.S.$130) double. Shoulder (Feb–Apr and Sept–Dec) A$175–$230 (U.S.$113.75–$149.50) double. Winter (May to early Sept) A$140–$185 (U.S.$91–$120.25) double. Additional person A$45 (U.S.$29.25) extra. AE, BC, DC, MC, V.

The Lakeside Units at this former colonial barracks and Aboriginal prison are Rottnest's most luxurious accommodation, with flagstone floors, cream painted brick walls, bright furnishings, and a living area. Some have salt-lake views, not always pretty when the water dries up. The remaining Deluxe, Standard, and Family rooms, which sleep from 2 to 10, are of a much lesser standard, mostly dark, viewless, and small. You are just a few minutes' stroll from the jetty and Visitor Centre. There is a decent restaurant, and a small, pretty swimming pool.

IN PURSUIT OF THE GRAPE IN THE SWAN VALLEY
20km (13 miles) NE of Perth

Twenty minutes from the city center is the Swan Valley, home to two of Australia's best wine labels. In all there are 30 or so wineries along with wildlife parks, antique shops, a few art and craft galleries, several good restaurants, and Australia's best golf resort. Some restaurants and wineries close Monday and Tuesday.

Lord Street from the Perth city center becomes Guildford Road and takes you to Guildford at the start of the Swan Valley. The **Swan Valley Visitor Information Centre** is in the Guildford Village Potters Studio at 22 Meadow St., Guildford (☎ **08/9279 9859;** www.swanvalley-holiday.com.au). It's open Monday through Friday 9:30am to 3pm, and Saturday and Sunday 9:30am to 4pm. Several companies (see "Whale-Watching Cruises, Tram Trips & Other Tours," above) run day cruises from Perth.

TOURING THE WINERIES & OTHER THINGS TO DO

Most Swan wineries are small family-run affairs, but an exception is **Houghton's,** Dale Road, Middle Swan (☎ **08/9274 5100**). This is Western Australia's oldest, biggest, and most venerable winery. The big-beamed timber cellar has old wine-making machinery on show, and there are beautiful picnic grounds (especially nice in Nov when mauve jacaranda trees blossom), a cafe, and an art gallery selling works by local artists. The other big-name winery is **Sandalford,** 3210 W. Swan Rd., Caversham (☎ **08/9274 5922**). It has a gift shop and pleasant vine-covered cafe; by the time you read this, it may be conducting tours at a fee. Both wineries' cellar doors are open daily for free tastings from 10am to 5pm.

If you have kids, stop at the **Caversham Wildlife Park,** Arthur Street, West Swan (☎ **08/9274 2202**). You can stroke koalas (but not hold them, because the owner believes it stresses them), feed kangaroos, pet farm animals, take a camel ride for A$4.50 (U.S.$2.95), and gawk at 200 species of mostly Western Australian wildlife. It's open daily 9am to 5pm. Admission is A$10 (U.S.$6.50) for adults, A$8 (U.S.$5.20) for seniors and students, and A$4.50 (U.S.$2.95) for children 2 to 14.

Lovers of old stuff should browse the junk-shop strip on **James Street, in Guildford** (most shops are open daily), or visit **Woodbridge,** a beautifully restored and furnished 1883 manor house at Ford Street, in West Midland (☎ **08/9274 2432**). The house is open to the public Monday through Saturday (closed Wed) 1 to 4pm, and Sunday and public holidays 11am to 5pm; closed all July for restorative maintenance, and Christmas, Boxing Day (Dec 26) and Good Friday. Admission is A$3.50 (U.S.$2.30) for adults, A$1.50 (U.S.$1) for seniors and school-age children, and A$8 (U.S.$5.20) for a family. Its tearoom opens at noon.

Ladies, one of Perth's best boutiques, **the Swan Valley Boutique** (☎ 08/9377 2070) is in the unlikely location of 4 Johnson St., Guildford; it serves coffee while you try on clothes by big-name Aussie fashion designers.

ACCOMMODATIONS

The Swan is too close to Perth to *require* an overnight stay, but you may want to treat yourself at one of these properties.

✪ **Hansons Swan Valley.** 60 Forest Rd., Henley Brook, WA 6055. ☎ **08/9296 3366.** Fax 08/9296 3332. www.members.iinet.net.au/~hansons. E-mail: hansons@iinet.net.au. 10 units (6 with Jacuzzis and shower, 4 with shower only). A/C MINIBAR TV TEL. A$155–$220 (U.S.$100.75–$143) double. Rates include full breakfast. AE, BC, DC, MC, V. Take West Swan Rd. to Henley Brook and turn right at Little River Winery into Forrest St. Hansons is on the left at the end of the road. No children under 15.

"At last!" some of you will cry as you step into the sleek entry hall—it's a B&B that's not down-on-the-farm hokey or drowning in chintz. Instead, these rooms have stark white walls and groovy furniture à la Philippe Starck. All rooms have bathrobes, VCRs, and minibars stocked with cheeses, chocolates, and other goodies. Former advertising executives Jon and Selina Hanson purpose-built their house to create a slick B&B of the kind they would like to stay in themselves, and it works. The house is set on a 10-hectare (25-acre) farm and has a small swimming pool. It also has great breakfasts and dinners. No smoking indoors.

Novotel Vines Resort. Verdelho Dr., Belhus near Upper Swan, WA 6069. ☎ **1300/ 65 6565** in Australia, 800/221 4542 in the U.S. and Canada, 020/8283 4500 in the U.K., 0800/44 4422 in New Zealand, or 08/9297 3000. Fax 08/9297 3333. www.vines.com.au. E-mail: novotelvines@bigpond.com. 103 units. A/C MINIBAR TV TEL. A$189–$403 (U.S.$122.85–$261.95) double, A$273 (U.S.$177.45) 2-bedroom apt, A$383 (U.S.$248.95) 3-bedroom apt. Extra person A$27.50 (U.S.$17.90). Children under 16 stay free in parents' room with existing bedding. Ask about packages. AE, BC, DC, JCB, MC, V. Take West Swan Rd. to the Upper Swan and turn left on to Millhouse Rd. The resort entrance is about 1.5 kilometers (1 mile) on the right.

This upscale rural retreat was rated the best golf resort in Australia by *Golf Australia* magazine in 2000. Every room or apartment in the low-rise accommodation has a balcony looking onto the two picturesque 18-hole courses where kangaroos often join the players. The rooms are too stiff and citified for my taste, but the facilities are good—day/night tennis courts and squash courts, a gym, a large swimming pool and sundeck, a children's pool, a Jacuzzi, a brasserie, and a formal restaurant.

DINING

✪ **Hansons** dining room (see "Accommodations," above) is only a small room at the rear of the house, but the flavors are big. It is open to the public daily from 8 to 10:30am and from 7pm until late. Main courses, such as veal medallions in a bagna cauda sauce of parsley, garlic, and anchovies, average A$25 (U.S.$16.25). Breakfast is a gourmet à la carte menu. Reservations are a good idea.

✪ **Lamont's.** 85 Bisdee Rd., Millendon near Upper Swan. ☎ **08/9296 4485.** Reservations recommended, especially for dinner. Main courses A$21.50–$25 (U.S.$14–$16.25). AE, BC, DC, MC, V. Wed–Sun 10am–5pm and Sat 6:30pm–late. Closed for 2 weeks from Dec 24. Take the Great Northern Hwy. to Baskerville near Upper Swan, take a right onto Haddrill Rd. for 1.6 kilometers (1 mile), right onto Moore Rd. for 1 kilometer (just over 1/2 mile), and right onto Bisdee Rd. MODERN AUSTRALIAN.

This highly regarded restaurant is housed in a rustic timber building at Lamont Winery. Full-flavored main courses such as roast lamb fillet with a mustard crust in a spinach and sweet-potato salad with honey vinaigrette, and gutsy desserts such as warm chocolate pudding with chocolate sauce and vanilla ice cream, ensure that lots of regulars make the drive from Perth. Marron, a local crustacean, is a specialty. A gallery on the grounds shows Western Australian art and crafts.

YORK: TAKING A STEP BACK IN HISTORY
97km (60 miles) E of Perth

The state's first inland settlement, this peaceful National Trust–classified village on the Avon River oozes charm from an unspoiled Victorian streetscape. There are lovely B&Bs, historic buildings of stone wrapped by wrought-iron lace verandas, art galleries, a rose garden, a medley of museums including one housing a A$30 million (U.S.$19.5 million) display of vintage cars, and one of the state's finest jarrah furniture shops. The rolling green hills (well, green for hot, dry Australia) round about are lovely. Bring a picnic and enjoy it on the shady grass by the river.

From downtown Perth, take Lord Street, which becomes Guildford Road, to Midland, where it becomes the Great Eastern Highway. Follow this for a further 32 kilometers (20 miles) to The Lakes, then take the York turnoff right onto the Great Southern Highway for 47 kilometers (29 miles). The whole drive takes about 75 minutes. **Westrail** (☎ **13 10 53** in Western Australia, 1800/099 150 from interstate, or 08/9326 2222) runs a daily coach service from Perth for A$9.70 (U.S.$6.30) adults, A$4.85 (U.S.$3.15) children under 16, one-way. Check ahead if you plan to travel on a public holiday or during Western Australian school vacations, because schedules sometimes change then.

The **York Tourist Bureau** is within the Town Hall, Avon Terrace at Joaquina Street, York, WA 6302 (☎ **08/9641 1301;** www.yorkwa.com.au.). It's open daily 9am to 5pm.

EXPLORING THE TOWN

Just wandering the streets is the best way to soak up the charm of York's old buildings, like the faithfully restored railway station, the impressive Town Hall (built in 1911), the library, the convent, old pubs like the York and the Castle, St. Patrick's church, the Uniting Church, the Holy Trinity Church (with its lovely stained-glass windows), the fire station, and the old hospital. Among the sights worth seeing is the **Old Gaol and Court House,** 132 Avon Terrace (☎ **08/9641 2072**), housing a colonial-era courtroom still in use, cells, stables, and a simple trooper's cottage. It's open Monday to Friday 11am to 4pm, and weekends and public holidays from 10am to 4pm, although these times can vary because the staff are volunteers; closed Christmas and Good Friday. Admission is A$3 (U.S.$1.95) for adults, A$1.50 (U.S.$1) for seniors and children under 14, and A$7.50 (U.S.$4.90) for families.

The short walk out of town to the excellent **Residency Museum,** Brook Street (☎ **08/9641 1751**), is well worth it for its displays of everything from prayer books, children's toys, needlework, and old kitchenware to antique furniture, farm tools, and other memorabilia of life in York in days gone by. It's open Tuesday to Thursday and public holidays from 1 to 3pm, Saturday and Sunday from noon to 4pm, and also Monday to Friday from 1 to 3pm during school vacations (times vary because the staff are volunteers; closed Christmas and Good Friday). Admission is A$2 (U.S.$1.30) for adults and A$1 (U.S.65¢) for children ages 5 to 16.

If you visit on a Friday, Saturday, Sunday, or Monday (10am to 4:30pm) in autumn or spring (usually the end of Sept to early Dec, and late Mar to early June), you can explore the evolution of the rose at the **Avon Valley Historical Rose Garden** (☎ **08/ 9641 1469**), 2 kilometers (1¼ miles) out of town on Osnaburg Road. Admission is A$4 (U.S.$2.60) adults, free for children under 15.

Of the several special-interest museums in York, the ❂ **York Motor Museum,** 116–124 Avon Terrace (☎ **08/9641 1288**), is the most spectacular. Among the 150 or so veteran, vintage, classic, and racing vehicles and motorcycles on display are the world's first car (an 1886 Benz), a 1904 Napier, and the Williams Formula 1 car in which Aussie Alan Jones won the world championship in 1980. The museum is open daily from 9:30am to 4pm. Admission is A$6 (U.S.$3.90) for adults, A$5 (U.S.$3.25) for seniors, and A$3 (U.S.$1.95) for children under 12.

Take a peek at the superb craftsmanship at ❂ **Jah-Roc Furniture** (☎ **08/9641 2522**) in the wonderful Old Flour Mill on Broome Street, even if you can't afford tens of thousands of dollars for a dining table handcrafted from a single slab of recycled jarrah. The showroom is open daily from 10am to 5pm.

ACCOMMODATIONS

❂ **Hillside Country Retreat.** Forrest St., York, WA 6302. ☎ **08/9641 1065.** Fax 08/9641 2417. E-mail: hillside@avon.net.au. 6 units (all with shower only). A/C TV. A$130 (U.S.$84.50) double. Rates include full breakfast. No credit cards.

When a U.S. diplomat stayed at this adorable historic homestead a few years ago, he said he'd never seen so much stuff in one place. He was referring to the old pogo sticks, farm machinery, wooden ice skates, original radios, old road signs, 1910 washing machine, and countless other relics of a bygone era that grace every spare inch of wall and floor space. So intrigued are guests by all this history that the owners conduct free tours after breakfast of the grand front rooms, likewise stocked with old books, precious china, and much besides. Each individually furnished room has a potbelly stove, VCR, hair dryer, and minifridge, and you get treated to fresh flowers in your room, complimentary port, sherry, chocolates, plunger coffee, and a daily newspaper. Whether you stay in the homestead or in the rustic mud-brick servants' quarters, your room has pretty antique furnishings. There is a tennis court and a small private pool. Breakfast is served in the garden from a deliciously quaint pagoda called the Morris Edwards Tea and Ginger Beer House. No smoking indoors.

NEW NORCIA: A TOUCH OF EUROPE IN AUSTRALIA
132km (83 miles) N of Perth

It's the last thing you expect to see in the Australian bush—a Benedictine monastery town with elegant European architecture, a fine museum, and a collection of Renaissance art—but New Norcia is no mirage. Boasting a population of 55 (when everyone's at home, that is), this pretty town and the surrounding 8,000-hectare (19,760-acre) farm were established in 1846 by Spanish Benedictine missionaries. Visitors can tour beautifully frescoed chapels, marvel at one of the finest religious art collections in Australia, stock up on famous New Norcia nutcake straight from the monastery's 120-year-old wood-fired ovens, and attend prayers with the 18 monks who live here.

New Norcia is an easy 2-hour drive from Perth. From downtown, take Lord Street, which becomes Guildford Road, to Midland; here join the Great Northern Highway to New Norcia. **Westrail** (☎ **13 10 53** in Western Australia, 1800/099 150 from interstate, or 08/9326 2222) runs a coach service Sunday, Tuesday, and Thursday from Perth for A$13 (U.S.$8.45) one-way. Check ahead if you plan to travel on a public holiday or during Western Australian school vacations, because schedules sometimes change then. **Greyhound Pioneer** (☎ **13 20 30** in Australia) coaches run from Perth Friday and Sunday, arriving at 5:20pm. The fare is A$37.40 (U.S.$24.30). Day tours from Perth are available. There is no train.

Conference groups can book the town solid, so reserve accommodations and tours in advance, especially in wildflower season from August to October.

You can get information at the **New Norcia Tourist Information Centre,** New Norcia, WA 6509 (☎ **08/9654 8056;** www.newnorcia.wa.edu.au), in the Museum and Art Gallery, just off the highway behind St. Joseph's, beside the Trading Post and Roadhouse. Its hours are those of the museum and gallery (see below).

EXPLORING THE TOWN & MONASTERY

The New Norcia Tourist Information Centre's intriguing 2-hour ✪ **walking tours** are a must. Tickets cost A$10 (U.S.$6.50) for adults and A$5 (U.S.$3.25) for children 12 to 17, free for younger children. Tours depart daily except Christmas at 11am and 1:30pm, and they allow time for you to attend prayers with the monks if you wish. The guide strolls you around some of the town's 27 National Trust–classified buildings and gives an insight into the monks' lifestyle. You will also see the delightful frescoes in the old monastery chapel and in St. Ildephonsus's and St. Gertrude's colleges. Much of the monastery is closed to visitors, but the tour does show you the fruit gardens and a glimpse of the men-only courtyard. Heritage walking-trail maps sold for A$3 (U.S.$1.95) at the Tourist Information Centre include more buildings not visited on the tour, such as the octagonal apiary.

The ✪ **museum and art gallery** is full of relics from the monks' past—old mechanical and musical instruments, artifacts from the days when New Norcia was an Aboriginal mission, gifts to the monks from the Queen of Spain, and an astounding collection of paintings by Spanish and Italian artists. The oldest I saw was dated 1492. Give yourself at least an hour here, easily more. The museum and gallery are open daily 9:30am to 5pm August through October, and 10am to 4:30pm November through July (closed Christmas). Admission is A$4 (U.S.$2.60) for adults, A$3 (U.S.$1.95) for seniors and students, and A$1 (U.S.65¢) for children 6 to 12.

Apart from joining the monks for 15-minute prayers in the monastery five times a day (midday and 2:30pm are the most convenient for day visitors), you can join them for Mass in the Holy Trinity Abbey Church Monday through Saturday at 7:30am and on Sunday at 9am.

ACCOMMODATIONS & DINING

New Norcia Hotel. Great Northern Hwy., New Norcia, WA 6509. ☎ **08/9654 8034.** Fax 08/9654 8011. 17 units (1 only with bathroom). A$60 (U.S.$39) double without bathroom, A$85 (U.S.$55.25) double with bathroom. Extra person A$10 (U.S.$6.50). AE, BC, MC, V.

When they thought a Spanish royal visit to New Norcia was imminent in 1926, the monks built this grandiose white hotel fit for, well, a king. Sadly, the royals never materialized, and the building fell into disrepair. Only the grand central staircase, soaring pressed-metal ceilings, and imposing Iberian facade hint at the splendor that was. Two years ago, new carpets, curtains, beds, and hair dryers were put in, but be prepared for rather grim rooms. Only one has an en suite, air-conditioning, and a TV. Still, it's kinda nice to eat a meal at the rather-dated bar (or take your plate into the charmingly faded Dining Room) and to sit on the football-sized front veranda upstairs. The bar gets jumping on Friday and Saturday nights when local farmers come to town. This is the only place to stay in town.

3 Margaret River & the Southwest: Wine Tasting in Australia's Prettiest Corner

Margaret River: 290km (181 miles) S of Perth

Say "Margaret River" to Australians and they reply "great wine!" with their eyes all lit up. The area's 38 wineries nestle among statuesque forests of karri, the world's third-tallest tree. The wineries contribute only around 1% to Australia's wine output, yet

---

Every February or March, **Leeuwin Estate Winery** (☎ **08/9757 6253;** www.leeuwinestate.com.au) stages a spectacular ✪ **outdoor concert** starring some leading showbiz light (Shirley Bassey, Julio Iglesias, or Diana Ross are past performers), attended by 6,000 picnicking guests. Tickets are A$104.50 (U.S.$67.95). This is a *big* local event, so book months ahead.

The Margaret River Wine Region Festival runs over a week in November.

---

they turn out 10% of the country's top-notch "premium" wines. Not even most Aussies know about the Southwest's other drawing cards, though—like the spectacular surf breaks on the 130-kilometer (81-mile) coast from Cape Naturaliste in the north to Cape Leeuwin on the southwest tip of Australia; the coastal cliffs, perfect for abseiling and rock climbing; and the honeycomb of limestone caves filled with stalagmites and stalactites. Whales pass by from June through December, wildflowers line the roads August through October, and wild birds, kangaroos, and cute shingleback lizards are everywhere. If you like hiking, pack your boots, because there are plenty of trails, from a 15-minute stroll around Margaret River township, to a ✪ **6-day Cape-to-Cape trek** along the sea cliffs. The Southwest is truly one of Australia's last great wildernesses, and one of my favorite parts of the country.

Like wine regions the world over, the Southwest has more than its fair share of cozy B&Bs, art and craft galleries, and some super restaurants. Plan to stay at least 2 days.

ESSENTIALS

GETTING THERE   It's a 3¹/₂-hour drive to Margaret River from Perth; take the inland South Western Highway (the quickest route) or the tad more scenic Old Coast Road to Bunbury, where you pick up the Bussell Highway to Margaret River.

Maroomba Airlines (☎ **1800/677 747** in Western Australia, or 08/9478 3850) flies to Margaret River from Perth once or twice daily, Monday to Friday only, in a 10-seater plane. The fare is A$200 (U.S.$130) round-trip, or A$169 (U.S.$109.85) for a 7-day advance-purchase ticket. After the baggage limit of 10 kilograms, excess luggage is charged at A80¢ per kilo. **Leeuwin Estate** winery (book through it Fremantle office ☎ **08/9430 4099**) does "Flying Visit" day and overnight trips from Perth. A day trip including return flights, three-course à la carte lunch at its excellent restaurant (wine costs extra), winery tour and tasting, and a district tour costs A$297 (U.S.$193.70) per person.

Southwest Coachlines (☎ **08/9324 2333**) runs a daily service, and two on weekends, to Margaret River from Perth for A$23 (U.S.$14.95). **Westrail** (☎ **13 10 53** in Western Australia, 1800/099 150 in Australia from interstate, or 08/9326 2222) runs a daily train from Perth to Bunbury with coach connections to Margaret River (taking just over 4¹/₂ hours), and a separate all-coach service from Perth, once or twice a day every day except Saturday. Westrail's coach service takes over 5 hours, and you transfer by local bus (which does not run Sun or public holidays) to a different coach in Bunbury. Fares are A$24.50 (U.S.$15.95) with either mode. Westrail schedules can differ on a public holiday or during Western Australian school vacations.

VISITOR INFORMATION   You will pass many wineries before you get to Margaret River township, but it's worth heading first to the **Augusta Margaret River Tourism Association** information center to pick up a winery guide. It's on the Bussell Highway at Tunbridge Street, Margaret River, WA 6285 (☎ **08/9757 2911;** www.margaretriverwa.com). It is open daily 9am to 5pm.

GETTING AROUND   Nine kilometers (5.5 miles) past Busselton, which marks the start of the Southwest, the Bussell Highway makes a sharp left and heads south among the wineries through Vasse, 25 kilometers (15¹/₂ miles) on through the tiny village of Cowaramup, 11 kilometers (7 miles) farther through Margaret River proper, and a farther 43 kilometers (27 miles) on to windswept Cape Leeuwin and the tiny fishing port of Augusta.

A car is close to essential. **Avis** (☎ **1800/679 880** within Australia for reservations in the Southwest, or 08/9757 3686 for the Margaret River office) has offices in Bunbury, Busselton, and Margaret River.

Margaret River Tour Company (☎ **0419/91 7166**) and **Milesaway Tours** (☎ **1800/818 102** in Australia, or 08/9754 2929) run sightseeing, adventure, and winery tours from Margaret River.

TOURING THE WINERIES

Fans of premium wines (and who isn't?) will have a field day in the Southwest. Cabernet sauvignon and merlot are the star red varieties, while Chardonnay, semillon, and sauvignon blanc are the pick of the bunch among whites. Most wineries offer free tastings from 10am to 4:30pm daily.

The "big three" are **Cape Mentelle,** 4 kilometers (2.5 miles) west of Margaret River on Wallcliffe Road (☎ **08/9757 3266**); ✪ **Leeuwin Estate,** Stevens Road, Margaret River (☎ **08/9757 6253**); and **Vasse Felix,** Caves Road at Harman's Road South, Cowaramup (☎ **08/9755 5242**). Leeuwin Estate in particular has a towering reputation, especially for Chardonnay. It does interesting winery tours three times a day. A relative newcomer, **Voyager Estate,** Stevens Road, Margaret River (☎ **08/9757 6358**), has exquisite rose gardens around a South African Cape Dutch–style cellar and does a highly drinkable shiraz grenache. Other good labels to look for are Arlewood Estate, Cullen Willyabrup Wines, Evans & Tate, Fermoy Estate, Lenton Brae, and Sandalford Wines.

BEYOND THE WINERIES: CAVES, BUSH TUCKER & MORE

Five of the Southwest's 350 or so limestone caves are open to the public, all with elaborate stalactite formations. Before or after you visit one, call at the excellent **CaveWorks** eco-interpretive center at Lake Cave, Caves Road, 15 kilometers (9 miles) south of Wallcliffe Road (☎ **08/9757 7411**), open daily except Christmas from 9am to 5pm. Entry is free if you tour Lake, Jewel, Mammoth, or Moondyne caves, or else A$5 (U.S.$3.25) for adults, A$3 (U.S.$1.95) for children ages 4 to 16.

Lake Cave, right outside CaveWorks and 300 steps down an ancient sinkhole, contains a tranquil pond in which exquisite stalactites are reflected. A few minutes north along Caves Road is **Mammoth Cave,** where you can inspect the fossilized jaw of a baby zygotaurus trilobus, an extinct giant wombat. **Jewel Cave,** 8 kilometers (5 miles)

A Wine-Buying Tip

The place to buy wine if you want to take it out of Australia is the **Margaret River Regional Wine Centre,** 9 Bussell Hwy., Cowaramup (☎ **08/9755-5501**), because most wineries don't deliver internationally. It stocks every local wine, does daily tastings of select vintages, sells maps and winery guides, and has an expert staff to help you purchase wisely, and even tailor your day's foray. It is open Monday through Saturday 10am to 8pm, and Sunday noon to 6pm (closed Christmas and Good Friday). Order off its Web site at www.mrwines.com.

north of Augusta on Caves Road, is the prettiest. Tours of Lake and Jewel and self-guided tours of Mammoth cost A$13 (U.S.$8.45) each for adults, A$5 (U.S.$3.25) for children 4 to 16. A 7-day Grand Pass to all three plus CaveWorks saves you money. Mammoth is open from 9am to 5pm (last tour at 4pm); tours of Lake and Jewel run hourly from 9:30am to the last tour at 3:30pm. Sometimes extra tours are scheduled in school vacations. The caves are open every day except Christmas. Book tours through CaveWorks.

Just next to Jewel Cave is **Moondyne Cave,** an "adventure cave" where you get down and dirty crawling on your hands and knees, in the protective clothing supplied. This 2-hour experience costs A$25 (U.S.$16.25) for adults and A$18 (U.S.$11.70) for kids 10 to 16 (kids under 10 are not permitted, and an adult must accompany kids). Tours depart daily at 2pm; book 24 hours ahead. Book through CaveWorks. A similar adventure tour taking about 3 hours is offered at **Ngilgi Cave,** Caves Road, Yallingup (☎ **08/9755 2152**), for A$35 (U.S.$22.75) for anyone over 14. It departs daily at 9:30am; book 24 hours ahead. Ngilgi's main chamber has beautiful translucent stalactite "shawls," which anyone can explore on a semiguided tour. This costs A$12 (U.S.$7.80) for adults and A$5 (U.S.$3.25) children 5 to 17, and runs half-hourly from 9:30am. The cave is open daily from 9:30am with the last tour at 3:30pm (4pm during school vacations, 4:30pm during Christmas school vacations).

You can pick your own kiwi, raspberries, and other fruit at **The Berry Farm,** 222 Bessell Rd. outside Margaret River (☎ **08/9757 5054**), or buy them ready-made as attractively packaged sparkling, dessert, and port wines; jams; and vinegars. The farm is open daily 10am to 4:30pm (closed Christmas, Boxing Day, New Year's Day, and Good Friday).

Art and craft galleries are thick on the ground in the Southwest. One of the most upscale is **Gunyulgup Galleries,** Gunyulgup Valley Drive near Yallingup (☎ **08/9755 2177**), which has top-of-the-line jewelry, glass, ceramics, and artworks.

Greg Miller of **Adventure Plus** (☎ **0419/961 716**) arranges all kinds of outdoor adventures from abseiling and rock climbing coastal cliffs, to caving, canoeing, hiking, and camping. He welcomes beginners. Prices vary with the activity; expect to pay around A$100 (U.S.$52) for a day's action. Plenty of hiking trails are suited to an afternoon's ramble. The tourist information center in Margaret River (see "Visitor Information") sells trail maps for a few dollars each, including maps to all the sections of the Cape-to-Cape cliff-edge walk from Cape Naturaliste to Cape Leeuwin.

Try to make time for one of two tours offered by ✪ **"Bushtucker Woman"** Helen Lee (☎ **0419/91 1971** or 9757 9084). On one tour, she has you canoeing up the

Scenic Drives & a Spectacular View

The picturesque 106-kilometer (66-mile) north–south drive along **Caves Road,** the length of the Southwest from Busselton in the north to Augusta on Cape Leeuwin in the south, is well worth doing.

Don't miss the magical ✪ **Boranup Drive,** a scenic detour off Caves Road through towering karris—although your rental car is not insured on its unpaved surface! It departs Caves Road 6 kilometers (3³/₄ miles) south of Mammoth Cave and rejoins it after a 14-kilometer (8³/₄-mile) meander. Near Augusta, a sweeping ocean view—sometimes even of seals, whales, and dolphins—awaits those who climb to the top of **Cape Leeuwin lighthouse.** It's open every day except Christmas 9am to 4pm (the stairs close 3:45pm). Entry is A$4 (U.S.$2.60) for adults and A$2 (U.S.$1.30) for children under 16.

river, exploring a cave, and eating smoked emu, grub pâté (I'm not kidding), and other Aboriginal delicacies on a river island. It runs from 10am to 2pm, and costs A$33 (U.S.$19) for adults and A$16.50 (U.S.$10.70) for kids. Highly recommended! Her **winery tour** has an alternative bent incorporating short karri-forest walks, insights into organic wine making, tastings at several wineries, a visit to Leeuwin Estate's herb garden, and a picnic lunch of bush tucker and local cheeses, hams, and dips. She'll teach you how vaporized peppermint oil from the native trees condenses on the grapes to create the distinctive flavor of Margaret River whites. The 5-hour tour departs at noon and costs A$44 (U.S.$28.60).

Surfing lessons from four-time Western Australian professional surfing champion ✪ **Josh Parmateer** (☎ **08/9757 3850** or 0418/958 264) are a must—take it from this surf virgin! Two-hour lessons in the gentle waist-deep surf at Prevelly Park Beach, 9 kilometers (5¹/₂ miles) west of Margaret River, run daily and cost A$80 (U.S.$52) per person, or A$30 (U.S.$19) per person if there are two of you. Josh supplies the boards and wet suits and a free round-trip pickup from your hotel. Lessons run October to June. If you are already a Master of the Surf Universe, try the legendary Smiths Beach or the Three Bears (Mama, Papa, and Baby) break at Yallingup, the double-barreled North Point at Gracetown, or the plentiful breaks at Prevelly Park. **Beach Life,** 117 Bussell Hwy., Margaret River (☎ **08/9757 2888**), rents boards for A$40 (U.S.$26) for 24 hours.

From June to December whales play just off-shore all along the coast. There is a whale lookout near the Cape Naturaliste lighthouse. Daily 3-hour whale-watching cruises with ✪ **Naturaliste Charters** (☎ **08/9755 2276**) depart June to September from Augusta. September to December, cruise departures switch to Dunsborough, where humpbacks rest their calves. Cruise costs were about to rise at press time; expect to pay around A$45 (U.S.$29.25) for adults and around A$30 (U.S.$19.50) for children 4 to 14. Children under 4 are free.

ACCOMMODATIONS

It's not the prettiest village in the Southwest, but Margaret River has the advantage of banks, a supermarket, and a few restaurants and shops. The blink-and-you'll-miss-it hamlet of Cowaramup is closer to more wineries and has a general store, a restaurant, and one or two interesting craft shops. Vasse is a tiny settlement at the northern edge of the Southwest. Some places may demand a minimum 2-night stay on weekends.

IN MARGARET RIVER

Basildene Manor. Lot 100 Wallcliffe Rd. (2km/1¹/₄ miles west of town), Margaret River, WA 6285. ☎ **08/9757 3140.** Fax 08/9757 3383. www.basildene.com.au. E-mail: stay@basildene.com.au. 17 units (all with shower only, 8 with Jacuzzis also). A/C TV TEL. A$181–$269 (U.S.$117.65–$174.85) double. Rates include full breakfast. AE, BC, DC, MC, V. No children under 15.

If we still lived in manor houses today, they would look like this lovely National Trust–classified farmhouse, built by the local lighthouse keeper in 1912 out of local stone. Following a supremely tasteful refurbishment in 1997 by friendly proprietors, Garry Nielsen and Julie Whittingham, it's now a gentrified B&B with plush bedrooms, gold-framed prints, and gorgeous flower arrangements. The bigger rooms have their own sitting areas and all have VCRs. Some lead off an impressive jarrah gallery overlooking the cozy "Main Hall" with its open fire; eight rooms added in 1999 have Jacuzzis. Hair dryers are available. A stylish cooked breakfast is served in the pretty conservatory overlooking the 14-acre grounds, and your hosts point you along a walking trail to spy on a mob of kangaroos. No smoking.

○ **Heritage Trail Lodge.** 31 Bussell Hwy. (400m north of town), Margaret River, WA 6285. ☎ **08/9757 9595.** Fax 08/9757 9596. www.heritage-trail-lodge.com.au. E-mail: enquiry@ heritage-trail-lodge.com.au. 10 units (all with shower and Jacuzzi). A/C MINIBAR TV TEL. A$198–$215 (U.S.$128.70–$139.75) double. Extra person A$30 (U.S.$19.50). Rates include continental breakfast. AE, BC, DC, MC, V.

Although they're on the highway and "in" Margaret River (within walking distance of restaurants), this cute row of salmon-pink cabin-style rooms, built in 1997, are huddled in a serene karri forest, out of sight of town. Inside, each spacious unit has king double or king twin beds and a fabulous double Jacuzzi (even the room with facilities for people with disabilities), from which you have a view of the forest. All but two have small decks backing onto a 35-minute bushwalk trail; the other two have balconies looking over the road into the bush. All have hair dryers, irons, and satellite TV to improve on Margaret River's poor reception. Welcoming proprietors Hugh and Maxine Beckingham serve up a delicious continental breakfast of cereals, Berry Farm jams, and local cheeses and breads in the sunny pine dining room. Roos even hop into the carpark sometimes. No smoking.

IN COWARAMUP

The Noble Grape. Lot 18, Bussell Hwy., Cowaramup, WA 6284. ☎ and fax **08/9755 5538.** www.babs.com.au/noblegrape. E-mail: noblegrape@netserv.net.au. 6 units (all with shower only). TV. A$99–$110 (U.S.$64.35–$71.50) double. Additional person A$22 (U.S.$14.30). Rates include continental breakfast. AE, BC, DC, MC, V.

English cottage gardens surround Louise and Chris Stokes's colonial-style B&B. Each well-maintained room is adorned with Australian antiques and has a modern bathroom, heating, ceiling fans, a comfy sitting area, and a small rear patio opening onto bird-filled trees. One caters to travelers with disabilities. Louise fixes a delicious breakfast buffet of homemade muffins, jams, muesli, yogurts, and plunger coffee every morning, and serves a cooked breakfast for an extra A$7 (U.S.$4.55). An inexpensive room-service menu is a welcome sight if you don't feel like dining out. Hair dryers are at reception. No smoking indoors.

IN VASSE

○ **Newtown House.** Bussell Hwy. (9km/5^1/$_2$ miles past Busselton), Vasse, WA 6280. ☎ and fax **08/9755 4485.** 4 units (all with shower only). MINIBAR TV. A$140 (U.S.$91) double. Rates include continental breakfast. AE, BC, DC, MC, V. The property is on the right just after the Bussell Hwy. turns left (south).

Set in lavender and rose gardens, this National Trust–listed 1851 homestead has four pretty rooms with "contemporary country" decor, furnished with wrought-iron table and chairs, pine furniture, and cute touches like potpourri "dream sacks" on your pillow. The fixings for a gourmet continental breakfast are sent up to your room the night before. Wander out back to chat with the resident painter in the barn-cum-studio, and don't miss the excellent restaurant (see "Dining," below). No smoking.

DINING

Good restaurants are attached to a number of wineries, including Vasse Felix, Amberley Estate, Driftwood Estate, and Brookland Valley Vineyard. Of all of them, the restaurant at **Leeuwin Estate,** Stevens Road, Margaret River (☎ **08/9757 6253**), is probably the best.

Stock up for a picnic at the supermarket in Margaret River. Cape Mentelle and Vasse Felix both have green shady picnic areas beside a brook.

✪ **Newtown House.** Bussell Hwy. (9km/5^1/$_2$ miles past Busselton), Vasse. ☎ **08/ 9755 4485.** Reservations recommended. Main courses A$9.50–$18 (U.S.$6.20–$11.70) at lunch, A$22.50–$26 (U.S.$14.65–$16.90) at dinner. AE, BC, DC, MC, V. Tues–Sat 10am–4:30pm and 6pm–late. MODERN FRENCH/AUSTRALIAN.

The Southwest boasts some of the best restaurants in Australia, and this is one of 'em. Folks come from far and wide to savor chef Stephen Reagan's skill in preparing such dishes as rare local venison with roast pears, beetroot, and red wine glaze. Desserts are no letdown, either—caramel soufflé with lavender ice cream and hot caramel sauce is typical. Located in a historic homestead, the restaurant consists of two simple, intimate rooms with sisal matting and contemporary, boldly colored walls. Even better, it's BYO.

The Valley Café. Carters Rd. (near Caves Rd.), Margaret River. ☎ **08/9757 3225.** Reservations recommended. Main courses A$16–$22.50 (U.S.$10.40–$14.65). Seafood market price. AE, BC, DC, MC, V. Daily 8:30am–4pm, Fri–Sat (and Sun on 3-day weekends) 6–10pm. MODERN AUSTRALIAN.

Voted most popular Southwest cafe in 1999, this pleasant place serves up stylish breakfasts, lunches, and dinners with views over the surrounding countryside. Lunch might be crispy squid salad, or risotto with Augusta smoked chicken, sun-dried capsicum (bell pepper), and shaved parmesan. Dinner might be cured Atlantic salmon with polenta, asparagus, and caramelized balsamic vinegar. BYO.

4 The Goldfields

595km (372 miles) E of Perth

After Paddy Hannan struck gold in 1893, the wheat-belt town of Kalgoorlie found itself sitting on the "Golden Mile," the richest square mile of gold-bearing earth in the world, at the time. Today ✪ **Kalgoorlie** (pop. 33,000) is still an Outback gold-rush boomtown, a mixture of yesteryear charm and 21st-century corporate gold fever. The town is perched literally on the edge of the Super Pit, the world's biggest open-cut gold mine currently 4.5 kilometers (3 miles) long, 1.5 kilometers (1 mile) wide, and 290 meters (951 ft.) deep. It yields around 680,000 ounces of the precious yellow stuff every year—a mere 1,863 ounces *a day.* An estimated 30 million ounces is still in the ground. Hardly surprisingly, **Kalgoorlie Consolidated Gold Mines,** which operates the pit, is Australia's biggest gold producer.

Walking down the wide streets fronted with wrought-iron lace verandas is like stumbling onto a Western movie set. Countless bars still do the roaring trade they notched up in the 1890s—only now they serve besuited gold-mining executives from Adelaide and Perth.

Life on the Golden Mile is not so lively for everyone, however. Just down the road 39 kilometers (24 miles) is **Coolgardie** (pop. 1,400), another 1890s gold-rush boomtown where the gold ran out in 1963. The town's semi-abandoned air is a sad foil to Kalgoorlie's brash energy; but much of the lovely architecture remains, so you can just wander the gracious streets for a pleasant nostalgia buzz.

ESSENTIALS

GETTING THERE   Between them, **Ansett** (☎ **13 13 00** in Australia), its subsidiary **Skywest Airlines** (☎ **1800/642 225** in Australia, 08/9478 9999, or book through Ansett), and **Airlink** (book through Qantas at ☎ **13 13 13** in Australia) fly to Kalgoorlie from Perth many times a day. Airlink flies direct from Adelaide daily.

Fun Fact

In Kalgoorlie's young days, its streets were paved with a blackish spoil from the mining process called "tellurides." When someone realized tellurides contain up to 40% gold and 10% silver, those streets were ripped up in one big hurry. The city fathers had paved the streets with gold and didn't even know it!

Greyhound Pioneer (☎ **13 20 30** in Australia) makes the 8-hour trip daily from Perth for A$103.40 (U.S.$67.20). Greyhound's daily service from Adelaide takes around 24¹/₂ hours and costs A$229.90 (U.S.$149.45). **Goldrush Tours** (☎ **1800/ 62 0440** in Australia, or 08/9021 2954) runs an express coach service from Perth five times a week for $65.

Kalgoorlie is a stop on the 3-day ✪ *Indian–Pacific* train service, which runs between Sydney and Perth through Adelaide twice a week in both directions. See section 11, "Getting Around Australia," in chapter 2, for contact details. The *Prospector* train makes 11 trips a week from Perth to Kalgoorlie for A$49.30 (U.S.$32.05). Call **Westrail** (☎ **13 10 53** in Western Australia, 1800/099 150 in Australia from interstate, or 08/9326 2222).

From Perth, take the Great Eastern Highway. If you want to make the 2,182-kilometer (1,364-mile) journey on the Eyre Highway from Adelaide, which features the longest straight stretch of highway in the world on the mind-numbingly empty Nullarbor Plain, contact the South Australian or Western Australian state auto clubs listed under "Getting Around Australia," in chapter 2, for advice. There are only a handful of small towns and gas stops en route. I don't recommend this drive, because it's boring landscape most of the way.

VISITOR INFORMATION   The **Kalgoorlie-Boulder Tourist Centre,** 250 Hannan St., Kalgoorlie, WA 6430 (☎ **08/9021 1966;** www.kalgoorlieandwagoldfields.com.au), dispenses information on Kalgoorlie, Coolgardie, and outlying regions. Boulder is a suburb of Kalgoorlie. The center's walking-trail map to the town's architecture, which sells for a few dollars, is worth buying. The center is open Monday through Friday 8:30am to 5pm, and Saturday, Sunday, and public holidays 9am to 5pm. The **Coolgardie Tourist Bureau,** 62 Bayley St., Coolgardie, WA 6429 (☎ **08/9026 6090**), is open daily 9am to 5pm.

GETTING AROUND   **Avis** (☎ 08/9021 1722), **Budget** (☎ 08/9093 2300), **Hertz** (☎ 08/9093 2211), and **Osborne Thrifty** (☎ 08/9021 4722) have offices in Kalgoorlie.

The **Kalgoorlie Adventure Bus** runs daily service to Hannans North Historic Mining Reserve and the Super Pit for A$5 (U.S.$3.25) per person per attraction, round-trip. It also runs to other attractions around town every second day. Buy tickets at the Tourist Centre, above. The Tourist Centre also sells an exclusive A$12 (U.S.$7.80) round-trip taxi fare to Hannans North Historic Mining Reserve.

As well as offering coach, 4WD, and guided self-drive 2WD and 4WD bush tours of Kalgoorlie, Coolgardie, and outlying ghost towns, local tour operators will take you gold prospecting in outlying regions from half a day for up to several days.

WHAT TO SEE & DO

As you might guess, gold is a common thread running through many of the town's attractions. The best is ✪ **Hannans North Historic Mining Reserve,** Broad Arrow Road, 6 kilometers (3³/₄ miles) north of the Tourist Centre on the Goldfields Highway (☎ **08/9091 4074**), where you can venture underground to see what was once a working gold mine, pan for gold, watch a gold pour, watch the interesting video in a re-created miner's tent, and pore over an extensive collection of mining memorabilia, old shaft heads, machinery, and huts in a re-created miners' village. I think the exhibits are well done. Underground tours, pouring, and panning each take place three times a day, one after the other. The admission fee, which includes all activities, is A\$16.50 (U.S.\$10.75) for adults, A\$14.30 (U.S.\$9.30) for seniors and students, A\$8.25 (U.S.\$5.40) for school-age kids, and A\$41.80 (U.S.\$27.20) for a family. It is open daily 9am to 4:30pm (closed Christmas). Wear enclosed shoes, and allow 3 to 4 hours to see the lot. In late 2001, the reserve will expand to include a new Australian Prospectors and Miners Hall of Fame, focusing on prospecting, the business of mining, minerals, and mining's role in the economy.

The Museum of the Goldfields, 17 Hannan St. (☎ **08/9021 8533**), contains the first 400-ounce gold bar minted in town, the Western Australian State Gold Collection, and some interesting historical displays on the region. The museum is open daily from 10am to 4:30pm, closed Christmas and Good Friday. Admission is by donation. Allow an hour.

Don't leave town without ogling the awesome **Super Pit open-cut mine.** There is a lookout platform at Outram Street in Boulder, off the Goldfields Highway (called the Eastern Bypass Road on some maps). It is open daily from 6am to 7pm except when blasting closes it temporarily (check with the tourist center). Entry is free.

When they're not digging money out of the ground, hard-bitten locals gamble for it at the **Bush Two-Up School,** a rusty and roofless corrugated-iron ring among the eucalypts, 7 kilometers (4 miles) north of town on the Goldfields Highway. The game is a simple bet on the 50-50 chance of a penny landing heads or tails. The ring opens daily around 5pm to dusk, or later if the crowds are big (closed Christmas and Good Friday). Admission is free. Kids under 18 are not permitted.

The **Royal Flying Doctor Service** (RFDS; ☎ **08/9093 7500**) base at Kalgoorlie-Boulder Airport is open for visitors to browse memorabilia, see a video, and look over an aircraft if one is in. It is open Monday to Friday from 11am to 3pm. Admission is by donation.

Full-blood Aboriginal Geoffrey Stokes of ✪ **Yamatji Bitja Aboriginal Bush Tours** (☎ **08/9093 3745** or 0407/378 602) grew up the Aboriginal way in the bush. On his full-day 4WD tours, you'll forage for bush tucker, eat witchetty grubs (if you're game!), cook kangaroo over a fire, track emus, and learn Aboriginal bushcraft. Tours cost A\$77 (U.S.\$50.05), half price for kids 4 to 12; he picks you up from your hotel. Geoff also does twilight campfire evenings, and overnight or longer tours in the bush.

Wandering Coolgardie's quiet streets, which are graced with historic facades, is a pleasant stroll back in time. One hundred fifty signboards erected around the place, many with photos, detail what each site was like in the town's heyday at the turn of the century.

The Goldfields Exhibition, 62 Bayley St. (☎ **08/9026 6090**), tells the town's story in a lovely 1898 building once used as the mining warden's courthouse (the Tourist Bureau is also here). It has a huge old bottle collection too. Admission is A\$3.30 (U.S.\$2.15) for adults, A\$2.75 (U.S.\$1.80) for seniors, A\$1.10 (U.S.75¢) for children under 16, or A\$7.70 (U.S.\$5) for a family. It's open daily except Christmas from 9am to 5pm.

The **Railway Station Museum** (☎ **08/9026 6388**) on Woodward Street houses gold-rush and transport memorabilia in the original 1896 station building and the engine, two carriages, and the guard's van of a turn-of-the-century steam train. It's open daily 9am to 4pm (closed Christmas, Boxing Day, and Good Friday). Admission is by donation.

If you like period architecture and interiors, browse the restored National Trust–owned **Warden Finnerty's Residence** (☎ 08/9026 6028) on McKenzie Street off Hunt Street. It was built in 1895 for the mining warden. It is open daily from 9am to 4pm; admission is A$2 (U.S.$1.30) adults, A$1 (U.S.65¢) seniors and school-age kids, A$4 (U.S.$2.60) for a family.

The **Coolgardie Camel Farm,** 4 kilometers (2¹/₂ miles) west of Coolgardie on the Great Eastern Highway (☎ 08/9026 6159), leads rides through the bush on the mode of transport they used in the goldfields in the old days—camels.

ACCOMMODATIONS

Mercure Hotel Plaza Kalgoorlie. 45 Egan St., Kalgoorlie, WA 6430. ☎ **1300/65 6565** in Australia, 800/221-4542 in the U.S. and Canada, 020/8283 4500 in the U.K., 0800/44 4422 in New Zealand, or 08/9021 4544. Fax 08/9091 2195. www.hotelweb.fr. Email: mercureplaza@bigpond.com.au. 100 units (all with shower only). A/C MINIBAR TV TEL. A$165–$178.20 (U.S.$107.25–$115.85) double, A$242 (U.S.$157.30) suite. Extra person A$22 (U.S.$14.30). Children under 17 free with existing bedding. Ask about weekend packages. AE, BC, DC, MC, V.

Mining execs like the practical comforts, upscale restaurant (which I can recommend), and walking distance to town at this four-story property. The rooms are smart and spacious and some have modest city views. There are a small swimming pool and room service, and the front desk books tours and rental cars and exchanges foreign currency. The cocktail lounge has a nice clubby buzz in the evenings.

Mercure Inn Overland Kalgoorlie. Lower Hannan St., Kalgoorlie, WA 6430. ☎ **1300/66 6565** in Australia, 800/221-4542 in the U.S. and Canada, 020/8283 4500 in the U.K., 0800/44 4422 in New Zealand, or 08/9021 1433. Fax 08/9021 1121. www.hotelweb.fr. E-mail: mercureoverland@bigpond.com.au. 87 units (all with shower only). A/C MINIBAR TV TEL. A$99 (U.S.$64.35) double, A$143 (U.S.$92.95) family. Extra person A$22 (U.S.$14.30). Children under 17 stay free in parents' room with existing bedding. AE, BC, DC, MC, V.

This serviceable motel is on the highway (but quiet) about 2 kilometers (1¹/₄ miles) from town, so you'll need to have your own wheels or be prepared to take a cab to go exploring on your own. Tours pick up from the door. The rooms are modern, clean, and a good size; family rooms have an extra bedroom and a kitchenette. There are a nice restaurant and cocktail bar, room service at dinner, free movies, a swimming pool, and a tour and car-rental desk.

DINING

Akudjura. 418 Hannan St. (next to Hannan's View Motel). ☎ **08/9091 3311.** Reservations recommended. Main courses A$11.95–$24 (U.S.$7.80–$15.60); seafood platter A$60 (U.S.$39); lunch from A$7.50 (U.S.$4.90). AE, BC, DC, MC, V. Daily 10:30am–late (kitchen closes at 8:30pm). MODERN AUSTRALIAN.

The Italianate outdoor terrace under sailcloth and the timber floors, curved silver bar, and blond-wood furniture make this Kalgoorlie's first groovy restaurant. Bright young waitstaff provide snappy service from a long and stylish menu featuring items like chicken Caesar salad, smoked salmon fettuccine, kangaroo steak, and seafood dishes (yep, even in the desert) like Tasmanian salmon in a citrus and coriander dressing. Lighter fare is available outside meal hours.

5 The Midwest & the Northwest: Where the Outback Meets the Sea

The Midwest and Northwest coasts of Western Australia are treeless, riverless semi-desert, occupied by vast sheep stations and only a handful of people. Temperatures soar into the 40s°C (over 115°F) in summer, and the sand burns bright orange in the blazing sun. But it's not the land you come here for—it's what's in the sea that you're interested in. Since the 1960s, a pod of **bottle-nosed dolphins** has been coming into shallow water at ✪ **Monkey Mia** in the World Heritage–listed Shark Bay Marine Park to greet delighted shore-bound humans. Their magical presence has generated worldwide publicity and drawn people from every corner of the globe. So popular are the dolphins that a resort has been built on the lonely shore just to accommodate the crowds.

Another 872 kilometers (545 miles) by road north on the Northwest Cape, adventure seekers from around the world come to ✪ **snorkel with awesome whale sharks**—measuring up to 18 meters (59 ft.) long—every fall (Mar to early June). The Cape's parched shore and green waters hide an even more dazzling secret though—a second barrier reef 260 kilometers (163 miles) long and 2 kilometers (1¹/₄ miles) wide called **Ningaloo Marine Park.** It protects 250 species of coral and 450 kinds of fish, dolphins, mantas, whales, and turtles in its 5,000 square kilometers (1,640 square miles). Even the Great Barrier Reef can't beat ✪ **Ningaloo Reef's** proximity to shore—just a step or two off the beach delivers you into a magical underwater garden. What is so amazing about the reef is not that it is here, but that so few people know about it—a mere 8,000 tourists a year. To you, that means beaches pretty much to yourself, seas teeming with life because pesky humans haven't scared it away, unspoiled scenery, and a genuine sense of the frontier.

The Midwest and Northwest are lonely, remote, and really too hot to visit between November and March, when some tour operators close down on account of the heat. The best time to visit is April to October, when it is still warm enough to swim, though snorkelers might want a wet suit from June through August. Both regions are too far south to get the Top End's Wet Season, so humidity is always low. Facilities are scarce and distances are immense in this neck of the woods, so be prepared.

SHARK BAY (MONKEY MIA)
853km (533 miles) N of Perth; 1,867km (1,167 miles) S of Broome

There is no guarantee that Monkey Mia's famous dolphins will show on time or at all, but they rarely miss a visit. Apart from these delightful sea mammals, Shark Bay's waters absolutely heave with fish, dolphins, turtles, the world's biggest population of dugongs (10,000 at last count), manta rays, sea snakes, and, June through October, whales. On the tip of the Peron Peninsula, which juts out like the middle prong of a "W" into the Shark Bay Marine Park, is **Francois Peron National Park,** home to many endangered species, white beaches composed entirely of shells, and "living fossils"—rocklike structures on the shore called stromatolites. The bay's only town is the one-time pearling town of **Denham** (pop. 500), 129 kilometers (81 miles) from the highway, which has a hotel or two, a restaurant or two, a couple of shops, and several fishing-charter operators. There is no settlement, only a pleasant but basic resort (see below), at Monkey Mia.

ESSENTIALS
GETTING THERE   **Skywest Airlines** (☎ **1800/642 225** in Australia, or 08/9478 9999, or book through Ansett) and **Western Airlines** (☎ **1800/998 097** in Australia, or 08/9277 4022) both fly two or three times a week from Perth to Shark Bay Airport (also called Monkey Mia Airport), 18 kilometers (11 miles) from Monkey Mia Dolphin Resort. The one-way fare with Western Airlines is A$261 (U.S.$169.65). Skywest Airlines offers fly/fly and fly/drive accommodation-inclusive packages. No airline operates from towns other than Perth. The **Shark Bay Airport Bus** (☎ **08/9948 1358**)

meets every flight and transfers you to **Monkey Mia Dolphin Resort** (see "Accommodations & Dining," below) for A$7.70 (U.S.$5) per person one-way.

There is no train to Shark Bay. **Greyhound Pioneer** (☎ **13 20 30** in Australia) travels once or twice a day from Perth, daily from Broome, and three times a week from Exmouth via Coral Bay, to the Overlander Roadhouse at the Shark Bay turnoff on the North West Coastal Highway. These services connect with a coach service to Monkey Mia Dolphin Resort coach service. The 9-hour trip from Perth costs A$155.10 (U.S.$100.80). From Exmouth, it's a 7-hour trip, and from Broome, 22¹/₂ hours through featureless landscape—not recommended!

The 9- to 10-hour drive from Perth is mostly uninteresting and lonely. Beware of wildlife on the road and keep the gas tank full. Take the Brand Highway to Geraldton, 424 kilometers (265 miles) north of Perth, then the North West Coastal Highway for 280 kilometers (175 miles) to the Overlander Roadhouse. Turn left onto the Denham–Hamelin Road. Monkey Mia is 152 kilometers (95 miles) from the turnoff, 27 kilometers (17 miles) past Denham. If you want to break the journey, the **Mercure Inn Geraldton,** Brand Highway, Geraldton, WA 6530 (☎ **08/9921 2455**), has smart, clean motel rooms. Rates are A$105 (U.S.$68.25) double; specials are available most nights. In spring, consider taking the Everlasting Trail wildflower route to Geraldton, described in "Tiptoeing Through the Wildflowers," in the introduction to this chapter.

Numerous coach and 4WD tours run from Perth. **Feature Tours** does 24-hour "express" overnight coach tours from Perth. **Kookaburra Air** and **Complete Aviation Services** do aerial day trips and multiday tours from Perth. These companies' contact details appear in "Exploring the State," at the start of this chapter.

VISITOR INFORMATION   Wide-ranging information on Shark Bay's natural history and local tours is available at the **Dolphin Visitor's Centre** (☎ **08/9948 1366**) within Monkey Mia Dolphin Resort (see "Accommodations & Dining," below). Videos run throughout the day, and researchers (who are mostly from American universities) give free talks and slide shows some nights. The official visitor information outlet is the **Shark Bay Tourist Association's Centre** at Knight Terrace, Denham, WA 6537 (☎ and fax **08/9948 1253;** www.sharkbay.asn.au), open daily 8am to 6:30pm. The state Department of Conservation and Land Management is a good source of information on the ecology of Shark Bay Marine Park, Francois Peron National Park, and Hamelin Pool Marine Nature Reserve; it has an office in Denham, or contact its "W.A. Naturally" information center in Perth (see section 1 of this chapter).

GETTING AROUND   Shark Bay Car Hire (☎ **08/9948 1247**) delivers cars and 4WDs to the airport and the resort from its Denham office. Several companies run tours to all the main attractions.

FAST FACTS   Admission to the Monkey Mia Reserve, in which Monkey Mia Dolphin Resort is located, is A$6 (U.S.$3.90) per adult, A$2 (U.S.$1.30) per child 7 to 16, and A$12 (U.S.$7.80) for a family. If you stay longer than a day, it is A$12 (U.S.$7.80) for adults and A$22 (U.S.$14.30) for a family.

ATMs and banks are nonexistent. Banking agencies are located within the tourist association center and the newsagent in Denham.

MEETING THE DOLPHINS

At 7am guests at Monkey Mia Dolphin Resort are already gathering on the beach in quiet anticipation of the dolphins' arrival. By 8am three or more dolphins usually show, and they come and go until the early afternoon. Because of the crowds the dolphins attract (about 40 people a session in low season, coachloads in high season), a park ranger instructs everyone to line up knee-deep in the water as the playful swimsters cruise by your legs. You may not approach them or reach out to pat them (research shows dolphins veer away from people trying to pat them, anyhow), but they do come up to touch people of their accord sometimes. (Rangers are very strict about monitoring everyone's behavior with the dolphins. It's a thrilling contact with nature; but it's a bit touristy, and it's not an interactive frolic in the water with the little guys.) Sometimes the dolphins even offer you a fish as a present! Feeding times are different each day so the dolphins won't become dependent on the food. Once the crowd disperses, savvy swimmers dive into the water just up the beach outside the no-swimmers-allowed Dolphin Interaction Area, because the dolphins may head there after the "show." Apart from the Monkey Mia Reserve entry fee, there is no charge to see the creatures.

A GREAT SEA-LIFE CRUISE, LIVING "FOSSILS" & MORE

Don't do what so many visitors do—come to Monkey Mia, see the dolphins, and then shoot back to Perth. I found my cruise to see Shark Bay's incredible marine life on the sailing catamaran ✪ *Shotover* (☎ **1800/24 1481** in Australia, or 08/9948 1481) to be even better than the dolphins! During a 2½-hour dugong (manatee) cruise, we saw a hammerhead shark, a baby great white, two very large sea snakes that we hauled out of the water for a closer look, three turtles, oodles of dolphins that came up to the boat, and a baby dugong riding on its mum's back. Every passenger is given Polaroid sunglasses, which help you spot underwater animals. Sometimes you see dozens of dugong (though they leave the area mid-May to Aug). The dugong cruise departs 1pm daily from Monkey Mia Dolphin Resort and costs A$44 (U.S.$28.60). The Shotover also does a daily 2-hour dolphin cruise at 10:30am (A$38.50/U.S.$25), a sunset cruise, and, September through March, a nightly "Astronomy Under Sail" cruise. Children 7 to 16 are half price on all cruises, free for younger kids.

On your way in or out of Monkey Mia, stop by the **Hamelin Pool Historic Telegraph Station** (☎ **08/9942 5905**), 41 kilometers (25½ miles) from the highway turnoff. A small museum houses old equipment, farming tools, and historical odds and sods from the 19th-century days when Monkey Mia was a repeater station on a telegraph line. Entry to the museum includes an explanation of the local **stromatolites,** rocky formations about a foot high that were created by the planet's first oxygen-breathing cells—Earth's first life, in other words. From the telegraph station, you can wander down to **Shell Beach** at Hamelin Pool and have a look at them. You may find them something of an anticlimax, but following the signposted boardwalk over their tidal zone proves them a little more interesting. The "sand" on the beach consists of zillions of teensy white shells, which were quarried as bricks to build some of the local buildings. The museum tour costs A$4.40 (U.S.$2.90) for adults, A$2.20 (U.S.$1.45) for kids under 16, and A$12.10 (U.S.$7.90) for families, and runs about every half hour daily. There is a cafe and gift store too.

You can explore the saltpans, dunes, coastal cliffs, short walking trails, and old homestead in the nearby 52,500-hectare (129,675-acre) **Francois Peron National Park,** either alone (you will need a 4WD) or on a half- or full-day tour—although not everyone will appreciate the park's harsh scenery. You should easily spot wallabies, birds, emus, turtles, dolphins, rays, dugongs, and, in season, whales from the cliffs.

Other activities in the region include half- and full-day sportfishing trips from Denham, and a couple of pearl-farm tours.

ACCOMMODATIONS & DINING

Monkey Mia Dolphin Resort. Monkey Mia Rd., Shark Bay (P.O. Box 119, Denham, WA 6537). ☎ **1800/653 611** in Australia, or 08/9948 1320. Fax 08/9948 1034. www.monkeymia. com.au. E-mail: sales@monkeymia.com.au. Tent sites; 58 powered sites; 10 on-site caravans; 6 "canvas condo" permanent tents to sleep 6, all with bathroom (shower only); 13 park homes to sleep 6, none with bathroom; 60 motel rooms, all with bathroom (shower only). A$38.50–$55 (U.S.$25–$35.75) up to 3 or 4 people sharing caravan rented from resort plus A$2 (U.S.$1.30) per night for power hookup; A$77 (U.S.$50.05) up to 4 people in canvas condo; A$88 (U.S.$57.20) up to 4 people in park home; A$154–$176 (U.S.$100.10–$114.40) double or triple, motel room. Extra person A$4.40–$11 (U.S.$2.90–$7.15). Linen A$11 (U.S.$7.15) per person in park homes, canvas condos, and caravans for duration of stay. Lower rates Feb 1–Mar 31 (excluding Easter) and May 1–Jun 30. Weekly rates available. AE, BC, DC, MC, V.

Set right on the very beach the dolphins visit daily, this pretty oasis of green lawns and palms doubles as a town settlement. Most comfortable are the spacious air-conditioned motel rooms (the deluxe kind look right onto the beach and have their own barbecues); safari tent "canvas condos" with carpeted floors, electricity, a fridge, and a separate kitchen/dining area from the bedroom (but no air-conditioning); and air-conditioned demountable "park homes" with cooking facilities. The resort has a tour desk, a well-stocked minimarket, two tennis courts, a volleyball court, a pool and Jacuzzi fed by naturally warm underground water, a cafe for takeout, and the pleasant Bough Shed Restaurant overlooking the sea. Most tours in the area depart from the resort.

THE NORTHWEST CAPE

1,272km (795 miles) N of Perth; 1,567km (979 miles) S of Broome

Driving along the only road on the ✪ **Northwest Cape** is like driving on the moon. Hundreds of red anthills taller than you march away to the horizon, sheep and 'roos threaten to get under the wheels, and the sun beats down from a harsh blue sky. On the Cape's western shore is coral-filled Coral Bay, a tiny cluster of dive shops, backpacker lodges, a low-key resort, and charter boats nestled on sand so white, water so blue, and ochre dust so orange you think the townsfolk computer-enhanced it. Stretching north of town are deserted sandy beaches edged by coral. On the Cape's east coast is **Exmouth** (pop. 3,500), born in 1967 as a support town to the nearby Harold E. Holt Naval Communications Station, a joint Australian/United States center. Apart from whale-shark diving, scuba diving, and snorkeling in Ningaloo Marine Park are the big activities on the Cape, along with 4WD trips over the arid Cape Range National Park and surrounding sheep stations.

Exmouth and Coral Bay are 150 kilometers (94 miles) apart. Coral Bay is several degrees cooler than Exmouth and has divine diving, swimming, and snorkeling right on the doorstep; a restaurant and takeout or two, and a bar; a small supermarket; and little else. Exmouth is hot, dusty, and charmless, but it has more facilities, including a supermarket, an ATM, and an outdoor cinema. Most tours not having to do with the reef, such as 4WD safaris, leave from Exmouth. Both places have plenty of dive and snorkel companies. Wherever you stay, book ahead in whale-shark season (Mar through early June).

ESSENTIALS

GETTING THERE　Skywest Airlines (☎ **1800/642 225** in Australia, or 08/9478 9999, or book through Ansett) flies about six times a week, usually twice a day, from Perth (via Monkey Mia) to Learmonth Airport, 35 kilometers (22 miles) from Exmouth. A shuttle bus meets every flight and takes you to your Exmouth hotel for A$15 (U.S.$9.75) one-way. It does not take bookings. **Coral Bay Adventures**

(☎ **08/9942 5955**) makes transfers, on demand, from Learmonth to Coral Bay, approximately 120 kilometers (75 miles) away, for A$75 (U.S.$48.75) per person one-way.

Greyhound Pioneer operates three services a week from Perth to Coral Bay and Exmouth. The trip is close to 17 hours and costs A$183.70 (U.S.$119.40) to Coral Bay and A$203.50 (U.S.$132.30) to Exmouth. Greyhound's daily Perth-Broome and Broome-Perth services connect with a local bus service to Exmouth at the turnoff on the highway at Giralia. The change happens in the wee hours of the morning.

There is no train to the Northwest Cape.

The 14-hour drive from Perth (plus rest stops) is through lonely country on a two-lane highway. Check whether your contract allows you to drive your rental car this far north of Perth. Wildlife will be thick on the ground, and gas stations thin. Take the Brand Highway to Geraldton, 424 kilometers (265 miles) north of Perth, then the North West Coastal Highway for 623 kilometers (389 miles) to Minilya gas station; the Exmouth turnoff is 7 kilometers (4 miles) north of here. Exmouth is a further 225 kilometers (141 miles) from the turnoff. Overnight at the Mercure Inn Geraldton, listed in "Getting There," under "Shark Bay (Monkey Mia)," above, or in Carnarvon, which is the only town between Geraldton and Exmouth. Everything else that looks like a town on your map is just a gas station.

VISITOR INFORMATION   The Exmouth Tourist Bureau, Murat Road, Exmouth, WA 6707 (☎ **08/9949 1176;** www.exmouth-australia.com), is open daily 8:30am to 5pm. The **Milyering Visitors Centre,** 52 kilometers (32¹/₂ miles) northwest of Exmouth, is the Cape Range National Park's information center, run by the Department of Conservation and Land Management (CALM). The **Coral Bay Supermarket,** Coral Bay Arcade, Robinson Street, Coral Bay, WA 6701 (☎ and fax **08/9942 5988**), doubles as the tourist information center there. There is only one ATM cash machine on the Cape, in Exmouth.

GETTING AROUND   Many tours and dive operators pick up from either Exmouth or Coral Bay accommodations, but not usually both. The roads along the cape to Exmouth and around the tip as far down as Turquoise Bay are paved, as is the road across the cape to Coral Bay. To explore more widely, rent a 4WD, available only from Avis and Budget. Avis (☎ **08/9949 2492**), Budget (☎ **08/9949 1534**), Hertz (☎ **08/9144 1221**), and local operator Allen's Car Hire (☎ **08/9949 2403**) have offices in Exmouth; there is no car rental in Coral Bay.

Ningaloo Reef Bus (☎ **08/9949 1776**) runs from Exmouth hotels around the cape as far as Turquoise Bay, stopping at the Milyering Visitors Centre en route. It departs at 9am and gets back around 3:30pm, running every day except Thursday from April to September, and 4 days a week from October to March. The round-trip fare to Turquoise Bay is A$20 (U.S.$13). Ask about the sea kayak-and-snorkeling day trip, or the overnight safari camp-out, offered by the bus's operator, Ningaloo Reef Retreat.

✪ DIVING WITH WHALE SHARKS

"Diving" is not really a correct term for this activity, because it's by snorkeling that you get close to these leviathans of the deep. Whale sharks are sharks, not whales, and they are the world's biggest fish, reaching an alarming 12 to 18 meters (39 to 59 ft.) in length. Terrified? Don't be. Their gigantic size belies a gentle nature (whew) and swimming speed, and despite having a mouth big enough to swallow a boatload of snorkelers in one go, they eat plankton (whew again). Several boat operators take people out to swim alongside the fish when they appear March through early June. A trip with **Exmouth Diving Centre** (☎ **1800/655 156** in Australia, or 08/9949 1201;

www.exmouthdiving.com.au) or its Coral Bay sister company, **Ningaloo Reef Diving Centre** (☎ **08/9942 5824;** www.users.bigpond.com/ningaloo), costs A$250 (U.S.$162.50) and takes a day. Shark-protection regulations limit your boat to 10 snorkelers and a maximum 90 minutes with any one fish; your boat is free to search for several fish in one day. Most boats stop at reefs for more snorkeling, and some incorporate optional scuba dives.

DIVING, SNORKELING, FISHING & FOUR-WHEEL-DRIVING

Scuba dive the unspoiled waters of the Cape and you will see marvelous reef formations, grouper, manta rays, angel fish, octopus, morays, potato cod (which you can hand-feed), and other underwater marvels. Divers often spot humpback and false killer whales, large sharks, dolphins, and turtles. Loads of dive companies in Exmouth and Coral Bay rent gear and run daily dive trips and learn-to-dive courses, including the two listed in "Diving with Whale Sharks," above. A two-dive day trip costs around A$110 (U.S.$71.50) with all gear supplied. Live-aboard trips also run.

Three great snorkeling spots are right off the shore at Coral Bay; Bundegi Beach, a short drive north of Exmouth; and at beautiful ✪ **Turquoise Bay,** approximately 60 kilometers (37¹⁄₂ miles) from Exmouth on the cape's western coast. Walk up the beach, wade in, and let the bay's gentle current carry you back over the fish. In deeper offshore waters off Coral Bay, you can snorkel with **manta rays** with a "wingspan" up to 7 meters (23 ft.). They are least common in August and September. Ningaloo Reef Diving Centre (above) runs a manta snorkel tour for A$80 (U.S.$52), or A$150 (U.S.$97.50) if you want to dive with the creatures. Snorkel gear from the numerous dive operators in either town rents for about A$12 (U.S.$7.80) per day, and Ningaloo Reef Bus passengers use it free on the day of travel! Tour companies run snorkel tours or glass-bottom boat rides from either town.

Reef fish, tuna, and Spanish mackerel are common catches in these waters, and black, blue, and striped marlin run outside the reef from September to January. Up to a dozen boats operate reef and **game-fishing day trips** out of Exmouth and Coral Bay, and tackle and tin fishing dinghies are easily rented in either town.

Green and loggerhead ✪ **turtles** nest at night from November through February or March on the Cape's beaches. Take a flashlight and go looking for them, or join one of several turtle-watch tours from either town. From August to November, boats run cruises from either town to spot migrating **humpback whales.** Dugong are a common sight for snorkelers and divers, too.

Because the Cape has few roads, which don't show you many sights anyhow, touring is best done on a "Top of the Range" off-road 240-kilometer (150-mile) 4WD escapade with ✪ **Neil McLeod's Ningaloo Safari Tours** (☎ **08/9949 1550**). Neil takes you over the arid limestone ridges of the 50,581-hectare (124,935-acre) Cape Range National Park, down to dazzling Turquoise Bay for snorkeling, climbing up an old lighthouse, cruising orange-walled Yardie Creek Gorge to spot rock wallabies, and scoffing his Mum's fruit cake. I have never seen so many 'roos in one place, including big reds. He knows heaps about the area's geology, wildlife, history, and Aboriginal culture too. This full-day trip departs your Exmouth hotel at 7:30am and costs A$125 (U.S.$81.25) for adults and A$90 (U.S.$58.50) for children under 12. Highly recommended.

ACCOMMODATIONS & DINING

In Exmouth

Potshot Hotel Resort. Murat Rd., Exmouth, WA 6707. ☎ **08/9949 1200.** Fax 08/9949 1486. potshot@nwc.net.au. 97 units (all with shower only). A/C TV. High season (Jul 1–Oct 15) A$93.50 (U.S.$60.80) double homestead room, A$126.50 (U.S.$82.20) 4 people in motel room, A$198 (U.S.$128.70) 4 people in 3-bedroom apt. Shoulder season (Oct 16–Dec 31 and Apr 1–Jun 30) A$82.50 (U.S.$53.65) double in homestead room, A$115.50 (U.S.$75.10) 4 people in motel room, A$187 (U.S.$121.55) 4 people in 3-bedroom apt. Slightly lower rates in low season (Jan 1–Mar 31) in motel rms and 3-bedroom apts. Year-round A$137.50 (U.S.$89.40) 4 people in 2-bedroom apt. Extra person A$11 year-round (U.S.$7.15). Servicing in apts A$22–$33 (U.S.$14.30–$21.45) per day. AE, BC, DC, MC, V.

The grounds here are hot and dusty, but the hotel itself is a bright, modern complex right in town, with three swimming pools, tennis courts, and minigolf. The pleasant cocktail bar around the pool is the only shady place in town to enjoy a drink, which explains its popularity with locals. The restaurant is devoid of much atmosphere but has a long menu, good food, and a nice wine list. The brick motel rooms are cool and spacious; the homestead rooms are smaller, older, and more basic; there are two-bedroom apartments; and across the road are new three-bedroom apartments. Most rooms have telephones.

In Coral Bay

Ningaloo Reef Resort. At the end of Robinson St., Coral Bay, WA 6701. ☎ **08/9942 5934.** Fax 08/9942 5953. www.williams.com.au/resort.htm. E-mail: WHALESHARK@Bigpond.com. 34 units, all with bathroom (shower only). A$126.50–$132 (U.S.$82.25–$85.80) double, A$159.50–$275 (U.S.$103.70–$178.75) apt. Extra person A$11 (U.S.$7.15) adults. Ask about weekly rates. BC, MC, V.

This low-rise complex of motel rooms, studios, and apartments stands out as the best place to stay among Coral Bay's profusion of backpacker hostels. Located on a blissfully green lawn with a swimming pool overlooking the bay, the rooms are not fancy, but they're clean, with aspects toward the bay and the pool. Hair dryers are available. The place has a restaurant and a nice communal air, thanks to the bar doubling as the local pub.

10

Adelaide & South Australia

by Marc Llewellyn

Adelaide has a major advantage over the other Australian state capitals: It has Outback, vineyards, major wetlands, animal sanctuaries, a major river, and mountain ranges virtually on its doorstep. Meals and lodgings are also cheaper in Adelaide than in Sydney or Melbourne, and it has the small-town advantage of being easy to get around.

If you plan to travel outside the city, then a trip to one of the wine-growing areas has to be on your itinerary, since Australian wines have been taking home international wine prizes over the past few years. Of all the wine areas, the ✪ **Barossa Valley** is the nearest to Adelaide and the most interesting. Centered on Tanunda, the Barossa features German architecture, including 19th-century Lutheran churches, as well as dozens of pretty hamlets, fine restaurants, and vineyards offering cellar-door tastings.

If you want to see animals in addition to grapes, you're in luck. You're likely to come across the odd kangaroo or wallaby near the main settlements, especially at dusk, or you could visit one of the area's many wildlife reserves. Otherwise, head out into the Outback where animals abound, or over to ✪ **Kangaroo Island,** which is without a doubt the best place in Australia to see many types of native animals in the wild without having to travel enormous distances.

Also well worth visiting are the craggy **Flinders Ranges,** some 460 kilometers (285 miles) north of Adelaide. Though the scenery along the way is mostly unattractive grazing properties devoid of trees, the Flinders Ranges offer an incredible landscape of multicolored rocks, rough-and-ready characters, and even camel treks though the semidesert. On the other side of the mountain ranges, the real Outback starts.

The **South Australian Outback** is serenely beautiful, with giant skies, wildflowers after the rains, red earth, and little water. Out here you'll find bizarre opal-mining towns, such as **Coober Pedy,** where summer temperatures can reach 50°C (122°F) and where most people live underground to escape the heat.

If you prefer your landscape with a little more moisture, head to the **Coorong,** a water-bird sanctuary rivaled only by Kakadu National Park in the Northern Territory (see chapter 8).

EXPLORING THE STATE

VISITOR INFORMATION   The **South Australia Travel Centre,** 18 King William St. (☎ **1300 655 276** in Australia, or 08/8303 2033; www.visit-southaustralia.com.au; e-mail: sthaustour@tourism.sa.gov.au),

is the best place to collect information on Adelaide and South Australia. It's open weekdays from 8:30am to 5pm and weekends from 9am to 2pm.

For general information about South Australia's national parks, contact the **Department of Environment and Natural Resources Information Centre,** Australis House, 77 Grenfell St., Adelaide, SA 5000 (☎ **08/8204 1910**). It's open Monday to Friday from 9am to 5pm.

GETTING AROUND   South Australia, at four times the size of the United Kingdom, has a lot of empty space between places of interest. The best way to see it is by car, though a limited rail service connects Adelaide with some areas. The **Stuart Highway** bisects the state from south to north; it runs from Adelaide through the industrial center of Port Augusta (gateway to the Flinders Ranges), and onward through Coober Pedy to Alice Springs in the Red Centre. The **Eyre Highway** travels westward along the coastline and into Western Australia, while the **Barrier Highway** enters New South Wales just before the mining city of Broken Hill (see chapter 4). The **Princes Highway** takes you east to Melbourne. You should seek travel advice from the

Royal Automobile Association of South Australia (RAA), 41 Hindmarsh Sq., Adelaide, SA 5000 (☎ **08/8202 4600,** or 13 11 11 in South Australia only, or 08/8202 4500; www.raa.net), if you plan to drive into the Outback regions. The RAA provides route maps and emergency breakdown service.

Both **Qantas** (☎ **13 13 13** in Australia) and **Ansett** (☎ **13 13 00** in Australia) fly to Adelaide from the other major state capitals. **Kendell Airlines** (☎ **1800/338 894** in Australia, or 08/8231 9567) is the largest regional airline serving the state.

Both **Greyhound Pioneer** (☎ **13 20 30** in Australia) and **McCafferty's** (☎ **13 14 99** in Australia) service South Australia. Within the state, the largest coach operator is **Stateliner** (☎ **08/8415 5555**).

1 Adelaide

Adelaide, "The City of Churches," has a reputation as a sleepy place, full of parkland and surrounded by vineyards. In many ways it's something of a throwback to 1950s Australia, with a lifestyle that the more progressive state capitals have left behind.

Numerous parks and gardens, wide tree-lined streets, the River Torrens running through its center, sidewalk cafes, colonial architecture, and, of course, the churches help make it a pleasant, open city, perfect for strolling or bicycling.

Though the immigrant population has added a cosmopolitan flair to the restaurant scene, Adelaide still has a feeling of old England about it. That's not surprising when you learn that Adelaide was the only capital settled entirely by English free settlers rather than convicts, and that it attracted plenty more after World War II, when Brits flocked here to work in the city's car-parts and domestic-appliance industries.

But it was earlier immigrants—from Germany—who gave Adelaide and the surrounding area a romantic twist. Arriving as refugees in the 1830s, fleeing a nation torn by religious strife, German immigrants brought with them their wine-making skills. Today, more than one-third of all Australian wine—including some of the world's best—comes from areas mostly within an hour's drive from Adelaide. As a result, Adelaidians of all socioeconomic groups are more versed in wine than even the French and regularly compare vintages, wine-growing regions, and wine-making trends.

Any time of the year is a good time to visit Adelaide, though May to August can be chilly and December and January hot.

ORIENTATION

ARRIVING   By Plane   Ansett (☎ **13 13 00** in Australia) and **Qantas** (☎ **13 13 13** in Australia) both fly to Adelaide, with frequent service from other state capitals. **Adelaide International Airport** is 5 kilometers (3 miles) west of the city center. Major car-rental companies (Avis, Budget, Hertz, and Thrifty) have desks in both the international and the domestic terminals. You can pick up a few tourist brochures here, but there is no official tourist help desk. Lockers are available, though you'll need exact change when you want to retrieve your luggage. In the domestic terminal you'll find a bank and a post office; there is a machine selling stamps in the international terminal. Both terminals have showers, currency-exchange desks, shops, and places to eat.

The **Transit Bus** (☎ **08/8381 5311;** www.transitregency.com.au) links the airport with major city hotels and the rail and bus stations. On weekdays, buses leave the terminals at 30-minute intervals from 5am to 9:30pm, and on weekends and public holidays hourly (on the half hour). Adult tickets are A$6 (U.S.$3.90) one-way and A$10 (U.S.$6.50) round-trip. Child tickets cost A$3 (U.S.$1.95) each way.

A **taxi** to the city will cost around A$15 (U.S.$9.75).

By Train   One of the great trains of Australia, *The Indian Pacific,* transports passengers from Sydney to Adelaide (trip time: 28 hr.) and from Adelaide to Perth (trip time: 36 hr.) twice a week on Monday and Thursday. Tickets from Sydney to Adelaide are A$499 (U.S.$324) for adults and A$334 (U.S.$217) for children in first class, A$360 (U.S.$234) for adults and A$241 (U.S.$156) for children in holiday class, and A$168 (U.S.$109) for adults and A$84 (U.S.$54) for children in coach class.

The other legendary Australian train is *The Ghan,* which runs from Melbourne to Adelaide and then up to Alice Springs weekly from November to April and twice a week from May to October. First-class tickets for the Melbourne-to-Adelaide leg of the trip are A$778 (U.S.$505.70) for adults, A$522 (U.S.$339.30) for children; holiday-class tickets are A$460 (U.S.$299) adults, A$308 (U.S.$200.20) children; economy-class tickets are A$197 (U.S.$128.05) adults, A$98 (U.S.$63.70) children.

The Overlander provides daily service between Adelaide and Melbourne (trip time: 12 hr.). Tickets are A$199 (U.S.$129) for adults and A$133 (U.S.$86) for children in first class, and A$64 (U.S.$42) for adults and A$43 (U.S.$28) for children in economy.

Call **Great Southern Railways** (☎ **08/8213 4530**) for more information and bookings, or check out the timetables and fares on their Web site (www.gsr.com.au/fares.htm).

The **Keswick Interstate Rail Passenger Terminal,** located 2 kilometers (1 1/2 miles) west of the city center, is Adelaide's main railway station. The terminal has a small snack bar and a cafe.

By Bus   Intercity coaches terminate at the central bus station, 101 Franklin St. (☎ **08/8415 5533**), near Morphett Street in the city center.

Adventurous types should consider traveling to Adelaide from Melbourne (or vice versa) on the ☉ **Wayward Bus,** operated by the Wayward Bus Touring Company (☎ **1800/882 823** in Australia, or 08/8232 6646; www.waywardbus.com.au). These 21-seat buses make the trip in 3 1/2 days via the Great Ocean Road; the fare is A$180 (U.S.$117) for adults and A$119 (U.S.$77) for children under 15. You spend around 4 to 5 hours a day on the bus, and the driver acts as your guide. A picnic or cafe lunch each day and entry to national parks are included in the fare. You must arrange your own accommodation in Port Fairy and Beachport and Apollo Bay. After July, packages are available including some accommodation options. You can leave the trip and rejoin another later. Reservations are essential.

VISITOR INFORMATION   Head to the **South Australia Travel Centre,** 18 King William St. (☎ **1300 655 276** in Australia, or 08/8303 2033; www.visit-southaustralia. com.au; e-mail: sthaustour@tourism.sa.gov.au), for maps and travel advice. It's open

The Adelaide Festival & Other Special Events

Adelaide is home to Australia's largest performing-arts festival, the **Adelaide Festival,** which takes place over 3 weeks in March during even-numbered years. The festival includes literary and visual arts, as well as dance, opera, classical music, jazz, cabaret, and comedy. The festival encompasses Writers' Week and a fringe comedy festival. For information, check the Web site at www.adelaidefestival.telstra.com.au.

In February and March of odd-numbered years, the 3-day **Womadelaide Festival** of world music takes place. Crowds of 60,000 or more turn up to watch Australian and international artists.

For more information, contact the Adelaide Festival, P.O. Box 8116, Station Arcade, Adelaide, SA 5000 (☎ **08/8216 4444;** www.adelaidefestival.telstra.com.au).

weekdays from 9am to 5pm and weekends from 9am to 2pm. There's also an information booth on Rundle Mall open daily from 10am to 5pm.

CITY LAYOUT   Adelaide is a simple city to negotiate because of its gridlike pattern, which was planned down to each wide street and airy square by Colonel William Light in 1836. The city's official center is **Victoria Square,** where you'll find the Town Hall. Bisecting the city from south to north is the city's main thoroughfare, **King William Street.** Streets running perpendicular to King William Street change their names on either side, so that Franklin Street, for example, changes into Flinders Street. Of these cross streets, the most interesting to the visitor are the restaurant strips of **Gouger Street** and **Rundle Street,** the latter running into the pedestrian-only shopping precinct of **Rundle Mall.** Another is **Hindley Street,** with its inexpensive restaurants and nightlife. On the banks of the River Torrens just north of the city center, you'll find **Adelaide Plaza,** the home of the Festival Centre, the Convention Centre, and the Adelaide Casino. Bordering the city center on the north and south are **North Terrace,** which is lined with galleries and museums and leads to the Botanic Gardens, and **South Terrace.**

Follow King William Street south and you'll be chasing the tram to the beachside suburb of **Glenelg;** follow it north and it crosses the River Torrens and flows into sophisticated **North Adelaide,** an area crammed with Victorian and Edwardian architecture. The main avenues in North Adelaide, **O'Connell and Melbourne streets,** are lined with restaurants, cafes, and bistros that offer the tastes of a multicultural city.

To the northwest of the city center is **Port Adelaide,** a seaport and the historic maritime heart of South Australia and the home to some of the finest colonial buildings in the state, as well as good pubs and restaurants.

GETTING AROUND

BY PUBLIC TRANSPORTATION   If you plan to get around the city via public transportation, it's a good idea to purchase a **Daytrip ticket,** which covers unlimited travel on buses, trams, and city trains within the metropolitan area for 1 day. The pass costs A$5.40 (U.S.$3.50) for adults and A$2.70 (U.S.$1.75) for children 5 to 15 and is available at most train stations, newsagents, and the **Passenger Transport Board Information Centre** (☎ 08/8210 1000).

By Bus   Adelaide's public bus network is divided into three zones, and fares are calculated according to the number of zones traveled. The city center is classed as Zone 1. The fare in Zone 1 is A$1.60 (U.S.$1) from 9am to 3pm on weekdays and A$2.80 (U.S.$1.80) most other times. You can buy tickets on board the bus or at newsagents around the city. You can pick up a free metro information and timetable booklet at the **Passenger Transport Board Information Centre** (☎ 08/8210 1000), on the corner of Currie and King William streets, open Monday to Saturday from 8am to 6pm and Sunday from 10:30am to 5:30pm. For timetable information over the phone, call the **Passenger Transport Infoline** (☎ 08/8210 1000).

The **City Loop bus** operates free bus service around the city center along North Terrace, East Terrace, Grenfell Street, Pulteney Street, Wakefield Street, Grote Street, Morphett Street, Light Square, Hindley Street, and West Terrace. All City Loop and some other buses are wheelchair accessible.

The **Adelaide Explorer bus** stops at 10 sights around town and costs A$27 (U.S.$17.55) for adults, A$18 (U.S.$11.70) for children, and A$65 (U.S.$42.25) for families of four. The bus stops at each destination every 1^1/$_2$ hours in summer and every 3 hours in winter. The full loop takes a leisurely 2^3/$_4$ hours, with commentary. Call ☎ 08/8364 1933 for details. Buy tickets on the bus.

By Tram   The **Glenelg Tram** runs between Victoria Square and the beachside suburb of Glenelg. Tickets are valid for 2 hours and cost A$1.60 (U.S.$1) for adults and A80¢ (U.S.52¢) for children 5 to 14 from 9am to 3pm, and A$2.80 (U.S.$1.80) for adults and A$1 (U.S.65¢) for children at other times. The journey takes 29 minutes.

BY TAXI   The major cab companies are **Yellow Cabs** (☎ 13 22 27 in South Australia only), **Suburban** (☎ 08/8211 8888), and **Amalgamated** (☎ 08/8223 3333). **Access Cabs** (☎ 1300/360 940 in South Australia only) offers wheelchair taxis. The base fare is A$2 (U.S.$1.30) Monday through Friday from 6am to 7pm and Saturday from 6am to 7pm; A$2.90 (U.S.$1.90) Monday through Friday from 7pm to 6am, Saturday after 7pm, and all day Sunday.

BY CAR   Major car-rental companies in the area are **Avis,** 136 N. Terrace (☎ 08/8410 5727); **Budget,** 274 N. Terrace (☎ 08/8223 1400); **Hertz,** 233 Morphett St. (☎ 08/8231 2856); and **Thrifty,** 296 Hindley St. (☎ 08/8211 8788). All four companies also operate at the airport.

Fast Facts: Adelaide

American Express   The AMEX office, at 13 Grenfell St. (☎ **08/8202 1400**), is open during normal business hours.

Business Hours   Generally, banks are open Monday to Thursday from 9:30am to 4pm and Friday from 9:30am to 5pm. Stores are generally open Monday to Thursday from 9am to 5:30pm, Friday from 9am to 9pm, Saturday from 9am to 5pm, and Sunday from 11am to 5pm.

Currency Exchange   Banks and hotels, the casino, and the Myer department store in Rundle Mall all cash traveler's checks. The **Thomas Cook** office is at 45 Grenfell St. (☎ **08/8212 3354**).

Dentist   Contact the **Australian Dental Association Emergency Information Service** (☎ **08/8272 8111**), open nightly 5 to 9pm, and Saturday and Sunday 9am to 9pm. It will put you in touch with a dentist. You can also contact the office of **Dr. Brook,** 231 N. Terrace (☎ **08/8223 6988**), open during normal business hours.

Doctor   The **Travellers' Medical & Vaccination Centre,** 29 Gilbert Place (☎ **08/8212 7522**), offers vaccinations and other travel-related medicines.

Emergencies   Dial ☎ **000** to call an ambulance, the fire department, or the police in an emergency.

Hospitals   The **Royal Adelaide Hospital,** North Terrace (☎ **08/8222 4000**), is located in the city center.

Hotlines   Call the **Crisis Care Centre** at ☎ **13 16 11,** or the **Disability Information and Resource Centre** at ☎ **08/8223 7522.**

Internet Access   The **Ngapartji Multimedia Centre,** 211 Rundle St. (☎ **08/8232 0839**), offers e-mail and Internet access Monday to Thursday 8:30am to 7pm, Friday 8:30am to 10pm, Saturday 10am to 10pm, Sunday noon to 7pm.

Pharmacies   Remember, they're "chemist shops" in Australia. **Burden Chemists,** Shop 11, Southern Cross Arcade, King William St. (☎ **08/8231 4701**), is open Monday to Thursday from 8am to 6pm, Friday from 8am to 8pm, and Saturday from 9am to 1pm.

Rest Rooms   Public rest rooms can be found at the Central Market Arcade, between Grote and Gouger streets, in both Hindmarsh and Victoria squares, and at James Place (off Rundle Mall).

Safety   Adelaide is a very safe city, though it's wise to avoid walking along the River Torrens and through side streets near Hindley Street after dark.

ACCOMMODATIONS

The **South Australia Travel Centre** (see "Visitor Information," above) can supply information on B&Bs and homestays around the state. Satellite or cable TV are rare in South Australian hotels, though some provide pay-per-view movies.

If you plan to be in town during the biennial Adelaide Festival, make sure you book your accommodations well in advance. Accommodations can also get pretty scarce during the Christmas and New Year's period, so it's wise to book well in advance then too.

IN THE CITY CENTER
Very Expensive

Hyatt Regency Adelaide. North Terrace, Adelaide, SA 5000. ☎ **800/233-1234** in the U.S. and Canada, 13 12 34 in Australia, or 08/8231 1234. Fax 08/8231 1120. www.hyatt.com. E-mail: adelaide@hyatt.com.au. 367 units. A/C MINIBAR TV TEL. A$240 (U.S.$156) double; A$260 (U.S.$169) river-view double; A$280 (U.S.$182) Regency Club City View (including breakfast); A$300 (U.S.$195) Regency Club River Park View (including breakfast); A$390 (U.S.$253.50) Executive Suite; A$840 (U.S.$546) Deluxe Suite. Extra person A$40 (U.S.$26). Ask about packages and lower weekend rates. Children under 18 stay free in parents' room. AE, BC, DC, JCB, MC, V. Parking A$15 (U.S.$9.75).

The 20-story Hyatt Regency is in the heart of the city and is part of the complex that includes the Adelaide Festival Centre, the Casino, the Exhibition Hall, and the Convention Centre. The five-star property overlooks the River Torrens and nearby parklands, and there are some wonderful views from the higher floors. The Hyatt doesn't cut corners, and pays attention to detail in the rooms. It also offers fantastic weekend deals, when rooms can go for as little as A$99 (U.S.$64.35). Guests staying in the club-level Regency rooms get a good complimentary breakfast and free evening drinks and canapés.

Dining/Diversions: Blake's Restaurant is a refined dining spot, with plenty of South Australian vintages on the wine list. Riverside Restaurant has good buffet food, while Shiki is an award-winning Japanese restaurant famous for its authentic tempura and teppanyaki dishes. Waves, a cabaret/nightclub, offers a combination of video, disco, and live music; it's free for hotel guests, though it can be dull and the drinks are expensive. Afternoon tea is served in the stylish Atrium Lounge, which gets surprisingly full as the night wears on.

Amenities: Concierge, 24-hour room service, shoe shine, free daily newspaper, laundry, valet, nightly turndown, baby-sitting, massage, business center. There are also an outdoor pool and a fitness center with sauna, solarium, sports shop, whirlpool, plunge pool, weight room, and juice bar; business center.

Expensive

Hilton Adelaide. 233 Victoria Sq., Adelaide, SA 5000. ☎ **1800 222 255** worldwide, or 08/8217 2000. Fax 08/8217 2001. www.hilton.com. E-mail: sales_adelaide@hilton.com. 380 units. A/C MINIBAR TV TEL. A$200–$260 (U.S.$130–$169) double; A$315–$345 (U.S.$205–$224) executive floor; A$360–$650 (U.S.$234–$422) suite. Extra person A$40 (U.S.$26). Children under 12 stay free in parents' room. AE, BC, DC, MC, V. Parking A$15 (U.S.$9.75). The tram stops in front of the hotel; a bus stop is adjacent.

The luxurious Hilton stands on Victoria Square, just around the corner from a whole host of restaurants on Gouger Street. The lobby is polished marble, with a cascading fountain and piano music tinkling throughout. Guest rooms are pleasant, with all you might expect from a classy establishment. There are 11 rooms specially equipped for travelers with disabilities. It's a tough call between staying here or at the Hyatt; since hotel rates often fluctuate, call both and go with whichever choice has the best deals during your stay.

Dining/Diversions: There's a coffee shop and the upscale Grange restaurant (see "Dining," later in the chapter). The Brasserie offers meals all day. I was surprised to find Charlie's Bar—full of photos of famous Charlies—virtually empty even on a Saturday night.

Amenities: Heated outdoor pool, spa pool, gym, sauna, tennis court, jogging track, concierge, 24-hour room service, free daily newspaper, laundry, valet, massage, dry cleaning, baby-sitting, business center, unisex hair salon.

Novotel Adelaide on Hindley. 65 Hindley St., Adelaide, SA 5000. ☎ **1800 882 633** in Australia, or 08/8231 5552. Fax 08/8237 3800. www.parkroyal.com.au. 217 units. A/C MINI-BAR TV TEL. Midweek A$280 (U.S.$182) double; A$310 (U.S.$201) suite. Weekend A$150 (U.S.$97.50) double; A$190 (U.S.$123.50) suite. Ask about package deals. Children under 15 stay free in parents' room. AE, BC, DC, MC, V, JCB. Parking A$6 (U.S.$3.90).

Only a short stroll from the center of town, the Novotel is good value if you happen to be staying on the weekend when business travelers go home and the rates go down. Otherwise, it's not as classy as either the Hyatt or the Hilton. What you get for your money is a good, recently renovated, bright room. Ask at the reception desk for a robe, because they don't come standard in the standard rooms. Some rooms have a fax, while all have fax/modem lines.

Dining: Meals are served in the casual Oli's Brasserie, where the Friday- and Saturday-night buffets are popular with guests and nonguests.

Amenities: Heated outdoor pool, well-equipped gym, spa, sauna, 24-hour room service, and good business center. You can rent mountain bikes for A$10 (U.S.$6.50) for a half day and A$15 (U.S.$9.75) for a full day.

Moderate

Barron Townhouse. 164 Hindley St., Adelaide, SA 5000. ☎ **800/624-3524** in the U.S. and Canada, 0800/892 407 in the U.K., 0800/803 524 in New Zealand, 1800/888 241 in Australia, or 08/8211 8255. Fax 08/8231 1179. www.barrontownhouse.com.au. E-mail: barron@chariot.net.au. 68 units. A/C MINIBAR TV TEL. A$129 (U.S.$83.85) standard double, A$172 (U.S.$111.80) deluxe double; A$182 (U.S.$118.30) executive room. Extra person A$18 (U.S.$11.70). Children under 12 stay free in parents' room. Lower rates in off-season and weekends. Ask about package deals. AE, BC, DC, JCB, MC, V. Free parking.

Friendly staff and garish china flamingos welcome you to this uninspiring-looking four-star concrete block. It's a 10- to 15-minute walk from the center of town, 5 minutes from the casino, and not far from the nightclub and red-light district. Rooms are spacious and comfortable enough, with everything, including hair dryers. There are a very nice pool and sauna on the rooftop. Downstairs is the informal Flamingos bistro. The cocktail lounge is more of the same, but with a better view of the traffic lights on the busy road outside.

City Park Motel. 471 Pulteney St., Adelaide, SA 5000. ☎ **08/8223 1444.** Fax 08/8223 1133. 18 units, 14 with bathroom (shower only). A/C TV TEL. A$50 (U.S.$32.50) double without bathroom; A$69 (U.S.$44.85) double with bathroom. Extra person A$10 (U.S.$6.50). AE, BC, DC, MC, V. Free parking. The tram to Glenelg stops just around the corner, and 3 streets up is a bus stop for the free City Loop bus.

The rooms in this first-floor motel just outside the city center have modern furnishings and nice bathrooms with a shower. Some rooms have private balconies. Also on the premises is a separate bathroom with a tub. The best room is number 45. Downstairs there's a new cocktail bar, nightclub, and bistro.

Saville Park Suites Adelaide. 255 Hindley St., Adelaide SA 5000. ☎ **1800/882 601** in Australia, or 08/8231 8333. Fax 08/8217 2519. www.savillesuites.com.au. Email: adelaide@ shg.com.au. 144 units. A/C MINIBAR TV TEL. A$138 (U.S.$89.70) 1-bedroom studio; A$182 (U.S.$118.30) 2-bedroom studio; A$210 (U.S.$136.50) 2-bedroom premium. AE, BC, CB, DC, MC, V. Parking A$5 (U.S.$3.25).

You can't miss this mass of russet-red bricks just on the outskirts of the city center (about a 10-min. walk away). Rooms are nice and spacious, if a bit formal, which is not surprising since the place is popular with business travelers. Each room has a fully equipped kitchen and laundry and a private balcony. Four units are equipped for travelers with disabilities. Everything you'd expect to find in a four-star hotel you'll find here. On the premises is the Zipp Restaurant and Wine Bar, where Tommy Chang serves up an innovative menu.

Inexpensive

Moore's Brecknock Hotel. 401 King William St., Adelaide, SA 5000. ☎ **08/8231 5467.** Fax 08/8410 1968. 10 units, none with private bathroom. A/C. A$50 (U.S.$32.50) double; A$65 (U.S.$42.25) triple. Rates include continental breakfast. AE, BC, DC, MC, V. Free parking. The tram to Glenelg stops in front of the hotel.

Adelaide's original Irish pub, built in 1851, still attracts a lot of Irish visitors, who drop in for the great selection of beer and reasonably priced home-style cooking—it reputedly serves Adelaide's best hamburgers. It's also very popular with American guests who use the accommodations upstairs as a base from which to discover Kangaroo Island and other parts of the state. The Brecknock is about 4 blocks from Victoria Square and is run by Kerry Moore and his Canadian wife, Tricia. There are live bands downstairs on Friday, Saturday, and Sunday evenings, but the music finishes at 1am on Friday and Saturday, and 10pm on Sunday, so you shouldn't have too much trouble sleeping. Rooms are large and pleasantly done out in old-world style. Each has a double and a single bed, and a sink, with the shared bathrooms down the hall.

IN NORTH ADELAIDE

This suburb across the river is an interesting place to stay because of its nice architecture and good restaurants. It's about a 10-minute bus ride from the city center.

✪ **North Adelaide Heritage Group.** Office: 109 Glen Osmond Rd., Eastwood, SA 5063. ☎ **08/8272 1355** or 0418/289 494 (mobile phone). Fax 08/8272 1355. www.adelaideheritage.com.au. E-mail: heritage@senet.com.au. 19 units. TV TEL. A$125–$337 (U.S.$81.25–$219) double, depending on accommodation. Rates include GST. Extra person A$60–$75 (U.S.$39–$48.75). Children under 12 A$25 (U.S.$16.25). AE, BC, DC, JCB, MC, V.

It's worth coming all the way to Adelaide just for the experience of staying in one of these out-of-this-world apartments, cottages, and suites. Each of these separate properties, in various locations around North Adelaide and Eastwood, is fabulous. I recommend particularly the former Friendly Meeting Chapel Hall, a small, simple gabled hall of blue-stone rubble trimmed with brick and resembling a small church. Built in 1878, it's stocked with period pieces and antiques and rounded off with a modern, fully stocked kitchen; a huge spa bath; a queen-size bed; and a CD player and TV.

Another standout place is George Lowe Esquire unit. This huge 19th-century apartment is also stocked with antiques, and has a huge four-poster bed, a separate bathroom, a lounge, and a full kitchen. Guests also have use of nice gardens. Owners Rodney and Regina Twiss have added all those little touches that make you feel like home, from magazines to bacon and eggs in the fridge. All properties are within easy walking distance of the main attractions in the area. The company has just bought the old North Adelaide Fire Station and has renovated it into three separate apartments.

Old Lion Apartments. 9 Jerningham St., North Adelaide, SA 5006. ☎ **08/8223 0500.** Fax 08/8223 0588. E-mail: reservations@majesticapartments.com.au. 57 units. A/C TV TEL. A$130 (U.S.$84.50) 1-bedroom apt; A$145 (U.S.$94.25) 2-bedroom apt; A$180 (U.S.$117) 3-bedroom apt. Extra adult A$15 (U.S.$9.75), extra child 3–12 A$5 (U.S.$3.25). AE, BC, CB, DC, MC, V. Parking $5 (U.S.$3.25). Bus: 184, 224, 226, 228, or 229.

These pleasant apartments are located inside a renovated brewery. The complex is about a 15-minute walk from the city center and is on a direct bus route. Rooms are spacious, with high ceilings, and come with a kitchenette, a living room, French doors separating bedrooms from living quarters, a shower and bathtub, and a good-sized balcony. All apartments also have use of a washing machine and dryer. VCRs and videos are available for rent at the front desk. Continental breakfast costs A$8.50 (U.S.$5.50) extra.

Princes Lodge Motel. 73 Lefevre Terrace, North Adelaide, SA 5006. ☎ **08/8267 5566.** Fax 08/8239 0787. E-mail: princeslodge@senet.com.au. 21 units. A/C TV TEL. A$66 (U.S.$42.90) double with attached private bathroom; A$55 (U.S.$35.75) double with separate private bathroom. Rates include continental breakfast and GST. AE, BC, DC, MC, V. Bus: 222 from Victoria Square (with pickups along King William St.).

One of the best motels in Adelaide, the Princes Lodge looks more like a large private home than your typical simple brick roadside structure. Rooms are nicely decorated and have the usual motel appliances, and generally come with a double and a single bed. Three family rooms are available, one of which has a double and three singles, while another has six beds in one room. The motel is within walking distance of the restaurant strip on O'Connell Street, and a A$5 (U.S.$3.25) taxi ride from the city center. There's a laundry on the premises.

In Glenelg

I recommend without hesitation that you stay in Glenelg rather than in the city center. The journey to the city center by car or tram takes less than 30 minutes, and the airport is less than 10 minutes away. Add to this the sea, the lovely beach, the fun fair, the great shops, the good pub, and the nice accommodations, and you have a perfect place for a holiday.

Atlantic Tower Motor Inn. 760 Anzac Hwy., Glenelg, SA 5045. ☎ **08/8294 1011.** Fax 08/8376 0964. 27 units (20 with shower only). A/C TV TEL. A$72 (U.S.$46.80) double; A$92 (U.S.$59.80) deluxe double; A$120–$135 (U.S.$78–$87.75) suite. Extra person A$10 (U.S.$6.50). Children under 15 stay free in parents' room. Free parking. Hotel is 1 block from the tram stop.

If you're looking for relatively inexpensive accommodations near the beach, here's your place. You can't miss this circular building not far from the sea, with its slowly revolving restaurant on the 12th floor. Rooms are simple, but very bright, and have nice park views through large windows. Each room has a double and a single bed—and even a toaster. The deluxe rooms are a bit nicer and come with bathtubs rather than just showers. Suites have two rooms and excellent views; the most expensive have a spa. The gently turning Rock Lobster Cafe upstairs is open for lunch on Thursday, Friday, and Sunday (no lunch on Sat) and dinner every evening.

Stamford Grand Adelaide. Moseley Square (P.O. Box 600), Glenelg, SA 5045. ☎ **1800/ 882 777** in Australia, or 08/8376 1222. Fax 08/8376 1111. 240 units. A/C MINIBAR TV TEL. A$178–$198 (U.S.$115.70–$128.70) double; A$258–$408 (U.S.$167.70–$265) suite. Children under 12 stay free in parents' room. AE, BC, DC, MC, V. Parking A$10 (U.S.$6.50). The tram from Adelaide stops in front of the hotel.

A classic Adelaide photo shows the trams awaiting passengers in front of the imposing facade of the Stamford Grand. Located right on the beach, this classy hotel offers nice rooms with modern furnishings; many overlook the beach, the ocean, and the pier.

Meals are served in Promenade, a popular restaurant overlooking the ocean. Even if you don't stay here, you can pop in for Devonshire tea at A$7.90 (U.S.$5.15) per head. There are also two walk-in cafes on the premises: Cafe Delorian, offering Thai food, and Tesoro, serving up Italian cuisine. The Pier and Pines is a very popular bar that's almost bursting with youngish crowds most nights; for a more mellow scene, there's Horizons piano bar, which offers quality live music, particularly on weekends.

DINING

With more than 600 restaurants, pubs, and cafes, Adelaide boasts more dining spots per capita than anywhere else in Australia. Many of them are clustered in particular areas, such as Rundle Street and Gouger Street in the city center, and in North Adelaide—where you'll find almost every style of cuisine you can imagine.

For cheap noodles, laksas, sushi, and cakes, head to Adelaide's popular **Central Markets** (☎ **08/8203 7494**), behind the Adelaide Hilton Hotel, between Gouger and Grote streets.

Because of South Australia's healthy wine industry, you'll find that many of the more expensive restaurants have extensive wine lists—though with spicier foods, it's probably wiser to stick with beer, or a fruity white in a pinch. Many Adelaide restaurants allow diners to bring their own wine (BYO), but most charge a steep corkage fee to open your bottle—A$6 (U.S.$3.90) or so is not uncommon.

IN THE CITY CENTRE

Expensive

✪ **The Grange.** In the Adelaide Hilton, 233 Victoria Square. ☎ **08/8217 2000.** Reservations required. 3-course menu A$75 (U.S.$48.75); 4-course menu A$90 (U.S.$58.50); 6-course menu A$90 (U.S.$58.50). AE, BC, DC, MC, V. Tues–Sat 7–10:30pm. MODERN AUSTRALIAN.

The Grange is a large restaurant with an open floor plan, specializing in contemporary food by Adelaide's most influential chef, Cheong Liew. Liew offers an innovative fusion of Western and Asian ingredients, rounded off with an extensive wine list. The menu begins with a choice of two starters, among them Liew's signature dish, "The four dances of the sea"—an antipasto of fish, octopus in a garlic sauce, prawn sushi, raw cuttlefish, and black noodles. For the next course, you could choose a shark-fin pouch in a venison consommé spiced with tarragon, or ostrich in spaghetti timbale with a vegetable and herb broth. Main courses might include Chinese-style roast duck breast with grilled mango and duck leg in a lotus pancake, or a lightly smoked kangaroo fillet with veal liver, black current compote, sweet potato puree, and parsleyed beans. If there are two of you dining, you might want to check the menu a day in advance, because some of the dishes for two require 24 hours' notice.

Moderate

Amalfi. 29 Frome St. (just off Rundle St.). ☎ **08/8223 1948.** Reservations recommended. Main courses A$13.50–$16.50 (U.S.$8.80–$10.70). AE, BC, DC, MC, V. Mon–Thurs 11:30am–3pm and 5:30–11pm (until midnight Fri); Sat 5:30pm–midnight. ITALIAN.

Come here for good Italian cooking at reasonable prices served up in a lively atmosphere. The pizzas are the best in Adelaide—though a little expensive—and consistently good veal and pasta dishes are always on the menu. Be sure to check out the daily specials board, where you can pick out a very good fish dish or two.

Jasmin Indian Restaurant. 31 Hindmarsh Square. ☎ **08/8223 7837.** Reservations recommended. Main courses A$14.50–$16.50 (U.S.$9.40–$10.70). Lunch banquet A$18 (U.S.$11.70), dinner banquet A$27 (U.S.$17.55). AE, BC, DC, JCB, MC, V. Tues–Fri noon–2:30pm; Tues–Sat 5:30–9:30pm. NORTH INDIAN.

Something Different: Dining Tours

If you like good food and wine but can't decide on just one restaurant, try one of **Graeme Andrews' tours** (☎ **08/8336 8333,** or 0412/842 242 mobile; e-mail: graeme@food-fun-wine.com.au; www.food-fun-wine.com.au). He offers eight food or food-and-wine tours showcasing the Central Market, Chinatown, and Gouger Street restaurants. Prices (including GST) start at A$28 (U.S.$18). Private tours are also available on request.

Prices have crept up as this place has gotten more popular, but this family-run Adelaide institution a block south of Rundle Mall is still a good value. Indian artifacts and signed cricket bats from visiting Indian teams decorate the walls. The atmosphere is comfortable yet busy, and the service is professional. The house special is the very hot beef vindaloo, but all the old favorites, such as tandoori chicken, butter chicken (a big seller here), lamb korma, and malabari beef with coconut cream, ginger and garlic, are here, too. Mop it all up with naan bread, and cool your palate with a side dish of raita. The suji halwa, a semolina pudding with nuts, is the best I've tasted. No smoking.

Jolleys Boathouse Restaurant. Jolleys Lane. ☎ **08/8223 2891.** Reservations recommended. Main courses A$20–$23 (U.S.$13–$14.95). Lunch A$19.50 (U.S.$12.70) for 1 course, A$29.50 (U.S.$19.20) for 2 courses, and A$38.50 (U.S.$25) for 3 courses. AE, BC, DC, MC, V. Daily noon–2:30pm; Mon–Sat 6:30–9:30pm. MODERN AUSTRALIAN.

Jolleys is nicely situated on the banks of the River Torrens, with views of boats, ducks, and black swans. Businesspeople and ladies who lunch rush for the three outside tables for a bit of alfresco dining may beat you, but if you miss out, the bright and airy interior, with its cream-colored tablecloths and director's chairs, isn't too much of a letdown. You might start with the intriguing goat's curd ravioli with red pesto and chives. Moving on, you could tuck into the roasted duck with hazelnut risotto (try to tune out the peaceful quacking out on the river if you can). The banana and cardamom soufflé for dessert is wicked.

✪ **Matsuri.** 167 Gouger St. ☎ **08/8231 3494.** Reservations recommended. Main courses A$9.50–$16.80 (U.S.$6.20–$10.90). AE, BC, DC, MC, V. Fri noon–2pm; Wed–Mon 5:30–10pm. JAPANESE.

I really like the atmosphere in this very good Japanese restaurant on the popular Gouger Street restaurant strip. The food is prepared by Takaomi Kitamura, world-famous ice sculptor and sushi master. The sushi and sashimi dishes are some of the best in Australia. Monday night is "sushi festival night," when sushi is half price. During happy hour Wednesday to Sunday, sushi is 30% off if you place your order before 7pm (you can preorder over the phone and eat later). Other popular dishes include vegetarian and seafood tempura, yose nobe (a hot pot of vegetables, seafood, and chicken), and chawan mushi (a steamed custard dish). The service is friendly and considerate. Corkage fee is A$4.50 (U.S.$2.90) a bottle.

Rigoni's Bistro. 27 Leigh St. ☎ **08/8231 5160.** Reservations recommended. Main courses A$10.90–$22 (U.S.$7–$14.30); antipasto bar (lunch only) A$10.50–$12.50 (U.S.$6.80–$8.10). AE, BC, DC, JCB, MC, V. Mon–Fri noon–2:30pm; Mon–Sat 6:30–10pm. ITALIAN.

Located on a narrow lane west of King William Street, this traditional Italian trattoria is often packed at lunch, though it's less frantic in the evening. It's big and bright with high ceilings and russet quarry tiles. A long bar runs through the middle of the dining room; brass plates mark the stools of regular diners. The food is very traditional and quite good. The chalkboard menu often changes, but you're likely to find lasagne, veal in white wine, marinated fish, and various pasta dishes. There's also an extensive salad bar with a variety of antipasto. An outside dining area should be completed by the time you read this.

Inexpensive

Austral Hotel. 205 Rundle St. ☎ **08/8223 4660.** Reservations recommended. Main courses A$7–$12 (U.S.$4.55–$7.80) in bistro, A$14–$20 (U.S.$9.10–$13) in restaurant. AE, BC, MC, V. Mon–Thurs noon–3pm and 5:30–9:30pm; Fri–Sun noon–10pm. MODERN AUSTRALIAN.

This large pub, with its dark timber and forest-colored wallpaper, is a pleasant place for a good-value pub meal. You can eat at the bar, outside on the street, or in the dining room. The bistro serves burgers, fish-and-chips, pastas, laksas, and Thai curries. The restaurant is a bit more upscale and offers risotto, handmade crab ravioli, beef fillets, chicken dishes, venison, paella, and baby octopus.

Golden Triangle. 106A Hindley St. ☎ **08/8211 8222.** Reservations recommended. Main courses A$9.50–$15 (U.S.$6.20–$9.75). AE, BC, DC, MC, V. Daily noon–2:30pm; 5pm–until last customer leaves. THAI/LAOS/BURMESE.

From Thai chicken laksa and Burmese beef curry to tom-yum soup and Indonesian nasee goreng, the Golden Triangle serves the lot. This grottolike joint is dark, cramped, and badly furnished—with sea-green walls, a Buddha in the corner, and just 10 tables—but all this only serves to emphasize the wonderfully authentic food that will knock your socks off. Dinner specials—including a starter; a main course (except seafood); a glass of wine, fruit juice, or coffee; and a ticket for the nearby movie complex—cost just A$22.50 (U.S.$14.60).

Mekong Thai. 68 Hindley St. ☎ **08/8231 2914.** Main courses A$9.60–$10.90 (U.S.$6.25–$7). AE, BC, DC, MC, V. Daily 5:15pm–late. THAI/MALAYSIAN/HALAL.

Though this place is not much to look at—with simple tables and chairs, some outside in a portico—it has a fiery reputation for good food among in-the-know locals. The food is spicy and authentic, and the portions are filling. It's also a vegetarian's paradise, with at least 16 meat-free mains on the ethnically varied menu. It's Adelaide's only fully halal (suitable for Muslims) restaurant.

Ruby's Café. 255b Rundle St. ☎ **08/8224 0365.** Main courses A$7.70–$15.20 (U.S.$5–$9.90). AE, BC, MC, V. Sun 9am–5pm; daily 6:30–11:30pm. MODERN AUSTRALIAN.

Situated in suitably unpretentious surroundings for a former market cafe catering to the local workers, Ruby's is an Adelaide institution. It still has its laminated tables and the NO SPITTING, NO COARSE LANGUAGE sign behind the bar, despite being far more upscale than that these days. Basically, you get a very good restaurant meal in an old cafe atmosphere at very good prices. Ruby's serves up filling curries and fancier pasta dishes, hearty meals such as lamb shanks, and quite a few vegetarian options. For dessert, I recommend the toffee pudding with toffee sauce. The menu changes every 6 weeks.

IN NORTH ADELAIDE

✪ **The Manse.** 142 Tynte St., North Adelaide. ☎ **08/8267 4636.** Reservations recommended. A$30 (U.S.$19.50) for 2 courses. Tues–Fri noon–3pm; Mon–Sat 6:30–10pm. AE, BC, DC, MC, V. Bus: 182, 224, 226, 228, or 229. SEAFOOD.

Swiss chef Bernhard Oehrli has a fine touch when it comes to seafood, and I recommend this place wholeheartedly. The surroundings are neat and gracious, with a log fire inside to keep you warm in winter and room to dine outside on the sidewalk on sunnier days. As for the food, the scallops here are almost fresh enough to waddle off the warmed cucumber base and head for sea, while the rare tuna in Japanese-style tempura is so delicate it literally melts in your mouth. If you want something other than seafood, then you can't go wrong with the duck or veal dishes. For dessert, try the warm chocolate gâteau or the rhubarb gratin with ice cream.

The Oxford. 101 O'Connell St., North Adelaide. ☎ **08/8267 2652.** Reservations recommended, especially for lunch and dinner Fri, and dinner Sat. Main courses A$14.50–$20.50 (U.S.$9.40–$13.30). AE, BC, DC, MC, V. Mon–Fri noon–3pm; Mon–Sat 6–10pm or later. Bus: 182, 222, 224, 226, 228, or 229. MODERN AUSTRALIAN.

This restaurant keeps racking up awards for its cooking. The Oxford is highly praised for its creative, contemporary food in a range of fusion styles. It's big and busy, housed in a renovated, character-filled 1870s building. Inside you'll find crisp white tablecloths, a single-page menu, and a stainless-steel kitchen whipping up steam. The signature dishes are the red-roasted spatchcock (a small chicken) with water chestnuts, a chicken-and-cashew-nut spring roll, black-bean mayonnaise, and coconut broth; and the wonderful Caesar salad. Other favorites include satay fried chicken; jellyfish with Moroccan-spiced salsa; and poached prawns with natural oysters, served with wasabi, nori rolls, and soy dressing. The wine list is extensive.

IN KENT TOWN

Chloe's Restaurant. 36 College Rd., Kent Town. ☎ **08/8362 2574.** Reservations recommended. Main courses A$24.90–$28.90 (U.S.$16.20–$18.80). AE, BC, DC, MC, V. Mon–Fri noon–2pm; Mon–Sat 7–10:30pm. CREATIVE FRENCH.

This aristocrat of Adelaide's restaurant scene is so good you hardly feel the pain arising from your hip pocket when you come to pay the bill. A meal here may well be one of the highlights of your trip to Adelaide. Located in a suburb on the edge of the city center, Chloe's has won awards for the best wine list in the state, the best chef in the state, and the best restaurant in the state. It's situated in a fine 1880s mansion stocked with antiques, chandeliers, and high-quality oil paintings. The menu changes every 3 months, but you're sure to find the signature dish—spiced caramel duck breast with wontons, black rice, tamarind glaze, and bok choy tempura—making an appearance. Other dishes might include slowly cooked pigeon breast with braised pigeon legs with a cabbage and truffle cream stuffing, or veal shank ravioli. Vegetarians have very limited options. Chloe's wine list is 20 pages long and offers some 600 domestic and imported wines; the cellar is stocked with some 22,000 bottles.

SEEING THE SIGHTS

Adelaide is a very laid-back city. It's not jam-packed with tourist attractions like some of the larger state capitals, though the Migration Museum (see below) is easily one of the best museums in Australia. The best way to enjoy this pleasant city is to take things nice and easy. Take a walk beside the River Torrens, take the tram to the beachside suburb of Glenelg, and spend the evenings sipping wine and sampling some of the country's best alfresco dining.

Festival Tours (☎ **08/8374 1270**) operates city sightseeing tours for A$32 (U.S.$20.80) for adults, A$22 (U.S.$14.30) for children. Tours operate from 9:30am to noon every day except Sunday. The bus can pick you up at your hotel.

The **Adelaide Explorer** (☎ **08/8364 1933**) is a replica tram that circles the city, stopping off at a number of attractions along the way, including Glenelg. The full route takes 2³/₄ hours to complete; you can get on or off along the route and rejoin another tram later on. Buses depart from 38 King William St. daily at 9am, 10:20am,

12:10pm, 1:30pm, and 3pm. Tickets are A$23 (U.S.$14.95) for adults, A$15 (U.S.$9.75) for children ages 6 to 14, and A$55 (U.S.$35.75) for families of four.

THE TOP ATTRACTIONS

Art Gallery of South Australia. North Terrace. ☎ **08/8207 7000.** Free admission. Daily 10am–5pm. Guided tours Mon–Fri 11am and 2pm; Sat–Sun 11am and 3pm. Closed Christmas Day.

Adelaide's premier public art gallery has a good range of local and international works and a fine Asian ceramics collection. Of particular interest are Charles Hall's *Proclamation of South Australia 1836;* Nicholas Chevalier's painting of the departure of explorers Burke and Wills from Melbourne; several examples of works by Australian painters Sidney Nolan, Albert Tucker, and Arthur Boyd; and some excellent contemporary art. The bookshop has an extensive collection of art publications.

✪ **The Migration Museum.** 82 Kintore Ave. ☎ **08/8207 7580.** Admission by donation. Mon–Fri 10am–5pm, Sat–Sun and public holidays 1–5pm. Closed Good Friday and Christmas. Bus: Any to North Terrace.

This tiny museum, dedicated to immigration and multiculturalism, is one of the most important and fascinating in Australia. With touching, personal displays, it tells the story of the waves of immigrants who have helped shape this multicultural society, from the boatloads of convicts who came here in 1788 to the ethnic groups who have been trickling in over the past 2 centuries. The migrant hostel setup is particularly interesting; it gives you an idea of the very basic accommodation options that were often the first home in Australia for the waves of immigrants who arrived here on government-sponsored schemes. Ironically, the museum is housed in the former Destitute Asylum, where many migrants ended up when they found starting life anew got too tough.

South Australian Maritime Museum. 126 Lipson St., Port Adelaide. ☎ **08/8207 6255.** Admission A$8.50 (U.S.$5.50) adults, A$3.50 (U.S.$2.30) children, A$22 (U.S.$14.30) families. Daily 10am–5pm. Closed Christmas. Bus 153 or 157 from North Terrace in the city to Stop 40 (Port Adelaide). Train: Port Adelaide.

Over 150 years of maritime history are commemorated in this Port Adelaide museum. Most of the exhibits can be found in the 1850s Bond Store, but the museum also incorporates an 1863 lighthouse and three vessels moored alongside Wharf No.1, just a short walk away. The fully rigged replica of the 54-foot ketch *Active II* is very impressive.

✪ **South Australian Museum.** On North Terrace between the State Library and the Art Gallery. ☎ **08/8207 7500.** Free admission. Daily 10am–5pm. Closed Good Friday and Christmas.

The star attraction of this interesting museum is the new Australian Aboriginal Cultures Gallery, which opened in March 2000. On display is an extensive collection of utensils, spears, tools, bush medicine, food samples, photographs, and the like. Also within the museum is a sorry-looking collection of stuffed native animals (sadly also including a few extinct marsupials, including the Tasmanian tiger), a good collection of Papua New Guinea artifacts, and excellent mineral and butterfly collections.

If you're interested in learning even more about the exhibits, take one of the Behind-the-Scenes Tours. They're conducted after museum hours and cost A$12 (U.S.$7.80) for adults.

✪ **Tandanya Aboriginal Cultural Institute.** 253 Grenfell St. ☎ **08/8223 2467.** Admission A$4 (U.S.$2.60) adults, A$3 (U.S.$1.95) children ages 13 and under, A$10 (U.S.$6.50) families. Daily 10am–5pm.

This place offers a great opportunity to experience Aboriginal life through Aboriginal eyes. Exhibits change regularly, but all give insight into Aboriginal art and cultural

Adelaide

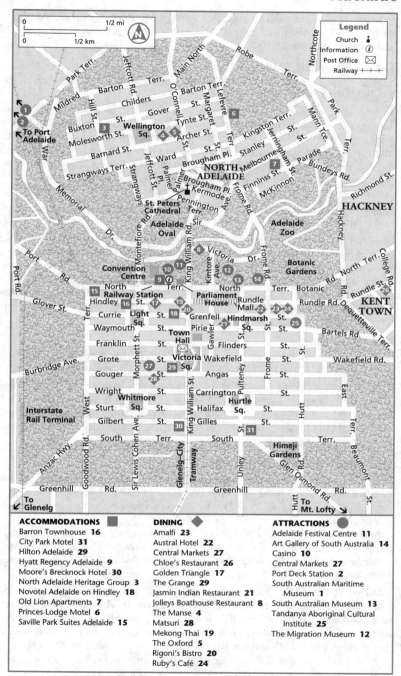

Legend
- Church
- Information *(i)*
- Post Office
- Railway ┼┼┼

0 — 1/2 mi
0 — 1/2 km

To Port Adelaide

Park Terr.
Mildred
Barton Terr.
Hill St.
Buxton St.
Childers
Molesworth St.
Gover St.
Wellington Sq.
Tynte St.
Archer St.
Barnard St.
Strangways Terr.
Ward St.
Brougham Pl.
NORTH ADELAIDE
Kermode St.
St. Peters Cathedral
Pennington Terr.
Adelaide Oval
Sir
Victoria Dr.
Kintore Ave.
Convention Centre
North Terr.
North Railway Station
Hindley St.
Currie St.
Light Sq.
Waymouth St.
Franklin St.
Grote St.
Town Hall
Victoria Sq.
Gouger St.
Wright St.
Whitmore Sq.
Sturt St.
Gilbert St.
South Terr.
Greenhill Rd.
To Glenelg

O'Connell St.
Barton Terr.
Margaret St.
Tynte St.
Lefevre Terr.
Robe Terr.
Main North Rd.
Jeffcott Rd.
Stanley St.
Melbourne St.
Finniss St.
Frome Rd.
McKinnon Parade
Brougham Pl.

Kingston Terr.
Jerningham St.
Mann Tce.
Northcote Terr.
Park Terr.
Richmond St.
HACKNEY
Hackney Rd.

Adelaide Zoo
Botanic Gardens
Botanic Rd.
North Terr.
Rundle St.
KENT TOWN
Rundle Rd.
Dequetteville Terr.
Bartels Rd.
Wakefield Rd.
East Terr.
Beaumont
Glen Osmond Rd.
To Mt. Lofty

Parliament House
Rundle Mall
Hindmarsh Sq.
Grenfell St.
Pirie St.
Flinders St.
Wakefield St.
Angas St.
Carrington St.
Halifax St.
Hurtle Sq.
Gilles St.
South Terr.
Himeji Gardens
Greenhill

Interstate Rail Terminal
Anzac Hwy.
Goodwood Rd.
Sir Lewis Cohen Ave.
Glenelg-City Tramway
King William St.
Pulteney St.
Hutt St.
Glover St.
Port Rd.
Memorial Dr.
Burbridge Ave.
West Terr.
Morphett St.
Gawler Pl.
Frome St.
College Rd.
Rundle St.
Strangways
Jeffcott St.
Palmer Pl.

ACCOMMODATIONS
Barron Townhouse **16**
City Park Motel **31**
Hilton Adelaide **29**
Hyatt Regency Adelaide **9**
Moore's Brecknock Hotel **30**
North Adelaide Heritage Group **3**
Novotel Adelaide on Hindley **18**
Old Lion Apartments **7**
Princes Lodge Motel **6**
Saville Park Suites Adelaide **15**

DINING
Amalfi **23**
Austral Hotel **22**
Central Markets **27**
Chloe's Restaurant **26**
Golden Triangle **17**
The Grange **29**
Jasmin Indian Restaurant **21**
Jolleys Boathouse Restaurant **8**
The Manse **4**
Matsuri **28**
Mekong Thai **19**
The Oxford **5**
Rigoni's Bistro **20**
Ruby's Café **24**

ATTRACTIONS
Adelaide Festival Centre **11**
Art Gallery of South Australia **14**
Casino **10**
Central Markets **27**
Port Deck Station **2**
South Australian Maritime Museum **1**
South Australian Museum **13**
Tandanya Aboriginal Cultural Institute **25**
The Migration Museum **12**

activities. At noon every day there's a didgeridoo performance. A shop sells Aboriginal art and books on Aboriginal culture, while a cafe on the premises serves up several bush tucker (native food) items.

THE FLORA & THE FAUNA

Adelaide Zoo. Frome Rd. ☎ **08/8267 3255.** Admission A$12 (U.S.$7.80) adults, A$7 (U.S.$4.55) children. Daily 9:30am–5pm.

To be honest, if you've already experienced the wonderful Melbourne Zoo, or even Taronga Zoo in Sydney, it's probably not worth your while coming here. But if this is going to be your only chance to see a kangaroo in captivity, then plan a visit here. Of course, other Australian animals live at the zoo, too, and the nicely landscaped gardens and lack of crowds make it a pleasant place for an entertaining stroll. The zoo houses the only Pygmy blue-tongue lizard in captivity in Australia, a species thought to be extinct since the 1940s, until a specimen was discovered inside the belly of a dead snake.

Botanic Gardens. North Terrace. ☎ **08/8228 2311.** Free admission. Mon–Fri 8am–sunset, Sat–Sun 9am–sunset.

You'll feel like you're at the true heart of the city when you stroll through the huddles of office workers having picnic lunch on the lawns here. Park highlights include a broad avenue of shady Moreton Bay figs, duck ponds, giant water lilies, an Italianate garden, a palm house, and the Bicentennial Conservatory—a large glass dome full of rain-forest species. You might want to have lunch in the Botanic Gardens Restaurant (☎ **08/8223 3526**), surrounded by bird song and lush vegetation, right in the center of the park; it's open daily from 10am to 5pm.

FOR TRAIN BUFFS

Port Dock Station. Lipton St., North Adelaide. ☎ **08/8341 1690.** Admission A$8 (U.S.$5.20) adults, A$3 (U.S.$1.95) children, A$19 (U.S.$12.35) families. Daily 10am–5pm.

This former Port Adelaide railway yard houses Australia's largest and finest collection of locomotives engines and rolling stock—with around 104 items on display, including some 30 engines. Among the most impressive trains on show are the gigantic "Mountain" class engines, and so-called "Tea and Sugar" trains that once ran between railway camps in remote parts of the desert. Entrance includes a train ride.

ENJOYING THE GREAT OUTDOORS

BIKING   Adelaide's parks and riverbanks are very popular with cyclists. Rent your own two wheels from **Linear Park Hire** (☎ **018/844 588** mobile phone). The going rate is A$15 to $20 (U.S.$9.75 to $13) for 24 hours, including helmet, lock, and baby seat (if needed).

   Recreation SA (☎ **08/8226 7301**) publishes a brochure showing Adelaide's bike routes. Pick one up at the South Australia Travel Centre (see "Visitor Information," earlier in the chapter). **The Map Shop,** 6 Peel St. (☎ **08/8231 2033**), is also a good source for maps.

HIKING & JOGGING   The banks of the River Torrens are a good place for a jog. The truly fit and/or adventurous might want to tackle the **Heysen Trail,** a spectacular 1,600-kilometer (992-mile) walk through bush, farmland, and rugged hill country that starts 80 meters (50 miles) south of Adelaide and goes to the Flinders Ranges by way of the Adelaide Hills and the Barossa Valley. For more information on the trail, visit the South Australia Travel Centre (see "Visitor Information," earlier in chapter).

GOLF   The **City of Adelaide Golf Course** (☎ **08/8267 2171**) is quite close to town and has two short 18-hole courses and a full-size championship course. Greens

A Trip to the Seaside

If you need a beach fix while in Adelaide, head to the lovely suburb of Glenelg, just a 30-minute tram ride from the city center. Glenelg has much more to offer than just a nice beach, the ocean, and a classic pier (as if these weren't enough). It's also where you catch the ferry to Kangaroo Island, and it's home to some interesting attractions. For maps and brochures on the area, head to the **Glenelg Tourist Information Centre** (☎ 08/8294 5833), in the Foreshore Building near the seafront. It's open daily from 9am to 5pm.

You can see pieces of **HMS *Buffalo***, Adelphi Terrace, Patawalonga Boat Haven, Glenelg (☎ **08/8294 7000**), a full-scale replica of the ship that brought the first settlers to South Australia, if you dine at the seafood restaurant here, where main courses cost around A$19 (U.S.$12.35).

The carousel and giant gray hillock you can see from the seafront are part of the **Magic Mountain** amusement park, Colley Reserve, Glenelg (☎ **08/8294 8199**). You can keep the kiddies happy for hours here on the water slides, bumper boats, miniature golf, shooting galleries, and video games. Water slides cost A$12 (U.S.$7.80) for an hour and A$7 (U.S.$4.55) for 30 minutes. A 3-hour lock-in on Saturday mornings and school holidays from 9am to noon, with unlimited use of supervised water slides and most other attractions, costs A$12 (U.S.$7.80).

Want to get face-to-face with one of South Australia's famous great white sharks (and live to tell the story)? The **Shark Museum,** The Glenelg Town Hall, Mosely Square, (☎ **08/8376 3373**), has full-size models of the terrors of the sea, as well as filming cages, shark jaws, photos, and fossils. Admission is A$8 (U.S.$5.20) for adults, A$4 (U.S.$2.60) for children, A$19 (U.S.$12.35) for a family. It's open from 10am to 6pm Wednesday to Friday (daily during school holidays and public holidays).

History buffs will want to visit the **Old Gum Tree.** It was under this tree that Governor Hindmarsh read the 1836 proclamation making South Australia a colony; it's on MacFarlane Street.

---

fees are A$12.50 to $15 (U.S.$8.10 to $9.75), depending on the course, Monday through Friday, plus A$3 (U.S.$1.95) extra on weekends. Club rental is available.

THE SHOPPING SCENE

Rundle Mall (between King Williams and Pulteney streets) is Adelaide's main shopping street. This pedestrian-only thoroughfare is home to all the big names in fashion.

Adelaide's Central Markets (☎ 08/8203 7494), behind the Adelaide Hilton Hotel between Gouger and Grote streets, make up the largest produce market in the Southern Hemisphere. They're a good place to shop for vegetables, fruit, meat, fish, and the like, although the colorful markets are worth popping into even if you're not looking for picnic fixings. The markets, held in a huge warehouselike structure, are open Tuesday from 7am to 5:30pm, Thursday from 11am to 5:30pm, Friday from 7am to 9pm, and Saturday from 7am to 3pm. **Market Adventures** (☎ 08/8336 8333, or mobile 0412/842 242) runs behind-the-scenes tours of the markets every Tuesday and Thursday at 10:30am and 1:30pm, Friday at 10am and 2pm, and Saturday at 8:30am. Tours cost A$28 (U.S.$18.20) for adults and A$15 (U.S.$9.75) for children 3 to 11. Phone for directions. The company also runs a Dawn Market Tour at 7:15am every

Shopping for Opals

South Australia is home to the world's largest sources of white opals (the more expensive black opals generally come from Lightning Ridge in northern New South Wales). There are plenty of places to buy around town, but **Opal Field Gems,** 33 King William St. (☎ **08/8212 5300**), is one of the best. As a rule, you're not going to find any bargains, so just buy what you like (and can afford—good opals cost many thousands of dollars).

Tuesday, Thursday, Friday, and Saturday for A$49 (U.S.$31.85), including GST and breakfast.

The six-story **Myer Centre,** next door to the Myer department store, 22–38 Rundle Mall, has a Body Shop (on the ground floor), for beauty products; an Australian Geographic shop (on level 3), for top-quality Australiana; and Exotica (level 2), where you can find unusual futuristic gifts.

Just off Rundle Mall, at Shop 6 in the City Cross Arcade, is **L'Unique** (☎ **08/8231 0030**), a good craft shop selling South Australian pottery, jewelry, woodcraft, handblown glass, and original paintings.

Elsewhere, the renowned **Jam Factory Craft and Design Centre,** in the Lions Art Centre, 19 Morphett St. (☎ **08/8410 0727**), sells an excellent range of locally made ceramics, glass, furniture, and metal items. You can also watch the craftspeople at work here.

For the best boots in Australia, head to the **R.M. Williams** shop on Gawler Place (☎ **08/8232 3611**) for the best simple boots you're ever likely to find, as well as other Aussie fashion icons, including Akubra hats, moleskin pants, and Driza-bone coats.

ADELAIDE AFTER DARK

The *Adelaide Advertiser* lists all performances and exhibitions in its entertainment pages. The free tourist guide *Today in Adelaide,* available in most hotels, also has information.

Tickets for theater and other entertainment events in Adelaide can be purchased from **BASS ticket outlets** at the following locations: Festival Theatre, Adelaide Festival Centre, King William Road; Centre Pharmacy, 19 Central Market Arcade; Verandah Music, 182 Rundle St.; and on the 5th floor of the Myer department store, Rundle Mall. Call BASS at ☎ **13 12 46** in South Australia, or 08/8400 2205.

THE PERFORMING ARTS   The major concert hall in town is the **Adelaide Festival Centre,** King William Road (☎ **08/8216 8600** for general inquiries; 08/8400 2205 for the box office). The Festival Centre encompasses three auditoriums: the 1,978-seat Festival Theatre, the 612-seat Playhouse, and the 350-seat Space Centre. This is the place in Adelaide to see opera, ballet, drama, orchestral concerts, the Adelaide Symphony Orchestra, plays, and experimental drama.

The complex also includes an outdoor amphitheater used for jazz, rock and roll, and country music concerts; an art gallery; a bistro; a piano bar; and the Silver Jubilee Organ, the world's largest transportable concert-hall organ (built in Austria to commemorate Queen Elizabeth II's Silver Jubilee).

The **Adelaide Repertory Festival** presents a season of five productions a year, ranging from drama to comedy, at the Arts Theatre, 53 Angus St. (☎ **08/8221 5644**). Playwrights Alan Ayckbourne and Terrence Ratagan are among the many who have had plays performed here. The theatre, which is just a short walk away from many hotels and restaurants, is also the home of the **Metropolitan Musical Theatre**

So Much Wine, So Little Time

If you have the choice of exploring either the Barossa or the Hunter Valley in New South Wales (see chapter 4), I recommend the Barossa, which, despite being a little more touristy, has more to offer in terms of history and architecture.

Another famous wine-producing region is the **Coonawarra,** 381 kilometers (236 miles) southeast of Adelaide and near the border with Victoria; it's particularly convenient if you're driving from Melbourne. The area is just 12 kilometers (7 miles) long and 2 kilometers (just over 1 mile) wide, but the scenic countryside is crammed with historic villages and 16 wineries. The **Clare Valley,** 135 kilometers (84 miles) north of Adelaide, is another pretty area; it produces some outstanding examples of cool-climate wine.

Company, which presents two musical comedy productions a year. Tickets cost around A$16 (U.S.$10.40) for adults and A$11 (U.S.$7.15) for children.

Her Majesty's Theatre, 58 Grote St. (☎ **08/8216 8600**), is a 1,000-seat venue opposite Central Markets that presents drama, comedy, smaller musicals, dance, opera, and recitals. Tickets are generally A$30 to $55 (U.S.$19.50 to $35.75).

THE BAR & CLUB SCENE   Adelaide's nightlife ranges from twiddling your thumbs to nude lapdancers. For adult entertainment (clubs with the word "strip" in the name) head to Hindley Street—there are a few pubs there, too, but I wouldn't recommend them. For information on gay and lesbian options, pick up a copy of the *Adelaide Gay Times.*

As for your basic pubs, the locals will point you toward **The Austral,** 205 Rundle St. (☎ **08/8223 4660**); **The Lion,** at the corner of Melbourne and Jerningham streets (☎ **08/8367 0222**); and the **British Hotel,** 58 Finniss St. (☎ **08/8267 2188**), in North Adelaide, where you can cook your own steak on the courtyard barbecue. Also popular with both visitors and locals alike is the **Earl of Aberdeen,** 316 Pulteney St., at Carrington Street (☎ **08/8223 6433**), a colonial-style pub popular for after-work drinks. **The Port Dock,** 10 Todd St., Port Adelaide (☎ **08/8240 0187**), was licensed as a pub in 1864 and has kept up with tradition ever since; it even brews four of its own beers and pumps them directly to its three bars with old English beer engines. Most pubs are open from 11am to midnight.

TRYING YOUR LUCK AT THE CASINO   Right next to the Adelaide Hyatt, and dwarfed by the old railway station it's situated in, is the **Adelaide Casino,** North Terrace (☎ **1800/888 711** in Australia, or 08/8212 2811). It has two floors of gaming tables and slot machines, as well as four bars and several dining options, including a fast-food station and the excellent Pullman buffet restaurant. The casino is open Sunday to Thursday from 10am to 4am and Friday and Saturday from 10am to 6am.

2 Side Trips from Adelaide
THE BAROSSA: ON THE TRAIL OF THE GRAPE

More than a quarter of Australia's wines, and a disproportionate number of top labels, originate in the Barossa and Eden valleys—collectively known as the Barossa. Beginning just 45 kilometers (28 miles) northeast of Adelaide and easily accessible, the area has had an enormous influence on the city's culture. In fact, Adelaidians of all socioeconomic levels partake in more wine talk than do the French. The area was first settled by German settlers from Silesia, who came to escape religious persecution. They brought with them their particular brand of culture, their food, and their vines. They also built the Lutheran churches that dominate the Barossa's skyline. With the help of wealthy English aristocrats, the wine industry went from strength to strength. Today, there are more than 50 wineries in an area that still retains its German flavor.

The focal points of the areas are **Angaston,** the farthest away from Adelaide; **Nuriootpa,** the center of the rural services industry; and **Tanunda,** the nearest town to the city. Each has interesting architecture, craft and antiques shops, and specialty food outlets.

If you're adventurous, you might want to rent a bike in Adelaide, take it on the train to Gawler, and bike through the Barossa. Other options are exploring the area by hot-air balloon, Harley-Davidson motorcycle, or limousine. **Balloon Adventures** (☎ 08/8389 3195) runs champagne breakfast flights daily, costing A$231 (U.S.$150.15) for adults and A$165 (U.S.$107.25) for children ages 6 to 16.

ESSENTIALS

WHEN TO GO   The best times to visit the Barossa are in the spring (Sept and Oct), when it's not too hot and there are plenty of flowering trees and shrubs, and in the fall (Apr and May), when the leaves turn red. The main wine harvest is late summer/early autumn (Feb and Mar). The least crowded time is winter (June, July, and Aug).

GETTING THERE   If you have a car (by far the most flexible way to visit the Barossa), I recommend taking the scenic route from Adelaide (the route doesn't have a specific name, but it's obvious on any map). It takes about half an hour longer than the Main North Road through Gawler, but the trip is well worthwhile. Follow the signs to Birdwood, Springton, Mount Pleasant, and Angaston.

Public buses run infrequently to the major centers from Adelaide. There are no buses between wineries.

ORGANIZED TOURS FROM ADELAIDE   Various companies run limited sightseeing tours. One of the best, **Festival Tours** (☎ 08/8374 1270), offers a day trip visiting three wineries and other attractions. It costs A$62 (U.S.$40.30) for adults and A$48 (U.S.$31.20) for children, including a restaurant lunch. The tour departs daily at the corner of Rundle Mall and King William Street at 9:20am and picks up at hotels beforehand.

VISITOR INFORMATION   The excellent **Barossa Wine and Visitor Centre,** 66–68 Murray St., Tanunda, SA 5352 (☎ **08/8563 0600;** e-mail: bwta@dove.net.au; www.barrosa-region.org), is open Monday to Friday from 9am to 5pm, and Saturday and Sunday from 10am to 4pm. It's worth popping into the center's small audiovisual display for an introduction to the world of wine; entry is A$2 (U.S.$1.30) for adults; children are free. You'll need a least an hour to look around.

TOURING THE WINERIES

With some 48 wineries offering free cellar-door tastings and/or daily tours charting the wine-making process, you won't be stuck for places to visit. All wineries are well signposted. Below are just a few of my favorite places, but don't be shy about just stopping whenever you come across a winery that strikes your fancy.

Drinking & Driving—Don't Do It!

Australia's drunk-driving laws are strict and rigidly enforced. If you'll be chasing the grape around the Barossa, choose a designated driver or take a guided tour.

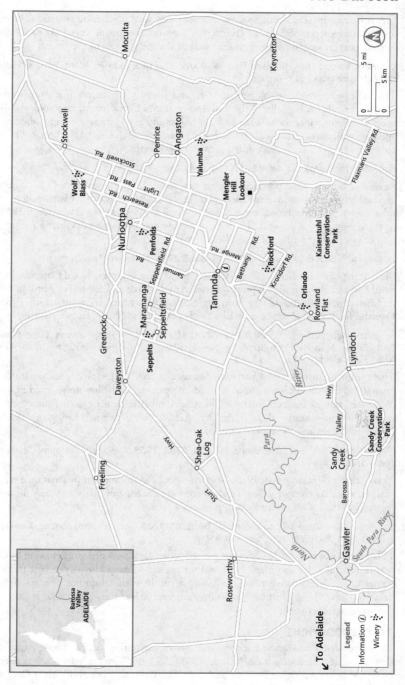

Legend

i Information

Winery

To Adelaide

A tip: Try a sparkling red. Some wine snobs may turn up their noses, and it takes some getting used to; but bear in mind that the world's wine industry now hangs on Australia's every new offering, so it may well be the great tipple of the future.

Orlando. Barossa Hwy., Rowland Flat. ☎ **08/8521 3140.** Mon–Fri 10am–5pm, Sat–Sun and public holidays 10am–4pm.

This large winery was established in 1847 and is today the home of many award-winning brands. Its big seller is the well-known Jacobs Creek brand, now sold world-wide. Premium wines include the Lawson Shiraz and the Jacaranda Ridge Cabernet, and new vintages of either will set you back at least A$45 (U.S.$29.25) a bottle. There are an opal shop, a craft shop, and a picnic area with BBQs.

Penfolds. Nuriootpa. ☎ **08/8301 5400.** Daily 10am–4:30pm.

Australia's biggest wine producer churns out some 22.5 million liters (5.8 million U.S. gal.) from this one winery every year. Penfolds also owns other wineries all over the country. It all started when Dr. Christopher Rawson planted a few vines in 1844 to make wine for his patients. The winery now houses the largest oak-barrel matura-tion cellars in the Southern Hemisphere.

Rockford. Krondorf Rd., Tanunda. ☎ **08/8563 2720.** Mon–Sat 11am–5pm.

Most of the buildings here were constructed in 1984 out of recycled local materials, but you'd never know. The wine is pressed between mid-March and the end of April, in the traditional way with machinery from the turn of the century. It's a fascinating sight. Demand for Rockford wines, especially the Basket Pressed Shiraz, far exceeds supply.

Seppelts. Seppeltsfield. ☎ **08/8562 8028.** Mon–Fri 10am–5pm, Sat–Sun 11am–5pm. Tours hourly Mon–Fri 11am–3pm; Sat–Sun 11:30am, 1:30pm, and 2:30pm. Adults A$5 (U.S.$3.25), children A$2 (U.S.$1.30).

This National Trust–listed property was founded in 1857 by Joseph Seppelt, an immi-grant from Silesia. The wine tour around the gardens and blue-stone buildings is considered one of the best in the world. Check out the family's giant Romanesque mausoleum on a nearby slope skirted by roadside palms planted during the 1930s recession to keep winery workers employed.

Wolf Blass. Sturt Hwy., Nuriootpa. ☎ **08/8562 1955.** Mon–Fri 9am–5pm, Sat–Sun 10am–5pm.

This winery's Germanic-style black-label vintages have an excellent international rep-utation, while its cheaper yellow-label vintages are the toast of many a Sydney dinner party. The small Wolf Blass museum is worth a peek.

Yalumba. Eden Valley Rd., Angaston. ☎ **08/8561 3200.** www.yalumba.com.au. Mon–Fri 8:30am–5pm, Sat 10am–5pm, Sun noon–5pm.

This winery was built in 1849, making it the oldest family-owned wine-making busi-ness in Australia. It's also huge. Look out for the sad-looking Himalayan bear in the corner of the large tasting room, following a run-in with a hunting rifle; it's been Yalumba's advertising gimmick. The winery's Signature Red Cabernet-Shiraz is among the best you'll ever taste.

ACCOMMODATIONS

There are plenty of standard motels and lots of interesting B&Bs throughout the Barossa, some with rooms for as little as A$60 (U.S.$39). Weekends are often booked solid, and prices are higher than on weekdays. The **Barossa Wine and Visitor Centre** (see "Visitor Information," above) can provide information on additional accommo-dation choices and off-season deals.

Barossa Park Motel. Barossa Valley Hwy., Lyndoch (P.O. Box 370), Lyndoch, SA 5351. ☎ **08/8524 4268.** Fax 08/8524 4725. 34 units. A/C MINIBAR TV TEL. A$83 (U.S.$53.95) double. Extra adult A$12 (U.S.$7.80), extra child under 12 A$7 (U.S.$4.55). Ask about packages. AE, BC, DC, MC, V.

Unlike your average motor inn, this one is set well back from the road within its own large grounds. The rooms are quite large, and some interconnect, which can be handy for families. All rooms are comfortable and clean, and have queen-size beds plus at least another twin. All have connecting bathrooms with a shower. There are a fully licensed restaurant, an outdoor pool and spa, and a game room on the premises.

Barossa Valley (SA) Tourist Park. Penrice Rd., Nuriootpa, SA 5355. ☎ **08/8562 1404.** Fax 08 85622 615. www.barossa.touristpark.com.au. E-mail: barpark@dove.net.au. 27 cabins, 19 with bathroom. A/C TV. A$30 (U.S.$19.50) double without private bathroom; A$45–$60 (U.S.$29.25–$39) double with bathroom. Extra adult A$5 (U.S.$3.25), extra child 3–15 A$3 (U.S.$1.95). AE, BC, DC, MC, V.

This very peaceful place is set way back from the road and abuts a lake and wildlife reserve. The cabins are simple affairs but come with just about everything you'll need for a pleasant-enough stay. Cabins have a combination of doubles, singles, and bunk beds. All units have small kitchenettes, although only the more expensive cabins have microwaves. There's a swimming pool just down the road, and a laundry, a barbecue, and tennis courts are on the property. If you don't have your own linen, you'll be charged A$5 (U.S.$3.25) per single bed and A$10 (U.S.$6.50) per double.

✪ **Collingrove Homestead.** Eden Valley Rd., Angaston, SA 5351. ☎ **08/8564 2061.** Fax 08/8564 3600. 5 units, 3 with bathroom. A$150 (U.S.$97.50) double without private bathroom; A$180 (U.S.$117) double with bathroom. Rates include full breakfast. AE, BC, DC, MC, V.

In my opinion, Collingrove is not just the best country-house experience in the Barossa but one of the best in Australia. This was the home of John Howard Angas, one of South Australia's initial settlers. It was originally built in 1856, and additions were made as Angas's successful sheep business prospered. The hallway is festooned with spears, artillery shells, rifles, oil-painted portraits, and the mounted heads of various stags and tigers. English oak paneling and creaky floorboards add a certain nuance, and the cedar kitchen, library, glorious dining room, and various other places are all bursting with antiques and knickknacks. What the quaint, individually decorated guest rooms lack in modern amenities (no phones or TVs), they make up for in charm. The modern communal spa is set in the old stables, with its flagstone floors and old horse harnesses; there's also a flagstone-floored tennis court.

Even if you don't stay here, you may want to indulge in Devonshire tea on the terrace (served daily for A$5/U.S.$3.25) or tour the property, which is possible Monday through Friday from 1 to 4:30pm and Saturday and Sunday from 11am to 4:30pm. The tour costs A$4 (U.S.$2.60) for adults and A$1.50 (U.S.$1) for children. Sunday brunch is also popular.

The Hermitage of Marananga. Corner of Seppltsfield and Stonewell Rd., Marananga, SA 5351. ☎ **08/8562 2722.** Fax 08/8562 3133. E-mail: thehermitage@dove.net.au. 11 units, including 1 apt. A/C MINIBAR TV TEL. A$190 (U.S.$123.50) double; A$230 (U.S.$149.50) spa room; $230 (U.S.$149.50) apt. Rates include GST and cooked breakfast. AE, BC, DC, MC, V.

This is far and away the best of the area's motels. The rooms are awkwardly shaped but have been recently renovated. Each has a small balcony, a fridge, and tea- and coffee-making facilities. The main building is old-fashioned and bursting with character. It's also cool in the heat of summer. Outside are a swimming pool and spa, and fantastic views over the valley and to the ranges beyond. A four-course, country-style dinner in the restaurant costs around A$45 (U.S.$29.25), including GST. There are good walks around the property and, at dusk, plenty of 'roos in the surrounding fields. The new apartment has a private balcony overlooking the vineyards, a separate bedroom, and a double sleeper sofa in the living room.

✪ **Marble Lodge.** 21 Dean St., Angaston, SA 5351. ☎ **08/8564 2478.** Fax 08/8564 2941. www.marblelodge.com.au. Reservations recommended. 2 units. A/C TV TEL. A$165 (U.S.$107.25) suite. Rate includes breakfast, bottle of champagne, and minibar drinks. AE, BC, DC, MC, V.

Wake up and smell the roses—there are plenty of them in the beautiful gardens surrounding this romantic historic property (as well as a tennis court, and several resident deer and kangaroos). Away from the main house is a lodge made of local marble that's divided into two suites. The larger suite has two rooms and an open fireplace. The second is basically a large bed/sitting room, with an open fireplace. Both suites have access to the shared spa bath and are tastefully furnished in antiques. There are always fresh fruit, homemade cookies, and chocolates in the room, and it's a 5-minute walk to three local restaurants. A double room, with shared bathroom, is sometimes available in the homestead itself.

DINING

The Barossa prides itself on its cuisine as well as its wine, so you'll find plenty of fine places to eat, many of them serving up traditional German foods that reflect the area's heritage.

Put the **1918 Bistro & Grill,** 94 Murray St., Tanunda (☎ **08/8563 0405**), at the top of your list. Appetizers, ranging in price from A$8.90 to $13 (U.S.$5.80 to $8.45), are enough to fill you up; I recommend the baked mushrooms. Another hot spot for lunch or dinner is the **Vintner's Bar & Grill,** Nuriootpa Road, Angaston (☎ **08/8564 2488**). The wine list here is six pages long! Main courses cost A$15 to $19 (U.S.$9.75 to $12.35). Both restaurants serve essentially Modern Australian cuisine.

The valley's best German-style bakery is in Lyndoch: the **Lyndoch Bakery,** on the Barossa Highway (☎ **08/8524 4422**). In Angaston, stop off at the **Angas Park Hotel,** 28 Murray St. (☎ **08/8562 1050**), which serves up home-cooked meals.

THE ADELAIDE HILLS

Only a 25-minute drive from Adelaide and visible even from the main shopping street, you'll find the tree-lined slopes and pretty valleys, the orchards, vineyards, winding roads, and historic townships of the Adelaide Hills. You might want to walk part of the **Heysen Trail** (see "Enjoying the Great Outdoors" in the "Adelaide" section, earlier in this chapter), browse through the shops in Hahndorf, stop in Melba's Chocolate Factory in Woodside, or visit Cleland Wildlife Park or Warrawong Sanctuary. Otherwise, it's a nice outing just to hit the road and drive. Should you decide to stay overnight, the area offers lots of cozy B&Bs.

ESSENTIALS

GETTING THERE   The Adelaide Hills are just 25 minutes from Adelaide by car via Greenhill and Glen Osmond roads. **Adelaide Sightseeing** (☎ **08/8231 4144**) runs outings to the gorgeous little town of Hahndorf (see below), as well as to Cleland Wildlife Park. An afternoon excursion to Hahndorf costs A$30 (U.S.$19.50) for adults and A$20 (U.S.$13) for children; the tour to Cleland costs A$26 (U.S.$16.90) for adults and A$20 (U.S.$13) for children, including park entry.

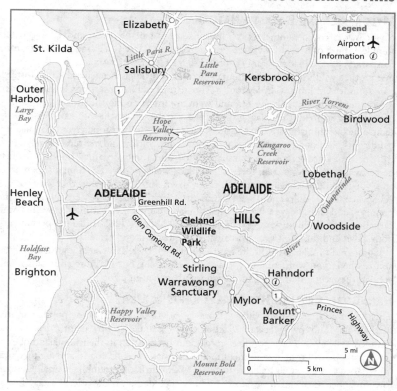

VISITOR INFORMATION   Visitor information and bookings are available through the **Adelaide Hills Tourist Information Centre,** 41 Main St., Hahndorf (☎ **08/8388 1185**). It's open Monday to Friday from 9am to 4pm. Otherwise, detailed maps are available at the South Australia Travel Centre in Adelaide.

BIRDWOOD: FOR VINTAGE CAR FANS

Birdwood, located 46 kilometers (28 miles) east and slightly north of Adelaide, is best known for the restored 1852 flour mill that now contains the **National Motor Museum** (☎ **08/8568 5006**). Here you'll find the best collection of vintage cars anywhere in Australia. Among them is the first vehicle to cross Australia (in 1908). The complex also includes tearooms and a gift shop, and you can picnic along banks of the upper reaches of the River Torrens. The museum is open daily from 9am to 5pm (closed Christmas). Admission is A$9 (U.S.$5.85) for adults, A$4 (U.S.$2.60) for children 5 to 15, and A$24 (U.S.$15.60) for a family of four.

WOODSIDE: CHOCOLATE LOVERS UNITE!

Visitors come here for **Melba's Chocolate Factory,** Henry Street (☎ **08/8389 7868**), where chocoholics will find a huge range of handmade chocolates to tempt the taste buds. Melba's is part of Heritage Park, a complex that includes a wood turner, a cheese maker, a ceramics studio, a leather maker, and a craft shop. It's open Monday to Friday from 10am to 4pm; and Saturday, Sunday, and public holidays from noon to 5pm.

MYLOR: GETTING BACK TO NATURE

Mylor is located 25 kilometers (15 miles) southeast of Adelaide, and 10 kilometers (6 miles) south of Mt. Lofty via the town of Crafters. Here you'll find the **Warrawong Sanctuary,** Stock Road, Mylor (☎ **08/8370 9197;** www.efl.com.au). Unlike those in many other wildlife parks, the animals here are not kept in enclosed runs. Instead, park founder Dr. John Wamsley took a 35-acre tract of former farming land, replanted it with natural bush, fenced it off, and went around shooting the introduced rabbits, cats, dogs, and foxes that plague much of Australia. Then the good doctor took to reintroducing animals native to the site—such as kangaroos, various types of wallabies, bandicoots, beetongs, platypuses, possums, frogs, birds, and reptiles. They are all thriving, not only because he eliminated their unnatural predators, but also because he re-created waterways, rain forests, and black-water ponds. The animals roam free, and you're guided through on 1¹/₂-hour dawn or sunset walks that costs A$18 (U.S.$11.70) for adults and A$12 (U.S.$7.80) for children. There's a restaurant on the premises, and you can even stay overnight in large cabins with bathrooms, wall-to-wall carpeting, and air-conditioning. The cabins cost A$125 (U.S.$81.25) per person with both dawn and dusk tours, a two-course dinner, and breakfast.

Compared to Cleland Wildlife Park (see below), there's not such a great variety of animals here (you won't find any koalas, for example), but it's more educational and you get the feeling that you're in the wild, rather than in a zoo.

HAHNDORF: GERMAN HERITAGE, CRAFTS & MORE

This historic German-style village is one of South Australia's most popular tourist destinations. The town, located 29 kilometers (18 miles) southeast of Adelaide, was founded in 1839 by Lutherans fleeing religious persecution in their homeland of eastern Prussia. They brought with them their wine-making skills, foods, and architectural inheritance and put it all together here. ✪ **Hahndorf** still resembles a small German town in appearance and atmosphere, and it is included on the World Heritage List as a Historical German Settlement. Strolling around, you'll notice **St. Paul's Lutheran Church,** erected in 1890. The **Wool Factory, L'Unique Fine Arts & Craft,** and **Bamfurlong Fine Crafts** are all worth checking out and are all within walking distance of Main Street.

Busway Travel (☎ **08/8410 6888**) operates half-day tours daily to Hahndorf, including a German lunch, and a visit to Mt. Lofty Summit (see below). Tours cost A$28 (U.S.$18.20) for adults and A$19 (U.S.$12.35) for children. Tours leave from the Busway Travel offices on Bank Street, off North Terrace, in Adelaide.

Accommodations

The Hahndorf Resort. 145A Main St., Hahndorf, SA 5245. ☎ **08/8388 7921.** Fax 08/8388 7282. 60 units, 80 caravan and tent sites. A/C TV TEL. A$55 (U.S.$35.75) cabin; A$89 (U.S.$57.85) motel room; A$89–$99 (U.S.$57.85–$64.35) chalet. AE, BC, DC, MC, V.

This large resort has a variety of accommodations plus approximately 80 caravan and tent sites. The fully self contained, air-conditioned cabins come with a private bathroom, a small kitchen area, a TV, and linen. Motel rooms are typical of their type and come with queen-size beds (some have an extra single) and a shower. The chalets look like they're straight out of Bavaria; each can accommodate from two to five people in either one or two bedrooms. All have full kitchens and attached private bathrooms with showers. Some of them overlook a small lake. The spa chalets are larger and, of course, come with a spa bath. There is a restaurant with main courses averaging around A$15 (U.S.$9.75), a swimming pool, a small gym, a couple of putting greens, a canoe lake, a half-size tennis court, a laundry, and a few emus, kangaroos, and horses running around in an animal sanctuary. Bicycles are available for rent.

Dining

✪ **Karl's German Coffee Shop.** 17 Main St., Hahndorf. ☎ **08/8388 7171.** Main courses A$3.90–$10.50 (U.S.$2.55–$6.80) at lunch; A$8.90–$13.90 (U.S.$5.80–$9) at dinner. AE, BC, DC, MC, V. Wed–Sun 11am–10pm and public holidays. GERMAN.

Pop into this Bavarian beer cellar–style eatery at any time of day for good homemade cakes and coffee. At lunch, the ploughman's lunch goes down well, as do the German sausages with sauerkraut. Dinner favorites include seafood, steaks, and chicken dishes.

OAKBANK: A DAY AT THE RACES

This is the spot for the Adelaide Hills' biggest event, the **Easter Oakbank Racing Carnival,** part of the Australia-wide "picnic races" that take place in small towns throughout the nation. The Oakbank horse races attract crowds in excess of 70,000 a day over the long Easter weekend. General admission is A$9 (U.S.$5.85), plus another A$5 (U.S.$3.25) for admission to the grandstand. The **Oakbank Racing Club** (☎ **08/8212 6279**) is just off the main road; you can't miss it.

Accommodations

Adelaide Hills Country Cottages. P.O. Box 100, Oakbank, SA 5243. ☎ **08/8388 4193.** Fax 08/8388 4733. www.ahcc.com.au. E-mail: relax@ahcc.com.au. 3 cottages. A/C TV. A$145–$230 (U.S.$94.25–$149.50) including GST. Extra person A$55 (U.S.$35.75). Rates include provisions for full breakfast. 1-night stays include A$30 (U.S.$19.50) surcharge. Ask about lower weekly rates. BC, MC, V. Oakbank is 35 min. from Adelaide, 7 min. from Hahndorf, and less than an hour from the Barossa Valley.

These three self-contained cottages have won several tourism awards, including the 1998 Australian Tourist Commission award for hosted accommodation in Australia—which is quite a big deal. They are 1 kilometer (0.6 miles) apart and are surrounded by 150 acres of scenic countryside. The Apple Tree cottage, circa 1860, sleeps up to five, has a spa bath and antiques, and overlooks an orchard and a lake; the Gum Tree Cottage sleeps four and has wonderful country views; and the Lavender Fields Cottage also sleeps up to four and overlooks a lily-fringed duck pond. All of the cottages have open fireplaces and fully equipped kitchens. This is a great place to relax and a good base for exploring the area. You'll get a couple of free drinks and a fruit basket upon arrival.

MT. LOFTY: VIEWS & 'ROOS

Visitors make the pilgrimage to the top of the 2,300-foot Mt. Lofty, 16 kilometers (10 miles) southeast of Adelaide, for the panoramic views over Adelaide, the surrounding Adelaide plains, and the Mt. Lofty Ranges. There are several nice bushwalks from the top. You can find the **Summit Restaurant** (☎ **08/8339 2600**) up here, too; it's open for lunch daily and dinner Wednesday through Sunday. Main courses cost between A$13.90 and $19.90 (U.S.$9 and $12.95) and include roasted field mushrooms on polenta, roast duck breast with black rice, and veal porterhouse. In the same building is the Summit Cafe, selling good sandwiches and cakes, and Devonshire tea for A$6 (U.S.$3.90). The restaurant runs a limo service to Adelaide and back for up to four people for A$80 (U.S.$52) round-trip.

Almost at the top of Mt. Lofty, off Summit Road, is the **Cleland Wildlife Park** (☎ **08/8339 2444**). Here you'll find all the usual Australian animals on offer—including the largest male red kangaroo I've ever seen. Though the park is not nearly as good as similar wildlife parks elsewhere in Australia, it does have a very good wetlands aviary. One of the drawbacks of Cleland is that it's got some unimaginative enclosures, most notably the one for the Tasmanian devils. The park is open daily from 9:30am to 4:30pm. Visitors can meet at the Tasmanian devil enclosure at 2pm and join the animal feed run by following a tractor around the park as it drops off food.

Admission to Cleland is A$7.50 (U.S.$4.90) for adults, A$4.50 (U.S.$2.90) for children 3 to 14, and A$18.50 (U.S.$12) for families. Koala holding is allowed during the photo sessions held daily from 2 to 4pm (but not on very hot summer days); on Sunday there's an additional session from 10am to noon. The privilege will cost you A$8 (U.S.$5.20) per photo. A kiosk and restaurant are on the premises.

3 Kangaroo Island

110km (68 miles) South of Adelaide

There is nowhere better than ✪ **Kangaroo Island** to see Australian marsupials in the wild. Period. Spend a couple of days on the island with the right guide and you can walk along a beach past a colony of sea lions; spot hundreds of New Zealand fur seals playing together in foreshore rock pools; creep through the bush on the trail of wallabies; stroke semitame kangaroos; spot sea eagles, black swans, sacred ibis, pelicans, fairy penguins, galahs, crimson rosellas, the rare glossy cockatoo, and the endangered stone curlew; come across goannas and the island's lone emu; pick out bunches of koalas hanging sleepily in the trees above your head; and, if you're lucky, see platypus, echidna, bandicoots, reclusive pygmy possums, and lots, lots more.

The secrets to Kangaroo Island's success are its perfect conditions—the most important of which is the fact that there are no introduced foxes or rabbits to take their toll on the native inhabitants or their environment. The island was also never colonized by the dingo (Australia's "native" dog), which was believed to have been introduced from Asia some 4,000 years ago. About one-third of the island is unspoiled national park, and there are plenty of wildlife corridors to give the animals a chance to move about the island, thus lessening the problems of inbreeding.

While the animals are what most people come to see, no one goes away without also being impressed by the scenery. Kangaroo Island has low mallee scrubland, dense eucalyptus forests, rugged coastal scenery, gorgeous beaches, caves, lagoons, and black-water swamps. The effect of 150 years of European colonization has taken its toll, though. In South Australia as a whole, some 27 mammal, 5 bird, 1 reptile, and 30 plant species have become extinct since the state was discovered by the English seafarer Matthew Flinders in 1802.

The island's history is a rugged one. Aboriginal people inhabited the island as early as 10,000 years ago, but abandoned it for unexplained reasons. In the 19th century it was settled by pirates; mutineers; cutthroats; deserters from English, French, and American ships; and escaped convicts from the eastern colonies. Sealers also arrived and took a heavy toll on the local seal and sea lion population—in just 1 year, 1803 to 1804, they managed to kill more than 20,000 of these animals. Between 1802 and 1836, Aboriginal women from both the mainland and Tasmania were kidnapped, brought to Kangaroo Island, and forced to work catching and skinning seals, kangaroos, and wallabies, and lugging salt from the salt mines.

In 1836, Kangaroo Island became the first place in South Australia to be officially settled. The state's capital was Kingscote, until it was abandoned a couple of years later in favor of Adelaide. In spite of its early settlement, Kangaroo Island had very few residents until after World War II, when returned soldiers set up farms here. Today, more than a million sheep are raised on the island. The island also acts as an official bee sanctuary to protect the genetic purity of the Lugurian bee, introduced in 1881 and believed to be the only place in the world where this strain of bee survives.

ISLAND ESSENTIALS

WHEN TO GO   The best time to visit Kangaroo Island is between November and March (though you'll have difficulty finding accommodations over the Christmas school holiday period). July and August tend to be rainy, and winter can be cold (though often milder than on the mainland around Adelaide).

Many companies offer 1-day trips to Kangaroo Island from Adelaide, but I would strongly advise you to tailor your holiday to spend at least 2 days here, though 3 or even 5 would be even better. There really is a lot to see, and you won't regret spending the extra time.

GETTING THERE   **Kendell Airlines** (☎ 1800/338 8894 in Australia, or 08/8231 9567) flies from Adelaide to Kingscote from the Ansett terminal at Adelaide Airport. The round-trip fare is about A$180 (U.S.$117), with 14-day advance purchase fares around A$98 (U.S.$63.70). Note that prices may change on a daily basis depending on availability. The flight to Kangaroo Island takes about 25 minutes. Luggage restrictions mean you can take only 10 kilograms (2.2 lb.) of luggage onboard these aircraft.

If you prefer to go there by sea, **Kangaroo Island SeaLink** (☎ 13 13 01 in Australia, or 08/8202 8688; www.sealink.com.au; e-mail: kiexpert@sealink.com.au) operates two vehicle and passenger ferries four times daily (sometimes 10 times in peak periods) from Cape Jervis on the tip of the mainland to Penneshaw on Kangaroo Island. The trip takes 40 minutes and costs A$60 (U.S.$39) round-trip for adults, A$30 (U.S.$19.50) for children 3 to 14, and A$130 (U.S.$84.50) for cars. Connecting bus service from Adelaide to Cape Jervis is provided at an extra A$30 (U.S.$19.50) for adults round-trip, and A$15 (U.S.$9.75) for children. Count on 3 hours for the whole trip from Adelaide if you take the connecting bus.

VISITOR INFORMATION   **Tourism Kangaroo Island,** The Gateway Information Centre, Howard Drive, Penneshaw (P.O. Box 336, Penneshaw, Kangaroo Island, SA 5222; ☎ 08/8553 1185; www.tourkangarooisland.com.au; e-mail: tourki@kin.on.net), has plenty of maps and information and can book accommodations and island tours.

For more information on the island's national parks, contact the **National Parks and Wildlife Service (NPWS)** office, 39 Dauncey St. (☎ 08/8553 2381), open Monday to Friday from 9am to 5pm.

In addition, hotel and motel staff generally carry a stack of tourist brochures and can point you in the right direction as far as where to go and what to see.

ISLAND LAYOUT   Kangaroo Island is Australia's third-largest island, at 156 kilometers (97 miles) long and 57 kilometers (35 miles) wide at its widest point. The distance across the narrowest point is only 2 kilometers (1.25 miles). Approximately

---

A Travel Tip

I'd advise buying an **NPWS Island Pass** if you'll be exploring the island on your own. It costs A$24 (U.S.$15.60) for adults, A$17 (U.S.$11) for children, and A$65 (U.S.$42.25) for families, and includes guided tours of Seal Bay, Kelly Hill Caves, Cape Borda, and Cape Willoughby. Also included is access to Flinders Chase National Park, where a A$9 (U.S.$5.85) charge per vehicle is usually levied. The pass doesn't cover penguin tours, or camping fees. You can purchase it at the visitor information office on Kangaroo Island, at the NPWS office in Kingscote, or at any park ranger station, like the one at Seal Bay.

Kangaroo Island

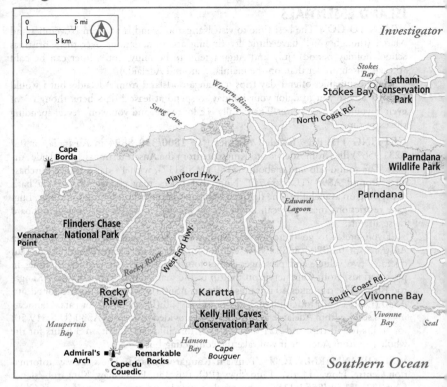

3,900 people live on the island. More than half the population lives on the northeast coast of the island in one of the three main towns: Kingscote (pop. 1,800), Penneshaw (pop. 250), and American River (pop. 200). The island's major attractions, however, are located farther from the mainland; Flinders Chase National Park is in the far west, Lathami Conservation Park is on the north coast, and Seal Bay and Kelly's Caves are on the south coast.

GETTING AROUND   Apart from a bus service that connects Kingscote, Penneshaw, and American River, there is no public transportation on the island. An **Airport Shuttle Service** (☎ **08/8553 2390**) can transport you from Kingscote Airport to your Kingscote accommodation. The 15-minute trip costs A$10 (U.S.$6.50) for adults and A$5 (U.S.$3.25) for children. The shuttle meets all Kendell flights.

Major roads between Penneshaw, American River, Kingscote, and Parndana are paved, as is the road to Seal Bay. But most other roads are made of ironstone gravel and can be very slippery if corners are approached too quickly. All roads are accessible by two-wheel-drive vehicles, but if you're bringing over a rental car from the mainland, make sure your policy allows you to drive on Kangaroo Island's roads. Avoid driving at night—animals rarely fare best in a collision with a car.

Car-rental agencies on the island include **Budget** (☎ **08/8553 3133,** or 08/8553 1034) and **Hertz & Kangaroo Island Rental Cars** (☎ **1800 088 296** in Australia, or 08/8553 2390). You can pick up cars at the airport or ferry terminals.

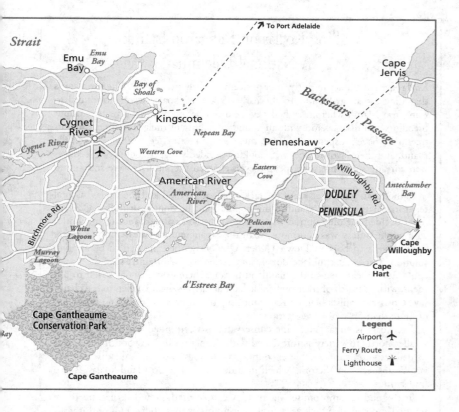

Strait

Emu Bay — *Emu Bay*

Bay of Shoals

Cygnet River

Cygnet River

To Port Adelaide

Cape Jervis

Backstairs Passage

Kingscote

Nepean Bay

Penneshaw

Western Cove

Eastern Cove

American River

American River

Willoughby Rd

Antechamber Bay

DUDLEY PENINSULA

Pelican Lagoon

Birchmore Rd.

White Lagoon

Murray Lagoon

Cape Willoughby

Cape Hart

d'Estrees Bay

Cape Gantheaume Conservation Park

Bay

Cape Gantheaume

Legend

Airport ✈
Ferry Route – – – –
Lighthouse ⚊

EXPLORING THE ISLAND

The island is much bigger than you might think, and you can spend a fair bit of time just getting from one place of interest to the next. Of the many, many places to see on the island, ✪ **Flinders Chase National Park** is one of the most important. It took 30 years of lobbying until reluctant politicians finally agreed to preserve this unique western region of the island in 1919. Today, it makes up around 17% of the island and is home to true wilderness, some beautiful coastal scenery, two old lighthouses, and plenty of animals. Bird-watchers have recorded at least 243 species of birds here. Koalas are so common in parts that they're almost falling out of the trees. Platypus have been seen, but you'll probably need to make a special effort and sit next to a stream in the dark for a few hours to have any chance of spotting one. In the works are plans to develop a series of walking trails, boardwalks, and platypus observation hides at the Rocky River Waterhole, which should greatly increase visitors' chances of viewing the elusive critters. Kangaroos, wallabies, and brush-tailed possums, on the other hand, are so tame and numerous that the authorities were forced to erect a barrier around the Rocky River Campground to stop them from bounding up and carrying away picnickers' sandwiches!

The most impressive coastal scenery can be found at **Cape du Couedic** at the southern tip of the park, where millions of years of crashing ocean have created curious structures—like the hollowed-out limestone promontory called **Admiral's Arch**

Culling Koalas on Kangaroo Island:
A National Dilemma

Koalas are cute. They're fluffy, they're sleepy, and they're cuddly. The problem is that they eat an awful lot. In the early 1920s, 18 koalas were introduced to Kangaroo Island, where they had never existed before. Over the years, without predators and disease, and with an abundant supply of their favorite eucalyptus trees, they have prospered. By 1996, there were an estimated 4,000 koalas on the island, and their favorite trees were looking decidedly ragged. Some of the koalas were already suffering; some people even claimed the animals were starving to death.

Rather than waiting to see if the lack of adequate food and the koalas' natural territorial nature would stabilize the population, the South Australian Government decided the only option was to shoot Australia's ambassador to the world. The public outcry was enormous, with the Japanese even threatening to advise their citizens to boycott Down Under. Obviously, there needed to be another solution. But what could be done? Some scientists maintained that the koalas could not be relocated to the mainland because there were few places left to put them, with so much of their preferable habitat having already fallen to the chainsaw. Conservationists blamed Kangaroo Island's farmers for depleting the island of more than 50% of its vegetation.

The koala is endangered, the conservationists reminded the politicians; the smaller northern variety is threatened with extinction in New South Wales due to deforestation, unfavorable encounters with dogs and cars, and disease. The larger subspecies in Victoria, which includes the Kangaroo Island koalas, is also under threat.

In the end a compromise was met. A couple of thousand koalas are to be trapped and neutered each year until their numbers are stabilized (as of this writing, there are now around 5,000 koalas). A few conscientious farmers will plant more trees. Other farmers will, no doubt, continue to see the koalas as pests.

When white man came to Australia, there were countless millions of koalas. In modern times, most Australians will never see one in the wild.

---

and the aptly named **Remarkable Rocks,** where you'll see huge boulders balancing on top of a massive granite dome. At Admiral's Arch, there is a colony of some 4,000 New Zealand fur seals that are easily spotted playing in the rock pools and resting on the rocks. During rough weather, this place can be spectacular. Recently, the road from Rocky River Park Headquarters to Admiral's Arch and Remarkable Rocks was paved to within 4 kilometers of Rocky River. A new parking lot and loop trail also have been developed at Remarkable Rocks. There are also a new road, parking lot, and trail system around the Cape du Couedic heritage lighthouse district.

Elsewhere on the island, you shouldn't miss out on the unforgettable experience of walking through a colony of Australian sea lions at **Seal Bay.** The Seal Bay Conservation Park was established in 1972, and these days some 100,000 people visit it each year. Boardwalks have been built through the dunes to the beach to reduce the impact of so many feet. The colony consists of about 500 animals, but at any one time you might see up to 100 basking with their pups here. The rangers who supervise the area lead guided trips throughout the day, every 15 to 30 minutes from 9am to 4:15pm.

Don't Feed the Animals, Please

Don't feed any native animals. Kangaroos and wallabies might beg for food, but they are lactose intolerant and can go blind, or catch disease, from being fed human food.

If you come here without a coach group, you must join a tour. Tours cost A$7.50 (U.S.$4.90) for an adult, A$5 (U.S.$3.25) for a child, and A$15 (U.S.$9.75) for a family.

Lathami Conservation Park, just to the east of Stokes Bay, is a wonderful place to see wallabies in the wild. Just dip in under the low canopy of casuarina pines and walk silently, keeping your eyes peeled, and you're almost certain to spot them. If you're fortunate, you may even come across a very rare glossy cockatoo—it's big and black and feeds mainly on casuarina nuts.

Another interesting spot, especially for bird-watchers, is **Murray Lagoon,** on the northern edge of Cape Gantheaume Conservation Park. It's the largest lagoon on the island and an important habitat for thousands of water birds. Contact the NPWS (see "Visitor Information," above) for information on a ranger-guided Wetland Wade.

If you want to see **fairy penguins**—tiny animals that stand just 33 centimeters (13 in.) tall—forget the touristy show at Phillip Island near Melbourne. On Kangaroo Island, you get to see them in a totally natural environment. Tours are conducted nightly by the NPWS (see "Visitor Information," above) and cost A$5 (U.S.$3.25) for adults, A$3.50 (U.S.$2.30) for children, and A$13.50 (U.S.$8.80) for families. Times of tours change seasonally, so call NPWS to confirm. Tours of a colony near Penneshaw gather at the Interpretive Centre adjacent to the penguins, and tours of the Kingscote colony meet at the reception desk of the Ozone Hotel.

For a fabulous day of boat fishing for everything from King George Whiting, trevally, and snapper to mullet and mackerel, contact **Kangaroo Island Fishing Charters** (☎ **08/8553 5247**). A day out costs $100 (U.S.$65) including lunch.

Finally, Kangaroo Island is renowned for its fresh food. Across the island, you'll see signs beckoning to you to come and have a taste of cheese, honey, wine, and the like. One place worth a stop is **Clifford's Honey Farm** (☎ **08/8553 8295**), which is open daily from 9am to 5pm. The farm sells pots of stringybark and canola- and mallee-flower honey, along with beeswax candles and honey ice cream. The farm is located roughly in the center of the island, but ring ahead for exact directions.

ADVENTURE TOUR OPERATORS

✪ **Kangaroo Island Wilderness Tours** (☎ **08/8559 2220**) operates several small four-wheel-drive vehicles (maximum six people) and takes visitors around the islands on very informative 1-day trips costing A$205 (U.S.$133.25) per person, including transfers, an excellent lunch with wine, and park entry fees. Two-, 3-, and 4-day trips, with all meals and accommodation included, cost A$513 (U.S.$333.45), A$821 (U.S.$533.65), and A$1,129 (U.S.$733.85) per person, respectively.

Another excellent operator is ✪ **Adventure Charters of Kangaroo Island,** Playford Highway, Cygnet River, SA 5223 (☎ **08/8553 9119**), with the knowledgeable and gregarious Craig Wickham, a former national park ranger, at the helm. Day trips cost A$225 (U.S.$146.25) a day with a big lunch, or A$402 (U.S.$261.30) for a 1-day safari including Kendell flights from and to Adelaide.

Kangaroo Island Odysseys (☎ **08/8553 1311**) offers a similar day trip in small vehicles for A$215 (U.S.$139.75) per person, including lunch.

ACCOMMODATIONS

If the choices below are full, check out **www.tourkangarooisland.com.au**, which lists additional options.

There are some 40 self-contained cottages or coastal lodgings on the island. Contact **Kangaroo Island Remote and Coastal Farm Accommodation** (☎ 08/8553 1233). Standards vary and prices range from A$40 to $100 (U.S.$26 to $65) for each property. The staff can also arrange lodgings in local farms, homes, and B&Bs for A$60 to $110 (U.S.$39 to $71.50) for a double with breakfast.

The **NPWS** (see "Visitor Information," above) also offers basic but comfortable lodgings for rent, including relatively isolated ✪ **lighthouse cottages** at Cape Willoughby, Cape Borda, and Cape du Couedic, from A$20 (U.S.$13) per adult per night (though the minimum charge per stay is between A$60 and A$90/U.S.$39 and $58.50 per cottage).

Camping is allowed only at designated sites for a minimal fee. The main sites are at Rocky River in Flinders Chase National Park.

IN & NEAR KINGSCOTE

Ozone Hotel. The Foreshore (P.O. Box 145), Kingscote, SA 5223. ☎ **08/8553 2011.** Fax 08/8553 2249. 37 units. A/C TV TEL. A$85–$105 (U.S.$55.25–$68.25) double; A$112 (U.S.$72.80) triple. Extra person A$7 (U.S.$4.55). AE, BC, DC, JCB, MC, V.

The best known of Kangaroo Island's lodging alternatives, the Ozone gets its name from the aroma of the sea—which virtually laps at its door. It's a nice, centrally located choice, with a restaurant, a casual bistro serving good meals, a couple of bars, a game room, a pool and sauna, and a laundry. Rooms are comfortable, with plenty of space; most of the more expensive ones have water views of Nepean Bay. Family rooms have a double bed and two single beds.

✪ **Wisteria Lodge.** 7 Cygnet Rd., Kingscote, SA 5223. ☎ **08/8553 2707.** Fax 08/8553 2200. Reservations can be made through Flag Inns (☎ 800/624-3524 in the U.S. and Canada, 0800/892 407 in the U.K., 0800/803 524 in New Zealand, 13 24 00 in Australia). 20 units. A/C MINIBAR TV TEL. A$120 (U.S.$78) double; A$136 (U.S. $88.40) triple. Spa room A$153 (U.S.$99.45) double; A$173 (U.S.$112.45) triple. Extra adult A$16–$20 (U.S.$10.40–$13); extra child 3–12 A$13–$17 (U.S.$8.45–$11.05). Breakfast A$9.60 (U.S.$6.25) extra. Ask about money-saving packages (with transport to the island, transfers, meals, and day tours). AE, BC, DC, MC, V.

All rooms at the modern and definitely unglamorous-looking Wisteria Lodge are standard motel-type, but ocean views over Nepean Bay are a plus. Deluxe rooms offer a spa and queen-size beds. There is a pool, a spa, a playground, and half-size tennis court here, too. Simple meals, such as pastas, steak, apricot chicken, or fish, are served in the Beachcomber restaurant, where reservations are essential.

IN AMERICAN RIVER

Popular with fishermen and located 37 kilometers (23 miles) from Kingscote, American River lacks a beach but offers black swans on Pelican Lagoon instead. Wild wallabies abound, and egrets, magpies, and cockatoos offer early-morning wake-up calls.

Casuarina Holiday Units. 9 Ryberg Rd., American River, SA 5221. TV. ☎ and fax **08/8553 7020.** 6 units. TV. A$50 (U.S.$32.50) double. BC, V.

These simple, country-style units are a good value. Each comes with a double bed, two singles, a fan, a heater, a TV, and an attached shower. There are a laundry, a barbecue, a children's playground, and fish-cleaning facilities if you manage to catch anything.

✪ **Kangaroo Island Lodge.** Scenic Rd., American River, SA 5221. ☎ **08/8553 7053.** Fax 08/8553 7030. www.kangarooislandlodge.com.au. 38 units. $142 (U.S.$92.30) water-view double; $115 (U.S.$74.75) poolside double, including GST. $17 (U.S.$11) extra person. AE, BC, DC, MC, V.

Though Kangaroo Island Lodge was originally built in 1801, renovations in late 1999 have so completely overhauled the place that you'd be hard-pressed to find anything rustic remaining. What you have, though, is a very nicely appointed property with pleasant, quiet motel-style rooms, a good swimming pool, a spa and sauna, and a nice restaurant and bar where main courses average A$17.50 (U.S.$11.40). The lodge looks over Pelican Lagoon (rightly famous for its pelicans), but it's a little too far away from it to make the water-view double rooms really worth the extra cost.

Wanderers Rest. Bayview Rd. (P.O. Box 34), American River, SA 5221. ☎ **08/8553 7140.** Fax 08/8553 7282. www.wanderersrest.com.au. E-mail: wanderers@kin.on.net. 9 units. MINI-BAR TV. A$174 (U.S.$113) double including GST; A$224 (U.S.$145.60) triple. Rates include full breakfast. Ask about their very good value packages and ferry transport deals. AE, BC, DC, MC, V. No children under 12.

This pleasant guest house is set on a hillside with panoramic views across the sea to the mainland. It has large, comfortably furnished rooms with balconies. All rooms come with king-size beds that convert to twins. You get a shower but no tub. There are a pool and spa in the garden, and a game room. Breakfasts are hearty, packed lunches are available, and dinnertime can be a hoot, with guests sipping beers and wine around the dining-room table and tucking into King George whiting caught that day. Other meals are available, such as steak, lamb chops, local oysters, and a vegetarian stir-fry. Main courses cost $19 (U.S.$12.35), including GST. The restaurant is fully licensed. No smoking.

IN PARNDANA

Developed by soldier-settlers after World War II, Parndana today is a rural service center situated a 25-minute drive from Seal Bay and Stokes Bay, and just around the corner from Parndana Wildlife Park, which has more than 50 aviaries with collections of native and other birds, some of them rare and protected.

✪ **The Open House.** 70 Smith St., Parndana, SA 5221. ☎ **08/8559 6113.** Fax 08/8559 6088. www.theopenhouse.com.au. E-mail: walls@arcom.com.au. 4 units. A$116 (U.S.$75.40) per person with dinner and breakfast included; A$88 (U.S.$57.20) per person with just breakfast included. A$88 (U.S.$57.20) per child under 14 with dinner and breakfast included; A$72 (U.S.$46.80) per child with just breakfast included. BC, MC, V.

The best thing about the Open House is mealtimes, when the guests get together and sit around a communal table and tuck into delicious home-cooked meals—and imbibe plenty of wine. The rooms—two with double beds, one with a queen-size bed, one with two singles, and a family room sleeping up to four—are comfortable and homey and come with private bathrooms with showers. The very friendly owner, Sarah Wall, will offer excellent advice on what to do around the island; she whips up a mean packed lunch for A$20 (U.S.$13).

OTHER PLACES

✪ **Hanson Bay Cabins.** Hanson Bay Company, P.O. Box 614, Kingscote, SA 5225. ☎ **08/8853 2603.** Fax 08/8853 2673. 6 cabins. A$100 (U.S.$65) cabin for 2. $12 (U.S.$7.80) each extra adult. A$10 (U.S.$6.50) extra child. AE, BC, DC, MC, V.

Located on the southwest coast of the island, on the South Coast Road, Hanson Bay Cabins is a row of six comfortable log cabins perched above a fabulous beach. The cabins each have a large picture window facing the southern ocean, and come with a full kitchen, a bathroom, two bedrooms (including a double bed and three singles in all), and a wood stove. Bring your own food and supplies from Kingscote, American River, or Penneshaw. The ocean can get really wild and dramatic around here with strong off-shore winds whipping up the sand and spray. The cottages are near to most of the major attractions and so make a good base. Salmon are often caught off the beach.

✪ **Stranraer Homestead.** Wheatons Rd., MacGillivray, SA 5221. ☎ **08/8553 8235.** Fax 08/8553 8226. 4 units. A$160 (U.S.$104) double. Prices include GST and gourmet breakfast. AE, BC, DC, MC, V.

Lyn and Graham Wheaton are your kind hosts at this federation homestead built in the 1920s by Graham's grandfather. Located 30 kilometers (19 miles) south of Kingscote off the Hundred Line Road on the way to the Estuary Bay, it has four individual country-style rooms with high molded ceilings, comfy double beds, and fireplaces. The two shared bathrooms are good-sized, each coming with a clawfoot bathtub and a shower. The owners prefer to rent out only two rooms a night so that guests essentially have private bathrooms. Single travelers pay less than a couple for a room. Also here is a guest lounge room with a small library. Excellent three-course local-produce dinners are served around a communal table and cost $52 (U.S.$33.80).

DINING

You'll find that most accommodations on Kangaroo Island provide meals for guests (at an additional cost, usually), and most day tours around the island include lunch. You'll find a few cheap take-out booths scattered around the island at the most popular tourist spots. For lunch you could get sandwiches at the deli on Dauncey Street, behind the Ozone Hotel, in Kingscote.

IN PENNESHAW

Dolphin Rock Café. 43 N. Terrace (next to the YHA). ☎ **08/8553 1284.** Main courses A$3–$9.50 (U.S.$1.95–$6.20). AE, BC, MC, V . Winter Wed–Mon 7:30am–7:30pm; summer daily 7am–8:30pm. FAST FOOD.

This place offers your basic plastic tables and chairs plus budget meals (very popular with backpackers), including individual pizzas and french fries and gravy. Also on offer are fish-and-chips, burgers, and roasted chicken. Across the road, the fairy penguins come in at dusk.

AT CAPE WILLOUGHBY

Cape Willoughby Café. Cape Willoughby. ☎ **08/8553 1333.** Main courses A$12–$17 (U.S.$7.80–$11). AE, BC, DC, MC, V. Call ahead for opening times and reservations policy, because ownership was changing hands as of this writing. LOCAL PRODUCE.

This fabulous restaurant is perched on a cliff-top on the far eastern tip of the island, right next to Cape Willoughby Lighthouse (an attraction in itself). One wall is all glass, and there's a veranda outside with terrific ocean views. King George Whiting is a specialty, as are the desserts (the sticky date pudding is mouth-watering).

Forty-five–minute tours of the lighthouse leave from the lighthouse office at 10am, 11am, 12:30pm, and 2pm daily. They cost $6 (U.S.$3.90) for adults, A$4.50 (U.S.$2.90) for children and A$16.50 (U.S.$10.70) for families.

4 Outback South Australia

South Australia is the driest state in the country. This is well borne out once you leave behind the parklands of Adelaide and head into the interior. The Outback is as harsh as it is beautiful. Much of it is made up of stony desert, salt pans, and sand hills, roamed by kangaroos and wild goats. After spring rains, though, the area can burst alive with wildflowers.

It was always difficult to travel through these parts, and even today there are only four main routes that traverse it. One of them, the **Birdsville Track,** is famed in Outback history as the trail along which stockman once drove their herds of cattle south from Queensland. Another, the **Strzelecki Track,** runs through remote sand-dune country to Innamincka and on to Coopers Creek. Both of these tracks cut through the "dog fence"—a 5,600-kilometer (3,500-mile) long barrier designed to keep dingoes out of the pastoral lands to the south.

If you follow the **Stuart Highway,** or the Oodnadatta Track, you'll pass the mining towns of Coober Pedy, Andamooka, and Mintabie, where people from all over the world have been turned loose in the mad search for opals. Out here, too, are national parks, such as the daunting **Simpson Desert Conservation Park,** with its seemingly endless blood-red sand dunes and spinifex plains, and **Lake Eyre National Park,** with its dried-up salt pan that, during the rare event of a flood, is a temporary home to thousands of water birds.

You can create a fabulous driving tour by renting a four-wheel-drive vehicle in Adelaide, and taking a day's drive north through the **Clare Valley wine region** (stop off for a traditional Aussie lunch at **Bluey Blundstone's Café** at Melrose; ☎ **08/ 8666 2173**). The next day it's a 3- or 4-hour drive to **William Creek,** an unusual Outback town with a pub/hotel. Just 20 kilometers (12 miles) before you reach town is the turnoff to Lake Eyre. (**Wrightsair** offers 1-hour flights over Lake Eyre for $110 per person; call ☎ **08/8670 7880.**) Camping beside the lake is a magical experience. The next day it's a 166-kilometer (103-mile) drive to Coober Pedy (see above), or a 9-hour drive back to Adelaide.

THE FLINDERS RANGES NATIONAL PARK
460km (285 miles) N of Adelaide

The dramatic craggy peaks and ridges that make up the Flinders Ranges rise out of the South Australian desert country. The colors of the rock vary from deep red to orange, with sedimentary lines easily visible as they run down the sides of cliffs. Much of the greenery around here is stunted arid land vegetation. Ever since the introduction of a devastating rabbit virus in 1996, and with the continued culling of hundreds of thousands of wild goats, shoots and saplings that for decades were nibbled away before they grew up have started to turn what was once bare land back into bush. The most remarkable attraction is **Wilpena Pound,** a natural circle of cliff faces that form a gigantic depression on top of a mountainous ledge. The wind whipping over the cliff edges can produce some exhilarating white-knuckle turbulence if you fly over it in a light aircraft. Kangaroos and emus can sometimes be seen wandering around the park, but outside the park, kangaroos are heavily culled.

The best tour operator to the national park from Adelaide is **Wallaby Tracks Adventure Tours** (☎ **1800/639 933** or 08/8648 6655; e-mail: headbush@dove.net.au;

An Outback Travel Warning

If you intend to drive through the Outback, take care. Distances between points of interest can be huge, and water supplies, petrol, food, and accommodations are far apart. Always travel with a good map and plenty of expert advice. If you plan to travel off-road, a 4WD vehicle is a must. Read "Road Conditions & Safety," in the "Getting Around Australia" section in chapter 2, before setting off.

http://headbush.mtx.net). The company's 3-night mountain safari, including camping, costs A$279 (U.S.$181.35), while a 2-night Weekend Escape package departing Adelaide every Friday afternoon and returning Sunday night costs A$199 (U.S.$129.35). It also runs trips to the Flinders from Port Augusta and Quorn, as well as a 10-day Australian bush expedition from Adelaide to Alice Springs called ✪ **Heading Bush Adventures.** On this tour you get to experience the Flinders Ranges, the Oodnatta Track, Coober Pedy, the Simpson Desert, Ayers Rock, the Olgas, Kings Canyon, and Aboriginal communities. This remarkable trip costs A$750 (U.S.$487.50), including meals and bush camping, and focuses on Aboriginal culture.

Kev's Kamel Kapers (☎ **0419/839 288** mobile phone) offers remarkable 2-hour sunset camel safaris for A$25 (U.S.$16.25), half-day excursions for A$50 (U.S.$32.50), and full-day safaris including a champagne lunch for A$80 (U.S.$52) for adults and A$60 (U.S.$39) for children under 16. Overnight camel treks are available, and on weekends and public holidays 15-minute rides cost just A$5 (U.S.$3.25). The tours run only from March to the end of October and leave from Hawker (call beforehand for exact pickup spot). Kev is often unreachable, so check with the tourist association for his whereabouts.

ESSENTIALS

GETTING THERE   By car, take either Highway 1 out of Adelaide to Port Augusta (3½ hr.), then head east on Route 47 via Quorn and Hawker (another 45 min.). It's another hour to Wilpena Pound. Alternatively, take the scenic route (it doesn't have a specific name) through the Clare Valley (around 5 hr.): From Adelaide head to Gawler and then through the Clare Valley; follow signs to Gladstone, Melrose, Wilmington, and Quorn.

Premier Stateliner (☎ **08/8415 5555**) runs five buses every day from Adelaide to Port Augusta for A$31.20 (U.S.$20.30) one-way. The company also runs buses to Wilpena Pound via Hawker and Quorn, leaving Adelaide at 8:30am on Wednesday and 11am on Friday. Fares each way are A$39.90 (U.S.$25.90) to Quorn, A$52.30 (U.S.$34) to Hawker, and A$56.30 (U.S.$36.60) to Wilpena Pound. Buses return to Adelaide from Wilpena Pound at 11am on Thursday, 7:15pm on Friday (arriving in Adelaide at 5am), and 3:05pm on Sunday.

VISITOR INFORMATION   Before setting off, contact the **Flinders Ranges and Outback of South Australia Regional Tourism Association (FROSATA)** at P.O. Box 2083, Port Augusta (☎ **1800/633 060** in Australia), for advice on roads and conditions.

I strongly recommend a visit to the **Wadlata Outback Centre** at 41 Flinders Terrace, Port Augusta (☎ **08/8642 4511**), an excellent, award-winning interactive museum and information center. The museum costs A$7 (U.S.$4.55) for adults and A$4.50 (U.S.$2.90) for children and is open Monday to Friday from 9am to 5:30pm, and Saturday and Sunday from 10am to 4pm.

In Hawker, both the Mobil service station and the post office also act as information outlets.

ENTRANCE FEES   Park entrance is A$7.50 (U.S.$4.90) per vehicle. The fee is payable at the National Parks and Wildlife Service office near the Wilpena Pound Resort, or by exchanging cash for a ticket at unmanned ticket booths around the park.

ACCOMMODATIONS

✪ **Andu Lodge.** 12 First St., Quorn, SA 5043. ☎ **1800/639 933** in Australia, or 08/8648 6655. Fax 08/8648 6898. E-mail: headbush@dove.net.au. 64 beds. A$43 (U.S.$27.95) double; A$51 (U.S.$33.15) family room (sleeps 4). A$20 (U.S.$13) dorm bed. AE, BC, DC, MC, V.

A Spectacular Bushwalk

The Heysen Trail, named after the painter Sir Hans Heysen, is a 2,000-kilometer (1,200-mile) track that starts in the northern Flinders Ranges, traverses the Flinders and the Lofty ranges, and ends up at the coast at Cape Jervis. The most interesting section of the trail is through the Flinders Ranges, where the dramatic reds of the Outback contrast at times with water holes and tree-lined creeks.

✪ **Ecotrek** (☎ **08/8383 7198;** e-mail: ecotrek@ozemail.com.au) runs 7-day walking tours of the Flinders Ranges part of the Heysen Trail, with overnight stays at sheep stations. It's a real Aussie adventure. Each day consists of 5 hours of walking; but you only carry a daypack, and the going is fairly easy. Treks cost A$890 (U.S.$578.50), including guide, accommodation, food, and transfers to and from Adelaide.

This fabulous backpackers' lodge is one of the best in Australia. Situated in Quorn, in the central Flinders Ranges (42km/26 miles from Port Augusta), this upscale former hotel is air-conditioned in summer, is heated in winter, and has nice clean rooms (dorms sleep six). There are also a nice TV room, a laundry, a computer for e-mailing, and a kitchen area. The hostel offers transfers from Port Augusta for A$6 (U.S.$3.90) each way and runs a range of outings, with an emphasis on Aboriginal culture and eco-tourism. Guests can also rent mountain bikes. Quorn (pop. 1,300) was where the old Ghan railway used to start and finish from, and where part of the movie Gallipoli was filmed. The town has four friendly pubs, all serving meals for A$5 (U.S.$3.25).

✪ **Prairie Hotel.** Corner of High St. and West Terrace, Parachilna, SA 5730. ☎ **08/8648 4844.** Fax 08/8648 4606. www.prairiehotel.com.au. 12 units. A/C MINIBAR. A$105–$145 (U.S.$68.25–$94.25) double; A$195 (U.S.$126.75) double with spa. Extra person A$35 (U.S.$22.75). Rates include light breakfast. AE, BC, DC, MC, V.

If you're going to stay anywhere near the Flinders Ranges, stay here. This tiny, tin-roofed, stone-walled pub offers a memorable experience and is well worth the dusty 89-kilometer (55-mile) drive north alongside the Ranges from Hawker on the A83. A new addition to the pub contains nice rooms, each with a queen-size bed and a shower. The older-style rooms are smaller and quaint. Three units have spa tubs.

The bar out front is a great place to meet the locals and other travelers (who all shake their heads in wonder that this magnificent place is still so undiscovered). Meals here, prepared by "Flinders Feral Food," are top-notch—very nearly the best I've had in Australia. Among their specialties are so-called "feral" foods, such as kangaroo tail soup to start and a mixed grill of emu sausages, camel steak, and kangaroo as a main course.

The owner's brother runs remarkable scenic flights over Wilpena Pound and out to the salt lakes. From here you could head to the township of William Creek for a side trip to see the giant salt-lake, Lake Eyre, and then onward west to Coober Pedy.

Wilpena Pound Resort. Wilpena Pound, SA 5434. ☎ **1800/805 802** in Australia, or 08/8648 0004. Fax 08/8648 0028. 60 units. A/C TV. A$95–$135 (U.S.$61.75–$87.75) double; A$145 (U.S.$94.25) self-contained units. Extra adult A$10 (U.S.$6.50); extra child 2–14 A$5 (U.S.$3.25). AE, BC, DC, MC, V.

The nearest place to the Wilpena Pound itself, this partly refurbished resort almost monopolizes the overnight tourist market around here. Standard rooms are adequate and offer respite from the summer heat. The self-contained units come with a stove-top, a microwave, a basin, and cooking utensils. There are also a rather tacky dining room and bar, a general store, and a swimming pool.

The resort also operates a campground. Campsites cost A$17 (U.S.$11) per night for two people with power and A$11 (U.S.$7.15) per night for two people without power, and A$3 (U.S.$1.95) for each extra person.

There are some good walks around the area. The resort also offers half-hour scenic flights over the Ranges for A$125 (U.S.$81.25) for one person, A$75 (U.S.$48.75) per person for two, or A$65 (U.S.$42.25) per person for three or more. They also operate 4WD tours with lunch for A$80 (U.S.$52) for a full day and A$65 (U.S.$42.25) for a half day.

DINING

The **Old Ghan Restaurant** on Leigh Creek Road, Hawker (☎ **08/8648 4176**), is open for lunch and dinner Wednesday through Sunday; the restaurant used to be a railway station on the *Ghan* railway line to Alice Springs before the line was shifted sideways due to flooding. The food here is unexciting, but the homemade pies have a following.

If you find yourself in Port Augusta, the area's main town, head to the **Standpipe Motor Inn** (☎ **08/8642 4033**) for excellent Indian food. The rooms here are nice enough, and quiet, and cost A$80 (U.S.$52) for a double.

COOBER PEDY

854km (529 miles) NW of Adelaide, 689km (427 miles) S of Alice Springs

Tourists come to this Outback opal-mining town for one thing: the people. More than 3,500 people, from 44 nations, work and sleep mainly underground here—the majority suffering from so-called opal fever, which keeps you digging and digging on the trail of the elusive shimmering rocks. Though some residents are secretive and like to keep themselves to themselves, many others are colorful characters, ready to stop for a chat and spin a few yarns.

Historically, ✪ **Coober Pedy** was a rough place, and it still has a certain Wild West air about it. The first opal was found here in 1915, but it wasn't until 1917, when the Trans Continental Railway was completed, that people began seriously digging for opal. Since then, they have mainly lived underground—not surprising when you encounter the heat, the dust, and the flies for yourself.

The town got its name from the Aboriginal words "kupa piti," commonly thought to mean "white man in a hole." Remnants of the holes left by early miners are every-where, mostly in the form of bleached-white hills of waste called "mullock heaps." It's a popular tourist activity to "noodle" (search through) these heaps in search of over-looked opals.

As for the town itself, there isn't that much to look at, except a couple of under-ground churches, some casual restaurants, a handful of opal stores, and the necessary service-type businesses. These places are all within walking distance of each other on the main highway.

ESSENTIALS

GETTING THERE   **Kendell Airlines** (☎ **1800/338 894** in Australia, or 08/8231 9567) has daily flights to Coober Pedy from Adelaide.

Greyhound-Pioneer (☎ **13 20 30** in Australia) runs services from Adelaide to Coober Pedy for A$76 (U.S.$49.40) for adults and A$61 (U.S.$39.65) for children one-way. The trip takes about 12 hours. The bus from Alice Springs to Coober Pedy costs A$75 (U.S.$48.75) for adults and A$60 (U.S.$39) for children. Passengers bound for Ayers Rock transfer at Erldunda.

If you drive from Adelaide, it will take you about 9 hours to reach Coober Pedy along the Stuart Highway. It will take you another 7 hours to drive the 700 kilometers (437 miles) to Alice Springs.

VISITOR INFORMATION The **Coober Pedy Tourist Information Centre,** Hutchinson St., Coober Pedy (☎ **08/8672 5298,** or 1800/637 076 in Australia), is open Monday to Friday from 8:30am to 5pm (closed public holidays).

SEEING THE TOWN

The **Desert Cave Hotel** (☎ **08/8672 5688**) runs tours for both guests and nonguests of the opal fields and township, including visits to an underground mine, a home, and various potteries, as well as a tour of the underground Serbian Church. You also get to witness an opal-cutting demonstration and "noodle" through the mullock heaps. The 4-hour tour costs A$39 (U.S.$25.35) for adults, A$19.50 (U.S.$12.70) for children, and A$95 (U.S.$61.75) for families.

If you want to see parts of Australia that most Australians never see, join a ✪ **Mail Run** for a 12-hour journey out into the bush. Tours leave every Monday and Thursday from **Underground Books** (☎ **08/8672 5558**) in Coober Pedy (yep, it's a bookshop underground) and travel along 600 kilometers (372 miles) of dirt roads to Oodnatta and William Creek cattle station, stopping off at five different stations along the route. It can get pretty hot and dusty outside, but it's relatively comfortable inside the air-conditioned 4WD. Bring your own lunch, or buy it along the way. Tours cost A$75 (U.S.$48.75) for adults and A$55 (U.S.$35.75) for children under 12, though kids might find the long trip difficult. This could easily be one of the most memorable experiences you have in Australia.

ACCOMMODATIONS & DINING

The **Opal Inn** (☎ **08/8672 5054**) offers good-value counter meals of the typical pub-grub variety. Head to **Traces** (☎ **08/8672 5147**), the township's favorite Greek restaurant, for something a bit different.

✪ **The Backpacker's Inn at Radeka's Downunder Motel.** 1 Oliver St., Coober Pedy, SA 5723. ☎ **08/8672 5223.** Fax 08/86725821. 150 beds, including 6 twins; 9 motel rooms. A$15 (U.S.$9.75) dorm bed; A$75 (U.S.$48.75) double motel room. Extra person A$19 ($12.35). AE, BC, MC, V. Free parking.

While other "underground" rooms in Coober Pedy are actually built into the side of a hill, the hostel part of this centrally located lodging is actually underground—some 6.5 meters directly below the topside building, that is. This makes for nice all-year-round temperatures. Dorms have no doors and contain just four beds, though there are two large dorms sleeping up to 20 people. The twin rooms are simply furnished but pleasant. Guests have the use of a TV and video room, a pool table, a new kitchen and dining room, and a bar. The motel rooms, all dug out of the side of a fill, are quite comfortable, and come with attached bathrooms with showers; some have kitchenettes. Room 9 is huge, with a double and two sets of bunk beds. Radeka's also runs a good opal tour.

The Desert Cave Hotel. Hutchison St., Coober Pedy (P.O. Box 223), Coober Pedy, SA 5723. ☎ **08/8672 5688.** Fax 08/8672 5198. 50 units (19 underground). A/C MINIBAR TV TEL. A$152 (U.S.$98.80) double; A$165 (U.S.$107.25) family room sleeping 5. Extra person A$15 (U.S.$9.75). 3-day package (all inclusive, including tours and round-trip airfare from Adelaide) A$340 (U.S.$221) per person. AE, BC, DC, MC, V. Free parking.

Though it's not the only underground hotel in the world, this is the only one with a pool and spa. It was dug out using tunneling machines brought in from the opal fields; they ground up the hard desert sandstone in the side of a cliff to make tunnels

3 meters high and 2 meters wide. The walls were then sealed to cut out dust and moisture. Personally, I find the place to be a little soulless and in need of refurbishment. The bar's "pokie" machines are noisy, and you can hear your neighbors in the next room. Staying underground is a unique experience, but for those who feel a little queasy about the idea, there are identically laid-out rooms above, reached from belowground by a winding staircase. It's also worth clambering up the staircase for the specialty char-grilled dishes served at Umbertos restaurant. There's also a cafe offering lighter meals for lunch, as well as a game room.

Desert View Underground Apartments. Shore Place, Catacombe Rd. (P.O. Box 272), Coober Pedy, SA 5723. ☎ **08/8672 3330.** Fax 08/8672 3331. 11 units. TV. A$80 (U.S.$52) double. Extra adult A$20 (U.S.$13); extra child 5–12 A$12 (U.S.$7.80). AE, BC, DC, MC, V.

The apartments here are dug into the side of a hill. Each unit has a separate lounge and kitchen area, an attached bathroom with shower, a master bedroom with a double bed, and a separate bedroom with two single beds. A family room comes with a double bed and four bunks. Outside you'll find a laundry, a small pool, and a barbecue area. Half-day tours of the township can be arranged for A$20 (U.S.$13).

5 The Coorong

Few places in the world attract as much wildfowl as the Coorong, one of Australia's most precious sanctuaries. The Coorong is made up of an area that includes the mouth of the Murray River, the huge Lake Alexandrina, the smaller Lake Albert, and a long, thin sand spit called the Younghusband Peninsula. A small, but by far the most scenic, part of this area is encompassed in the Coorong National Park. The area is under constant environmental threat due to pollutants coming south via the Murray River from the farmlands to the north. It still manages, however, to play host to large colonies of native and visiting birds, such as the Australian pelican, black swans, royal spoonbills, greenshank, and the extremely rare hooded plover. The national park, which stands out starkly against the degraded farmland surrounding it, is also home to several species of marsupials, including wombats.

The best time to visit the Coorong is in December and January, when the lakes are full of migratory birds from overseas. However, plenty of birds can be spotted year-round. *Note:* Binoculars are highly recommended.

The best operator in the area is ✪ **Coorong Nature Tours** (☎ **08/8574 0037,** or 0428 714 793 mobile phone), based in Narrung. The tours are run by David Dadd, a delightful, unassuming Cockney who fell in love with the Coorong when he arrived at the age of 11. He offers memorable 1-, 2-, and 3-day tours of the area, with pickup in either Meningie or Adelaide. Full-day tours cost A$120 (U.S.$78) per person from Meningie or A$175 (U.S.$113.75) per person from Adelaide. Reservations are essential.

ESSENTIALS

GETTING THERE The best way to visit the Coorong is by car, though a guided tour of the area is highly recommended once you arrive at either the main settlement of Goolwa on the western fringe of the waterways or, more preferably, in Meningie, on the eastern boundary. From Adelaide, follow the Princes Highway along the coast. The Coorong is about 140 kilometers (87 miles) southeast of Adelaide; it's an easy 2-hour drive on a good road.

VISITOR INFORMATION The **Goolwa Tourist Information Centre,** BF Lawrie Lane, Goolwa (☎ **08/8555 1144**), has information on the area and can book accommodations.

ACCOMMODATIONS

There are plenty of hotels, B&Bs, campgrounds, and caravan parks in Goolwa and along the main road that runs parallel to the national park.

✪ **Poltalloch.** P.M.B.3, Narrung via Tailem Bend, SA 5260. ☎ **08/8574 0088.** Fax 08/8574 0065. 5 cottages. TV. A$95–$165 (U.S.$61.75–$107.25), including GST, per cottage. Extra person A$25 (U.S.$16.25). BC, MC, V.

Located smack dab in the middle of nowhere on the eastern edge of the Coorong, Poltalloch is a working farm property—with plenty of cows, ducks, chickens, and dogs wandering about—that seems more like a village. The whole place is classified by the National Trust of South Australia, and history is evident everywhere, from the cottages once used by farmhands to the giant wooden shearing shed and other outbuildings crammed with relics from the past.

You can stay in a choice of five cottages scattered across the property. The Shearer's Hut is a stone cottage that sleeps up to nine people; the Overseers stone cottage sleeps up to eight people; the Boundary Rider's Cottage is built of timber, iron, and stone, and sleeps five; and the Station Hand's Cottage sleeps four. The Shearer's Quarters is mainly for large groups and sleeps 12. All of the units are modern and comfortable inside and have their own kitchen facilities and barbecues. I stayed in the Station Hand's Cottage, which was once the home of Aboriginal workers. I loved the mix of rural feeling and modern conveniences.

There's a private beach on the property if you want to swim in the lake, and guests have the use of a dingy, a canoe, a tennis court, and a Ping-Pong table. Fascinating historical tours of the property cost A$9 (U.S.$5.85) for adults, and A$4.50 (U.S.$2.90) for children with a minimum charge of A$27 (U.S.$17.55). Bookings are essential. Breakfast provisions are available for A$13 (U.S.$8.45) per person. Coorong Nature Tours will pick you up from here for no extra charge. There's plenty of bird life on and around the property.

11

Melbourne

by Marc Llewellyn

Australia's second-largest city, with a population well over 3 million, is a melting pot of cultures. For starters, there are more people of Greek descent living here than in any other city in the world, except Athens. Then there are the Chinese, the Italians, the Vietnamese, and the Lebanese—they've all added something to Melbourne. In fact, almost a third of Melburnites were born overseas or have parents who were born overseas. With such a diverse population, and with trams rattling through the streets and stately European architecture surrounding you, you could easily forget you're in Australia at all. Melbourne (pronounced *Mel*-bun) feels like a cosmopolitan mix of Rome, Lisbon, and Hong Kong, with a dash of London thrown in. It's a restless, image-conscious city that's always exciting and always changing.

Throughout Australia, Melbourne has a reputation of being at the head of the pack when it comes to shopping, restaurants, fashion, music, and cafe culture. Time after time, it has beaten out other state capitals in bids for major international concerts, plays, exhibitions, and sporting events. The city also revels in its healthy rivalry with its northern neighbor (when Sydney won the Olympic Games and was in the throes of mass delirium, you could've heard a pin drop in Melbourne).

Melbourne's roots go back to the 1850s, when gold was found in the surrounding hills. British settlers flocked here and took up residence and have since prided themselves in coming freely to their city, rather than being forced here in convict chains. The city grew wealthy and remained largely a conservative bastion until World War II, when another wave of immigration, this time mainly from southern Europe, made it a more relaxed place. As further waves of migrants arrived, Melbourne evolved into the exciting, cosmopolitan city it is today.

1 Orientation

ARRIVING

BY PLANE Melbourne is served by two airports: **Essendon Airport** and **Melbourne Tullamarine Airport.** Major international and domestic airlines fly into the latter. Airlines serving Melbourne include Ansett, Qantas, British Airways, United, and Air New Zealand. If you're traveling from Sydney, the flight will take you around 1 hour and 20 minutes. Tullamarine Airport is 22 kilometers (14 miles) northwest of the city center. There's an information desk open from 7am to 7pm daily in the international terminal, but surprisingly not

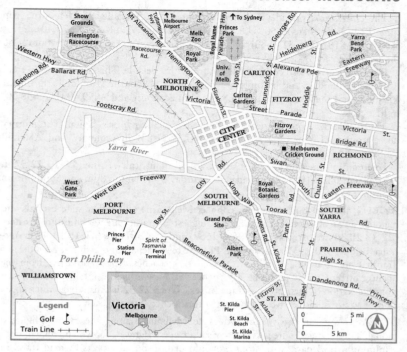

Legend
Golf
Train Line ++++

Victoria
Melbourne

one in the domestic terminal. There are snack bars, a restaurant, currency-exchange facilities, and duty-free shops in the international terminal. Baggage trolleys are free in the international baggage-claim hall, but they cost A$2 (U.S.$1.30) if hired in the car park, departure lounge, or domestic terminal. Baggage lockers cost A$4 (U.S.$2.60) per day.

Thrifty (☎ **1800 652 008** in Australia, or 03/9330 1522), **Budget** (☎ **13 27 27** in Australia), **Avis** (☎ **1800 225 533** in Australia, or 03/9338 1800), and **Hertz** (☎ **13 30 39** in Australia, or 03/9379 9955) all have rental desks at the airport.

Skybus (☎ **03/9662 9275**) picks up passengers in front of the baggage-claim area every 30 minutes from 5:30am to 11pm. The trip into the center takes around 35 minutes and costs A$10 (U.S.$6.50) one way and A$18 (U.S.$11.70) round-trip. The service travels direct to the Skybus terminal on Spencer Street and then continues to Spencer Street Railway Station. Most passengers disembark at the Skybus terminal and take a free shuttle bus to their hotel. When you want to return to the airport, book the Skybus service at least 1 hour in advance and allow at least 40 minutes for traveling time.

A taxi to the city center takes about 30 minutes and costs between A$25 and $30 (U.S.$16.25 and $19.50).

BY TRAIN Interstate trains arrive at **Spencer Street Railway Station,** at Spencer and Little Collins Streets (5 blocks from Swanston Street in the city center). Taxis and buses connect with the city.

The **Sydney–Melbourne *XPT*** travels between Australia's two largest cities daily; trip time is 10¹/₂ hours. The fares are A$96 (U.S.$62.50) in economy, A$134 (U.S.$87) in first class, and A$229 (U.S.$148.85) for a first-class sleeper. If you book well in advance, you can get discounts of up to 10% to 40% off these fares.

The *Overlander* provides daily service to and from Adelaide and Melbourne (trip time: 12 hr.). Fares are A$58 (U.S.$37.70) in economy, A$116 (U.S.$75.40) in first class, and A$182 (U.S.$118.30) for a first-class sleeper. You can transport your car on the *Overlander* for A$100 (U.S.$65).

Daylink services also connect Melbourne with Adelaide. This trip is by train from Adelaide to Bendigo and by bus from Bendigo to Melbourne. The total trip time is 11 hours, and the fare is A$51 (U.S.$33.15) in economy and A$59.40 (U.S.$38.60) in first class.

The *Canberra Link* connects Melbourne with the nation's capital. The journey takes around 11 hours and costs A$49 (U.S.$31.85) in economy, and A$64.50 (U.S.$41.90) in first class.

For train information and reservations for all trains, call **V/Line** (☎ **13 22 32** in Australia, or 03/9619 5000) Monday to Saturday from 8am to 8pm and Sunday from 10am to 6pm.

BY BUS   Several bus companies connect Melbourne with other state capitals and regional areas of Victoria. Among the biggest operators are **Greyhound Pioneer** (☎ **13 20 30** in Australia, or 03/9600 1687) and **McCafferty's** (☎ **13 14 99** in Australia, or 03/9670 2533). Greyhound Pioneer buses depart and arrive at Melbourne's Transit Centre, at 58 Franklin St. McCafferty's coaches depart and arrive from the Spencer Street Coach Station at 205 Spencer St. New arrivals can take a tram or taxi from the station to their hotel. **V/Line buses** (☎ **13 22 32** in Australia), which travel all over Victoria, also arrive and depart at the Spencer Street Coach Station.

BY CAR   You can drive from Sydney to Melbourne along the Hume Highway, though a much nicer route is via the coastal Princes Highway, for which you will need a minimum of 2 days, with stops. For information on all aspects of road travel in Victoria, contact the **Royal Automotive Club of Victoria,** 360 Bourke St. (☎ **03/ 9790 3333**).

VISITOR INFORMATION

The first stop on any visitor's itinerary should be the **Victorian Visitors Information Center,** Melbourne Town Hall, Swanston Street, at the corner of Little Collins Street (☎ **13 28 42** in Australia; www.tourism.vic.gov.au). You'll find everything you need here, and the staff can make reservations for accommodations and tours. The Melbourne Greeter Service operates from the Town Hall, too. This service connects visitors to enthusiastic local volunteers who offer free one-on-one orientation tours of the city. Advance bookings for this service are essential, and make sure you state your interests. The center is open Monday to Friday from 9am to 6pm and Saturday and Sunday from 9am to 5pm.

You'll find some information services at **The National Trust Shop,** Shop 21, Block Arcade, 282 Collins St. (☎ **03/9654 7448**), and at **Information Victoria,** 356 Collins St. (☎ **1300/366 356**). Staffed information booths are also found in Bourke Street Mall, at Flinders Street Station (on the corner of Flinders Street and Swanston Walk), and at the Queen Victoria Markets (on the corner of Therry and Queen streets).

Good Web sites on the city include **CitySearch Melbourne (melbourne.citysearch. com.au)** and **www.melbourne.org**.

CITY LAYOUT

Melbourne is situated on the **Yarra River** and stretches inland from **Port Philip Bay,** which lies to its south. Look at a map, and you'll see a distinct central oblong area surrounded by Flinders Street to the south, Latrobe Street to the north, Spring Street to the east, and Spencer Street to the west. Cutting north-to-south through its center are the two main shopping thoroughfares, **Swanston Street** and **Elizabeth Street.** A series of cross streets, including **Bourke Street Mall,** a pedestrians-only shopping thoroughfare, runs between the major thoroughfares. If you continue south along Swanston Street, it turns into **St. Kilda Road,** which runs to the coast. The central area is surrounded by Melbourne's various urban "villages," including South Yarra, Richmond, Carlton, and Fitzroy. The seaside suburb of St. Kilda has a rather scruffy beach. If you've visited Sydney, you'll find Melbourne's city center to be much smaller and far less congested with people and cars.

The Neighborhoods in Brief

Melbourne is huge. At more than 6,110 square kilometers (92,359 square miles), it's one of the biggest cities in the world. Below are the areas of most interest to visitors:

City Centre   Made up of a grid of streets north of the Yarra River, the city center is bordered to the south by Flinders Street and to the north by Latrobe Street. The eastern and western borders are Spring Street and Spencer Street, respectively.

Chinatown, with plenty of cheap restaurants, is a colorful section of the city center that's centered on Little Bourke Street between Swanston and Exhibition streets.

Carlton   North of the city center, Carlton is a tourist mecca famous for the Italian restaurants strung along Lygon Street. It has a distinct Mediterranean flair. It's also the home of the University of Melbourne, so there's a healthy student scene. Tram: 1 or 22 from Swanston Street.

Fitzroy   A ruggedly bohemian place, 2 kilometers (1 1/4 miles) north of the city center, Fitzroy is filled with students and artists—great for people-watching. Fitzroy revolves around Brunswick Street, with its cheap restaurant scene, busy cafes, art galleries, and pubs. Around the corner, on Johnston Street, are tapas bars and Spanish clubs. Tram: 11 from Collins Street; 86 from Bourke Street.

Richmond   One of Melbourne's earliest settlements is a multicultural quarter based around historic streets and back lanes. Victoria Street is reminiscent of Ho Chi Minh City, with Vietnamese sights, sounds, aromas, and restaurants everywhere. Bridge Road is a bustling fashion precinct. Tram: 48 or 75 from Flinders Street to Bridge Road; 70 from Batmans Avenue at Princes Bridge to Swan Street; 109 from Bourke Street to Victoria Street.

St. Kilda   Very hip and bohemian in a shabby sort of way, this seaside suburb (6km/4 miles south of the city center) has Melbourne's highest concentration of dining spots, ranging from glitzy to cheap, and some superb cake shops and delis. The Esplanade, which hugs the beach, is the scene of a lively Sunday market filled with arts and crafts stalls. Ackland Street houses many of St Kilda's restaurants, ranging from Chinese to Jewish. Brush up on your in-line skating skills and wear your Ray-Bans. Tram: 12 from Collins Street; 16 from Swanston Street; 94 or 96 from Bourke Street.

South Yarra/Prahan   This posh part of town is crammed with chic boutiques, cinemas, nightclubs, and galleries. Chapel Street is famous for its sidewalk eateries and designer fashion houses. Commercial Road is popular with the gay community. Tram: 6, 8, or 72 from Swanston Street.

South Melbourne   One of the oldest working-class districts of the city, South Melbourne is known for its historic buildings, old-fashioned pubs and hotels, and markets. Tram: 12 from Collins Street; 1 from Swanston Street.

Williamstown A lack of extensive development has left this outer waterfront suburb with a rich architectural heritage centered on Ferguson Street and Nelson Place—both reminiscent of old England. On the Strand, overlooking the sea, are a line of bistros and restaurants, and a World War II warship museum. Ferry: From Southgate, the World Trade Center, or St. Kilda Pier.

2 Getting Around

BY PUBLIC TRANSPORTATION

Trams, trains, and buses are operated by **The Met.** Melbourne has the oldest tram network in the world. Trams are still an essential part of the city, as well as being a major cultural icon. There are some 700 mostly green-and-yellow trams running over 325 kilometers (200 miles) of track. Instead of phasing out this nonsmoggy method of transport, Melbourne is busily expanding the network.

Tram travel within the city costs A$1.50 (U.S.$1) for adults, A80¢ (U.S.52¢) for children, for a single journey. Or you could buy a **2-Hour Metcard** good for unlimited transport on buses or trains in the central zone for up to 2 hours. The 2-Hour Metcards cost A$2.30 (U.S.$1.50) for adults and A$1.30 (U.S.85¢) for children. A better deal may be the **Zone 1 Metcard Daily ticket,** which allows travel on all transport within the city center from 5:30am to midnight (when transportation stops) and costs A$4.40 (U.S.$2.90) for adults and A$2.30 (U.S.$1.50) for children. **Metcard Weekly tickets** cost A$19.10 (U.S.$12.40) for adults and A$9.50 (U.S.$6.20) for children. The weekly ticket is good for travel within the city center and to all suburbs mentioned in this chapter.

Buy single-trip and 2-hour tram tickets at ticket machines, at special ticket offices (such as at the tram terminal on Elizabeth Street, near the corner of Flinders Street), at most newsagents, and at Metcard vending machines at many railway stations and on trams. A Metcard needs to be validated by the Metcard Validator machine on station platforms, buses, and trams before each journey; the only exception to this is a ticket purchased from a vending machine on a tram, which is automatically validated for that journey only. Vending machines on trams accept only coins, whereas larger vending machines at train stations give change up to A$10 (U.S.$6.50).

You can pick up a free route map from the Victorian Visitors Information Center, in the Town Hall on Swanston Street, or at the **Met Information Centre,** 103 Elizabeth St., at the corner of Collins Street (☎ **13 16 38** in Australia, or 03/9617 0900). The latter is open Monday to Friday from 8:30am to 4:30pm, and Saturday from 9am to 1pm.

The **City Circle Tram** is the best way to get around the very center of Melbourne—and it's free. These burgundy-and-cream trams travel a circular route between all the major central attractions, and past shopping malls and arcades. The trams run, in both directions, every 10 minutes between 10am and 6pm, except Good Friday and Christmas Day. City Circle Tram stops are marked with a burgundy sign.

Popular tram routes from the city include numbers **94, 96, and 16 to St. Kilda Beach;** numbers **48, 75, and 70 to East Melbourne;** number **57 to North Melbourne;**

A Money-Saving Transit Pass

The **Getabout Travelcard,** which can be used by two adults and up to four children, is good 1 day of travel on Saturday and Sunday only. It costs A$9.10 to $15.60 (U.S.$5.90 to $10.15), depending on how far you want to go. Buy it at newsagents.

and number **8 to South Yarra.** Trams can be hailed at numbered green-and-gold tram-stop signs. To get off the tram, press the red button located near handrails, or pull the cord running above your head.

BY EXPLORER BUS

City Explorer (☎ **03/9563 9788**) operates double-decker London-style buses that pick up and drop off at 16 stops around the city, including Queen Victoria Markets, Crown Casino, Captain Cook's Cottage, Chinatown, the Melbourne Zoo, and the Botanic Gardens, among others. There is full commentary on board. You can hop on and off as often as you want during the day. A bus returns to each stop hourly. The first bus leaves Town Hall on Swanston Street at 10am and the last leaves at 4pm. Tickets cost A$22 (U.S.$14.30) for adults, A$10 (U.S.$6.50) for children, and A$50 (U.S.$32.50) for families.

The **City Wanderer** is owned by the same company and travels a similar route, but it makes trips to historic Williamstown and the Scienceworks Museum instead of to Melbourne Zoo and Carlton.

BY TAXI

Cabs are plentiful in the city, but it may be difficult to hail one in the city center late Friday and Saturday nights. Taxi companies include **Silver Top** (☎ **13 10 08** or 03/9345 3455), **Embassy** (☎ **13 17 55** or 03/9277 3444), and **Black Cabs** (☎ **13 22 27**).

BY CAR

Driving in Melbourne is not fun. Roads can be confusing, there are trams and aggressive drivers everywhere, and there's a strange rule about turning right from the left lane. Add to this the general lack of parking spaces and expensive hotel valet-parking charges, and you'll know why it's better to get on a tram instead.

If you do want to rent a car (say, for when you're ready to move on), you'll find the big four companies represented at the airport, in additional to these city branches: **Avis,** 400 Elizabeth St. (☎ 03/9663 6366); **Budget,** 398 Elizabeth St. (☎ 03/9203 4844); **Delta,** 110 Abeckett St. (☎ 03/9600 9025); **Hertz,** 97 Franklin St. (☎ 03/9698 2555); and **Thrifty,** 390 Elizabeth St. (☎ 03/9663 5200). Expect to pay from A$30 (U.S.$19.50) a day for a small car.

Fast Facts: Melbourne

American Express   The main AMEX office is at 233 Collins St. (☎ **03/9633 6333**). It's open Monday to Friday from 9am to 5:30pm, and Saturday from 9am to noon.

Business Hours   In general, stores are open Monday to Thursday, Friday from 9am to 9pm, Saturday from 9am to 5:30pm, and Sunday from 10am to 5pm. The larger department stores stay open on Thursday evening until 9pm. Banks are open Monday to Thursday from 9:30am to 4pm, and Friday from 9:30am to 5pm.

Camera Repair   Vintech Camera Repairs, 358 Lonsdale St., 5th floor (☎ **03/9602 1820**), is well regarded.

Consulates   The following English-speaking countries have consulates in Melbourne: **United States,** 553 St. Kilda Rd. (☎ **03/9526 5900**); **United**

Kingdom, 90 Collins St., Level 17 (☎ **03/9650 4155**); and **Canada,** 123 Camberwell Rd., 1st floor, Hawthorn (☎ **03/9811 9999**).

Dentist   Call the **Dental Emergency Service** (☎ **03/9341 0222**) for emergency referral to a local dentist.

Doctor   The "casualty" department at the **Royal Melbourne Hospital,** Grattan Street, Parkville (☎ **03/9342 7000**), responds to emergencies. The **Traveller's Medical & Vaccination Centre,** 393 Little Bourke St., 2nd floor, (☎ **03/9602 5788**), offers full vaccination and travel medical services.

Emergencies   In an emergency, call ☎ **000** for police, ambulance, or the fire department.

Internet Access   **Melbourne Central Internet,** Level 2, Melbourne Central, at the corner of Elizabeth and Latrobe streets (☎ **03/9663 8410**) is open Monday to Thursday 10am to 6pm, Friday 10am to 7pm, Saturday 10am to 5:30pm, and Sunday 11am to 5pm. Another option is **Global Gossip,** 440 Elizabeth St. (☎ **03/9663 0511**), which is open daily from 8am to 1am.

Pharmacies   The **McGibbony & Beaumont Pharmacy** is in the Grand Hyatt hotel complex, 123 Collins St. (☎ **03/9650 1823**). It's open Monday to Thursday from 8am to 6:30pm, Friday from 8am to 7pm, Saturday from 9:30am to 2:30pm, and Sunday from 9:30am to noon.

Safety   St. Kilda might be coming up in the world, but it's still wise not to walk around there late at night. Parks and gardens can also be risky at night, as can the area around the King Street nightclubs.

Taxes   Sales tax, where it exists, is included in the price. There is no hotel tax as yet in Melbourne.

Weather   Call ☎ **1196** for recorded weather information.

3 Accommodations

Getting a room is generally easy enough on weekends, when business travelers are back at home with the kids. You need to book well in advance, however, for the better hotels when the city's hallmark events are taking place (say, the weekend before the Melbourne Cup horse race in Nov, and during the Grand Prix in Mar and the Australia Open in Jan—see the "Australia Calendar of Events," in chapter 2, for dates).

Though once considered dead after the office blocks closed down for the day, the city center has been rejuvenated in recent years, and you'll feel right in the heart of the action if you stay here. Otherwise, the various suburbs are all exciting satellites with good street life, restaurants, and pubs. Staying outside the city center will also let you experience the city as the natives do—commuting to the city on a tram.

The rates listed below are "rack rates," the hotels' official published rates. Hardly anybody pays the rack rate, though, so be sure to ask about any discounts or package deals before you book a room. Don't automatically rule out a place because it seems out of your price range; even the top hotels offer some amazing package deals, especially on weekends.

We've listed rates that include the new GST wherever it was possible, though some hotels had not published their new post-GST rates at the time of this writing. For now, it's best to ask carefully and clarify whether the rates you're quoted include GST.

Melbourne Accommodations

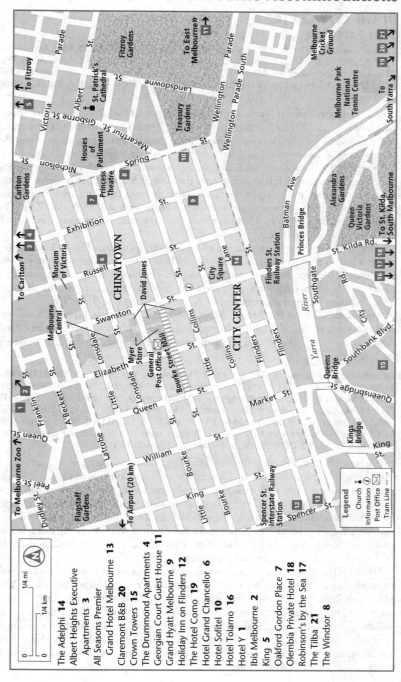

The Adelphi **14**
Albert Heights Executive
    Apartments **3**
All Seasons Premier
    Grand Hotel Melbourne **13**
Claremont B&B **20**
Crown Towers **15**
The Drummond Apartments **4**
Georgian Court Guest House **11**
Grand Hyatt Melbourne **9**
Holiday Inn on Flinders **12**
The Hotel Como **19**
Hotel Grand Chancellor **6**
Hotel Sofitel **10**
Hotel Tolarno **16**
Hotel Y **1**
Ibis Melbourne **2**
King **5**
Oakford Gordon Place **7**
Olembia Private Hotel **18**
Robinson's by the Sea **17**
The Tilba **21**
The Windsor **8**

Legend

Church
Information
Post Office
Tram Line

0   1/4 mi
0   1/4 km

IN THE CITY CENTRE
VERY EXPENSIVE

Crown Towers. 8 Whiteman St., Southbank, Melbourne 3006. ☎ **13 21 38** in Australia, or 03/9292 6868. Fax 03/9292 6600. www.crownltd.com.au. 500 units. A/C MINIBAR TV TEL. A$560 (U.S.$364) double; A$900–$1,500 (U.S.$585–$975) suite. Extra person A$50 (U.S.$32.50). Children under 12 stay free in parents' room. AE, BC, DC, JCB, MC, V. Parking A$20 (U.S.$13).

One of Melbourne's finest hotels, Crown Towers is part of the Crown Casino complex, which opened in 1997 on the banks of the Yarra River. The hotel itself is very grand and very impressive. People are often heard to let out an audible gasp as they enter the huge glittering lobby paved in black marble. Superior guest rooms occupy floors 5 through to 15; those above the 10th floor have spectacular city views. Deluxe rooms, which run up to the 28th floor, are exactly the same except with better views. Rooms are very large, with thick carpets, walk-in closets, in-room faxes and safes, voice mail, and enormous bathrooms with spa tubs, separate showers, and their own TVs. The hotel's only fault is that it's a 15-minute walk from the main shopping streets, though trams do stop right outside.

Dining/Diversions: Crown Casino offers 24-hour gambling. The 900-seat Showroom offers live entertainment nightly. A 24-hour 14-screen cinema complex and three cabaret theaters are also part of the complex. The hotel's signature restaurants are Koko, which offers traditional Japanese food (see "Dining," later in this chapter); Silks, featuring Cantonese cuisine; and Cecconi's, offering fine Italian fare.

Amenities: Olympic-size heated indoor pool, sauna, gym, spa, massage, concierge, 24-hour room service, shoe shine, laundry, valet, free daily newspaper, nightly turndown, baby-sitting, postal and business services, boutiques, newsstand, currency exchange.

Grand Hyatt Melbourne. 123 Collins St., Melbourne, VIC 3000. ☎ **1800/339 494** in Australia, 800/233-1234 in the U.S. and Canada, or 03/9657 1234. Fax 03/9650 3491. www.melbourne.hyatt.com. Email: melbourne@hyatt.com.au. 547 units. A/C MINIBAR TV TEL. A$550 (U.S.$357) Hyatt Guest double; A$570 (U.S.$370) deluxe double; A$600 (U.S.$390) Regency Club double; A$840–$3,300 (U.S.$546–$2,145) suite. Extra person A$50 (U.S.$32.50). Children under 18 stay free in parents' room. Ask about lower weekend rates and packages. AE, BC, DC, JCB, MC, V. Parking A$21 (U.S.$13.65).

The Grand Hyatt is a glitzy, glamorous affair, situated in the best part of town, just a short walk from Swanston Street, Elizabeth Street, and Chinatown. Rooms are large and luxurious and come with a nice-sized marble bathroom and all those details you'd expect from a five-star establishment, including multiple phones, dataports, tea and coffee facilities, and hair dryers (though, oddly, no irons and ironing boards). Prices vary with the view, which can almost make you feel like you're in Hong Kong as you look over the city from the top floors. Regency Club guests get free sushi and drinks in the evening, snacks all day, and a complimentary breakfast.

Dining/Diversions: The dress-up-to-dine Max's Restaurant is one of Melbourne's most glamorous spots, serving modern Australian food and expensive wines. The Plane Tree Cafe Restaurant is more relaxed. Monsoon's is a late-night disco. Downstairs, the Hyatt Food Court offers a range of casual options plus shopping.

Amenities: Concierge, 24-hour room service, laundry, valet, nightly turndown, shoe shine, baby-sitting, massage, business center. The City Club has a very large gym, a small indoor pool, a huge spa, a sauna, aerobics lessons, and a solarium. A tennis court costs A$22 (U.S.$14.30) per hour.

Hotel Sofitel. 25 Collins St., Melbourne, VIC 3000. ☎ **1300/65 65 65** in Australia, 800/ 221-4542 in the U.S. and Canada; 0800/44 4422 in New Zealand, or 03/9653 0000. Fax 03/ 9650 4261. www.sofitelmelbourne.com.au. E-mail reservations@sofitelmelbourne.com.au. 363 units. A/C MINIBAR TV TEL. A$560–$605 (U.S.$365–$393) double; A$725–$1,700 (U.S.$471–$1,105) suite. Extra person A$40 (U.S.$26). Children under 16 stay free in parents' room. Ask about lower weekend rates and other packages. AE, BC, DC, JCB, MC, V. Parking A$24 (U.S.$15.60).

I guarantee you'll like this beautiful luxury hotel, located on the best stretch of Collins Street, just a short walk from the major shopping and business area. The hotel features a glass-topped atrium that allows natural light to flood in. Rooms are large and very pleasant, with high-quality furniture, two TVs (no cable, though), VCRs, dataports, tea and coffee facilities, irons, bathrobes, safes, and large bathrooms with tub/shower combinations and hair dryers. More expensive rooms have two walls of tall windows and magnificent views over the city. The service is very impressive.

Dining/Diversions: Le Restaurant is an award-winning fine-dining choice (see "Dining," later in chapter). Café La offers fabulous good food from an all-day brasserie-style menu, and The Atrium is good for a gourmet lunch. Sofi's offers brunch and late-night cocktails.

Amenities: Concierge, 24-hour room service, laundry, valet, nightly turndown, baby-sitting, free daily newspapers, shoe shine, doctor on call, business center, hairdresser, gift shops and restaurants in same complex. Though there are a small spa and a gym in the basement, surprisingly, there's no pool.

✪ **The Windsor.** 103 Spring St., Melbourne, VIC 3000. ☎ **1800 033 100** in Australia, or 03/9633 6000. Fax 03/9633 6001. www.thewindsor.com.au. E-mail: info@thewindsor.com.au. 180 units. A/C MINIBAR TV TEL. $357 (U.S.$232) standard double; $418 (U.S.$271.70) superior double; A$473 (U.S.$307.45) deluxe double; from A$605 (U.S.$393) suite. AE, BC, DC, MC, V. Parking A$18 (U.S.$11.70).

The Windsor is Australia's only surviving authentic "grand" hotel. It opened in 1883 as, literally, The Grand and was restored to its original condition by Oberoi Hotels International. The charmingly upper-crust establishment oozes sophistication and has hosted such notables as Lauren Bacall, Douglas Fairbanks Jr., Katharine Hepburn, Sir Anthony Hopkins, Muhammad Ali, Vivien Leigh, and Omar Sharif. The lobby is luxuriously carpeted, and the staff is very friendly and efficient. Standard rooms are comfortable, with high ceilings, tasteful furnishings, and good-sized bathrooms with hair dryers. Deluxe rooms are twice as big, and many have good views of Parliament House and the Melbourne Cathedral. Superior rooms are more sumptuous still. Suites are huge and furnished with antiques. All rooms have dataports suitable for a fax or modem, and tea and coffee facilities. Guests can choose from among 10 types of pillows, including an aromatherapy version filled with rose petals and herbs. The Windsor is a member of both Leading Hotels of the World and Small Luxury Hotels of the World.

Dining/Diversions: The Grand Ballroom, with its ornate ceilings, leather furniture, gorgeous carpets, and plenty of gold leaf, is perhaps the most impressive place to eat in all of Melbourne; it's open to nonguests for an unlimited buffet lunch on Fridays at noon. One Eleven Spring Street restaurant and cocktail bar is reminiscent of a grand colonial dining room and serves lunch, dinner, and afternoon tea. The Cricketers' Club Bar is suitably upscale and traditional.

Amenities: Concierge, 24-hour room service, laundry, valet, nightly turndown, baby-sitting, free daily newspapers, health club, business center, gift shop. No pool, though.

EXPENSIVE

The Adelphi. 187 Flinders Lane, Melbourne, VIC 3000. ☎ **1800 800 177** in Australia, or 03/9650 7555. Fax 03/9650 2710. www.adelphi.com.au. E-mail: info@adelphi.com.au. 34 units (most with shower only). A/C MINIBAR TV TEL. A$270 (U.S.$175.50) standard double; A$290 (U.S.$188.50) deluxe double; A$435 (U.S.$282.75) executive double. Rates include breakfast. AE, BC, DC, MC, V. Extra person A$30 (U.S.$19.50). Free on-street parking.

It may be worth staying in this designer boutique hotel, a minute's walk from the city center, just for the experience of taking a dip in its top-floor 25-meter lap pool, which juts out from the end of the building and hangs over the city streets below. The pool has a glass bottom, so you can watch pedestrians below as you float upside down. The rooms are similarly modernist, with colorful leather seating and lots of burnished metal. While I highly recommend this place for its architectural intrigue, on my last stay the front desk staff was as spiky as the furniture. There's a reasonable restaurant downstairs.

✪ **All Seasons Premier Grand Hotel Melbourne.** 33 Spencer St., Melbourne, VIC 3000. ☎ **1300/361 455** in Australia, or 03/9611 4567. Fax 03/9611 4655. www.allseasons. com.au. E-mail: grandres@iaccess.com.au. 118 units. A/C MINIBAR TV TEL. A$220–$385 (U.S.$143–$250.25) studio suite; A$242–$440 (U.S.$157–$286) 1-bedroom suite; A$357–$605 (U.S.$232–$393) 2-bedroom suite; A$418–$715 (U.S.$271.70–$464.75) 3-bedroom suite. Extra person A$44 (U.S.$28.60). Children under 14 stay free in parents' room. Ask about weekend and seasonal packages. AE, BC, DC, JCB, MC, V. Parking A$12 (U.S.$7.80). Tram: 48 or 75 from Flinders St.

This majestic former railway department headquarters is striking for its remarkable scale and imposing Italianate facade. Building started on the six-story site in 1887, and additions were still being made in 1958. It finally became a hotel in late 1997. Suites have plush red Pullman carpets, full kitchens with dishwashers, CD players, second TVs in the bedrooms, and great views over the railway tracks. All rooms are similar but vary in size, though some have balconies. Many of the suites are split level, with bedrooms on the second floor. Guests have use of a free laundry, gym, sauna, Jacuzzi, indoor pool, and BBQs.

Holiday Inn on Flinders. Flinders Lane at Spencer St., Melbourne, VIC 3000. ☎ **800/ HOLIDAY** from North America, 1800/039 099 in Australia, or 03/9629 4111. Fax 03/ 9629 4300. www.holiday-inn.com\hotels\melsf. E-mail: info@malvern.starway.net.au. 202 units. A/C MINIBAR TV TEL. A$230 (U.S.$149.50) standard double; A$240 (U.S.$156) executive double; $340 (U.S.$221) suite. Extra person A$25 (U.S.$16.25). Children under 19 stay free in parents' room. AE, BC, DC, JCB, MC, V. A$10 (U.S.$6.50) parking. Tram: 48 or 75 from Flinders St.

If you like your hotels neat, compact, and predictable, then the Holiday Inn might be for you, though I feel it's rather expensive for what you get. It's nothing spectacular; the lobby is small, and there is a bar (with happy hour from 5 to 7pm) and a separate restaurant overlooking the road. The hotel also has a sauna, a gym, and a small but nice heated outdoor pool on the first floor. The rooms are also quite small. The City Circle tram goes right past the front door, and it's a 10-minute walk to the heart of the city.

MODERATE

Hotel Grand Chancellor. 131 Lonsdale St., Melbourne, VIC 3000. ☎ **1800/331 006** in Australia, or 03/9656 4000. Fax 03/9662 3479. www.hgcmelbourne.com.au. E-mail: reshgc@ hgcmelbourne.com.au. 160 units. A/C MINIBAR TV TEL. A$200–$250 (U.S.$130–$162.50) double. Extra person A$25 (U.S.$16.25). Ask about weekend packages and lower rates through Aussie auto clubs. Children under 15 stay free in parents' room. AE, BC, DC, JCB, MC, V. Parking A$11 (U.S.$7.15)

The great advantage of this hotel is that it's right in the heart of the action, on the very edge of Chinatown. The staff is very friendly, the heated swimming pool on the roof is pleasant on a hot summer day, and the views from the roof and some of the higher rooms are noteworthy. Furnishings are simple—you get two single beds pushed together to form a double—and you may have an interminable wait for the elevator to get to your room. It's not quite as nice as the Holiday Inn on Flinders, but it's a bit cheaper and it has a much better location.

✪ **Ibis Melbourne.** 15–21 Therry St., Melbourne, VIC 3000. ☎ **1300/65 65 65** in Australia, 800/221-4542 in the U.S. and Canada, 0800/44 4422 in New Zealand, or 03/9639 2399. Fax 03/9639 1988. 250 units. A/C TV TEL. A$155 (U.S.$100.75) standard double; A$185 (U.S.$120.25) 1-bedroom apt; A$235–$265 (U.S.$152.75–$172.25) 2-bedroom apt. Extra person A$25 (U.S.$16.25). Children under 18 stay free in parents' room. Ask about package deals. AE, BC, DC, MC, V. No parking available.

The Ibis is right next door to the bus station and a short walk from the central shopping areas. The four-star rooms are spacious, immaculate, and bright, and have an attached shower. Apartments come with kitchenettes and a tub. All guests have free use of the swimming pool, sauna, and spa just up the road at the Melbourne City Baths. There is a restaurant, a bar, and a business center on the premises.

Oakford Gordon Place. 24 Little Bourke St., Melbourne, VIC 3000. ☎ **1800/818 236** in Australia, or 03/9663 2888. Fax 03/9639 1537. www.oakford.com. E-mail: res.ogp@oakford. com. 82 apts. A/C MINIBAR TV TEL. A$140–$270 (U.S.$91–$175.50) studio; A$176–$271 (U.S.$114.40–$176.15) 1-bedroom apt; A$211–$325 (U.S.$137.15–$211.25) 2-bedroom apt; A$226–$325 (U.S.$146.90–$211.25) split-level 3-bedroom apt. Extra person A$22 (U.S.$14.30). Rates include GST. Ask about weekend packages, corporate rates, and long-term stays. AE, BC, DC, MC, V. Parking A$10–$20 (U.S.$6.50–$13).

These serviced apartments, located inside an 1884 National Trust–listed building, are some of the best I've seen, and are a good alternative if you want to do a bit of your own cooking. The spacious apartments come with full kitchens, including dishwasher. Those in the south block are older in style but still have contemporary furnishings. Those in the north block are very new and a bit more upscale; they are set farther back from the road, too. More than half of the units have a tub, but specify when booking to make sure.

The Terrace Cafe and Bar sits under a retractable glass roof, making alfresco dining possible year-round. Breakfast is served daily, but lunch is served Monday to Friday only. The hotel also features a heated saltwater pool, a spa, a sauna, a small gym, a hair salon, laundry facilities, nightly turndown, and free daily newspaper. There's a supermarket just 1 block away. All units are serviced daily.

INEXPENSIVE

Hotel Y. YWCA Melbourne, 489 Elizabeth St., Melbourne, VIC 3000. ☎ **03/9329 5188.** Fax 03/9329 1469. E-mail: hotely@ywca.net. 60 units. A$79–$110 (U.S.$51.35–$71.50) double; A$99–$120 (U.S.$64.35–$78) triple; A$170 (U.S.$110.50) apt for 4. A$30 (U.S.$19.50) dorm bed. Extra person A$15 (U.S.$9.75). AE, BC, DC, MC, V. No parking.

The Y welcomes both women and men. All rooms are sparsely furnished and not overly large. The most expensive rooms have been refurbished recently and have TVs, refrigerators, and air-conditioning. There used to be a gym here, and when I was there, a swimming pool too, but the management was planning to get rid of it. The hotel is near the Queen Victoria Markets and a short tram ride down Elizabeth Street, or a 10-minute walk, from the city center.

IN CARLTON & EAST MELBOURNE

✪ **Albert Heights Executive Apartments.** 83 Albert St., East Melbourne, VIC 3002. ☎ **1800/800 117** in Australia, or 03/9419 0955. Fax 03/9419 9517. www.albertheights. com.au. E-mail: enq@albertheights.com.au. 34 units. A/C TV TEL. A$122 (U.S.$79.30) double, including GST. Extra adult A$20 (U.S.$13), extra child A$15 (U.S.$9.75). Rates include light breakfast on first morning. Ask about special deals. AE, BC, DC, MC, V. Free parking. Tram 42 or 109; or a 10-min. walk to city.

For good moderately priced accommodations, with all the facilities you need to reduce the expense of eating out, you can't go wrong with the Albert Heights, a favorite with American travelers. It's in a very nice area of Melbourne, a few minutes' walk from the city center, and there are parks at each end of the street. Each unit in this neat brick building is large, clean, and attractive. If you want your own space, or are traveling with your family, you can use the sofa bed in the living room. Each unit comes with a full kitchen with a microwave (no conventional oven), a dining area, a large bathroom, a VCR, and two phones. There are a very popular Jacuzzi and a laundry on the premises. The hotel was renovated in 1999.

The Drummond Apartments. 371 Drummond St., Carlton, VIC 3053. ☎ **03/9345 3888.** Fax 03/9349 1250. 10 units. TV TEL. A$99 (U.S.$64.35) studio apt; A$108 (U.S.$70.20) 1-bedroom apt. AE, BC, DC, MC, V. Off-street parking. Tram: 1 or 22 from Swanston St.

You'll find very nice and functional apartments at a decent price here, giving you the option of cooking your own meals. All units are modern and clean, and come with full kitchens, hair dryers, and irons. One-bedroom apartments also have sofa beds. There's a communal laundry, and breakfast packs are available on request. It's within walking distance of the city center.

Georgian Court Guest House. 21 George St., East Melbourne, VIC 3002. ☎ **03/9419 6353.** Fax 03/9416 0895. www.georgiancourt.aunz.com. E-mail: georgian@dataline.net.au. 31 units, 21 with private bathroom. A/C TV. A$77 (U.S.$50) double without bathroom; A$97 (U.S.$63) double with bathroom; A$117 (U.S.$76) spa room. A$10–$20 (U.S.$6.50–$13) surcharge during busy periods, such as the Melbourne Grand Prix and other major sporting events. Extra adult A$20 (U.S.$13); extra child under 15 A$10 (U.S.$6.50). Rates include special buffet breakfast. AE, BC, DC, MC, V. Free parking. Tram: 78 or 45; Georgian Court is behind the Hilton, a 15-min. walk from the city center.

The Georgian Court hasn't changed much since it was built in 1910. The sitting room and the dining room both have high ceilings and offer a bit of old-world atmosphere. The bedrooms are nice, though furnished with little more than plain pine furniture and a double bed. Most rooms have air-conditioning, though some doubles without bathrooms just have fans.

IN FITZROY

The King. 122 Nicholson St., Fitzroy, VIC 3065. ☎ **03/9417 1113.** Fax 03/9417 1116. www.kingaccom.com.au. E-mail: kingaccomm@bigpond.com. 3 units (2 with shower only). A$145–$175 (U.S.$94.25–$113.75) double. Rates include breakfast. BC, MC, V. On-street parking. Tram: 96 (2 stops from top of Bourke St.).

Belying its ornate, Italianate facade, the King offers sophisticated and modern B&B-style accommodations that combine the elegance of grandly proportioned, high-ceilinged rooms with an airy minimalist decor. The three rooms vary in size. The smallest room is in the attic, and it comes with air-conditioning and a shower. The two larger rooms on the first floor have luxury marble bathrooms (one with shower only) but no air-conditioning. A TV and phone are available in the comfortable guest lounge. There are also a sunny breakfast room and a balcony overlooking the local park. A hair dryer is available. It's a short stroll to the city center.

IN ST. KILDA

✪ **Hotel Tolarno.** 42 Fitzroy St., St. Kilda, Melbourne, VIC 3182. ☎ **03/9537 0200.** Fax 03/9534 7800. www.hoteltolarno.com.au. E-mail: hoteltolarno.com.au. 35 units. TV TEL. A$100 (U.S.$65) standard double; A$122 (U.S.$79.30) balcony double; A$165–$235

(U.S.$107.25–$152.75) suite (sleeps up to 4). Extra person A$20 (U.S.$13). AE, BC, DC, MC, V. On-street parking. Tram: 16 from Swanston St.; 96 from Flinders St. (about a 15-min. ride from city center).

The Hotel Tolarno is right in the middle of St. Kilda's cafe and restaurant strip and a long stone's throw away from the beach. The whole place was renovated and expanded in 1998 and has a new foyer and breakfast/lounge room. Rich red carpets cover the corridors throughout this 1950s–1960s retro-style building. Rooms vary, but all are modern and nice. Some of the most popular rooms face the front and have balconies overlooking the main street. All rooms have showers, and some have Jacuzzi tubs. Breakfast costs A$8 (U.S.$5.20) per person. There's a restaurant and bar on the property.

Olembia Private Hotel. 96 Barkly St., St Kilda, Melbourne, VIC 3182. ☎ **03/9537 1412.** Fax 03/9537 1600. www.olembia.com.au. E-mail: stay@olembia.com.au. 23 units, none with private bathroom. A$60 (U.S.$39) double. AE, BC, MC, V. Free parking. Tram: 16 from Swanston St., 96 from Bourke St. The Frankston Airport bus will also drop you off here.

This sprawling Edwardian house, built in 1922, is set back from this busy St. Kilda street behind a leafy courtyard. It's popular with tourists, business travelers, and young families, and everyone gets together for frequent evening video nights, wine and cheese parties, and barbecues. The bedrooms are clean and simply furnished, with little more than beds, desks, hand basins, and wardrobes, but they've been recently repainted and upgraded. Guests share six bathrooms. There are a guest kitchen, a dining room, a very comfortable sitting room, and a courtyard area with BBQs. The Olembia is near St. Kilda beach and the restaurants on Acland Street. It also has 24 dorm beds that go for A$21 (U.S.$13.65), including GST.

✪ **Robinson's by the Sea.** 335 Beaconsfield Parade, St. Kilda, Melbourne, VIC 3182. ☎ **03/9534 2683.** Fax 03/9534 2683. www.babs.com.au/vic/robinsons. E-mail: wendyr@ alphalink.com.au. 5 units, 3 with private bathroom. A$130–$175 (U.S.$84.50–$113.75) double. Rates include cooked breakfast. AE, BC, DC, JCB, MC, V. Free parking. Tram: 12, 16, or 96.

If you want something very special, Robinson's by the Sea fits the bill. The management (and pet dog) at this 1870s heritage B&B just across the road from the beach are incredibly friendly. They encourage an evening social scene, and downstairs you'll find a comfortable, antique-filled living room and dining room, where you can mix and mingle with other guests. Four of the five bedrooms are located upstairs. Each unit is unique; for example, the Eastern Room has a four-poster queen-size bed and Indian and Chinese furniture, whereas the Roses room is decorated with flower patterns and pastel colors. The units all share three communal bathrooms, one with a Jacuzzi tub. There are wood floorboards and fireplaces throughout.

IN SOUTH YARRA

Claremont B&B. 189 Toorak Rd., South Yarra, VIC 3141. ☎ **03/9826 8000** or 03/9286 8222. Fax 03/9827 8652. 80 units, none with private bathroom. TV. A$68 (U.S.$44.20) double. Rates include continental breakfast. Extra person A$10 (U.S.$6.50). Children under 10 stay free in parents' room. AE, BC, DC, MC, V. On-street parking.

The high ceilings and mosaic tiles in the lobby welcome visitors into the interior of this old-world hotel, which reopened in 1995 after a complete overhaul. It's an attractive place, with sparsely furnished but comfortable rooms, each with either a double or a single bed, a TV, a refrigerator, and a heater for those cold winter nights. On the premises you'll find a coin-op laundry and 24-hour tea and coffee. There's no elevator in this three-story building, so it could be a bad choice for travelers with mobility issues.

✪ **The Hotel Como.** 630 Chapel St., South Yarra, Melbourne, VIC 3141. ☎ **1800/ 033 400** in Australia, 800/552-6844 in the U.S. and Canada, or 0800/389 7791 in the U.K., 0800/446 110 in New Zealand, or 03/9825 2222. Fax 03/9824 1263. www.hotelcomo. com.au. E-mail: resv@hotelcomo.com.au. 107 units. A$520 (U.S.$338) studio; A$600 (U.S.$390) 1-bedroom suite; A$720 (U.S.$468) 2-bedroom suite; A$850 (U.S.$552.50) penthouse; A$1,220 (U.S.$793) Como/Executive Suite. Ask about weekend package deals. AE, BC, DC, MC, V. Parking $15 (U.S.$9.75).

Winner of many tourism awards, the Hotel Como, which just completed a multi-million-dollar sprucing up, deservedly basks in its reputation for excellent service and terrific accommodations. Rooms include studios (some with showers only, all with tea and coffee facilities), one-room suites (some with kitchens or kitchenettes), one- or two-bedroom suites (all with kitchens, some with offices), and luxurious (and pricey) penthouse and executive suites. Some units have private Japanese gardens. The hotel is especially adept at accommodating business travelers: All rooms have video-conferencing capability, and three complimentary limousines carry guests to the city center each weekday morning. Weekend packages are a very good value.

Dining/Diversions: Maxim's, the hotel's fine-dining venue, is the doyen of the Melbourne scene. The Brasserie offers casual dining. The contemporary bar also serves up light meals.

Amenities: Heated indoor pool, sauna, gym, spa, concierge, 24-hour room service, shoe shine, laundry, valet, free daily newspaper, nightly turndown, baby-sitting, massage, postal and business services, currency exchange.

The Tilba. 30 W. Toorak Rd. (at Domain St.), South Yarra, VIC 3141. ☎ **03/9867 8844.** Fax 03/9867 6567. 15 units and 1 cottage. TV TEL. A$140–$195 (U.S.$91–$126.75) double. Rates include breakfast. AE, BC, DC, MC, V. Closed the first week of Jan and the last week of Dec. Free parking. Tram: 6, 8, or 72 from Swanston St. No children under 12.

With its turreted facade, antique furniture, and lead-glass windows, the Tilba is the city's most elegant and romantic small hotel. The 1907 building started life as a private mansion and was used as an army hostel during World War II; it has been an exclusive hotel since the mid-1980s. The tranquil Tilba, which overlooks Faulkner Park, attracts mostly business travelers, who appreciate its homelike atmosphere. The bedrooms, some of which were former stables or lofts, are unique in size, design, and color. The sitting and breakfast rooms are richly decorated with antiques and have open fireplaces.

4 Dining

Melbourne's ethnically diverse population ensures a healthy selection of international cooking styles. Chinatown, in the city center, is a fabulous hunting ground for authentic Chinese, Malaysian, Thai, Indonesian, Japanese, and Vietnamese fare, often at bargain prices. Carlton has plenty of Italian trattorias; Richmond is crammed with Greek and Vietnamese restaurants; and Fitzroy has cheap Asian, Turkish, Mediterranean, Spanish, and vegetarian food. To see and be seen, head for Chapel Street, Toorak Road in South Yarra, or Fitzroy and Ackland streets in St. Kilda.

In Melbourne, bad restaurants don't last long, because the competition soon weeds them out. That said, Melbourne's restaurant-goers are a fickle lot, and what is crowded to the point of bursting one week can find itself almost empty the next.

The currently trendy Modern Australian cuisine (a fusion of local fresh produce with Mediterranean and Asian influences) has attracted quite a bit of criticism recently, with famous Australian chefs suggesting that everyone is jumping on the bandwagon and trying to get away with serving up tiny, often inferior-tasting meals. The restaurants serving such cuisine below are exceptions to that trend.

Melbourne Dining

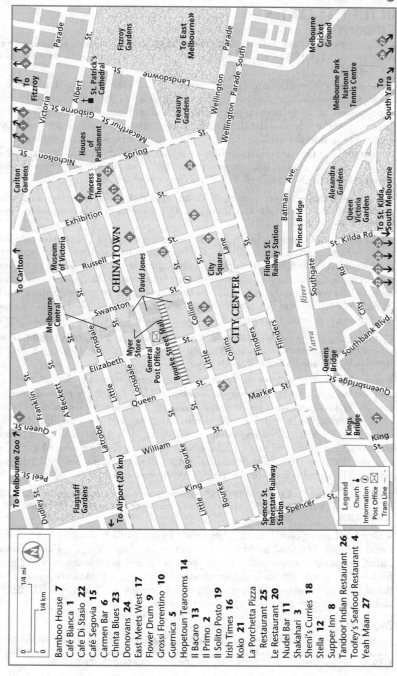

Bamboo House **7**
Café Bianca **1**
Cafe Di Stasio **22**
Café Segovia **15**
Carmen Bar **6**
Chinta Blues **23**
Donovans **24**
East Meets West **17**
Flower Drum **9**
Grossi Florentino **10**
Guernica **5**
Hopetoun Tearooms **14**
Il Bacaro **13**
Il Primo **2**
Il Solito Posto **19**
Irish Times **16**
Koko **21**
La Porchetta Pizza
  Restaurant **25**
Le Restaurant **20**
Nudel Bar **11**
Shakahari **3**
Sheni's Curries **18**
Stella **12**
Supper Inn **8**
Tandoor Indian Restaurant **26**
Toofey's Seafood Restaurant **4**
Yeah Maan **27**

IN THE CITY CENTER
EXPENSIVE

✪ **Flower Drum.** 17 Market Lane. ☎ **03/9662 3655.** Reservations required. Main courses A$25–$42 (U.S.$16.25–$27.30). AE, BC, DC, MC, V. Mon–Sat noon–3pm; daily 6–10pm. CANTONESE.

Praise pours in from all quarters for this upscale choice situated just off Little Bourke Street, Chinatown's main drag. Take a slow elevator up to the restaurant, which has widely spaced tables (perfect for politicians and businesspeople clinching their deals). Take note of the specials—the chefs are extremely creative and utilize the best ingredients they find in the markets each day. The signature dish here is the Peking duck, though the king-crab dumplings in soup are a great starter, and the buttered garfish is my favorite main course. You can also prearrange a banquet for two or more with unusual dishes (such as abalone), but give a day or two's advance notice.

Koko. Level 3, Crown Towers, Southbank. ☎ **03/9292 6886.** Reservations required. Main courses A$25–$30 (U.S.$16.25–$19.50). AE, BC, DC, JCB, MC, V. Daily noon–2:30pm and 6:30–10:30pm. JAPANESE.

A visit to Crown Casino can be a memorable experience in itself, but stop off here and you'll remember these tastes forever. The restaurant has a mixed contemporary/traditional decor, with a goldfish pond in the center of the main dining room and wonderful views over the city. There are separate teppanyaki grills and screened tatami rooms where you sit on the matted floor. The sushi selection is great, or perhaps you'll go for the boiled eel with rice. Otherwise, the yaki udon, or the cooked "sushi" of roast chicken, duck, prawns, and rare beef, is popular. A choice of 10 sakes helps digestion.

✪ **Le Restaurant.** In the Hotel Sofitel, 35th floor, 25 Collins St. ☎ **03/9653 0000.** Reservations recommended. Main courses A$32–$40 (U.S.$20.80–$26). AE, BC, DC, JCB, MC, V. Tues–Sat 7–10:30pm. MODERN AUSTRALIAN.

You might not want to leave the hotel once you've experienced the Sofitel's magnificent dining options. As if having the wonderful Café La on the premises weren't enough, it is blessed with Le Restaurant, one of Melbourne's premier fine-dining choices. The service is exquisite, the cuisine inventive, and the view fixating. The dishes here are well crafted and combine wonderful flavors and colors. The menu changes regularly, but you might find the King Island crayfish in a crust of kaffir leaf and morel dust served up with scallop ravioli, shiitake mushroom, and tarragon essence. The wine list is enormous, though mostly very expensive.

Stella. 159 Spring St. ☎ **03/9639 1555.** Reservations required. Main courses A$23–$28 (U.S.$14.95–$18.20). AE, BC, DC, MC, V. Mon–Fri noon–3pm; Mon–Sat 6–11pm. MODERN AUSTRALIAN.

This relaxed eating spot is made all the nicer by the cushion-scattered benches and mood lighting. The food is imaginative; you could end up eating the likes of barramundi on kipfler potatoes with a rocket pesto, or cumin- and coriander-scented pork fillet with spinach, potatoes, and green tomato chutney. The desserts, such as the baked chocolate pudding, are quite expensive at between A$15 and $18 (U.S.$9.75 and $11.70) but are a taste sensation.

MODERATE

Bamboo House. 47 Little Bourke St. ☎ **03/9662 1565.** Reservations recommended. Main courses A$17–$24 (U.S.$11–$15.60). AE, BC, DC, MC, V. Mon–Fri noon–3pm; Mon–Sat 5:30–11pm, Sun 5:30–10pm. NORTHERN REGIONAL CHINESE/CANTONESE.

If Flower Drum is full (or breaks your budget), try this Chinese restaurant, which is highly esteemed by both the Chinese community and local business big shots. The

A Special Meal on Wheels

Talk about eating on the move! A fully refurbished 1927 tram featuring the **Colonial Tramcar Restaurant** trundles through the streets of Melbourne, while all aboard tuck into a silver-service feast and sip champagne. It's very romantic, with velvet seats, lots of polished brass, and fresh flowers on the tables. Stabilizers have been fitted to ensure you won't spill your drink, and one-way windows mean you can enjoy the passing scenery knowing you're not on display. The limited menu might begin with foie gras, a choice of appetizer (perhaps either Tasmanian salmon or pepper-crusted kangaroo), and either steak mignon or chicken breast for the main course. A cheese platter, desserts, coffee, and liqueurs top it all off.

Reservations are recommended well in advance (☎ **03/9696 4000**). The early three-course dinner (at 5:45pm) is A$60 (U.S.$39); a later five-course dinner (at 8:35pm) costs A$85 (U.S.$55.25) Sunday to Thursday, A$95 (U.S.$61.75) Friday and Saturday, with all drinks included. The tram departs from and returns to Stop 125 on Normandy Road (on the corner of Clarendon Street), opposite the Crown Casino.

service here really is a pleasure, and the food (especially the delicious chicken with shallot sauce) is worth writing home about. The waiters are all eager to help you construct a feast from the myriad Cantonese and northern Chinese dishes. (Don't leave without a taste of the duck in plum sauce!) Other popular dishes include panfried dumplings, spring onion pancakes, and the signature dish, Szechuan smoked duck.

Grossi Florentino. 80 Bourke St. ☎ **03/9662 1811.** Reservations recommended. Main courses $16–$35 (U.S.$10.40–22.75). AE, BC, DC, MC, V. Mon–Fri noon–3pm; Mon–Sat 6–11pm. ITALIAN.

Under the management of the Grossi family, this restaurant has perked up considerably; it's now probably the best Italian restaurant in Melbourne. It's split into three separate sections, with a casual bistro downstairs, next to the Cellar bar (where you can pick up a bowl of pasta for around A$10/U.S.$6.50), and upstairs, a fine-dining restaurant with chandeliers and murals. On the menu here, you could find veal shanks braised with tomato and red wine on a bed of saffron, as well as typical Italian risotto, seafood, and steak dishes.

Il Bacaro. 168–170 Little Collins St. ☎ **03/9654 6778.** Reservations recommended. Main courses A$19.80–$26.80 (U.S.$12.85–$17.40). Mon–Fri noon–4pm; Mon–Sat 6pm–midnight. ITALIAN.

Walk into Il Bacaro and you'll feel you've been transported to Venice. Dominated by a horseshoe-shaped bar, it's jam-packed with small tables and weaving waiters carrying dishes like carpaccio of tuna or semolina gnocchetti with duck ragout. The pasta dishes and the risotto of the day always go down well, as do the salad side dishes. Il Bacaro is often crowded at lunch with local businesspeople digging deep into the excellent wine list.

Il Solito Posto. 113 Collins St. (in the basement; enter via George Parade). ☎ **03/9654 4466.** Reservations recommended. Main courses A$8.50–$13 (U.S.$5.50–$8.45) in bistro, A$18.50–$27.50 (U.S.$12–$17.90) in trattoria. AE, BC, DC, MC, V. Bistro Mon–Sat 7:30am–1am. Trattoria Mon–Fri noon–2:30pm, Mon–Sat 6–10pm. NORTHERN ITALIAN.

This lower-level restaurant is divided into two parts. The casual bistro has a blackboard menu offering good pastas, soups, and salads. In the more upscale trattoria, there's an à la carte menu offering steak, fish, spaghetti, and veal dishes. The coffee is good.

Irish Times. 427 Little Collins St. ☎ **03/9642 1699.** Reservations recommended. Main courses $8.50–$18 (U.S.$5.50–$11.70). AE, BC, DC, MC, V. Sun–Tues 11am–midnight; Wed–Sat 11am–3am. IRISH/MODERN AUSTRALIAN.

An Irish bar that's more authentic than most, the Irish Times is a character-filled escape from the rush of the city outside. There's the mandatory Guinness on tap, plus generous portions of dishes like warm chicken salad, mussels in a creamy broth, Caesar salad, and Irish specialties such as boxty (patties of mashed potato, leek, and onion, with an accompanying tomato relish). There's a live band on Thursday and Friday evenings from 9:30pm and on Saturday from 10:30pm.

Nudel Bar. 76 Bourke St. ☎ **03/9662 9100.** Reservations recommended Fri–Sat evenings. Main courses $12.50–$14.50 (U.S.$8.10–$9.40). AE, BC, DC, MC, V. Sun–Thurs 11am–11pm, Fri–Sat 11am–midnight. NOODLES.

A favorite with city slickers, the Nudel Bar serves up a variety of noodle dishes to the crowded tables and bar. Check out the cold spicy green tea noodles or the mee goreng; sticky rice pudding is a favorite for dessert.

INEXPENSIVE

✪ Café Bianca. Store 97–98 Queen Victoria Markets. No phone. Main courses A$2.60–$3.80 (U.S.$1.70–$2.50). No credit cards. Tues–Thurs 10am–2pm, Fri 10am–6pm, Sat 10am–3pm, Sun 9am–4pm. PIZZA.

Inside the main market building, past the meat and fish sellers and the cake and deli stalls, is the best little take-out pizza joint in Australia. It's tiny and there's nowhere to sit, but who has time to hang around with so much to see anyway? Unusual offerings include chicken tandoori pizza, fresh asparagus pizza, and potato and herb pizza, among others. Don't be fooled by the pretenders to the pizza crown that can be found nearby.

✪ Café Segovia. 33 Block Arcade. ☎ **03/9650 2373.** Main courses A$8–$15.50 (U.S.$5.20–$10). AE, BC, DC, MC, V. Mon–Fri 7:30am–late, Sat 8am–late, Sun 9am–7pm. CAFE.

Café Segovia is one of the most atmospheric cafes in Australia, with a smoky, sensual interior reminiscent of Spain. Seating is also available outside in an arcade, but you'll have to come early at lunchtime to nab a chair. Typical cafe food is on offer, such as focaccias, cakes, and light meals.

East Meets West. 271 Flinders Lane. ☎ **03/9650 8877.** Main courses A$5.50–$7 (U.S.$3.60–$4.55). No credit cards. Mon–Fri 11am–6pm. ASIAN/FAST FOOD.

This little place is great for a quick Indian curry, a plate of noodles, some spring rolls, or fish-and-chips. It's simple and cheap, with a few small tables. The curries are delicious and come in medium and large portions.

Hopetoun Tearooms. Shops 1 and 2, Block Arcade. ☎ **03/9650 2777.** Main courses A$4.50–$8.50 (U.S.$2.90–$5.50). Minimum charge A$5 (U.S.$3.25) per person noon–2pm. AE, BC, DC, MC, V. Mon–Thurs 8:30am–5pm, Fri 8:30am–6pm, Sat 10am–3:30pm. CAFE.

The first cup of coffee served in this Melbourne institution left the pot in 1891. It's all very civilized here, with green-and-white Regency wallpaper and marble tables. The cakes are very good. There are also sandwiches, focaccias, scones, croissants, and grilled items.

Sheni's Curries. Shop 16, 161 Collins St. (on the corner of Flinders Lane and Russell St., across from the Grand Hyatt). ☎ **03/9654 3535.** Lunch specials A$4.50–$7 (U.S.$2.90–$4.55). No credit cards. Mon–Fri 8am–4pm. SRI LANKAN.

This tiny, very busy place (it seats 30) offers a small range of authentic Sri Lankan curries for lunch. Choose from vegetable, meat, or seafood dishes. All meals come with rice, three types of chutney, and a papadam. You can also buy extra items such as samosas and roti.

Supper Inn. 15 Celstial Ave. ☎ **03/9663 4759.** Reservations recommended. Main courses A$9–A$12 (U.S.$5.85–$7.80). AE, BC, DC, MC, V. Daily 5:30pm–2:30am. CANTONESE.

Head here if you get the late-night munchies for Chinese food. It's a friendly place with a mixed crowd of locals and tourists chowing down on steaming bowls of congee (a rice-based porridge), barbecued suckling pig, mud crab, or stuffed scallops. Everything's authentic, not like some of the Westernized stuff you often get served elsewhere.

IN CARLTON

Il Primo. 242 Lygon St. ☎ **03/9663 6100.** Reservations recommended. Main courses A$16.80–$23.50 (U.S.$10.90–$15.20). AE, BC, DC, MC, V. Sun–Tues 6:30am–1am, Wed–Sat 6:30am–3am. Tram: 1, 15, 21, or 22 traveling north on Swanston St. (Stop 12). SOUTHERN EUROPEAN.

This restaurant is tucked away in a pair of historic houses in the Italian sector of Carlton. There are three dining areas in all, all cozy, with antique bricks, wood-beamed ceilings, and tiled floors. It feels like you're dining in a wine cellar, and indeed, there's a great wine list, including a range of unlabeled local wines at rock-bottom prices. The menu changes regularly, but classic dishes include the charcoal-grilled marinated quail with a warm eggplant salad, and rack of lamb filled with bacon, fresh herbs, toasted pine nuts, and tomato concassé. Live jazz brings in the customers every night from 10 or 11pm to closing time.

Shakahari. 201–203 Faraday St. ☎ **03/9347 3848.** Main courses A$12.50 (U.S.$8.10). AE, BC, DC, MC, V. Mon–Sat noon–3:30pm; Sun–Thurs 6–9:30pm; Fri–Sat 6–10:30pm. Any tram going north along Swanston St. toward Melbourne University. VEGETARIAN.

Good vegetarian food isn't just a meal without meat; it's a creation in its own right. At Shakahari you are assured of a creative meal that's not at all bland. The restaurant is quite large and low key, although the service can be a bit inconsistent. The Sate Samsara (skewered, lightly fried vegetables and tofu pieces with a peanut dip) is a winner, as is the couscous served in a vast earthenware pot. Also on offer are curry, croquets, couscous, laksa, and polenta. Though the menu is quite small, it was voted the Best Vegetarian Restaurant in Melbourne by *The Age Good Food Guide* (produced by the local upscale newspaper) from 1985 to 2000.

✪ **Toofey's Seafood Restaurant.** 162 Elgin St. ☎ **03/9347 9838.** Reservations recommended. Main courses A$20–$28 (U.S.$13–$18.20). AE, BC, DC, MC, V. Tues–Fri noon–3pm, Tues–Sun 6–10pm. Tram: 1, 15, 21, or 22 traveling north on Swanston St. SEAFOOD.

Some of Melbourne's best seafood makes its way to Toofeys, a highly recommended restaurant a fair way from the sea. The food, if not the industrial concrete surroundings, is inspired. The appetizer of sweet mud crab in Pernod and mayonnaise is irresistible, as is the consommé with mussels and saffron. Main courses of real note include the garfish and prawn nori rolls, and the salmon in red wine sauce. Don't leave Melbourne without eating here.

IN FITZROY

Carmen Bar. 74 Johnston St. ☎ **03/9417 4794.** Reservations recommended Fri–Sat evenings. Main courses A$8–$14 (U.S.$5.20–$9.10). BC, MC, V. Tues–Sun 6pm–1am. SPANISH.

Right in the heart of the Spanish quarter, this great little eatery offers seating around tables or beside the bar (the bar is always the best place to eat tapas, which are little dishes of Spanish goodies). Six to eight bowls of tapas should do you. The *gambas* (prawns) with garlic, the octopus in its ink, the *patatas bravas* (spicy potatoes), the grilled sardines—well, everything is nice, and even better when washed down with a jug of sangria.

✪ **Guernica.** 257 Brunswick St. ☎ **03/9416 0969.** Reservations recommended. Main courses A$17.90–$22.90 (U.S.$11.60–$14.80). AE, BC, DC, MC, V. Mon–Fri 11am–3pm, Sat–Sun and holidays 11am–4pm; daily 6–10:30pm. Tram: 11 from Collins St., or 86 from Bourke St. 5–10 min. taxi ride from city. MODERN AUSTRALIAN.

Dimly lit and featuring a giant print of Picasso's famous 1936 painting, this restaurant serves up some exciting dishes, many jazzed up with a healthy tingle of spice or pepper. Choices range from coconut-fried garfish with Vietnamese fried noodles to spiced lamb cutlets with creamed feta, roasted eggplant, and lemon and pomegranate molasses. The desserts are some of the best in town, including the marvelous palm sugar caramelized rice pudding served with toasted coconut ice cream. Check out the blackboard selections of good Australian wines by the glass. The restaurant is non-smoking in the evenings until 10pm.

IN ST. KILDA

Cafe Di Stasio. 31 Fitzroy St. ☎ **03/9525 3999.** Reservations recommended. Main courses A$21–$28 (U.S.$13.60–$18.20). AE, BC, DC, MC, V. Daily noon–3pm and 6–11pm. Tram: 16 from Swanston St., 96 from Bourke St. ITALIAN.

Wildly popular among Melbourne's trendsetters, St. Kilda's hottest restaurant has prices to match its lofty reputation. Two brass, hand-shaped door handles pull you into an interior of stressed-paint walls and cozy candlelight. Artists, musicians, and the wealthy come here to see and be seen—but only the struggling painters get a discount (they pay a reduced rate for their meals in return for looking a bit avant-garde). Some of the specials on offer might include roast duckling; char-grilled baby calamari with vegetables; rabbit loin stuffed with fresh herbs, pancetta, and prosciutto; or fillet of lamb with rosemary, anchovies, and vinegar.

Chinta Blues. 6 Ackland St. ☎ **03/9534 9233.** Main courses A$7.50–$16 (U.S.$4.90–$10.40). AE, BC, MC, V. Mon–Wed noon–2:30pm and 6–10pm; Thurs–Sat noon–2:30pm and 6–10:45pm; Sun noon–9:45pm. Tram: 16 from Swanston St. or 96 from Bourke St. MALAYSIAN.

Head to this very popular spot if you're looking for simple, satisfying food with a healthy touch of spice. The big sellers are the laksa, the mei goreng, the curry chicken, the sambal spinach, and a chicken dish called ayam blues. It's especially busy at lunch.

✪ **Donovans.** 40 Jacka Blvd. ☎ **03/9534 8221.** Reservations recommended. Main courses A$23–$32 (U.S.$14.90–$20.80). AE, BC, DC, MC, V. Daily noon–10:30pm. Tram: 12 from Collins St., 16 from Swanston St., 94 or 96 from Bourke St. SEAFOOD.

Donovans is so near the sea that you expect the fish to jump through the door and onto the plate, and indeed, you do get extremely fresh seafood. The restaurant is all higgledy-piggledy and charming, with lots of cushions, a log fire, and the sound of jazz and breakers on the beach filling the air. The menu offers 53 dishes, so you're sure to find something to suit your fancy. Favorites include the home-style fish stew, which is big enough for two. If you're not a big fish eater, choose from among several pasta and meat dishes.

La Porchetta Pizza Restaurant. 80 Acland St. ☎ **03/9534 1888.** Main courses A$5–$13.50 (U.S.$3.25–$8.80). Sun–Thurs 11am–midnight, Fri–Sat 11am–1am. Tram: 16 from Swanston St. or 96 from Bourke St. PIZZA.

This large, bustling pizza joint is a very good value. There are some 22 different styles to choose from, with the largest just large enough to feed two. The menu also includes pasta, steaks, and chicken, seafood, and veal dishes.

IN SOUTH YARRA

Tandoor Indian Restaurant. 517 Chapel St. ☎ **03/9827 8247.** Reservations recommended Fri–Sat nights. Main courses A$9–$17 (U.S.$5.85–$11). AE, BC, DC, MC, V. Wed–Sun noon–2:30pm; daily 6–11pm. Tram: 6, 8, or 72 from Swanston St. INDIAN.

This simple Indian restaurant was far less crowded than many of the others on the Chapel Street strip when I last visited, but all I can say is that the crowds didn't know what they were missing. The curries here are rich and spicy. Some dishes, such as the crab masala curry, are truly inspirational. The main courses are quite large, so you probably won't need a first course; but I highly recommend side dishes of naan bread (one per person) and a cucumber raita to cool the palate.

✪ **Yeah Maan.** 340 Punt Rd. (at the corner of Fawkner St.). ☎ **03/9820 2707.** Reservations not accepted. Main courses A$8.60–$13 (U.S.$5.60–$8.45). AE, BC, DC, MC, V. Tues–Sat 6–10:30pm, Sun 5–9:30pm. Tram: 6, 8, or 72 from Swanston St. CARIBBEAN.

Is this the coolest restaurant in Australia, or what? Calypso music fills the air, palm trees sway—and the food! Wow! The whole place is rockin', with the 75 seats almost continually occupied. The authentic Trinidadian goat curry is a must, as is the Barbados burrito. The Jamaican KFC (chicken marinated for 2 days in about 30 spices, and then smoked) and the jumbo-jumbie cassava shoe-string fries (cassava is similar to a potato) are very, very popular. The staff is ultrafriendly.

5 Seeing the Sights

Melbourne may not have as many major "attractions" as Sydney, but visitors come here to experience the contrasts of old-world architecture and the exciting feel of a truly multicultural city.

A leisurely boat trip might be a nice introduction to all that the city has to offer. **Melbourne River Cruises** (☎ 03/9614 1215 or 03/9650 2055) offers three cruises on the Yarra River, lasting between 1 and 2¹/₂ hours. Cruises run at various times throughout the morning and afternoon; call ahead to check the schedule. Shorter cruises cost A$15 (U.S.$9.75) for adults, A$8 (U.S.$5.20) for children between 3 and 12, and A$38 (U.S.$24.70) for families. Longer cruises cost A$27 (U.S.$17.55) for adults, A$14 (U.S.$9.10) for children, and A$68 (U.S.$44.20) for families.

Suggested Itineraries

If you have time to see only one major attraction in Melbourne, then by all means make it the Melbourne Zoo. If you have the luxury to follow a more leisurely itinerary, here are my suggestions:

If You Have 1 Day   Take a trip up to the top of the Rialto Towers Observation Deck to get your bearings, then visit the National Gallery of Victoria, walk through the Botanic Gardens, and stroll around the city streets. If you have time, head to Phillip Island to see the fairy penguins.

If You Have 2 Days   Visit the Queen Victoria Markets and take a tram to the Melbourne Zoo. Head out to St. Kilda in the evening for a great choice of restaurants.

If You Have 3 Days Rent a car or take a bus trip to explore the environs of Melbourne. I'd suggest that you either tour the Yarra Valley wineries and the Healesville Sanctuary, or go to the Mornington Peninsula, staying overnight in Portsea. Another option is a 2-day excursion down The Great Ocean Road (see chapter 12).

If You Have 4 Days Head out to the Dandenong Ranges (see "Side Trips from Melbourne," later in this chapter) or the goldfield town of Ballarat (see chapter 12).

THE TOP ATTRACTIONS

✪ **Gold Treasury Museum.** Old Treasury Building, Spring St. (top of Collins St.). ☎ **03/9651 2233.** Mon–Fri 9am–5pm; weekends and holidays 10am–4pm. A$7 (U.S.$4.55) adults; $3.50 (U.S.$2.30) children; A$18 (U.S.$11.70) family. Tram: City Circle tram to Spring St. and top of Collins St.

Designed by architect J.J. Clarke (when he was only 19) and built in 1857, The Old Treasury Building is an imposing neoclassical sandstone building that once housed precious metal from the Ballarat and Bendigo gold rushes. The gold was stored in eight thick-walled vaults underground and protected by iron bars. The "Built on Gold" exhibition within the vaults themselves is a high-tech multimedia show featuring videos and displays showing how the gold was dug up, sold, transported, and housed. In the basement is the restored living quarters of a caretaker who lived there from 1916 to 1928. The ground floor is taken up by the "Melbourne: A City Built on Gold" display, which shows how Melbourne was built using the profits from the gold rushes. A temporary exhibition gallery on the premises can feature anything from prints to gold-thread embroidery.

IMAX Theatre. Melbourne Museum Complex, Rathdowne St., Carlton. ☎ **03/9663 5454.** Admission from A$13.95 (U.S.$9) adults, A$9.95 (U.S.$6.50) children. Daily 10am–10pm. Tram: 1 or 22 from Swanston St.

This eight-story movie screen rivals the world's largest screen at Sydney's Darling Harbour. The movies shown here are shot with special giant-format cameras. Recent subjects have been outer space, the African Serengeti, and the deep oceans.

✪ **Melbourne Zoo.** Elliot Ave., Parkville. ☎ **03/9285 9300** or 03/9347 9530. Admission A$14.50 (U.S.$9.40) adults, A$7.20 (U.S.$4.70) children 4–15; family ticket A$39.30 (U.S.$25.50). Daily 9am–5pm (open later Thurs–Sun in Jan–Feb). Free guided tours Mon–Fri 10am–3pm, Sat–Sun 11am–4pm (go to the Friends of the Zoo Office to arrange tours). Tram: 55 or 56 going north on William St. to stop 25; 18, 19, 20 from Elizabeth St. to Stop 16 (then a short walk to your left following signposts). Train: Royal Park Station. Bus: City Explorer.

This place is a must-see. Built in 1862, it's the oldest zoo in the world, and still among the best. There are some 3,000 animals here, including the ever-popular kangaroos, wallabies, echidnas, koalas, wombats, and platypuses. Rather than being locked up in tiny cages, most animals are set in almost-natural surroundings or well-tended gardens. Don't miss the wonderful butterfly house, with its thousands of colorful Australian species flying around; the enormous free-flight aviary; the lowland gorilla exhibit; and the treetop monkey displays. Allow at least an hour if you just want to see the Australian natives, or around 2¹/₂ hours for the whole zoo.

National Gallery of Victoria. 285–321 Russell St. ☎ **03/9208 0203.** Free general admission; call about special exhibits. Daily 10am–5pm. Closed Good Friday and Christmas. Any southbound tram on Swanston St.

This is the best place in Victoria to view Aboriginal art, as well as colonial Australian, Asian, and European works. Look for works by artists such as Sidney Nolan, Russell Drysdale, and Tom Roberts; there are also a few works by Rembrandt, Picasso, Manet, and Turner. A free Aboriginal arts tour starts at 2pm every Thursday. There are a cafe

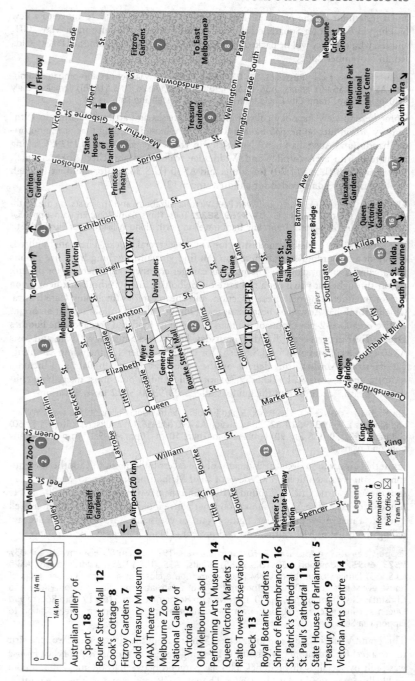

Australian Gallery of
    Sport **18**
Bourke Street Mall **12**
Cook's Cottage **8**
Fitzroy Gardens **7**
Gold Treasury Museum **10**
IMAX Theatre **4**
Melbourne Zoo **1**
National Gallery of
    Victoria **15**
Old Melbourne Gaol **3**
Performing Arts Museum **14**
Queen Victoria Markets **2**
Rialto Towers Observation
    Deck **13**
Royal Botanic Gardens **17**
Shrine of Remembrance **16**
St. Patrick's Cathedral **6**
St. Paul's Cathedral **11**
State Houses of Parliament **5**
Treasury Gardens **9**
Victorian Arts Centre **14**

and a restaurant on the premises. The Australian collection is due to move to a new building in Federation Square, on the corner of Flinders and Swanston in May 2001, and the whole gallery will be packed up and moved to its original home at 180 St. Kilda Rd. in November 2002.

Old Melbourne Gaol. Russell St. ☎ **03/9663 7228.** www.vicnet.net.au/~omgaol. Admission A$9 (U.S.$5.90) adults, A$6 (U.S.$3.90) children, A$26 (U.S.$16.90) families. Daily 9:30am–4:30pm. Tram: City Circle tram to corner of Russell and Latrobe sts.

Come here to view a spooky collection of death masks and artifacts relating to 19th-century prison life. Some 135 hangings took place here, including that of the notorious bandit (and Australian hero) Ned Kelly, in 1880. The jail closed in 1929. Chilling night tours run every Sunday and Wednesday (call ahead and check the schedule); they cost A$18 (U.S.$11.70) for adults and A$10 (U.S.$6.50) for children (though the tour is not recommended for children under 12).

✪ Queen Victoria Markets. Between Peel, Victoria, Elizabeth, and Therry sts. on the northern edge of the city center. ☎ **03/9269 5822.** Tues–Thurs 6am–2pm, Fri 6am–6pm, Sat 6am–3pm, Sun 9am–4pm. Tram: Any tram traveling north along William St. or Elizabeth St.

The Queen Vic is a Melbourne institution covering several blocks. There are hundreds of indoor and outdoor stalls, where you can find virtually anything from live rabbits to bargain-basement clothes. The markets can get cramped, and there's a lot of junk to sort through; but you'll get a real taste of Melbourne and its ethnic mix here. Look out for the interesting delicatessen section, and cheap eateries (including Café Bianca, which I think has Australia's best pizza; see "Dining," above). Allow at least an hour.

Two organized 2-hour tours of the market take in its food and heritage. The **Foodies Dream Tour** departs every Tuesday, Thursday, Friday, and Saturday at 10am and costs A$20 (U.S.$13) and A$15 (U.S.$9.75) for children under 15, including sampling. The **Heritage Market Tour** departs on the same days but at 10:30am and includes morning tea. It costs A$15 (U.S.$9.75) for adults and "would most likely bore children to death," according to the guide. Call ☎ **03/9320 5822** for reservations.

Rialto Towers Observation Desk. Rialto Building, 55th Floor, Collins St. (between William and King sts.). ☎ **03/9629 8222.** Admission A$9.90 (U.S.$6.40) adults, A$5.50 (U.S.$3.60) children, A$27.50 (U.S.$17.90) families. Sun–Thurs 10am–10pm, Fri–Sat 10am–11pm. Any tram on Collins St.

From this observation deck, near the top of the tallest building in the Southern Hemisphere, you get magnificent 360° views of all of Melbourne and beyond. See if you can spot the Melbourne Cricket Ground (MCG) and the new Crown Casino. A 20-minute film costing A$2 (U.S.$1.30) shows you what you're looking at, but you might as well just take a map up with you and figure it out for yourself. Of interest are the displays telling about life in Melbourne, past and present. There's a licensed cafe here, too.

Rippon Lea House Museum & Historic Garden. 192 Hotham St., Elsternwick. ☎ **03/9523 6095.** Admission A$9 (U.S.$5.85) adults, A$5 (U.S.$3.25) children 5–16, A$20 (U.S.$13) families of up to 6. Daily 10am–5pm (house closes at 4:45pm). Guided tours of house every half hour 10:30am–4pm and tour of estate at 2pm. Closed Good Friday and Christmas Day. Tram: 67 to Stop 40, then walk up Hotham St. Bus: 216/219 from Bourke and Queen sts. in the city to Stop 4. Train: Sandringham Line from Flinders Street Station to Rippon Lea Station.

This grand Victorian house, 8 kilometers (5 miles) from the city center, is worth a visit to get a feel for old-money Melbourne. Boasting dozens of rooms, Rippon Lea House was built by socialite Sir Frederick Thomas Sargood between 1868 and 1903; a pool and ballroom were added in the 1930s. Though the Romanesque architecture is interesting (note the stained glass and polychrome brickwork), the real attraction is the

A City Center Walk

A good place to start any stroll in Melbourne is from **Southgate,** on the south side of the Yarra River. You could pop into the **Victorian Arts Centre** while you're in the vicinity. Cross the Princes Bridge, with the **Melbourne Cricket Ground** to your right, and you enter the city center.

At the corner of Finders Street and Swanston Street to your right is **Flinders Street Station,** the Edwardian hub of Melbourne's rail network and a popular meeting point for Melburnians. Walk up the pedestrian Swanston Street (avoiding the trams) and you pass **St. Paul's Cathedral** on your right, followed by **City Square.** The square, which was redeveloped in 1998–1999, incorporates a series of lifelike modernist bronze statues of tall, thin men striding among the crowds, as well as a statues of Robert Burke and William Wills, who were the first to cross Australia from south to north in 1860–1861.

Turn left into Collins Street and you come to **Block Arcade,** with its boutiques and cafes. Then, walk north to Little Collins Street, where to your left you'll find the **Royal Arcade,** guarded by the mythical giants Gog and Magog on either side of Gaunte's Clock (which tolls on the hour). Running between Swanston and Elizabeth Streets is **Bourke Street Mall,** a pedestrian precinct crammed with shops and musicians. Again, watch out for the trams.

Bourke Street proper runs off eastward and ends at Spring Street, right next to the **Windsor Hotel,** a great place for an elegant lunch or afternoon tea. Opposite The Windsor on the other side of the road are the **State Houses of Parliament,** which are worth popping into for a tour, or to sit up in the public gallery if parliament is in session. Walk right down Spring Street and you come to the **Old Treasury Building,** which houses some interesting exhibits on Melbourne's gold-rush history. The **Treasury Gardens** and the **Fitzroy Gardens** (look out for Cook's Cottage) farther east offer a nice respite from the city bustle. From here, you can head up Landsdown Street and turn left into Cathedral Place for a visit to **St. Patrick's Cathedral.**

The walking tour should take an hour or so nonstop, but it can occupy your whole day if you take time out to shop or tour some of the sights along the way.

surrounding 5.3 hectares (13 acres) of gorgeous landscaped gardens, which include a conservatory, a lake, a lookout tower, an orchard, and extensive flower beds and ornate shrubbery. If you're here on a weekend, on a public holiday, or during school vacations, you might like to drop into the tearoom, which is open from 11am to 4pm.

St. Patrick's Cathedral. Cathedral Place. ☎ **03/9662 2233.** Mon–Fri 6:30am–6pm; weekends 7:15am–7:30pm.

Though lacking the intricacy of design of St. Paul's, the Roman Catholic St. Patrick's is another interesting Gothic Revival construction with exceptional stained-glass windows. Built between 1858 and 1940 (consecrated in 1897), St. Patrick's was closely associated with immigrants from Ireland who were escaping the mid–19th-century potato famine back home. In the courtyard out front is a statue of the Irish patriot Daniel O'Connell.

St. Paul's Cathedral. Flinders and Swanston sts. ☎ **03/9650 3791.** Daily 7:30am–6pm.

Built from 1880 to 1892 from the designs of William Butterfield, a famous English Gothic revival architect, the Anglican St. Paul's Cathedral is noteworthy for its highly decorative interior and English organ built by T.S. Lewis. Gold mosaics cover the walls and Victorian tiles cover the floors, there are intricate wood carvings and wonderful stained-glass windows, and the cathedral sports the second-highest spire (at 98m/321.5 ft.) in the Anglican Communion. The tallest spire, by the way, is on top of Salisbury Cathedral in England (123m/403.5 ft.). A boy's choir sings at 5:10pm Monday to Friday during school times, and twice on Sunday, at 10:30am and 6pm. Outside is a statue of Matthew Flinders, who became the first sailor to navigate the Australian mainland between 1801 and 1803 in the *Tom Thumb*.

State Houses of Parliament. Spring St. ☎ **03/9651 8911.** Mon–Fri 9am–4pm. Free guided tours 10am, 11am, noon, 2pm, 3pm, and 3:45pm on weekdays when parliament is not in session; reservations recommended.

Now the home of the Victorian (as in the state of Victoria) Parliament, this imposing monument to Victorian (as in Queen Victoria) architecture at the top of a run of sandstone steps was built in 1856. Between the time of Australian Federation, in 1900, to 1927, it was used as the National Parliament. When the State Government is in session (generally on Tues afternoon and all day Wed and Thurs between Mar and July, and again between Aug and Nov), you can view the proceedings from the public gallery. But call ahead and check, because sitting times do vary. During non–sitting times, both the extremely opulent Upper House and the less ornate Lower House chambers are open to the public.

PARKS & GARDENS

The ✪ **Royal Botanic Gardens,** 2 kilometers (1¼ miles) south of the city on Birdwood Avenue, off St. Kilda Road (☎ **03/9252 2300**), are the best of their type in Australia. More than 100 acres of gardens are lush and blooming with more than 12,000 plant species from all over the world. Don't miss a visit to the oldest part of the garden, the Tennyson Lawn, with its 120-year-old English elm trees. Other special corners include a fern gully, camellia gardens, rain forests, and ponds full of ducks and black swans. You can either discover the gardens by wandering at your own pace (most plant species are labeled, so you'll know what you're seeing), or take one of the free guided walks that leave the national Herbarium Building, F Gate, Sunday to Friday at 11am and noon. Bring snacks and your picnic blanket to **Shakespeare in the Park,** a popular summer event in the gardens, with performances in January and February. Tickets cost around A$30 (U.S.$19.50). Call ☎ **03/9252 2300** for details. The gardens are open daily: November to March from 7:30am to 8:30pm, in April from 7:30am to 6pm, May to August from 7:30am to 5:30pm, September and October 7:30am to 6pm. Admission is free. To get there, catch the tram on route 8, traveling south on St. Kilda Road, and get off at Stop 21.

Nearby, in King's Domain, take a look at Victoria's first **Government House,** Latrobe's Cottage (☎ **03/9654 5528**). It was built in England and transported to Australia brick by brick in 1836. Admission is A$2 (U.S.$1.30) per person. The cottage is open from 11am to 4pm every Monday, Wednesday, Saturday, and Sunday. On the other side of Birdwood Avenue is the **Shrine of Remembrance,** a memorial to the servicemen lost in Australia's wars. It's designed so that at 11am on Remembrance Day (the 11th of Nov), a beam of sunlight hits the Stone of Remembrance in the Inner Shrine. Note the eternal flame in the forecourt. King's Domain is Stop 12 on the route 15 tram traveling south along St. Kilda Road.

In **Fitzroy Gardens,** off Wellington Parade, is **Cook's Cottage** (☎ **03/9419 4677**), which was moved to Melbourne from Great Ayton, in Yorkshire, England, in 1934 to mark Victoria's centenary. It's claimed (with some debate) that Captain Cook lived here between his long voyages. Inside, it's spartan and cramped, not unlike a ship's cabin. Admission is A$3 (U.S.$1.95) for adults, A$1.50 (U.S.$1) for children 5 to 15, and A$7.50 (U.S.$4.90) for families of up to six. It's open daily from 9am to 5pm. Also east of the central business district are the **Treasury Gardens.** Look out for the memorial to John F. Kennedy near the lake. Treasury Gardens and Fitzroy Gardens can be reached by Tram 75 traveling east along Flinders Street. Get off at Stop 14 for Treasury Gardens and Stop 14A for Fitzroy Gardens.

6 Outdoor Pursuits & Spectator Sports

OUTDOOR PURSUITS

BALLOONING   Melbourne by Balloon, Balloon Sunrise Office, 41 Dover St., Richmond (☎ **03/9427 7596**), offers flights over the city plus a champagne breakfast once you've hit the ground again. Dawn flights cost A$225 (U.S.$146.25) for adults, and A$155 (U.S.$100.75) for children under 12 (but if they're under 4 ft. tall they won't be able to see over the basket). Advance reservations are essential.

BIKING   Extensive bicycle paths wind through the city and suburbs. For details on the 20 most popular routes, pick up a copy of *Melbourne Bike Tours,* published by **Bicycle Victoria** (☎ **03/9328 3000;** www.bv.com.au), available at most bookshops. Bicycle Victoria also runs several major cycling tours throughout the state every year.

Bike Now, 320 Toorak Rd., South Yarra (☎ **03/9826 6870**), will rent you two wheels for A$15 (U.S.$9.75) for 2 hours, A$20 (U.S.$13) for 4 hours, A$30 (U.S.$19.50) for a full day, and A$70 (U.S.$45.50) for a week. The shop is open weekdays from 9am to 7pm, Saturday from 9am to 5pm, and Sunday from 11am to 5pm. Take tram 8 to Toorak Road.

You can also rent a bike from **Hire a Bike** at St. Kilda Pier (☎ **03/9531 7403**); non-Australians must show their passports.

GOLF   One of the best public golf courses in Australia is **Yarra Bend,** Yarra Bend Road, Fairfield (☎ **03/9481 3729**). Greens fees are about A$15 (U.S.$9.75), and club rental is an extra A$10 (U.S.$6.50) for a half-set and A$25 (U.S.$16.25) for a full set.

The exclusive ✪ **Royal Melbourne Golf Club,** in the suburb of Black Rock, 24 kilometers (15 miles) from the city center (☎ **03/9598 6755**), is rated as one of the world's 10 best golf courses. It's open to members only, but if you belong to a top-notch golf club at home, you might be able to wheedle your way in. Call ahead for greens fees.

For more information on golf in Victoria, contact the **Victorian Golf Association,** 15 Bardolph St., Burwood (☎ **03/9889 6731**).

IN-LINE SKATING   The promenade in St. Kilda is the most popular place to strap on a pair of skates. You can rent all you need at **Rock'n'n'Roll'n,** 11a Fitzroy St., St. Kilda (☎ **03/9525 3434**). The first hour costs A$8 (U.S.$5.20). Successive hours are less expensive.

TENNIS   The venue for the Australian Open, the **Melbourne Park National Tennis Centre,** on Batman Avenue (☎ **03/9286 1244**), is a great place to play tennis. When tournaments are not scheduled, its 22 outdoor courts and 4 indoor courts are open to the public. You can rent courts Monday to Friday from 7am to 11pm, and Saturday and Sunday from 9am to 6pm. Charges range from A$14 (U.S.$9.10) to A$30 (U.S.$19.50) per hour, depending on the court and time of day (outdoor courts are cheapest). Show courts 1, 2, and 3 are also for hire at the same prices. Racquets are also available for A$3 (U.S.$1.95).

SPECTATOR SPORTS

AUTO RACING   The annual **Australian Formula One Grand Prix** takes place in early March. Call **Ticketmaster** (☎ **13 61 22** in Australia) or the **Grand Prix Hotline** (☎ **13 16 41** in Australia, or 03/9258 7100) for information on tickets, accommodations, and airfares. Also check out the Grand Prix's Web site at **www. grandprix.com.au**.

CRICKET   From October to March, cricket's the name of the game in Melbourne. The **Melbourne Cricket Ground (MCG),** Brunton Avenue, Yarra Park, Jolimont (☎ **03/9657 8879**), once the main stadium for the 1956 Melbourne Olympic Games, is perhaps Australia's most hallowed cricket field. The stadium can accommodate 97,500 people. For the uninitiated, "1-day" games are the ones to look out for; "test" games take several days to complete. Buy tickets at the gate or in advance from **Ticketmaster** (☎ **13 61 22** in Australia; www.ticketmaster.com.au).

Tours of the MCG and its museum leave every half hour daily from 10am to 3pm. The **Australian Gallery of Sport** and the **Olympic Museum** are also at the MCG. The Olympic Museum traces the development of the modern Olympics with individual display sections for each city.

FOOTBALL   Melbourne's number-one sport is Australian Rules Football, a skillful—but often violent—ball game the likes of which you've never seen (unless you have ESPN). This game has rules that most Australians don't understand! It's played either at the **Melbourne Cricket Ground** (see above) or at **Waverley Park,** Wellington Road, Mulgrave. The season starts on the 3rd weekend in March and ends with the Grand Final on the last Saturday in September. For game information, call **AFL Headquarters** at ☎ **03/9643 1999.** Buy tickets at **Ticketmaster** (☎ **13 61 22** in Australia; www.ticketmaster.com.au).

HORSE RACING   The ✪ **Melbourne Cup,** run on the first Tuesday in November, has been fought for by the best of Australia's thoroughbreds (and a few from overseas) since 1861. Melbourne society puts on a show when they all dress up for the occasion, and it seems that the entire nation stops in its tracks to at least tune in on TV.

The city has four racetracks: **Flemington** (which holds the Melbourne Cup), on Epson Road in Flemington (☎ **03/9371 7171**); **Moonee Valley,** on McPherson Street in Mooney Ponds (☎ **03/9373 2222**); **Caulfield,** on Station Street in Caulfield (☎ **03/9257 7200**); and **Sandown,** on Racecourse Drive in Springvale (☎ **03/9518 1300**). If you're staying in the city center, Flemington and Moonee Valley tracks are the easiest to get to. Take tram 57 from Flinders Street to reach the Flemington racetrack, and catch tram 59 from Elizabeth Street to travel to Moonee Valley.

TENNIS   The ✪ **Australian Open,** one of the world's four Grand Slam events, is played during the last 2 weeks of January every year at the **Melbourne Park National Tennis Center,** on Batman Avenue (☎ **03/9286 1234**). Tickets for the Australian Open go on sale in mid-October and are available through **Ticketek** (☎ **03/ 9299-9079**) and also on the Open's Web site, **www.ausopen.org**. Guided tours of the center are offered from April to October, Wednesday to Friday, when events aren't scheduled. Tours cost A$5 (U.S.$3.25) for adults and A$2.50 (U.S.$1.60) for children. To get there, take a train from the Flinders Street Station to Richmond Station and catch the special Tennis Center tram from there.

7 Shopping

Ask almost any Melbournite to help you plan your time in the city, and they'll advise you to shop 'til you drop. All of Australia regards Melbourne as a shopping mecca—it's got everything. If you're coming from Sydney, I say, save your money until you get to Melbourne, and then indulge!

Start at the magnificent city arcades, such as the **Block Arcade** (running between Collins and Little Collins streets), which has more than 30 shops, including the historic Hopetoun Tearooms (see "Dining" above), and the **Royal Arcade** (stretching from Little Collins Street to the Bourke Street Mall). Then hit the courts and lanes around **Swanston Street** and the huge **Melbourne Central shopping complex** between Latrobe and Lonsdale streets.

Next, take your wallet with you as you fan out across the city, taking in **Chapel Street in South Yarra,** for its Australian fashions; and **The Jam Factory,** 500 Chapel St., South Yarra (☎ **03/9826 0537**), which is a series of buildings with a range of shops and food outlets, including a branch of the U.S.-based Borders Books, as well as 16 cinema screens. Get there on tram no. 8, or no. 72 from Swanston Street.

There's also **Toorak Road in Toorak,** for Gucci and other high-priced, high-fashion names; **Bridge Road in Richmond** for budget fashions; **Lygon Street in Carlton** for Italian fashion, footwear, and accessories; and **Brunswick Street in Fitzroy** for a more alternative scene.

Serious shoppers might like to contact **Shopping Spree Tours** (☎ **03/9596 6600**), a company that takes you to all those exclusive and alternative shopping venues, manufacturers, and importers you wouldn't be likely to find by yourself. Tours depart Monday to Saturday at 8:30am and cost A$60 (U.S.$39) per person, including GST, lunch, and a visit to the Rialto Observation Deck.

See also the listing for the **Queen Victoria Markets** in section 5, "Seeing the Sights," earlier in this chapter.

ABORIGINAL CRAFTS

The Aboriginal Gallery of the Dreaming. 73–77 Bourke St., City. ☎ **03/9650 3277.**

This place stocks an extensive range of acrylic dot paintings and represents more than 120 artists. Boomerangs, didgeridoos, pottery, jewelry, bark paintings, prints, books, and music are also available.

Aboriginal Handcrafts. Mezzanine floor, 130 Little Collins St. ☎ **03/9650 4717.**

Didgeridoos, bark paintings, boomerangs, and so forth are sold here, with the profits going to Aboriginal colleges.

CRAFTS

An interesting **Art & Crafts Market** is held on The Esplanade in St. Kilda on Sunday from 9am to 4pm. Take tram 16 from Swanston Street or no. 96 from Bourke Street.

The Australian Geographic Shop. Shop 130, Melbourne Central, 300 Londsdale St. ☎ **03/9639 2478.**

Head here for high-quality Australiana, including crafts, books, and various gadgets.

DEPARTMENT STORES

Daimaru. In the Central Melbourne complex. ☎ **03/9660 6666.**

With six floors of interesting merchandise, including Asian foodstuffs and top-label fashions, Daimaru is giving the more established department stores a run for shoppers' money.

David Jones. 310 Bourke St. Mall, City. ☎ **03/9643 2222.**

Like Myer, its direct competition, David Jones (or DJ's, as it's affectionately known) spans 2 blocks and offers similar goods.

Georges. 162 Collins St., City. ☎ **03/9929 9999.**

Melbourne's glitziest and out-of-the-ordinary department store offers very exclusive men's and women's fashions, top-end stationery and pens, stylish knickknacks, perfumes, and more. There are a cafe and cheap dining spot here, too.

✪ **Myer.** 314 Bourke St. Mall, City. ☎ **03/9661 1111.**

The grand dame of Melbourne's department stores has 12 floors of household goods, perfume, jewelry, and fashions stretching over 2 blocks. (It claims to be the fifth-largest store in the world.) There's a good food section on the ground floor offering, among other things, good sushi.

FASHION

Of course, you can always head to one of the major department stores (see above) if you're looking for fashions. High-fashion boutiques also line the eastern stretch of **Collins Street** between the Grand Hyatt and the Hotel Sofitel, and **Chapel Street** in South Yarra.

In addition, many thousands of retail shops and factory outlets are dotted around the city, many of them concentrated on **Bridge Road** near Punt Road and **Swan Street** near Church Street in Richmond. You'll be able to find designer clothes, many just last season's fashions, at a fraction of the original price.

Country Road. 252 Toorak Rd., and other sites, including Chapel St., South Yarra. ☎ **1800/801 911** in Australia, or 03/9824 0133.

County Road is one of Australia's best-known names for men's and women's fashion. The cool, classic looks don't come cheap, but the quality is worth it. County Road also sells designer cooking equipment and housewares.

Mortisha's. Shop 8–10, Royal Arcade, City. ☎ **03/9654 1586.**

Looking for something to wear to your next Goth party? Then don't miss this satin-lined, coffinlike store selling everything from vampy velvet dresses to original bridal wear. You can also find some very unusual jewelry and accessories to complete your Addams Family look.

Death by Chocolate

If you love chocolate, sign up now for the **Chocolate Indulgence Walk** and the **Chocolates & Other Desserts Walk** by calling ☎ **03/9815 1228,** or 0412/158 017. The former takes you on a tasting tour of Cadbury's, Myer, New Zealand Natural Ice Creamery, Chocolate Box, and Darrell Lea, and finishes off over chocolate cake at a cafe. This 2-hour tour leaves every Saturday at 12:30pm and costs A$22 (U.S.$14.30) for adults (children under 6 are free). The latter tour includes sampling plenty of ice creams and chocolates around town as you tour kitchens and talk to chefs. The tour finishes with afternoon tea at the Grand Hyatt. This tour leaves every Saturday at 2:30pm and also costs A$22 (U.S.$14.30). A third tour has been recently added, the **Coffee and Café Walk,** during which you try coffee and pastries at some of Melbourne's grooviest cafes. This tour also costs A$22 (U.S.$14.30). Advance reservations are essential.

Overseas Designer Warehouse. 18 Ellis St., South Yarra (off Chapel St., between Toorak and Commercial Rd.). ☎ **03/9824 0399.**

This place sells end-of-run and last season's high fashions. The stuff is still pretty expensive, but you can find a few bargains if you really search.

Paddington Coat Factory. 461–463 Chapel St., South Yarra. ☎ **03/9827 4004.**

Exquisite, high-fashion clothes made by young Australian designers, such as Andrea Yasmin, Susie Mooratoff, and Lara Agnew, go for between A$39 and $500 (U.S.$25.30 and $325) at this Melbourne sister store of the one in Paddington, Sydney.

R.M. Williams. In the Melbourne Central complex. ☎ **03/9663 7126.**

Head here for genuine Australian gear: great boots, Driza-bone coats, and Akubra hats.

Saba. 132 Bourke St., City. ☎ **03/9654 6176.**

Australian designer Joseph Saba has several very vogue, very expensive boutiques for men and women in Melbourne, including one for each sex on Chapel Street (nos. 538 and 548) in South Yarra. This store caters to both men and women.

Sam Bear. 225 Russell St., City. ☎ **03/9663 2191.**

Sam Bear is another good bet for Outback-style fashions: Driza-bone coats, Akubra bush hats, R.M. Williams boots and clothing, and Blundstone boots (my favorite). They also sell a solid range of camping equipment.

Surf, Dive 'N Ski Australia. The Jam Factory, Chapel St., South Yarra. ☎ **03/9826 4071.**

As well as surfboards, boogie boards, and sunglasses, this store stocks a wide range of hip and happening beachwear—all at reasonable prices. All the big names in Australian surf wear can be found here, including Ripcurl, Quicksilver, and Billabong.

Vegan Wares. 78 Smith St., Collingwood. ☎ **03/9417 0230.**

Instead of leather, Vegan Wares uses microfiber to create tough, stylish shoes, handbags, and belts. It's not just for vegetarians; carnivores enjoy browsing here, too.

FOODSTUFFS

Haigh's Chocolates. 26 Collins St. ☎ **03/9650 2114.**

Indulge in some 50 manifestations of Australia's best chocolate, from milk to dark, some with fruit flavors, and in all kinds of shapes. I recommend the Sparkling Shiraz truffle if you need a serious treat. There's another location in Shop 26, the Block Arcade, 282 Collins St. (☎ **03/9654 7673**).

Suga–Melbourne Candy Kitchen. Shop 20, Royal Arcade, City. ☎ **03/9663 5654.**

If you have a sweet tooth, you're likely to spend a fortune at this traditional little candy shop that makes its goodies right before your very eyes. Rock candy is a specialty, and you can even get your name (or the name of someone back home) spelled out in its center.

JEWELRY

Altman & Cherny. 120 Exhibition St. (at the corner of Little Collins St.). ☎ **03/9650 9685.**

Even if you're not in the market to buy, it's worth coming here to check out "Olympic Australia," the largest precious-gem opal in the world. It was found in Coober Pedy in South Australia in 1956 and is valued at U.S.$1.6 million. The store offers tax-free shopping for tourists armed with a passport and international airline ticket.

✪ Dinosaur Designs. 562 Chapel St., South Yarra. ☎ **03/9827 2600.**

Dinosaur Designs is taking the jewelry design world by storm with its range of very artistic jewelry made out of resin. The shop has modern housewares as well. None of it's cheap, but the odd item won't break the bank.

Portobello Lane of South Yarra. 405 Chapel St., South Yarra. ☎ **03/9827 5708.**

Proprietor Robyn Meate specializes in locally produced and imported sterling-silver jewelry with lots of beads and glass. Some of the designs are quite intricate. Pieces cost from A$40 to $200 (U.S.$26 to $130).

8 Melbourne After Dark

Melbourne can be an exciting place once the sun has set. The pubs here are far better than those in Sydney, though they are definitely split between the very trendy and the very down-to-earth. Friday and Saturday nights will see most pubs packed to the rafters, and at lunchtime, those that serve food are pretty popular, too. To find out what's hot and happening, check the entertainment guide included in *The Age* each Friday.

THE PERFORMING ARTS

As far as the performing arts go, Melbourne is the most dynamic city in Australia. Its theaters run the gamut from off-beat independent productions to large-scale musicals like what you'd find on Broadway. The city is also the home of the most prestigious festivals, with the annual **Melbourne Fringe Festival** (held over the first 3 weeks in Oct) and the annual **Melbourne International Comedy Festival** (from the end of Mar to roughly the end of Apr) attracting the best of Australian and international talent. If you're in town during these times, you'll be well advised to pick up a few tickets (hotel rooms might also be more difficult to find, because people flood in from all over Australia and beyond).

The Melbourne International Comedy Festival sees venues all over the city putting on performances, while the Fringe Festival sees the streets, pubs, theaters, and restaurants playing host to everyone from jugglers and fire-eaters to musicians and independent productions covering all art forms. For more information, look up the relevant Web sites (**www.melbournefringe.org.au** and **www.comedyfestival.com.au**).

Another good time to plan your visit is during the annual **Melbourne International Film Festival** (from mid-July to the end of the 1st week in Aug), when new releases, shorts, and avant-garde movies are shown at varying venues around the city. For details, look up the schedules on the net (**www.melbournefilmfestival.com.au**).

For information on upcoming theater productions and reviews, check out **www.stageleft.com.au** or the official government entertainment information site (**www.melbourne.vic.gov.au/news/events/events/**). The latter site shows what's on in the theater world for 2 months in advance, as well as what's happening in dance, film, comedy, music, exhibitions, sports, and tours.

The best place to buy tickets over the net for everything from theater to major sporting events, as well as obtain details on schedules, is via **Ticketmaster** (**www.ticketmaster.com.au**); you can also call them at ☎ **13 28 849** or 1800/062 849 in Australia, or ☎ **61-3-9299 9079** (international number).

THE HEART OF MELBOURNE'S CULTURAL LIFE

✪ Victorian Arts Centre. 100 St. Kilda Rd. ☎ **03/9281 8000,** or 13 61 66 for ticket purchase. www.artscentre.net.au. Tickets for State Theatre A$40–$110 (U.S.$26–$71.50); Playhouse and Fairfax A$30–$59 (U.S.$19.50–$38.35); Concert Hall A$40–$80 (U.S.$26–$52).

Half-Price Tickets

Buy your tickets for entertainment events, including opera, dance, and drama, on the day of the performance from the **Half-Tix Kiosk** in Bourke Street Mall (☎ **03/9650 9420**). The booth is open Monday from 10am to 2pm, Tuesday to Thursday from 11am to 6pm, Friday from 11am to 6:30pm, and Saturday from 10am to 2pm. Tickets must be paid for in cash. The available shows are displayed each day on the booth door, and you can't get show information over the phone.

The towering spire atop the Theaters Building of the Victorian Arts Center, on the banks of the Yarra River, crowns the city's leading performing-arts complex. Beneath it, the State Theatre, the Playhouse, and the Fairfax present performances that represent the focal point of Melbourne's cultural life.

The State Theater, seating 2,079 on three levels, can accommodate elaborate stagings of opera, ballet, musicals, and more. The Playhouse is a smaller venue that often hosts the **Melbourne Theatre Company.** The Fairfax is more intimate still and is often used for experimental theater or cabaret.

Adjacent to the Theaters Building is the Melbourne Concert Hall, home of the **Melbourne Symphony Orchestra** and the **State Orchestra of Victoria,** and often host to visiting orchestras. Many international stars have graced this stage, which is known for its excellent acoustics.

Guided 1-hour tours of the Concert Hall and the theaters are offered Monday to Saturday at noon and 2:30pm and Saturday at 10:30am and noon. They cost A$10 (U.S.$6.50) for adults, A$7.50 (U.S.$4.90) for children, and A$23 (U.S.$14.95) for families. Backstage tours on Sunday at 12:15pm cost A$13.50 (U.S.$8.80). Children under 11 are not allowed. Call ☎ 03/9281 8000 between 9:30am and 5pm for information.

ADDITIONAL VENUES & THEATERS

Check *The Age* to see what productions are scheduled during your visit. Odds are that the leading shows will be produced in one of the following venues.

The enormous outdoor **Sydney Myer Music Bowl,** King's Domain, Alexandra Avenue (☎ **03/9281 8360**), is run under the auspices of the Victorian Arts Centre Trust and hosts opera, jazz, and ballet in the warmer months (and ice skating in the winter!). It underwent extensive renovations in 2000.

The Princess Theatre, 163 Spring St. (☎ **03/9299 9800**), is a huge facility that hosts extravaganza productions. It opened its doors in 1886, and it still retains a dramatic marble staircase and ornate plaster ceilings.

Built in 1929, the **Regent Theatre,** 191 Collins St. (☎ **03/9299 9800**), fell into disrepair, and its stage was dark for 25 years. Now, after a recent A$35 million (U.S.$22.75 million) renovation, it's been restored to its former glory. It recently staged lavish production of *Showboat.* Tickets are available in the United States through **ATS Tours** at ☎ 800/423-2880. The theater offers a range of dining packages.

A fire destroyed the original **Her Majesty's Theatre,** 219 Exhibition St. (☎ 03/9663 3211), but the current structure still retains the original facade and the art deco interior added during a 1936 renovation. Musicals, such as the Australian premiere of *Chicago,* frequent the boards.

The **Forum Theatre,** 154 Flinders St. (☎ 03/9299 9700), hosts well-known bands and international comedians. Tables and chairs are set up in cabaret-style booths, from which you can order drinks and meals from the bar.

The **Comedy Theatre,** 240 Exhibition St. (☎ **03/9209 9000**), with its ornate Spanish rococo interior, manages to feel intimate even though it seats more than 1,000 people. Plays and musicals usually fill the bill, but dance companies and comedians also appear.

THE CLUB & MUSIC SCENE

Melbourne's nightclub scene is centered along **King Street,** though hip places come and go month by month. It's best just to follow the crowds. Otherwise, the following options are more enduring in their appeal.

✪ **Bobby McGee's Entertainment Lounge.** In the Rydges Melbourne Hotel, 186 Exhibition St. ☎ **03/9639 0630.** Cover A$5 (U.S.$3.25) Mon and Thurs–Sat after 8pm; free for hotel guests.

If you want a fun night out, head for the restaurant section of Bobby McGee's, then hit the dance floor at the disco. The restaurant has good American-style food served by waiters in fancy dress, while the disco area is open from 5pm to the wee hours (the music, a mix of the popular dance hits of the moment, starts pounding at 9pm). The disco is popular with the 22-to-35 crowd after work, while the younger set flocks in after 10pm. You'll see lots of business suits on Thursday and Friday nights; dress is casual but smart on other nights.

✪ **The Comedy Club.** Level 1, 380 Lygon St., Carlton. ☎ **03/9348 1622.** Dinner and show Fri–Sat A$40–$45 (U.S.$26–$29.25) depending on performer; show only Thurs–Sat approx. A$20 (U.S.$13).

The Comedy Club is another Melbourne institution. Come here to see local and international comedy acts, musicals, and special shows.

Monsoon's Entertainment Studio. In the Grand Hyatt Melbourne, 123 Collins St. ☎ **03/9657 1234.** Cover A$15 (U.S.$9.75); free for hotel guests.

Dress up a bit if you want to blend in with the crowd at the upscale Monsoon's. Hotel guests and well-heeled locals dance to Top 40 tunes, or check out visiting jazz or cabaret performers on Friday and Saturday nights (Thurs night is funk night). One Sunday and Wednesday every month the nightclub is also open for special theme nights.

WHERE TO SHARE A PINT

If you want to enjoy a few drinks and meet a few people, take one of the **City Pub Walks** (☎ **03/9384 0655** or 0412/085 661). The 2¹/₂- to 3-hour walks stop off at a variety of interesting pubs and bars where you can sample the local brews (at your own expense). Tours leave from "under the clocks" at Flinders Railway Station at 6:30pm Tuesday and Thursday.

Bridie O'Reillys. 62 Little Collins St. (just off Exhibition St.). ☎ **03/9650 0840.**

Bridie O'Reillys is one of Melbourne's best Irish pubs, complete with traditional dark wood decor and good beer. The two-level pub has 19 different beers on tap (7 of them Irish). There's live Irish music every night from around 9pm. The place gets quite crowded on weekends.

Cocktails, Anyone?

For a touch of sophistication and spectacular views, drop into the cocktail bar on the 35th floor of the **Hotel Sofitel,** at 25 Collins St. (☎ **03/9653 0000**). Otherwise, the **Windsor Hotel,** at 103 Spring St. (☎ **03/9653 0653**), offers cocktails in an atmosphere of Old World charm.

The Charles Dickens Tavern. 290 Collins St. (between Elizabeth and Swanston sts.). ☎ **03/9654 1821.**

Come here for a touch of Olde England in the heart of the city center. The homey pub has two bars and a restaurant serving good pub grub (traditional roasts and pies as well as some lighter dishes).

Cricketers Bar. In the Windsor Hotel, 103 Spring St. ☎ **03/9653 0653.**

Locals come to this popular English-style pub in this five-star hotel to lift a glass surrounded by the relics of Australia's summer passion. Glass cases are packed full of cricket bats, pads, and stumps, whereas the plush green carpets and solid mahogany woodwork give the place a touch of class.

The Mitre Tavern. 5 Bank Place (between Queen and William sts. and Collins and Little Collins sts.). ☎ **03/9670 5644.**

This place is almost as good as a traditional English pub—if they'd only put some good carpets on the floor. Still, it's atmospheric and centrally located. The outdoor courtyard is perfect for lunch on a sunny day.

The Prince St. Kilda. 29 Fitzroy St., St. Kilda. ☎ **03/9536 1111.**

This pub is a legend among the locals. Though it was recently refurbished, it has kept its original rough-at-the-edges appearance. Bands play most nights, some of them big names.

Young & Jacksons. At the corner of Flinders and Swanston sts. ☎ **03/9650 3884.**

You probably won't think much of the rough-and-tumble downstairs here, but you'll want to head upstairs, anyway, to get a peek at the naked *Chloe*. The famous painting was brought to Melbourne for the Great Exhibition in 1880. The pub, which was built in 1853 and started selling beer in 1861, has a few years on the *Chloe*, which was painted in Paris in 1875. She has a special place in the hearts of customers and has spawned hundreds of copies that have found their way to far-flung places worldwide.

THE CASINO

Crown Casino. Clarendon St., Southbank. ☎ **03/9292 6868.**

Australia's largest casino is a plush affair open 24 hours. You'll find all the usual roulette and blackjack tables and so on, as well as an array of poker machines. There are some 25 restaurants and 40 bars on the premises. Casual clothes are fine, but no shorts.

9 Side Trips from Melbourne

DANDENONG RANGES
40km (25 miles) E of Melbourne

Melburnites traditionally do a "day in the Dandenongs" from time to time, topping off their getaway with Devonshire tea with scones and jam at one of the many cafes en route. Up in the cool, high country you'll find native bush, famous gardens, the Dandenong Ranges National Park, historic attractions such as the Puffing Billy vintage steam train, and plenty of restaurants and cozy B&Bs. The Dandenong Ranges National Park is one of the state's oldest, having been set aside in 1882 to protect its Mountain Ash forests and lush tree-fern gullies.

Auswalk (☎ 02/6457 2220; e-mail: monica@auswalk.com.au) offers a 4-day/3-night self-guided tour of the Dandenongs for two or more people, including accommodations, most meals, a ride on the Puffing Billy steam train (see below), national-park entrance fees, vehicle transfers, and an itinerary and maps. The tour costs around A$590 (U.S.$383) per person but could be a little cheaper depending on the season.

ESSENTIALS

GETTING THERE To get to the area, take the Burwood Highway from Melbourne, then the Mt. Dandenong Tourist Road, which starts at Upper Ferntree Gully and then winds its way through the villages of Sassafras, Olinda, Mount Dandenong, and Kalorama to Montrose. If you take a turnoff to Sherbrook, or extend your journey into a loop taking in Seville, Woori Yallock, Emerald, and Belgrave, you'll see a fair slice of the local scenery.

VISITOR INFORMATION The **Dandenong Ranges & Knox Visitor Information Center,** 1211 Burwood Hwy., Upper Ferntree Gully, VIC 3156 (☎ **1800/ 645 505** in Australia, or 03/9758 7522), is open daily from 9am to 5pm.

NATURE WALKS

Most people come here to get out of the city for a pleasant bushwalk (hike), much like Sydneysiders escape to the Blue Mountains. Some of the better walks include the easy 2.5-kilometer (1½-mile) stroll from the **Sherbrook Picnic Ground** through the forest, and the **Thousand Steps** and the **Kokoda Track Memorial Walk,** a challenging rain-forest track from the Fern Tree Gully Picnic Ground up One Tree Hill. Along the way are plaques commemorating Australian troops who fought and died in Papua New Guinea in World War II.

FOR GARDENING BUFFS

Bonsai Farm. Mt. Dandenong Tourist Rd., Mt. Dandenong. ☎ **03/9751 1150.** Free admission. Wed–Sun 11am–5pm. Transportation: See William Ricketts Sanctuary, above.

If you don't like to crane your neck when it comes to looking at trees, then visit this large display of petite bonsai. Some of them are many decades old and cost a pretty penny.

National Rhododendron Gardens. The Georgian Rd., Olinda. ☎ **03/9751 1980.** Admission Sept–Nov A$6.50 (U.S.$4.20) adults, A$2 (U.S.$1.30) children 12–16, A$15 (U.S.$ 9.75) family of 5; Dec–Aug A$5 (U.S.$3.25) adults, A$2 (U.S.$1.30) children, A$12 (U.S.$7.80) family. Closed Christmas Day. Train to Croydon and then bus no. 688 to the gardens.

From September to November, thousands of rhododendrons and azaleas burst into bloom in these magnificent gardens. There are 103 lovely acres in all, with a 3-kilometer (2-mile) walking path leading past flowering exotics and native trees, as well as great vistas over the Yarra Valley. A tearoom is open every day during spring and on weekends at other times. Visitors flock here in summer for the glorious walks, and again in autumn when the leaves are turning.

Tesselaar's Bulbs and Flowers. 357 Monbulk Rd., Silvan. ☎ **03/9737 9305.** Admission during tulip festival A$9.50 (U.S.$6.20) for adults, children under 16 free if accompanied by an adult; free for everyone rest of the year. During tulip festival (approx. Sept 12–Oct 11) daily 10am–5pm; rest of year Mon–Fri 8am–4:30pm, Sat–Sun 1–5pm. Take the train to Lilydale and then bus no. 679.

There are literally tens of thousands of flowers on display here, all putting on a flamboyantly colorful show in the spring (Sept and Oct). Expect to see a dazzling variety of tulips, daffodils, rhododendrons, azaleas, fuchsias, and ranunculi. Bulbs are on sale at discount prices at other times.

William Ricketts Sanctuary. Mt. Dandenong Tourist Rd., Mt. Dandenong. ☎ **03/9751 1300.** Admission A$5 (U.S.$3.25) adults, A$2 (U.S.$1.30) children 10–16, A$12 (U.S.$7.80) families of 4. Daily 10am–4:30pm. Closed Christmas. Train to Croydon then bus no. 688 to the sanctuary.

This wonderful garden, set in a forest of mountain ash, features clay figures representing the Aboriginal Dreamtime. The sculptures were all created over the lifetime of

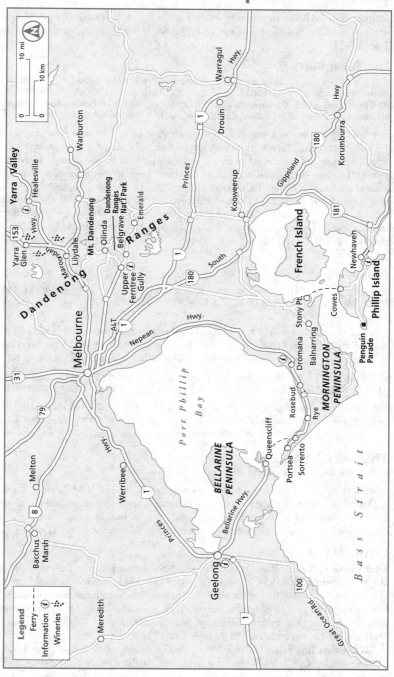

Warragul

Hwy.

Drouin

1

Korumburra

Hwy.

180

Kooweerup

Gippsland

Warburton

Yarra Valley

Healesville

181

Princes

i

Hwy.

153

Yarra Glen

Maroondah

Lilydale

Mt. Dandenong

Olinda

Dandenong Ranges Nat'l Park

Emerald

Belgrave

Dandenong Ranges

1

French Island

Newhaven

i

Phillip Island

Upper Ferntree Gully

i

180

South

Stony Pt.

Cowes

Penguin Parade

Melbourne

ALT 1

Nepean

Hwy.

Dromana

i

Balnarring

MORNINGTON PENINSULA

31

Port Phillip Bay

Rosebud

Rye

79

Hwy.

Melton

Werribee

1

Queenscliff

Portsea

Sorrento

8

Princes

BELLARINE PENINSULA

Bacchus Marsh

Bass Strait

Bellarine Hwy.

Meredith

Geelong

i

100

1

Great Ocean Rd.

Legend

Ferry ---

Information i

Wineries

0 10 mi

0 10 km

sculptor William Ricketts, who died in 1993 at the age of 94. The garden encompasses fern gullies and waterfalls spread out over 33 acres, though the sculptures occupy just 2 acres.

FOR TRAIN BUFFS

Puffing Billy Railway. Belgrave Station, Belgrave. ☎ **03/9754 6800** for 24-hr. recorded information. Admission A$18 (U.S.$11.70) adults, A$10 (U.S.$6.50) children 4–16, A$51 (U.S.$33) families of 5. Operates daily except Christmas. Train from Flinders Street Station in Melbourne to Belgrave; the Puffing Billy station is a short walk away.

For just about a century, the Puffing Billy steam railway has been chugging over a 13-kilometer (8-mile) track from Belgrave to Emerald Lake. Passengers take trips on open carriages and are treated to lovely views as the train passes through forests and fern gullies and over a National Trust–classified wooden trestle bridge. Trips take around an hour each way. Trains leave at 10:30am, 11:15am, noon, and 2:30pm on weekdays; and at 10:30am, 11:45am, 1:30pm, and 3:15pm on Saturday and Sunday. A further stretch of track to Gembrook was opened in 1998. Daily trips to Gembrook take an extra 45 minutes and cost A$25 (U.S.$16.25) for adults, A$14 ($9.10) for children, and A$72 (U.S.$46.80) for families. Night trains also run on occasional Saturday nights.

DINING

Churinga Café. 1381 Mt. Dandenong Tourist Rd., Mt. Dandenong. ☎ **03/9751 1242.** Main courses A$12.95–$13.95 (U.S.$8.40–$9). AE, BC, DC, MC, V. Sat–Wed 10:30am–4:30pm. CAFE.

This is a pleasant place for a quick lunch or morning or afternoon tea. It has nice gardens and is just across from the William Ricketts Sanctuary. You can get everything here from curries to traditional British fare. Devonshire tea costs A$6 (U.S.$3.90).

Wild Oak Café. 232 Ridge Rd., Mt. Dandenong. ☎ **03/9751 2033.** Main courses A$16–$19 (U.S.$10.40–$12.35). BC, DC, MC, V. Daily 10am–10pm. MODERN AUSTRALIAN.

For good home cooking, you can't beat this cozy cafe. The food could include the likes of char-grilled steak, smoked Atlantic salmon risotto, linguini with prawns, and Cajun chicken. The restaurant has a few vegetarian selections and a roaring log fire in winter.

THE YARRA VALLEY

61km (38 miles) E of Melbourne

The Yarra Valley is a well-known wine-growing region just east of Melbourne. It's dotted with villages, historic houses, gardens, craft shops, antiques centers, and restaurants, as well as dozens of wineries. There are some good bushwalks around here, and the Healesville Sanctuary is one of the best places in Australia to see native animals.

ESSENTIALS

GETTING THERE   If you're driving, pick up a detailed map of the area from the **Royal Automotive Club of Victoria** (☎ **03/9790 3333**) in Melbourne. Maps here are free if you're a member of an auto club in your home country, but remember to bring along your membership card. Alternatively, you can pick up a map at the tourist office. Take the Maroondah Highway from Melbourne to Lilydale and on to Healesville. The trip takes around an hour and 15 minutes.

McKenzie's Bus Lines (☎ **03/9853 6264**) operates a bus service from Lilydale Railway Station to Healesville (catch a train from Melbourne's Spencer Street Station to Lilydale; the trip takes about an hour). Buses connect with trains approximately 12 times a day; call for exact connection times.

VISITOR INFORMATION   Pick up details on what to see and where to stay at the **Yarra Valley Visitor Information Center,** Old Court House, Harker Street, Healesville (☎ **03/5962 2600**). It's open daily from 9am to 5pm.

EXPLORING THE VALLEY

There are three principal roads in the valley: the Melba Highway, the Maroondah Highway, and Myers Creek Road, which together form a triangle. Within the triangle are three smaller roads, the Healesville Yarra Glen Road, Old Healesville Road, and Chum Creek Road, which all access wineries. Most people start their tour of the Yarra Valley from Lilydale and take in several cellar-door tastings at vineyards along the route.

   Balloon Aloft (☎ **1800/028 568** in Australia) offers dawn balloon rides over the wineries for A$195 (U.S.$126.75) for adults and A$130 (U.S.$84.50) for children over 8. The flight includes a champagne breakfast. **Peregrin Adventures** (☎ **03/9662 2800;** e-mail: travelcentre@peregrin.net.au; www.peregrin.net.au) also has balloon flights over the valley, with free pickup from Adelaide for A$195 (U.S.$126.75) on weekends and A$175 (U.S.$113.75) on weekdays. Peregrin can also arrange accommodations.

   Parkwood Personalised Tours (☎ **03 5334 2428;** www.oztour.com; e-mail: info@oztour.com) runs personalized 1-day and multiday tours of the Yarra Valley, as well as other places in Victoria, including the Great Ocean Road, staying at quaint B&B guest houses or boutique hotels, from $60 (U.S.$39) per hour.

Healesville Sanctuary. Badger Creek Rd., Healesville. ☎ **03/5957 2800.** www.zoo.org.au. Admission A$17 (U.S.$11) adults, A$9 (U.S.$5.80) children 4–15, A$45 (U.S.$29.25) families. Daily 9am–5pm (to 7:30pm Jan–Feb). Train from Flinders Street Station to Lilydale, then bus no. 685 to the sanctuary.

Forget about seeing animals in cages—this preserve is a great place to spot native animals in almost-natural surroundings. You can see wedge-tailed eagles, dingoes, koalas, wombats, reptiles, and more, all while strolling through the peppermint-scented gum forest, which rings with the chiming of bell birds. The sanctuary was started in 1921 by Sir Colin McKenzie, who set it up as a center to preserve endangered species and educate the public. There are a gift shop, a cafe serving light meals, and picnic grounds.

ACCOMMODATIONS & DINING

Melba Lodge. 939 Melba Hwy., Yarra Glen, VIC 3775. ☎ **03/9730 1511.** Fax 03/9730 1566. www.melbalodge.citysearch.com.au. E-mail: melba@onthe.net.au. 6 units. A/C TV. A$150 (U.S.$97.50) queen room; A$180 (U.S.$117) king room. Rates include cooked breakfast. AE, BC, DC, MC, V. Transportation: See the Healesville Sanctuary above.

These stylish, modern accommodations opened in Yarra Glen, in the heart of the Yarra Valley wine region, in early 1999. Of the six luxurious bedrooms, four have queen-size beds and two have king-size beds and spas; all have private bathrooms. There's a comfortable lounge with an open fire. The lodge is only a few minutes' walk from historic Yarra Glen, which has antique shops and a craft market. There are plenty of restaurants and wineries around too. It's a short drive to the Healesville Sanctuary.

Sanctuary House Motel Healesville. Badger Creek Rd. (P.O. Box 162), Healesville, VIC 3777. ☎ **03/5962 5148.** Fax 03/5962 5392. 12 units. A/C TV. A$65–$75 (U.S.$42.25–$48.75) double. Extra adult A$20 (U.S.$13); extra child A$10 (U.S.$6.50). AE, BC, DC, MC, V. Transportation: See the Healesville Sanctuary, above.

This place is very handy for visiting the sanctuary and even better if you want to relax and sample some good Yarra Valley wine. Just 400 meters (440 yd.) from the

Healesville Sanctuary, Sanctuary House is set in some 10 acres of beautiful bushland. The rooms are motel style and come with all the essentials. On the grounds are also a pool, a Jacuzzi, a sauna, a half-court tennis court, a game room, a phone booth, and a casual restaurant serving three-course home-cooked meals.

PHILLIP ISLAND: PENGUINS ON PARADE
139km (86 miles) S of Melbourne

Philip Island's penguin parade, which you can see every evening at dusk, is one of Australia's most popular animal attractions. There are places to watch penguins elsewhere in Australia that are less crowded and feel less staged (Kangaroo Island in South Australia comes to mind), but at least the little guys and their nesting holes are protected from the throngs of curious tourists by guides and boardwalks. Nevertheless, the commercialism of the Penguin Parade puts a lot of people off—busloads of tourists squashed into a sort of amphitheater is hardly being one with nature. Phillip Island also offers nice beaches, good bushwalking, and a seagull rookery. If you have the time, you should spend at least 2 days here.

ESSENTIALS
GETTING THERE   Most visitors come to Phillip Island on a day trip from Melbourne and arrive in time for the Penguin Parade and dinner. Several tour companies run day trips. Among them are **Gray Line** (☎ **03/9663 4455**), which operates penguin trips daily departing Melbourne at 1:30pm and returning at around 11:30pm. Tours cost A$79.50 (U.S.$51.60) for adults and A$39.75 (U.S.$25.80) for children. Gray line also offers full-day trips, including the Dandenong Ranges and a ride on the Puffing Billy Steam Train.

Down Under Day Tours (☎ **03/9650 2600**) offers a similar half-day tour for A$79.50 (U.S.$51.70) for adults and A$39.50 (U.S.$25.70) for children; tours depart Melbourne at 1:30pm and return at 11:30pm. It also offers a daylong trip that combines a Melbourne sightseeing tour with the penguin tour for A$106 (U.S.$68.90) for adults and A$53 (U.S.$34.45) for children, and a half-day combined Dandenong Ranges/Phillip Island tour costing A$96 (U.S.$62.40) for adults and A$48 (U.S.$31.20) for children.

An excellent budget option is a half-day trip with **Melbourne Sightseeing** (☎ **03/9663 3388**). Tours depart Melbourne daily at 1:30pm and include visits to a cattle farm (where you can hand-feed kangaroos), the Koala Conservation Centre, and a seal colony, as well as the Penguin Parade. The coach returns to Melbourne at 10:30pm. The trip costs A$75 (U.S.$48.75) for adults (A$49/U.S.$31.85 with a YHA card) and A$38 (U.S.$24.70) for children. For the same price, an express bus leaves Melbourne at 5:30pm (returning at 11pm) and travels directly to the Penguin Parade.

Auswalk (☎ **02/6457 2220;** e-mail: monica@auswalk.com.au) offers a 4-night self-guided tour of Phillip Island for two or more people for A$760 (U.S.$494) per person. The price includes accommodations, most meals, park and entrance fees to the main places of interest, some vehicle transfers, an itinerary, and maps.

If you're driving on your own, it's an easy 2-hour trip from Melbourne along the South Gippsland Highway and then the Bass Highway. A bridge connects the highway to the mainland.

V/Line trains (☎ **13 22 32** in Australia, or 03/9619 5000) run in summer from Flinders Street Station to Phillip Island via Dandenong. The trip takes 2 hours and 15 minutes and costs A$13.40 (U.S.$8.70).

VISITOR INFORMATION   The **Phillip Island Information Center,** Phillip Island Tourist Road, Newhaven (☎ **1300/366 422** in Australia, or 03/5956 7447), is an attraction in itself, with interactive computer displays, relevant information, dioramas giving visitors a glimpse into the penguin's world, and a theaterette. It's open daily 9am to 5pm (to 6pm in the summer).

EXPLORING THE AREA

Visitors approach the island from the east, passing through the town of **Newhaven.** Just a little past Newhaven is the Phillip Island Information Center.

The main town on the island, **Cowes** (pop. 2,400), is on the far north coast. It's worth taking a stroll along its Esplanade. The Penguin Parade is on the far southwest coast.

The tip of the west coast of the Summerland Peninsula ends in a particularly inter-esting rock formation called **The Nobbies.** This strange-looking outcropping can be reached at low tide by a basalt causeway. You'll get some spectacular views of the coast-line and two offshore islands from here. On the farthest of these islands is a popula-tion of up to **12,000 Australian fur seals,** the largest colony in Australia (bring your binoculars). This area is also home to thousands of nesting silver gulls.

On the north coast you can explore **Rhyll Inlet,** an inter-tidal mangrove wetland, where you can see wading birds such as spoonbills, oyster catchers, herons, egrets, cor-morants, and the rare bar-tailed godwit and the whimbrel.

Bird-watchers will also love **Swan Lake,** another important breeding habitat for wetland birds.

Elsewhere, walking trails lead through heath and pink granite to **Cape Woolamai,** the island's highest point, where there are fabulous coastal views. From September to April the cape is home to thousands of short-tailed shearwaters, or muttonbirds as they are sometimes called.

If you really want to see a bit of the island (instead of just seeing the parade and dashing off), consider taking one of the 15 different tours offered by Mike Cleeland and his **Island Nature Tours,** RMB 6080, Cowes, Phillip Island, VIC 3922 (☎ **03/5956 7883**).

Phillip Island Penguin Reserve. Summerland Beach, Phillip Island. ☎ **03/5956 8300.** Admission A$10.50 (U.S.$6.80) adults, A$6.50 (U.S.$4.20) children 4–13, A$26.50 (U.S.$17.20) families. Visitor center opens 10am; penguins arrive at sunset. Reservations essential in summer, when tickets can be difficult to get, and on weekends and public holi-days throughout the year.

The Penguin Parade takes place every night of the year at dusk, when hundreds of Little Penguins appear at the water's edge, gather together in the shallows, and waddle up the beach toward their burrows in the dunes. They're the smallest of the world's 17 species of penguins, standing just 33 centimeters (13 in.) high, and they're the only penguins that breed on the Australian mainland. Fences and viewing stands were erected in the 1960s to protect the nesting areas. Flash photography is banned because it scares the little guys. Wear a sweater or jacket, since it gets chilly after the sun goes down. A kiosk selling food opens an hour before the penguins turn up.

If you get to Phillip Island on your own and don't have your own car, the **Penguin Parade Bus** (☎ **03/5952 1042,** or 0417/360 370) will pick you up from your accommodation in time to see the action. The round-trip price is A$19 (U.S.$12.40) for adults and A$11 (U.S.$7.10) for children and includes a prebooked ticket for the Penguin Parade.

Koala Conservation Centre. Fiveways, Phillip Island. ☎ **03/5956 8300.** A$4 (U.S.$2.60) adults, A$1.50 (U.S.$1) children, A$10 (U.S.$6.50) family. Daily 10am–5pm.

Koalas were introduced to Phillip Island in the 1880s. At first they thrived in the predator-free environment, but overpopulation, the introduction of foxes and dogs, and the clearing of land for farmland, townships, and roads have all taken their toll. Though today you can still see a few koalas in the wild, the best place to find them is at this sanctuary, which was set up for research and breeding purposes. Visitors can get quite close to them, especially on the elevated boardwalk, which lets you peek into their treetop homes. For the best viewing come around 4pm, when the ordinarily sleepy koalas are on the move.

ACCOMMODATIONS

Penguin Hill Country House B&B. At Backbeach and Ventnor Rd. (RMB 1093, Cowes), Phillip Island, VIC 3922. ☎ and fax **03/5956 8777.** 3 units. A$125 (U.S.$81.25) double. Rates include cooked breakfast and GST. BC, MC, V. Not suitable for children.

This private home with views over sheep paddocks to Bass Strait is within walking distance of the Penguin Parade. Each room has good views and is stocked with antiques (as is much of the house) and queen-size beds. Two have an attached bathroom with shower, and the third has a private bathroom across the hall. There are a TV and a phone in the cozy lounge. The hosts can pick you up from Cowes.

Rothsaye on Lovers Walk. 2 Roy Court, Cowes 3922. ☎ and fax **03/5952 2057.** www.rothsaye.com. E-mail: rothsaye@nex.net.au. 2 suites, 1 cottage. A$125–$145 (U.S.$81.25–$94.25) suite; A$130–$150 (U.S.$84.50–$97.50) cottage. Rates include GST. BC, MC, V. No children allowed.

The penguins are just down the road and the beach is right on your doorstep—who could ask for anything more? The two suites here are adjuncts to the owner's home and the one-bedroom cottage is set slightly apart. All rooms are very nice and come with antiques and king-size beds. You also get a fruit basket, free fishing gear, beach chairs and umbrellas, magazines, and fresh flowers. Lovers Walk, a romantic floodlit path, leads from the doorstep to the center of Cowes. The owners also have a new beachside property nearby called Abaleigh on Lovers Walk. The two apartments here come with a kitchen, BBQ, and good water views. They cost $205 (U.S.$133.25) a night.

AROUND PORT PHILLIP BAY

West of Melbourne, the Princes Freeway (or M1) heads toward Geelong via a bypass at Werribee. To the east of Melbourne, the Nepean Highway travels along the coast to the Mornington Peninsula as far as Portsea. If you have time to stay the night, you can combine the two options, first heading down to the Mornington Peninsula (see below) and then taking the car and passenger ferry from Sorrento to Queenscliff (see below).

WERRIBEE

This small country town is located 32 kilometers (20 miles) southwest of Melbourne, a 30-minute drive away along the Princes Freeway. Trains run from Melbourne to Werribee station; a taxi from the station to the zoo will cost around A$5 (U.S.$3.25).

Victoria's Open Range Zoo at Werribee. K Rd., Werribee. ☎ **03/9731 9600.** www.zoo.org.au. Admission A$14.50 (U.S.$9.40) adults, A$7.20 (U.S.$4.70) children under 14, A$42 (U.S.$27.30) families. Daily 10:30am–5pm (the entrance gate closes at 3:30pm). Safari tours hourly 10am–4pm.

From inside your zebra-striped safari bus, you can almost touch the mainly African animals that wander almost freely over the plains—no depressing cages here. This high-caliber open-air zoo is closely associated with the Melbourne Zoo. There's also a walk-through section featuring African cats, including cheetahs, and monkeys.

Werribee Park Mansion. K Rd., Werribee. ☎ **13 19 63** in Australia, or 03/9741 2444. Park and picnic grounds free; admission to mansion A$10 (U.S.$6.50) adults, A$5 (U.S.$3.25) children 5–15, A$26 (U.S.$16.90) families. Nov–Mar daily 10am–5pm; Apr–Oct daily 10am–4pm. Closed Christmas.

Known as "the palace in the paddock," this 60-room Italianate mansion was built in 1877. It was quite the extravagant project in its day. In addition to touring the house, you may like to stroll around the grounds and have a picnic; it's surrounded by 325 acres of bushland fronting the Werribee River. You can also prearrange to take one of the popular carriage rides that make their way through the property.

GEELONG

Victoria's second-largest city, Geelong, lies 72 kilometers (45 miles) southwest of Melbourne. It's an industrial center, not really of note to visitors except as the home of the National Wool Museum. Geelong is a 45-minute drive from Melbourne. There's a regular train service, and the museum is a couple of blocks from the station.

You can pick up brochures and book accommodations through the **Geelong Great Ocean Road Visitor Information Center,** Stead Park, Princes Highway, Geelong (☎ **1800/620 888** in Australia, or 03/5275 5797; www.greatoceanroad.org.au). The office is open daily from 9am to 5pm.

National Wool Museum. 26 Moorabool St., Geelong. ☎ **1800/620 888** in Australia, or 03/5227 0701. A$7 (U.S.$4.50) adults, A$3.50 (U.S.$2.30) children under 16; A$18 (U.S.$11.70) families. Daily 9:30am–5pm. Closed Christmas and Good Friday.

For Australians in colonial times, the sheep was the lifeblood of the nation, providing food and warm wool, profits to the landlords, and jobs to shearers, stockmen, and farmhands. This fascinating museum tells the story, from how sheepdogs work to how the sheep are sheared. You'll also see an interesting collection of gadgets used to create products from wool. There is also a reconstructed shearers' hut and a 1920s mill workers' cottage, as well as a specialty wool store, a gift shop, and a bistro.

THE MORNINGTON PENINSULA

The Mornington Peninsula, a scenic 40-kilometer-long (25-mile-long) stretch of windswept coastline and hinterland some 80 kilometers (50 miles) south of Melbourne, is one of Melbourne's favorite day-trip and weekend-getaway destinations. The coast is lined with good beaches and thick bush consisting almost entirely of tea trees (early colonists used it as a tea substitute). The Cape Schanck Coastal Park stretches along the peninsula's Bass Strait foreshore from Portsea to Cape Schanck. It's home to gray kangaroos, Southern Brown bandicoots, echidnas, native rats, mice, reptiles, bats, and many forest and ocean birds. The park has many interconnecting walking trails providing access to some remote beaches.

Along the route south you could stop off at the **Morning Peninsula Regional Gallery,** 4 Vancouver St., Mornington (☎ **03/5975 4395**), to check out the work of famous Australian artists (open Tues to Sun 10am to 5pm), or visit **Arthurs Seat State Park** to take a short hike or ride a chairlift to a 1,000-foot summit, which offers glorious views over the surrounding bush. At **Sorrento,** take time out to spot pelicans on the jetty or visit the town's many galleries.

Also on the Mornington Peninsula is Australia's oldest and most famous maze, **Ashcombe Maze & Water Gardens,** Red Hill Road, Shoreham (☎ **03/5989 8387**), which also has extensive water and woodland gardens. There's even a rose maze made out of 1,300 rose bushes, which is spectacular when in full bloom over the spring and summer months. There's also pleasant cafe with indoor and outdoor dining. The park is open daily from 10am to 5pm; admission is A$7 (U.S.$4.60) for adults and A$4 (U.S.$2.60) for children.

ESSENTIALS

GETTING THERE   From Melbourne, take the Mornington Peninsula Freeway to Rosebud, and then the Point Nepean Road. If you want to cross Port Phillip Bay from Sorrento to Queenscliff, take the Queenscliff Sea Road Ferry (☎ **03/5258 3255**), which operates daily every 2 hours from 8am to 6pm (there's an 8pm ferry on Fri and Sat from mid-Sept to mid-Dec and daily from mid-Dec until Easter Thurs). Ferries from Queenscliff operate from 7am to 5pm (plus a 7pm ferry on days listed above). The fare is A$32 to A$34 (U.S.$20.80 to $22.10) for cars, depending on season, plus A$3 (U.S.$1.90) for adults, A$2 (U.S.$1.30) for children 5 to 15, and A$1 (U.S.65¢) for children 4 and under. Passenger-only fares are A$7 (U.S.$4.50) for adults, A$5 (U.S.$3.25) for children 5 to 15, and A$1 (U.S.65¢) for children under 4. The crossing takes 35 to 40 minutes.

VISITOR INFORMATION   The **Peninsula Visitor Information Center,** Point Nepean Road, Dromana (☎ **1800/804 009** in Australia, or 03/5987 3078), has plenty of maps and information on the area and can also help book accommodations. It's open daily from 9am to 5pm. You can get more information on this and all the other **Victorian National Parks** at ☎ **13 19 63,** or on the Web at www. parks.vic.gov.au.

ACCOMMODATIONS & DINING

The Portsea Hotel. 3746 Point Nepean Rd., Portsea, VIC 3944. ☎ **03/5984 2213.** Fax 03/5984 4066. www.portseahotel.com.au. 34 units, 8 with private bathroom. A$60 (U.S.$39) double without bathroom; A$110 (U.S.$71.50) double with bathroom; A$140 (U.S.$91) bay-view suite. AE, BC, DC, MC. V.

The rooms in this typical Australian motel right on the seafront are done up in country-style furnishings. The standard twin rooms are quite basic and all share bathrooms. None has a TV, but all have tea- and coffee-making facilities. En suite doubles have a double bed and TV, and an attached bathroom with shower. There is a reasonable bistro and three bars downstairs, as well as a terraced beer garden and another outdoor bar.

Victoria 12

by Marc Llewellyn

Australia's southernmost mainland state is astoundingly diverse. Within its boundaries are 35 national parks, encompassing every possible terrain, from rain forest and snowcapped mountain ranges to sunbaked Outback desert and a coast where waves crash dramatically onto rugged sandstone outcroppings.

Melbourne (see chapter 11) may be this rugged state's heart, but the mighty Murray River, which separates Victoria from New South Wales, is its lifeblood, providing irrigation for vast tracts of semidesert land.

Most visitors to Victoria start out exploring Melbourne's cosmopolitan streets, then visit a few local wineries, before heading for the gold fields around the historic city of Ballarat. Lots of them experience only a fraction of Victoria as a blur whizzing by the window of their rental car, but this wonderful and not overly touristy region is worth a closer look.

Visitors with more time might make their way inland to the mountains (perhaps for skiing or bushwalking at Mt. Hotham or Falls Creek), or seek out the wilderness of the Snowy River National Park. You could also head to the Outback, to the Grampians National Park, and onward to Mildura through open deserts and past pink lakes and red sand dunes. Lots of options await you, and because much of it is out in the country, you'll find prices for accommodations very affordable. Whatever itinerary you choose, you're sure to find adventure and dramatic scenery.

See "Side Trips from Melbourne," in chapter 11, for information on **Phillip Island,** the **Mornington Peninsula,** the **Dandenong Ranges,** and the **Yarra Valley.**

EXPLORING THE STATE

VISITOR INFORMATION   While you're in Melbourne (see chapter 11), pick up brochures and maps at the **Victorian Visitors Information Centre,** Melbourne Town Hall, Swanston Street, at the corner of Little Collins Street (☎ **13 28 42** in Australia; www.tourism. vic.gov.au), open Monday to Friday from 9am to 6pm, Saturday and Sunday from 9am to 5pm. Or call the **Victorian Tourism Information Service** (☎ **13 28 42**) from anywhere in Australia to talk to a consultant about your plans. The service, open daily from 8am to 6pm, will also send out brochures. If you need information along the way, look for blue road signs with a yellow information symbol.

GETTING AROUND   V/Line (☎ **13 61 96** in Victoria, 13 22 32 in NSW, or 03/9619 5000) runs a limited network of trains to various places in Victoria, continuing trips to most major centers with connecting buses.

Several bus companies connect Melbourne with regional areas of Victoria; the biggest operators are **Greyhound Pioneer** (☎ **13 20 30** in Australia, or 03/9600 1687) and **McCafferty's** (☎ **13 14 99** in Australia, or 03/9670 2533).

One of Australia's most famous train trips is aboard *The Ghan*. It leaves Melbourne every Wednesday night at 10:30pm, arrives in Adelaide at 10:10am on Thursday, and arrives in Alice Springs at 10am on Friday. (While the Melbourne–Alice service goes only once a week, there is daily service from Melbourne to Adelaide which can then link up to the Sydney–Alice *Ghan* service.) The one-way fare to Alice Springs is A$930 (U.S.$604) in first class, A$555 (U.S.$360) in holiday class (also with a sleeper), and A$279 (U.S.$181) in coach class (in a recliner chair). Contact the **Great Southern Railway** (☎ **13 21 47** in Australia, or 08/8213 4592; www.gsr.com.au) for details.

If you'll be doing a lot of driving, contact the **Royal Automobile Club of Victoria (RACV)** at ☎ **13 19 55** in Australia, or 03/9790 2211). You could also stop into their office at 360 Bourke St., Melbourne (☎ **03/9790 3333**).

1 Ballarat: Gold-Rush City

113km (70 miles) W of Melbourne

Ballarat, Victoria's largest inland city (pop. 90,000), is all about gold. In 1851, two prospectors found gold nuggets scattered on the ground at a place known as, ironically, Poverty Point. Within a year, 20,000 people had drifted into the area and Australia's El Dorado gold rush had begun.

In 1858, the second-largest chunk of gold ever discovered in Australia (the Welcome Nugget) was found, but by the early 1860s, most of the easily obtainable yellow metal was gone. Larger operators continued digging until 1918, and by then Ballarat had developed enough industry to survive without mining.

Today, you can still see the gold rush's effects in the impressive buildings, built from the miners' fortunes, lining Ballarat's streets. If you're interested in seeing another former mining town, head 1¹/₂ hours north to Bendigo, a small city filled with elaborate public buildings constructed with the gains from the gold rush.

ESSENTIALS

GETTING THERE   **From Melbourne, Ballarat is a 1¹/₂-hour drive via the **Great Western Highway.

V/Line (☎ **13 61 96** in Victoria, 13 22 32 in NSW, or 03/9619 5000) runs trains between the cities every day; the trip takes less than 2 hours. The one-way fare is A$13.80 (U.S.$9) for adults and A$6.90 (U.S.$4.50) for children. A public bus connects the Ballarat train station with the town center.

Several sightseeing companies offer day trips to Ballarat from Melbourne. **Melbourne Sightseeing** (☎ **03/9663 3388**) offers one of the most affordable choices, a full-day tour that costs A$81 (U.S.$52.65) for adults and A$41 (U.S.$26.65) for children.

VISITOR INFORMATION   **The **Ballarat Visitor Information Centre, 39 Sturt St. (at the corner of Albert Street), Ballarat, VIC 3350 (☎ **1800/648 450** in Australia, or 03/5320 5741; www.ballarat.com), is open daily from 9am to 5pm.

SEEING THE SIGHTS

Ballarat contains many reminders of the gold-rush era, but it all really comes to life in the colonial-era re-creation on Sovereign Hill.

Victoria

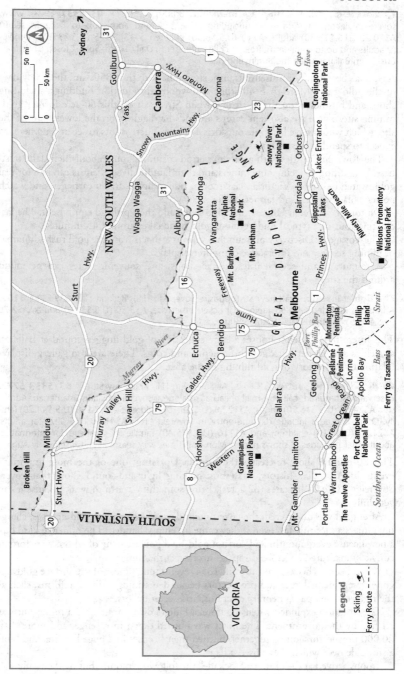

✪ Sovereign Hill Goldmining Township. Bradshaw St. ☎ **03/5331 1944.** www. sovereignhill.com.au. Admission (including mine tour and admission to Gold Museum) A$20.50 (U.S.$13.30) adults, A$10 (U.S.$6.50) children 5–15, A$55 (U.S.$35.75) families (2 adults and up to 4 children), free for children under 5. Daily 10am–5pm. Closed Christmas. Bus: From Ballarat catch the Buninyong bus.

Australia's best outdoor museum transports you back to the 1850s and the heady days of the gold rush. More than 40 stone-and-wood reproduction buildings, including shops and businesses on the re-created Main Street, sit on this 60-acre former gold-mining site. There are also tent camps around the diggings on the lowest part of the site, which would have been the outskirts of town. There is lots to see and do here, so expect to spend at least 4 hours.

The Township bustles with actors in period costumes going about their daily business. In addition to seeing how miners and their families lived, visitors can pan for real gold, watch lessons in Victorian classrooms, ride in horse-drawn carriages, and watch potters, blacksmiths, and tanners make their wares.

On top of Sovereign Hill are the mine shafts and their pithead equipment. The fascinating tour of a typical underground gold mine takes around 45 minutes.

The Voyage to Discovery museum has various artifacts from the gold rush, dioramas of mining scenes, and interactive computer displays.

A restaurant and several cafes, coffee shops, and souvenir stores can be found around the site.

The Gold Museum. Bradshaw St. (opposite Sovereign Hill), Ballarat. ☎ **03/5337 1107.** Admission included with Sovereign Hill ticket; otherwise, A$5.50 (U.S.$3.60) adults, A$2.70 (U.S.$1.75) children. Daily 10am–5:30pm.

This interesting museum houses a large collection of gold nuggets found at Ballarat, as well as alluvial deposits, gold ornaments, and coins. There are also gallery displays relating to the history of gold mining in the area.

✪ Blood on the Southern Cross. At Sovereign Hill, Bradshaw St. ☎ **03/5333 5777.** Reservations required; call or e-mail ahead at rmaloney@sovereignhill.austasia.net.au. Admission A$24.50 (U.S.$15.90) adults; A$12.50 (U.S.$8.10) children 5–15; A$68 (U.S.$44.20) family. Other packages include daytime entry to Sovereign Hill: A$41.50 (U.S.$27) for adults, A$21.50 (U.S.$14) children, and A$116 (U.S.$75.40) families. Call ahead for information about other packages. 2 shows nightly Mon–Sat (times vary seasonally). Closed early Aug.

This 80-minute show re-creates the **Eureka Uprising,** one of the most important events in Australia's history, in a breathtaking light-and-sound show that covers Sovereign Hill's 25 hectares (62 acres). Bring something warm to wear, because it can get chilly.

After gold was discovered, the government devised a system of gold licenses, charging miners a monthly fee, even if they came up empty-handed. The miners had to buy a new license every month, and corrupt gold-field police (many of whom were former convicts) instituted a vicious campaign to extract the money.

When license checks intensified in 1854, even though most of the surface gold was gone, resentment flared, and prospectors began demanding political reforms, such as the right to vote, parliamentary elections, and secret ballots.

The situation exploded when the Eureka Hotel's owner murdered a miner but was set free by the government. The hotel was burned down in revenge, and more than 20,000 prospectors joined together, burned their licenses in a huge bonfire, and built a stockade over which they raised a flag.

Troops arrived at the "Eureka Stockade" the following month, but by then only 150 miners remained behind its walls. The stockade was attacked at dawn, and in the 15-minute skirmish, 24 miners were killed and 30 wounded. The civil uprising forced the government to act: The licenses were replaced with "miners' rights" and cheaper fees, and the vote was introduced to Victoria.

Eureka Stockade Centre. Eureka St. ☎ **03/5333 1854.** Admission A$8 (U.S.$5.20) adults, A$4 (U.S.$2.60) children, and A$22 (U.S.$71.50) families of 6. Open every day 9am–5pm. Closed Christmas and Mon except public holidays.

You can't miss this building with its huge sail, signifying the flag of the Southern Cross, which was raised above the original miners' stockade in the Eureka Uprising. Relive the action of the battle through multimedia displays. The Contemplation Room, where you are asked to think about Australian history while listening to a trickling water soundscape, is a bit too hokey for me.

Ballarat Fine Art Gallery. 40 Lydiard St. N., Ballarat. ☎ **03/5331 5622.** Admission A$4 (U.S.$2.60) adults, A$1 (U.S.65¢) children 6–16. Daily 10:30am–5pm. Closed Good Friday and Christmas.

After you've learned the story of the Eureka uprising (see above), you may find it moving to come here and see the original Eureka flag. This provincial gallery also houses a large collection of Australian art, including works by Sydney Nolan, Fred Williams, and Russell Drysdale. Look out for Tom Roberts's *Charcoal Burners* and Phillip Fox's *Love Story.*

ACCOMMODATIONS

The Ansonia. 32 Lydiard St. S., Ballarat 3350. ☎ **03/5332 4678.** Fax 03/5332 4698. www.ballarat.com/ansonia. E-mail: ansonia@ansonia.ballarat.net.au. 20 units. TV TEL. A$115 (U.S.$74.75) double, A$130 (U.S.$84.50) executive double; A$150 (U.S.$97.50) suite; A$180 (U.S.$117) family room; A$180 (U.S.$117) apt. AE, BC, DC, MC, V. Free parking.

This boutique hotel in a restored Victorian building sports a glass atrium that runs the length of the property and is filled with plants and wicker chairs. Studio rooms are simply but comfortably furnished, and have nice polished floorboards. The executive doubles are larger and a little plusher. The two family rooms can sleep four people in two bedrooms. There is a comfortable library and sitting room, and plenty of flowers and art are scattered everywhere. No smoking on the property.

The restaurant serves as a cafe during the day and a Mediterranean-style restaurant at night. It serves up such fare as homemade pies, soups, curries, meat dishes, and a great gorgonzola soufflé on a bed of forest mushrooms.

Ballarat Heritage Homestay. 185 Victoria St. (P.O. Box 1360), Ballarat Mail Centre, VIC 3354. ☎ **1800/813 369** in Australia, or 03/5332 8296. Fax 03/5331 3358. www.ballarat. com/homestay.htm. E-mail: ball.heritage@netconnect.com.au. 5 cottages, 1 B&B unit. TV TEL (available on request). A$270–$340 (U.S.$175.50–$221) for 2 people for 2-night weekend stay; A$130–$160 (U.S.$84.50–$104) weekday night. Rates include breakfast. Extra adult A$25 (U.S.$16.25); extra child under 18 A$15 (U.S.$9.65). AE, BC, DC, MC, V.

If you'd enjoy staying in a historic cottage, you might want to try Ballarat Heritage Homestay. Some of these Victorian and Edwardian cottages date back to the gold-rush days. All of them are very different. Three cottages have clawfoot tubs, and one has a Jacuzzi. Generally there are a queen, a double, and two singles in each cottage.

The Sovereign Hill Lodge. Magpie St., Ballarat, VIC 3350. ☎ **03/5333 3409.** Fax 03/5333 5861. E-mail: istiff@sovereignhill.austasia.net. 29 motel units, 2 dorms. A/C TV TEL. A$98 (U.S.$63.70) double or family room; A$110–$125 (U.S.$71.50–$81.25) heritage room. Extra person A$11 (U.S.$7.15). Ask about packages. AE, BC, DC, JCB, MC, V. Free parking.

The colonial-style wooden buildings adjacent to the Sovereign Hill Goldmining Township were built to resemble an 1850s Government Camp that was used to control (and tax) the mine fields. The Residence building has rooms with queen-size beds and a set of single bunks, and the Offices building has heritage rooms with four-poster beds and plenty of Baltic pine furnishings, some with Jacuzzis. There are eight double rooms in the Superintendent's house, while the Barracks houses dorm rooms that sleep up to 10 people (A$16/U.S.$10.40 for YHA members; A$18/U.S.$11.70 for non-members). There is a bar, 24-hour reception, and a game room on the grounds. Guests get a 10% discount off entry to Sovereign Hill.

DINING

Lake Pavilion Restaurant Café. Wendouree Parade (across from the Botanical Gardens). ☎ **03/5334 1811.** All main courses around A$11 (U.S.$7.15). AE, BC, MC, V. Daily 9am–6pm. Bus: 15 Mon–Sat. INTERNATIONAL.

I like this restaurant across from the Botanical Gardens and on the shores of Lake Wendouree. The Lake Pavilion was constructed in 1890 and still has that old-world atmosphere, with polished floorboards and high ceilings. You can eat either indoors or outside, but either way you have some good views across the gardens and the lake. The menu includes pizzas, focaccia sandwiches, various pasta dishes, salads, steaks, and seafood. It's licensed but you can also bring your own wine. A kiosk adjacent to the restaurant sells cheap snacks.

Robin Hood Family Bistro. 33 Peel St. N. ☎ **03/5331 3348.** Reservations recommended Fri–Sat. Main courses A$8.95–$17.95 (U.S.$5.80–$11.65). AE, BC, DC, MC, V. Daily 11:30am–2pm and 5:30–8pm. BISTRO.

The Robin Hood is located in a big old pub—not exactly a place where you'd expect to find a bistro catering to healthy eating. The bistro, though, is a past winner of the Real Meal Award, handed out by the Australian Hoteliers Association and aimed at promoting healthier pub food. Everything here is made with low-fat/low-cholesterol ingredients. On the menu you'll find steak-and-kidney pie, beef curry, and several types of steak. Not healthy so far, perhaps; but there's an extensive salad bar, and all main courses come with a healthy dollop of vegetables.

2 The Great Ocean Road: One of the World's Most Scenic Drives

Geelong: 75km (46¹/₂ miles) SW of Melbourne; Torquay: 94km (58 miles) SW of Melbourne; Port Campbell National Park: 285km (177 miles) SW of Melbourne; Peterborough: 200km (160 miles) SW of Melbourne

The ✪ **Great Ocean Road**—which hugs the coast from Torquay, and onward through Anglesea, Lorne, Apollo Bay, and Port Campbell, until it ends at Peterborough—is one of Australia's most spectacular drives (many say it's the best). The scenery along the 106-kilometer (64¹/₂-mile) route includes huge cliffs, ocean vistas, beaches, rain forests, and some incredible rock formations. The settlements along the highway are small, but they offer a number of accommodation choices.

The best way to travel along the Great Ocean Road is to drive yourself at a leisurely pace, stopping off wherever your fancy takes you. The main attractions are in the coastal **Port Campbell National Park,** so don't be surprised if you're not overly impressed until you get there. If you are traveling on to Adelaide, you could stop off for 1 night along the Great Ocean Road, and spend another night in the Coorong in South Australia (see chapter 10).

ESSENTIALS

ORGANIZED TOURS **Melbourne Sightseeing** (☎ 03/9663 3388) offers a bus trip featuring the highlights of the Great Ocean Road. The buses leave from

Melbourne daily at 8:15am and return at 8:30pm—a journey I wouldn't like to attempt in a day. Tours cost A$89 (U.S.$57.85) for adults (A$50/U.S.$32.50 if you have a YHA card) and A$44 (U.S.$28.60) for children (A$38/U.S.$24.70 with a YHA card). The trip can be stretched out over 2 days with overnight accommodation in the YHA in Lorne; the price for the overnight trip is A$129 (U.S.$83.85). **Grayline Sightseeing Tours** (☎ 03/9663 4455) also has daily trips that cost A$91 (U.S.$59.15) for adults.

Another option worth considering is a 2-day excursion with **Let's Go Bush Tours** (☎ 03/9662 3969), which departs Melbourne every Wednesday and Saturday. The trip is less rushed than others, and you get to stay in the company's own house situated on the highest point of the Great Ocean Road. The trip costs A$89 (U.S.$57.85), including dinner, breakfast, and accommodation.

Wild-Life Tours (☎ 03/9747 1882; www.wildlifetours.com.au; e-mail: wildlife@eisa.net.au) also offers a 2-day Great Ocean Road tour for A$75 (U.S.$48.75) and a 3-day tour that includes the Grampians for A$126 (U.S.$81.90). The company also offers a 2-day trip from Melbourne to Adelaide along the Great Ocean Road for A$125 (U.S.$81.25) one-way, and various other offerings. Prices do not include accommodation or food.

V/Line (☎ 13 61 96 in Victoria, 13 22 32 in NSW, or 03/9619 5000) runs a special combined train/coach Coast Link service as far as Warr-nambool, via Geelong, Lorne, Apollo Bay, and Port Campbell. The train leaves Melbourne every Friday at 8:49am; you transfer onto a bus at Geelong. The bus tours the Great Ocean Road, stopping off at various lookout points (and for lunch) and then carries on to Warr-nambool. At 5:35pm, passengers catch the train back to Melbourne. There's an extra service every Monday in December and January. The trip costs A$66.40 (U.S.$43) for adults and A$33.20 (U.S.$21.60) for children.

VISITOR INFORMATION   Most places along the route have their own information centers. If you're coming from Melbourne, stop at the **Geelong & Great Ocean Road Visitors Centre,** Stead Park, Princess Highway, Geelong, VIC 3220 (☎ 03/5275 5797; www.greatoceanrd.org.au), which is open daily from 9am to 5pm. You can book accommodations here, which you should do in advance, especially in summer. There's also a visitor center at the **National Wool Museum,** 26 Moorabool St., Geelong (☎ 1800/620 888 in Australia, or 03/5222 2900).

Along the route, the **Park Information Centre,** at Port Campbell National Park, Norris Street, Port Campbell (☎ 03/5598 6382), is also a good place to pick up brochures. It also has some interesting displays and an audiovisual show of the area. It's open from 10am to 4:30pm daily.

If you're approaching from the north, visit the **Camperdown Visitor Information Centre,** "Court House," Manifold Street, Princes Highway, Camperdown (☎ 03/5593 3390). It's open Monday to Friday from 9:30am to 5pm, Saturday from 9:30am to 4pm, and Sunday from 11am to 4pm.

EXPLORING THE COASTAL ROAD

Along the route, you might want to stop off at **Torquay,** a township dedicated to surfing. The main surf beach here is much nicer than the one farther down the coast in Lorne. While in Torquay, you might want to stop off at **Surfworld,** Surfcoast Plaza Beach Road, West Torquay (☎ 03/5261 4606), which has interactive exhibits dealing with surfboard design and surfing history, and video of the world's best surfers. Admission is A$6 (U.S.$3.90) for adults, A$4 (U.S.$2.60) for children, and A$16 (U.S.$10.40) for families. **Bells Beach,** just down the road, is world famous in surfing circles for its perfect waves.

Lorne has some nice boutiques and is a good place to stop off for lunch or stay the night (see recommendations below). The stretch from **Lorne to Apollo Bay** is one of the most spectacular sections of the route, as the road narrows and twists and turns along a cliff edge with the ocean on the other side. **Apollo Bay** itself is a pleasant town that was once a whaling station. It has good sandy beaches and is much more low-key than Lorne.

Next, you come to the **Angahook-Lorne State Park,** which protects most of the coastal section of the Otway Ranges from Aireys Inlet, just south of Anglesea, to Kennett River. It has plenty of well-marked rain-forest walks and picnic areas at Shelly Beach, Elliot River, and Blanket Bay. There's plenty of wildlife around here.

About 13 kilometers (8 miles) past Apollo Bay, just off the main road, you can take a stroll through the rain forest on the **Maits Rest Rainforest Boardwalk.** A little farther along the main road, an unsealed road branches off and leads north past Hopetoun Falls and Beauchamp Falls to the settlement of **Beech Forest.** Seven kilometers farther along the main road, another unsealed road heads off south for 15 kilometers (9 miles) to a windswept headland and the **Cape Otway Lighthouse.** Built by convicts in 1848, the 100-meter-tall (328-ft.) lighthouse is open to tourists daily from 9am to 5pm. Admission is A$6 (U.S.$3.90) for adults and A$3 (U.S.$1.95) for children. Ask about guided tours.

Back on the main road again, your route heads inland through an area known as **Horden Vale,** before running to the sea again at **Glenaire** (there's good surfing and camping at Johanna, 6km north of here). Then the Great Ocean Road heads north again to **Lavers Hill,** a former timber town. Five kilometers (3 miles) southwest of Lavers Hill is the small **Melba Gully State Park,** where you can spot glowworms at night and walk along routes of rain-forest ferns. Keep an eye out for one of the last giant gum trees that escaped the loggers—it's some 27 meters (88$^1/_2$ ft.) in circumference and is estimated to be more than 300 years old.

The next place of note is **Moonlight Head,** which marks the start of the "Shipwreck Coast"—a 120-kilometer (74-mile) stretch of coastline running to Port Fairy that claimed more than 80 ships in only 40 years at the end of the 19th century and the beginning of the 20th.

Just past Princetown starts the biggest attraction of the entire trip, ✪ **Port Campbell National Park.** With its sheer cliffs and coastal rock sculptures, it's one of the most immediately recognizable images of natural Australia. You can't miss the **Twelve Apostles,** a series of rock pillars that stand in the foam just offshore. Other attractions are the **Blowhole,** which throws up huge sprays of water; the **Grotto,** a baroque rock formation intricately carved by the waves; **London Bridge,** which looked quite like the real thing until the center crashed into the sea in 1990, leaving a bunch of tourists stranded on the wrong end; and the **Loch Ard Gorge. Port Fairy,** a lovely fishing town once known as Belfast by Irish immigrants who settled here to escape the potato famine, is also on the Shipwreck Coast.

Not far past the town of **Peterborough,** the Great Ocean Road heads inland to Warr-nambool to eventually join the Princes Highway heading toward Adelaide.

ACCOMMODATIONS ALONG THE WAY

The **Great Ocean Road Accommodation Centre,** 136 Mountjoy Parade, Lorne, VIC 3232 (☎ **03/5289 1800**), rents out cottages and units along the route.

IN LORNE

Lorne is a good option for a night's rest. Though the beach and water are nothing special, there are plenty of restaurants.

⚫ **Cumberland Lorne Conference & Leisure Resort.** 150–178 Mountjoy Parade, Lorne, VIC 3232. ☎ **1800/037 010** in Australia, or 03/5289 2400. Fax 03/5289 2256. www. cumberland.com.au. E-mail: reservations@cumberland.com.au. 99 units. TV TEL. Summer A$265–$285 (U.S.$172.25–$185.25) 1-bedroom apt; A$315–$335 (U.S.$204.75–$217.75) 2-bedroom apt; A$370–$390 (U.S.$240.50–$253.50) penthouse. Off-season A$200–$220 (U.S.$130–$143) 1-bedroom apt.; A$255–$275 (U.S.$165.75–$178.75) 2-bedroom apt.; A$310–$330 (U.S.$201.50–$214.50) penthouse. Prices include GST. Ask about packages. AE, BC, DC, MC, V.

This sporty resort, built in 1988 but already crumbling around the edges, stands out like a sore thumb from its location between the sea and the foothills of the Otway Ranges. Still, I highly recommend it, because it's a good value for your money and quite luxurious. Every apartment has a queen-size bed and a foldout sofa bed, a large kitchen, a laundry, a Jacuzzi, a balcony, and free in-house movies. All units have large bathrooms with combination shower/tubs. More than half of the rooms have panoramic ocean views, while the rest look out onto gardens. Two-bedroom apartments have two extra single beds, and split-level penthouses have two Jacuzzis and two balconies. There is an indoor heated pool, a spa, a sauna, a gym, barbecues, two squash courts, two tennis courts, and free bicycle, surfboard, and body-board rentals. A kid's club makes life easier for Mom and Dad, and there's a good restaurant on the premises, too.

Great Ocean Road Cottages. 10 Erskine Ave. (P.O. Box 60), Lorne, VIC 3232. ☎ **03/5289 1070.** Fax 03/5289 2508. E-mail: greatoecanrd_cots@iprimus.com.au. 10 cottages, 7 apts, dorms sleeping 33. Cottages A$175 (U.S.$113.75) in summer, A$95 (U.S.$61.75) off-season. Depending on season, A$100–$150 (U.S.$65–$97.50) standard apts, A$160–$185 (U.S.$104–$120.25) spa apts, A$230–$265 (U.S.$149.50–$172.25) suite. Dorm beds A$17.60 (U.S.$11.50) for YHA members, A$20.90 (U.S.$13.60) nonmembers. AE, BC, DC, MC, V.

This complex has it all, although with so many people around (and quite a few children), it can be a little noisy in summer. There's a set of self-contained cottages, set away from each other in a quiet patch of bushland, about a 5-minute walk from the town center. Each cottage is a two-story wooden hut with a double bed, two twin beds, a pull-out mattress, a private bathroom, and a full kitchen. Just down the road is Waverley House, a historic mansion that's been divided into seven apartments. All of them are nice, but they vary enormously.

Also on the property is Great Ocean Road Backpackers, which offers dorm-style accommodation. They also have a few family rooms (discounts apply to all backpacker beds for YHA members).

IN APOLLO BAY

Bayside Gardens. 219 Great Ocean Rd., Apollo Bay, VIC 3233. ☎ and fax **03/5237 6248.** 10 units. TV. A$60–$110 (U.S.$39–$71.50) 1-bedroom apts. Higher rates apply Christmas, Jan, Easter, and public holidays. Minimum 1-week stay in Jan. BC, MC, V.

Right opposite the beach, with good ocean views from the front rooms, Bayside Gardens is a pleasant place to stay—and you can save money on meals by cooking in your own kitchen. Each unit has a separate bedroom with a double bed, a lounge area, a full kitchen, and an attached bathroom with shower. Rooms at the front can be noisy if you're not used to living beside an ocean. There are wood fires in some of the units, and all rooms are centrally heated. Wash your clothes at the coin-op laundry and fry your fish on the barbecues scattered around in the $1^{1}/_{2}$-acre grounds. It's a 10-minute walk to town.

IN PORT CAMPBELL

Macka's Farm. RSD 2305 Princetown Rd., Princetown, VIC 3269. ☎ **03/5598 8261.**
Fax 03/5598 8201. E-mail: macka's@netcam.com.au. 3 units. A$85–$100 (U.S.$55.25–$65)
double, depending on season. Extra person A$15 (U.S.$9.75). BC, MC. V.

This working farm is located inland from the Twelve Apostles (continue on from the
Twelve Apostles for 2km/1¼ miles and turn off at the sign for Macka's farm—it's
another 4km/2½ miles inland from there). The units all have kitchens, so you can
cook up your own feast. Otherwise, you can order meals by prior arrangement outside
peak season, or visit one of the nearby restaurants. Rooms sleep between six and eight
people in a mixture of singles and doubles. There's no TV—but who needs it when
there are lots of pigs, cows, ducks, and chickens running around? Overall, it's a great
farm experience.

WHERE TO DINE IN LORNE

Arab Restaurant. Mount Joy Parade. ☎ **03/5289 1435.** Reservations recommended.
Main courses A$10.50–$18.50 (U.S.$6.80–$12). AE, BC, DC, MC, V. Mon–Fri 9am–9pm, Sat
8am–11pm, Sun 7:30am–10pm. Closed Christmas. INTERNATIONAL.

This popular bistro serves some of the best food along this part of the coast. The house
specialty is chicken Kiev, but you can also tuck into dishes such as the fish of the day
or chicken schnitzel. The apple crumble is delicious.

Marks. Mount Joy Parade. ☎ **03/5289 2787.** Main courses A$9–$17.50
(U.S.$5.85–$11.40). AE, BC, DC, MC, V. Daily noon–2:30pm (only Sat–Sun in winter) and
6–8:30pm. INTERNATIONAL.

Lorne's best restaurant is a classy joint with simple wooden chairs and tables set in an
elegant fashion in a cool, yellow-walled interior. Dishes includes fried calamari salad,
spicy octopus, risotto, and the intriguing oven-baked vine-wrapped goat cheese and
macadamia nut parcel on eggplant pâté with red capsicum puree. The bar is open for
coffee and drinks all day.

Ozone Milk Bar. Mount Joy Parade. ☎ **03/5289 1780.** Menu items A$1.80–$4
(U.S.$1.20–$2.60). No credit cards. Daily 7am–6pm (to 11pm Christmas to the end of Jan).
AUSTRALIAN MILK BAR.

An Ozzie icon, the milk bar is a kind of down-market cafe selling everything from
milk shakes and pies to newspapers. This one sells good pies and quiche, a limp-looking
and bland-tasting veggie burger I wouldn't recommend, chicken fillet burgers, cookies,
ice cream, and small homemade cakes. The milk shakes are particularly good. You can
sit inside or around three small tables outside. There's a Thai place next door, but it's
very unwelcoming.

3 The Murray River

Mildura: 544km (337 miles) NW of Melbourne; Albury-Wadonga: 305km (189 miles) N of
Melbourne; Echuca: 210km (130 miles) N of Melbourne

The Murray is Australia's version of the Mississippi River. Though it's a rushing
torrent of white water at its source in the Snowy Mountains, it becomes slow moving
and muddy brown by the time it becomes the meandering border between Victoria
and New South Wales. The Murray is watered by the Darling River, which starts off
in Queensland, and together the two combine to make Australia's longest river.

The Murray was once used by Aborigines as a source of food and transportation,
and later the water was plied by paddle steamers, laden with wool and crops from the
land it helped irrigate. In 1842, the Murray was "discovered" by explorers Hamilton
Hume and William Howell on the first overland trek from Sydney to Port Phillip, near

Melbourne. As Hume later wrote, on their trek the explorers "suddenly arrived at the bank of a very fine river—at least 200 feet wide, apparently deep, the bank being 8 or 9 feet above the level, which is overflowed at the time of flood. . . . In the solid wood of a healthy tree I carved my name." You can still see the carved initials on a tree standing by the river bank in Albury, on the border between the two states.

ESSENTIALS

GETTING THERE   Most visitors cross the river during an overland drive between cities. There are two routes to get to the Murray from Melbourne: Either take the Calder Highway to Mildura, which is a 6-hour drive, or take the $2^{1}/_{2}$-hour route down the Midland Highway to Echuca. Traveling from Melbourne to Mildura is practical only if you're continuing on to Broken Hill, which is 297 kilometers (184 miles) north of Mildura. Those in a hurry to get to and from Sydney can travel via the river-straddling twin towns of Albury-Wadonga on the Hume Highway (about a 12-hr. trip with short stops).

V/Line (☎ **13 61 96** in Victoria, 13 22 32 in NSW, or 03/9619 5000) runs regular train services to Mildura, Echuca, and Albury-Wadonga.

VISITOR INFORMATION   The **Echuca and Moama and District Visitor Information Centre,** 2 Heygarth St., Echuca, VIC 3564 (☎ **1800/804 446** in Australia, or 03/5480 7555; www.echucamoama.com; e-mail: emt@river.net.au), has plenty of maps and detailed information about local accommodations and river cruises. It's open daily from 9am to 5pm.

The **Mildura Visitor Information & Booking Centre,** 180–190 Deakin Ave., Mildura, VIC 3502 (☎ **1800/039 043** or 03/5021 4424; e-mail: tourism@mildura. vic.gov.au), offers similar services. It's open Monday to Friday from 9am to 5:30pm and weekends from 9am to 5pm.

If you're passing through Albury, you might want to contact the **Gateway Visitors Information Centre,** Gateway Village, Lincoln Causeway, Wadonga, VIC 3690 (☎ **1800/800 743** or 02/6041 3875), open daily from 9am to 5pm.

RIVER CRUISES & OTHER FUN STUFF
IN MILDURA

Mildura is one of Australia's most important fruit-growing areas. There was a time, however, when this was just semi-arid red dust country. The area bloomed due to a little ingenuity and, of course, the Murray. The original irrigation system consisted of two imported English water pumps and the manual labor of hundreds of newly arrived immigrants, who were put to work clearing the scrub and digging channels through the new fields. Today, the hungry land soaks up the water.

Several paddle steamers leave from Mildura wharf. One of the nicest boats is the **P.S. *Melbourne*** (☎ **03/5023 2200**), which was built in 1912 and is still powered by steam. It offers 2-hour trips leaving 10:50am and 1:50pm. The fare is A$17 (U.S.$11) for adults and A$6 (U.S.$3.90) for children. Children under 5 are free.

The P.S. *Melbourne*'s sister ship, the ***Rothbury,*** was built in 1881, but its steam-driven engine has been replaced by a conventional engine. It offers a winery cruise every Thursday from 10:30am to 3:30pm, stopping off at a winery for tastings and a barbecue lunch. The trip costs A$38 (U.S.$24.70) for adults and A$18 (U.S.$11.70) for children. The *Rothbury* has evening dinner cruises every Thursday from 7 to 10pm for the same price. You can also take the paddleboat to the Golden River Zoo (see below) during school holiday periods; it leaves Mildura Wharf at 9:50am on Wednesday morning, returning at 3pm. The trip costs A$32 (U.S.$20.80) for adults and A$16 (U.S.$10.40) for children 5 to 14, including entry to the zoo.

If you have more time, I recommend an all-inclusive cruise on the *Murray Princess,* run by Captain Cook Cruises in Sydney (☎ **02/9206 1144;** www. captaincook.com.au; e-mail:cruise@captaincook.com.au). A 2-night weekend cruise costs from A$350 to $490 (U.S.$227.50 to $318.50) per person, depending on the cabin; a 3-night cruise costs from A$525 to $615 (U.S.$341.25 to $399.75); and a 5-night cruise costs from A$825 to $1,175 (U.S.$536.25 to $763.75). Round-trip transfers from Adelaide are A$50 to $75 (U.S.$32.50 to $48.75) extra.

On dry land, the **Golden River Zoo,** Flora Avenue, Mildura (☎ **03/5023 5540;** www.goledriverzoo.com.au), is a pleasant place to see native animals. The zoo fronts onto the river 4 kilometers (2¹/₂ miles) from the city center down 11th Street. The animals here virtually follow you around (on the lookout for food) as you walk through their large enclosures. Admission is A$14 (U.S.$9.10) for adults and A$7 (U.S.$4.55) for children, including a free barbecue lunch at noon and a free tractor-train ride down to the river at 1:30pm and an animal show. The zoo is open daily, except Christmas Day, from 10am to 5pm.

Side Trips from Mildura into the Outback

If you want to get out into the Outback, then trips from Mildura with **Mallee Outback Experiences** (☎/fax **03/5021 1621,** or mobile 0418/521 0030) are well worth the effort. The company offers two trips. The first goes to Mungo National Park, which is famous for its red sand dunes and shifting sands, and which I highly recommend you go and see. The second is to Hattah National Park, which has some gorgeous river plains, Murray River lakes, pine forests, and more mallee scrub. The Mungo trip leaves every Wednesday and Saturday, and the Hattah National Park trip leaves every Friday. All trips cost A$50 (U.S.$32.50) for adults, A$30 (U.S.$19.50) for children, and A$120 (U.S.$78) for a family of five.

You can get to these two national parks on your own, but it's best to have a 4-wheel-drive vehicle—even better is to go with an experienced guide. ✪ **Mungo National Park** is a unique, arid region located 110 kilometers (68 miles) northeast of Mildura, off the Sturt Highway. People come here to see the "Walls of China," a strangely weathered moonscape of intricately weathered red sand. The walls edge onto Lake Mungo, which is now dry but was once a huge freshwater lake during the last Ice Age. A 60-kilometer (37-mile) driving tour starting at the visitor center at the park's entrance takes you across the lake bed to the Walls of China. There are several short walks in the park leading off from the visitor center (☎ **03/5023 1278**), and camp sites at the park entrance. Just outside the park, the **Mungo Lodge** (☎ **03/5029 7297;** www.mungoldg@ruralnet.net.au) offers affordable motel accommodation and a casual restaurant.

In Echuca

In Echuca, another paddle-steamer option is the *Emmylou* (☎ **03/5480 2237;** www.emmylou.com.au). A 2-day/2-night cruise leaves the Port of Echuca Wednesday at 6pm and returns at noon on Friday (but check sailings beforehand). The cruise includes a visit to the Barmah, an area famous for its wetlands and the largest red gum trees in the world, or, depending on river levels, a stop at Perricoota Station. The trip costs A$365 to $395 (U.S.$237 to $256) per person, depending on the cabin. Children 4 to 14 receive a 25% discount. An overnight trip also leaves on Saturday at 6pm and returns at 10am on Sunday. It costs A$135 to $155 (U.S.$87.75 to $100.75) per person including breakfast; dinner is extra. The *Emmylou* also offers various day trips costing A$14 (U.S.$9.10) for 1 hour and A$17 (U.S.$11.05) for 1¹/₂ hours for adults. Children are half price.

The **Port of Echuca** (☎ **03/5482 4248;** www.portofechuca.org.au; e-mail: port@ portofechuca.org.au) is definitely worth a look. The three-level red gum wharf was built in 1865 and is still used by paddle steamers. The Port owns the PS *Adelaide,* the oldest operating wooden-hulled paddle steamer in the world (1866), the PS *Pevensey* (1911), and the PS *Alexander Arbuthnot* (1923). One-hour cruises on the latter two are offered daily at 10:15am, 11:30am, 1pm, 2:15pm, and 3:30pm for A$14 (U.S.$9.10) for adults and A$5.50 (U.S.$3.60) for children. You can also take a look around the wharf on a guided tour, priced at A$9 (U.S.$5.85) for adults, A$5.50 (U.S.$3.60) for children, and A$25 (U.S.$16.25) for families. Inquire about combined prices for a further discount. Outside the Port, in the Echuca Port Precinct, there are various things to do, including horse and carriage rides and old penny arcade machines in Sharpes Magic Movies, located in an old riverboat warehouse.

ACCOMMODATIONS
In Mildura

Mildura Grand Hotel Resort. Seventh St., Mildura, VIC 3500. ☎ **1800/034 228** in Australia, or 03/5023 0511. Fax 03/5022 1801. 104 units (most with shower only). A/C MINI-BAR TV TEL. A$81–$127 (U.S.$52.65–$82.55) double; A$127 (U.S.$82.55) "Grand Room" double; A$146–$420 (U.S.$94.90–$273) suite. Rates include breakfast. Ask about packages. AE, BC, DC, MC, V.

This huge 19th-century hotel is right in the center of Mildura, overlooking the Murray. Standard double rooms are comfortable, and many have been recently refurbished. There are 21 "Grand" rooms, which are a little bigger, and some have balconies and garden views. The State Suite (A$250/U.S.$162.50 per night) has also been refurbished and matches anything you're likely to find in a five-star hotel. If money's no object, you could indulge in the huge, luxurious Presidential Suite for a mere A$420 (U.S.$273) a night. Guests have use of laundry facilities, a pool, a sauna, a hot tub, a game room, a pool room, and five restaurants, including the excellent Stefano's, which serves Italian cuisine with zingy Asian accents.

In Echuca

Echuca Gardens B&B and YHA. 103 Mitchell St., Echuca, VIC 3564. ☎ **03/5480 6522.** Fax 03/5482 6951. 6 units (3 in B&B and 3 in hostel). B&B room A$120 (U.S.$78) weekends, A$100 (U.S.$65) weekdays. Rates include breakfast. BC, MC, V.

There are evening gatherings around the piano at this popular two-story log cabin B&B, as well as a pretty neat hot tub in the front yard surrounded by murals and landscaped water gardens. Rooms are decorated in native flower themes, and all of them have balconies. Two rooms have showers in the bathroom, and another has a shower on the second floor. It's a short stroll from the B&B to either the river or a state forest. The YHA has a basic twin room inside and three tentlike cabins outside, one with a double bed and the other with two singles. There are also three basic dorm rooms with beds going for A$16 (U.S.$10.40) for YHA members and A$19 (U.S.$12.35) for nonmembers.

In Albury

Hume Country Golf Club Motor Inn. 736 Logan Rd., Albury, NSW 2640. ☎ **02/6025 8233.** Fax 02/6040 4999. E-mail: humegolfmotel@primus.com.au. 25 units. A/C TV TEL. A$75 (U.S.$48.75) double; A$85 (U.S.$55.25) family room; A$115 (U.S.$74.75) suite. Extra person A$10 (U.S.$6.50). AE, BC, DC, MC, V.

This is a good place to stop if you're making the long trip north to Sydney. Just on the New South Wales side of the border, this motor inn has typical motel rooms with everything you'd expect, plus a toaster thrown in for good measure. There are also two very large family rooms, one sleeping five, the other seven. Suites are also large and come with a Jacuzzi tub. All rooms overlook the 27-hole golf course, where a round of golf costs A$18 (U.S.$11.70).

4 The Southeast Coast

The Princes Highway wanders down the coast from Sydney just past Eden, then darts across into Victoria, passing through the logging town of Orbost and then dipping down toward Lakes Entrance. The highway continues to the southwest, swooping in an arch to Melbourne.

This region's most interesting sights are Wilsons Promontory National Park, and— to a lesser extent—Lakes Entrance and the Snowy River National Park.

WILSONS PROMONTORY NATIONAL PARK
200km (124 miles) SE of Melbourne

"The Prom," as it's called, is Victoria's best-loved national park. Dipping down into Bass Strait, the park—which was named after a prominent London businessman— marks the southernmost point on Australia's mainland. It's thought to once have been joined to Tasmania by a land bridge. The best time to visit the park is from late September to early December, when all the bush flowers are in bloom.

Visitors come here for the spectacular granite mountains, the thick forests and vast plains, and some of the country's best beaches. Wildlife abounds in the park, including plenty of koalas, kangaroos, wallabies, possums, echidnas, wombats, and emus. You can hand-feed crimson rosellas at the capital of the Prom, **Tidal River,** but you'll find little more here than the national park's **Tourist Information Center** (☎ **1800/350 552** in Australia, or 03/5680 9555) and camping and caravan grounds.

There are plenty of **trails** leading away into the mountains. Following the longer trails can turn into a 2- or 3-day excursion, though shorter day hikes are possible. One of the best trails is the 1-hour Mt. Oberon walk, which starts from the Mt. Oberon parking lot and offers superb views. Visitors also rave about the Squeaky Beach Nature Walk, a 1^1/$_2$-hour walk from Tidal River to the next bay and back.

There are some 30 **beaches** in the park, some of which are easily accessible. Norman's Beach in Tidal River is the most popular, and it's the only one recommended for swimming. There's no snorkeling or lifeguards at these beaches, but they're gorgeous.

ESSENTIALS

ENTRY FEES   Park entry costs A$8 (U.S.$5.20) for cars, which you pay at the park entrance gate, 30 kilometers (18 miles) north of Tidal River. The gate is open 24 hours, but if you arrive late and the collection station is closed, pay the following morning at Tidal River.

GETTING THERE   From Melbourne, take the South Gippsland Highway (B440), turning south at Meeniyan and again at Fish Creek or Foster. The route is well sign-posted. Tidal River is 30 kilometers inside the park boundary.

There's no public transportation to the park. You can, however, take the **V/Line bus** from Melbourne to Foster (fare: A$21.30/U.S.$13.85), which is 60 kilometers (37 miles) north of the park. In Foster, you can stay at the **Foster Backpackers Hostel,** 17 Pioneer St., Foster, VIC 3960 (☎ **03/5682 2614**). It's basically a private home with a few spare rooms; the two doubles cost A$40 (U.S.$26), and dorm beds go for A$17 (U.S.$11.05). There are also two fully self-contained apartments for $50 (U.S.$32.50). The owner offers daily transport to Tidal River for A$20 (U.S.$13) each way; the trip takes around 45 minutes.

ACCOMMODATIONS

The national park's Tourist Information Center operates 17 self-contained **cabins** costing A$115 (U.S.$74.75) a night for two (they can accommodate up to six people; each extra person costs A$16/U.S.$10.40), as well as five "Lorikeet" units costing A$82 (U.S.$53.30) a night for two and A$118 (U.S.$76.70) for four. For bookings, call ☎ **03/5680 9500** or fax 03/568 09516.

Waratah Park Country House. Thomson Rd., Waratah Bay, VIC 3959. ☎ **03/5683 2575.** Fax 03/5683 2275. 6 units. A/C TV TEL. A$75 (U.S.$48.75) including breakfast; A$110 (U.S.$71.50) Sun–Thurs (including 4-course dinner and breakfast); A$259 (U.S.$168.35) for weekend package including 2 nights' lodgings, 2 breakfasts, and 2 4-course dinners. All rates are per person. AE, BC, MC, V.

If you don't feel like roughing it, this is the only place within the park that will do. Rooms, with king-size beds and double spas, offer stunning views over Wilsons Promontory and a dozen or so islands. The food here is excellent, too. The hotel is also next to the new Cape Liptrap Coastal Park, home to some 120 species of birds.

It's a very friendly place, where the hosts will sit down with you and go through the things you want to do while in the area. A V/Line coach operates from Melbourne to Fish Creek, and the owner will pick you up from the bus station.

LAKES ENTRANCE

316km (189½ miles) E of Melbourne; 792km (491 miles) SW of Sydney

Lakes Entrance (pop. 4,200) is Victoria's fishing capital and a popular summer resort town. People come here for three things: the surrounding **national parks;** the vast **Gippsland Lakes** (Australia's largest enclosed waterway, separated from the coast by sand spits and dunes crossed by walkways); and the **beaches,** the most famous of which is **Ninety Mile Beach.** Most of Ninety Mile Beach is encompassed within the **Gippsland Lakes Coastal Park**—a bird lovers' paradise. Lake Entrance's beaches never get crowded, so grab a blanket and head for your own personal stretch of white sand.

The town is situated at the eastern end of the lake system and attracts lots of anglers, windsurfers, boaters, and water-skiers. If you're hurrying on down to Melbourne from Sydney, you might want to pull over here and admire the ocean views from **Jemmy Point,** 2 kilometers (1 mile) west of town on the Princes Highway.

ESSENTIALS

GETTING THERE   It's a fairly easy drive from Melbourne. Or take **V/Line** (☎ **13 61 96** in Victoria, 13 22 32 in NSW, or 03/9619 5000), which operates daily buses from Melbourne to Bairnsdale for around A$34.20 (U.S.$22.25), with a connection to Lakes Entrance for an additional A$7.10 (U.S.$4.60).

VISITOR INFORMATION   The **Lakes Entrance Visitor Information Centre** (☎ **03/5155 1966**) is on the Princes Highway, just as you enter the town from the west.

ACCOMMODATIONS

Abel Tasman Motor Lodge. 643 Esplanade (Princes Hwy.), Lakes Entrance, VIC 3909. ☎ **03/5155 1655.** Fax 03/5155 1603. www.lakes-entrance.com/abletasman. E-mail: tas@net-tech. 16 units (2 with spa). A/C TV TEL. A$65–$115 (U.S.$42.25–$74.75) double; A$100–$280 (U.S.$65–$182) apt. Rates are highest Christmas to the end of Jan, Easter, and long weekends. AE, BC, DC, MC, V.

The rooms at this modern motel, which was totally refurbished in 1998, are the best in Lakes Entrance. Furnished in typical motel style, standard rooms on the top floor also have private balconies. All have views across the lake. The apartments were built in 1998 and are quite classy. Guests have the use of a swimming pool, barbecues, and a coin-op laundry.

Déjà Vu. Clara St. (P.O. Box 750), Lakes Entrance, VIC 3909. ☎ **03/5155 4330.** Fax 03/ 5155 3718. www.dejavu.com.au. E-mail: dejavu@dejavu.com.au. 6 units. TV. A$120 (U.S.$75) standard double; A$135–$185 (U.S.$87.75–$120.25) spa double. Rates include cooked breakfast. Ask about midweek packages. BC, DC, JCB, MC, V.

This waterfront retreat is set in 6 acres of rain forest and wetlands and has panoramic ocean views. Rooms are large and comfortable (four have Jacuzzis), each with a sitting room and a balcony (from which you might spot pelicans, black swans, and other feathered friends). There is also a meditation room, and massages are available. Seafood platter meals are served on your balcony, or you can paddle a canoe the 2 minutes it takes to get to the shops and restaurants in town. Tours of the area can be arranged. There's also a waterfront apartment suitable for two couples with its own private beach costing A$240 (U.S.$156) for four people or A$145 (U.S.$94.25) for one couple. A minimum 2-night stay is required in the apartment, and the rates include breakfast provisions. Cruises by arrangement are available; a happy-hour cruise provides light refreshments or a full dinner cruise is available. Cruises are subject to availability and weather.

5 The High Country

Victoria's High Country is made up of the hills and mountains of the **Great Dividing Range,** which runs from Queensland, through New South Wales, to just before Ballarat, where it drops away and reappears in the dramatic mountains of the **Grampians,** in the western part of Victoria. The range separates inland Australia from the greener coastal belt. The highest mountain in the Victorian segment of the range is **Mt. Bogong,** which, at just 1,988 meters (6,621 ft.), is minuscule by world mountain standards.

The main attractions of the High Country are its natural features, which include moorland and typical mountainous alpine scenery. It's also popular for its outdoor activities, including hiking, canoeing, white-water rafting, and rock climbing. The High Country is also the home of the Victorian **ski fields,** based around Mt. Buller, Mt. Stirling, Falls Creek, Mt. Buffalo, and Mt. Hotham. If you plan to go walking here, make sure you have plenty of water and sunscreen, as well as a tent and a good-quality sleeping bag. As in any alpine region, temperatures can plummet dramatically. In summer, days can be very hot, and nights very cold.

SNOWY RIVER NATIONAL PARK
390km (242 miles) NE of Melbourne

The Snowy River National Park, with its lovely river scenery and magnificent gorges, protects Victoria's largest forest wilderness areas. The Snowy River was once a torrent worthy of Banjo Patterson's famous poem, but since the Snowy Mountain Hydro-Electric came along and erected a series of dams, it's become a mere trickle of its former self.

ESSENTIALS
GETTING THERE & GETTING AROUND   There are two main access roads to the park: the Gelantipy Road from Buchan and the Bonang Freeway from the logging township of Orbost. MacKillop's Road (also known as Deddick River Road) runs across the park's northern border from Bonang to a little south of Wulgulmerang.

Around MacKillop's Bridge, along MacKillop's Road, is some spectacular scenery, and the park's best campgrounds, set beside some nice swimming holes and sandy river beaches. The Barry Way leads through the main township of Buchan, where you'll find some of Australia's best caves.

VISTOR INFORMATION   The main place to get information on Snowy River National Park and Alpine National Park is the **Buchan Caves Information Centre,** in the Buchan Caves complex. It's open daily from 9am to 4pm (closed Christmas). Otherwise, call **Parks Victoria** (☎ **13 19 63** in Victoria, or 03/5155 9264).

EXPLORING THE BUCHAN CAVES & MORE

The ✪ **Buchan Caves** (☎ **03/5155 9264**) are set in a scenic valley that's particularly beautiful in autumn, when all the European trees are losing their leaves. Tourists can visit the Royal and Fairy caves (which are quite similar), with their fabulous stalactites and stalagmites. There are several tours daily: April to September at 11am, 1pm, and 3pm; October to March at 10am, 11:15am, 1pm, 2:15pm, and 3:30pm. Entry to one cave costs A$10 (U.S.$6.50) for adults, A$5 (U.S.$3.25) for children ages 5 to 16, and A$25 (U.S.$16.25) for families of five.

To reach the caves from the Princes Highway, turn off at Nowa Nowa (it's well sign-posted), or if you're coming south from Jindabyne in New South Wales (see chapter 4), follow the Barry Way, which runs alongside the Snowy River.

Want to feel like the Man from Snowy River? **Snowy Mountain Rider Tours,** Karoonda Park, Gelantipy (☎ **03/5155 0220**), offers half-day rides in the Snowy River National Park for A$60 (U.S.$39), and full-day tours for A$120 (U.S.$78) including lunch. Four-day trips including camping and all meals costs A$520 (U.S.$338). The company also arranges rafting on Snowy River for A$120 (U.S.$78) a day including lunch.

There are no hotels or cabins in the park, but there are plenty of **camping** spots beside the Snowy River at McKillops Bridge north of Buchan (ask at Buchan Caves for directions). Otherwise, the three-star **Karoonda Park** (☎ **03/5155 0220;** e-mail: karoonda@net-nettech.com.au) offers several self-contained houses (A$65/U.S.$42.25 for two), 40 dorm beds (A$18/U.S.$11.70 for YHA members, A$20/U.S.$13 for nonmembers), and six double rooms (A$40/U.S.$26 double). There's a home-style eatery on the premises. Karronda Park is 30 minutes north of Buchan and 3 hours south of Jindabyne, in New South Wales on the Barrier Way.

ALPINE NATIONAL PARK

333km (200 miles) NE of Melbourne, 670km (402 miles) SW of Sydney

Victoria's largest national park at 646,000 hectares (2494 square miles), the Alpine National Park connects the High Country areas of New South Wales and the ACT. The park's scenery is spectacular, encompassing most of the state's highest mountains, wild rivers, impressive escarpments, forests, and high plains. The flora is diverse; in all, some 1,100 plant species have been recorded within the park's boundaries, including 12 not found anywhere else.

Hiking here is particularly good in spring and summer, when the **Bogong High Plains** are covered in a carpet of wildflowers. Other impressive walking trails include the 5.7-kilometer (3¹/₂-mile) route through **Bryce Gorge** to **The Bluff,** a 200-meter (356-ft.) high rocky escarpment with panoramic views. Of the numerous other walking trails in the park, the most well known is the **Alpine Walking Track,** which bisects the park for 400 kilometers (240 miles) from Walhalla to the township of Tom Groggin, on the New South Wales border. There are plenty of access roads into the park, though some close in winter.

Ecotrek (☎ 08/8383 7198; e-mail: ecotrek@ozE-mail.com.au) offers an 8-day Bogong Alpine Traverse trek, including 4 nights camping and 3 nights in ski lodges. You carry your own pack, but the pain is worth it for the incredible panoramic views of peaks, plains, and forested valleys. The trek costs A$1,150 (U.S.$747.50), including round-trip transport from Melbourne. The company also offers a 5-day trek that involves camping and day walks through extremely rugged country. It costs A$630 (U.S.$409.50), including round-trip transport to Melbourne.

The Alpine National Park can be accessed by several routes from Melbourne, including the Great Alpine Road (B500), the Kiewa Valley Highway (C531), and the Lincoln Road from Heyfield. Get to The Bluff from Mansfield along the Maroodah Highway.

If you'd like to spend a couple of days exploring the park, see the sections on the ski resorts that follow for accommodations information.

HITTING THE SLOPES: THE HIGH COUNTRY SKI RESORTS

Most of the Victoria's ✪ **ski areas** are in, or on the edge of, the Alpine National Park (see above). The ski season in the Victorian High Country lasts from June to October, with July and August being the most popular months.

MT. HOTHAM
373km (231 miles) NE of Melbourne

Mt. Hotham (1,750m/5,740 ft.) is an intimate ski resort, significantly smaller than those at Falls Creek (see below). There are eight lifts, offering runs from beginner to advanced. It also offers some good off-trail cross-country skiing, including a route across the Bogong High Plains to Falls Creek. Some of the lifts are quite far apart, although there's a free "zoo cart" and bus transport system in winter along the main road.

Essentials
GETTING THERE   From Melbourne, take the Hume Highway via Harrietville, or the Princes Highway via Omeo. The trip takes around 5½ hours (the trip is slightly quicker on the Hume Highway).

Trekset Mount Hotham Snow Service (☎ 03/9370 9055) runs buses to Mt. Hotham daily during the ski season departing Melbourne's Spencer Street Coach Terminal at 9am. The trip takes 6 hours and costs A$70 (U.S.$45.50) one-way or A$105 (U.S.$68.25) round-trip. You need to book in advance.

ENTRY FEES & LIFT TICKETS   Resort entry costs A$18 (U.S.$11.70) per car for a day, payable at the resort entry gates, or at the Mount Hotham Resort Management office (see "Visitor Information," below). Ski tickets are available from **Mount Hotham Skiing Company** (☎ 03/5759 4444). Full-day **lift tickets** cost A$64 (U.S.$41.60) for adults and A$33 (U.S.$21.45) for children. Combined lift and ski-lesson tickets cost A$87 (U.S.$56.55) for adults and A$59 (U.S.$38.35) for children.

VISITOR INFORMATION   **Mount Hotham Resort Management,** Great Alpine Road, Mt. Hotham (☎ 03/5759 3550), is as close as you'll come to an information office. It has plenty of brochures. It's open daily from 8am to 5pm during the ski season, and Monday to Friday from 9am to 5pm at other times.

Accommodations
The **Mt. Hotham Accommodation Service** (☎ 1800/032 061 in Australia; www.mt-hotham-accommodation.com.au; e-mail: hotham@netc.net.com) can book rooms and advise you on special deals during both off-peak and peak periods. Another option is **Mt. Hotham Central Reservations** (☎ 1800/032 061 in Australia;

www.hotham.net.au). During the ski season, most places will want you to book for an entire week. Prices are significantly lower in the non–ski season.

FALLS CREEK
375km (225 miles) NE of Melbourne

One of Victoria's best ski resorts, and my favorite, Falls Creek is situated on the edge of the Bogong High Plains overlooking the Kiewa Valley. This compact alpine village is the only one in Australia where you can ski from your lodge to the lifts and back again from the ski slopes. The nightlife is also very good in the ski season, with plenty of party options as well as a range of walk-in lodge restaurants.

The ski fields are split into two parts, the **Village Bowl** and **Sun Valley,** with 22 lifts in all. There are plenty of intermediate and advanced runs, as well as a sprinkling for beginners. Plans are afoot to create Australia's only double-black-diamond ski run by around 2001. You'll also find some of Australia's best cross-country skiing here; Australia's major cross-country skiing event, the **Kangaroo Hoppet,** is held here on the last Saturday in August every year.

Falls Creek is also a pleasant place to visit in summer, when you can go bushwalking, horseback riding, and trout fishing. **Angling Expeditions** (☎ and fax **03/ 5754 1466**) is the best option for fly-fishing for trout in the alpine area during spring, summer, and fall. Trips last from 3 hours to all day and are suitable for everyone from beginners to experts. Overnight trips are also available. Horseback-riding operators include **Falls Creek Trail Rides** (☎ **03/5758 3655**) and **Bogong Horseback Adventures** (☎ **03/5754 4849**).

Essentials

GETTING THERE **Pyles Coaches** (☎ **03/5754 4024**) runs buses to the ski resort from Melbourne every day during the ski season (from the end of June to the end of Sept), departing Melbourne at 9am and Falls Creek at 5pm. The round-trip fare is A$100 (U.S.$65) for adults and A$75 (U.S.$48.75) for children and includes the resort entrance fee. The company also runs shuttle buses to and from Albury just over the border in New South Wales, and between Mt. Beauty and Falls Creek. Bookings are essential.

Alternatively, **Kendell Airlines** (☎ **1800/338 8894** in Australia) flies to Albury, a 1¹/₂-hour drive from Falls Creek. Avis, Budget, Thrifty, and Hertz have desks at Albury airport.

If you're driving from Melbourne, take the Hume Highway to Wangaratta, and then through Myrtleford and Mt. Beauty to Falls Creek. The trip takes around 4¹/₂ hours. From Sydney, take the Hume Highway to Albury-Wodonga and follow the signs to Mt. Beauty and the snow fields.

ENTRY FEES & LIFT TICKETS Entry to the resort costs A$6 (U.S.$3.90). Full-day lift tickets cost A$64 (U.S.$41.60) for adults and A$33 (U.S.$21.45) for children. Combined lift and ski-lesson tickets cost from A$37 (U.S.$24.05) for adults and from A$29 (U.S.$18.85) for children. Call the **Falls Creek Ski Lifts** (☎ **03/5758 3280**) for details. The ski lifts can also organize accommodation options.

VISITOR INFORMATION The **Falls Creek Information Centre** at 1 Bogong High Plains Rd., Falls Creek (☎ **03/5758 3490**), is open daily from 8am to 5pm. Buy your lift tickets in the booth next door, between mid-June and October.

Accommodations & Dining

Falls Creek is a year-round resort, with a good range of accommodations available at all times, though it tends to fill up fast during the ski season. As you might expect, room rates are significantly higher during the ski season. The **Falls Creek Reservation Centre** (☎ **1800/45 35 25** in Australia, or 03/5758 3100; www.fallscreek.net; e-mail: accom@fallscreek.albury.net.au) can tell you what deals are on offer and can book rooms for you.

○ **Feathertop Alpine Lodge.** Parallel St. (P.O. Box 259), Falls Creek, VIC 3699. ☎ **03/5758 3232.** Fax 03/5758 3514. www.ski.com.au/feathertop. E-mail: feathertop@fallscreek. albury.net.au. 10 units. Winter A$95–$165 (U.S.$61.75–$107.25) per person; summer A$70 (U.S.$45.50) per person. Rates include dinner and breakfast. AE, BC, MC, V.

I really like this pleasant old-fashioned ski lodge nestled among the gum trees. Hosts Pip and Mark Whittaker have made it into one of the friendliest getaways in the mountains, and its relatively small size makes it easy to get to know a few of the other guests. Rooms are functional yet cozy, and sleep two to four people. All have showers attached. The lounge room is large and comfortable with good views, a well-stocked bar, and a library. The restaurant has a pretty good reputation for country cooking. Relax after a day on the slopes or the walking trails in the sauna or swimming pool. There are a guest laundry and a drying room too.

Summit Ridge Alpine Lodge. Schuss St., Falls Creek, VIC 3699. ☎ **03/5758 3800.** Fax 03/5758 3833. E-mail: sunridge@fallscreek.albury.net.au. TV. Winter A$110–$195 (U.S.$71.50–$126.75) queen room per person; A$120–$210 (U.S.$78–$136.50) mezzanine suite. Summer A$100 (U.S.$65) mezzanine suite per person. AE, BC, DC, MC, V. Rates include breakfast and dinner. Children 5–14 25% off adult rate. No children under 5.

Summit Ridge is a large four-star property made from local rock and timber. It caters to discerning guests. All rooms are quite nice, if a little stark. The mezzanine suites are split-level with the bedroom upstairs; they have king-size beds and an attached bathroom with tub. There are a large lounge and dining room on the ground floor and a small library on the second. If the mist holds out, there are some fine valley views. The hosts pay a lot of attention to detail, and the homemade bread is worth an early rise. The restaurant offers fine dining. The owner can take you out on early-morning ski runs.

MT. BUFFALO NATIONAL PARK
350km (210 miles) NE of Melbourne

Based around Mt. Buffalo, this is the oldest national park in the Victorian High Country, declared in 1898. The scenery around here is spectacular, with huge granite outcrops and plenty of waterfalls. As you ascend the mountain, you pass through dramatic vegetation changes, from tall snow gum forests to subalpine grasslands. In summer, carpets of silver snow daisies, royal bluebells, and yellow Billy Button flowers bloom on the plateau. Animals and birds here include wallabies and wombats, cockatoos, lyrebirds, and mobs of crimson rosellas, which congregate around the campsite at Lake Catani (popular for swimming and canoeing). Other popular sports around and about include advanced hang gliding and some very serious rock climbing. There are also more than 90 kilometers (54 miles) of walking trails.

Mt. Buffalo is also home to Victoria's smallest **ski resort,** with just five lifts and a vertical drop of 157 meters (515 ft.). There are also 11 kilometers (6¹/2 miles) of marked **cross-country ski trails.**

ESSENTIALS
GETTING THERE   From Melbourne, take the Hume Freeway (M31) to Wangaratta, then follow the Great Alpine Road to Porepunkah. From there, follow the Mount Buffalo Tourist Road.

ENTRY FEES & LIFT TICKETS Entry to Mt. Buffalo ski resort is A$10 (U.S.$6.50) per car. Full-day **lift tickets** cost around A$35 (U.S.$22.75) for adults, A$21 (U.S.$13.65) for children under 15, and A$10 (U.S.$6.50) for children under 8. Combination lift and ski-lesson packages cost A$37 to $49 (U.S.$24 to $31.85) for adults, and A$27 to $34 (U.S.$17.55 to $22.10) for children. Buy lift tickets at the park offices (☎ **13 19 63** in Victoria or 03/5756 2328) or between 9am and 3pm.

VISITOR INFORMATION The nearest visitor information center is in the town of Bright. Find the **Bright Visitor Information Centre** at 1A Delaney Ave., Bright (☎ **03/5755 2275**).

ACCOMMODATIONS

✪ **Mt. Buffalo Chalet.** Mt. Buffalo National Park, VIC 3740. ☎ **1800/037 038** in Australia, or 03/5755 1500. Fax 03/5755 1892. 97 units, 72 with private bathroom (some with shower only). A$119 (U.S.$77.35) guest house without bathroom; A$145 (U.S.$94.25) room with bathroom; A$170 (U.S.$110.50) view room with bathroom; A$185 (U.S.$120.25) suite. Rates are per person and include all meals, guided walks, evening activities, and park entry. Higher rates Christmas to mid-Jan and Easter weekend. AE, BC, DC, MC, V.

This rambling mountain guest house was built in 1910 and retains a wonderful old-world feel. Guest-house rooms, which have a mixture of double, twin, and bunk beds, are period style, reminiscent of the 1930s. They have tea and coffee facilities but no TV. View rooms have better furnishings and views across the valley. There are a large lounge room and a game room, both with open fireplaces. You'll also find a sauna, a spa, tennis courts, a cafe, and a bar. During summer the chalet operates canoeing, mountain biking, and abseiling. Meals are available for nonguests for A$35 (U.S.$22.75) for three courses.

6 The Northwest: Grampians National Park

260km (161 miles) NW of Melbourne

One of Victoria's most popular attractions, the rugged Grampians National Park rises some 1,000 meters (3,280 ft.) from the plains, appearing from the distance like some kind of monumental island. The park, which is an ecological meeting place of Victoria's western volcanic plains and the forested Great Dividing Range, contains one-third of all the wildflowers native to Victoria and most of the surviving Aboriginal rock art in southeastern Australia. Almost 200 species of birds, 35 species of mammals, 28 species of reptiles, 11 species of amphibians, and 6 species of freshwater fish have been discovered here. Kangaroos, koalas, emus, gliders, and echidnas can be easily spotted.

There are some awesome sights in the Grampians, including **Reeds Lookout** and **The Balconies,** which are both accessible by road, and the **Wonderland Range,** which offers walking trails leading past striking rock formations and massive cliffs to waterfalls and more spectacular lookouts.

The main town in the Grampians is **Halls Gap,** which is situated in a valley between the southern tip of the Mt. Difficult Range and the northern tip of the Mt. William Range. It's a good place to stock up on supplies. The Wonderland Range, with its stunning scenery, is close to Halls Gap, too. Plenty of short strolls and longer bushwalks are available.

A don't-miss stop in the park is the **Brambuk Aboriginal Living Cultural Centre** (☎ **03/5356 4452**), adjacent to the park visitor center (see below). It offers an excellent introduction to the area's Aboriginal history and accessible rock art sites. A 15-minute movie highlighting the local Aboriginal history costs A$4 (U.S.$2.60) for adults and A$2.50 (U.S.$1.60) for children. Otherwise, entrance to the center is free. The center is open daily from 10am to 5pm.

ESSENTIALS

GETTING THERE   By car, the park is accessed from the Western Highway at Ararat, Stawell (pronounced "Storl"), or Horsham. Alternatively, you can access the southern entrance from the Glenelg Highway at Dunkeld. The western areas of the park are reached from the Henty Highway (A200).

V/Line (☎ **13 61 96** in Victoria, 13 22 32 in NSW, or 03/9619 5000) has a daily train and bus service to Halls Gap from Melbourne (the train goes to Stawell, and a connecting bus takes you to your destination). The trip takes around 4 hours.

GETTING AROUND   Sealed (paved) roads include the Grampians Tourist Road, which cuts through the park from Dunkeld to Halls Gap; the Mt. Victory Road from Halls Gap to Wartook; and the Roses Gap Road, which runs from Wartook across to Dadswells Bridge on the Western Highway. Many other roads in the park are unsealed, but most are passable with a 2WD car.

Grampians National Park Tours (☎ **03/5356 6221**) offers all-day, 4WD tours of the park, stopping off at Aboriginal rock art sites, waterfalls, and lookouts. There's not much walking involved, but you certainly get the chance to spot native animals and ferret around among the native flora. The tour includes lunch, and morning and afternoon tea, and costs A$75 (U.S.$48.75).

Auswalk, P.O. Box 516, Jindabyne, NSW 2627 (☎ **02/6457 2220;** e-mail: monica@ auswalk.com.au), organizes self-guided tours through the park. A 6-night tour for two or more people costs A$1,090 (U.S.$708) per person including accommodation, most meals, national-park fees, some vehicle transfers, a half-day 4WD tour, an itinerary, and maps.

VISITOR INFORMATION   The **Grampians National Park Visitor Centre** (☎ **03/5356 4379**), 2.5 kilometers (1½ miles) south of Halls Gap, is open daily from 9am to 5pm. It has plenty of maps and brochures, and the rangers can advise you on walking trails and camping spots.

ACCOMMODATIONS

You can rent a campervan or a cabin for the night at **Halls Gap Caravan Park** (☎ **03/5356 4251**). Caravans cost A$30 (U.S.$19.50) and cabins A$35 (U.S.$22.75). Another option is the **Halls Gap Lakeside Caravan Park** (☎ **03/5356 4281**), which is 5 kilometers (3 miles) from town on the shores of Lake Bellfield. Cabins cost A$35 (U.S.$22.75) and holiday units from A$42 (U.S.$27.30).

The Mountain Grand Guesthouse and Business Retreat. Grampians Tourist Rd. ☎ **03/5356 4232.** Fax 03/5356 4254. E-mail: mtgrand@netconnect.co.au. 10 units. A/C. A$49 (U.S.$31.85) per person twin. Rates include breakfast. AE, BC, DC, MC, V.

A couple of years ago, this old-fashioned guesthouse was pretty run-down, but recent refurbishment by the new owners has brought it up to a comfortable 3½-star standard. These days it's promoting itself as a business retreat, so tourists who turn up get all the benefits of those added little corporate extras, such as exceptional service. The guest house specializes in a weekend getaway package, costing A$90 (U.S.$58.50) per person in a twin share, with a Devonshire tea, a three-course dinner, a buffet breakfast, a gourmet picnic lunch, and champagne and chocolates thrown in.

The rooms are quite small, but furnished with nice country-style furniture and double beds. All have an attached bathroom. Larger family rooms, some of which have a spa, were renovated in 1999. There are several lounge rooms and "conversion nooks," all with TVs, as well as a guest laundry, a bar, a cafe, and a restaurant serving good home-cooked meals.

by Marc Llewellyn

If you mention you're heading to Canberra (pronounced *Can*-bra, with very open vowels), most Australians will raise an eyebrow and say, "Why bother?" Even many Canberrans will admit that it's a great place to live but they wouldn't want to visit.

So what is it about Canberra that draws so much lackluster comment? Simply put, Australians aren't used to having things so nice and ordered. In many ways, Canberra is like Washington, D.C., or any new town that was a planned community from the start. Some see its virtues as of the bland variety: The roads are wide and in good order, the buildings are modern, and the suburbs are pleasant and leafy. Canberra is also the seat of government and the home of thousands of civil servants—enough to make almost any free-thinking, individualist Aussie with a hint of convict in him or her to shudder.

But to me, Canberra's differences from other Australian cities are the very things that make it special. The streets aren't clogged with traffic, and there are plenty of opportunities for safe biking—try that in almost any other city center and you'll be dusting the sides of cars and pushed onto the sidewalks in no time. There are plenty of open spaces, parklands, and fascinating monuments, and there is an awful lot to see and do—from museum and gallery hopping to ballooning with a champagne glass in your hand or boating on Lake Burley Griffin.

Canberra was born after the Commonwealth of Australia was officially created in 1901. Melbourne and Sydney, even then jockeying for preeminence, each put in their bid to become the new federal capital. In the end, Australian leaders decided to follow the example of their U.S. counterparts by creating a federal district; in 1908 they chose an undeveloped area between the two cities.

Designing the new capital fell to Chicago landscape architect Walter Burley Griffin, a contemporary of Frank Lloyd Wright. The city he mapped out was christened Canberra (a local Aboriginal word meaning "meeting place"), and by 1927, the first meeting of parliament took place. The business of government was underway.

1 Orientation

ARRIVING

BY PLANE   **Ansett** (☎ **13 13 00** in Australia, or 02/6249 7641) and **Qantas** (☎ **13 13 13** in Australia, or 02/9691 3636) both run frequent daily services to Canberra. The Canberra Airport is about

10 minutes from the city center. It has car-rental desks, a gift shop, a newsagent (newsstand), a currency exchange, a bar, and a bistro. Stamps are sold at the newsagent and a mailbox is provided for cards and letters. **Canberra City Sites and Tours (☎ 02/ 6294 3171,** or mobile phone 041/262 5552) meets most planes, but make sure you phone them before you arrive. They charge A$6 (U.S.$3.90) per person for a trip to city center hotels.

BY TRAIN **Countrylink (☎ 13 22 32** in Australia) runs three *Canberra Xplorer* trains daily between Sydney and Canberra. The 4-hour trip costs A$63 (U.S.$40.95) in first class and A$45 (U.S.$29.25) in economy; children are charged half price, and a return trip costs double. Many people make use of Countrylink transportation/hotel packages (call **Countrylink Holidays** at **☎ 13 28 29),** which can save you quite a bit of money. There's a range of hotels to choose from in Canberra costing between A$85 and A$186 (U.S.$55.25 and $121) a night for a couple, and if you book in advance (they recommend 2 weeks) you can save up to 40% on the train fare (through a Rail Escape package).

From Melbourne, V/Line's *Canberra Link* involves a 5-hour bus trip and a $3^{1}/_{2}$-hour train trip: it costs A$47 (U.S.$30.55) for adults and A$23.50 (U.S.$15.30) for children.

Canberra Railway Station (☎ 02/6239 7039) is on Wentworth Avenue, Kingston, about 5 kilometers (3 miles) southeast of the city center.

BY BUS **Greyhound Pioneer (☎ 13 20 30** in Australia, or 07/3258 1600; www.greyhound.com.au) runs eight services a day from Sydney to Canberra. Tickets cost A$30 (U.S.$19.50) for adults and A$15 (U.S.$9.75) for children; the trip takes 4 to $4^{1}/_{2}$ hours. From Melbourne, tickets to Canberra cost A$57 (U.S.$37) Express and A$48 (U.S.$31) Standard for adults, and A$46 (U.S.$30) Express and A$39 (U.S.$25.35) Standard for children, and the trip takes around 10 hours. (Advanced purchase fares can save you up to 35%.)

Murrays Australia (☎ 13 22 51 in Australia, or 02/9252 3590) runs three services a day from Sydney to Canberra for A$32 (U.S.$20.80) for adults and A$17 (U.S.$11) for children. YHA members travel for A$22 (U.S.$14.30). Several sightseeing companies in Sydney, including AAT King's, Murrays, and Australia Pacific Tours, offer day trips to Canberra.

Intercity buses arrive at **Jolimont Tourist Centre,** at the corner of Northbourne Avenue and Alinga Street, in Canberra City.

BY CAR The ACT is surrounded by the state of New South Wales. Sydney is 306 kilometers (190 miles) northeast and Melbourne is 651 kilometers (404 miles) southwest of Canberra. If you drive from Sydney via the Hume and Federal Highways, the trip will take $3^{1}/_{2}$ to 4 hours. From Melbourne, take the Hume Highway to Yass, then switch to the Barton Highway; the trip will take about 8 hours.

Special Events

A host of free events—from concerts to competitions—are part of the annual **Canberra National Multicultural Festival** held in the first 3 weeks of March. The fun includes **Canberra Day** (always the third Mon in Mar), a hot-air balloon fiesta, firework displays, food and wine promotions, plenty of music, and a large range of activities organized by Australia's large ethnic mix. Visitors could find it a little more difficult to book accommodations during this time, but you should always be able to find something.

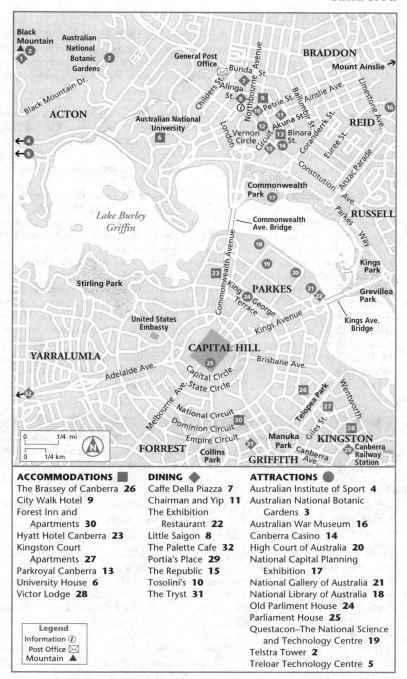

Canberra

Black Mountain ▲ 1
Telstra Tower 2
Australian National Botanic Gardens 3
Australian National University 6
General Post Office
Bunda St.
Childers St. 7
Alinga St. 8
9
10
11
Petrie St.
12
13 Binara St.
14
15
Vernon Circle
Northbourne Avenue
Ballumbir St.
Ainslie Ave.
Akuna St.
Coranderrk St.
Euree St.
Limestone Ave.
Mount Ainslie →
BRADDON
REID
RUSSELL
16 Australian War Museum
Anzac Parade
Parkes Way
Constitution Ave.
Commonwealth Park 17
Commonwealth Ave. Bridge
Lake Burley Griffin
Stirling Park
United States Embassy
18
19
20
21
22
23
24
King George Terrace
Commonwealth Avenue
Kings Avenue
PARKES
Kings Park
Grevillea Park
Kings Ave. Bridge
CAPITAL HILL
25
Capital Circle
State Circle
Brisbane Ave.
26
27
28
Telopea Park
Wentworth
YARRALUMLA
Adelaide Ave.
Melbourne Ave.
National Circuit
Dominion Circuit
Empire Circuit
30
31
29
FORREST
Collins Park
Manuka Park
Giles St.
KINGSTON
Canberra Ave.
GRIFFITH
Canberra Railway Station
ACTON
Black Mountain Dr.

0 1/4 mi
0 1/4 km

591

ACCOMMODATIONS ■
The Brassey of Canberra 26
City Walk Hotel 9
Forest Inn and Apartments 30
Hyatt Hotel Canberra 23
Kingston Court Apartments 27
Parkroyal Canberra 13
University House 6
Victor Lodge 28

DINING ◆
Caffe Della Piazza 7
Chairman and Yip 11
The Exhibition Restaurant 22
Little Saigon 8
The Palette Cafe 32
Portia's Place 29
The Republic 15
Tosolini's 10
The Tryst 31

ATTRACTIONS ●
Australian Institute of Sport 4
Australian National Botanic Gardens 3
Australian War Museum 16
Canberra Casino 14
High Court of Australia 20
National Capital Planning Exhibition 17
National Gallery of Australia 21
National Library of Australia 18
Old Parliment House 24
Parliament House 25
Questacon–The National Science and Technology Centre 19
Telstra Tower 2
Treloar Technology Centre 5

Legend
Information ⓘ
Post Office ✉
Mountain ▲

VISITOR INFORMATION

The **Canberra Visitors' Centre,** 330 Northbourne Ave., Dickson (☎ **1800/026 166** in Australia, or 02/6205 0044; www.canberratourism.com.au; e-mail: canberravisitorscentre@ msn.com.au), dispenses information and books accommodations. The office is open Monday to Friday from 9am to 5:30pm, and Saturday and Sunday from 9am to 4pm.

CITY LAYOUT

The first thing that strikes you about Canberra is its parklike feel (amazing, since there was barely a tree on the original site). Half a dozen avenues radiate from **Capital Hill,** where the **Parliament House** stands. Each of these broad, tree-shaded streets leads to a traffic circle, from which yet more streets emanate. Around each hub, the streets form a pattern of concentric circles—not the easiest layout for visitors trying to find their way.

Another of Canberra's most notable features is **Lake Burley Griffin,** a man-made lake created by damming the Molonglo River. The centerpiece of the lake is the Captain Cook Memorial Jet, a spire of water that reaches 147 meters (162 yd.) into the air. Wedged between Commonwealth Avenue and Kings Avenue is the suburb of **Parkes,** also known as the **Parliamentary Triangle.** Here you'll find many of the city's most impressive attractions, such as the National Gallery of Australia, the High Court of Australia, and the National Science and Technology Center.

Canberra's main shopping district is on the other side of the lake, centered around Northbourne Avenue, one of the city's main thoroughfares. Officially labeled **Canberra City,** this area is more commonly known as **"Civic."** Northeast of Civic is **Mount Ainslie,** with the Australian War Memorial at its foot; from its summit there are spectacular views of the city and beyond. Another good lookout point is from the top of the Telstra Tower on **Black Mountain,** reached by Black Mountain Drive. All the embassies and consulates are concentrated in the suburb of **Yarralumla,** east of Capital Hill, while most of the other suburbs are filled with pleasant homes and small retail areas.

2 Getting Around

BY CAR **Advantage Car Rentals,** 74 Northbourne Ave. (corner of Barry Drive; ☎ **1800 504 460** in Australia, or 02/6257 6888), has cars from A$35 (U.S.$22.75) per day, including 200 kilometers (124 miles) per day. **Budget** (☎ **02/6257 1305**), **Hertz** (☎ **02/6249 6211**), and **Thrifty** (☎ **02/6247 7422**) have desks at the airport.

If you have your own wheels, you could follow one or more of the six tourist drives marked with signs; pick up details from the Canberra Visitors' Centre.

BY TAXI Canberra's only taxi company is **Canberra Cabs** (☎ **02/6285 9222**).

BY BUS Canberra's bus system is coordinated by **ACTION** (☎ **02/6207 7611;** www.action.gov.au). The central bus terminal is on Alinga Street, in Civic, at 200 Scollay St. As far as the bus system goes, Canberra is divided into three zones; travel within the city center is in Zone One, which will cost A$2 (U.S.$1.30) for adults one-way and A$1 (U.S.65¢) for children 5 to 15. If you travel through more than one zone, it will cost A$4 (U.S.$2.60) for adults and A$2 (U.S.$1.30) for children. Ask the driver when you board the bus just to make sure how much you should pay.

Weekly tickets cost A$17 (U.S.$11) for Zone One and A$34 (U.S.$22) for all three zones; children are half price. Ten-Ride tickets also cost A$17 (U.S.$11). Purchase all tickets on the bus, or from most newsagents and ACTION interchanges.

For timetable information, call ACTION Monday to Friday from 6:30am to 11:30pm, Saturday from 7:30am to 11pm, and Sunday from 8:30am to 6pm. Pick up bus route maps at bus interchanges, newsagents, and the Canberra Visitors' Center.

Canberra City Sightseeing Tours (☎ **0500 505 012**) pulls in at 11 attractions around the city. Visitors can get off and on when they like. An all-day ticket costs A$25 (U.S.$16.25) for adults and A$12.50 (U.S.$8.15) for children.

BY BICYCLE   Canberra is unique in Australia for its extensive system of cycle tracks—some 120 kilometers (74 miles) of bike trails—which makes sightseeing on two wheels a very pleasurable experience. See "Outdoor Pursuits," later in this chapter, for details on bike rentals.

Fast Facts: Canberra

American Express   The office at Centerpoint, Shop 1, 185 City Walk (at the corner of Petrie Plaza), Civic (☎ **02/6247 2333**), is open Monday to Friday from 9am to 5pm, and Saturday from 9am to noon.

Car Rentals   See "Getting Around," above.

Climate   The best time to visit Canberra is in spring (Sept to Nov) or autumn (Mar to May). Summers are hot and winters can get pretty cold.

Currency Exchange   Cash traveler's checks at banks, at **American Express** (above), or at **Thomas Cook,** at the Petrie Plaza entrance of the Canberra Centre (☎ **02/6257 2222**), open Monday to Friday from 9am to 5pm and Saturday from 9:30am to 12:30pm.

Dentist   Canberra lacks a dental-emergency referral service. A reputable dentist in the center of town is **Lachland B. Lewis,** Level 3, 40 Allara St., Civic (☎ **02/6257 2777** after hours, and 02/6295 2319 or 02/6295 9495 weekends).

Doctor   The **Capital Medical Centre,** 2 Mort St., Civic (☎ **02/6257 3766**), is open Monday to Friday from 8:30am to 5pm. The **Travellers' Medical & Vaccination Centre,** Level 5, 8–10 Hobart Place (☎ **02/6257 7154**), offers vaccinations and travel medicines. A consultation here costs A$36 (U.S.$23.40).

E-mail   **Cyberchino Café,** 33 Kennedy St., Kingston (☎ **02/6295 7844**), is open daily from 10am to 9pm (it opens at 8:30am on Sat). The **National Library,** Parkes Place, Parkes (☎ **02/6262 1111**), has e-mail facilities available Monday to Thursday from 9am to 9pm, Friday and Saturday from 9am to 5pm, and Sunday 1:30 to 5pm.

Embassies/Consulates   The **British High Commission** is located at Old Parliament House Annex, Parkes (☎ **02/6270 6666**). The **Canadian High Commission** is at Commonwealth Ave., Yarralumla (☎ **02/6270 4000**); the **U.S. Embassy** is found at Moonah Place, Yarralumla (☎ **02/6214 5600**); and the **New Zealand High Commission** is at Commonwealth Ave., Yarralumla (☎ **02/6270 4211**). The **Embassy of Ireland** is at 20 Arkana St., Yarralumla (☎ **02/6273 3022**). The **South African High Commission** (☎ **02/6273 2424**) is right around the corner from the Irish embassy.

Emergencies   Call **000** for an ambulance, the police, or the fire department.

Eyeglasses   For repairs, glasses, and contact lenses, try **OPSM Express,** shop 5, Lower Ground Floor, The Canberra Centre, Civic (☎ **02/6249 7344**). It's open 9am to 5:30pm weekdays (to 9pm on Fri),and 9am to 4pm on Saturday.

Hospitals   For medical attention, go to the **Canberra Hospital,** Yamba Drive, Garran (☎ **02/6244 2222**), or call the **Accident & Emergency Department** on ☎ **02/6244 2324** (24 hr.).

Hot Lines   Rape Crisis Centre (☎ **02/6247 2525**); **Drug/Alcohol Crisis Line** (☎ **02/6205 4545** 24 hr.); **Lifeline Crisis Counseling** (☎ **13 11 14**); **Poison Information Centre** (☎ **02/6285 2852**); **National Roads & Motorists Association** (NRMA; ☎ **13 21 32**).

Pharmacies   The **Canberra Centre Pharmacy,** Civic (☎ **02/6249 8074**), is open general shopping hours.

Photographic Needs   Fletchers Fotographics, Shop 2, 38 Akuna St., Civic (☎ **02/6247 8460**), is the best place to buy camera gear and film. They also repair cameras and sell secondhand equipment.

Rest Rooms   You'll find public rest rooms near the city bus exchange, City Hall, London Circuit.

Transit Information   Call **ACTION timetable information** at ☎ **02/6207 7611.**

3   Accommodations

Canberra has a good selection of places to stay, and generally accommodations are much cheaper than in most other state capitals. Many people travel to Canberra during the week, so many hotels offer cheaper weekend rates to put heads on beds.

VERY EXPENSIVE

✪ **Hyatt Hotel Canberra.** Commonwealth Ave., Yarralumla, ACT 2600. ☎ **800/233-1234** in the U.S. and Canada, 13 12 34 in Australia, 0181/335 1220 in London or 0845/758 1666 elsewhere in the U.K., 0800/44 1234 in New Zealand, or 02/6270 1234. Fax 02/6281 5998. www.hyatt.com. 249 units A/C MINIBAR TV TEL. A$300 (U.S.$195) standard double; A$360 (U.S.$234) deluxe double; A$670 (U.S.$435.50) executive suite; A$1,200 (U.S.$780) Diplomatic Suite. Extra person A$28 (U.S.$18.20). Children under 18 stay free in parents' room. Ask about weekend packages and special rates. AE, BC, DC, JCB, MC, V. Free parking.

Visiting heads of state and pop stars make this their residence of choice when staying in Canberra, and it's not hard to see why. It has a great location, only a 2-minute drive from the city center, in the shadow of Parliament House and between Lake Burley Griffin and the Parliamentary Triangle. Originally the Hotel Canberra, it opened in 1924 and was based on the low-slung "prairie" design of the now-destroyed Imperial Hotel in Tokyo. For many years the Hyatt was an important part of Canberra's social and political life, with key decisions affecting all Australians being consistently made over drinks in the bar. All staff members wear 1920s costumes to add to the atmosphere.

Some 39 rooms are in the original two-story section. These have more historic appeal, but they are darker than their more modern counterparts, which were added in the 1980s. Standard rooms have king-size beds and large marble bathrooms; deluxe rooms come with balconies and have good views over the lake. All units come with all the little luxuries you'd expect from a hotel of this class.

Dining/Diversions: Meals and drinks are served in the Promenade Cafe, the Tea Lounge, the Speaker's Corner, Griffin's, and the Oak Room.

Amenities: Indoor pool, extensive fitness center, gym, sauna, spa, tennis court, business center, bike rental, concierge, 24-hour room service, free daily newspaper, massage, laundry, valet, nightly turndown, shoe shine.

EXPENSIVE

Parkroyal Canberra. 1 Binara St., Canberra, ACT 2601. ☎ **1800/020 055** in Australia, or 02/6247 8999. Fax 02/6257 4903. www.parkroyal.com.au. E-mail: prc@canberra.parkroyal. com.au. 295 units. A/C MINIBAR TV TEL. From A$255 (U.S.$165.75) standard double; from A$265 (U.S.$172.25) parkview double; A$455–$605 (U.S.$295.75–$393.25) suite. Extra person A$30 (U.S.$19.50). Lower weekend rates. Children under 15 stay free in parents' room. AE, BC, DC, MC, V. Free parking.

The Parkroyal, right in the city center, is part of the National Convention Centre and is also hitched onto Canberra Casino. It's nice if you're driving, but its long, long drive-way is rather inconvenient for pedestrians (even if its nice gardens in the back are good for early-morning strolls). Rooms face onto oval internal balconies that look down onto the restaurants below. Standard rooms are user-friendly and comfortable; most come with one queen-size bed or two doubles. There are in-room movies but there's no cable TV.

Dining: The hotel has one restaurant, the Brindabella Buffet, which serves buffet and à la carte lunch and dinners.

Amenities: Pool, health club, gym, sauna, concierge, 24-hour room service, nightly turndown, free daily newspaper, laundry, valet, baby-sitting, business center.

MODERATE

The Brassey of Canberra. Belmore Gardens, Barton, ACT 2600. ☎ **1800 659 191** in Australia, or 02/6273 3766. Fax 02/6273 2791. www.brassey.net.au. E-mail: info@brassey.net.au. 81 units. MINIBAR TV TEL. A$120 (U.S.$78) double, or A$150 (U.S.$97.50) for a family room; A$145 (U.S.$94.25) heritage double, or A$195 (U.S.$126.75) for a heritage family room; A$185 (U.S.$120.25) suite. Rates include full breakfast. AE, BC, DC, MC, V. Free parking. Bus: 36 (get off outside the National Press Club).

Rooms in this 1927 heritage-listed building, formerly a boardinghouse for visiting government officials, are large, quiet, and almost plush. The garden bar and piano lounge are popular. Other good points include its proximity to Parliament House and other major attractions, and the hearty breakfasts. The hotel underwent extensive reno-vations in early 2000, which included the remodeling of many of the doubles into larger heritage rooms.

Forest Inn and Apartments. 30 National Circuit, Forrest, ACT 2603. ☎ **1800/676 372** in Australia, or 02/6295 3433. Fax 02/6295 2119. www.forestinn.com.au. E-mail: reservations@ forestinn.com.au. 102 units. A/C TV TEL. A$105 (U.S.$68.25) motel room; A$115 (U.S.$74.75) 1-bedroom-apt; A$145 (U.S.$94.25) 2-bedroom apt. AE, BC, DC, MC, V. Free parking. Bus: 39 (get off at the Rydges Hotel).

The Forest Inn is far from fancy, but it's close to the Manuka shops and restaurants and Parliament House. The outside of this 1960s property looks tacky, but the inte-rior has been recently refurbished. The motel-style rooms are small and colorless, but clean; the apartments are nicer and have full-size kitchens (since the price isn't that much higher, I'd go for one of these). Two-bedroom apartments are perfect for fami-lies, and even the one-bedroom apartments have a single bed in the living room.

Kingston Court Apartments. 4 Tench St., Kingston, ACT 2604. ☎ **02/6295 2244.** Fax 02/6295 5300. www.kingstonterrace.com.au. E-mail: csa@kingstonterrace.com.au. 36 units. A/C TV TEL. A$125 (U.S.$81.25) apt for 2 including GST. Extra adult A$15 (U.S.$9.75), extra child A$7 (U.S.$4.55). AE, BC, DC, MC, V. Free parking. Bus: 38.

Kingston Court, situated about 1 kilometer (½ mile) from the Parliamentary Trian-gle and 6 kilometers (3½ miles) from Civic, is a good option if you're looking for the comforts of home. The apartments are modern and very spacious and come with a full kitchen, a washing machine and dryer, a balcony, and a courtyard. There are also a pool, a gas barbecue, and a half-court tennis court on the grounds. The rooms underwent a full renovation in 2000.

University House. At Australian National University, Balmain Crescent, Acton (GPO Box 1535, Canberra, ACT 2601). ☎ **1800/814 864** in Australia, or 02/6249 5211. Fax 02/6249 5252. 100 units. (146 units) TV TEL. A$106 (U.S.$68.90) twin; A$111 (U.S.$75.40) suite; A$116 (U.S.$75.40) 1-bedroom apt.; A$161 (U.S.$104.65) 2-bedroom apt. Ask about packages, especially during low season. AE, BC, DC, MC, V. Free security parking. Bus: 34.

University House, situated less than 2 kilometers (1¼ miles) from the city center, offers a pleasant alternative to run-of-the-mill hotels in a similar price bracket. Large twin rooms come with two single beds; suites have a sitting room and a queen-size bed; the one-bedroom apartments have a bedroom with a queen-size bed, a sitting room, and a kitchenette; and the two-bedroom apartments are huge, with two large bedrooms, a dining room, a lounge room, and a full kitchen. All units have bathrooms with a shower and a tub. Meals are served in Boffins Restaurant and the Cellar Café Monday to Friday. Breakfast, baby-sitting, and bicycles are available. University House also has tennis courts and easy access to walking and jogging tracks.

INEXPENSIVE

City Walk Hotel. 2 Mort St., Civic, ACT 2601. ☎ **02/6257 0124.** Fax 02/6257 0116. E-mail: citywalk@ozemail.com.au. 55 units, 18 with bathroom (shower only). A$55 (U.S.$35.75) double without private bathroom; A$65 (U.S.$42.25) double with bathroom; A$90–$110 (U.S.$58.50–$71.50) family room. Extra adult A$10 (U.S.$6.50); extra child A$5 (U.S.$3.25). A$19–$21 (U.S.$12.35–$13.65) dorm bed. BC, MC, V.

You can hardly get closer to the city center than at this "former YWCA turned budget hotel." Being right near the Jolimont Tourist Centre bus interchange, it gets a lot of business from backpackers and budget travelers arriving by bus from other parts of the country. The rooms are pretty basic, but clean. There are five double rooms with shared bathrooms, though three of these also have two extra single beds. Six rooms have air-conditioning. All rooms with bathrooms have their own TV. Family rooms sleep up to seven people, all in one room (one has its own kitchen). There are also a guest lounge, a laundry, a kitchen, a communal telephone, an air-conditioned common room with TV and video, and tea- and coffee-making facilities.

Victor Lodge. 29 Dawes St., Kingston, ACT 2604. ☎ **02/6295 7777.** Fax 02/6295 2466. www.victorlodge.com.au. 28 units, none with bathroom. A$52 (U.S.$33.80) double. A$21 (U.S.$13.65) dorm bed. Rates include continental breakfast. BC, MC, V. Free parking. Bus: 38, 39, 50.

Backpackers, parliamentary staff, and budget travelers frequent this friendly place, which is situated right next to Kingston shops and about a 15-minute drive from the city center. Rooms vary from dorms with three, four, or five beds to modern, simple doubles. There are communal showers and toilets, a laundry, a guest refrigerator, a TV room, free tea and coffee, and a courtyard. The staff picks up guests from the train and bus stations daily and drops off guests in town every morning. It's a nice place overall, but you'll have to decide whether you want to put up with the short trek into the city. Bike rental costs A$12 (U.S.$7.80) for a full day and A$8 (U.S.$5.20) for a half day after 2pm.

The owners also own the Best Western motel next door, which has standby rates of A$70 (U.S.$45.50) for a double. Apparently, long-suffering parents often dump their teenage kids at the lodge and live it up at the motel.

4 Dining

EXPENSIVE

✪ **Chairman and Yip.** 108 Bunda St., Civic. ☎ **02/6248 7109.** Reservations required. Main courses A$16–$22 (U.S.$10.40–$14.30). AE, BC, DC, MC, V. Sun–Fri noon–3pm; daily 6–11pm. ASIAN AUSTRALIAN.

This is, without doubt, Canberra's best restaurant. Upbeat and popular with political bigwigs, it really is the place to see and be seen. The fish specials are good and spicy, with combinations of chili, coriander, lemongrass, and galangal perking up your taste buds. I always go for the prawns with homemade chili jam, served on vermicelli noodles with mango salsa. Abalone and lobster also find their way onto the menu. The pannacotta is the signature dessert.

The Exhibition Restaurant. In the Sculpture Garden of the National Gallery of Australia, Parkes. ☎ **02/6273 2836.** Reservations recommended. All main courses A$20 (U.S.$13). AE, BC, DC, MC, V. Daily noon–2:30pm (but closing times vary depending on patronage). MODERN AUSTRALIAN.

The Exhibition Restaurant sits on a lake edged with rushes and sculptures and full of goldfish. Add smoke machines (they call it a fog sculpture) on the far bank to send mysterious white eddies across the lake's surface toward your lakeside table, and you have a charming fantasy world in which to dine. The menu is small, with only a choice of four first courses, main courses, and desserts. Main courses could include roasted pheasant, panfried lamb loin stuffed with an almond mousse, a vegetarian option, and a veal fillet.

The Republic. 20 Allara St., Civic. ☎ **02/6247 1717.** www.republic-restaurant.com.au. Reservations recommended. Main courses A$19–$26 (U.S.$12.35–$16.90). AE, BC, DC, MC, V. Tues–Fri noon–3pm; Mon–Sat 6–10pm. MODERN AUSTRALIAN.

With stylish looks and a cutting-edge menu, The Republic is a top-flight brasserie, serving up big, bold flavors in small nouvelle cuisine–size servings. Specializing in seafood, chef Marcia Branson adds Asian accents to her creations for a bit of zing—try the yellowfin tuna with deliciously smooth garlicky potatoes, or the Atlantic salmon. The vegetarian options, such as the field mushrooms wok-seared in a honey-and-soy sauce with coriander, are well worth giving up meat. To finish off, you shouldn't miss the homemade ice creams. A two-course dinner special with a glass of wine costs just A$22.50 (U.S.$14.60) if you're in and out by 8pm.

MODERATE

Caffe Della Piazza. 19 Garema Place, Civic. ☎ **02/6248 9711.** Reservations recommended, especially for Fri–Sat evenings. Main courses A$11–$16 (U.S.$7.15–$10.40). AE, BC, DC, MC, V. Daily 10am–midnight. ITALIAN/CAFE.

Good eating isn't hard to find in Canberra, but this place is up there with the best. It won several awards for its Italian-inspired cooking, including the catering industry's award for the best restaurant in the state (there's nothing like being judged by your peers). The restaurant offers both indoor and outdoor dining in pleasant surroundings, and it is a good place to pop in for a light meal and a coffee, or something more substantial, like the pastas or the best seller, the king prawn and chicken tenderloin salad.

The Palette Cafe. Beaver Gallery, 81 Denison St., Deakin. ☎ **02/6282 8416.** Main courses A$12–$18 (U.S.$7.80–$11.70). AE, BC, MC, V. Daily 10am–5pm. CAFE/MODERN AUSTRALIAN.

This is a great choice for lunch, especially since it's in the same building as Canberra's largest private art gallery. You can either eat inside, surrounded by artwork, or claim a table outside in the sunny courtyard. Standout dishes include grilled asparagus spears with Japanese scallops and almond hollandaise, and the chili-salted baby octopus. The Caesar salads are particularly good, as are the field mushrooms with a sauce of soy, Japanese rice wine, honey, and coriander. The etchings, paintings, and sculptures on display are of high quality and are well priced.

Tosolini's. Corner of London Circuit at East Row, Civic. ☎ **02/6247 4317.** Main courses A$14–$16 (U.S.$9.10–$10.40). AE, BC, DC, MC, V. Mon–Sat 7:30am–10:30pm, Sun 9am–5pm. CAFE/MODERN AUSTRALIAN.

Since it's situated right next to the busy central bus terminal and close to the major shopping areas, Tosolini's really pulls in the passing crowd. You can sit out on the sidewalk terrace and watch the world go by. The eggs Benedict served here at breakfast could be the best A$7.50 (U.S.$4.90) you've ever spent. Lunchtime fare is almost as good. Both the battered flathead and the panfried broad bill (both are local fish) are tasty, but Tosolini's really made its name with its pastas and focaccias.

✪ **The Tryst.** Bougainville St., Manuka. ☎ **02/6239 4422.** Reservations recommended. Main courses A$15–$18 (U.S.$9.75–$11.70). AE, BC, DC, MC, V. Daily noon–2:30pm and 6–10pm. MODERN AUSTRALIAN.

The personal touches and the service really shine through at The Tryst, and the food is consistently delicious. The restaurant is tastefully decorated in an upscale cafe style, with the kitchen staff on show as they rustle up some of the capital's best tucker. It's relaxed, feeling more communal than intimate on busy nights. My favorite dish is the Atlantic salmon served with beurre blanc sauce and potatoes, but the oven-roasted spatchcock (a small chicken) with traditional herb stuffing on stir-fried vegetables gets a big thumbs-up, too. If you have room left for dessert, don't miss out on the sticky date pudding served with hot butterscotch sauce, pralines, and ice cream—it's as good as it sounds. Otherwise, the long list of daily specials that complement the extensive menu could keep you busy for weeks.

INEXPENSIVE

✪ **Little Saigon.** Alinga St. and Northbourne Ave., Civic. ☎ **02/6230 5003.** Main courses A$10–$12 (U.S.$6.50–U.S.$7.80). AE, BC, DC, MC, V. Daily 10am–3pm and 5–10:30pm. VIETNAMESE.

This spacious restaurant has minimalist decor and floor-to-ceiling windows offering views of the busy city center. Tables are set up on either side of an indoor pond, and there's a bar in the back of the restaurant. The menu is vast, with lots of noodle dishes, as well as spicy seafood, duck, chicken, pork, beef, and lamb selections.

Portia's Place. 11 Kennedy St., Kingston. ☎ **02/6239 7970.** Main courses A$9.80–$18.80 (U.S.$6.40–$12.20). AE, BC, DC, MC, V. Daily noon–2:30pm; Sun–Wed 5–10pm, Thurs–Sat 5–10:30pm. CANTONESE/MALAYSIAN/PEKING.

A small restaurant serving up excellent traditional cookery, Portia's Place often fills up early and does a roaring lunchtime trade. The best things on the menu are the shang tung sauce lamb ribs, the King Island fillet steak in pepper sauce, the flaming pork (brought to your table wrapped in foil and bursting with flames), and the Queensland trout stir-fried with snow peas.

5 Seeing the Sights

Australian Institute of Sport. Leverrier Crescent, Bruce. ☎ **02/6214 1111.** Admission A$8 (U.S.$5.20) adults, A$4 (U.S.$2.60) children, A$20 (U.S.$13) families; tours leave the AIS shop Mon–Fri at 11:30am and 2:30pm, and Sat–Sun at 10am, 11:30am, 1pm, and 2:30pm. Bus: 80 from city center.

Up, Up & Away

Balloon Aloft (☎ **02/6285 1540**) offers fabulous 45-minute sunrise flights over Canberra Monday to Friday for A$155 (U.S.$100.75) for adults and A$100 (U.S.$65) for children 6 to 12, including a champagne breakfast on touchdown. On weekends an hourlong trip costs A$220 (U.S.$143) for adults and A$140 (U.S.$91) for children, including breakfast at the Hyatt Hotel. It costs A$25 (U.S.$16.25) less each day if you don't want breakfast. **Dawn Drifters** (☎ **02/6285 4450;** e-mail: ballooning@dawndrifters.com.au; www.dawndrifters.com.au) will also send you soaring over the city. One-hour champagne flights with breakfast cost A$155 (U.S.$100.75) for adults Monday to Friday and A$195 (U.S.$126.75) on weekends and public holidays. Children go for 40% of the adult price. Breakfast is A$15 (U.S.$9.75) extra.

This institution provides first-class training and facilities for Australia's elite athletes. Tours, led by one of the institute's athletes, include visits to the gymnasium, basketball courts, and Olympic swimming pool to see training in progress. There is also a fascinating interactive sports display where visitors can test their sporting skills.

✪ **Australian National Botanic Gardens.** Clunies Ross St., Black Mountain, Acton. ☎ **02/6250 9540.** Free admission. Daily 9am–5pm (to 8pm in summer). Visitor center daily 9:30am–4:30pm. No bus service.

The gardens are home to the best collection of Australian native plants anywhere. They're situated on 125 acres on the lower slopes of Black Mountain and feature a Eucalyptus Lawn containing more than 600 species of eucalyptus, a rain-forest area, a Tasmanian alpine garden, and self-guided walking trails. Free guided tours depart from the visitor center at 11am on weekdays and 11am and 2pm on weekends.

✪ **Australian War Memorial.** At the head of Anzac Parade on Limestone Ave. ☎ **02/ 6243 4211.** Free admission. Daily 10am–5pm (when the Last Post is played). Closed Christmas. Guided tours at 10am, 10:30am, 11am, 1:30pm, and 2pm. Bus: 233, 302, 303, 362, 436, or 901.

This monument to Australian troops who gave their lives for their country is truly moving, and well worth a visit. Artifacts and displays tell the story of Australia's conflicts abroad. You won't soon forget the exhibit on Gallipoli, the bloody World War I battle in which so many Anzac (Australian and New Zealand Army Corps) servicemen were slaughtered. The Hall of Memory is the focus of the memorial, where the body of the Unknown Soldier lies entombed after his remains were brought back from a WWI battlefield in 1993. There's a good art collection at the memorial, too. The memorial underwent a A$20 million (U.S.$13 million) upgrade in 1999; new interactive exhibits include a film showing the surrender of Singapore projected onto the very table on which the surrender was signed and a simulated ride aboard an original Lancaster bomber.

✪ **Canberra Deep Space Communication Complex.** Tidbinbilla, 39km (23¹/₄ miles) southwest of Civic. ☎ **02/6201 7880.** www.cdscc.nasa.gov. Free admission. Summer daily 9am–8pm; rest of year daily 9am–5pm. No public bus service, but several tour companies offer programs that include the complex.

This information center, which stands beside huge tracking dishes, is a must for anyone interested in outer space. There are plenty of models, audio-visual recordings, and displays, including a genuine space suit, space food, and archive film footage of the Apollo moon landings. The complex is still active and is tracking and recording results from the Mars Pathfinder, Voyager 1 and 2, and the Cassini, Soho, Galileo, and Ulysses space exploration projects, as well as providing a vital link with NASA spacecraft. This is a great stop off on the way back from the Tidbinbilla Nature Reserve just up the road (see below).

High Court of Australia. Overlooking Lake Burley Griffin, Parkes Place. ☎ **02/6270 6811.** Free admission. Mon–Fri 9:45am–4:30pm. Closed public holidays. Bus: 34.

The High Court, an impressive concrete-and-glass building that overlooks Lake Burley Griffin and stands next to the National Gallery of Australia, was opened by Elizabeth II in 1980. It is home to the highest court in Australia's judicial system and contains three courtrooms, a video display, and a huge seven-story-high public hall. When the court is in session, visitors can observe the proceedings from the public gallery. Call for session details.

National Capital Planning Exhibition. On the lakeshore at Regatta Point in Commonwealth Park. ☎ **02/6257 1068.** Free admission. Daily 9am–6pm (5pm in winter).

If you want to find out more about Canberra's beginnings—and get a memorable view of Lake Burley Griffin, the Captain Cook Memorial Water Jet, and the Carillon in the bargain—then head here. The displays are well done, and a film provides an overview of the city's design.

National Gallery of Australia. Parkes Place. ☎ **02/6240 6502.** Free admission (except for major touring exhibitions). Daily 10am–5pm. Guided tours daily at 11am and 2pm; Thurs and Sun at 11am, free tour focusing on Aboriginal art. Bus: 36 and 39 from Old Parliament House, or 34 from Parkes Place in front of the High Court.

Linked to the High Court by a pedestrian bridge, the National Gallery showcases both Australian and international art. The permanent collection and traveling exhibitions are displayed in 11 separate galleries. You'll find paintings by big names such as Claude Monet and Jackson Pollock, and Australian painters Arthur Boyd, Sidney Nolan, Arthur Streeton, Charles Condor, Tom Roberts, and Albert Tucker. The exhibition of Tiwi islander burial poles in the foyer is also interesting (the Tiwi Islands include Melville and Bathurst islands off Darwin), and there's a large collection of Aboriginal bark paintings from central Australia. A sculpture garden surrounding the gallery has 24 sculptures and is always open to the public.

Old Parliament House. On King George Terrace, midway between the new Parliament House (below) and the lake. ☎ **02/6273 4723.** Admission A$2 (U.S.$1.30) adults, A$1 (U.S.65¢) children. Daily 9am–5pm. Bus: 39.

The seat of government from 1927 to 1988, the Old Parliament House is now home to regular exhibitions from the National Museum and the Australian Archives. The National Portrait Gallery is also here, and outside on the lawn is the Aboriginal Tent Embassy, which was set up in 1972 in a bid to persuade the authorities to recognize the land ownership claims of Aboriginal and Torres Strait Islander people. The red, black, and yellow Aboriginal flag first came to prominence here. Interestingly, the Australian Heritage Commission now recognizes the campsite as a place of special cultural significance.

Parliament House. Capital Hill. ☎ **02/6277 7111.** Free admission. Daily 9am–5pm. Closed Christmas. Bus: 39.

Conceived by American architect Walter Burley Griffin in 1912, but not built until 1988, Canberra's unmistakable centerpoint was designed to blend organically into its setting at the top of Capital Hill; only a national flag supported by a giant four-footed flagpole rises above the peak of the hill. In good weather, picnickers crowd the grass that covers the roof, where the view is spectacular. Inside are more than 3,000 works of Australian arts and crafts, and extensive areas of the building are open to the general public. Be sure to look out for a mosaic by Michael Tjakamarra Nelson entitled *Meeting Place,* which represents a gathering of various Aboriginal tribes, and can be found just inside the main entrance. There's also a 20-meter-long tapestry by Arthur Boyd in the Great Hall on the first floor and one of the four known versions of the **Magna Carta** in the Great Hall directly beneath the flag pole. Free 50-minute guided tours are offered throughout the day.

Parliament usually is in session Monday to Thursday between mid-February and late June, and mid-August to mid-December. Both the lower house (the House of Representatives, where the prime minister sits) and the upper house (the Senate) have public viewing galleries. The best time to see the action is during Question Time, which starts at 2pm in the lower house. If you turn up early enough, you might be lucky and get a seat; otherwise, make reservations for gallery tickets via the sergeant-at-arms (☎ **02/6277 4889**) at least a day in advance.

Questacon—The National Science and Technology Centre. King Edward Terrace, Parkes. ☎ **02/6270 2800.** Admission A$8 (U.S.$5.20) adults, A$4 (U.S.$2.60) children, A$20 (U.S.$13) families. Daily 10am–5pm. Closed Christmas. Bus: 34.

Questacon offers some 170 hands-on exhibits that can keep you and your inner child occupied for hours. Exhibits are clustered into six galleries, each representing a different aspect of science. The artificial earthquake is a big attraction. The center is great for kids, but give it a miss if you've already visited the Powerhouse Museum in Sydney (see chapter 5).

Telstra Tower. Black Mountain Dr. ☎ **02/6248 1911.** Admission A$3 (U.S.$1.95) adults, A$1 (U.S.65¢) children. Daily 9am–10pm. No bus service.

The tower, which rises 195 meters (644 ft.) above the summit of Black Mountain, has both open-air and enclosed viewing galleries that provide magnificent 360° views over Canberra and the surrounding countryside. Those who dine in the pricey, revolving Tower Restaurant (☎ **02/6248 7096**) are entitled to a refund of their admission charge.

Tidbinbilla Nature Reserve. Tidbinbilla. ☎ **02/6237 5120.** Admission A$8 (U.S.$5.20) per vehicle per day. Daily 9am–6pm (8pm in summer). Visitor center Mon–Fri 9am–4:30pm, Sat–Sun 9am–5:30pm. No public bus service, but several tour companies offer programs that include the reserve.

This is a great place to see native animals such as kangaroos, wallabies, koalas, platypus, and birds in their natural environment. Unlike other wildlife parks around the country, this one has plenty of space, so sometimes you'll have to look hard to spot the animals. (On a recent quick visit, I saw a few birds and not much else, but on previous visits I've been almost stomped on by kangaroos.) A guide is available from the visitor's center. If you want to be sure to spot some animals, contact **Round About Tours** (☎ **02/6259 5999**), which runs day tours of the reserve for A$55 (U.S.$35.75), which includes a picnic lunch and afternoon tea. It also offers 2-hour kangaroo-spotting night tours for A$20 (U.S.$13).

A Taste of the Grape

National Capital Wine Tours (☎ **02/6231 3330**) offers wine-tasting trips with gourmet lunches and tastings on Saturday and Sunday for A$59 (U.S.$38.35), including hotel pickup. Tours leave at 10am and return at 4pm and visit three local wineries.

Treloar Technology Centre. Corner of Vickers and Callan sts. ☎ **02/6243 4450.** Admission A$3 (U.S.$1.95) to walkway above exhibition floor. Floor tours A$15 (U.S.$9.75) adults, A$10 (U.S.$6.50) children (1 week's advance notice required). Sun and Wed 11am–4pm (other times by appointment). Bus: 312–317 from city to Belconnen, and 48 from there.

Aviation buffs will want to book a floor tour of this facility, which you have to do well in advance. Last time I was there, the technicians in the workshop were stripping down a Lancaster bomber. Also on display are plenty of war relics: German V1 and V2 rockets, a Gallipoli landing craft, a Soviet T34 tank, Vietnam War helicopters, a Korean War Meteor, a Japanese Zero once flown by the 4th-ranked Japanese Ace (with 68 kills to his credit), miniature submarines, a Messerschmitt 163b Komet, and much more.

6 Outdoor Pursuits

The **Namadgi National Park** covers almost half of the Australian Capital Territory. Parts of the park, which has high rolling plateaus, good trout-fishing streams, and dense forest, are just 30 kilometers (19 miles) from Canberra. There are marked hiking trails throughout the park. Spring is the best time of year to visit for the prolific display of bush flowers. In the past, sections of the park were cleared for sheep grazing, but these days the pastures are popular with hundreds of gray kangaroos (they're easiest to spot in the early morning and late afternoon). At Yankee Hat, off the Nass/Boboyan Road, is an Aboriginal rock art site. The **Namadgi Visitors Center** (☎ **02/6207 2900**), on the Nass/Boboyan Road, 3 kilometers (1³/₄ miles) south of the township of Tharwa, has maps and information on walking trails.

BIKING   With 120 kilometers (74 miles) of bike paths, Canberra is made for exploring on two wheels. Rent a bike from **Mr. Spoke's Bike Hire** on Barrine Drive near the ferry terminal in Acton (☎ **02/6257 1188**). Bikes for adults cost A$8 (U.S.$5.20) for the 1st hour and A$7 (U.S.$4.55) for each hour afterward; rates are A$7 (U.S.$4.55) for kids, going down to A$6 (U.S.$3.90) for each subsequent hour.

BOATING   Burley Griffin Boat Hire, on Barrine Drive near the ferry terminal in Acton (☎ **02/6249 6861**), rents paddleboats for A$9 (U.S.$5.85) per hour and canoes for A$15 (U.S.$9.75) per hour. **Row 'n' Ride,** near the MacDermott Place Boat Ramp, Belconnen (☎ **02/6254 7838**), is open on weekends and school and public holidays and offers canoes from A$9 (U.S.$5.85) per hour, kayaks for A$10 (U.S.$6.50) per hour, and mountain bikes for A$9 (U.S.$5.85) per hour.

GOLF   With 11 golf courses, Canberra offers varied opportunities for serious golfers. The nearest to the city center is the **Yowani Country Club** on the Federal Highway in the suburb of Lyneham (☎ **02/6241 3377**). Greens fees are A$35 (U.S.$22.75) for 18 holes and A$20 (U.S.$13) for 9 holes. Club rental costs an additional A$13 to 20 (U.S.$8.45 to $13). Dress restrictions apply, and advance reservations are essential. The **Federal Golf Course,** Red Hills Lookout Road, Red Hill (☎ **02/6281 1888**), is regarded as the capital's most challenging course. Nonmembers are welcome on most weekdays. Greens fees are A$40 (U.S.$26) for 18 holes. The **Royal Canberra Golf Course** (☎ **02/6282 7000**) is the most exclusive, costing A$200 (U.S.$130) for 18 holes. Guests, who must be a member of another golf club, can play Monday and Thursday only.

HORSEBACK RIDING   The **National Equestrian Centre,** 919 Cotter Rd., Weston Creek, Canberra (☎ **02/6288 5555**), 15 minutes from Parliament House, offers trail rides through rolling rural countryside hopping with kangaroos and cattle. Rides cost around A$21 (U.S.$13.65) for 1 hour, A$37 (U.S.$24) for 2 hours, A$51

(U.S.$33) for a half day (minimum four people), and A$95 (U.S.$61.75) for a full day (minimum 4 people).

7 Shopping

The **Canberra Centre,** 4 square blocks between City Walk and Ballumbir Street between Petrie and Akuna Streets in Civic, is the place to shop till you drop. You can spend hours browsing through the dozens of boutiques or the department stores in the three-story atrium. The City Market section, which includes a bakery, fruit and vegetable sellers, a deli, and more, is the place to take a break; it's open Monday to Thursday from 9am to 6pm, Friday from 9am to 9pm, and Saturday and Sunday from 9am to 5pm.

The centrally located **Gorman House Markets,** Ainslie Avenue (☎ **02/6249 7377**), are spread around the courtyard of a heritage building. You can pick up good arts and crafts here, as well as clothing, jewelry, essential oils, books, and secondhand clothes. The markets are open Saturday from 10am to 4pm and Sunday from noon to 4pm.

8 Canberra After Dark

The "Good Time" section in Thursday's *Canberra Times* has listings on what's on offer around town.

Of the pubs in town, the best in the city center are the British-style **Wig & Pen,** on the corner of Limestone and Alinga Street (☎ **02/6248 0171**); the very popular **Moosehead's Pub,** at 105 London Circuit in the south of the city (☎ **02/6257 6496**); the **Phoenix,** at 21 East Row (☎ **02/6247 1606**), which has live music upstairs for a small cover charge; and **P.J. O'Reileys,** on the corner of West Row and Alinga Street (☎ **02/6230 4752**), an authentic-style Irish pub.

If you're looking to roll some dice, the **Casino Canberra,** in Glebe Park, 21 Binara St., Civic (☎ **1800/806 833** in Australia, or 02/6257 7074), is a small, older-style casino offering all the usual casino games from noon to 6am. Dress regulations prohibit leisure wear, running shoes, and jeans, but overall it's a casual place to lose some money.

14 Tasmania

by Marc Llewellyn

The very name "Tasmania" has an exotic ring about it. It suggests an unspoiled place, with vast stretches of wilderness at the ends of the earth roamed by strange creatures like the Tasmanian Devil. Many mainland residents still half-jokingly refer to their "country cousins" as rednecks. In truth, most Tasmanians are hospitable and friendly people, lacking the harsh edge that big cities can foster. Most also care passionately for the magnificent environment they've inherited, and lay scorn on the pockets of the population who still believe that anything that moves deserves a bullet and anything that stands still needs chopping down.

Visitors to Tasmania are surprised by its size, though when compared to the rest of Australia, the distances are certainly more manageable. Dense rain forests, stony mountain peaks, alpine meadows, pine plantations, vast eucalyptus stands, and fertile stretches of farmland are all easily accessible, but you should still be prepared for several hours of concentrated driving to get you between the main attractions. Tasmania's main drawing cards are twofold. First, there's the natural environment. More than 20% of the island has been declared a World Heritage Area, and nearly a third of the island is protected within its 14 national parks. Wherever you go, wilderness is always within reach, and though part of it can be viewed from the road, you really need to shake off your city clothes and step out into the bush to get the best out of it.

Tasmania's second drawing card is its history. Remains of the Aboriginal people that lived here for tens of thousands of years are evident in isolated rock paintings, engravings, stories, and a general feeling of spirituality that still holds tight in places where modern civilization has not yet reached.

Europeans discovered Tasmania (or Van Diemen's Land, as it was once known) in 1642, when the great seafarer Abel Tasman set anchor off its southwest coast, although it wasn't identified as an island until 1798. Tasmania soon became a dumping ground for convicts, who were more often than not transported for petty crimes committed in their homeland. The brutal system of control, still evident in the ruins at Port Arthur and elsewhere, soon spilled over into persecution of the native population. Tragically, the last full-blooded Tasmanian Aborigine died in 1876, just 15 years after the last convict transportation. Most of the rest had already died of disease and maltreatment at the hands of the settlers.

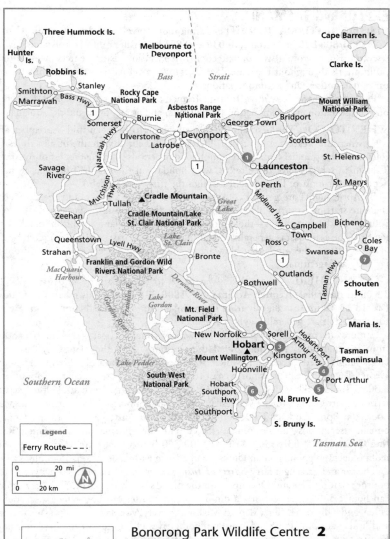

Three Hummock Is.

Cape Barren Is.

Hunter Is.

Melbourne to Devonport

Clarke Is.

Robbins Is.

Bass   Strait

Stanley

Smithton
Marrawah
Bass Hwy

Rocky Cape National Park

Mount William National Park

Somerset
Burnie

Asbestos Range National Park

George Town
Bridport

Ulverstone
Devonport

Scottsdale

Latrobe

Waratah Hwy

St. Helens

Savage River

Launceston

Perth

St. Marys

Cradle Mountain

Great Lake

Murchison Hwy

Tullah

Cradle Mountain/Lake St. Clair National Park

Midland Hwy

Bicheno

Zeehan

Campbell Town

Coles Bay

Queenstown
Lyell Hwy

Lake St. Clair

Ross

Swansea

Strahan

Bronte

Schouten Is.

MacQuarie Harbour

Franklin and Gordon Wild Rivers National Park

Derwent River

Outlands

Bothwell

Tasman Hwy

Gordon River

Franklin R.

Lake Gordon

Mt. Field National Park

Maria Is.

New Norfolk
Sorell

Hobart-Port Arthur Hwy

Hobart

Tasman Penninsula

Southern Ocean

Lake Pedder

Mount Wellington
Kingston

Huonville

Port Arthur

South West National Park

Hobart-Southport Hwy

N. Bruny Is.

Southport

S. Bruny Is.

Tasman Sea

Legend

Ferry Route — — —

0   20 mi

0   20 km

TASMANIA

Bonorong Park Wildlife Centre **2**
Cataract Gorge **1**
Freycinet National Park **7**
Port Arthur Penal Settlement Ruins **5**
Royal Tasmanian Botanical Gardens **3**
Talune Wildlife Park and Koala Gardens **6**
Tasmanian Devil Park Wildlife
        Rescue Centre **4**

EXPLORING TASMANIA

VISITOR INFORMATION   The **Tasmanian Travel and Information Centre** (☎ **1800/806 846** in Australia, or 03/6230 8233; e-mail: tasinfo@tourism.tas.gov.au; www.tourism.tas.gov.au) is a private company operating visitor centers in more than 30 locations throughout the state. It can arrange travel passes, ferry and bus tickets, car rental, cruises, and accommodations.

Pick up a copy of *Travelways,* Tourism Tasmania's excellent tourist tabloid, for details on transportation, accommodations, restaurants, and attractions around Tasmania.

WHEN TO GO   The best time to visit Tasmania is between mid-September and May, when the weather is at its best. December to February are the busiest times for tourism, as are public holiday and school holiday periods. (Unlike the rest of Australia, Tasmanian schools have three terms, with holidays in the first half of June, in mid-Sept, and for most of Dec straight through the first week in Feb.)

By April, nights are getting cold, the days are getting shorter, and the deciduous trees are starting to turn golden. Winters (June through Aug), especially in the high country, can be quite harsh—though that's the best time to curl up in front of a blazing log fire. The east coast is generally milder than the west coast, which is buffered by the "Roaring 40s"—the winds that blow across the ocean and the 40° meridian, from as far away as Argentina.

GETTING THERE   The quickest way to get to Tasmania is by air. **Ansett** (☎ **13 13 00** in Australia), **Kendell Airlines** (☎ **1800/338 894** in Australia), and **Qantas** (☎ **13 13 13** in Australia) fly from the mainland to Hobart and Launceston. Flights to Launceston are generally slightly cheaper.

A more adventurous way to reach Tasmania is to take a boat across the Bass Strait from the mainland. The quickest of these options is on the **_DevilCat,_** Australia's largest high-speed catamaran, which runs between Melbourne's Station Pier and George Town on Tasmania's north coast (trip time: 6 hr.). Ferries depart Melbourne at 8:30am Tuesday, Thursday, and Saturday, arriving in George Town at 2:30pm. Return ferries depart George Town Wednesday, Friday, and Sunday at 2pm, arriving in Melbourne at 8pm. Contact **TT-Line** (☎ **13 20 10** in Australia; www.tt-line.com.au; e-mail: reservations@tt-line.com.au) for current fare information. **Tasmanian Redline Coaches** (☎ **03/6336 1446,** or 1300 360 000 from within Tasmania; e-mail: redlinecoach@bigpond.com.au) links George Town with Launceston, 35 minutes away.

The car and passenger ferry **_Spirit of Tasmania_** plies the Tasman Sea between Melbourne's Station Pier and Devonport on the island's northwest coast. The ferry, which can hold 1,300 passengers, has a dining room, a buffet bistro, a cafeteria, a pool, a sauna, and a disco. The ferry departs Melbourne every Monday at 7:30pm, Wednesday and Friday at 6pm, and Sunday at 9pm and arrives in Devonport the next morning. Return trips leave Devonport every Saturday at 4pm, Monday at 2am, and Tuesday and Thursday at 6pm. One-way adult fares range from A$110 to $241 (U.S.$71.50 to $156.50) in winter (depending on the type of accommodation) and from A$152 to $354 (U.S.$98.80 to $230) at peak times in summer. To transport a car costs an extra A$55 (U.S.$35.75) in the peak season, and A$30 (U.S.$19.50) in winter. Prices are highest during the school holiday periods of mid-December to January, and during the 2 weeks over Easter. Make reservations through **TT-Line** (see above). You can also book tickets by calling **Inta-Aussie** at ☎ **800/531-9222** in the United States or Canada.

Tasmanian Redline Coaches (☎ **03/6336 1446**) connects with each ferry. Standard single fares are A$34.80 (U.S.$22.60) for adults and A$17.40 (U.S.$11.30) for children 15 years and under to Hobart, and A$14.40 (U.S.$9.40) for adults and A$7.20 (U.S.$4.70) for children to Launceston.

Driving Safety Tips

Driving in Tasmania can be dangerous; there are more accidents involving tourists on Tasmania's roads than just about anywhere else in Australia. Many roads are narrow and bends can be tight, especially in the mountainous inland regions—where you may also come across black ice early in the morning or anytime in winter. Marsupials are also very common around dusk, and hitting or swerving to avoid them has caused countless crashes.

McCafferty's (☎ **13 14 99** in Australia) can organize coach travel from the eastern mainland states, with transfers to Tasmania by ferry.

GETTING AROUND   Regional airline **Tasair** (☎ **1800 062 900** in Australia; www.tasair.com.au; e-mail: flights@tasair.com.au) flies to most major settlements in Tasmania. **Par Avion** (☎ **03/6248 5390;** www.paravion.com.au) concentrates on the southwest World Heritage areas of the state and also operates tours.

Bus service is provided by **Tasmanian Redline Coaches** (☎ 03/6336 1446), **TWT Tassie Link** (formally Tasmanian Wilderness Travel; ☎ 03/6272 7300; www.tassie.net.au/wildtour), **Tasmanian Tours & Travel Tigerland** (☎ 03/6272 6611), and **Hobart Coaches** (☎ 1800/030 620 in Australia, or 03/6234 4077). The cheapest way to get around by coach is to buy a **Tassie Link Explorer Pass,** which can be used on all TWT Tassie Link routes. Passes come in four categories, including a 7-day pass that's good for travel within 10 days for A$130 (U.S.$84.50), and a 10-day pass that's good for travel within 15 days for A$160 (U.S.$104). Passes are available through **TWT Tassie Link,** Hobart Head Office, 212 Main Rd., Moonah (☎ 03/6272 7300), or by calling ☎ **1300/300 520** toll-free in Australia. Tasmanian Travel and Information Centres and the *Spirit of Tasmania* also sell the passes.

Driving a car from Devonport on the north coast to Hobart on the south coast takes less than 4 hours. From Hobart to Strahan on the west coast also takes around 4 hours, while the journey from Launceston to Hobart takes just under 3 hours. The **Royal Automobile Club of Tasmania (RACT),** at Murray and Patrick streets in Hobart (☎ **13 27 22** in Tasmania, or 03/6232 6300; www.aaa.asn.au), can supply you with touring maps.

There are no passenger trains in Tasmania.

TOUR OPERATORS   Dozens of operators run organized hiking, horse trekking, sailing, caving, fishing, bushwalking, diving, biking, rafting, climbing, kayaking, or canoeing trips in Tasmania. For a full selection, see the "Outdoor Adventure" section of *Travelways,* the Tasmanian tourist board's publication (see "Visitor Information," above).

One of the best operators in Tasmania is **Peregrin Adventures** (☎ **03/9662 2800;** www.peregrin.net.au; e-mail: travelcentre@peregrin.net.au). They run rafting tours of the Franklin River, which carves its way through some of the most beautiful, rugged, and inaccessible wilderness in the world. Two other good operators are **Rafting Tasmania** (☎ **03/6239 1080;** e-mail: raftingtas@ozE-mail.com.au; www.tasmanianadventures.com.au) and the **Roaring 40's Ocean Kayaking Company** (☎ **1800/653 712** in Australia); both companies offer paddling expeditions lasting from 1 to 11 days. **Tasmanian Expeditions,** based in Launceston (☎ **1800/030 230** in Australia, or 03/6334 3477; e-mail: tazzie@tassie.net.au; www.tas-ex.com), runs a whole range of cycling, trekking, and rafting trips around the country, some starting or finishing in Hobart.

A SUGGESTED ITINERARY If I were heading to Tasmania for the first time again, I'd pack my walking boots, raincoat, and shorts, and head off first to either Launceston or Hobart, the island's two main cities. I'd take in Freycinet National Park for its wonderful scenery and abundant wildlife, stop in at Port Arthur for its beautiful setting and fascinating though disturbing convict past, and head to the central highlands for a tramp around Cradle Mountain. If I had a lot more time, I'd drive to Strahan on the far west coast to discover the great southwest wilderness, take some time off to go trout fishing in the central lakes, and head off to the quaint coastal towns of the north.

HOMESTAYS & BED-AND-BREAKFAST RESERVATIONS For something different, you can stay with a Tasmanian family either in town or at a farm in the country or arrange accommodations in one of the many boutique bed-and-breakfasts found throughout Tasmania. Contact **Heritage Tasmania Pty Ltd.,** P.O. Box 780, Sandy Bay, TAS 7005 (☎ **03/6233 5511**). Nightly bed-and-breakfast rates range from about A$60 to $160 (U.S.$39 to $104) for a double.

1 Hobart

198km (123 miles) S of Launceston

Tasmania's capital (pop. 126,000) is an appealing place that's well worth visiting for a couple of days. Hobart's main features are its wonderful harbor and the colonial cottages that line the narrow lanes of Battery Point. As with Sydney, Hobart's harbor is the city's focal point, attracting yachts from all over the world. Down by the waterfront, picturesque Salamanca Place bursts with galleries, pubs, cafes, and an excellent market on Saturdays. Europeans first settled at Hobart in 1804, a year after Tasmania's first colony was set up at Risdon (10km/6 miles up the Derwent River).

ESSENTIALS

GETTING THERE **Ansett** (☎ 13 13 00 in Australia), **Qantas** (☎ 13 13 13 in Australia), and **Kendell Airlines** (☎ 1800/338 894 in Australia) carry passengers from the mainland. The trip from the airport to the city center takes about 20 minutes and costs about A$25 (U.S.$16.25) by taxi and A$7.50 (U.S.$4.90) by Tasmanian Redline Coaches (☎ 03/6336 1446). **Tasmanian Redline Coaches** (☎ **03/6233 9466**) drops you off at the Collins Street bus terminal or at any central city hotel.

Car-rental offices at the airport include **Hertz** (☎ 03/6237 1155), **Avis** (☎ 03/6248 5424), **Budget** (☎ 1300/362 848 in Australia, or 03/6248 5333), and **Thrifty** (☎ 1800/030 730 in Australia, or 03/6234 1341). Cars cost around A$50 (U.S.$32.50) for 1 day, A$45 (U.S.$29.25) per day for 2 days, A$40 (U.S.$26) per day for 4 days, and A$35 (U.S.$22.75) per day for a week or more.

VISITOR INFORMATION Information is available from the **Tasmanian Travel and Information Centre,** at Davey and Elizabeth streets (☎ **03/6230 8233**). It's open Monday through Friday from 8:30am to 5:15pm, Saturday and public holidays from 9am to 4pm, and Sunday from 9am to 1pm (longer hours in summer). You can also obtain information by calling ☎ **1800/806 846** from anywhere in the rest of Australia.

You can pick up information on Tasmania's national parks at the **Lands Information Bureau,** 134 Macquarie St. (☎ **03/6233 8011**).

CITY LAYOUT Hobart straddles the Derwent River on the south coast of Tasmania. Historic **Salamanca Place** and nearby Battery Point abut Sullivan's Cove, home to hundreds of yachts. The row of sandstone warehouses that dominate Salamanca

Hobart

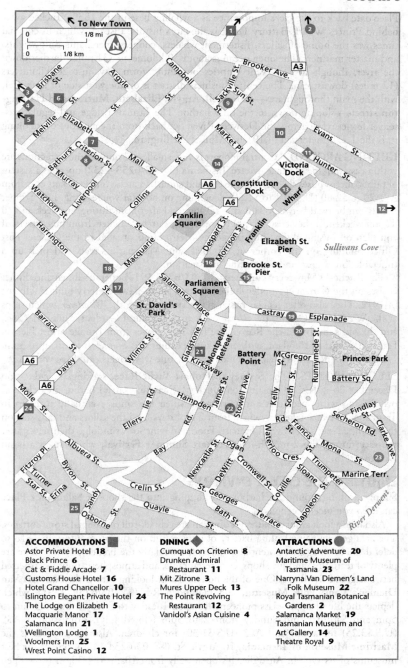

ACCOMMODATIONS ■
Astor Private Hotel **18**
Black Prince **6**
Cat & Fiddle Arcade **7**
Customs House Hotel **16**
Hotel Grand Chancellor **10**
Islington Elegant Private Hotel **24**
The Lodge on Elizabeth **5**
Macquarie Manor **17**
Salamanca Inn **21**
Wellington Lodge **1**
Woolmers Inn **25**
Wrest Point Casino **12**

DINING ◆
Cumquat on Criterion **8**
Drunken Admiral
   Restaurant **11**
Mit Zitrone **3**
Mures Upper Deck **13**
The Point Revolving
   Restaurant **12**
Vanidol's Asian Cuisine **4**

ATTRACTIONS ●
Antarctic Adventure **20**
Maritime Museum of
   Tasmania **23**
Narryna Van Diemen's Land
   Folk Museum **22**
Royal Tasmanian Botanical
   Gardens **2**
Salamanca Market **19**
Tasmanian Museum and
   Art Gallery **14**
Theatre Royal **9**

Place date back to the city's importance as a whaling base in the 1830s. Tucked away behind Princes Wharf, **Battery Point** is the city's historic district, which in colonial times was the home of sailors, fishermen, whalers, coopers, merchants, shipwrights, and master mariners. The open ocean is about 50 kilometers (31 miles) farther down the river, though the Derwent empties out into Storm Bay, just 20 kilometers (12 miles) downstream. The central business district is on the west side of the water, with the main thoroughfares—**Campbell, Argyle, Elizabeth, Murray, and Harrington streets**—sloping down to the busy harbor. The Tasman Bridge and regular passenger ferries reach across the Derwent River. Set back from the city, but overlooking it, is the 1,270-meter-tall (4,191-ft.) **Mount Wellington.**

GETTING AROUND   Central Hobart is very small, and most of the attractions are within easy walking distance. **Metro Tasmania** (☎ **03/6233 4232**) operates a system of public metro buses throughout the city and suburban areas. Single tickets cost from A$1.20 to $2.80 (U.S.80¢ to $1.80) depending on how far you're going. Day Tripper tickets can be used between 9am and 4:30pm and after 6pm during the week and all day on weekends; they cost A$1.90 (U.S.$1.25). Purchase tickets from bus drivers. If you plan on busing about, stop off at the Metro Shop situated in the General Post Office building on the corner of Elizabeth and Macquarie streets and pick up a timetable, brochures, and sightseeing information.

The **Roche-O'May ferry company** (☎ **03/6223 1914**) operates lunch and dinner cruises on the *Cartela,* a wooden-hulled, former steam-powered ferry built in Hobart in 1912. They also offer regular passenger ferry service on the *Wanderer,* which stops at the Wrest Point Casino, the Royal Tasmanian Botanical Gardens, Sullivan's Cove, and the old suburb of Belle Reeve. The first ferry leaves from Brooke Street Pier on Franklin Wharf at 10:30am, with other trips heading out every 1¹/₂ hours until 3pm.

Parking is difficult in the city center, and the one-way streets can drive you crazy.

SPECIAL EVENTS   The **Sydney-to-Hobart Yacht Race,** starting in Sydney on December 26, fills the Constitution Dock Marina and general harbor area close to overflowing with spectators and partygoers when the ships eventually turn up in Tasmania. The race takes anywhere from 2 to 4 days, and the sailors and fans stay on to celebrate New Year's Eve in Hobart. Food and wine lovers indulge themselves after the race during the 2-month-long **Hobart Summer Festival,** which starts around December 28.

ENJOYING THE CITY & ENVIRONS

Simply strolling around the harbor and popping into the shops at **Salamanca Place** can keep you nicely occupied.

Also take a look around **Battery Point,** an area chock-full of colonial stone cottages. The area gets its name from a battery of guns set up on the promontory in 1818 to defend the town against potential invaders (particularly the French). Today, there are plenty of tearooms, antique shops, cozy restaurants, and atmospheric pubs interspersed between grand dwellings. One of the houses worth looking into is the **Narryna Van Diemen's Land Folk Museum,** 103 Hampden Rd. (☎ **03/6234 2791**), which depicts the life of upper-class pioneers. It's open Tuesday to Friday from 10:30am to 5pm and Saturday and Sunday from 2 to 5pm (closed July). Admission is A$5 (U.S.$3.25) for adults and A$2 (U.S.$1.30) for children. Also in this area is the **Maritime Museum of Tasmania,** 16 Argyle St. (☎ 03/6234 1427), one of the best museums of its type in Australia. It's open daily from 10am to 4:30pm (now open until 5pm daily), and admission is A$6 (U.S.$3.90) for adults, A$4 (U.S.$2.60) for children 4 to 16, and A$16 (U.S.$10.40) for a family.

The National Trust (☎ **03/6223 7570**) offers a 3-hour **Battery Point Heritage Walk** leaving at 9:30am every Saturday from the wishing well in Franklin Square. It costs A$10 (U.S.$6.50) for adults and A$2.50 (U.S.$1.60) for children 6 to 16, and includes morning tea.

For magnificent views over Hobart and across a fair-sized chunk of Tasmania, drive to **The Pinnacle** on top of Mount Wellington, about 40 minutes from the city center. (Take a warm coat, though; the wind in this alpine area can bite.) An extensive network of walking trails offers good hiking around the mountain. Pick up a copy of *Mt. Wellington Day Walk Map and Notes* from the Department of Environment Tasmap Centre, on the ground floor of the Lands Building, 134 Macquarie St. (☎ **03/6233 3382**).

THE TOP ATTRACTIONS

✪ **Antarctic Adventure.** 2 Salamanca Sq. ☎ **03/6220 8220.** Admission A$16 (U.S.$10.40) adults, A$8 (U.S.$5.20) children ages 4–13, A$40 (U.S.$26) families. Daily 10am–5pm. Closed Christmas.

Hobart is the last port of call for expeditions to Antarctica. You can experience the cold continent yourself at this highly recommended attraction. It doesn't look like much at first, but I promise you'll be sucked in. You can experience an Antarctic blizzard, climb all over heavy machinery, experience a downhill ski simulator (I'm not sure how that fits in), and get computer access to Antarctic weather conditions and communications. The photos and other displays are also interesting. The irresistible stuffed huskies in the souvenir shop will take a hefty bite out of your wallet.

Bonorong Park Wildlife Centre. Briggs Rd., Brighton. ☎ **03/6268 1184.** Admission A$8 (U.S.$5.20) adults, A$4 (U.S.$2.60) children under 15. Daily 9am–5pm. Closed Christmas Day. Bus to Glenorchy from the central bus terminal in Hobart (about 10 min.), then take bus 125 or 126 to the park. Drive north on route 1 to Brighton; it's about 25 min. north of Hobart and well signposted.

I don't think I've ever seen so many wallabies in one place as I saw here—they were hopping all over the place. There are lots of other native animals around too, including snakes, koalas, Tasmanian devils, and wombats. The Bush Tucker shed serves lunch, billy teas, and damper. Koala cuddling isn't allowed in Tasmania, but if you're around at feeding times it's possible to stroke one—they're not as shy as you might think. Feeding times are 12:30 and 3pm daily. The park is on the side of a steep hill, so travelers in wheelchairs and anyone who likes things flat are likely to fare badly.

Cadbury Chocolate Factory. Claremont, 12km (7 miles) north of Hobart. ☎ **1800/ 627 367** in Australia, or 03/6249 0333. Tours A$10 (U.S.$6.50) adults, A$5 (U.S.$3.25) children, A$25 (U.S.$16.25) families. Mon–Fri 8am (summer only), 9am, 9:30am, 10:30am, and 1pm.

Eat chocolates till they make you sick on this Willy Wonka–type trip. Book well ahead, because chocolate tours are very popular. See "Organized Tours," below, for information on how to get there by boat.

Cascade Brewery Tours. Cascade Rd. ☎ **03/6221 8300.** Tours A$7.50 (U.S.$4.90) adults, A$1.50 (U.S.$1) children 5–16. Mon–Fri 9:30am and 1pm. Closed public holidays. Reservations required. Bus: 44, 46, and 49; get off at stop 18.

Cascade Premium is one of the best beers in the country, in my humble opinion. To see how this heady amber nectar is produced, head to Australia's oldest brewery and tag along on a fascinating 2-hour tour, which includes a stroll through the grand old Woodstock Gardens behind the factory.

Fudge Factory and Historic Garden Tours. Island Produce Confectionery, 16 Degraves St., South Hobart. ☎ **03/6223 3233.** Tours A$6 (U.S.$3.90) adults, A$3 (U.S.$1.95) children, A$15 (U.S.$9.75) families. Mon–Fri 8am–4pm. Closed Sat as of this writing, though they hope to change this. Tours begin at 10:30am (and 1:30pm during summer) Mon–Fri; reservations essential. (You can look around the gardens free anytime if you make a purchase in the shop.) Bus: 44, 46, or 49 to South Hobart and Cascade Rd.; get off at stop 16.

This is an interesting stopover if you're visiting either the Cascade Brewery or Mount Wellington. You get not only a trip around a very successful fudge-making factory, but also a guided tour around the remains of the women's prison next door. The tales told around here will make the hairs on your neck stand on end—like the fact that 17 out of every 20 children born within the walls of the institution died soon after birth, and that women who died were simply tossed into an unmarked mass grave. All the proceeds of the tour goes into preserving the prison.

Royal Tasmanian Botanical Gardens. On the Queens Domain near Government House. ☎ **03/6234 6299.** Admission to gardens free; conservatory A$2 (U.S.$1.30) donation. Daily 8am–6:30pm (until 4:45pm in winter). Bus: 17.

Established in 1818, these gardens are known for English-style plant and tree layouts, a Japanese garden dominated by a miniature Mt. Fuji, and colorful seasonal blooming plants housed in the conservatory. A restaurant provides lunch and teas. There are also a Botanical Discovery Centre (admission A$2/U.S.$1.30) and a Sub-Antarctic plant house.

Tasmanian Museum and Art Gallery. 40 Macquarie St. ☎ **03/6223 1422.** Free admission. Daily 10am–5pm.

Come here to find out more about Tasmania's Aboriginal heritage, its history since settlement, and the island's wildlife. Traveling art exhibitions are mounted from time to time, but always on display are the paintings of the colonial era. The art gallery has a particularly impressive collection of paintings by Tom Roberts and by several convict artists. The pride of the entire collection, though, is *The Conciliation* by Benjamin Duttereau, the painting of second-most historical significance in Australia, after Tom Roberts' *Shearing of the Rams,* which you can see in the National Gallery of Victoria in Melbourne.

ORGANIZED TOURS

You'll get a good introduction to the city on the daily **Hobart Historic Walk** (☎ 03/ 6225 4806), a 2-hour leisurely stroll through historic Sullivan's Cove and Battery Point. Tours start at 10am daily from September to May and on request from June to August and cost A$17 (U.S.$11) for adults. Children under 12 are free. Be advised that there is now a minimum of six people for a walk to go ahead, and they do provide group discounts.

Several companies run boat tours of the harbor. **Captain Fells Ferries** (☎ 03/ 6223 5893) offers a wide range of morning tea, lunch, afternoon, and dinner cruises. The company also runs **Cadbury Factory Tours,** which include coach transfers, a tour of the factory, a harbor cruise, and a two-course lunch for A$32 (U.S.$20.80) for adults and A$18 (U.S.$11.70) for children; these tours leave at 9:45am Monday through Thursday. Cruises depart from Franklin Wharf behind the wooden cruise-sales booths beside Elizabeth Street Wharf at the bottom of Elizabeth Street.

The **Cruise Company** (☎ 03/6234 9294) operates river trips along the Derwent to the Cadbury Chocolate Factory. Cruises depart at 10am Monday to Friday, returning at 2:30pm, and cost A$33 (U.S.$21.45) for adults, A$16 (U.S.$10.40) for children 5 to 15, and A$93 (U.S.$60.45) for a family, including entry and a guided tour of the factory. Children under 5 are free. The boat leaves from Brooke Street Pier. Also of interest is the company's 2-hour Ironpot Cruise (to the lighthouse of that name at the mouth of the Derwent). The scenic tour of the river leaves Brooke Street Pier at 2pm every Saturday and costs A$20 (U.S.$13) for adults, free for children under 15.

THE SHOPPING SCENE

If you're in Hobart on a Saturday, don't miss the **Salamanca Market,** in Salamanca Place—it's one of the best markets in Australia. Some 200 stalls offer everything from fruit and vegetables to crafts made from pottery, glass, and native woods. The market is open from 8:30am to 3pm.

Salamanca Place, 65 Salamanaca Place, itself has plenty of craft and souvenir shops that are worth exploring, though you pay for the privilege of buying them in such a fashionable area. You could try **The Salamanca Collection** (☎ 03/6224 1341) for good-quality decorative arts. The **Handmark Gallery,** 77 Salamanca Place (☎ 03/6223 7895), has a fine selection of wooden jewelry boxes and art deco–style jewelry and pottery. The best bookshop in town is a beauty and sells a large range of new and secondhand books, many relating to Tasmania. Find the **Hobart Bookshop** at 22 Salamanca Sq. (☎ **03/6223 1803**).

For great chocolate and the best licorice, head to **Darrell Lea,** shop 36 in the Cat & Fiddle Arcade between Collins and Liverpool streets. There are plenty of other interesting shops here, too.

Store hours are Monday through Thursday from 9am to 6pm, Friday from 9am to 9pm, and Saturday from 9am to noon.

ACCOMMODATIONS

Hobart has some of the best hotels, guest houses, and B&Bs in Australia.

VERY EXPENSIVE

Hotel Grand Chancellor. 1 Davey St., Hobart, TAS 7000. ☎ **1800 625 138** in Australia, or 03/6235 4535. Fax 03/6223 8175. www.hgchobart.com.au. 234 units. A/C MINIBAR TV TEL. A$235–$265 (U.S.$152.75–$172.25) double; A$365 (U.S.$237.25) executive suite. Extra person A$30 (U.S.$19.50). Children under 15 stay free in parents' room. AE, BC, DC, MC, V. Free parking.

If you prefer the reliability of standard hotel accommodations to a stately old homestead, then book a room at this imposing property overlooking the yachts and fishing boats parked in Victoria Dock (the impressive marble-and-granite lobby has a large curved window to catch all the action). Standard rooms are large and comfortable, with large polished granite bathrooms. More than 50% of the rooms have water views. Eight rooms are equipped for travelers with disabilities.

Dining/Diversions: Meehans First Class Restaurant specializes in innovative Tasmanian cuisine, while the Atrium Cocktail Lounge is relaxed and has good views.

Amenities: Heated indoor pool, sauna, health club (with gym equipment and massage), concierge, 24-hour room service, laundry, valet, baby-sitting, massage, unisex hair salon, business facilities, newsstand.

Wrest Point Casino. 410 Sandy Bay Rd., Sandy Bay, TAS 7005. ☎ **1800/030 611** in Australia, or 03/6225 0112. Fax 03/6225 3744. www.wrestpoint.com.au. E-mail: mail@ wrestpoint.com.au. 197 units. A/C MINIBAR TV TEL. A$220–$240 (U.S.$143–$156) double; A$300 (U.S.$195) spa suite. AE, BC, DC, MC, V. Free parking.

An A$23 million (U.S.$15 million) facelift in 1998 completely transformed this Hobart icon, which was built in 1973, and gave birth to Australia's A$2-billion-a-year (U.S.$1.3-billion-a-year) casino industry. Situated beside the Derwent River,

3 kilometers (almost 2 miles) from the city center, the hotel complex looks out across the harbor and the city and up to Mount Wellington. All rooms feature fine Tasmanian oak furniture and plush carpets. Adjacent to the casino is the 61-room Wrest Point Motor Inn, which has nice rooms for A$109 (U.S.$70.85). Taxis from Wrest Point to the city cost around A$6 (U.S.$3.90), and the bus operates to and from the city every 15 minutes for A$1.20 (U.S.80¢).

Dining/Diversions: Wrest Point features an intimate casino, a harbor boardwalk with indoor and outdoor entertainment, the Birdcage cocktail bar, the spectacular Riverview Lounge and bar, a nightclub, and a sports bar. There are three restaurants, including The Point Revolving Restaurant (see "Dining," below).

Amenities: Heated indoor pool, sauna, health club with gym, tennis courts, nine-hole putting course, concierge, 24-hour room service, laundry, valet, baby-sitting, massage, business facilities, newsstand, barbecue areas, children's playground.

EXPENSIVE

Islington Elegant Private Hotel. 321 Davey St., Hobart, TAS 7004. ☎ **03/6223 3900.** Fax 03/6224 3167. 8 units. TV TEL. A$150 (U.S.$97.50) standard double; A$170 (U.S.$110) grand double. Rates include continental breakfast. AE, BC, DC, MC, V. Free parking. The Islington is 1.5km (1 mile) from the city on the way to Mt. Wellington. Take the A6 Hwy. from the airport to Davey St.; it's important to stay in the right lane and go straight ahead when the road turns left. Bus: 44, 46, 48, or 49 from the city. No children under age 16.

This quiet 1845 private home is very popular with American travelers. Rooms are large and simple, each with a queen-size bed and an older-style TV. The Grand rooms are slightly roomier. Antiques, cedar woodwork, and elegant furnishings contribute to an air of gentility. French doors open onto a nice garden and a pool. The breakfast room is small and sunny, and the chessboard, piano, and open fire add charm to the front parlor. When I went there, the guests had found the place so relaxing they'd all retired for their afternoon snooze. No smoking.

✪ **Macquarie Manor.** 172 Macquarie St. (2 blocks from central bus terminal), Hobart, TAS 7000. ☎ **1800/243 044** in Australia, or 03/6224 4999. Fax 03/6224 4333. 18 units (most with shower only). MINIBAR TV TEL. A$140 (U.S.$91) Heritage room; A$170 (U.S.$110) Heritage suite; A$185 (U.S.$120) Macquarie suite. Rates include full breakfast. AE, BC, DC, MC, V. Free parking (just to the left down the side of the main building).

As soon as you walk into this place, you'll know you want to stay. Macquarie Manor was built in 1875 as a doctor's surgery and residence, and extra rooms were added in 1950. Thick carpets and double-glazed windows keep the place very quiet, even though the Manor is on the main road. Rooms, which vary enormously, are comfortable and elegantly furnished. One room is suitable for people with disabilities. The staff is very friendly and will be happy to escort you around the premises in search of your favorite room. Check out the delightful dining room, and the drawing room, which is complete with old couches and a grand piano. No smoking.

Salamanca Inn. 10 Gladstone St., Hobart, TAS 7000. ☎ **1800/030 944** in Australia, or 03/6223 3300. Fax 03/6223 7167. www.salamancainn.com.au. E-mail: salamancainn@southcom.com.au. 68 units. MINIBAR TV TEL. A$176 (U.S.$110.50) 1-bedroom apt; A$198 (U.S.$128.70) 2-bedroom suite; A$240 (U.S.$156) 2-bedroom deluxe suite. Extra adult A$25 (U.S.$16.25), extra child 3–14 A$15 (U.S.$9.75). Ask about weekend and long-stay packages. AE, BC, DC, MC, V. Free parking. Bus: Sandy Bay Rd.

This property is right on the edge of the central business district and toward the waterfront near Battery Point. The apartments are modern and pleasant. Many were fully refurbished in 1998 and now feature queen-size beds, modern leather couches, Tasmanian oak furniture, galley-style kitchens, and spacious living areas. The more expensive suites are a bit plusher. On the premises is a complimentary self-service laundry, a rooftop heated pool, a spa, and a restaurant. Room service and baby-sitting are available, and free in-house videos are provided.

MODERATE

The Lodge on Elizabeth. 249 Elizabeth St., Hobart, TAS 7000. ☎ **03/6231 3830.** Fax 03/ 6234 2566. 13 units (some with shower only). A$115 (U.S.$74.75) standard double; A$125 (U.S.$81.25) deluxe double. AE, BC, DC, MC, V.

The Lodge on Elizabeth is located in the second-oldest building in Tasmania, with some parts of it dating back to 1810. Originally a gentleman's residence, it later became the first private boy's school in Tasmania. It's well situated, just a 12-minute walk from Salamanca Place and surrounded by restaurants. All rooms are decorated with antiques, and many are quite romantic, with four-poster beds. Standard rooms have just a shower; the deluxe rooms come with more antiques and a large granite bathroom with a tub. Complimentary drinks are served in the communal living room in the evenings, and a good continental breakfast buffet goes for A$9.50 (U.S.$6.20).

Wellington Lodge. 7 Scott St., Hobart, TAS 7000. ☎ **03/6231 0614.** Fax 03/6234 1551. 4 units, 2 with tub and shower, 2 with shower only. TV. A$85–$110 (U.S.$55.25–$71.50) double. Extra person A$30 (U.S.$19.50). Rates include full breakfast. BC, MC, V. Free parking. The airport bus will drop you off here, as will any bus to the Aquatic Center. No children under age 11.

This charming Victorian-style townhouse (ca. 1885) is just a 10-minute walk (through Hobart's Rose Garden) from the main shopping area and Salamanca Place. It was refurbished in 1997 and decorated with period antiques. Two rooms have their own shower attached; the other two have their own separate private bathrooms. All rooms have wicker chairs, hair dryers, and tea- and coffee-making facilities. Complimentary port is served every evening in the guest lounge. No smoking.

Woolmers Inn. 123–127 Sandy Bay Rd., Hobart, TAS 7000. ☎ **1800/030 780** in Australia, or 03/6223 7355. Fax 03/6223 1981. 36 units. TV TEL. A$99 (U.S.$64.35) 1-bedroom apt; A$130 (U.S.$84.50) 2-bedroom apt. Extra adult A$15 (U.S.$9.75); extra child A$8 (U.S.$5.20). Rates 10% higher Christmas/Jan. AE, BC, DC, MC, V. Free parking. Bus: Catch the Sandy Bay (no number) bus from Elizabeth Street Mall on Elizabeth St.

Situated 2 kilometers (1¼ miles) south of the city, Woolmers Inn offers cozy one- or two-bedroom units with fully equipped kitchens and VCRs. One unit is suitable for travelers with disabilities. Sandy Bay is Hobart's main suburb; it's halfway between the casino and the city (within walking distance of Salamanca Place) and features a "golden mile" of boutique shopping. You'll find a coin-op laundry and a travel center on the property. The inn was upgraded throughout 1999 and went from a three-star to a four-star government rating.

INEXPENSIVE

Astor Private Hotel. 157 Macquarie St., Hobart, TAS 7000. ☎ **03/6234 6611.** Fax 03/ 6234 6384. 21 units, none with bathroom. A$65–$80 (U.S.$42.25–$52) double, depending on season. Extra person A$25 (U.S.$16.25). BC, MC, V.

Built in 1922 right in the heart of the city, this homey three-story property fell from grace following a few years of neglectful management. That's all changed now, and minor renovations are gradually proceeding with a new owner at the helm. It's a friendly place, with lots of natural timber, and two floors of accommodation upstairs. On the ground floor is the Astor Grill, an upscale fish and steak restaurant. There are a guest lounge with a TV and a laundry on the premises, too.

Black Prince. 145 Elizabeth St., Hobart, TAS 7000. ☎ **03/6234 3501.** Fax 03/6234 3502. 10 units. TV. A$56 (U.S.$36.50) double. Rates include breakfast. AE, BC, DC, MC, V.

If you're looking for centrally located, clean, and unfussy accommodations, then I recommend the Black Prince, an American-influenced pub with a 1950s bent. All rooms come with a shower and a bathtub, and a TV. Room 8 is the landlord's favorite here, because "it's nearer to the stairs so you don't have to walk too far" (presumably beneficial when you've had a few beers). Downstairs, the American-style bar called Joe's Garage is popular, especially on weekends. The American-influenced restaurant serves up budget-priced steaks and chicken dishes. Lunch is offered from Monday to Friday, and dinner Monday to Saturday.

Customs House Hotel. 1 Murray St., Hobart, TAS 7000. ☎ **03/6234 6645.** Fax 03/6223 8750. 13 units, 2 with bathroom. A$65 (U.S.$42.25) double without private bathroom; A$70 (U.S.$45.50) double with bathroom. Rates include continental breakfast. AE, BC, DC, MC, V.

You won't find a better value than the rooms above this historic sandstone pub overlooking the waterfront. Built in 1846, the property offers simple, colonial-style rooms. Four have water views overlooking the old sailing ship the May Queen, which used to carry wood up the Derwent River. Other rooms look across Parliament House. Guests make the best of a shared TV room. Downstairs, a friendly public bar overlooks the water, and at the back of the building is a popular seafood restaurant known for its scallops.

DINING

Tasmania is known for its fresh seafood, including oysters, crab, crayfish, salmon, and trout. It all used to be cheap, though in recent years, prices have crept up to match or even surpass those on the mainland. Generally, though, the food is good quality—as long as you avoid some of the cheaper fish-and-chip take-away joints on the waterfront (Flippers on Constitution Dock is an exception).

EXPENSIVE

Mures Upper Deck. Between Victoria and Constitution docks, Hobart. ☎ **03/6231 2121.** Reservations recommended. Main courses A$19.50–$25 (U.S.$12.70–$16.25). AE, BC, DC, MC, V. Daily noon–10pm. SEAFOOD.

This large and bustling waterfront restaurant offers great views of bobbing yachts as well as very fine seafood caught on the owner's own fishing boats. I recommend starting with a bowl of potato soup, or the signature Mures Oysters topped with smoked salmon, sour cream, and salmon caviar. The most popular main courses are the blue-eye fillet Martinique—a Creole-inspired sweet fish curry with coconut cream and banana sauce—or the giant seafood platter for two. The best summer dessert on the menu is the restaurant's famous summer pudding, which almost bursts with berries. In winter, come here if only for the Granny Leatherwood Pudding—made of apples and Australian leatherwood honey and served with cinnamon ice cream. The complex also includes Lower Deck, a very popular self-service family restaurant where you can dine very well for under A$15 (U.S.$9.75).

The Point Revolving Restaurant. In the Wrest Point Hotel Casino, 410 Sandy Bay Rd. ☎ **03/6225 0112.** Reservations recommended. Main courses from A$11.50 (U.S.$7.50) at lunch, from $17 (U.S.$11) at dinner. Set 3-course lunch menu A$25.50 (U.S.$16.60); set 3-course dinner menu A$43 (U.S.$27.95) Fri–Sat, A$34 (U.S.$22) Sun–Thurs. AE, BC, DC, MC, V. Daily noon–2pm and 6:30–9:30pm. TASMANIAN/AUSTRALIAN.

This revolving restaurant on the 17th floor of the Wrest Point Hotel Casino is known for its spectacular harbor and mountain views. Criticism of its consistency has led to a complete review of its cuisine over the past couple of years, but fortunately its specialties—prawns flambé in a curry sauce and the Caesar salad—have remained through regular menu upgrades. The crêpes suzette is a wonderful signature dessert. The service is friendly and relaxed. This place is packed on weekends. The cheaper fixed-price dinner has fewer options.

MODERATE

Drunken Admiral Restaurant. 17–19 Hunter St. ☎ **03/6234 1903.** Reservations required. Main courses A$13.50–$22.90 (U.S.$8.80–$15). AE, BC, DC, MC, V. Daily 6pm–late. SEAFOOD.

The Drunken Admiral, opposite the Hotel Grand Chancellor on the waterfront, is an extremely popular spot with tourists and can get quite raucous on very busy evenings. The main attraction is its famous seafood chowder, swimming with anything that was on sale at the docks that morning. The large Yachties seafood grill is made up of plenty of squid, scallops, fish, mussels, and prawns, but there are plenty of simpler fish dishes on the menu, too. Otherwise, splash into Sperm Whale Sally's Shellfish Platter, or perhaps Captain Nimrod's Depth Charge Platter. The salad bar is spread in a sailing dingy and can be raided as often as you want; but it's rather uninteresting, so you'll probably be content with just one dip.

✪ **Mit Zitrone.** 333 Elizabeth St., North Hobart. ☎ **03/6234 8113.** Reservations recommended. Main courses A$15.50–$17 (U.S.$10–$11). AE, BC, DC, MC, V. Mon–Sat 10am–2pm; Tues–Sat 6–10pm. MODERN AUSTRALIAN.

Chef and owner Chris Jackman has earned quite a reputation in Tasmania. His twice-cooked eggs with chili-palm sugar are a huge seller, while the hot smoked blue-eye cod with ginger and wok-fried greens, and the chicken and mushroom sausages with wide noodles, spinach, and anchovy sauce are sensational. The informal restaurant, which is basically an old shop, has bright yellow citrus walls and wooden floors and furniture. You can also drop in for just coffee and cake.

Vanidol's Asian Cuisine. 353 Elizabeth St., North Hobart. ☎ **03/6234 9307.** Reservations recommended. Main courses A$11.90–$16.50 (U.S.$7.75–$9.75). Tues–Sun 6–around 11pm. AE, BC, MC, V. PAN-ASIAN.

Very popular with both locals and tourists, Vanidol's serves up a variety of Thai, Indonesian, and Indian dishes (though it's probably better to stick to one cuisine instead of swapping between styles). The beef salad with basil, chili, and mint is very good, as are the barbecue prawns served with a sweet tamarind sauce. The fish cooked in a light red curry sauce is another specialty. No smoking between 6 and 9pm.

INEXPENSIVE

Cumquat on Criterion. 10 Criterion St. ☎ **03/6234 5858.** Reservations recommended. Main courses A$7.50–$15 (U.S.$4.90–$9.75). No credit cards. Mon–Fri 8am–6pm. PAN-ASIAN/AUSTRALIAN.

This cafe is an excellent breakfast venue, offering everything from eggs on toast to traditional porridge with brown sugar. On the menu for lunch and dinner, you could find Thai beef curry, laksa, a daily risotto, and chermoula marinated fish. The desserts can be great. Vegetarians and vegans, and those on a gluten-free diet, will find lots of options, as will your average carnivores.

Sisco's on the Pier. Upper Level, Murray Street Pier. ☎ **03/6223 2059.** Reservations recommended. Main courses A$17–$18 (U.S.$11–$11.70). AE, BC, DC, MC V. Mon–Fri noon–3pm; Mon–Sat 6–12pm. SPANISH/MEDITERRANEAN/INTERNATIONAL.

Light and bright, with a large outdoor balcony, Sisco's has transformed itself from a typical Spanish eatery with roving guitar players to a more upscale international affair

Tasmania by Raft

A good way to experience Tasmania's natural beauty is to take a raft trip with **Rafting Tasmania,** P.O. Box 403, Sandy Bay, Tasmania 7006 (☎ **03/6239 1080;** e-mail: raftingtas@ozE-mail.com.au). This company supplies all equipment, including high-quality rubber rafts for four or more people, trained guides, and camping equipment. The Franklin River is the company's specialty, and they have trips lasting 4, 7, and 10 days departing from Hobart. Each trip leaves on specific dates between mid-November and the first week or so of April, so you'll have to make plans in advance or take potluck when you arrive. The Franklin River offers a real wilderness experience, with gorges, waterfalls, rain forests, pebble beaches, limestone cliffs, and some fairly difficult rapids along the way. Trips cost A$950 (U.S.$617) for 4 days, A$1,250 (U.S.$812) for 7 days, and A$1,650 (U.S.$1,075) for 10 days.

An alternative is to take the company's 1-day rafting trip down the Picton River, not too far from Hobart. This trip costs A$115 (U.S.$80.50) and leaves Hobart Sundays year-round (also Tues and Fri between Nov and Mar).

in recent years. Today it's known for its paella, Morton Bay bugs (a kind of small crayfish) with chocolate, garlic prawns with squid ink spaghetti, and char-grilled octopus.

HOBART AFTER DARK

Built in 1837, the 747-seat **Theatre Royal,** 29 Campbell St. (☎ **03/6233 2299**), is the oldest theater in the country. It's known for its excellent acoustics and its classic Victorian decor. Ticket prices vary depending on the performance, but A$25 (U.S.$16.25) is average.

The **Hobart Historic Pub Tour** (☎ **03/6225 4806**) traces the city's early development through hotel drinking holes—an important part of life in Hobart early in the 1800s. The 2-hour tour takes in four pubs; visitors enjoy a drink in each as guides give a lively account of the building's unique place in Hobart's drinking history. Tours depart Sunday to Thursday at 5pm, and cost A$35 (U.S.$22.75), including a drink at each pub.

Opened in 1829 as a tavern and a brothel frequented by whalers, **Knopwood's Retreat,** 39 Salamanca Place (☎ **03/6223 5808**), is still a raucous place to be on Friday and Saturday evenings, when crowds cram the historic interior and spill out onto the streets. Light lunches are popular throughout the week, and occasionally you'll find jazz or blues on the menu.

My favorite watering hole in Hobart is **Irish Murphy's,** 21 Salamanca Place (☎ **03/6223 1119**), an atmospheric pub with stone walls and lots of dark wood. Local bands play Friday and Saturday evenings.

If you want to tempt Lady Luck, head to the **Wrest Point Casino,** in the Wrest Point Hotel, 410 Sandy Bay Rd. (☎ **03/6225 0112**), Australia's first legal gambling club. Smart, casual attire required (collared shirts for men).

A SIDE TRIP TO MOUNT FIELD NATIONAL PARK
80km (50 miles) NW of Hobart

Mount Field National Park is one of the prettiest spots in Tasmania. It was proclaimed a national park in 1916 to protect a plateau dominated by dolerite-capped mountains and dramatic glaciated valleys. Mount Field West is the highest point, and in the central and western regions of the park in particular there are examples of lakes and tarns formed in the ice age of 30,000 years ago. The most mountainous regions support alpine moorlands of cushion plants, pineapple and sword grass, waratahs, and giant pandani. You can get a good look at these changing environments on a 16km drive from the park entrance to Lake Dobson along an unsealed and often highly corrugated road, which is not suitable for conventional vehicles in winter or after heavy rain.

Bennett's and rufous wallabies are common in the park, as are wombats, barred bandicoots, Tasmanian devils, and quolls. Platypus inhabit the lakes. Birds common to the park include black cockatoos, olive whistlers, green rosellas, honeyeaters, curra-wongs, wedge-tailed eagles, and lyrebirds, which were introduced from Victoria in the 1930s. Also here are rare native hens, yellow wattlebirds, and dusky robins.

There are many walking trails throughout the park, including one to Tasmania's most photographed waterfall, the spectacular 45-meter **Russell Falls,** near the park's entrance. The walk to the falls along a sealed, wheelchair-accessible track takes 15 minutes and passes ferns and forests, with some of Tasmania's tallest trees, mighty swamp gums up to 85 meters high.

ESSENTIALS

GETTING THERE   **Tasmanian Redline Coaches** (☎ **03/6336 1446**) runs day tours to the park from Hobart, and **TWT Tassie Link** (☎ **03/6272 7300;** www. tassie.net.au/wildtour) offers a daily service from December to March for A$35 (U.S.$22.75) one-way.

By car, take the Lyall Highway from Hobart to the Gordon River and follow the signs after the township of Westerway.

VISITOR INFORMATION   As this book went to press, a brand-new **visitor center** was due to open in late 2000 at the only entrance to the park. It will feature interpretive displays of the park's wildlife and geology, offer maps and guides, and include a cafe. It will be open daily from 8:30am to 4:30pm.

ACCOMMODATIONS

National Park Hotel. 2366 Gordon River Rd., National Park, TAS 7140. ☎ **03/6288 1103.** 7 units, none with private bathroom. A$60 (U.S.$39) double. Rates include full breakfast. BC, MC, V.

Located 300 meters inside the national park, this typical one-story Aussie hotel has basic rooms with tea- and coffee-making facilities; some rooms have sinks. There's a TV in the lounge bar. The hotel can book horseback-riding expeditions within the park, and there's a golf course nearby.

Russell Falls Holiday Cottages. Lake Dobson Rd., National Park, TAS 7140. ☎ **03/6288 1198.** 4 units. TV. A$50 (U.S.$32.50) for 2 people. Extra adult A$12 (U.S.$7.80), extra child under 16 A$7 (U.S.$4.55). BC, MC, V.

These cottages are right at the entrance to the national park in a rural setting with rolling fields. Each is spacious and comfortable, with an attached toilet and shower and an open kitchen, lounge, and dining area. All cottages come with a TV and gas heating.

2 Port Arthur: Discovering Tasmania's Convict Heritage

102km (63 miles) SE of Hobart

Port Arthur, on the Tasman Peninsula, is one of Australia's prettiest harbors, though it was the site of one of the darkest chapters in the nation's history. Here stand the extensive remains of Tasmania's largest penal colony—essentially Australia's version of

Devil's Island. It's the state's number-one tourist destination (easily seen from your base in Hobart), and you really should plan to spend at least a whole day in this incredibly picturesque yet haunting place.

From 1830 to 1877, Port Arthur was one of the harshest institutions of its type anywhere in the world. It was built to house the settlement's most notorious prisoners, often prisoners who had escaped into the bush from lesser institutions. Nearly 13,000 convicts found their way here, and nearly 2,000 died while incarcerated. Port Arthur was, and still is, connected to the rest of Tasmania by a narrow strip of land called Eaglehawk Neck. Guards and rows of dogs kept watch over this narrow path, while the authorities circulated rumors that the waters around the peninsula were shark infested. Only a few convicts ever managed to escape, and most of those either perished in the bush or were tracked down and hanged. Look out for the blowhole and other coastal formations, including Tasman's Arch, Devil's Kitchen, and the Tessellated Pavement, as you pass through Eaglehawk Neck.

Port Arthur is a 1¹/₂-hour drive from Hobart via the Lyell and Arthur highways. **Tasmanian Tours & Travel Tigerland** (☎ **03/6272 6611;** www.tigerline.com.au) runs trips from Hobart to the former penal settlement every day; tours depart from 199 Collins St. at 9am and return around 5:30pm. Tours cost between A$50 and $60 (U.S.$32.50 to $39) for adults, and A$32 to $37 (U.S.$20.80 to $24) for children 4 to 16, depending on which tour you take. Children under 4 are free. Both trips include a guided tour of the Port Arthur site.

Experience Tasmania (☎ **03/6234 3336**) also runs coach trips from Hobart to Port Arthur every Monday, Wednesday, Friday, and Sunday, leaving the Cruise Company ferry offices on Franklin Wharf at 9:15am and returning around 5pm. One tour option goes straight to Port Arthur. The second option takes in the Tasmanian Devil Park, and the third tour features both the Tasmanian Devil Park and the **Bushmill Steam Railway and Settlement** (☎ **03/6250 2221**), a complex featuring a narrow-gauge railway, a replica steam-powered sawmill, and buildings from a typical late 19th–century township. Tours cost A$50 (U.S.$32.50), A$60 (U.S.$39), or A$65 (U.S.$42.25) for adults, respectively; and A$32 (U.S.$20.80), A$37 (U.S.$24), or A$40 (U.S.$26) for children 5 to 16, respectively. Children under 5 are free. All trips include a guided tour of the prison complex.

EN ROUTE TO PORT ARTHUR

On the way to Port Arthur from Hobart, you might want to stop off at the historic village of Richmond and at the Tasmanian Devil Park Wildlife Rescue Centre.

Richmond is just 26 kilometers (16 miles) northeast of Hobart and is the site of the country's oldest bridge (1823), the best preserved convict jail in Australia (1825), and several old churches, including St. John's Church (1836), the oldest Catholic church in the country. Richmond also has plenty of tearooms, craft shops, galleries, and antique stores.

Eighty kilometers (50 miles) from Hobart is the **Tasmanian Devil Park Wildlife Rescue Centre,** Port Arthur Highway, Taranna (☎ **03/6250 3230**), which houses orphaned or injured native animals, including Tasmanian devils, quolls, kangaroos, eagles, and owls. The park is open daily from 9am to 5pm. Admission is A$12 (U.S.$7.80) for adults, A$6 (U.S.$3.90) for children, and A$30 (U.S.$19.50) for a family. The Devils are fed (roadkill) daily at 10am, 11am, and 5pm. The adjoining World Tiger Snake Centre, a unique medical research project, contains some 1,500 highly venomous snakes.

Excellent **Ghost Tours** of Port Arthur by lantern (reservations are essential; call ☎ **1800/659 101** in Australia) leave nightly at 6:30 and 8:30pm. The cost is A$13 (U.S.$8.45) for adults and A$8 (U.S.$5.20) for children. A family ticket for two adults and up to six children is A$34 (U.S.$22).

EXPLORING THE SITE

The sprawling ✪ **Port Arthur Historic Site** (☎ **03/6251 2310**) is scattered with some 30 19th-century buildings (most of the main ones were damaged during bushfires in 1877, shortly after the property ceased to be a penal institution). You can tour the remains of the church, guard tower, model prison, and several other buildings. It's best to tour the area with a guide, who can graphically describe what the buildings were originally used for. Don't miss the fascinating museum in the old lunatic asylum, which has a scale model of the prison complex, as well as leg irons and chains.

The site is open daily from 9am to 5pm; admission is A$18 (U.S.$11.70) for adults, A$9 (U.S.$5.85) for children 4 to 7. The admission price includes a walking tour and a boat cruise around the harbor leaving eight times daily in summer. There is also a separate cruise to the Isle of the Dead off the coast of Port Arthur twice a day; some 1,769 convicts and 180 free settlers were buried here, mostly in mass graves with no headstones. The cruise costs an extra A$5 (U.S.$3.25) per person.

A new Visitor Centre opened in January 1999. The main feature is a fabulous Interpretive Gallery, which takes visitors through the process of sentencing in England to transportation to Van Dieman's Land. The gallery contains a courtroom, a section of a transport ship's hull, a blacksmith's shop, a lunatic asylum, and much more. Allow between 3 and 4 hours to explore the site and the gallery.

ACCOMMODATIONS & DINING

Port Arthur Motor Inn. Port Arthur Historic Site, Arthur Hwy., Port Arthur, TAS 7182. ☎ **1800/030 747** in Australia, or 03/6250 2101. Fax 03/6250 2417. E-mail: portarthur@ fc-hotels.com.au. 35 units. MINIBAR TV TEL. A$110 (U.S.$71.50) double. Extra person A$15 (U.S.$9.75). Children 11 and under stay free in parents' room. AE, BC, DC, MC, V. Free parking. Bus: Hobart Coaches run from Hobart on weekdays.

If you decide to stop over rather than drive all the way back to Hobart, which is a good idea if you'll be taking the Ghost Tour (remember marsupials get killed all the time on the roads at night—and they can do a lot of damage to a rental car), then this is a good choice. The rooms are attractive and overlook the historic site. There are also a self-service laundry and a kids' playground. Port Arthur ghost-tour packages are available from here. The restaurant here is quite formal, with main courses costing between A$12 and $19 (U.S.$7.80 to $12.35).

3 Freycinet National Park

206km (129miles) NE of Hobart, 214km (134 miles) SW of Launceston

If you have time to visit only one place in Tasmania, make sure it's Freycinet National Park. The Freycinet Peninsula hangs down off the eastern coast of Tasmania. It's a place of craggy pink granite peaks, spectacular white beaches, wetlands, heathlands, coastal dunes, and dry eucalyptus forests. This is the place to come to spot sea eagles, wallabies, seals, pods of dolphins, and humpback and southern right whales during their migration to and from the warmer waters of northern New South Wales from

May to August. The township of **Coles Bay** is the main gateway, and there are many bush walks in the area. The walk to the spectacular ✪ **Wineglass Bay,** named as one of the world's top 10 beaches by *Outside* magazine, will be one of the nicest you'll ever do.

ESSENTIALS

GETTING THERE   Tasmanian Redline Coaches (☎ **03/6336 1446**) runs between Hobart (199 Collins St.) and Bicheno, leaving Hobart at 10am on Monday and Wednesday, 12:30pm on Tuesday and Thursday, 2pm on Friday, and 10:30am on Sunday. The trip takes about 4¹/₂ hours. From Launceston (112 George St.), buses leave at 2pm Monday to Thursday, 3:45pm on Friday, and 11am on Sunday, and take less than 3 hours. From Bicheno, you can catch a local bus run by **Bicheno Coach Services** (☎ **03/6257 0293,** or mobile 0419 570 293). Buses leave at 9am and 3pm every day (except Sat when there's no 3pm service). Buses also meet every coach from Hobart or Launceston, but you need to book in advance. **TWT Tassie Link** (☎ **03/6272 7300**) runs buses from Launceston to Bicheno on Monday, Wednesday, Friday, and Sunday leaving at 8:30am.

From Hobart, it's about a 3-hour drive to the park.

VISITOR INFORMATION   The **Visitor Information Centre** (☎ **03/6375 1333**) on the Tasman Highway at Bicheno can arrange tour bookings. Otherwise, the **Tasmanian Travel and Information Centre** in Hobart (☎ **03/6230 8383**) can supply you with maps and details.

ENTRANCE FEES   Daily entry to the park costs A$9 (U.S.$5.85) per vehicle.

EXPLORING THE PARK

If you have time to do only one hike, then head out from Freycinet Lodge on the 30-minute uphill hike past spectacularly beautiful pink granite outcrops to **Wineglass Bay** Lookout for breathtaking views. You can then head down to Wineglass Bay itself and back up again. This walk takes around 2¹/₂ hours. A longer walk takes you along the length of **Hazards Beach,** where you'll find plenty of shell middens—seashell refuge heaps—left behind by the Aborigines who once lived here. This walk takes 6 hours.

The **Moulting Lagoon Game Reserve,** an important breeding ground for black swans and wild ducks, is signposted along the highway into Coles Bay from Bicheno. Some 10,000 black swans inhabit the lake, so it's very rare not to see them.

Six kilometers outside town and inside the national park is the **Cape Tourville Lighthouse,** from where there are extensive views north and south along the coast and out across several of the small islands in the Tasman Ocean.

The ✪ **Freycinet Experience,** with offices in Hobart at 36 St. Georges Terrace, Battery Point (☎ **1800/506 003** in Australia; www.freycinet.com.au; e-mail: walk@ freycinet.com.au), is well worth considering if you have the time. The "experience" is

National Park Entry Fees

A **Tassie Holiday Pass** costs $30 (U.S.$19.50) and allows entry for a car and passengers to all of Tasmania's 18 national parks for a period of 2 months. Also valid for the same period is a **Backpackers Pass,** available to pedestrians, cyclists, and motorcyclists for $12 (U.S.$7.80). Occasional users can buy a 24-hour pass costing $9 (U.S.$5.85) per car, while walkers, cyclists, motorcyclists, and coach passengers pay $3 (U.S.$1.95) per day. Passes are available at all major national parks and Tasmanian Visitor Information Centres. For more information, contact the Parks and Wildlife Service at ☎ **03/6233 8203** or www.parks.tas.gov.au.

a 40-kilometer (25-mile), 4-day trek along the entire length of the Freycinet Peninsula from Schouten Island to Friendly Beaches Lodge, an award-winning, environmentally sensitive building where you'll spend your last night. Accommodations the first 2 nights are standing camps on elevated wooden platforms with comfortable beds. The journey starts with a boat trip to Schouten Island, where you can go fishing. The next 2 days are spent walking along the dramatic sea cliffs. Wildlife, including wombats, wallabies, quolls, and sea eagles, abound. The meals and wines are outstanding. The trip costs from A$1,080 to $1,200 (U.S.$702 to $780), including all meals and GST.

Tasmanian Expeditions (☎ **1800/030 230** in Australia, or 03/6334 3477; www.tas-ex.com; e-mail: tazzie@tassie.net.au) offers a 3-day trip from Launceston and back that includes 2 nights in cabins at Coles Bay. The trip includes guided walks to Wineglass Bay and Mt. Amor. The company also offers 6- and 12-night walking, rafting, and cycling trips.

Not to be missed is a trip aboard **Freycinet Sea Charter's** vessel *Kahala* (☎ **03/6257 0355**), which offers whale watching between June and September, bay and game fishing, dolphin watching, diving, scenic and marine wildlife cruises, and sunset cruises. Half-day cruises cost A$60 (U.S.$39) per person with a minimum of four adults on board. Full-day cruises cost A$100 (U.S.$65) per person.

ACCOMMODATIONS & DINING

Camping is available in the national park itself for A$10 (U.S.$6.50) a tent, though water is scarce. For inquiries, call the **Parks and Wildlife Service** (☎ **03/6257 0107**).

✪ **Freycinet Lodge.** Freycinet National Park, Coles Bay, TAS 7215. ☎ **03/6257 0101.** Fax 03/6257 0278. www.freycinetlodge.com.au. E-mail: info@freycinetlodge.com.au. 60 units. A$160 (U.S.$104) standard cabin; A$200 (U.S.$130) spa cabin. AE, BC, DC, MC, V.

I can't praise the eco-friendly lodge enough. Comfortable one- and two-room cabins are spread unobtrusively through the bush and connected by raised walking tracks. Each has a balcony, and some have huge spa bathtubs. The main part of the lodge houses a lounge room and a truly excellent restaurant that sweeps out onto a veranda overlooking the limpid green waters of Great Oyster Bay. From here it's an easy stroll to the start of the Wineglass Bay walk, and the lodge is right next to the white sands of Hazards Beach. Orchids bloom in October; you may see dolphins and whales migrating from May through August; and diving and charter-boat expeditions to see seal and penguin colonies can be arranged.

4 From Hobart to Launceston via the Heritage Highway

By the 1820s, several garrison towns had been built between Launceston and Hobart, and by the middle of the 19th century, convict labor had produced what was considered to be the finest highway of its time in Australia. Today, many of the towns along the route boast magnificent examples of Georgian and Victorian architecture. It takes about 2 hours to drive between Launceston and Hobart on the Heritage Highway (officially known as the A1, or the Midland Highway), but allow yourself a whole day or two to relax and explore at your own pace.

OATLANDS

84km north of Hobart; 117km south of Launceston

Oatlands, a former military garrison, has the largest number of colonial-era sandstone buildings of any village in Australia. Eighty-seven of them are situated in Main Street, the most notable being the convict-built courthouse (1829) and Callington Mill (1837), once the largest flour producer in the region. This site consists of a five-story windmill, a granary, the steam mill, a stable, and the miller's cottage. There are pleasant picnic grounds along the lakefront, and waterfowl breed in the lake's marshland wildlife sanctuary.

For additional information, stop by the **Central Tasmania Tourism Centre,** 77 High St. (☎ **03/6254 1212**); it's open daily from 9am to 5pm.

ROSS

121km north of Hobart; 78km south of Launceston

One of Tasmania's best-preserved historic villages, picturesque Ross was established as a garrison town in 1812 on a strategically important crossing point on the Macquarie River. **Ross Bridge,** the third oldest in Australia, was built in 1836 to replace an earlier one made of logs. The bridge is decorated with Celtic symbols, animals, and faces of notable people of the time. It's lit up at night, and there are good views of it from a dirt track that runs alongside the river's north bank.

The town's main crossroads is edged by four historic buildings, humorously known as "temptation" (represented by the Man-o'-Ross Hotel), "salvation" (the Catholic church), "recreation" (the town hall), and "damnation" (the old gaol, or jail). The **Ross Female Factory,** built in the early 1840s, consists of ruins, a few interpretive signs, and a model of the original site and buildings inside the original Overseer's Cottage. Entry is free. Women convicts were imprisoned here from 1847 to 1854.

At the **Tasmanian Wool Centre** and tourist information center on Church Street (☎ **03/6381 5466**), there's an exhibit detailing the growth of the region and the wool industry since settlement. It's open daily from 9am to 5pm (until 6pm Jan to Mar), and entry costs A$4 (U.S.$2.60) for adults, A$2 (U.S.$1.30) for children, and A$10 (U.S.$6.50) for a families.

ACCOMMODATIONS & DINING

Colonial Cottages of Ross. 12 Church St., Ross, TAS 7209. ☎ **03/6381 5354.** Fax 03/6381 5408. E-mail: tim@tasmania.com. 4 cottages. TV. A$110–$130 (U.S.$77.50–$84.50) for 2 (depending on cottage and season). A$20–$30 (U.S.$13–$19.50) extra person. BC, MC, V.

Here's a collection of delightful historic cottages, each with a modern bathroom and kitchen facilities. The Apple Dumpling Cottage (ca. 1880) is a two-bedroom wooden cottage that sleeps four, with impressive sandstone fireplaces set on the edge of the village in a rural setting. The spacious Church Mouse Cottage (ca. 1840), set in an old Sunday School, sleeps just two. Captain Samuel's Cottage (ca. 1830) accommodates six people in three bedrooms, with two double and two single beds. Finally, Hudson Cottage (ca. 1850) sleeps four.

The Ross Village Bakery and Inn. 15 Church St., Ross, TAS 7209. ☎ **03/6381 5246.** Fax 03/6381 5360. 4 units. A$95 (U.S.$61.75) double. AE, MC, V.

This old coaching inn, built in 1832, offers four homey rooms done out old English style. One room has a double bed; another has a double and two singles. The third room is a double, and it opens up onto a fourth room with two singles (a great arrangement for a family). A separate lounge room has a TV and free tea, coffee, sherry, and cakes. The bakery on the premises is an excellent place for lunch, serving up things like filled baked potatoes and some of the best pies in Australia, baked in a wood-fired oven dating from 1860.

LONGFORD

27km (17 miles) S of Launceston; 188km (116 miles) N of Hobart

About 6km (3.7 miles) west of the Midland Highway, Longford is best known for its Georgian architecture, much of which was built using convict labor. "The Path to

History" brochure, available at the visitor center, is great for a self-guided tour of many of the colonial buildings. The **Longford Visitor Information Centre,** 3 Malborough St. (☎ **03/6391 1181**), is open from 10am to 5pm daily.

If you follow Wellington Street south out of town, you'll find the historic houses of Woolmers and Brickendon, both established by Thomas Archer, who became a major landowner in the area.

The oldest part of the **Woolmers** homestead dates from 1818, and a new Italianate front was added in 1845. At its peak, the estate consisted of some 24,000 acres, but much of it was acquired by the government in 1911 and 1945 and given to settlers and returned soldiers. The great thing about Woolmers for the visitor is that all its contents are original to the house. The outbuildings and gardens (and the view across the fields and English trees) are worth seeing, even if you miss out on the guided tours, which are the only way you'll get to see inside the house. There's a good restaurant on-site and three cottages are available for overnight stays. Woolmers (☎ **03/6391 2230**) is open from 10am to 4:30pm daily, with guided tours at 11am, 12:30pm, 2pm, and 3:30pm. Admission costs A$10 (U.S.$6.50) for adults, A$2.50 (U.S.$1.60) for children, and A$25 (U.S.$16.25) for a family.

Brickendon was built by Thomas Archer's older brother, William, in 1829. The house itself is not open to the general public, but the gardens and convict-made buildings that surround it are. There are 16 of these buildings in all, including Dutch barns, a blacksmith shop, a cook's house, a Gothic chapel, a poultry shed, and a shearing shed. The gardens were established in the 1830s and planted with exotic tree species from around the world. Today, the property is still the center of a working farm, so there are plenty of animals grazing about, too. You can stay in one of the historic worker's cottages or farm cottages for between A$130 and $150 (U.S.$84.50 to U.S.$97.50) a night. Brickendon (☎ **03/6391 1251**) is open Wednesday to Sunday 9:30am to 5pm. Entry costs A$7.50 (U.S.$4.90) for adults, A$3.50 (U.S.$2.30) for children, and A$20 (U.S.$13) for families.

Another historic house of note is **Clarendon,** located 12km (7.5 miles) off the Heritage Highway via Evandale on the B41. One of the great Georgian houses of Australia, Clarendon (☎ **03/6398 6220**) was completed in 1838 for wealthy wool grower and merchant James Cox. Set on the banks of the South Esk River, Clarendon has extensive formal gardens featuring rows of giant elm trees. It was restored to its original appearance in 1974, with the addition of a portico and parapet. Most of the furniture and knickknacks came from other Tasmanian collections, but together they give you a good insight into the life of a prosperous 19th-century landowner. The collection of dolls and children's toys on the second floor and the period dresses are fascinating. It's open daily 10am to 5pm (to 4pm June, July, and Aug). Entry costs A$7 (U.S.$4.55) for adults, A$5 (U.S.$3.25) for children under 16, and $14 (U.S.$9) for families.

5 Launceston

198km (123 miles) N of Hobart

Tasmania's second city is Australia's third oldest (after Sydney and Hobart). Situated at the head of the Tamar River, 50km (31 miles) inland from the north coast, and surrounded by delightful undulating farmland, ✪ **Launceston** is a pleasant city crammed with elegant Victorian and Georgian architecture and plenty of remnants from convict days. Unfortunately, short-sighted local and state governments are gradually chipping away at the city's great architectural heritage in favor of the usual parking garages and ugly concrete monoliths. However, Launceston (pop. 104,000) is still one of Australia's most beautiful cities and has plenty of delightful parks and churches. It's also well placed as the gateway to the wineries of the Tamar Valley, the highlands and alpine lakes of the north, and the stunning beaches to the east.

ESSENTIALS

GETTING THERE Both **Ansett** (☎ **13 13 00** in Australia) and **Qantas** (☎ **13 13 13** in Australia) fly to Launceston from Melbourne and Sydney.

Tasmanian Redline Coaches depart Hobart for Launceston several times daily (trip time: around 2 hr., 40 min.). The one-way fare is A$19 (U.S.$12.35). Launceston is 1¹/₂ hours from Devonport if you take the *Spirit of Tasmania* **ferry** across Bass Strait to Devonport. The bus ride from Devonport costs around A$13 (U.S.$8.45).

The drive from Hobart to Launceston takes just over 2 hours on Highway 1.

VISITOR INFORMATION The **Gateway Tasmania Travel Centre,** on the corner of St. John and Paterson streets (☎ **03/6336 3133;** fax 03/6336 3118; e-mail: gateway.tas@microtech.com.au), is open Monday to Friday from 9am to 5pm, Saturday from 9am to 3pm, and Sunday and public holidays from 9am to noon.

CITY LAYOUT The main pedestrian shopping mall, **Brisbane Street,** along with St. John and Charles streets on either side, forms the heart of the central area. The Victorian-Italianate Town Hall is 2 blocks north on **Civic Square,** opposite the red brick Post Office building, which dates from 1889. The **Tamar River** slips quietly past the city's northern edge and is crossed at two points by Charles Bridge and Tamar Street. **City Park,** to the northeast of the central business district, is a nice place for a stroll.

EXPLORING THE CITY & ENVIRONS

Launceston is easily explored by foot. I highly recommend a stroll with ✪ **Launceston Historic Walks** (☎ **03/6331 3679;** e-mail: harris.m@bigpond.com), which leave from the Gateway Tasmania Travel Centre Monday to Friday at 9:45am (weekend walks can also be arranged). The hourlong walk gives a fascinating insight into Launceston's history and costs A$10 (U.S.$6.50). **City Sights** (☎ **03/6336 3122**), on the corner of St. John and Paterson streets, runs city tours daily by replica tram. Tours cost A$23 (U.S.$14.95) for adults and A$16 (U.S.$10.40) for children under 16.

A must-see is ✪ **Cataract Gorge,** the result of violent earthquakes that rattled Tasmania some 40 million years ago. It's a wonderfully scenic area just 10 minutes from Launceston, on Paterson Street, at Kings Bridge. The South Esk River flows through the gorge and collects in a small lake traversed by a striking yellow suspension bridge and the longest single-span chairlift in the world. The **chairlift** (☎ **03/6331 5915**) is open daily from 9am to 4:30pm (except from June 23 to Aug 11, when it operates on Sat and Sun only), and it costs A$5 (U.S.$3.25) for adults and A$3 (U.S.$1.95) for children under 16. Outdoor concerts are sometimes held on the lake bank. The hike to the Duck Reach Power Station takes about 45 minutes (take good footwear and a raincoat); other walks in the area are shorter and easier. The **Gorge Restaurant** (☎ **03/6331 3330**) and the kiosk next door serve meals with glorious views from the outdoor tables.

Tamar River Cruises (☎ **03/6334 9900**) offers lunch, afternoon, and evening buffet dinner cruises up the Tamar River from Home Point Wharf in Launceston.

Mountain biking is popular in this area. Contact **Tasmanian Expeditions** (☎ **1800/030 230** in Australia, or 03/6334 3477; www.tassie.net.au/tas_ex/; e-mail: tazzie@tassie.net.au) for information on its 4- to 7-day trips along the east coast in summer.

You can **rent bicycles** from the youth hostel at 36 Thistle St. (☎ **03/6344 9779**) for A$11 (U.S.$7.15) per day for a touring bike or A$18 (U.S.$11.70) per day for a mountain bike. They also rent camping equipment, such as boots, tents, sleeping bags, and stoves.

The **Trevallyn State Recreation Area,** on the outskirts of Launceston off Reatta Road, is a man-made lake surrounded by a beautiful wildlife reserve with several walking tracks. There are also barbecue facilities, picnic areas, and even a beach.

OTHER ATTRACTIONS

If you're in Launceston on a Sunday, try to visit the **York Town Square Market,** at the rear of the Launceston International Hotel. There are plenty of craft items on sale. The market is open from 9am to 5pm.

Aquarius Roman Baths. 127 George St. ☎ **03/6331 2255.** www.romanbaths. tastourism.com.au. Admission to baths and hot rooms A$20 (U.S.$13) for 1, A$30 (U.S.$19.50) for 2. Treatments extra. Mon–Fri 8:30am–10pm, Sat–Sun 9am–6pm.

Adorned with gold, Italian marble, and works of art, this remarkable Romanesque structure is worth visiting just for the architectural experience. Indulge in warm-, hot-, and cold-water baths; visit the steam room; or get a massage or a beauty makeover. Massages cost A$38.50 (U.S.$25) for half an hour, A$55 (U.S.$37.75) for 1 hour; book them well in advance.

National Automobile Museum of Tasmania. 86 Cimitiere St. ☎ **03/6334 8888.** Admission A$7.50 (U.S.$4.90) adults, A$4 (U.S.$2.60) children under 16, A$19 (U.S.$12.35) families. Daily 9am–5pm summer, 10am–4pm winter. Closed Christmas.

More than 80 classic automobiles and motorbikes are on display here, some unique to this exhibition. Children particularly enjoy the model-car collection.

The Old Umbrella Shop. 60 George St. ☎ **03/6331 9248.** Free admission. Mon–Fri 9am–5pm, Sat 9am–noon.

Built in the 1860s, this unique shop is the last genuine store from this period left in Tasmania; it's been operated by the same family since the early 1900s. Umbrellas spanning the past 100 years are on display, while modern "brollies" and souvenirs are for sale.

The Penny Royal World & Gunpowder Mill. Off Bridge Rd. ☎ **03/6331 6699.** Admission A$19.50 (U.S.$12.70) adults, A$9.50 (U.S.$6.20) children, A$49.50 (U.S.$32.20) family ticket for 2 adults and up to 6 children. Daily 9am–4:30pm. Closed Christmas.

This amusement park, with its sailboat, barges, and trams, and historic gunpowder mills, is large enough to occupy an entire day, even if most of the rides are pretty tame. Admission also includes a tram ride and a trip up Cataract Gorge and the Tamar River on the paddle steamer M.V. *Lady Stelfox.*

The Queen Victoria Museum & Art Gallery. Corner of Wellington and Paterson sts. ☎ **03/6323 3777.** Free admission. Mon–Sat 10am–5pm, Sun 2–5pm.

Opened in honor of Queen Victoria's Golden Jubilee in 1891, this museum houses a large collection of stuffed wildlife, including the extinct Tasmanian Tiger, or Thylacine. There are also temporary exhibits and historical items on display.

Waverley Woollen Mills. Waverley Rd. ☎ **03/6339 1106.** Tours A$4 (U.S.$2.60) adults, A$2 (U.S.$1.30) children, A$12 (U.S.$7.80) families. Tours daily 9am–4pm (there's usually a 20-min. wait).

Established in 1874 on a site 5 kilometers (3 miles) northeast of town, this business still uses a waterwheel to turn the looms that help make Woollen blankets and rugs.

Tours show how the process works. Everything from woolen hats to ties is sold on the premises.

ACCOMMODATIONS
EXPENSIVE

✪ **Alice's Place & Ivy Cottage.** 129 Balfour St., Launceston, TAS 7250. ☎ **03/6334 2231.** Fax 03/6334 2696. 2 cottages, plus 9 more also mentioned below. TV. A$170 (U.S.$110) for 1 or 2 people. Extra person A$30–$50 (U.S.$19.50–$32.50). Rates include breakfast provisions. AE, BC, DC, MC, V. Free parking.

I highly recommend these two delightful cottages, owned by the hard-working Helen Poynder. She made Alice's Place, which sleeps four, entirely from bits and pieces of razed historic buildings. Ivy Cottage, on the other hand, is a restored Georgian house (ca. 1831). Both places are furnished with antiques and fascinating period bric-a-brac. Kitchens are fully equipped, and both units have large spa bathtubs. Guests come and go as they please and stay here on their own (check in at the reception at 129 Balfour St.). Both cottages share the same garden.

Also available for rent are five other spa cottages called Alice's Hideaways, which cost A$170 (U.S.$110) a night for one or two people, and four cottages collectively known as The Shambles, which cost A$140 (U.S.$91) for one or two people.

Novotel Launceston. 29 Cameron St., Launceston, TAS 7250. ☎ **800/221-4542** from North America, 1300/656 565 in Australia, or 03/6334 3434. Fax 03/6331 7347. www.accorhotel.com. 162 units. MINIBAR TV TEL. A$200 (U.S.$130) double; A$260 (U.S.$169) spa room. Children stay free in parents' room. Ask about packages. AE, BC, DC, MC, V. Free parking.

The Novotel has some of the most comfortable and homey rooms of any major chain hotel in Australia. The rooms have everything you'd expect from a four-star hotel except cable TV, though a good series of free in-room movies is thrown in. Standard rooms have two double beds or a king-size bed. Jackson's Tavern, just off the lobby, is a popular watering hole. Services include concierge, 24-hour room service, laundry, valet parking, and baby-sitting. There are also a self-service laundry, a business center, a beauty salon, and a gift shop. No smoking.

✪ **York Mansions.** 9–11 York St., Launceston, TAS 7250. ☎ **03/6334 2933.** Fax 03/6334 2870. www.yorkmansions.com.au. E-mail: yorkmansions@tassie.net.au. 5 units. TV TEL. A$162 (U.S.$105) 2-bedroom apt, A$45 (U.S.$29.25) extra person; A$178 (U.S.$115) 3-bedroom apt, A$45–$50 (U.S.$29–$32.50) extra person. Rates include breakfast provisions. AE, BC, DC, MC, V. Free parking.

If you feel that where you stay is as important to your visit as what you see, then you have to stay here. Within the walls of the National Trust–classified York Mansions, built in 1840, are five very spacious apartments, each with a distinctly individual character. The Duke of York apartment is fashioned after a gentleman's drawing room, complete with rich leather sofa, antiques, and an extensive collection of historic books. The light and airy Duchess of York unit has hand-painted silk panels. Each apartment is self-contained and has its own separate kitchen, dining room, living room, bedrooms, bathroom, and laundry. A CD player and large-screen TV add modern touches. The ingredients for a hearty breakfast can be found in the refrigerator. There's also a delightful cottage garden.

MODERATE

Innkeepers Colonial Motor Inn. 31 Elizabeth St., Launceston, TAS 7250. ☎ **03/6331 6588.** Fax 03/6334 2765. 63 units. A/C MINIBAR TV TEL. A$120 (U.S.$78) double; A$195 (U.S.$126.75) suite. Extra person A$15 (U.S.$9.75). Lower weekend rates. Children under 3 stay free in parents' room. AE, BC, DC, MC, V. Free parking.

If you just want a tried-and-true motel, you'll feel right at home at the Colonial, a place that combines old-world ambience with modern facilities. The rooms are quite large and have attractive furnishings. The Old Grammar School that stands next door has been incorporated into the complex, with the Quill and Cane Restaurant operating in what once was a schoolroom, and Three Steps On George, Launceston's liveliest nightspot, making use of the former boys' gym. Rooms are fairly standard and attract a large corporate clientele.

✪ **Waratah on York.** 12 York St., Launceston, TAS 7250. ☎ **03/6331 2081.** Fax 03/ 6331 9200. E-mail: waratahonyork@bigpond.com. 9 units. TV TEL. A$148 (U.S.$96.20) standard double; A$168 (U.S.$109.20) spa room; A$198 (U.S.$128.70) executive spa suite. Rates include continental breakfast. AE, BC, DC, MC, V. Free off-street parking.

The Waratah on York is a carefully renovated Victorian mansion, originally built in 1862 for Alexander Webster, an ironmonger by trade and mayor of Launceston in the 1860s and 1870s. The current owners have spent considerable time and energy restoring the property to its former glory. Some of the original features—pressed brass ceiling roses and a staircase with a cast-iron balustrade—remain, while others have been faithfully re-created. Of the nine rooms, six come with spa bathtubs, one with a private balcony, and another with a private sunroom. All have high ceilings, large-screen TVs, hair dryers, and ornate (but nonfunctional) fireplaces. The executive rooms have four-poster beds and sweeping views down upon the Tamar River. There's also a comfortable lounge with an open fireplace and a bar.

INEXPENSIVE

Hillview House. 193 George St., Launceston, TAS 7250. ☎ **03/6331 7388.** Fax 03/ 6331 7388. 9 units. A$90 (U.S.$58.50) double; A$105 (U.S.$68.25) family room for 3. Rates include full breakfast. MC, V.

The rooms at this restored farmhouse are nothing fancy but are quite comfortable. They come with a double bed, a TV, and a shower. The family room has an extra single bed; it's the nicest room and has the best views. The hotel overlooks the city, and the large veranda and colonial dining room both have extensive views over the city and the Tamar River.

Hotel Tasmania. 191 Charles St., Launceston, TAS 7250. ☎ **03/6331 7355.** Fax 03/ 6331 5589. 18 units. A$58 (U.S.$37.70) double. Rates include continental breakfast. Extra person A$17 (U.S.$11). BC, MC, V. Free on-street parking.

Situated right in the heart of town, this hotel offers simple rooms with modern furnishings, a TV, coffee- and tea-making facilities, and attached showers. All the rooms were renovated in 1998, which helped this place win the Australian Hoteliers Association's award for the best budget pub-style accommodation in Tasmania. Downstairs there's a saloon-style bar with a cowboy theme. There's also a bistro.

Lloyd's Hotel. 23 George St., Launceston, TAS 7250. ☎ **03/6331 4966.** Fax 03/ 6331 5589. 18 units (some with shower only). A$54 (U.S.$35) double. Rates include full breakfast. Extra person A$20 (U.S.$13). BC, MC, V. Free parking.

This older-style property offers comfortable lodging at bargain prices. It's centrally located, and the owners are friendly and interesting, and have traveled extensively, mainly through the United States. Each room comes with a refrigerator, and tea- and coffee-making facilities. Most rooms have TVs.

DINING

You'll find that most places to eat in Launceston don't have a fixed closing time, rather they close up shop when the last customer has been served.

If you crave good coffee, bypass every other place in Launceston and head to
✪ **Croplines Coffee Bar,** Brisbane Court, off Brisbane Street (☎ **03/6331 4023**),
open daily from 8am to 5:30pm. It's a bit hard to find, and you may have to ask for
directions; but basically it's behind the old Brisbane Arcade. The owners are dedicated
to coffee, grinding their beans on the premises daily. If coffee's not your cup of tea,
then try the hot chocolate—it's the best I've tasted.

Fee & Me Restaurant. Corner of Charles and Frederick sts. ☎ **03/6331 3195.** Reserva-
tions recommended. A$42 (U.S.$27.30) for 3 courses, A$48 (U.S.$31.20) for 4 courses,
A$50 (U.S.$32.50) for 5 courses. AE, BC, DC, MC, V. Mon–Sat 7pm–late. MODERN
AUSTRALIAN.

What is perhaps Launceston's best restaurant is found in a grand old mansion. The
menu is structured so that diners choose a selection from five categories, each one
moving from light to rich. An extensive wine list has been designed to complement
selections for each course. A five-course meal could go something like this: Tasmanian
smoked salmon with salad, capers, and a soft poached egg; followed by chili oysters
with a coconut sauce and vermicelli noodles; then ricotta and goat cheese gnocchi
with creamed tomato and red capsicum; followed by Asian-style duck on bok choy
with a citrus sauce; finally topped off with a coffee and chicory soufflé. This is just a
sample, because the dishes change very frequently.

Konditorei Cafe Manfred. 106 George St. ☎ **03/6334 2490.** Reservations not accepted.
Light meals A$4–$5 (U.S.$2.60–$3.25); main courses A$9–$18 (U.S.$5.85–$11.70). AE, BC,
DC, MC, V. Mon–Thurs 9am–5:30pm, Fri 9am–late, Sat 10am–late. PATISSERIE.

This German patisserie has recently moved to larger premises to keep up with demand
for its sensational cakes and breads. It's also added an à la carte restaurant serving up
the likes of pastas and steaks. Light meals include croissants, salads, and cakes. You can
eat in or outside.

O'Keefe's Hotel. 124 George St. ☎ **03/6331 4015.** Reservations recommended. Main
courses A$10.50–$14.50 (U.S.$6.80–$9.40). AE, BC, MC, V. Daily 11:30am–2pm and
5:30pm–late. ASIAN/TASMANIAN.

This pub-style place earns high praise for its variety of well-prepared dishes. You can
choose from Thai curry and laksa; seafood dishes such as scallops, prawns, and sushi;
and plenty of pastas and grills. There's also a range of good salads.

✪ **Shrimps.** 72 George St. (at the corner of Paterson St.). ☎ **03/6334 0584.** Reservations
recommended. Main courses A$14–$19 (U.S.$9.10–$12.35). AE, BC, DC, MC, V. Mon–Sat
noon–2pm and 6:30pm–late. SEAFOOD.

Shrimps offers the best selection of seafood in Launceston. Built in 1824 by convict
labor, it has a classic Georgian exterior. Tables are small and well spaced, and the best
meals are off the blackboard menu, which generally includes at least eight fish dishes.
Usually available are wonderful Tasmanian mussels, whitebait, Thai-style fishcakes,
and freshly split oysters. Everything is very fresh and seasonal.

Star Bar Cafe. 113 Charles St. ☎ **03/6331 9659.** Reservations recommended. Main
courses A$10.50–$17.50 (U.S.$6.80–$11.40). AE, BC, MC, V. Mon–Wed 11am–11pm,
Thurs–Sat 11am–midnight, Sun noon–10pm. MEDITERRANEAN.

Many consider this Tasmania's best bistro. It offers a range of dishes, such as mee
goreng, beetroot, and quail risotto; grilled octopus, steaks, and chicken livers; and
popular pizzas and breads cooked in the large wood-fired oven. In winter, guests
congregate around a large open fire.

6 Cradle Mountain & Lake St. Clair National Park

85km (53 miles) S of Devonport; 175km (107 miles) NW of Hobart

The national park and World Heritage area, which encompasses both Cradle Mountain and Lake St. Clair, is one of the most spectacular regions in Australia and, after Hobart and Port Arthur, the most visited place in Tasmania. The 1,545-meter (5,199-ft.) mountain dominates the north part of the island, and the long, deep lake is to its south. Between them lie more steep slopes, button grass plains, majestic alpine forests, dozens of lakes filled with trout, and several rivers. Mount Ossa, in the center of the park, is Tasmania's highest point at 1,617 meters (5,336 ft.). The Overland Track (see below) links Cradle Mountain with Lake St. Clair and is the best known of Australia's walking trails.

Another option in the area is a visit to the **Walls of Jerusalem National Park,** a high alpine area with spectacular granite walls, small lakes, and old-growth forest.

ESSENTIALS

GETTING THERE   **TWT Tassie Link** (☎ 03/6272 7300) runs buses to Cradle Mountain from Hobart, Launceston, Devonport, and Strahan (see "Exploring Tasmania," at the beginning of this chapter, for more details). Round-trip coach transfers from Launceston cost A$69 (U.S.$44.80) and leave daily in the summer at 8:30am. A special Overland Track service drops off passengers at the beginning of the walk and picks them up at the end; it costs A$69 (U.S.$44.80) round-trip from Hobart. All coaches have commentary on board.

Maxwells Cradle Mountain–Lake St. Clair Charter Bus and Taxi Service (☎ 03/6492 1431) runs buses from Devonport and Launceston to Cradle Mountain from A$35 (U.S.$22.75), depending on how many people are on board. The buses also travel to other areas nearby, such as the Walls of Jerusalem and Lake St. Clair. Buses also run from Cradle Mountain campground to the start of the Overland Track.

Motorists enter the park via the Lyall Highway from Hobart, via Deloraine or Poatina from Launceston, and via Sheffield or Wilmot from Devonport. Both Cradle Mountain and Lake St. Clair are well signposted.

VISITOR INFORMATION   The park headquarters, **Cradle Mountain Visitor Centre** (☎ 03/6492 1133; www.parks.tas.gov.au), on the northern edge of the national park just outside Cradle Mountain Lodge, offers the best information on local walks and treks. It's open 8am to 5pm (6pm in summer) daily.

EXPLORING THE PARK

Cradle Mountain Lodge (see "Accommodations & Dining," below) runs a daily program of guided walks, abseiling, rock climbing, and trout-fishing excursions for lodge guests. There are also plenty of trails in the area that can be attempted by people equipped with directions from the staff at the park headquarters (see "Visitor Information," above). Be warned, though, that the weather changes quickly in the high country; so go prepared with wet-weather gear and always tell someone where you are headed. Of the shorter walks, the stroll to Pencil Pines and the 5-kilometer (3-mile) walk to Dove Lake are the most pleasant.

Between June and October, it's sometimes possible to cross-country ski in the park.

HIKING THE OVERLAND TRACK

The most well-known hiking trail in Australia is the ✪ **Overland Track,** an 85-kilometer (53-mile) route between Cradle Mountain and Lake St. Clair. The trek takes between 5 and 10 days and goes through high alpine plateaus, buttongrass plains, heathland, and dense rain forests and passes glacial lakes, ice-carved crags, and waterfalls. The trek gives you a good look at the wild beauty of Tasmania's pristine wilderness, and although the first day is quite tough walking, you soon get into the rhythm. After climbing to Pelion Gap, the track gradually descends southward toward the towering myrtle forests on the shores of Lake St Clair. There are many rewarding side trips, including the 1-day ascent of Mt. Ossa (1,617m, or 5,305 ft.), Tasmania's highest peak.

Several companies offer guided walks of the Overland Track from October to April, although simple public huts, on a first-come-first-served basis, and camping areas are available for those who wish to do it solo. Every summer, up to 200 people a day start the trek. Most trekking companies employ at least two guides who carry tents and cooking gear, while you carry your sleeping bag, lunch, and personal belongings. Wet-weather gear is essential, because heavy downpours can be frequent, and make sure your boots are well worn in to avoid blisters.

✪ **Tasmanian Expeditions** (☎ **1800/030 230** in Australia, or 03/6334 3477; www.tassie.net.au/tas_ex/; e-mail tazzie@tassie.net.au) offers 3-day walking tours around Cradle Mountain, staying at Waldheim Cabins. The tours depart from Launceston and cost A$430 (U.S.$279), all-inclusive. The company also offers a full 8-day trek on the Overland Track for A$995 (U.S.$646.75), all-inclusive from Launceston (wet-weather gear costs A$55/U.S.$35.75 extra to rent). Another trip, a 6-day Cradle Mountain and Walls of Jerusalem National Park trip, includes 3 nights' wilderness camping and 3 nights in a cabin. It costs A$840 (U.S.$546); many people have reported this trek to be the highlight of their trip to Australia.

Craclair Tours (☎ **03/6424 7833;** www.southcom.com.au/~craclair; e-mail: craclair@southcom.com.au) also offers an 8-day Overland Track tour, including 5 nights of camping, between October and mid-April for A$1,085 (U.S.$705).

Another alternative is to go on an organized trek with **Cradle Mountain Huts** (☎ **03/6331 2006;** e-mail: cradle@tassie.net.au), staying in heated and well-equipped huts. Six-day walks cost A$1,450 (U.S.$942) for adults and A$1,350 (U.S.$877) for children 12 to 16; rates are all-inclusive and include transfers to and from Launceston. Children under 12 are not permitted. The huts are fully equipped and quite comfortable, with showers, a main living area, and a full kitchen. You get a good three-course meal every night.

LAKE ST. CLAIR

Australia's deepest natural freshwater lake is a narrow, 15-kilometer-long waterway, fully enclosed within the Cradle Mountain–Lake St. Clair National Park. On the lake's southern edge is **Cynthia Bay,** site of an informative ranger station where you must register if you're attempting the Overland Track from this end, as well as a restaurant, cabin accommodations, and a backpackers' hostel (the latter are operated by Lakeside St. Clair; ☎ **03/6289 1137**). National park rangers run several tours between Boxing Day and the end of February, including spotlighting tours and guided walks around the local area. Call ahead for details (☎ **03/6289 1172**).

At the kiosk near the ranger station, you can book a seat on the small **M.V. *Idaclair* ferry,** which stops off at Echo Point and Narcissus Bay at the lake's northern tip. From Echo Point, the lovely hike back to Cynthia Bay along the lakeshore takes 3 to 4 hours (5 to 6 hours from Narcissus Bay). Other walks include a 1¹/₂-hour Woodland Nature Walk and the 45-minute Watersmeet Track, which both run to and from the ranger station and take in pockets of rain forest and sphagnum moorland.

The M.V. *Idaclair* departs Cynthia Bay at 9am, 12:30pm, and 3pm (a minimum of four people are required for the ferry to run, but in summer that's not usually a problem). Tickets cost A$15 (U.S.$9.75) one-way for adults, and A$10 (U.S.$6.50) for children 4 to 14. The trip time to Narcissus Bay is 30 minutes. A scenic cruise (basically a round-trip back to Cynthia Bay so you don't hike back) costs A$20 (U.S.$13) for adults and A$12 (U.S.$7.80) for children.

ACCOMMODATIONS & DINING

✪ **Cradle Mountain Lodge.** GPO Box 478, Sydney, NSW 2001. ☎ **13 24 69** in Australia, 800/225-9849 in the U.S., 0171/805-3875 in the U.K., or 03/6492 1303. Fax 02/9299 2477. www.poresorts.com.au. 96 cabins. Pencil Pine cabins A$186 (U.S.$120.90) per cabin; spa cabins A$240 (U.S.$156) per cabin. Extra person A$26 (U.S.$22). Children under 3 stay free in parents' room. Ask about special winter packages. AE, BC, DC, MC, V. Free parking.

If you like luxury in your rain forests, then this award-winning lodge is the place for you. Cradle Mountain Lodge is simply marvelous. Just minutes from your bed are the giant buttresses of 1,500-year-old trees, moss forests, craggy mountain ridges, limpid pools and lakes, and hordes of scampering marsupials. The cabins are comfortable, the food is excellent, the staff is friendly, and the big open fireplaces invite you to cuddle up for a couple of days. Each modern wood cabin has a pot-bellied stove as well as an electric heater for chilly evenings, a shower, and a small kitchen. There are no telephones or TVs in the rooms—but who needs them! Spa cabins come with carpets, spa tubs, and balconies offering scenic views. Some have separate bedrooms. Two cabins have limited facilities for travelers with disabilities. Guests have the use of the casual and comfortable main lodge, where there is a large dining room, a guest lounge with TV and VCR, cozy bars, a tavern, and a cafe. Almost every room in the lodge has a blazing log fire.

7 The West Coast

Strahan: 296km (184 miles) NW of Hobart, 245km (152 miles) SW of Devonport

Tasmania's west coast is wild and mountainous, with a scattering of mining and logging towns and plenty of wilderness. The pristine Franklin and Gordon rivers tumble through World Heritage Areas once bitterly contested by loggers, politicians, and environmentalists, whereas the bare, poisoned hills that make up the eerily beautiful "moonscape" of Queenstown show the results of intensive mining and industrial activity. Strahan (pronounced "Strawn"), the only town of any size in the area, is the starting point for cruises up the Gordon River and ventures into the rain forest.

ESSENTIALS

GETTING THERE   TWT Tassie Link (☎ **03/6272 7300**) runs coaches between Strahan and Launceston, Devonport, and Cradle Mountain every Tuesday, Thursday, and Saturday (and also Sun to and from Hobart). The trip from Launceston takes over 8 hours. The drive from Hobart to Strahan takes about 4^1/$_2$ hours without stops. From Devonport, allow 3^1/$_2$ hours. Although the roads are good, they twist and turn quite dramatically and are particularly hazardous at night, when marsupials come out to feed.

The cheapest way to travel between these places is via bus with a Tassie Wilderness Pass (see "Exploring Tasmania," at the beginning of this chapter, for details).

VISITOR INFORMATION   Strahan Visitors Centre, on The Esplanade (☎ **03/ 6471 7622**), is open daily from 10am to 6pm in winter and to 8pm in spring and summer. It has good information on local activities.

CRUISING THE RIVERS & OTHER ADVENTURES

Gordon River Cruises, based in Strahan (☎ 03/6471 7187) offers a half-day trip daily at 9am, an afternoon cruise sailing at 2pm in the first 3 weeks of January, and a full-day trip from October 1 to the end of May. Cruises take passengers across Macquarie Harbour and up the Gordon River past historic Sarah Island, where convicts—working in horrendous conditions—were once used to log valuable Huon pine. A stop is made at **Heritage Landing,** where you can get a taste of the rain forest on a half-hour walk. The full-day cruise in the high season (Oct through May) includes lunch and a guided tour through the convict ruins on Sarah Island. Cruises depart from the Main Wharf on The Esplanade, in the town center.

World Heritage Cruises (☎ 03/6471 7174; www.worldheritagecruises.com.au; e-mail: worldheritagecruises@tassie.net.au) offers daily Gordon River trips leaving Strahan Wharf at 9am and returning at 3:30pm. The company's M.V. *Wanderer III* stops at Sarah Island, Heritage Landing, and the salmon and trout farm at Liberty Point. Meals and drinks are available on board.

West Coast Yacht Charters (☎ 03/6471 7422) runs fishing trips from 9am to noon for A$40 (U.S.$26; negotiable) with fishing gear, bait, and morning tea included. They also offer evening crayfish dinner and fishing cruises for A$50 (U.S.$32.50), and 2-day, 2-night sailing cruises for A$320 (U.S.$208) all-inclusive.

Although cruises are the main attraction in the area, you can also enjoy jet-boat rides, flight-seeing in a seaplane that lands on the Gordon River, helicopter flights, and 4WD tours, all easily arranged in Strahan.

MINE TOURS & OTHER ATTRACTIONS

Zeehan's West Coast Pioneers Memorial Museum (☎ 03/6471 6225), 42 kilometers (26 miles) north of Strahan, is worth a visit for its mining relics and fascinating local history. It's open daily from 8:30am to 5pm from April 1 to October 1, and until 6pm at other times. Admission is A$5 (U.S.$3.25) for adults, A$3 (U.S.$1.95) for children, and A$10 (U.S.$6.50) for families.

Worth seeing, too, are the 103-meter (338-ft.) Montezuma Falls, the highest falls in Tasmania. A highly recommended 5-kilometer (3-mile) walk to the falls starts off at the Montezuma Falls signpost at Williamstown, 5km south of Rosebury. The walk is mostly through rain forest, following an old railway track. It's flat and easy, though it can be slippery at times; the journey takes about 3 hours round-trip. **Hays Bus Service** (☎ 03/6473 1247) runs 4WD trips to the falls if you don't fancy the walk. The drive takes around 3 hours (it's slow going along that track) and costs A$40 (U.S.$26), including lunch.

The **Queenstown Chairlift** in Queenstown is also interesting. It's open daily from 8am to 6pm and costs A$6 (U.S.$3.90) for adults, A$4 (U.S.$ 2.60) for children, and A$15 (U.S.$9.75) for families. The chairlift offers panoramic views across the surrounding starkness of the hillsides. The ride takes 15 minutes to the top of the 537-meter (1,760-ft.) Limestone Quarry Hill. You can walk around on top before coming back down. There's a cafe in the chairlift building.

Lyell Tours (☎ 03/6471 2388; e-mail: romanabt@tassie.net.au) runs surface and underground tours of a Queenstown mine, operated by Copper Mines of Tasmania (CMT). The 1-hour surface tour takes in the enormous open-cut mine, the lunar landscape around Queenstown, and Queenstown's main street. Tours leave from the company's offices below the Empire Hotel in Driffield Street, Queenstown. They run at 9:15am and 4pm and cost A$12 (U.S.$7.80) for adults and A$6.50 (U.S.$4.20) for

Dune Buggy Rides

What's more fun than scooting across the sand in a dune buggy? **Four-Wheelers** (☎ **03/6471 7622,** or mobile 0419/508 175) offers exhilarating 40-minute rides across the ❍ **Henty Sand Dunes,** about 10 minutes north of Strahan. Trips cost just A$30 (U.S.$19.50) for one adult and A$55 (U.S.$35.75) for two. Longer trips are also offered outside the hot summer months.

children. The company's underground tour of the mine (3.5 hr.) starts at 8:30am and 1:30pm. It really is world-class. Visitors dress as miners and get taken 5km (3 miles) underground in a cage. It costs A$50 (U.S.$32.50) per person, and there's a maximum of seven people. Children under 12 are not allowed. The company also runs an excellent Bird River Rainforest Tour, taking in some of Australia's most spectacular rain forest. The 4¹/₂-hour tour leaves at 8:30am and 2pm daily and costs A$60 (U.S.$39) for adults and A$40 (U.S.$26) for children.

ACCOMMODATIONS

Franklin Manor. The Esplanade, Strahan, TAS 7468. ☎ **03/6471 7311.** Fax 03/6471 7267. 14 units, 4 cottages. TV TEL. A$150 (U.S.$97.50) standard double, A$170 (U.S.$110.50) deluxe double or cottage. Rates include breakfast. Ask about winter deals. AE, BC, DC, MC, V.

Built in 1886 as the home of the harbormaster, this B&B offers a comfortable main lounge that's warmed by a log fire. Standard rooms have queen-size beds; deluxe rooms have kings. The simple Huon pine bar in the foyer and the wine cellar operate on the honor system. A three-course dinner costs A$39 (U.S.$25.35) per person. The specialties are salmon, duck, and lobster, with venison and wallaby served in winter. Though nice, Franklin Manor has come up against strong competition from the more upscale Ormiston House.

Gordon Gateway Chalets. Grining St., Strahan, TAS 7468. ☎ **03/6471 7165.** Fax 03/6471 7588. 12 units. TV. Jan–Apr A$110 (U.S.$71.50) studio double, May–Dec A$72 (U.S.$46.80) studio double. Sept–Apr A$150 (U.S.$97.50) 2-bedroom; May–Aug A$125 (U.S.$81.25) 2-bedroom. BC, MC, V.

These modern self-contained units are on a hill with good views of the harbor and Strahan township. Each has cooking facilities so you can save on meal costs. The two-bedroom apartments have bathtubs, while the studios just have showers. Breakfast is provided on request for A$8.50 (U.S.$5.50) per person. Guests have the use of a self-service laundry, a barbecue area, and a children's playground. One unit is equipped for travelers with disabilities.

❍ **Ormiston House.** The Esplanade, Strahan, TAS 7468. ☎ **03/6471 7077.** Fax 03/6471 7007. www.ormistonhouse.com.au. E-mail: ormiston@tassie.net.au. 6 units. TV TEL. A$180–$225 (U.S.$117–$146.25) double. Extra person A$44 (U.S.$28.60). Rates include breakfast. AE, BC, DC, MC, V.

Ormiston House is a five-star gem. Built in 1899 for the family that gave it its name, the present owners have made it into a sort of shrine to their predecessors. Each of the four rooms is styled to represent one of the original family members. Each room is intricately furnished and wallpapered in busy designs and comes with a good-size private bathroom. There are a nice morning room and a restaurant serving good food. The owners are very friendly and have plenty of time for their guests. No smoking.

8 The Central Highland Lakes

Tasmania's extensive hydroelectric schemes have transformed the island state, creating many new lakes, all of which have been seeded with trout. Some of the most popular trout fishing and recreation lakes are Arthur's Lake, Great Lake, Lake Sorell, and Lake St. Clair (see section 6 of this chapter). The Bronte lakes, between Bronte Park and Tarraleah, are also favorites, especially because they are about halfway between Strahan and Hobart and offer accommodation options. The lakes around here hold some of the biggest wild brown and rainbow trout in the world. Monsters of well over 9 pounds are not uncommon, while anglers frequently pull out 5- to 6-pound fish. The water is clear and very shallow, making spotting the trout an easy affair.

To fish, you need an **angling license** costing A$12 (U.S.$7.80) for 1 day, A$20 (U.S.$13) for 3 days, A$35 (U.S.$22.75) for 2 weeks, and A$45 (U.S.$29.25) for a full season. The trout-fishing season is from the beginning of August to the end of April. Call **Inland Fisheries** (☎ 03/6233 4140), or pick up a license at a tourist information office, aboard the *Spirit of Tasmania* ferry, in tackle shops, and in general stores in small towns.

For more information on fishing guides, contact the **Tasmanian Professional Trout Guides Association** (☎ 03/6229 5896; e-mail: tastroutguides@vision.net.au).

ACCOMMODATIONS
VERY EXPENSIVE

✪ **London Lakes Lodge.** Post Office, Bronte Park, TAS 7140. ☎ **03/6289 1159.** Fax 03/6289 1122. www.londonlakes.com.au. E-mail: garrette@londonlakes.com.au. 5 units. Advance reservations mandatory. A$650–$840 (U.S.$422.50–$546) per night per angler with guide (depending on season, Oct 1–Mar 31 is most expensive); A$370–$510 (U.S.$240–$331) per night per nonguided angler; A$290–$350 (U.S.$188–$227) per night per person accompanying angler. All meals, tackle, rods, clothing, and transportation included. Prepayment required, by personal check or traveler's checks only. Closed May–July.

This place is so exclusive that the owners decline to put up a road sign to tell you where it is (you'll find the London Lakes Lodge off the first dirt track after the Bronte Park turnoff on the road from Strahan to Hobart). Three of the nearby lakes are personally owned by the lodge's proprietors and along with more than 30 other lakes in the vicinity hold some of the biggest wild brown and rainbow trout in the world. The lodge is all about low-key, high-action trout fishing. China trout leap from every wall and from atop the fireplace, while fishing rods, flies, and waders are stocked in vast quantities around the lodge. Guides (one to every two guests) take you out on the lakes, rivers, and streams in the area, offering personal tips and lessons. The owner, the current captain of the Australian Fly-Fishing Team, regularly passes on his knowledge, too. The lodge caters to just 10 guests in five simple twin-bedded rooms. The socializing goes on in the main living areas, where you may even be able to pet the latest in a line of baby wombats found in the woods outside. The chef here, Greg Howitt, produces marvelous food. Highly recommended if you can afford it.

INEXPENSIVE

Bronte Park Highland Village. Bronte Park, TAS 7140. ☎ **03/6289 1126.** Fax 03/6289 1109. 17 cottages, 12 rms in chalet, 9 hostel rms. A$65 (U.S.$42.25) standard cottage, A$12 (U.S.$7.80) extra adult, A$5 (U.S.$3.25) child. A$88 (U.S.$57.20) superior cottage, A$17 (U.S.$11) extra adult, A$10 (U.S.$6.50) extra child. A$66 (U.S.$42.90) standard double, A$15 (U.S.$9.75) extra adult, A$10 (U.S.$6.50) extra child; A$75 (U.S.$48.75) superior double. A$120 (U.S.$78) spa cottage. Ask about specials. AE, BC, DC, MC, V. Free parking.

Village by name, village by nature, Bronte Park offers everything for a passer-through or for those after the local trout. Cottages are self-contained and comfortably warmed by log fires, and can sleep between 4 and 10. Chalet rooms within the main house are old-pub style in appearance, with attached bathrooms. The spa cottage has a double and two singles and is rated as four stars. Caravans and camping facilities are also on-site. The main building also has a gift shop, a good restaurant, a family bar, even bigger log fires, a TV room, and games rooms. The village store acts as a post office, a service station, and food take-away. You can also hire your trout-fishing gear here. Find Bronte Park just off the Lyell Highway between Queenstown and Hobart.

Tullah Lakeside Chalet. Farrell St., Tullah, TAS 7321 (90km/56 miles northeast of Strahan, 164km/101 miles south of Devonport). ☎ **03/6473 4121.** Fax 03/6473 4130. 51 units. A$55 (U.S.$35.75) standard double, A$75 (U.S.$48.75) superior double, A$90 (U.S.$58.50) Lakeside double. Children ages 2–12 A$10 (U.S.$6.50) extra. AE, BC, DC, MC, V. Free parking.

This place is a good stopover for lunch on the way to and from the north coast from Strahan, or an excellent base from which to discover Tasmania's lake district. Standard rooms are cheap and cheerful, although quite small, and come with a double bed and a shower. Superior rooms are slightly larger and come with a queen-size bed. Guests also have the use of a laundry, a kitchenette, and a TV lounge. Devonshire teas, for A$5 (U.S.$3.25), are available in the bar or dining room or in front of the huge fireplace. Lunch and dinner menus could include marinated quail as a starter, and spinach and ricotta cannelloni or a big chunk of salmon served with a simple salad and french fries for a main course. Mains go for between A$12 and $18 (U.S.$7.80 to $11.70).

The chalet runs horseback tours, trout-fishing tours, boating trips on the lake, and horse and wagon rides around the village. Mountain bikes and canoes are also available for rent. Among the most popular walks in the area are the 5-hour round-trip hike to the top of Mount Murchison, which offers fabulous 360° views, and the 3-hour walk to the top of Mount Farrel, which overlooks Tullah and Lake Rosebury. Ask at the chalet for directions. **Hays Bus Service** (☎ **03/6473 1247**) runs half-day and full-day trout-fishing tours of the area's lakes.

Appendix:
Australia in Depth

by Marc Llewellyn

The land "Down Under" is a modern nation coming to terms with its identity. The umbilical cord with mother England has been cut, and the nation is still trying to find its position within Asia.

One thing it realized early on, though, was the importance of tourism to its economy. Millions of visitors flock to Australia every year. You'll find Aussies generally impressively helpful and friendly; and services, tours, and food and drink the rival of any in the world. And then, of course, there is the landscape, the native Australian culture, the sunshine, the animals, and some of the world's best cities—what more could you ask for?

1 Australian History 101

Dateline

- **120,000 B.C.** Evidence suggests Aborigines living in Australia.
- **60,000 B.C.** Aborigines living in Arnham Land in the far north fashion stone tools.
- **24,500 B.C.** The world's oldest known ritual cremation takes place at Lake Mungo.
- **1606** Dutch explorer Willem Jansz lands on far north coast of Van Diemen's Land (Tasmania).
- **1622** First English ship to reach Australia wrecks on the west coast.
- **1642** Abel Tasman charts the Tasmanian coast.
- **1770** Capt. James Cook lands at Botany Bay.
- **1787** Capt. Arthur Phillip's First Fleet leaves England with convicts aboard.

continues

IN THE BEGINNING In the beginning there was the **Dreamtime**—at least according to the Aborigines of Australia. Between then and now, perhaps, the supercontinent referred to as **Pangaea** split into two huge continents called **Laurasia** and **Gondwanaland.** Over millions of years, continental drift carried the landmasses apart. Laurasia gradually broke up and formed North America, Europe, and most of Asia. Meanwhile, Gondwanaland divided into South America, Africa, India, Australia and New Guinea, and Antarctica. **Giant marsupials** evolved to roam the continent of Australia. Among them were a plant-eating animal that looked like a wombat the size of a rhinoceros; a giant squashed-face kangaroo standing 3 meters (10 ft.) high; a giant wombat the size of a donkey; and a flightless bird the same size as an emu but four times heavier. The last of these giant marsupials are believed to have died out some 40,000 years ago.

EARLY EXPLORERS The existence of Australia had been in the minds of Europeans since the Ancient Greek astronomer Ptolemy drew a map of the world in about A.D. 150 showing a large landmass in the south, which he believed had to be there to balance out the land in the northern hemisphere. He called it Terra Australia Incognita—the unknown south land.

There's evidence to suggest **Portuguese** ships reached Australia at least as early as **1536** and even charted part of its coastline. In 1606, William Jansz was sent by the **Dutch East India Company** to open up a new route to the spice island, and to find New Guinea, which was supposed to be rich in gold. He landed on the north coast of Queensland and fought with local Aborigines. Between 1616 and 1640, many more Dutch ships made contact with Australia as they hugged the west coast of what they called "New Holland," after sailing with the westerlies from the Cape of Good Hope.

In **1642,** the Dutch East India Company, through the Governor General of the Indies, Anthony Van Diemen, sent Abel Tasman to search out and map the great south land. During two voyages he charted the northern Australian coastline and discovered **Tasmania,** which he named Van Diemen's Land.

THE ARRIVAL OF THE BRITISH In **1697,** the English pirate **William Dampier** published a book about his adventures. In it, he mentioned Shark Beach on the northwest coast of Australia as the place the pirate ship he sailed on made its repairs after robbing ships on the Pacific Ocean. The king of England was so impressed with Dampier that he sent him back to Australia to find out more. On his return he reported that he found little to recommend.

Captain James Cook turned up more than 70 years later, in 1770, and charted the whole east coast, claiming it for Britain and naming it New South Wales. On the 29th of April, Cook landed at **Botany Bay,** which he named after the plant-collecting expedition led by the ship's botanist, Joseph Banks. Back in Britain, King George III was convinced Australia could make a good colony. It would also help reduce Britain's overflowing prison population, caused by the refusal of the new United States of America to take any more transported British convicts following the War of Independence.

The **First Fleet** left England in May 1787, made up of 11 store and transport ships led by

- **1788** Captain Phillip raises British flag at Port Jackson (Sydney Harbour).
- **1788–1868** Convicts are transported from England to the colony of Australia.
- **1793** The first free settlers arrive.
- **1830** Governor Arthur lines up 5,000 settlers across Van Diemen's Land to walk the length of the island to capture and rid it of all Aborigines.
- **1850** Gold discovered in Bathurst, New South Wales.
- **1852** Gold rush begins in Ballarat, Victoria.
- **1853** The last convict arrives in Van Diemen's Land, and to celebrate, the colony is renamed Tasmania after Abel Tasman.
- **1860** The white population of Australia jumps to more than one million.
- **1872** England and Australia exchange their first telephone call.
- **1875** Silver found at Broken Hill, New South Wales.
- **1889** Australian troops fight in the Boer War in South Africa.
- **1895** Banjo Patterson's *The Man from Snowy River* published.
- **1901** The six states join together to become the Commonwealth of Australia.
- **1902** Women gain the right to vote.
- **1908** Canberra is chosen as the site for the federal capital.
- **1911** Australian (non-Aboriginal) population reaches 4,455,005.
- **1915** Australian and New Zealand troops massacred at Gallipoli.
- **1927** Federal capital is moved from Melbourne to Canberra.
- **1931** First airmail letters are delivered to England by Charles Kingsford Smith and Charles Ulm.

continues

- **1931** The Arnham Land Aboriginal Reserve is proclaimed.
- **1932** The Sydney Harbour Bridge opens.
- **1942** Darwin bombed, and Japanese minisubmarines found in Sydney Harbour.
- **1950** Australian troops fight alongside Americans in Korea.
- **1953** British nuclear tests at Emu in South Australia lead to a radioactive cloud killing and injuring many Aborigines.
- **1956** Olympic Games held in Melbourne.
- **1962** Commonwealth government gives Aborigines the right to vote.
- **1965** Australian troops start fighting in Vietnam.
- **1967** Aborigines granted Australian citizenship and are counted in census.
- **1968** Australia's population passes 12 million following heavy immigration.
- **1971** Australia pulls out of Vietnam following mass demonstrations the previous year.
- **1971** The black, red, and yellow Aboriginal flag flown for the first time.
- **1973** The Sydney Opera House completed.
- **1974** Cyclone Tracy devastates Darwin.
- **1976** The Aboriginal Land Rights (Northern Territory) Act gives some land back to native people.
- **1983** Ayres Rock given back to local Aborigines, who rename it Uluru.
- **1983** Australia wins the Americas Cup, ending 112 years of American domination of the event.
- **1986** Queen Elizabeth II severs the Australian Constitution from Great Britain's.

continues

Arthur Phillip. (It's interesting to note that none of the ships was bigger than the regular passenger ferries that ply modern-day Sydney Harbour.) Aboard were 1,480 people, including 759 convicts. Phillip's flagship, The Supply, reached Botany Bay in January 1788, but Phillip decided the soil was poor and the surrounds too swampy. On **January 26,** now celebrated as Australia Day, he settled for Port Jackson (Sydney Harbour) instead.

SETTLING DOWN The **convicts** were immediately put to work clearing land, planting crops, and constructing buildings. The early food harvests were failures, and by early 1790 the fledgling colony was facing starvation.

Phillip decided to give some convicts pardons if they were good and worked hard, and even grant small land parcels to those who were really industrious. In **1795,** coal was discovered; in **1810,** Governor Macquarie began extensive city building projects; and in **1813,** the explorers Gregory Blaxland, William Charles Wentworth, and William Lawson forged a passage over the Blue Mountains to the fertile plains beyond.

When **gold** was discovered in Victoria in 1852, and in Western Australia 12 years later, hundreds of thousands of immigrants from Europe, America, and China flooded into the country in search of their fortunes. By **1860,** more than a million non-Aboriginal people were living in Australia.

The **last 10,000 convicts** were transported to Western Australia between 1850 and 1868, bringing the total shipped out to Australia to **168,000.**

FEDERATION & THE GREAT WARS On January 1, 1901, the six states that made up Australia proclaimed themselves to be part of one nation, and the **Commonwealth of Australia** was formed. In the same ceremony, the first **Governor General** was sworn in as the representative of the Queen, who remained head of state. In 1914, Australia joined the mother country in war. In April the following year, the Australian and New Zealand Army Corps (ANZAC) formed a beachhead on the peninsula of **Gallipoli** in Turkey. The Turkish troops had been forewarned, and 8 months of fighting ended with 8,587 Australian dead and more than 19,000 wounded.

Australians were fighting again in **World War II,** this time in North Africa, Greece, and the Middle East. In March 1942, Japanese aircraft bombed Broome in Western Australia and Darwin in the Northern Territory. In May of that year, Japanese midget submarines entered Sydney Harbour and torpedoed a ferry, before being destroyed. Later that year, Australian volunteers fought a fighting retreat through the jungles of Papua New Guinea on the Kokoda Trail against superior Japanese forces. Australian troops fought alongside Americans in subsequent wars in Korea and Vietnam and sent military support to the Persian Gulf conflicts.

RECENT TIMES Following World War II, **mass immigration** to Australia, primarily from Europe, boosted the population. In 1974, the left-of-center Whitlam government put an end to the White Australia policy that had largely restricted black and Asian immigration since 1901. In 1986, the official umbilical cord to Britain was cut when the **Australian Constitution** was separated from that of its motherland. Australia had begun the march to complete independence.

In 1992, the High Court handed down the **"Mabo" decision,** which ruled that Aborigines had a right to claim government-owned land if they could prove a continued connection with it. The following year, huge crowds filled Sydney's Circular Quay to hear that the city had won the **2000 Olympic Games.** In 1998, debate began to rage over continued Asian immigration, Aboriginal land claims, restrictive gun laws (following a 1996 massacre in which gunman Martin Bryant killed 35 people in Port Arthur, Tasmania), and a feeling among parts of the community that the government was ignoring the electorate. As the world looked on with concern at the events unfolding in Australia, a new right-wing political party, called **One Nation,** began making stunning electoral gains. The party won more than 10% of the vote in Queensland during the 1998 general election, in which the Liberal/National Party Coalition was returned with John Howard as the Prime Minister.

In 1999, Howard courted controversy by announcing that he would open the Sydney 2000 Olympics, an honor that traditionally belongs to the head of state of the host country, which in this case would be the Queen of England, because she is also officially the Queen of Australia. With his announcement, the idea of Australia breaking all ties with England and becoming a republic has been once again thrust into the forefront of public debate.

The Olympic city undertook preparations for the Games in earnest. Olympic venues emerged, a new expressway and train link were built to connect the spruced-up airport to the city center, all the city center's sidewalks

- **1988** Aborigines demonstrate as Australia celebrates its Bicentennial with a reenactment of the First Fleet's entry into Sydney Harbour.
- **1991** Australia's population reaches 17 million.
- **1993** Sydney chosen as the site of 2000 Olympics.
- **1994** High Court "Mabo" decision overturns the principle of *Terra Nullius,* which suggested Australia was unoccupied at time of white settlement.
- **1995** Australians protest as France explodes nuclear weapons in the South Pacific.
- **1996** High Court hands down "Wik" decision, which allows Aborigines the right to claim some Commonwealth land.
- **1998** The right-wing One Nation Party, led by Pauline Hanson, holds the balance of power in Queensland elections on a platform of anti-immigration and anti-Aboriginal policies.
- **1999** A 10% Goods and Services tax becomes the major debate within Australia, with a minor party, the Australian Democrats, and a single independent senator rejecting the new tax in the upper house and threatening to throw Australia into constitutional crisis.
- **2000** Sydney hosts the Olympic Games.

were dug up and replaced—in fact, wherever you look, something in Sydney has had a recent makeover. Its moment in the sun, September of 2000, put Sydney firmly on the map.

2 The People of Oz

It's generally believed that more races live in Australia at the present time than anywhere else in the world, including America. Eighteen million people, from some 165 nations, make the country their home. In general, relations between the different ethnic groups have been peaceful. Australia is a shining example of a multicultural society, despite an increasingly vocal minority which believes that Australia has come too far in welcoming people from races other than their own.

ABORIGINAL AUSTRALIA   When Captain James Cook landed at Botany Bay in 1770 determined to claim the land he surveyed for the British Empire, at least 300,000 Aborigines were already living on the continent. Whether you believe a version of history that suggests the Aboriginal people were descendants of migrants from Indonesia to the north, or the Aboriginal belief that they have occupied Australia since the beginning of time, there is scientific evidence that people were using fire for cooking in present-day New South Wales at least 120,000 years ago.

At the time of the white "invasion" of their lands, there were in Australia at least 600 different largely nomadic communities, each linked to its ancestral land by **"sacred sites"** (certain features of the land, such as hills or rock formations). They were hunter-gatherers, spending about 20 hours a week harvesting the resources of the land, the rivers, and the ocean. Much of the rest of the time was taken up by a complex social and belief system, as well as the practicalities of life, such as making utensils, weapons, and unique musical instruments such as didgeridoos, and clapsticks.

The basis of Aboriginal spirituality rests in the **Dreamtime** stories, in which everything, including the land, stars, mountains, moon, sun, oceans, water holes, and both animals and humans, was created by spirits. Much Aboriginal art is related to the land and the sacred sites where the Dreamtime spirits reside. Some Aboriginal groups believe these spirits came in giant human form, others believed they were animals, still more believe they were huge snakes. Some even believe in a single Western God–like figure. According to Aboriginal custom, individuals can draw on the power of the Dreamtime spirits by reenacting various stories and practicing certain ceremonies.

Aboriginal groups had encountered people from other lands before the British arrived. Dutch records from 1451 show that the Macassans, from islands now belonging to Indonesia, had a long relationship trading Dutch glass, smoking pipes, and alcoholic liqueur for edible sea slugs from Australia's northern coastal waters, which they sold to the Chinese in the Canton markets. Dutch, Portuguese, French, and Chinese vessels also encountered Australia—with the Dutch fashion for pointy beards catching on through northern Australia long before the invasion of 1770.

When the British came, they brought with them **diseases** that the Aborigines had never encountered, and thus had no natural defenses against. Entire coastal communities were virtually wiped out by smallpox. Even as late as the 1950s, large numbers of Aborigines in remote regions of South Australia and the Northern Territory succumbed to deadly influenza and measles outbreaks.

Though it seems relationships were initially peaceful between the settlers and local Aborigines, conflicts over land and food soon led to skirmishes in which Aborigines were massacred, and settlers and convicts were turned against—even the colony's first governor, Arthur Phillip, who had been the commander of the First Fleet of settlers to Australia, was speared in the back by an Aborigine in 1790.

Within a few years, some 10,000 Aborigines and 1,000 Europeans were killed in Queensland alone, while in Tasmania a campaign to rid the island entirely of local Aborigines was ultimately successful. By the turn of the century, it was widely regarded that the Aboriginal people were a race doomed for extinction. Most that were left alive were living in government-owned reserves or church-controlled missions.

Massacres of Aborigines continued to go largely or wholly unpunished into the 1920s, by which time it became official government policy to remove light-skinned Aboriginal children from their families and to forcibly sterilize young women. Many children of this "stolen generation" were brought up in white foster homes or church refuges and were never reunited with their parents.

Today, there are some 283,000 Aborigines living in Australia, and the great divide still exists between them and the rest of the population. Aboriginal life expectancy is much lower than that of other Australians, with overall death rates between two and four times higher. A far higher percentage of Aboriginal people than other Australians also fill Australian prisons, and despite a Royal Commission into Aboriginal Deaths in Custody, Aborigines continue to die while incarcerated.

A landmark in Aboriginal affairs occurred in 1992 when the High Court determined that Australia was not an empty land (*terra nullius*) as it had been seen officially since the British invasion. The so-called **"Mabo" decision** resulted in the **1993 Native Title Act,** which allowed Aboriginal groups, and the ethnically distinct people living in the Torres Strait islands off northern Queensland, to claim government-owned land if they could prove continual association with it since 1788. The later **"Wik" decision** determined that Aborigines could make claims on Government land leased to agriculturists.

In response to concerns from powerful farming and mining interests, the federal government then went on to severely curtail Aboriginal rights to their land. In response, Aboriginal groups threatened major demonstrations to coincide with the Sydney 2000 Olympics.

But worse was to follow. Mandatory sentencing laws, enacted in West Australia and the Northern Territory state governments in 1996 and 1997, respectively, came to the forefront of international attention in 2000. The laws were perceived by the Aboriginal community as being aimed squarely at them. Then, when a 15-year-old Aboriginal boy allegedly committed suicide in February 2000, less than a week before he was due to be released from a Northern Territory prison, and a 21-year-old Aboriginal youth was imprisoned for a year for stealing A$23 (U.S.$14.95) worth of fruit cordial and biscuits from a store in the same month, all hell broke loose. Aboriginal people protested, activists of all colors came out in support, and even the United Nations weighed in with heavy criticism.

Added to this was the simmering issue of the federal government's decision not to apologize to the Aboriginal people for the "stolen generation." The Aboriginal people in general believed that an apology would go a long way toward reconciliation, but in March 2000, a government-sponsored report stated there was never a "stolen generation" after all and, according to respected researchers on both sides of the fence, went on to markedly underestimate the number of people personally affected. Aboriginal activists remain up in arms, and tensions are far from over.

THE REST OF AUSTRALIA "White" was always used to distinguish the Anglo-Saxon population from that of the Aboriginal population. These days, though, a walk through any of the major cities would show that things have changed dramatically. On average, around 100,000 people emigrate to Australia each year. Of these, approximately 12% were born in the U.K. or Ireland; 11% in New Zealand; and more than 21% in China, Hong Kong, Vietnam, or the Philippines. Waves of immigration have brought in millions of people since the end of World War II. At the last census in 1996, more than a quarter of a million Australia residents were born in Italy, for example, some 186,000 in the former Yugoslavia, 144,000 in Greece, 118,000 in Germany, and 103,000 in China. So what's the typical Australian like? Well, hardly Crocodile Dundee.

3 Aussie Eats & Drinks

THE EATS

It took a long time for the average Australian to realize there was more to food than English-style sausage and mashed potatoes, "meat and three veg," lamb chops, and a good old Sunday roast. It wasn't so long ago that spaghetti was something foreigners ate, and zucchini and eggplant were considered exotic vegetables. Then came mass immigration, and with it all sorts of foods that people had only read about in *National Geographic.*

The first big wave of Italian immigrants in the 1950s caused a national scandal. The great Aussie dream was to have a quarter-acre block of land with a Hills Hoist (one of those revolving circular clothesline implements) in the backyard. When the Italians started hanging their freshly made pasta out to dry on this Aussie icon, it caused a national uproar, and more than a few clamored for the new arrivals to be shipped back. As Australia matured, Southern European cuisine became increasingly popular, until olive oil was greasing frying pans the way only lard had previously done.

In the 1980s, everything was turned on its head again, this time as waves of Asian immigrants hit Australia's shores. Suddenly, everyone was cooking with woks, and newly discovered spices and herbs were causing a sensation at dinner parties across the land. These days, this fusion of flavors and styles has melded into what's now commonly referred to as "Modern Australian," or "Mod Oz"—a distinctive cuisine blending the spices of the east with the flavors of the west.

Aboriginal people, of course, have been living off the land for tens of thousands of years, but it was only recently that Australian restaurateurs began looking into the possibilities of native foods ("bush tucker"). **Kangaroo** is now a common sight on menus around the country, with **wallaby, emu,** and **crocodile** also making regular appearances. Native berries and nuts, such as the **quandong** (a tart-tasting fruit the size of a grape) and the now–world-famous **macadamia nut,** commonly find their way into new-wave Australian cuisine. Less widely eaten by squeamish Australians are **witchetty grubs**—large white insect larvae that look like puffed-up bald caterpillars that Aborigines traditionally eat either raw or cooked over embers. Australia's introduced species have also become semipopular eating, with Northern Territory buffalo, in particular, lumbering onto restaurant menus.

THE DRINKS

THE AMBER NECTAR The great Aussie drink is a "tinnie" (a can) of beer. Barbecues would not be the same without a case of tinnies, or "stubbies" (small bottles). In the hotter parts of the country, you may be offered a Styrofoam cup in which to place your beer to keep it cool. *Warning:* Don't pour the beer into the cup and expect to get away without everyone collapsing into laughter—place your tinnie or stubbie into it instead.

Australian beers vary considerably in quality, but, of course, there's no accounting for tastes. Among the most popular are **Victoria Bitter** (known as "VB"), **XXXX** (pronounced "four ex"), **Fosters,** and various brews produced by the **Tooheys** company. All are popular in cans, in bottles, or on tap (draft).

If I had to recommend a choice brew, I'd go for the XXXX (popular in Queensland) in a can or draft, and Tooheys Red from the bottle. If you prefer slightly darker beers, then go for Tooheys Old. My favorite beer is **Cascade,** a German-style beer that you will usually find only in a bottle. It's light in color, is strong in taste, and is made from Tasmanian water straight off a mountain. If you want to get plastered, try **Coopers**—it's rather cloudy in looks, is very strong, and usually ends up causing a terrific hangover. Most Australian beers range from 4.8% to 5.2% alcohol.

In New South Wales, beer is served by the glass in a "schooner" or a smaller "midi"—though in a few places it's also sold in British measurements, by pints and half-pints. In Victoria, you should ask for a "pot," or the less copious "glass." Elsewhere in the country, the terminology differs, sometimes from town to town. My advice is to ask for a beer and gesture with your hands like a local to show whether you want a small glass or a larger one.

Pub opening times vary significantly depending on their licenses. But as a rule, most will be open from around 10am to midnight most nights, with many extending their drinking hours to the small hours on Friday and Saturday nights. A few pubs in major cities are open 24 hours.

THE VINO   Australian wine making has come a long way since the first grape vines were brought to Australia on the First Fleet in 1788. These days, more than 550 major companies and small wine makers produce wine commercially in Australia. It comes as no surprise—at least not to Australians, anyway—that vintages from Down Under consistently beat competitors from other wine-producing nations in major international shows. It's widely believed, and not without justification, that it takes a very good bottle of old-world wine to beat an average bottle from Australia. The demand for Australian wine overseas has increased so dramatically in the past few years that domestic prices have risen, and new vineyards are being planted at a frantic pace.

Australian wines are generally named after the grape varieties from which they are made. Of the white wines, the fruity **chardonnay** and **Riesling** varieties, the "herbaceous" or "grassy" **sauvignon blanc,** and the dry **semillon** are big favorites. Of the reds, the dry **cabernet sauvignon,** the fruity **merlot,** the burgundy-type **pinot noir,** and the big and bold **shiraz** come out tops.

4 Recommended Reading

The earliest Australian literature consists mostly of poems and shanties that generally go on about how difficult it was to travel all the way over to the new land to find it full of flies, dusty plains, and hard work. Of the 19th-century writers, the one that stands head and shoulders above anyone else is "Banjo" Patterson, whose epic poem *The Man from Snowy River* hit the best-seller list in 1895.

A big name of the 20th century is Miles Franklin, who wrote *My Brilliant Career* (1901), which tells the story of a young woman faced with the dilemma of choosing between marriage and a career. Outback adventures were at the heart of three classic Australian books printed later in the century. Colleen McCullough's *Thorn Birds* is a romantic epic about a Catholic priest who falls in love with a girl; *We of the Never Never* tells the story of a young woman who leaves the comfort of her Melbourne home to go and live on a cattle station in the Northern Territory; and *Walkabout,* by James V. Marshall, shows the relationship between an Aborigine and two children who get lost in the bush. *Walkabout* was later made into one of Australia's most influential films.

The critics' choice, and the winner of the Nobel Prize for Literature in 1973 for *The Eye of the Storm,* is novelist Patrick White. This novelist and scholar also wrote *Voss.* Though not Australian, D. H. Lawrence spent a lot of time Down Under, and his novel *Kangaroo* is worth a read.

Travel writer Bruce Chatwin really got to the heart of Australia with his book *Songlines,* while another travel scribe, Jan Morris, summed up the Emerald City well in her book *Sydney.* Bill Bryson's newest book, *In a Sunburned Country,* chronicles his adventures Down Under. If you can find it anywhere, *The Long Farewell* by Don Charlwood tells amazing first-hand diary accounts of long journeys from Europe to Australia in the 1800s.

Additional modern novelists of note include David Ireland, Elizabeth Jolley, Helen Garner, Sue Woolfe, and Peter Carey, who wrote the classic *Oscar and Lucinda.*

Index

Index

FROMMER'S® COMPLETE TRAVEL GUIDES

Alaska
Amsterdam
Arizona
Atlanta
Australia
Austria
Bahamas
Barcelona, Madrid &
 Seville
Beijing
Belgium, Holland &
 Luxembourg
Bermuda
Boston
British Columbia & the
 Canadian Rockies
Budapest & the Best of
 Hungary
California
Canada
Cancún, Cozumel &
 the Yucatán
Cape Cod, Nantucket &
 Martha's Vineyard
Caribbean
Caribbean Cruises & Ports
 of Call
Caribbean Ports of Call
Carolinas & Georgia
Chicago
China
Colorado
Costa Rica
Denmark
Denver, Boulder & Colorado
 Springs
England
Europe

European Cruises & Ports
 of Call
Florida
France
Germany
Greece
Greek Islands
Hawaii
Hong Kong
Honolulu, Waikiki & Oahu
Ireland
Israel
Italy
Jamaica
Japan
Las Vegas
London
Los Angeles
Maryland & Delaware
Maui
Mexico
Montana & Wyoming
Montréal & Québec City
Munich & the Bavarian
 Alps
Nashville & Memphis
Nepal
New England
New Mexico
New Orleans
New York City
New Zealand
Nova Scotia, New Brunswick
 & Prince Edward Island
Oregon
Paris
Philadelphia & the
 Amish Country

Portugal
Prague & the Best of the
 Czech Republic
Provence & the Riviera
Puerto Rico
Rome
San Antonio & Austin
San Diego
San Francisco
Santa Fe, Taos & Albuquerque
Scandinavia
Scotland
Seattle & Portland
Shanghai
Singapore & Malaysia
South Africa
Southeast Asia
South Florida
South Pacific
Spain
Sweden
Switzerland
Thailand
Tokyo
Toronto
Tuscany & Umbria
USA
Utah
Vancouver & Victoria
Vermont, New Hampshire
 & Maine
Vienna & the Danube Valley
Virgin Islands
Virginia
Walt Disney World &
 Orlando
Washington, D.C.
Washington State

FROMMER'S® DOLLAR-A-DAY GUIDES

Australia from $50 a Day
California from $60 a Day
Caribbean from $70 a Day
England from $70 a Day
Europe from $70 a Day

Florida from $70 a Day
Hawaii from $70 a Day
Ireland from $60 a Day
Italy from $70 a Day
London from $85 a Day

New York from $80 a Day
Paris from $80 a Day
San Francisco from $60 a Day
Washington, D.C.,
 from $70 a Day

FROMMER'S® PORTABLE GUIDES

Acapulco, Ixtapa &
 Zihuatanejo
Alaska Cruises & Ports of Call
Bahamas
Baja & Los Cabos
Berlin
California Wine Country
Charleston & Savannah
Chicago
Dublin

Hawaii: The Big Island
Las Vegas
London
Los Angeles
Maine Coast
Maui
Miami
New Orleans
New York City
Paris

Puerto Vallarta, Manzanillo
 & Guadalajara
San Diego
San Francisco
Sydney
Tampa & St. Petersburg
Venice
Washington, D.C.

FROMMER'S® NATIONAL PARK GUIDES

Family Vacations in the
National Parks
Grand Canyon

National Parks of the
American West
Rocky Mountain

Yellowstone & Grand Teton
Yosemite & Sequoia/
Kings Canyon
Zion & Bryce Canyon

FROMMER'S® MEMORABLE WALKS

Chicago
London

New York
Paris

San Francisco
Washington, D.C.

FROMMER'S® GREAT OUTDOOR GUIDES

New England
Northern California

Southern California & Baja
Southern New England

Washington & Oregon

FROMMER'S® BORN TO SHOP GUIDES

Born to Shop: France
Born to Shop: Italy

Born to Shop: London
Born to Shop: New York

Born to Shop: Paris

FROMMER'S® IRREVERENT GUIDES

Amsterdam
Boston
Chicago
Las Vegas

London
Los Angeles
Manhattan
New Orleans

Paris
San Francisco
Seattle & Portland
Vancouver

Walt Disney World
Washington, D.C.

FROMMER'S® BEST-LOVED DRIVING TOURS

America
Britain
California

Florida
France
Germany

Ireland
Italy
New England

Scotland
Spain
Western Europe

THE UNOFFICIAL GUIDES®

Bed & Breakfasts in
California
Bed & Breakfasts in
New England
Bed & Breakfasts in
the Northwest
Bed & Breakfasts in
Southeast
Beyond Disney
Branson, Missouri

California with Kids
Chicago
Cruises
Disneyland
Florida with Kids
Golf Vacations in the
Eastern U.S.
The Great Smoky &
Blue Ridge
Mountains

Inside Disney
Hawaii
Las Vegas
London
Miami & the Keys
Mini Las Vegas
Mini-Mickey
New Orleans
New York City
Paris

San Francisco
Skiing in the West
Southeast with Kids
Walt Disney World
Walt Disney World
for Grown-ups
Walt Disney World
for Kids
Washington, D.C.

SPECIAL-INTEREST TITLES

Frommer's Britain's Best Bed & Breakfasts and
Country Inns
Frommer's Britain's Best Bike Rides
The Civil War Trust's Official Guide
to the Civil War Discovery Trail
Frommer's Caribbean Hideaways
Frommer's Adventure Guide to Central America
Frommer's Adventure Guide to South America
Frommer's Adventure Guide to Southeast Asia
Frommer's Food Lover's Companion to France
Frommer's Gay & Lesbian Europe
Frommer's Exploring America by RV
Hanging Out in Europe

Israel Past & Present
Mad Monks' Guide to California
Mad Monks' Guide to New York City
Frommer's The Moon
Frommer's New York City with Kids
The New York Times' Unforgettable
Weekends
Places Rated Almanac
Retirement Places Rated
Frommer's Road Atlas Britain
Frommer's Road Atlas Europe
Frommer's Washington, D.C., with Kids
Frommer's What the Airlines Never Tell You